Bowes and Church's

# Food Values of Portions Commonly Used

**15**th edition     revised by

Jean A. T. Pennington, Ph.D., R.D.

**J. B. Lippincott Company**

**Philadelphia**

Cambridge   New York   St. Louis   San Francisco

London   Singapore   Sydney   Tokyo

Acquisitions Editor: Patti Cleary
Manuscript Editor: Linda J. Stewart
Indexer: Ann Cassar
Cover Photography: Dennis Deghan/UNIPHOTO
Cover Designer: Anthony Frizano
Database Design: Barrie Eichhorn
Production Supervisor: Niels Malmquist
Compositor: Tapsco, Inc
Printer: Semline

15th Edition

9 8 7 6 5 4 3 2

**Library of Congress Cataloging-in-Publication Data**

Bowes, Anna De Planter.
    Bowes and Church's Food values of portions commonly
used.

    1. Food—Composition—Tables.   2. Nutrition—Tables.
I. Pennington, Jean A. Thompson.   II. Title.
TX551.B64 1989          641.1          88-13519
ISBN 0-397-54727-7

The author has attempted to provide readers with the most
accurate food composition data available as of the date of
manuscript submission. However, the field of food
composition is a dynamic one. Because of changes in product
formulation, changes in product size, development of new
products, discontinuation of products, sampling concerns,
and advances in analytical methodologies, the information in
these tables should be used as reasonable approximations.
Individuals who are on restricted diets for medical purposes
may need to contact food manufacturers for more specific
information.

# Dedication

This edition of *Food Values of Portions Commonly Used* is dedicated to **Helen Nichols Church**, who was coauthor with her husband, Charles F. Church, M.D., on the ninth through twelfth editions (1963 to 1975) of this book.

Helen N. Church earned her bachelor's degree in home economics from the University of Illinois. She served as the clinical dietitian at Cornell University Medical College Clinic and the New York Hospital Clinic. She also directed field work in nutrition for Columbia University graduate students, served as dietitian-in-charge for the first Howard Johnson Restaurant (in Quincy, Massachusetts), worked with agricultural experimental stations in the northeastern United States, and provided dietetic counseling to numerous patients. Her research in nutrition has concerned methods to measure dietary intake, reliability of dietary data obtained by interviewers, and the nutritional and dietary status of industrial workers.

The contribution of Helen N. Church to the field of nutrition and dietetics, and particularly to *Food Values of Portions Commonly Used*, is gratefully acknowledged.

# Preface

The tradition of *Bowes and Church's Food Values of Portions Commonly Used* now spans more than 50 years. The purpose of this edition remains the same as that of the first and subsequent editions—"to supply authoritative data on the nutritional values of foods in a form for quick and easy reference."

The nutrient values in this edition have been revised according to the most recent data available from the food industry, USDA food composition publications, and the scientific literature. There are two major changes from the previous edition:

■ Values for dietary fiber, which were previously listed in a supplementary table, are now included in the main table. Values for crude fiber, which were previously listed in the main table, have been deleted.

■ Following the listing of sources used to compile data for this edition (page 287), there is an extended listing of recent literature references that provides additional data on the composition of foods and some information about methods used to analyze foods for various substances.

I would like to express my gratitude to the many companies and trade associations who responded to my request for food composition data for this edition. I gratefully acknowledge the reviews of this book provided by Kathryn Fleming, Ph.D., Carolyn Miles, Ph.D., and Suzanne Murphy, Ph.D., and I thank Patricia Cleary and the staff at J. B. Lippincott for their editorial assistance and support.

*Jean A. T. Pennington, Ph.D., R.D.*

*June 1987*

# Preface to the First Edition

The purpose of this book is to supply authoritative data on the nutritional values of foods in a form for quick and easy reference.

In teaching nutrition to students of medicine, dentistry, dental hygiene and public health nursing, food values based on common measures or portions frequently served have been found most useful. This basis of calculation is particularly well suited to the practical study of comparative food values, as well as to the approximate analysis of diets from records of daily food intake. For calculations of diets from weighed portions the actual weight of each food is given in grams or ounces.

*Anna dePlanter Bowes*
*Charles F. Church*

*November 1937*

# Contents

## Supplementary Tables

# Explanatory Notes

In the main table, entitled "Nutrient Content of Foods," foods are grouped on the basis of food type with concerns for common usage. To conserve space, each food is listed only once, although some foods may be applicable to several sections. Please use the index if you cannot locate an item.

For most sections in the main table, each food has two lines of nutrient data. The heading at the top of the page indicates the nutrients and units of measurement for the numerical values listed in the two lines. For two sections—"Infant Formulas" and "Special Dietary Formulas, Commercial and Hospital"—there are four lines of nutrient data per food because of the complete nutrient profiles that were available for these formulated products.

The abbreviated heading names and other abbreviations and symbols used throughout the text are listed on pages xxi–xxii.

Each food is identified by name, description, brand name (if applicable), and serving portion. Foods are presented primarily in their table-ready form, although ingredient items (e.g., flour, baking soda, herbs) are also listed. Where available, brand names are used to help identify products such as ready-to-eat breakfast cereals, candy bars, and entrees.

The serving portion for most foods is listed in both household units and grams. Serving portions are those suggested by the food manufacturer or USDA food composition tables, or are practical sizes adopted by the author.

Supplementary tables are used to present information on nutrients or substances where there was not enough data to warrant a listing in the main table. Information provided in the supplementary tables is also listed by food groups. Most of the foods in the supplementary tables are also listed in the main table and the serving portions are usually consistent.

The data in the tables presented in this book have been taken directly from the sources indicated on pages 288–297. Values from various sources have not been averaged, and values for multi-ingredient foods have not been calculated from ingredients.

# Precautionary Notes

For those unfamiliar with the use of food composition tables, please note the following:

■ These tables should be used as approximate guides to the nutrient content of foods. Persons on special diets for various disease conditions may require more specific nutrient composition data from food manufacturers.

■ Blank spaces denote lack of information. Do not assume that missing values are zeros.

■ The nutrient values presented here are mean values; some of these values may have large standard deviations and wide ranges. Causes for nutrient variations in foods include soil type, season, geography, genetics, diet, processing, method of preparation, sampling scheme, and method of analysis. Because of nutrient variation and the fact that the data are collected from various sources (the food industry, USDA publications, and the scientific literature), apparent inconsistencies may occur. For example, portion sizes and gram weights of similar foods may vary among sources, and nutrient values may vary according to analytical methodology.

■ The values presented here may not be representative of the entire food supply. Representativeness depends upon the sampling scheme and the number of samples collected and analyzed.

■ The mineral content of water varies from one location to another. The mineral content of beverages made by addition of water to powders or frozen concentrates and of foods cooked in water (for example, rice, oatmeal, pasta, vegetables) may vary depending on the mineral content of the water used. Likewise, the mineral content of commercial beverages (for example, beer, carbonated sodas, juice drinks) depends on the mineral content of the water in the area where the beverages are bottled. Individuals on medically restricted diets may need to obtain information on the mineral content of their home tap water and on the mineral content of the specific beverages they consume.

■ Information presented in these tables may not be the same as that provided on food labels. There are several reasons for such differences.
  • Portions sizes may differ. The household portions and gram weights presented here may differ from those used on the label.
  • Nutrient values on food labels are rounded and adjusted to be in compliance with government labeling regulations. Values presented here are generally mean values that have not been adjusted.
  • The product may have been reformulated with different ingredients or different proportions of ingredients.

**Food and Nutrition Board, National Academy of Sciences—National Research Council**

# Recommended Daily Dietary Allowances,[a] Revised 1980

**Designed for the Maintenance of Good Nutrition of Practically All Healthy People in the U.S.A.**

| | Age (years) | Weight (kg) (lb) | Height (cm) (in) | Protein (g) | Vitamin A (µg RE)[b] | Vitamin D (µg)[c] | Vitamin E (mg α TE)[d] | Vitamin C (mg) | Thiamin (mg) | Riboflavin (mg) | Niacin (mg NE)[e] | Vitamin B$_6$ (mg) | Folacin (µg)[f] | Vitamin B$_{12}$ (µg) | Calcium (mg) | Phosphorus (mg) | Magnesium (mg) | Iron (mg) | Zinc (mg) | Iodine (µg) |
|---|---|---|---|---|---|---|---|---|---|---|---|---|---|---|---|---|---|---|---|---|
| **Infants** | 0.0–0.5 | 6   13 | 60   24 | kg × 2.2 | 420 | 10 | 3 | 35 | 0.3 | 0.4 | 6 | 0.3 | 30 | 0.5[g] | 360 | 240 | 50 | 10 | 3 | 40 |
| | 0.5–1.0 | 9   20 | 71   28 | kg × 2.0 | 400 | 10 | 4 | 35 | 0.5 | 0.6 | 8 | 0.6 | 45 | 1.5 | 540 | 360 | 70 | 15 | 5 | 50 |
| **Children** | 1–3 | 13   29 | 90   35 | 23 | 400 | 10 | 5 | 45 | 0.7 | 0.8 | 9 | 0.9 | 100 | 2.0 | 800 | 800 | 150 | 15 | 10 | 70 |
| | 4–6 | 20   44 | 112   44 | 30 | 500 | 10 | 6 | 45 | 0.9 | 1.0 | 11 | 1.3 | 200 | 2.5 | 800 | 800 | 200 | 10 | 10 | 90 |
| | 7–10 | 28   62 | 132   52 | 34 | 700 | 10 | 7 | 45 | 1.2 | 1.4 | 16 | 1.6 | 300 | 3.0 | 800 | 800 | 250 | 10 | 10 | 120 |
| **Males** | 11–14 | 45   99 | 157   62 | 45 | 1000 | 10 | 8 | 50 | 1.4 | 1.6 | 18 | 1.8 | 400 | 3.0 | 1200 | 1200 | 350 | 18 | 15 | 150 |
| | 15–18 | 66   145 | 176   69 | 56 | 1000 | 10 | 10 | 60 | 1.4 | 1.7 | 18 | 2.0 | 400 | 3.0 | 1200 | 1200 | 400 | 18 | 15 | 150 |
| | 19–22 | 70   154 | 177   70 | 56 | 1000 | 7.5 | 10 | 60 | 1.5 | 1.7 | 19 | 2.2 | 400 | 3.0 | 800 | 800 | 350 | 10 | 15 | 150 |
| | 23–50 | 70   154 | 178   70 | 56 | 1000 | 5 | 10 | 60 | 1.4 | 1.6 | 18 | 2.2 | 400 | 3.0 | 800 | 800 | 350 | 10 | 15 | 150 |
| | 51+ | 70   154 | 178   70 | 56 | 1000 | 5 | 10 | 60 | 1.2 | 1.4 | 16 | 2.2 | 400 | 3.0 | 800 | 800 | 350 | 10 | 15 | 150 |
| **Females** | 11–14 | 46   101 | 157   62 | 46 | 800 | 10 | 8 | 50 | 1.1 | 1.3 | 15 | 1.8 | 400 | 3.0 | 1200 | 1200 | 300 | 18 | 15 | 150 |
| | 15–18 | 55   120 | 163   64 | 46 | 800 | 10 | 8 | 60 | 1.1 | 1.3 | 14 | 2.0 | 400 | 3.0 | 1200 | 1200 | 300 | 18 | 15 | 150 |
| | 19–22 | 55   120 | 163   64 | 44 | 800 | 7.5 | 8 | 60 | 1.1 | 1.3 | 14 | 2.0 | 400 | 3.0 | 800 | 800 | 300 | 18 | 15 | 150 |
| | 23–50 | 55   120 | 163   64 | 44 | 800 | 5 | 8 | 60 | 1.0 | 1.2 | 13 | 2.0 | 400 | 3.0 | 800 | 800 | 300 | 18 | 15 | 150 |
| | 51+ | 55   120 | 163   64 | 44 | 800 | 5 | 8 | 60 | 1.0 | 1.2 | 13 | 2.0 | 400 | 3.0 | 800 | 800 | 300 | 10 | 15 | 150 |
| *Pregnant* | | | | +30 | +200 | +5 | +2 | +20 | +0.4 | +0.3 | +2 | +0.6 | +400 | +1.0 | +400 | +400 | +150 | [h] | +5 | +25 |
| *Lactating* | | | | +20 | +400 | +5 | +3 | +40 | +0.5 | +0.5 | +5 | +0.5 | +100 | +1.0 | +400 | +400 | +150 | [h] | +10 | +50 |

[a] The allowances are intended to provide for individual variations among most normal persons as they live in the United States under usual environmental stresses. Diets should be based on a variety of common foods in order to provide other nutrients for which human requirements have been less well defined.

[b] Retinol equivalents. 1 Retinol equivalent = 1 µg retinol or 6 µg β carotene.

[c] As cholecalciferol. 10 µg cholecalciferol = 400 IU vitamin D.

[d] α-tocopherol equivalents. 1 mg d-α-tocopherol = 1 α TE

[e] 1 NE (niacin equivalent) is equal to 1 mg of niacin or 60 mg of dietary tryptophan.

[f] The folacin allowances refer to dietary sources as determined by *Lactobacillus casei* assay after treatment with enzymes (conjugases) to make polyglutamyl forms of the vitamin available to the test organism.

[g] The RDA for Vitamin B$_{12}$ in infants is based on average concentration of the vitamin in human milk. The allowances after weaning are based on energy intake (as recommended by the American Academy of Pediatrics) and consideration of other factors such as intestinal absorption.

[h] The increased requirement during pregnancy cannot be met by the iron content of habitual American diets nor by the existing iron stores of many women; therefore the use of 30–60 mg of supplemental iron is recommended. Iron needs during lactation are not substantially different from those of nonpregnant women, but continued supplementation of the mother for 2 to 3 months after parturition is advisable in order to replenish stores depleted by pregnancy.

Reproduced from National Academy of Sciences: Recommended Dietary Allowances, 9th rev. ed., Washington, D.C., 1980.

**Food and Nutrition Board, National Academy of Sciences—National Research Council**

# Estimated Safe and Adequate Daily Dietary Intakes of Selected Vitamins and Minerals[a]

| | Age (years) | Vitamin K (µg) | Biotin (µg) | Pantothenic Acid (mg) | Copper (mg) | Manganese (mg) | Fluoride (mg) | Chromium (mg) | Selenium (mg) | Molybdenum (mg) | Sodium (mg) | Potassium (mg) | Chloride (mg) |
|---|---|---|---|---|---|---|---|---|---|---|---|---|---|
| | | | | | | Vitamins | | Trace Elements[b] | | | Electrolytes | | |
| **Infants** | 0–0.5 | 12 | 35 | 2 | 0.5–0.7 | 0.5–0.7 | 0.1–0.5 | 0.01–0.04 | 0.01–0.04 | 0.03–0.06 | 115–350 | 350–925 | 275–700 |
| | 0.5–1 | 10–20 | 50 | 3 | 0.7–1.0 | 0.7–1.0 | 0.2–1.0 | 0.02–0.06 | 0.02–0.06 | 0.04–0.08 | 250–750 | 425–1275 | 400–1200 |
| **Children** | 1–3 | 15–30 | 65 | 3 | 1.0–1.5 | 1.0–1.5 | 0.5–1.5 | 0.02–0.08 | 0.02–0.08 | 0.05–0.1 | 325–975 | 550–1650 | 500–1500 |
| **and** | 4–6 | 20–40 | 85 | 3–4 | 1.5–2.0 | 1.5–2.0 | 1.0–2.5 | 0.03–0.12 | 0.03–0.12 | 0.06–0.15 | 450–1350 | 775–2325 | 700–2100 |
| **Adolescents** | 7–10 | 30–60 | 120 | 4–5 | 2.0–2.5 | 2.0–3.0 | 1.5–2.5 | 0.05–0.2 | 0.05–0.2 | 0.10–0.3 | 600–1800 | 1000–3000 | 925–2775 |
| | 11+ | 50–100 | 100–200 | 4–7 | 2.0–3.0 | 2.5–5.0 | 1.5–2.5 | 0.05–0.2 | 0.05–0.2 | 0.15–0.5 | 900–2700 | 1525–4575 | 1400–4200 |
| **Adults** | | 70–140 | 100–200 | 4–7 | 2.0–3.0 | 2.5–5.0 | 1.5–4.0 | 0.05–0.2 | 0.05–0.2 | 0.15–0.5 | 1100–3300 | 1875–5625 | 1700–5100 |

[a] Because there is less information on which to base allowances, these figures are not given in the main table of the RDA and are provided here in the form of ranges of recommended intakes.

[b] Since the toxic levels for many trace elements may be only several times usual intakes, the upper levels for the trace elements given in this table should not be habitually exceeded.

Reproduced from National Academy of Sciences: Recommended Dietary Allowances, 9th rev. ed., Washington, D.C., 1980.

**Food and Nutrition Board, National Academy of Sciences—National Research Council**

# Mean Heights and Weights and Recommended Energy Intake[a]

| | Age (years) | Weight (kg) | Weight (lb) | Height (cm) | Height (in) | Energy Needs (with range) (kcal) | (MJ) |
|---|---|---|---|---|---|---|---|
| Infants | 0.0–0.5 | 6 | 13 | 60 | 24 | kg × 115 (95–145) | kg × .48 |
| | 0.5–1.0 | 9 | 20 | 71 | 28 | kg × 105 (80–135) | kg × .44 |
| Children | 1–3 | 13 | 29 | 90 | 35 | 1300 (900–1800) | 5.5 |
| | 4–6 | 20 | 44 | 112 | 44 | 1700 (1300–2300) | 7.1 |
| | 7–10 | 28 | 62 | 132 | 52 | 2400 (1650–3300) | 10.1 |
| Males | 11–14 | 45 | 99 | 157 | 62 | 2700 (2000–3700) | 11.3 |
| | 15–18 | 66 | 145 | 176 | 69 | 2800 (2100–3900) | 11.8 |
| | 19–22 | 70 | 154 | 177 | 70 | 2900 (2500–3300) | 12.2 |
| | 23–50 | 70 | 154 | 178 | 70 | 2700 (2300–3100) | 11.3 |
| | 51–75 | 70 | 154 | 178 | 70 | 2400 (2000–2800) | 10.1 |
| | 76+ | 70 | 154 | 178 | 70 | 2050 (1650–2450) | 8.6 |
| Females | 11–14 | 46 | 101 | 157 | 62 | 2200 (1500–3000) | 9.2 |
| | 15–18 | 55 | 120 | 163 | 64 | 2100 (1200–3000) | 8.8 |
| | 19–22 | 55 | 120 | 163 | 64 | 2100 (1700–2500) | 8.8 |
| | 23–50 | 55 | 120 | 163 | 64 | 2000 (1600–2400) | 8.4 |
| | 51–75 | 55 | 120 | 163 | 64 | 1800 (1400–2200) | 7.6 |
| | 76+ | 55 | 120 | 163 | 64 | 1600 (1200–2000) | 6.7 |
| Pregnant | | | | | | +300 | |
| Lactating | | | | | | +500 | |

[a] The data in this table have been assembled from the observed median heights and weights of children together with desirable weights for adults for the mean heights of men (70 inches) and women (64 inches) between the ages of 18 and 34 years as surveyed in the U. S. population (HEW/NCHS data).

The energy allowances for the young adults are for men and women doing light work. The allowances for the two older groups represent mean energy needs over these age spans, allowing for a 2% decrease in basal (resting) metabolic rate per decade and a reduction in activity of 200 kcal/day for men and women between 51 and 75 years, 500 kcal for men over 75 years and 400 kcal for women over 75 years. The customary range of daily energy output is shown in parentheses for adults, and is based on a variation in energy needs of ±400 kcal at any one age, emphasizing the wide range of energy intakes appropriate for any group of people.

Energy allowances for children through age 18 are based on median energy intakes of children of these ages followed in longitudinal growth studies. The values in parentheses are 10th and 90th percentiles of energy intake, to indicate the range of energy consumption among children of these ages.

Reproduced from National Academy of Sciences: Recommended Dietary Allowances, 9th rev. ed., Washington, D.C., 1980.

# United States Recommended Daily Allowances (U.S. RDA)[a]

| | Unit | Infants (birth–12 mo.) | Children under 4 yrs. | Adults and children 4 or more yrs. | Pregnant or lactating women |
|---|---|---|---|---|---|
| Protein[b] | g | 25 | 28 | 65 | — |
| Protein[c] | g | 18 | 20 | 45 | — |
| Vitamin A | IU | 1500 | 2500 | 5000 | 8000 |
| Vitamin D | IU | 400 | 400 | 400 | 400 |
| Vitamin E | IU | 5 | 10 | 30 | 30 |
| Vitamin C | mg | 35 | 40 | 60 | 60 |
| Folic Acid | mg | 0.1 | 0.2 | 0.4 | 0.8 |
| Thiamin ($B_1$) | mg | 0.5 | 0.7 | 1.5 | 1.7 |
| Riboflavin ($B_2$) | mg | 0.6 | 0.8 | 1.7 | 2.0 |
| Niacin | mg | 8 | 9 | 20 | 20 |
| Vitamin $B_6$ | mg | 0.4 | 0.7 | 2.0 | 2.5 |
| Vitamin $B_{12}$ | mcg | 2 | 3 | 6 | 8 |
| Biotin | mg | 0.05 | 0.15 | 0.3 | 0.3 |
| Pantothenic Acid | mg | 3 | 5 | 10 | 10 |
| Calcium | g | 0.6 | 0.8 | 1.0 | 1.3 |
| Phosphorus | g | 0.5 | 0.8 | 1.0 | 1.3 |
| Iodine | mcg | 45 | 70 | 150 | 150 |
| Iron | mg | 15 | 10 | 18 | 18 |
| Magnesium | mg | 70 | 200 | 400 | 450 |
| Copper | mg | 0.6 | 1.0 | 2.0 | 2.0 |
| Zinc | mg | 5 | 8 | 15 | 15 |

[a] The U.S. RDAs are nutrient standards set by the Food and Drug Administration in 1973 using the Recommended Dietary Allowances of the National Academy of Sciences, National Research Council. The U.S. RDAs are established for four age–sex groups. Generally, the highest values in the RDA table were selected for use within each U.S. RDA category. The nutritional information on food labels is expressed as percent of the U.S. RDA.

[b] Protein efficiency ratio less than casein.
[c] Protein efficiency ratio greater than or equal to casein.

Reproduced from the FDA consumer memo, "Nutrition Labels and U.S. RDA." 81-2146, 1981.

# Abbreviations and Symbols

| | |
|---|---|
| am | American |
| amt | amount |
| ap | as purchased |
| arg | arginine |
| avg | average |
| bbq | barbeque |
| bio | biotin |
| blank space | insufficient information for nutrient values |
| Ca | calcium |
| caff | caffeine |
| cal | calorie(s) |
| calif | California |
| chln | choline |
| cho | carbohydrate |
| choc | chocolate |
| chol | cholesterol |
| cinn | cinnamon |
| ckd | cooked |
| Cl | chloride |
| cnd* | canned |
| combo | combination |
| conc | concentrate |
| cond | condensed |
| Cr | chromium |
| crm | cream |
| Cu | copper |
| cys | cystine |
| dfibr | dietary fiber |
| enr | enriched |
| Fe | iron |
| fl oz | fluid ounce |
| fol | folate |
| frzn* | frozen |
| g | gram(s) |
| his | histidine |
| $H_2O$ | water |
| hp | heaping |
| I | iodine |
| imit | imitation |
| inos | myo-inositol |
| inst | instant |

| | |
|---|---|
| iso | isoleucine |
| IU | international unit |
| jce | juice |
| jr | junior food |
| K | potassium |
| kcal | calorie(s) |
| lb | pound |
| leu | leucine |
| lys | lysine |
| marb | marbled |
| marg | margarine |
| mcg | microgram(s) |
| mct | medium-chain triglycerides |
| med | medium |
| met | methionine |
| mg | milligram(s) |
| Mg | magnesium |
| Mn | manganese |
| micro ckd | microwave cooked |
| Mo | molybdenum |
| Na | sodium |
| nfdm | nonfat dry milk solids |
| nia | niacin |
| orig | original |
| oz | ounce |
| P | phosphorus |
| pant | pantothenic acid |
| phe | phenylalanine |
| pkg | package |
| pkt | packet |
| prep | prepared |
| pro | protein |
| pufa | polyunsaturated fatty acids |
| rd | round |
| RE | retinol equivalents |
| recon | reconstituted |
| reg | regular |
| rib | riboflavin |
| rte | ready-to-eat |
| rts | ready-to-serve |
| sce | sauce |
| Se | selenium |
| sec | second |

* *Canned (cnd)* and *frozen (frzn)* refer to commercially canned and frozen foods.

(*continued*)

| | | | |
|---|---|---|---|
| sep | separable | vit B-1 | vitamin B-1 (thiamine) |
| sfa | saturated fatty acids | vit B-2 | vitamin B-2 (riboflavin) |
| std | standard | vit B-6 | vitamin B-6 (pyridoxine) |
| str | strained baby food | vit B-12 | vitamin B-12 (cobalamin) |
| sub | substitute | vit C | vitamin C (ascorbic acid) |
| t | teaspoon | vit D | vitamin D |
| T | tablespoon | vit E | vitamin E (tocopherol) |
| thi | thiamin | vit K | vitamin K |
| thr | threonine | vol | volume |
| tr | trace | whpd | whipped |
| try | tryptophan | wt | weight |
| tyr | tyrosine | w/ | with |
| unenr | unenriched | w/o | without |
| val | valine | Zn | zinc |
| van | vanilla | & | and |
| veg | vegetable | 0 | zero/none |
| vit A | vitamin A | / | per/or |

# Conversion Tables

**Volume Measures**

|  |  |  |  |
|---|---|---|---|
| 1 t = ⅓ T | = ⅙ fl oz | = 4.9 ml |
| 3 t = 1 T | = ½ fl oz | = 14.8 ml |
| 2 T = ⅛ cup | = 1 fl oz | = 29.6 ml |
| 4 T = ¼ cup | = 2 fl oz | = 59.1 ml |
| 5⅓ T = ⅓ cup | = 2⅔ fl oz | = 78.9 ml |
| 8 T = ½ cup | = 4 fl oz | = 118.3 ml |
| 10⅔ T = ⅔ cup | = 5⅓ fl oz | = 157.7 ml |
| 12 T = ¾ cup | = 6 fl oz | = 177.4 ml |
| 14 T = ⅞ cup | = 7 fl oz | = 207.0 ml |
| 16 T = 1 cup | = 8 fl oz | = 236.6 ml |

1 ml = .034 fl oz = 1 cc = .001 liter
1 liter = 34 fl oz = 1000 ml

1 pint = 2 cups = .473 liter = 473 ml
1 quart = 2 pt = .946 liter = 946 ml
1 gallon = 4 quarts = 3.785 liter = 3785 ml
1 liter = 1.057 quarts = 0.264 gallon = 1000 ml

**Weight Measures**

1 g = .035 oz = .001 kg = 1000 mg = 1,000,000 mcg
1 mg = .001 g = 1000 mcg
1 oz = 28.35 g (often rounded to 28 g)
1 lb = 16 oz = 453.59 g = .454 kg
1 kg = 2.21 lb = 1000 g
.1 kg = 100 g = 3.52 oz

**Heat Measures**

1 kilojoule = 0.239 kilocalories
1 kilocalorie = 4.184 kilojoules

The relationship between volume measures and weight measures is variable depending on the food. For example, note the weights of 1 cup of the following foods:

| Food | Weight of 1 level cup |
|---|---|
| almonds, chopped | 127 g |
| cottage cheese | 233 g |
| orange juice | 244 g |
| peas, green, canned | 172 g |
| pickle relish | 243 g |
| chicken noodle soup | 230 g |
| milk, whole | 244 g |
| mayonnaise | 221 g |
| shredded wheat | 35 g |
| puffed wheat | 12 g |
| peanut butter | 251 g |

The volume weight of water is a commonly used reference point for other food measures.

1 T water = 15 g = 15 cc
1 cup water = 237 g
1 fl oz water = 29.54 g (often rounded to 30 g)
1 cc water = 1 g = 1 ml
1 liter water = 1 kg = 1000 g
1 quart water = 946 g = .946 kg

# Nutrient Content of Foods

| | KCAL | H₂O (g) | FAT (g) | PUFA (g) | CHOL (mg) | **Vitamins** | | | | | **Minerals** | | | | |
|---|---|---|---|---|---|---|---|---|---|---|---|---|---|---|---|
| | | | | | | A (RE) | C (mg) | B-2 (mg) | B-6 (mg) | FOL (mcg) | Na (mg) | Ca (mg) | Mg (mg) | Zn (mg) | Mn (mg) |
| | WT (g) | PRO (g) | CHO (g) | SFA (g) | DFIB (g) | A (IU) | B-1 (mg) | NIA (mg) | B-12 (mcg) | PANT (mg) | K (mg) | P (mg) | Fe (mg) | Cu (mg) | |

# 1. BEVERAGES
## 1.1. ALCOHOLIC BEVERAGES
### 1.1.1. ALES, BEERS & MALT LIQUORS

| Item | KCAL / WT | H₂O / PRO | FAT / CHO | PUFA / SFA | CHOL / DFIB | A(RE) / A(IU) | C / B-1 | B-2 / NIA | B-6 / B-12 | FOL / PANT | Na / K | Ca / P | Mg / Fe | Zn / Cu | Mn |
|---|---|---|---|---|---|---|---|---|---|---|---|---|---|---|---|
| **ale, Blatz Cream** | 155 | | 0.0 | 0.0 | 0 | | | | | | 14 | 17 | | | |
| *12 fl oz* | 360 | 1.1 | 11.1 | 0.0 | | | | | | | 77 | | .02 | | |
| **beer** | 146 | 328.8 | 0.0 | 0.0 | 0 | 0 | 0 | .09 | .18 | 21 | 19 | 18 | 23 | .06 | .043 |
| *12 fl oz* | 356 | 0.9 | 13.2 | 0.0 | | 0 | .02 | 1.6 | .06 | .21 | 89 | 44 | .11 | .032 | |
| Anheuser-Busch | 153 | 327.0 | 0.0 | 0.0 | 0 | | 0 | .14 | .16 | | 9 | 16 | 22 | .01 | .040 |
| *12 fl oz* | 355 | 1.5 | 13.2 | 0.0 | 0.0 | | .01 | 1.4 | | .41 | 142 | 57 | .01 | .014 | |
| Black Label | 136 | | 0.0 | 0.0 | 0 | | | | | | 17 | 15 | | | |
| *12 fl oz* | 360 | 1.2 | 11.2 | 0.0 | | | | | | | 81 | | .02 | | |
| Blatz | 142 | | 0.0 | 0.0 | 0 | | | | | | 14 | 16 | | | |
| *12 fl oz* | 360 | 1.1 | 11.8 | 0.0 | | | | | | | 82 | | .02 | | |
| Coors Premium | 141 | | | | | | | .09 | | | 15 | 12 | | | |
| *12 fl oz* | 360 | 1.0 | 11.6 | | | | .04 | 1.4 | | | 83 | | | | |
| Heileman's Old Style | 146 | | 0.0 | 0.0 | 0 | | | | | | 10 | 17 | | | |
| *12 fl oz* | 360 | 1.1 | 11.5 | 0.0 | | | | | | | 81 | | .02 | | |
| Heileman's Special Export | 155 | | 0.0 | 0.0 | 0 | | | | | | 14 | 17 | | | |
| *12 fl oz* | 360 | 1.1 | 11.1 | 0.0 | | | | | | | 77 | | .02 | | |
| Heileman's Special Export Dark | 155 | | 0.0 | 0.0 | 0 | | | | | | 14 | 17 | | | |
| *12 fl oz* | 360 | 1.1 | 11.1 | 0.0 | | | | | | | 77 | | .02 | | |
| Herman Joseph's | 157 | | | | | | | | | | 14 | 9 | | | |
| *12 fl oz* | 360 | 1.3 | 13.5 | | | | | | | | 124 | | | | |
| Killian's | 172 | | | | | | | | | | 15 | 10 | | | |
| *12 fl oz* | 360 | 1.4 | 14.9 | | | | | | | | 116 | | | | |
| Rainier | 142 | | 0.0 | 0.0 | 0 | | | | | | 13 | 23 | | | |
| *12 fl oz* | 360 | 1.2 | 11.6 | 0.0 | | | | | | | 61 | | .02 | | |
| Schmidt | 142 | | 0.0 | 0.0 | 0 | | | | | | 15 | 29 | | | |
| *12 fl oz* | 360 | 1.1 | 11.8 | 0.0 | | | | | | | 61 | | .02 | | |
| Stroh's American Lager | 145 | 323.0 | 0.0 | 0.0 | 0 | 0 | 0 | .07 | .18 | | 25 | 22 | 25 | .03 | |
| *12 fl oz* | 355 | 9.9 | 13.4 | 0.0 | 0.0 | 0 | .01 | 1.8 | | .17 | 64 | 48 | .00 | .000 | |
| **beer, light** | 100 | 337.0 | 0.0 | 0.0 | 0 | 0 | 0 | .11 | .12 | 15 | 10 | 18 | 17 | .11 | .057 |
| *12 fl oz* | 354 | 0.7 | 4.8 | 0.0 | | 0 | .03 | 1.4 | .02 | .13 | 64 | 43 | .12 | .085 | |
| Anheuser-Busch | 117 | 334.0 | 0.0 | 0.0 | 0 | | 0 | .10 | .16 | | 9 | 15 | 23 | .01 | .040 |
| *12 fl oz* | 355 | 1.1 | 9.2 | 0.0 | 0.0 | | .00 | 0.1 | | .29 | 128 | 46 | .01 | .014 | |
| Blatz | 96 | | 0.0 | 0.0 | 0 | | | | | | 15 | 17 | | | |
| *12 fl oz* | 360 | 0.9 | 3.2 | 0.0 | | | | | | | 61 | | .02 | | |
| Coors | 103 | | | | | | | .09 | | | 18 | 13 | | | |
| *12 fl oz* | 360 | 0.7 | 4.9 | | | | .04 | 0.1 | | | 67 | | | | |
| Heileman's Old Style | 99 | | 0.0 | 0.0 | 0 | | | | | | 7 | 17 | | | |
| *12 fl oz* | 360 | 0.9 | 6.4 | 0.0 | | | | | | | 54 | | .02 | | |
| Heileman's Special Export | 115 | | 0.0 | 0.0 | 0 | | | | | | 7 | 17 | | | |
| *12 fl oz* | 360 | 1.0 | 7.5 | 0.0 | | | | | | | 68 | | .02 | | |
| **beer, LA (low alcohol)** | | | | | | | | | | | | | | | |
| Anheuser-Busch | 111 | 330.0 | 0.0 | 0.0 | 0 | | 0 | .09 | | | 9 | 18 | 18 | .00 | .030 |
| *12 fl oz* | 355 | 0.7 | 15.6 | 0.0 | 0.0 | | .04 | 0.2 | .00 | .00 | 174 | 39 | .01 | .014 | |
| Blatz | 73 | | 0.0 | 0.0 | 0 | | | | | | 8 | 16 | | | |
| *12 fl oz* | 360 | 0.9 | 7.0 | 0.0 | | | | | | | 45 | | .02 | | |
| Heileman's Old Style | 73 | | 0.0 | 0.0 | 0 | | | | | | 8 | 16 | | | |
| *12 fl oz* | 360 | 0.7 | 7.0 | 0.0 | | | | | | | 45 | | .02 | | |
| **malt liquor** | | | | | | | | | | | | | | | |
| Blatz Old Fashioned Private Stock | 149 | | 0.0 | 0.0 | 0 | | | | | | 14 | 17 | | | |
| *12 fl oz* | 360 | 1.1 | 11.5 | 0.0 | | | | | | | 80 | | .02 | | |
| Colt 45 | 156 | | 0.0 | 0.0 | 0 | | | | | | 14 | 17 | | | |
| *12 fl oz* | 360 | 1.2 | 11.0 | 0.0 | | | | | | | 93 | | .02 | | |

| | KCAL / WT (g) | $H_2O$ / PRO (g) | FAT / CHO (g) | PUFA / SFA (g) | CHOL / DFIB (mg / g) | A (RE) / A (IU) | C / B-1 (mg) | B-2 / NIA (mg) | B-6 / B-12 (mg / mcg) | FOL / PANT (mcg / mg) | Na / K (mg) | Ca / P (mg) | Mg / Fe (mg) | Zn / Cu (mg) | Mn (mg) |
|---|---|---|---|---|---|---|---|---|---|---|---|---|---|---|---|

### 1.1.2. COCKTAILS & COCKTAIL MIXES

**bloody mary (tomato jce, vodka & lemon jce)—5 fl oz cocktail**

| | KCAL/WT | $H_2O$/PRO | FAT/CHO | PUFA/SFA | CHOL/DFIB | A(RE)/A(IU) | C/B-1 | B-2/NIA | B-6/B-12 | FOL/PANT | Na/K | Ca/P | Mg/Fe | Zn/Cu | Mn |
|---|---|---|---|---|---|---|---|---|---|---|---|---|---|---|---|
| bloody mary (tomato jce, vodka & lemon jce) | 116 | 127.3 | 0.1 | 0.0 | 0 | 51 | 20 | .03 | .11 | 20 | 332 | 10 | 11 | .14 | .073 |
| 5 fl oz cocktail | 148 | 0.8 | 4.8 | 0.0 | | 508 | .05 | 0.6 | .00 | .24 | 216 | 21 | .55 | .102 | |
| bourbon & soda | 105 | 100.8 | 0.0 | 0.0 | 0 | 0 | 0 | .00 | .00 | 0 | 16 | 4 | 1 | .09 | |
| 4 fl oz cocktail | 116 | 0.0 | 0.0 | 0.0 | | 0 | .00 | 0.0 | .00 | .00 | 2 | 2 | | | |
| daiquiri cnd | | 154.4 | | | | | | | | | 83 | 1 | | | |
| 6.8 fl oz can | 207 | | | | | | | | | | 22 | | .02 | | |
| rum, lime jce & sugar | 111 | 41.9 | 0.0 | 0.0 | 0 | 0 | 1 | .00 | .00 | 1 | 3 | 2 | 1 | .04 | |
| 2 fl oz cocktail | 60 | 0.0 | 4.1 | 0.0 | | 2 | .01 | 0.0 | .00 | .01 | 13 | 4 | .09 | .026 | |
| gin & tonic (tonic water, gin & lime jce) | 171 | 193.0 | 0.0 | 0.0 | 0 | 0 | 1 | .00 | .01 | 1 | 10 | 4 | 2 | | |
| 7.5 fl oz cocktail | 225 | 0.0 | 15.8 | 0.0 | | 2 | .01 | 0.0 | .00 | .01 | 12 | 2 | | | |
| manhattan (whiskey & vermouth) | 128 | 37.7 | 0.0 | 0.0 | 0 | | 0 | .00 | .00 | 0 | 2 | 1 | 1 | .03 | .024 |
| 2 fl oz cocktail | 57 | 0.0 | 1.8 | 0.0 | | | .01 | 0.1 | 0 | .01 | 15 | 4 | .05 | .016 | |
| martini (gin & vermouth) | 156 | 47.3 | 0.0 | 0.0 | 0 | | 0 | .00 | .00 | 0 | 2 | 1 | 1 | .01 | |
| 2.5 fl oz cocktail | 70 | 0.0 | 0.2 | 0.0 | | | .00 | 0.0 | .00 | .00 | 13 | 2 | .06 | .004 | |
| pina colada cnd | 525 | 121.8 | 16.9 | 0.3 | | | | | | | 158 | 1 | | | |
| 6.8 fl oz can | 222 | 1.3 | 61.3 | 14.6 | | | | | | | 184 | | .07 | | |
| pineapple jce, rum, sugar & coconut cream | 262 | 91.7 | 2.6 | 0.5 | 0 | 0 | 7 | .02 | | 14 | 9 | 11 | | .19 | |
| 4.5 fl oz cocktail | 141 | 0.6 | 39.9 | 1.2 | | 3 | .04 | 0.2 | .00 | | 100 | 10 | .31 | .116 | |
| screwdriver (orange jce & vodka) | 174 | 178.6 | 0.1 | 0.0 | 0 | 13 | 67 | .03 | .08 | 75 | 2 | 16 | 17 | .09 | .023 |
| 7 fl oz cocktail | 213 | 1.2 | 18.4 | 0.0 | | 133 | .14 | 0.3 | .00 | .27 | 325 | 29 | .17 | .079 | |
| tequila sunrise cnd | | 166.2 | | | | | | | | | 119 | 1 | | | |
| 6.8 fl oz can | 211 | | | | | | | | | | 22 | | .04 | | |
| orange jce, tequila, lime jce & grenadine | 189 | 137.2 | 0.2 | 0.0 | 0 | 17 | 33 | .03 | .09 | | 7 | 10 | 12 | .11 | |
| 5.5 fl oz cocktail | 172 | 0.6 | 14.7 | 0.0 | | 166 | .07 | 0.3 | .00 | | 178 | 17 | .47 | .072 | |
| tom collins (club soda, gin, lemon jce & sugar) | 121 | 202.9 | 0.0 | 0.0 | 0 | 0 | 4 | .00 | .01 | 2 | 39 | 10 | 3 | .17 | |
| 7.5 fl oz cocktail | 222 | 0.1 | 3.0 | 0.0 | | 2 | .01 | 0.0 | .00 | .01 | 18 | 1 | | | |
| whiskey sour cnd | | 160.7 | | | | | | | | | 91 | 1 | | | |
| 6.8 fl oz cocktail | 209 | | | | | | | | | | 22 | | .02 | | |
| lemon jce, whiskey & sugar | 123 | 69.3 | 0.1 | 0.0 | 0 | 1 | 11 | .01 | .02 | 5 | 10 | 5 | 4 | .05 | .015 |
| 3 fl oz cocktail | 90 | 0.2 | 5.0 | 0.0 | | 7 | .19 | 0.1 | .00 | .04 | 48 | 6 | .07 | .027 | |
| prep from bottled mix | 158 | 76.9 | 0.0 | 0.0 | 0 | 1 | 2 | .01 | .00 | 0 | 66 | 1 | 1 | .06 | .006 |
| 2 fl oz mix & 1.5 fl oz whiskey | 106 | 0.0 | 13.8 | 0.0 | 0.1 | 14 | .01 | 0.0 | .00 | .01 | 19 | 6 | .08 | .010 | |
| prep from powdered mix—17 g pkt w/ | 169 | 71.2 | 0.0 | 0.0 | 0 | 1 | 1 | .00 | .00 | 0 | 48 | 47 | 4 | .05 | .006 |
| 1.5 fl oz water & 1.5 fl oz whiskey | 103 | 0.1 | 16.4 | 0.0 | 0.1 | 5 | .00 | 0.0 | .00 | .01 | 4 | 5 | .08 | .034 | |
| whiskey sour mix bottled[a] | 55 | 50.5 | 0.0 | 0.0 | 0 | 1 | 2 | .01 | .00 | 0 | 66 | 1 | | .05 | .000 |
| 2 fl oz cocktail | 65 | 0.0 | 13.8 | 0.0 | 0.1 | 14 | .01 | 0.0 | .00 | .01 | 18 | 4 | .07 | .000 | |
| powder[a] | 64 | 0.1 | 0.0 | 0.0 | 0 | 1 | 1 | .00 | .00 | 0 | 46 | 45 | 3 | .02 | .000 |
| 1 pkt | 17 | 0.1 | 16.2 | 0.0 | 0.1 | 5 | .00 | 0.0 | | .01 | 3 | 2 | .07 | .022 | |

### 1.1.3. DISTILLED SPIRITS

| | KCAL/WT | $H_2O$/PRO | FAT/CHO | PUFA/SFA | CHOL/DFIB | A(RE)/A(IU) | C/B-1 | B-2/NIA | B-6/B-12 | FOL/PANT | Na/K | Ca/P | Mg/Fe | Zn/Cu | Mn |
|---|---|---|---|---|---|---|---|---|---|---|---|---|---|---|---|
| gin, 90 proof | 110 | 26.1 | 0.0 | 0.0 | 0 | 0 | 0 | .00 | .00 | 0 | 1 | 0 | 0 | .00 | |
| 1.5 fl oz jigger | 42 | 0.0 | 0.0 | 0.0 | | 0 | .00 | 0.0 | .00 | .00 | 0 | 0 | .00 | .002 | |
| gin/rum/vodka/whiskey, 94 proof | 116 | 25.3 | 0.0 | 0.0 | 0 | 0 | 0 | .00 | .00 | 0 | 0 | 0 | 0 | .02 | .008 |
| 1.5 fl oz jigger | 42 | 0.0 | 0.0 | 0.0 | | 0 | .00 | 0.0 | .00 | .00 | 1 | 2 | .02 | .009 | |
| gin/rum/vodka/whiskey, 100 proof | 124 | 24.2 | 0.0 | 0.0 | 0 | 0 | 0 | .00 | .00 | 0 | 0 | 0 | 0 | .02 | .008 |
| 1.5 fl oz jigger | 42 | 0.0 | 0.0 | 0.0 | | 0 | .00 | 0.0 | .00 | .00 | 1 | 2 | .02 | .009 | |

[a] Contains no alcohol.

| | KCAL | H₂O (g) | FAT (g) | PUFA (g) | CHOL (mg) | A (RE) | C (mg) | B-2 (mg) | B-6 (mg) | FOL (mcg) | Na (mg) | Ca (mg) | Mg (mg) | Zn (mg) | Mn (mg) |
|---|---|---|---|---|---|---|---|---|---|---|---|---|---|---|---|
| | WT (g) | PRO (g) | CHO (g) | SFA (g) | DFIB (g) | A (IU) | B-1 (mg) | NIA (mg) | B-12 (mcg) | PANT (mg) | K (mg) | P (mg) | Fe (mg) | Cu (mg) | |
| rum, 80 proof | 97 | 28.0 | 0.0 | 0.0 | 0 | 0 | 0 | .00 | .00 | 0 | 0 | 0 | 0 | .03 | |
| *1.5 fl oz jigger* | 42 | 0.0 | 0.0 | 0.0 | | 0 | .00 | 0.0 | .00 | .00 | 1 | 2 | .05 | .021 | |
| vodka, 80 proof | 97 | 28.0 | 0.0 | 0.0 | 0 | 0 | 0 | .00 | .00 | 0 | 0 | 0 | 0 | .00 | .000 |
| *1.5 fl oz jigger* | 42 | 0.0 | 0.0 | 0.0 | | 0 | .00 | 0.0 | .00 | ,.00 | 0 | 2 | .00 | .004 | |
| whiskey, 86 proof | 105 | 26.8 | 0.0 | 0.0 | 0 | 0 | 0 | .00 | .00 | 0 | 0 | 0 | 0 | .02 | .006 |
| *1.5 fl oz jigger* | 42 | 0.0 | 0.1 | 0.0 | | 0 | .00 | 0.0 | .00 | .00 | 1 | 2 | .01 | .009 | |

## 1.1.4. LIQUEURS

| | KCAL | H₂O (g) | FAT (g) | PUFA (g) | CHOL (mg) | A (RE) | C (mg) | B-2 (mg) | B-6 (mg) | FOL (mcg) | Na (mg) | Ca (mg) | Mg (mg) | Zn (mg) | Mn (mg) |
|---|---|---|---|---|---|---|---|---|---|---|---|---|---|---|---|
| | WT (g) | PRO (g) | CHO (g) | SFA (g) | DFIB (g) | A (IU) | B-1 (mg) | NIA (mg) | B-12 (mcg) | PANT (mg) | K (mg) | P (mg) | Fe (mg) | Cu (mg) | |
| coffee, 53 proof | 174 | 16.1 | 0.1 | 0.1 | 0 | 0 | 0 | .01 | | 0 | 4 | 1 | 1 | .01 | |
| *1.5 fl oz* | 52 | 0.0 | 24.4 | 0.1 | | 0 | .00 | 0.1 | | .00 | 15 | 3 | .03 | .021 | |
| coffee, 63 proof | 160 | 21.5 | 0.1 | 0.1 | 0 | 0 | 0 | .01 | | 0 | 4 | 1 | 1 | .01 | |
| *1.5 fl oz* | 52 | 0.0 | 16.7 | 0.1 | | 0 | .00 | 0.1 | | .00 | 15 | 3 | .03 | .021 | |
| coffee w/ cream, 34 proof | 154 | 21.9 | 7.4 | 0.3 | | | 0 | .03 | | 0 | 43 | 7 | 1 | .08 | |
| *1.5 fl oz* | 47 | 1.3 | 9.8 | 4.5 | | | .00 | 0.0 | | .04 | 15 | 23 | .06 | .019 | |
| creme de menthe | 186 | 14.2 | 0.1 | 0.1 | 0 | 0 | | .00 | .00 | 0 | 3 | 0 | 0 | | .020 |
| *1.5 fl oz* | 50 | 0.0 | 20.8 | 0.0 | | 0 | .00 | 0.0 | .00 | .00 | 0 | 0 | .04 | .040 | |

## 1.1.5. WINES & WINE BEVERAGES

| | KCAL | H₂O (g) | FAT (g) | PUFA (g) | CHOL (mg) | A (RE) | C (mg) | B-2 (mg) | B-6 (mg) | FOL (mcg) | Na (mg) | Ca (mg) | Mg (mg) | Zn (mg) | Mn (mg) |
|---|---|---|---|---|---|---|---|---|---|---|---|---|---|---|---|
| | WT (g) | PRO (g) | CHO (g) | SFA (g) | DFIB (g) | A (IU) | B-1 (mg) | NIA (mg) | B-12 (mcg) | PANT (mg) | K (mg) | P (mg) | Fe (mg) | Cu (mg) | |
| sparkling cooler, citrus, La Croix | 215 | | 0.0 | 0.0 | 0 | | | | | | 10 | | | | |
| *12 fl oz* | 360 | 0.5 | 30.0 | 0.0 | | | | | | | | | .07 | | |
| sparkling cooler, strawberry, La Croix | 215 | | 0.0 | 0.0 | 0 | | | | | | 10 | | | | |
| *12 fl oz* | 360 | 0.5 | 30.0 | 0.0 | | | | | | | | | .07 | | |
| wine, dessert, dry | 74 | 42.7 | 0.0 | 0.0 | 0 | | 0 | .01 | .00 | 0 | 5 | 5 | 5 | .04 | .070 |
| *2 fl oz* | 59 | 0.1 | 2.4 | 0.0 | | | .01 | 0.1 | .00 | .02 | 54 | 6 | .14 | .027 | |
| wine, dessert, sweet | 90 | 42.7 | 0.0 | 0.0 | 0 | | 0 | .01 | .00 | 0 | 5 | 5 | 5 | .04 | .070 |
| *2 fl oz* | 59 | 0.1 | 7.0 | 0.0 | | | .01 | 0.1 | .00 | .02 | 54 | 6 | .14 | .027 | |
| wine, table, all types | 72 | 91.6 | 0.0 | 0.0 | 0 | 0 | 0 | .02 | .03 | 1 | 8 | 9 | 10 | .07 | .149 |
| *3.5 fl oz* | 103 | 0.2 | 1.4 | 0.0 | | 0 | .00 | 0.1 | .01 | .03 | 91 | 14 | .42 | .014 | |
| wine, table, red | 74 | 91.1 | 0.0 | 0.0 | 0 | 0 | 0 | .03 | .04 | 2 | 6 | 8 | 13 | .10 | .615 |
| *3.5 fl oz* | 103 | 0.2 | 1.8 | 0.0 | | 0 | .01 | 0.1 | .01 | .04 | 115 | 14 | .44 | .021 | |
| wine, table, rose | 73 | 91.6 | 0.0 | 0.0 | 0 | | 0 | .02 | .03 | 1 | 5 | 9 | 10 | .06 | .108 |
| *3.5 fl oz* | 103 | 0.2 | 1.5 | 0.0 | | | .00 | 0.1 | .01 | .03 | 102 | 15 | .39 | .054 | |
| wine, table, white | 70 | 92.3 | 0.0 | 0.0 | 0 | 0 | 0 | .01 | .01 | 0 | 5 | 9 | 11 | .07 | .473 |
| *3.5 fl oz* | 103 | 0.1 | 0.8 | 0.0 | | 0 | .00 | 0.1 | .00 | .02 | 82 | 14 | .33 | .022 | |

## 1.2. CARBONATED BEVERAGES

| | KCAL | H₂O (g) | FAT (g) | PUFA (g) | CHOL (mg) | A (RE) | C (mg) | B-2 (mg) | B-6 (mg) | FOL (mcg) | Na (mg) | Ca (mg) | Mg (mg) | Zn (mg) | Mn (mg) |
|---|---|---|---|---|---|---|---|---|---|---|---|---|---|---|---|
| | WT (g) | PRO (g) | CHO (g) | SFA (g) | DFIB (g) | A (IU) | B-1 (mg) | NIA (mg) | B-12 (mcg) | PANT (mg) | K (mg) | P (mg) | Fe (mg) | Cu (mg) | |
| apple Slice | 196 | 308.4 | 0.0 | 0.0 | | | | | | | 5 | 0 | | | |
| *12 fl oz* | 360 | 0.0 | 48.0 | 0.0 | 0.0 | | | | | | 67 | 0 | .00 | | |
| cherry coke, Coca-Cola | 154 | | 0.0 | | | | | | | | 14 | | | | |
| *12 fl oz* | 370 | 0.0 | 40.0 | | | | | | | | 0 | 54 | | | |
| cherry cola Slice | 164 | 313.2 | 0.0 | 0.0 | | | | | | | 5 | 0 | | | |
| *12 fl oz* | 360 | 0.0 | 43.2 | 0.0 | 0.0 | | | | | | 67 | 0 | .00 | | |
| cherry RC | 171 | | 0.0 | | | | | | | | 1 | | | | |
| *12 fl oz* | 360 | 0.0 | 42.8 | | | | | | | | 12 | 47 | | | |
| Coca-Cola | 155 | | 0.0 | | | | | | | | 6 | | | | |
| *12 fl oz* | 370 | 0.0 | 40.0 | | | | | | | | 0 | 54 | | | |
| Coca-Cola Classic | 144 | | 0.0 | | | | | | | | 14 | | | | |
| *12 fl oz* | 369 | 0.0 | 38.0 | | | | | | | | 0 | 60 | | | |
| cola | 151 | 330.8 | 0.1 | | 0 | 0 | 0 | .00 | .00 | 0 | 14 | 9 | 3 | .05 | .130 |
| *12 fl oz* | 370 | 0.1 | 38.5 | | | 0 | .00 | 0.0 | .00 | .00 | 4 | 46 | .13 | .041 | |
| cola, RC | 171 | | 0.0 | | | | | | | | 1 | | | | |
| *12 fl oz* | 360 | 0.0 | 42.8 | | | | | | | | 12 | 47 | | | |
| cola, RC 100, caffeine-free | 171 | | 0.0 | | | | | | | | 1 | | | | |
| *12 fl oz* | 360 | 0.0 | 42.8 | | | | | | | | 12 | 47 | | | |
| cream soda | 191 | 321.5 | 0.0 | 0.0 | 0 | 0 | 0 | .00 | .00 | 0 | 43 | 19 | 3 | .24 | |
| *12 fl oz* | 371 | 0.0 | 49.3 | 0.0 | | 0 | .00 | 0.0 | .00 | .00 | 4 | 0 | .19 | .030 | |
| Dr. Nehi | 163 | | 0.0 | | | | | | | | 26 | | | | |
| *12 fl oz* | 360 | 0.0 | 40.8 | | | | | | | | 1 | 46 | | | |

| | KCAL / WT (g) | H₂O (g) / PRO (g) | FAT (g) / CHO (g) | PUFA (g) / SFA (g) | CHOL (mg) / DFIB (g) | A (RE) / A (IU) | C (mg) / B-1 (mg) | B-2 (mg) / NIA (mg) | B-6 (mg) / B-12 (mcg) | FOL (mcg) / PANT (mg) | Na (mg) / K (mg) | Ca (mg) / P (mg) | Mg (mg) / Fe (mg) | Zn (mg) / Cu (mg) | Mn (mg) |
|---|---|---|---|---|---|---|---|---|---|---|---|---|---|---|---|
| fruit punch, Nehi | 200 | | 0.0 | | | | | | | | 16 | | | | |
| 12 fl oz | 360 | 0.0 | 49.9 | | | | | | | | 0 | 0 | | | |
| ginger ale | 124 | 333.9 | 0.0 | 0.0 | 0 | 0 | 0 | .00 | .00 | 0 | 25 | 12 | 3 | .18 | |
| 12 fl oz | 366 | 0.1 | 31.9 | 0.0 | | 0 | .00 | 0.0 | .00 | .00 | 5 | 1 | .66 | .066 | |
| ginger ale, Fanta | 126 | | 0.0 | | | | | | | | 28 | | | | |
| 12 fl oz | 367 | 0.0 | 32.0 | | | | | | | | 0 | 0 | | | |
| ginger ale, Nehi | 152 | | 0.0 | | | | | | | | 1 | | | | |
| 12 fl oz | 360 | 0.0 | 37.9 | | | | | | | | 0 | 0 | | | |
| grape, Fanta | 172 | | 0.0 | | | | | | | | 14 | | | | |
| 12 fl oz | 372 | 0.0 | 44.0 | | | | | | | | 0 | 0 | | | |
| grape, Nehi | 192 | | 0.0 | | | | | | | | 15 | | | | |
| 12 fl oz | 360 | 0.0 | 47.9 | | | | | | | | 0 | 0[a] | | | |
| grape soda | 161 | 330.3 | 0.0 | 0.0 | 0 | 0 | 0 | .00 | .00 | 0 | 57 | 12 | 4 | .26 | |
| 12 fl oz | 372 | 0.0 | 41.7 | 0.0 | | 0 | .00 | | .00 | .00 | 3 | 0 | .31 | .082 | |
| Kick | 195 | | 0.0 | | | | | | | | 49 | | | | |
| 12 fl oz | 360 | 0.0 | 48.7 | | | | | | | | 0 | 0 | | | |
| lemon-lime soda | 149 | 329.4 | 0.0 | 0.0 | 0 | 0 | 0 | .00 | .00 | 0 | 41 | 9 | 2 | .18 | .048 |
| 12 fl oz | 368 | 0.0 | 38.4 | 0.0 | | 0 | .00 | 0.1 | .00 | .00 | 4 | 1 | .25 | .044 | |
| mandarin orange Slice | 193 | 307.2 | 0.0 | 0.0 | | | | | | | 22 | 0 | | | |
| 12 fl oz | 360 | 0.0 | 50.4 | 0.0 | 0.0 | | | | | | 85 | 0 | .00 | | |
| Mello Yello | 174 | | 0.0 | | | | 0 | | | | 24 | | | | |
| 12 fl oz | 372 | 0.0 | 44.0 | | | | | | | | 8 | 0 | | | |
| Mr. Pibb | 142 | | 0.0 | | | | | | | | 22 | | | | |
| 12 fl oz | 369 | 0.0 | 38.0 | | | | | | | | 0 | 42 | | | |
| Mountain Dew | 179 | 326.4 | 0.0 | 0.0 | | | | | | | 31 | | | | |
| 12 fl oz | 360 | 0.0 | 44.4 | 0.0 | 0.0 | | | | | | 10 | 0 | | | |
| orange, Fanta | 176 | | 0.0 | | | | | | | | 14 | | | | |
| 12 fl oz | 372 | 0.0 | 46.0 | | | | | | | | 0 | 0 | | | |
| orange, Nehi | 209 | | 0.0 | | | | | | | | 22 | | | | |
| 12 fl oz | 360 | 0.0 | 52.1 | | | | | | | | 0 | 60 | | | |
| orange soda | 177 | 325.9 | 0.0 | 0.0 | 0 | 0 | 0 | .00 | .00 | 0 | 46 | 19 | 4 | .38 | |
| 12 fl oz | 372 | 0.0 | 45.8 | 0.0 | | 0 | .00 | | .00 | .00 | 9 | 4 | .23 | .056 | |
| peach, Nehi | 203 | | 0.0 | | | | | | | | 33 | | | | |
| 12 fl oz | 360 | 0.0 | 50.8 | | | | | | | | 0 | 0 | | | |
| pepper type soda | 151 | 328.9 | 0.4 | | 0 | 0 | 0 | .00 | .00 | 0 | 38 | 12 | 1 | .15 | |
| 12 fl oz | 368 | 0.0 | 38.2 | | | 0 | .00 | 0.0 | .00 | .00 | 2 | 41 | .14 | .022 | |
| Pepsi Cola | 160 | 328.8 | 0.0 | 0.0 | | | | | | | 2 | 0 | | | |
| 12 fl oz | 360 | 0.0 | 39.6 | 0.0 | 0.0 | | | | | | | 55 | .00 | | |
| Pepsi Free | 160 | 328.8 | 0.0 | 0.0 | | | | | | | 2 | 0 | | | |
| 12 fl oz | 360 | 0.0 | 39.6 | 0.0 | 0.0 | | | | | | 13 | 55 | .00 | | |
| quinine water, Nehi | 142 | | 0.0 | | | | | | | | 0 | | | | |
| 12 fl oz | 360 | 0.0 | 35.5 | | | | | | | | 0 | 0 | | | |
| root beer | 152 | 330.4 | 0.0 | 0.0 | 0 | 0 | 0 | .00 | .00 | 0 | 49 | 19 | 4 | .26 | |
| 12 fl oz | 370 | 0.1 | 39.2 | 0.0 | | 0 | .00 | 0.0 | .00 | .00 | 3 | 2 | .18 | .026 | |
| root beer, Fanta | 156 | | 0.0 | | | | | | | | 20 | | | | |
| 12 fl oz | 370 | 0.0 | 40.0 | | | | | | | | 0 | 0 | | | |
| root beer, Nehi | 193 | | 0.0 | | | | | | | | 18 | | | | |
| 12 fl oz | 360 | 0.0 | 48.0 | | | | | | | | 0 | 0 | | | |
| root beer, Ramblin' | 176 | | 0.0 | | | | | | | | 20 | | | | |
| 12 fl oz | 373 | 0.0 | 46.0 | | | | | | | | 0 | 0 | | | |
| Slice | 152 | 328.8 | 0.0 | 0.0 | | | | | | | 11 | 0 | | | |
| 12 fl oz | 360 | 0.0 | 39.6 | 0.0 | 0.0 | | | | | | 100 | 0 | .00 | | |
| Sprite | 142 | | 0.0 | | | | | | | | 46 | | | | |
| 12 fl oz | 368 | 0.0 | 36.0 | | | | | | | | 0 | 0 | | | |
| strawberry, Nehi | 192 | | 0.0 | | | | | | | | 14[b] | | | | |
| 12 fl oz | 360 | 0.0 | 47.9 | | | | | | | | 0 | 0 | | | |
| tonic water/quinine water | 125 | 333.6 | 0.0 | 0.0 | 0 | 0 | 0 | .00 | .00 | 0 | 15 | 5 | 1 | | |
| 12 fl oz | 366 | 0.0 | 32.2 | 0.0 | | 0 | .00 | 0.0 | .00 | .00 | 1 | 0 | | | |
| Upper 10 | 169 | | 0.0 | | | | | | | | 40 | | | | |
| 12 fl oz | 360 | 0.0 | 42.2 | | | | | | | | 0 | 0 | | | |
| Upper 10, salt-free | 173 | | 0.0 | | | | | | | | 0 | | | | |
| 12 fl oz | 360 | 0.0 | 43.2 | | | | | | | | 25 | 0 | | | |

[a] For cnd soda; if in bottles P is 73 mg.

[b] For cnd soda; if in bottles Na is 0 mg & P is 94 mg.

| | KCAL / WT (g) | H₂O (g) / PRO (g) | FAT (g) / CHO (g) | PUFA (g) / SFA (g) | CHOL (mg) / DFIB (g) | A (RE) / A (IU) | C (mg) / B-1 (mg) | B-2 (mg) / NIA (mg) | B-6 (mg) / B-12 (mcg) | FOL (mcg) / PANT (mg) | Na (mg) / K (mg) | Ca (mg) / P (mg) | Mg (mg) / Fe (mg) | Zn (mg) / Cu (mg) | Mn (mg) |
|---|---|---|---|---|---|---|---|---|---|---|---|---|---|---|---|

## 1.3. CARBONATED BEVERAGES, LOW CALORIE

| Item | KCAL / WT(g) | H₂O / PRO | FAT / CHO | PUFA / SFA | CHOL / DFIB | A(RE) / A(IU) | C / B-1 | B-2 / NIA | B-6 / B-12 | FOL / PANT | Na / K | Ca / P | Mg / Fe | Zn / Cu | Mn |
|---|---|---|---|---|---|---|---|---|---|---|---|---|---|---|---|
| club soda | 0 | 354.8 | 0.0 | 0.0 | 0 | 0 | 0 | .00 | .00 | 0 | 75 | 17 | 4 | | .36 |
| *12 fl oz* | 355 | 0.0 | 0.0 | 0.0 | | 0 | .00 | 0.0 | .00 | .00 | 6 | 0 | | | |
| diet apple Slice[a] | 20 | 349.2 | 0.0 | 0.0 | | | | | | | 5 | 0 | | | |
| *12 fl oz* | 360 | 0.0 | 4.8 | 0.0 | 0.0 | | | | | | 67 | 0 | .00 | | |
| diet cherry coke, Coca-Cola | 1 | | 0.0 | | | | | | | | 8 | | | | |
| *12 fl oz* | 354 | 0.0 | 0.3 | | | | | | | | 19 | 28 | | | |
| diet cherry cola Slice[b] | 20 | 349.2 | 0.0 | 0.0 | | | | | | | 5 | 0 | | | |
| *12 fl oz* | 360 | 0.0 | 4.8 | 0.0 | 0.0 | | | | | | 67 | 0 | .00 | | |
| diet cherry RC | 2 | | 0.0 | | | | | | | | 1 | | | | |
| *12 fl oz* | 360 | 0.0 | 0.4 | | | | | | | | 60 | 41 | | | |
| diet coke, Coca-Cola | 1 | | 0.0 | | | | | | | | 8 | | | | |
| *12 fl oz* | 354 | 0.0 | 0.3 | | | | | | | | 18 | 24 | | | |
| diet cola, aspartame sweetened | 2 | 354.3 | 0.0 | 0.0 | 0 | 0 | 0 | .08 | .00 | 0 | 21[c] | 12 | 4 | | .28 |
| *12 fl oz* | 355 | 0.2 | 0.3 | 0.0 | | 0 | .02 | 0.0 | .00 | .00 | 0 | 30 | .11 | | |
| diet grape, Nehi | 3 | | 0.0 | | | | | | | | 0 | | | | |
| *12 fl oz* | 360 | 0.0 | 0.8 | | | | | | | | 44 | 0 | | | |
| diet lemon-lime, Nehi | 5 | | 0.0 | | | | | | | | 0 | | | | |
| *12 fl oz* | 360 | 0.0 | 1.1 | | | | | | | | 83 | 0 | | | |
| diet mandarin orange Slice[d] | 19 | 349.2 | 0.0 | 0.0 | | | | | | | 22 | 0 | | | |
| *12 fl oz* | 360 | 0.0 | 4.2 | 0.0 | 0.0 | | | | | | 85 | 0 | .00 | | |
| diet orange, Nehi | 2 | | 0.0 | | | | | | | | 0 | | | | |
| *12 fl oz* | 360 | 0.0 | 0.6 | | | | | | | | 63 | 0 | | | |
| diet Pepsi[e] | 1 | 354.0 | 0.0 | 0.0 | | | | | | | 2 | 0 | | | |
| *12 fl oz* | 360 | 0.0 | 0.2 | 0.0 | 0.0 | | | | | | 30 | 29 | .00 | | |
| diet Pepsi Free[e] | 1 | 354.0 | 0.0 | 0.0 | | | | | | | 2 | 0 | | | |
| *12 fl oz* | 360 | 0.0 | 0.2 | 0.0 | 0.0 | | | | | | 100 | 50 | .00 | | |
| diet RC | 1 | | 0.0 | | | | | | | | 1 | | | | |
| *12 fl oz* | 360 | 0.0 | 0.4 | | | | | | | | 60 | 41 | | | |
| diet RC, caffeine-free | 1 | | 0.0 | | | | | | | | 1 | | | | |
| *12 fl oz* | 360 | 0.0 | 0.4 | | | | | | | | 60 | 41 | | | |
| diet RC 100 | 2 | | 0.0 | | | | | | | | 1 | | | | |
| *12 fl oz* | 360 | 0.0 | 0.4 | | | | | | | | 60 | 41 | | | |
| diet Rite cola, salt-free | 2 | | 0.0 | | | | | | | | 1 | | | | |
| *12 fl oz* | 360 | 0.0 | 0.4 | | | | | | | | 60 | 41 | | | |
| diet Slice[f] | 26 | 348.0 | 0.0 | 0.0 | | | | | | | 11 | 0 | | | |
| *12 fl oz* | 360 | 0.0 | 6.0 | 0.0 | 0.0 | | | | | | 100 | 0 | .00 | | |
| diet soda, sodium saccharin sweetened | 2 | 354.3 | 0.0 | 0.0 | 0 | 0 | 0 | .00 | .00 | 0 | 57 | 14 | 3 | .18 | .060 |
| *12 fl oz* | 355 | 0.1 | 0.3 | 0.0 | | 0 | .00 | 0.0 | .00 | .00 | 7 | 38[g] | .14 | .089 | |
| diet Sprite | 4 | | 0.0 | | | | | | | | 0 | | | | |
| *12 fl oz* | 354 | 0.0 | 0.0 | | | | | | | | 56 | 0 | | | |
| diet strawberry, Nehi | 3 | | 0.0 | | | | | | | | 0 | | | | |
| *12 fl oz* | 360 | 0.0 | 0.7 | | | | | | | | 44 | 0 | | | |
| diet Upper 10 | 5 | | 0.0 | | | | | | | | 0 | | | | |
| *12 fl oz* | 360 | 0.0 | 1.1 | | | | | | | | 83 | 0 | | | |
| Fresca | 4 | | 0.0 | | | | 0 | | | | 0 | | | | |
| *12 fl oz* | 354 | 0.0 | 0.3 | | | | | | | | 76 | 0 | | | |
| Pepsi Light[e] | 1 | 354.0 | 0.0 | 0.0 | | | | | | | 2 | 0 | | | |
| *12 fl oz* | 360 | 0.0 | 0.1 | 0.0 | 0.0 | | | | | | 46 | 26 | .00 | | |
| Tab | 1 | | 0.0 | | | | | | | | 8 | | | | |
| *12 fl oz* | 354 | 0.0 | 0.3 | | | | | | | | 18 | 46 | | | |

[a] Contains 170.0 mg aspartame.
[b] Contains 168.5 mg aspartame.
[c] Cola w/aspartame & sodium saccharine contains 32 mg Na.
[d] Contains 187.1 mg aspartame.
[e] Contains 177.0 mg aspartame.
[f] Contains 136.6 mg aspartame.
[g] For cola & pepper types: other flavors have 0 mg P.

| | KCAL | H₂O (g) | FAT (g) | PUFA (g) | CHOL (mg) | A (RE) | C (mg) | B-2 (mg) | B-6 (mg) | FOL (mcg) | Na (mg) | Ca (mg) | Mg (mg) | Zn (mg) | Mn (mg) |
|---|---|---|---|---|---|---|---|---|---|---|---|---|---|---|---|
| | WT (g) | PRO (g) | CHO (g) | SFA (g) | DFIB (g) | A (IU) | B-1 (mg) | NIA (mg) | B-12 (mcg) | PANT (mg) | K (mg) | P (mg) | Fe (mg) | Cu (mg) | |

### 1.4. CEREAL GRAIN BEVERAGES

| | KCAL | H₂O | FAT | PUFA | CHOL | A(RE) | C | B-2 | B-6 | FOL | Na | Ca | Mg | Zn | Mn |
|---|---|---|---|---|---|---|---|---|---|---|---|---|---|---|---|
| powder | 9 | 0.1 | 0.1 | 0.0 | 0 | | | .00 | | | 2 | 1 | 6 | .01 | .025 |
| *1 t* | 2.3 | 0.1 | 1.9 | 0.0 | | | | 0.4 | .00 | | 42 | 13 | .11 | .005 | |
| **prep from powder** | | | | | | | | | | | | | | | |
| w/ water | 9 | 177.7 | 0.1 | 0.0 | 0 | | | .00 | | | 7 | 5 | 7 | .06 | .027 |
| *6 fl oz water & 1 t powder* | 180 | 0.1 | 1.9 | 0.0 | | | | 0.4 | .00 | | 43 | 13 | .12 | .016 | |
| w/ water, Postum | 11 | 178.0 | 0.0 | 0.0 | 0 | | 0 | .01 | .02 | 5 | 3 | 8 | 10 | .25 | |
| *6 fl oz* | 181 | 0.2 | 2.6 | 0.0 | | 0 | .02 | 0.7 | .00 | .05 | 97 | 20 | .20 | .055 | |
| w/ water, Postum, coffee flavored | 11 | 177.0 | 0.0 | 0.0 | 0 | | 0 | .01 | .01 | 5 | 3 | 8 | 10 | .25 | |
| *6 fl oz* | 180 | 0.2 | 2.6 | 0.0 | | 0 | .02 | 0.7 | .00 | .05 | 96 | 20 | .20 | .055 | |
| w/ whole milk | 121 | 160.9 | 6.2 | 0.3 | 25 | 57 | 2 | .30 | .08 | 9 | 91 | 219 | 30 | .71 | .030 |
| *6 fl oz milk & 1 t powder* | 185 | 6.1 | 10.4 | 3.8 | | 230 | .07 | 0.5 | .65 | .57 | 319 | 184 | .20 | .022 | |

### 1.5. COFFEE

| | KCAL | H₂O | FAT | PUFA | CHOL | A(RE) | C | B-2 | B-6 | FOL | Na | Ca | Mg | Zn | Mn |
|---|---|---|---|---|---|---|---|---|---|---|---|---|---|---|---|
| brewed | 4 | 175.7 | 0.0 | 0.0 | 0 | | 0 | .00 | .00 | 0 | 4 | 3 | 10 | .03 | .048 |
| *6 fl oz* | 177 | 0.1 | 0.8 | 0.0 | | | .00 | 0.4 | .00 | | 96 | 2 | .72 | .012 | |
| inst powder | 4 | 0.1 | 0.0 | 0.0 | 0 | 0 | 0 | .00 | .00 | 0 | 1 | 3 | 6 | .01 | .031 |
| *1 rd t* | 1.8 | 0.2 | 0.7 | 0.0 | | 0 | .00 | 0.5 | .00 | .00 | 64 | 5 | .08 | .003 | |
| cappuccino flavor, sugar sweetened | 62 | 0.2 | 2.1 | 0.0 | | 0 | 0 | .01 | .00 | 0 | 98 | 4 | 7 | .04 | .028 |
| *2 rd t* | 14 | 0.4 | 10.7 | 1.8 | 0.0 | 0 | .02 | 0.3 | .00 | .01 | 118 | 26 | .14 | .016 | |
| decaffeinated | 4 | 0.1 | 0.0 | 0.0 | 0 | 0 | 0 | .02 | .00 | 0 | 0 | 3 | 6 | .00 | .022 |
| *1 rd t* | 1.8 | 0.2 | 0.8 | 0.0 | | 0 | .00 | 0.5 | .00 | .00 | 63 | 5 | .07 | .001 | |
| french flavor, sugar sweetened | 57 | 0.3 | 3.4 | 0.1 | | | | | | | | 4 | | | |
| *2 rd t* | 11.5 | 0.5 | 6.6 | 2.9 | | | | 0.7 | | | 136 | 41 | | | |
| mocha flavor, sugar sweetened | 51 | 0.2 | 1.9 | 0.0 | | 0 | 0 | .00 | .00 | 0 | 31 | 4 | 8 | .11 | .051 |
| *2 rd t* | 11.5 | 0.5 | 8.4 | 1.6 | 0.0 | 0 | .00 | 0.3 | .00 | .01 | 119 | 29 | .23 | .050 | |
| w/ chicory | 6 | 0.1 | 0.0 | 0.0 | 0 | | 0 | .39 | | | 5 | 2 | 4 | .01 | .022 |
| *1 rd t* | 1.8 | 0.2 | 1.3 | 0.0 | | | .01 | | .00 | | 61 | 5 | .09 | .001 | |
| **prep from inst powder** | 4 | 177.2 | 0.0 | 0.0 | 0 | 0 | 0 | .00 | .00 | 0 | 6 | 6 | 8 | .05 | .032 |
| *6 fl oz water & 1 rd t powder* | 179 | 0.2 | 0.7 | 0.0 | | 0 | .00 | 0.5 | .00 | .00 | 64 | 6 | .09 | .013 | |
| amaretto, General Foods | 51 | 177.8 | 2.4 | 0.0 | 0 | | 0 | .03 | .00 | 0 | 23 | 4 | 10 | .02 | |
| *6 fl oz water & 11.5 g powder[a]* | 189 | 0.2 | 6.8 | 2.0 | | 0 | .00 | 0.8 | .00 | .00 | 230 | 57 | .14 | .029 | |
| amaretto, sugar-free, General Foods | 36 | 177.5 | 2.6 | 0.0 | 0 | | 0 | .03 | .00 | 0 | 21 | 4 | 9 | .01 | |
| *6 fl oz water & 7.7 g powder[a]* | 185 | 0.3 | 3.0 | 2.1 | | 0 | .00 | 0.7 | .00 | .00 | 253 | 35 | .06 | .020 | |
| cappuccino flavor, sugar sweetened | 62 | 177.9 | 2.1 | 0.0 | 0 | 0 | 0 | .01 | .00 | 0 | 104 | 7 | 9 | .08 | .029 |
| *6 fl oz water & 2 rd t powder* | 192 | 0.4 | 10.7 | 1.8 | | 0 | .02 | 0.3 | .00 | .01 | 119 | 26 | .15 | .027 | |
| decaffeinated | 4 | 177.2 | 0.0 | 0.0 | 0 | 0 | 0 | .03 | .00 | 0 | 6 | 6 | 7 | .05 | .023 |
| *6 fl oz water & 1 rd t powder* | 179 | 0.2 | 0.8 | 0.0 | | 0 | .00 | 0.5 | .00 | .00 | 63 | 5 | .08 | .013 | |
| francais, General Foods | 55 | 177.7 | 3.2 | 0.1 | 0 | | 0 | .02 | .00 | 0 | 27 | 3 | 11 | .01 | |
| *6 fl oz water & 11.5 g powder[a]* | 189 | 0.3 | 6.0 | 2.6 | | 0 | .00 | 0.2 | .00 | .00 | 278 | 73 | .13 | .029 | |
| francais, sugar-free, General Foods | 36 | 177.5 | 2.5 | 0.0 | 0 | | 0 | .03 | .00 | 0 | 22 | 4 | 9 | .01 | |
| *6 fl oz water & 7.7 g powder[a]* | 185 | 0.3 | 3.1 | 2.1 | | 0 | .00 | 0.7 | .00 | .00 | 260 | 34 | .06 | .020 | |
| french flavor, sugar sweetened | 57 | 177.7 | 3.4 | 0.1 | | | | | | | 8 | 2 | .05 | .000 | |
| *6 fl oz water & 2 rd t powder* | 189 | 0.5 | 6.6 | 2.9 | | | | 0.7 | | | 137 | 41 | .01 | .011 | |
| irish creme, General Foods | 55 | 177.5 | 2.4 | 0.0 | 0 | | 0 | .03 | .00 | | 19 | 8 | 10 | .04 | |
| *6 fl oz water & 12.8 g powder[a]* | 190 | 0.3 | 8.1 | 2.0 | | 0 | .00 | 0.6 | .00 | .00 | 243 | 52 | .18 | .039 | |
| irish creme, sugar-free, General Foods | 32 | 178.1 | 2.2 | 0.0 | 0 | | 0 | .02 | .00 | 0 | 14 | 4 | 9 | .03 | |
| *6 fl oz water & 7.1 g powder[a]* | 185 | 0.3 | 3.0 | 1.8 | | 0 | .00 | 0.5 | .00 | .00 | 234 | 31 | .09 | .027 | |
| irish mocha mint, General Foods | 52 | 177.7 | 2.2 | 0.0 | 0 | | 0 | .02 | .00 | | 22 | 5 | 14 | .00 | |
| *6 fl oz water & 11.5 g powder[a]* | 189 | 0.2 | 7.6 | 1.8 | | 0 | .00 | 0.1 | .00 | .00 | 248 | 65 | .36 | .015 | |
| irish mocha mint, sugar-free, General Foods—*6 fl oz water & 6.4 g powder[a]* | 27 | 177.8 | 1.9 | 0.0 | 0 | | 0 | .02 | .00 | 0 | 18 | 4 | 11 | .11 | |
| | 184 | 0.5 | 2.8 | 1.5 | | 1 | .00 | 0.2 | .00 | .01 | 211 | 33 | .30 | .066 | |

[a] 2 rd t.

| | KCAL | H₂O (g) | FAT (g) | PUFA (g) | CHOL (mg) | A (RE) | C (mg) | B-2 (mg) | B-6 (mg) | FOL (mcg) | Na (mg) | Ca (mg) | Mg (mg) | Zn (mg) | Mn (mg) |
|---|---|---|---|---|---|---|---|---|---|---|---|---|---|---|---|
| | WT (g) | PRO (g) | CHO (g) | SFA (g) | DFIB (g) | A (IU) | B-1 (mg) | NIA (mg) | B-12 (mcg) | PANT (mg) | K (mg) | P (mg) | Fe (mg) | Cu (mg) | |
| mocha flavor, sugar sweetened | 51 | 176.7 | 1.9 | 0.0 | | 0 | 0 | .00 | .00 | 0 | 36 | 7 | 9 | .15 | .053 |
| *6 fl oz water & 2 rd t powder* | 188 | 0.5 | 8.4 | 1.6 | | 0 | .00 | 0.3 | .00 | .01 | 119 | 29 | .24 | .060 | |
| orange cappuccino, General Foods | 59 | 177.3 | 2.0 | 0.0 | 0 | 0 | | .03 | .00 | 0 | 106 | 4 | 12 | .02 | |
| *6 fl oz water & 14 g powder*[a] | 191 | 0.2 | 9.7 | 1.7 | | 0 | .00 | 0.3 | .00 | .00 | 125 | 51 | .24 | .032 | |
| orange cappuccino, sugar-free, General | 29 | 177.6 | 1.9 | 0.0 | 0 | 0 | | .03 | .00 | 0 | 62 | 4 | 10 | .01 | |
| *Foods—6 fl oz water & 6.7 g powder*[a] | 184 | 0.2 | 2.8 | 1.6 | | 0 | .00 | 0.6 | .00 | .00 | 128 | 30 | .15 | .022 | |
| suisse mocha, General Foods | 53 | 177.7 | 2.5 | 0.0 | 0 | 0 | | .02 | .00 | | 23 | 4 | 11 | .01 | |
| *6 fl oz water & 11.5 g powder*[a] | 189 | 0.2 | 7.5 | 1.7 | | 0 | .00 | 0.2 | .00 | .00 | 153 | 57 | .02 | .019 | |
| suisse mocha, sugar-free, General Foods | 30 | 177.8 | 2.1 | 0.0 | 0 | 0 | | .02 | .00 | 0 | 20 | 3 | 9 | .05 | |
| *6 fl oz water & 6.4 g powder*[a] | 184 | 0.4 | 2.8 | 1.7 | | 1 | .00 | 0.3 | .00 | .00 | 151 | 31 | .19 | .038 | |
| vienna, General Foods | 59 | 177.2 | 2.0 | 0.0 | 0 | 0 | | .00 | .00 | 0 | 105 | 4 | 11 | .01 | |
| *6 fl oz water & 14 g powder*[a] | 191 | 0.2 | 9.9 | 1.7 | | 0 | .00 | 0.4 | .00 | .00 | 112 | 32 | .04 | .027 | |
| vienna, sugar-free, General Foods | 30 | 177.6 | 2.0 | 0.0 | 0 | 0 | | .00 | .00 | 0 | 95 | 0 | 9 | .01 | |
| *6 fl oz water & 6.7 g powder*[a] | 184 | 0.2 | 2.7 | 1.7 | | 0 | .00 | 0.7 | .00 | .00 | 122 | 21 | .00 | .020 | |
| w/ chicory | 6 | 177.2 | 0.0 | 0.0 | 0 | | | .01 | | | 10 | 6 | 6 | .05 | .023 |
| *6 fl oz water & 1 rd t powder* | 179 | 0.2 | 1.3 | | | | .00 | 0.4 | .00 | | 61 | 5 | .09 | .013 | |

## 1.6. FRUIT JUICE DRINKS & FRUIT FLAVORED BEVERAGES[b]

| | KCAL | H₂O (g) | FAT (g) | PUFA (g) | CHOL (mg) | A (RE) | C (mg) | B-2 (mg) | B-6 (mg) | FOL (mcg) | Na (mg) | Ca (mg) | Mg (mg) | Zn (mg) | Mn (mg) |
|---|---|---|---|---|---|---|---|---|---|---|---|---|---|---|---|
| | WT (g) | PRO (g) | CHO (g) | SFA (g) | DFIB (g) | A (IU) | B-1 (mg) | NIA (mg) | B-12 (mcg) | PANT (mg) | K (mg) | P (mg) | Fe (mg) | Cu (mg) | |
| **appleberry jce works, Campbell's** | 96 | | 0.0 | | | | 0 | .00 | | | 39 | 28 | | | |
| *6 fl oz* | 182 | 0.3 | 23.8 | | | 0 | .01 | 0.1 | | | 215 | | 1.30 | | |
| **apple, Hawaiian Punch** | 90 | | 0.0 | | | | 60[c] | .00 | | | 13 | 1 | | | |
| *6 fl oz* | 185 | 0.0 | 22.0 | | | 1 | .00 | 0.0 | | | 21 | 2 | | | |
| **apple jce works, Campbell's** | 97 | | 0.1 | | | | 5 | .00 | | | 30 | 19 | | | |
| *6 fl oz* | 182 | 0.3 | 23.7 | | | 0 | .00 | 0.3 | | | 125 | | .90 | | |
| **berry blend, from powder, Crystal Light** | 3 | 236.6 | 0.0 | 0.0 | 0 | | 6 | .00 | .00 | 0 | 0 | 17 | | .00 | |
| *8 fl oz* | 238 | 0.1 | 0.2 | 0.0 | 0.0 | 0 | .00 | 0.0 | .00 | .00 | 46 | 0 | | | |
| **caribbean cooler, from powder, Crystal** | 3 | 236.7 | 0.0 | 0.0 | 0 | | 6 | .00 | .00 | 0 | 1 | 16 | | .00 | |
| *Light—8 fl oz* | 238 | 0.1 | 0.3 | 0.0 | 0.0 | 0 | .00 | 0.0 | .00 | .00 | 46 | | | | |
| **cherry, Hawaiian Punch** | 90 | | 0.0 | | | | 60[c] | .00 | | | 17 | 5 | | | |
| *6 fl oz* | 185 | 0.0 | 23.0 | | | 5 | .00 | 0.0 | | | 26 | 3 | | | |
| **cherry jce works, Campbell's** | 96 | | 0.1 | | | | 7 | .01 | | | 18 | 20 | | | |
| *6 fl oz* | 182 | 0.2 | 23.6 | | | 0 | .01 | 0.4 | | | 118 | | .90 | | |
| **citrus blend, from powder, Crystal Light** | 3 | 236.5 | 0.0 | 0.0 | 0 | | 6 | .00 | .00 | 0 | 0 | 21 | | .00 | |
| *8 fl oz* | 238 | 0.1 | 0.2 | 0.0 | 0.0 | 0 | .00 | 0.0 | .00 | .00 | 46 | 0 | | | |
| **citrus fruit jce drink, from frozn conc** | 114 | 217.9 | 0.0 | 0.0 | 0 | 10 | 67[c] | | .06 | 5 | 7 | 21 | 16 | .13 | .181 |
| *8 fl oz* | 248 | 0.8 | 28.4 | 0.0 | 0.2 | 103 | .04 | 0.4 | .00 | .33 | 277 | 25 | 2.79 | .079 | |
| **cranapple drink, Ocean Spray** | 130 | | 0.0 | | | | 60 | | | | 4 | 13 | 4 | .07 | |
| *6 fl oz* | | 0.0 | 32.0 | | | | | | | | 51 | 5 | .10 | .014 | |
| **cranberry jce cocktail** | | | | | | | | | | | | | | | |
| bottled | 108 | 162.4 | 0.1 | | 0 | 1 | 67[c] | .02 | .04 | 1 | 4 | 7 | 4 | .14 | .367 |
| *6 fl oz* | 190 | 0.0 | 27.4 | | | 7 | .02 | 0.1 | .00 | .11 | 34 | 4 | .28 | .034 | |
| from frozn conc | 102 | 160.6 | 0.0 | | 0 | 2 | 18[c] | .02 | .02 | 0 | 6 | 9 | 4 | .07 | .077 |
| *6 fl oz* | 187 | 0.0 | 26.2 | | | 18 | .01 | 0.0 | .00 | .26 | 27 | 3 | .17 | .019 | |
| low cal, bottled[d] | 33 | 169.5 | 0.0 | | 0 | | 57[c] | | | | 6 | 16 | 3 | .04 | |
| *6 fl oz* | 178 | 0.0 | 8.5 | | | | | | .00 | | 39 | 1 | .07 | | |
| **cranberry-apple jce drink, bottled** | 123 | 152.4 | 0.0 | | 0 | | 59[c] | .04 | | | 4 | 13 | 3 | .08 | |
| *6 fl oz* | 184 | 0.1 | 31.5 | | | | .01 | 0.1 | .00 | | 50 | 5 | .11 | .013 | |
| **cranberry-apricot jce drink, bottled** | 118 | 153.6 | 0.0 | | 0 | | 0 | .02 | | | 4 | 17 | 6 | .07 | |
| *6 fl oz* | 184 | 0.3 | 29.9 | | | | .01 | 0.2 | | | 113 | 10 | .28 | .028 | |
| **cranberry-grape jce drink, bottled** | 103 | 157.5 | 0.2 | 0.1 | 0 | | 59[c] | .03 | | | 5 | 15 | 6 | .07 | |
| *6 fl oz* | 184 | 0.3 | 25.8 | 0.1 | | | .02 | 0.2 | .00 | | 44 | 7 | .02 | .013 | |
| **crangrape drink, Ocean Spray** | 110 | | 0.0 | | | | 60 | .03 | | | 7 | 7 | 4 | | |
| *6 fl oz* | | 0.0 | 26.0 | | | | .02 | 0.2 | | | 37 | 7 | .25 | .022 | |
| **cranraspberry drink, Ocean Spray** | 110 | | 0.0 | | | | 60 | | | | 6 | | | | |
| *6 fl oz* | | 0.0 | 27.0 | | | | | | | | 35 | | | | |
| **fruit juicy red, Hawaiian Punch** | 90 | | 0.0 | | | | 60[c] | .00 | | | 17 | 3 | | | |
| *6 fl oz* | 185 | 0.0 | 22.0 | | | 10 | .00 | 0.0 | | | 30 | 2 | | | |
| **fruit punch, from powder, Crystal Light** | 3 | 236.8 | 0.0 | 0.0 | 0 | | 6 | .00 | .00 | 0 | 0 | 33 | | .00 | |
| *8 fl oz* | 238 | 0.1 | 0.1 | 0.0 | 0.0 | 0 | .00 | 0.0 | .00 | .00 | 45 | 15 | | | |

[a] 2 rd t.
[b] Fruit & veg juices are listed in section 14.
[c] Vit C added.
[d] Sweetened w/ calcium saccharin & corn sweeteners.

| | | | | | | Vitamins | | | | | Minerals | | | | |
|---|---|---|---|---|---|---|---|---|---|---|---|---|---|---|---|
| | KCAL | $H_2O$ (g) | FAT (g) | PUFA (g) | CHOL (mg) | A (RE) | C (mg) | B-2 (mg) | B-6 (mg) | FOL (mcg) | Na (mg) | Ca (mg) | Mg (mg) | Zn (mg) | Mn (mg) |
| | WT (g) | PRO (g) | CHO (g) | SFA (g) | DFIB (g) | A (IU) | B-1 (mg) | NIA (mg) | B-12 (mcg) | PANT (mg) | K (mg) | P (mg) | Fe (mg) | Cu (mg) | |
| **fruit punch drink** | | | | | | | | | | | | | | | |
| cnd | 87 | 163.7 | 0.0 | 0.0 | 0 | 3 | 55ª | .04 | .00 | 2 | 41 | 14 | 4 | .23 | .372 |
| *6 fl oz* | 186 | 0.1 | 22.1 | 0.0 | 0.2 | 26 | .04 | 0.0 | .00 | .03 | 47 | 2 | .38 | .095 | |
| from frzn conc | 113 | 217.8 | 0.0 | 0.0 | 0 | 3 | 108ª | .03 | .02 | 2 | 11 | 9 | 6 | .09 | .252 |
| *8 fl oz* | 247 | 0.1 | 28.8 | 0.2 | 0.0 | 27 | .03 | 0.1 | .00 | .02 | 31 | 2 | .22 | .074 | |
| from powder | 97 | 236.8 | 0.0 | 0.0 | 0 | 0 | 31ª | .01 | .00 | 0 | 38 | 41 | 3 | .09 | .008 |
| *2 rd t in 8 fl oz water* | 262 | 0.0 | 24.8 | 0.0 | 0.0 | 1 | .00 | 0.0 | .00 | .00 | 2 | 52 | .14 | .047 | |
| **fruit punch jce drink, from frozn conc** | 123 | 216.5 | 0.5 | 0.1 | 0 | 1 | 14 | .16 | .03 | 0 | 12 | 18 | 9 | .54 | .149 |
| *8 fl oz* | 248 | 0.2 | 30.4 | 0.1 | 0.2 | 15 | .00 | 0.1 | .00 | .07 | 191 | 0 | .57 | .060 | |
| **fruit punch, low sugar, Hawaiian Punch** | 30 | | 0.0 | | | | 60ª | .00 | | | 20 | 5 | | | |
| *6 fl oz* | 185 | 0.0 | 8.0 | | | 32 | .00 | 0.0 | | | 30 | 2 | | | |
| **grape drink, cnd** | 84 | 166.3 | 0.0 | 0.0 | 0 | 0 | 64ª | .01 | .01 | 1 | 12 | | | .21 | |
| *6 fl oz* | 188 | 0.0 | 21.6 | 0.0 | | 2 | .01 | 0.0 | .00 | .01 | 10 | | .31 | .023 | |
| **grape, from powder, Crystal Light** | 3 | 236.8 | 0.0 | 0.0 | 0 | | 6 | .00 | .00 | 0 | 0 | | 14 | .00 | |
| *8 fl oz* | 238 | 0.1 | 0.3 | 0.0 | 0.0 | 0 | .00 | 0.0 | .00 | .00 | 0 | 0 | | | |
| **grape, Hawaiian Punch** | 90 | | 0.0 | | | | 60ª | .00 | | | 13 | 7 | | | |
| *6 fl oz* | 185 | 0.0 | 23.0 | | | 15 | .00 | 0.1 | | | 30 | 7 | | | |
| **grape jce drink, cnd** | 94 | 163.6 | 0.0 | | 0 | 0 | 30ª | .02 | .04 | 2 | 2 | 6 | | | |
| *6 fl oz* | 188 | 0.2 | 24.2 | | | 4 | .02 | 0.2 | .00 | .02 | 66 | 8 | .19 | | |
| **grape jce works, Campbell's** | 98 | | 0.2 | | | | 15 | .02 | | | 15 | 14 | | | |
| *6 fl oz* | 182 | 0.4 | 23.5 | | | 0 | .00 | 0.3 | | | 71 | | .70 | | |
| **island fruit cocktail, Hawaiian Punch** | 90 | | 0.0 | | | | 60ª | .00 | | | 19 | 2 | | | |
| *6 fl oz* | 185 | 0.0 | 22.0 | | | 19 | .00 | 0.0 | | | 29 | 2 | | | |
| **kool-aid, from powder, all flavors** | 98 | 220.2 | 0.0 | 0.0 | 0 | | 6 | .00 | .00 | 0 | 8 | 15 | | .00 | |
| *8 fl oz* | 246 | 0.0 | 25.1 | 0.0 | 0.0 | 0 | .00 | 0.0 | .00 | .00 | 1 | 8 | | | |
| **kool-aid, from sugar sweetened powder, all flavors—8 fl oz** | 80 | 220.0 | 0.0 | 0.0 | 0 | | 6 | .00 | .00 | 0 | 8 | 26 | | .00 | |
| | 241 | 0.0 | 20.4 | 0.0 | 0.0 | 0 | .00 | 0.0 | .00 | .00 | 1 | 9 | | | |
| **kool-aid kooler, from powder, all flavors** | 127 | 227.5 | 0.0 | 0.0 | 0 | | 60 | .01 | .02 | 3 | 2 | 4 | 3 | .03 | |
| *8.5 fl oz* | 262 | 0.2 | 33.2 | 0.0 | 0.0 | 5 | .01 | 0.1 | .00 | .03 | 51 | 4 | .11 | .018 | |
| **kool-aid, sugar-free, from powder, all flavors—8 fl oz** | 3 | 236.8 | 0.0 | 0.0 | 0 | | 7 | .00 | .00 | 0 | 8 | 27 | | .00 | |
| | 238 | 0.1 | 0.3 | 0.0 | 0.0 | 0 | .00 | 0.0 | .00 | .00 | 4 | 26 | | | |
| **lemonade** | | | | | | | | | | | | | | | |
| from frzn conc | 100 | 221.6 | 0.1 | 0.0 | 0 | 5 | 10ᵇ | .05 | .02 | 6 | 8 | 8 | 5 | .09 | .012 |
| *6 fl oz* | 248 | 0.1 | 26.0 | 0.0 | | 53 | .02 | 0.0 | .00 | .03 | 38 | 5 | .41 | .045 | |
| from powder | 102 | 236.7 | 0.0 | 0.0 | 0 | 0 | 9 | | .01 | 4 | 13 | 71 | 3 | .10 | |
| *8 fl oz* | 240 | 0.0 | 26.9 | 0.0 | | 0 | .01 | 0.0 | .00 | .02 | 33 | 34 | .15 | | |
| from powder, aspartame sweetened | 5 | 236.5 | 0.0 | | 0 | 0 | 6ª | .00 | .00 | | 7 | 51 | 3 | .06 | .002 |
| *8 fl oz* | 238 | 0.1 | 1.3 | | | 0 | .00 | 0.0 | .00 | .00 | 1 | 23 | .10 | .017 | |
| from powder, Country Time | 82 | 220.0 | 0.0 | 0.0 | 0 | 0 | 9 | .00 | .00 | 0 | 21 | | | .00 | |
| *8 fl oz* | 242 | 0.0 | 20.5 | 0.0 | | 0 | .00 | 0.0 | .00 | .00 | 12 | 0 | | .000 | |
| from powder, Country Time sugar-free | 5 | 237.0 | 0.0 | 0.0 | 0 | 0 | 9 | .00 | .00 | 0 | 0 | 33 | | .00 | |
| *8 fl oz* | 239 | 0.1 | 0.2 | 0.0 | 0.0 | 0 | .00 | 0.0 | .00 | .00 | 28 | 15 | | .000 | |
| from powder, Crystal Light | 5 | 237.0 | 0.0 | 0.0 | 0 | 0 | 6 | .00 | .00 | 0 | 0 | | 25 | .00 | |
| *8 fl oz* | 239 | 0.1 | 0.2 | 0.0 | 0.0 | 0 | .00 | 0.0 | .00 | .00 | 62 | | | | |
| **lemonade flavored drink, from powder** | 113 | 236.9 | 0.1 | 0.0 | 0 | 0 | 34ª | .00 | .00 | 0 | 19 | 29 | 3 | .07 | |
| *2 T powder in 8 fl oz water* | 266 | 0.0 | 28.8 | 0.0 | | 0 | .00 | 0.0 | .00 | .00 | 1 | 3 | .04 | .027 | |
| **lemonade, pink** | | | | | | | | | | | | | | | |
| from powder, Country Time | 82 | 220.1 | 0.0 | 0.0 | 0 | 0 | 9 | .00 | .00 | 0 | 21 | | | .00 | |
| *8 fl oz* | 242 | 0.0 | 20.4 | 0.0 | 0.0 | 0 | .00 | 0.0 | .00 | .00 | 12 | 0 | | | |
| from powder, Country Time sugar-free | 5 | 237.0 | 0.0 | 0.0 | 0 | 0 | 9 | .00 | .00 | 0 | 0 | 33 | | | |
| *8 fl oz* | 239 | 0.1 | 0.2 | 0.0 | 0.0 | 0 | .00 | 0.0 | .00 | .00 | 28 | 15 | | | |
| **lemon lime** | | | | | | | | | | | | | | | |
| from powder, Country Time | 82 | 220.1 | 0.0 | 0.0 | 0 | 0 | 9 | .00 | .00 | 0 | 20 | | | .00 | |
| *8 fl oz* | 242 | 0.0 | 20.5 | 0.0 | 0.0 | 0 | .00 | 0.0 | .00 | .00 | 7 | 0 | | | |
| from powder, Country Time sugar-free | 5 | 237.0 | 0.0 | 0.0 | 0 | 0 | 9 | .00 | .00 | 0 | 0 | 33 | | .00 | |
| *8 fl oz* | 239 | 0.1 | 0.2 | 0.0 | 0.0 | 0 | .00 | 0.0 | .00 | .00 | 17 | 15 | | | |
| from powder, Crystal Light | 4 | 236.3 | 0.0 | 0.0 | 0 | 0 | 6 | .00 | .00 | 0 | 0 | | 11 | .00 | |
| *8 fl oz* | 238 | 0.1 | 0.1 | 0.0 | 0.0 | 0 | .00 | 0.0 | .00 | .00 | 6 | 0 | | | |

ª Vit C added.   ᵇ Range is 1 to 18 mg.

| | KCAL | H₂O (g) | FAT (g) | PUFA (g) | CHOL (mg) | A (RE) | C (mg) | B-2 (mg) | B-6 (mg) | FOL (mcg) | Na (mg) | Ca (mg) | Mg (mg) | Zn (mg) | Mn (mg) |
|---|---|---|---|---|---|---|---|---|---|---|---|---|---|---|---|
| | WT (g) | PRO (g) | CHO (g) | SFA (g) | DFIB (g) | A (IU) | B-1 (mg) | NIA (mg) | B-12 (mcg) | PANT (mg) | K (mg) | P (mg) | Fe (mg) | Cu (mg) | |
| limeade, from frozn conc | 102 | 219.6 | 0.1 | 0.0 | 0 | | 7 | .01 | | | 6 | 7 | 2 | .05 | .000 |
| 8 fl oz | 247 | 0.1 | 27.1 | 0.0 | | | .01 | 0.1 | | | 33 | 3 | .06 | .012 | |
| orange & apricot jce drink, cnd | 128 | 216.8 | 0.3 | 0.1 | 0 | 145 | 50[a] | .03 | | | | 13 | | | |
| 8 fl oz | 250 | 0.8 | 31.8 | 0.0 | | 1450 | .05 | 0.5 | .00 | | 201 | 20 | .25 | | |
| orange breakfast drink, from frozn conc | 84 | 165.7 | 0.0 | 0.0 | 0 | 1 | 104[b] | 2.0 | .13[b] | 61[b] | 18 | 221[b] | 20 | .10 | |
| 6 fl oz | 188 | 0.2 | 21.3 | 0.0 | 0.2 | 11 | .20[b] | 0.5[b] | .00 | .36[b] | 254 | 63 | .15 | .182 | |
| orange drink, cnd | 94 | 161.6 | 0.0 | 0.0 | 0 | 3 | 64[a] | .01 | .02 | | 31 | 12 | 3 | .16 | .028 |
| 6 fl oz | 186 | 0.0 | 24.0 | 0.0 | | 33 | .01 | 0.1 | .00 | .03 | 33 | 3 | .53 | .006 | |
| orange drink, from powder, Crystal Light | 4 | 236.2 | 0.0 | 0.0 | 0 | | 6 | .00 | .00 | 0 | 0 | 57 | | .00 | |
| 8 fl oz | 238 | 0.1 | 0.3 | 0.0 | 0.0 | 0 | .00 | 0.0 | .00 | .00 | 46 | 27 | | | |
| orange flavor breakfast drink | | | | | | | | | | | | | | | |
| from frzn conc | 91 | 162.2 | 0.3 | 0.1 | 0 | 0 | 129[a] | .07 | .00 | | 17 | 61 | 2 | .07 | |
| 6 fl oz | 186 | 0.0 | 22.7 | 0.0 | | 0 | .22[c] | 0.0 | .00 | .01 | 231 | 40 | .15 | | |
| prep from powder | 86 | 163.8 | 0.0 | 0.0 | 0 | 413[d] | 91[a] | .03 | .00 | 107[e] | 9 | 46 | 2 | .07 | .011 |
| 3 rd t in 6 fl oz water | 186 | 0.0 | 21.9 | 0.0 | | 1376[d] | .00 | 0.0 | .00 | .00 | 37 | 29 | .15 | .028 | |
| orange flavor gelatin drink, prep from | 67 | 118.9 | 0.2 | 0.1 | | | 50[a] | | | | 32 | 1 | | .03 | .000 |
| powder—1 pkt in 4 fl oz water | 136 | 6.2 | 10.5 | 0.0 | | | | | | | 3 | | .01 | .007 | |
| orange, Hawaiian Punch | 100 | | 0.0 | | | | 60[a] | .00 | | | 19 | 6 | | | |
| 6 fl oz | 185 | 0.0 | 24.0 | | | 37 | .00 | 0.0 | | | 37 | 5 | | | |
| orange jce works, Campbell's | 90 | | 0.3 | | | | 20 | .02 | | | 56 | 15 | | | |
| 6 fl oz | 182 | 0.5 | 21.4 | | | 23 | .01 | 0.5 | | | 185 | | 1.10 | | |
| paradise punch, from powder, Crystal Light—8 fl oz | 3 | 236.9 | 0.0 | 0.0 | 0 | | 6 | .00 | .00 | 0 | 0 | 13 | | .00 | |
| | 238 | 0.1 | 0.1 | 0.0 | 0.0 | 0 | .00 | 0.0 | .00 | .00 | 45 | 0 | | | |
| pineapple & grapefruit jce drink, cnd | 117 | 219.7 | 0.2 | 0.1 | 0 | 9 | 115[a] | .04 | .11 | 26 | 34 | 18 | 15 | .15 | 1.033 |
| 8 fl oz | 250 | 0.6 | 29.0 | 0.0 | | 88 | .08 | 0.7 | .00 | .13 | 154 | 14 | .77 | .113 | |
| pineapple & pink grapefruit jce drink, cnd, Dole—6 fl oz | 101 | | 0.1 | | | | 60[a] | .02 | | | 0 | 9 | | | |
| | 188 | 0.4 | 25.4 | | | 20 | .04 | 0.2 | | | 116 | 9 | .40 | | |
| pineapple & orange jce drink, cnd | 125 | 217.0 | 0.0 | | 0 | 133[f] | 56[a] | .05 | .12 | 27 | 9 | 13 | 14 | .14 | .903 |
| 8 fl oz | 250 | 3.1 | 29.4 | | | 1328[f] | .08 | 0.5 | .00 | .14 | 116 | 10 | .67 | .103 | |
| pink grapefruit jce cocktail, Ocean Spray | 80 | | 0.0 | | | | 100 | | | | 15 | 14 | 8 | .11 | |
| 6 fl oz | | 0.0 | 20.0 | | | | | | | | 125 | 16 | .24 | .060 | |
| strawberry jce works, Campbell's | 94 | | 0.0 | | | | 2 | .00 | | | 53 | 56 | | | |
| 6 fl oz | 182 | 0.7 | 22.8 | | | 0 | .00 | 0.1 | | | 289 | | 1.60 | | |
| tang, orange, from powder | 88 | 161.5 | 0.0 | 0.0 | 0 | | 60 | .17 | .20 | 80 | 2 | 20 | | .00 | |
| 6 fl oz | 185 | 0.0 | 21.9 | 0.0 | 0.0 | 501 | .00 | 2.0 | .00 | .00 | 45 | 12 | 1.80 | | |
| tang, orange, sugar-free, from powder | 5 | 177.9 | 0.0 | 0.0 | 0 | | 60 | .00 | .00 | 80 | 1 | 20 | | .00 | |
| 6 fl oz | 180 | 0.1 | 0.4 | 0.0 | 0.0 | 501 | .00 | 0.0 | .00 | .00 | 51 | 21 | .00 | | |
| thirst quencher, bottled | 60 | 225.3 | 0.1 | 0.0 | 0 | 0 | 0 | .00 | .00 | 0 | 96 | 0 | 1 | .05 | .000 |
| 8 fl oz | 241 | 0.0 | 15.2 | 0.0 | | 0 | .01 | 0.0 | .00 | .00 | 26 | 22 | .12 | .048 | |
| tropical fruit, Hawaiian Punch | 90 | | 0.0 | | | | 60[a] | .00 | | | 8 | 3 | | | |
| 6 fl oz | 185 | 0.0 | 22.0 | | | 14 | .00 | 0.1 | | | 31 | 2 | | | |
| very berry, Hawaiian Punch | 90 | | 0.0 | | | | 60[a] | .00 | | | 22 | 6 | | | |
| 6 fl oz | 185 | 0.0 | 22.0 | | | 9 | .00 | 0.0 | | | 28 | 3 | | | |
| wild fruit, Hawaiian Punch | 90 | | 0.0 | | | | 60[a] | .00 | | | 19 | 2 | | | |
| 6 fl oz | 185 | 0.0 | 23.0 | | | 14 | .00 | 0.0 | | | 26 | 2 | | | |

## 1.7. MALT BEVERAGES, NONALCOHOLIC

| | KCAL | H₂O (g) | FAT (g) | PUFA (g) | CHOL (mg) | A (RE) | C (mg) | B-2 (mg) | B-6 (mg) | FOL (mcg) | Na (mg) | Ca (mg) | Mg (mg) | Zn (mg) | Mn (mg) |
|---|---|---|---|---|---|---|---|---|---|---|---|---|---|---|---|
| malt beverage | 32 | 353.2 | 0.0 | 0.0 | 0 | | | | | | | 25 | 31 | .03 | .047 |
| 12 fl oz | 360 | 1.1 | 5.1 | 0.0 | | | | | | | | 110 | .05 | .040 | |
| malt beverage, Kingsbury | 60 | | 0.0 | 0.0 | 0 | | | | | | 20 | 25 | | | |
| 12 fl oz | 360 | 0.6 | 12.8 | 0.0 | | | | | | | 50 | | .02 | | |

[a] Vit C added.
[b] Added nutrients.
[c] Thiamin added.
[d] Vit A added.
[e] Folacin added.
[f] Carotene added for color.

| | KCAL | H₂O (g) | FAT (g) | PUFA (g) | CHOL (mg) | A (RE) | C (mg) | B-2 (mg) | B-6 (mg) | FOL (mcg) | Na (mg) | Ca (mg) | Mg (mg) | Zn (mg) | Mn (mg) |
|---|---|---|---|---|---|---|---|---|---|---|---|---|---|---|---|
| | WT (g) | PRO (g) | CHO (g) | SFA (g) | DFIB (g) | A (IU) | B-1 (mg) | NIA (mg) | B-12 (mcg) | PANT (mg) | K (mg) | P (mg) | Fe (mg) | Cu (mg) | |

## 1.8. TEA, HOT/ICED

**tea, black**

| | KCAL | H₂O | FAT | PUFA | CHOL | A(RE) | C | B-2 | B-6 | FOL | Na | Ca | Mg | Zn | Mn |
|---|---|---|---|---|---|---|---|---|---|---|---|---|---|---|---|
| brewed 3 min | 2 | 177.4 | 0.0 | 0.0 | 0 | 0 | 0 | .03 | .00 | 9 | 5 | 0 | 5 | .04 | |
| *6 fl oz* | 178 | 0.0 | 0.4 | 0.0 | | 0 | .00 | 0.0 | .00 | | 66 | 1 | .04 | .018 | |
| inst powder | 2 | 0.0 | 0.0 | 0.0 | 0 | 0 | 0 | .01 | .01 | 1 | 1 | 0 | 3 | .02 | .518 |
| *1 t* | 0.7 | 0.1 | 0.4 | 0.0 | | 0 | .00 | 0.1 | .00 | .03 | 46 | 3 | .03 | .006 | |
| w/ lemon flavor | 4 | 0.1 | 0.0 | 0.0 | 0 | 0 | 0 | .02 | | | 7 | 0 | 2 | .02 | .429 |
| *1 rd t* | 1.4 | 0.1 | 1.1 | 0.0 | | 0 | .00 | 0.1 | .00 | | 48 | 1 | .01 | .005 | |
| w/ sugar & lemon flavor | 87 | 0.1 | 0.1 | 0.0 | 0 | 0 | 0 | .05 | | 10 | | 1 | 3 | .02 | .673 |
| *3 rd t* | 23 | 0.1 | 22.1 | 0.0 | | 0 | .00 | 0.1 | .00 | | 49 | 3 | .04 | .006 | |
| w/ sodium saccharin & lemon flavor | 5 | 0.1 | 0.0 | 0.0 | 0 | 0 | 0 | .01 | | 5 | 17 | 0 | 2 | .01 | .486 |
| *2 t* | 1.6 | 0.1 | 1.3 | 0.0 | | 0 | .00 | 0.1 | .00 | | 41 | 2 | .14 | .002 | |
| prep from inst powder | 2 | 236.2 | 0.0 | 0.0 | 0 | 0 | 0 | .01 | .01 | 1 | 8 | 5 | 5 | .08 | .519 |
| *1 t powder in 8 fl oz water* | 237 | 0.1 | 0.4 | 0.0 | | 0 | .00 | 0.1 | .00 | .03 | 47 | 3 | .04 | .019 | |
| berry, Crystal Light | 3 | 236.8 | 0.0 | 0.0 | 0 | | 6 | .00 | .00 | 0 | 1 | | 8 | .00 | |
| *8 fl oz* | 238 | 0.1 | 0.5 | 0.0 | 0.0 | 0 | .00 | 0.0 | .00 | .00 | 15 | 0 | | | |
| citrus, Crystal Light | 3 | 236.8 | 0.0 | 0.0 | 0 | | 6 | .00 | .00 | 0 | 1 | | 8 | .00 | |
| *8 fl oz* | 238 | 0.1 | 0.5 | 0.0 | 0.0 | 0 | .00 | 0.0 | .00 | .00 | 15 | 0 | | | |
| Crystal Light | 3 | 236.9 | 0.0 | 0.0 | 0 | | 6 | .00 | .00 | 0 | 1 | | 10 | .00 | |
| *8 fl oz* | 238 | 0.1 | 0.4 | 0.0 | 0.0 | 0 | .00 | 0.0 | .00 | .00 | 15 | 0 | | | |
| tropical, Crystal Light | 3 | 236.8 | 0.0 | 0.0 | 0 | | 6 | .00 | .00 | 0 | 1 | | 8 | .00 | |
| *8 fl oz* | 238 | 0.1 | 0.5 | 0.0 | 0.0 | 0 | .00 | 0.0 | .00 | .00 | 15 | 0 | | | |
| w/ lemon, Crystal Light | 2 | 237.0 | 0.0 | 0.0 | 0 | | 6 | .00 | .00 | 0 | 0 | | 8 | .00 | |
| *8 fl oz* | 238 | 0.1 | 0.3 | 0.0 | 0.0 | 0 | .00 | 0.0 | .00 | .00 | 15 | 0 | | | |
| w/ lemon flavor | 4 | 236.5 | 0.0 | 0.0 | 0 | 0 | 0 | .02 | | | 14 | 5 | 4 | .08 | .431 |
| *1 rd t powder in 8 fl oz water* | 238 | 0.1 | 1.1 | 0.0 | | 0 | .00 | 0.1 | .00 | | 49 | 2 | .02 | .019 | |
| w/ sugar & lemon flavor | 87 | 236.3 | 0.1 | 0.0 | 0 | 0 | 0 | .05 | | 10 | | 6 | 5 | .08 | .673 |
| *3 rd t powder in 8 fl oz water* | 259 | 0.1 | 22.1 | 0.0 | | 0 | .00 | 0.1 | .00 | | 50 | 3 | .05 | .021 | |
| w/ sodium saccharin & lemon flavor | 5 | 236.3 | 0.0 | 0.0 | 0 | 0 | 0 | .01 | | 5 | 24 | 5 | 4 | .07 | .488 |
| *2 t powder in 8 fl oz water* | 238 | 0.1 | 1.3 | 0.0 | | 0 | .00 | 0.1 | .00 | | 41 | 2 | .15 | .017 | |
| **tea, herb, brewed** | 1 | 177.5 | 0.0 | 0.0 | 0 | 0 | 0 | .01 | .00 | 1 | 2 | 4 | 2 | .06 | .078 |
| *6 fl oz* | 178 | 0.1 | 0.3 | 0.0 | | 0ᵃ | .02 | 0.0 | .00 | .02 | 15 | 0 | .14 | .027 | |

## 1.9. WATER

| | KCAL | H₂O | FAT | PUFA | CHOL | A(RE) | C | B-2 | B-6 | FOL | Na | Ca | Mg | Zn | Mn |
|---|---|---|---|---|---|---|---|---|---|---|---|---|---|---|---|
| **bottled, Perrier** | 0 | 191.9 | 0.0 | 0.0 | 0 | 0 | 0 | .00 | .00 | 0 | 3 | 26 | 1 | .00 | .000 |
| *6.5 fl oz bottled* | 192 | 0.0 | 0.0 | 0.0 | | 0 | .00 | 0.0 | .00 | .00 | 0 | 0 | .00 | .000 | |
| **bottled, Poland Spring** | 0 | 237.0 | 0.0 | 0.0 | 0 | 0 | 0 | .00 | .00 | 0 | 1 | 3 | 2 | | |
| *8 fl oz* | 237 | 0.0 | 0.0 | 0.0 | | 0 | .00 | 0.0 | .00 | .00 | 0 | | .01 | | |
| **mineral, La Croix** | 0 | | 0.0 | 0.0 | 0 | | | | | | 1 | 20 | | | |
| *12 fl oz* | 360 | 0.0 | 0.0 | 0.0. | | | | | | | 1 | | .01 | | |
| **municipal** | 0 | 236.9 | 0.0 | 0.0 | 0 | 0 | 0 | .00 | .00 | 0 | 7 | 5 | 2 | .06 | .002 |
| *8 fl oz* | 237 | 0.0 | 0.0 | 0.0 | | 0 | .00 | 0.0 | .00 | .00 | 1 | 0 | .01 | .014 | |

## 2. CANDY

| | KCAL | H₂O | FAT | PUFA | CHOL | A(RE) | C | B-2 | B-6 | FOL | Na | Ca | Mg | Zn | Mn |
|---|---|---|---|---|---|---|---|---|---|---|---|---|---|---|---|
| **almond joy, Peter Paul** | 136 | 2.6 | 2.3 | | 1 | | | .04 | | | 58 | 20 | | | |
| *1 oz* | 28 | 1.5 | 16.4 | 0.4 | | | .01 | 0.2 | | | | | .44 | | |
| **baby ruth** | 260 | | 12.0 | | | | | | | | 120 | | | | |
| *2 oz bar* | 57 | 4.0 | 36.0 | | | | | | | | 120 | | | | |
| **bonkers fruit candyᵇ** | 20 | | 0.0 | | | | | | | | 0 | | | | |
| *1 piece* | | 0.0 | 5.0 | | | | | | | | 0 | | | | |

ᵃ Chamomile tea contains 36 IU of vitamin A.　　　　ᵇ Grape, orange, strawberry or watermelon.

| | KCAL / WT (g) | H₂O (g) / PRO (g) | FAT (g) / CHO (g) | PUFA (g) / SFA (g) | CHOL (mg) / DFIB (g) | A (RE) / A (IU) | C (mg) / B-1 (mg) | B-2 (mg) / NIA (mg) | B-6 (mg) / B-12 (mcg) | FOL (mcg) / PANT (mg) | Na (mg) / K (mg) | Ca (mg) / P (mg) | Mg (mg) / Fe (mg) | Zn (mg) / Cu (mg) | Mn (mg) |
|---|---|---|---|---|---|---|---|---|---|---|---|---|---|---|---|
| **bridge mix** | 140 | | 6.0 | | | | | | | | 15 | | | | |
| *14 pieces (1 oz)* | 28 | 1.0 | 20.0 | | | | | | | | 55 | | | | |
| **butterfinger** | 260 | | 12.0 | | | | | | | | 100 | | | | |
| *2 oz bar* | 57 | 4.0 | 38.0 | | | | | | | | 120 | | | | |
| **butterscotch candy** | 113 | 0.4 | 1.0 | | | | 0 | .00 | | | 19 | 5 | | | |
| *1 oz* | 28 | 0.0 | 26.9 | 0.5 | | 40 | .00 | 0.0 | | | 1 | 2 | .40 | | |
| | | | | | | | | | | | | | | | |
| **candied** | | | | | | | | | | | | | | | |
| apricots | 94 | 3.4 | 0.1 | | | | | | | | | | | | |
| *1 oz* | 28 | 0.2 | 24.2 | | | | | | | | | | | | |
| cherries | 96 | 3.4 | 0.1 | | | | | | | | | | | | |
| *1 oz (8 cherries)* | 28 | 0.1 | 24.6 | | | | | | | | | | | | |
| citron | 89 | 5.0 | 0.1 | | | | | | | | 82 | 24 | | | |
| *1 oz* | 28 | 0.1 | 22.7 | | | | | | | | 34 | 7 | .20 | | |
| figs | 84 | 5.9 | 0.1 | | | | | | | | | | | | |
| *1 oz* | 28 | 1.0 | 20.6 | | | | | | | | | | | | |
| ginger root | 96 | 3.4 | 0.1 | | | | | | | | | | | | |
| *1 oz* | 28 | 0.1 | 24.7 | | | | | | | | | | | | |
| grapefruit peel | 90 | 4.9 | 0.1 | | | | | | | | | | | | |
| *1 oz* | 28 | 0.1 | 22.9 | | | | | | | | | | | | |
| lemon peel | 90 | 4.9 | 0.1 | | | | | | | | | | | | |
| *1 oz* | 28 | 0.1 | 22.9 | | | | | | | | | | | | |
| orange peel | 90 | 4.9 | 0.1 | | | | | | | | | | | | |
| *1 oz* | 28 | 0.1 | 22.9 | | | | | | | | | | | | |
| pear | 85 | 5.9 | 0.2 | | | | | | | | | | | | |
| *1 oz* | 28 | 0.4 | 21.3 | | | | | | | | | | | | |
| pineapple | 90 | 5.0 | 0.1 | | | | | | | | | | | | |
| *1 oz* | 28 | 0.2 | 22.7 | | | | | | | | | | | | |
| sweet potato | 143 | 51.0 | 2.8 | | | | 9 | .03 | | | 36 | 31 | | | |
| *1 piece* | 85 | 1.1 | 29.1 | | | 5360 | .05 | 0.3 | | | 162 | 37 | .80 | | |
| **candy corn** | 182 | 3.8 | 1.0 | | | | 0 | .00 | | | 106 | 7 | | | |
| *1/4 cup* | 50 | 0.1 | 44.8 | 0.3 | | 0 | .00 | 0.0 | | | 2 | 3 | .55 | | |
| **caramello, Cadbury** | 141 | 1.2 | 6.7 | | 6 | | | .07 | | | 54 | 58 | | | |
| *1 oz* | 28 | 1.8 | 18.4 | | 0.1 | 31 | .02 | 0.0 | | | | | .28 | | |
| **caramels** | 113 | 2.1 | 2.9 | | | | 0 | .05 | | | 64 | 42 | | | |
| *1 oz* | 28 | 1.1 | 21.7 | 1.6 | | 0 | .01 | 0.1 | | | 54 | 35 | .40 | | |
| **caramels w/ nuts** | 121 | 2.0 | 4.6 | | | | 0 | .05 | | | 58 | 40 | | | |
| *1 oz* | 28 | 1.3 | 20.0 | 1.6 | | 10 | .03 | 0.1 | | | 66 | 39 | .40 | | |
| **charleston chew, choc/strawberry/van** | 240 | | 6.0 | | | | | | | | 80 | | | | |
| *2 oz* | 57 | 2.0 | 44.0 | | | | | | | | 60 | | | | |
| **cherry candy, Y & S Bites** | 100 | | 1.0 | | | | | | | | 85 | | | | |
| *1 oz* | 28 | 1.0 | 23.0 | | | | | | | | | | | | |
| | | | | | | | | | | | | | | | |
| **chocolate** | | | | | | | | | | | | | | | |
| bittersweet | 135 | 0.5 | 11.3 | | | | 0 | .05 | | | 1 | 16 | | | |
| *1 oz* | 28 | 2.2 | 13.3 | 6.3 | | 10 | .01 | 0.3 | | | 174 | 81 | 1.40 | | |
| german sweet, Bakers | 141 | 0.2 | 9.4 | 0.3 | 0 | | 0 | .02 | .00 | 1 | 1 | 7 | 27 | .35 | |
| *1 oz square* | 28 | 1.0 | 16.9 | 5.6 | | 6 | .00 | 0.1 | .00 | .02 | 78 | 36 | .64 | .201 | |
| semi-sweet | 144 | 0.3 | 10.1 | | | | 0 | .02 | | | 1 | 9 | | | |
| *1 oz* | 28 | 1.2 | 16.2 | 5.7 | | 10 | .00 | 0.1 | | | 92 | 43 | .70 | | |
| semi-sweet, Bakers | 134 | 0.3 | 9.1 | 0.4 | 0 | | 0 | .03 | .00 | 1 | 1 | 11 | 40 | .53 | |
| *1 oz square* | 28 | 1.5 | 16.3 | 5.4 | | 8 | .01 | 0.2 | .00 | .03 | 115 | 56 | .94 | .294 | |
| special dark, Hershey | 221 | | 12.4 | | | | | .10 | | | 4 | 8 | 47 | .62 | .328 |
| *1.45 oz bar* | 41 | 2.5 | 24.8 | | | 8 | .01 | 0.3 | | | 139 | 66 | .86 | .328 | |
| sweet | 150 | 0.3 | 10.0 | | | | 0 | .04 | | | 9 | 27 | | | |
| *1 oz* | 28 | 1.2 | 16.4 | 5.6 | | 0 | .01 | 0.1 | | | 76 | 40 | .40 | | |
| | | | | | | | | | | | | | | | |
| **choc chips** | | | | | | | | | | | | | | | |
| Bakers | 196 | 0.4 | 8.8 | 0.3 | 0 | | 0 | .09 | .03 | 2 | 26 | 65 | 35 | .46 | |
| *1/4 cup* | 43 | 1.7 | 31.3 | 6.9 | | 4 | .03 | 0.1 | .08 | .21 | 222 | 81 | .87 | .204 | |
| german sweet, Bakers | 203 | 0.3 | 12.3 | 0.4 | 0 | | 0 | .04 | .01 | 2 | 1 | 13 | 50 | .64 | |
| *1/4 cup* | 43 | 1.8 | 27.7 | 7.2 | | 10 | .01 | 0.3 | .00 | .03 | 144 | 69 | 1.18 | .465 | |

| | KCAL / WT (g) | H₂O (g) / PRO (g) | FAT (g) / CHO (g) | PUFA (g) / SFA (g) | CHOL (mg) / DFIB (g) | A (RE) / A (IU) | C (mg) / B-1 (mg) | B-2 (mg) / NIA (mg) | B-6 (mg) / B-12 (mcg) | FOL (mcg) / PANT (mg) | Na (mg) / K (mg) | Ca (mg) / P (mg) | Mg (mg) / Fe (mg) | Zn (mg) / Cu (mg) | Mn (mg) |
|---|---|---|---|---|---|---|---|---|---|---|---|---|---|---|---|
| semi-sweet, Bakers | 202 | 0.2 | 11.8 | 0.4 | 0 | | 0 | .04 | .01 | 1 | 1 | 13 | 47 | .60 | |
| 1/4 cup | 43 | 1.7 | 28.4 | 6.9 | | 9 | .01 | 0.2 | .00 | .03 | 136 | 65 | 1.11 | .439 | |
| semi-sweet, Hershey | 228 | | 12.5 | | | | | .04 | | | 4 | 13 | 47 | .73 | .344 |
| 1/4 cup (1.5 oz) | 43 | 2.4 | 26.1 | | | 26 | .02 | 0.1 | | | 129 | 45 | 1.29 | .301 | |
| **choc coated** | | | | | | | | | | | | | | | |
| almonds | 161 | 0.6 | 12.4 | | | | 0 | .15 | | | 17 | 58 | | | |
| 1 oz (6-8 almonds) | 28 | 3.5 | 11.2 | 2.1 | | 0 | .03 | 0.5 | | | 155 | 97 | .80 | | |
| choc fudge | 122 | 1.7 | 4.5 | | | | 0 | .04 | | | 65 | 29 | | | |
| 1 oz | 28 | 1.1 | 20.7 | 1.5 | | 0 | .01 | 0.1 | | | 55 | 31 | .40 | | |
| choc fudge w/ nuts | 128 | 1.7 | 5.9 | | | | 0 | .04 | | | 58 | 29 | | | |
| 1 oz | 28 | 1.4 | 19.1 | 1.5 | | 0 | .02 | 0.1 | | | 62 | 39 | .40 | | |
| coconut | 124 | 1.8 | 5.0 | | | | 0 | .02 | | | 56 | 14 | | | |
| 1 oz | 28 | 0.8 | 20.4 | 2.9 | | 0 | .01 | 0.1 | | | 47 | 22 | .30 | | |
| mint | 45 | 0.6 | 1.2 | | | | 0 | .01 | | | 20 | 6 | | | |
| 1 small | 11 | 0.2 | 8.9 | 0.4 | | 0 | .00 | 0.0 | | | 10 | 6 | .10 | | |
| fondant | 116 | 1.6 | 3.0 | | | | 0 | .02 | | | 52 | 16 | | | |
| 1 oz | 28 | 0.5 | 23.0 | 0.9 | | 0 | .01 | 0.0 | | | 26 | 15 | .30 | | |
| fudge, caramel & peanuts | 123 | 2.3 | 5.1 | | | | 0 | .06 | | | 58 | 51 | | | |
| 1 oz | 28 | 2.2 | 18.2 | 1.4 | | 0 | .05 | 0.5 | | | 85 | 53 | .40 | | |
| nougat & caramel | 118 | 2.2 | 3.9 | | | | 0 | .05 | | | 49 | 36 | | | |
| 1 oz | 28 | 1.1 | 20.6 | 1.2 | | 10 | .02 | 0.1 | | | 60 | 35 | .50 | | |
| peanuts | 159 | 0.3 | 11.7 | | | | 0 | .05 | | | 17 | 33 | | | |
| 1 oz (8-16 peanuts) | 28 | 4.6 | 11.1 | 3.0 | | 0 | .10 | 2.1 | | | 143 | 84 | .40 | | |
| peanuts, Nabisco | 160 | | 9.0 | | | | | | | | 15 | | | | |
| 14 pieces (1 oz) | 28 | 4.0 | 14.0 | | | | | | | | 120 | | | | |
| raisins | 120 | 1.3 | 4.8 | | | | 0 | .06 | | | 18 | 43 | | | |
| 1 oz | 28 | 1.5 | 20.0 | 2.7 | | 40 | .02 | 0.1 | | | 171 | 49 | .70 | | |
| raisins, Nabisco | 130 | | 5.0 | | | | | | | | 20 | | | | |
| 29 pieces (1 oz) | 28 | 1.0 | 21.0 | | | | | | | | 150 | | | | |
| van creams | 123 | 2.1 | 4.8 | | | | 0 | .02 | | | 52 | 36 | | | |
| 1 oz | 28 | 1.1 | 19.9 | 1.4 | | 0 | .01 | 0.0 | | | 50 | 31 | .20 | | |
| **choc covered cherries, Welch's Cortina** | 175 | | 4.5 | | | | | | | | 20 | | | | |
| 2 pieces | 43 | 1.0 | 32.0 | | | | | | | | 35 | | | | |
| **choc disks, sugar-coated** | 132 | 0.3 | 5.6 | | | | 0 | .06 | | | 20 | 38 | | | |
| 1 oz | 28 | 1.5 | 20.6 | 3.1 | | 30 | .02 | 0.1 | | | 71 | 40 | .40 | | |
| **choc flavored roll** | 112 | 1.6 | 2.3 | | | | 0 | .02 | | | 56 | 19 | | | |
| 1 oz | 28 | 0.6 | 23.4 | 0.7 | | 0 | .01 | 0.0 | | | 35 | 34 | .50 | | |
| **choc fudgies, Kraft** | 33 | 0.6 | 1.0 | 0.5 | 0 | | 0 | .02 | .00 | 5 | 19 | 8 | 1 | | |
| 1 piece | 8 | 0.2 | 6.2 | 0.1 | | 0 | .00 | 0.0 | .02 | .04 | 20 | 7 | .05 | | |
| **choc kisses, Hershey** | 222 | | 12.5 | | | | | .14 | | | 33 | 83 | 27 | .53 | .123 |
| 9 pieces (1.5 oz) | 41 | 3.4 | 23.7 | | | 25 | .03 | 0.1 | | | 168 | 127 | .53 | .164 | |
| **chuckles candy[a]** | 105 | | 0.3 | | | | | | | | 12 | | | | |
| 1 oz | 28 | 0.0 | 24.1 | | | | | | | | 0 | | | | |
| **cough drops** | | | | | | | | | | | | | | | |
| Beech-Nut | 10 | | 0.0 | | | | | | | | 0 | | | | |
| 1 piece | | 0.0 | 3.0 | | | | | | | | 0 | | | | |
| honey & wild cherry, Pine Brothers | 130 | | 0.0 | | | | | | | | 0 | | | | |
| 13 pieces | 28 | 0.0 | 31.0 | | | | | | | | 75 | | | | |
| **fudge bar, Nabisco** | 170 | | 5.0 | | | | | | | | 40 | | | | |
| 2 pieces | 39 | 1.0 | 29.0 | | | | | | | | 50 | | | | |
| **fudge, choc** | 113 | 2.3 | 3.5 | | | | 0 | .03 | | | 54 | 22 | | | |
| 1 oz | 28 | 0.8 | 21.3 | 1.2 | | 0 | .01 | 0.1 | | | 42 | 24 | .30 | | |
| fudge, choc w/ nuts | 121 | 2.2 | 4.9 | | | | 0 | .03 | | | 48 | 22 | | | |
| 1 oz | 28 | 1.1 | 19.6 | 1.2 | | 0 | .01 | 0.1 | | | 50 | 32 | .30 | | |
| **fudge squares w/ nuts, Nabisco** | 130 | | 5.0 | | | | | | | | 25 | | | | |
| 2 pieces (1 oz) | 28 | 1.0 | 21.0 | | | | | | | | 30 | | | | |
| fudge, van | 113 | 2.8 | 3.1 | | | | 0 | .04 | | | 59 | 32 | | | |
| 1 oz | 28 | 0.9 | 21.2 | 0.8 | | 0 | .01 | 0.0 | | | 36 | 24 | .10 | | |
| **fudge, van w/ nuts** | 120 | 2.6 | 4.6 | | | | 0 | .04 | | | 53 | 31 | | | |
| 1 oz | 28 | 1.2 | 19.5 | 0.8 | | 0 | .01 | 0.0 | | | 32 | 32 | .20 | | |

[a] Includes fruit jellies & jells, jelly candy, jujubes, licorice jellies & jelly eggs, marshmallow eggs, nougat centers & eggs, orange slices, spearmint leaves, drops, strings, berries & softies.

| | KCAL | H₂O (g) | FAT (g) | PUFA (g) | CHOL (mg) | Vitamins A (RE) | C (mg) | B-2 (mg) | B-6 (mg) | FOL (mcg) | Minerals Na (mg) | Ca (mg) | Mg (mg) | Zn (mg) | Mn (mg) |
|---|---|---|---|---|---|---|---|---|---|---|---|---|---|---|---|
| | WT (g) | PRO (g) | CHO (g) | SFA (g) | DFIB (g) | A (IU) | B-1 (mg) | NIA (mg) | B-12 (mcg) | PANT (mg) | K (mg) | P (mg) | Fe (mg) | Cu (mg) | |
| **good stuff bar** | 250 | | 14.0 | | | | | | | | 90 | | | | |
| *1.79 oz bar* | 51 | 4.0 | 29.0 | | | | | | | | 150 | | | | |
| **gum drops** | 98 | 3.3 | 0.2 | | | | 0 | .00 | | | 10 | 2 | | | |
| *1 oz* | 28 | 0.0 | 24.8 | | | 0 | .00 | 0.0 | | | 1 | 0 | .10 | | |
| **hard candy** | 109 | 0.4 | 0.3 | | | | 0 | .00 | | | 9 | 6 | | | |
| *1 oz* | 28 | 0.0 | 27.6 | | | 0 | .00 | 0.0 | | | 1 | 2 | .50 | | |
| **jelly beans** | 104 | 1.8 | 0.1 | | | | 0 | .00 | | | 3 | 3 | | | |
| *1 oz* | 28 | 0.0 | 26.4 | | | 0 | .00 | 0.0 | | | 0 | 1 | .30 | | |
| **junior mints** | 120 | | 3.0 | | | | | | | | 10 | | | | |
| *12 pieces (1 oz)* | 28 | 1.0 | 24.0 | | | | | | | | 25 | | | | |
| **kit kat wafer, Hershey** | 244 | | 13.2 | | | | | .13 | | | 53 | 101 | 21 | .46 | .138 |
| *1.625 oz bar* | 46 | 3.1 | 28.5 | | | 32 | .02 | 0.2 | | | 138 | 83 | .41 | .092 | |
| **krackel bar, Hershey** | 249 | | 13.6 | | | | | .17 | | | 73 | 95 | 28 | .52 | .141 |
| *1.65 oz bar* | 47 | 3.1 | 28.6 | | | 33 | .02 | 0.3 | | | 160 | 113 | .33 | .188 | |
| **life savers, all flavors[a]** | 9.1 | | 0.0 | | | | | | | | 1 | | | | |
| *1 piece* | | 0.0 | 3.0 | | | | | | | | 0 | | | | |
| **life savers flavor pop, all flavors** | 40 | | 0.0 | | | | | | | | 0 | | | | |
| *1 pop* | | 0.0 | 10.0 | | | | | | | | 0 | | | | |
| **life savers sours** | 10 | | 0.0 | | | | | | | | 0 | | | | |
| *1 piece* | | 0.0 | 3.0 | | | | | | | | 0 | | | | |
| **lollipop, life savers[b]** | 45 | | 0.0 | | | | | | | | 10 | | | | |
| *1 pop* | | 0.0 | 11.0 | | | | | | | | 0 | | | | |
| **maple sugar** | 99 | 2.2 | 0.0 | 0.0 | | | | | | | 4 | 41 | | | |
| *1 oz piece* | 28 | 0.0 | 25.5 | 0.0 | | | | | | | 69 | 3 | .40 | | |
| **marshmallow** | 19 | 1.0 | 0.0 | | | | 0 | .00 | | | 2 | 1 | | | |
| *1 large* | 6 | 0.1 | 4.8 | | | 0 | .00 | 0.0 | | | 0 | 0 | .10 | | |
| **marshmallows, miniature** | 147 | 8.0 | 0.0 | | | | 0 | .00 | | | 18 | 8 | | | |
| *1 cup, not packed* | 46 | 0.9 | 37.0 | | | 0 | .00 | 0.0 | | | 3 | 3 | .70 | | |
| **milk choc** | 147 | 0.3 | 9.2 | | | | 0 | .10 | | | 27 | 65 | | | |
| *1 oz* | 28 | 2.2 | 16.1 | 5.1 | | 80 | .02 | 0.1 | | | 109 | 65 | .30 | | |
| **milk choc, Cadbury** | 151 | 0.2 | 8.2 | 1.0 | 7 | | | .09 | | | 46 | 70 | 16 | .06 | |
| *1 oz* | 28 | 2.2 | 17.2 | 4.9 | 0.1 | 71 | .02 | 0.2 | | | 123 | 70 | .78 | .090 | |
| **milk choc bar, Hershey** | 254 | | 14.5 | | | | | .17 | | | 35 | 94 | 31 | .61 | .141 |
| *1.65 oz bar* | 47 | 3.8 | 27.1 | | | 28 | .04 | 0.2 | | | 193 | 156 | .52 | .188 | |
| **milk choc chips** | 148 | | 7.8 | | | | | .06 | | | 34 | 43 | 15 | .25 | .084 |
| *1 oz* | 28 | 1.6 | 17.8 | | | 17 | .01 | 0.2 | | | 90 | 76 | .31 | .084 | |
| **milk choc stars, Nabisco** | 160 | | 8.0 | | | | | | | | 35 | | | | |
| *13 pieces (1 oz)* | 28 | 2.0 | 19.0 | | | | | | | | 85 | | | | |
| **milk choc w/ almonds** | 151 | 0.4 | 10.1 | | | | 0 | .12 | | | 23 | 65 | | | |
| *1 oz* | 28 | 2.6 | 14.5 | 4.5 | | 70 | .02 | 0.2 | | | 125 | 77 | .50 | | |
| **milk choc w/ almonds, Cadbury** | 153 | 0.3 | 8.9 | | 6 | | | .12 | | | 41 | 74 | | | |
| *1 oz* | 28 | 2.9 | 15.4 | | 0.3 | 65 | .02 | 0.2 | | | | | .44 | | |
| **milk choc bar w/ almonds, Hershey** | 246 | | 15.4 | | | | | .13 | | | 55 | 116 | 40 | .70 | .264 |
| *1.55 oz bar* | 44 | 5.0 | 21.7 | | | 40 | .01 | 0.2 | | | 189 | 132 | .75 | .220 | |
| **milk choc w/ fruit & nuts, Cadbury** | 148 | 0.6 | 8.0 | | 6 | | | .09 | | | 39 | 67 | | | |
| *1 oz* | 28 | 2.4 | 16.7 | | 0.2 | 40 | .02 | 0.5 | | | | | .68 | | |
| **milk choc w/ hazel nuts, Cadbury** | 153 | 0.3 | 8.7 | | 4 | | | .10 | | | 44 | 70 | | | |
| *1 oz* | 28 | 2.6 | 16.1 | | 0.3 | | .02 | 0.2 | | | | | .39 | | |
| **milk choc w/ peanuts** | 154 | 0.3 | 10.8 | | | | 0 | .07 | | | 19 | 49 | | | |
| *1 oz* | 28 | 4.0 | 12.6 | 4.5 | | 50 | .07 | 1.4 | | | 138 | 83 | .40 | | |
| **mints** | 100 | 2.1 | 0.6 | | | | 0 | .00 | | | 58 | 4 | | | |
| *1/4 cup* | 28 | 0.0 | 24.7 | | | 0 | .00 | 0.0 | | | 1 | 2 | .30 | | |
| **mints, Breath Savers, sugar-free[c]** | 8 | | 0.0 | | | | | | | | 0 | | | | |
| *1 piece* | | 0.0 | 2.0 | | | | | | | | 0 | | | | |
| **mounds, Peter Paul** | 135 | 2.8 | 7.0 | | 0 | | | .01 | | | 53 | 5 | | | |
| *1 oz* | 28 | 1.1 | 16.8 | | 0.4 | | .00 | 0.1 | | | | | .56 | | |
| **Mr. Goodbar, Hershey** | 296 | | 19.4 | | | | | .14 | | | 18 | 58 | 49 | .94 | .416 |
| *1.85 oz bar* | 52 | 7.2 | 23.7 | | | 21 | .03 | 2.4 | | | 234 | 146 | .62 | .260 | |
| **naturally nut 'n fruit bars, all flavors, Planters[d]—1 oz** | 143 | | 7.0 | | | | | | | | 79 | | | | |
| | 28 | 2.5 | 17.0 | | | | | | | | 100 | | | | |
| **nips, coffee/carmel/licorice, Pearson's** | 120 | | 3.0 | | | | | | | | 70 | | | | |
| *1 oz* | 28 | 1.0 | 23.0 | | | | | | | | 57 | | | | |

[a] Values are averages for 17 flavors.
[b] Values are for assorted, carnival & swirled flavors.
[c] Values are for 4 flavors.
[d] Values are averages for almond apricot, almond pineapple, peanut raisin & walnut apple.

| | KCAL / WT (g) | H₂O (g) / PRO (g) | FAT (g) / CHO (g) | PUFA (g) / SFA (g) | CHOL (mg) / DFIB (g) | A (RE) / A (IU) | C (mg) / B-1 (mg) | B-2 (mg) / NIA (mg) | B-6 (mg) / B-12 (mcg) | FOL (mcg) / PANT (mg) | Na (mg) / K (mg) | Ca (mg) / P (mg) | Mg (mg) / Fe (mg) | Zn (mg) / Cu (mg) | Mn (mg) |
|---|---|---|---|---|---|---|---|---|---|---|---|---|---|---|---|
| parfait, choc/coffioca/mint/peanut butter, Pearson's—*1 oz* | 120 / 28 | / 1.0 | 3.0 / 23.0 | | | | | | | | 70 / 69 | | | | |
| peanut, Planters *1 oz* | 140 / 28 | / 4.0 | 9.0 / 13.0 | | | | | | | | 70 / 130 | | | | |
| peanut bar, Planters *1.6 oz bar* | 240 / 45 | / 8.0 | 14.0 / 21.0 | | | | | | | | 110 / 130 | | | | |
| peanut brittle *1 oz* | 119 / 28 | 0.6 / 1.6 | 2.9 / 23.0 | / 0.6 | | 0 | 0 / .05 | .01 / 1.0 | | | 9 / 43 | 10 / 27 | / .70 | | |
| peanut butter chips, Reese's *1/4 cup (1.5 oz)* | 228 / 43 | / 8.9 | 12.8 / 19.3 | | | 9 | / .02 | .09 / 3.5 | | | 108 / 217 | 47 / 133 | 47 / .73 | .86 / .172 | .602 |
| peanut butter cups, Reese's *2 pieces (1.8 oz)* | 281 / 51 | / 6.4 | 16.7 / 25.9 | | | 10 | / .02 | .11 / 2.0 | | | 148 / 204 | 40 / 122 | 43 / .56 | .71 / .204 | .408 |
| peppermint patty, Nabisco *2 patties (1 oz)* | 110 / 28 | / 1.0 | 0.0 / 25.0 | | | | | | | | 10 / 25 | | | | |
| peppermint patty, York *1 oz* | 120 / 28 | 2.3 / 0.5 | 3.2 / 22.2 | | 0 / 0.1 | | / .00 | .01 / 0.0 | | | 10 / | 4 / | / .30 | | |
| pom pom caramels *2 oz box* | 200 / 57 | / 2.0 | 6.0 / 30.0 | | | | | | | | 140 / 90 | | | | |
| reese's pieces, Hershey *1.95 oz pkg* | 270 / 55 | / 8.0 | 11.4 / 33.5 | | | | / .03 | .13 / 3.1 | | | 83 / 215 | 73 / 132 | 50 / .83 | .83 / .165 | .330 |
| rolo caramels in milk choc, Hershey *9 pieces (1.93 oz)* | 264 / 55 | / 2.8 | 12.0 / 37.1 | | | 33 | / .03 | .14 / 0.0 | | | 94 / 143 | 74 / 88 | 17 / .28 | .39 / .055 | .110 |
| skor toffee bar, Hershey *1.4 oz bar* | 220 / 40 | / 1.9 | 13.8 / 22.6 | | | | / .01 | .14 / .04 | | | 92 / | 45 / | / .16 | | |
| strawberry twizzlers *1 oz* | 100 / 28 | / 1.0 | 1.0 / 23.0 | | | | | | | | 95 / | | | | |
| sugar babies milk caramels *1 pkg* | 180 / 46 | / 1.0 | 2.0 / 40.0 | | | | | | | | 85 / 50 | | | | |
| sugar-coated almonds *1 oz* | 129 / 28 | 0.6 / 2.2 | 5.3 / 19.9 | / 0.4 | | 0 | 0 / .01 | .08 / 0.3 | | | 6 / 72 | 28 / 47 | / .50 | | |
| sugar daddy milk caramel pop *1 pop* | 150 / 39 | / 1.0 | 1.0 / 33.0 | | | | | | | | 85 / 50 | | | | |
| sugar mama milk caramel candy *3/4 oz piece* | 90 / 21 | / 0.0 | 3.0 / 17.0 | | | | | | | | 30 / 30 | | | | |
| thin mints, Cortina *3 pieces* | 120 / 28 | / 1.0 | 2.0 / 23.0 | | | | | | | | 10 / 20 | | | | |
| whatchamacallit bar, Hershey *1.8 oz bar* | 270 / 51 | / 5.7 | 14.9 / 28.8 | | | | / .03 | .12 / 1.7 | | | 122 / 179 | 69 / 102 | 33 / .41 | .71 / .153 | .306 |

# 3. CEREALS, COOKED OR TO-BE-COOKED

| | KCAL / WT (g) | H₂O (g) / PRO (g) | FAT (g) / CHO (g) | PUFA (g) / SFA (g) | CHOL (mg) / DFIB (g) | A (RE) / A (IU) | C (mg) / B-1 (mg) | B-2 (mg) / NIA (mg) | B-6 (mg) / B-12 (mcg) | FOL (mcg) / PANT (mg) | Na (mg) / K (mg) | Ca (mg) / P (mg) | Mg (mg) / Fe (mg) | Zn (mg) / Cu (mg) | Mn (mg) |
|---|---|---|---|---|---|---|---|---|---|---|---|---|---|---|---|
| bulgur (parboiled wheat), cnd *1 cup* | 227 / 135 | 75.6 / 8.4 | 0.9 / 47.3 | | | 0 | 0 / .07 | .04 / 3.2 | | | 809 / 117 | 27 / 270 | / 1.80 | | |
| corn grits, inst, white hominy, enr *1 pkt prep* | 82 / 137 | 116.4 / 2.1 | 0.2 / 17.8 | | | 0 | / .17 | .09 / 1.3 | .05 / .00 | 1 / .43 | 344 / 29 | 7 / 17 | 5 / 1.02 | .09 / .014 | |
| Quaker *1 pkt (4/5 cup ckd)* | 79 / 23 | 1.9 / 1.9 | 0.1 / 17.7 | | | 0 | / .12 | .07 / 1.0 | .05 / .00 | 2 / .00 | 385 / 28 | 7 / 17 | 5 / .81 | .00 / .010 | .000 |
| w/ cheddar cheese flavor, Quaker *1 oz pkt* | 104 / 28 | 1.9 / 2.2 | 1.0 / 21.6 | | | 0 | / .12 | .07 / 1.0 | .07 / .00 | 10 / .00 | 497 / 40 | 14 / 38 | 10 / .81 | .00 / .020 | .000 |
| w/ cheese flavor *1 pkt prep* | 107 / 142 | 115.6 / 2.8 | 0.9 / 21.3 | | | 0 | / .17 | .13 / 1.5 | | | 481 / 40 | 14 / | / 1.16 | | |
| w/ imit bacon bits *1 pkt prep* | 104 / 141 | 114.2 / 3.0 | 0.5 / 21.5 | | | 0 | / .20 | .12 / 1.6 | .05 / .00 | 8 / .06 | 531 / 60 | 6 / 28 | 9 / 1.29 | .18 / .034 | |
| w/ imit bacon bits, Quaker *1 oz pkt* | 101 / 28 | 2.0 / 2.7 | 0.4 / 21.6 | | | 0 | / .12 | .07 / 1.0 | .05 / .00 | 2 / .00 | 544 / 62 | 7 / 28 | 9 / .81 | .00 / .030 | .000 |
| w/ imit ham bits *1 pkt prep* | 103 / 141 | 114.2 / 2.9 | 0.4 / 21.4 | | | 0 | / .25 | .15 / 1.7 | .06 / .00 | 10 / .74 | 657 / 52 | 7 / 33 | 9 / 1.51 | .17 / .027 | |

| | KCAL | H₂O (g) | FAT (g) | PUFA (g) | CHOL (mg) | A (RE) | C (mg) | B-2 (mg) | B-6 (mg) | FOL (mcg) | Na (mg) | Ca (mg) | Mg (mg) | Zn (mg) | Mn (mg) |
|---|---|---|---|---|---|---|---|---|---|---|---|---|---|---|---|
| | WT (g) | PRO (g) | CHO (g) | SFA (g) | DFIB (g) | A (IU) | B-1 (mg) | NIA (mg) | B-12 (mcg) | PANT (mg) | K (mg) | P (mg) | Fe (mg) | Cu (mg) | |
| w/ imit ham bits, Quaker | 99 | 2.1 | 0.3 | | | | | .07 | .06 | 1 | 665 | 7 | 9 | .00 | .000 |
| *1 oz pkt* | 28 | 2.7 | 21.3 | | | 0 | .12 | 1.0 | .00 | 1.00 | 56 | 33 | .81 | .030 | |
| corn grits, quick, yellow hominy, enr, | 101 | 3.0 | 0.2 | | | | | .07 | .05 | 3 | 1 | 1 | 6 | .00 | .000 |
| Quaker—*3 T (1 oz)* | 28 | 2.4 | 22.4 | | | 161 | .12 | 1.0 | .00 | .00 | 45 | 20 | .81 | .010 | |
| **corn grits, reg/quick** | | | | | | | | | | | | | | | |
| enr, ckd | 146 | 206.5 | 0.5 | | | | | .15 | .06 | 1 | 0ᵃ | 1 | 11 | .17 | .041 |
| *1 cup* | 242 | 3.5 | 31.4 | 0.6 | | ᵇ | .24 | 2.0 | | | 54 | 29 | 1.55 | .029 | |
| unenr, ckd | 146 | 206.4 | 0.5 | | | | | .02 | .06 | 1 | 0ᵃ | 1 | 11 | .17 | .041 |
| *1 cup* | 242 | 3.5 | 31.4 | 0.6 | | ᵇ | .05 | 0.5 | | | 54 | 29 | .48 | .029 | |
| white hominy, enr, Quaker/Aunt | 101 | 3.0 | 0.2 | | | | | .07 | .03 | 3 | 1 | 1 | 6 | .00 | .000 |
| Jemima—*3 T (1 oz)* | 28 | 2.4 | 22.4 | | | 0 | .12 | 1.0 | .00 | .00 | 39 | 20 | .81 | .010 | |
| **cream of rice, ckd** | 95 | 160.1 | 0.1 | | | | | .00 | .05 | 6 | 1ᶜ | 6 | 6 | .29 | .264 |
| *3/4 cup* | 183 | 1.6 | 21.1 | | | | .10 | 0.8 | | | 37 | 32 | .30 | .062 | |
| **cream of wheat, inst** | | | | | | | | | | | | | | | |
| ckd | 115 | 152.8 | 0.4 | | | | | .10 | | 8 | 5ᵈ | 44 | 11 | .31 | |
| *3/4 cup* | 181 | 3.3 | 23.8 | | | | .20 | 1.3 | | | 36 | 32 | 9.00 | .069 | |
| mix & eat | 102 | 116.4 | 0.3 | | | 375 | | .30 | .50 | 100 | 241 | 20 | 8 | .24 | |
| *1 pkt prep* | 142 | 2.8 | 21.4 | | | 1250 | .40 | 5.0 | | .13 | 38 | 20 | 8.10 | .041 | |
| mix & eat, flavoredᵉ | 132 | 117.2 | 0.4 | | | 375 | | .20 | .50 | 100 | 241 | 40 | 9 | .23 | |
| *1 pkt prep* | 150 | 2.5 | 28.9 | | | 1250 | .40 | 5.0 | | | 55 | 20 | 8.10 | .057 | |
| **cream of wheat, quick, ckd** | 96 | 155.1 | 0.4 | | | | | .10 | | 7 | 104ᶠ | 38 | 9 | .26 | |
| *3/4 cup* | 179 | 2.7 | 20.0 | | | | .10 | 1.1 | | .13 | 35 | 75 | 7.60 | .050 | |
| **cream of wheat, reg, ckd** | 100 | 163.8 | 0.4 | | | | | .10 | | 7 | 2ᵍ | 38 | 7 | .24 | |
| *3/4 cup* | 188 | 2.9 | 20.8 | | | | .10 | 1.1 | | .14 | 33 | 31 | 7.70 | .056 | |
| **farina** | | | | | | | | | | | | | | | |
| ckd, enr | 87 | 153.8 | 0.1 | | | | | .09 | .02 | 4 | 1ʰ | 3 | 3 | .12 | .00 |
| *3/4 cup* | 175 | 2.5 | 18.5 | | | 0 | .14 | 1.0 | .00 | .10 | 22 | 21 | .88 | .019 | |
| ckd, unenr | 87 | 153.8 | 0.1 | | | | | .02 | .02 | 4 | 1ʰ | 3 | 3 | .12 | .00 |
| *3/4 cup* | 175 | 2.5 | 18.5 | | | 0 | .02 | 0.1 | .00 | .098 | 22 | 21 | .04 | .019 | |
| dry, quick, creamy wheat, Quaker | 101 | 3.1 | 0.2 | | | | | .08 | .02 | 19 | 1 | 6 | 6 | .00 | .000 |
| *2 1/2 T (1 oz)* | 28 | 3.1 | 21.7 | | | 0 | .12 | 1.0 | .00 | .00 | 31 | 26 | .81 | .060 | |
| **maltex, ckd** | 135 | 151.5 | 0.8 | | | | | .07 | .06 | 16 | 7ⁱ | 14 | 43 | 1.40 | |
| *3/4 cup* | 187 | 4.3 | 29.7 | | | | .19 | 1.8 | | .17 | 200 | 134 | 1.35 | .252 | |
| **malt-o-meal, plain/choc, ckd** | 92 | 157.6 | 0.2 | | | 0 | 0 | .20 | .01 | 4 | 2ʲ | 4 | | .13 | |
| *3/4 cup* | 180 | 2.6 | 19.4 | | | 0 | .30 | 4.4 | | .104 | 35 | 18 | 7.10 | .020 | |
| **maypo, ckd** | 128 | 148.9 | 1.8 | | | 527 | 21 | .60 | .70 | 7 | 6ᵏ | 94 | 38 | 1.12 | |
| *3/4 cup* | 180 | 4.4 | 23.9 | | | 1754 | .50 | 7.0 | 2.10 | .25 | 158 | 186 | 6.30 | .119 | |
| **oatmeal, inst** | 104 | 151.8 | 1.7 | | 0 | 455 | | .29 | .74 | 150 | 286 | 163 | 35 | | |
| *1 pkt prep* | 177 | 4.4 | 18.1 | | | 1514 | .53 | 5.5 | .00 | .35 | 100 | 133 | 6.32 | | |
| Quaker | 105 | 2.7 | 1.7 | | | | | .17 | .40 | 80 | 281 | 100 | 35 | 1.00 | 1.000 |
| *1 pkt (3/4 cup ckd)* | 28 | 4.5 | 18.1 | | | 1000 | .30 | 3.0 | .00 | .00 | 101 | 128 | 8.10 | .130 | |
| w/ apples & cinn | 135 | 115.9 | 1.6 | | | 435 | | .28 | .70 | 137 | 222 | 158 | 31 | | |
| *1 pkt prep* | 149 | 3.9 | 26.3 | | | 1450 | .48 | 5.1 | .00 | .35 | 107 | 117 | 6.07 | | |
| w/ apples & cinn, Quaker | 134 | 2.5 | 1.6 | | | | | .17 | .40 | 80 | 181 | 100 | 31 | 1.00 | 1.000 |
| *1 pkt (3/4 cup ckd)* | 35 | 3.9 | 26.0 | | | 1000 | .30 | 3.0 | .00 | .00 | 108 | 110 | 4.50 | .120 | |
| w/ bran & raisins | 158 | 155.7 | 1.9 | | | 479 | | .63 | .76 | 155 | 247 | 173 | 57 | 1.35 | 1.587 |
| *1 pkt prep* | 195 | 4.9 | 30.4 | | | 1596 | .56 | 8.1 | .00 | .45 | 236 | 206 | 7.61 | .284 | |
| w/ bran & raisins, Quaker | 153 | 3.5 | 1.7 | | | | | .17 | .40 | 80 | 240 | 100 | 71 | 1.00 | 2.000 |
| *1 pkt (3/4 cup ckd)* | 43 | 5.2 | 29.2 | | | 1000 | .30 | 3.0 | .00 | .00 | 227 | 156 | 4.50 | .220 | |

ᵃ Na is 540 mg if salt is added according to label directions.
ᵇ White corn grits contain only a trace of vitamin A; yellow corn grits contain 145 IU.
ᶜ Na is 317 mg if salt is added according to label directions.
ᵈ Na is 273 mg if salt is added according to label directions.
ᵉ Apple w/cinn, banana & spice, or maple & brown sugar.
ᶠ Na is 347 mg if salt is added according to label directions.
ᵍ Na is 252 mg if salt is added according to label directions.
ʰ Na is 576 mg if salt is added according to label directions.
ⁱ Na is 142 mg if salt is added according to label directions.
ʲ Na is 243 mg if salt is added according to label directions.
ᵏ Na is 194 mg if salt is added according to label directions.

| | KCAL / WT (g) | H₂O (g) / PRO (g) | FAT (g) / CHO (g) | PUFA (g) / SFA (g) | CHOL (mg) / DFIB (g) | A (RE) / A (IU) | C (mg) / B-1 (mg) | B-2 (mg) / NIA (mg) | B-6 (mg) / B-12 (mcg) | FOL (mcg) / PANT (mg) | Na (mg) / K (mg) | Ca (mg) / P (mg) | Mg (mg) / Fe (mg) | Zn (mg) / Cu (mg) | Mn (mg) |
|---|---|---|---|---|---|---|---|---|---|---|---|---|---|---|---|
| w/ cinn & spice | 177 | 118.0 | 1.9 | | | 475 | | .34 | .77 | 153 | 280 | 172 | 51 | .97 | 1.476 |
| · *1 pkt prep* | 161 | 4.8 | 35.1 | | | 1581 | .56 | 5.7 | .00 | .38 | 104 | 146 | 6.65 | .119 | |
| w/ cinn & spice, Quaker | 176 | 2.9 | 1.8 | | | | | .17 | .40 | 80 | 258 | 100 | 40 | 1.00 | 1.000 |
| *1 pkt (3/4 cup ckd)* | 46 | 5.0 | 34.8 | | | 1000 | .30 | 3.0 | .00 | .00 | 106 | 143 | 8.10 | .130 | |
| w/ honey & graham, Quaker | 136 | 2.1 | 1.7 | | | | | .17 | .40 | 80 | 224 | 100 | 35 | 1.00 | 1.000 |
| *1 pkt (3/4 cup ckd)* | 35 | 3.6 | 26.6 | | | 1000 | .30 | 3.0 | .00 | .00 | 87 | 113 | 4.50 | .120 | |
| w/ maple & brown sugar | 163 | 115.3 | 1.9 | | | 451 | | .32 | .74 | 145 | 280 | 162 | 85 | | |
| *1 pkt prep* | 155 | 4.6 | 31.9 | | | 1503 | .53 | 5.4 | .00 | .32 | 102 | 143 | 6.35 | | |
| w/ maple & brown sugar, Quaker | 163 | 2.7 | 1.9 | | | | | .17 | .40 | 80 | 228 | 100 | 85 | 1.00 | 1.000 |
| *1 pkt (3/4 cup ckd)* | 43 | 4.6 | 31.9 | | | 1000 | .30 | 3.0 | .00 | .00 | 98 | 136 | 8.10 | .200 | |
| w/ peaches & cream, Quaker | 136 | 2.0 | 2.0 | | | | | .17 | .40 | 80 | 134 | 100 | 35 | 1.00 | 1.000 |
| *1 pkt (3/4 cup ckd)* | 35 | 3.5 | 26.0 | | | 1000 | .30 | 3.0 | .00 | .00 | 130 | 60 | 4.50 | .110 | |
| w/ raisins & spice | 161 | 118.4 | 1.8 | | | 440 | | .36 | .75 | 150 | 225 | 165 | 57 | | |
| *1 pkt prep* | 158 | 4.3 | 31.8 | | | 1466 | .51 | 5.5 | .00 | .37 | 150 | 133 | 6.58 | | |
| w/ raisins & spice, Quaker | 159 | 3.4 | 1.8 | | | | | .17 | .40 | 80 | 217 | 100 | 57 | 1.00 | 1.000 |
| *1 pkt (3/4 cup ckd)* | 43 | 4.5 | 31.4 | | | 1000 | .30 | 3.0 | .00 | .00 | 155 | 123 | 4.50 | .160 | |
| w/ raisins, dates & walnuts, Quaker | 150 | 2.5 | 3.6 | | | | | .17 | .40 | 80 | 155 | 100 | 39 | 1.00 | 1.000 |
| *1 pkt (3/4 cup)* | 37 | 4.0 | 25.4 | | | 1000 | .30 | 3.0 | .00 | .00 | 128 | 128 | 4.50 | .160 | |
| w/ strawberries & cream, Quaker | 136 | 2.0 | 1.9 | | | | | .17 | .40 | 80 | 172 | 100 | 34 | 1.00 | 1.000 |
| *1 pkt (3/4 cup)* | 35 | 3.4 | 26.3 | | | 1000 | .30 | 3.0 | .00 | .00 | 158 | 121 | 4.50 | .100 | |
| **oatmeal, quick/old fashioned, Quaker** | 109 | 2.6 | 1.9 | | | | | .03 | .06 | 29 | 1 | 14 | 40 | 1.00 | 1.000 |
| *1/3 cup dry (2/3 cup ckd)* | 28 | 4.6 | 18.4 | | | 0 | .19 | 0.2 | .00 | .00 | 105 | 128 | 1.08 | .090 | |
| **oatmeal, quick/reg, ckd** | 108 | 149.3 | 1.8 | 0.7 | 0 | | | .04 | .04 | 7 | 1ᵃ | 15 | 42 | .86 | 1.024 |
| *3/4 cup (from 1/3 cup or 1 oz dry)* | 175 | 4.5 | 18.9 | 0.3 | 1.6 | 29 | .19 | 0.2 | .00 | .35 | 99 | 133 | 1.19 | .096 | |
| **oatmeal, quick/reg, Ralston Purina** | 100 | | 1.8 | | | | 1 | .06 | .06 | 14 | 8 | 15 | 41 | .95 | |
| *1 oz dry* | 28 | 4.6 | 18.0 | | 3.4 | 8 | .23 | 0.3 | .00 | .26 | 103 | 132 | 1.25 | .147 | |
| **ralston, ckd** | 100 | 163.5 | 0.6 | | | | 1 | .13 | .09 | 13 | 3ᵇ | 10 | 45 | 1.06 | |
| *3/4 cup* | 190 | 4.2 | 21.2 | | 3.2 | 35 | .15 | 1.5 | .08 | .25 | 115 | 111 | 1.24 | .150 | |
| **roman meal, ckd** | 111 | 149.7 | 0.7 | | | | | .09 | .09 | 18 | 2ᶜ | 22 | 82 | 1.34 | |
| *3/4 cup* | 181 | 4.9 | 24.8 | | | | .18 | 2.3 | | .28 | 227 | 162 | 1.59 | .241 | |
| **roman meal w/ oats, ckd** | 127 | 146.8 | 1.5 | | | | | .16 | .28 | | 7ᵈ | 21 | 56 | | |
| *3/4 cup* | 180 | 5.4 | 25.6 | | | | .23 | 2.4 | | .19 | | 176 | 1.05 | .112 | |
| **wheatena, ckd** | 101 | 155.4 | 0.8 | | | | | .04 | .04 | 13 | 4ᵉ | 8 | 37 | 1.26 | 1.496 |
| *3/4 cup* | 182 | 3.7 | 21.5 | | | | .02 | 1.0 | | .08 | 140 | 109 | 1.02 | .095 | |
| **wheat hearts, ckd, Ralston Purina** | 110 | | 1.0 | | | | | | | | 0ᶠ | | | | |
| *3/4 cup (from 1 oz dry)* | | 4.0 | 21.0 | | | | | | | | 110 | | | | |
| **whole wheat hot natural cereal, ckd,** | 113 | 152.1 | 0.7 | | | | | .09 | .05 | 19 | 1ᵍ | 13 | 40 | .87 | 1.061 |
| **Quaker**—*3/4 cup* | 182 | 3.7 | 24.9 | | | 0 | .13 | 1.6 | .00 | .30 | 129 | 126 | 1.13 | .151 | |

## 4. CEREALS, READY-TO-EAT

| | KCAL / WT (g) | H₂O (g) / PRO (g) | FAT (g) / CHO (g) | PUFA (g) / SFA (g) | CHOL (mg) / DFIB (g) | A (RE) / A (IU) | C (mg) / B-1 (mg) | B-2 (mg) / NIA (mg) | B-6 (mg) / B-12 (mcg) | FOL (mcg) / PANT (mg) | Na (mg) / K (mg) | Ca (mg) / P (mg) | Mg (mg) / Fe (mg) | Zn (mg) / Cu (mg) | Mn (mg) |
|---|---|---|---|---|---|---|---|---|---|---|---|---|---|---|---|
| **almond delight, Ralston Purina** | 110 | | 1.6 | | | | 15 | | .50 | 100 | 199 | 24 | | 1.50 | |
| *3/4 cup (1 oz)* | 28 | 2.1 | 23.0 | | 1.5 | | .38 | 5.0 | 1.50 | | | | 1.80 | | |
| **alpha-bits, Post** | 110 | 0.3 | 0.7 | 0.2 | 0 | 371 | 0 | .42 | .49 | 99 | 178 | 9 | 22 | 1.48 | |
| *1 cup (1 oz)* | 28 | 2.3 | 24.1 | 0.2 | 0.6 | 1235 | .37 | 4.9 | 1.48 | .15 | 59 | 57 | 2.67 | .086 | |
| **apple jacks, Kellogg's** | 110 | 0.7 | 0.1 | | | 375 | 15 | .40 | .50 | 100 | 125 | 3 | 6 | 3.70 | |
| *1 cup (1 oz)* | 28 | 1.5 | 25.7 | | 0.2 | 1250 | .40 | 5.0 | | .10 | 23 | 30 | 4.50 | .099 | |
| **body buddies, brown sugar & honey,** | 110 | | 1.0 | | | | | | | | 290 | | | | |
| **General Mills**—*1 cup (1 oz)* | 28 | 2.0 | 24.0 | | | | | | | | 50 | | | | |
| **body buddies, natural fruit flavor, General** | 110 | | 1.0 | | | | | | | | 280 | | | | |
| **Mills**—*1 cup (1 oz)* | 28 | 2.0 | 24.0 | | | | | | | | 40 | | | | |
| **booberry, General Mills** | 110 | | 1.0 | | | | | | | | 210 | | | | |
| *1 cup (1 oz)* | 28 | 1.0 | 24.0 | | | | | | | | 45 | | | | |

ᵃ Na is 280 mg if salt is added according to label directions.
ᵇ Na is 357 mg if salt is added according to label directions.
ᶜ Na is 148 mg if salt is added according to label directions.
ᵈ Na is 405 mg if salt is added according to label directions.
ᵉ Na is 433 mg if salt is added according to label directions.
ᶠ Na is 190 mg if salt is added according to label directions.
ᵍ Na is 424 mg if salt is added according to label directions.

| | KCAL | H₂O (g) | FAT (g) | PUFA (g) | CHOL (mg) | A (RE) | C (mg) | B-2 (mg) | B-6 (mg) | FOL (mcg) | Na (mg) | Ca (mg) | Mg (mg) | Zn (mg) | Mn (mg) |
|---|---|---|---|---|---|---|---|---|---|---|---|---|---|---|---|
| | WT (g) | PRO (g) | CHO (g) | SFA (g) | DFIB (g) | A (IU) | B-1 (mg) | NIA (mg) | B-12 (mcg) | PANT (mg) | K (mg) | P (mg) | Fe (mg) | Cu (mg) | |
| **bran** | | | | | | | | | | | | | | | |
| Kellogg's all-bran | 71 | 0.9 | 0.5 | | | 375 | 15 | .40 | .50 | 100 | 320 | 23 | 106 | 3.70 | |
| *1/3 cup (1 oz)* | 28 | 4.0 | 21.1 | | 8.5 | 1250 | .40 | 5.0 | | .49 | 350 | 264 | 4.50 | .324 | |
| Loma Linda | 60 | 1.0 | 1.0 | | 0 | | | .08 | .08 | | 115 | 31 | | .95 | |
| *1/3 cup (1 oz)* | 28 | 4.0 | 19.0 | | | | .11 | 0.8 | .00 | .25 | 220 | | 1.70 | | |
| 100% | 76 | 0.8 | 1.4 | 0.8 | | | 27 | .80 | .90 | | 196 | 20 | 134 | 2.46 | |
| *1/2 cup (1 oz)* | 28 | 3.5 | 20.7 | 0.3 | 8.4 | | .70 | 9.0 | 2.70 | .55 | 354 | 344 | 3.49 | .447 | |
| **bran buds, Kellogg's** | 73 | 0.8 | 0.7 | | | 375 | 15 | .40 | .50 | 100 | 174 | 19 | 90 | 3.70 | |
| *1/3 cup (1 oz)* | 28 | 3.9 | 21.6 | | 7.9 | 1250 | .40 | 5.0 | | .55 | 474 | 246 | 4.50 | .300 | |
| **bran chex, Ralston Purina** | 90 | 0.7 | 0.7 | | | 6 | 15 | .16 | .50 | 100 | 299 | 17 | 73 | 3.75 | |
| *2/3 cup (1 oz)* | 28 | 2.9 | 23.0 | | 6.1 | 62 | .38 | 5.0 | 1.50 | .29 | 203 | 290 | 4.50 | .209 | |
| **bran flakes** | | | | | | | | | | | | | | | |
| Kellogg's | 93 | 0.9 | 0.5 | | | 375 | | .40 | .50 | 100 | 264 | 14 | 52 | 3.70 | |
| *3/4 cup (1 oz)* | 28 | 3.6 | 22.2 | | 4.0 | 1250 | .40 | 5.0 | 1.50 | | 180 | 139 | 8.10 | .210 | |
| Post | 87 | 0.9 | 0.4 | 0.2 | 0 | 371 | 0 | .42 | .49 | 99 | 227 | 16 | 68 | 1.48 | |
| *2/3 cup (1 oz)* | 28 | 3.0 | 22.2 | 0.1 | 5.6 | 1235 | .37 | 4.9 | 1.48 | | 199 | 166 | 8.00 | .240 | |
| Ralston Purina | 92 | 0.7 | 0.4 | | | 375 | 15 | .40 | .50 | 100 | 264 | 22 | 68 | 1.18 | |
| *3/4 cup (1 oz)* | 28 | 3.3 | 22.6 | | 3.5 | 1250 | .40 | 5.0 | 1.50 | .12 | 184 | 158 | 4.50 | .207 | |
| **bran muffin crisp, General Mills** | 130 | | 1.0 | | | | | | | | 250 | | | | |
| *2/3 cup (1.2 oz)* | 35 | 3.0 | 30.0 | | 4.0 | | | | | | 190 | | | | |
| **cap'n crunch, Quaker** | 121 | 0.7 | 2.6 | 0.4 | | 0 | | .26 | .50 | 100 | 185 | 5 | 8 | 2.00 | .000 |
| *3/4 cup (1 oz)* | 28 | 1.4 | 22.9 | 1.7 | 0.3 | 0 | .37 | 5.0 | 1.00 | 2.00 | 37 | 20 | 4.50 | .020 | |
| **cap'n crunch's** | | | | | | | | | | | | | | | |
| choco crunch, Quaker | 116 | 0.6 | 1.7 | | | | | .26 | .50 | 100 | 172 | 5 | 8 | 2.00 | .000 |
| *3/4 cup (1 oz)* | 28 | 1.5 | 23.8 | | | 0 | .37 | 5.0 | 1.00 | 2.00 | 45 | 20 | 4.50 | .040 | |
| crunchberries, Quaker | 120 | 0.7 | 2.6 | 0.4 | | | | .26 | .50 | 100 | 166 | 9 | 8 | 2.00 | .000 |
| *3/4 cup (1 oz)* | 28 | 1.4 | 22.9 | 1.6 | 0.3 | 0 | .37 | 5.0 | 1.00 | 2.00 | 40 | 20 | 4.50 | .010 | |
| peanut butter, Quaker | 127 | 0.5 | 3.8 | 0.8 | | 0 | | .26 | .50 | 100 | 210 | 6 | 8 | 2.00 | .000 |
| *3/4 cup (1 oz)* | 28 | 2.3 | 20.9 | 1.5 | 0.3 | 0 | .37 | 5.0 | 1.00 | 2.00 | 54 | 20 | 4.50 | .050 | |
| **cheerios, General Mills** | 111 | 1.4 | 1.8 | 0.8 | | 375 | 15 | .42 | .50 | 6 | 290 | 48 | 39 | .79 | .763 |
| *1 1/4 cups (1 oz)* | 28 | 4.3 | 19.6 | 0.3 | 2.0 | 1250 | .37 | 5.0 | 1.50 | .29 | 105 | 134 | 4.45 | .143 | |
| **cinnamon toast crunch, General Mills** | 120 | | 3.0 | | | | | | | | 220 | | | | |
| *3/4 cup (1 oz)* | 28 | 1.0 | 23.0 | | | | | | | | 40 | | | | |
| **circus fun, General Mills** | 110 | | 1.0 | | | | | | | | 160 | | | | |
| *1 cup (1 oz)* | 28 | 1.0 | 24.0 | | | | | | | | 25 | | | | |
| **cocoa krispies, Kellogg's** | 110 | 0.7 | 0.4 | | | 375 | 15 | .40 | .50 | 100 | 217 | 5 | 9 | 1.50 | |
| *3/4 cup (1 oz)* | 28 | 1.5 | 25.2 | | 0.1 | 1250 | .40 | 5.0 | | | 42 | 37 | 1.80 | .090 | |
| **cocoa pebbles, Post** | 112 | 0.6 | 1.1 | 0.0 | 0 | 371 | 0 | .42 | .49 | 99 | 158 | 5 | 11 | 1.48 | |
| *7/8 cup (1 oz)* | 28 | 1.3 | 24.5 | 1.0 | 0.1 | 1235 | .37 | 4.9 | 1.48 | | 41 | 22 | 1.78 | .056 | |
| **cocoa puffs, General Mills** | 110 | | 1.0 | | | | | | | | 200 | | | | |
| *1 cup (1 oz)* | 28 | 1.0 | 25.0 | | | | | | | | 45 | | | | |
| **cookie crisp, choc chip, Ralston Purina** | 110 | 0.5 | 1.0 | | | 375 | 15 | .26 | .50 | 100 | 190 | 9 | 8 | 2.25 | |
| *1 cup (1 oz)* | 28 | 1.5 | 25.0 | | 1.0 | 1250 | .38 | 5.0 | 1.50 | 2.00 | 42 | 30 | 4.50 | .005 | |
| **cookie crisp, vanilla wafer, Ralston Purina** | 110 | 0.5 | 1.1 | | | | | .26 | .50 | 100 | 203 | 8 | 7 | 2.25 | |
| *1 cup (1 oz)* | 28 | 1.5 | 25.0 | | 1.0 | | .38 | 5.0 | 1.50 | 2.00 | 29 | 47 | 4.50 | .047 | |
| **corn bran, Quaker** | 109 | 0.4 | 0.9 | | | 0 | | .26 | .50 | 100 | 244 | 23 | 8 | 3.00 | .000 |
| *2/3 cup (1 oz)* | 28 | 2.2 | 23.3 | | 5.4 | 0 | .37 | 5.0 | 1.00 | 2.00 | 62 | 20 | 8.10 | .060 | |
| **corn chex, Ralston Purina** | 110 | 0.5 | 0.2 | | | | 15 | .10 | .50 | 100 | 293 | 2 | 3 | .12 | .024 |
| *1 cup (1 oz)* | 28 | 2.0 | 25.0 | | 1.1 | | .38 | 5.0 | 1.50 | .03 | 23 | 10 | 1.80 | .023 | |
| **corn flakes** | | | | | | | | | | | | | | | |
| country, General Mills | 110 | | 1.0 | | | | | | | | 310 | | | | |
| *1 cup (1 oz)* | 28 | 2.0 | 25.0 | | | | | | | | 30 | | | | |
| Kellogg's | 110 | 0.7 | 0.1 | | | 375 | 15 | .40 | .50 | 100 | 351 | 1 | 3 | .08 | .023 |
| *1 1/4 cups (1 oz)* | 28 | 2.3 | 24.4 | | 0.3 | 1250 | .40 | 5.0 | | .05 | 26 | 18 | 1.80 | .019 | |
| low sodium | 113 | 0.9 | 0.1 | | | | | | .05 | | 3 | 12 | 3 | .08 | |
| *1 cup (1 oz)* | 28 | 2.2 | 25.2 | | | | .00 | 0.1 | | | 21 | 14 | .63 | .025 | |
| Post Toasties, Post | 108 | 1.0 | 0.3 | 0.1 | 0 | 371 | 0 | .42 | .49 | 99 | 277 | 2 | 3 | .27 | |
| *1 cup (1 oz)* | 28 | 1.9 | 24.0 | 0.2 | 0.4 | 1235 | .37 | 4.9 | 1.48 | | 31 | 11 | .36 | .023 | |

| | KCAL / WT (g) | H₂O (g) / PRO (g) | FAT (g) / CHO (g) | PUFA (g) / SFA (g) | CHOL (mg) / DFIB (g) | A (RE) / A (IU) | C (mg) / B-1 (mg) | B-2 (mg) / NIA (mg) | B-6 (mg) / B-12 (mcg) | FOL (mcg) / PANT (mg) | Na (mg) / K (mg) | Ca (mg) / P (mg) | Mg (mg) / Fe (mg) | Zn (mg) / Cu (mg) | Mn (mg) |
|---|---|---|---|---|---|---|---|---|---|---|---|---|---|---|---|
| Ralston Purina | 110 | 0.8 | 0.1 | | | | 15 | | .50 | 100 | 274 | 1 | 3 | .05 | |
| *1 cup (1 oz)* | 28 | 2.0 | 25.0 | | 1.4 | 1250 | .38 | 5.0 | 1.50 | .06 | 25 | 10 | 1.00 | .023 | |
| **corn total, General Mills** | 110 | | 1.0 | | | | | | | | 310 | | | | |
| *1 cup (1 oz)* | 28 | 2.0 | 24.0 | | | | | | | | 30 | | | | |
| **count chocula, General Mills** | 110 | | 1.0 | | | | | | | | 210 | | | | |
| *1 cup (1 oz)* | 28 | 2.0 | 24.0 | | | | | | | | 65 | | | | |
| **cracklin bran, Kellogg's** | 108 | 1.0 | 4.1 | | | 375 | 15 | .40 | .50 | 100 | 230 | 19 | 55 | 1.50 | |
| *1/3 cup (1 oz)* | 28 | 2.6 | 19.4 | | 4.3 | 1250 | .40 | 5.0 | | .32 | 168 | 114 | 1.80 | .159 | |
| **crisp rice, low Na** | 114 | 0.9 | 0.1 | | | | | .05 | | | 3 | 19 | 11 | .43 | |
| *1 cup (1 oz)* | 28 | 1.6 | 25.8 | | | | .00 | 0.4 | | | 22 | 29 | .87 | .069 | |
| **crispy oatmeal & raisin chex, Ralston Purina**—*3/4 cup (1.3 oz)* | 140 | | 0.5 | | | | 4 | .32 | .50 | 100 | 168 | 12 | 27 | 3.75 | |
| | 38 | 3.0 | 31.0 | | 1.7 | | .38 | 5.0 | 1.50 | .08 | 111 | 85 | | .124 | |
| **crispy rice** | 112 | 0.7 | 0.1 | | | | 1 | .00 | .05 | 3 | 208 | 5 | 12 | .47 | |
| *1 cup (1 oz)* | 28 | 1.8 | 25.1 | | 0.4 | 1250 | .10 | 2.0 | .08 | .11 | 27 | 31 | .70 | .062 | |
| **crispy wheats & raisins, General Mills** | 99 | 2.0 | 0.5 | | | 375 | | .40 | .50 | | 180 | 47 | 23 | .34 | |
| *3/4 cup (1 oz)* | 28 | 2.0 | 23.1 | | 1.3 | 1250 | .40 | 5.0 | 1.50 | | 100 | 77 | 4.50 | .085 | |
| **C.W. Post** | 126 | 0.7 | 4.4 | 0.4 | | 375 | | .40 | .50 | 100 | 49 | 14 | 20 | .48 | |
| *1/4 cup (1 oz)* | 28 | 2.6 | 20.3 | 3.3 | 0.7 | 1250 | .40 | 5.0 | 1.50 | | 58 | 66 | 4.50 | .110 | |
| **C.W. Post w/ raisins** | 123 | 1.1 | 4.0 | 0.4 | | 375 | | .40 | .50 | 100 | 44 | 14 | 20 | .45 | |
| *1/4 cup (1 oz)* | 28 | 2.4 | 20.3 | 3.0 | 0.5 | 1250 | .40 | 5.0 | 1.50 | | 72 | 64 | 4.50 | .109 | |
| **dairy crisp, Pet** | 120 | | 4.0 | | | | | | | | 140 | | | | |
| *1/4 cup (1 oz)* | 28 | 3.0 | 19.0 | | | | | | | | | | | | |
| **fiber one, General Mills**[a] | 60 | | 1.0 | | | | | | | | 230 | | | | |
| *1/2 cup (1 oz)* | 28 | 4.0 | 21.0 | | 12.0 | | | | | | 340 | | | | |
| **fortified oat flakes, Post** | 105 | 0.8 | 0.5 | 0.2 | 0 | 371 | 0 | .42 | .49 | 99 | 247 | 33 | 41 | 1.02 | |
| *2/3 cup (1 oz)* | 28 | 6.4 | 19.9 | 0.1 | 0.8 | 1235 | .37 | 4.9 | 1.48 | | 144 | 95 | 8.00 | .170 | |
| **frankenberry, General Mills** | 110 | | 1.0 | | | | | | | | 210 | | | | |
| *1 cup (1 oz)* | 28 | 1.0 | 24.0 | | | | | | | | 45 | | | | |
| **froot loops, Kellogg's** | 111 | 0.7 | 0.5 | | | 375 | 15 | .40 | .50 | 100 | 145 | 3 | 7 | 3.70 | |
| *1 cup (1 oz)* | 28 | 1.7 | 25.0 | | 0.2 | 1250 | .40 | 5.0 | | .10 | 26 | 24 | 4.50 | .060 | |
| **frosted mini-wheats, Kellogg's**[b] | 102 | 1.4 | 0.3 | | | 375 | 15 | .40 | .50 | 100 | 8 | 9 | 23 | 1.50 | |
| *4 biscuits (1 oz)* | 28 | 2.9 | 23.4 | | 2.1 | 1250 | .40 | 5.0 | | | 97 | 74 | 1.80 | .130 | |
| **frosted rice krinkles** | 109 | 0.5 | 0.1 | | | 375 | | .40 | .50 | 100 | 179 | 4 | 8 | 1.50 | |
| *7/8 cup (1 oz)* | 28 | 1.4 | 25.8 | | | 1250 | .40 | 5.0 | 1.50 | | 14 | 20 | 1.80 | .047 | |
| **fruit & fiber, Post** | | | | | | | | | | | | | | | |
|   harvest medley | 91 | 1.3 | 1.0 | 0.3 | 0 | | 0 | .42 | .49 | 99 | 192 | 18 | 61 | 1.48 | |
| *1/2 cup (1 oz)* | 28 | 2.8 | 21.7 | 0.1 | 4.2 | 1235 | .37 | 4.9 | 1.48 | .06 | 201 | 147 | 4.44 | .222 | |
|   mountain trail | 91 | 1.4 | 1.2 | 0.3 | 0 | | 2 | .42 | .49 | 99 | 177 | 16 | 59 | 1.48 | |
| *1/2 cup (1 oz)* | 28 | 2.8 | 21.4 | 0.5 | 4.2 | 1235 | .37 | 4.9 | 1.48 | .06 | 200 | 141 | 4.44 | .226 | |
|   tropical fruit | 93 | 1.1 | 1.4 | 0.3 | 0 | | 0 | .42 | .49 | 99 | 178 | 15 | 59 | 1.48 | |
| *1/2 cup (1 oz)* | 28 | 2.6 | 21.7 | 0.8 | 4.3 | 1235 | .37 | 4.9 | 1.48 | | 207 | 136 | 4.45 | .224 | |
|   w/ dates, raisins & walnuts | 89 | 1.5 | 0.8 | 0.5 | 0 | | 0 | .42 | .49 | 99 | 178 | 15 | 57 | 1.48 | |
| *1/2 cup (1 oz)* | 28 | 2.7 | 21.9 | 0.1 | 4.2 | 1235 | .37 | 4.9 | 1.48 | | 197 | 138 | 4.44 | .214 | |
| **fruity pebbles, Post** | 112 | 0.8 | 1.0 | 0.0 | 0 | 371 | 0 | .42 | .49 | 99 | 144 | 4 | 7 | 1.48 | |
| *7/8 cup (1 oz)* | 28 | 1.1 | 24.6 | 1.0 | 0.2 | 1235 | .37 | 4.9 | 1.48 | | 21 | 17 | 1.78 | .039 | |
| **golden grahams, General Mills** | 109 | 0.6 | 1.1 | 0.2 | | 375 | 15 | .42 | .50 | | 280 | 17 | 12 | .25 | |
| *3/4 cup (1 oz)* | 28 | 1.6 | 24.1 | 0.8 | 0.5 | 1250 | .37 | 5.0 | 1.50 | .12 | 55 | 41 | 4.45 | .226 | |
| **graham crackos, Kellogg's** | 102 | 0.9 | 0.2 | | | 375 | 15 | .40 | .50 | 100 | 185 | 13 | 24 | 1.50 | |
| *3/4 cup (1 oz)* | 28 | 2.1 | 24.5 | | 1.7 | 1250 | .40 | 5.0 | | | 102 | 62 | 1.80 | .074 | |
| **granola** | | | | | | | | | | | | | | | |
|   hearty, Post | 127 | 0.5 | 4.1 | 0.4 | 0 | | 0 | .42 | .49 | 99 | 76 | 11 | 23 | .71 | |
| *1/4 cup (1 oz)* | 28 | 2.4 | 20.7 | 3.0 | 0.9 | 1235 | .37 | 4.9 | 1.48 | | 62 | 60 | 4.44 | .116 | |
|   hearty w/ raisins, Post | 123 | 0.8 | 3.8 | 0.4 | 0 | | 0 | .42 | .49 | 99 | 79 | 11 | 22 | .66 | |
| *1/4 cup (1 oz)* | 28 | 2.2 | 20.8 | 2.7 | 0.9 | 1235 | .37 | 4.9 | 1.48 | | 74 | 57 | 4.44 | .113 | |
|   homemade | 138 | 0.9 | 7.7 | 4.0 | | | 0 | .07 | .10 | 23 | 3 | 18 | 33 | 1.04 | |
| *1/4 cup (1 oz)* | 28 | 3.5 | 15.6 | 1.4 | | 10 | .17 | 0.5 | | .17 | 142 | 115 | 1.13 | .162 | |
| **Kretschmer Sun Country** | | | | | | | | | | | | | | | |
|   w/ almonds | 130 | | 5.0 | | | | | .04 | | | 10 | 23 | | | |
| *1/4 cup (1 oz)* | 28 | 3.0 | 19.0 | | 1.0 | | .10 | | | | | 85 | .85 | | |

[a] Contains aspartame.  
[b] Sugar frosted, brown sugar cinnamon or apple flavored.

| Food | KCAL / WT (g) | H₂O (g) / PRO (g) | FAT (g) / CHO (g) | PUFA (g) / SFA (g) | CHOL (mg) / DFIB (g) | A (RE) / A (IU) | C (mg) / B-1 (mg) | B-2 (mg) / NIA (mg) | B-6 (mg) / B-12 (mcg) | FOL (mcg) / PANT (mg) | Na (mg) / K (mg) | Ca (mg) / P (mg) | Mg (mg) / Fe (mg) | Zn (mg) / Cu (mg) | Mn (mg) |
|---|---|---|---|---|---|---|---|---|---|---|---|---|---|---|---|
| w/ raisins | 130 | | 5.0 | | | | | | | .04 | 10 | 23 | | | |
| *1/4 cup (1 oz)* | 28 | 3.0 | 20.0 | | | | .10 | | | | | 85 | .85 | | |
| w/ raisins & dates | 130 | | 4.0 | | | | | | | .04 | 10 | 23 | | | |
| *1/4 cup (1 oz)* | 28 | 3.0 | 20.0 | | | | .10 | | | | | 85 | .85 | | |
| Nature Valleyᵃ | 126 | 1.1 | 4.9 | 0.7 | | | | .05 | | 21 | 58 | 18 | 29 | .55 | |
| *1/3 cup (1 oz)* | 28 | 2.9 | 18.9 | 3.3 | 1.0 | | .10 | 0.2 | | .23 | 98 | 89 | .95 | .092 | |
| grape-nut flakes, Post | 104 | 0.9 | 0.8 | 0.2 | 0 | 371 | 0 | .42 | .49 | 99 | 158 | 10 | 30 | 1.19 | |
| *7/8 cup (1 oz)* | 28 | 2.8 | 22.7 | 0.4 | 1.9 | 1235 | .37 | 4.9 | 1.48 | .29 | 94 | 82 | 8.00 | .128 | |
| grape-nuts, Post | 104 | 1.0 | 0.1 | 0.1 | 0 | 371 | 0 | .42 | .49 | 99 | 188 | 11 | 27 | 1.19 | |
| *1/4 cup (1 oz)* | 28 | 3.1 | 23.1 | 0.0 | 1.8 | 1235 | .37 | 4.9 | 1.48 | .27 | 85 | 71 | 2.67 | .118 | |
| grape-nuts w/ raisins, Post | 98 | 2.3 | 0.3 | 0.1 | 0 | | 0 | .42 | .49 | 99 | 138 | 11 | 22 | .64 | |
| *1/4 cup (1 oz)* | 28 | 2.7 | 22.1 | 0.1 | 1.7 | 1235 | .37 | 4.9 | 1.48 | | 97 | 64 | .71 | .103 | |
| halfsies, Quaker | 113 | 0.7 | 1.1 | | | | | .26 | .50 | 100 | 243 | 12 | 8 | 2.00 | .000 |
| *3/4 cup (1 oz)* | 28 | 1.8 | 24.0 | | | 0 | .37 | 5.0 | 1.00 | 2.00 | 37 | 29 | 8.10 | .050 | |
| heartland natural | 123 | 1.2 | 4.4 | | | | | .04 | | 16 | 72 | 19 | 36 | .75 | |
| *1/4 cup (1 oz)* | 28 | 2.9 | 19.4 | | 1.3 | | .09 | 0.4 | | | 95 | 103 | 1.07 | | |
| w/ coconut | 125 | 0.9 | 4.6 | | | | | .04 | | 15 | 57 | 18 | 37 | .74 | |
| *1/4 cup (1 oz)* | 28 | 3.0 | 19.2 | | 1.4 | | .09 | 0.5 | | | 104 | 103 | 1.45 | | |
| w/ raisins | 120 | 1.4 | 4.0 | | | | | .04 | | 11 | 58 | 17 | 36 | .73 | |
| *1/4 cup (1 oz)* | 28 | 2.8 | 19.6 | | 1.3 | | .08 | 0.4 | | | 107 | 97 | 1.04 | | |
| honey & nut corn flakes, Kellogg's | 113 | 1.1 | 1.5 | | | 375 | 15 | .40 | .50 | 100 | 225 | 3 | 6 | .11 | |
| *3/4 cup (1 oz)* | 28 | 1.8 | 23.3 | | 0.3 | 1250 | .40 | 5.0 | | | 36 | 13 | 1.80 | .050 | |
| honey bran | 97 | 0.7 | 0.6 | | | 375 | 15 | .40 | .50 | 19 | 164 | 13 | 37 | .73 | |
| *7/8 cup (1 oz)* | 28 | 2.5 | 23.2 | | 3.1 | 1250 | .40 | 5.0 | 1.50 | .16 | 122 | 107 | 4.50 | .135 | |
| honey buc wheat crisp, General Mills | 110 | | 1.0 | | | | | | | | 260 | | | | |
| *3/4 cup (1 oz)* | 28 | 2.0 | 24.0 | | | | | | | | 50 | | | | |
| honeycomb, Post | 110 | 0.4 | 0.3 | | | 371 | 0 | .42 | .49 | 99 | 158 | 4 | 10 | 1.48 | |
| *1 1/3 cups (1 oz)* | 28 | 1.4 | 25.4 | | 0.4 | 1235 | .37 | 4.9 | 1.48 | .11 | 32 | 23 | 2.67 | .057 | |
| honey nut cheerios, General Mills | 107 | 0.9 | 0.7 | 0.3 | | 375 | 15 | .42 | .50 | | 250 | 20 | 33 | .74 | |
| *3/4 cup (1 oz)* | 28 | 3.1 | 22.8 | 0.1 | | 1250 | .37 | 5.0 | 1.50 | | 95 | 105 | 4.45 | .198 | |
| ice cream cones, choc chip, General Mills—*3/4 cup (1 oz)* | 110 | | 2.0 | | | | | | | | 190 | | | | |
| | 28 | 1.0 | 23.0 | | | | | | | | 40 | | | | |
| ice cream cones, vanilla, General Mills | 110 | | 2.0 | | | | | | | | 190 | | | | |
| *3/4 cup (1 oz)* | 28 | 1.0 | 23.0 | | | | | | | | 45 | | | | |
| kaboom, General Mills | 110 | | 1.0 | | | | | | | | 290 | | | | |
| *1 cup (1 oz)* | 28 | 2.0 | 23.0 | | | | | | | | 65 | | | | |
| king vitamin, Quaker | 112 | 0.7 | 1.1 | | | | | .68 | .60 | 160 | 250 | 6 | 14 | .00 | .000 |
| *1 1/4 cups (1 oz)* | 28 | 2.2 | 23.4 | | | 1500 | .60 | 8.0 | 2.00 | .00 | 49 | 40 | 8.10 | .040 | |
| kix, General Mills | 110 | 0.9 | 0.7 | 0.3 | | 375 | 15 | .42 | .50 | | 290 | 35 | 12 | .25 | |
| *1 1/2 cups (1 oz)* | 28 | 2.5 | 23.4 | 0.2 | 0.4 | 1250 | .37 | 5.0 | 1.50 | | 45 | 39 | 8.10 | .047 | |
| life, cinn, Quaker | 110 | 1.4 | 1.6 | | | 0 | | .42 | .06 | 21 | 150 | 60 | 47 | 1.00 | 1.400 |
| *2/3 cup (1 oz)* | 28 | 5.2 | 18.8 | | 0.9 | 0 | .37 | 5.0 | .00 | .00 | 175 | 100 | 8.10 | .160 | |
| life, Quaker | 111 | 1.3 | 1.8 | | | 0 | | .42 | .04 | 21 | 150 | 60 | 12 | 1.00 | .000 |
| *2/3 cup (1 oz)* | 28 | 5.2 | 18.6 | | 0.9 | 0 | .37 | 5.0 | .00 | .00 | 172 | 100 | 8.10 | .170 | |
| life w/ raisins, Quaker | 105 | 2.4 | 1.8 | | | | | .42 | .04 | 18 | 161 | 60 | 45 | 1.00 | 1.000 |
| *2/3 cup (1 oz)* | 28 | 5.5 | 16.8 | | | 0 | .37 | 5.0 | .00 | .00 | 232 | 100 | 8.10 | .210 | |
| lucky charms, General Mills | 110 | 0.8 | 1.1 | 0.4 | | 375 | 15 | .40 | .50 | | 180 | 32 | 24 | .50 | |
| *1 cup (1 oz)* | 28 | 2.6 | 23.2 | 0.2 | 0.6 | 1250 | .40 | 5.0 | 1.50 | .18 | 75 | 78 | 4.50 | .098 | |
| most, Kellogg's | 95 | 1.3 | 0.3 | | | 1502 | 60 | 1.70 | 2.00 | 400 | 150 | 43 | 56 | 1.50 | |
| *2/3 cup (1 oz)* | 28 | 4.0 | 21.6 | | 3.5 | 5000 | 1.50 | 20.0 | 6.00 | | 185 | 197 | 18.00 | .159 | |
| Mr. T, Quaker | 121 | 0.6 | 2.6 | | | | | .34 | .60 | 8 | 189 | 9 | 10 | .00 | .000 |
| *1 cup (1 oz)* | 28 | 1.3 | 23.1 | | | 0 | .30 | 3.0 | 1.00 | .00 | 37 | 24 | 2.70 | .010 | |
| nutri-grain, Kellogg's | | | | | | | | | | | | | | | |
| barley | 106 | 0.8 | 0.2 | | | 375 | 15 | .40 | .50 | 100 | 192 | 8 | 22 | 3.70 | |
| *3/4 cup (1 oz)* | 28 | 3.1 | 23.5 | | 1.7 | 1250 | .40 | 5.0 | 1.50 | | 75 | 87 | 1.00 | .170 | |
| corn | 108 | 0.8 | 0.7 | | | 375 | 15 | .40 | .50 | 100 | 187 | 1 | 18 | 3.70 | |
| *2/3 cup (1 oz)* | 28 | 2.3 | 23.9 | | 1.8 | 1250 | .40 | 5.0 | 1.50 | | 66 | 81 | .60 | .082 | |
| rye | 102 | 0.9 | 0.2 | | | 375 | 15 | .40 | .50 | 100 | 193 | 6 | 22 | 3.70 | |
| *3/4 cup (1 oz)* | 28 | 2.5 | 24.0 | | 1.8 | 1250 | .40 | 5.0 | 1.50 | | 51 | 74 | .80 | .097 | |
| wheat | 102 | 0.9 | 0.3 | | | 375 | 15 | .40 | .50 | 100 | 193 | 8 | 22 | 3.70 | |
| *3/4 cup (1 oz)* | 28 | 2.5 | 24.0 | | 1.8 | 1250 | .40 | 5.0 | 1.50 | | 77 | 106 | .80 | .153 | |

ᵃ Cinn & raisin, coconut & honey, fruit & nut or toasted oat.

| | KCAL / WT (g) | H₂O (g) / PRO (g) | FAT (g) / CHO (g) | PUFA (g) / SFA (g) | CHOL (mg) / DFIB (g) | A (RE) / A (IU) | C (mg) / B-1 (mg) | B-2 (mg) / NIA (mg) | B-6 (mg) / B-12 (mcg) | FOL (mcg) / PANT (mg) | Na (mg) / K (mg) | Ca (mg) / P (mg) | Mg (mg) / Fe (mg) | Zn (mg) / Cu (mg) | Mn (mg) |
|---|---|---|---|---|---|---|---|---|---|---|---|---|---|---|---|
| pac man, General Mills | 110 | | 1.0 | | | | | | | | 200 | | | | |
| *1 cup (1 oz)* | 28 | 1.0 | 25.0 | | | | | | | | 30 | | | | |
| product 19, Kellogg's | 108 | 0.9 | 0.2 | | | 1502 | 60 | 1.70 | 2.00 | 400 | 325 | 3 | 11 | .43 | |
| *3/4 cup (1 oz)* | 28 | 2.8 | 23.5 | | 0.3 | 5000 | 1.50 | 20.0 | 6.00 | .18 | 44 | 40 | 18.00 | .079 | |
| puffed rice | 57 | 0.4 | 0.1 | | | | | .01 | .01 | 3 | 0 | 1 | 3 | .15 | .213 |
| *1 cup (1/2 oz)* | 14 | 0.9 | 12.8 | | 0.1 | | .02 | 0.4 | | .05 | 16 | 14 | .15 | .024 | |
| puffed rice, Quaker | 55 | 0.4 | 0.1 | | | | | .02 | .01 | 3 | 1 | 3 | 6 | .00 | .000 |
| *1 cup (1/2 oz)* | 14 | 0.9 | 12.7 | | | 0 | .10 | 1.2 | .00 | .00 | 16 | 26 | .41 | .020 | |
| puffed wheat | 52 | 0.4 | 0.2 | | | | | .03 | .02 | 5 | 1 | 4 | 21 | .33 | |
| *1 cup (1/2 oz)* | 14 | 2.1 | 11.3 | | 0.5 | | .03 | 1.5 | | .07 | 49 | 50 | .67 | .058 | |
| puffed wheat, Quaker | 54 | 0.4 | 0.2 | | | | | .10 | .01 | 5 | 1 | 3 | 13 | .00 | .000 |
| *1 cup (1/2 oz)* | 14 | 2.2 | 10.8 | | | 0 | .08 | 2.0 | .00 | .00 | 50 | 48 | .67 | .060 | |
| Quaker 100% natural | 136 | 0.5 | 5.6 | | | 0 | | .07 | .05 | 14 | 11 | 38 | 34 | 1.00 | 1.000 |
| *1/4 cup (1 oz)* | 28 | 3.7 | 17.8 | | 1.0 | 0 | .09 | 0.5 | .00 | .00 | 150 | 99 | .85 | .120 | |
| w/ apples & cinn | 133 | 0.5 | 5.3 | 0.4 | | | | .07 | .03 | 5 | 15 | 40 | 29 | 1.00 | 1.000 |
| *1/4 cup (1 oz)* | 28 | 3.2 | 18.2 | 4.2 | 1.3 | 0 | .11 | 0.4 | .00 | .00 | 141 | 104 | .89 | .140 | |
| w/ raisins & dates | 132 | 0.8 | 5.0 | 0.4 | | | | .03 | .04 | 12 | 11 | 36 | 32 | 1.00 | 1.000 |
| *1/4 cup (1 oz)* | 28 | 3.5 | 18.2 | 3.5 | 1.1 | 0 | .08 | 0.4 | .00 | .00 | 156 | 99 | .86 | .120 | |
| quisp, Quaker | 121 | 0.6 | 2.6 | 0.3 | | 0 | | .34 | .60 | 8 | 189 | 9 | 10 | .00 | .000 |
| *1 cup (1 oz)* | 28 | 1.3 | 23.1 | 1.4 | 0.4 | 0 | .30 | 3.0 | 1.00 | .00 | 37 | 24 | 2.70 | .010 | |
| **raisin bran** | | | | | | | | | | | | | | | |
| Kellogg's | 115 | 3.1 | 0.7 | | | 375 | | .40 | .50 | 100 | 269 | 13 | 48 | 3.80 | |
| *3/4 cup (1.3 oz)* | 37 | 4.0 | 27.9 | | 4.0 | 1250 | .40 | 5.0 | 1.50 | | 192 | 137 | 4.50 | .214 | |
| Post | 86 | 2.0 | 0.4 | 0.1 | 0 | 371 | 0 | .42 | .49 | 99 | 178 | 15 | 52 | 1.48 | |
| *1/2 cup (1 oz)* | 28 | 2.5 | 22.0 | 0.0 | 3.7 | 1235 | .37 | 4.9 | 1.48 | | 200 | 129 | 4.44 | .199 | |
| Ralston Purina | 120 | 2.8 | 0.2 | | | 375 | 1 | .40 | .50 | 100 | 328 | 18 | 57 | 1.13 | |
| *3/4 cup (1.3 oz)* | 38 | 3.0 | 31.4 | | 4.8 | 1250 | .40 | 5.0 | 1.50 | .28 | 194 | 167 | 4.50 | .206 | |
| raisin nut bran, General Mills | 110 | | 3.0 | | | | | | | | 140 | | | | |
| *1/2 cup (1 oz)* | 28 | 3.0 | 20.0 | | 3.0 | | | | | | 150 | | | | |
| raisins, rice & rye, Kellogg's | 124 | 2.2 | 0.1 | | | 375 | 0 | .40 | .50 | 100 | 280 | 8 | 16 | 3.80 | |
| *1 cup (1.3 oz)* | 37 | 2.1 | 31.5 | | | 1250 | .40 | 5.0 | 1.50 | | 115 | 40 | 4.50 | .130 | |
| rice chex, Ralston Purina | 110 | 0.7 | 0.3 | | | | 15 | .04 | .50 | 100 | 252 | 4 | 7 | .32 | |
| *1 1/8 cups (1 oz)* | 28 | 1.7 | 25.0 | | 0.5 | 17 | .38 | 5.0 | 1.50 | .10 | 32 | 28 | 1.80 | .068 | |
| rice krispies, Kellogg's | 112 | 0.7 | 0.2 | | | 375 | 15 | .40 | .50 | 100 | 340 | 4 | 10 | .48 | .281 |
| *1 cup (1 oz)* | 28 | 1.9 | 24.8 | | 0.1 | 1250 | .40 | 5.0 | | .20 | 30 | 34 | 1.80 | .071 | |
| rice krispies, frosted, Kellogg's | 109 | 0.7 | 0.1 | | | 375 | 15 | .40 | .50 | 100 | 240 | 1 | 5 | .31 | |
| *1 cup (1 oz)* | 28 | 1.3 | 25.7 | | 0.1 | 1250 | .40 | 5.0 | | .13 | 21 | 27 | 1.80 | .071 | |
| rice toasties, Post | 108 | 1.1 | 0.1 | 0.1 | 0 | | 0 | | | | 238 | 4 | 12 | .38 | |
| *3/4 cup (1 oz)* | 28 | 2.0 | 23.9 | 0.0 | 0.4 | | .30 | 4.0 | | | 34 | 30 | .83 | .070 | |
| rocky road, General Mills | 120 | | 2.0 | | | | | | | | 110 | | | | |
| *2/3 cup (1 oz)* | 28 | 2.0 | 23.0 | | | | | | | | 50 | | | | |
| ruskets biscuits, Loma Linda | 110 | 2.0 | 1.0 | | 0 | | | .43 | | | 85 | 14 | | .59 | |
| *2 biscuits* | 30 | 4.0 | 23.0 | | | | .31 | 3.0 | | | 100 | | 3.10 | | |
| seven grain cereal, crunchy, Loma Linda | 110 | 1.0 | 2.0 | | 0 | | | .04 | .03 | | 90 | 13 | | .36 | |
| *1/2 cup (1 oz)* | 28 | 2.0 | 21.0 | | | | .01 | 0.7 | .00 | .15 | 85 | | .42 | | |
| seven grain cereal, Loma Linda | 110 | 1.0 | 1.0 | | 0 | | | .04 | .06 | | 75 | 17 | | .56 | |
| *1 cup (1 oz)* | 28 | 5.0 | 20.0 | | | | .03 | 1.1 | .00 | .34 | 140 | | .56 | | |
| shredded wheat | 102 | 1.5 | 0.6 | | | | | .08 | .07 | 14 | 3 | 11 | 37 | .93 | |
| *1 oz* | 28 | 3.1 | 22.6 | | 2.6 | | .07 | 1.5 | | .24 | 102 | 100 | 1.20 | .188 | |
| | 83 | 1.5 | 0.3 | | | | | .06 | .06 | 12 | 0 | 10 | 40 | .59 | .725 |
| *1 biscuit* | 24 | 2.6 | 18.8 | | 2.2 | | .07 | 1.1 | | .19 | 77 | 86 | .74 | .118 | |
| Quaker | 104 | 1.8 | 0.4 | | | | | .08 | .05 | 19 | 1 | 11 | 32 | 1.00 | 1.000 |
| *1 oz* | 28 | 3.1 | 22.0 | | | 0 | .07 | 1.3 | .00 | .00 | 107 | 116 | .86 | .140 | |
| shredded wheat 'n bran, Nabisco | 110 | | 1.0 | | | | | | | | 0 | | | | |
| *1 oz* | 28 | 3.0 | 23.0 | | | | | | | | 135 | | | | |
| s'mores crunch, General Mills | 120 | | 2.0 | | | | | | | | 250 | | | | |
| *3/4 cup (1 oz)* | 28 | 1.0 | 24.0 | | | | | | | | 230 | | | | |

| | KCAL | H₂O (g) | FAT (g) | PUFA (g) | CHOL (mg) | A (RE) | C (mg) | B-2 (mg) | B-6 (mg) | FOL (mcg) | Na (mg) | Ca (mg) | Mg (mg) | Zn (mg) | Mn (mg) |
|---|---|---|---|---|---|---|---|---|---|---|---|---|---|---|---|
| | WT (g) | PRO (g) | CHO (g) | SFA (g) | DFIB (g) | A (IU) | B-1 (mg) | NIA (mg) | B-12 (mcg) | PANT (mg) | K (mg) | P (mg) | Fe (mg) | Cu (mg) | |
| **special K, Kellogg's** | 111 | 0.6 | 0.1 | | | 375 | 15 | .40 | .50 | 100 | 265 | 8 | 16 | 3.70 | |
| *1 1/3 cups (1 oz)* | 28 | 5.6 | 21.3 | | 0.2 | 1250 | .40 | 5.0 | | .15 | 49 | 55 | 4.50 | .128 | |
| **sugar corn pops, Kellogg's** | 108 | 1.0 | 0.1 | | | 375 | 15 | .40 | .50 | 100 | 103 | 1 | 2 | 1.50 | |
| *1 cup (1 oz)* | 28 | 1.4 | 25.6 | | 0.2 | 1250 | .40 | 5.0 | | .06 | 17 | 28 | 1.80 | .060 | |
| **sugar frosted flakes** | | | | | | | | | | | | | | | |
|   Kellogg's | 108 | 0.7 | 0.1 | | | 375 | 15 | .40 | .50 | 100 | 230 | 1 | 2 | .04 | |
| *3/4 cup (1 oz)* | 28 | 1.4 | 25.7 | | 0.3 | 1250 | .40 | 5.0 | | .060 | 18 | 21 | 1.80 | .060 | |
|   Ralston Purina | 111 | 0.4 | 0.4 | | | 375 | 15 | .40 | .50 | 2 | 184 | 3 | 2 | .61 | |
| *3/4 cup (1 oz)* | 28 | 1.5 | 25.5 | | 0.4 | 1250 | .40 | 5.0 | 1.50 | .01 | 18 | 7 | .70 | .019 | |
| **sugar smacks, Kellogg's** | 106 | 0.9 | 0.5 | | | 375 | 15 | .40 | .50 | 100 | 75 | 3 | 13 | .28 | |
| *3/4 cup (1 oz)* | 28 | 2.0 | 24.7 | | 0.4 | 1250 | .40 | 5.0 | | .13 | 42 | 31 | 1.80 | .079 | |
| **sugar sparkled flakes, Post** | 108 | 0.5 | 0.1 | 0.0 | 0 | 371 | 0 | .42 | .49 | 99 | 170 | 3 | 3 | .05 | |
| *3/4 cup (1 oz)* | 28 | 1.2 | 25.7 | 0.0 | 0.3 | 1235 | .37 | 4.9 | 1.48 | | 27 | 7 | .36 | .044 | |
| **sun flakes, Ralston Purina** | | | | | | | | | | | | | | | |
|   corn & rice | 110 | | 0.9 | | | | 15 | .13 | .50 | 100 | 237 | 9 | 12 | .19 | |
| *1 cup (1 oz)* | 28 | | 24.0 | | 1.0 | 1250 | .38 | 5.0 | 1.50 | .34 | 31 | 25 | 1.80 | | |
|   wheat & rice | 135 | | 3.4 | | | | 15 | | .50 | 100 | 182 | | | | |
| *1 cup (1 oz)* | 28 | 2.3 | 24.0 | | | 1250 | .38 | 5.0 | 1.50 | .48 | 70 | | 1.80 | | |
| **super golden crisp, Post** | 104 | 0.4 | 0.2 | 0.1 | 0 | | 0 | .42 | .49 | 99 | 44 | 5 | 19 | 1.48 | |
| *7/8 cup (1 oz)* | 28 | 2.0 | 25.2 | 0.0 | 0.4 | 1235 | .37 | 4.9 | 1.48 | | 48 | 47 | 2.67 | .089 | |
| **super sugar crisp** | 106 | 0.4 | 0.3 | | | 375 | | .40 | .50 | 100 | 25 | 6 | 17 | 1.50 | |
| *7/8 cup (1 oz)* | 28 | 1.8 | 25.6 | | 0.4 | 1250 | .40 | 5.0 | 1.50 | .10 | 105 | 51 | 1.80 | .077 | |
| **tasteeos, Ralston Purina** | 111 | 0.6 | 0.8 | | | 375 | 15 | .40 | .50 | 11 | 216 | 13 | 31 | .81 | |
| *1 1/4 cups (1 oz)* | 28 | 3.6 | 22.4 | | 1.0 | 1250 | .40 | 5.0 | 1.50 | .14 | 84 | 113 | 4.50 | .167 | |
| **team flakes** | 111 | 1.1 | 0.5 | | | 375 | 15 | .40 | .50 | | 175 | 4 | 13 | .39 | |
| *1 cup (1 oz)* | 28 | 1.8 | 24.3 | | 0.3 | 1250 | .40 | 5.0 | 1.50 | .21 | 48 | 44 | 1.74 | .146 | |
| **toasted wheat & raisins, Nabisco** | 100 | | 1.0 | | | | | | | | 0 | | | | |
| *1 oz* | 28 | 2.0 | 23.0 | | | | | | | | 110 | | | | |
| **total, General Mills** | 100 | 1.1 | 0.6 | 0.3 | | 1502 | 60 | 1.68 | 2.00 | 400 | 280 | 48 | 32 | .67 | .425 |
| *1 cup (1 oz)* | 28 | 2.8 | 22.3 | 0.1 | 2.0 | 5000 | 1.48 | 19.8 | 6.20 | .20 | 110 | 110 | 18.00 | .122 | |
| **trix, General Mills** | 109 | | 0.4 | | | 375 | 15 | .42 | .50 | | 170 | 6 | 6 | .13 | |
| *1 cup (1 oz)* | 28 | 1.5 | 25.2 | | 0.1 | 1250 | .37 | 5.0 | 1.50 | .08 | 25 | 19 | 4.45 | .045 | |
| **waffelos, Ralston Purina** | 115 | 0.7 | 1.2 | | | 375 | 15 | .40 | .50 | 3 | 118 | 8 | 6 | .23 | |
| *1 cup (1 oz)* | 28 | 1.0 | 24.5 | | 0.3 | 1250 | .40 | 5.0 | 1.50 | .05 | 25 | 231 | 4.50 | .032 | |
| **wheat & raisin chex, Ralston Purina** | 130 | | 0.3 | | | | | .58 | .50 | 100 | 198 | 25 | 34 | .88 | |
| *3/4 cup (1.3 oz)* | 37 | 3.4 | 31.0 | | 3.4 | | .38 | 5.0 | 1.50 | .12 | 150 | 112 | 5.40 | .156 | |
| **wheat chex, Ralston Purina** | 100 | 0.7 | 0.7 | | | | 15 | .10 | .50 | 100 | 200 | 11 | 33 | .74 | |
| *2/3 cup (1 oz)* | 28 | 2.9 | 23.0 | | 3.7 | | .38 | 5.0 | 1.50 | .12 | 107 | 109 | 4.50 | .135 | |
| **wheaties, General Mills** | 99 | 1.3 | 0.5 | 0.2 | | 375 | 15 | .42 | .50 | 9 | 270 | 43 | 31 | .63 | .425 |
| *1 cup (1 oz)* | 28 | 2.7 | 22.6 | 0.1 | 2.0 | 1250 | .37 | 5.0 | 1.50 | .21 | 110 | 98 | 4.45 | .131 | |

# 5. CHEESE & CHEESE PRODUCTS
## 5.1. CHEESE

| | KCAL | H₂O | FAT | PUFA | CHOL | A (RE) | C | B-2 | B-6 | FOL | Na | Ca | Mg | Zn | Mn |
|---|---|---|---|---|---|---|---|---|---|---|---|---|---|---|---|
| | WT | PRO | CHO | SFA | DFIB | A (IU) | B-1 | NIA | B-12 | PANT | K | P | Fe | Cu | |
| **american, processed** | 106 | 11.1 | 8.9 | 0.3 | 27 | 82 | 0 | .10 | .02 | 2 | 406 | 124 | 6 | .85 | |
| *1 oz* | 28 | 6.3 | 0.5 | 5.6 | 0.0 | 343 | .01 | 0.0 | .20 | .14 | 46 | 211 | .11 | | |
| **blue** | 100 | 12.0 | 8.2 | 0.2 | 21 | 65 | 0 | .11 | .05 | 10 | 396 | 150 | 7 | .75 | |
| *1 oz* | 28 | 6.1 | 0.7 | 5.3 | 0.0 | 204 | .01 | 0.3 | .35 | .49 | 73 | 110 | .09 | | |
| **brick** | 105 | 11.7 | 8.4 | 0.2 | 27 | 86 | 0 | .10 | .02 | 6 | 159 | 191 | 7 | .74 | |
| *1 oz* | 28 | 6.6 | 0.8 | 5.3 | 0.0 | 307 | .00 | 0.0 | .36 | .08 | 38 | 128 | .07 | | |
| **brie** | 95 | 13.7 | 7.9 | | 28 | | 0 | .15 | .07 | 18 | 178 | 52 | | | |
| *1 oz* | 28 | 5.9 | 0.1 | | 0.0 | 189 | .02 | 0.1 | .47 | .20 | 43 | 53 | .14 | | |
| **camembert** | 85 | 14.7 | 6.9 | 0.2 | 20 | 71 | 0 | .14 | .06 | 18 | 239 | 110 | 6 | .68 | |
| *1 oz* | 28 | 5.6 | 0.1 | 4.3 | 0.0 | 262 | .01 | 0.2 | .37 | .39 | 53 | 98 | .09 | | |
| **caraway** | 107 | 11.1 | 8.3 | | | 82 | 0 | .13 | | | 196 | 191 | 6 | | |
| *1 oz* | 28 | 7.1 | 0.9 | | 0.0 | 299 | .01 | 0.1 | .08 | .05 | | 139 | | | |
| **cheddar** | 114 | 10.4 | 9.4 | 0.3 | 30 | 86 | 0 | .11 | .02 | 5 | 176 | 204 | 8 | .88 | |
| *1 oz* | 28 | 7.1 | 0.4 | 6.0 | 0.0 | 300 | .01 | 0.0 | .23 | .12 | 28 | 145 | .19 | | |

| | KCAL / WT (g) | H₂O (g) / PRO (g) | FAT (g) / CHO (g) | PUFA (g) / SFA (g) | CHOL (mg) / DFIB (g) | A (RE) / A (IU) | C (mg) / B-1 (mg) | B-2 (mg) / NIA (mg) | B-6 (mg) / B-12 (mcg) | FOL (mcg) / PANT (mg) | Na (mg) / K (mg) | Ca (mg) / P (mg) | Mg (mg) / Fe (mg) | Zn (mg) / Cu (mg) | Mn (mg) |
|---|---|---|---|---|---|---|---|---|---|---|---|---|---|---|---|
| cheddar | 403 | 36.8 | 33.1 | 0.9 | 105 | 303 | 0 | .38 | .07 | 18 | 620 | 721 | 28 | 3.11 | |
| *3.5 oz* | 100 | 24.9 | 1.3 | 21.1 | 0.0 | 1059 | .03 | 0.1 | .83 | .41 | 98 | 512 | .68 | | |
| cheddar, grated | 455 | 41.5 | 37.5 | 1.1 | 119 | 342 | 0 | .42 | .08 | 21 | 701 | 815 | 31 | 3.51 | |
| *1 cup, not packed* | 113 | 28.1 | 1.5 | 23.8 | 0.0 | 1197 | .03 | 0.1 | .94 | .47 | 111 | 579 | .77 | | |
| cheddar, med, Kraft | 114 | 10.5 | 9.3 | 0.3 | 28 | | 0 | .11 | .02 | 6 | 174 | 208 | 7 | 1.01 | .010 |
| *1 oz* | 28 | 7.1 | 0.5 | 5.4 | | 366 | .01 | 0.1 | .23 | .11 | 20 | 143 | .07 | .004 | |
| cheshire | 110 | 10.7 | 8.7 | | 29 | 69 | 0 | .08 | | | 198 | 182 | 6 | | |
| *1 oz* | 28 | 6.6 | 1.4 | | 0.0 | 279 | .01 | | | | 27 | 131 | .06 | | |
| colby | 112 | 10.8 | 9.1 | 0.3 | 27 | 78 | 0 | .11 | .02 | | 171 | 194 | 7 | .87 | |
| *1 oz* | 28 | 6.7 | 0.7 | 5.7 | 0.0 | 293 | .00 | 0.0 | .23 | .06 | 36 | 129 | .22 | | |
| cottage cheese, creamed | 29 | 22.3 | 1.3 | 0.0 | 4 | 14 | 0 | .00 | .02 | 4 | 114 | 17 | 2 | .20 | |
| *1 rd T* | 28 | 3.5 | 0.8 | 0.8 | 0.0 | 48 | .00 | 0.0 | .18 | .06 | 24 | 37 | .07 | | |
| cottage cheese, creamed | 117 | 89.2 | 5.1 | 0.2 | 17 | 54 | 0 | .18 | .08 | 14 | 457 | 68 | 6 | .42 | |
| *4 oz* | 113 | 14.1 | 3.0 | 3.2 | 0.0 | 184 | .02 | 0.1 | .70 | .24 | 95 | 149 | .16 | | |
| cottage cheese, creamed | 217 | 165.8 | 9.5 | 0.3 | 31 | 101 | 0 | .34 | .14 | 26 | 850 | 126 | 11 | .78 | |
| *1 cup, not packed* | 210 | 26.2 | 5.6 | 6.0 | 0.0 | 342 | .04 | 0.3 | 1.31 | .45 | 177 | 277 | .29 | | |
| cottage cheese, creamed w/ fruit | 279 | 163.0 | 7.7 | 0.2 | 25 | | 0 | .29 | .12 | 22 | 915 | 108 | 9 | .66 | |
| *1 cup* | 226 | 22.4 | 30.1 | 4.9 | 0.0 | 139 | .04 | 0.2 | 1.12 | .38 | 151 | 236 | .25 | | |
| cottage cheese, dry curd | 123 | 115.7 | 0.6 | 0.0 | 10 | 12 | 0 | .21 | .12 | 21 | 19 | 46 | 6 | .68 | |
| *1 cup, not packed* | 145 | 25.0 | 2.7 | 0.4 | 0.0 | 44 | .04 | 0.2 | 1.20 | .24 | 47 | 151 | .33 | | |
| cottage cheese, low fat, 1% fat | 164 | 186.4 | 2.3 | 0.0 | 10 | 25 | 0 | .37 | .15 | 28 | 918 | 138 | 12 | .80 | |
| *1 cup* | 226 | 28.0 | 6.2 | 1.5 | 0.0 | 84 | .05 | 0.3 | 1.43 | .49 | 183 | 302 | .32 | | |
| cottage cheese, low fat, 2% fat | 203 | 179.2 | 4.4 | 0.1 | 19 | 45 | 0 | .42 | .17 | 30 | 918 | 155 | 14 | .95 | |
| *1 cup* | 226 | 31.1 | 8.2 | 2.8 | 0.0 | 158 | .05 | 0.3 | 1.61 | .55 | 217 | 340 | .36 | | |
| cream cheese | 99 | 15.2 | 9.9 | 0.4 | 31 | 124 | 0 | .06 | .01 | 0 | 84 | 23 | 2 | .15 | |
| *1 oz (2T)* | 28 | 2.1 | 0.8 | 6.2 | 0.0 | 405 | .01 | 0.0 | .12 | .08 | 34 | 30 | .34 | | |
| cream cheese, light, Philadelphia Brand | 62 | 18.3 | 4.7 | 0.1 | 16 | | 0 | .07 | .01 | 5 | 160 | 38 | 3 | .21 | .005 |
| *1 oz* | 28 | 2.9 | 1.8 | 2.8 | | 168 | .01 | 0.0 | .09 | .16 | 52 | 45 | .04 | .008 | |
| cream cheese, Philadelphia Brand | 98 | 15.5 | 9.5 | 0.3 | 28 | | 0 | .04 | .01 | 5 | 86 | 20 | 2 | .17 | .010 |
| *1 oz* | 28 | 2.3 | 0.7 | 5.4 | | 349 | .01 | 0.1 | .06 | .10 | 25 | 27 | .02 | .009 | |
| cream cheese w/ herb & garlic, Cremerie | 103 | 14.4 | 9.9 | 0.3 | 29 | | 0 | .05 | .01 | 4 | 216 | 29 | 3 | .17 | |
| *1 oz* | 28 | 0.9 | 2.5 | 5.5 | | 373 | .01 | 0.1 | .07 | .10 | 37 | 30 | .10 | .015 | |
| edam | 101 | 11.8 | 7.9 | 0.2 | 25 | 72 | 0 | .11 | .02 | 5 | 274 | 207 | 8 | 1.06 | |
| *1 oz* | 28 | 7.1 | 0.4 | 5.0 | 0.0 | 260 | .01 | 0.0 | .44 | .08 | 53 | 152 | .12 | | |
| feta | 75 | 15.7 | 6.0 | 0.2 | 25 | | 0 | | | | 316 | 140 | 5 | .82 | |
| *1 oz* | 28 | 4.0 | 1.2 | 4.2 | 0.0 | | | | | | 18 | 96 | .18 | | |
| fontina | 110 | 10.8 | 8.8 | 0.5 | 33 | | 0 | .06 | | | | 156 | 4 | .99 | |
| *1 oz* | 28 | 7.3 | 0.4 | 5.4 | 0.0 | 333 | .01 | 0.0 | | | | | .06 | | |
| gjetost | 132 | 3.8 | 8.4 | 0.3 | | | | | | | 170 | 113 | | | |
| *1 oz* | 28 | 2.7 | 12.1 | 5.3 | 0.0 | | | 0.2 | | | | 126 | | | |
| gouda | 101 | 11.8 | 7.8 | 0.2 | 32 | 49 | 0 | .10 | .02 | 6 | 232 | 198 | 8 | 1.11 | |
| *1 oz* | 28 | 7.1 | 0.6 | 5.0 | 0.0 | 183 | .01 | 0.0 | | .10 | 34 | 155 | .07 | | |
| gruyere | 117 | 9.4 | 9.2 | 2.4 | 31 | | 0 | .08 | .02 | 3 | 95 | 287 | | | |
| *1 oz* | 28 | 8.5 | 0.1 | 5.4 | 0.0 | 346 | .02 | 0.0 | .45 | .16 | 23 | 172 | | | |
| havarti, Casino | 121 | 10.4 | 10.6 | 0.3 | 34 | | 0 | .09 | .01 | 11 | 144 | 176 | 5 | .85 | .005 |
| *1 oz* | 28 | 6.1 | 0.3 | 6.5 | | 361 | .01 | 0.0 | .16 | .08 | 13 | 114 | .04 | .015 | |
| limburger | 93 | 13.7 | 7.7 | 0.1 | 26 | | 0 | .14 | .02 | 16 | 227 | 141 | 6 | .60 | |
| *1 oz* | 28 | 5.7 | 0.1 | 4.8 | 0.0 | 363 | .02 | 0.1 | .30 | .33 | 36 | 111 | .04 | | |
| monterey | 106 | 11.6 | 8.6 | | | | 0 | .11 | | | 152 | 212 | 8 | .85 | |
| *1 oz* | 28 | 6.9 | 0.2 | | 0.0 | 269 | | | | | 23 | 126 | .20 | | |
| mozzarella | 80 | 15.4 | 6.1 | 0.2 | 22 | 68 | 0 | .07 | .02 | 2 | 106 | 147 | 5 | .63 | |
| *1 oz* | 28 | 5.5 | 0.6 | 3.7 | 0.0 | 225 | .00 | 0.0 | .19 | .02 | 19 | 105 | .05 | | |
| mozzarella, low moisture | 90 | 13.7 | 7.0 | 0.2 | 25 | 78 | 0 | .08 | .02 | 2 | 118 | 163 | 6 | .70 | |
| *1 oz* | 28 | 6.1 | 0.7 | 4.4 | 0.0 | 256 | .01 | 0.0 | .21 | .02 | 21 | 117 | .06 | | |
| mozzarella, part skim | 72 | 15.3 | 4.5 | 0.1 | 16 | 50 | 0 | .09 | .02 | 2 | 132 | 183 | 7 | .78 | |
| *1 oz* | 28 | 6.9 | 0.8 | 2.9 | 0.0 | 166 | .01 | 0.0 | .23 | .02 | 24 | 131 | .06 | | |
| mozzarella, part skim, low moisture | 79 | 13.8 | 4.9 | 0.1 | 15 | 54 | 0 | .10 | .02 | 3 | 150 | 207 | 7 | .89 | |
| *1 oz* | 28 | 7.8 | 0.9 | 3.1 | 0.0 | 178 | .01 | 0.0 | .26 | .03 | 27 | 149 | .07 | | |
| muenster | 104 | 11.8 | 8.5 | 0.2 | 27 | 90 | 0 | .09 | .02 | 3 | 178 | 203 | 8 | .80 | |
| *1 oz* | 28 | 6.6 | 0.3 | 5.4 | 0.0 | 318 | .00 | 0.0 | .42 | .05 | 38 | 133 | .12 | | |
| neufchatel | 74 | 17.6 | 6.6 | 0.2 | 22 | 75 | 0 | .06 | .01 | 3 | 113 | 21 | 2 | .15 | |
| *1 oz* | 28 | 2.8 | 0.8 | 4.2 | 0.0 | 321 | .00 | 0.0 | .08 | .16 | 32 | 39 | .08 | | |

| | KCAL | H₂O (g) | FAT (g) | PUFA (g) | CHOL (mg) | A (RE) | C (mg) | B-2 (mg) | B-6 (mg) | FOL (mcg) | Na (mg) | Ca (mg) | Mg (mg) | Zn (mg) | Mn (mg) |
|---|---|---|---|---|---|---|---|---|---|---|---|---|---|---|---|
| | WT (g) | PRO (g) | CHO (g) | SFA (g) | DFIB (g) | A (IU) | B-1 (mg) | NIA (mg) | B-12 (mcg) | PANT (mg) | K (mg) | P (mg) | Fe (mg) | Cu (mg) | |
| **parmesan, grated** | 23 | 0.9 | 1.5 | 0.0 | 4 | | 0 | .02 | .01 | 0 | 93 | 69 | 3 | .16 | |
| *1 T* | 5 | 2.1 | 0.2 | 1.0 | 0.0 | 35 | .00 | 0.0 | | .03 | 5 | 40 | .05 | | |
| **parmesan, hard** | 111 | 8.3 | 7.3 | 0.2 | 19 | | 0 | .09 | .03 | 2 | 454 | 336 | 12 | .78 | |
| *1 oz* | 28 | 10.1 | 0.9 | 4.7 | 0.0 | 171 | .01 | 0.1 | | .13 | 26 | 197 | .23 | | |
| **pimento, processed** | 106 | 11.1 | 8.8 | 0.3 | 27 | | | .10 | .02 | 2 | 405 | 174 | 6 | .84 | |
| *1 oz* | 28 | 6.3 | 0.5 | 5.6 | | 358 | .01 | 0.0 | .20 | .14 | 46 | 211 | .12 | | |
| **port du salut** | 100 | 12.9 | 8.0 | 0.2 | 35 | | 0 | .07 | .02 | 5 | 151 | 184 | | | |
| *1 oz* | 28 | 6.7 | 0.2 | 4.7 | 0.0 | 378 | | 0.0 | .43 | .06 | | 102 | | | |
| **provolone** | 100 | 11.6 | 7.6 | 0.2 | 20 | 75 | 0 | .09 | .02 | 3 | 248 | 214 | 8 | .92 | |
| *1 oz* | 28 | 7.3 | 0.6 | 4.8 | 0.0 | 231 | .01 | 0.0 | .42 | .14 | 39 | 141 | .15 | | |
| **ricotta, part skim** | 171 | 92.3 | 9.8 | 0.3 | 38 | 140 | 0 | .23 | .03 | | 155 | 337 | 18 | 1.66 | |
| *1/2 cup* | 124 | 14.1 | 6.4 | 6.1 | 0.0 | 536 | .03 | 0.1 | .36 | | 155 | 226 | .55 | | |
| **ricotta, whole milk** | 216 | 88.9 | 16.1 | 0.5 | 63 | 166 | 0 | .24 | .05 | | 104 | 257 | 14 | 1.44 | |
| *1/2 cup* | 124 | 14.0 | 3.8 | 10.3 | 0.0 | 608 | .02 | 0.1 | .42 | | 130 | 196 | .47 | | |
| **romano** | 110 | 8.8 | 7.6 | | 29 | | 0 | .11 | | 2 | 340 | 302 | | | |
| *1 oz* | 28 | 9.0 | 1.0 | | 0.0 | 162 | | 0.0 | | | | 215 | | | |
| **roquefort, sheep's milk** | 105 | 11.2 | 8.7 | 0.4 | 26 | | 0 | .17 | .04 | 14 | 513 | 188 | 8 | .59 | |
| *1 oz* | 28 | 6.1 | 0.6 | 5.5 | 0.0 | 297 | .01 | 0.2 | .18 | .49 | 26 | 111 | .16 | | |
| **swiss** | 107 | 10.6 | 7.8 | 0.3 | 26 | 72 | 0 | .10 | .02 | 2 | 74 | 272 | 10 | 1.11 | |
| *1 oz* | 28 | 8.1 | 1.0 | 5.0 | 0.0 | 240 | .01 | 0.0 | .48 | .12 | 31 | 171 | .05 | | |
| **swiss, processed** | 95 | 12.0 | 7.1 | 0.1 | 15 | 65 | 0 | .08 | .01 | | 388 | 219 | 8 | 1.02 | |
| *1 oz* | 28 | 7.0 | 0.6 | 2.9 | 0.0 | 229 | .00 | 0.0 | .35 | .07 | 61 | 216 | .17 | | |
| **tilsit, whole milk** | 96 | 12.2 | 7.4 | 0.2 | 29 | | 0 | .10 | | | 213 | 198 | 4 | .99 | |
| *1 oz* | 28 | 6.9 | 0.5 | 4.8 | 0.0 | 296 | .02 | 0.1 | .60 | .10 | 18 | 142 | .06 | | |

## 5.2. CHEESE PRODUCTS

| | KCAL | H₂O (g) | FAT (g) | PUFA (g) | CHOL (mg) | A (RE) | C (mg) | B-2 (mg) | B-6 (mg) | FOL (mcg) | Na (mg) | Ca (mg) | Mg (mg) | Zn (mg) | Mn (mg) |
|---|---|---|---|---|---|---|---|---|---|---|---|---|---|---|---|
| | WT (g) | PRO (g) | CHO (g) | SFA (g) | DFIB (g) | A (IU) | B-1 (mg) | NIA (mg) | B-12 (mcg) | PANT (mg) | K (mg) | P (mg) | Fe (mg) | Cu (mg) | |
| **cheese food** | | | | | | | | | | | | | | | |
| american | 93 | 12.2 | 7.0 | 0.2 | 18 | | 0 | .13 | | | 337 | 163 | 9 | .85 | |
| *1 oz* | 28 | 5.6 | 2.1 | 4.4 | 0.0 | 259 | .01 | 0.0 | .32 | .16 | 79 | 130 | .24 | | |
| american, cold pack | 94 | 12.2 | 6.9 | 0.2 | 18 | | 0 | .13 | .04 | 2 | 274 | 141 | 8 | .85 | |
| *1 oz* | 28 | 5.6 | 2.4 | 4.4 | 0.0 | 200 | .01 | 0.0 | .36 | .28 | 103 | 113 | .24 | | |
| american, grated, Kraft | 131 | 1.1 | 7.1 | 0.2 | 18 | | 0 | .31 | .07 | 10 | 790 | 266 | 20 | .76 | |
| *1 oz* | 28 | 7.8 | 9.0 | 4.1 | | 260 | .06 | 0.1 | .91 | .90 | 310 | 312 | .20 | .030 | |
| hot pepper, Land O'Lakes | 92 | | 6.9 | 0.3 | 18 | | 0 | .13 | | | 357 | 169 | | | |
| *1 oz* | 28 | 5.6 | 1.9 | 4.3 | | 126 | .01 | 0.1 | | | | | .18 | | |
| jalapeno, Land O'Lakes | 90 | | 7.0 | 1.0 | 20 | | | | | | 360 | | | | |
| *1 oz* | 28 | 6.0 | 2.0 | 4.0 | | | | | | | | | | | |
| la chedda, Land O'Lakes | 90 | | 7.0 | 1.0 | 20 | | | | | | 335 | | | | |
| *1 oz* | 28 | 6.0 | 2.0 | 4.0 | | | | | | | 80 | | | | |
| onion, Land O'Lakes | 90 | | 7.0 | 1.0 | 15 | | | | | | 330 | | | | |
| *1 oz* | 28 | 6.0 | 2.0 | 4.0 | | | | | | | | | | | |
| pepperoni, Land O'Lakes | 90 | | 7.0 | 1.0 | 20 | | | | | | 395 | | | | |
| *1 oz* | 28 | 6.0 | 1.0 | 4.0 | | | | | | | 65 | | | | |
| salami, Land O'Lakes | 100 | | 8.0 | 1.0 | 20 | | | | | | 400 | | | | |
| *1 oz* | 28 | 5.0 | 2.0 | 5.0 | | | | | | | | | | | |
| sharp cheddar w/ wine, cold pack, Land O'Lakes—*1 oz* | 93 | | 6.9 | 0.2 | 18 | | 0 | .12 | | | 270 | 139 | | | |
| | 28 | 5.5 | 2.3 | 4.3 | | 197 | .01 | 0.0 | | | 102 | 112 | .24 | | |
| swiss | 92 | 12.4 | 6.8 | | 23 | | 0 | .11 | | | 440 | 205 | 8 | 1.01 | |
| *1 oz* | 28 | 6.2 | 1.3 | | 0.0 | 243 | .00 | 0.0 | .65 | .14 | 81 | 149 | .17 | | |
| **cheese nuggets** | | | | | | | | | | | | | | | |
| cheddar, breaded, frzn, Banquet | 414 | | 30.0 | | | | 0 | .01 | | | 1015 | 328 | | | |
| *3 oz* | 85 | 13.0 | 24.0 | | | 300 | .02 | 0.3 | | | 46 | | .50 | | |
| mozzarella, breaded, frzn, Banquet | 288 | | 16.0 | | | | 0 | .16 | | | 750 | 355 | | | |
| *3 oz* | 85 | 15.0 | 21.0 | | | 310 | .02 | 0.3 | | | 81 | | .50 | | |
| **cheese products** | | | | | | | | | | | | | | | |
| Light n' Lively, sharp cheddar | 72 | 14.0 | 4.1 | 0.1 | 12 | | 0 | .12 | .03 | 5 | 404 | 192 | 11 | .92 | |
| *1 oz* | 28 | 5.9 | 2.9 | 2.4 | | 205 | .02 | 0.1 | .22 | .21 | 64 | 141 | .08 | .008 | |

|  | KCAL | H₂O (g) | FAT (g) | PUFA (g) | CHOL (mg) | A (RE) | C (mg) | B-2 (mg) | B-6 (mg) | FOL (mcg) | Na (mg) | Ca (mg) | Mg (mg) | Zn (mg) | Mn (mg) |
|---|---|---|---|---|---|---|---|---|---|---|---|---|---|---|---|
|  | WT (g) | PRO (g) | CHO (g) | SFA (g) | DFIB (g) | A (IU) | B-1 (mg) | NIA (mg) | B-12 (mcg) | PANT (mg) | K (mg) | P (mg) | Fe (mg) | Cu (mg) |  |
| Light n' Lively, singles | 73 | 13.9 | 4.3 | 0.1 | 15 |  | 0 | .12 | .03 | 6 | 411 | 190 | 9 | .88 | .010 |
| *1 oz* | 28 | 6.4 | 2.1 | 2.5 |  | 196 | .02 | 0.1 | .33 | .19 | 75 | 157 | .08 | .014 |  |
| Light n' Lively, swiss | 71 | 13.9 | 3.7 | 0.1 | 12 |  | 0 | .11 | .03 | 3 | 366 | 214 | 11 | .93 |  |
| *1 oz* | 28 | 6.3 | 3.1 | 2.0 |  | 100 | .02 | 0.1 | .32 | .21 | 69 | 150 | .09 | .032 |  |
| **cheese sce** |  |  |  |  |  |  |  |  |  |  |  |  |  |  |  |
| cnd, Campbell's | 60 |  | 4.1 |  |  |  | 0 | .04 |  |  | 288 | 63 |  |  |  |
| *2 oz* | 57 | 2.3 | 3.5 |  |  | 161 | .00 | 0.1 |  |  | 23 |  | .20 |  |  |
| from dry mix | 158 | 108.0 | 8.5 | 0.8 | 26 |  | 1 | .28 |  |  | 783 | 285 | 23 | .48 |  |
| *1/2 cup* | 139 | 8.0 | 11.6 | 4.6 | 0.0 |  | .07 | 0.1 |  |  | 277 | 218 | .13 |  |  |
| Land O'Lakes | 41 |  | 2.9 |  | 6 |  | 0 | .05 |  |  | 205 | 47 |  |  |  |
| *1 oz* | 28 | 1.5 | 2.2 |  |  | 57 | .01 | 0.0 |  |  | 29 | 100 | .05 |  |  |
| aged cheddar | 50 |  | 3.7 |  | 8 |  | 0 | .05 |  |  | 232 | 69 |  |  |  |
| *1 oz* | 28 | 2.3 | 1.8 |  |  | 84 | .01 | 0.0 |  |  | 29 | 124 | .06 |  |  |
| la chedda cheddar | 37 |  | 2.5 |  | 4 |  | 0 | .04 |  |  | 181 | 39 |  |  |  |
| *1 oz* | 28 | 1.2 | 2.4 |  |  | 45 | .01 | 0.0 |  |  | 28 | 80 | .04 |  |  |
| **cheese spread** |  |  |  |  |  |  |  |  |  |  |  |  |  |  |  |
| american | 47 | 7.7 | 3.4 | 0.1 | 9 |  | 0 | .03 | .01 | 1 | 218 | 91 | 5 | .16 |  |
| *1 T* | 16 | 2.7 | 1.4 | 2.2 | 0.0 | 127 | .00 | 0.0 | .06 | .11 | 39 | 115 | .05 |  |  |
| american | 82 | 13.5 | 6.0 | 0.2 | 16 |  | 0 | .12 | .03 | 2 | 381 | 159 | 8 | .73 |  |
| *1 oz* | 28 | 4.7 | 2.5 | 3.8 | 0.0 | 223 | .01 | 0.0 | .11 | .19 | 69 | 202 | .09 |  |  |
| Cheez Whiz, Kraft | 77 | 14.5 | 5.7 | 0.1 | 16 |  | 0 | .11 | .02 | 4 | 370 | 147 | 8 | .69 |  |
| *1 oz* | 28 | 4.6 | 1.8 | 3.1 |  | 193 | .02 | 0.1 | .18 | .16 | 52 | 255 | .06 | .019 |  |
| Easy Cheese, all flavors[a] | 80 |  | 6.0 |  |  |  |  |  |  |  | 345 |  |  |  |  |
| *1 oz* | 28 | 4.0 | 2.0 |  |  |  |  |  |  |  | 73 |  |  |  |  |
| Land O'Lakes, golden velvet | 80 |  | 6.0 | 1.0 | 15 |  |  |  |  |  | 380 |  |  |  |  |
| *1 oz* | 28 | 5.0 | 2.0 | 4.0 |  |  |  |  |  |  | 70 |  |  |  |  |
| Velveeta sharp | 84 | 13.0 | 6.1 | 0.2 | 21 |  | 0 | .13 | .02 | 6 | 454 | 154 | 8 | .61 | .010 |
| *1 oz* | 28 | 5.2 | 2.2 | 3.6 |  | 343 | .02 | 0.0 | .33 | .19 | 88 | 292 | .06 | .015 |  |

# 6. CHIPS, PRETZELS, POPCORN & SIMILAR SNACK FOODS

|  | KCAL | H₂O (g) | FAT (g) | PUFA (g) | CHOL (mg) | A (RE) | C (mg) | B-2 (mg) | B-6 (mg) | FOL (mcg) | Na (mg) | Ca (mg) | Mg (mg) | Zn (mg) | Mn (mg) |
|---|---|---|---|---|---|---|---|---|---|---|---|---|---|---|---|
|  | WT (g) | PRO (g) | CHO (g) | SFA (g) | DFIB (g) | A (IU) | B-1 (mg) | NIA (mg) | B-12 (mcg) | PANT (mg) | K (mg) | P (mg) | Fe (mg) | Cu (mg) |  |
| **bugles, General Mills** | 150 |  | 8.0 |  |  |  |  |  |  |  | 290 |  |  |  |  |
| *1 oz* | 28 | 2.0 | 18.0 |  |  |  |  |  |  |  | 20 |  |  |  |  |
| **bugles, nacho cheese, General Mills** | 160 |  | 9.0 |  |  |  |  |  |  |  | 270 |  |  |  |  |
| *1 oz* | 28 | 2.0 | 17.0 |  |  |  |  |  |  |  | 35 |  |  |  |  |
| **cheese balls/curls, Planters** | 160 |  | 11.0 |  |  |  |  |  |  |  | 280 |  |  |  |  |
| *1 oz* | 28 | 2.0 | 14.0 |  |  |  |  |  |  |  | 40 |  |  |  |  |
| **cheese 'n crunch, Nabisco** | 160 |  | 11.0 |  |  |  |  |  |  |  | 190 |  |  |  |  |
| *41 pieces (1 oz)* | 28 | 2.0 | 15.0 |  |  |  |  |  |  |  | 55 |  |  |  |  |
| **cheese straws** | 272 | 13.0 | 17.9 |  |  |  | 0 | .10 |  |  | 433 | 155 |  |  |  |
| *10 pieces* | 60 | 6.7 | 20.7 | 6.4[b] |  | 230 | .01 | 0.2 |  |  | 38 | 124 | .40 |  |  |
| **chex party mix** | 130 |  | 4.7 |  |  |  | 6 | .10 | .30 | 60 | 320 |  | 16 | .30 |  |
| *2/3 cup (1 oz)* | 28 | 3.0 | 19.0 |  |  |  | .30 | 4.0 | .90 |  |  | 40 | 1.80 | .080 |  |
| nacho | 120 |  | 4.3 |  |  |  | 6 | .10 | .30 | 60 | 430 |  | 16 | .30 |  |
| *2/3 cup (1 oz)* | 28 | 2.9 | 18.0 |  |  |  | .30 | 4.0 | .90 |  |  | 40 | 1.80 | .080 |  |
| sweet & nutty | 130 |  | 4.1 |  |  |  | 9 | .07 | .30 | 60 | 240 |  | 8 | .30 |  |
| *3/4 cup (1 oz)* | 28 | 3.1 | 20.0 |  |  |  | .30 | 4.0 | .90 |  |  | 40 | 1.80 | .080 |  |
| **chipsters light 'n crispy potato snacks, Nabisco—57 pieces (1 oz)** | 120 |  | 5.0 |  |  |  |  |  |  |  | 580 |  |  |  |  |
|  | 28 | 1.0 | 19.0 |  |  |  |  |  |  |  | 180 |  |  |  |  |
| **corn chips** | 153 | 0.3 | 8.8 |  |  |  | 0 | 0.3 |  |  | 218 | 2 | 22 | .43 |  |
| *1 oz* | 28 | 1.7 | 16.6 |  |  | 65 | .05 | 0.0 | .00 |  |  | 31 | .039 |  |  |
| **corn diggers, Nabisco** | 150 |  | 8.0 |  |  |  |  |  |  |  | 260 |  |  |  |  |
| *36 pieces (1 oz)* | 28 | 2.0 | 17.0 |  |  |  |  |  |  |  | 25 |  |  |  |  |

[a] Values are averages for american, cheddar, cheddar 'n chives, cheese 'n bacon, nacho & sharp cheddar.

[b] If made w/ veg shortening; 7.9 g if made w/ lard.

| | KCAL | H₂O (g) | FAT (g) | PUFA (g) | CHOL (mg) | A (RE) | C (mg) | B-2 (mg) | B-6 (mg) | FOL (mcg) | Na (mg) | Ca (mg) | Mg (mg) | Zn (mg) | Mn (mg) |
|---|---|---|---|---|---|---|---|---|---|---|---|---|---|---|---|
| | WT (g) | PRO (g) | CHO (g) | SFA (g) | DFIB (g) | A (IU) | B-1 (mg) | NIA (mg) | B-12 (mcg) | PANT (mg) | K (mg) | P (mg) | Fe (mg) | Cu (mg) | |
| **doo dads, all flavors, Nabisco[a]** | 140 | | 6.0 | | | | | | | | 393 | | | | |
| *1/2 cup (1 oz)* | 28 | 3.0 | 18.0 | | | | | | | | 80 | | | | |
| **peanut butter boppers, General Mills[b]** | 166 | | 10.2 | | | | | | | | 115 | | | | |
| *1 oz bar* | 28 | 4.0 | 14.4 | | | | | | | | 108 | | | | |
| **pizza crunchies, Planters** | 160 | | 10.0 | | | | | | | | 160 | | | | |
| *1 oz* | 28 | 2.0 | 15.0 | | | | | | | | 45 | | | | |
| **popcorn, popped** | 23 | 0.2 | 0.3 | | | | 1 | .01 | | | 0 | 1 | | | |
| *1 cup* | 6 | 0.8 | 4.6 | 0.0 | | | | 0.1 | | | | 17 | .20 | | |
| fat & salt added | 41 | 0.3 | 2.0 | | | | 0 | .01 | | | 175 | 1 | | | |
| *1 cup* | 9 | 0.9 | 5.3 | 0.9[c] | | | | 0.2 | | | | 19 | .20 | | |
| Pillsbury microwave, frzn | | | | | | | | | | | | | | | |
| butter flavor | 192 | 0.9 | 11.5 | | | | 3 | .03 | | | 273 | 9 | | | |
| *3 cups* | 37 | 2.8 | 18.9 | | | 51 | .04 | 0.6 | | | 91 | 69 | .63 | | |
| original flavor | 192 | 0.9 | 11.5 | | | | 2 | .03 | | | 301 | 9 | | | |
| *3 cups* | 37 | 2.8 | 18.9 | | | 51 | .05 | 0.6 | | | 91 | 69 | .63 | | |
| salt free | 139 | 0.8 | 5.9 | | | | 2 | .03 | | | 5 | 2 | | | |
| *3 cups* | 30 | 2.8 | 18.9 | | | 51 | .03 | 0.6 | | | 90 | 66 | .60 | | |
| pop secret, natural/butter flavor, | 230 | | 13.5 | | | | | | | | 430 | | | | |
| General Mills—*4 cups* | 50 | 4.0 | 27.5 | | | | | | | | 95 | | | | |
| sugar-coated | 134 | 1.4 | 1.2 | | | | 0 | .02 | | | 0 | 2 | | | |
| *1 cup* | 35 | 2.1 | 29.9 | 0.4 | | | | 0.4 | | | | 47 | .50 | | |
| **potato chips** | 148 | 0.7 | 10.1 | 5.2 | 0 | 0 | 12 | .01 | .14 | 13 | 133[d] | 7 | 17 | .30 | .125 |
| *1 oz* | 28 | 1.8 | 14.7 | 2.6 | | 0 | .04 | 1.2 | .00 | .11 | 369 | 43 | .34 | .057 | |
| from dried potatoes | 164 | 0.5 | 13.1 | 0.9 | 0 | | 2 | .02 | | | 216 | 6 | 16 | .17 | |
| *1 oz* | 28 | 1.6 | 12.4 | 4.0 | | | .04 | 0.9 | | | 312 | 40 | .43 | .028 | |
| Pringle's | 167 | 0.5 | 13.0 | | 0 | | 2 | .02 | | | 215 | 7 | 16 | .17 | |
| *1 oz* | 28 | 1.6 | 10.8 | | | | .04 | 0.9 | | | 312 | 40 | .43 | .028 | |
| cheez-ums | 167 | 0.5 | 13.0 | | 2 | | 2 | .03 | | | 240 | 31 | | | |
| *1 oz* | 28 | 1.9 | 10.5 | | | | .05 | 0.7 | | | | | .45 | | |
| light style | 147 | 0.6 | 8.2 | | 0 | | 4 | .02 | | | 152 | 8 | 16 | .20 | |
| *1 oz* | 28 | 1.9 | 16.5 | | | | .05 | 1.0 | | | 301 | 48 | .45 | .028 | |
| rippled | 167 | 0.6 | 11.9 | | 0 | | 2 | .02 | | | 249 | 9 | 18 | .20 | |
| *1 oz* | 28 | 1.7 | 13.3 | | | | .04 | 0.9 | | | 286 | 48 | .34 | .057 | |
| sour cream 'n onion | 167 | 0.6 | 13.0 | | 0 | | 3 | .03 | | | 146 | 18 | | | |
| *1 oz* | 28 | 1.8 | 10.8 | | | | .05 | 0.7 | | | | | .40 | | |
| **potato sticks** | 148 | 0.6 | 9.8 | 5.0 | 0 | 0 | 13 | .03 | .09 | 11 | 71 | 5 | 18 | .28 | .119 |
| *1 oz* | 28 | 1.9 | 15.2 | 2.5 | | 0 | .03 | 1.4 | .00 | .11 | 351 | 49 | .65 | .090 | |
| **pretzels** | 111 | 0.7 | 1.0 | | | | 0 | .07 | .01 | 4 | 451 | 7 | 7 | .30 | |
| *1 oz* | 28 | 2.6 | 22.4 | | | 0 | .09 | 1.2 | .00 | .08 | 28 | 25 | .55 | .041 | |
| **pretzels, all shapes, Mister Salty[e]** | 110 | | 1.2 | | | | | | | | 543 | | | | |
| *1 oz* | 28 | 3.0 | 21.5 | | | | | | | | 37 | | | | |
| **sour cream & onion puffs, Planters** | 160 | | 10.0 | | | | | | | | 300 | | | | |
| *1 oz* | 28 | 1.0 | 16.0 | | | | | | | | 45 | | | | |
| **taro chips** | 110 | 0.6 | 5.9 | 0.8 | 0 | 0 | | .01 | | | 85 | 10 | 19 | | |
| *10 chips* | 23 | 0.5 | 15.5 | 1.8 | | 0 | .01 | 0.0 | .00 | | 189 | 30 | .31 | | |
| **tortilla chips, reg/nacho, Planters** | 150 | | 8.0 | | | | | | | | 155 | | | | |
| *1 oz* | 28 | 2.0 | 18.0 | | | | | | | | 63 | | | | |

# 7. CREAMS & CREAM SUBSTITUTES

| **creamers** | | | | | | | | | | | | | | |
|---|---|---|---|---|---|---|---|---|---|---|---|---|---|---|
| liquid | | | | | | | | | | | | | | |
| coffee rich, non-dairy creamer | 22 | 10.4 | 1.6 | 0.5 | 0 | | | | | | 7 | 0 | 0 | .00 |
| *1/2 oz* | 14 | 0.0 | 2.1 | 0.3 | | | | | | | 5 | 5 | .02 | .000 |

[a] Values are averages for cheddar 'n bacon, cheddar 'n herb, original & zesty cheese.
[b] Values are averages for cookie crunch, fudge chip, fudge graham, honey crisp & peanut crunch.
[c] If butter; 1.4 g if coconut oil.
[d] If no salt is added, Na is 2 mg.
[e] Values are averages for 15 shapes.

| | KCAL | $H_2O$ (g) | FAT (g) | PUFA (g) | CHOL (mg) | A (RE) | C (mg) | B-2 (mg) | B-6 (mg) | FOL (mcg) | Na (mg) | Ca (mg) | Mg (mg) | Zn (mg) | Mn (mg) |
|---|---|---|---|---|---|---|---|---|---|---|---|---|---|---|---|
| | WT (g) | PRO (g) | CHO (g) | SFA (g) | DFIB (g) | A (IU) | B-1 (mg) | NIA (mg) | B-12 (mcg) | PANT (mg) | K (mg) | P (mg) | Fe (mg) | Cu (mg) | |
| poly rich, non-dairy creamer | 22 | 10.5 | 1.4 | 0.7 | 0 | | | | | | 5 | 0 | 0 | .00 | |
| 1/2 oz | 14 | 0.0 | 2.1 | 0.3 | | | | | | | 11 | 5 | .00 | .003 | |
| liquid/frzn[a] | 20 | 11.6 | 1.5 | 0.0 | 0 | 1 | 0 | .00 | .00 | 0 | 12 | 1 | 0 | .00 | |
| 1/2 fl oz | 15 | 0.2 | 1.7 | 0.3 | 0.0 | 13 | .00 | 0.0 | .00 | .00 | 29 | 10 | .00 | | |
| liquid/frzn[b] | 20 | 11.6 | 1.5 | 0.0 | 0 | 1 | 0 | .00 | .00 | 0 | 12 | 1 | 0 | .00 | |
| 1/2 fl oz | 15 | 0.2 | 1.7 | 1.4 | 0.0 | 13 | .00 | 0.0 | .00 | .00 | 29 | 10 | .00 | | |
| powdered[b] | 11 | 0.0 | 0.7 | 0.0 | 0 | 0 | 0 | .00 | .00 | 0 | 4 | 0 | 0 | .00 | |
| 1 t | 2 | 0.1 | 1.1 | 0.7 | 0.0 | 4 | .00 | 0.00 | .00 | .00 | 16 | 8 | .00 | | |
| powdered, coffee-mate, Carnation | 10 | | 1.0 | 0.0 | 0 | | | | | | 2 | 1 | | | |
| 1 t | 2 | 1.0 | 1.0 | 0.7 | 0.0 | | | | | | 18 | 1 | | | |
| half & half cream | 20 | 12.1 | 1.7 | 0.0 | 6 | 16 | 0 | .02 | .01 | 0 | 6 | 16 | 2 | .08 | |
| 1 T | 15 | 0.4 | 0.6 | 1.1 | 0.0 | 65 | .01 | 0.0 | .05 | .04 | 19 | 14 | .01 | | |
| light (coffee/table) cream | 29 | 11.1 | 2.9 | 0.1 | 10 | 27 | 0 | .02 | .01 | 0 | 6 | 14 | 1 | .04 | |
| 1 T | 15 | 0.4 | 0.6 | 1.8 | 0.0 | 108 | .01 | 0.0 | .03 | .04 | 18 | 12 | .01 | | |
| medium (25% fat) cream | 37 | 10.3 | 3.8 | 0.1 | 13 | 35 | 0 | .02 | .01 | 0 | 6 | 14 | 1 | .04 | |
| 1 T | 15 | 0.4 | 0.5 | 2.3 | 0.0 | 141 | .00 | 0.0 | .03 | .04 | 17 | 11 | .01 | | |
| **sour cream** | | | | | | | | | | | | | | | |
| cultured | 26 | 8.5 | 2.5 | 0.0 | 5 | 23 | 0 | .02 | .00 | 1 | 6 | 14 | 1 | .03 | |
| 1 T | 12 | 0.4 | 0.5 | 1.6 | 0.0 | 95 | .00 | 0.0 | .04 | .04 | 17 | 10 | .01 | | |
| half & half, cultured | 20 | 12.0 | 1.8 | 0.0 | 6 | 17 | 0 | .02 | .00 | 2 | 6 | 16 | 2 | .08 | |
| 1 T | 15 | 0.4 | 0.6 | 1.1 | 0.0 | 68 | .01 | 0.0 | .05 | .05 | 19 | 14 | .01 | | |
| imitation | 59 | 20.2 | 5.5 | 0.0 | 0 | 0 | 0 | .00 | .00 | 0 | 29 | 1 | | | |
| 1 oz | 28 | 0.7 | 1.9 | 5.0 | 0.0 | 0 | .00 | 0.0 | .00 | .00 | 46 | 13 | | | |
| **sour cream dip, flavored, Land O'Lakes** | 70 | | 5.0 | 1.0 | 10 | | | | | | 315 | | | | |
| 1.7 oz | 48 | 2.0 | 4.0 | 3.0 | | | | | | | | | | | |
| **whipped cream, pressurized** | 8 | 1.8 | 0.7 | 0.0 | 2 | 6 | 0 | .00 | .00 | | 4 | 3 | 0 | .01 | |
| 1 T | 3 | 0.1 | 0.4 | 0.4 | 0.0 | 27 | .00 | 0.0 | .01 | .01 | 4 | 3 | .00 | | |
| **whipping cream** | | | | | | | | | | | | | | | |
| heavy, fluid | 52 | 8.7 | 5.6 | 0.2 | 21 | 63 | 0 | .02 | .00 | 1 | 6 | 10 | 1 | .03 | |
| 1 T | 15 | 0.3 | 0.4 | 3.5 | 0.0 | 220 | .00 | 0.0 | .03 | .04 | 11 | 9 | .00 | | |
| light, fluid | 44 | 9.5 | 4.6 | 0.1 | 17 | 44 | 0 | .02 | .00 | 1 | 5 | 10 | 1 | .04 | |
| 1 T | 15 | 0.3 | 0.4 | 2.9 | 0.0 | 169 | .00 | 0.0 | .03 | .04 | 15 | 9 | .00 | | |
| **whipped topping** | | | | | | | | | | | | | | | |
| from mix, Dream Whip | 9 | 3.3 | 0.4 | 0.0 | 1 | | 0 | .00 | .00 | 0 | 3 | 5 | 1 | .02 | |
| 1 T | 5 | 0.2 | 1.0 | 0.3 | | 10 | .00 | 0.0 | .01 | .01 | 6 | 4 | .00 | .001 | |
| from mix, w/ nutrasweet, D-Zerta | 7 | 3.9 | 0.6 | 0.0 | 0 | | 0 | .01 | .00 | 0 | 7 | 3 | 1 | .01 | |
| 1 T (from 1.112 g dry mix) | 5 | 0.1 | 0.3 | 0.5 | | 9 | .00 | 0.0 | .01 | .02 | 8 | 5 | .00 | .000 | |
| from mix, prep w/ whole milk | 8 | 2.7 | 0.5 | 0.0 | 0 | 2 | 0 | .01 | .00 | 0 | 3 | 4 | 0 | .01 | |
| 1 T | 4 | 0.1 | 0.7 | 0.4 | DFIB | 14 | B-1 | NIA | .01 | .01 | 6 | 3 | .00 | | |
| frzn | 13 | 2.0 | 1.0 | 0.0 | 0 | 3 | 0 | .00 | .00 | 0 | 1 | 0 | 0 | .00 | |
| 1 T | 4 | 0.1 | 0.9 | 0.9 | 0.0 | 34 | .00 | 0.0 | .00 | .00 | 1 | 0 | .00 | | |
| frzn, Cool Whip extra creamy, dairy | 16 | 2.4 | 1.2 | 0.0 | 0 | | 0 | .00 | .00 | 0 | 4 | 2 | 0 | .01 | |
| 1 T | 5 | 0.1 | 1.2 | 1.2 | | 38 | .00 | 0.0 | .00 | .00 | 2 | 3 | .00 | .000 | |
| frzn, Cool Whip non-dairy | 11 | 2.1 | 0.8 | 0.0 | 0 | | 0 | .00 | | | 1 | 0 | 0 | .00 | |
| 1 T | 4 | 0.1 | 1.0 | 0.8 | | 27 | .00 | 0.0 | .00 | | 0 | 0 | .00 | | |
| liquid, non-dairy topping, Richwhip[c] | 20 | 4.2 | 1.6 | | | | | | | | 4 | 0 | 0 | .00 | |
| 1/4 oz | 7 | | 1.2 | 1.3 | | | | | | | 0 | 0 | .00 | .000 | |
| pressurized | 11 | 2.4 | 0.9 | 0.0 | 0 | 2 | 0 | .00 | .00 | 0 | 2 | 0 | 0 | .00 | |
| 1 T | 4 | 0.0 | 0.6 | 0.8 | 0.0 | 19 | .00 | 0.0 | .00 | .00 | 1 | 1 | .00 | | |
| pressurized, non-dairy topping, Richwhip—1/4 oz | 20 | 4.2 | 1.7 | | | | | | | | 3 | 0 | 0 | .00 | |
| | 7 | 0.0 | 1.1 | 1.4 | | | | | | | 1 | 0 | .00 | .000 | |
| prewhipped, non-dairy topping, Richwhip—1 T | 12 | 2.0 | 0.9 | | 0 | | | .00 | | | 1 | 0 | 0 | .00 | |
| | 4 | 0.1 | 1.0 | 0.9 | | | .00 | 0.0 | | | 1 | 2 | .01 | .003 | |

[a] Contains hydrogenated veg oil & soy protein; veg oils are usually soybean, cottonseed, safflower, or blends thereof.

[b] Contains lauric acid oils and Na caseinate; lauric oils include modified coconut oil, hydrogenated coconut oil, and/or palm kernel oil.

[c] 1 fl oz if whipped.

| | KCAL | H₂O (g) | FAT (g) | PUFA (g) | CHOL (mg) | A (RE) | C (mg) | B-2 (mg) | B-6 (mg) | FOL (mcg) | Na (mg) | Ca (mg) | Mg (mg) | Zn (mg) | Mn (mg) |
|---|---|---|---|---|---|---|---|---|---|---|---|---|---|---|---|
| | WT (g) | PRO (g) | CHO (g) | SFA (g) | DFIB (g) | A (IU) | B-1 (mg) | NIA (mg) | B-12 (mcg) | PANT (mg) | K (mg) | P (mg) | Fe (mg) | Cu (mg) | |

# 8. DESSERTS

## 8.1. BROWNIES & OTHER BAR COOKIES

**brownie**

| | KCAL / WT | H₂O / PRO | FAT / CHO | PUFA / SFA | CHOL / DFIB | A(RE) / A(IU) | C / B-1 | B-2 / NIA | B-6 / B-12 | FOL / PANT | Na / K | Ca / P | Mg / Fe | Zn / Cu | Mn |
|---|---|---|---|---|---|---|---|---|---|---|---|---|---|---|---|
| black forest, from mix, Pillsbury | 160 | | 6.0 | | | | | | | | 100 | | | | |
| *2" square* | | 2.0 | 25.0 | | | | | | | | 65 | | | | |
| double fudge, from mix, Pillsbury | 160 | | 6.0 | | | | | | | | 105 | | | | |
| *2" square* | | 2.0 | 24.0 | | | | | | | | 60 | | | | |
| from mix | 86 | 2.1 | 4.0 | | | | 0 | .02 | | | 33 | 9 | | | |
| *1 brownie* | 20 | 1.0 | 12.6 | 0.8 | | 20 | .03 | 0.1 | | | 34 | 27 | .40 | | |
| frzn, Am Hosp Co | 216 | | 2.1 | | 50 | | | .06 | | | 180 | 10 | | | |
| *2.25 oz* | 64 | 5.8 | 43.5 | | | 50 | .04 | 1.4 | | | 24 | | 1.20 | | |
| fudge, from mix, Pillsbury | 150 | | 6.0 | | | | | | | | 100 | | | | |
| *2" square* | | 2.0 | 21.0 | | | | | | | | 35 | | | | |
| fudge 'n nut, Almost Home | 160 | | 7.0 | | | | | | | | 75 | | | | |
| *1 brownie* | 35 | 1.0 | 23.0 | | | | | | | | 50 | | | | |
| fudge, refrig dough, Pillsbury | 139 | 5.4 | 5.3 | | | | 0 | .05 | | | 112 | 12 | | | |
| *1 bar* | 34 | 1.3 | 21.6 | | | 0 | .04 | 0.8 | | | 60 | 20 | .85 | | |
| Rainbo Snacks | 230 | | 12.0 | | | | | | | | | | | | |
| *1 brownie* | 51 | 2.0 | 30.0 | | | | | | | | | | | | |
| rocky road fudge, from mix, Pillsbury | 170 | | 7.0 | | | | | | | | 100 | | | | |
| *2" square* | | 2.0 | 24.0 | | | | | | | | 50 | | | | |
| w/ nuts, homemade | 97 | 2.0 | 6.3 | | | | 0 | .02 | | | 50 | 8 | | | |
| *1 brownie (3x1x7/8")* | 20 | 1.3 | 10.2 | 1.4 | | 40 | .04 | 0.1 | | | 38 | 30 | .40 | | |
| w/ nuts & choc icing | 81 | 2.6 | 3.5 | | | | 0 | .05 | .03 | 2 | 47 | 10 | 8 | .29 | |
| *1 brownie* | 20 | 0.9 | 12.7 | | | 59 | .06 | 0.3 | .04 | .10 | 40 | 21 | .48 | .091 | |
| w/ nuts & choc icing, frzn | 103 | 3.1 | 5.0 | | | | 0 | .02 | | | 49 | 10 | | | |
| *1 brownie (1 1/2x 1 3/4x7/8")* | 25 | 1.2 | 14.9 | 1.7 | | 50 | .02 | 0.1 | | | 44 | 31 | .40 | | |
| w/ walnuts, from mix, PIllsbury | 150 | | 8.0 | | | | | | | | 90 | | | | |
| *2" square* | | 2.0 | 19.0 | | | | | | | | 40 | | | | |
| **brownie mix, Duncan Hines** | 120 | 1.0 | 2.8 | 0 | | | | .04 | | | 98 | 6 | 12 | .17 | |
| *1/24 pkg (1 brownie)* | 28 | 1.4 | 22.1 | | | | .04 | 0.5 | | | | 22 | 1.15 | .056 | |
| **choc chip oatmeal fudge jumbles, from mix, Pillsbury**—*1 bar* | 100 | | 4.0 | | | | | | | | 60 | | | | |
| | | 1.0 | 14.0 | | | | | | | | 30 | | | | |
| **coconut bar** | 45 | 0.3 | 2.2 | | | | 0 | .01 | | | 13 | 7 | | | |
| *1 bar (3x1 1/4x1/4")* | 9 | 0.6 | 5.8 | 0.8 | | 14 | .00 | 0.0 | | | 21 | 11 | .13 | | |
| **peanut butter oatmeal fudge jumbles, from mix, Pillsbury**—*1 bar* | 100 | | 4.0 | | | | | | | | 55 | | | | |
| | | 1.0 | 14.0 | | | | | | | | 55 | | | | |

## 8.2. CAKES

| | KCAL / WT | H₂O / PRO | FAT / CHO | PUFA / SFA | CHOL / DFIB | A(RE) / A(IU) | C / B-1 | B-2 / NIA | B-6 / B-12 | FOL / PANT | Na / K | Ca / P | Mg / Fe | Zn / Cu | Mn |
|---|---|---|---|---|---|---|---|---|---|---|---|---|---|---|---|
| **amaretto bundt, frzn, Am Hosp Co** | 289 | | 13.2 | | 48 | | | .04 | | | 288 | 28 | | | |
| *2.5 oz* | 71 | 7.3 | 32.6 | | | 52 | .08 | 0.1 | | | 92 | | .19 | | |
| **angel food** | | | | | | | | | | | | | | | |
| cake mix, Duncan Hines | 131 | 1.0 | 0.2 | 0 | | | | .14 | | | 119 | 20 | 3 | .02 | |
| *1/12 pkg* | 34 | 3.4 | 28.9 | | | | .00 | 0.1 | | | 85 | 32 | .05 | .003 | |
| homemade | 161 | 18.9 | 0.1 | | | | 0 | .14 | .01 | 5 | 161 | 7 | 7 | .12 | |
| *1 piece* | 60 | 4.8 | 35.7 | | | 0 | .07 | 0.7 | .02 | .14 | 59 | 17 | .51 | .023 | |
| from mix | 126 | 20.0 | 0.2 | | | | 0 | .11 | .01 | 4 | 269 | 44 | 4 | .05 | |
| *1/12 cake* | 53 | 3.2 | 28.6 | | | 0 | .03 | 0.1 | .00 | .12 | 70 | 91 | .23 | .032 | |
| **apple crumb, frzn, Am Hosp Co** | 214 | | 8.7 | | | | | .11 | | | 213 | 49 | | | |
| *2 oz* | 57 | 2.5 | 31.2 | | | 51 | .06 | 0.4 | | | 68 | | .60 | | |
| **applesce spice, from mix, Pillsbury** | 250 | | 11.0 | | | | | | | | 300 | | | | |
| *1/12 cake* | | 3.0 | 36.0 | | | | | | | | 80 | | | | |
| **apple spice, frzn, Am Hosp Co** | 316 | | 12.9 | | 9 | | 2 | .11 | | | 472 | 35 | | | |
| *3 oz* | 85 | 3.6 | 46.0 | | | 910 | .05 | 1.7 | | | 60 | | .93 | | |
| **banana, from mix, Pillsbury** | 250 | | 11.0 | | | | | | | | 290 | | | | |
| *1/12 cake* | | 3.0 | 36.0 | | | | | | | | 80 | | | | |

| | KCAL / WT (g) | H₂O (g) / PRO (g) | FAT (g) / CHO (g) | PUFA (g) / SFA (g) | CHOL (mg) / DFIB (g) | A (RE) / A (IU) | C (mg) / B-1 (mg) | B-2 (mg) / NIA (mg) | B-6 (mg) / B-12 (mcg) | FOL (mcg) / PANT (mg) | Na (mg) / K (mg) | Ca (mg) / P (mg) | Mg (mg) / Fe (mg) | Zn (mg) / Cu (mg) | Mn (mg) |
|---|---|---|---|---|---|---|---|---|---|---|---|---|---|---|---|
| banana, frzn, Am Hosp Co | 308 | | 13.7 | | 39 | | 0 | .12 | | | 306 | 71 | | | |
| *3 oz* | 85 | 6.3 | 40.3 | | | 280 | .01 | 0.8 | | | 103 | | .70 | | |
| blueberry crumb, frzn, Am Hosp Co | 210 | | 7.7 | | | | | .10 | | | 200 | 35 | | | |
| *2 oz* | 57 | 2.8 | 32.3 | | | 46 | .05 | 0.7 | | | 47 | | .60 | | |
| boston cream pie, homemade[a] | 311 | 35.5 | 9.7 | | | | 0 | .11 | | | 192 | 69 | | | |
| *1/8 cake* | 103 | 5.2 | 51.4 | 3.0[b] | | 220 | .03 | 0.2 | | | 92 | 104 | .50 | | |
| bundt ring, from mix, Pillsbury[c] | 248 | | 9.8 | | | | | | | | 295 | | | | |
| *1/16 cake* | | 2.8 | 37.4 | | | | | | | | 73 | | | | |
| butter recipe, from mix, Pillsbury | 260 | | 12.0 | | | | | | | | 370 | | | | |
| *1/12 cake* | | 3.0 | 34.0 | | | | | | | | 35 | | | | |
| caramel w/ caramel icing, homemade | 398 | 21.9 | 15.5 | | | | 0 | .07 | | | 265 | 88 | | | |
| *1/12 cake* | 105 | 3.9 | 62.1 | 4.7 | | 210 | .02 | 0.1 | | | 67 | 100 | 1.60 | | |
| carrot cake mix, Duncan Hines Deluxe | 187 | 1.0 | 4.0 | | 0 | | | .06 | | | 253 | 62 | 3 | .09 | |
| *1/12 pkg* | 44 | 1.6 | 36.1 | | | 1175 | .08 | 0.7 | | | 48 | 110 | .62 | .022 | |
| carrot, frzn, Am Hosp Co | 326 | | 17.1 | | 24 | | 0 | .10 | | | 310 | 28 | | | |
| *3 oz* | 85 | 5.6 | 36.8 | | | 442 | .00 | 0.9 | | | 122 | | 1.10 | | |
| carrot 'n spice, from mix, Pillsbury | 260 | | 11.0 | | | | | | | | 330 | | | | |
| *1/12 cake* | | 3.0 | 36.0 | | | | | | | | 85 | | | | |
| cheesecake | 257 | 39.0 | 16.3 | | | | 4 | .11 | .05 | 15 | 189 | 48 | 9 | .36 | |
| *1 piece* | 85 | 4.6 | 24.3 | | | 216 | .03 | 0.4 | .42 | .49 | 83 | 75 | .41 | .051 | |
| **cheesecake, from mix** | | | | | | | | | | | | | | | |
| Jell-O[d] | 278 | 43.0 | 12.9 | 1.0 | 28 | | 0 | .21 | .03 | 6 | 350 | 142 | 18 | .29 | |
| *1/8 cheesecake* | 99 | 4.9 | 36.3 | 8.0 | | 357 | .10 | 0.5 | .18 | .22 | 199 | 187 | .39 | .038 | |
| Royal[d] | 225 | | 9.0 | | | | | | | | 370 | | | | |
| *1/8 cheesecake* | | 5.0 | 31.0 | | | | | | | | 210 | | | | |
| cheesecake, lite, from mix, Royal[e] | 210 | | 10.0 | | | | | | | | 380 | | | | |
| *1/8 cheesecake* | | 5.0 | 23.0 | | | | | | | | 250 | | | | |
| cheese crumb, frzn, Am Hosp Co | 202 | | 9.3 | | | | | .08 | | | 191 | 27 | | | |
| *2 oz* | 57 | 4.3 | 25.5 | | | 124 | .02 | 0.2 | | | 40 | | .60 | | |
| cherry crumb, frzn, Am Hosp Co | 193 | | 7.3 | | | | | .10 | | | 168 | 37 | | | |
| *2 oz* | 57 | 3.1 | 29.0 | | | 159 | .05 | 0.6 | | | 65 | | .70 | | |
| choc chip cake mix, Duncan Hines Deluxe | 189 | 1.2 | 4.4 | | 0 | | | .08 | | | 249 | 57 | 6 | .13 | |
| *1/12 pkg* | 44 | 1.8 | 35.6 | | | | .11 | 1.0 | | | | 119 | .92 | .040 | |
| choc chip crumb, frzn, Am Hosp Co | 260 | | 13.8 | | | | | | | | 231 | 30 | | | |
| *2 oz* | 57 | 3.7 | 30.3 | | | 89 | .03 | 0.5 | | | 127 | | .80 | | |
| choc chip, from mix, Pillsbury | 270 | | 14.0 | | | | | | | | 290 | | | | |
| *1/12 cake* | | 3.0 | 33.0 | | | | | | | | 60 | | | | |
| choc chip pudding, frzn, Am Hosp Co | 355 | | 17.8 | | 9 | | 0 | .18 | | | 336 | 33 | | | |
| *3 oz* | 85 | 3.5 | 45.1 | | | 1 | .00 | 0.3 | | | 108 | 68 | | | |
| choc, frzn, Am Hosp Co | 326 | | 13.7 | | 27 | | 0 | .21 | | | 293 | 35 | | | |
| *3 oz* | 85 | 7.5 | 43.7 | | | 201 | .02 | 1.3 | | | 234 | | 4.20 | | |
| choc mint, from mix, Pillsbury | 250 | | 12.0 | | | | | | | | 370 | | | | |
| *1/12 cake* | | 3.0 | 32.0 | | | | | | | | 85 | | | | |
| choc mousse, frzn, Nutra Choice | 150 | | 6.0 | | 5 | | | | | | 273 | 65 | | | |
| *2.2 oz serving* | 62 | 2.8 | 21.0 | | | | | | | | | | .79 | | |
| **coffee cake** | | | | | | | | | | | | | | | |
| apple cinn, from mix, Pillsbury | 240 | | 7.0 | | | | | | | | 160 | | | | |
| *1/8 cake* | | 3.0 | 40.0 | | | | | | | | 90 | | | | |
| from mix | 232 | 21.6 | 6.9 | | | | 0 | .12 | | | 310 | 44 | | | |
| *1/6 cake* | 72 | 4.5 | 37.7 | 2.0 | | 120 | .13 | 1.0 | | | 78 | 125 | 1.20 | | |
| mix, Aunt Jemima | 162 | 1.1 | 4.4 | | | | | .04 | .01 | 28 | 225 | 58 | 13 | .00 | .000 |
| *1.3 oz dry mix* | 37 | 1.8 | 28.7 | | | 8 | .12 | 1.0 | .00 | .00 | 32 | 94 | .73 | .080 | |
| **cottage pudding** | | | | | | | | | | | | | | | |
| homemade | 186 | 14.4 | 6.1 | | | | 0 | .09 | | | 161 | 49 | | | |
| *1/8 cake* | 54 | 3.5 | 29.3 | 1.7 | | 80 | .08 | 0.6 | | | 48 | 62 | .80 | | |
| w/ choc sce, homemade | 235 | 20.6 | 6.5 | | | | 0 | .10 | | | 172 | 53 | | | |
| *1/8 cake & 1 T sce* | 74 | 3.9 | 42.0 | 2.0 | | 70 | .09 | 0.7 | | | 104 | 81 | 1.00 | | |
| w/ strawberry sce, homemade | 204 | 25.6 | 6.2 | | | | 8 | .11 | | | 163 | 51 | | | |
| *1/8 cake & 1 T sce* | 70 | 3.6 | 33.9 | 1.7 | | 80 | .08 | 0.8 | | | 65 | 65 | .80 | | |

[a] Layer cake w/ custard filling & powdered sugar topping.
[b] Made w/ veg shortening; 4.5 g if made w/ butter.
[c] Values are averages for boston cream, choc macaroon, choc mousse, lemon blueberry, pineapple cream, pound, tunnel of fudge & tunnel of lemon.
[d] Prepared w/ vitamin D fortified whole milk.
[e] Prepared w/ vitamin D fortified 2% low fat milk.

| | KCAL / WT (g) | H₂O (g) / PRO (g) | FAT (g) / CHO (g) | PUFA (g) / SFA (g) | CHOL (mg) / DFIB (g) | A (RE) / A (IU) | C (mg) / B-1 (mg) | B-2 (mg) / NIA (mg) | B-6 (mg) / B-12 (mcg) | FOL (mcg) / PANT (mg) | Na (mg) / K (mg) | Ca (mg) / P (mg) | Mg (mg) / Fe (mg) | Zn (mg) / Cu (mg) | Mn (mg) |
|---|---|---|---|---|---|---|---|---|---|---|---|---|---|---|---|
| **dark choc, from mix, Pillsbury** | 250 | | 12.0 | | | | | | | | 380 | | | | |
| *1/12 cake* | | 3.0 | 32.0 | | | | | | | | 65 | | | | |
| **date nut roll, Dromedary** | 80 | | 2.0 | | | | | | | | 160 | | | | |
| *1/2" slice* | | 1.0 | 13.0 | | | | | | | | 60 | | | | |
| **dessert cup, Hostess** | 60 | | 0.0 | | 9 | | 0 | | | | 120 | | | | |
| *1 dessert cup* | 21 | 1.0 | 14.0 | | | 0 | | | | | | | | | |
| **devil's food** | | | | | | | | | | | | | | | |
| cake mix, Duncan Hines Deluxe | 189 | 0.6 | 4.1 | | 0 | | | .07 | | | 363 | 66 | 21 | .35 | |
| *1/12 pkg* | 44 | 2.5 | 35.6 | | | | .07 | 0.7 | | | 145 | 119 | 1.98 | .176 | |
| from mix | 312 | 21.7 | 11.3 | | | | 0 | .07 | | | 241 | 54 | | | |
| *1/12 cake* | 92 | 4.0 | 53.6 | 4.4 | | 140 | .03 | 0.3 | | | 120 | 97 | .70 | | |
| from mix, Pillsbury | 270 | | 14.0 | | | | | | | | 370 | | | | |
| *1/12 cake* | | 4.0 | 32.0 | | | | | | | | 130 | | | | |
| homemade | 227 | 13.8 | 11.3 | | | | 0 | .11 | .02 | 6 | 160 | 68 | 23 | .48 | |
| *1 piece* | 60 | 3.4 | 30.4 | | | 53 | .08 | 0.7 | .13 | .24 | 95 | 76 | 1.03 | .142 | |
| pudding type, from mix | 191 | 21.7 | 9.3 | | | | 0 | .08 | .03 | 6 | 341 | 54 | 16 | .41 | |
| *1 piece* | 60 | 2.9 | 24.8 | | | 47 | .06 | 0.8 | .26 | .12 | 129 | 128 | 1.21 | .101 | |
| w/ choc icing, frzn | 323 | 17.9 | 15.0 | | | | 0 | .07 | | | 357 | 46 | | | |
| *1/6 cake* | 85 | 3.7 | 47.3 | 7.7 | | 370 | .02 | 0.2 | | | 101 | 78 | .70 | | |
| w/ choc icing, homemade | 233 | 11.6 | 10.8 | | | | 0 | .08 | .02 | 4 | 108 | 50 | 21 | .40 | |
| *1 piece* | 60 | 2.6 | 34.2 | | | 39 | .05 | 0.5 | .10 | .17 | 87 | 62 | .83 | .140 | |
| w/ whipped cream filling & choc icing, | 315 | 25.2 | 18.6 | | | | 0 | .07 | | | 162 | 68 | | | |
| *frzn—1/6 cake* | 85 | 3.0 | 37.2 | 6.2 | | 230 | .02 | 0.2 | | | 96 | 104 | .50 | | |
| **french crumb, frzn, Am Hosp Co** | 229 | | 8.5 | | | | | .14 | | | 173 | 26 | | | |
| *2 oz* | 57 | 3.4 | 34.6 | | | 35 | .07 | 0.8 | | | 58 | | .80 | | |
| **fruitcake** | | | | | | | | | | | | | | | |
| dark, homemade | 163 | 7.8 | 6.6 | | | | 0 | .06 | | | 68 | 31 | | | |
| *1 piece* | 43 | 2.1 | 25.7 | 1.4 | | 50 | .06 | 0.3 | | | 213 | 49 | 1.10 | | |
| light, homemade | 167 | 8.0 | 7.1 | | | | 0 | .05 | | | 83 | 29 | | | |
| *1 piece* | 43 | 2.6 | 24.7 | 1.6 | | 30 | .04 | 0.3 | | | 100 | 49 | .70 | | |
| **fudge cake mix, Duncan Hines Butter** | 185 | 1.6 | 4.2 | | 0 | | | .12 | | | 242 | 22 | 17 | .26 | |
| **Recipe**—*1/12 pkg* | 44 | 2.5 | 34.8 | | | | .09 | 1.0 | | | 176 | 53 | 1.14 | .088 | |
| **fudge marble, from mix, Pillsbury** | 270 | | 12.0 | | | | | | | | 300 | | | | |
| *1/12 cake* | | 4.0 | 36.0 | | | | | | | | 55 | | | | |
| **german choc, from mix, Pillsbury** | 250 | | 11.0 | | | | | | | | 340 | | | | |
| *1/12 cake* | | 3.0 | 36.0 | | | | | | | | 60 | | | | |
| **gingerbread** | | | | | | | | | | | | | | | |
| from mix | 174 | 23.3 | 4.3 | | | | 0 | .06 | | | 192 | 57 | | | |
| *1/9 cake* | 63 | 2.0 | 32.2 | 1.1 | | 0 | .02 | 0.5 | | | 173 | 63 | 1.00 | | |
| from mix, Dromedary | 100 | | 2.0 | | | | | | | | 190 | | | | |
| *2" square* | | 1.0 | 19.0 | | | | | | | | 90 | | | | |
| from mix, Pillsbury | 190 | | 4.0 | | | | | | | | 310 | | | | |
| *3" square* | | 2.0 | 36.0 | | | | | | | | 160 | | | | |
| homemade | 267 | 17.1 | 12.9 | | | | 0 | .11 | .05 | 6 | 99 | 48 | 15 | .32 | |
| *1 piece* | 70 | 3.0 | 35.0 | | | 28 | .13 | 1.1 | .07 | .27 | 237 | 41 | 2.11 | .134 | |
| **golden cake mix, Duncan Hines Butter** | 185 | 1.5 | 3.9 | | 0 | | | .08 | | | 158 | 35 | 2 | .09 | |
| **Recipe**—*1/12 pkg* | 44 | 1.6 | 36.5 | | | | .09 | 0.8 | | | 23 | 57 | .53 | .018 | |
| **honey spice, from mix** | 363 | 23.4 | 11.1 | | | | 0 | .09 | | | 252 | 73 | | | |
| *1/12 cake* | 103 | 4.2 | 62.7 | 3.3 | | 160 | .02 | 0.2 | | | 84 | 199 | .80 | | |
| **lemon delight, frzn, Am Hosp Co** | 271 | | 15.1 | | 18 | | | .05 | | | 50 | 38 | | | |
| *3 oz* | 85 | 3.0 | 34.1 | | | 5 | .02 | 0.2 | | | 113 | | .30 | | |
| **lemon, from mix, Pillsbury** | 220 | | 9.0 | | | | | | | | 260 | | | | |
| *1/12 cake* | | 3.0 | 31.0 | | | | | | | | 30 | | | | |
| **marble streusel w/ icing, from mix** | 224 | 19.0 | 9.8 | | | | 0 | .08 | .03 | 6 | 278 | 34 | 9 | .26 | |
| *1 piece* | 65 | 2.5 | 32.7 | | | 38 | .07 | 0.6 | .13 | .22 | 71 | 129 | .88 | .061 | |
| **mocha, from mix, Pillsbury** | 250 | | 12.0 | | | | | | | | 380 | | | | |
| *1/12 cake* | | 3.0 | 33.0 | | | | | | | | 75 | | | | |
| **oats 'n brown sugar, from mix, Pillsbury** | 260 | | 12.0 | | | | | | | | 310 | | | | |
| *1/12 cake* | | 3.0 | 35.0 | | | | | | | | 80 | | | | |

| | KCAL | $H_2O$ (g) | FAT (g) | PUFA (g) | CHOL (mg) | A (RE) | C (mg) | B-2 (mg) | B-6 (mg) | FOL (mcg) | Na (mg) | Ca (mg) | Mg (mg) | Zn (mg) | Mn (mg) |
|---|---|---|---|---|---|---|---|---|---|---|---|---|---|---|---|
| | WT (g) | PRO (g) | CHO (g) | SFA (g) | DFIB (g) | A (IU) | B-1 (mg) | NIA (mg) | B-12 (mcg) | PANT (mg) | K (mg) | P (mg) | Fe (mg) | Cu (mg) | |
| **pineapple upside-down, homemade** | 236 | 25.0 | 9.1 | | | | 4 | .08 | .05 | 9 | 179 | 54 | 13 | .41 | |
| *1 piece* | 75 | 2.5 | 37.4 | | | 291 | .12 | 0.8 | .06 | .25 | 128 | 47 | 1.19 | .090 | |
| **pound** | | | | | | | | | | | | | | | |
| from mix, Dromedary | 150 | | 6.0 | | | | | | | | 340 | | | | |
| *1/2" slice* | 65 | 2.0 | 21.0 | | | | | | | | | | | | |
| frzn, Am Hosp Co | 256 | | 14.8 | | 8 | | 2 | .22 | | | 290 | 34 | | | |
| *2.25 oz* | 64 | 3.2 | 27.5 | | | 0 | .11 | 1.1 | | | 61 | | 1.10 | | |
| modified, homemade | 119 | 5.6 | 5.4 | | | | 0 | .03 | | | 52 | 12 | | | |
| *1 piece* | 29 | 1.9 | 15.9 | 1.4 | | 80 | .01 | 0.1 | | | 23 | 30 | .20 | | |
| old fashioned, homemade | 142 | 5.2 | 8.9 | | | | 0 | .03 | | | 33 | 6 | | | |
| *1 piece* | 30 | 1.7 | 14.1 | 2.3 | | 80 | .01 | 0.1 | | | 18 | 24 | .20 | | |
| **snackin' cake mix[a]** | 192 | | 5.8 | | | | | | | | 252 | | | | |
| *1/9 cake* | 89 | 2.0 | 32.8 | | | | | | | | | | | | |
| sponge, homemade | 188 | 21.6 | 3.1 | | | | 0 | .13 | .04 | 15 | 164 | 25 | 7 | .80 | |
| *1 piece* | 66 | 4.8 | 35.7 | | | 125 | .09 | 0.7 | .33 | .53 | 59 | 65 | 1.11 | .033 | |
| **strawberry** | | | | | | | | | | | | | | | |
| delight mousse, frzn, Nutra Choice | 135 | | 4.1 | | 4 | | | | | | 179 | 54 | | | |
| *2.2 oz serving* | 62 | 2.0 | 15.8 | | | | | | | | | | .56 | | |
| from mix, Pillsbury | 260 | | 11.0 | | | | | | | | 300 | | | | |
| *1/12 cake* | 85 | 3.0 | 37.0 | | | | | | | | | | | | |
| **stir 'n frost cake mix w/ frosting[b]** | 237 | | 6.6 | | | | | | | | 246 | | | | |
| *1/6 pkg* | 103 | 2.0 | 42.0 | | | | | | | | | | | | |
| **streusel swirl, from mix, Pillsbury[c]** | 263 | | 11.0 | | | | | | | | 235 | | | | |
| *1/16 cake* | 44 | 3.0 | 38.0 | | | | | | | | | | | | |
| **white** | | | | | | | | | | | | | | | |
| cake mix, Duncan Hines Deluxe | 189 | 1.2 | 4.0 | | 0 | | | .09 | | | 251 | 75 | 3 | .13 | |
| *1/12 pkg* | 44 | 2.1 | 36.1 | | | | .12 | 1.0 | | | | 145 | .70 | .022 | |
| from mix | 333 | 20.0 | 10.2 | | | | 0 | .08 | | | 216 | 94 | | | |
| *1/12 cake* | 95 | 3.7 | 59.7 | 3.7 | | 60 | .02 | 0.2 | | | 110 | 170 | .50 | | |
| from mix, Pillsbury | 240 | | 10.0 | | | | | | | | 290 | | | | |
| *1/12 cake* | 75 | 3.0 | 35.0 | | | | | | | | | | | | |
| homemade | 285 | 19.4 | 11.6 | | | | 0 | .16 | .02 | 5 | 346 | 87 | 11 | .27 | |
| *1 piece* | 78 | 4.6 | 40.9 | | | 29 | .12 | 1.1 | .08 | .22 | 80 | 66 | .84 | .031 | |
| pudding type, from mix | 219 | 26.6 | 9.8 | | | | 0 | .08 | .01 | 4 | 293 | 34 | 4 | .11 | |
| *1 piece* | 71 | 2.5 | 31.2 | | | 0 | .06 | 0.7 | .04 | .21 | 34 | 115 | .46 | .026 | |
| w/ choc icing, homemade | 298 | 15.8 | 12.1 | | | | 0 | .12 | .02 | 4 | 219 | 62 | 15 | .29 | |
| *1 piece* | 78 | 3.3 | 45.8 | | | 23 | .08 | 0.7 | .06 | .15 | 84 | 58 | .75 | .086 | |
| **yellow** | | | | | | | | | | | | | | | |
| cake mix, Duncan Hines Deluxe | 189 | 0.6 | 3.6 | | 0 | | | .09 | | | 271 | 53 | 3 | .09 | |
| *1/12 pkg* | 44 | 1.9 | 37.0 | | | | .12 | 0.9 | | | | 110 | .66 | .022 | |
| from mix | 310 | 23.6 | 10.4 | | | | 0 | .07 | | | 209 | 84 | | | |
| *1/12 cake* | 92 | 3.8 | 53.0 | 3.7 | | 130 | .02 | 0.2 | | | 100 | 167 | .60 | | |
| from mix, Pillsbury | 250 | | 11.0 | | | | | | | | 290 | | | | |
| *1/12 cake* | 30 | 3.0 | 34.0 | | | | | | | | | | | | |
| homemade | 283 | 17.9 | 12.4 | | | | 0 | .15 | .03 | 9 | 329 | 89 | 11 | .41 | |
| *1 piece* | 75 | 4.3 | 38.9 | | | 74 | .13 | 1.1 | .19 | .35 | 72 | 80 | 1.02 | .033 | |
| pudding type, from mix | 231 | 23.6 | 10.8 | | | | 0 | .11 | .02 | 7 | 299 | 43 | 5 | .41 | |
| *1 piece* | 69 | 3.1 | 30.5 | | | 56 | .12 | 1.0 | .18 | .23 | 39 | 139 | .87 | .066 | |
| w/ choc icing, homemade | 292 | 14.6 | 12.3 | | | | 0 | .11 | .02 | 6 | 208 | 62 | 14 | .37 | |
| *1 piece* | 75 | 3.2 | 43.8 | | | 52 | .08 | 0.7 | .13 | .24 | 79 | 66 | .86 | .085 | |

## 8.3. CAKES, CUPCAKES & SNACK CAKES

| | KCAL | $H_2O$ (g) | FAT (g) | PUFA (g) | CHOL (mg) | A (RE) | C (mg) | B-2 (mg) | B-6 (mg) | FOL (mcg) | Na (mg) | Ca (mg) | Mg (mg) | Zn (mg) | Mn (mg) |
|---|---|---|---|---|---|---|---|---|---|---|---|---|---|---|---|
| | WT (g) | PRO (g) | CHO (g) | SFA (g) | DFIB (g) | A (IU) | B-1 (mg) | NIA (mg) | B-12 (mcg) | PANT (mg) | K (mg) | P (mg) | Fe (mg) | Cu (mg) | |
| **choco bliss, Hostess** | 200 | | 7.0 | 0 | | | 0 | | | | 170 | | | | |
| *1 piece* | 50 | 2.0 | 34.0 | | | 0 | .00 | | | | | | | | |
| **choco diles, Hostess** | 240 | | 11.0 | | 22 | | 0 | | | | 280 | | | | |
| *1 piece* | 57 | 2.0 | 35.0 | | | 0 | | 0.0 | | | | | | | |
| **cinn nut rolls, Rainbo Snacks** | 330 | | 11.0 | | | | | | | | | | | | |
| *2 rolls* | 85 | 5.0 | 52.0 | | | | | | | | | | | | |

[a] Values are averages for 5 flavors.
[b] Values are averages for 7 flavors.
[c] Values are averages for cinn, dutch apple, lemon & pecan brown sugar.

| | KCAL | H₂O (g) | FAT (g) | PUFA (g) | CHOL (mg) | A (RE) | C (mg) | B-2 (mg) | B-6 (mg) | FOL (mcg) | Na (mg) | Ca (mg) | Mg (mg) | Zn (mg) | Mn (mg) |
|---|---|---|---|---|---|---|---|---|---|---|---|---|---|---|---|
| | WT (g) | PRO (g) | CHO (g) | SFA (g) | DFIB (g) | A (IU) | B-1 (mg) | NIA (mg) | B-12 (mcg) | PANT (mg) | K (mg) | P (mg) | Fe (mg) | Cu (mg) | |
| **crumb cake, Hostess** | 130 | | 4.0 | | 10 | | 0 | | | | 95 | | | | |
| *1 piece* | 35 | 1.0 | 22.0 | | | 0 | | | | | | | | | |
| **cupcakes** | | | | | | | | | | | | | | | |
| choc, Hostess | 170 | | 6.0 | | 3 | | 0 | | | | 250 | | | | |
| *1 cupcake* | 50 | 2.0 | 29.0 | | | 0 | | | | | | | | | |
| choc, Rainbo Snacks | 350 | | 10.0 | | | | | | | | | | | | |
| *2 cupcakes* | 68 | 4.0 | 62.0 | | | | | | | | | | | | |
| orange, Hostess | 150 | | 5.0 | | 13 | | 0 | | | | 175 | | | | |
| *1 cupcake* | 43 | 1.0 | 28.0 | | | 0 | | | | | | | | | |
| w/ choc icing, from mix | 172 | 10.7 | 6.0 | | | | 0 | .05 | | | 161 | 62 | | | |
| *1 cupcake* | 48 | 2.2 | 28.4 | | | 80 | .02 | 0.1 | | | 56 | 95 | .40 | | |
| w/ choc icing, homemade | 173 | 10.1 | 6.5 | | | | 0 | .04 | | | 108 | 30 | | | |
| *1 cupcake* | 47 | 2.0 | 27.9 | | | 80 | .01 | 0.1 | | | 54 | 49 | .30 | | |
| w/ white icing, homemade | 172 | 9.7 | 5.5 | | | | 0 | .03 | | | 107 | 24 | | | |
| *1 cupcake* | 47 | 1.6 | 29.8 | | | 90 | .01 | 0.0 | | | 29 | 35 | .10 | | |
| **ding dongs/big wheels, Hostess** | 170 | | 9.0 | | 6 | | 0 | | | | 130 | | | | |
| *1 piece* | 38 | 1.0 | 21.0 | | | 0 | .00 | | | | | | | | |
| **filled twins, Rainbo Snacks** | 300 | | 7.0 | | | | | | | | | | | | |
| *2 twins* | 85 | 3.0 | 56.0 | | | | | | | | | | | | |
| **fruitcake, supreme, Rainbo Snacks** | 110 | | 5.0 | | | | | | | | | | | | |
| *1 oz* | 28 | 1.0 | 16.0 | | | | | | | | | | | | |
| **fruit loaf, Hostess** | 400 | | 9.0 | | 7 | | 0 | | | | 520 | | | | |
| *1 piece* | 142 | 4.0 | 77.0 | | | 0 | | | | | | | | | |
| **ho hos, Hostess** | 120 | | 6.0 | | 13 | | 0 | | | | 90 | | | | |
| *1 piece* | 28 | 1.0 | 17.0 | | | 0 | .00 | 0.0 | | | | | | | |
| **honey buns, glazed, Hostess** | 450 | | 27.0 | | 24 | | 0 | | | | 650 | | | | |
| *1 piece* | 106 | 5.0 | 49.0 | | | 0 | | | | | | | | | |
| **honey buns, Rainbo Snacks** | 380 | | 23.0 | | | | | | | | | | | | |
| *1 piece* | 85 | 4.0 | 41.0 | | | | | | | | | | | | |
| **hoot 'n toots, Rainbo Snacks** | 450 | | 16.0 | | | | | | | | | | | | |
| *2 pieces* | 92 | 3.0 | 73.0 | | | | | | | | | | | | |
| **hostess O's, Hostess** | 240 | | 11.0 | | 14 | | 0 | | | | 265 | | | | |
| *1 piece* | 64 | 3.0 | 33.0 | | | 0 | | | | | | | | | |
| **lil' angles, Hostess** | 90 | | 2.0 | | 2 | | 0 | | | | 95 | | | | |
| *1 piece* | 28 | 1.0 | 14.0 | | | 0 | | 0.0 | | | | | | | |
| **sno balls, Hostess** | 150 | | 4.0 | | 2 | | 0 | | | | 170 | | | | |
| *1 piece* | 43 | 1.0 | 28.0 | | | 0 | | | | | | | | | |
| **suzy Q's, banana, Hostess** | 240 | | 9.0 | | 21 | | 0 | | | | 195 | | | | |
| *1 piece* | 64 | 2.0 | 38.0 | | | 0 | | | | | | | | | |
| **suzy Q's, choc, Hostess** | 240 | | 10.0 | | 16 | | 0 | | | | 300 | | | | |
| *1 piece* | 64 | 2.0 | 37.0 | | | 0 | | | | | | | | | |
| **tiger tail, Hostess** | 210 | | 6.0 | | 25 | | 0 | | | | 240 | | | | |
| *1 piece* | 64 | 2.0 | 38.0 | | | 0 | | | | | | | | | |
| **twinkies, Hostess** | 160 | | 5.0 | | 20 | | 0 | | | | 150 | | | | |
| *1 piece* | 43 | 1.0 | 26.0 | | | 0 | | | | | | | | | |

## 8.4. COOKIES (COMMERCIAL UNLESS OTHERWISE INDICATED)

| | KCAL | H₂O (g) | FAT (g) | PUFA (g) | CHOL (mg) | A (RE) | C (mg) | B-2 (mg) | B-6 (mg) | FOL (mcg) | Na (mg) | Ca (mg) | Mg (mg) | Zn (mg) | Mn (mg) |
|---|---|---|---|---|---|---|---|---|---|---|---|---|---|---|---|
| | WT (g) | PRO (g) | CHO (g) | SFA (g) | DFIB (g) | A (IU) | B-1 (mg) | NIA (mg) | B-12 (mcg) | PANT (mg) | K (mg) | P (mg) | Fe (mg) | Cu (mg) | |
| **animal crackers** | 112 | 0.8 | 2.4 | | | | 0 | .03 | | | 79 | 14 | | | |
| *10 pieces* | 26 | 1.7 | 20.8 | 0.6 | | 30 | .01 | 0.1 | | | 25 | 30 | .10 | | |
| **animal crackers, Barnum's** | 130 | | 4.0 | | | | | | | | 120 | | | | |
| *11 cookies* | 28 | 2.0 | 21.0 | | | | | | | | 30 | | | | |
| **apple/blueberry/cherry fruit sticks, Almost Home—*1 cookie*** | 70 | | 2.0 | | | | | | | | 73 | | | | |
| | 19 | 0.0 | 14.0 | | | | | | | | 23 | | | | |
| **apple newtons** | 147 | | 2.7 | | | | | | | | 60 | | | | |
| *2 cookies* | 37 | 1.3 | 28.0 | | | | | | | | 47 | | | | |
| **applesce raisin, iced, Almost Home** | 140 | | 8.0 | | | | | | | | 70 | | | | |
| *2 cookies* | 28 | 2.0 | 17.0 | | | | | | | | 60 | | | | |
| **arrowroot biscuit, National** | 130 | | 4.0 | | | | | | | | 80 | | | | |
| *6 cookies* | 28 | 2.0 | 21.0 | | | | | | | | 25 | | | | |
| **blueberry newtons** | 147 | | 2.6 | | | | | | | | 107 | | | | |
| *2 cookies* | 38 | 1.3 | 28.0 | | | | | | | | 33 | | | | |

| | KCAL / WT (g) | H₂O (g) / PRO (g) | FAT (g) / CHO (g) | PUFA (g) / SFA (g) | CHOL (mg) / DFIB (g) | A (RE) / A (IU) | C (mg) / B-1 (mg) | B-2 (mg) / NIA (mg) | B-6 (mg) / B-12 (mcg) | FOL (mcg) / PANT (mg) | Na (mg) / K (mg) | Ca (mg) / P (mg) | Mg (mg) / Fe (mg) | Zn (mg) / Cu (mg) | Mn (mg) |
|---|---|---|---|---|---|---|---|---|---|---|---|---|---|---|---|
| **brown edge wafers, Nabisco** | 140 | | 6.0 | | | | | | | | 80 | | | | |
| *5 cookies* | 28 | 1.0 | 20.0 | | | | | | | | 30 | | | | |
| **butter cookies** | 229 | 2.3 | 8.5 | | | | 0 | .03 | | | 209 | 63 | | | |
| *10 cookies* | 50 | 3.1 | 35.5 | | | 330 | .02 | 0.2 | | | 30 | 47 | .30 | | |
| **butter flavored, Nabisco** | 130 | | 5.0 | | | | | | | | 140 | | | | |
| *6 cookies* | 28 | 2.0 | 20.0 | | | | | | | | 35 | | | | |
| **cherry newtons** | 147 | | 2.7 | | | | | | | | 107 | | | | |
| *2 cookies* | 38 | 1.3 | 26.7 | | | | | | | | 40 | | | | |
| **choc cakes, Mallomars** | 130 | | 6.0 | | | | | | | | 35 | | | | |
| *2 cookies* | 28 | 1.0 | 18.0 | | | | | | | | 55 | | | | |
| **choc chip** | 99 | 0.6 | 4.4 | | | | 0 | .01 | | | 84 | 8 | | | |
| *2 cookies* | 21 | 1.1 | 14.6 | | | 26 | .01 | 0.1 | | | 28 | 24 | .38 | | |
| Almost Home | 130 | | 5.0 | | | | | | | | 100 | | | | |
| *2 cookies* | 28 | 1.0 | 20.0 | | | | | | | | 35 | | | | |
| Chips Ahoy | 130 | | 6.0 | | | | | | | | 110 | | | | |
| *2 cookies* | 28 | 1.0 | 18.0 | | | | | | | | 25 | | | | |
| Chips Ahoy Chewy | 140 | | 7.0 | | | | | | | | 95 | | | | |
| *3 cookies* | 28 | 2.0 | 18.0 | | | | | | | | 35 | | | | |
| Chips 'n More original/coconut | 150 | | 7.5 | | | | | | | | 83 | | | | |
| *2 cookies* | 28 | 1.5 | 18.0 | | | | | | | | 40 | | | | |
| cookie mix, Duncan Hines | 144 | 0.9 | 7.3 | | 0 | | | .06 | | | 81 | 11 | 10 | .17 | |
| *1/18 pkg (2 cookies)* | 28 | 1.3 | 18.2 | | | | .04 | 0.5 | | | 50 | 21 | .50 | .084 | |
| from refrig dough | 47 | 0.5 | 2.3 | | | | 0 | .02 | .00 | 1 | 36 | 3 | 2 | .05 | |
| *1 cookie* | 10 | 0.5 | 6.6 | | | 6 | .01 | 0.2 | | .02 | 13 | 7 | .22 | .011 | |
| frzn, Am Hosp Co | 250 | | 14.0 | | 18 | | 0 | .03 | | | 194 | 20 | | | |
| *1.75 oz* | 50 | 2.0 | 30.0 | | | 329 | .04 | 0.2 | | | 61 | | .90 | | |
| homemade | 46 | 0.3 | 2.7 | | | | 0 | .02 | .00 | 1 | 21 | 3 | 4 | .04 | |
| *1 cookie* | 10 | 0.5 | 6.4 | | | 4 | .02 | 0.1 | .01 | .03 | 21 | 8 | .25 | .032 | |
| refrig dough, Continental | 110 | | 5.0 | | | | | | | | 75 | | | | |
| *2 cookies* | 25 | 1.0 | 16.0 | | | | | | | | 25 | | | | |
| refrig dough, Pillsbury | 208 | 6.5 | 9.7 | | | | 0 | .17 | | | 151 | 9 | | | |
| *3 cookies* | 47 | 1.8 | 28.4 | | | 0 | .05 | 0.6 | | | 74 | 30 | .93 | | |
| w/ pecans refrig dough | 110 | | 5.0 | | | | | | | | 95 | | | | |
| *2 cookies* | 25 | 1.0 | 15.0 | | | | | | | | 25 | | | | |
| **choc chip macaroons, frzn, Am Hosp Co** | 327 | | 16.1 | | 9 | | 4 | .01 | | | 218 | 33 | | | |
| *2.5 oz* | 71 | 4.8 | 40.6 | | | | .00 | 1.1 | | | 315 | | | | |
| **choc chip snaps, Nabisco** | 130 | | 4.0 | | | | | | | | 100 | | | | |
| *6 cookies* | 28 | 2.0 | 21.0 | | | | | | | | 30 | | | | |
| **choc choc chip, frzn, Am Hosp Co** | 240 | | 14.0 | | 18 | | 0 | .04 | | | 144 | 21 | | | |
| *1.75 oz* | 50 | 2.0 | 29.0 | | | 330 | .04 | 0.2 | | | 125 | | 1.00 | | |
| **choc coated graham crackers** | 124 | 0.5 | 6.2 | | | | 0 | .08 | | | 106 | 30 | | | |
| *2 cookies* | 26 | 1.4 | 17.6 | 1.8 | | 20 | .02 | 0.4 | | | 84 | 54 | .60 | | |
| Nabisco | 150 | | 7.0 | | | | | | | | 70 | | | | |
| *3 cookies* | 28 | 2.0 | 19.0 | | | | | | | | 80 | | | | |
| **choc middles, Nabisco** | 150 | | 8.0 | | | | | | | | 65 | | | | |
| *2 cookies* | 28 | 2.0 | 18.0 | | | | | | | | 50 | | | | |
| **choc peanut bar, Ideal** | 150 | | 8.0 | | | | | | | | 130 | | | | |
| *2 cookies* | 28 | 2.0 | 17.0 | | | | | | | | 80 | | | | |
| **choc sandwich** | 49 | 0.2 | 2.1 | | | | | .02 | .00 | 0 | 63 | 3 | 5 | .09 | |
| *1 cookie* | 10 | 0.5 | 7.1 | | | | .02 | 0.2 | .00 | | 22 | 10 | .36 | .040 | |
| Oreo | 140 | | 6.0 | | | | | | | | 170 | | | | |
| *3 cookies* | 28 | 1.0 | 20.0 | | | | | | | | 50 | | | | |
| Oreo double stuff | 140 | | 7.0 | | | | | | | | 120 | | | | |
| *2 cookies* | 28 | 1.0 | 19.0 | | | | | | | | 35 | | | | |
| Oreo mint creme | 140 | | 6.0 | | | | | | | | 160 | | | | |
| *2 cookies* | 28 | 1.0 | 20.0 | | | | | | | | 50 | | | | |

| | KCAL | H₂O (g) | FAT (g) | PUFA (g) | CHOL (mg) | A (RE) | C (mg) | B-2 (mg) | B-6 (mg) | FOL (mcg) | Na (mg) | Ca (mg) | Mg (mg) | Zn (mg) | Mn (mg) |
|---|---|---|---|---|---|---|---|---|---|---|---|---|---|---|---|
| | WT (g) | PRO (g) | CHO (g) | SFA (g) | DFIB (g) | A (IU) | B-1 (mg) | NIA (mg) | B-12 (mcg) | PANT (mg) | K (mg) | P (mg) | Fe (mg) | Cu (mg) | |
| choc snaps, Nabisco | 130 | | 4.0 | | | | | | | | 140 | | | | |
| 7 cookies | 28 | 2.0 | 21.0 | | | | | | | | 50 | | | | |
| choc/van double dip creme sandwich, I Scream—2 cookies | 150 | | 7.0 | | | | | | | | 70 | | | | |
| | 28 | 1.0 | 20.0 | | | | | | | | 37 | | | | |
| choc/van sandwich, Giggles | 140 | | 6.0 | | | | | | | | 60 | | | | |
| 2 cookies | 28 | 1.0 | 17.0 | | | | | | | | 17 | | | | |
| choc wafers, Famous | 130 | | 4.0 | | | | | | | | 200 | | | | |
| 5 cookies | 28 | 2.0 | 21.0 | | | | | | | | 75 | | | | |
| cinn raisin, Almost Home | 140 | | 7.0 | | | | | | | | 95 | | | | |
| 2 cookies | 28 | 3.0 | 16.0 | | | | | | | | 85 | | | | |
| coconut macaroon soft cakes, Nabisco | 190 | | 9.0 | | | | | | | | 65 | | | | |
| 1 cookie | 38 | 1.0 | 23.0 | | | | | | | | 95 | | | | |
| cone for ice cream | 45 | 1.1 | 0.3 | | | 0 | | .03 | | | 28 | 19 | | | |
| 1 cone | 12 | 1.2 | 9.3 | 0.1 | | 0 | .01 | 0.1 | | | 29 | 24 | .05 | | |
| Comet Cups | 20 | | 0.0 | | | | | | | | 5 | | | | |
| 1 cone | | 0.0 | 4.0 | | | | | | | | 5 | | | | |
| Comet Cups, choc flavored | 25 | | 0.0 | | | | | | | | 5 | | | | |
| 1 cone | | 0.0 | 5.0 | | | | | | | | 10 | | | | |
| Comet Cups, sugar | 40 | | 0.0 | | | | | | | | 35 | | | | |
| 1 cone | | 1.0 | 9.0 | | | | | | | | 15 | | | | |
| creme sandwich, Baronet/Cameo | 140 | | 5.5 | | | | | | | | 80 | | | | |
| 3 cookies | 28 | 1.0 | 20.0 | | | | | | | | 35 | | | | |
| devil's food cakes, Nabisco | 140 | | 1.0 | | | | | | | | 90 | | | | |
| 1 cookie | 38 | 1.0 | 30.0 | | | | | | | | 50 | | | | |
| double choc cookie mix, Duncan Hines | 135 | 2.0 | 6.2 | | 0 | | | .06 | | | 77 | 4 | 11 | .16 | |
| 1/18 pkg (2 cookies) | 27 | 1.4 | 18.4 | | | | .05 | 0.6 | | | 84 | 22 | .78 | .081 | |
| dutch apple fruit sticks, iced, Almost Home—1 cookie | 70 | | 1.0 | | | | | | | | 40 | | | | |
| | 19 | 0.0 | 14.0 | | | | | | | | 40 | | | | |
| fig bars | 53 | 1.7 | 1.0 | | | | 0 | .02 | .02 | 1 | 45 | 10 | 4 | .09 | |
| 1 bar | 14 | 0.5 | 10.6 | | 0.2 | 16 | .02 | 0.2 | .00 | .05 | 41 | 8 | .34 | .041 | |
| fig newtons | 100 | | 2.0 | | | | | | | | 100 | | | | |
| 2 cookies | 28 | 1.0 | 20.0 | | | | | | | | 60 | | | | |
| fudge, caramel & peanut bar, Heyday | 140 | | 8.0 | | | | | | | | 45 | | | | |
| 1 cookie | 28 | 2.0 | 15.0 | | | | | | | | 80 | | | | |
| fudge choc chip, Almost Home | 130 | | 5.0 | | | | | | | | 130 | | | | |
| 2 cookies | 28 | 1.0 | 20.0 | | | | | | | | 60 | | | | |
| fudge choc chip, Chips 'n More | 140 | | 6.0 | | | | | | | | 90 | | | | |
| 3 cookies | 28 | 2.0 | 19.0 | | | | | | | | 45 | | | | |
| fudge choc chip raisin, Almost Home | 130 | | 5.0 | | | | | | | | 85 | | | | |
| 2 cookies | 28 | 1.0 | 18.0 | | | | | | | | 60 | | | | |
| fudge choc sandwich, Gaiety | 150 | | 7.0 | | | | | | | | 120 | | | | |
| 3 cookies | 28 | 2.0 | 19.0 | | | | | | | | 50 | | | | |
| fudge 'n choc/van creme sandwich, Almost Home—1 cookie | 140 | | 6.0 | | | | | | | | 115 | | | | |
| | 32 | 1.5 | 20.0 | | | | | | | | 38 | | | | |
| fudge striped shortbread, Nabisco | 150 | | 7.0 | | | | | | | | 110 | | | | |
| 3 cookies | 28 | 1.0 | 19.0 | | | | | | | | 30 | | | | |
| gingersnaps | 59 | 0.4 | 1.2 | | | | 0 | .01 | | | 80 | 10 | | | |
| 2 cookies | 14 | 0.8 | 11.2 | 0.3 | | 10 | .01 | 0.1 | | | 65 | 7 | .32 | | |
| homemade | 34 | 0.2 | 1.6 | | | | 0 | .01 | .00 | 1 | 20 | 3 | 1 | .03 | |
| 1 cookie | 7 | 0.3 | 4.7 | | | 3 | .01 | 0.1 | .01 | .02 | 14 | 4 | .16 | .009 | |
| Nabisco | 120 | | 3.0 | | | | | | | | 200 | | | | |
| 4 cookies | 28 | 2.0 | 22.0 | | | | | | | | 100 | | | | |
| golden sugar cookie mix, Duncan Hines | 118 | 0.8 | 5.0 | | 0 | | | .05 | | | 66 | 4 | 1 | .02 | |
| 1/18 pkg (2 cookies) | 24 | 1.2 | 16.8 | | | | .06 | 0.6 | | | 10 | 10 | .26 | .000 | |
| graham, Bugs Bunny | 120 | | 4.0 | | | | | | | | 130 | | | | |
| 9 cookies | 28 | 2.0 | 20.0 | | | | | | | | 60 | | | | |
| imported danish, Nabisco | 150 | | 8.0 | | | | | | | | 70 | | | | |
| 5 cookies | 28 | 1.0 | 18.0 | | | | | | | | 25 | | | | |

| | KCAL / WT (g) | H₂O (g) / PRO (g) | FAT (g) / CHO (g) | PUFA (g) / SFA (g) | CHOL (mg) / DFIB (g) | A (RE) / A (IU) | C (mg) / B-1 (mg) | B-2 (mg) / NIA (mg) | B-6 (mg) / B-12 (mcg) | FOL (mcg) / PANT (mg) | Na (mg) / K (mg) | Ca (mg) / P (mg) | Mg (mg) / Fe (mg) | Zn (mg) / Cu (mg) | Mn (mg) |
|---|---|---|---|---|---|---|---|---|---|---|---|---|---|---|---|
| **ladyfingers** | 79 | 4.2 | 1.7 | | | | 0 | .03 | | | 15 | 9 | | | |
| *2 ladyfingers* | 22 | 1.7 | 14.2 | 0.5 | | 145 | .01 | 0.0 | | | 15 | 36 | .35 | | |
| **macaroons** | 181 | 1.7 | 8.8 | | | | 0 | .06 | | | 13 | 10 | | | |
| *2 cookies* | 38 | 2.0 | 25.1 | | | 0 | .02 | 0.2 | | | 176 | 32 | .30 | | |
| **macaroons, frzn, Am Hosp Co** | 390 | | 22.0 | | 15 | | 0 | .08 | | | 225 | 63 | | | |
| *3 oz* | 85 | 4.0 | 48.0 | | | 55 | .03 | 0.2 | | | 235 | | 1.20 | | |
| **marshmallow**[a] | 147 | 3.5 | 4.7 | | | | 0 | .02 | | | 75 | 8 | | | |
| *2 cookies* | 36 | 1.4 | 26.0 | | | 95 | .00 | 0.0 | | | 33 | 20 | .20 | | |
| **marshmallow puffs, Nabisco** | 120 | | 4.0 | | | | | | | | 55 | | | | |
| *1 cookie* | 28 | 1.0 | 20.0 | | | | | | | | 50 | | | | |
| **marshmallow sandwich, Nabisco** | 120 | | 3.0 | | | | | | | | 80 | | | | |
| *4 cookies* | 28 | 1.0 | 22.0 | | | | | | | | 20 | | | | |
| **marshmallow twirls cakes, Nabisco** | 130 | | 5.0 | | | | | | | | 55 | | | | |
| *1 cookie* | 28 | 1.0 | 19.0 | | | | | | | | 55 | | | | |
| **molasses** | 137 | 1.3 | 3.4 | | | | 0 | .02 | | | 125 | 17 | | | |
| *1 cookie* | 33 | 2.0 | 24.7 | 0.9 | | 30 | .01 | 0.2 | | | 45 | 27 | .70 | | |
| **molasses, Pantry** | 130 | | 4.0 | | | | | | | | 130 | | | | |
| *2 cookies* | 28 | 2.0 | 21.0 | | | | | | | | 120 | | | | |
| **mystic mint sandwich** | 150 | | 8.0 | | | | | | | | 95 | | | | |
| *2 cookies* | 28 | 1.0 | 19.0 | | | | | | | | 70 | | | | |
| **nilla wafers, Nabisco** | 130 | | 4.0 | | | | | | | | 95 | | | | |
| *7 cookies* | 28 | 1.0 | 21.0 | | | | | | | | 30 | | | | |
| **nutter butter peanut butter sandwich,** | 140 | | 6.0 | | | | | | | | 100 | | | | |
| Nabisco—*2 cookies* | 28 | 3.0 | 18.0 | | | | | | | | 55 | | | | |
| **nutter butter peanut creme patties,** | 150 | | 8.0 | | | | | | | | 95 | | | | |
| Nabisco—*4 cookies* | 28 | 3.0 | 17.0 | | | | | | | | 70 | | | | |
| **oatmeal, Bakers Bonus** | 130 | | 5.0 | | | | | | | | 90 | | | | |
| *2 cookies* | 28 | 2.0 | 20.0 | | | | | | | | 35 | | | | |
| **oatmeal creme sandwich, Almost Home** | 140 | | 5.0 | | | | | | | | 150 | | | | |
| *1 cookie* | 32 | 2.0 | 21.0 | | | | | | | | 60 | | | | |
| **oatmeal, homemade** | 62 | 0.4 | 2.6 | | | | 0 | .02 | .01 | 2 | 45 | 11 | 5 | .13 | |
| *1 cookie* | 13 | 0.8 | 8.9 | | | 5 | .03 | 0.2 | .01 | .07 | 31 | 18 | .41 | .014 | |
| **oatmeal raisin** | 235 | 1.5 | 8.0 | | | | 0 | .04 | | | 84 | 11 | | | |
| *4 cookies* | 52 | 3.2 | 38.2 | 2.1 | | 30 | .06 | 0.3 | | | 192 | 53 | 1.50 | | |
| cookie mix, Duncan Hines | 134 | 1.3 | 6.2 | | 0 | | | .04 | | | 63 | 20 | 13 | .22 | |
| *1/18 pkg (2 cookies)* | 28 | 1.9 | 18.2 | | | | .07 | 0.4 | | | 70 | 42 | .50 | .056 | |
| from refrig dough | 61 | 0.6 | 2.6 | | | | 0 | .02 | .01 | 2 | 37 | 4 | 4 | .08 | |
| *1 cookie* | 13 | 0.7 | 8.9 | | | 10 | .02 | 0.2 | | .06 | 23 | 14 | .28 | .014 | |
| frzn, Am Hosp Co | 191 | | 7.8 | | 13 | | 1 | .00 | | | 160 | 22 | | | |
| *1.6 oz* | 45 | 3.0 | 26.4 | | | 222 | .02 | 0.4 | | | 80 | | 1.20 | | |
| iced/uniced, Almost Home | 130 | | 5.0 | | | | | | | | 90 | | | | |
| *2 cookies* | 28 | 2.0 | 19.5 | | | | | | | | 55 | | | | |
| refrig dough, Pillsbury | 200 | 7.7 | 8.4 | | | | 0 | .18 | | | 198 | 11 | | | |
| *3 cookies* | 48 | 3.1 | 28.1 | | | 0 | .11 | 1.6 | | | 80 | 52 | 1.01 | | |
| **party grahams, Nabisco** | 140 | | 7.0 | | | | | | | | 100 | | | | |
| *3 cookies* | 28 | 1.0 | 19.0 | | | | | | | | 50 | | | | |
| **peanut butter** | | | | | | | | | | | | | | | |
| Almost Home | 140 | | 7.0 | | | | | | | | 95 | | | | |
| *2 cookies* | 28 | 3.0 | 16.0 | | | | | | | | 85 | | | | |
| cookie mix, Duncan Hines | 135 | 0.8 | 7.3 | | 0 | | | .04 | | | 111 | 9 | 11 | .16 | |
| *1/18 pkg (2 cookies)* | 26 | 2.5 | 15.1 | | | | .03 | 1.1 | | | 60 | 25 | .31 | .052 | |
| from refrig dough | 50 | 0.5 | 2.6 | | | | 0 | .02 | .00 | 2 | 57 | 12 | 4 | .08 | |
| *1 cookie* | 10 | 0.8 | 5.9 | | | 15 | .02 | 0.4 | | .01 | 19 | 24 | .19 | .016 | |
| refrig dough, Continental | 110 | | 5.0 | | | | | | | | 135 | | | | |
| *2 cookies* | 25 | 2.0 | 15.0 | | | | | | | | 40 | | | | |
| refrig dough, Pillsbury | 199 | 7.2 | 8.5 | | | | 0 | .17 | | | 193 | 11 | | | |
| *3 cookies* | 47 | 3.1 | 27.4 | | | 0 | .12 | 1.5 | | | 71 | 53 | 1.08 | | |
| **peanut butter choc chip, frzn, Am Hosp** | 231 | | 13.0 | | 35 | | 0 | .03 | | | 58 | | | | |
| Co—*1.75 oz* | 50 | 4.4 | 25.7 | | | 64 | .07 | 1.1 | | | 104 | | | | |

[a] Choc coated cookie w/ marshmallow.

| | KCAL / WT (g) | H₂O (g) / PRO (g) | FAT (g) / CHO (g) | PUFA (g) / SFA (g) | CHOL (mg) / DFIB (g) | A (RE) / A (IU) | C (mg) / B-1 (mg) | B-2 (mg) / NIA (mg) | B-6 (mg) / B-12 (mcg) | FOL (mcg) / PANT (mg) | Na (mg) / K (mg) | Ca (mg) / P (mg) | Mg (mg) / Fe (mg) | Zn (mg) / Cu (mg) | Mn (mg) |
|---|---|---|---|---|---|---|---|---|---|---|---|---|---|---|---|
| **peanut butter creme sandwich, Almost Home**—*1 cookie* | 140 | 6.0 | | | | | | | | | 120 | | | | |
| | 32 | 2.0 | 20.0 | | | | | | | | 60 | | | | |
| **peanut butter fudge, Almost Home** | 140 | 7.0 | | | | | | | | | 90 | | | | |
| *2 cookies* | 28 | 3.0 | 16.0 | | | | | | | | 85 | | | | |
| **pecan shortbread, Nabisco** | 150 | 9.0 | | | | | | | | | 80 | | | | |
| *2 cookies* | 28 | 2.0 | 16.0 | | | | | | | | 20 | | | | |
| **pinwheels, choc & marshmallow cakes** | 130 | 5.0 | | | | | | | | | 35 | | | | |
| *1 cookie* | 28 | 1.0 | 20.0 | | | | | | | | 40 | | | | |
| **raisin nut, frzn, Am Hosp Co** | 270 | 11.0 | | 20 | | | 0 | .04 | | | 213 | 19 | | | |
| *2 oz* | 58 | 4.0 | 41.0 | | | 354 | .04 | 0.3 | | | 145 | | 1.10 | | |
| **sandwich type** | | | | | | | | | | | | | | | |
| choc/van | 198 | 0.9 | 9.0 | | | | 0 | .02 | | | 193 | 10 | | | |
| *4 cookies* | 40 | 1.9 | 27.7 | 2.4 | | 0 | .02 | 0.2 | | | 15 | 96 | .30 | | |
| w/ peanut butter filling | 116 | 0.6 | 4.7 | | | | 0 | .02 | | | 42 | 10 | | | |
| *2 cookies* | 25 | 2.4 | 16.4 | | | 50 | .01 | 0.7 | | | 43 | 28 | .20 | | |
| shortbread | 75 | 0.5 | 3.5 | | | | 0 | .01 | | | 9 | 11 | | | |
| *2 cookies* | 15 | 1.1 | 9.8 | 0.9 | | 6 | .01 | 0.1 | | | 10 | 23 | .08 | | |
| homemade | 42 | 0.2 | 2.3 | | | | 0 | .02 | .00 | 1 | 36 | 2 | 1 | .04 | |
| *1 cookie* | 8 | 0.5 | 4.9 | | | 85 | .02 | 0.2 | .00 | .02 | 5 | 9 | .15 | .005 | |
| Lorna Doone | 140 | 7.0 | | | | | | | | | 135 | | | | |
| *4 cookies* | 28 | 2.0 | 18.0 | | | | | | | | 30 | | | | |
| **social tea biscuits, Nabisco** | 130 | 4.0 | | | | | | | | | 105 | | | | |
| *6 cookies* | 28 | 2.0 | 21.0 | | | | | | | | 30 | | | | |
| **sugar** | | | | | | | | | | | | | | | |
| from refrig dough | 35 | 0.3 | 1.7 | | | | 0 | .01 | .00 | 1 | 38 | 7 | 1 | .02 | |
| *1 cookie* | 7 | 0.3 | 4.6 | | | 5 | .01 | 0.2 | | .02 | 5 | 13 | .14 | .003 | |
| homemade | 71 | 1.3 | 2.7 | | | | 0 | .02 | | | 51 | 12 | | | |
| *2 cookies* | 16 | 1.0 | 10.9 | 0.7 | | 18 | .02 | 0.2 | | | 12 | 16 | .22 | | |
| refrig dough, Continental | 110 | 6.0 | | | | | | | | | 85 | | | | |
| *2 cookies* | 25 | 1.0 | 15.0 | | | | | | | | 15 | | | | |
| refrig dough, Pillsbury | 201 | 7.4 | 8.1 | | | | 0 | .18 | | | 192 | 4 | | | |
| *3 cookies* | 48 | 1.8 | 30.2 | | | 0 | .12 | 1.1 | | | 72 | 21 | .98 | | |
| **sugar rings, Bakers Bonus** | 130 | 5.0 | | | | | | | | | 100 | | | | |
| *2 cookies* | 28 | 2.0 | 20.0 | | | | | | | | 25 | | | | |
| **sugar wafers** | 92 | 0.3 | 3.7 | | | | 0 | .01 | | | 36 | 7 | | | |
| *2 cookies* | 19 | 0.9 | 13.9 | 0.9 | | 26 | .00 | 0.0 | | | 11 | 15 | .06 | | |
| Biscos | 150 | 7.0 | | | | | | | | | 35 | | | | |
| *8 cookies* | 28 | 1.0 | 20.0 | | | | | | | | 15 | | | | |
| w/ peanut butter filling | 66 | 0.3 | 2.7 | | | | 0 | .01 | | | 24 | 6 | | | |
| *2 cookies* | 14 | 1.4 | 9.4 | | | 28 | .01 | 0.4 | | | 25 | 16 | .12 | | |
| **super heroes, Nabisco** | 135 | 5.0 | | | | | | | | | 120 | | | | |
| *11 cookies* | 28 | 2.0 | 20.0 | | | | | | | | 50 | | | | |
| **van flavored creme sandwiches, Cookie Break**—*3 cookies* | 140 | 6.0 | | | | | | | | | 95 | | | | |
| | 28 | 1.0 | 20.0 | | | | | | | | 20 | | | | |
| **van wafers** | 92 | 0.6 | 3.2 | | | | 0 | .01 | | | 50 | 8 | | | |
| *5 cookies* | 20 | 1.1 | 14.9 | | | 25 | .00 | 0.0 | | | 15 | 12 | .10 | | |
| **waffle cremes, Biscos** | 150 | 7.0 | | | | | | | | | 30 | | | | |
| *3 cookies* | 28 | 1.0 | 20.0 | | | | | | | | 5 | | | | |

| | KCAL | H₂O (g) | FAT (g) | PUFA (g) | CHOL (mg) | A (RE) | C (mg) | B-2 (mg) | B-6 (mg) | FOL (mcg) | Na (mg) | Ca (mg) | Mg (mg) | Zn (mg) | Mn (mg) |
|---|---|---|---|---|---|---|---|---|---|---|---|---|---|---|---|
| | WT (g) | PRO (g) | CHO (g) | SFA (g) | DFIB (g) | A (IU) | B-1 (mg) | NIA (mg) | B-12 (mcg) | PANT (mg) | K (mg) | P (mg) | Fe (mg) | Cu (mg) | |

## 8.5. CUSTARDS

| | KCAL | H₂O | FAT | PUFA | CHOL | A(RE) | C | B-2 | B-6 | FOL | Na | Ca | Mg | Zn | Mn |
|---|---|---|---|---|---|---|---|---|---|---|---|---|---|---|---|
| **baked, homemade** | 305 | 204.6 | 14.6 | | | | 1 | .50 | | | 209 | 297 | | | |
| *1 cup* | 265 | 14.3 | 29.4 | 6.8 | | 9.30 | .11 | 0.3 | | | 387 | 310 | 1.10 | | |

## 8.6. DOUGHNUTS

| | KCAL | H₂O | FAT | PUFA | CHOL | A(RE) | C | B-2 | B-6 | FOL | Na | Ca | Mg | Zn | Mn |
|---|---|---|---|---|---|---|---|---|---|---|---|---|---|---|---|
| **cake** | 105 | 5.3 | 5.8 | | | | 0 | .05 | .01 | 2 | 139 | 11 | 6 | .13 | |
| *1 doughnut* | 25 | 1.3 | 12.2 | | | 14 | .06 | 0.4 | | .10 | 27 | 55 | .37 | .033 | |
| **cake, Hostess** | 110 | | 7.0 | | 7 | | 0 | | | | 135 | | | | |
| *1 doughnut* | 28 | 1.0 | 12.0 | | | 0 | | | | | | | | | |
| **choc coated donette, Hostess** | 60 | | 3.0 | | 4 | | 0 | | | | 50 | 0 | | | |
| *1 piece* | 13 | 1.0 | 6.0 | | | 0 | | 0.0 | | | | | .00 | | |
| **choc coated, Hostess** | 130 | | 8.0 | | 4 | | 0 | | | | 150 | | | | |
| *1 doughnut* | 28 | 1.0 | 14.0 | | | 0 | | | | | | | | | |
| **cinn, Hostess** | 110 | | 6.0 | | 6 | | 0 | | | | 140 | | | | |
| *1 doughnut* | 28 | 1.0 | 15.0 | | | 0 | | | | | | | | | |
| **cinn apple, Earth Grains** | 310 | | 17.0 | | 25 | | | | | | 270 | | | | |
| *1 doughnut* | 71 | 3.0 | 35.0 | | | | | | | | 75 | | | | |
| **devil's food, Earth Grains** | 330 | | 21.0 | | 20 | | | | | | 320 | | | | |
| *1 doughnut* | 74 | 3.0 | 33.0 | | | | | | | | 125 | | | | |
| **glazed old fashioned, Earth Grains** | 310 | | 18.0 | | 20 | | | | | | 270 | | | | |
| *1 doughnut* | 71 | 3.0 | 34.0 | | | | | | | | 65 | | | | |
| **glazed old fashioned, Hostess** | 230 | | 12.0 | | 11 | | 0 | | | | 200 | | | | |
| *1 doughnut* | 57 | 2.0 | 30.0 | | | 0 | | | | | | | | | |
| **krunch, Hostess** | 110 | | 4.0 | | 4 | | 0 | | | | 130 | | | | |
| *1 doughnut* | 28 | 1.0 | 16.0 | | | 0 | | | | | | | | | |
| **old fashioned, Hostess** | 180 | | 10.0 | | 9 | | 0 | | | | 220 | | | | |
| *1 doughnut* | 43 | 2.0 | 22.0 | | | 0 | | | | | | | | | |
| **powdered sugar, Hostess** | 110 | | 5.0 | | 6 | | 0 | | | | 140 | | | | |
| *1 doughnut* | 28 | 1.0 | 15.0 | | | 0 | | | | | | | | | |
| **powdered sugar donette, Hostess** | 40 | | 2.0 | | 2 | | 0 | .00 | | | 40 | 0 | | | |
| *1 piece* | 9 | 0.0 | 5.0 | | | 0 | | 0.0 | | | | | .00 | | |
| **powdered sugar old fashioned, Earth Grains**—*1 doughnut* | 290 | | 19.0 | | 20 | | | | | | 260 | | | | |
| | 61 | 3.0 | 27.0 | | | | | | | | 60 | | | | |
| **sugar gem, Rainbo Snacks** | 310 | | 16.0 | | | | | | | | | | | | |
| *6 doughnuts* | 71 | 3.0 | 38.0 | | | | | | | | | | | | |
| **yeast** | 176 | 11.9 | 11.3 | | | | 0 | .07 | | | 99 | 16 | | | |
| *1 doughnut* | 42 | 2.7 | 16.0 | 2.8 | | 30 | .07 | 0.6 | | | 34 | 32 | .60 | | |

## 8.7. FROZEN DESSERTS

| | KCAL | H₂O | FAT | PUFA | CHOL | A(RE) | C | B-2 | B-6 | FOL | Na | Ca | Mg | Zn | Mn |
|---|---|---|---|---|---|---|---|---|---|---|---|---|---|---|---|
| **bon bon ice cream nuggets, Carnation** | | | | | | | | | | | | | | | |
| bavarian mint | 163 | | 12.1 | | | | 0 | .06 | .01 | 2 | 28 | 39 | 6 | .18 | .019 |
| *5 nuggets* | 48 | 1.3 | 13.0 | | | 137 | .01 | 0.0 | .11 | .11 | 58 | 36 | .17 | .051 | |
| choc | 179 | | 12.9 | | | | 0 | .08 | .02 | 2 | 50 | 44 | 7 | .19 | .019 |
| *5 nuggets* | 49 | 1.6 | 15.4 | | | 160 | .02 | 0.1 | .12 | .14 | 78 | 49 | .31 | .050 | |
| choc peanut butter | 192 | | 14.7 | | | | 0 | .09 | .02 | 2 | 53 | 55 | 7 | .22 | .011 |
| *5 nuggets* | 49 | 2.4 | 13.8 | | | 142 | .03 | 0.5 | .16 | .15 | 101 | 62 | .27 | .044 | |
| van | 167 | | 12.1 | | | | 0 | .06 | .01 | 1 | 28 | 39 | 6 | .18 | .019 |
| *5 nuggets* | 48 | 1.3 | 13.0 | | | 137 | .01 | 0.0 | .11 | .11 | 58 | 36 | .17 | .051 | |
| **dreamy tofu, Giant Foods**[a] | 135 | | 4.8 | | 0 | | | | | | 46 | | | | |
| *1/2 cup* | | 1.8 | 21.5 | | | | | | | | | | | | |
| **frozen dessert, Weight Watchers** | | | | | | | | | | | | | | | |
| choc mint treat | 60 | | 1.0 | | | | 1 | .11 | | | 50 | 90 | | | |
| *1.75 fl oz* | | 3.0 | 12.0 | | | 12 | .04 | 0.2 | | | 125 | 72 | .10 | | |
| choc treat | 100 | | 1.0 | | | | 1 | .17 | | | 75 | 135 | | | |
| *2.75 fl oz* | | 4.0 | 18.0 | | | 17 | .06 | 0.4 | | | 190 | 112 | .20 | | |

[a] Values are averages for 4 flavors, choc, mint choc swirl, peanut butter swirl & wildberry swirl.

| | KCAL | H₂O (g) | FAT (g) | PUFA (g) | CHOL (mg) | A (RE) | C (mg) | B-2 (mg) | B-6 (mg) | FOL (mcg) | Na (mg) | Ca (mg) | Mg (mg) | Zn (mg) | Mn (mg) |
|---|---|---|---|---|---|---|---|---|---|---|---|---|---|---|---|
| | WT (g) | PRO (g) | CHO (g) | SFA (g) | DFIB (g) | A (IU) | B-1 (mg) | NIA (mg) | B-12 (mcg) | PANT (mg) | K (mg) | P (mg) | Fe (mg) | Cu (mg) | |
| cookies 'n cream | 120 | | 1.0 | | | | 2 | .18 | | | 105 | 151 | | | |
| *4.6 fl oz* | | 4.0 | 22.0 | | | 19 | .03 | 0.3 | | | | 98 | .40 | | |
| double fudge | 60 | | 1.0 | | | | 0 | .10 | | | 45 | 82 | | | |
| *1.75 fl oz* | | 3.0 | 12.0 | | | 10 | .05 | 0.2 | | | 140 | 69 | .10 | | |
| dutch choc | 100 | | 1.0 | | | | 1 | .16 | | | 75 | 135 | | | |
| *4.4 fl oz* | | 4.0 | 18.0 | | | 17 | .07 | 0.4 | | | | 111 | .20 | | |
| golden van | 100 | | 1.0 | | | | 1 | .17 | | | 75 | 142 | | | |
| *4.6 fl oz* | | 4.0 | 18.0 | | | 21 | .05 | 0.1 | | | | 109 | .10 | | |
| neapolitan | 100 | | 1.0 | | | | 2 | .17 | | | 75 | 140 | | | |
| *4.6 fl oz* | | 4.0 | 18.0 | | | 20 | .06 | 0.2 | | | | 110 | .10 | | |
| orange-van treat | 60 | | 1.0 | | | | 1 | .11 | | | 50 | 92 | | | |
| *1.75 fl oz* | | 3.0 | 12.0 | | | 14 | .03 | 0.1 | | | 130 | 71 | .00 | | |
| van sandwich bar | 130 | | 2.0 | | | | 0 | .14 | | | 170 | 98 | | | |
| *2.75 fl oz* | | 3.0 | 26.0 | | | 10 | .10 | 0.7 | | | | 54 | .60 | | |
| **frozen yogurt, Honey Hill Farms**[a] | 118 | | 3.5 | | | | | | | | | | | | |
| *4.5 fl oz* | 100 | 3.5 | 18.7 | | | | | | | | | | | | |
| | | | | | | | | | | | | | | | |
| **fruit & cream bar, Dole** | | | | | | | | | | | | | | | |
| blueberry | 90 | 44.9 | 1.4 | | 5 | | 2 | .06 | | | 20 | 31 | | | |
| *1 bar* | 68 | 1.1 | 19.4 | | | 21 | .01 | 0.1 | | | 57 | | .17 | | |
| peach | 90 | 45.0 | 1.4 | | 5 | | 16 | .07 | | | 19 | 27 | | | |
| *1 bar* | 68 | 1.0 | 19.4 | | | 226 | .01 | 0.2 | | | 67 | | .07 | | |
| strawberry | 90 | 45.0 | 1.4 | | 5 | | 6 | .06 | | | 22 | 32 | | | |
| *1 bar* | 68 | 1.1 | 19.3 | | | 11 | .01 | 0.1 | | | 73 | | .17 | | |
| | | | | | | | | | | | | | | | |
| **fruit ice** | | | | | | | | | | | | | | | |
| boysenberry, Haagen-Dazs | 90 | | 0.0 | | | | | | | | 20 | | | | |
| *1/2 cup* | | 0.0 | 22.0 | | | | | | | | | | | | |
| cassis, Haagen-Dazs | 130 | | 0.0 | | | | | | | | 10 | | | | |
| *1/2 cup* | | 0.0 | 32.0 | | | | | | | | | | | | |
| lemon, Haagen-Dazs | 140 | | 0.0 | | | | | | | | 20 | | | | |
| *1/2 cup* | | 0.0 | 34.0 | | | | | | | | | | | | |
| lime | 247 | 129.1 | 0.0 | | | | 2 | .00 | | | 0 | 0 | | | |
| *1 cup* | 193 | 0.8 | 62.9 | | | 0 | .00 | 0.0 | | | 6 | 0 | .00 | | |
| orange, Haagen-Dazs | 140 | | 0.0 | | | | | | | | 20 | | | | |
| *1/2 cup* | | 0.0 | 34.0 | | | | | | | | | | | | |
| raspberry, Haagen-Dazs | 100 | | 0.0 | | | | | | | | 20 | | | | |
| *1/2 cup* | | 1.0 | 24.0 | | | | | | | | | | | | |
| | | | | | | | | | | | | | | | |
| **fruit juice bar** | | | | | | | | | | | | | | | |
| all flavors, Jell-O[b] | 42 | 40.7 | 0.0 | 0.0 | 0 | | 5 | .01 | .01 | 3 | 4 | 3 | 2 | .03 | |
| *1 bar* | 52 | 0.6 | 10.1 | 0.0 | | 15 | .00 | 0.1 | .00 | .02 | 35 | 3 | .10 | .012 | |
| banana, Dole | 80 | 53.9 | 0.0 | | | | 0 | .02 | | | 13 | 2 | 3 | | |
| *1 bar* | 75 | 0.4 | 19.7 | | | 61 | .00 | 0.2 | | | 119 | 9 | .11 | | |
| dark sweet cherry, Dole | 70 | 59.0 | 0.0 | | | | 4 | | | | 13 | 0 | | | |
| *1 bar* | 75 | 0.0 | 17.0 | | | 0 | | | | | 55 | | | | |
| gelatin pops, all flavors, Jell-O[c] | 31 | 36.1 | 0.0 | 0.0 | 0 | | 0 | .00 | .00 | 0 | 20 | 0 | 0 | .00 | |
| *1 pop* | 44 | 0.5 | 6.9 | 0.0 | | 0 | .00 | 0.0 | .00 | .00 | 1 | 0 | .00 | .000 | |
| grape/raspberry/strawberry, Weight Watchers—*1.7 oz bar* | 35 | | 0.0 | | | | [d] | .02 | | | 10 | 10 | | | |
| | | 0.0 | 9.0 | | | 2 | .00 | 0.0 | | | | | .10 | | |
| mandarin orange, Dole | 70 | 55.4 | 0.1 | | | | 20 | .02 | | | 14 | 2 | 2 | | |
| *1 bar* | 75 | 0.4 | 18.2 | | | 113 | .05 | 0.1 | | | 87 | 10 | .11 | | |
| orange, Dole | 70 | 53.5 | 0.0 | | | | 18 | .02 | | | 6 | 6 | 6 | | |
| *1 bar* | 75 | 0.3 | 16.2 | | | 190 | .01 | 0.1 | | | 70 | 9 | .33 | | |
| pina colada, Dole | 90 | 60.0 | 3.0 | | | | 4 | | | | 2 | 0 | | | |
| *1 bar* | 79 | 0.0 | 16.0 | | | 0 | .06 | | | | 48 | | .04 | | |
| pineapple, Dole | 70 | 52.4 | 0.0 | | | | 5 | .02 | | | 4 | 9 | 8 | | |
| *1 bar* | 75 | 0.3 | 17.1 | | | 17 | .00 | 0.1 | | | 51 | 5 | .28 | | |
| raspberry, Dole | 70 | 57.7 | 0.0 | | | | 2 | .02 | | | 14 | 1 | 1 | | |
| *1 bar* | 75 | 0.2 | 16.1 | | | 11 | .01 | 0.1 | | | 20 | 3 | .28 | | |
| strawberry, Dole | 70 | 53.3 | 0.0 | | | | 3 | .02 | | | 6 | 6 | 4 | | |
| *1 bar* | 75 | 0.2 | 16.3 | | | 6 | .00 | 0.1 | | | 64 | 8 | .20 | | |

[a] Values are averages for 26 flavors.
[b] Values are averages for 8 flavors.
[c] Values are averages for 12 flavors.
[d] 6 mg for grape, 7 mg for raspberry, and 27 mg for strawberry.

| | KCAL / WT (g) | H₂O (g) / PRO (g) | FAT (g) / CHO (g) | PUFA (g) / SFA (g) | CHOL (mg) / DFIB (g) | A (RE) / A (IU) | C (mg) / B-1 (mg) | B-2 (mg) / NIA (mg) | B-6 (mg) / B-12 (mcg) | FOL (mcg) / PANT (mg) | Na (mg) / K (mg) | Ca (mg) / P (mg) | Mg (mg) / Fe (mg) | Zn (mg) / Cu (mg) | Mn (mg) |
|---|---|---|---|---|---|---|---|---|---|---|---|---|---|---|---|
| **ice bean frzn dessert**[a] | 137 | | 7.8 | | 0 | | | | | | 68 | | | | |
| *4 fl oz* | | 2.6 | 15.0 | | | | | | | | | | | | |
| **ice cream** | | | | | | | | | | | | | | | |
| butter pecan, Haagen-Dazs | 310 | | 24.0 | | | | | | | | 100 | | | | |
| *1/2 cup* | | 5.0 | 19.0 | | | | | | | | | | | | |
| carob, Haagen-Dazs | 260 | | 17.0 | | | | | | | | 100 | | | | |
| *1/2 cup* | | 6.0 | 20.0 | | | | | | | | | | | | |
| cherry van, Haagen-Dazs | 260 | | 17.0 | | | | | | | | 45 | | | | |
| *1/2 cup* | | 4.0 | 22.0 | | | | | | | | | | | | |
| choc, Haagen-Dazs | 280 | | 17.0 | | | | | | | | 120 | | | | |
| *1/2 cup* | | 6.0 | 25.0 | | | | | | | | | | | | |
| choc chip, Haagen-Dazs | 310 | | 18.0 | | | | | | | | 180 | | | | |
| *1/2 cup* | | 7.0 | 25.0 | | | | | | | | | | | | |
| choc swiss almond, Haagen-Dazs | 250 | | 17.0 | | | | | | | | 70 | | | | |
| *1/2 cup* | | 3.0 | 21.0 | | | | | | | | | | | | |
| coffee, Haagen-Dazs | 270 | | 17.0 | | | | | | | | 90 | | | | |
| *1/2 cup* | | 6.0 | 24.0 | | | | | | | | | | | | |
| cookies 'n cream, Haagen-Dazs | 270 | | 17.0 | | | | | | | | 90 | | | | |
| *1/2 cup* | | 5.0 | 24.0 | | | | | | | | | | | | |
| elberta peach, Haagen-Dazs | 250 | | 16.0 | | | | | | | | 100 | | | | |
| *1/2 cup* | | 4.0 | 27.0 | | | | | | | | | | | | |
| french van, soft serve | 377 | 103.4 | 22.5 | 1.0 | 153 | 199 | 1 | .45 | .10 | 9 | 153 | 236 | 25 | 1.99 | |
| *1 cup* | 173 | 7.0 | 38.3 | 13.5 | 0.0 | 794 | .08 | 0.2 | 1.00 | 1.07 | 338 | 199 | .43 | | |
| honey van, Haagen-Dazs | 270 | | 17.0 | | | | | | | | 100 | | | | |
| *1/2 cup* | | 5.0 | 24.0 | | | | | | | | | | | | |
| macadamia nut, Haagen-Dazs | 260 | | 19.0 | | | | | | | | 40 | | | | |
| *1/2 cup* | | 4.0 | 20.0 | | | | | | | | | | | | |
| maple walnut, Haagen-Dazs | 290 | | 19.0 | | | | | | | | 70 | | | | |
| *1/2 cup* | | 6.0 | 23.0 | | | | | | | | | | | | |
| mocha chip, Haagen-Dazs | 270 | | 18.0 | | | | | | | | 70 | | | | |
| *1/2 cup* | | 5.0 | 22.0 | | | | | | | | | | | | |
| oreo cookies 'n cream, choc/mint/van | 140 | | 8.0 | | | | | | | | 100 | | | | |
| *3 fl oz* | | 2.0 | 16.0 | | | | | | | | 110 | | | | |
| pralines 'n cream, Haagen-Dazs | 260 | | 16.0 | | | | | | | | 110 | | | | |
| *1/2 cup* | | 4.0 | 26.0 | | | | | | | | | | | | |
| rum raisin, Haagen-Dazs | 260 | | 16.0 | | | | | | | | 220 | | | | |
| *1/2 cup* | | 4.0 | 25.0 | | | | | | | | | | | | |
| strawberry, Haagen-Dazs | 270 | | 16.0 | | | | | | | | 80 | | | | |
| *1/2 cup* | | 5.0 | 25.0 | | | | | | | | | | | | |
| van, Haagen-Dazs | 270 | | 17.0 | | | | | | | | 60 | | | | |
| *1/2 cup* | | 5.0 | 24.0 | | | | | | | | | | | | |
| van, reg (10% fat) | 269 | 80.9 | 14.3 | 0.5 | 59 | 133 | 1 | .33 | .06 | 3 | 116 | 176 | 18 | 1.41 | |
| *1 cup* | 133 | 4.8 | 31.7 | 8.9 | 0.0 | 543 | .05 | 0.1 | .63 | .65 | 257 | 134 | .12 | | |
| van, rich (16% fat) | 349 | 87.1 | 23.7 | 0.9 | 88 | 219 | 1 | .28 | .05 | 2 | 108 | 151 | 16 | 1.21 | |
| *1 cup* | 148 | 4.1 | 32.0 | 14.7 | 0.0 | 897 | .04 | .12 | .54 | .56 | 221 | 115 | .10 | | |
| van chip, Haagen-Dazs | 280 | | 17.0 | | | | | | | | 50 | | | | |
| *1/2 cup* | | 5.0 | 25.0 | | | | | | | | | | | | |
| van swiss almond, Haagen-Dazs | 340 | | 24.0 | | | | | | | | 80 | | | | |
| *1/2 cup* | | 7.0 | 28.0 | | | | | | | | | | | | |
| **ice cream bar** | | | | | | | | | | | | | | | |
| choc coated w/ dark choc, Haagen-Dazs—1 bar | 360 | | 25.0 | | | | | | | | 50 | | | | |
| | | 5.0 | 35.0 | | | | | | | | 270 | | | | |
| cookies 'n cream on a stick | 220 | | 15.0 | | | | | | | | 100 | | | | |
| *1 bar* | | 3.0 | 19.0 | | | | | | | | 120 | | | | |
| oreo cookies 'n cream sandwich | 240 | | 11.0 | | | | | | | | 300 | | | | |
| *1 sandwich* | | 4.0 | 31.0 | | | | | | | | 175 | | | | |
| van coated w/ dark choc, Haagen-Dazs | 330 | | 23.0 | | | | | | | | 60 | | | | |
| *1 bar* | | 4.0 | 28.0 | | | | | | | | 200 | | | | |
| van coated w/ milk choc, Haagen-Dazs | 330 | | 23.0 | | | | | | | | 60 | | | | |
| *1 bar* | | 4.0 | 28.0 | | | | | | | | 200 | | | | |

[a] Avg of 12 flavors, almond espresso, carob, choc, honey van, mocha, peanut butter carob chip, strawberry, toasted almond fudge, tofu almond fudge, tofu strawberry, tofu van & wildberry.

| | KCAL | H₂O (g) | FAT (g) | PUFA (g) | CHOL (mg) | A (RE) | C (mg) | B-2 (mg) | B-6 (mg) | FOL (mcg) | Na (mg) | Ca (mg) | Mg (mg) | Zn (mg) | Mn (mg) |
|---|---|---|---|---|---|---|---|---|---|---|---|---|---|---|---|
| | WT (g) | PRO (g) | CHO (g) | SFA (g) | DFIB (g) | A (IU) | B-1 (mg) | NIA (mg) | B-12 (mcg) | PANT (mg) | K (mg) | P (mg) | Fe (mg) | Cu (mg) | |
| **ice milk** | | | | | | | | | | | | | | | |
| van | 184 | 89.9 | 5.6 | 0.2 | 18 | 52 | 1 | .35 | .09 | 3 | 105 | 176 | 19 | .55 | |
| *1 cup* | 131 | 5.2 | 29.0 | 3.5 | 0.0 | 214 | .08 | 0.1 | .88 | .66 | 256 | 129 | .18 | | |
| van, soft serve | 223 | 121.9 | 4.6 | 0.2 | 13 | 44 | 1 | .54 | .13 | 5 | 162 | 274 | 29 | .86 | |
| *1 cup* | 175 | 8.0 | 38.4 | 2.9 | 0.0 | 175 | .12 | 0.2 | 1.37 | 1.03 | 412 | 202 | .28 | | |
| **le tofu, frzn desserts, Brightsong Light Foods** | | | | | | | | | | | | | | | |
| choc | 155 | 70.4 | 7.7 | | | | | | | | 33 | 12 | | | |
| *3.5 oz* | 100 | 1.4 | 20.0 | | | | | | | | | | .20 | | |
| strawberry | 163 | 69.5 | 8.5 | | | | | | | | 24 | 22 | | | |
| *3.5 oz* | 100 | 0.9 | 20.0 | | | | | | | | | | .20 | | |
| van | 155 | 70.6 | 7.8 | | | | | | | | 33 | 12 | | | |
| *3.5 oz* | 100 | 0.8 | 20.6 | | | | | | | | | | .20 | | |
| **mellorine, Fresh 'n Frosty** | | | | | | | | | | | | | | | |
| choc | 372 | 127.8 | 13.6 | | 6 | | | .49 | | | 142 | 214 | 41 | .76 | |
| *12 fl oz* | 206 | 9.0 | 53.2 | | | 639 | .10 | 0.3 | | | 395 | 195 | 1.44 | .210 | |
| strawberry | 376 | 126.4 | 13.2 | | 6 | | | .51 | | | 166 | 247 | 28 | .68 | |
| *12 fl oz* | 205 | 9.2 | 54.8 | | | 620 | .12 | 0.4 | | | 349 | 212 | .41 | .100 | |
| van | 368 | 127.6 | 12.8 | | 6 | | | .51 | | | 166 | 247 | 26 | .66 | |
| *12 fl oz* | 206 | 9.4 | 53.9 | | | 602 | .12 | 0.3 | | | 351 | 214 | .31 | .120 | |
| **mocha mix frzn dessert[a]** | 144 | | 8.0 | 3.1 | 0 | | | | | | 80 | | | | |
| *1/2 cup* | | 0.6 | 17.5 | 2.1 | | | | | | | | | | | |
| **pudding pops, Jell-O** | | | | | | | | | | | | | | | |
| choc | 75 | 29.9 | 1.9 | 0.0 | 2 | | 0 | .09 | .01 | 1 | 80 | 69 | 10 | .18 | |
| *1 pop* | 47 | 2.0 | 12.7 | 1.8 | | 51 | .02 | 0.1 | .11 | .17 | 91 | 54 | .28 | .037 | |
| choc caramel swirl | 73 | 30.4 | 1.9 | 0.0 | 1 | | 0 | .09 | .01 | 1 | 63 | 64 | 7 | .14 | |
| *1 pop* | 47 | 1.9 | 12.3 | 1.8 | | 67 | .02 | 0.1 | .17 | .17 | 74 | 49 | .16 | .019 | |
| choc fudge | 69 | 30.9 | 2.1 | 0.0 | 1 | | 0 | .08 | .02 | 1 | 78 | 66 | 10 | .18 | |
| *1 pop* | 47 | 1.9 | 11.3 | 2.0 | | 53 | .01 | 0.1 | .29 | .16 | 113 | 53 | .22 | .046 | |
| choc van swirl | 73 | 30.4 | 1.9 | 0.0 | 1 | | 0 | .09 | .01 | 1 | 63 | 64 | 7 | .14 | |
| *1 pop* | 47 | 1.9 | 12.4 | 1.8 | | 66 | .02 | 0.1 | .17 | .17 | 74 | 49 | .16 | .021 | |
| choc w/ choc chips | 79 | 29.9 | 2.7 | 0.0 | 1 | | 0 | .08 | .02 | 1 | 75 | 64 | 12 | .20 | |
| *1 pop* | 48 | 1.9 | 12.8 | 2.3 | | 51 | .01 | 0.1 | .28 | .15 | 127 | 55 | .27 | .068 | |
| choc w/ choc coating | 127 | 24.5 | 7.4 | 0.5 | 1 | | 0 | .08 | .01 | 1 | 75 | 63 | 12 | .22 | |
| *1 pop* | 49 | 2.0 | 14.4 | 5.4 | | 54 | .02 | 0.1 | .26 | .16 | 124 | 56 | .26 | .064 | |
| double choc swirl | 70 | 30.9 | 2.1 | 0.0 | 1 | | 0 | .08 | .02 | 1 | 78 | 66 | 9 | .16 | |
| *1 pop* | 47 | 1.9 | 11.3 | 2.0 | | 53 | .01 | 0.1 | .29 | .16 | 104 | 52 | .18 | .038 | |
| milk choc | 70 | 30.9 | 2.1 | 0.0 | 1 | | 0 | .08 | .02 | 1 | 78 | 67 | 8 | .15 | |
| *1 pop* | 47 | 1.9 | 11.4 | 2.0 | | 54 | .01 | 0.0 | .29 | .16 | 95 | 51 | .14 | .030 | |
| van | 71 | 31.0 | 2.0 | 0.0 | 1 | | 0 | .09 | .02 | 1 | 46 | 60 | 5 | .10 | |
| *1 pop* | 47 | 1.7 | 12.1 | 1.9 | | 81 | .02 | 0.0 | .22 | .17 | 57 | 44 | .04 | .004 | |
| van w/ choc chips | 79 | 30.5 | 2.7 | 0.0 | 1 | | 0 | .08 | .01 | 1 | 50 | 63 | 8 | .15 | |
| *1 pop* | 48 | 1.8 | 12.4 | 2.3 | | 52 | .01 | 0.1 | .28 | .15 | 88 | 48 | .13 | .036 | |
| van w/ choc coating | 127 | 25.0 | 7.4 | 0.5 | 1 | | 0 | .08 | .01 | 1 | 52 | 62 | 8 | .17 | |
| *1 pop* | 49 | 1.8 | 14.1 | 5.5 | | 56 | .02 | 0.0 | .26 | .16 | 89 | 50 | .13 | .036 | |
| **sherbet** | | | | | | | | | | | | | | | |
| fruit flavors, Land O'Lakes | 127 | | 1.7 | 0.1 | 4 | | 1 | .06 | | | 24 | 44 | | | |
| *1/4 cup* | 97 | 1.2 | 27.3 | 1.0 | | 66 | | | | | 174 | 34 | | | |
| orange | 270 | 127.5 | 3.8 | 0.1 | 14 | 39 | 4 | .09 | .03 | 14 | 88 | 103 | 15 | 1.33 | |
| *1 cup* | 193 | 2.2 | 58.7 | 2.4 | | 185 | .03 | 0.1 | .16 | .06 | 198 | 74 | .31 | | |
| **sorbet, Dole** | | | | | | | | | | | | | | | |
| mandarin orange | 110 | 75.3 | 0.1 | | | | 25 | .05 | | | 9 | | | | |
| *1/2 cup* | 104 | 0.5 | 28.0 | | | 312 | .02 | | | | 138 | | .38 | | |
| peach | 120 | 73.7 | 0.1 | | | | 13 | .05 | | | 11 | 3 | 3 | | |
| *1/2 cup* | 104 | 0.6 | 29.6 | | | 314 | .01 | 0.3 | | | 61 | 3 | .57 | | |
| pineapple | 120 | 75.0 | 0.1 | | | | 12 | .06 | | | 11 | 9 | 8 | | |
| *1/2 cup* | 104 | 0.5 | 28.0 | | | 12 | .05 | 0.1 | | | 79 | 5 | .47 | | |

[a] Avg of 8 flavors, choc chip, dutch choc, mocha, almond fudge & neapolitan.

| | | Vitamins | | Minerals | |
|---|---|---|---|---|---|

| | KCAL / WT (g) | H₂O (g) / PRO (g) | FAT (g) / CHO (g) | PUFA (g) / SFA (g) | CHOL (mg) / DFIB (g) | A (RE) / A (IU) | C (mg) / B-1 (mg) | B-2 (mg) / NIA (mg) | B-6 (mg) / B-12 (mcg) | FOL (mcg) / PANT (mg) | Na (mg) / K (mg) | Ca (mg) / P (mg) | Mg (mg) / Fe (mg) | Zn (mg) / Cu (mg) | Mn (mg) |
|---|---|---|---|---|---|---|---|---|---|---|---|---|---|---|---|
| raspberry | 110 | 75.7 | 0.0 | | | | 1 | .04 | | | 12 | | | | |
| *1/2 cup* | 104 | 0.4 | 27.9 | | | | | | | | 37 | | .43 | | |
| strawberry | 110 | 75.3 | 0.1 | | | | 4 | .04 | | | 11 | 8 | 3 | | |
| *1/2 cup* | 104 | 0.5 | 27.9 | | | 6 | .02 | 0.2 | | | 62 | 6 | .52 | | |
| **sorbet & cream, Haagen-Dazs** | | | | | | | | | | | | | | | |
| orange & van | 210 | | 9.0 | | | | | | | | 45 | | | | |
| *1/2 cup* | | 3.0 | 29.0 | | | | | | | | | | | | |
| raspberry & van | 180 | | 9.0 | | | | | | | | 40 | | | | |
| *1/2 cup* | | 3.0 | 24.0 | | | | | | | | | | | | |
| **tofulite, Barricini Foods**[a] | 165 | | 8.5 | | 0 | | | | | | 70 | | | | |
| *4 fl oz* | | 1.5 | 23.5 | | | | | | | | | | | | |
| **tofutti, Tofu Time** | | | | | | | | | | | | | | | |
| hard pack[b] | 220 | | 13.3 | | 0 | | | | | | 105 | | | | |
| *4 fl oz* | | 2.8 | 21.3 | | | | | | | | 29 | 47 | | | |
| soft serve[c] | 158 | | 8.0 | | 0 | | | | | | 64 | | | | |
| *4 fl oz* | | 1.3 | 19.8 | | | | | | | | 28 | 24 | | | |

## 8.8. FRUIT BETTYS/TURNOVERS

| | KCAL / WT (g) | H₂O (g) / PRO (g) | FAT (g) / CHO (g) | PUFA (g) / SFA (g) | CHOL (mg) / DFIB (g) | A (RE) / A (IU) | C (mg) / B-1 (mg) | B-2 (mg) / NIA (mg) | B-6 (mg) / B-12 (mcg) | FOL (mcg) / PANT (mg) | Na (mg) / K (mg) | Ca (mg) / P (mg) | Mg (mg) / Fe (mg) | Zn (mg) / Cu (mg) | Mn (mg) |
|---|---|---|---|---|---|---|---|---|---|---|---|---|---|---|---|
| apple brown betty, homemade | 325 | 138.7 | 7.5 | | | | 2 | .09 | | | 329 | 39 | | | |
| *1 cup* | 215 | 3.4 | 63.9 | 3.2 | | 220 | .13 | 0.9 | | | 215 | 47 | 1.30 | | |
| turnover, apple, Pillsbury | 170 | 23.4 | 7.8 | | | | 0 | .06 | | | 320 | 6 | | | |
| *1 turnover* | 57 | 2.1 | 23.1 | | | 0 | .09 | 0.9 | | | 32 | 123 | .74 | | |
| turnover, blueberry, Pillsbury | 166 | 23.9 | 7.8 | | | | 0 | .06 | | | 316 | 6 | | | |
| *1 turnover* | 57 | 2.0 | 21.4 | | | 5 | .09 | 0.9 | | | 23 | 123 | .57 | | |
| turnover, cherry, Pillsbury | 173 | 22.2 | 7.8 | | | | 5 | .07 | | | 314 | 6 | | | |
| *1 turnover* | 57 | 2.1 | 23.4 | | | 52 | .09 | 0.9 | | | 32 | 124 | .80 | | |

## 8.9. GELATIN DESSERTS, ALL FLAVORS, FROM MIX

| | KCAL / WT (g) | H₂O (g) / PRO (g) | FAT (g) / CHO (g) | PUFA (g) / SFA (g) | CHOL (mg) / DFIB (g) | A (RE) / A (IU) | C (mg) / B-1 (mg) | B-2 (mg) / NIA (mg) | B-6 (mg) / B-12 (mcg) | FOL (mcg) / PANT (mg) | Na (mg) / K (mg) | Ca (mg) / P (mg) | Mg (mg) / Fe (mg) | Zn (mg) / Cu (mg) | Mn (mg) |
|---|---|---|---|---|---|---|---|---|---|---|---|---|---|---|---|
| **Jell-O**[d] | 81 | 118.9 | 0.0 | 0.0 | 0 | | 0 | .00 | .00 | 0 | 54 | 0 | 0 | .00 | |
| *1/2 cup* | 140 | 1.6 | 18.8 | 0.0 | | 0 | .00 | 0.0 | .00 | .00 | 0 | 30 | .02 | .004 | |
| **Royal**[e] | 80 | | 0.0 | | | | | | | | 95 | | | | |
| *1/2 cup* | | 2.0 | 19.0 | | | | | | | | 0 | | | | |
| sugar-free, D-Zerta[f] | 8 | 118.7 | 0.0 | 0.0 | 0 | | 0 | .00 | .00 | 0 | 4 | | | .00 | |
| *1/2 cup* | 121 | 1.6 | 0.1 | 0.0 | 0.0 | 0 | .00 | 0.0 | .00 | .00 | 50 | 0 | | | |
| sugar-free, Featherweight | 10 | | 0.0 | | | | 9 | | | | | | | | |
| *1/2 cup* | | 2.0 | 1.0 | | | | | | | | | | | | |
| sugar-free, Jell-O[g] | 8 | 118.6 | 0.0 | 0.0 | 0 | | 0 | .00 | .00 | 0 | 55 | | | .00 | |
| *1/2 cup* | 121 | 1.4 | 0.2 | 0.0 | | 0 | .00 | 0.0 | .00 | .00 | 0 | 33 | | | |
| sugar-free, Royal[h] | 12 | | 0.0 | | | | | | | | 71 | | | | |
| *1/2 cup* | | 2.0 | 0.0 | | | | | | | | 0 | | | | |
| w/ bananas & grapes, from mix | 161 | 196.3 | 0.2 | | | | 7 | | | | 82 | | | | |
| *1 cup* | 240 | 3.1 | 39.4 | | | | | | | | | | | | |

[a] Values are averages for banana pecan, choc, rum raisin, strawberry, van & wildberry.

[b] Values are averages for choc supreme, maple walnut, van almond bark & wildberry supreme.

[c] Values are averages for banana pecan, choc, maple walnut, peanut butter, van & wildberry.

[d] Values are averages for 16 flavors.

[e] Values are averages for 13 flavors.

[f] Values are averages for cherry, lemon, lime, orange, raspberry & strawberry.

[g] Values are averages for 11 flavors.

[h] Values are averages for 5 flavors.

| | KCAL | H₂O (g) | FAT (g) | PUFA (g) | CHOL (mg) | A (RE) | C (mg) | B-2 (mg) | B-6 (mg) | FOL (mcg) | Na (mg) | Ca (mg) | Mg (mg) | Zn (mg) | Mn (mg) |
|---|---|---|---|---|---|---|---|---|---|---|---|---|---|---|---|
| | WT (g) | PRO (g) | CHO (g) | SFA (g) | DFIB (g) | A (IU) | B-1 (mg) | NIA (mg) | B-12 (mcg) | PANT (mg) | K (mg) | P (mg) | Fe (mg) | Cu (mg) | |

## 8.10. GRANOLA DESSERTS

**all flavors**

| | KCAL/WT | H₂O/PRO | FAT/CHO | PUFA/SFA | CHOL/DFIB | A(RE)/A(IU) | C/B-1 | B-2/NIA | B-6/B-12 | FOL/PANT | Na/K | Ca/P | Mg/Fe | Zn/Cu | Mn |
|---|---|---|---|---|---|---|---|---|---|---|---|---|---|---|---|
| dandy bar, Nature Valley[a] | 163 | | 7.3 | | | | | | | | 108 | | | | |
| *1 bar* | 31 | 2.3 | 22.5 | | | | | | | | 105 | | | | |
| granola bar | 109 | 1.0 | 4.2 | | | | | .03 | | | 67 | 14 | | | |
| *1 bar* | 24 | 2.3 | 16.0 | | | | .07 | | .00 | .13 | 78 | 66 | .76 | | |
| granola bar, Nature Valley[b] | 120 | | 5.1 | | | | | | | | 73 | | | | |
| *1 bar* | 24 | 2.1 | 16.1 | | | | | | | | 66 | | | | |
| caramel grand slam, New Trail | 245 | | 11.8 | | | | | .14 | | | 117 | 58 | | | |
| *1.8 oz bar* | 51 | 4.2 | 31.0 | | | | .07 | 0.2 | | | | | .59 | | |
| caramel nut dipps, Quaker | 148 | 1.4 | 6.3 | | | | | .06 | .00 | 10 | 63 | 30 | 16 | .00 | .000 |
| *1.1 oz bar* | 31 | 1.9 | 21.0 | | | 0 | .02 | 0.4 | .00 | .00 | 87 | 51 | .56 | .120 | |
| caramel nut, Smores | 120 | | 3.9 | | | | | .10 | .04 | 8 | 81 | 14 | 15 | .50 | |
| *1 oz bar* | 28 | 2.0 | 21.0 | | 0.7 | 31 | .04 | 0.7 | | .10 | 53 | 47 | 1.16 | .082 | |
| choc chip, chewy, Quaker | 129 | 1.4 | 4.7 | | | | | .03 | .03 | 6 | 79 | 26 | 22 | 1.00 | .000 |
| *1 oz bar* | 28 | 2.2 | 19.4 | | | 0 | .07 | 0.3 | .00 | .00 | 99 | 65 | .74 | .110 | |
| choc chip dipps, Quaker | 138 | 0.9 | 6.4 | | | | | .06 | .00 | 7 | 65 | 29 | 18 | .00 | .000 |
| *1 oz bar* | 29 | 1.8 | 18.4 | | | 0 | .02 | 0.2 | .00 | .00 | 90 | 56 | .77 | .100 | |
| choc chip, New Trail | 185 | | 8.9 | | | | | .06 | | | 89 | 19 | | | |
| *1.3 oz bar* | 37 | 2.7 | 23.5 | | | | .04 | 0.4 | | | | | .54 | | |
| choc chip, Smores | 120 | | 2.9 | | | | | .11 | .03 | 9 | 60 | 11 | 16 | .27 | |
| *1 oz bar* | 28 | 1.5 | 22.0 | | 1.0 | 36 | .06 | 0.5 | | .06 | 73 | 38 | 1.17 | .085 | |
| choc chip raisin, Smores | 120 | | 3.9 | | | | | .07 | | | 60 | | | | |
| *1 oz bar* | 28 | 2.3 | 21.0 | | | | .03 | | | | | | .10 | | |
| choc fudge, Smores | 130 | | 4.1 | | | | | .07 | | | 65 | | | | |
| *1 oz bar* | 28 | 2.1 | 22.0 | | | | .03 | | | | | | .10 | | |
| choc, graham & marshmallow, chewy, Quaker—*1 oz bar* | 126 | 1.7 | 4.4 | | | | | .05 | .01 | 6 | 93 | 25 | 20 | .00 | .000 |
| | 28 | 1.9 | 19.6 | | | 0 | .04 | 0.3 | .00 | .00 | 79 | 57 | .79 | .080 | |
| chunky nut & raisin, chewy, Quaker | 133 | 1.6 | 6.1 | | | | | .03 | .03 | 8 | 81 | 24 | 26 | 1.00 | .000 |
| *1 oz bar* | 28 | 2.4 | 17.2 | | | 0 | .05 | 0.8 | .00 | .00 | 118 | 68 | .64 | .110 | |
| cocoa, choc covered, New Trail | 200 | | 11.6 | | | | | .06 | | | 59 | 43 | | | |
| *1.3 oz bar* | 37 | 2.1 | 21.4 | | | | .02 | 0.1 | | | | | .40 | | |
| honey & oats, chewy, Quaker | 125 | 1.7 | 4.4 | | | | | .03 | .02 | 7 | 93 | 28 | 21 | 1.00 | 1.000 |
| *1 oz bar* | 28 | 2.4 | 19.0 | | | 0 | .08 | 0.3 | .00 | .00 | 97 | 65 | .76 | .080 | |
| honey & oats dipps, Quaker | 137 | 1.1 | 6.1 | | | | | .07 | .00 | 5 | 66 | 30 | 16 | .00 | .000 |
| *1 oz bar* | 28 | 1.7 | 18.8 | | | 0 | .03 | 0.2 | .00 | .00 | 82 | 51 | .62 | .080 | |
| honey graham, choc covered, New Trail | 200 | | 11.7 | | | | | .04 | | | 52 | 26 | | | |
| *1.3 oz bar* | 37 | 1.9 | 21.4 | | | | .04 | 0.1 | | | | | .36 | | |
| mint choc chip dipps, Quaker | 140 | 0.8 | 6.4 | | | | | .06 | .00 | 4 | 56 | 30 | 18 | .00 | .000 |
| *1 oz bar* | 28 | 1.8 | 18.8 | | | 0 | .03 | 0.2 | .00 | .00 | 86 | 49 | .70 | .120 | |
| peanut butter & choc chip, chewy, Quaker | 131 | 1.6 | 5.5 | | | | | .03 | .03 | 9 | 92 | 23 | 25 | 1.00 | .000 |
| *1 oz bar* | 28 | 3.0 | 17.4 | | | 0 | .04 | 0.8 | .00 | .00 | 108 | 74 | .49 | .110 | |
| peanut butter & choc chip, New Trail | 185 | | 9.4 | | | | | .11 | | | 85 | 19 | | | |
| *1.3 oz bar* | 37 | 3.9 | 20.9 | | | | .03 | 0.5 | | | | | .63 | | |
| peanut butter & choc chip, Smores | 130 | | 4.4 | | | | | .09 | .04 | 9 | 69 | 11 | 18 | .45 | |
| *1 oz bar* | 28 | 2.2 | 20.0 | | 0.9 | 30 | .07 | 0.7 | | .07 | 76 | 49 | 1.58 | .088 | |
| peanut butter, chewy, Quaker | 130 | 1.4 | 5.0 | | | | | .03 | .03 | 9 | 106 | 26 | 24 | 1.00 | .000 |
| *1 oz bar* | 28 | 3.2 | 18.0 | | | 0 | .07 | 0.9 | .00 | .00 | 109 | 71 | .62 | .190 | |
| peanut butter dipps, Quaker | 141 | 1.0 | 7.0 | | | | | .06 | .00 | 7 | 89 | 23 | 19 | .00 | .000 |
| *1 oz bar* | 28 | 2.5 | 17.0 | | | 0 | .02 | 0.6 | .00 | .00 | 87 | 54 | .62 | .090 | |
| peanut butter, New Trail | 185 | | 8.8 | | | | | .07 | | | 89 | 28 | | | |
| *1.3 oz bar* | 37 | 4.6 | 21.3 | | | | .06 | 1.0 | | | | | .67 | | |
| peanut butter, Smores | 120 | | 3.9 | | | | | .10 | .04 | 9 | 65 | 14 | 18 | .30 | |
| *1 oz bar* | 28 | 2.1 | 20.0 | | 0.7 | 31 | .04 | 0.8 | | .10 | 64 | 50 | 1.44 | .068 | |
| peanut, choc covered, New Trail | 196 | | 11.2 | | | | | .06 | | | 78 | 40 | | | |
| *1.3 oz bar* | 37 | 3.4 | 20.2 | | | | .04 | 0.1 | | | | | .34 | | |
| raisin & almond dipps, Quaker | 139 | 1.0 | 6.4 | | | | | .07 | .00 | 5 | 84 | 26 | 16 | .00 | .000 |
| *1 oz bar* | 28 | 1.7 | 18.6 | | | 0 | .02 | 0.2 | .00 | .00 | 81 | 49 | .75 | .080 | |

[a] Values are averages for choc almond, dark choc, milk choc & peanut butter.

[b] Values are averages for almond, choc chip, cinnamon, coconut, oats 'n honey, peanut & peanut butter.

| | KCAL | H₂O (g) | FAT (g) | PUFA (g) | CHOL (mg) | A (RE) | C (mg) | B-2 (mg) | B-6 (mg) | FOL (mcg) | Na (mg) | Ca (mg) | Mg (mg) | Zn (mg) | Mn (mg) |
|---|---|---|---|---|---|---|---|---|---|---|---|---|---|---|---|
| | WT (g) | PRO (g) | CHO (g) | SFA (g) | DFIB (g) | A (IU) | B-1 (mg) | NIA (mg) | B-12 (mcg) | PANT (mg) | K (mg) | P (mg) | Fe (mg) | Cu (mg) | |
| raisin & cinn, chewy, Quaker | 130 | 1.7 | 5.1 | | | | | .03 | .03 | 6 | 83 | 28 | | .00 | .000 |
| *1 oz bar* | 28 | 2.3 | 18.6 | | | 0 | .08 | 0.3 | .00 | .00 | 104 | 62 | .71 | .080 | |
| rocky road dipps, Quaker | 140 | 0.9 | 6.5 | | | | | .05 | .00 | 5 | 60 | 30 | 17 | .00 | .000 |
| *1 oz bar* | 28 | 2.2 | 18.2 | | | 0 | .02 | 0.5 | .00 | .00 | 87 | 50 | .57 | .100 | |

## 8.11. PASTRIES (DANISH PASTRIES/FILLED PASTRIES/SWEET ROLLS/TOASTER PASTRIES)

| | KCAL | H₂O (g) | FAT (g) | PUFA (g) | CHOL (mg) | A (RE) | C (mg) | B-2 (mg) | B-6 (mg) | FOL (mcg) | Na (mg) | Ca (mg) | Mg (mg) | Zn (mg) | Mn (mg) |
|---|---|---|---|---|---|---|---|---|---|---|---|---|---|---|---|
| | WT (g) | PRO (g) | CHO (g) | SFA (g) | DFIB (g) | A (IU) | B-1 (mg) | NIA (mg) | B-12 (mcg) | PANT (mg) | K (mg) | P (mg) | Fe (mg) | Cu (mg) | |
| bear claw, Earth Grains | 250 | | 15.0 | | | | | | | | | | | | |
| *2 oz claw* | 58 | 4.0 | 27.0 | | | | | | | | | | | | |
| charlotte russe w/ whipped cream filling, homemadeᵃ—*1 serving* | 326 | 51.9 | 16.6 | | | | 0 | .11 | | | 49 | 52 | | | |
| | 114 | 6.7 | 38.2 | 8.3 | | 840 | .03 | 0.1 | | | 73 | 104 | .80 | | |
| cream puff w/ custard filling | 303 | 75.8 | 18.1 | | | | 0 | .22 | | | 108 | 105 | | | |
| *1 cream puff* | 130 | 8.5 | 26.7 | 5.6 | | 460 | .05 | 0.1 | | | 157 | 148 | .90 | | |
| cream puff, bavarian, Rich's | 146 | 11.7 | 7.6 | | 35 | | | .06 | | | 66 | 9 | 8 | .24 | |
| *1 cream puff* | 38 | 2.1 | 17.0 | | | | .03 | 0.3 | | | 34 | 17 | .62 | .010 | |
| danish pastry | 161 | 11.2 | 8.8 | | | | 0 | .10 | | | 161 | 45 | 6 | .35 | |
| *1 piece* | 42 | 2.6 | 18.8 | | | 45 | .10 | 0.9 | | | 39 | 43 | .78 | | |
| apple cinn, frzn, Am Hosp Co | 455 | | 24.2 | | 37 | | 4 | .03 | | | 522 | 71 | | | |
| *4 oz* | 113 | 10.9 | 48.5 | | | 183 | .05 | 3.3 | | | 157 | | 2.90 | | |
| apple, Earth Grains | 230 | | 13.0 | | | | | | | | | | | | |
| *2 oz danish* | 58 | 3.0 | 26.0 | | | | | | | | | | | | |
| apple, Hostess | 360 | | 20.0 | | 19 | | 0 | | | | 410 | | | | |
| *1 piece* | 99 | 4.0 | 43.0 | | | 0 | | | | | | | | | |
| apple w/ icing, refrig dough, Pillsbury—*1 roll* | 240 | 25.9 | 11.1 | | | | 0 | .10 | | | 260 | 16 | | | |
| | 74 | 2.2 | 31.8 | | | 6 | | 1.1 | | | 47 | 44 | .98 | | |
| butterhorn, Hostess | 330 | | 18.0 | | 8 | | 0 | | | | 520 | | | | |
| *1 piece* | 81 | 5.0 | 39.0 | | | 0 | | | | | | | | | |
| caramel w/ nuts, refrig dough, Pillsbury | 311 | 17.9 | 16.4 | | | | 0 | .12 | | | 488 | 18 | | | |
| *2 rolls* | 78 | 3.9 | 38.2 | | | 0 | .19 | 1.6 | | | 58 | 211 | 1.18 | | |
| cherry, Earth Grains | 230 | | 13.0 | | | | | | | | | | | | |
| *2 oz danish* | 56 | 4.0 | 26.0 | | | | | | | | | | | | |
| cinn, Earth Grains | 220 | | 10.0 | | | | | | | | | | | | |
| *2 oz danish* | 58 | 4.0 | 29.0 | | | | | | | | | | | | |
| cinn, refrig dough | 125 | | 4.0 | | | | | | | | 360 | | | | |
| *1 roll* | 39 | 2.0 | 21.0 | | | | | | | | 35 | | | | |
| cinn raisin, frzn, Am Hosp Co | 419 | | 17.8 | | 29 | | 4 | .03 | | | 591 | 95 | | | |
| *4 oz* | 113 | 9.2 | 55.4 | | | 430 | .05 | 2.5 | | | 199 | | 2.60 | | |
| cinn raisin w/ icing, refrig dough, Pillsbury—*2 rolls* | 291 | 20.0 | 13.8 | | | | 0 | .12 | | | 442 | 16 | | | |
| | 77 | 3.1 | 38.9 | | | 6 | .17 | 1.4 | | | 54 | 190 | .95 | | |
| orange, refrig dough | 130 | | 5.0 | | | | | | | | 320 | | | | |
| *1 roll* | 39 | 2.0 | 18.0 | | | | | | | | 25 | | | | |
| orange w/ icing, refrig dough, Pillsbury | 289 | 20.8 | 13.9 | | | | 2 | .12 | | | 477 | 10 | | | |
| *2 rolls* | 77 | 3.2 | 37.7 | | | 8 | .18 | 1.5 | | | 33 | 200 | 1.00 | | |
| raspberry, Hostess | 270 | | 7.0 | | 20 | | 0 | | | | 295 | | | | |
| *1 piece* | 81 | 5.0 | 46.0 | | | 0 | | | | | | | | | |
| raisin, refrig dough | 135 | | 5.0 | | | | | | | | 290 | | | | |
| *1 roll* | 39 | 2.0 | 21.0 | | | | | | | | 50 | | | | |
| eclair, choc, Rich's | 205 | 19.3 | 9.7 | | 35 | | | .08 | | | 113 | 10 | 10 | .26 | |
| *1 eclair* | 57 | 2.3 | 27.3 | | | | .03 | 0.4 | | | 47 | 33 | .84 | .120 | |
| eclair w/ custard filling & choc icing | 239 | 56.2 | 13.6 | | | | 0 | .16 | | | 82 | 80 | | | |
| *1 eclair* | 100 | 6.2 | 23.2 | 4.4 | | 340 | .04 | 0.1 | | | 122 | 112 | .70 | | |
| raisin bun | 179 | 20.8 | 1.9 | | | | 0 | .07 | | | 250 | 49 | | | |
| *1 bun* | 65 | 4.5 | 36.7 | | | 0 | .04 | 0.5 | | | 159 | 59 | .91 | | |
| sweet roll | 154 | 10.5 | 6.8 | | | | 0 | .13 | .04 | 13 | 170 | 11 | 8 | .20 | |
| *1 roll* | 42 | 2.6 | 21.4 | | | 0 | .16 | 0.9 | | .16 | 47 | 30 | .76 | .020 | |
| **sweet roll, refrig dough** | | | | | | | | | | | | | | | |
| cinn | 110 | | 3.0 | | | | | | | | 300 | | | | |
| *1 roll* | 34 | 2.0 | 18.0 | | | | | | | | 35 | | | | |

ᵃ 4 ladyfingers w/ 1/3 cup whipped cream filling.

| | KCAL | H₂O (g) | FAT (g) | PUFA (g) | CHOL (mg) | A (RE) | C (mg) | B-2 (mg) | B-6 (mg) | FOL (mcg) | Na (mg) | Ca (mg) | Mg (mg) | Zn (mg) | Mn (mg) |
|---|---|---|---|---|---|---|---|---|---|---|---|---|---|---|---|
| | WT (g) | PRO (g) | CHO (g) | SFA (g) | DFIB (g) | A (IU) | B-1 (mg) | NIA (mg) | B-12 (mcg) | PANT (mg) | K (mg) | P (mg) | Fe (mg) | Cu (mg) | |
| cinn, butter flavored | 130 | | 7.0 | | | | | | | | 320 | | | | |
| *1 roll* | 34 | 2.0 | 15.0 | | | | | | | | 30 | | | | |
| cinn, frzn, Am Hosp Co | 520 | | 14.5 | | 12 | | 7 | .03 | | | 695 | 100 | | | |
| *4.75 oz* | 135 | 12.5 | 84.0 | | | 438 | .13 | 4.5 | | | 200 | | 2.70 | | |
| cinn w/ icing, Hungry Jack | 291 | 22.1 | 14.2 | | | | 0 | .13 | | | 580 | 13 | | | |
| *2 rolls* | 79 | 3.3 | 37.9 | | | 5 | .18 | 1.5 | | | 32 | 234 | .95 | | |
| cinn w/ icing, Pillsbury | 230 | 19.4 | 9.4 | | | | 0 | .13 | | | 517 | 13 | | | |
| *2 rolls* | 67 | 2.9 | 33.6 | | | 3 | .17 | 1.5 | | | 40 | 215 | 1.27 | | |
| cinn w/ icing, Pillsbury Best Quick | 211 | 13.7 | 9.3 | | | | 0 | .11 | | | 266 | 13 | | | |
| *1 roll* | 57 | 2.4 | 29.4 | | | 13 | | 1.1 | | | 29 | 82 | 1.08 | | |
| **toaster pastry** | 195 | 6.4 | 5.7 | | | | | .17 | .19 | 40 | 229 | 96 | 9 | .29 | |
| *1 pastry* | 50 | 1.9 | 35.2 | | | 482 | .16 | 2.1 | .00 | .11 | 84 | 96 | 2.00 | .075 | |
| **toaster strudel, Pillsbury** | | | | | | | | | | | | | | | |
| apple spice | 187 | 14.8 | 8.6 | | | | 0 | .11 | | | 190 | 8 | | | |
| *1 pastry* | 54 | 2.8 | 28.1 | | | 11 | .16 | 1.4 | | | 38 | 69 | .97 | | |
| blueberry | 194 | 12.3 | 7.6 | | | | 0 | .11 | | | 201 | 6 | | | |
| *1 pastry* | 54 | 2.2 | 27.9 | | | 1 | .11 | 1.1 | | | 39 | 45 | .70 | | |
| cherry | 194 | 15.4 | 8.6 | | | | 0 | .11 | | | 201 | 8 | | | |
| *1 pastry* | 54 | 2.8 | 26.2 | | | 12 | .16 | 1.4 | | | 41 | 71 | 1.03 | | |
| cinnamon | 193 | 17.3 | 8.4 | | | | 0 | .11 | | | 198 | 5 | | | |
| *1 pastry* | 54 | 2.2 | 25.9 | | | 0 | .13 | 1.1 | | | 36 | 45 | .70 | | |
| raspberry | 187 | 17.8 | 7.5 | | | | 0 | .11 | | | 201 | 6 | | | |
| *1 pastry* | 54 | 2.2 | 26.5 | | | 2 | .13 | 1.1 | | | 41 | 46 | .70 | | |
| strawberry | 199 | 12.2 | 7.5 | | | | 1 | .11 | | | 202 | 6 | | | |
| *1 pastry* | 54 | 2.2 | 27.1 | | | 1 | .13 | 1.1 | | | 41 | 46 | .70 | | |
| **toastettes, all flavors, Nabisco[a]** | 200 | | 5.1 | | | | | | | | 193 | | | | |
| *1 pastry* | | 2.0 | 35.9 | | | | | | | | 45 | | | | |

## 8.12. PIES & PIE CRUSTS

| | KCAL | H₂O (g) | FAT (g) | PUFA (g) | CHOL (mg) | A (RE) | C (mg) | B-2 (mg) | B-6 (mg) | FOL (mcg) | Na (mg) | Ca (mg) | Mg (mg) | Zn (mg) | Mn (mg) |
|---|---|---|---|---|---|---|---|---|---|---|---|---|---|---|---|
| | WT (g) | PRO (g) | CHO (g) | SFA (g) | DFIB (g) | A (IU) | B-1 (mg) | NIA (mg) | B-12 (mcg) | PANT (mg) | K (mg) | P (mg) | Fe (mg) | Cu (mg) | |
| **apple** | | | | | | | | | | | | | | | |
| frzn, baked | 231 | 43.5 | 9.1 | | | | 1 | .01 | | | 195 | 8 | | | |
| *1/6 pie* | 92 | 1.8 | 36.5 | 2.3 | | 10 | .01 | 0.2 | | | 66 | 19 | .20 | | |
| frzn, Banquet | 253 | | 11.0 | | | | 3 | .03 | | | 282 | 12 | | | |
| *1/6 of 20 oz pie* | 94 | 2.0 | 37.0 | | | 15 | .02 | 0.3 | | | 49 | | 1.00 | | |
| homemade | 282 | 60.0 | 11.9 | | | | 0 | .09 | .03 | 6 | 181 | 11 | 9 | .20 | |
| *1/8 pie* | 118 | 2.4 | 43.0 | | | 22 | .13 | 1.1 | .00 | .17 | 100 | 27 | 1.06 | .063 | |
| **banana cream** | | | | | | | | | | | | | | | |
| from mix, Jell-O[b] | 233 | 46.9 | 11.9 | 0.7 | 28 | | 0 | .13 | .03 | 6 | 267 | 67 | 11 | .31 | |
| *1/8 pie* | 92 | 3.3 | 28.8 | 7.3 | | 375 | .09 | 0.7 | .20 | .24 | 104 | 154 | .43 | .039 | |
| from mix, Banquet | 177 | | 10.0 | | | | 1 | .06 | | | 146 | 32 | | | |
| *1/6 of 14 oz pie* | 66 | 2.0 | 21.0 | | | 7 | .02 | 0.2 | | | 94 | | 1.00 | | |
| **banana custard, homemade** | 252 | 62.0 | 10.6 | | | | 1 | .15 | | | 221 | 75 | | | |
| *1/8 pie* | 114 | 5.1 | 35.0 | 3.4 | | 290 | .05 | 0.3 | | | 231 | 93 | .60 | | |
| **blackberry** | | | | | | | | | | | | | | | |
| frzn, Banquet | 268 | | 11.0 | | | | 5 | .03 | | | 342 | 23 | | | |
| *1/6 of 20 oz pie* | 94 | 3.0 | 40.0 | | | 49 | .02 | 0.3 | | | 65 | | 1.00 | | |
| homemade | 287 | 60.2 | 13.0 | | | | 5 | .02 | | | 316 | 22 | | | |
| *1/8 pie* | 118 | 3.1 | 40.6 | 3.2 | | 110 | .02 | 0.4 | | | 118 | 31 | .60 | | |
| **blueberry** | | | | | | | | | | | | | | | |
| frzn, Banquet | 266 | | 11.0 | | | | 3 | .03 | | | 342 | 17 | | | |
| *1/6 of 20 oz pie* | 94 | 3.0 | 40.0 | | | 25 | .03 | 0.3 | | | 45 | | 1.00 | | |
| homemade | 286 | 60.2 | 12.7 | | | | 4 | .02 | | | 316 | 13 | | | |
| *1/8 pie* | 118 | 2.8 | 41.2 | 3.2 | | 40 | .02 | 0.4 | | | 77 | 27 | .70 | | |
| **butterscotch, homemade** | 304 | 51.4 | 12.5 | | | | 0 | .11 | | | 244 | 86 | | | |
| *1/8 pie* | 114 | 5.0 | 43.7 | 4.5 | | 300 | .03 | 0.2 | | | 108 | 92 | 1.00 | | |

[a] Values are averages for apple, blueberry, brown sugar, cinn, cherry, fudge & strawberry, frosted & unfrosted.

[b] Prepared w/ vitamin D fortified whole milk.

| | KCAL | H₂O (g) | FAT (g) | PUFA (g) | CHOL (mg) | A (RE) | C (mg) | B-2 (mg) | B-6 (mg) | FOL (mcg) | Na (mg) | Ca (mg) | Mg (mg) | Zn (mg) | Mn (mg) |
|---|---|---|---|---|---|---|---|---|---|---|---|---|---|---|---|
| | WT (g) | PRO (g) | CHO (g) | SFA (g) | DFIB (g) | A (IU) | B-1 (mg) | NIA (mg) | B-12 (mcg) | PANT (mg) | K (mg) | P (mg) | Fe (mg) | Cu (mg) | |
| **cherry** | | | | | | | | | | | | | | | |
| frzn, baked | 282 | 39.4 | 11.7 | | | | 2 | .02 | | | 222 | 12 | | | |
| *1/6 pie* | 97 | 2.1 | 42.9 | 2.9 | | 280 | .02 | 0.2 | | | 79 | 23 | .20 | | |
| frzn, Banquet | 252 | | 11.0 | | | | 2 | .04 | | | 258 | 13 | | | |
| *1/6 of 20 oz pie* | 94 | 3.0 | 36.0 | | | 185 | .03 | 0.3 | | | 72 | | 1.00 | | |
| homemade | 308 | 55.0 | 13.3 | | | | 0 | .02 | | | 359 | 17 | | | |
| *1/8 pie* | 118 | 3.1 | 45.3 | 3.5 | | 520 | .02 | 0.6 | | | 124 | 30 | .40 | | |
| **choc chiffon** | 266 | 26.7 | 12.4 | | | | 0 | .08 | | | 204 | 19 | | | |
| *1/8 pie* | 81 | 5.5 | 35.4 | 4.2 | | 250 | .02 | 0.2 | | | 89 | 79 | 1.00 | | |
| **choc cream** | | | | | | | | | | | | | | | |
| frzn, Banquet | 185 | | 10.0 | | | | 0 | .05 | | | 106 | 38 | | | |
| *1/6 of 14 oz pie* | 66 | 2.0 | 24.0 | | | 7 | .02 | 0.2 | | | 86 | | 1.00 | | |
| homemade | 301 | 56.4 | 17.3 | | | | 0 | .19 | .05 | 10 | 311 | 96 | 29 | .75 | |
| *1/8 pie* | 114 | 5.2 | 33.6 | | | 301 | .11 | 0.8 | .42 | .55 | 162 | 124 | 1.23 | .136 | |
| **choc mint, from mix, Royal**[a] | 260 | | 15.0 | | | | | | | | 280 | | | | |
| *1/8 pie* | | 5.0 | 25.0 | | | | | | | | 260 | | | | |
| **choc mousse, from mix, Jell-O**[a] | 249 | 47.2 | 14.6 | 0.5 | 29 | | 0 | .14 | .03 | 3 | 437 | 74 | 30 | .57 | |
| *1/8 pie* | 95 | 3.6 | 27.5 | 8.3 | | 392 | .05 | 0.6 | .20 | .19 | 270 | 220 | 1.03 | .193 | |
| **coconut cream** | | | | | | | | | | | | | | | |
| from mix, Jell-O[a] | 260 | 46.8 | 16.5 | 0.7 | 29 | | 1 | .10 | .04 | 4 | 309 | 67 | 16 | .36 | |
| *1/8 pie* | 94 | 2.7 | 26.6 | 11.1 | | 381 | .03 | 0.1 | .20 | .24 | 132 | 159 | .37 | .078 | |
| frzn, Banquet | 187 | | 11.0 | | | | 0 | .05 | | | 113 | 30 | | | |
| *1/6 of 14 oz pie* | 66 | 2.0 | 22.0 | | | 1 | .01 | 0.2 | | | 77 | | 1.00 | | |
| **coconut custard** | | | | | | | | | | | | | | | |
| frzn, baked | 249 | 51.2 | 12.0 | | | | 0 | .16 | | | 252 | 95 | | | |
| *1/6 pie* | 100 | 6.0 | 29.5 | 5.0 | | 160 | .04 | 0.2 | | | 172 | 115 | .60 | | |
| homemade | 268 | 63.2 | 14.3 | | | | 0 | .22 | | | 282 | 107 | | | |
| *1/8 pie* | 114 | 6.8 | 28.4 | 5.7 | | 260 | .07 | 0.3 | | | 186 | 132 | .80 | | |
| **custard, homemade** | 249 | 66.2 | 12.7 | | | | 0 | .18 | | | 327 | 109 | | | |
| *1/8 pie* | 114 | 7.0 | 26.7 | 4.3 | | 260 | .06 | 0.3 | | | 156 | 129 | .70 | | |
| **lemon chiffon** | 254 | 28.8 | 10.2 | | | | 2 | .06 | | | 211 | 19 | | | |
| *1/8 pie* | 81 | 5.7 | 35.5 | 2.7 | | 140 | .02 | 0.2 | | | 66 | 67 | .70 | | |
| **lemon cream, frzn, Banquet** | 173 | | 9.0 | | | | 2 | .04 | | | 111 | 30 | | | |
| *1/6 of 14 oz pie* | 66 | 2.0 | 23.0 | | | 2 | .02 | 0.2 | | | 70 | | 1.00 | | |
| **lemon meringue, homemade** | 350 | 66.4 | 13.1 | | | | 4 | .14 | .03 | 13 | 260 | 18 | 8 | .39 | |
| *1/6 pie* | 140 | 4.5 | 55.1 | | | 195 | .11 | 0.8 | .22 | 0.4 | 62 | 56 | 1.05 | .032 | |
| **mince, homemade** | 320 | 50.7 | 13.6 | | | | 1 | .05 | | | 529 | 33 | | | |
| *1/8 pie* | 118 | 3.0 | 48.6 | 3.6 | | 0 | .08 | 0.5 | | | 210 | 45 | 1.20 | | |
| **mincemeat, frzn, Banquet** | 258 | | 11.0 | | | | 1 | .03 | | | 364 | 19 | | | |
| *1/6 of 20 oz pie* | 94 | 3.0 | 38.0 | | | 2 | .03 | 0.3 | | | 110 | | 1.00 | | |
| **peach** | | | | | | | | | | | | | | | |
| frzn, Banquet | 244 | | 11.0 | | | | 14 | .03 | | | 275 | 11 | | | |
| *1/6 of 20 oz pie* | 94 | 3.0 | 35.0 | | | 232 | .02 | 0.5 | | | 69 | | 1.00 | | |
| homemade | 301 | 56.1 | 12.6 | | | | 4 | .05 | | | 316 | 12 | | | |
| *1/8 pie* | 118 | 3.0 | 45.1 | 3.1 | | 860 | .02 | 0.8 | | | 176 | 34 | .60 | | |
| **pecan, homemade** | 431 | 20.1 | 23.6 | | | | 0 | .07 | | | 228 | 48 | | | |
| *1/8 pie* | 103 | 5.3 | 52.8 | 3.3 | | 160 | .16 | 0.3 | | | 127 | 106 | 2.90 | | |
| **pie crust** | | | | | | | | | | | | | | | |
| from mix | 742 | 29.9 | 46.5 | | | 0 | | .05 | | 1301 | 65 | | | | |
| *1/2 yield from 10 oz pkg* | 160 | 10.2 | 70.4 | 11.5 | | 0 | .05 | 0.8 | | | 89 | 136 | .65 | | |
| from sticks/mix, Pillsbury | 270 | | 16.8 | | | 0 | | .15 | | | 416 | 10 | | | |
| *1/6 of 2 crust pie* | | 4.2 | 24.8 | | | 0 | .26 | 1.9 | | | 77 | 36 | 1.02 | | |
| homemade, enr, baked | 900 | 26.8 | 60.1 | | | 0 | | .25[b] | | 1100 | 25 | | | | |
| *1 pie shell* | 180 | 11.0 | 78.8 | 14.9 | | 0 | .36[b] | 3.2[b] | | | 89 | 90 | 3.10[b] | | |
| mix, Flako | 244 | 4.1 | 14.4 | | | | | .09 | .01 | 10 | 314 | 48 | 9 | .00 | .000 |
| *1.7 oz dry mix* | 48 | 3.4 | 25.0 | | | 0 | .17 | 1.3 | .00 | .00 | 35 | 55 | 1.12 | .060 | |

[a] Prepared w/ vitamin D fortified whole milk.

[b] Unenr pie shell contains .05 mg thiamin, .05 mg riboflavin, 0.9 mg niacin & .90 mg iron.

| | KCAL | H₂O (g) | FAT (g) | PUFA (g) | CHOL (mg) | Vitamins A (RE) | C (mg) | B-2 (mg) | B-6 (mg) | FOL (mcg) | Minerals Na (mg) | Ca (mg) | Mg (mg) | Zn (mg) | Mn (mg) |
|---|---|---|---|---|---|---|---|---|---|---|---|---|---|---|---|
| | WT (g) | PRO (g) | CHO (g) | SFA (g) | DFIB (g) | A (IU) | B-1 (mg) | NIA (mg) | B-12 (mcg) | PANT (mg) | K (mg) | P (mg) | Fe (mg) | Cu (mg) | |
| ready-to-eat, Pillsbury | 241 | 12.4 | 14.9 | | | | | | | | 214 | | | | |
| *1/8 of 2 crust pie* | 54 | 1.7 | 23.8 | | | | | | | | 30 | | | | |
| pineapple, homemade | 299 | 56.6 | 12.6 | | | | 1 | .02 | | | 320 | 15 | | | |
| *1/8 pie* | 118 | 2.6 | 45.0 | 3.1 | | 20 | .05 | 0.5 | | | 85 | 25 | .60 | | |
| pineapple chiffon, homemade | 233 | 33.3 | 9.8 | | | | 1 | .07 | | | 207 | 19 | | | |
| *1/8 pie* | 81 | 5.3 | 31.7 | 2.6 | | 280 | .03 | 0.3 | | | 79 | 62 | .70 | | |
| pineapple custard | 251 | 61.9 | 9.9 | | | | 1 | .10 | | | 212 | 57 | | | |
| *1/8 pie* | 114 | 4.6 | 36.6 | 3.0 | | 210 | .05 | 0.5 | | | 111 | 74 | .50 | | |
| **pumpkin** | | | | | | | | | | | | | | | |
| frzn, Banquet | 197 | | 8.0 | | | | 2 | .07 | | | 341 | 53 | | | |
| *1/6 of 20 oz pie* | 94 | 3.0 | 29.0 | | | 1938 | .04 | 0.4 | | | 138 | | 1.00 | | |
| homemade | 241 | 67.5 | 12.8 | | | | 0 | .11 | | | 244 | 58 | | | |
| *1/8 pie* | 114 | 4.6 | 27.9 | 4.5 | | 2810 | .03 | 0.6 | | | 182 | 79 | .60 | | |
| raisin, homemade | 319 | 50.2 | 12.6 | | | | 1 | .04 | | | 336 | 21 | | | |
| *1/8 pie* | 118 | 3.1 | 50.7 | 3.1 | | 10 | .04 | 0.4 | | | 227 | 47 | 1.10 | | |
| rhubarb, homemade | 299 | 55.9 | 12.6 | | | | 4 | .05 | | | 319 | 76 | | | |
| *1/8 pie* | 118 | 3.0 | 45.1 | 3.1 | | 60 | .02 | 0.4 | | | 188 | 31 | .80 | | |
| strawberry cream, frzn, Banquet | 168 | | 9.0 | | | | 6 | .05 | | | 112 | 30 | | | |
| *1/6 of 14 oz pie* | 66 | 2.0 | 22.0 | | | 4 | .02 | 0.2 | | | 80 | | 1.00 | | |
| strawberry, homemade | 184 | 54.3 | 7.3 | | | | 23 | .04 | | | 180 | 15 | | | |
| *1/8 pie* | 93 | 1.8 | 28.7 | 1.8 | | 40 | .02 | 0.4 | | | 112 | 23 | .70 | | |
| sweet potato, homemade | 243 | 67.6 | 12.9 | | | | 5 | .14 | | | 249 | 79 | | | |
| *1/8 pie* | 114 | 5.1 | 27.0 | 4.6 | | 2730 | .06 | 0.3 | | | 186 | 96 | .60 | | |

## 8.13. PIES, SNACK (FRIED)

| | KCAL | H₂O (g) | FAT (g) | PUFA (g) | CHOL (mg) | A (RE) | C (mg) | B-2 (mg) | B-6 (mg) | FOL (mcg) | Na (mg) | Ca (mg) | Mg (mg) | Zn (mg) | Mn (mg) |
|---|---|---|---|---|---|---|---|---|---|---|---|---|---|---|---|
| | WT (g) | PRO (g) | CHO (g) | SFA (g) | DFIB (g) | A (IU) | B-1 (mg) | NIA (mg) | B-12 (mcg) | PANT (mg) | K (mg) | P (mg) | Fe (mg) | Cu (mg) | |
| **apple, fried** | 258 | 40.6 | 13.1 | | | | 0 | .11 | | | 288 | 9 | 10 | .24 | |
| *1 snack pie* | 90 | 2.7 | 32.6 | | | | .18 | 1.2 | | | 74 | 68 | 1.25 | .045 | |
| **apple, Hostess** | 390 | | 20.0 | | 18 | | | | | | 540 | | | | |
| *1 snack pie* | 128 | 5.0 | 45.0 | | | 0 | | | | | | | | | |
| **berry, Hostess** | 390 | | 20.0 | | 18 | | | | | | | | | | |
| *1 snack pie* | 128 | 3.0 | 48.0 | | | 0 | | | | | | | | | |
| **blueberry, Hostess** | 390 | | 20.0 | | 18 | | | | | | 450 | | | | |
| *1 snack pie* | 128 | 3.0 | 49.0 | | | 0 | | | | | | | | | |
| **cherry, Hostess** | 420 | | 20.0 | | 18 | | | | | | 530 | | | | |
| *1 snack pie* | 128 | 5.0 | 55.0 | | | 0 | | | | | | | | | |
| **fried, Rainbo Snacks** | 410 | | 19.0 | | | | | | | | | | | | |
| *1 snack pie* | | 5.0 | 57.0 | | | | | | | | | | | | |
| **lemon, Hostess** | 400 | | 22.0 | | 30 | | 0 | | | | 470 | | | | |
| *1 snack pie* | 128 | 3.0 | 53.0 | | | 0 | | | | | | | | | |
| **peach, Hostess** | 400 | | 20.0 | | 18 | | | | | | 445 | | | | |
| *1 snack pie* | 128 | 4.0 | 53.0 | | | 0 | | | | | | | | | |
| **pudding, Hostess** | 470 | | 17.0 | | 18 | | 0 | | | | 360 | | | | |
| *1 snack pie* | 142 | 4.0 | 75.0 | | | | | | | | | | | | |
| **strawberry, Hostess** | 340 | | 14.0 | | 13 | | | | | | 400 | | | | |
| *1 snack pie* | 128 | 3.0 | 56.0 | | | 0 | | | | | | | | | |

## 8.14. PUDDINGS

| | KCAL | H₂O (g) | FAT (g) | PUFA (g) | CHOL (mg) | A (RE) | C (mg) | B-2 (mg) | B-6 (mg) | FOL (mcg) | Na (mg) | Ca (mg) | Mg (mg) | Zn (mg) | Mn (mg) |
|---|---|---|---|---|---|---|---|---|---|---|---|---|---|---|---|
| | WT (g) | PRO (g) | CHO (g) | SFA (g) | DFIB (g) | A (IU) | B-1 (mg) | NIA (mg) | B-12 (mcg) | PANT (mg) | K (mg) | P (mg) | Fe (mg) | Cu (mg) | |
| **all flavors** | | | | | | | | | | | | | | | |
| from inst mix, Royal[a] | 181 | | 4.4 | | | | | | | | 375 | | | | |
| *1/2 cup* | | 3.7 | 31.5 | | | | | | | | 208 | | | | |
| from reg mix, Royal[a] | 162 | | 3.7 | | | | | | | | 160 | | | | |
| *1/2 cup* | | 3.6 | 27.7 | | | | | | | | 191 | | | | |
| sugar-free, from inst mix, Royal[b] | 103 | | 2.3 | | | | | | | | 473 | | | | |
| *1/2 cup* | | 4.3 | 16.3 | | | | | | | | 243 | | | | |
| **apple tapioca, homemade** | 293 | 175.0 | 0.3 | | | | 0 | .00 | | | 128 | 8 | | | |
| *1 cup* | 250 | 0.5 | 73.5 | | | 30 | .00 | 0.0 | | | 65 | 10 | .50 | | |

[a] Values are averages for 11 flavors; pudding is prepared w/ vitamin D fortified whole milk.

[b] Values are averages for 3 flavors; pudding is prepared w/ vitamin D fortified 2% low fat milk.

| | KCAL / WT (g) | H₂O (g) / PRO (g) | FAT (g) / CHO (g) | PUFA (g) / SFA (g) | CHOL (mg) / DFIB (g) | A (RE) / A (IU) | C (mg) / B-1 (mg) | B-2 (mg) / NIA (mg) | B-6 (mg) / B-12 (mcg) | FOL (mcg) / PANT (mg) | Na (mg) / K (mg) | Ca (mg) / P (mg) | Mg (mg) / Fe (mg) | Zn (mg) / Cu (mg) | Mn (mg) |
|---|---|---|---|---|---|---|---|---|---|---|---|---|---|---|---|
| **banana cream** | | | | | | | | | | | | | | | |
| from inst mix, Jell-O[a] | 165 | 108.3 | 4.3 | 0.2 | 17 | | 1 | .20 | .05 | 6 | 443 | 147 | 17 | .47 | |
| *1/2 cup* | 147 | 4.0 | 28.4 | 2.6 | | 154 | .05 | 0.1 | .44 | .39 | 187 | 314 | .09 | .017 | |
| sugar-free, from inst mix, Jell-O[b] | 88 | 108.9 | 2.4 | 0.1 | 9 | | 1 | .20 | .05 | 6 | 426 | 150 | 17 | .47 | |
| *1/2 cup* | 130 | 4.2 | 12.6 | 1.5 | | 250 | .05 | 0.1 | .44 | .39 | 192 | 302 | .08 | .013 | |
| **bread, homemade** | 496 | 155.3 | 16.2 | | | | 3 | .50 | | | 533 | 289 | | | |
| *1 cup* | 265 | 14.8 | 75.3 | 7.7 | | 800 | .16 | 1.3 | | | 570 | 302 | 2.90 | | |
| **butter pecan, from inst mix, Jell-O[a]** | 170 | 107.8 | 4.8 | 0.3 | 17 | | 1 | .21 | .05 | 7 | 443 | 150 | 19 | .48 | |
| *1/2 cup* | 147 | 4.2 | 28.1 | 2.6 | | 154 | .05 | 0.1 | .44 | .39 | 195 | 319 | .14 | .027 | |
| **butterscotch** | | | | | | | | | | | | | | | |
| from inst mix, Jell-O[a] | 164 | 108.3 | 4.3 | 0.2 | 17 | | 1 | .20 | .05 | 6 | 481 | 147 | 17 | .47 | |
| *1/2 cup* | 147 | 4.0 | 28.3 | 2.6 | | 154 | .05 | 0.1 | .44 | .39 | 187 | 340 | .09 | .017 | |
| Rich's | 133 | 58.6 | 5.9 | | | | | .09 | | | 128 | 26 | 5 | .14 | |
| *3 oz* | 85 | 1.7 | 18.3 | | | | .02 | | | | 85 | 47 | .20 | .020 | |
| sugar-free, from inst mix, D-Zerta[c] | 68 | 112.3 | 0.2 | 0.0 | 2 | | 1 | .17 | .05 | 6 | 66 | 154 | 14 | .49 | |
| *1/2 cup* | 130 | 4.3 | 12.1 | 0.1 | | 251 | .04 | 0.1 | .46 | .40 | 237 | 124 | .05 | .016 | |
| sugar-free, from inst mix, Jell-O[b] | 90 | 109.5 | 2.4 | 0.1 | 9 | | 1 | .20 | .05 | 6 | 426 | 150 | 17 | .48 | |
| *1/2 cup* | 131 | 4.2 | 12.8 | 1.5 | | 251 | .05 | 0.1 | .45 | .39 | 193 | 303 | .08 | .010 | |
| **choc** | | | | | | | | | | | | | | | |
| from inst mix | 325 | 178.6 | 6.5 | | | | 2 | .39 | | | 322 | 374 | | | |
| *1 cup* | 260 | 7.8 | 63.4 | 3.6 | | 340 | .08 | 0.3 | | | 335 | 237 | 1.30 | | |
| from inst mix, Jell-O[a] | 176 | 107.5 | 4.5 | 0.2 | 17 | | 1 | .21 | .06 | 6 | 514 | 149 | 27 | .61 | |
| *1/2 cup* | 150 | 4.4 | 31.0 | 2.7 | | 155 | .05 | 0.1 | .44 | .39 | 297 | 379 | .43 | .096 | |
| from non-inst mix | 322 | 182.0 | 7.8 | | | | 2 | .39 | | | 335 | 265 | | | |
| *1 cup* | 260 | 8.8 | 59.3 | | | 340 | .05 | 0.3 | | | 354 | 247 | .80 | | |
| homemade | 385 | 171.1 | 12.2 | | | | 1 | .36 | | | 146 | 250 | | | |
| *1 cup* | 260 | 8.1 | 66.8 | 6.7 | | 390 | .05 | 0.3 | | | 445 | 255 | 1.30 | | |
| Rich's | 141 | 57.4 | 7.1 | | | | | .08 | | | 136 | 22 | 13 | .25 | |
| *3 oz* | 85 | 1.7 | 18.2 | | | | .02 | 0.2 | | | 111 | 53 | .64 | .030 | |
| sugar-free, from inst mix, D-Zerta[c] | 65 | 112.3 | 0.4 | 0.0 | 2 | | 1 | .18 | .05 | 6 | 68 | 159 | 23 | .60 | |
| *1/2 cup* | 130 | 4.6 | 11.3 | 0.3 | | 252 | .05 | 0.1 | .46 | .41 | 324 | 136 | .31 | .076 | |
| sugar-free, from inst mix, Featherweight—*1/2 cup* | 80 | | 0.5 | | 2 | | 1 | .17 | .05 | 10 | 100 | 190 | 20 | .50 | |
| | 134 | 5.0 | 15.0 | | | 240 | .05 | 0.2 | .46 | .42 | 440 | 194 | 1.85 | .010 | |
| sugar-free, from inst mix, Jell-O[b] | 96 | 109.4 | 2.7 | 0.1 | 9 | | 1 | .21 | .06 | 6 | 414 | 153 | 25 | .59 | |
| *1/2 cup* | 133 | 4.5 | 14.1 | 1.6 | | 252 | .05 | 0.1 | .45 | .40 | 281 | 303 | .34 | .074 | |
| **choc fudge** | | | | | | | | | | | | | | | |
| from inst mix, Jell-O[a] | 174 | 107.5 | 4.6 | 0.2 | 17 | | 1 | .21 | .06 | 6 | 479 | 150 | 31 | .67 | |
| *1/2 cup* | 150 | 4.6 | 30.7 | 2.7 | | 156 | .05 | 0.2 | .44 | .39 | 356 | 387 | .58 | .130 | |
| sugar-free, from inst mix, Jell-O[b] | 100 | 109.7 | 3.0 | 0.1 | 9 | | 1 | .22 | .06 | 6 | 366 | 155 | 35 | .72 | |
| *1/2 cup* | 135 | 4.9 | 15.2 | 1.7 | | 254 | .05 | 0.2 | .45 | .41 | 404 | 318 | .66 | .147 | |
| **choc fudge mousse, from inst mix, Jell-O[a]** | 139 | 54.2 | 5.6 | 0.2 | 9 | | 1 | .17 | .05 | 5 | 84 | 119 | 36 | .72 | |
| *1/2 cup* | 86 | 5.2 | 19.6 | 4.0 | | 82 | .04 | 0.2 | .39 | .36 | 369 | 137 | .81 | .184 | |
| **choc mousse, from inst mix, Jell-O[a]** | 141 | 54.2 | 5.4 | 0.1 | 9 | | 1 | .17 | .05 | 5 | 83 | 119 | 31 | .66 | |
| *1/2 cup* | 86 | 4.9 | 20.2 | 3.9 | | 81 | .04 | 0.2 | .39 | .35 | 233 | 129 | .58 | .142 | |
| **choc tapioca, from inst mix, Jell-O[a]** | 169 | 108.5 | 4.6 | 0.2 | 17 | | 1 | .21 | .06 | 6 | 169 | 150 | 31 | .67 | |
| *1/2 cup* | 147 | 4.7 | 27.6 | 2.9 | | 157 | .05 | 0.2 | .44 | .39 | 294 | 143 | .49 | .123 | |
| **coconut cream, from inst mix, Jell-O[a]** | 178 | 107.8 | 6.4 | 0.2 | 17 | | 1 | .20 | .05 | 6 | 356 | 148 | 20 | .46 | |
| *1/2 cup* | 147 | 4.3 | 26.7 | 4.5 | | 154 | .05 | 0.1 | .44 | .38 | 209 | 293 | .22 | .038 | |
| **french van, from inst mix, Jell-O[a]** | 165 | 108.3 | 4.3 | 0.2 | 17 | | 1 | .20 | .05 | 6 | 439 | 149 | 17 | .47 | |
| *1/2 cup* | 147 | 4.0 | 28.4 | 2.6 | | 154 | .05 | 0.1 | .44 | .39 | 187 | 315 | .09 | .017 | |
| **golden egg custard, from inst mix, Jell-O[a]** | 160 | 107.5 | 5.4 | 0.3 | 73 | | 1 | .31 | .09 | 11 | 197 | 199 | 26 | .69 | |
| *1/2 cup* | 143 | 5.2 | 23.1 | 3.0 | | 230 | .08 | 0.2 | .69 | .80 | 283 | 173 | .34 | .027 | |
| **lemon, from inst mix, Jell-O[a]** | 168 | 107.7 | 4.3 | 0.2 | 17 | | 1 | .20 | .05 | 6 | 396 | 147 | 17 | .46 | |
| *1/2 cup* | 147 | 4.0 | 29.1 | 2.6 | | 154 | .05 | 0.1 | .44 | .38 | 187 | 314 | .10 | .019 | |
| **milk choc, from inst mix, Jell-O[a]** | 178 | 107.5 | 4.7 | 0.2 | 17 | | 1 | .21 | .06 | 6 | 506 | 154 | 26 | .60 | |
| *1/2 cup* | 150 | 4.5 | 30.9 | 2.8 | | 161 | .05 | 0.1 | .45 | .40 | 281 | 381 | .39 | .090 | |
| **pineapple cream, from inst mix, Jell-O[a]** | 165 | 108.3 | 4.3 | 0.2 | 17 | | 1 | .20 | .05 | 6 | 395 | 147 | 17 | .47 | |
| *1/2 cup* | 147 | 4.0 | 28.6 | 2.6 | | 154 | .05 | 0.1 | .44 | .39 | 187 | 314 | .09 | .017 | |

[a] Prepared w/ vitamin D fortified whole milk.
[b] Prepared w/ vitamin A & D fortified 2% low fat milk.
[c] Prepared w/ vitamin A & D fortified skim milk.

| | KCAL / WT (g) | H₂O (g) / PRO (g) | FAT (g) / CHO (g) | PUFA (g) / SFA (g) | CHOL (mg) / DFIB (g) | A (RE) / A (IU) | C (mg) / B-1 (mg) | B-2 (mg) / NIA (mg) | B-6 (mg) / B-12 (mcg) | FOL (mcg) / PANT (mg) | Na (mg) / K (mg) | Ca (mg) / P (mg) | Mg (mg) / Fe (mg) | Zn (mg) / Cu (mg) | Mn (mg) |
|---|---|---|---|---|---|---|---|---|---|---|---|---|---|---|---|
| **pistachio** | | | | | | | | | | | | | | | |
| from inst mix, Jell-O[a] | 170 | 107.8 | 4.8 | 0.3 | 17 | | 1 | .21 | .05 | 7 | 442 | 149 | 19 | .46 | |
| *1/2 cup* | 147 | 4.2 | 28.2 | 2.6 | | 154 | .05 | 0.1 | .44 | .39 | 195 | 319 | .15 | .027 | |
| sugar-free, from inst mix, Jell-O[b] | 95 | 108.9 | 3.0 | 0.2 | 9 | | 1 | .21 | .05 | 7 | 427 | 152 | 20 | .48 | |
| *1/2 cup* | 131 | 4.3 | 12.8 | 1.5 | | 250 | .05 | 0.1 | .44 | .39 | 200 | 307 | .13 | .021 | |
| **prune whip, homemade** | 203 | 74.4 | 0.3 | | | | 3 | .18 | | | 213 | 29 | | | |
| *1 cup* | 130 | 5.7 | 48.0 | | | 600 | .03 | 0.7 | | | 377 | 43 | 1.70 | | |
| **rennin dessert** | | | | | | | | | | | | | | | |
| caramel/fruit/van, from mix | 238 | 199.3 | 9.0 | | | | 3 | .40 | | | 115 | 293 | | | |
| *1 cup* | 250 | 8.0 | 32.0 | 5.0 | | 380 | .08 | 0.3 | | | 320 | 230 | .00 | | |
| choc, from mix | 260 | 198.6 | 9.7 | | | | 3 | .38 | | | 133 | 311 | | | |
| *1 cup* | 255 | 8.7 | 36.0 | 5.3 | | 360 | .08 | 0.3 | | | 319 | 245 | .00 | | |
| homemade | 227 | 206.8 | 8.9 | | | | 3 | .38 | | | 209 | 283 | | | |
| *1 cup* | 255 | 7.9 | 29.6 | 4.9 | | 360 | .08 | 0.3 | | | 321 | 212 | .00 | | |
| **rice, from inst mix, Jell-O[a]** | 175 | 108.9 | 4.1 | 0.2 | 17 | | 1 | .20 | .05 | 6 | 158 | 150 | 20 | .55 | |
| *1/2 cup* | 149 | 4.8 | 30.0 | 2.6 | | 154 | .11 | 0.6 | .44 | .41 | 187 | 125 | .54 | .016 | |
| **rice w/ raisins, homemade** | 387 | 174.4 | 8.2 | | | | 0 | .37 | | | 188 | 260 | | | |
| *1 cup* | 265 | 9.5 | 70.8 | 4.5 | | 290 | .08 | 0.5 | | | 469 | 249 | 1.10 | | |
| **tapioca cream, homemade** | 221 | 118.5 | 8.4 | | | | 2 | .30 | | | 257 | 173 | | | |
| *1 cup* | 165 | 8.3 | 28.2 | 3.9 | | 480 | .07 | 0.2 | | | 223 | 180 | .70 | | |
| **vanilla** | | | | | | | | | | | | | | | |
| (blancmange), homemade | 283 | 193.8 | 9.9 | | | | 2 | .41 | | | 166 | 298 | | | |
| *1 cup* | 255 | 8.9 | 40.5 | 5.5 | | 410 | .08 | 0.3 | | | 352 | 232 | .00 | | |
| from inst mix, Jell-O[a] | 168 | 107.7 | 4.3 | 0.2 | 17 | | 1 | .20 | .05 | 6 | 441 | 147 | 17 | .48 | |
| *1/2 cup* | 147 | 4.0 | 29.0 | 2.6 | | 154 | .05 | 0.1 | .44 | .38 | 187 | 313 | .10 | .019 | |
| Rich's | 129 | 58.5 | 5.9 | | | | | .08 | | | 162 | 26 | 5 | .17 | |
| *3 oz* | 85 | 1.6 | 18.4 | | | | .02 | 0.0 | | | 85 | 48 | .17 | .030 | |
| sugar-free, from inst mix, D-Zerta | 69 | 112.4 | 0.2 | 0.0 | 2 | | 1 | .17 | .05 | 6 | 66 | 154 | 14 | .49 | |
| *1/2 cup* | 130 | 4.3 | 12.1 | 0.1 | | 251 | .04 | 0.1 | .46 | .40 | 205 | 124 | .05 | .016 | |
| sugar-free, from inst mix, Jell-O[b] | 90 | 109.5 | 2.4 | 0.1 | 9 | | 1 | .20 | .05 | 6 | 425 | 150 | 17 | .48 | |
| *1/2 cup* | 131 | 4.2 | 12.9 | 1.5 | | 251 | .05 | 0.1 | .45 | .39 | 193 | 304 | .08 | .010 | |
| **vanilla/butterscotch. sugar-free, from inst mix, Featherweight—*1/2 cup*** | 80 | | 0.3 | | 2 | | 1 | .17 | .05 | 10 | 100 | 190 | 14 | .49 | |
| | 134 | 4.0 | 16.0 | | | 240 | .05 | 0.1 | .46 | .40 | 330 | 170 | 1.60 | .010 | |
| **vanilla tapioca, from inst mix, Jell-O[a]** | 160 | 108.3 | 4.1 | 0.2 | 17 | | 1 | .20 | .05 | 6 | 170 | 147 | 17 | .48 | |
| *1/2 cup* | 145 | 4.0 | 27.4 | 2.6 | | 154 | .05 | 0.1 | .44 | .38 | 186 | 115 | .09 | .055 | |

## 8.15. SAUCES, SYRUPS & TOPPINGS FOR DESSERTS

| | KCAL / WT (g) | H₂O (g) / PRO (g) | FAT (g) / CHO (g) | PUFA (g) / SFA (g) | CHOL (mg) / DFIB (g) | A (RE) / A (IU) | C (mg) / B-1 (mg) | B-2 (mg) / NIA (mg) | B-6 (mg) / B-12 (mcg) | FOL (mcg) / PANT (mg) | Na (mg) / K (mg) | Ca (mg) / P (mg) | Mg (mg) / Fe (mg) | Zn (mg) / Cu (mg) | Mn (mg) |
|---|---|---|---|---|---|---|---|---|---|---|---|---|---|---|---|
| **cake & cookies decorator, Pillsbury** | | | | | | | | | | | | | | | |
| all flavors except choc | 71 | 2.5 | 2.0 | | | | 0 | .00 | | | 0 | 0 | | | |
| *1 T* | 18 | 0.0 | 13.7 | | | 0 | .00 | 0.0 | | | 5 | 0 | .00 | | |
| choc | 61 | 2.8 | 1.8 | | | | 0 | .00 | | | 0 | 0 | | | |
| *1 T* | 16 | 0.1 | 11.4 | | | 0 | .00 | 0.0 | | | 27 | 11 | .13 | | |
| **choc syrup** | 92 | 11.9 | 0.8 | | | | 0 | .03 | | | 20 | 6 | | | |
| *2 T* | 38 | 0.9 | 23.5 | 0.4 | | 0 | .01 | 0.2 | | | 106 | 35 | .60 | | |
| **choc flavored syrup, Hershey** | 73 | | 0.4 | | | | | .01 | | | 18 | 4 | 20 | .22 | .112 |
| *2 T (1 oz)* | 28 | 0.9 | 16.4 | | | 6 | .01 | 0.1 | | | 48 | 36 | .50 | .140 | |
| **choc fudge topping, Hershey** | 95 | | 3.8 | | | | | .06 | | | 36 | 28 | 13 | .22 | .084 |
| *2 T (1 oz)* | 28 | 1.3 | 14.3 | | | 25 | .01 | 0.1 | | | 60 | 48 | .34 | .084 | |
| **fudge topping** | 124 | 9.5 | 5.1 | | | | 0 | .08 | | | 33 | 48 | | | |
| *2 T* | 38 | 1.9 | 20.3 | 2.9 | | 60 | .02 | 0.2 | | | 107 | 60 | .50 | | |
| **fudge topping, Kraft** | 65 | 6.1 | 2.5 | 0.5 | 0 | | 0 | .02 | .00 | | 41 | 15 | 1 | .10 | |
| *1 T* | 20 | 0.4 | 10.3 | 0.2 | | 1 | .00 | 0.0 | .03 | .02 | 20 | 19 | .03 | .042 | |
| **icing/frosting, from mix** | | | | | | | | | | | | | | | |
| choc fudge | 293 | 11.9 | 11.1 | | | | 0 | .03 | | | 121 | 13 | | | |
| *1/4 cup* | 78 | 1.7 | 51.9 | 2.7 | | 210 | .00 | 0.1 | | | 49 | 51 | .78 | | |
| coconut almond, Pillsbury | 160 | | 10.0 | | | | | | | | 85 | | | | |
| *amt for 1/12 cake* | | 1.0 | 16.0 | | | | | | | | 85 | | | | |

[a] Prepared w/ vitamin D fortified whole milk.   [b] Prepared w/ vitamin A & D fortified 2% low fat milk.

| | | | | | | | Vitamins | | | | | Minerals | | |
|---|---|---|---|---|---|---|---|---|---|---|---|---|---|---|
| KCAL | H₂O (g) | FAT (g) | PUFA (g) | CHOL (mg) | A (RE) | C (mg) | B-2 (mg) | B-6 (mg) | FOL (mcg) | Na (mg) | Ca (mg) | Mg (mg) | Zn (mg) | Mn (mg) |
| WT (g) | PRO (g) | CHO (g) | SFA (g) | DFIB (g) | A (IU) | B-1 (mg) | NIA (mg) | B-12 (mcg) | PANT (mg) | K (mg) | P (mg) | Fe (mg) | Cu (mg) | |
| **coconut pecan, Pillsbury** | | | | | | | | | | | | | | |
| 150 | | 7.0 | | | | | | | | 105 | | | | |
| *amt for 1/12 cake* — | 1.0 | 20.0 | | | | | | | | 60 | | | | |
| **fluffy white, Pillsbury** | | | | | | | | | | | | | | |
| 60 | | 0.0 | | | | 0 | .01 | | | 63 | 1 | | | |
| *amt for 1/12 cake* — | 0.3 | 14.6 | | | 0 | .00 | 0.0 | | | 4 | 1 | .00 | | |
| **icing/frosting, homemade** | | | | | | | | | | | | | | |
| choc — 259 | 9.9 | 9.6 | | | | 0 | .07 | | | 42 | 41 | | | |
| *1/4 cup* — 69 | 2.2 | 46.4 | 5.3 | | 145 | .01 | 0.1 | | | 134 | 76 | .83 | | |
| white — 300 | 8.9 | 5.2 | | | | 0 | .01 | | | 39 | 12 | | | |
| *1/4 cup* — 80 | 0.4 | 65.1 | 2.9 | | 215 | .00 | 0.0 | | | 16 | 10 | .00 | | |
| **icing/frosting mix** | | | | | | | | | | | | | | |
| choc, Duncan Hines — 160 | 7.0 | 6.6 | | 7 | | | .02 | | | 82 | 6 | | | |
| *1/12 pkg* — 39 | 0.5 | 24.6 | | | | .01 | 0.1 | | | | | .90 | | |
| dark dutch fudge, Duncan Hines — 156 | 7.4 | 6.6 | | 7 | | | .01 | | | 94 | 7 | | | |
| *1/12 pkg* — 39 | 0.6 | 23.8 | | | | .00 | 0.1 | | | | | .78 | | |
| milk choc, Duncan Hines — 156 | 7.0 | 6.6 | | 7 | | | .02 | | | 82 | 7 | | | |
| *1/12 pkg* — 39 | 0.7 | 24.2 | | | | | 0.1 | | | | | .66 | | |
| van, Duncan Hines — 158 | 7.0 | 6.6 | | 7 | | | .01 | | | 84 | 4 | | | |
| *1/12 pkg* — 39 | 0.1 | 25.0 | | | | .00 | 0.0 | | | | | .16 | | |
| **icing/frosting, ready-to-spread** | | | | | | | | | | | | | | |
| all flavors, creamy deluxe, General Mills[a] *1/12 tub* — 164 | | 7.3 | | | | | | | | 89 | | | | |
| 33 | 1.0 | 23.9 | | | | | | | | 53 | | | | |
| caramel pecan, Pillsbury — 159 | 9.5 | 8.7 | | | | 0 | .00 | | | 70 | 2 | | | |
| *amt for 1/12 cake* — 38 | 0.2 | 21.3 | | | 3 | .02 | 0.0 | | | 35 | 6 | .06 | | |
| choc chip, Pillsbury — 151 | 5.0 | 5.2 | | | | 0 | .00 | | | 67 | 1 | | | |
| *amt for 1/12 cake* — 37 | 0.1 | 26.3 | | | 1 | .00 | 0.0 | | | 19 | 5 | .08 | | |
| choc fudge, Pillsbury — 150 | 6.8 | 6.5 | | | | 0 | .00 | | | 82 | 1 | | | |
| *amt for 1/12 cake* — 38 | 0.5 | 23.7 | | | 0 | .00 | 0.1 | | | 93 | 39 | .46 | | |
| choc mint, Pillsbury — 148 | 7.6 | 6.5 | | | | 0 | .00 | | | 83 | 1 | | | |
| *amt for 1/12 cake* — 38 | 0.5 | 22.8 | | | 0 | .00 | 0.1 | | | 106 | 16 | .91 | | |
| coconut almond, Pillsbury — 151 | 7.4 | 9.1 | | | | 0 | .02 | | | 59 | 7 | | | |
| *amt for 1/12 cake* — 35 | 0.6 | 17.1 | | | 0 | .01 | 0.1 | | | 59 | 17 | .23 | | |
| coconut pecan, Pillsbury — 160 | 7.8 | 10.0 | | | | 0 | .00 | | | 63 | 5 | | | |
| *amt for 1/12 cake* — 37 | 0.5 | 17.8 | | | 3 | .02 | 0.0 | | | 57 | 14 | .19 | | |
| cream cheese, Pillsbury — 160 | 5.3 | 6.2 | | | | 0 | .00 | | | 117 | 1 | | | |
| *amt for 1/12 cake* — 38 | 0.0 | 26.2 | | | 0 | .00 | 0.0 | | | 10 | 1 | .02 | | |
| double dutch, Pillsbury — 141 | 8.1 | 6.3 | | | | 0 | .00 | | | 45 | 1 | | | |
| *amt for 1/12 cake* — 37 | 0.7 | 21.1 | | | 0 | .00 | 0.1 | | | 134 | 21 | 1.18 | | |
| lemon, Pillsbury — 160 | 5.3 | 6.2 | | | | 0 | .00 | | | 79 | 0 | | | |
| *amt for 1/12 cake* — 38 | 0.0 | 26.2 | | | 0 | .00 | 0.0 | | | 10 | 1 | .02 | | |
| milk choc, Pillsbury — 149 | 6.7 | 6.2 | | | | 0 | .00 | | | 59 | 1 | | | |
| *amt for 1/12 cake* — 37 | 0.4 | 22.9 | | | 0 | .00 | 0.1 | | | 77 | 14 | .38 | | |
| mocha, Pillsbury — 149 | 5.7 | 6.1 | | | | 0 | .00 | | | 58 | 1 | | | |
| *amt for 1/12 cake* — 37 | 0.2 | 23.7 | | | 0 | .00 | 0.1 | | | 63 | 9 | .48 | | |
| sour cream van, Pillsbury — 158 | 4.4 | 5.9 | | | | 1 | .00 | | | 76 | 0 | | | |
| *amt for 1/12 cake* — 37 | 0.0 | 26.3 | | | 31 | .00 | 0.0 | | | 17 | 5 | .00 | | |
| strawberry, Pillsbury — 160 | 5.3 | 6.1 | | | | 0 | .00 | | | 78 | 0 | | | |
| *amt for 1/12 cake* — 38 | 0.0 | 26.2 | | | 0 | .00 | 0.0 | | | 10 | 1 | .02 | | |
| van, Pillsbury — 160 | 5.3 | 6.1 | | | | 0 | .00 | | | 74 | 0 | | | |
| *amt for 1/12 cake* — 38 | 0.0 | 26.2 | | | 0 | .00 | 0.0 | | | 10 | 0 | .02 | | |
| **marshmallow creme, Kraft** — 90 | 4.9 | 0.0 | 0.0 | 0 | 0 | .01 | | .00 | 5 | 17 | 9 | 0 | | |
| *1 oz* — 28 | 0.3 | 23.0 | 0.0 | | 0 | .00 | 0.0 | .00 | .00 | 9 | 3 | .00 | | |

[a] Values are averages for 20 flavors.

| | | | | | | Vitamins | | | | | Minerals | | | | |
|---|---|---|---|---|---|---|---|---|---|---|---|---|---|---|---|
| | **KCAL** / **WT** (g) | **H₂O** (g) / **PRO** (g) | **FAT** (g) / **CHO** (g) | **PUFA** (g) / **SFA** (g) | **CHOL** (mg) / **DFIB** (g) | **A** (RE) / **A** (IU) | **C** (mg) / **B-1** (mg) | **B-2** (mg) / **NIA** (mg) | **B-6** (mg) / **B-12** (mcg) | **FOL** (mcg) / **PANT** (mg) | **Na** (mg) / **K** (mg) | **Ca** (mg) / **P** (mg) | **Mg** (mg) / **Fe** (mg) | **Zn** (mg) / **Cu** (mg) | **Mn** (mg) |

# 9. EGGS, EGG DISHES & EGG SUBSTITUTES

## 9.1. EGGS, CHICKEN

| Item | KCAL/WT | H₂O/PRO | FAT/CHO | PUFA/SFA | CHOL/DFIB | A(RE)/A(IU) | C/B-1 | B-2/NIA | B-6/B-12 | FOL/PANT | Na/K | Ca/P | Mg/Fe | Zn/Cu | Mn |
|---|---|---|---|---|---|---|---|---|---|---|---|---|---|---|---|
| **boiled, hard/soft** | 79 | 37.3 | 5.6 | 0.7 | 274 | 78 | 0 | .14 | .06 | 24 | 69 | 28 | 6 | .72 | |
| *1 large* | 50 | 6.1 | 0.6 | 1.7 | 0.0 | 260 | .04 | 0.0 | .66 | .86 | 65 | 90 | 1.04 | | |
| **fried** | 83 | 33.1 | 6.4 | 0.7 | 246 | 83 | 0 | .13 | .05 | 22 | 144 | 26 | 5 | .64 | |
| *1 large* | 46 | 5.4 | 0.5 | 2.4 | 0.0 | 286 | .03 | 0.0 | .58 | .76 | 58 | 80 | .92 | | |
| **omelet, plain** | 95 | 48.8 | 7.1 | 0.7 | 248 | 89 | 0 | .16 | .06 | 22 | 155 | 47 | 8 | .70 | |
| *1 large egg* | 64 | 6.0 | 1.4 | 2.8 | 0.0 | 311 | .04 | 0.0 | .64 | .82 | 85 | 97 | .93 | | |
| **poached** | 79 | 37.1 | 5.6 | 0.7 | 273 | 78 | 0 | .13 | .05 | 24 | 146 | 28 | 6 | .72 | |
| *1 large* | 50 | 6.0 | 0.6 | 1.7 | 0.0 | 259 | .04 | 0.0 | .62 | .86 | 65 | 90 | 1.04 | | |
| **scrambled w/ milk & fat** | 95 | 48.8 | 7.1 | 0.7 | 248 | 89 | 0 | .16 | .06 | 22 | 155 | 47 | 8 | .70 | |
| *1 large egg* | 64 | 6.0 | 1.4 | 2.8 | 0.0 | 311 | .04 | 0.0 | .64 | .82 | 85 | 97 | .93 | | |
| **white, fresh/frzn** | 16 | 29.1 | 0.0 | 0.0 | 0 | 0 | 0 | .09 | .00 | 5 | 50 | 4 | 3 | .01 | .002 |
| *white of 1 large egg* | 33 | 3.4 | 0.4 | 0.0 | 0.0 | 0 | .00 | 0.0 | .02 | .08 | 45 | 4 | .01 | .009 | |
| **whole, dried, stabilized (glucose reduced)** | 31 | 0.1 | 2.2 | 0.3 | 101 | 31 | 0 | .06 | .02 | 10 | 27 | 11 | 2 | .28 | |
| *1 T* | 5 | 2.4 | 0.1 | 0.7 | 0.0 | 102 | .02 | 0.0 | .53 | .34 | 26 | 86 | .41 | | |
| **whole, fresh/frzn** | 79 | 37.3 | 5.6 | 0.7 | 274 | 78 | 0 | .15 | .06 | 32 | 69 | 28 | 6 | .72 | .021 |
| *1 large* | 50 | 6.1 | 0.6 | 1.7 | 0.0 | 260 | .04 | 0.0 | .77 | .86 | 65 | 90 | 1.04 | .033 | |
| **yolk, fresh** | 63 | 8.3 | 5.6 | 0.7 | 272 | 94 | 0 | .07 | .05 | 26 | 8 | 26 | 3 | .58 | .019 |
| *yolk of 1 large egg* | 17 | 2.8 | 0.0 | 1.7 | 0.0 | 313 | .04 | 0.0 | .65 | .75 | 15 | 86 | .95 | .024 | |

## 9.2. EGGS, OTHER

| Item | KCAL/WT | H₂O/PRO | FAT/CHO | PUFA/SFA | CHOL/DFIB | A(RE)/A(IU) | C/B-1 | B-2/NIA | B-6/B-12 | FOL/PANT | Na/K | Ca/P | Mg/Fe | Zn/Cu | Mn |
|---|---|---|---|---|---|---|---|---|---|---|---|---|---|---|---|
| **duck, whole** | 130 | 49.6 | 9.6 | 0.9 | 619 | | 0 | .28 | .18 | 56 | 102 | 45 | 12 | .99 | |
| *1 egg* | 70 | 9.0 | 1.0 | 2.6 | 0.0 | 930 | .11 | 0.1 | 3.78 | | 156 | 154 | 2.70 | | |
| **goose, whole** | 276 | 101.4 | 19.1 | 2.4 | | | 0 | | | | | | | | |
| *1 egg* | 144 | 20.0 | 1.9 | 5.2 | 0.0 | | | | | | | | | | |
| **quail, whole** | 14 | 6.7 | 1.0 | 0.1 | 76 | | 0 | .07 | .01 | | | 6 | | | |
| *1 egg* | 9 | 1.2 | 0.0 | 0.3 | 0.0 | 27 | .01 | 0.0 | | | | 20 | .33 | | |
| **turkey, whole** | 135 | 57.3 | 9.4 | 1.3 | 737 | | 0 | .37 | | | | | | | |
| *1 egg* | 79 | 10.8 | 0.9 | 2.9 | 0.0 | | .09 | 0.0 | | | | 134 | 3.24 | | |

## 9.3. EGG (CHICKEN) DISHES

| Item | KCAL/WT | H₂O/PRO | FAT/CHO | PUFA/SFA | CHOL/DFIB | A(RE)/A(IU) | C/B-1 | B-2/NIA | B-6/B-12 | FOL/PANT | Na/K | Ca/P | Mg/Fe | Zn/Cu | Mn |
|---|---|---|---|---|---|---|---|---|---|---|---|---|---|---|---|
| **omelette** | | | | | | | | | | | | | | | |
| cheddar cheese, frzn, Am Hosp Co | 313 | | 27.1 | | 328 | | 0 | .00 | | | 398 | 245 | | | |
| *4 oz* | 113 | 15.9 | 1.3 | | | | .07 | | | | 128 | | 1.58 | | |
| mushroom & cheese, frzn, Am Hosp Co—3 oz | 152 | | 11.6 | | 245 | | 0 | .16 | | | 138 | 59 | | | |
| *(3 oz)* | 85 | 9.8 | 1.9 | | | 334 | .04 | 0.3 | | | 101 | | .90 | | |
| mushroom, cheese & onion, frzn, Am Hosp Co—4 oz | 252 | | 20.2 | | 373 | | 1 | .29 | | | 310 | 145 | | | |
| *(4 oz)* | 113 | 15.3 | 2.3 | | | 653 | .07 | | | | 160 | | 1.60 | | |
| plain, frzn, Am Hosp Co | 199 | | 17.7 | | 298 | | 0 | .03 | | | 222 | 41 | | | |
| *3 oz* | 85 | 8.9 | 0.9 | | | 767 | .07 | 0.1 | | | 100 | | 1.39 | | |
| spanish, frzn, Am Hosp Co[a] | 199 | | 16.3 | | 365 | | 6 | .23 | | | 197 | 47 | | | |
| *4 oz* | 113 | 10.3 | 2.8 | | | 671 | .07 | 0.3 | | | 164 | | 1.60 | | |
| western, frzn, Am Hosp Co[b] | 207 | | 16.7 | | 366 | | 9 | .24 | | | 281 | 46 | | | |
| *4 oz* | 113 | 11.1 | 3.0 | | | 611 | .09 | 0.4 | | | 164 | | 1.60 | | |
| **quiche** | | | | | | | | | | | | | | | |
| bacon & onion, Pour-a-Quiche | 230 | | 18.0 | | 240 | | | | | | 385 | | | | |
| *4.3 oz* | 123 | 13.0 | 6.0 | | | | | | | | 170 | | | | |
| florentine, frzn, Am Hosp Co | 410 | | 19.6 | | 113 | | | | | | 652 | | | | |
| *7 oz* | 198 | 28.1 | 30.2 | | | | | | | | 448 | | | | |
| ham, Pour-a-Quiche | 230 | | 17.0 | | 235 | | | | | | 360 | | | | |
| *4.3 oz* | 123 | 13.0 | 4.0 | | | | | | | | 165 | | | | |
| lorraine, frzn, Am Hosp Co | 531 | | 19.9 | | 210 | | | | | | 1313 | | | | |
| *7 oz* | 198 | 24.8 | 63.3 | | | | | | | | 421 | | | | |
| spinach & onion, Pour-a-Quiche | 220 | | 16.0 | | 230 | | | | | | 365 | | | | |
| *4.3 oz* | 123 | 12.0 | 6.0 | | | | | | | | 210 | | | | |

[a] Contains tomatoes, onions, mushrooms, green peppers & celery.

[b] Contains onions, mushrooms, ham, red & green peppers & tomatoes.

| | KCAL / WT (g) | H2O (g) / PRO (g) | FAT (g) / CHO (g) | PUFA (g) / SFA (g) | CHOL (mg) / DFIB (g) | A (RE) / A (IU) | C (mg) / B-1 (mg) | B-2 (mg) / NIA (mg) | B-6 (mg) / B-12 (mcg) | FOL (mcg) / PANT (mg) | Na (mg) / K (mg) | Ca (mg) / P (mg) | Mg (mg) / Fe (mg) | Zn (mg) / Cu (mg) | Mn (mg) |
|---|---|---|---|---|---|---|---|---|---|---|---|---|---|---|---|
| **three cheeses, Pour-a-Quiche** | 236 | | 18.7 | | 250 | | 1 | .30 | | | 326 | 289 | | | |
| *4.3 oz* | 123 | 12.9 | 4.2 | | | 696 | .06 | 0.1 | | | 154 | 253 | .96 | | |
| **scrambled egg croquette, frzn, Am Hosp Co—3 oz** | 190 | | 13.2 | | 289 | | 3 | .14 | | | 272 | 110 | | | |
| | 85 | 8.3 | 9.6 | | | 819 | .23 | 1.3 | | | 113 | | 1.88 | | |
| **scrambled egg w/ bacon pastry wrap, frzn, Am Hosp Co—4.5 oz** | 277 | | 19.8 | | 247 | | 11 | .23 | | | 363 | 41 | | | |
| | 128 | 7.9 | 16.7 | | | 369 | .17 | | | | 119 | | 1.99 | | |
| **souffle** | | | | | | | | | | | | | | | |
| cheese, homemade | 207 | 61.8 | 16.2 | | | | 0 | .23 | | | 346 | 191 | | | |
| *1 cup* | 95 | 9.4 | 5.9 | 8.2 | | 760 | .05 | 0.2 | | | 115 | 185 | 1.00 | | |
| spinach[a] | 218 | 100.6 | 18.4 | 3.1 | 184 | 675 | 3 | .31 | .12 | 62 | 763 | 230 | 37 | 1.29 | |
| *1 cup* | 136 | 11.0 | 2.8 | 7.1 | | 3461 | .09 | 0.5 | .68 | | 202 | 231 | 1.34 | .120 | |

## 9.4. EGG SUBSTITUTES

| | KCAL / WT (g) | H2O (g) / PRO (g) | FAT (g) / CHO (g) | PUFA (g) / SFA (g) | CHOL (mg) / DFIB (g) | A (RE) / A (IU) | C (mg) / B-1 (mg) | B-2 (mg) / NIA (mg) | B-6 (mg) / B-12 (mcg) | FOL (mcg) / PANT (mg) | Na (mg) / K (mg) | Ca (mg) / P (mg) | Mg (mg) / Fe (mg) | Zn (mg) / Cu (mg) | Mn (mg) |
|---|---|---|---|---|---|---|---|---|---|---|---|---|---|---|---|
| **by type** | | | | | | | | | | | | | | | |
| frzn[b] | 96 | 43.9 | 6.7 | 3.7 | 1 | 81 | | .23 | .08 | | 120 | 44 | | | .59 |
| *1/4 cup* | 60 | 6.8 | 1.9 | 1.2 | 0.0 | 810 | .07 | | | 1.00 | 128 | 43 | 1.19 | | |
| liquid[c] | 40 | 38.9 | 1.6 | 0.8 | 0 | 102 | 0 | .14 | | | 33 | 25 | | | .61 |
| *1.5 fl oz* | 47 | 5.6 | 0.3 | 0.3 | 0.0 | 1015 | .05 | .05 | .14 | 1.27 | 155 | 57 | .99 | | |
| powdered[d] | 44 | 0.4 | 1.3 | 0.2 | 57 | | 0 | .17 | | | 79 | 32 | | | |
| *0.35 oz* | 10 | 5.5 | 2.2 | 0.4 | 0.0 | 122 | .02 | 0.0 | | | 74 | 47 | .31 | | |
| **by brand** | | | | | | | | | | | | | | | |
| country morning, Land O'Lakes | 173 | | 12.1 | | 594 | | 0 | .52 | | | 180 | 52 | | | |
| *1/2 cup* | 121 | 14.6 | 1.3 | | | 1138 | .06 | | | | 133 | 197 | 2.07 | | |
| egg beaters, Fleischmann's | 25 | | 0.0 | | 0 | | | | | | 80 | | | | |
| *1/4 cup* | | 5.0 | 1.0 | | | | | | | | 85 | | | | |
| egg beaters w/ cheez, Fleischmann's | 130 | | 6.0 | | 5 | | | | | | 440 | | | | |
| *1/2 cup* | | 14.0 | 3.0 | | | | | | | | 110 | | | | |
| egg vantage lite, frzn, Am Hosp Co[e] | 25 | | 0.0 | | 0 | | | | | | 100 | | | | |
| *1 serving* | 50 | 6.0 | 0.0 | | | | | | | | | | | | |
| scrambled, Land O'Lakes | 143 | | 9.1 | | 466 | | 0 | .38 | | | 173 | 77 | | | |
| *1/2 cup* | 121 | 12.1 | 3.0 | | | 1071 | .06 | | | | 150 | 190 | 1.67 | | |
| scramblers, Morningstar | 58 | 44.5 | 2.4 | 1.5 | 1 | | | .63 | .15 | | 94 | 46 | | | .77 |
| *1/4 cup* | 57 | 6.5 | 2.7 | 0.3 | | 1144 | .33 | | 2.39 | 1.84 | 98 | | 1.28 | | |

# 10. ENTREES & MEALS
## 10.1. BOX MIX ENTREES

| | KCAL / WT (g) | H2O (g) / PRO (g) | FAT (g) / CHO (g) | PUFA (g) / SFA (g) | CHOL (mg) / DFIB (g) | A (RE) / A (IU) | C (mg) / B-1 (mg) | B-2 (mg) / NIA (mg) | B-6 (mg) / B-12 (mcg) | FOL (mcg) / PANT (mg) | Na (mg) / K (mg) | Ca (mg) / P (mg) | Mg (mg) / Fe (mg) | Zn (mg) / Cu (mg) | Mn (mg) |
|---|---|---|---|---|---|---|---|---|---|---|---|---|---|---|---|
| **chicken helper main dishes[f]**—1/5 pkg w/ | 530 | | 27.8 | | | | | | | | 1166 | | | | |
| *chicken & other ingredients* | | 32.6 | 36.8 | | | | | | | | 498 | | | | |
| **chili con carne, concentrate, Oscar Mayer** | 78 | 14.5 | 5.8 | | 14 | 1 | .08 | .06 | 3 | | 426 | 6 | 8 | .65 | |
| *1 oz* | 28 | 3.9 | 2.5 | | | | .02 | 1.1 | 1.05 | .12 | 98 | 37 | .81 | .060 | |
| **burgers, ckd, made w/ burger stuffin, Oscar Mayer** | | | | | | | | | | | | | | | |
| bacon & cheese | 265 | 44.4 | 19.8 | | 71 | | | | | | 588 | 75 | 18 | 4.05 | |
| *1 burger* | 88 | 21.3 | 0.5 | | | | | | | | 246 | 276 | 1.95 | .230 | |
| mexican style | 233 | 52.3 | 18.4 | | 53 | | | | | | 701 | 90 | 18 | 2.94 | |
| *1 burger* | 90 | 15.6 | 1.1 | | | | | | | | 198 | 210 | 2.24 | .350 | |
| mushroom | 224 | 50.6 | 17.3 | | 65 | | | | | | 440 | 75 | 14 | 3.19 | |
| *1 burger* | 87 | 16.1 | 1.2 | | | | | | | | 192 | 217 | 1.62 | .230 | |
| onion | 229 | 48.0 | 16.9 | | 88 | | | | | | 452 | 81 | 17 | 4.10 | |
| *1 burger* | 86 | 16.9 | 2.4 | | | | | | | | 185 | 236 | 1.75 | .160 | |
| pizza | 244 | 51.0 | 18.0 | | 62 | | | | | | 615 | 109 | 16 | 3.32 | |
| *1 burger* | 92 | 18.2 | 2.3 | | | | | | | | 263 | 205 | 2.28 | .220 | |
| **hamburger helper main dishes[g]** | 335 | | 14.9 | | | | | | | | 1027 | | | | |
| *1/5 pkg w/ 1/5 lb ground beef* | | 19.4 | 30.8 | | | | | | | | 436 | | | | |

[a] Contains whole milk, spinach, egg white, cheddar cheese, egg yolk, butter, flour, salt & pepper.
[b] Contains egg white, corn oil & nfdm.
[c] Contains egg white, hydrogenated soybean oil & soy protein.
[d] Contains egg white solids, whole egg solids, sweet whey solids, nfdm & soy protein.
[e] Contains egg white, flavors & colors.
[f] Values are averages for 5 main dishes.
[g] Values are averages for 15 main dishes.

| | KCAL | H₂O (g) | FAT (g) | PUFA (g) | CHOL (mg) | A (RE) | C (mg) | B-2 (mg) | B-6 (mg) | FOL (mcg) | Na (mg) | Ca (mg) | Mg (mg) | Zn (mg) | Mn (mg) |
|---|---|---|---|---|---|---|---|---|---|---|---|---|---|---|---|
| | WT (g) | PRO (g) | CHO (g) | SFA (g) | DFIB (g) | A (IU) | B-1 (mg) | NIA (mg) | B-12 (mcg) | PANT (mg) | K (mg) | P (mg) | Fe (mg) | Cu (mg) | |
| **macaroni & cheese deluxe dinner, prep, Kraft—3/4 cup** | 255 | 90.3 | 7.5 | 0.6 | 18 | | 0 | .24 | .05 | 12 | 652ᵃ | 123 | 29 | 1.27 | .300 |
| | 147 | 10.8 | 36.3 | 4.2 | | 388 | .26 | 1.7 | .23 | .35 | 94 | 345 | 1.94 | .116 | |
| **pasta shells & cheese, prep, Velvetta 3/4 cup** | 261 | 93.9 | 9.8 | 0.7 | 25 | | 0 | .26 | .05 | 22 | 858ᵇ | 186 | 30 | 1.46 | .330 |
| | 150 | 12.1 | 31.8 | 5.4 | | 372 | .23 | 1.8 | .39 | .36 | 117 | 434 | 1.91 | .135 | |
| **pizza, cheese, from Contadina Pizzeria Kit** | | | | | | | | | | | | | | | |
| thick crust 1/4 pizza | 295 | 56.0 | 3.8 | 0.7 | 0 | | 12 | .38 | .00 | 0 | 820 | 63 | 1 | | .01 |
| | 128 | 8.8 | 56.0 | 0.2 | | 782 | .69 | 4.8 | .02 | .04 | 322 | 163 | 3.88 | | |
| thin crust 1/4 pizza | 209 | 53.0 | 3.0 | 0.7 | 0 | | 12 | .26 | .00 | 0 | 650 | 44 | 1 | | .01 |
| | 104 | 6.2 | 39.2 | 0.2 | | 782 | .48 | 3.4 | .01 | .03 | 285 | 114 | 2.87 | | |
| **tuna helper main dishes^c 1/5 pkg w/ 1.3 oz tuna** | 300 | | 13.8 | | | | | | | | 943 | | | | |
| | | 14.8 | 29.0 | | | | | | | | 253 | | | | |

## 10.2. CANNED ENTREES

| | KCAL | H₂O (g) | FAT (g) | PUFA (g) | CHOL (mg) | A (RE) | C (mg) | B-2 (mg) | B-6 (mg) | FOL (mcg) | Na (mg) | Ca (mg) | Mg (mg) | Zn (mg) | Mn (mg) |
|---|---|---|---|---|---|---|---|---|---|---|---|---|---|---|---|
| | WT (g) | PRO (g) | CHO (g) | SFA (g) | DFIB (g) | A (IU) | B-1 (mg) | NIA (mg) | B-12 (mcg) | PANT (mg) | K (mg) | P (mg) | Fe (mg) | Cu (mg) | |
| **beans, baked** | | | | | | | | | | | | | | | |
| w/ bacon, Special Recipe 6.9 oz | 316 | | 12.6 | | | | 5 | .12 | | | 1024 | 120 | | | |
| | 195 | 10.5 | 40.2 | | | 194 | .12 | 0.6 | | | 311 | | 4.20 | | |
| w/ beef 1 cup | 321 | 189.7 | 9.2 | 0.5 | 59 | 57 | 5 | .12 | .24 | | 1264 | 119 | 67 | 3.19 | 1.596 |
| | 266 | 17.0 | 45.0 | 4.5 | | 565 | .14 | 2.5 | .67 | | 851 | 215 | 4.26 | .798 | |
| w/ beef in bbq sce, Special Recipe 6.9 oz | 262 | | 5.7 | | | | 8 | .13 | | | 814 | 85 | | | |
| | 195 | 15.7 | 36.9 | | | 707 | .12 | 1.6 | | | 493 | | 3.70 | | |
| w/ chicken in bbq sce, Special Recipe 6.9 oz | 254 | | 5.4 | | | | 8 | .11 | | | 803 | 90 | | | |
| | 195 | 14.7 | 36.6 | | | 761 | .12 | 1.4 | | | 535 | | 3.20 | | |
| w/ franks 1 cup | 366 | 178.2 | 16.9 | 2.1 | 15 | 40 | 6 | .14 | .12 | 77 | 1105 | 123 | 71 | 4.79 | 1.079 |
| | 257 | 17.3 | 39.6 | 6.0 | 5.9 | 395 | .15 | 2.3 | .87 | .36 | 604 | 267 | 4.45 | .547 | |
| w/ franks, Campbell's 8 oz | 352 | | 13.8 | | | | 5 | .11 | | | 1154 | 122 | | | |
| | 227 | 14.6 | 42.5 | | | 293 | .08 | 2.1 | | | 463 | | 3.90 | | |
| w/ franks in tomato sce, Campbell's 7.9 oz | 346 | | 13.5 | | | | 5 | .11 | | | 1134 | 119 | | | |
| | 223 | 14.4 | 41.8 | | | 288 | .08 | 2.1 | | | 455 | | | | |
| w/ franks, Van Camp's beanee weenee 1 cup | 326 | 173.1 | 15.4 | | | | | .17 | | | 990 | 95 | | | |
| | 235 | 15.2 | 31.7 | | | 294 | .13 | 2.0 | | | 565 | | 4.27 | | |
| w/ pork 1 cup | 268 | 180.8 | 3.9 | 0.5 | 17 | 45 | 5 | .10 | .16 | 92 | 1048 | 133 | 85 | 3.69 | .913 |
| | 253 | 13.1 | 50.6 | 1.5 | 6.6 | 451 | .13 | 1.1 | .06 | .25 | 781 | 274 | 4.31 | .544 | |
| **beef & veg stew 1 cup** | 194 | 202.1 | 7.6 | | | | 7 | .12 | | | 1007 | 29 | | | |
| | 245 | 14.2 | 17.4 | | | 2380 | .07 | 2.5 | | | 426 | 110 | 2.20 | | |
| Bounty 7.6 oz | 144 | | 3.4 | | | | 6 | .10 | | | 987 | 21 | | | |
| | 216 | 12.1 | 16.2 | | | 3936 | .03 | 2.4 | | | 287 | | 2.20 | | |
| Campbell's 7.5 oz | 144 | | 3.5 | | | | 9 | .11 | | | 962 | 23 | | | |
| | 213 | 12.0 | 16.2 | | | 4233 | .02 | 2.1 | | | 337 | | 2.10 | | |
| Wolf Brand scant cup | 179 | 173.8 | 7.5 | | | | | .30 | .17 | 13 | 1043 | 34 | 26 | 2.00 | .000 |
| | 213 | 9.6 | 18.3 | | | 8090 | .02 | 3.5 | 2.00 | .00 | 417 | 136 | 1.89 | .110 | |
| **beef ravioli, Franco-American 7.5 oz** | 223 | | 4.7 | | | | 5 | .18 | | | 1092 | 35 | | | |
| | 213 | 9.0 | 36.1 | | | 1692 | .15 | 2.8 | | | 324 | | 2.30 | | |
| **beef raviolio's, Franco-American 7.5 oz** | 243 | | 7.3 | | | | 8 | .18 | | | 900 | 38 | | | |
| | 213 | 10.2 | 34.2 | | | 467 | .25 | 3.3 | | | 436 | | 2.40 | | |
| **beef sirloin w/ onions, Prego Plus 4 oz** | 150 | | 6.2 | | | | 12 | .05 | | | 402 | 48 | | | |
| | 113 | 4.5 | 19.1 | | | 830 | .05 | 0.8 | | | 285 | | 1.60 | | |
| **chicken a la king, Swanson 5.3 oz** | 182 | | 11.7 | | | | 0 | .15 | | | 657 | 45 | | | |
| | 149 | 10.9 | 8.3 | | | 39 | .04 | 2.8 | | | 177 | | .90 | | |
| **chicken & dumplings, Swanson 7.5 oz** | 220 | | 11.2 | | | | 0 | .12 | | | 963 | 25 | | | |
| | 213 | 11.4 | 18.4 | | | 674 | .03 | 2.7 | | | 151 | | 1.10 | | |
| **chicken & veg stew** | | | | | | | | | | | | | | | |
| Bounty 7.5 oz | 166 | | 7.0 | | | | 5 | .09 | | | 1055 | 29 | | | |
| | 213 | 10.5 | 15.1 | | | 7317 | .03 | 3.4 | | | 315 | | 1.20 | | |
| Swanson 7.6 oz | 164 | | 7.1 | | | | 6 | .09 | | | 962 | 27 | | | |
| | 216 | 9.7 | 15.4 | | | 6236 | .04 | 3.2 | | | 289 | | 1.00 | | |

ᵃ 585 mg Na if prepared w/ unsalted cooking water.
ᵇ 717 mg Na if prepared w/ unsalted cooking water.
ᶜ Values are averages for 6 main dishes.

| Food | KCAL / WT (g) | H₂O (g) / PRO (g) | FAT (g) / CHO (g) | PUFA (g) / SFA (g) | CHOL (mg) / DFIB (g) | A (RE) / A (IU) | C (mg) / B-1 (mg) | B-2 (mg) / NIA (mg) | B-6 (mg) / B-12 (mcg) | FOL (mcg) / PANT (mg) | Na (mg) / K (mg) | Ca (mg) / P (mg) | Mg (mg) / Fe (mg) | Zn (mg) / Cu (mg) | Mn (mg) |
|---|---|---|---|---|---|---|---|---|---|---|---|---|---|---|---|
| chicken w/ veg & pasta, Prego | 120 | | 2.4 | | | | 5 | .07 | | | 965 | 50 | | | |
| 9.49 oz | 269 | 10.8 | 13.7 | | | 2467 | .05 | 2.9 | | | 195 | | 1.30 | | |
| chilee weenee, Van Camp's | 309 | 178.1 | 15.7 | | | | | .20 | | | 1057 | 68 | | | |
| 1 cup | 236 | 14.4 | 27.6 | | | 2228 | .11 | 2.1 | | | 527 | | 4.63 | | |
| **chili-mac** | | | | | | | | | | | | | | | |
| Bounty | 232 | | 10.2 | | | | 4 | .14 | | | 1250 | 74 | | | |
| 7.8 oz | 220 | 10.2 | 25.0 | | | 374 | .11 | 2.3 | | | 306 | | 2.70 | | |
| Wolf Brand | 317 | 154.2 | 19.9 | | | | | .53 | .13 | 40 | 854 | 28 | 28 | 2.00 | .000 |
| scant cup | 213 | 11.5 | 22.9 | | | 2450 | .08 | 3.5 | 2.00 | .00 | 337 | 136 | 1.87 | .170 | |
| **chili w/ beans** | 286 | 192.6 | 14.0 | 0.9 | 43 | 86 | 4 | .27 | .34 | | 1330 | 119 | 115 | 5.10 | |
| 1 cup | 255 | 14.6 | 30.4 | 6.0 | | 860 | .12 | 0.9 | .03 | 3.62 | 932 | 393 | 8.75 | | |
| Bounty | 292 | | 13.4 | | | | 4 | .11 | | | 1101 | 82 | | | |
| 7.8 oz | 220 | 16.2 | 26.7 | | | 1290 | .08 | 1.8 | | | 477 | | 3.40 | | |
| Bounty, hot | 287 | | 12.5 | | | | 3 | .10 | | | 1189 | 88 | | | |
| 7.8 oz | 220 | 16.3 | 27.3 | | | 1356 | .08 | 1.7 | | | 477 | | 3.50 | | |
| Van Camp's | 352 | 176.3 | 23.2 | | | | | .22 | | | 1215 | 63 | | | |
| 1 cup | 235 | 14.9 | 20.9 | | | 3428 | .09 | 2.4 | | | 537 | | 4.83 | | |
| Wolf Brand | 345 | 161.6 | 22.0 | | | | | .82 | .25 | 32 | 1013 | 59 | 57 | 2.00 | .000 |
| 1 cup | 227 | 15.0 | 21.8 | | | 3940 | .09 | 2.7 | .00 | .00 | 633 | 252 | 2.54 | .230 | |
| Wolf Brand, extra spicy | 324 | 151.5 | 20.6 | | | | | .77 | .23 | 30 | 926 | 55 | 53 | 2.00 | .000 |
| scant cup | 213 | 14.1 | 20.6 | | | 3690 | .08 | 2.5 | .00 | .00 | 593 | 236 | 2.38 | .220 | |
| **chili w/o beans** | | | | | | | | | | | | | | | |
| Van Camp's | 412 | 169.6 | 33.5 | | | | | .28 | | | 1499 | 46 | | | |
| 1 cup | 231 | 15.4 | 12.1 | | | 4934 | .06 | 3.2 | | | 370 | | 3.48 | | |
| Wolf Brand | 387 | 157.5 | 26.6 | | | | | 1.27 | .10 | 25 | 1042 | 64 | 30 | 2.00 | .000 |
| 1 cup | 227 | 20.7 | 16.2 | | | 4770 | .11 | 3.9 | 1.00 | .00 | 717 | 146 | 3.86 | .130 | |
| Wolf Brand, extra spicy | 363 | 147.7 | 24.9 | | | | | 1.19 | .09 | 23 | 962 | 60 | 28 | 2.00 | .000 |
| scant cup | 213 | 19.4 | 15.3 | | | 4470 | .10 | 3.6 | 1.00 | .00 | 672 | 137 | 3.62 | .120 | |
| cowpeas, common w/ pork | 199 | 186.2 | 3.8 | 0.6 | 17 | 0 | 1 | .12 | | | 840 | 41 | 104 | 2.49 | .941 |
| 1 cup | 240 | 6.6 | 39.7 | 1.5 | | 0 | .15 | 1.0 | .03 | | 427 | 231 | 3.41 | .408 | |
| dumplings & chicken, Bounty | 200 | | 9.2 | | | 0 | | .10 | | | 1047 | 26 | | | |
| 7.5 oz | 213 | 9.5 | 19.7 | | | 2708 | .03 | 2.6 | | | 131 | | 1.10 | | |
| linguini w/ white clam sce, Prego | 391 | | 10.5 | | | | 3 | .20 | | | 753 | 45 | | | |
| 11 oz | 312 | 17.8 | 56.4 | | | 0 | .60 | 2.5 | | | 107 | | 6.20 | | |
| macaroni & cheese | 228 | 192.5 | 9.6 | | | | 0 | .24 | | | 730 | 199 | | | |
| 1 cup | 240 | 9.4 | 25.7 | 4.2 | | 260 | .12 | 1.0 | | | 139 | 182 | 1.00 | | |
| Franco-American | 168 | | 5.4 | | | | 0 | .21 | | | 876 | 93 | | | |
| 7.4 oz | 209 | 6.4 | 23.5 | | | 567 | .25 | 2.2 | | | 103 | | 1.50 | | |
| macaroni w/ meat sce, Hearty | 192 | | 4.8 | | | | 5 | .18 | | | 814 | 97 | | | |
| 7.5 oz | 213 | 9.8 | 27.4 | | | 270 | .21 | 3.3 | | | 390 | | 2.30 | | |
| noodles & chicken, Bounty | 204 | | 11.7 | | | | 1 | .15 | | | 1020 | 61 | | | |
| 7.5 oz | 213 | 7.9 | 16.8 | | | 728 | .09 | 2.3 | | | 145 | | 1.50 | | |
| noodle weenee, Van Camp's | 245 | 187.2 | 8.5 | | | | | .20 | | | 1245 | 47 | | | |
| 1 cup | 238 | 9.3 | 32.9 | | | 672 | .12 | 2.1 | | | 289 | | 5.98 | | |
| pasta twists w/ meat sce, Hearty | 208 | | 6.1 | | | | 5 | .20 | | | 873 | 43 | | | |
| 7.5 oz | 213 | 9.6 | 28.7 | | | 481 | .14 | 3.3 | | | 458 | | 2.10 | | |
| pasta w/ chicken cacciatore sce, Prego | 359 | | 9.1 | | | | 6 | .22 | | | 933 | 57 | | | |
| 12.2 oz | 347 | 26.1 | 43.0 | | | 1140 | .49 | 6.4 | | | 577 | | 4.60 | | |
| pizzo's, Franco-American | 163 | | 0.6 | | | | 7 | .19 | | | 1048 | 22 | | | |
| 7.5 oz | 213 | 5.0 | 34.3 | | | 778 | .18 | 2.4 | | | 352 | | 1.60 | | |
| potatoes & beef in gravy, Bounty | 142 | | 0.9 | | | | 9 | .09 | | | 822 | 26 | | | |
| 7.5 oz | 213 | 10.4 | 23.0 | | | 0 | .04 | 2.0 | | | 362 | | 1.60 | | |
| **ravioli w/ meat sce** | | | | | | | | | | | | | | | |
| Franco-American | 284 | | 10.8 | | | | 7 | .21 | | | 995 | 75 | | | |
| 7.5 oz | 213 | 11.3 | 35.4 | | | 1091 | .23 | 3.4 | | | 495 | | 1.80 | | |

| | KCAL / WT (g) | H₂O (g) / PRO (g) | FAT (g) / CHO (g) | PUFA (g) / SFA (g) | CHOL (mg) / DFIB (g) | A (RE) / A (IU) | C (mg) / B-1 (mg) | B-2 (mg) / NIA (mg) | B-6 (mg) / B-12 (mcg) | FOL (mcg) / PANT (mg) | Na (mg) / K (mg) | Ca (mg) / P (mg) | Mg (mg) / Fe (mg) | Zn (mg) / Cu (mg) | Mn (mg) |
|---|---|---|---|---|---|---|---|---|---|---|---|---|---|---|---|
| Hearty | 284 | | 10.8 | | | | 7 | .21 | | | 995 | 75 | | | |
| *7.5 oz* | 213 | 11.3 | 35.4 | | | 1091 | .23 | 3.4 | | | 495 | | 1.80 | | |
| **sausage, italian & green peppers, Prego Plus—4 oz** | 164 | | 8.2 | | | | 19 | .05 | | | 478 | 48 | | | |
| | 113 | 3.4 | 19.1 | | | 1058 | .07 | 1.0 | | | 362 | | 1.30 | | |
| **skettee weenee, Van Camp's** | 243 | 186.6 | 7.4 | | | | | .20 | | | 1128 | 44 | | | |
| *1 cup* | 238 | 9.4 | 34.7 | | | 644 | .11 | 2.2 | | | 253 | | 6.31 | | |
| **spaghetti 'n beef, Franco-American** | 213 | | 8.2 | | | | 5 | .20 | | | 1075 | 32 | | | |
| *7.5 oz* | 213 | 9.0 | 25.8 | | | 819 | .20 | 3.3 | | | 395 | | 2.30 | | |
| **spaghettio's, Franco-American** | | | | | | | | | | | | | | | |
| w/ franks | 210 | | 8.4 | | | | 4 | .18 | | | 974 | 32 | | | |
| *7.4 oz* | 209 | 7.6 | 26.1 | | | 519 | .20 | 3.2 | | | 302 | | 2.20 | | |
| w/ meatballs | 204 | | 7.5 | | | | 4 | .18 | | | 946 | 29 | | | |
| *7.4 oz* | 209 | 9.1 | 24.9 | | | 524 | .19 | 3.1 | | | 318 | | 2.20 | | |
| w/ tomato & cheese sce | 165 | | 1.3 | | | | 0 | .16 | | | 912 | 29 | | | |
| *7.5 oz* | 213 | 4.9 | 33.5 | | | 707 | .23 | 2.4 | | | 219 | | 1.50 | | |
| **spaghetti w/ meatballs & tomato sce** | 258 | 195.0 | 10.3 | | | | 5 | .18 | | | 1220 | 53 | | | |
| *1 cup* | 250 | 12.3 | 28.5 | 2.2 | | 1000 | .15 | 2.3 | | | 245 | 113 | 3.30 | | |
| Franco-American | 215 | | 7.4 | | | | 4 | .20 | | | 834 | 29 | | | |
| *7.4 oz* | 209 | 9.6 | 27.5 | | | 567 | .18 | 3.2 | | | 338 | | 2.30 | | |
| Prego | 450 | | 13.4 | | | | 11 | .31 | | | 919 | 90 | | | |
| *13 oz* | 369 | 20.2 | 62.1 | | | 1779 | .87 | 7.6 | | | 686 | | 9.30 | | |
| **spaghetti w/ meat sce** | | | | | | | | | | | | | | | |
| Franco-American | 211 | | 8.1 | | | | 5 | .21 | | | 1101 | 28 | | | |
| *7.5 oz* | 213 | 8.5 | 26.2 | | | 928 | .22 | 3.5 | | | 391 | | 2.20 | | |
| Hearty | 176 | | 4.8 | | | | 5 | .17 | | | 797 | 37 | | | |
| *7.4 oz* | 209 | 9.5 | 23.5 | | | 389 | .20 | 3.2 | | | 397 | | 2.10 | | |
| Prego | 390 | | 8.3 | | | | 11 | .38 | | | 870 | 50 | | | |
| *12.5 oz* | 354 | 21.1 | 57.7 | | | 1376 | .92 | 8.0 | | | 641 | | 6.60 | | |
| **spaghetti w/ tomato sce & cheese** | 190 | 200.3 | 1.5 | | | | 10 | .28 | | | 955 | 40 | | | |
| *1 cup* | 250 | 5.5 | 38.5 | | | 930 | .35 | 4.5 | | | 303 | 88 | 2.80 | | |
| Franco-American | 180 | | 1.3 | | | | 0 | .19 | | | 958 | 28 | | | |
| *7.8 oz* | 220 | 5.4 | 36.9 | | | 768 | .28 | 2.8 | | | 227 | | 1.60 | | |
| **spaghetti w/ tomato sce, Franco-American** | 171 | | 1.2 | | | | 0 | .18 | | | 910 | 27 | | | |
| *7.4 oz* | 209 | 5.1 | 35.0 | | | 730 | .27 | 2.6 | | | 215 | | 1.60 | | |
| **spanish rice, Van Camp's** | 150 | 188.2 | 2.7 | | | | | .10 | | | 1358 | 35 | | | |
| *1 cup* | 227 | 3.1 | 28.2 | | | 1228 | .05 | 1.2 | | | 260 | | 2.92 | | |
| **tamales, Wolf Brand** | 328 | 150.4 | 24.5 | | | | | .49 | .26 | 23 | 1181 | 68 | 43 | 2.00 | .000 |
| *scant cup* | 213 | 8.3 | 24.9 | | | 2150 | .08 | 1.9 | .00 | .00 | 279 | 141 | 2.19 | .110 | |
| **tamales w/ sce, Van Camp's** | 293 | 153.8 | 16.2 | | | | | .16 | | | 1132 | 36 | | | |
| *1 cup* | 227 | 8.3 | 28.6 | | | 1906 | .05 | 2.1 | | | 236 | | 2.71 | | |
| **UFO's, Franco-American** | 185 | | 2.3 | | | | 8 | .24 | | | 781 | 38 | | | |
| *7.5 oz* | 213 | 5.8 | 35.1 | | | 697 | .22 | 3.6 | | | 341 | | 2.30 | | |
| **UFO's w/ meteors, Franco-American** | 234 | | 8.5 | | | | 7 | .24 | | | 784 | 28 | | | |
| *7.5 oz* | 213 | 9.2 | 30.0 | | | 637 | .17 | 3.6 | | | 361 | | 2.40 | | |
| **veal & mushrooms, Prego Plus** | 143 | | 5.0 | | | | 14 | .05 | | | 395 | 45 | | | |
| *4 oz* | 113 | 5.1 | 19.5 | | | 856 | .04 | 0.8 | | | 338 | | 1.30 | | |

## 10.3. FROZEN ENTREES (1-2 ITEMS/ENTREE)

| | KCAL / WT (g) | H₂O (g) / PRO (g) | FAT (g) / CHO (g) | PUFA (g) / SFA (g) | CHOL (mg) / DFIB (g) | A (RE) / A (IU) | C (mg) / B-1 (mg) | B-2 (mg) / NIA (mg) | B-6 (mg) / B-12 (mcg) | FOL (mcg) / PANT (mg) | Na (mg) / K (mg) | Ca (mg) / P (mg) | Mg (mg) / Fe (mg) | Zn (mg) / Cu (mg) | Mn (mg) |
|---|---|---|---|---|---|---|---|---|---|---|---|---|---|---|---|
| **beef & macaroni, Am Hosp Co** | 191 | | 6.3 | | 35 | | 12 | .19 | | | 770 | 23 | | | |
| *6 oz entree* | 170 | 16.6 | 16.9 | | | 792 | .17 | 4.3 | | | 521 | | 3.00 | | |
| **beef & noodles w/ sce, Am Hosp Co** | 186 | | 7.2 | | 35 | | 1 | .23 | | | 72 | 12 | | | |
| *6 oz entree* | 170 | 19.8 | 9.6 | | | 78 | .11 | 6.0 | | | 109 | | 3.60 | | |
| **beef & peppers w/ sce, Am Hosp Co** | 155 | | 3.0 | | 32 | | 46 | .17 | | | 614 | 16 | | | |
| *6 oz entree* | 170 | 19.8 | 11.4 | | | 816 | .08 | 3.4 | | | 362 | | 2.40 | | |

| | KCAL | H₂O (g) | FAT (g) | PUFA (g) | CHOL (mg) | A (RE) | C (mg) | B-2 (mg) | B-6 (mg) | FOL (mcg) | Na (mg) | Ca (mg) | Mg (mg) | Zn (mg) | Mn (mg) |
|---|---|---|---|---|---|---|---|---|---|---|---|---|---|---|---|
| | WT (g) | PRO (g) | CHO (g) | SFA (g) | DFIB (g) | A (IU) | B-1 (mg) | NIA (mg) | B-12 (mcg) | PANT (mg) | K (mg) | P (mg) | Fe (mg) | Cu (mg) | |
| beef & veg szechwan style, Van de | 370 | | 15.0 | | | | | | | | 940 | | | | |
| Kamp's—*11 oz entree* | 312 | 20.0 | 35.0 | | | | | | | | | | | | |
| beef brisket bbq pastry wrap, Am Hosp | 301 | | 18.0 | | 24 | | 0 | .16 | | | 347 | | | | |
| Co—*4.5 oz entree* | 128 | 12.8 | 22.0 | | | 194 | .14 | 3.0 | | | 326 | | 2.41 | | |
| beef burgundy, Am Hosp Co | 131 | | 4.3 | | 45 | | 1 | .15 | | | 279 | 15 | | | |
| *6 oz entree* | 170 | 20.4 | 2.6 | | | 86 | .05 | 3.3 | | | 297 | | 2.88 | | |
| beef burgundy w/ parsley noodles, frzn, | 230 | | 4.0 | | 55 | | 1 | .23 | | | 1240 | 14 | | | |
| Light & Elegant—*9 oz entree* | 255 | 23.0 | 25.0 | | | 906 | .15 | 1.7 | | | 200 | 172 | 3.10 | | |
| beef, chipped & creamed, Banquet | 90 | | 2.0 | | 25 | | 0 | .18 | | | 818 | 107 | | | |
| *4 oz entree* | 113 | 9.0 | 10.0 | | | 15 | .06 | 0.9 | | | 206 | | 1.10 | | |
| beef julienne w/ rice & peppers, frzn, | 260 | | 7.0 | | | | 4 | .10 | | | 990 | 27 | | | |
| Light & Elegant—*8.5 oz entree* | 241 | 21.0 | 27.0 | | | 1781 | .09 | 3.5 | | | 240 | 152 | 4.90 | | |
| beef marsala w/ noodles, Prego | 384 | | 15.0 | | | | 3 | .24 | | | 849 | 37 | | | |
| *11.3 oz* | 319 | 27.5 | 34.7 | | | 467 | .18 | 4.7 | | | 187 | | 4.00 | | |
| beef patties, charbroiled w/ mushroom | 210 | | 15.0 | | | | 1 | .12 | | | 850 | 38 | | | |
| gravy, Banquet—*1/6 of 32 oz pkg* | 151 | 10.0 | 8.0 | | | 57 | .10 | 1.1 | | | 170 | | 1.50 | | |
| beef pot roast w/ sce & mixed veg, Am | 139 | | 4.1 | | 43 | | 5 | .17 | | | 341 | 19 | | | |
| Hosp Co—*6 oz entree* | 170 | 20.0 | 5.7 | | | 906 | .09 | 4.0 | | | 313 | | 2.64 | | |
| beef ravioli, Am Hosp Co | 185 | | 5.7 | | 59 | | 6 | .16 | | | 446 | 83 | | | |
| *5 oz entree* | 142 | 9.2 | 24.4 | | | 895 | .08 | 1.2 | | | 348 | | 1.15 | | |
| beef short ribs w/ bbq sce, Am Hosp Co | 345 | | 20.9 | | 59 | | 5 | .16 | | | 702 | 19 | | | |
| *5.6 oz entree* | 159 | 26.0 | 13.3 | | | 716 | .09 | 4.6 | | | 266 | | 3.50 | | |
| **beef, sliced** | | | | | | | | | | | | | | | |
| & veg, frzn, Banquet | 300 | | 9.0 | | 100 | | 1 | .27 | | | 770 | 78 | | | |
| *10 oz entree* | 284 | 38.0 | 17.0 | | | 520 | .45 | 4.1 | | | 382 | | 4.30 | | |
| w/ bbq sce, Am Hosp Co | 225 | | 8.4 | | 40 | | 0 | .13 | | | 378 | 53 | | | |
| *5 oz* | 142 | 18.9 | 18.5 | | | 592 | .04 | 3.7 | | | 590 | | 2.60 | | |
| w/ bbq sce, Banquet | 90 | | 2.0 | | 40 | | 0 | .09 | | | 789 | 16 | | | |
| *4 oz entree* | 113 | 9.0 | 10.0 | | | 339 | .05 | 1.1 | | | 137 | | 1.50 | | |
| w/ gravy, Banquet | 90 | | 3.0 | | 40 | | 0 | .10 | | | 426 | 10 | | | |
| *4 oz entree* | 113 | 12.0 | 4.0 | | | 29 | .03 | 1.2 | | | 81 | | 2.00 | | |
| w/ gravy, Banquet | 160 | | 6.0 | | | | 2 | .21 | | | 900 | 17 | | | |
| *1/4 of 32 oz pkg* | 227 | 19.0 | 9.0 | | | 73 | .07 | 2.2 | | | 150 | | 2.50 | | |
| w/ mustard & tomato sce, Am Hosp | 240 | | 10.9 | | 48 | | 8 | .15 | | | 678 | 38 | | | |
| Co—*6 oz entree* | 170 | 17.5 | 17.9 | | | 828 | .07 | 3.1 | | | 378 | | 2.82 | | |
| beef stew, Am Hosp Co | 150 | | 6.0 | | 45 | | 8 | .11 | | | 846 | 26 | | | |
| *6 oz entree* | 170 | 12.0 | 12.0 | | | 1530 | .07 | 2.7 | | | 222 | | 1.86 | | |
| beef stew, Banquet | 254 | | 13.0 | | | | 7 | .10 | | | 977 | 23 | | | |
| *1/4 of 32 oz pkg* | 227 | 12.0 | 21.0 | | | 1862 | .08 | 2.7 | | | 308 | | 2.00 | | |
| beef stroganoff, Am Hosp Co | 185 | | 9.1 | | 44 | | 1 | .22 | | | 350 | 20 | | | |
| *6 oz* | 170 | 20.5 | 5.3 | | | 189 | .06 | | | | 277 | | 3.20 | | |
| beef stroganoff w/ parsley noodles, Light | 260 | | 6.0 | | 65 | | 2 | .26 | | | 790 | 45 | | | |
| & Elegant—*9 oz entree* | 255 | 24.0 | 27.0 | | | 944 | .20 | 2.1 | | | 230 | 79 | 3.00 | | |
| beef tamale pie, Am Hosp Co | 178 | | 6.6 | | 37 | | 24 | | | | 429 | 154 | | | |
| *6 oz entree* | 170 | 12.6 | 16.8 | | | 915 | | 2.4 | | | 446 | | 2.10 | | |
| beef teriyaki, Am Hosp Co | 154 | | 4.4 | | 18 | | 20 | .15 | | | 816 | 46 | | | |
| *6 oz entree* | 170 | 12.3 | 16.1 | | | 1290 | .07 | 1.7 | | | 382 | | 2.20 | | |
| beef teriyaki w/ rice & pea pods, Light & | 240 | | 3.0 | | 45 | | 2 | .10 | | | 625 | 30 | | | |
| Elegant—*8 oz entree* | 227 | 18.0 | 37.0 | | | 122 | .40 | 2.5 | | | 215 | 152 | 5.60 | | |
| beef wellington, Am Hosp Co | 245 | | 15.5 | | 113 | | | | | | 427 | | | | |
| *6.5 oz entree* | 184 | 24.2 | 2.1 | | | | | | | | 641 | | | | |
| **burrito** | | | | | | | | | | | | | | | |
| beef, red hot, El Charrito | 340 | | 17.0 | | 20 | | | | | | 780 | | | | |
| *5 oz burrito* | 142 | 10.0 | 39.0 | | | | | | | | 260 | | | | |
| crispy fried, Van de Kamp's | 365 | | 15.0 | | | | | | | | 825 | | | | |
| *6 oz entree* | 170 | 10.0 | 40.0 | | | | | | | | 540 | | | | |
| grande, El Charrito | 430 | | 16.0 | | 25 | | | | | | 820 | | | | |
| *6 oz burrito* | 170 | 17.0 | 53.0 | | | | | | | | 540 | | | | |
| green chili, El Charrito | 370 | | 16.0 | | 20 | | | | | | 650 | | | | |
| *5 oz burrito* | 142 | 12.0 | 51.0 | | | | | | | | 380 | | | | |

| | KCAL / WT (g) | H₂O (g) / PRO (g) | FAT (g) / CHO (g) | PUFA (g) / SFA (g) | CHOL (mg) / DFIB (g) | A (RE) / A (IU) | C (mg) / B-1 (mg) | B-2 (mg) / NIA (mg) | B-6 (mg) / B-12 (mcg) | FOL (mcg) / PANT (mg) | Na (mg) / K (mg) | Ca (mg) / P (mg) | Mg (mg) / Fe (mg) | Zn (mg) / Cu (mg) | Mn (mg) |
|---|---|---|---|---|---|---|---|---|---|---|---|---|---|---|---|
| green chili grande, El Charrito | 410 | | 14.0 | | 20 | | | | | | 1030 | | | | |
| 6 oz entree | 170 | 16.0 | 56.0 | | | | | | | | 510 | | | | |
| jalapeno grande, El Charrito | 410 | | 15.0 | | 25 | | | | | | 1060 | | | | |
| 6 oz burrito | 170 | 16.0 | 53.0 | | | | | | | | 560 | | | | |
| red chili, El Charrito | 380 | | 18.0 | | 20 | | | | | | 620 | | | | |
| 5 oz burrito | 142 | 12.0 | 40.0 | | | | | | | | 380 | | | | |
| red chili grande, El Charrito | 410 | | 15.0 | | 25 | | | | | | 830 | | | | |
| 6 oz burrito | 170 | 16.0 | 53.0 | | | | | | | | 570 | | | | |
| red hot, El Charrito | 374 | | 18.0 | | 20 | | | | | | 650 | | | | |
| 5 oz burrito | 142 | 12.0 | 41.0 | | | | | | | | 410 | | | | |
| sirloin, grande, Van de Kamp's | 440 | | 15.0 | | | | | | | | 1120 | | | | |
| 11 oz entree | 312 | 25.0 | 45.0 | | | | | | | | | | | | |
| **cabbage stuffed w/ rice, grd beef & tom** | 172 | | 6.1 | | 43 | | 39 | .16 | | | 479 | 43 | | | |
| **sce, Am Hosp Co**—7.4 oz entree | 210 | 10.9 | 18.3 | | | 1113 | .11 | 2.6 | | | 447 | | 2.56 | | |
| **cabbage stuffed w/ rice, tom, corn & crm** | 211 | | 6.1 | | 105 | | 20 | | | | 930 | 73 | | | |
| **sce, Am Hosp Co**—7.1 oz entree | 201 | 11.3 | 27.6 | | | 2570 | .13 | 3.4 | | | 585 | | 1.60 | | |
| **cannelloni florentine (veal, spinach &** | 362 | | 21.6 | | 89 | | 18 | .48 | | | 689 | 120 | | | |
| **beef), Am Hosp Co**—8 oz entree | 227 | 16.6 | 25.3 | | | 3360 | .62 | 6.5 | | | 272 | | 4.20 | | |
| **cheese blintz, Am Hosp Co** | 432 | | 25.6 | | 436 | | | 2.00 | | | 246 | 336 | | | |
| 8 oz entree | 227 | 19.2 | 31.2 | | | 1568 | .33 | 3.9 | | | 312 | | 4.80 | | |
| **chicken a la kiev, Am Hosp Co** | 400 | | 27.6 | | 140 | | | | | | 395 | | | | |
| 6 oz entree | 170 | 31.2 | 6.6 | | | | | | | | 501 | | | | |
| chicken a la king | | | | | | | | | | | | | | | |
| Am Hosp Co | 150 | | 4.3 | | 42 | | 11 | | | | 404 | 46 | | | |
| 6 oz entree | 170 | 15.5 | 12.4 | | | 468 | .06 | 4.3 | | | 251 | | 1.02 | | |
| Banquet | 110 | | 5.0 | | 40 | | 0 | .14 | | | 551 | 64 | | | |
| 4 oz entree | 113 | 8.0 | 9.0 | | | 72 | .06 | 1.0 | | | 137 | | .60 | | |
| **chicken a la reine pastry wrap, Am Hosp** | 266 | | 17.2 | | 27 | | 1 | .15 | | | 387 | 19 | | | |
| **Co**—4.5 oz entree | 128 | 9.8 | 17.9 | | | 213 | .14 | 3.4 | | | 160 | | 1.43 | | |
| **chicken almond, cantonese w/ rice, Van** | 440 | | 15.0 | | | | | | | | 1220 | | | | |
| **de Kamp's**—11 oz entree | 312 | 25.0 | 50.0 | | | | | | | | | | | | |
| **chicken & biscuits, Am Hosp Co** | 265 | | 12.5 | | 46 | | 0 | .22 | | | 962 | 84 | | | |
| 6.6 oz entree | 187 | 15.2 | 22.4 | | | 349 | .12 | 3.8 | | | 250 | | 1.30 | | |
| chicken & dumplings | 430 | | 25.0 | | | | 0 | .14 | | | 928 | 18 | | | |
| 1/4 of 32 oz pkg | 227 | 18.0 | 31.0 | | | 77 | .06 | 3.5 | | | 133 | | .90 | | |
| **chicken & noodles w/ sce, Am Hosp Co** | 169 | | 6.8 | | 41 | | 6 | .30 | | | 456 | 55 | | | |
| 6 oz entree | 170 | 15.0 | 12.0 | | | 348 | .31 | 4.3 | | | 144 | | 1.50 | | |
| **chicken breast, Am Hosp Co** | | | | | | | | | | | | | | | |
| hawaiian (w/ pineapple stuffing) | 231 | | 2.8 | | 107 | | | | | | 303 | | | | |
| 8 oz entree | 227 | 35.6 | 16.0 | | | | | | | | 731 | | | | |
| jamaica (w/ chili sce, green peppers, | 287 | | 5.6 | | 84 | | 20 | .25 | | | 1018 | 126 | | | |
| raisins & almonds)—7.5 oz entree | 213 | 24.7 | 34.5 | | | | .15 | 9.5 | | | 1022 | | 2.90 | | |
| mandarin (w/ stuffing & orange sce) | 253 | | 10.7 | | 87 | | 27 | .23 | | | 270 | 37 | | | |
| 8 oz entree | 227 | 26.0 | 13.1 | | | 460 | .13 | 9.3 | | | 476 | | 2.20 | | |
| new englander (w/ stuffing & crm sce) | 335 | | 14.4 | | 101 | | | | | | 330 | | | | |
| 7 oz entree | 198 | 35.5 | 16.0 | | | | | | | | 500 | | | | |
| pilgrim (w/ cranberry stuffing & crm | 243 | | 5.4 | | 84 | | | | | | 185 | | | | |
| sce)—7 oz entree | 198 | 30.6 | 18.1 | | | | | | | | 448 | | | | |
| w/ cornbread stuffing & gravy | 360 | | 20.9 | | 46 | | 1 | .22 | | | 630 | 33 | | | |
| 8 oz entree | 227 | 28.4 | 14.6 | | | 712 | .09 | 9.7 | | | 387 | | 1.84 | | |
| w/ wild rice stuffing | 318 | | 16.5 | | 107 | | | | | | 189 | | | | |
| 8 oz entree | 227 | 35.9 | 6.5 | | | | | | | | 672 | | | | |
| **chicken cacciatore, Banquet** | 260 | | 5.0 | | 40 | | 1 | .21 | | | 510 | 42 | | | |
| 10 oz entree | 284 | 17.0 | 35.0 | | | 678 | .19 | 2.3 | | | 191 | | 3.00 | | |
| **chicken cordon blue, Am Hosp Co** | 272 | | 10.3 | | 108 | | 17 | | | | 327 | | | | |
| 6.5 oz entree | 184 | 25.7 | 19.2 | | | | | | | | 411 | | | | |
| **chicken, french, Banquet** | 190 | | 4.0 | | 35 | | 1 | .16 | | | 850 | 52 | | | |
| 10 oz entree | 284 | 12.0 | 25.0 | | | 1084 | .14 | 2.2 | | | 455 | | 1.90 | | |
| **chicken fricassee, Am Hosp Co** | 152 | | 6.4 | | 41 | | 118 | .12 | | | 152 | 34 | | | |
| 6 oz entree | 170 | 16.6 | 7.1 | | | 301 | .07 | 4.7 | | | 250 | | 1.20 | | |

| | KCAL / WT (g) | $H_2O$ (g) / PRO (g) | FAT (g) / CHO (g) | PUFA (g) / SFA (g) | CHOL (mg) / DFIB (g) | A (RE) / A (IU) | C (mg) / B-1 (mg) | B-2 (mg) / NIA (mg) | B-6 (mg) / B-12 (mcg) | FOL (mcg) / PANT (mg) | Na (mg) / K (mg) | Ca (mg) / P (mg) | Mg (mg) / Fe (mg) | Zn (mg) / Cu (mg) | Mn (mg) |
|---|---|---|---|---|---|---|---|---|---|---|---|---|---|---|---|
| chicken, glazed w/ veg rice, Light & Elegant—*8 oz entree* | 240 | | 4.0 | | 75 | | 1 | .16 | | | 660 | 15 | | | |
| | 227 | 29.0 | 23.0 | | | 156 | .15 | 7.9 | | | 300 | 348 | 1.90 | | |
| chicken in bbq sce w/ corn & pecan rice, Light & Elegant—*8 oz entree* | 300 | | 6.0 | | | | 5 | .15 | | | 900 | 22 | | | |
| | 227 | 26.0 | 35.0 | | | 943 | .19 | 6.9 | | | 450 | 896 | 1.50 | | |
| chicken in cheese sce w/ rice & broccoli, Light & Elegant—*8.75 oz entree* | 293 | | 11.0 | | 50 | | 11 | .21 | | | 800 | 204 | | | |
| | 248 | 19.0 | 30.0 | | | 377 | .12 | 1.9 | | | 170 | | 1.60 | | |
| chicken kiev, Am Hosp Co *6.5 oz entree* | 240 | | 9.5 | | 126 | | 11 | .14 | | | 442 | | | | |
| | 184 | 23.6 | 14.9 | | | | .00 | | | | 451 | | | | |
| **chicken leg, Am Hosp Co** | | | | | | | | | | | | | | | |
| hawaiian (w/ pineapple stuffing) *6 oz entree* | 226 | | 7.9 | | 62 | | 4 | .27 | | | 277 | 28 | | | |
| | 170 | 24.6 | 14.0 | | | 114 | .14 | 6.8 | | | 273 | | 1.61 | | |
| normandy (w/ grain-based onion & apple stuffing)—*6 oz entree* | 222 | | 7.5 | | 61 | | 1 | .28 | | | 309 | 35 | | | |
| | 170 | 24.7 | 14.0 | | | 66 | .13 | 6.7 | | | 279 | | 1.60 | | |
| saint laurent (w/ ham, broccoli & cheese stuffing)—*6 oz entree* | 222 | | 11.8 | | 73 | | 10 | .32 | | | 309 | 115 | | | |
| | 170 | 27.4 | 1.6 | | | 549 | .14 | 6.8 | | | 304 | | 1.60 | | |
| w/ apple bread, almond & raisin stuffing—*6 oz entree* | 326 | | 17.9 | | 92 | | 1 | .25 | | | 266 | 254 | | | |
| | 170 | 27.9 | 13.4 | | | 73 | .10 | 13.3 | | | 297 | | 2.00 | | |
| w/ cranberry & crouton stuffing *6 oz entree* | 254 | | 11.2 | | 61 | | 2 | .26 | | | 247 | 25 | | | |
| | 170 | 24.2 | 14.3 | | | 72 | .10 | 6.7 | | | 244 | | 1.60 | | |
| chicken parmigiana w/ parsley noodles, Light & Elegant—*8 oz entree* | 260 | | 6.0 | | | | 7 | .20 | | | 680 | 73 | | | |
| | 227 | 28.0 | 23.0 | | | 640 | .33 | 6.6 | | | 320 | | 2.80 | | |
| chicken piccata w/ rice, Prego *11 oz* | 342 | | 18.5 | | | | 6 | .14 | | | 1148 | 96 | | | |
| | 312 | 21.0 | 22.9 | | | 893 | .18 | 8.0 | | | 135 | | 2.90 | | |
| chicken princess, Am Hosp Co[a] *6 oz entree* | 110 | | 4.2 | | 34 | | 3 | .08 | | | 433 | 12 | | | |
| | 170 | 12.0 | 9.0 | | | 53 | .04 | 2.8 | | | 250 | | 1.20 | | |
| chicken salad, Am Hosp Co *1 oz entree* | 45 | | 2.3 | | 8 | | 1 | .02 | | | 78 | 5 | | | |
| | 28 | 4.2 | 1.8 | | | 15 | .01 | 1.4 | | | 67 | | 3.40 | | |
| chicken stew, Am Hosp Co *6 oz entree* | 126 | | 2.4 | | 28 | | 3 | .08 | | | 107 | 18 | | | |
| | 170 | 16.2 | 10.2 | | | 530 | .05 | 2.2 | | | 306 | | 4.60 | | |
| chicken tortilla casserole, Am Hosp Co *6 oz entree* | 215 | | 10.8 | | 20 | | 14 | .09 | | | 415 | 269 | | | |
| | 170 | 14.4 | 14.4 | | | 524 | .08 | 5.9 | | | 209 | | .66 | | |
| chicken wellington, Am Hosp Co[b] *7.5 oz entree* | 386 | | 20.8 | | 79 | | 1 | .24 | | | 534 | 21 | | | |
| | 213 | 26.3 | 23.3 | | | 148 | .15 | 8.4 | | | 331 | | 2.11 | | |
| chicken w/ bbq sce, Am Hosp Co *5 oz entree* | 175 | | 4.5 | | 51 | | 8 | .20 | | | 132 | 12 | | | |
| | 142 | 27.5 | 6.0 | | | 581 | .07 | 10.4 | | | 498 | | 1.70 | | |
| chicken w/ broccoli, Light & Elegant *9.5 oz entree* | 290 | | 11.0 | | | | 1 | .21 | | | 805 | 204 | | | |
| | 270 | 19.0 | 30.0 | | | 377 | .11 | 1.8 | | | 180 | 240 | 1.60 | | |
| chicken w/ crm sce & veg, Am Hosp Co[c] *6 oz entree* | 179 | | 8.3 | | 44 | | 52 | .17 | | | 410 | 47 | | | |
| | 170 | 15.4 | 10.5 | | | 666 | .08 | | | | 329 | | .90 | | |
| chicken w/ veloute sce *5 oz entree* | 165 | | 4.0 | | 55 | | 0 | .44 | | | 64 | 41 | | | |
| | 142 | 27.0 | 5.5 | | | 79 | .06 | 11.6 | | | 338 | | 1.30 | | |
| chili & cheese pastry wrap, Am Hosp Co *4.5 oz entree* | 339 | | 25.3 | | 15 | | 10 | .12 | | | 548 | 67 | | | |
| | 128 | 7.1 | 20.7 | | | 545 | .15 | 2.0 | | | 233 | | 2.09 | | |
| chili relleno casserole, Am Hosp Co *6 oz entree* | 377 | | 27.5 | | 124 | | 101 | .26 | | | 679 | 483 | | | |
| | 170 | 18.9 | 13.4 | | | 2118 | .13 | 1.0 | | | 208 | | 1.38 | | |
| chili w/ meat sce, Am Hosp Co *6 oz entree* | 176 | | 6.0 | | 28 | | 8 | | | | 1140 | 16 | | | |
| | 170 | 9.6 | 21.0 | | | 472 | | 3.1 | | | 429 | | | | |
| **chow mein** | | | | | | | | | | | | | | | |
| beef, Am Hosp Co *6 oz entree* | 83 | | 3.3 | | 15 | | 17 | .08 | | | 658 | 22 | | | |
| | 170 | 8.0 | 5.2 | | | 251 | .07 | 1.1 | | | 100 | | 1.08 | | |
| beef mandarin, Van de Kamp's *11 oz entree* | 310 | | 10.0 | | | | | | | | 1700 | | | | |
| | 312 | 20.0 | 40.0 | | | | | | | | | | | | |
| chicken mandarin, Van de Kamp's *11 oz entree* | 340 | | 10.0 | | | | | | | | 1180 | | | | |
| | 312 | 20.0 | 40.0 | | | | | | | | | | | | |
| vegetable, Am Hosp Co *6 oz entree* | 56 | | 1.0 | | | | 38 | .11 | | | 597 | 24 | | | |
| | 170 | 2.1 | 9.5 | | | 358 | .09 | 0.6 | | | 213 | | .90 | | |
| coquille saint-jacques, Am Hosp Co[d] *4 oz entree* | 126 | | 4.9 | | 25 | | | | | | 115 | | | | |
| | 113 | 10.1 | 10.2 | | | | | | | | 199 | | | | |
| crepes a la reine, Am Hosp Co[e] *4.5 oz entree* | 130 | | 5.7 | | 106 | | | | | | 144 | | | | |
| | 128 | 13.5 | 7.0 | | | | | | | | 295 | | | | |

[a] Chicken w/ oyster sce, bamboo shoots, mushrooms, snow peas, water chestnuts & scallions.
[b] Breast meat wrapped in pastry dough w/ madeira wine sce.
[c] Vegetables include mashed potatoes, mushrooms & red peppers.
[d] Scallops, potatoes & mushrooms w/ sce.
[e] Contains chicken & cream sce.

| | KCAL / WT (g) | H₂O (g) / PRO (g) | FAT (g) / CHO (g) | PUFA (g) / SFA (g) | CHOL (mg) / DFIB (g) | A (RE) / A (IU) | C (mg) / B-1 (mg) | B-2 (mg) / NIA (mg) | B-6 (mg) / B-12 (mcg) | FOL (mcg) / PANT (mg) | Na (mg) / K (mg) | Ca (mg) / P (mg) | Mg (mg) / Fe (mg) | Zn (mg) / Cu (mg) | Mn (mg) |
|---|---|---|---|---|---|---|---|---|---|---|---|---|---|---|---|
| **crepes de la mer, Am Hosp Co[a]** | 187 | | 9.3 | | | | | | | | 436 | | | | |
| 5 oz entree | 142 | 13.3 | 14.2 | | | | | | | | 128 | | | | |
| **eggplant parmigiana, Am Hosp Co** | 223 | | 12.0 | | 5 | | 19 | .19 | | | 982 | 218 | | | |
| 6.4 oz entree | 181 | 10.8 | 17.9 | | | 1436 | .15 | 1.7 | | | 462 | | 2.16 | | |
| **egg rolls, cantonese, Van de Kamp's** | 280 | | 5.0 | | | | | | | | 550 | | | | |
| 5.25 oz | 149 | 10.0 | 40.0 | | | | | | | | | | | | |
| **enchilada casserole, Am Hosp Co[b]** | 270 | | 15.9 | | 31 | | 9 | .16 | | | 847 | 97 | | | |
| 6 oz entree | 170 | 15.5 | 16.3 | | | 1302 | .10 | 2.8 | | | 463 | | 1.86 | | |
| **enchiladas** | | | | | | | | | | | | | | | |
| beef & cheese, El Charrito | 880 | | 42.0 | | 70 | | | | | | 2520 | | | | |
| 6 enchiladas (16.25 oz entree) | 461 | 23.0 | 96.0 | | | | | | | | 880 | | | | |
| beef, Banquet | 264 | | 8.0 | | | | 0 | .13 | | | 1477 | 52 | | | |
| 1/4 of 32 oz pkg | 227 | 11.0 | 37.0 | | | 179 | .19 | 1.9 | | | 92 | | 1.00 | | |
| beef, El Charrito | 560 | | 31.0 | | 55 | | | | | | 1550 | | | | |
| 3 enchiladas (11 oz entree) | 312 | 17.0 | 53.0 | | | | | | | | 490 | | | | |
| beef, El Charrito | 880 | | 49.0 | | 75 | | | | | | 2130 | | | | |
| 6 enchiladas (16.25 oz entree) | 461 | 27.0 | 85.0 | | | | | | | | 770 | | | | |
| beef, shredded, Van de Kamp's | 180 | | 10.0 | | | | | | | | 930 | | | | |
| 5.5 oz entree | 156 | 10.0 | 15.0 | | | | | | | | | | | | |
| beef, Van de Kamp's | 250 | | 15.0 | | | | | | | | 1200 | | | | |
| 7.5 oz entree | 213 | 10.0 | 20.0 | | | | | | | | | | | | |
| beef, Van de Kamp's | 340 | | 15.0 | | | | | | | | 1480 | | | | |
| 4 enchiladas (8.5 oz) | 241 | 15.0 | 30.0 | | | | | | | | | | | | |
| cheese, El Charrito | 470 | | 20.0 | | 30 | | | | | | 1720 | | | | |
| 3 enchiladas (11 oz entree) | 312 | 12.0 | 64.0 | | | | | | | | 540 | | | | |
| cheese, El Charrito | 780 | | 30.0 | | 45 | | | | | | 2680 | | | | |
| 6 enchiladas (16.25 oz entree) | 461 | 19.0 | 109.0 | | | | | | | | 880 | | | | |
| cheese ranchero, Van de Kamp's | 250 | | 15.0 | | | | | | | | 540 | | | | |
| 5.5 oz entree | 156 | 10.0 | 20.0 | | | | | | | | | | | | |
| cheese, Van de Kamp's | 270 | | 15.0 | | | | | | | | 965 | | | | |
| 7.5 oz entree | 213 | 10.0 | 25.0 | | | | | | | | | | | | |
| cheese, Van de Kamp's | 370 | | 20.0 | | | | | | | | 1175 | | | | |
| 4 enchiladas (8.5 oz) | 241 | 15.0 | 30.0 | | | | | | | | | | | | |
| chicken, El Charrito | 440 | | 13.0 | | 60 | | | | | | 1550 | | | | |
| 3 enchiladas (11 oz entree) | 312 | 23.0 | 59.0 | | | | | | | | 630 | | | | |
| chicken suiza, Van de Kamp's | 220 | | 10.0 | | | | | | | | 590 | | | | |
| 5.5 oz entree | 156 | 10.0 | 20.0 | | | | | | | | | | | | |
| chicken, Van de Kamp's | 250 | | 10.0 | | | | | | | | 1105 | | | | |
| 7.5 oz entree | 213 | 15.0 | 25.0 | | | | | | | | | | | | |
| **fettuccini & chicken w/ sce, Am Hosp Co** | 122 | | 4.3 | | 18 | | 2 | .08 | | | 182 | 40 | | | |
| 4 oz entree | 113 | 7.2 | 13.6 | | | 358 | .08 | 1.8 | | | 126 | | .88 | | |
| **fettuccini primavera, Am Hosp Co[c]** | 305 | | 14.2 | | 45 | | 10 | .15 | | | 1410 | 251 | | | |
| 6 oz entree | 170 | 11.6 | 32.3 | | | 1588 | .19 | 1.5 | | | 165 | | 1.43 | | |
| **fish, batter-dipped & chips, Van de Kamp's—7 oz entree** | 440 | | 25.0 | | | | | | | | 640 | | | | |
| | 198 | 20.0 | 35.0 | | | | | | | | | | | | |
| **french bread pizza** | | | | | | | | | | | | | | | |
| cheese, Am Hosp Co | 417 | | 18.5 | | 38 | | 8 | .40 | | | 941 | 316 | | | |
| 5.75 oz entree | 163 | 17.8 | 44.9 | | | 635 | .47 | 3.6 | | | 238 | | 3.10 | | |
| cheese, Pillsbury Microwave | 339 | 83.1 | 13.5 | | | | 6 | .31 | | | 574 | 281 | | | |
| 1 piece | 155 | 14.1 | 40.3 | | | 1319 | .31 | 3.6 | | | 256 | 214 | 2.95 | | |
| pepperoni, Am Hosp Co | 425 | | 20.1 | | 59 | | 7 | .45 | | | 1165 | 189 | | | |
| 5.6 oz entree | 159 | 16.1 | 44.8 | | | 574 | .62 | 5.4 | | | 275 | | 4.40 | | |
| pepperoni, Pillsbury Microwave | 410 | 88.9 | 20.2 | | | | 5 | .51 | | | 1163 | 245 | | | |
| 1 piece | 171 | 16.6 | 40.5 | | | 607 | .63 | 6.5 | | | 316 | 207 | 4.79 | | |
| sausage, Pillsbury Microwave | 409 | 95.6 | 19.1 | | | | 6 | .34 | | | 1018 | 239 | | | |
| 1 piece | 177 | 18.1 | 40.0 | | | 598 | .46 | 4.4 | | | 329 | 228 | 3.19 | | |
| sausage & pepperoni, Pillsbury Microwave—1 piece | 429 | 97.3 | 21.9 | | | | 11 | .31 | | | 1149 | 246 | | | |
| | 185 | 18.1 | 41.1 | | | 670 | .37 | 4.6 | | | 346 | 228 | 3.15 | | |
| **green pepper steak, Banquet** | 310 | | 5.0 | | 50 | | 1 | .19 | | | 1125 | 28 | | | |
| 10 oz entree | 284 | 21.0 | 44.0 | | | 307 | .21 | 2.7 | | | 221 | | 3.30 | | |

[a] Contains shrimp, crab, langostinos & scallops w/ cream sce.
[b] Contains ground beef, tortillas, jack cheese & sce.
[c] Contains peas, broccoli, carrots & mushrooms.

| | KCAL | H₂O (g) | FAT (g) | PUFA (g) | CHOL (mg) | A (RE) | C (mg) | B-2 (mg) | B-6 (mg) | FOL (mcg) | Na (mg) | Ca (mg) | Mg (mg) | Zn (mg) | Mn (mg) |
|---|---|---|---|---|---|---|---|---|---|---|---|---|---|---|---|
| | WT (g) | PRO (g) | CHO (g) | SFA (g) | DFIB (g) | A (IU) | B-1 (mg) | NIA (mg) | B-12 (mcg) | PANT (mg) | K (mg) | P (mg) | Fe (mg) | Cu (mg) | |
| **green pepper, stuffed, Am Hosp Co** | | | | | | | | | | | | | | | |
| w/ beef, rice & sce | 227 | | 10.2 | | 64 | | 74 | .16 | | | 465 | 27 | | | |
| 7.5 oz entree | 213 | 15.5 | 18.2 | | | 325 | .09 | 2.6 | | | 330 | | 2.11 | | |
| w/ ground beef, rice & tomatoes | 172 | | 6.1 | | 54 | | 26 | .16 | | | 188 | 28 | | | |
| 7.5 oz entree | 213 | 13.9 | 15.4 | | | 980 | .14 | 6.1 | | | 590 | | 2.80 | | |
| **ham & potato casserole, Am Hosp Co** | 176 | | 8.6 | | | 47 | 12 | .12 | | | 811 | 76 | | | |
| 6 oz entree | 170 | 9.8 | 14.8 | | | 189 | .25 | 1.7 | | | 391 | | 1.40 | | |
| **italian sausage & peppers, Am Hosp Co** | 327 | | 29.4 | | 59 | | 361 | .13 | | | 665 | 14 | | | |
| 6 oz entree | 170 | 7.2 | 9.6 | | | 934 | .28 | 1.9 | | | 155 | | 1.80 | | |
| **lasagna** | | | | | | | | | | | | | | | |
| Am Hosp Co | 244 | | 10.8 | | 21 | | 19 | .30 | | | 816 | 167 | | | |
| 6 oz entree | 170 | 15.6 | 21.0 | | | 1308 | .53 | 4.4 | | | 271 | | 2.80 | | |
| beef & mushroom, Van de Kamp's | 430 | | 25.0 | | | | | | | | 970 | | | | |
| 11 oz entree | 312 | 25.0 | 30.0 | | | | | | | | | | | | |
| florentine, Light & Elegant | 280 | | 5.0 | | 25 | | 23 | .38 | | | 980 | 280 | | | |
| 11.25 oz entree | 319 | 24.0 | 35.0 | | | 4080 | .39 | 1.8 | | | 720 | 387 | 3.60 | | |
| italian sausage, Van de Kamp's | 440 | | 25.0 | | | | | | | | 1190 | | | | |
| 11 oz entree | 312 | 25.0 | 35.0 | | | | | | | | | | | | |
| primavera (spinach), Am Hosp Co | 178 | | 9.6 | | 30 | | 14 | .10 | | | 378 | 126 | | | |
| 6 oz entree | 170 | 7.4 | 15.5 | | | 3558 | .11 | 2.3 | | | 245 | | 1.38 | | |
| w/ meat sce, Am Hosp Co | 256 | | 11.4 | | 35 | | 7 | .17 | | | 496 | 142 | | | |
| 6 oz entree | 170 | 16.8 | 21.6 | | | 1416 | .19 | 2.9 | | | 475 | | 2.22 | | |
| w/ meat sce, Banquet | 330 | | 11.0 | | | | 1 | .30 | | | 1000 | 244 | | | |
| 1/4 of 32 oz pkg | 227 | 19.0 | 39.0 | | | 1291 | .50 | 3.2 | | | 340 | | 2.40 | | |
| **lumache, Am Hosp Co** | | | | | | | | | | | | | | | |
| w/ italian sausage & tomato sce | 138 | | 8.7 | | 35 | | 0 | .04 | | | 531 | 51 | | | |
| 3 oz entree | 85 | 6.3 | 8.1 | | | 83 | .05 | 0.4 | | | 201 | | .90 | | |
| w/ ricotta cheese & tomato sce | 139 | | 7.3 | | 19 | | 1 | .08 | | | 313 | 121 | | | |
| 3.58 oz entree | 101 | 8.0 | 10.4 | | | 491 | .07 | 5.3 | | | 169 | | .58 | | |
| **macaroni & cheese** | | | | | | | | | | | | | | | |
| Am Hosp Co | 196 | | 7.1 | | 17 | | 4 | .24 | | | 358 | 269 | | | |
| 6 oz entree | 170 | 11.0 | 21.8 | | | 88 | .18 | 0.9 | | | 73 | | .69 | | |
| Banquet | 344 | | 17.0 | | | | 0 | .13 | | | 930 | 210 | | | |
| 8 oz entree | 227 | 11.0 | 36.0 | | | 605 | .05 | 0.7 | | | 135 | | 1.00 | | |
| Banquet | 230 | | 8.0 | | | | 0 | .19 | | | 790 | 153 | | | |
| 1/4 of 32 oz pkg | 227 | 9.0 | 31.0 | | | 127 | .26 | 0.9 | | | 40 | | 1.40 | | |
| w/ bread crumb topping, Light & | 300 | | 9.0 | | 5 | | 0 | .43 | | | 1010 | 328 | | | |
| Elegant—9 oz entree | 255 | 16.0 | 38.0 | | | 302 | .34 | 1.5 | | | 216 | 334 | 2.00 | | |
| **manicotti, Am Hosp Co** | | | | | | | | | | | | | | | |
| vegetarian w/ tomato sce | 192 | | 6.7 | | 31 | | 0 | .16 | | | 403 | 257 | | | |
| 5.6 oz entree | 159 | 8.9 | 24.0 | | | 470 | .12 | 0.1 | | | 158 | | .78 | | |
| w/ ricotta cheese & tomato sce | 229 | | 13.5 | | 56 | | 2 | .04 | | | 421 | 18 | | | |
| 5 oz entree | 142 | 13.0 | 12.5 | | | 163 | .04 | 0.3 | | | 225 | | .10 | | |
| **meatballs** | | | | | | | | | | | | | | | |
| swedish w/ sce, Am Hosp Co | 220 | | 13.2 | | 42 | | 3 | .18 | | | 528 | 36 | | | |
| 6 oz entree | 170 | 12.0 | 13.2 | | | 204 | .16 | 7.2 | | | 294 | | 1.20 | | |
| w/ tomato sce, Am Hosp Co | 186 | | 8.4 | | 58 | | 0 | .17 | | | 942 | 38 | | | |
| 6 oz entree | 170 | 15.6 | 12.6 | | | 2214 | .14 | 4.2 | | | 198 | | 3.00 | | |
| **meatloaf** | | | | | | | | | | | | | | | |
| Am Hosp Co | 147 | | 7.2 | | 58 | | 4 | .12 | | | 465 | 11 | | | |
| 3 oz entree | 85 | 17.1 | 3.4 | | | 90 | .06 | 3.4 | | | 285 | | 2.10 | | |
| Banquet | 240 | | 15.0 | | 45 | | 19 | .15 | | | 827 | 55 | | | |
| 5 oz entree | 142 | 12.0 | 12.0 | | | 303 | .14 | 1.6 | | | 385 | | 2.50 | | |
| w/ brown gravy, Am Hosp Co | 169 | | 7.8 | | 58 | | 5 | .13 | | | 742 | 11 | | | |
| 5 oz entree | 142 | 18.0 | 6.8 | | | 90 | .07 | 5.7 | | | 304 | | 2.10 | | |

| | KCAL | H₂O (g) | FAT (g) | PUFA (g) | CHOL (mg) | A (RE) | C (mg) | B-2 (mg) | B-6 (mg) | FOL (mcg) | Na (mg) | Ca (mg) | Mg (mg) | Zn (mg) | Mn (mg) |
|---|---|---|---|---|---|---|---|---|---|---|---|---|---|---|---|
| | WT (g) | PRO (g) | CHO (g) | SFA (g) | DFIB (g) | A (IU) | B-1 (mg) | NIA (mg) | B-12 (mcg) | PANT (mg) | K (mg) | P (mg) | Fe (mg) | Cu (mg) | |
| w/ tomato sce, Am Hosp Co | 182 | | 8.1 | | 58 | | 16 | .14 | | | 623 | 12 | | | |
| *5 oz entree* | 142 | 17.9 | 9.3 | | | 722 | .10 | 4.0 | | | 458 | | | | |
| **mostaccioli w/ meat sce, Banquet** | 240 | | 4.0 | | | | 1 | .23 | | | 1180 | 35 | | | |
| *1/4 of 32 oz pkg* | 227 | 12.0 | 38.0 | | | 1092 | .43 | 2.8 | | | 330 | | 3.60 | | |
| **noodles & beef, Banquet** | 283 | | 18.0 | | | | 1 | .12 | | | 877 | 18 | | | |
| *1/4 of 32 oz pkg* | 227 | 10.0 | 21.0 | | | 100 | .19 | 2.3 | | | 99 | | 1.50 | | |
| **osso bucco (veal shank w/ veg & sce), Am** | 321 | | 17.2 | | 119 | | 5 | .39 | | | 673 | 32 | | | |
| **Hosp Co**—*11.7 oz entree* | 332 | 32.8 | 8.8 | | | 1102 | .30 | 10.4 | | | 754 | | 4.90 | | |
| **pasta shells & sce, Banquet** | 310 | | 8.0 | | 35 | | 0 | .28 | | | 950 | 178 | | | |
| *10 oz entree* | 284 | 17.0 | 41.0 | | | 687 | .37 | 2.9 | | | 335 | | 3.50 | | |
| **pizza, bacon, Totino's Party** | 271 | 49.4 | 12.7 | | | | 4 | .21 | | | 721 | 114 | | | |
| *1/3 pizza* | 103 | 7.7 | 28.8 | | | 467 | .21 | 2.3 | | | 173 | 97 | 1.34 | | |
| **pizza, canadian style bacon** | | | | | | | | | | | | | | | |
| Big Slice Lite | 61 | 15.7 | 2.3 | | 1 | | 1 | .04 | | | 74 | 74 | | | |
| *1 oz slice* | 28 | 2.9 | 6.9 | | | 144 | .03 | 1.5 | | | | | .50 | | |
| Celeste | 541 | 112.0 | 26.0 | | | | | .73 | .29 | 141 | 1593 | 491 | 62 | 4.00 | .000 |
| *7.75 oz pizza* | 220 | 27.3 | 49.6 | | | 1553 | .37 | 2.9 | 2.00 | .00 | 444 | 684 | 1.89 | .260 | |
| Celeste | 329 | 69.8 | 16.9 | | | | | .44 | .19 | 100 | 976 | 301 | 35 | 3.00 | .000 |
| *1/4 of 19 oz pizza* | 135 | 16.6 | 27.7 | | | 900 | .20 | 2.0 | 1.00 | .00 | 290 | 418 | 1.21 | .160 | |
| Totino's Classic | 320 | 71.5 | 11.9 | | | | 6 | .86 | | | 817 | 212 | | | |
| *1/4 pizza* | 143 | 15.9 | 37.2 | | | 183 | 1.00 | 3.3 | | | 225 | 232 | 2.29 | | |
| Totino's Party | 230 | 55.2 | 8.4 | | | | 3 | .21 | | | 670 | 112 | | | |
| *1/3 pizza* | 103 | 10.1 | 28.3 | | | 383 | .21 | 2.1 | | | 169 | 62 | 1.24 | | |
| **pizza, cheese** | | | | | | | | | | | | | | | |
| Celeste | 497 | 84.4 | 24.5 | | | | | .44 | .15 | 35 | 828 | 375 | 48 | 4.00 | .000 |
| *6.5 oz pizza* | 184 | 21.2 | 48.0 | | | 927 | .15 | 1.2 | 2.00 | .00 | 342 | 386 | 1.36 | .240 | |
| Celeste | 317 | 62.1 | 16.6 | | | | | .39 | .10 | 14 | 673 | 204 | 30 | 3.00 | .000 |
| *1/4 of 18 oz pizza* | 126 | 14.2 | 27.8 | | | 779 | .08 | 1.1 | 1.00 | .00 | 268 | 266 | 1.00 | .140 | |
| Fox Deluxe | 170 | 46.5 | 6.1 | | | | 2 | .17 | | | 504 | 117 | | | |
| *1/3 pizza* | 83 | 6.6 | 21.6 | | | 337 | .17 | 1.8 | | | 106 | 159 | 1.16 | | |
| Pillsbury Heat 'n Eat Microwave | 269 | 54.2 | 10.4 | | | | 5 | .22 | | | 667 | 241 | | | |
| *4.1 oz* | 116 | 12.8 | 31.3 | | | 537 | .16 | 1.7 | | | 202 | 204 | 1.16 | | |
| Pillsbury Microwave | 480 | | 19.0 | | | | | | | | 1190 | | | | |
| *7.1 oz* | 201 | 21.0 | 56.0 | | | | | | | | 360 | | | | |
| Totino's Classic | 351 | 58.0 | 14.8 | | | | 6 | .26 | | | 811 | 282 | | | |
| *1/4 pizza* | 138 | 15.2 | 40.0 | | | 722 | .18 | 2.5 | | | 273 | 239 | 1.66 | | |
| Totino's Extra | 251 | 44.7 | 12.2 | | | | 3 | .19 | | | 462 | 229 | | | |
| *1/4 pizza* | 94 | 11.3 | 24.4 | | | 451 | .12 | 1.3 | | | 185 | 182 | 1.03 | | |
| Totino's Microwave | 254 | 51.8 | 9.4 | | | | 5 | .21 | | | 638 | 194 | | | |
| *3.9 oz* | 111 | 11.1 | 31.1 | | | 501 | .16 | 1.9 | | | 199 | 171 | 1.22 | | |
| Totino's Party | 255 | 47.5 | 11.8 | | | | 3 | .17 | | | 635 | 151 | | | |
| *1/3 pizza* | 97 | 8.9 | 27.2 | | | 458 | .15 | 1.6 | | | 131 | 190 | 1.07 | | |
| Totino's Slices | 170 | 35.9 | 6.8 | | | | 2 | .13 | | | 346 | 125 | | | |
| *1 slice* | 71 | 7.2 | 19.9 | | | 258 | .11 | 1.1 | | | 87 | 110 | .78 | | |
| **pizza, combination** | | | | | | | | | | | | | | | |
| Pillsbury Microwave | 673 | 114.8 | 36.2 | | | | 18 | .43 | | | 1550 | 390 | | | |
| *9 oz* | 255 | 27.0 | 59.4 | | | 1025 | .43 | 4.6 | | | 500 | 390 | 3.06 | | |
| Totino's Classic | 461 | 68.9 | 25.4 | | | | 12 | .30 | | | 1033 | 271 | | | |
| *1/4 pizza* | 164 | 18.0 | 39.4 | | | 758 | .28 | 3.1 | | | 342 | 262 | 2.13 | | |
| **pizza, deluxe** | | | | | | | | | | | | | | | |
| Celeste | 582 | 123.8 | 31.8 | | | | | .82 | .26 | 80 | 1308 | 332 | 61 | 5.00 | .000 |
| *8.25 oz pizza* | 234 | 22.7 | 51.2 | | | 1226 | .30 | 3.5 | 2.00 | 2.00 | 498 | 480 | 2.57 | .350 | |
| Celeste | 378 | 86.3 | 22.1 | | | | | .55 | .17 | 57 | 953 | 267 | 38 | 3.00 | .000 |
| *1/4 of 22 oz pizza* | 158 | 15.5 | 29.3 | | | 950 | .20 | 2.7 | 2.00 | 2.00 | 352 | 357 | 1.85 | .220 | |
| **pizza, ground beef** | | | | | | | | | | | | | | | |
| Am Hosp Co | 300 | | 12.9 | | 22 | | 8 | .18 | | | 320 | 118 | | | |
| *5.66 oz entree* | 160 | 19.7 | 26.3 | | | 536 | .16 | 5.1 | | | 671 | | 2.52 | | |

| | KCAL / WT (g) | H₂O (g) / PRO (g) | FAT (g) / CHO (g) | PUFA (g) / SFA (g) | CHOL (mg) / DFIB (g) | A (RE) / A (IU) | C (mg) / B-1 (mg) | B-2 (mg) / NIA (mg) | B-6 (mg) / B-12 (mcg) | FOL (mcg) / PANT (mg) | Na (mg) / K (mg) | Ca (mg) / P (mg) | Mg (mg) / Fe (mg) | Zn (mg) / Cu (mg) | Mn (mg) |
|---|---|---|---|---|---|---|---|---|---|---|---|---|---|---|---|
| Fox Deluxe | 180 | 45.7 | 6.2 | | | | 2 | .17 | | | 457 | 69 | | | |
| *1/3 pizza* | 83 | 8.1 | 22.4 | | | 221 | .17 | 2.2 | | | 144 | 66 | 1.66 | | |
| Totino's Party | 279 | 51.9 | 13.3 | | | | 3 | .21 | | | 650 | 111 | | | |
| *1/3 pizza* | 106 | 11.7 | 27.9 | | | 413 | .15 | 2.1 | | | 193 | 86 | 1.70 | | |
| **pizza, mexican style, Totino's Party** | 239 | 38.5 | 13.9 | | | | 6 | .18 | | | 590 | 113 | | | |
| *1/3 pizza* | 89 | 7.6 | 21.0 | | | 348 | .18 | 1.9 | | | 163 | 82 | 1.78 | | |
| **pizza, nacho, Totino's Party** | 230 | 47.6 | 12.5 | | | | 7 | .18 | | | 480 | 191 | | | |
| *1/3 pizza* | 92 | 8.6 | 20.2 | | | 362 | .14 | 1.5 | | | 98 | 121 | 1.29 | | |
| **pizza, pepperoni** | | | | | | | | | | | | | | | |
| Big Slice Lite | 67 | 14.7 | 2.3 | | 1 | | 1 | .04 | | | 57 | 74 | | | |
| *1 oz slice* | 28 | 3.1 | 7.0 | | | 144 | .03 | 1.5 | | | | | .57 | | |
| Celeste | 546 | 86.1 | 29.6 | | | | | .71 | .21 | 97 | 1417 | 336 | 53 | 4.00 | .000 |
| *6.75 oz pizza* | 191 | 20.2 | 49.7 | | | 1316 | .25 | 2.6 | 2.00 | .00 | 416 | 443 | 2.04 | .290 | |
| Celeste | 368 | 65.4 | 21.3 | | | | | .57 | .18 | 101 | 1061 | 186 | 39 | 4.00 | .000 |
| *1/4 of 19 oz pizza* | 135 | 15.0 | 29.2 | | | 1343 | .14 | 1.6 | 1.00 | .00 | 284 | 386 | 1.42 | .160 | |
| Fox Deluxe | 169 | 46.9 | 5.8 | | | | 2 | .17 | | | 505 | 67 | | | |
| *1/3 pizza* | 83 | 6.6 | 22.4 | | | 232 | .17 | 2.2 | | | 116 | 62 | 1.41 | | |
| Pillsbury Heat 'n Eat Microwave | 346 | 58.1 | 18.2 | | | | 5 | .29 | | | 1070 | 217 | | | |
| *4.6 oz* | 130 | 13.4 | 31.2 | | | 673 | .20 | 2.5 | | | 226 | 228 | 1.69 | | |
| Pillsbury Microwave | 595 | 110.9 | 28.0 | | | | 18 | .43 | | | 1571 | 390 | | | |
| *8.5 oz* | 241 | 26.8 | 59.5 | | | 901 | .39 | 4.6 | | | 458 | 381 | 2.89 | | |
| Totino's Classic | 409 | 63.2 | 19.9 | | | | 7 | .27 | | | 1104 | 245 | | | |
| *1/4 pizza* | 152 | 17.2 | 40.3 | | | 711 | .26 | 3.2 | | | 333 | 234 | 1.82 | | |
| Totino's Extra | 260 | 40.0 | 13.7 | | | | 4 | .17 | | | 686 | 159 | | | |
| *1/4 pizza* | 94 | 10.2 | 24.1 | | | 507 | .15 | 1.9 | | | 115 | 175 | 1.50 | | |
| Totino's Microwave | 292 | 50.2 | 14.1 | | | | 5 | .23 | | | 1267 | 130 | | | |
| *4 oz* | 113 | 9.9 | 30.5 | | | 571 | .23 | 2.5 | | | 191 | 163 | 1.70 | | |
| Totino's Party | 259 | 53.0 | 12.4 | | | | 3 | .15 | | | 739 | 114 | | | |
| *1/3 pizza* | 105 | 9.7 | 28.0 | | | 302 | .17 | 2.0 | | | 156 | 162 | 1.26 | | |
| Totino's Slices | 190 | 36.7 | 9.2 | | | | 3 | .15 | | | 526 | 84 | | | |
| *1 slice* | 74 | 6.7 | 20.0 | | | 312 | .15 | 1.5 | | | 87 | 106 | 1.11 | | |
| **pizza, sausage** | | | | | | | | | | | | | | | |
| Am Hosp Co | 342 | | 20.8 | | 40 | | 26 | .24 | | | 698 | 146 | | | |
| *6 oz entree* | 170 | 10.6 | 28.1 | | | 1155 | .26 | 2.2 | | | 170 | | 2.20 | | |
| Big Slice Lite | 65 | 15.0 | 2.5 | | 1 | | 1 | .04 | | | 74 | 80 | | | |
| *1 oz slice* | 28 | 3.1 | 7.2 | | | 113 | .03 | 1.5 | | | | | .60 | | |
| Celeste | 571 | 103.7 | 31.7 | | | | | .77 | .23 | 109 | 1374 | 371 | 60 | 4.00 | .000 |
| *7.5 oz pizza* | 213 | 22.6 | 48.8 | | | 1359 | .30 | 2.9 | 2.00 | .00 | 456 | 505 | 2.28 | .340 | |
| Celeste | 376 | 70.6 | 21.7 | | | | | .51 | .17 | 89 | 988 | 322 | 40 | 3.00 | .000 |
| *1/4 of 20 oz pizza* | 142 | 15.6 | 29.7 | | | 1048 | .18 | 2.0 | 1.00 | .00 | 311 | 385 | 1.52 | .180 | |
| Fox Deluxe | 180 | 42.9 | 6.5 | | | | 2 | .17 | | | 532 | 71 | | | |
| *1/3 pizza* | 85 | 6.5 | 23.0 | | | 234 | .26 | 2.1 | | | 129 | 65 | 1.36 | | |
| Pillsbury Heat 'n Eat Microwave | 360 | 53.0 | 19.7 | | | | 5 | .27 | | | 1127 | 219 | | | |
| *4.8 oz* | 136 | 13.3 | 31.3 | | | 681 | .26 | 2.3 | | | 262 | 241 | 1.90 | | |
| Pillsbury Microwave | 647 | 112.1 | 34.2 | | | | 21 | .40 | | | 1421 | 387 | | | |
| *8.75 oz* | 248 | 25.3 | 59.0 | | | 1019 | .42 | 4.2 | | | 476 | 377 | 2.98 | | |
| Totino's Classic | 439 | 68.0 | 23.5 | | | | 7 | .26 | | | 974 | 240 | | | |
| *1/4 pizza* | 162 | 16.2 | 40.5 | | | 757 | .29 | 2.9 | | | 366 | 238 | 2.11 | | |
| Totino's Extra | 279 | 34.1 | 15.5 | | | | 4 | .20 | | | 767 | 141 | | | |
| *1/4 pizza* | 98 | 9.8 | 24.3 | | | 472 | .20 | 2.0 | | | 176 | 166 | 1.57 | | |
| Totino's Microwave | 301 | 47.6 | 14.9 | | | | 5 | .24 | | | 925 | 132 | | | |
| *4.2 oz* | 119 | 10.1 | 31.2 | | | 534 | .24 | 2.3 | | | 242 | 162 | 1.67 | | |
| Totino's Party | 270 | 46.2 | 13.1 | | | | 3 | .21 | | | 772 | 114 | | | |
| *1/3 pizza* | 105 | 9.8 | 28.4 | | | 391 | .21 | 1.9 | | | 174 | 85 | 1.37 | | |
| Totino's Slices | 200 | 34.3 | 10.1 | | | | 3 | .16 | | | 558 | 86 | | | |
| *1 slice* | 78 | 6.9 | 20.3 | | | 282 | .16 | 1.4 | | | 121 | 107 | 1.09 | | |
| **pizza, sausage & mushroom** | | | | | | | | | | | | | | | |
| Celeste | 592 | 127.7 | 32.3 | | | | | .87 | .34 | 82 | 1347 | 362 | 60 | 5.00 | .000 |
| *8.5 oz pizza* | 241 | 23.9 | 51.3 | | | 1200 | .34 | 3.9 | 2.00 | 2.00 | 549 | 504 | 2.41 | .340 | |

| | KCAL / WT (g) | H₂O (g) / PRO (g) | FAT (g) / CHO (g) | PUFA (g) / SFA (g) | CHOL (mg) / DFIB (g) | A (RE) / A (IU) | C (mg) / B-1 (mg) | B-2 (mg) / NIA (mg) | B-6 (mg) / B-12 (mcg) | FOL (mcg) / PANT (mg) | Na (mg) / K (mg) | Ca (mg) / P (mg) | Mg (mg) / Fe (mg) | Zn (mg) / Cu (mg) | Mn (mg) |
|---|---|---|---|---|---|---|---|---|---|---|---|---|---|---|---|
| Celeste | 387 | 85.2 | 22.4 | | | | | .51 | .19 | 102 | 1033 | 310 | 45 | 3.00 | .000 |
| *1/4 of 25 oz pizza* | 177 | 16.9 | 29.4 | | | 1065 | .24 | 2.9 | 2.00 | .00 | 361 | 407 | 1.61 | .220 | |
| **pizza, sausage & pepperoni** | | | | | | | | | | | | | | | |
| Fox Deluxe | 170 | 42.1 | 6.2 | | | | 2 | .20 | | | 505 | 67 | | | |
| *1/3 pizza* | 81 | 6.3 | 21.9 | | | 223 | .22 | 2.0 | | | 120 | 62 | 1.30 | | |
| Pillsbury Heat 'n Eat Microwave | 378 | 55.0 | 21.3 | | | | 5 | .28 | | | 1202 | 218 | | | |
| *4.9 oz* | 139 | 13.9 | 31.3 | | | 678 | .25 | 2.6 | | | 270 | 243 | 1.95 | | |
| Totino's Extra | 289 | 37.4 | 16.2 | | | | 4 | .20 | | | 793 | 160 | | | |
| *1/4 pizza* | 101 | 10.8 | 24.7 | | | 503 | .20 | 2.0 | | | 199 | 183 | 1.62 | | |
| Totino's Microwave | 307 | 48.9 | 15.5 | | | | 5 | .23 | | | 1091 | 140 | | | |
| *4.2 oz* | 119 | 10.5 | 30.9 | | | 562 | .24 | 2.4 | | | 227 | 171 | 1.74 | | |
| Totino's Party | 278 | 50.1 | 13.2 | | | | 4 | .22 | | | 791 | 125 | | | |
| *1/3 pizza* | 109 | 10.5 | 29.4 | | | 421 | .19 | 2.0 | | | 172 | 88 | 1.42 | | |
| Totino's Slices | 200 | 35.9 | 9.9 | | | | | .16 | | | 645 | 92 | | | |
| *1 slice* | 78 | 7.0 | 20.3 | | | 307 | .15 | 1.5 | | | 108 | 112 | 1.17 | | |
| **pizza, suprema** | | | | | | | | | | | | | | | |
| Celeste | 678 | 130.8 | 39.3 | | | | | .92 | .28 | 120 | 1693 | 454 | 64 | 5.00 | .000 |
| *9 oz pizza* | 255 | 26.5 | 54.0 | | | 1943 | .33 | 3.7 | 3.00 | 3.00 | 528 | 602 | 2.73 | .360 | |
| Celeste | 381 | 87.9 | 24.1 | | | | | .68 | .20 | 67 | 1043 | 295 | 41 | 3.00 | .000 |
| *1/4 of 23 oz pizza* | 163 | 16.8 | 29.2 | | | 1167 | .20 | 2.2 | 2.00 | .00 | 342 | 408 | 1.78 | .230 | |
| **pizza, vegetable, Totino's Party** | 219 | 61.6 | 7.9 | | | | 10 | .22 | | | 631 | 118 | | | |
| *1/3 pizza* | 108 | 7.9 | 29.2 | | | 591 | .14 | 1.8 | | | 158 | 72 | 1.40 | | |
| **pork chops w/ bbq sce, Am Hosp Co** | 293 | | 13.0 | | 80 | | 6 | .26 | | | 499 | 56 | | | |
| *7.2 oz entree* | 204 | 21.6 | 22.3 | | | 529 | 1.0 | 5.1 | | | 725 | | 3.30 | | |
| **pork chops w/ brown gravy, Am Hosp Co** | 252 | | 16.2 | | | | 1 | .20 | | | 367 | 9 | | | |
| *6.5 oz entree* | 184 | 22.1 | 4.4 | | | 33 | .43 | 4.3 | | | 339 | | 2.50 | | |
| **pork, ground** | | | | | | | | | | | | | | | |
| w/ cheese sce & veg, Am Hosp Co[a] | 217 | | 13.1 | | 48 | | 10 | .19 | | | 365 | 167 | | | |
| *6 oz entree* | 170 | 16.0 | 8.8 | | | 2184 | .32 | 2.3 | | | 286 | | 2.10 | | |
| w/ brown sce, apple stuffing & mixed | 227 | | 13.9 | | 48 | | 1 | .16 | | | 612 | 17 | | | |
| veg, Am Hosp Co—*6 oz entree* | 170 | 15.5 | 10.2 | | | 698 | .36 | 3.1 | | | 318 | | .96 | | |
| **pork rib shaped patties, char-broiled w/** | 467 | | 20.3 | | 191 | | 9 | .17 | | | 1506 | 63 | | | |
| bbq sce, Am Hosp Co—*6.7 oz entree* | 190 | 19.5 | 51.6 | | | 697 | .35 | 4.6 | | | 766 | | 3.01 | | |
| **pot pie** | | | | | | | | | | | | | | | |
| beef, Banquet | 449 | | 24.0 | | | | 1 | .05 | | | 1292 | 23 | | | |
| *8 oz pie* | 227 | 14.0 | 44.0 | | | 655 | .18 | 0.9 | | | 113 | | 2.00 | | |
| chicken, Banquet | 450 | | 24.0 | | | | 1 | .07 | | | 966 | 38 | | | |
| *8 oz pie* | 227 | 15.0 | 44.0 | | | 669 | .21 | 2.0 | | | 109 | | 1.90 | | |
| tuna, Banquet | 395 | | 18.0 | | | | 0 | .06 | | | 565 | 58 | | | |
| *8 oz pie* | 227 | 16.0 | 43.0 | | | 170 | .19 | 3.5 | | | 162 | | .70 | | |
| turkey, Banquet | 437 | | 23.0 | | | | 0 | .07 | | | 1263 | 45 | | | |
| *8 oz pie* | 227 | 13.0 | 46.0 | | | 134 | .20 | 2.2 | | | 159 | | 1.60 | | |
| **rigatoni w/ ham & peas, Banquet** | 280 | | 8.0 | | 45 | | 1 | .31 | | | 1215 | 110 | | | |
| *10 oz entree* | 284 | 16.0 | 36.0 | | | 91 | .67 | 2.6 | | | 212 | | 2.40 | | |
| **salisbury steak** | | | | | | | | | | | | | | | |
| Banquet | 230 | | 18.0 | | 35 | | 0 | .12 | | | 766 | 49 | | | |
| *5 oz entree* | 142 | 10.0 | 7.0 | | | 29 | .09 | 1.1 | | | 180 | | 1.90 | | |
| champignon, Am Hosp Co | 194 | | 9.9 | | 111 | | 0 | .11 | | | 253 | 20 | | | |
| *5.5 oz entree* | 156 | 17.6 | 8.7 | | | 80 | .06 | 3.6 | | | 253 | | 3.30 | | |
| w/ gravy, Banquet | 210 | | 15.0 | | | | 1 | .12 | | | 850 | 38 | | | |
| *1/6 of 32 oz pkg* | 151 | 10.0 | 8.0 | | | 57 | .10 | 1.1 | | | 170 | | 1.50 | | |
| w/ onion sce, Am Hosp Co | 280 | | 19.3 | | 68 | | 1 | .13 | | | 1165 | 7 | | | |
| *6.7 oz entree* | 190 | 16.7 | 9.9 | | | 105 | .07 | 2.4 | | | 386 | | 1.90 | | |
| **scrod fillet, Seafood Elites** | | | | | | | | | | | | | | | |
| w/ broccoli & mozzarella | 140 | | 7.0 | | 66 | | | | | | 180 | | | | |
| *5 oz entree* | 142 | 19.0 | 1.0 | | | | | | | | | | | | |

[a] Vegetables include butternut squash, green beans & red peppers.

| | KCAL | H₂O (g) | FAT (g) | PUFA (g) | CHOL (mg) | A (RE) | C (mg) | B-2 (mg) | B-6 (mg) | FOL (mcg) | Na (mg) | Ca (mg) | Mg (mg) | Zn (mg) | Mn (mg) |
|---|---|---|---|---|---|---|---|---|---|---|---|---|---|---|---|
| | WT (g) | PRO (g) | CHO (g) | SFA (g) | DFIB (g) | A (IU) | B-1 (mg) | NIA (mg) | B-12 (mcg) | PANT (mg) | K (mg) | P (mg) | Fe (mg) | Cu (mg) | |
| w/ lemon & wild rice | 150 | | 5.0 | | 49 | | | | | | 320 | | | | |
| 5 oz entree | 142 | 20.0 | 7.0 | | | | | | | | | | | | |
| w/ spinach & cheddar | 140 | | 6.0 | | 63 | | | | | | 225 | | | | |
| 5 oz entree | 142 | 21.0 | 1.0 | | | | | | | | | | | | |
| seafood (cod & surimi) w/ rice, spinach & crm sce, Am Hosp Co—6 oz entree | 198 | | 9.1 | | 37 | | 5 | .08 | | | 356 | 75 | | | |
| | 170 | 16.9 | 12.3 | | | 2512 | .08 | 1.2 | | | 282 | | .90 | | |
| seafood natural herbs, Armour Classic Lites—11.5 oz entree | 250 | | 6.0 | | 20 | | | | | | 1240 | | | | |
| | 326 | 12.0 | 38.0 | | | | | | | | 340 | | | | |
| seafood (scallops) creole, Am Hosp Co / 6 oz entree | 137 | | 3.8 | | 21 | | 38 | .10 | | | 372 | 223 | | | |
| | 170 | 10.4 | 15.4 | | | 1220 | .11 | 1.8 | | | 537 | | 1.56 | | |
| seafood (shrimp, cod & surimi) & pasta w/ sce, Am Hosp Co—6 oz entree | 180 | | 8.4 | | 56 | | 1 | .08 | | | 316 | 26 | | | |
| | 170 | 10.6 | 15.6 | | | 287 | .09 | 1.3 | | | 140 | | .78 | | |
| shrimp creole w/ rice & peppers, Light & Elegant—10 oz entree | 218 | | 2.0 | | 120 | | 1 | .09 | | | 1050 | 68 | | | |
| | 283 | 14.0 | 36.0 | | | 720 | .17 | 1.2 | | | 220 | 225 | 1.80 | | |
| sirloin tips supreme, Banquet / 10 oz entree | 160 | | 1.0 | | 40 | | 1 | .20 | | | 1030 | 49 | | | |
| | 284 | 13.0 | 24.0 | | | 2200 | .14 | 2.2 | | | 365 | | 3.20 | | |
| **sole fillet, Seafood Elites** | | | | | | | | | | | | | | | |
| w/ broccoli & mozzarella | 150 | | 7.0 | | 53 | | | | | | 205 | | | | |
| 5 oz entree | 142 | 18.0 | 2.0 | | | | | | | | | | | | |
| w/ lemon & wild rice | 150 | | 7.0 | | 47 | | | | | | 325 | | | | |
| 5 oz entree | 142 | 16.0 | 8.0 | | | | | | | | | | | | |
| w/ spinach & cheddar | 130 | | 6.0 | | 58 | | | | | | 200 | | | | |
| 5 oz entree | 142 | 16.0 | 2.0 | | | | | | | | | | | | |
| **spaghetti w/ meat sce** | | | | | | | | | | | | | | | |
| Am Hosp Co / 6 oz entree | 173 | | 4.5 | | 26 | | 14 | .30 | | | 654 | 30 | | | |
| | 170 | 14.4 | 18.6 | | | 702 | .57 | 5.8 | | | 612 | | 3.40 | | |
| Banquet / 8 oz entree | 270 | | 8.0 | | | | 14 | .12 | | | 1242 | 29 | | | |
| | 227 | 14.0 | 35.0 | | | 898 | .12 | 3.2 | | | 421 | | 3.00 | | |
| Light & Elegant / 10.25 oz entree | 290 | | 8.0 | | 35 | | 10 | .15 | | | 700 | 100 | | | |
| | 290 | 16.0 | 40.0 | | | 787 | .25 | 3.4 | | | 794 | 252 | 6.00 | | |
| sweet & sour pork, Am Hosp Co / 6 oz entree | 222 | | 9.7 | | 38 | | 44 | .08 | | | 801 | 19 | | | |
| | 170 | 12.6 | 21.0 | | | 660 | .09 | 2.6 | | | 300 | | 1.33 | | |
| sweet & sour pork w/ rice, Van de Kamp's—11 oz entree | 430 | | 15.0 | | | | | | | | 790 | | | | |
| | 312 | 15.0 | 65.0 | | | | | | | | | | | | |
| swiss steak w/ brown sce, Am Hosp Co / 5.7 oz entree | 224 | | 11.8 | | 60 | | 5 | | | | 738 | 5 | | | |
| | 162 | 25.8 | 3.7 | | | 0 | .06 | 6.1 | | | 298 | | 1.60 | | |
| taquitos, beef, shredded w/ guacamole, Van de Kamp's—8 oz entree | 490 | | 25.0 | | | | | | | | 990 | | | | |
| | 227 | 15.0 | 45.0 | | | | | | | | | | | | |
| tortellini besciamella (ham), Am Hosp Co / 6 oz entree | 276 | | 15.8 | | 94 | | 2 | .16 | | | 650 | 149 | | | |
| | 170 | 13.4 | 19.9 | | | 485 | .23 | 2.0 | | | 200 | | 1.62 | | |
| tostada, beef supreme, Van de Kamp's / 8.5 oz entree | 530 | | 30.0 | | | | | | | | 900 | | | | |
| | 241 | 25.0 | 40.0 | | | | | | | | | | | | |
| tuna & cheese pastry wrap, Am Hosp Co / 4.5 oz entree | 287 | | 18.8 | | 14 | | 10 | .12 | | | 387 | 74 | | | |
| | 128 | 12.3 | 17.0 | | | 386 | .14 | 4.5 | | | 68 | | 1.63 | | |
| tuna & noodles, Am Hosp Co / 6 oz entree | 135 | | 3.1 | | 14 | | 1 | .04 | | | 518 | 23 | | | |
| | 170 | 13.8 | 12.9 | | | 77 | .10 | 3.8 | | | 140 | | 1.30 | | |
| turkey breast, sliced w/ apple stuffing & gravy, Am Hosp Co—6 oz entree | 339 | | 14.8 | | 55 | | 2 | .14 | | | 333 | 33 | | | |
| | 170 | 23.1 | 28.5 | | | 302 | .16 | 7.2 | | | 304 | | 1.32 | | |
| turkey, carrots & peas w/ supreme sce, Am Hosp Co—6 oz entree | 132 | | 3.6 | | 33 | | 6 | .15 | | | 80 | 57 | | | |
| | 170 | 17.8 | 7.8 | | | 4122 | .11 | 3.8 | | | 178 | | 7.80 | | |
| turkey, sliced w/ gravy / 5 oz entree | 95 | 120.8 | 3.7 | 0.7 | | | | .18 | .14 | | 786 | 20 | 12 | | .99 |
| | 142 | 8.4 | 6.6 | 2.2 | | 59 | .03 | 2.6 | | | | 114 | 1.31 | | |
| Banquet / 5 oz entree | 110 | | 5.0 | | 45 | | 0 | .09 | | | 586 | 19 | | | |
| | 142 | 8.6 | 7.0 | | | 8 | .04 | 1.7 | | | 83 | | .70 | | |
| Banquet / 1/4 of 32 oz pkg | 160 | | 8.0 | | | | 2 | .14 | | | 1010 | 31 | | | |
| | 227 | 14.0 | 8.0 | | | 45 | .01 | 2.9 | | | 150 | | 1.00 | | |
| w/ cranberry dressing, Am Hosp Co / 6 oz entree | 283 | | 17.0 | | 83 | | 2 | .15 | | | 441 | 30 | | | |
| | 170 | 18.7 | 13.8 | | | 846 | .06 | 3.9 | | | 224 | | 1.20 | | |

| | KCAL | H$_2$O (g) | FAT (g) | PUFA (g) | CHOL (mg) | A (RE) | C (mg) | B-2 (mg) | B-6 (mg) | FOL (mcg) | Na (mg) | Ca (mg) | Mg (mg) | Zn (mg) | Mn (mg) |
|---|---|---|---|---|---|---|---|---|---|---|---|---|---|---|---|
| | WT (g) | PRO (g) | CHO (g) | SFA (g) | DFIB (g) | A (IU) | B-1 (mg) | NIA (mg) | B-12 (mcg) | PANT (mg) | K (mg) | P (mg) | Fe (mg) | Cu (mg) | |
| w/ white & wild rice stuffing, Light & Elegant—*8 oz entree* | 230 | | 5.0 | | 55 | | 1 | .14 | | | 1020 | 18 | | | |
| | 227 | 20.0 | 25.0 | | | 857 | .12 | 4.6 | | | 280 | 121 | 1.00 | | |
| **turkey tetrazzini** | | | | | | | | | | | | | | | |
| Am Hosp Co | 228 | | 9.0 | | 23 | | 0 | .17 | | | 66 | 250 | | | |
| *6 oz entree* | 170 | 20.8 | 15.9 | | | 238 | .06 | 3.5 | | | 196 | | .66 | | |
| Banquet | 270 | | 4.0 | | 25 | | 0 | .32 | | | 1025 | 138 | | | |
| *10 oz entree* | 284 | 19.0 | 38.0 | | | 286 | .20 | 3.3 | | | 247 | | 2.60 | | |
| **veal & beef patties, Am Hosp Co** | 136 | | 6.3 | | 41 | | 2 | .15 | | | 189 | 14 | | | |
| *3 oz entree* | 85 | 14.4 | 5.4 | | | 69 | .18 | 6.9 | | | 206 | | .09 | | |
| **veal & peppers w/ tomato sce, Am Hosp Co**—*6 oz entree* | 106 | | 1.4 | | 31 | | 62 | .66 | | | 569 | 22 | | | |
| | 170 | 15.0 | 8.4 | | | 2148 | .06 | 4.1 | | | 365 | | | | |
| **veal blanquette (veal, onion & mushrooms w/ sce), Am Hosp Co**—*6 oz entree* | 148 | | 5.6 | | 61 | | 3 | .18 | | | 419 | 37 | | | |
| | 170 | 18.6 | 5.7 | | | 606 | .09 | 3.5 | | | 467 | | 1.50 | | |
| **veal cordon blue, Am Hosp Co** | 242 | | 9.0 | | 96 | | | | | | 416 | | | | |
| *5.5 oz entree* | 156 | 33.0 | 7.3 | | | | | | | | 634 | | | | |
| **veal florentine, Am Hosp Co**[a] | 208 | | 11.1 | | 60 | | 6 | .13 | | | 315 | 106 | | | |
| *6 oz entree* | 170 | 15.5 | 11.6 | | | 1767 | .13 | 3.9 | | | 418 | | 2.80 | | |
| **veal italiano, Am Hosp Co**[b] | 195 | | 9.1 | | 47 | | 11 | .21 | | | 267 | 75 | | | |
| *5.83 oz entree* | 165 | 17.8 | 10.5 | | | 718 | .24 | 9.7 | | | 472 | | .61 | | |
| **veal marsala, Am Hosp Co** | 164 | | 9.1 | | 52 | | 2 | .17 | | | 366 | 14 | | | |
| *6 oz entree* | 170 | 13.0 | 7.7 | | | 226 | .11 | 4.5 | | | 288 | | 2.22 | | |
| **veal parmigiana** | | | | | | | | | | | | | | | |
| Am Hosp Co | 279 | | 17.9 | | 67 | | 2 | .15 | | | 858 | 133 | | | |
| *5 oz entree* | 142 | 17.0 | 11.8 | | | 122 | .11 | 2.0 | | | 429 | | 1.67 | | |
| Banquet | 282 | | 18.0 | | | | 5 | .10 | | | 961 | 92 | | | |
| *1/5 of 32 oz pkg* | 181 | 15.0 | 21.0 | | | 378 | .06 | 2.3 | | | 213 | | 1.40 | | |
| breaded, Banquet | 230 | | 11.0 | | 35 | | 0 | .12 | | | 842 | 66 | | | |
| *5 oz entree* | 142 | 10.0 | 20.0 | | | 478 | .13 | 1.6 | | | 237 | | 1.70 | | |
| **veal stew, Am Hosp Co**[c] | 108 | | 1.8 | | 39 | | 5 | .22 | | | 108 | 24 | | | |
| *6 oz entree* | 170 | 15.6 | 7.2 | | | 4002 | .19 | 6.6 | | | 156 | | 3.00 | | |

## 10.4. FROZEN MEALS (USUALLY 3 COURSE MEALS)

| | KCAL | H$_2$O (g) | FAT (g) | PUFA (g) | CHOL (mg) | A (RE) | C (mg) | B-2 (mg) | B-6 (mg) | FOL (mcg) | Na (mg) | Ca (mg) | Mg (mg) | Zn (mg) | Mn (mg) |
|---|---|---|---|---|---|---|---|---|---|---|---|---|---|---|---|
| | WT (g) | PRO (g) | CHO (g) | SFA (g) | DFIB (g) | A (IU) | B-1 (mg) | NIA (mg) | B-12 (mcg) | PANT (mg) | K (mg) | P (mg) | Fe (mg) | Cu (mg) | |
| **beans & franks, Banquet** | 500 | | 19.0 | | | | 20 | .23 | | | 1377 | 153 | | | |
| *10.25 oz meal* | 291 | 19.0 | 64.0 | | | 4741 | .33 | 3.1 | | | 685 | | 5.00 | | |
| **beef, Banquet Extra Helping** | 864 | | 46.0 | | | | 13 | .39 | | | 1731 | 97 | | | |
| *16 oz meal* | 454 | 40.0 | 72.0 | | | 4864 | .24 | 8.2 | | | 904 | | 5.00 | | |
| **beef burgundy, Armour Dinner Classics** | 330 | | 15.0 | | 95 | | | | | | 990 | | | | |
| *10.5 oz meal* | 298 | 28.0 | 23.0 | | | | | | | | 540 | | | | |
| **beef, chopped, Banquet** | 434 | | 30.0 | | | | 9 | .20 | | | 1199 | 69 | | | |
| *11 oz meal* | 312 | 19.0 | 23.0 | | | 6803 | .12 | 4.1 | | | 658 | | 3.00 | | |
| **beef pepper steak, rice & green beans, Armour Classic Lites**—*10 oz meal* | 240 | | 7.0 | | 60 | | | | | | 1020 | | | | |
| | 284 | 16.0 | 28.0 | | | | | | | | 380 | | | | |
| **beef short ribs** | | | | | | | | | | | | | | | |
| boneless w/ bbq sce, Armour Dinner Classics—*10.5 oz meal* | 460 | | 26.0 | | 95 | | | | | | 1180 | | | | |
| | 298 | 25.0 | 33.0 | | | | | | | | 870 | | | | |
| boneless w/ horseradish sce, Armour Dinner Classics—*10.5 oz meal* | 370 | | 21.0 | | 100 | | | | | | 1160 | | | | |
| | 298 | 25.0 | 21.0 | | | | | | | | 720 | | | | |
| **beef stroganoff, Armour Dinner Classics** | 370 | | 17.0 | | 85 | | | | | | 1330 | | | | |
| *11.25 oz meal* | 319 | 30.0 | 25.0 | | | | | | | | 590 | | | | |
| **beef w/ gravy, Banquet** | 345 | | 19.0 | | | | 8 | .22 | | | 1009 | 59 | | | |
| *10 oz meal* | 284 | 23.0 | 19.0 | | | 6531 | .13 | 5.0 | | | 624 | | 3.00 | | |
| **burrito, grande w/ rice & corn, Van de Kamp's**—*14.75 oz meal* | 530 | | 20.0 | | | | | | | | 1210 | | | | |
| | 418 | 20.0 | 70.0 | | | | | | | | | | | | |
| **chicken a la king, rice & green beans almondine, Le Menu**—*10.25 oz meal* | 320 | | 13.0 | | | | | | | | 1170 | | | | |
| | 291 | 22.0 | 29.0 | | | | | | | | | | | | |
| **chicken & dumplings, Banquet** | 286 | | 13.0 | | | | 7 | .12 | | | 944 | 55 | | | |
| *9 oz meal* | 255 | 13.0 | 28.0 | | | 3101 | .11 | 4.2 | | | 396 | | 1.10 | | |

[a] Ground veal, spinach & rice w/ cream sce.
[b] Veal & beef patties w/ tomato sce & cheese.
[c] Veal, carrots, green peas & mushrooms.

| | KCAL / WT (g) | H₂O (g) / PRO (g) | FAT (g) / CHO (g) | PUFA (g) / SFA (g) | CHOL (mg) / DFIB (g) | A (RE) / A (IU) | C (mg) / B-1 (mg) | B-2 (mg) / NIA (mg) | B-6 (mg) / B-12 (mcg) | FOL (mcg) / PANT (mg) | Na (mg) / K (mg) | Ca (mg) / P (mg) | Mg (mg) / Fe (mg) | Zn (mg) / Cu (mg) | Mn (mg) |
|---|---|---|---|---|---|---|---|---|---|---|---|---|---|---|---|
| **chicken breast medallions marsala, Armour Classic Lites**—*11 oz meal* | 270 | | 7.0 | | 85 | | | | | | 970 | | | | |
| | 312 | 22.0 | 28.0 | | | | | | | | 470 | | | | |
| **chicken breast, sherried, Armour Dinner Classics**—*10 oz meal* | 300 | | 12.0 | | 90 | | | | | | 830 | | | | |
| | 284 | 29.0 | 19.0 | | | | | | | | 390 | | | | |
| **chicken burgundy, Armour Classic Lites** *11.25 oz meal* | 230 | | 5.0 | | 70 | | | | | | 1220 | | | | |
| | 319 | 21.0 | 26.0 | | | | | | | | 530 | | | | |
| **chicken fricassee, rice & broccoli, Armour Dinner Lites**—*11.75 oz meal* | 340 | | 12.0 | | 70 | | | | | | 1210 | | | | |
| | 333 | 23.0 | 35.0 | | | | | | | | 440 | | | | |
| **chicken fricassee, veg w/ sce, rice & green beans, Nutra Choice**—*12.5 oz meal* | 349 | | 9.5 | | 58 | | 12 | .36 | | | 167 | 166 | | | |
| | 354 | 27.3 | 36.8 | | | 2746 | .19 | 6.5 | | | 580 | 279 | 2.26 | | |
| **chicken** | | | | | | | | | | | | | | | |
| fried, Banquet *11 oz meal* | 359 | | 11.0 | | | | 11 | .18 | | | 1831 | 89 | | | |
| | 312 | 18.0 | 46.0 | | | 7589 | .16 | 5.5 | | | 674 | | 2.00 | | |
| hawaiian, Armour Dinner Classics—*11.5 oz meal* | 360 | | 10.0 | | 75 | | | | | | 700 | | | | |
| | 326 | 21.0 | 47.0 | | | | | | | | 540 | | | | |
| marsala, potatoes, carrots & green beans, Nutra Choice—*12.25 oz meal* | 304 | | 8.6 | | 68 | | 11 | .31 | | | 193 | 133 | | | |
| | 347 | 26.2 | 29.2 | | | 9497 | .16 | 7.7 | | | 728 | 248 | 2.04 | | |
| milan, Armour Dinner Classics *11.5 oz meal* | 350 | | 12.0 | | 75 | | | | | | 1360 | | | | |
| | 326 | 24.0 | 38.0 | | | | | | | | 540 | | | | |
| oriental, Armour Classic Lites *10 oz meal* | 250 | | 6.0 | | 65 | | | | | | 880 | | | | |
| | 284 | 24.0 | 26.0 | | | | | | | | 330 | | | | |
| parmigiana, fettucini alfredo & green beans, Le Menu—*11.5 oz meal* | 380 | | 18.0 | | | | | | | | 890 | | | | |
| | 326 | 27.0 | 28.0 | | | | | | | | | | | | |
| roasted breast, Armour Classic Lites *11 oz meal* | 270 | | 9.0 | | 85 | | | | | | 1220 | | | | |
| | 312 | 22.0 | 26.0 | | | | | | | | 560 | | | | |
| supreme w/ sce, parsleyed ndls, mxd veg, Nutra Choice—*12 oz meal* | 377 | | 11.4 | | 75 | | 23 | .31 | | | 176 | 141 | | | |
| | 340 | 34.5 | 32.2 | | | 6678 | .15 | 12.8 | | | 652 | 353 | 2.17 | | |
| tetrazzini, Armour Dinner Classics *11.5 oz meal* | 320 | | 14.0 | | 75 | | | | | | 850 | | | | |
| | 326 | 23.0 | 26.0 | | | | | | | | 490 | | | | |
| **chopped sirloin w/ mushroom gravy potatoes & green beans, Le Menu** *12.25 oz meal* | 410 | | 23.0 | | | | | | | | 1080 | | | | |
| | 347 | 26.0 | 28.0 | | | | | | | | | | | | |
| **chow mein, chicken, Armour Dinner Classics**—*10.5 oz meal* | 220 | | 4.0 | | 60 | | | | | | 1180 | | | | |
| | 298 | 20.0 | 25.0 | | | | | | | | 240 | | | | |
| **cod** | | | | | | | | | | | | | | | |
| almondine, Armour Dinner Classics *12 oz meal* | 360 | | 15.0 | | 95 | | | | | | 1440 | | | | |
| | 340 | 23.0 | 33.0 | | | | | | | | 590 | | | | |
| w/ lemon sce, rice, green peas & carrots, Nutra Choice—*12 oz meal* | 279 | | 8.0 | | 85 | | | | | | 196 | | | | |
| | 340 | 23.0 | 27.0 | | | | | | | | 632 | | | | |
| **enchilada** | | | | | | | | | | | | | | | |
| beef & cheese w/ rice & beans, Van de Kamp's—*14.75 oz meal* | 540 | | 20.0 | | | | | | | | 1380 | | | | |
| | 418 | 25.0 | 60.0 | | | | | | | | | | | | |
| beef, Banquet *12 oz meal* | 497 | | 15.0 | | | | 7 | .19 | | | 1805 | 109 | | | |
| | 340 | 19.0 | 72.0 | | | 376 | .44 | 3.0 | | | 419 | | 4.00 | | |
| beef, El Charrito *13.75 oz meal* | 620 | | 31.0 | | 45 | | | | | | 2130 | | | | |
| | 390 | 19.0 | 63.0 | | | | | | | | 790 | | | | |
| beef grande, El Charrito *21 oz meal* | 950 | | 49.0 | | 70 | | | | | | 2730 | | | | |
| | 595 | 29.0 | 93.0 | | | | | | | | 1290 | | | | |
| beef, 4 grande, El Charrito *16.5 oz meal* | 890 | | 47.0 | | 65 | | | | | | 2250 | | | | |
| | 468 | 28.0 | 83.0 | | | | | | | | 1140 | | | | |
| beef, 2 grande, 2 cheese tacos & beans, El Charrito—*16.5 oz meal* | 800 | | 35.0 | | 45 | | | | | | 2460 | | | | |
| | 468 | 23.0 | 92.0 | | | | | | | | 1220 | | | | |
| beef, shredded w/ rice & corn, Van de Kamp's—*14.75 oz meal* | 490 | | 15.0 | | | | | | | | 1170 | | | | |
| | 418 | 25.0 | 60.0 | | | | | | | | | | | | |
| beef, Van de Kamp's *12 oz meal* | 390 | | 15.0 | | | | | | | | 2175 | | | | |
| | 340 | 20.0 | 45.0 | | | | | | | | | | | | |
| cheese, Banquet *12 oz meal* | 543 | | 19.0 | | | | 7 | .27 | | | 2166 | 281 | | | |
| | 340 | 22.0 | 71.0 | | | 711 | .44 | 2.5 | | | 429 | | 3.00 | | |

| | KCAL / WT (g) | H₂O (g) / PRO (g) | FAT (g) / CHO (g) | PUFA (g) / SFA (g) | CHOL (mg) / DFIB (g) | A (RE) / A (IU) | C (mg) / B-1 (mg) | B-2 (mg) / NIA (mg) | B-6 (mg) / B-12 (mcg) | FOL (mcg) / PANT (mg) | Na (mg) / K (mg) | Ca (mg) / P (mg) | Mg (mg) / Fe (mg) | Zn (mg) / Cu (mg) | Mn (mg) |
|---|---|---|---|---|---|---|---|---|---|---|---|---|---|---|---|
| cheese, El Charrito | 570 | | 24.0 | | 30 | | | | | | 2330 | | | | |
| *13.75 oz meal* | 390 | 16.0 | 72.0 | | | | | | | | 860 | | | | |
| cheese, Van de Kamp's | 450 | | 20.0 | | | | | | | | 1665 | | | | |
| *12 oz meal* | 340 | 20.0 | 45.0 | | | | | | | | | | | | |
| cheese w/ rice & beans, Van de Kamp's | 620 | | 30.0 | | | | | | | | 1460 | | | | |
| *14.75 oz meal* | 418 | 25.0 | 60.0 | | | | | | | | | | | | |
| chicken, El Charrito | 510 | | 17.0 | | 50 | | | | | | 2150 | | | | |
| *13.75 oz meal* | 390 | 22.0 | 69.0 | | | | | | | | 940 | | | | |
| chicken suiza w/ rice & beans, Van de Kamp's—*14.75 oz meal* | 550 | | 20.0 | | | | | | | | 1210 | | | | |
| | 418 | 25.0 | 65.0 | | | | | | | | | | | | |
| fillet of fish, Van de Kamp's | 300 | | 10.0 | | | | | | | | 1820 | | | | |
| *12 oz meal* | 340 | 25.0 | 25.0 | | | | | | | | | | | | |
| fish, Banquet | 553 | | 33.0 | | | | 18 | .26 | | | 927 | 62 | | | |
| *8.75 oz meal* | 248 | 18.0 | 45.0 | | | 5305 | .34 | 3.7 | | | 601 | | 6.00 | | |
| grande mexican style, El Charrito | 850 | | 47.0 | | 65 | | | | | | 3100 | | | | |
| *20 oz meal* | 567 | 26.0 | 87.0 | | | | | | | | 1200 | | | | |
| grand satillo, El Charrito | 820 | | 34.0 | | 45 | | | | | | 3160 | | | | |
| *20.75 oz meal* | 588 | 22.0 | 103.0 | | | | | | | | 1380 | | | | |
| ham, Banquet | 532 | | 22.0 | | | | 10 | .28 | | | 1148 | 80 | | | |
| *10 oz meal* | 284 | 21.0 | 61.0 | | | 7176 | .51 | 4.1 | | | 530 | | 4.00 | | |
| italian style, Banquet | 597 | | 26.0 | | | | 23 | .24 | | | 1783 | 79 | | | |
| *12 oz meal* | 340 | 21.0 | 71.0 | | | 1391 | .34 | 4.0 | | | 527 | | 4.00 | | |
| imperial chicken w/ mushrooms in sce & veg, Weight Watchers[a] | 240 | | 4.0 | | | | | | | | 840 | | | | |
| *9.25 oz meal* | 262 | 22.0 | 29.0 | | | | | | | | | | | | |
| lasagna, Armour Dinner Classics | 380 | | 16.0 | | 70 | | | | | | 1120 | | | | |
| *10 oz meal* | 284 | 17.0 | 42.0 | | | | | | | | 580 | | | | |
| macaroni & cheese, Banquet | 334 | | 16.0 | | | | 12 | .16 | | | 940 | 184 | | | |
| *9 oz meal* | 255 | 11.0 | 37.0 | | | 5109 | .19 | 1.5 | | | 295 | | 2.60 | | |
| meat loaf, Banquet | 437 | | 27.0 | | | | 18 | .21 | | | 1525 | 80 | | | |
| *11 oz meal* | 312 | 20.0 | 30.0 | | | 5044 | .19 | 4.0 | | | 702 | | 3.00 | | |
| **mexican style** | | | | | | | | | | | | | | | |
|   Banquet | 483 | | 18.0 | | | | 8 | .16 | | | 1995 | 110 | | | |
|   *12 oz meal* | 340 | 18.0 | 62.0 | | | 358 | .39 | 2.8 | | | 439 | | 3.00 | | |
|   Banquet Extra Helping | 777 | | 27.0 | | | | 13 | .43 | | | 4778 | 411 | | | |
|   *21.25 oz meal* | 602 | 31.0 | 105.0 | | | 1261 | .65 | 3.8 | | | 712 | | 5.00 | | |
|   combination, Banquet | 518 | | 17.0 | | | | 7 | .23 | | | 1978 | 194 | | | |
|   *12 oz meal* | 340 | 20.0 | 72.0 | | | 539 | .44 | 2.7 | | | 423 | | 3.00 | | |
|   El Charrito | 690 | | 35.0 | | 45 | | | | | | 2430 | | | | |
|   *14.25 oz meal* | 404 | 30.0 | 70.0 | | | | | | | | 870 | | | | |
|   Van de Kamp's | 420 | | 20.0 | | | | | | | | 1040 | | | | |
|   *11.5 oz meal* | 326 | 20.0 | 45.0 | | | | | | | | | | | | |
| noodles & chicken, Banquet | 361 | | 11.0 | | | | 4 | .16 | | | 964 | 62 | | | |
| *9.5 oz meal* | 269 | 13.0 | 50.0 | | | 4923 | .16 | 3.1 | | | 295 | | 2.60 | | |
| oriental beef, veg & rice, Lean Cuisine | 270 | | 8.0 | | | | | | | | 1150 | | | | |
| *8.6 oz meal* | 245 | 20.0 | 30.0 | | | | | | | | | | | | |
| pork sliced w/ orange sce, rice & veg medley, Nutra Choice | 354 | | 10.3 | | 81 | | 34 | .40 | | | 99 | 46 | | | |
| *11 oz meal* | 312 | 26.4 | 38.4 | | | 812 | .53 | 5.6 | | | 525 | 230 | 2.68 | | |
| queso, El Charrito | 490 | | 16.0 | | 15 | | | | | | 2540 | | | | |
| *13.25 oz meal* | 376 | 14.0 | 74.0 | | | | | | | | 970 | | | | |
| **salisbury steak** | | | | | | | | | | | | | | | |
|   Banquet | 395 | | 26.0 | | | | 10 | .15 | | | 1333 | 62 | | | |
|   *11 oz meal* | 312 | 17.0 | 24.0 | | | 4203 | .14 | 3.1 | | | 514 | | 2.00 | | |
|   Banquet Extra Helping | 1024 | | 65.0 | | | | 13 | .35 | | | 2175 | 127 | | | |
|   *19 oz meal* | 539 | 39.0 | 72.0 | | | 4662 | .22 | 6.0 | | | 851 | | 4.00 | | |
|   italian style sce & veg, Lean Cuisine | 270 | | 13.0 | | | | | | | | 820 | | | | |
|   *9.5 oz meal* | 269 | 25.0 | 14.0 | | | | | | | | | | | | |

[a] Vegetables include rice & broccoli.

| | KCAL / WT (g) | H₂O (g) / PRO (g) | FAT (g) / CHO (g) | PUFA (g) / SFA (g) | CHOL (mg) / DFIB (g) | A (RE) / A (IU) | C (mg) / B-1 (mg) | B-2 (mg) / NIA (mg) | B-6 (mg) / B-12 (mcg) | FOL (mcg) / PANT (mg) | Na (mg) / K (mg) | Ca (mg) / P (mg) | Mg (mg) / Fe (mg) | Zn (mg) / Cu (mg) | Mn (mg) |
|---|---|---|---|---|---|---|---|---|---|---|---|---|---|---|---|
| roman w/ rotini noodles, Weight Watchers—*8.75 oz meal* | 300 / 248 | / 25.0 | 12.0 / 24.0 | | | | | | | | 990 / | | | | |
| whipped potatoes, corn & cherry apple crmb cke, Swanson's—*10.75 oz meal* | 350 / 305 | / 18.0 | 14.0 / 38.0 | | | | | | | | 1025 / | | | | |
| **salisbury steak w/ mushroom gravy,** | | | | | | | | | | | | | | | |
| broccoli & potatoes, Armour Classic Lites—*10 oz meal* | 290 / 284 | / 20.0 | 13.0 / 25.0 | | 75 / | | | | | | 870 / 780 | | | | |
| potatoes, peas & corn, Armour Dinner Classics—*11 oz meal* | 480 / 312 | / 20.0 | 27.0 / 39.0 | | 110 / | | | | | | 1400 / 740 | | | | |
| **salisbury steak w/ mushroom sce,** | | | | | | | | | | | | | | | |
| escalloped potatoes & peas w/ sce, Nutra Choice—*12 oz meal* | 378 / 340 | / 26.2 | 19.0 / 35.7 | | 97 / | / 891 | 19 / .32 | .40 / 5.3 | | | 244 / 824 | 135 / 284 | / 4.57 | | |
| satillo, El Charrito *13.5 oz meal* | 570 / 383 | / 16.0 | 24.0 / 70.0 | | 30 / | | | | | | 2200 / 860 | | | | |
| seafood newburg, Armour Dinner Classics *10.5 oz meal* | 280 / 298 | / 11.0 | 10.0 / 36.0 | | 70 / | | | | | | 1500 / 330 | | | | |
| shrimp americana, Armour Dinner Classics—*11.5 oz meal* | 280 / 326 | / 18.0 | 10.0 / 31.0 | | 110 / | | | | | | 1210 / 490 | | | | |
| shrimp creole, peas w/ sce & rice w/ sce, Nutra Choice—*12 oz meal* | 261 / 340 | / 18.3 | 3.9 / 38.2 | | 80 / | / 1333 | 32 / .27 | .17 / 4.7 | | | 142 / 558 | 83 / 214 | / 3.41 | | |
| shrimp in sherried crm sce, Armour Classic Lites—*10.5 oz meal* | 280 / 298 | / 17.0 | 8.0 / 34.0 | | 110 / | | | | | | 1220 / 490 | | | | |
| sirloin roast, Armour Dinner Classics *11 oz meal* | 280 / 312 | / 25.0 | 9.0 / 24.0 | | 100 / | | | | | | 780 / 730 | | | | |
| **sirloin tips w/ mushroom gravy,** | | | | | | | | | | | | | | | |
| potatoes, grn beans & carrots, Armour Dinner Classics—*11 oz meal* | 370 / 312 | / 29.0 | 16.0 / 27.0 | | 100 / | | | | | | 1180 / 710 | | | | |
| potatoes & broccoli w/ cheese sce, Le Menu—*11.5 oz meal* | 390 / 326 | / 29.0 | 19.0 / 26.0 | | | | | | | | 825 / | | | | |
| **sirloin tips w/ mushroom sce,** | | | | | | | | | | | | | | | |
| parsleyed noodles & mixed veg, Nutra Choice—*11 oz meal* | 297 / 312 | / 27.9 | 7.6 / 27.2 | | 69 / | / 5565 | 29 / .12 | .28 / 5.7 | | | 177 / 529 | 52 / 265 | / 4.01 | | |
| **spaghetti & meatballs** | | | | | | | | | | | | | | | |
| Armour Dinner Classics *11 oz meal* | 350 / 312 | / 14.0 | 21.0 / 27.0 | | 95 / | | | | | | 1130 / 760 | | | | |
| Banquet *9.5 oz meal* | 418 / 269 | / 15.0 | 14.0 / 57.0 | | / | / 4918 | 14 / .22 | .20 / 2.8 | | | 1317 / 473 | 73 / | / 3.60 | | |
| steak diane mignonettes, Armour Classic Lites—*10 oz meal* | 290 / 284 | / 29.0 | 9.0 / 23.0 | | 90 / | | | | | | 770 / 760 | | | | |
| stuffed cabbage, Armour Classic Lites *12 oz meal* | 290 / 340 | / 13.0 | 8.0 / 43.0 | | 40 / | | | | | | 600 / 780 | | | | |
| stuffed green peppers, Armour Dinner Classics—*12 oz meal* | 390 / 340 | / 16.0 | 18.0 / 41.0 | | 70 / | | | | | | 1750 / 580 | | | | |
| swedish meatballs, Armour Dinner Classics—*11.5 oz meal* | 470 / 326 | / 23.0 | 28.0 / 32.0 | | 105 / | | | | | | 1560 / 760 | | | | |
| **sweet & sour chicken** | | | | | | | | | | | | | | | |
| Armour Classic Lites *11 oz meal* | 250 / 312 | / 23.0 | 3.0 / 33.0 | | 70 / | | | | | | 640 / 400 | | | | |
| Armour Dinner Classics *11 oz meal* | 450 / 312 | / 16.0 | 20.0 / 51.0 | | 65 / | | | | | | 1240 / 450 | | | | |
| szechuan beef, Armour Classic Lites *10 oz meal* | 280 / 284 | / 23.0 | 9.0 / 26.0 | | 70 / | | | | | | 1010 / 520 | | | | |
| teriyaki chicken, Armour Dinner Classics *10.5 oz meal* | 250 / 298 | / 22.0 | 5.0 / 28.0 | | 80 / | | | | | | 1120 / 350 | | | | |
| teriyaki steak, Armour Dinner Classics *10 oz meal* | 360 / 284 | / 24.0 | 16.0 / 32.0 | | 95 / | | | | | | 1445 / 540 | | | | |

| | KCAL | H$_2$O (g) | FAT (g) | PUFA (g) | CHOL (mg) | A (RE) | C (mg) | B-2 (mg) | B-6 (mg) | FOL (mcg) | Na (mg) | Ca (mg) | Mg (mg) | Zn (mg) | Mn (mg) |
|---|---|---|---|---|---|---|---|---|---|---|---|---|---|---|---|
| | WT (g) | PRO (g) | CHO (g) | SFA (g) | DFIB (g) | A (IU) | B-1 (mg) | NIA (mg) | B-12 (mcg) | PANT (mg) | K (mg) | P (mg) | Fe (mg) | Cu (mg) | |
| **turf & surf, Armour Classic Lites** | 250 | | 7.0 | | 80 | | | | | | 890 | | | | |
| *10 oz meal* | 284 | 31.0 | 14.0 | | | | | | | | 520 | | | | |
| **turkey** | | | | | | | | | | | | | | | |
| Banquet | 320 | | 9.0 | | | | 8 | .25 | | | 1416 | 98 | | | |
| *11 oz meal* | 312 | 19.0 | 41.0 | | | 5656 | .20 | 5.1 | | | 639 | | 2.00 | | |
| Banquet Extra Helping | 723 | | 23.0 | | | | 14 | .44 | | | 2165 | 176 | | | |
| *19 oz meal* | 539 | 31.0 | 98.0 | | | 4940 | .34 | 7.6 | | | 946 | | 4.00 | | |
| **turkey parmesan w/ veg, butter sce & spaghetti, Armour Classic Lites** | 240 | | 8.0 | | 70 | | | | | | 480 | | | | |
| *11 oz meal* | 312 | 19.0 | 25.0 | | | | | | | | 770 | | | | |
| **veal parmigiana** | | | | | | | | | | | | | | | |
| Banquet | 413 | | 21.0 | | | | 19 | .18 | | | 1310 | 121 | | | |
| *11 oz meal* | 312 | 14.0 | 43.0 | | | 889 | .26 | 3.5 | | | 468 | | 3.00 | | |
| fettucine alfredo, green beans & apple crumb, Swanson's—*12.25 oz meal* | 490 | | 19.0 | | | | | | | | 965 | | | | |
| | 347 | 23.0 | 56.0 | | | | | | | | | | | | |
| pasta primavera, Nutra Choice | 354 | | 16.4 | | 76 | | 25 | .30 | | | 149 | 106 | | | |
| *11 oz meal* | 312 | 24.7 | 26.9 | | | 6534 | .15 | 5.3 | | | 571 | 289 | 4.04 | | |
| spaghetti & italian mixed veg, Armour Dinner Classics—*10.75 oz meal* | 400 | | 22.0 | | 75 | | | | | | 1430 | | | | |
| | 305 | 17.0 | 34.0 | | | | | | | | 520 | | | | |
| w/ veg medley, Weight Weighters | 230 | | 9.0 | | | | | | | | 1040 | | | | |
| *8 oz meal* | 229 | 24.0 | 9.0 | | | | | | | | | | | | |
| **western, Banquet** | 513 | | 29.0 | | | | 7 | .16 | | | 1548 | 93 | | | |
| *11 oz meal* | 312 | 22.0 | 43.0 | | | 57 | .14 | 3.6 | | | 643 | | 4.00 | | |
| **yankee pot roast** | | | | | | | | | | | | | | | |
| w/ gravy & parsleyed potatoes, Armour Dinner Classics—*11 oz meal* | 380 | | 15.0 | | 90 | | | | | | 820 | | | | |
| | 312 | 30.0 | 32.0 | | | | | | | | 770 | | | | |
| w/ mushroom grvy, potatoes, carrots & pearl onions, Le Menu—*11 oz meal* | 360 | | 15.0 | | | | | | | | 810 | | | | |
| | 312 | 28.0 | 28.0 | | | | | | | | | | | | |
| w/ sce, parsleyed potatoes & veg, Nutra Choice—*12 oz meal* | 281 | | 5.5 | | 67 | | 24 | .28 | | | 131 | 49 | | | |
| | 340 | 29.4 | 27.1 | | | 9562 | .28 | 6.9 | | | 733 | 284 | 4.48 | | |

## 10.5. HOMEMADE ENTREES

| | KCAL | H$_2$O (g) | FAT (g) | PUFA (g) | CHOL (mg) | A (RE) | C (mg) | B-2 (mg) | B-6 (mg) | FOL (mcg) | Na (mg) | Ca (mg) | Mg (mg) | Zn (mg) | Mn (mg) |
|---|---|---|---|---|---|---|---|---|---|---|---|---|---|---|---|
| | WT (g) | PRO (g) | CHO (g) | SFA (g) | DFIB (g) | A (IU) | B-1 (mg) | NIA (mg) | B-12 (mcg) | PANT (mg) | K (mg) | P (mg) | Fe (mg) | Cu (mg) | |
| **beef & veg stew** | 218 | 201.9 | 10.5 | | | | 17 | .17 | | | 91[a] | 29 | | | |
| *1 cup* | 245 | 15.7 | 15.2 | 4.9 | | 2400 | .15 | 4.7 | | | 613 | 184 | 2.90 | | |
| **beef, dried, chipped, ckd, creamed** | 377 | 176.4 | 25.2 | | | | 1 | .47 | | | 1754 | 257 | | | |
| *1 cup* | 245 | 20.1 | 17.4 | 13.7 | | 880 | .15 | 1.5 | | | 375 | 343 | 2.00 | | |
| **chicken a la king** | 468 | 167.1 | 34.3 | | | | 12 | .42 | | | 760 | 127 | | | |
| *1 cup* | 245 | 27.4 | 12.3 | 12.7 | | 1130 | .10 | 5.4 | | | 404 | 358 | 2.50 | | |
| **chicken & noodles** | 367 | 170.6 | 18.5 | | | | 0 | .17 | | | 600 | 26 | | | |
| *1 cup* | 240 | 22.3 | 25.7 | 5.9 | | 430 | .05 | 4.3 | | | 149 | 247 | 2.20 | | |
| **chicken fricassee** | 386 | 171.1 | 22.3 | | | | | .17 | | | 370 | 14 | | | |
| *1 cup* | 240 | 36.7 | 7.4 | 7.2 | | 170 | .05 | 5.8 | | | 336 | 271 | 2.20 | | |
| **chop suey** | 300 | 188.5 | 17.0 | | | | 33 | .38 | | | 1053 | 60 | | | |
| *1 cup* | 250 | 26.0 | 12.8 | 8.5 | | 600 | .28 | 5.0 | | | 425 | 248 | 4.80 | | |
| **chow mein** | 255 | 195.0 | 10.0 | | | | 10 | .23 | | | 718 | 58 | | | |
| *1 cup* | 250 | 31.0 | 10.0 | 2.4 | | 280 | .08 | 4.3 | | | 473 | 293 | 2.50 | | |
| **clam fritter** | 124 | 16.1 | 6.0 | | | | | .05 | | | | 30 | | | |
| *1 fritter* | 40 | 4.6 | 12.4 | | | | .01 | 0.4 | | | 59 | 78 | 1.40 | | |
| **corn fritter** | 132 | 10.2 | 7.5 | | | | 1 | .07 | | | 167 | 22 | | | |
| *1 fritter* | 35 | 2.7 | 13.9 | 2.0 | | 140 | .06 | 0.6 | | | 47 | 54 | .60 | | |
| **crab, deviled**[b] | 451 | 151.9 | 22.6 | | | | 14 | .26 | | | 2081 | 113 | | | |
| *1 cup* | 240 | 27.4 | 31.9 | | | | .19 | 3.5 | | | 398 | 329 | 2.90 | | |
| **crab, imperial**[c] | 323 | 158.2 | 16.7 | | | | 11 | .26 | | | 1602 | 132 | | | |
| *1 cup* | 220 | 32.1 | 8.6 | | | | .13 | 2.4 | | | 288 | 365 | 2.00 | | |

[a] W/o added salt.

[b] Prepared w/ bread crumbs, butter or marg, parsley, eggs, lemon jce & catsup.

[c] Prepared w/ butter or margarine, flour, milk, onion, green pepper, eggs & lemon jce.

| | KCAL | H₂O (g) | FAT (g) | PUFA (g) | CHOL (mg) | A (RE) | C (mg) | B-2 (mg) | B-6 (mg) | FOL (mcg) | Na (mg) | Ca (mg) | Mg (mg) | Zn (mg) | Mn (mg) |
|---|---|---|---|---|---|---|---|---|---|---|---|---|---|---|---|
| | WT (g) | PRO (g) | CHO (g) | SFA (g) | DFIB (g) | A (IU) | B-1 (mg) | NIA (mg) | B-12 (mcg) | PANT (mg) | K (mg) | P (mg) | Fe (mg) | Cu (mg) | |
| **fish cake, fried[a]** | 103 | 39.6 | 4.8 | | | | | | | | | | | | |
| *1 piece* | 60 | 8.8 | 5.6 | | | | | | | | | | | | |
| **fish loaf, ckd[b]** | 186 | 108.3 | 5.6 | | | | | | | | | | | | |
| *1 slice* | 150 | 21.2 | 11.0 | | | | | | | | | | | | |
| **green pepper stuffed w/ beef & crumbs** | 315 | 116.7 | 10.2 | | | | 74 | .81 | | | 581 | 78 | | | |
| *1 stuffed pepper* | 185 | 24.1 | 31.1 | 4.8 | | 520 | .17 | 4.6 | | | 477 | 224 | 3.90 | | |
| **ham croquette** | 163 | 35.1 | 9.8 | | | | 0 | .14 | | | 222 | 45 | | | |
| *1 croquette* | 65 | 10.6 | 7.6 | 3.9 | | 170 | .18 | 1.6 | | | 54 | 104 | 1.40 | | |
| **lobster thermidor** | 405 | | 26.6 | | | | 0 | .51 | | | | 290 | | | |
| *5.5 oz* | 157 | 28.5 | 14.8 | | 0.5 | 984 | .15 | 4.8 | | | | 451 | 1.90 | | |
| **lobster newburg[c]** | 485 | 160.0 | 26.5 | | | | | .28 | | | 573 | 218 | | | |
| *1 cup* | 250 | 46.3 | 12.8 | | | | .18 | | | | 428 | 480 | 2.30 | | |
| **macaroni & cheese** | 430 | 116.4 | 22.2 | | | | 0 | .40 | | | 1086 | 362 | | | |
| *1 cup* | 200 | 16.8 | 40.2 | 11.9 | | 860 | .20 | 1.8 | | | 240 | 322 | 1.80 | | |
| **oyster stew[d]** | 233 | 196.8 | 15.4 | | | | | .43 | | | 812 | 274 | | | |
| *1 cup* | 240 | 12.5 | 10.8 | | | 820 | .14 | 2.2 | | | 319 | 266 | 4.60 | | |
| **pizza** | | | | | | | | | | | | | | | |
| cheese | 153 | 31.4 | 5.4 | | | | 5 | .13 | | | 456 | 144 | | | |
| *1 piece* | 65 | 7.8 | 18.4 | 2.1 | | 410 | .04 | 0.7 | | | 85 | 127 | .70 | | |
| sausage | 157 | 33.9 | 6.2 | | | | 6 | .08 | | | 488 | 11 | | | |
| *1 piece* | 67 | 5.2 | 19.8 | 1.8 | | 380 | .06 | 1.0 | | | 113 | 62 | .80 | | |
| **pot pie** | | | | | | | | | | | | | | | |
| beef | 517 | 115.7 | 30.5 | | | | 6 | .25 | | | 596 | 29 | | | |
| *1 piece* | 210 | 21.2 | 39.5 | 8.4 | | 1720 | .23 | 4.2 | | | 334 | 149 | 3.80 | | |
| chicken | 545 | 131.3 | 31.3 | | | | 5 | .26 | | | 594 | 70 | | | |
| *1 piece* | 232 | 23.4 | 42.5 | 10.9 | | 3090 | .26 | 4.2 | | | 343 | 232 | 3.00 | | |
| turkey | 550 | 130.4 | 31.3 | | | | 5 | .30 | | | 633 | 63 | | | |
| *1 piece* | 232 | 24.1 | 42.9 | 10.5 | | 3090 | .26 | 5.8 | | | 459 | 234 | 3.20 | | |
| **salmon patty** | 239 | | 12.4 | | 64 | | 4 | .22 | .07 | 13 | 96 | 78 | 34 | .84 | |
| *3.5 oz* | 100 | 15.8 | 16.1 | | 0.8 | 66 | .12 | 4.0 | 3.00 | .66 | 89 | 104 | 1.24 | | |
| **salmon rice loaf** | 212 | 129.5 | 7.8 | | | | | | | | | | | | |
| *1 slice* | 174 | 20.9 | 12.7 | | | | | | | | | | | | |
| **spanish rice** | 213 | 192.3 | 4.2 | | | | 37 | .07 | | | 774 | 34 | | | |
| *1 cup* | 245 | 4.4 | 40.7 | | | 1620 | .10 | 1.7 | | | 566 | 96 | 1.50 | | |
| **spaghetti in tomato sce** | 260 | 192.5 | 8.8 | | | | 13 | .18 | | | 955 | 80 | | | |
| *1 cup* | 250 | 8.8 | 37.0 | 2.0 | | 1080 | .25 | 2.3 | | | 408 | 135 | 2.30 | | |
| **spaghetti w/ meatballs & tomato sce** | 332 | 173.8 | 11.7 | | | | 22 | .30 | | | 1009 | 124 | | | |
| *1 cup* | 248 | 18.6 | 38.7 | 3.3 | | 1590 | .25 | 4.0 | | | 665 | 236 | 3.70 | | |
| **tuna patty** | 209 | | 10.6 | 0.7 | 47 | | 1 | .16 | | | 154 | 56 | 25 | | |
| *3.5 oz* | 100 | 19.8 | 7.4 | | | 78 | .08 | 7.4 | | | 64 | 173 | 1.70 | | |
| **welsh rarebit** | 415 | 162.9 | 31.6 | | | | 0 | .53 | | | 770 | 582 | | | |
| *1 cup* | 232 | 18.8 | 14.6 | 17.3 | | 1230 | .09 | 0.2 | | | 320 | 432 | .70 | | |

# 11. FAST FOODS
## 11.1. GENERIC FAST FOODS[e]

| | KCAL | H₂O (g) | FAT (g) | PUFA (g) | CHOL (mg) | A (RE) | C (mg) | B-2 (mg) | B-6 (mg) | FOL (mcg) | Na (mg) | Ca (mg) | Mg (mg) | Zn (mg) | Mn (mg) |
|---|---|---|---|---|---|---|---|---|---|---|---|---|---|---|---|
| | WT (g) | PRO (g) | CHO (g) | SFA (g) | DFIB (g) | A (IU) | B-1 (mg) | NIA (mg) | B-12 (mcg) | PANT (mg) | K (mg) | P (mg) | Fe (mg) | Cu (mg) | |
| **bacon cheeseburger** | 464 | 65.4 | 27.3 | | 68 | | 2 | .27 | .24 | 26 | 660 | 116 | 35 | 5.25 | |
| *1 sandwich* | 150 | 25.1 | 29.1 | | | 368 | .15 | 4.9 | 1.80 | .27 | 339 | 302 | 3.74 | .120 | |
| **burrito** | 392 | 89.3 | 13.6 | | 56 | | 2 | .30 | .17 | 29 | 1030 | 191 | 70 | 2.37 | |
| *1 burrito* | 174 | 15.5 | 51.9 | | | 209 | .37 | 5.4 | 1.04 | .31 | 501 | 235 | 2.70 | .313 | |
| **cheeseburger** | 299 | 51.3 | 15.1 | | 45 | | 1 | .24 | .11 | 18 | 672 | 136 | 22 | 2.24 | |
| *1 reg sandwich* | 112 | 14.8 | 28.3 | | | 340 | .26 | 3.7 | .90 | .27 | 220 | 174 | 2.33 | .112 | |
| **cheeseburger w/ 4 oz meat** | 524 | 88.3 | 31.4 | | 105 | | 2 | .49 | .23 | 23 | 1224 | 237 | 43 | 5.23 | |
| *1 sandwich* | 194 | 30.1 | 39.6 | | | 671 | .33 | 7.4 | 2.33 | .64 | 407 | 320 | 4.46 | .155 | |
| **chicken, fried** | | | | | | | | | | | | | | | |
| dark meat | 234 | 43.4 | 14.6 | | 51 | | 0 | .29 | | | 414 | 13 | 21 | 1.86 | |
| *3 oz* | 85 | 19.0 | 6.5 | | | 119 | .07 | 4.5 | | | 230 | 138 | 1.02 | .068 | |
| light & dark meat | 235 | 41.6 | 13.6 | | 72 | | 0 | .15 | .26 | 11 | 394 | 12 | 21 | 1.11 | |
| *3 oz* | 85 | 14.3 | 13.2 | | | 97 | .08 | 4.8 | .17 | | 223 | 146 | .78 | .060 | |

[a] Prepared w/ cnd flaked fish, potato & egg.
[b] Prepared w/ cnd flaked fish, bread cubes, egg, tomatoes, onions & butter or margarine.
[c] Prepared w/ butter or margarine, egg yolks, sherry & cream.
[d] Approximately 6 med oysters/cup.
[e] Averages of data covering a number of chains sampled in different locations.

| | KCAL | H₂O (g) | FAT (g) | PUFA (g) | CHOL (mg) | A (RE) | C (mg) | B-2 (mg) | B-6 (mg) | FOL (mcg) | Na (mg) | Ca (mg) | Mg (mg) | Zn (mg) | Mn (mg) |
|---|---|---|---|---|---|---|---|---|---|---|---|---|---|---|---|
| | WT (g) | PRO (g) | CHO (g) | SFA (g) | DFIB (g) | A (IU) | B-1 (mg) | NIA (mg) | B-12 (mcg) | PANT (mg) | K (mg) | P (mg) | Fe (mg) | Cu (mg) | |
| light meat | 224 | 42.8 | 12.1 | | 81 | | 0 | .09 | .26 | 11 | 366 | 10 | 21 | .61 | |
| *3 oz* | 85 | 12.6 | 16.1 | | | 66 | .07 | 5.7 | .17 | | 218 | 149 | .52 | .051 | |
| **chili** | 268 | 198.6 | 9.1 | | 26 | | 3 | 1.17 | .34 | 31 | 1061 | 70 | 52 | 3.90 | |
| *1 cup* | 260 | 23.9 | 23.9 | | | 1708 | .16 | 2.5 | 1.30 | | 731 | 187 | 4.16 | .416 | |
| **coffee** | 4 | 179.3 | 0.0 | | 0 | | 0 | .02 | | 0 | 2 | 4 | 13 | .05 | |
| *6 fl oz* | 180 | 0.2 | 0.0 | | | 0 | .00 | 0.4 | .00 | | 124 | 2 | .02 | .018 | |
| **cola** | 159 | 328.0 | 0.0 | | 0 | | 0 | .00 | .00 | | 18 | 11 | 4 | .15 | |
| *12 fl oz* | 369 | 0.0 | 40.6 | | | 0 | .00 | 0.0 | | | 7 | 63 | .18 | .111 | |
| **coleslaw** | 122 | 72.8 | 11.5 | | | | 1 | .02 | .11 | 39 | 232 | 44 | 14 | .21 | |
| *1/2 cup* | 100 | 1.7 | 11.7 | | | | .03 | 0.0 | .20 | .15 | 196 | | .54 | .030 | |
| **cookies** | | | | | | | | | | | | | | | |
| choc chip | 307 | 3.3 | 13.2 | | 18 | | 1 | .39 | .03 | 6 | 309 | 29 | 29 | .49 | |
| *13 cookies* | 68 | 3.9 | 46.4 | | | 75 | .10 | 2.3 | .14 | .15 | 168 | 106 | 1.54 | .170 | |
| plain | 313 | 2.8 | 10.7 | | 12 | | 1 | .24 | .02 | 6 | 359 | 12 | 11 | .31 | |
| *21 cookies* | 68 | 4.8 | 48.8 | | | 27 | .25 | 2.5 | .07 | .22 | 57 | 65 | 1.50 | .054 | |
| **enchilada** | 396 | 157.1 | 20.9 | | | | | .25 | .25 | | 1332 | 97 | 76 | 1.29 | |
| *1 enchilada* | 230 | 17.3 | 34.7 | | | | .18 | | 2.07 | .60 | 653 | 198 | 3.29 | .299 | |
| **english muffin w/ egg, cheese & bacon** | 359 | 67.5 | 18.1 | | 214 | | 1 | .50 | .15 | 41 | 832 | 197 | 28 | 1.86 | |
| *1 sandwich* | 138 | 17.9 | 31.1 | | | 654 | .47 | 3.7 | .83 | .69 | 201 | 290 | 3.11 | .124 | |
| **fish, breaded & fried** | 196 | 38.0 | 11.4 | | | | | .04 | .10 | 9 | 334 | 9 | 16 | .32 | |
| *1 portion* | 73 | 10.5 | 11.8 | | | 64 | .05 | 1.1 | .73 | .14 | 230 | 124 | .22 | | |
| **fish sandwich** | 469 | 81.8 | 26.7 | | 90 | | 0 | .24 | .12 | 43 | 621 | 61 | 34 | .88 | |
| *1 large sandwich* | 170 | 18.0 | 41.1 | | | 109 | .34 | 3.5 | 1.53 | | 374 | 247 | 2.23 | .136 | |
| **fish sandwich w/ cheese** | 421 | 60.2 | 22.7 | | 196 | | 3 | .27 | .10 | 24 | 668 | 132 | 29 | .95 | |
| *1 reg sandwich* | 140 | 15.8 | 38.5 | | | 160 | .32 | 3.3 | .84 | .48 | 274 | 223 | 1.85 | .098 | |
| **french fries** | 274 | 32.8 | 14.2 | | 14 | | 5 | .03 | .22 | 23 | 30ᵃ | 14 | 29 | .33 | |
| *3 oz* | 85 | 3.4 | 33.1 | | | 25 | .11 | 1.8 | .09 | .37 | 598 | 100 | .71 | .085 | |
| **ham & cheese sandwich** | 372 | 78.6 | 16.0 | | 70 | | 2 | .64 | | | 1118 | 217 | | | |
| *1 sandwich* | 155 | 24.2 | 32.4 | | | 186 | .19 | 2.5 | | | 332 | | 3.98 | | |
| **hamburger** | 245 | 44.8 | 11.1 | | 32 | | 1 | .25 | .10 | 17 | 463 | 56 | 20 | 1.86 | |
| *1 reg sandwich* | 98 | 12.1 | 28.4 | | | 77 | .24 | 3.8 | .78 | .30 | 202 | 107 | 2.16 | .098 | |
| w/ 4 oz meat | 444 | 87.5 | 21.1 | | 71 | | 2 | .38 | .28 | 24 | 762 | 75 | 40 | | |
| *1 sandwich* | 174 | 24.9 | 37.6 | | | 157 | .38 | 7.8 | 2.26 | .52 | 404 | 226 | 4.84 | | |
| w/ 4 oz meat on large roll | 668 | 139.7 | 37.2 | | 114 | | 3 | .37 | .40 | 55 | 1019 | 106 | 48 | 4.62 | |
| *1 sandwich* | 264 | 26.1 | 56.8 | | | 507 | .48 | 6.8 | 2.11 | | 560 | 243 | 4.73 | .264 | |
| w/ double meat | 370 | 67.8 | 20.8 | | 81 | | | .27 | | | 459 | 59 | 29 | 3.70 | |
| *1 sandwich* | 137 | 21.2 | 24.9 | | | 459 | .22 | 4.3 | | | 336 | 181 | 3.53 | .123 | |
| w/ double meat & 3 piece roll | 524 | 89.5 | 29.6 | | 78 | | 2 | .36 | .21 | 19 | 893 | 154 | 34 | 3.99 | |
| *1 sandwich* | 190 | 24.9 | 42.8 | | | 296 | .95 | 7.0 | 1.71 | .25 | 323 | 281 | 3.52 | .152 | |
| **hash brown potatoes** | 282 | 52.9 | | | | | | | | | 73ᵇ | 9 | 19 | .26 | |
| *3 oz* | 85 | | | | | | | | | | 282 | 70 | .54 | .093 | |
| **hot chocolate** | 47 | 177.8 | 0.4 | | 0 | | 0 | .08 | 2.06 | 2 | 68 | 43 | 24 | .39 | |
| *6 fl oz* | 206 | 1.6 | 11.1 | | | 2 | .00 | 0.0 | .41 | .25 | 107 | 43 | .14 | .103 | |
| **hot dog** | 214 | 43.7 | 13.7 | | 37 | | 0 | .23 | | | 636 | 27 | 13 | 2.05 | |
| *1 hot dog* | 82 | 9.1 | 13.6 | | | | .20 | 3.1 | | | 140 | 84 | 1.53 | .107 | |
| **hush puppies** | 153 | 17.9 | 5.5 | | | | 0 | .01 | .06 | 12 | | | | | |
| *3 pieces* | 45 | 3.2 | 17.5 | | | | .00 | 1.2 | .09 | .13 | | | | | |
| **lemon-lime soda** | 153 | 332.6 | 0.0 | | 0 | | 0 | .00 | | | 33 | 7 | 4 | .15 | |
| *12 fl oz* | 372 | 0.0 | 39.1 | | | 0 | .00 | 0.0 | .00 | | 4 | 0 | .45 | .037 | |
| **omelet w/ ham & cheese** | 255 | 74.3 | 17.7 | | 446 | | 6 | .55 | .19 | 41 | 399 | 116 | 19 | 2.17 | |
| *2 eggs* | 118 | 17.1 | 6.7 | | | 743 | .14 | 0.7 | 1.18 | 1.01 | 189 | 287 | 2.94 | .094 | |
| **onion rings** | 285 | 30.4 | 15.6 | | 16 | | 1 | .10 | .07 | 11 | 485 | 23 | 16 | .37 | |
| *3 oz* | 85 | 3.8 | 33.5 | | | 9 | .09 | 0.9 | .26 | .20 | 141 | 81 | .78 | .077 | |
| **orange jce** | 56 | 110.1 | 0.1 | | 0 | | 49 | .03 | .05 | 55 | 1 | 11 | 13 | .05 | |
| *1/2 cup* | 125 | 0.9 | 13.5 | | | 98 | .10 | 0.3 | .00 | .20 | 238 | 20 | .13 | .063 | |
| **orange soda** | 179 | 325.9 | 0.0 | | 0 | | 0 | .00 | .00 | | 52 | 15 | 4 | .26 | |
| *12 fl oz* | 372 | 0.0 | 45.8 | | | 0 | .00 | 0.0 | | | 37 | 11 | .26 | .074 | |
| **pancakes w/ butter & syrup** | 468 | 97.8 | 10.4 | | 46 | | 4 | .38 | .08 | 8 | 1020 | 122 | 28 | .62 | |
| *3 pancakes* | 200 | 7.0 | 82.2 | | | 244 | .28 | 3.0 | .20 | .22 | 216 | 430 | 2.20 | .100 | |

ᵃ 152 mg if salted.   ᵇ 453 mg if salted.

| | KCAL | H₂O (g) | FAT (g) | PUFA (g) | CHOL (mg) | A (RE) | C (mg) | B-2 (mg) | B-6 (mg) | FOL (mcg) | Na (mg) | Ca (mg) | Mg (mg) | Zn (mg) | Mn (mg) |
|---|---|---|---|---|---|---|---|---|---|---|---|---|---|---|---|
| | WT (g) | PRO (g) | CHO (g) | SFA (g) | DFIB (g) | A (IU) | B-1 (mg) | NIA (mg) | B-12 (mcg) | PANT (mg) | K (mg) | P (mg) | Fe (mg) | Cu (mg) | |
| **pizza** | | | | | | | | | | | | | | | |
| cheese | 290 | 54.6 | 8.6 | | 56 | | 2 | .29 | .12 | 55 | 698 | 220 | 31 | 1.67 | |
| 1 slice | 120 | 14.6 | 39.1 | | | 750 | .34 | 4.2 | .48 | .42 | 230 | 216 | 1.61 | .144 | |
| pepperoni | 306 | 56.2 | 11.5 | | | | 2 | .29 | .10 | 78 | 817 | 196 | | | |
| 1 slice | 120 | 13.0 | 36.7 | | | 532 | .32 | 5.1 | .36 | .42 | 216 | | 2.52 | | |
| **roast beef sandwich** | 347 | 78.0 | 13.4 | | 56 | | 3 | .33 | .29 | 42 | 756 | 60 | 38 | 3.66 | |
| 1 sandwich | 150 | 22.4 | 33.8 | | | 240 | .39 | 6.0 | 1.35 | .75 | 338 | 222 | 4.04 | .195 | |
| **salad bar items** | | | | | | | | | | | | | | | |
| alfalfa sprouts, raw | 2 | 5.5 | 0.0 | | 0 | | 0 | .01 | .00 | 2 | 0 | 2 | 2 | .06 | |
| 2 T | 6 | 0.2 | 0.2 | | | 9 | .00 | 0.0 | .00 | .03 | 5 | 4 | .06 | .010 | |
| bacon bits | 27 | 0.2 | 1.6 | | 0 | | 0 | .02 | | | 165 | 8 | | | |
| 1 T | 6 | 1.9 | 1.7 | | | 0 | .02 | 0.1 | | | | 18 | .30 | | |
| beets, pickled, cnd | 18 | 22.9 | 0.0 | | | | 1 | .01 | | | 74 | 3 | 4 | .07 | |
| 1/8 cup | 28 | 0.2 | 4.6 | | | 0 | .01 | 0.1 | .00 | | 41 | 5 | .11 | .034 | |
| broccoli, raw | 3 | 10.0 | 0.0 | | 0 | | 10 | .01 | .02 | 8 | 3 | 5 | 3 | .04 | |
| 1/8 cup | 11 | 0.3 | 0.6 | | | 170 | .01 | 0.1 | .00 | .06 | 36 | 7 | .10 | .004 | |
| carrots, raw | 6 | 12.3 | 0.0 | | 0 | | 1 | .01 | .02 | 2 | 5 | 4 | 2 | .03 | |
| 1/8 cup | 14 | 0.1 | 1.4 | | | 394 | .01 | 0.1 | .00 | .03 | 45 | 6 | .07 | .007 | |
| cheese, cheddar, shredded | 56 | 5.2 | 4.6 | | 15 | | 0 | .05 | .01 | 3 | 87 | 101 | 4 | .44 | |
| 2 T | 14 | 3.5 | 0.2 | | | 148 | .00 | 0.0 | .11 | .06 | 14 | 72 | .10 | | |
| cheese, cottage | 116 | 89.3 | 5.1 | | 17 | | 0 | .18 | .08 | 14 | 458 | 68 | 6 | .42 | |
| 1/2 cup | 113 | 14.1 | 3.1 | | | 184 | .02 | 0.1 | .68 | .24 | 95 | 149 | .16 | | |
| cheese, parmesan | 46 | 1.8 | 3.0 | | 1 | | 0 | .04 | .01 | 1 | 186 | 138 | 5 | .32 | |
| 2 T | 10 | 4.2 | 0.4 | | | 70 | .00 | 0.0 | | .05 | 11 | 81 | .10 | | |
| chickpeas (garbanzo beans) | 21 | 19.6 | 0.4 | | 0 | | 0 | .02 | | | 75 | 10 | | | |
| 2 T | 25 | 1.2 | 3.5 | | | 16 | .02 | 0.1 | .00 | | 43 | 23 | .30 | | |
| croutons | 60 | | 3.0 | | | | | | | | 155 | | | | |
| 1/2 oz | 14 | 2.0 | 8.0 | | | | | | | | 30 | | | | |
| cucumber, raw | 2 | 12.5 | 0.0 | | 0 | | 0 | .00 | .01 | 2 | 0 | 2 | 1 | .03 | |
| 2 T | 13 | 0.1 | 0.4 | | | 6 | .00 | 0.0 | .00 | .03 | 19 | 2 | .04 | .005 | |
| eggs, ckd, chopped | 27 | 12.7 | 1.9 | | 93 | | 0 | .05 | .02 | 8 | 23 | 10 | 2 | .24 | |
| 2 T | 17 | 2.1 | 0.2 | | | 88 | .01 | 0.0 | .22 | .29 | 22 | 31 | .36 | | |
| lettuce | 2 | 13.4 | 0.0 | | 0 | | 1 | .00 | .01 | 8 | 1 | 3 | 1 | | |
| 1/4 cup | 14 | 0.1 | 0.3 | | | 46 | .01 | 0.0 | .00 | .01 | 22 | 3 | .07 | | |
| mushrooms, raw | 2 | 8.3 | 0.0 | | 0 | | 0 | .04 | .01 | 2 | 0 | 0 | 1 | .07 | |
| 2 T | 9 | 0.2 | 0.4 | | | 0 | .01 | 0.4 | .00 | .20 | 33 | 9 | .11 | .044 | |
| onion, raw | 7 | 18.2 | 0.1 | | 0 | | 2 | .00 | .03 | 4 | 0 | 5 | 2 | .04 | |
| 2 T | 20 | 0.2 | 1.5 | | | | .01 | 0.0 | .00 | .03 | 31 | 6 | .07 | .008 | |
| pepper, green, raw | 3 | 11.1 | 0.0 | | 0 | | 23 | .01 | .02 | 2 | 0 | 1 | 2 | .02 | |
| 2 T | 12 | 0.1 | 0.6 | | | 684 | .01 | 0.1 | .00 | .00 | 23 | 3 | .15 | .012 | |
| potato salad | 179 | 95.0 | 10.3 | | 85 | | 13 | .08 | .18 | 9 | 661 | 24 | 19 | .39 | |
| 1/2 cup | 125 | 3.4 | 14.0 | | | 261 | .10 | 1.1 | .00 | .66 | 318 | 65 | .81 | .150 | |
| **salad dressing** | | | | | | | | | | | | | | | |
| blue cheese | 76 | 4.8 | 7.8 | | | | 0 | .02 | | | | 12 | | | |
| 1 T | 15 | 0.7 | 1.1 | | | 32 | .00 | 0.0 | | | | 11 | .03 | | |
| french | 79 | 5.2 | 8.7 | | 0 | | 0 | .00 | .00 | 0 | 176 | 2 | 0 | .01 | |
| 1 T | 15 | 0.0 | 0.6 | | | 1 | .00 | 0.0 | .00 | .00 | 2 | 1 | .03 | .002 | |
| italian | 79 | 5.2 | 8.6 | | 0 | | 0 | .00 | | | 162 | 1 | | | |
| 1 T | 15 | 0.1 | 0.9 | | | 29 | .00 | 0.0 | | | 5 | 1 | .03 | | |
| italian, low calorie | 7 | 12.9 | 0.0 | | 0 | | 0 | .00 | | | 136 | 1 | | | |
| 1 T | 15 | 0.0 | 1.7 | | | 0 | .00 | 0.0 | | | 4 | 1 | .02 | | |
| oil & vinegar | 72 | 7.6 | 8.0 | | | | | | | | 0 | | | | |
| 1 T | 16 | 0.0 | 0.4 | | | | | | | | 1 | | | | |
| thousand island | 57 | 6.9 | 5.4 | | | | | | | | 105 | 2 | | .02 | |
| 1 T | 15 | 0.1 | 2.3 | | | 48 | | | | | 17 | 3 | .09 | | |
| tomato, raw | 2 | 11.3 | 0.0 | | 0 | | 2 | .01 | .00 | 1 | 1 | 1 | 1 | .01 | |
| 2 slices | 12 | 0.1 | 0.5 | | | 136 | .01 | 0.1 | .00 | .03 | 25 | 3 | .06 | .010 | |
| **sausage** | 198 | 17.1 | 17.2 | | 39 | | 0 | .11 | .13 | 1 | 418 | 8 | 9 | 1.30 | |
| 1 patty | 46 | 8.4 | 1.9 | | | 31 | .20 | 2.3 | .51 | .30 | 136 | 74 | .81 | .046 | |

| | KCAL / WT (g) | H₂O (g) / PRO (g) | FAT (g) / CHO (g) | PUFA (g) / SFA (g) | CHOL (mg) / DFIB (g) | A (RE) / A (IU) | C (mg) / B-1 (mg) | B-2 (mg) / NIA (mg) | B-6 (mg) / B-12 (mcg) | FOL (mcg) / PANT (mg) | Na (mg) / K (mg) | Ca (mg) / P (mg) | Mg (mg) / Fe (mg) | Zn (mg) / Cu (mg) | Mn (mg) |
|---|---|---|---|---|---|---|---|---|---|---|---|---|---|---|---|
| **scrambled eggs** | 175 | 63.5 | 14.7 | | 346 | | 1 | .60 | .19 | 63 | 226 | 60 | 13 | 1.64 | |
| *2 eggs* | 95 | 13.2 | 2.5 | | | 632 | .08 | 0.3 | .95 | .72 | 154 | 230 | 2.59 | .067 | |
| **shake** | | | | | | | | | | | | | | | |
| choc | 360 | 202.3 | 10.5 | 0.4 | 37 | 64 | 1 | .69 | .14 | 10 | 273 | 319 | 47 | 1.15 | .110 |
| *10 fl oz* | 283 | 9.6 | 57.9 | 6.5 | | 263 | .16 | 0.5 | .97 | 1.10 | 567 | 288 | .88 | .184 | |
| strawberry | 319 | 209.7 | 8.0 | | 31 | 83 | 2 | .55 | .13 | 9 | 234 | 320 | 36 | 1.00 | .042 |
| *10 fl oz* | 283 | 9.5 | 53.4 | | | 340 | .13 | 0.5 | .88 | 1.39 | 516 | 283 | .30 | .062 | |
| van | 314 | 211.5 | 8.4 | 0.3 | 32 | 90 | 2 | .52 | .15 | 9 | 232 | 344 | 35 | 1.01 | .040 |
| *10 fl oz* | 283 | 9.8 | 50.8 | 5.3 | | 368 | .13 | 0.5 | 1.01 | 1.19 | 492 | 289 | .26 | .144 | |
| **sundae** | | | | | | | | | | | | | | | |
| caramel | 328 | 93.2 | 9.9 | | 26 | | 3 | .31 | .05 | 13 | 196 | 201 | 30 | .87 | |
| *1 sundae* | 165 | 7.3 | 53.0 | | | 281 | .07 | 1.0 | .66 | .40 | 338 | 231 | .23 | .083 | |
| hot fudge | 312 | 98.5 | 10.9 | | 18 | | 3 | .31 | .13 | 10 | 176 | 85 | 35 | .99 | |
| *1 sundae* | 165 | 7.3 | 46.5 | | | 231 | .07 | 1.1 | .66 | .35 | 413 | 238 | .24 | .132 | |
| strawberry | 285 | 101.6 | 8.9 | | 20 | | 3 | .30 | .05 | 20 | 97 | 175 | 28 | .31 | |
| *1 sundae* | 165 | 6.9 | 46.0 | | | 231 | .07 | 1.0 | .66 | .41 | 292 | 182 | .38 | .099 | |
| **taco** | 187 | 45.5 | 10.4 | | 21 | | 1 | .06 | .12 | 11 | 456 | 109 | 36 | 1.56 | |
| *1 taco* | 81 | 10.6 | 12.7 | | | 420 | .09 | 1.4 | .41 | .11 | 263 | 134 | 1.15 | .105 | |
| **tea** | 2 | 239.0 | 0.0 | | 0 | | 0 | .00 | | | 2 | 0 | 2 | .05 | |
| *8 fl oz* | 240 | 0.0 | 0.0 | | | | .02 | 0.0 | .00 | | 35 | 2 | .07 | .000 | |
| **tomato jce** | 21 | 114.6 | 0.1 | | 0 | | 22 | .04 | .13 | 24 | 440 | 11 | 13 | .17 | |
| *1/2 cup* | 122 | 1.0 | 5.1 | | | 678 | .06 | 0.8 | .00 | .31 | 268 | 23 | .71 | .122 | |
| **tuna submarine sandwich** | 566 | 142.3 | 27.8 | | | | | | | | 1288 | 74 | 79 | 1.86 | |
| *1 sandwich* | 255 | 28.8 | 52.0 | | | | | | | | 334 | 219 | 2.63 | .434 | |
| **turnover** | | | | | | | | | | | | | | | |
| apple | 255 | 36.5 | 14.1 | | 4[a] | | 1 | .06 | .03 | 3 | 326 | 12 | 8 | .16 | |
| *3 oz* | 85 | 2.2 | 31.3 | | | 34 | .09 | 1.0 | .09 | .13 | 42 | 34 | .94 | .043 | |
| cherry | 251 | 35.4 | 14.2 | | 13 | | 1 | .06 | .02 | 3 | 371 | 11 | 8 | .17 | |
| *3 oz* | 85 | 2.0 | 32.2 | | | 186 | .06 | 0.6 | .00 | .26 | 61 | 41 | .70 | .051 | |
| lemon | 279 | 32.0 | 15.0 | | 20 | | 0 | .09 | .02 | 3 | 286 | 11 | 9 | .24 | |
| *3 oz* | 85 | 2.7 | 34.3 | | | | .18 | 1.7 | .17 | .10 | 43 | 53 | 1.17 | .043 | |

## 11.2. BURGER KING

| | KCAL / WT (g) | H₂O (g) / PRO (g) | FAT (g) / CHO (g) | PUFA (g) / SFA (g) | CHOL (mg) / DFIB (g) | A (RE) / A (IU) | C (mg) / B-1 (mg) | B-2 (mg) / NIA (mg) | B-6 (mg) / B-12 (mcg) | FOL (mcg) / PANT (mg) | Na (mg) / K (mg) | Ca (mg) / P (mg) | Mg (mg) / Fe (mg) | Zn (mg) / Cu (mg) | Mn (mg) |
|---|---|---|---|---|---|---|---|---|---|---|---|---|---|---|---|
| **cheeseburger** | 317 | | 15.0 | | 48 | | 3 | .29 | | | 651 | 102 | 26 | 2.63 | |
| *1 sandwich* | 120 | 17.3 | 30.0 | 7.0 | | 341 | .23 | 3.9 | | | 247 | 186 | 2.74 | .060 | |
| **cheeseburger, double w/ bacon** | 510 | | 31.0 | | 104 | | | .42 | | | 728 | 168 | 37 | 5.06 | |
| *1 sandwich* | 159 | 31.9 | 27.0 | 15.0 | | 384 | .31 | 6.3 | | | 314 | 328 | 3.80 | .090 | |
| **chicken sandwich** | 688 | | 40.0 | | 82 | | | .31 | | | 1423 | 79 | 54 | 1.15 | |
| *1 sandwich* | 230 | 26.0 | 56.0 | 8.0 | | 126 | .45 | 9.6 | | | 375 | 274 | 3.30 | .160 | |
| **chicken tenders** | 204 | | 10.0 | | 47 | | | .08 | | | 636 | 18 | 24 | .56 | |
| *6 pieces* | 95 | 20.2 | 10.0 | 2.0 | | 95 | .08 | 7.3 | | | 200 | 236 | .67 | .070 | |
| **croissandwich** | | | | | | | | | | | | | | | |
| w/ bacon, egg & cheese | 355 | | 24.0 | | | | | .30 | | | 762 | 136 | 20 | 1.51 | |
| *1 croissandwich* | 119 | 14.6 | 20.0 | 8.0 | | 426 | .32 | 2.1 | | | 182 | 249 | 2.01 | | |
| w/ ham, egg & cheese | 335 | | 20.0 | | | | | .32 | | | 987 | 136 | 24 | 1.87 | |
| *1 croissandwich* | 145 | 17.5 | 20.0 | 6.0 | | 426 | .49 | 3.2 | | | 256 | 317 | 2.16 | | |
| w/ sausage, egg & cheese | 538 | | 41.0 | | | | | .32 | | | 1042 | 145 | 19 | 2.43 | |
| *1 croissandwich* | 163 | 19.4 | 20.0 | 14.0 | | 426 | .36 | 4.2 | | | 285 | 292 | 2.89 | | |
| **french fries** | 227 | | 13.0 | | 14 | | | .30 | | | 160 | | 21 | | |
| *1 reg serving* | 74 | 2.6 | 24.0 | 7.0 | | | .10 | 1.5 | | | 360 | 114 | .52 | .080 | |
| **french toast platter** | | | | | | | | | | | | | | | |
| w/ bacon | 469 | | 30.0 | | 73 | | | .24 | | | 448 | 59 | 19 | 1.30 | |
| *1 platter* | 117 | 11.0 | 41.0 | 7.0 | | | .24 | 3.3 | | | 151 | 118 | 2.72 | .010 | |
| w/ sausage | 635 | | 46.0 | | 115 | | | .27 | | | 686 | 70 | 18 | 2.32 | |
| *1 platter* | 158 | 16.1 | 41.0 | 13.0 | | | .29 | 5.5 | | | 242 | 164 | 3.71 | | |
| **ham & cheese sandwich** | 471 | | 24.0 | | 70 | | 7 | .42 | | | 1534 | 195 | 42 | 2.36 | |
| *1 sandwich* | 230 | 23.7 | 44.0 | 9.0 | | 725 | .87 | 6.1 | | | 419 | 384 | 3.19 | .120 | |

[a] If fried, cholesterol is 14 mg.

| | KCAL / WT (g) | H₂O (g) / PRO (g) | FAT (g) / CHO (g) | PUFA (g) / SFA (g) | CHOL (mg) / DFIB (g) | A (RE) / A (IU) | C (mg) / B-1 (mg) | B-2 (mg) / NIA (mg) | B-6 (mg) / B-12 (mcg) | FOL (mcg) / PANT (mg) | Na (mg) / K (mg) | Ca (mg) / P (mg) | Mg (mg) / Fe (mg) | Zn (mg) / Cu (mg) | Mn (mg) |
|---|---|---|---|---|---|---|---|---|---|---|---|---|---|---|---|
| **hamburger** | 275 | | 12.0 | | 37 | | 3 | .25 | | | 509 | 37 | 23 | 2.36 | |
| *1 sandwich* | 109 | 15.0 | 29.0 | 5.0 | | 150 | .23 | 3.9 | | | 235 | 124 | 2.73 | .060 | |
| **hot chocolate** | 131 | | 4.0 | | 1 | | | | | | 172 | 27 | 17 | | |
| *1 serving* | 244 | 1.3 | 22.0 | | | | | | | | 140 | 59 | .71 | .070 | |
| **onion rings** | 274 | | 16.0 | | 0 | | | | | | 665 | 124 | 18 | .37 | |
| *1 reg serving* | 79 | 3.6 | 28.0 | 3.0 | | | | | | | 173 | 195 | .80 | .090 | |
| **pie** | | | | | | | | | | | | | | | |
| apple | 305 | | 12.0 | | 4 | | 5 | .16 | | | 412 | | | | |
| *1 snack pie* | 125 | 3.1 | 44.0 | 4.0 | | | .27 | 0.6 | | | 122 | 31 | 1.18 | | |
| cherry | 357 | | 13.0 | | 6 | | 8 | .16 | | | 204 | | 12 | | |
| *1 snack pie* | 128 | 3.6 | 55.0 | 4.0 | | 370 | .24 | 0.5 | | | 166 | 37 | 1.12 | | |
| pecan | 459 | | 20.0 | | 4 | | | .18 | | | 374 | 24 | 16 | | |
| *1 snack pie* | 113 | 5.0 | 64.0 | 16.0 | | | .28 | | | | 204 | 84 | 1.13 | .140 | |
| **salad w/ dressing[a]** | 160 | | 13.2 | | 10 | | 42 | .13 | | | 322 | 45 | 28 | .49 | |
| *1 salad* | 176 | 2.6 | 8.5 | 2.0 | | 1630 | .06 | 1.3 | | | 396 | 68 | 1.34 | .120 | |
| **scrambled egg platter** | 468 | | 30.0 | | 370 | | 3 | .35 | | | 808 | 101 | 32 | 1.51 | |
| *1 platter* | 195 | 14.2 | 33.0 | | | 375 | .31 | 2.9 | | | 487 | 271 | 2.69 | .060 | |
| w/ bacon | 536 | | 36.0 | | 378 | | 3 | .38 | | | 975 | 103 | 35 | 1.85 | |
| *1 platter* | 206 | 18.0 | 33.0 | | | 375 | .39 | 3.6 | | | 532 | 299 | 2.82 | .060 | |
| w/ sausage | 702 | | 52.0 | | 420 | | 3 | .40 | | | 1213 | 112 | 33 | 2.69 | |
| *1 platter* | 247 | 21.9 | 33.0 | | | 375 | .42 | 5.5 | | | 623 | 335 | 3.66 | .060 | |
| **shake** | | | | | | | | | | | | | | | |
| choc | 320 | | 12.0 | | | | | .55 | | | 202 | 260 | 46 | .95 | |
| *1 med shake* | 273 | 8.0 | 46.0 | | | | .13 | | | | 567 | 262 | 1.61 | .090 | |
| choc w/ added syrup | 374 | | 11.0 | | | | | .51 | | | 225 | 248 | 56 | 1.05 | |
| *1 med shake* | 284 | 8.3 | 60.0 | | | | .12 | | | | 590 | 264 | 1.55 | .160 | |
| van | 321 | | 10.0 | | | | | .57 | | | 205 | 295 | 32 | .98 | |
| *1 med shake* | 273 | 8.7 | 49.0 | | | | .11 | | | | 508 | 284 | | | |
| **whaler sandwich** | 488 | | 27.0 | | 84 | | | .21 | | | 592 | 46 | 40 | .82 | |
| *1 sandwich* | 189 | 18.6 | 45.0 | 6.0 | | 36 | .28 | 4.0 | | | 369 | 249 | 2.22 | .110 | |
| w/ cheese | 530 | | 30.0 | | 95 | | | .24 | | | 734 | 112 | 43 | 1.10 | |
| *1 sandwich* | 201 | 20.9 | 46.0 | 8.0 | | 227 | .27 | 4.0 | | | 381 | 311 | 2.24 | .110 | |
| **whopper jr sandwich** | 322 | | 17.0 | | 41 | | 6 | .25 | | | 486 | 40 | 24 | 2.34 | |
| *1 sandwich* | 136 | 15.2 | 30.0 | 6.0 | | 296 | .23 | 4.0 | | | 278 | 127 | 2.81 | .070 | |
| w/ cheese | 364 | | 20.0 | | 52 | | 6 | .29 | | | 628 | 105 | 27 | 2.62 | |
| *1 sandwich* | 147 | 17.4 | 31.0 | 8.0 | | 488 | .23 | 4.0 | | | 290 | 189 | 2.82 | .070 | |
| **whopper sandwich** | 640 | | 41.0 | | 94 | | 14 | .41 | | | 842 | 80 | 43 | 4.54 | |
| *1 sandwich* | 265 | 26.9 | 42.0 | 14.0 | | 618 | .33 | 6.8 | | | 547 | 237 | 4.88 | .140 | |
| double beef | 850 | | 52.0 | | | | 14 | .56 | | | | 91 | 60 | 8.54 | |
| *1 sandwich* | 351 | 46.4 | 52.0 | | | 617 | .34 | 10.4 | | | | 387 | 7.31 | .180 | |
| double beef w/ cheese | 950 | | 60.0 | | | | 14 | .63 | | | | 222 | 65 | 9.07 | |
| *1 sandwich* | 374 | 50.8 | 54.0 | | | 1001 | .35 | 10.4 | | | | 510 | 7.34 | .180 | |
| w/ cheese | 723 | | 48.0 | | 117 | | 14 | .48 | | | 1126 | 210 | 48 | 5.09 | |
| *1 sandwich* | 289 | 31.4 | 43.0 | 19.0 | | 1001 | .34 | 6.8 | | | 570 | 361 | 4.91 | .140 | |

## 11.3. JACK-IN-THE-BOX

| | KCAL / WT (g) | H₂O (g) / PRO (g) | FAT (g) / CHO (g) | PUFA (g) / SFA (g) | CHOL (mg) / DFIB (g) | A (RE) / A (IU) | C (mg) / B-1 (mg) | B-2 (mg) / NIA (mg) | B-6 (mg) / B-12 (mcg) | FOL (mcg) / PANT (mg) | Na (mg) / K (mg) | Ca (mg) / P (mg) | Mg (mg) / Fe (mg) | Zn (mg) / Cu (mg) | Mn (mg) |
|---|---|---|---|---|---|---|---|---|---|---|---|---|---|---|---|
| **bacon cheeseburger** | 667 | | 39.0 | 7.0 | 65 | | | | | | 1127 | | | | |
| *1 sandwich* | 230 | 11.0 | 67.0 | 15.0 | | | | | | | | | | | |
| **breakfast jack** | 307 | | 13.0 | 2.5 | 203 | | | | | | 871 | | | | |
| *1 sandwich* | 126 | 18.0 | 30.0 | 5.2 | | | | | | | | | | | |
| **cheeseburger** | 325 | | 17.0 | 2.7 | 41 | | | | | | 746 | | | | |
| *1 sandwich* | 113 | 15.0 | 28.0 | 7.5 | | | | | | | | | | | |

[a] Avg values for 6 types of dressing. If reduced calorie dressing is used, SFA is 0.0 g, fat is 1.0 g, chol is 0 mg & Kcal are 42.

| | KCAL | H₂O (g) | FAT (g) | PUFA (g) | CHOL (mg) | A (RE) | C (mg) | B-2 (mg) | B-6 (mg) | FOL (mcg) | Na (mg) | Ca (mg) | Mg (mg) | Zn (mg) | Mn (mg) |
|---|---|---|---|---|---|---|---|---|---|---|---|---|---|---|---|
| | WT (g) | PRO (g) | CHO (g) | SFA (g) | DFIB (g) | A (IU) | B-1 (mg) | NIA (mg) | B-12 (mcg) | PANT (mg) | K (mg) | P (mg) | Fe (mg) | Cu (mg) | |
| cheesecake | 309 | | 17.5 | 1.0 | 63 | | | | | | 208 | | | | |
| *1 serving* | 99 | 8.0 | 29.0 | 9.0 | | | | | | | | | | | |
| chef salad | 295 | | 18.0 | 1.0 | 107 | | | | | | 812 | | | | |
| *1 salad* | 369 | 32.0 | 3.0 | 9.4 | | | | | | | | | | | |
| chicken breast tenderloins, wedge fries, garlic roll & dressing—*1 dinner* | 689 | | 30.0 | 7.3 | 100 | | | | | | 1213 | | | | |
| | 321 | 40.0 | 65.0 | 11.5 | | | | | | | | | | | |
| chicken supreme | 575 | | 36.0 | 7.6 | 62 | | | | | | 1525 | | | | |
| *1 sandwich* | 231 | 27.0 | 34.0 | 14.3 | | | | | | | | | | | |
| club pita | 277 | | 8.0 | 1.0 | 43 | | | | | | 931 | | | | |
| *1 sandwich* | 179 | 23.0 | 28.0 | 3.6 | | | | | | | | | | | |
| crescent, canadian | 452 | | 31.0 | 7.0 | 226 | | | | | | 851 | | | | |
| *1 sandwich* | 134 | 19.0 | 25.0 | 9.7 | | | | | | | | | | | |
| crescent, sausage | 584 | | 43.0 | 5.7 | 187 | | | | | | 1012 | | | | |
| *1 sandwich* | 156 | 22.0 | 28.0 | 15.5 | | | | | | | | | | | |
| crescent, supreme | 547 | | 40.0 | 7.8 | 178 | | | | | | 1053 | | | | |
| *1 sandwich* | 146 | 20.0 | 27.0 | 13.2 | | | | | | | | | | | |
| **dressing** | | | | | | | | | | | | | | | |
| blue cheese | 131 | | 11.0 | 6.3 | 9 | | | | | | 459 | | | | |
| *1 pkt* | 35 | 1.0 | 7.0 | 2.0 | | | | | | | | | | | |
| buttermilk house | 181 | | 18.0 | 10.8 | 10 | | | | | | 347 | | | | |
| *1 pkt* | 35 | 1.0 | 4.0 | 2.9 | | | | | | | | | | | |
| french, low calorie | 80 | | 4.0 | 2.4 | 0 | | | | | | 300 | | | | |
| *1 pkt* | 35 | 1.0 | 13.0 | 0.6 | | | | | | | | | | | |
| thousand island | 156 | | 15.0 | 8.8 | 11 | | | | | | 350 | | | | |
| *1 pkt* | 35 | 1.0 | 6.0 | 2.5 | | | | | | | | | | | |
| french fries | 221 | | 12.0 | 1.7 | 8 | | | | | | 164 | | | | |
| *reg serving* | 68 | 2.0 | 27.0 | 5.0 | | | | | | | | | | | |
| french fries | 353 | | 19.0 | 2.7 | 13 | | | | | | 262 | | | | |
| *large serving* | 109 | 3.0 | 43.0 | 7.9 | | | | | | | | | | | |
| grape jelly | 38 | | 0.0 | 0.0 | 0 | | | | | | 3 | | | | |
| *1 pkt* | 14 | 0.0 | 9.0 | 0.0 | | | | | | | | | | | |
| ham & swiss burger | 754 | | 49.0 | 7.0 | 106 | | | | | | 1217 | | | | |
| *1 sandwich* | 259 | 13.0 | 65.0 | 21.0 | | | | | | | | | | | |
| hamburger | 288 | | 13.0 | 2.4 | 26 | | | | | | 556 | | | | |
| *1 sandwich* | 103 | 13.0 | 29.0 | 5.1 | | | | | | | | | | | |
| hot chocolate | 133 | | 4.0 | | | | | | | | 180 | | | | |
| *8 fl oz* | | 1.3 | 24.0 | | | | | | | | | | | | |
| jumbo jack | 573 | | 34.0 | 8.0 | 73 | | | | | | 733 | | | | |
| *1 sandwich* | 222 | 16.0 | 50.0 | 11.0 | | | | | | | | | | | |
| jumbo jack w/ cheese | 665 | | 40.0 | 9.0 | 102 | | | | | | 1090 | | | | |
| *1 sandwich* | 242 | 19.0 | 58.0 | 14.0 | | | | | | | | | | | |
| moby jack | 444 | | 25.0 | 8.7 | 47 | | | | | | 820 | | | | |
| *1 sandwich* | 137 | 16.0 | 39.0 | 8.4 | | | | | | | | | | | |
| monterey burger | 865 | | 57.0 | 4.0 | 152 | | | | | | 1124 | | | | |
| *1 sandwich* | 281 | 17.0 | 72.0 | 28.0 | | | | | | | | | | | |
| mushroom burger | 470 | | 24.0 | 2.0 | 64 | | | | | | 910 | | | | |
| *1 sandwich* | 182 | 10.0 | 54.0 | 10.0 | | | | | | | | | | | |
| nachos, cheese | 571 | | 35.0 | 8.0 | 37 | | | | | | 1154 | | | | |
| *1 serving* | 170 | 15.0 | 49.0 | 12.7 | | | | | | | | | | | |
| nachos, supreme | 639 | | 36.0 | 6.5 | 37 | | | | | | 2187 | | | | |
| *1 serving* | 284 | 21.0 | 59.0 | 13.6 | | | | | | | | | | | |
| onion rings | 382 | | 23.0 | 1.3 | 27 | | | | | | 407 | | | | |
| *1 serving* | 108 | 5.0 | 39.0 | 11.1 | | | | | | | | | | | |
| pancake platter | 630 | | 27.0 | 3.3 | 85 | | | | | | 1670 | | | | |
| *1 platter* | 232 | 16.0 | 79.0 | 12.6 | | | | | | | | | | | |
| pancake syrup | 121 | | 0.0 | 0.0 | 0 | | | | | | 6 | | | | |
| *1 pkt* | 42 | 0.0 | 30.0 | 0.0 | | | | | | | | | | | |
| pasta & seafood salad | 394 | | 22.0 | 11.9 | 48 | | | | | | 1570 | | | | |
| *1 salad* | 417 | 15.0 | 32.0 | 4.0 | | | | | | | | | | | |
| pizza pocket sandwich | 497 | | 28.0 | 2.0 | 32 | | | | | | 940 | | | | |
| *1 sandwich* | 162 | 19.0 | 42.0 | 13.1 | | | | | | | | | | | |

| | KCAL | H₂O (g) | FAT (g) | PUFA (g) | CHOL (mg) | A (RE) | C (mg) | B-2 (mg) | B-6 (mg) | FOL (mcg) | Na (mg) | Ca (mg) | Mg (mg) | Zn (mg) | Mn (mg) |
|---|---|---|---|---|---|---|---|---|---|---|---|---|---|---|---|
| | WT (g) | PRO (g) | CHO (g) | SFA (g) | DFIB (g) | A (IU) | B-1 (mg) | NIA (mg) | B-12 (mcg) | PANT (mg) | K (mg) | P (mg) | Fe (mg) | Cu (mg) | |
| **sauce** | | | | | | | | | | | | | | | |
| A-1 steak sauce | 35 | | 0.0 | 0.0 | 0 | | | | | | 809 | | | | |
| *1 pkt* | 50 | 0.0 | 9.0 | 0.0 | | | | | | | | | | | |
| barbeque | 78 | | 0.0 | 0.0 | 0 | | | | | | 535 | | | | |
| *1 pkt* | 50 | 0.7 | 19.0 | 0.0 | | | | | | | | | | | |
| mayo-mustard | 124 | | 13.0 | | 10 | | | | | | 247 | | | | |
| *1 pkt* | 21 | 0.5 | 2.0 | | | | | | | | | | | | |
| mayo-onion | 143 | | 15.0 | | 20 | | | | | | 140 | | | | |
| *1 pkt* | 21 | 0.3 | 1.0 | | | | | | | | | | | | |
| seafood cocktail | 57 | | 0.0 | 0.0 | 0 | | | | | | 367 | | | | |
| *1 pkt* | 50 | 1.5 | 12.2 | 0.0 | | | | | | | | | | | |
| **scrambled egg platter** | 720 | | 44.0 | 1.6 | 260 | | | | | | 1110 | | | | |
| *1 platter* | 267 | 26.0 | 55.0 | 21.1 | | | | | | | | | | | |
| **shake** | | | | | | | | | | | | | | | |
| choc | 330 | | 7.0 | 1.0 | 25 | | | | | | 270 | | | | |
| *1 shake* | 322 | 11.0 | 55.0 | 4.3 | | | | | | | | | | | |
| strawberry | 320 | | 7.0 | 1.0 | 25 | | | | | | 240 | | | | |
| *1 shake* | 328 | 10.0 | 55.0 | 4.3 | | | | | | | | | | | |
| van | 320 | | 6.0 | 1.0 | 25 | | | | | | 230 | | | | |
| *1 shake* | 317 | 10.0 | 57.0 | 3.6 | | | | | | | | | | | |
| **side salad** | 51 | | 3.0 | 0.0 | 1 | | | | | | 84 | | | | |
| *1 salad* | 111 | 7.0 | 1.0 | 2.0 | | | | | | | | | | | |
| **sirloin steak, wedge fries, garlic roll & sce** | 699 | | 27.0 | 6.1 | 75 | | | | | | 969 | | | | |
| *1 dinner* | 334 | 38.0 | 75.0 | 10.0 | | | | | | | | | | | |
| **shrimp, breaded, wedge fries, garlic roll & seafood cocktail sce—**1 dinner | 731 | | 37.0 | 4.8 | 157 | | | | | | 1510 | | | | |
| | 301 | 22.0 | 77.0 | 16.6 | | | | | | | | | | | |
| **swiss & bacon burger** | 681 | | 47.0 | 7.0 | 92 | | | | | | 1458 | | | | |
| *1 sandwich* | 187 | 5.0 | 61.0 | 20.0 | | | | | | | | | | | |
| **taco** | 191 | | 11.0 | 1.0 | 21 | | | | | | 406 | | | | |
| *1 taco* | 81 | 8.0 | 16.0 | 5.2 | | | | | | | | | | | |
| **taco salad** | 377 | | 24.0 | 2.5 | 102 | | | | | | 1436 | | | | |
| *1 salad* | 358 | 31.0 | 10.0 | 10.4 | | | | | | | | | | | |
| **taco, super** | 288 | | 17.0 | 1.2 | 37 | | | | | | 765 | | | | |
| *1 taco* | 135 | 12.0 | 21.0 | 8.0 | | | | | | | | | | | |
| **turnover, hot apple** | 410 | | 24.0 | 2.0 | 15 | | | | | | 350 | | | | |
| *1 turnover* | 119 | 4.0 | 45.0 | 10.8 | | | | | | | | | | | |

## 11.4. KENTUCKY FRIED CHICKEN

| | KCAL | H₂O (g) | FAT (g) | PUFA (g) | CHOL (mg) | A (RE) | C (mg) | B-2 (mg) | B-6 (mg) | FOL (mcg) | Na (mg) | Ca (mg) | Mg (mg) | Zn (mg) | Mn (mg) |
|---|---|---|---|---|---|---|---|---|---|---|---|---|---|---|---|
| | WT (g) | PRO (g) | CHO (g) | SFA (g) | DFIB (g) | A (IU) | B-1 (mg) | NIA (mg) | B-12 (mcg) | PANT (mg) | K (mg) | P (mg) | Fe (mg) | Cu (mg) | |
| **beans, baked** | 105 | | 1.2 | 0.3 | 0 | | 2 | .04 | | | 387 | 54 | | | |
| *1 serving* | 89 | 5.1 | 18.4 | 0.4 | | | .06 | 0.5 | | | | | 1.43 | | |
| **biscuit, buttermilk** | 269 | | 13.6 | 1.1 | 0 | | 0 | .13 | | | 521 | 77 | | | |
| *1 biscuit* | 75 | 5.1 | 31.6 | 3.5 | | | .28 | 1.8 | | | | | 1.22 | | |
| **coleslaw** | 103 | | 5.7 | 2.9 | 4 | | 19 | .03 | | | 171 | 29 | | | |
| *1 serving* | 79 | 1.3 | 11.5 | 0.8 | | 269 | .03 | 0.2 | | | | | .19 | | |
| **corn-on-the-cob** | 176 | | 3.1 | 1.5 | 0 | | 2 | .11 | | | | 7 | | | |
| *1 ear* | 143 | 5.1 | 31.9 | 0.5 | | 272 | .14 | 1.8 | | | | | .79 | | |
| **chicken, fried, extra crispy** | | | | | | | | | | | | | | | |
| breast, center | 353 | | 20.9 | 2.0 | 93 | | | .16 | | | 842 | 35 | | | |
| *1 center breast* | 120 | 26.9 | 14.4 | 5.3 | | | .10 | 10.0 | | | | | .86 | | |
| breast, side | 354 | | 23.7 | 2.3 | 66 | | | .13 | | | 797 | 32 | | | |
| *1 side breast* | 98 | 17.7 | 17.3 | 6.0 | | | .08 | 6.5 | | | | | .86 | | |
| drumstick | 173 | | 10.9 | 1.3 | 65 | | | .14 | | | 346 | 15 | | | |
| *1 drumstick* | 60 | 12.7 | 5.9 | 2.8 | | | .05 | 2.8 | | | | | .61 | | |
| thigh | 371 | | 26.3 | 3.4 | 121 | | | .27 | | | 766 | 46 | | | |
| *1 thigh* | 112 | 19.6 | 13.8 | 6.9 | | | .09 | 5.2 | | | | | 1.21 | | |
| wing | 218 | | 15.6 | 1.8 | 63 | | | .07 | | | 437 | 21 | | | |
| *1 wing* | 57 | 11.5 | 7.8 | 4.0 | | | .03 | 2.8 | | | | | .52 | | |

| | KCAL | H₂O (g) | FAT (g) | PUFA (g) | CHOL (mg) | A (RE) | C (mg) | B-2 (mg) | B-6 (mg) | FOL (mcg) | Na (mg) | Ca (mg) | Mg (mg) | Zn (mg) | Mn (mg) |
|---|---|---|---|---|---|---|---|---|---|---|---|---|---|---|---|
| | WT (g) | PRO (g) | CHO (g) | SFA (g) | DFIB (g) | A (IU) | B-1 (mg) | NIA (mg) | B-12 (mcg) | PANT (mg) | K (mg) | P (mg) | Fe (mg) | Cu (mg) | |

**chicken, fried, original recipe**

| | KCAL/WT | H₂O/PRO | FAT/CHO | PUFA/SFA | CHOL/DFIB | A(RE)/A(IU) | C/B-1 | B-2/NIA | Na/K | Ca/P | Mg/Fe |
|---|---|---|---|---|---|---|---|---|---|---|---|
| breast, center | 257 | | 13.7 | 1.6 | 93 | | | .14 | 532 | 39 | |
| *1 center breast* | 107 | 25.5 | 8.0 | 3.6 | | | .09 | 10.0 | | | .63 |
| breast, side | 276 | | 17.3 | 2.3 | 96 | | | .18 | 654 | 48 | |
| *1 side breast* | 95 | 20.0 | 10.1 | 4.6 | | | .07 | 6.8 | | | .79 |
| drumstick | 147 | | 8.8 | 1.1 | 81 | | | .13 | 269 | 13 | |
| *1 drumstick* | 58 | 13.6 | 3.4 | 2.3 | | | .06 | 2.9 | | | .60 |
| thigh | 278 | | 19.2 | 2.6 | 122 | | | .28 | 517 | 28 | |
| *1 thigh* | 96 | 18.0 | 8.4 | 5.3 | | | .08 | 4.6 | | | 1.05 |
| wing | 181 | | 12.3 | 1.7 | 67 | | | .06 | 387 | 38 | |
| *1 wing* | 56 | 11.8 | 5.8 | 3.3 | | 56 | .03 | 3.2 | | | .45 |
| **chicken nuggets** | 46 | | 2.9 | 0.3 | 12 | | | .03 | 140 | 2 | |
| *1 nugget* | 16 | 2.8 | 2.2 | 0.7 | | | .02 | 1.0 | | | .13 |

**chicken nugget sce**

| | KCAL/WT | H₂O/PRO | FAT/CHO | PUFA/SFA | CHOL/DFIB | A(RE)/A(IU) | C/B-1 | B-2/NIA | Na/K | Ca/P | Mg/Fe |
|---|---|---|---|---|---|---|---|---|---|---|---|
| barbeque | 35 | | 0.6 | 0.3 | 0 | | 0 | .01 | 450 | 6 | |
| *1 oz* | | 0.3 | 7.1 | 0.1 | | 370 | .01 | 0.2 | | | .24 |
| honey | 49 | | 0.0 | 0.0 | 0 | | | .00 | | 1 | |
| *1/2 oz* | | 0.0 | 12.1 | 0.0 | | | .00 | 0.0 | | | .11 |
| mustard | 36 | | 0.9 | | 0 | | 0 | .01 | 346 | 10 | |
| *1 oz* | | 0.9 | 6.0 | 0.1 | | | .02 | 0.2 | | | .26 |
| sweet & sour | 58 | | 0.6 | 0.3 | 0 | | 0 | | 148 | 5 | |
| *1 oz* | | 0.1 | 13.0 | 0.1 | | 60 | .01 | 0.0 | | | .16 |
| **fries** | 268 | | 12.8 | 0.7 | 2 | | 3 | .06 | 81 | 24 | |
| *1 serving* | 119 | 4.8 | 33.3 | 3.1 | | | .17 | 2.7 | | | .94 |
| **gravy, chicken** | 59 | | 3.7 | 0.3 | 2 | | | .03 | 398 | 9 | |
| *1 serving* | 78 | 2.0 | 4.4 | 1.0 | | | .00 | 0.5 | | | .48 |
| **potatoes, mashed** | 59 | | 0.6 | 0.0 | 0 | | 0 | .04 | | 21 | |
| *1 serving* | 80 | 1.9 | 11.6 | 0.2 | | | .00 | 1.0 | | | .28 |
| **potatoes, mashed w/ gravy** | 62 | | 1.4 | 0.1 | 0 | | 0 | .04 | 297 | 19 | |
| *1 serving* | 86 | 2.1 | 10.3 | 0.4 | | | .00 | 1.0 | | | .35 |
| **potato salad** | 141 | | 9.3 | 4.9 | 11 | | 3 | .02 | 396 | 10 | |
| *1 serving* | 90 | 1.8 | 12.6 | 1.4 | | 90 | .07 | 0.6 | | | .32 |

## 11.5. MCDONALDS

| | KCAL/WT | H₂O/PRO | FAT/CHO | PUFA/SFA | CHOL/DFIB | A(RE)/A(IU) | C/B-1 | B-2/NIA | Na/K | Ca/P | Mg/Fe |
|---|---|---|---|---|---|---|---|---|---|---|---|
| **big mac** | 570 | | 35.0 | | 83 | | 3 | .38 | 979 | 203 | |
| *1 sandwich* | 200 | 24.6 | 39.2 | | | 380 | .48 | 7.2 | | | 4.90 |

**biscuit**

| | KCAL/WT | H₂O/PRO | FAT/CHO | PUFA/SFA | CHOL/DFIB | A(RE)/A(IU) | C/B-1 | B-2/NIA | Na/K | Ca/P | Mg/Fe |
|---|---|---|---|---|---|---|---|---|---|---|---|
| plain | 330 | | 18.2 | | 9 | | | .15 | 786 | 74 | |
| *1 biscuit* | 85 | 4.9 | 36.6 | | | 179 | .21 | 1.7 | | | 1.30 |
| w/ bacon, egg & cheese | 483 | | 31.6 | | 263 | | 2 | .43 | 1269 | 2 | |
| *1 biscuit* | 145 | 16.5 | 33.2 | | | 653 | .30 | 2.3 | | | 2.57 |
| w/ sausage | 467 | | 30.9 | | 48 | | | .22 | 1147 | 82 | |
| *1 biscuit* | 121 | 12.1 | 35.3 | | | 61 | .56 | 3.4 | | | 2.05 |
| w/ sausage & egg | 585 | | 39.9 | | 285 | | | .49 | 1301 | 119 | |
| *1 biscuit* | 175 | 19.8 | 36.4 | | | 420 | .53 | 3.9 | | | 3.43 |
| **cheeseburger** | 318 | | 16.0 | | 41 | | 2 | .24 | 743 | 169 | |
| *1 sandwich* | 114 | 15.0 | 28.5 | | | 353 | .30 | 4.3 | | | 2.84 |
| **chicken mcnuggets** | 323 | | 21.3 | | 73 | | 2 | .14 | 512 | 11 | |
| *1 serving* | 109 | 19.1 | 13.7 | | | | .16 | 7.5 | | | 1.25 |

**chicken mcnugget sce**

| | KCAL/WT | H₂O/PRO | FAT/CHO | PUFA/SFA | CHOL/DFIB | A(RE)/A(IU) | C/B-1 | B-2/NIA | Na/K | Ca/P | Mg/Fe |
|---|---|---|---|---|---|---|---|---|---|---|---|
| barbeque | 60 | | 0.4 | | 0 | | 0 | .01 | 309 | 4 | |
| *1 container* | 32 | 0.4 | 13.7 | | | 45 | .01 | 0.1 | | | .12 |
| honey | 50 | | 0.0 | | 0 | | 0 | .00 | 2 | 1 | |
| *1 container* | 14 | 0.0 | 12.4 | | | | .00 | 0.0 | | | .02 |
| hot mustard | 63 | | 2.1 | | 3 | | 0 | .00 | 259 | 8 | |
| *1 container* | 30 | 0.6 | 10.5 | | | 9 | .01 | 0.1 | | | .17 |
| sweet & sour | 64 | | 0.3 | | 0 | | 0 | .00 | 186 | 2 | |
| *1 container* | 32 | 0.2 | 15.0 | | | 200 | .01 | 0.1 | | | .08 |

| | KCAL | H₂O (g) | FAT (g) | PUFA (g) | CHOL (mg) | A (RE) | C (mg) | B-2 (mg) | B-6 (mg) | FOL (mcg) | Na (mg) | Ca (mg) | Mg (mg) | Zn (mg) | Mn (mg) |
|---|---|---|---|---|---|---|---|---|---|---|---|---|---|---|---|
| | WT (g) | PRO (g) | CHO (g) | SFA (g) | DFIB (g) | A (IU) | B-1 (mg) | NIA (mg) | B-12 (mcg) | PANT (mg) | K (mg) | P (mg) | Fe (mg) | Cu (mg) | |
| **cookies** | | | | | | | | | | | | | | | |
| chocolaty chip | 342 | | 16.3 | | 18 | | 1 | .21 | | | 313 | 29 | | | |
| *1 box* | 69 | 4.2 | 44.8 | | | 76 | .12 | 1.7 | | | | | 1.56 | | |
| mcdonaldland | 308 | | 10.8 | | 10 | | | .23 | | | 358 | 12 | | | |
| *1 box* | 67 | 4.2 | 48.7 | | | | .23 | 2.9 | | | | | 1.47 | | |
| egg mcmuffin | 340 | | 15.8 | | 259 | | | .44 | | | 885 | 226 | | | |
| *1 mcmuffin* | 138 | 18.5 | 31.0 | | | 591 | .47 | 3.8 | | | | | 2.93 | | |
| english muffin w/ butter | 186 | | 5.3 | | 15 | | 1 | .49 | | | 310 | 117 | | | |
| *1 muffin* | 63 | 5.0 | 29.5 | | | 164 | .28 | 2.6 | | | | | 1.51 | | |
| filet-o-fish sandwich | 435 | | 25.7 | | 45 | | | .23 | | | 799 | 133 | | | |
| *1 sandwich* | 143 | 14.7 | 35.9 | | | 186 | .36 | 3.0 | | | | | 2.47 | | |
| french fries | 220 | | 11.5 | | 9 | | 13 | .02 | | | 109 | 9 | | | |
| *1 reg serving* | 68 | 3.0 | 26.1 | | | | .12 | 2.3 | | | | | .61 | | |
| hamburger | 263 | | 11.3 | | 29 | | 2 | .22 | | | 506 | 84 | | | |
| *1 sandwich* | 100 | 12.4 | 28.3 | | | 100 | .31 | 4.1 | | | | | 2.85 | | |
| hash brown potatoes | 125 | | 7.0 | | 7 | | 4 | .00 | | | 325 | 5 | | | |
| *1 serving* | 55 | 1.5 | 14.0 | | | | .06 | 0.8 | | | | | .40 | | |
| hotcake w/ butter & syrup | 500 | | 10.3 | | 47 | | 5 | .36 | | | 1070 | 103 | | | |
| *1 serving* | 214 | 7.9 | 93.9 | | | 257 | .26 | 2.3 | | | | | 2.23 | | |
| ice cream in cone | 185 | | 5.2 | | 24 | | | .36 | | | 109 | 183 | | | |
| *1 serving* | 115 | 4.3 | 30.2 | | | 218 | .06 | 0.4 | | | | | .12 | | |
| Mc D.L.T. | 680 | | 44.0 | | 101 | | 8 | .46 | | | 1030 | 230 | | | |
| *1 sandwich* | 254 | 30.0 | 40.0 | | | 508 | .56 | 8.0 | | | | | 6.60 | | |
| **pie** | | | | | | | | | | | | | | | |
| apple | 253 | | 14.3 | | 12 | | | .02 | | | 398 | 14 | | | |
| *1 snack pie* | 85 | 1.9 | 29.3 | | | | .02 | 0.2 | | | | | .62 | | |
| cherry | 260 | | 13.6 | | 13 | | | .02 | | | 427 | 12 | | | |
| *1 snack pie* | 88 | 2.0 | 32.1 | | | 114 | .03 | 0.3 | | | | | .59 | | |
| quarter pounder | 427 | | 23.5 | | 81 | | 3 | .32 | | | 718 | 98 | | | |
| *1 sandwich* | 160 | 24.6 | 29.3 | | | 128 | .35 | 7.2 | | | | | 4.30 | | |
| w/ cheese | 525 | | 31.6 | | 107 | | 3 | .41 | | | 1220 | 255 | | | |
| *1 sandwich* | 186 | 29.6 | 30.5 | | | 614 | .37 | 7.1 | | | | | 4.84 | | |
| sausage | 210 | | 18.6 | | 39 | | | .11 | | | 423 | 16 | | | |
| *1 serving* | 53 | 9.8 | 0.6 | | | | .27 | 2.1 | | | | | .82 | | |
| sausage mcmuffin | 427 | | 26.3 | | 59 | | 1 | .25 | | | 942 | 168 | | | |
| *1 mcmuffin* | 115 | 17.6 | 30.0 | | | 380 | .70 | 4.1 | | | | | 2.25 | | |
| sausage mcmuffin w/ egg | 517 | | 32.9 | | 287 | | | .50 | | | 1044 | 196 | | | |
| *1 mcmuffin* | 165 | 22.9 | 32.2 | | | 660 | .84 | 4.5 | | | | | 3.47 | | |
| scrambled eggs | 180 | | 13.0 | | 514 | | 1 | .47 | | | 205 | 61 | | | |
| *1 serving* | 98 | 13.2 | 2.5 | | | 652 | .08 | 0.2 | | | | | 2.53 | | |
| **shake** | | | | | | | | | | | | | | | |
| choc | 383 | | 9.0 | | 30 | | | .44 | | | 300 | 320 | | | |
| *1 shake* | 291 | 9.9 | 65.5 | | | 349 | .12 | 0.5 | | | | | .84 | | |
| strawberry | 362 | | 8.7 | | 32 | | 4 | .44 | | | 207 | 322 | | | |
| *1 shake* | 290 | 9.0 | 62.1 | | | 377 | .12 | 0.4 | | | | | .17 | | |
| van | 352 | | 8.4 | | 31 | | 3 | .70 | | | 201 | 329 | | | |
| *1 shake* | 291 | 9.3 | 59.6 | | | 349 | .12 | 0.4 | | | | | .18 | | |
| **sundae** | | | | | | | | | | | | | | | |
| caramel | 361 | | 10.0 | | 31 | | 4 | .31 | | | 145 | 200 | | | |
| *1 sundae* | 165 | 7.2 | 60.8 | | | 279 | .07 | 1.0 | | | | | .23 | | |
| hot fudge | 357 | | 10.8 | | 27 | | 2 | .31 | | | 170 | 215 | | | |
| *1 sundae* | 164 | 7.0 | 58.0 | | | 230 | .07 | 1.1 | | | | | .61 | | |
| strawberry | 320 | | 8.7 | | 25 | | 3 | .30 | | | 90 | 174 | | | |
| *1 sundae* | 164 | 6.0 | 54.0 | | | 230 | .07 | 1.0 | | | | | .38 | | |

| | KCAL | H₂O (g) | FAT (g) | PUFA (g) | CHOL (mg) | A (RE) | C (mg) | B-2 (mg) | B-6 (mg) | FOL (mcg) | Na (mg) | Ca (mg) | Mg (mg) | Zn (mg) | Mn (mg) |
|---|---|---|---|---|---|---|---|---|---|---|---|---|---|---|---|
| | WT (g) | PRO (g) | CHO (g) | SFA (g) | DFIB (g) | A (IU) | B-1 (mg) | NIA (mg) | B-12 (mcg) | PANT (mg) | K (mg) | P (mg) | Fe (mg) | Cu (mg) | |

**11.6. ROY ROGERS**

| | KCAL | H₂O | FAT | PUFA | CHOL | A(RE) | C | B-2 | B-6 | FOL | Na | Ca | Mg | Zn | Mn |
|---|---|---|---|---|---|---|---|---|---|---|---|---|---|---|---|
| **bacon cheeseburger** | 581 | | 39.2 | | 103 | | | | | | 1536 | | | | |
| *1 sandwich* | 180 | 32.3 | 25.0 | | | | | | | | | | | | |
| **bar burger** | 611 | | 39.4 | | 115 | | | | | | 1826 | | | | |
| *1 sandwich* | 208 | 36.1 | 28.0 | | | | | | | | | | | | |
| **biscuit** | 231 | | 12.1 | | | | | | | | 575 | | | | |
| *1 biscuit* | 63 | 4.4 | 26.2 | | | | | | | | | | | | |
| **breakfast crescent sandwich** | 401 | | 27.3 | | 148 | | | | | | 867 | | | | |
| *1 sandwich* | 127 | 13.1 | 25.3 | | | | | | | | | | | | |
| w/ bacon | 431 | | 29.7 | | 156 | | | | | | 1035 | | | | |
| *1 sandwich* | 133 | 15.4 | 25.5 | | | | | | | | | | | | |
| w/ ham | 557 | | 41.7 | | 189 | | | | | | 1192 | | | | |
| *1 sandwich* | 165 | 19.8 | 25.3 | | | | | | | | | | | | |
| w/ sausage | 449 | | 29.4 | | 168 | | | | | | 1289 | | | | |
| *1 sandwich* | 162 | 19.9 | 25.9 | | | | | | | | | | | | |
| **brownie** | 264 | | 11.4 | | 10 | | | | | | 150 | | | | |
| *1 brownie* | 64 | 3.3 | 37.3 | | | | | | | | | | | | |
| **cheeseburger** | 563 | | 37.3 | | 95 | | | | | | 1404 | | | | |
| *1 sandwich* | 173 | 29.5 | 27.4 | | | | | | | | | | | | |
| **chicken, fried** | | | | | | | | | | | | | | | |
| breast | 412 | | 23.7 | | 118 | | | | | | 609 | | | | |
| *1 breast* | 144 | 33.0 | 16.9 | | | | | | | | | | | | |
| leg | 140 | | 8.0 | | 40 | | | | | | 190 | | | | |
| *1 leg* | 53 | 11.5 | 5.5 | | | | | | | | | | | | |
| thigh | 296 | | 19.5 | | 85 | | | | | | 406 | | | | |
| *1 thigh* | 98 | 18.4 | 11.7 | | | | | | | | | | | | |
| wing | 192 | | 12.8 | | 47 | | | | | | 285 | | | | |
| *1 wing* | 52 | 10.5 | 8.5 | | | | | | | | | | | | |
| **coleslaw** | 110 | | 6.9 | | | | | | | | 261 | | | | |
| *1 serving* | 99 | 1.0 | 11.0 | | | | | | | | | | | | |
| **crescent roll** | 287 | | 17.7 | | | | | | | | 547 | | | | |
| *1 roll* | 70 | 4.7 | 27.2 | | | | | | | | | | | | |
| **danish** | | | | | | | | | | | | | | | |
| apple | 249 | | 11.6 | | 15 | | | | | | 255 | | | | |
| *1 danish* | 71 | 4.5 | 31.6 | | | | | | | | | | | | |
| cheese | 254 | | 12.2 | | 11 | | | | | | 260 | | | | |
| *1 danish* | 71 | 4.9 | 31.4 | | | | | | | | | | | | |
| cherry | 271 | | 14.4 | | 11 | | | | | | 242 | | | | |
| *1 danish* | 71 | 4.4 | 31.7 | | | | | | | | | | | | |
| **egg & biscuit platter** | 394 | | 26.5 | | 284 | | | | | | 734 | | | | |
| *1 platter* | 165 | 16.9 | 21.9 | | | | | | | | | | | | |
| w/ bacon | 435 | | 29.6 | | 294 | | | | | | 957 | | | | |
| *1 platter* | 173 | 19.7 | 22.1 | | | | | | | | | | | | |
| w/ ham | 442 | | 28.6 | | 304 | | | | | | 1156 | | | | |
| *1 platter* | 200 | 23.5 | 22.5 | | | | | | | | | | | | |
| w/ sausage | 550 | | 40.9 | | 325 | | | | | | 1059 | | | | |
| *1 platter* | 203 | 23.4 | 21.9 | | | | | | | | | | | | |
| **french fries** | 268 | | 13.5 | | 42 | | | | | | 165 | | | | |
| *1 reg serving* | 85 | 3.9 | 32.0 | | | | | | | | | | | | |
| **french fries** | 357 | | 18.4 | | 56 | | | | | | 221 | | | | |
| *1 large serving* | 113 | 5.3 | 42.7 | | | | | | | | | | | | |
| **hamburger** | 456 | | 28.3 | | 73 | | | | | | 495 | | | | |
| *1 sandwich* | 143 | 23.8 | 26.6 | | | | | | | | | | | | |

| | KCAL | H₂O (g) | FAT (g) | PUFA (g) | CHOL (mg) | A (RE) | C (mg) | B-2 (mg) | B-6 (mg) | FOL (mcg) | Na (mg) | Ca (mg) | Mg (mg) | Zn (mg) | Mn (mg) |
|---|---|---|---|---|---|---|---|---|---|---|---|---|---|---|---|
| | WT (g) | PRO (g) | CHO (g) | SFA (g) | DFIB (g) | A (IU) | B-1 (mg) | NIA (mg) | B-12 (mcg) | PANT (mg) | K (mg) | P (mg) | Fe (mg) | Cu (mg) | |
| **hot chocolate** | 123 | | 2.0 | | 35 | | | | | | 125 | | | | |
| *6 fl oz* | | 3.0 | 22.0 | | | | | | | | | | | | |
| **macaroni salad** | 186 | | 10.7 | | | | | | | | 603 | | | | |
| *1 serving* | 100 | 3.1 | 19.4 | | | | | | | | | | | | |
| **pancake platter w/ butter & syrup** | 452 | | 15.2 | | 53 | | | | | | 842 | | | | |
| *1 platter* | 165 | 7.7 | 71.8 | | | | | | | | | | | | |
| w/ bacon | 493 | | 18.3 | | 63 | | | | | | 1065 | | | | |
| *1 platter* | 173 | 10.4 | 72.0 | | | | | | | | | | | | |
| w/ ham | 506 | | 17.3 | | 73 | | | | | | 1264 | | | | |
| *1 platter* | 200 | 14.3 | 72.4 | | | | | | | | | | | | |
| w/ sausage | 608 | | 29.6 | | 94 | | | | | | 1167 | | | | |
| *1 platter* | 203 | 14.2 | 71.8 | | | | | | | | | | | | |
| **potato, baked** | | | | | | | | | | | | | | | |
| w/ bacon & cheese | 397 | | 21.7 | | 34 | | | | | | 778 | | | | |
| *1 potato* | 248 | 17.1 | 33.3 | | | | | | | | | | | | |
| w/ broccoli & cheese | 376 | | 18.1 | | | | | | | | 523 | | | | |
| *1 potato* | 312 | 13.7 | 39.6 | | | | | | | | | | | | |
| w/ sour cream & chives | 408 | | 20.9 | | 31 | | | | | | 138 | | | | |
| *1 potato* | 297 | 7.3 | 47.6 | | | | | | | | | | | | |
| w/ taco beef & cheese | 463 | | 21.8 | | 37 | | | | | | 726 | | | | |
| *1 potato* | 359 | 21.8 | 45.0 | | | | | | | | | | | | |
| **potato salad** | 107 | | 6.1 | | | | | | | | 696 | | | | |
| *1 serving* | 100 | 2.0 | 10.9 | | | | | | | | | | | | |
| **roast beef sandwich** | 317 | | 10.1 | | 55 | | | | | | 785 | | | | |
| *1 sandwich* | 154 | 27.2 | 29.1 | | | | | | | | | | | | |
| | 360 | | 11.9 | | 73 | | | | | | 1044 | | | | |
| *1 large sandwich* | 182 | 33.9 | 29.6 | | | | | | | | | | | | |
| w/ cheese | 424 | | 19.2 | | 77 | | | | | | 1694 | | | | |
| *1 sandwich* | 182 | 32.9 | 29.9 | | | | | | | | | | | | |
| w/ cheese | 467 | | 20.9 | | 95 | | | | | | 1953 | | | | |
| *1 large sandwich* | 211 | 39.6 | 30.3 | | | | | | | | | | | | |
| **shake** | | | | | | | | | | | | | | | |
| choc | 358 | | 10.2 | | 37 | | | | | | 290 | | | | |
| *1 shake* | 319 | 7.9 | 61.3 | | | | | | | | | | | | |
| strawberry | 315 | | 10.2 | | 37 | | | | | | 261 | | | | |
| *1 shake* | 312 | 7.6 | 49.4 | | | | | | | | | | | | |
| van | 306 | | 10.7 | | 40 | | | | | | 282 | | | | |
| *1 shake* | 306 | 8.0 | 45.0 | | | | | | | | | | | | |
| **strawberry shortcake** | 447 | | 19.2 | | 28 | | | | | | 674 | | | | |
| *1 serving* | 205 | 10.1 | 59.3 | | | | | | | | | | | | |
| **sundae** | | | | | | | | | | | | | | | |
| caramel | 293 | | 8.5 | | 23 | | | | | | 193 | | | | |
| *1 sundae* | 145 | 7.0 | 51.5 | | | | | | | | | | | | |
| hot fudge | 337 | | 12.5 | | 23 | | | | | | 186 | | | | |
| *1 sundae* | 151 | 6.5 | 53.3 | | | | | | | | | | | | |
| strawberry | 216 | | 7.1 | | 23 | | | | | | 99 | | | | |
| *1 sundae* | 142 | 5.7 | 33.1 | | | | | | | | | | | | |

## 11.7. WENDY'S

| | KCAL | H₂O (g) | FAT (g) | PUFA (g) | CHOL (mg) | A (RE) | C (mg) | B-2 (mg) | B-6 (mg) | FOL (mcg) | Na (mg) | Ca (mg) | Mg (mg) | Zn (mg) | Mn (mg) |
|---|---|---|---|---|---|---|---|---|---|---|---|---|---|---|---|
| | WT (g) | PRO (g) | CHO (g) | SFA (g) | DFIB (g) | A (IU) | B-1 (mg) | NIA (mg) | B-12 (mcg) | PANT (mg) | K (mg) | P (mg) | Fe (mg) | Cu (mg) | |
| **bacon cheeseburger** | 455 | | 25.0 | | 98 | | | | | | 843 | | | | |
| *1 sandwich* | 154 | 31.0 | 26.0 | | | | | | | | | | | | |
| **big classic hamburger** | 470 | | 25.0 | | 80 | | | | | | 900 | | | | |
| *1 sandwich* | 241 | 26.0 | 36.0 | | | | | | | | 470 | | | | |
| **big classic double hamburger** | 680 | | 39.0 | | 155 | | | | | | 1005 | | | | |
| *1 sandwich* | 317 | 46.0 | 36.0 | | | | | | | | 740 | | | | |

| | KCAL | H₂O (g) | FAT (g) | PUFA (g) | CHOL (mg) | Vitamins | | | | | Minerals | | | | |
|---|---|---|---|---|---|---|---|---|---|---|---|---|---|---|---|
| | | | | | | A (RE) | C (mg) | B-2 (mg) | B-6 (mg) | FOL (mcg) | Na (mg) | Ca (mg) | Mg (mg) | Zn (mg) | Mn (mg) |
| | WT (g) | PRO (g) | CHO (g) | SFA (g) | DFIB (g) | A (IU) | B-1 (mg) | NIA (mg) | B-12 (mcg) | PANT (mg) | K (mg) | P (mg) | Fe (mg) | Cu (mg) | |
| **breakfast potatoes** | 360 | | 22.0 | | 20 | | | | | | 745 | | | | |
| *1 serving* | 103 | 4.0 | 37.0 | | | | | | | | 615 | | | | |
| **breakfast sandwich (white bread, egg & cheese)**—*1 sandwich* | 370 | | 19.0 | | 200 | | | | | | 770 | | | | |
| | 129 | 17.0 | 33.0 | | | | | | | | 155 | | | | |
| **buttermilk biscuit** | 320 | | 17.0 | | 0 | | | | | | 860 | | | | |
| *1 biscuit* | 94 | 5.0 | 37.0 | | | | | | | | 125 | | | | |
| **chicken club sandwich** | 479 | | 25.0 | | 78 | | | | | | 813 | | | | |
| *1 sandwich* | 187 | 29.0 | 30.0 | | | | | | | | 365 | | | | |
| **chicken fried steak** | 580 | | 41.0 | | 95 | | | | | | 1040 | | | | |
| *1 serving* | 176 | 28.0 | 25.0 | | | | | | | | 390 | | | | |
| **chicken nuggets** | 290 | | 21.0 | | 55 | | | | | | 615 | | | | |
| *6 pieces* | 95 | 16.0 | 11.0 | | | | | | | | 165 | | | | |
| **chicken nugget sce** | | | | | | | | | | | | | | | |
| barbeque | 50 | | 0.0 | | 0 | | | | | | 100 | | | | |
| *1 pkt* | 28 | 0.0 | 11.0 | | | | | | | | 95 | | | | |
| honey | 45 | | 0.0 | | 0 | | | | | | 0 | | | | |
| *1 pkt* | 14 | 0.0 | 12.0 | | | | | | | | 0 | | | | |
| sweet & sour | 45 | | 0.0 | | 0 | | | | | | 55 | | | | |
| *1 pkt* | 28 | 0.0 | 11.0 | | | | | | | | 40 | | | | |
| sweet mustard | 50 | | 1.0 | | 0 | | | | | | 140 | | | | |
| *1 pkt* | 28 | 0.0 | 9.0 | | | | | | | | 30 | | | | |
| **chili** | 240 | | 8.0 | | 25 | | | | | | 990 | | | | |
| *1 reg serving* | 236 | 19.0 | 24.0 | | | | | | | | 540 | | | | |
| **chili** | 360 | | 12.0 | | 38 | | | | | | 1485 | | | | |
| *1 large serving* | 354 | 29.0 | 36.0 | | | | | | | | 810 | | | | |
| **coleslaw** | 80 | | 5.0 | | 40 | | | | | | 165 | | | | |
| *1/4 cup* | 57 | 0.0 | 9.0 | | | | | | | | 85 | | | | |
| **cookie, choc chip** | 320 | | 17.0 | | 5 | | | | | | 235 | | | | |
| *1 cookie* | 64 | 3.0 | 40.0 | | | | | | | | 100 | | | | |
| **danish, apple/cheese/cinn raisin** | 400 | | 17.7 | | | | | | | | 437 | | | | |
| *1 danish* | 95 | 7.0 | 53.3 | | | | | | | | | | | | |
| **double cheeseburger** | 620 | | 36.0 | | 165 | | | | | | 760 | | | | |
| *1 sandwich* | 221 | 48.0 | 26.0 | | | | | | | | | | | | |
| **double hamburger** | 560 | | 30.0 | | 150 | | | | | | 465 | | | | |
| *1 sandwich* | 203 | 44.0 | 26.0 | | | | | | | | 590 | | | | |
| **egg, fried** | 90 | | 6.0 | | 230 | | | | | | 95 | | | | |
| *1 egg* | 44 | 6.0 | 1.0 | | | | | | | | 65 | | | | |
| **eggs, scrambled** | 190 | | 12.0 | | 450 | | | | | | 160 | | | | |
| *2 eggs* | 91 | 14.0 | 7.0 | | | | | | | | 130 | | | | |
| **fish fillet** | 210 | | 11.0 | | 45 | | | | | | 475 | | | | |
| *1 serving* | 92 | 14.0 | 13.0 | | | | | | | | 255 | | | | |
| **french fries** | 310 | | 15.0 | | 15 | | | | | | 105 | | | | |
| *1 reg serving* | 106 | 4.0 | 38.0 | | | | | | | | 675 | | | | |
| **french fries** | 403 | | 19.5 | | 20 | | | | | | 137 | | | | |
| *1 large serving* | 138 | 5.2 | 49.4 | | | | | | | | 878 | | | | |
| **french toast** | 400 | | 19.0 | | 115 | | | | | | 850 | | | | |
| *2 slices* | 135 | 11.0 | 45.0 | | | | | | | | 175 | | | | |
| **frosty dairy dessert** | 400 | | 14.0 | | 50 | | | | | | 220 | | | | |
| *1 small* | 243 | 8.0 | 59.0 | | | | | | | | 585 | | | | |
| | 520 | | 18.2 | | 65 | | | | | | 286 | | | | |
| *1 med* | 316 | 10.4 | 76.7 | | | | | | | | 761 | | | | |
| | 680 | | 23.8 | | 85 | | | | | | 374 | | | | |
| *1 large* | 413 | 13.6 | 100.3 | | | | | | | | 995 | | | | |
| **kid's hamburger** | 200 | | 9.0 | | 35 | | | | | | 225 | | | | |
| *1 sandwich* | 72 | 13.0 | 17.0 | | | | | | | | 170 | | | | |
| **omelet** | | | | | | | | | | | | | | | |
| w/ ham & cheese | 290 | | 21.0 | | 355 | | | | | | 570 | | | | |
| *1 serving* | 118 | 18.0 | 7.0 | | | | | | | | 190 | | | | |

| | KCAL | H₂O (g) | FAT (g) | PUFA (g) | CHOL (mg) | A (RE) | C (mg) | B-2 (mg) | B-6 (mg) | FOL (mcg) | Na (mg) | Ca (mg) | Mg (mg) | Zn (mg) | Mn (mg) |
|---|---|---|---|---|---|---|---|---|---|---|---|---|---|---|---|
| | WT (g) | PRO (g) | CHO (g) | SFA (g) | DFIB (g) | A (IU) | B-1 (mg) | NIA (mg) | B-12 (mcg) | PANT (mg) | K (mg) | P (mg) | Fe (mg) | Cu (mg) | |
| w/ ham, cheese & mushrooms | 250 | | 17.0 | | 450 | | | | | | 405 | | | | |
| *1 serving* | 114 | 18.0 | 6.0 | | | | | | | | 180 | | | | |
| w/ ham, cheese, onion & green pepper | 280 | | 19.0 | | 525 | | | | | | 485 | | | | |
| *1 serving* | 128 | 19.0 | 7.0 | | | | | | | | 200 | | | | |
| w/ mushrooms, green pepper & onion | 210 | | 15.0 | | 460 | | | | | | 200 | | | | |
| *1 serving* | 114 | 14.0 | 7.0 | | | | | | | | 190 | | | | |
| pasta salad | 130 | | 6.0 | | 5 | | | | | | 190 | | | | |
| *1/4 cup* | 57 | 3.0 | 18.0 | | | | | | | | 70 | | | | |
| potato, baked | 250 | | 2.0 | | 0 | | | | | | 60 | | | | |
| *1 potato* | 250 | 6.0 | 52.0 | | | | | | | | 1360 | | | | |
| w/ bacon & cheese | 570 | | 30.0 | | 22 | | | | | | 1180 | | | | |
| *1 potato* | 350 | 19.0 | 57.0 | | | | | | | | 1380 | | | | |
| w/ broccoli & cheese | 500 | | 25.0 | | 22 | | | | | | 430 | | | | |
| *1 potato* | 365 | 13.0 | 54.0 | | | | | | | | 1550 | | | | |
| w/ cheese | 590 | | 34.0 | | 22 | | | | | | 450 | | | | |
| *1 potato* | 350 | 17.0 | 55.0 | | | | | | | | 1380 | | | | |
| w/ chili & cheese | 510 | | 20.0 | | 22 | | | | | | 610 | | | | |
| *1 potato* | 400 | 22.0 | 63.0 | | | | | | | | 1590 | | | | |
| w/ sour cream & chives | 460 | | 24.0 | | 15 | | | | | | 230 | | | | |
| *1 potato* | 310 | 6.0 | 53.0 | | | | | | | | 1420 | | | | |
| sausage | 200 | | 18.0 | | 45 | | | | | | 405 | | | | |
| *1 patty* | 45 | 8.0 | 0.0 | | | | | | | | 115 | | | | |
| sausage gravy | 440 | | 36.0 | | 85 | | | | | | 1300 | | | | |
| *6 oz* | 214 | 17.0 | 13.0 | | | | | | | | 340 | | | | |
| single cheeseburger | 410 | | 22.0 | | 90 | | | | | | 655 | | | | |
| *1 sandwich* | 145 | 28.0 | 26.0 | | | | | | | | | | | | |
| single hamburger | 350 | | 16.0 | | 75 | | | | | | 360 | | | | |
| *1 sandwich* | 127 | 24.0 | 26.0 | | | | | | | | 320 | | | | |
| syrup | 140 | | 0.0 | | 0 | | | | | | 5 | | | | |
| *1 pkt* | 43 | 0.0 | 37.0 | | | | | | | | 0 | | | | |
| taco salad | 430 | | 19.0 | | 45 | | | | | | 1260 | | | | |
| *1 serving* | 398 | 22.0 | 43.0 | | | | | | | | 760 | | | | |
| tartar sce | 80 | | 9.0 | | | | | | | | 75 | | | | |
| *1 T* | 14 | 0.0 | 0.0 | | | | | | | | | | | | |

# 12. FATS, OILS & SHORTENINGS
## 12.1. ANIMAL FATS

| | KCAL | H₂O (g) | FAT (g) | PUFA (g) | CHOL (mg) | A (RE) | C (mg) | B-2 (mg) | B-6 (mg) | FOL (mcg) | Na (mg) | Ca (mg) | Mg (mg) | Zn (mg) | Mn (mg) |
|---|---|---|---|---|---|---|---|---|---|---|---|---|---|---|---|
| beef suet, raw | 242 | 1.1 | 26.7 | 0.9 | 19 | | | | | | | | | | |
| *1 oz* | 28 | 0.4 | 0.0 | 14.8 | | | | | | | 5 | | | | |
| beef tallow, raw | 116 | 0.0 | 12.8 | 0.5 | 14 | | | | | | 0 | | | | |
| *1 T* | 13 | 0.0 | 0.0 | 6.4 | 0.0 | | | | | | 0 | | | | |
| chicken fat, raw | 115 | 0.0 | 12.8 | 2.7 | 11 | | | | | | | | | | .002 |
| *1 T* | 13 | 0.0 | 0.0 | 3.8 | | | | | | | | | | | |
| duck fat, raw | 115 | 0.0 | 12.8 | 1.7 | 13 | | | | | | | | | | |
| *1 T* | 13 | 0.0 | 0.0 | 4.3 | 0.0 | | | | | | | | | | |
| goose fat, raw | 115 | 0.0 | 12.8 | 1.4 | 13 | | | | | | | | | | |
| *1 T* | 13 | 0.0 | 0.0 | 3.5 | 0.0 | | | | | | | | | | |
| mutton tallow, raw | 116 | 0.0 | 12.8 | 1.0 | 13 | | | | | | | | | | |
| *1 T* | 13 | 0.0 | 0.0 | 6.1 | 0.0 | | | | | | | | | | |
| pork fat (lard), raw | 115 | 0.0 | 12.8 | 1.4 | 12 | | | | | | 0 | 0 | 0 | .01 | |
| *1 T* | 13 | 0.0 | 0.0 | 5.0 | 0.0 | | | | | | 0 | | | | |
| pork separable fat | 200 | 5.1 | 21.3 | 2.3 | 26 | 1 | 0 | .03 | .17 | 0 | 9 | 1 | 2 | .17 | .001 |
| *1 oz* | 28 | 1.9 | 0.0 | 7.8 | 0.0 | 4 | .09 | 0.7 | .17 | .04 | 23 | 17 | .09 | .015 | |
| salt pork, raw | 212 | 3.1 | 22.8 | 2.7 | 25 | 0 | | .02 | .02 | 0 | 404 | 2 | 2 | .26 | .001 |
| *1 oz* | 28 | 1.4 | 0.0 | 8.3 | 0.0 | 0 | .06 | 0.5 | .08 | .06 | 19 | 15 | .12 | .014 | |
| turkey fat, raw | 115 | 0.0 | 12.8 | 3.0 | 13 | | | | | | | | | | |
| *1 T* | 13 | 0.0 | 0.0 | 3.8 | 0.0 | | | | | | | | | | |

| | KCAL | H₂O (g) | FAT (g) | PUFA (g) | CHOL (mg) | A (RE) | C (mg) | B-2 (mg) | B-6 (mg) | FOL (mcg) | Na (mg) | Ca (mg) | Mg (mg) | Zn (mg) | Mn (mg) |
|---|---|---|---|---|---|---|---|---|---|---|---|---|---|---|---|
| | WT (g) | PRO (g) | CHO (g) | SFA (g) | DFIB (g) | A (IU) | B-1 (mg) | NIA (mg) | B-12 (mcg) | PANT (mg) | K (mg) | P (mg) | Fe (mg) | Cu (mg) | |

## 12.2. VEGETABLE OILS

| | KCAL | H₂O/PRO | FAT/CHO | PUFA/SFA | CHOL/DFIB | A | C/B-1 | B-2/NIA | B-6/B-12 | FOL/PANT | Na/K | Ca/P | Mg/Fe | Zn/Cu | Mn |
|---|---|---|---|---|---|---|---|---|---|---|---|---|---|---|---|
| almond oil | 120 | 0.0 | 13.6 | 2.4 | | | | | | | | | | | |
| 1 T | 14 | 0.0 | 0.0 | 1.1 | 0.0 | | | | | | | | | | |
| coconut oil | 120 | 0.0 | 13.6 | 0.2 | | | | | | | | | | | |
| 1 T | 14 | 0.0 | 0.0 | 11.8 | 0.0 | | | | | | | | | | |
| corn oil | 120 | 0.0 | 13.6 | 8.0 | | | | | | | | | | | |
| 1 T | 14 | 0.0 | 0.0 | 1.7 | 0.0 | | | | | | | | | | |
| corn oil, Fleischmann's | 120 | | 14.0 | 8.0 | 0 | | | | | | 0 | | | | |
| 1 T | | 0.0 | 0.0 | 2.0 | | | | | | | 0 | | | | |
| corn oil, Mazola | 125 | 0.0 | 14.0 | 8.3 | 0 | | | | | | 0 | | | | |
| 1 T | 14 | 0.0 | 0.0 | 1.8 | | | | | | | | | | | |
| cottonseed oil | 120 | 0.0 | 13.6 | 7.1 | | | | | | | | | | | |
| 1 T | 14 | 0.0 | 0.0 | 3.5 | 0.0 | | | | | | | | | | |
| Crisco oil | 124 | 0.0 | 14.0 | 7.3 | 0 | | | | | | | | | | |
| 1 T | 14 | 0.0 | 0.0 | 1.8 | 0.0 | | | | | | | | | | |
| olive oil | 119 | 0.0 | 13.5 | 1.1 | | | | | | | 0 | 0 | 0 | .01 | |
| 1 T | 14 | 0.0 | | 1.8 | 0.0 | | | | | | | 0 | .05 | | |
| palm oil | 120 | 0.0 | 13.6 | 1.3 | | | | | | | | | | | |
| 1 T | 14 | 0.0 | 0.0 | 6.7 | 0.0 | | | | | | | 0 | .00 | | |
| palm kernel oil | 120 | 0.0 | 13.6 | 0.2 | | | | | | | | | | | |
| 1 T | 14 | 0.0 | 0.0 | 11.1 | 0.0 | | | | | | | | | | |
| peanut oil | 119 | 0.0 | 13.5 | 4.3 | | | | | | | 0 | 0 | 0 | .00 | |
| 1 T | 14 | 0.0 | 0.0 | 2.3 | 0.0 | | | | | | 0 | 0 | .00 | | |
| peanut oil, Planters | 130 | | 14.0 | 4.0 | 0 | | | | | | 0 | | | | |
| 1 T | | 0.0 | 0.0 | 2.0 | | | | | | | 0 | | | | |
| popcorn oil, Planters | 130 | | 14.0 | 4.0 | 0 | | | | | | 0 | | | | |
| 1 T | | 0.0 | 0.0 | 0.2 | | | | | | | 0 | | | | |
| Puritan oil | 124 | 0.0 | 14.0 | 9.5 | 0 | | | | | | | | | | |
| 1 T | 14 | 0.0 | 0.0 | 1.7 | 0.0 | | | | | | | | | | |
| safflower oil | 120 | 0.0 | 13.6 | 10.1 | | | | | | | | | | | |
| 1 T | 14 | 0.0 | 0.0 | 1.2 | 0.0 | | | | | | | | | | |
| sesame oil | 120 | 0.0 | 13.6 | 5.7 | | | | | | | | | | | |
| 1 T | 14 | 0.0 | 0.0 | 1.9 | 0.0 | | | | | | | | | | |
| soybean oil | 120 | 0.0 | 13.6 | 7.9 | | | | | | | 0 | 0 | 0 | .00 | |
| 1 T | 14 | 0.0 | 0.0 | 2.0 | 0.0 | | | | | | 0 | .00 | | | |
| soybean oil, hydrogenated | 120 | 0.0 | 13.6 | 5.1 | | | | | | | | | | | |
| 1 T | 14 | 0.0 | 0.0 | 2.0 | 0.0 | | | | | | | | | | |
| soybean (hydrogenated) & cottonseed oil | 120 | 0.0 | 13.6 | 6.5 | | | | | | | | | | | |
| 1 T | 14 | 0.0 | 0.0 | 2.4 | 0.0 | | | | | | | | | | |
| soybean lecithin[a] | 120 | 0.0 | 13.6 | 6.1 | | | | | | | | | | | |
| 1 T | 14 | 0.0 | 0.0 | 2.1 | 0.0 | | | | | | | | | | |
| sunflower oil | 120 | 0.0 | 13.6 | 8.9 | | | | | | | | | | | |
| 1 T | 14 | 0.0 | 0.0 | 1.4 | 0.0 | | | | | | | | | | |
| veg oil spray, Mazola No Stick | 6 | 0.0 | 0.7 | 0.4 | 0 | | | | | | 0 | | | | |
| 2.5 sec spray | 0.7 | 0.0 | 0.0 | 0.1 | | | | | | | | | | | |
| wheat germ oil | 120 | 0.0 | 13.6 | 8.5 | | | | | | | | | | .50 | |
| 1 T | 14 | 0.0 | 0.0 | 2.6 | 0.0 | | | | | | | | | | |

## 12.3. SHORTENINGS

| | KCAL | H₂O/PRO | FAT/CHO | PUFA/SFA | CHOL/DFIB | A | C/B-1 | B-2/NIA | B-6/B-12 | FOL/PANT | Na/K | Ca/P | Mg/Fe | Zn/Cu | Mn |
|---|---|---|---|---|---|---|---|---|---|---|---|---|---|---|---|
| Crisco, reg/butter flavor | 106 | 0.0 | 12.0 | 3.6 | 0 | | | | | | | | | | |
| 1 T | 12 | 0.0 | 0.0 | 3.1 | 0.0 | 0[b] | | | | | | | | | |
| lard & veg oil | 115 | 0.0 | 12.8 | 1.4 | | | | | | | | | | | |
| 1 T | 13 | 0.0 | 0.0 | 5.2 | 0.0 | | | | | | | | | | |
| soybean & cottonseed | 113 | 0.0 | 12.8 | 3.3 | | | | | | | | | | | |
| 1 T | 13 | 0.0 | 0.0 | 3.2 | 0.0 | | | | | | | | | | |
| soybean & palm | 113 | 0.0 | 12.8 | 1.8 | | | | | | | | | | | |
| 1 T | 13 | 0.0 | 0.0 | 3.9 | 0.0 | | | | | | | | | | |

[a] 70% soybean phosphatide in 30% soybean oil.

[b] Butter flavor contains 190 IU Vit A.

| | KCAL | H₂O (g) | FAT (g) | PUFA (g) | CHOL (mg) | A (RE) | C (mg) | B-2 (mg) | B-6 (mg) | FOL (mcg) | Na (mg) | Ca (mg) | Mg (mg) | Zn (mg) | Mn (mg) |
| --- | --- | --- | --- | --- | --- | --- | --- | --- | --- | --- | --- | --- | --- | --- | --- |
| | WT (g) | PRO (g) | CHO (g) | SFA (g) | DFIB (g) | A (IU) | B-1 (mg) | NIA (mg) | B-12 (mcg) | PANT (mg) | K (mg) | P (mg) | Fe (mg) | Cu (mg) | |

## 13. FISH, SHELLFISH & CRUSTACEA

| | KCAL / WT | H₂O / PRO | FAT / CHO | PUFA / SFA | CHOL / DFIB | A(RE) / A(IU) | C / B-1 | B-2 / NIA | B-6 / B-12 | FOL / PANT | Na / K | Ca / P | Mg / Fe | Zn / Cu | Mn |
| --- | --- | --- | --- | --- | --- | --- | --- | --- | --- | --- | --- | --- | --- | --- | --- |
| **abalone** | | | | | | | | | | | | | | | |
| raw | 89 | 63.4 | 0.6 | 0.1 | 72 | | | | | 4 | 255 | 27 | 41 | .69 | .034 |
| 3 oz | 85 | 14.5 | 5.1 | 0.1 | | | | | | 2.55 | | | 2.71 | .167 | |
| friedᵃ | 161 | 51.1 | 5.8 | 1.4 | 80 | | | | | 5 | 502 | 32 | 47 | .80 | |
| 3 oz | 85 | 16.7 | 9.4 | 1.4 | | | | | | | | | 3.23 | .194 | |
| **alewife** | | | | | | | | | | | | | | | |
| raw | 127 | 79.4 | 4.9 | | | | | | | | | | | | |
| 3.5 oz | 100 | 19.4 | 0.0 | | 0.0 | | | | | | | 218 | | | |
| cnd | 141 | 73.0 | 8.0 | | | | | | | | | | | | |
| 3.5 oz | 100 | 16.2 | 0.0 | | 0.0 | | | | | | | | | | |
| **anchovy** | | | | | | | | | | | | | | | |
| raw | 111 | 62.4 | 4.1 | 1.4 | | | | .22 | .12 | | 88 | 125 | 35 | 1.46 | |
| 3 oz | 85 | 17.3 | 0.0 | 1.1 | | | .05 | 11.9 | .53 | | 325 | 148 | 2.76 | .179 | |
| cnd in olive oil | 42 | 10.1 | 1.9 | 0.5 | | | | .07 | .04 | | 734 | 46 | 14 | .49 | |
| 5 anchovies | 20 | 5.8 | 0.0 | 0.4 | | | .02 | 4.0 | .18 | | 109 | 50 | .93 | .068 | |
| paste | 14 | | 0.8 | 0.5 | | | | | | | | | | | |
| 1 t | 7 | 1.4 | 0.3 | | 0.0 | | | | | | | | | | |
| pickled | 49 | 16.4 | 2.9 | | | | | | | | | 47 | | | |
| 1 oz | 28 | 5.4 | 0.1 | | 0.0 | | | | | | | 59 | | | |
| **barracuda, pacific, raw** | 113 | 75.4 | 2.6 | | | | | | | | | | | | |
| 3.5 oz | 100 | 21.0 | 0.0 | | 0.0 | | | | | | | | | | |
| **bass, black** | | | | | | | | | | | | | | | |
| raw | 93 | 79.3 | 1.2 | | | | | | | | 68 | | | | |
| 3.5 oz | 100 | 19.2 | 0.0 | | 0.0 | | | | | | 256 | | | | |
| baked | 287 | | 19.4 | | | | 0 | .16 | | | 68 | 96 | | | |
| 4 oz | 113 | 23.6 | 3.0 | | 0.0 | 97 | .07 | 3.5 | | | 256 | 269 | 1.20 | | |
| stuffed, bakedᵇ | 259 | 52.9 | 15.8 | | | | | | | | | | | | |
| 3.5 oz | 100 | 16.2 | 11.4 | | 0.0 | | | | | | | | | | |
| **bass, freshwater, raw** | 97 | 64.3 | 3.1 | 0.9 | 58 | | | | | | 59 | 68 | 26 | .56 | .756 |
| 3 oz | 85 | 16.0 | 0.0 | 0.7 | | | | | | | 303 | 170 | 1.27 | .079 | |
| **bass, striped, raw** | 82 | 67.3 | 2.0 | 0.7 | 68 | | | | | | 59 | | | .34 | .013 |
| 3 oz | 85 | 15.1 | 0.0 | 0.4 | | | | | 3.25 | | | | .71 | .026 | |
| **bluefish, raw** | 105 | 60.2 | 3.6 | 0.9 | 50 | 338 | | .07 | .34 | 1 | 51 | 6 | 28 | .69 | .018 |
| 3 oz | 85 | 17.0 | 0.0 | 0.8 | | 101 | .05 | 5.1 | 4.58 | .70 | 316 | 193 | .41 | .045 | |
| **bonito, cnd** | 257 | | 19.1 | | | | | .09 | | | 514 | 8 | 28 | | |
| 3.5 oz | 100 | 19.8 | 0.0 | | 0.0 | | .01 | 9.8 | | | 302 | 193 | 1.00 | | |
| **bullhead, black, raw** | 84 | 81.3 | 1.6 | | | | | | | | | | | | |
| 3.5 oz | 100 | 16.3 | 0.0 | | 0.0 | | | | | | | | | | |
| **burbot, raw** | 76 | 67.4 | 0.7 | 0.3 | 51 | | | | | | 82 | 43 | 27 | .64 | .595 |
| 3 oz | 85 | 16.4 | 0.0 | 0.1 | | | | | | | 343 | 170 | .77 | .170 | |
| **butterfish, raw** | 124 | 63.0 | 6.8 | | 55 | | | | | | 75 | | | .65 | .013 |
| 3 oz | 85 | 14.7 | 0.0 | | | | | | | | 318 | | .42 | .046 | |
| **carp** | | | | | | | | | | | | | | | |
| raw | 108 | 64.9 | 4.8 | 1.2 | 56 | 25 | 1 | | .16 | | 42 | 35 | 25 | 1.26 | |
| 3 oz | 85 | 15.2 | 0.0 | 0.9 | | 7 | | | 1.30 | | 283 | 352 | 1.05 | .048 | |
| ckd by dry heat | 138 | 59.2 | 6.1 | 1.6 | 72 | 27 | 1 | | .19 | 1 | 54 | 44 | 32 | 1.62 | |
| 3 oz | 85 | 19.4 | 0.0 | 1.2 | | 8 | | | | | 363 | 452 | 1.35 | .062 | |
| **catfish, channel** | | | | | | | | | | | | | | | |
| raw | 99 | 64.9 | 3.6 | 0.9 | 49 | | | .09 | | | 54 | 34 | 21 | .61 | .013 |
| 3 oz | 85 | 15.5 | 0.0 | 0.8 | | | .04 | 1.8 | | | 296 | 181 | .83 | .080 | |
| breaded & friedᶜ | 194 | 50.0 | 11.3 | 2.8 | 69 | 24 | 0 | .11 | | | 238 | 37 | 23 | .73 | |
| 3 oz | 85 | 15.4 | 6.8 | 2.8 | | 7 | .06 | 1.9 | | | 289 | 183 | 1.22 | .086 | |

ᵃ Dipped in flour & salt before frying.
ᵇ Stuffed w/ bacon, butter, celery, onion & bread cubes.
ᶜ Breading consists of cornmeal, egg, milk & salt.

| | KCAL / WT(g) | H₂O(g) / PRO(g) | FAT(g) / CHO(g) | PUFA(g) / SFA(g) | CHOL(mg) / DFIB(g) | A(RE) / A(IU) | C(mg) / B-1(mg) | B-2(mg) / NIA(mg) | B-6(mg) / B-12(mcg) | FOL(mcg) / PANT(mg) | Na(mg) / K(mg) | Ca(mg) / P(mg) | Mg(mg) / Fe(mg) | Zn(mg) / Cu(mg) | Mn(mg) |
|---|---|---|---|---|---|---|---|---|---|---|---|---|---|---|---|
| **caviar, black & red, granular** | 40 | 7.6 | 2.9 | | 94 | | | | | | 240 | | | | |
| *1 T* | 16 | 3.9 | 0.6 | | | | | | | | | | | | |
| **chub, raw** | 145 | 74.9 | 8.8 | | 50 | | | | | | | | | | |
| *3.5 oz* | 100 | 15.3 | 0.0 | | 0.0 | | | | | | | | | | |
| **cisco** | | | | | | | | | | | | | | | |
| raw | 84 | 67.1 | 1.6 | 0.5 | | | | | | | 47 | | | | |
| *3 oz* | 85 | 16.1 | 0.0 | 0.4 | | | | | | | 301 | | .31 | | |
| smoked | 151 | 59.3 | 10.1 | 1.9 | 27 | 802 | | .14 | .23 | 2 | 409 | 22 | 14 | .25 | .018 |
| *3 oz* | 85 | 13.9 | 0.0 | 1.5 | | 240 | .04 | 2.0 | 3.62 | .26 | 249 | 128 | .41 | .183 | |
| **clam liquid, cnd** | 6 | 234.5 | 0.1 | | | | | | | | 516 | 31 | 26 | .24 | .178 |
| *1 cup* | 240 | 1.0 | 0.2 | | | | | | | | | | | .934 | |
| **clams** | | | | | | | | | | | | | | | |
| raw | 63 | 69.6 | 0.8 | 0.2 | 29 | 255 | | .18 | | | 47 | 39 | 8 | 1.16 | .425 |
| *3 oz (4 large or 9 small)* | 85 | 10.9 | 2.2 | 0.1 | | 77 | | 1.5 | 42.03 | .31 | 267 | 144 | 11.88 | .292 | |
| breaded & fried[a] | 171 | 52.3 | 9.5 | 2.4 | 52 | 257 | | .21 | | | 309 | 54 | 12 | 1.24 | |
| *3 oz (9 small)* | 85 | 12.1 | 8.8 | 2.3 | | 77 | | 1.8 | 34.23 | | 277 | 160 | 11.83 | .303 | |
| cnd | 126 | 54.1 | 1.7 | 0.5 | 57 | 484 | | .36 | | | 95 | 78 | 16 | 2.32 | |
| *3 oz* | 85 | 21.7 | 4.4 | 0.2 | | 145 | | 2.9 | 84.06 | | 534 | 287 | 23.76 | .585 | |
| ckd by moist heat | 126 | 54.1 | 1.7 | 0.5 | 57 | 484 | | .36 | | | 95 | 78 | .16 | 2.32 | |
| *3 oz (9 small)* | 85 | 21.7 | 4.4 | 0.2 | | 145 | | 2.9 | 84.06 | | 534 | 287 | 23.76 | .585 | |
| **cod, atlantic** | | | | | | | | | | | | | | | |
| raw | 70 | 69.0 | 0.6 | 0.2 | 37 | 34 | 1 | .06 | .21 | | 46 | 13 | 27 | .38 | .013 |
| *3 oz* | 85 | 15.1 | 0.0 | 0.1 | | 10 | .07 | 1.8 | .77 | .13 | 351 | 173 | .32 | .024 | |
| cnd | 89 | 64.3 | 0.7 | 0.2 | 47 | 39 | 1 | .07 | .24 | | 185 | 18 | 35 | .49 | |
| *3 oz* | 85 | 19.4 | 0.0 | 0.1 | | 12 | .07 | 2.1 | .89 | | 449 | 221 | .41 | .031 | |
| ckd by dry heat | 89 | 64.5 | 0.7 | 0.2 | 47 | 39 | 1 | .07 | .24 | | 66 | 12 | 36 | .49 | |
| *3 oz* | 85 | 19.4 | 0.0 | 0.1 | | 12 | .08 | 2.1 | .89 | | 208 | 117 | .41 | .031 | |
| dried & salted | 246 | 13.7 | 2.0 | 0.7 | 129 | 120 | 3 | .20 | .73 | | 5973 | 136 | 113 | 1.35 | |
| *3 oz* | 85 | 53.4 | 0.0 | 0.4 | | 36 | .23 | 6.4 | 8.50 | 1.42 | 1239 | 808 | 2.13 | .150 | |
| **cod, frzn** | | | | | | | | | | | | | | | |
| almondine, Am Hosp Co | 347 | | 21.7 | | 49 | 1 | | .18 | | | 312 | 91 | | | |
| *5.5 oz* | 156 | 26.4 | 11.4 | | | 307 | .13 | 4.3 | | | 511 | | 1.70 | | |
| breaded, Van de Kamp's | 290 | | 20.0 | | | | | | | | 370 | | | | |
| *5 oz piece* | 142 | 20.0 | 10.0 | | | | | | | | | | | | |
| w/ creole sce, Am Hosp Co | 158 | | 5.6 | | 38 | | 28 | .14 | | | 498 | 42 | | | |
| *6.44 oz* | 183 | 20.5 | 6.4 | | | 875 | .12 | 3.4 | | | 621 | | 1.42 | | |
| w/ fish-based crm sce, Am Hosp Co | 188 | | 9.3 | | 72 | | 1 | .05 | | | 497 | 81 | | | |
| *6 oz* | 170 | 15.8 | 10.2 | | | 343 | .05 | 1.7 | | | 282 | | 1.08 | | |
| w/ lemon sce, Am Hosp Co | 237 | | 11.4 | | 63 | | 4 | .13 | | | 165 | 42 | | | |
| *6.5 oz* | 184 | 29.2 | 4.4 | | | 431 | .09 | 3.0 | | | 436 | | 1.01 | | |
| **cod, pacific, raw** | 70 | 69.1 | 0.5 | 0.2 | 31 | 24 | | .04 | | | 60 | 6 | 21 | .34 | .010 |
| *3 oz* | 85 | 15.2 | 0.0 | 0.1 | | 7 | .02 | 1.7 | | .12 | 342 | 148 | .22 | .022 | |
| **crab, alaska king** | | | | | | | | | | | | | | | |
| raw | 71 | 67.6 | 0.5 | | 35 | 20 | | .04 | | | 711 | 39 | | 5.05 | .030 |
| *3 oz* | 85 | 15.6 | 0.0 | | | 6 | .04 | 0.9 | | | 173 | 186 | .50 | .784 | |
| ckd by moist heat | 82 | 65.9 | 1.3 | 0.5 | 45 | 25 | | .05 | | | 911 | 50 | | 6.48 | |
| *3 oz* | 85 | 16.5 | 0.0 | 0.1 | | 7 | .05 | 1.1 | | | 222 | 238 | .64 | 1.01 | |
| imitation, made from surimi | 87 | 62.3 | 1.1 | | 17 | | | .02 | | | 715 | 11 | | | |
| *3 oz* | 85 | 10.2 | 8.7 | | | | .03 | 0.2 | | | 77 | | .33 | | |
| **crab, blue** | | | | | | | | | | | | | | | |
| raw | 74 | 67.2 | 0.9 | 0.3 | 66 | | | | | | 249 | 76 | 29 | 3.00 | 1.28 |
| *3 oz* | 85 | 15.4 | 0.0 | 0.2 | | | | | | | 280 | 195 | .63 | .569 | |
| cnd | 84 | 64.7 | 1.0 | 0.4 | 76 | | | .07 | | | 283 | 86 | 33 | 3.41 | |
| *3 oz* | 85 | 17.4 | 0.0 | 0.2 | | | | 1.2 | .39 | | 318 | 221 | .71 | .646 | |
| ckd by moist heat | 87 | 65.8 | 1.5 | | | 0.6 | 85 | | | | 237 | 88 | 28 | 3.58 | |
| *3 oz* | 85 | 17.2 | 0.0 | | | 0.2 | | | 6.21 | | 275 | 175 | .77 | .548 | |

[a] Prepared w/ bread crumbs, egg, milk & salt.

|  | KCAL | $H_2O$ (g) | FAT (g) | PUFA (g) | CHOL (mg) | A (RE) | C (mg) | B-2 (mg) | B-6 (mg) | FOL (mcg) | Na (mg) | Ca (mg) | Mg (mg) | Zn (mg) | Mn (mg) |
|---|---|---|---|---|---|---|---|---|---|---|---|---|---|---|---|
|  | WT (g) | PRO (g) | CHO (g) | SFA (g) | DFIB (g) | A (IU) | B-1 (mg) | NIA (mg) | B-12 (mcg) | PANT (mg) | K (mg) | P (mg) | Fe (mg) | Cu (mg) |  |
| **crab cakes[a]** | 93 | 42.6 | 4.5 | 1.4 | 90 |  |  |  |  |  | 198 | 63 | 20 | 2.46 |  |
| *1 cake* | 60 | 12.1 | 0.3 | 0.9 |  |  |  |  | 3.56 |  | 195 | 128 | .65 | .366 |  |
| **crab, dungeness, raw** | 73 | 67.3 | 0.8 | 0.3 | 50 |  |  | .14 |  |  | 251 | 39 | 39 | 3.63 | .068 |
| *3 oz* | 85 | 14.8 | 0.6 | 0.1 |  |  | .04 | 2.7 |  |  | 301 | 154 | .31 | .573 |  |
| **crab, queen, raw** | 76 | 68.5 | 1.0 | 0.4 | 47 |  |  |  |  |  | 458 | 22 |  |  |  |
| *3 oz* | 85 | 15.7 | 0.0 | 0.1 |  |  |  |  |  |  | 147 | 113 |  |  |  |
| **crayfish** |  |  |  |  |  |  |  |  |  |  |  |  |  |  |  |
| raw | 76 | 68.7 | 0.9 | 0.3 | 118 | 3 |  | .05 |  |  | 45 | 20 | 21 | 1.11 |  |
| *3 oz* | 85 | 15.9 | 0.0 | 0.2 |  |  |  | 2.0 | 2.30 | .35 | 233 | 219 | 2.08 | .371 |  |
| ckd by moist heat | 97 | 64.1 | 1.2 | 0.3 | 151 | 3 |  | .07 |  |  | 58 | 26 | 27 | 1.42 |  |
| *3 oz* | 85 | 20.3 | 0.0 | 0.2 |  |  |  | 2.5 | 2.94 |  | 298 | 280 | 2.67 | .475 |  |
| **croaker, atlantic** |  |  |  |  |  |  |  |  |  |  |  |  |  |  |  |
| raw | 89 | 66.3 | 2.7 | 0.4 | 52 |  |  |  |  |  | 47 | 13 | 34 | .35 | .021 |
| *3 oz* | 85 | 15.1 | 0.0 | 0.9 |  |  |  |  |  |  | 293 | 178 | .31 | .036 |  |
| breaded & fried[b] | 188 | 50.8 | 10.8 | 2.5 | 71 |  |  |  |  |  | 296 | 27 | 35 | .44 |  |
| *3 oz* | 85 | 15.5 | 6.4 | 3.0 |  |  |  |  |  |  | 289 | 184 | .73 | .055 |  |
| **cusk, raw** | 74 | 64.9 | 0.6 |  | 35 |  |  | .11 | .33 |  | 27 | 9 | 27 | .32 | .013 |
| *3 oz* | 85 | 16.1 | 0.0 |  |  |  |  | 2.3 | .89 | .24 | 333 | 173 | .71 | .015 |  |
| **cuttlefish, raw** | 67 | 68.5 | 0.6 | 0.1 | 95 | 5 |  | .77 |  |  | 316 | 77 |  | 1.47 |  |
| *3 oz* | 85 | 13.8 | 0.7 | 0.1 |  |  | .01 | 1.0 | 2.55 |  | 301 | 329 | 5.11 | .499 |  |
| **dogfish, spiny, raw** | 156 | 72.3 | 9.0 |  |  |  |  |  |  |  |  |  |  |  |  |
| *3.5 oz* | 100 | 17.6 | 0.0 |  | 0.0 |  | .05 |  |  |  |  |  |  |  |  |
| **dolphinfish, raw** | 73 | 65.9 | 0.6 | 0.1 | 62 |  |  |  |  |  | 74 |  |  | .39 | .013 |
| *3 oz* | 85 | 15.7 | 0.0 | 0.2 |  |  |  |  |  |  | 354 |  | .96 | .035 |  |
| **drum, freshwater, raw** | 101 | 65.7 | 4.2 | 1.0 | 54 |  |  |  |  |  | 64 | 51 | 26 | .56 | .595 |
| *3 oz* | 85 | 14.9 | 0.0 | 1.0 |  |  |  |  |  |  | 234 | 153 | .77 | .197 |  |
| **fish fillets, frzn** |  |  |  |  |  |  |  |  |  |  |  |  |  |  |  |
| batter-dipped, Van de Kamp's | 180 |  | 10.0 |  |  |  |  |  |  |  | 230 |  |  |  |  |
| *3 oz piece* | 85 | 10.0 | 15.0 |  |  |  |  |  |  |  |  |  |  |  |  |
| country seasoned, Van de Kamp's | 200 |  | 10.0 |  |  |  |  |  |  |  | 335 |  |  |  |  |
| *2 oz piece* | 57 | 10.0 | 10.0 |  |  |  |  |  |  |  |  |  |  |  |  |
| light & crispy, Van de Kamp's | 180 |  | 15.0 |  |  |  |  |  |  |  | 175 |  |  |  |  |
| *2 oz piece* | 57 | 5.0 | 10.0 |  |  |  |  |  |  |  |  |  |  |  |  |
| **fish kabobs, frzn, batter-dipped, Van de Kamp's—4 oz** | 240 |  | 15.0 |  |  |  |  |  |  |  | 430 |  |  |  |  |
|  | 113 | 10.0 | 15.0 |  |  |  |  |  |  |  |  |  |  |  |  |
| **fish nuggets, frzn, light & crispy, Van de Kamp's—2 oz** | 130 |  | 10.0 |  |  |  |  |  |  |  | 160 |  |  |  |  |
|  | 57 | 10.0 | 10.0 |  |  |  |  |  |  |  |  |  |  |  |  |
| **fish pieces, frzn, reheated[c]** | 155 | 26.4 | 7.0 | 1.8 | 64 | 60 |  | .10 | .03 | 10 | 332 | 11 | 14 | .38 | .135 |
| *1 piece (4"x2"x1/2")* | 57 | 8.9 | 13.5 | 1.8 |  | 18 | .07 | 1.2 | 1.02 |  | 149 | 103 | .42 | .058 |  |
| **fish sticks** |  |  |  |  |  |  |  |  |  |  |  |  |  |  |  |
| frzn[c] | 76 | 13.0 | 3.4 | 0.9 | 31 | 30 |  | .05 | .02 | 5 | 163 | 6 | 7 | .19 | .066 |
| *1 stick (4"x2"x1/2")* | 28 | 4.4 | 6.7 | 0.9 |  | 9 | .04 | 0.6 | .50 |  | 73 | 51 | .21 | .028 |  |
| frzn, batter-dipped, Van de Kamp's | 220 |  | 15.0 |  |  |  |  |  |  |  | 330 |  |  |  |  |
| *4 pieces (4 oz)* | 113 | 10.0 | 15.0 |  |  |  |  |  |  |  |  |  |  |  |  |
| frzn, light & crispy, Van de Kamp's | 270 |  | 20.0 |  |  |  |  |  |  |  | 300 |  |  |  |  |
| *4 pieces (3.75 oz)* | 106 | 10.0 | 15.0 |  |  |  |  |  |  |  |  |  |  |  |  |
| **flatfish** |  |  |  |  |  |  |  |  |  |  |  |  |  |  |  |
| raw | 78 | 67.2 | 1.0 | 0.3 | 41 | 28 |  | .07 | .18 |  | 69 | 15 | 27 | .39 | .014 |
| *3 oz* | 85 | 16.0 | 0.0 | 0.2 |  | 8 | .08 | 2.5 | 1.29 | .43 | 307 | 156 | .30 | .027 |  |
| ckd by dry heat | 99 | 62.2 | 1.3 | 0.4 | 58 | 32 |  | .10 | .20 |  | 89 | 16 | 50 | .53 |  |
| *3 oz* | 85 | 20.5 | 0.0 | 0.3 |  | 10 | .07 | 1.9 | 2.13 |  | 292 | 246 | .28 | .022 |  |
| **flounder/sole** |  |  |  |  |  |  |  |  |  |  |  |  |  |  |  |
| raw | 68 |  | 0.5 |  |  |  |  | .05 |  |  | 56 | 61 | 30 |  |  |
| *3.5 oz* | 100 | 14.9 | 0.0 |  | 0.0 |  | .06 | 1.7 |  |  | 366 | 195 | .80 |  |  |
| baked | 202 | 58.1 | 8.2 |  |  | 2 |  | .08 |  |  | 237 | 23 | 30 |  |  |
| *3.5 oz* | 100 | 30.0 | 0.0 |  | 0.0 |  | .07 | 2.5 |  |  | 587 | 344 | 1.40 |  |  |

[a] Prepared w/ crab meat, egg, onion & margarine.
[b] Breading consists of bread crumbs, egg, milk & salt.
[c] Prepared from walleye pollock, bread crumbs, egg, milk & salt.

| Food | KCAL / WT (g) | H₂O (g) / PRO (g) | FAT (g) / CHO (g) | PUFA (g) / SFA (g) | CHOL (mg) / DFIB (g) | A (RE) / A (IU) | C (mg) / B-1 (mg) | B-2 (mg) / NIA (mg) | B-6 (mg) / B-12 (mcg) | FOL (mcg) / PANT (mg) | Na (mg) / K (mg) | Ca (mg) / P (mg) | Mg (mg) / Fe (mg) | Zn (mg) / Cu (mg) | Mn (mg) |
|---|---|---|---|---|---|---|---|---|---|---|---|---|---|---|---|
| frzn, breaded, Van de Kamp's | 300 | | 15.0 | | | | | | | | 410 | | | | |
| 5 oz piece | 142 | 15.0 | 15.0 | | | | | | | | | | | | |
| gefiltefish w/ broth, sweet | 35 | 33.7 | 0.7 | 0.1 | 12 | 37 | | .03 | .08 | 1 | 220 | 10 | 4 | .35 | .031 |
| 1 piece | 42 | 3.8 | 3.1 | 0.2 | | 11 | .03 | | .35 | | 38 | 31 | 1.04 | .082 | |
| **grouper** | | | | | | | | | | | | | | | |
| raw | 78 | 67.3 | 0.9 | 0.3 | 31 | | | .00 | | | 45 | 23 | 26 | .41 | .012 |
| 3 oz | 85 | 16.5 | 0.0 | 0.2 | | | .06 | 0.3 | 51 | | 410 | 138 | .75 | .017 | |
| ckd by dry heat | 100 | 62.4 | 1.1 | 0.3 | 40 | | | .01 | | | 45 | 18 | 32 | .43 | .010 |
| 3 oz | 85 | 21.1 | 0.0 | 0.3 | | | .07 | 0.3 | .59 | | 403 | 121 | .96 | .038 | |
| **haddock** | | | | | | | | | | | | | | | |
| raw | 74 | 67.9 | 0.6 | 0.2 | 49 | 47 | | .03 | .26 | | 58 | 28 | 33 | .32 | .021 |
| 3 oz | 85 | 16.1 | 0.0 | 0.1 | | 14 | .03 | 3.2 | 1.02 | .11 | 264 | 160 | .89 | .022 | |
| ckd by dry heat | 95 | 63.1 | 0.8 | 0.3 | 63 | 54 | | .04 | .29 | | 74 | 36 | 43 | .41 | |
| 3 oz | 85 | 20.6 | 0.0 | 0.1 | | 16 | .03 | 3.9 | 1.18 | | 339 | 205 | 1.14 | .028 | |
| frzn, batter-dipped, Van de Kamp's | 240 | | 10.0 | | | | | | | | 430 | | | | |
| 2 pieces (4 oz) | 113 | 10.0 | 20.0 | | | | | | | | | | | | |
| frzn, breaded, Van de Kamp's | 300 | | 20.0 | | | | | | | | 310 | | | | |
| 5 oz piece | 142 | 15.0 | 15.0 | | | | | | | | | | | | |
| frzn fillet, light & crispy, Van de Kamp's—2 oz piece | 180 | | 15.0 | | | | | | | | 160 | | | | |
| | 57 | 5.0 | 10.0 | | | | | | | | | | | | |
| smoked | 99 | 60.8 | 0.8 | 0.3 | 65 | 62 | | .04 | .34 | | 649 | 41 | 46 | .42 | |
| 3 oz | 85 | 21.4 | 0.0 | 0.1 | | 19 | .04 | 4.3 | 1.36 | | 353 | 214 | 1.19 | .036 | |
| **halibut, atlantic & pacific** | | | | | | | | | | | | | | | |
| raw | 93 | 66.2 | 2.0 | 0.7 | 27 | 132 | | .06 | .29 | | 46 | 40 | 71 | .35 | .013 |
| 3 oz | 85 | 17.7 | 0.0 | 0.3 | | 40 | .05 | 5.0 | 1.01 | .28 | 382 | 189 | .71 | .023 | |
| ckd by dry heat | 119 | 60.9 | 2.5 | 0.8 | 35 | 152 | | .08 | .34 | | 59 | 51 | 91 | .45 | |
| 3 oz | 85 | 22.7 | 0.0 | 0.4 | | 46 | .06 | 6.1 | 1.16 | | 490 | 242 | .91 | .030 | |
| **halibut, frzn** | | | | | | | | | | | | | | | |
| batter-dipped, Van de Kamp's | 260 | | 15.0 | | | | | | | | 440 | | | | |
| 3 pieces (4 oz) | 113 | 10.0 | 15.0 | | | | | | | | | | | | |
| breaded, Van de Kamp's | 220 | | 10.0 | | | | | | | | 520 | | | | |
| 4 oz piece | 113 | 15.0 | 15.0 | | | | | | | | | | | | |
| **halibut, greenland, raw** | 158 | 59.7 | 11.8 | 1.2 | 39 | 47 | | .07 | | 1 | 68 | 3 | | | |
| 3 oz | 85 | 12.2 | 0.0 | 2.1 | | 14 | .05 | 1.3 | 1.00 | .21 | 228 | 139 | .56 | | |
| **herring, atlantic** | | | | | | | | | | | | | | | |
| raw | 134 | 61.2 | 7.7 | 1.8 | 51 | 80 | 1 | .20 | .26 | | 76 | 49 | 27 | .84 | .030 |
| 3 oz | 85 | 15.3 | 0.0 | 1.7 | | 24 | .08 | 2.7 | 11.62 | .55 | 278 | 201 | .94 | .078 | |
| ckd by dry heat | 172 | 54.9 | 9.9 | 2.3 | 65 | 87 | 1 | .25 | .30 | | 98 | 63 | 35 | 1.08 | |
| 3 oz | 85 | 19.6 | 0.0 | 2.2 | | 26 | .10 | 3.5 | 11.17 | | 356 | 258 | 1.20 | .100 | |
| kippered | 87 | 23.9 | 5.0 | 1.2 | 33 | 51 | 0 | .13 | .17 | | 367 | 33 | 18 | .54 | |
| 1 piece (4 3/8"x1 3/4"x 1/4") | 40 | 9.8 | 0.0 | 1.1 | | 15 | .05 | 1.8 | 7.48 | | 179 | 130 | .60 | .054 | |
| pickled | 39 | 8.3 | 2.7 | 0.3 | 2 | 129 | | .02 | | 0 | 131 | 12 | 1 | .08 | .006 |
| 1 piece (1 3/4"x7/8"x1/2") | 15 | 2.1 | 1.5 | 0.4 | | 39 | .01 | | .64 | .01 | 10 | 13 | .18 | .016 | |
| **herring, pacific, raw** | 166 | 60.8 | 11.8 | 2.1 | 65 | 90 | | | | | 63 | | | .45 | .038 |
| 3 oz | 85 | 13.9 | 0.0 | 2.8 | | 27 | | | | | 359 | | .95 | .066 | |
| **inconnu, raw** | 146 | 72.0 | 6.8 | | | | | | | | | | | | |
| 3.5 oz | 100 | 19.9 | 0.0 | | 0.0 | | | | | | | | | | |
| **kingfish** | | | | | | | | | | | | | | | |
| raw | 105 | 77.3 | 3.0 | | | | | | | | 83 | | | | |
| 3.5 oz | 100 | 18.3 | 0.0 | | 0.0 | | | | | | 250 | | | | |
| ckd | 255 | | 13.4 | | | | 0 | .13 | | | 101 | 80 | 56 | | |
| 3.5 oz | 100 | 22.3 | 11.7 | | 0.0 | 93 | .11 | 2.9 | | | 293 | 287 | 1.90 | | |
| ling, raw | 74 | 67.7 | 0.5 | | | 85 | | .16 | .26 | | 115 | 29 | 53 | | |
| 3 oz | 85 | 16.1 | 0.0 | | | 26 | .09 | 2.0 | .48 | .27 | 322 | 169 | .55 | | |
| lingcod, raw | 72 | 68.9 | 0.9 | 0.3 | 44 | | | .10 | | | 50 | 12 | 22 | .39 | .017 |
| 3 oz | 85 | 15.0 | 0.0 | 0.2 | | | .03 | 1.6 | | | 371 | 171 | .27 | .023 | |

| | KCAL / WT (g) | H₂O (g) / PRO (g) | FAT (g) / CHO (g) | PUFA (g) / SFA (g) | CHOL (mg) / DFIB (g) | A (RE) / A (IU) | C (mg) / B-1 (mg) | B-2 (mg) / NIA (mg) | B-6 (mg) / B-12 (mcg) | FOL (mcg) / PANT (mg) | Na (mg) / K (mg) | Ca (mg) / P (mg) | Mg (mg) / Fe (mg) | Zn (mg) / Cu (mg) | Mn (mg) |
|---|---|---|---|---|---|---|---|---|---|---|---|---|---|---|---|
| **lobster, northern** | | | | | | | | | | | | | | | |
| raw | 77 | 65.2 | 0.8 | | 81 | | | .04 | | | | | | 2.57 | .047 |
| 3 oz | 85 | 16.0 | 0.4 | | | | | 1.2 | .79 | 1.39 | | | | 1.414 | |
| ckd by moist heat | 83 | 64.6 | 0.5 | 0.1 | 61 | 74 | | .06 | .07 | 9 | 323 | 52 | 30 | 2.48 | .052 |
| 3 oz | 85 | 17.4 | 1.1 | 0.1 | | 22 | .01 | 0.9 | 2.64 | .24 | 299 | 157 | .33 | 1.649 | |
| **lobster paste** | | | | | | | | | | | | | | | |
| 1 t | 13 | 4.3 | 0.7 | | | | | .02 | | | | 5 | | | |
| | 7 | 1.5 | 0.1 | | | | .01 | | | | | 13 | .10 | | |
| **lobster salad**[a] | | | | | | | | | | | | | | | |
| | 110 | 80.3 | 6.4 | 0.9 | | | 18 | .08 | | | 124 | 36 | | | |
| 3.5 oz | 100 | 10.1 | 2.3 | | | | .09 | | | | 264 | 95 | .90 | | |
| **mackerel, atlantic** | | | | | | | | | | | | | | | |
| raw | 174 | 54.0 | 11.8 | 4.0 | 60 | 140 | 0 | .27 | .34 | | 76 | 10 | 64 | .53 | .013 |
| 3 oz | 85 | 15.8 | 0.0 | 2.8 | | 42 | .15 | 7.7 | 7.40 | .73 | 267 | 184 | 1.38 | .063 | |
| ckd by dry heat | 223 | 45.3 | 15.1 | 3.7 | 64 | 153 | 0 | .35 | .39 | | 71 | 13 | 83 | .80 | |
| 3 oz | 85 | 20.3 | 0.0 | 3.6 | | 46 | .14 | 5.8 | 16.15 | | 341 | 236 | 1.33 | .080 | |
| **mackerel, jack, cnd** | 296 | 131.4 | 12.0 | 0.2 | 150 | 825 | 2 | .40 | .40 | 10 | 720 | 458 | 70 | 1.94 | .076 |
| 1 cup | 190 | 44.1 | 0.0 | 3.4 | | 247 | .08 | 11.7 | 13.19 | .58 | 369 | 572 | 3.88 | .279 | |
| **mackerel, king, raw** | 89 | 64.5 | 1.7 | 0.4 | 45 | 618 | | .41 | .38 | 6 | 134 | 26 | 27 | .48 | .004 |
| 3 oz | 85 | 17.2 | 0.0 | 0.3 | | 185 | .09 | 7.3 | 13.26 | .71 | 370 | 211 | 1.51 | .220 | |
| **mackerel, pacific & jack, raw** | 133 | 59.6 | 6.7 | 2.1 | 40 | 37 | | .36 | .28 | 2 | 73 | 19 | 24 | .57 | .013 |
| 3 oz | 85 | 17.1 | 0.0 | 1.9 | | 11 | .09 | 7.1 | 3.74 | .27 | 345 | 106 | .99 | .079 | |
| **mackerel, spanish** | | | | | | | | | | | | | | | |
| raw | 118 | 60.9 | 5.4 | 1.5 | 65 | | | .15 | | | 50 | 10 | 28 | .42 | .012 |
| 3 oz | 85 | 16.4 | 0.0 | 1.6 | | | .11 | 2.0 | 2.04 | | 379 | 175 | .37 | .047 | |
| ckd by dry heat | 134 | 58.2 | 5.4 | 1.5 | 62 | | | .18 | | | 56 | 11 | 32 | .53 | .010 |
| 3 oz | 85 | 20.1 | 0.0 | 1.5 | | | .11 | 4.3 | 5.95 | | 471 | 231 | .63 | .055 | |
| **menhaden, atlantic, cnd** | 172 | 67.9 | 10.2 | | | | | | | | | | | | |
| 3.5 oz | 100 | 18.7 | 0.0 | | 0.0 | | | | | | | | | | |
| **milkfish, raw** | 126 | 60.2 | 5.7 | | 44 | | | .05 | .36 | | | 43 | | .70 | |
| 3 oz | 85 | 17.5 | 0.0 | | | | .01 | 5.5 | 2.89 | | | 138 | .27 | .029 | |
| **monkfish, raw** | 64 | 70.8 | 1.3 | | 21 | | | .05 | | | 16 | 7 | 18 | .35 | .020 |
| 3 oz | 85 | 12.3 | 0.0 | | | | .02 | | | | | | .27 | .024 | |
| **mullet, striped** | | | | | | | | | | | | | | | |
| raw | 99 | 65.5 | 3.2 | 0.6 | 42 | 104 | 1 | | .36 | 7 | 55 | 34 | 24 | .44 | .014 |
| 3 oz | 85 | 16.5 | 0.0 | 0.9 | | 31 | | | | .65 | 304 | 188 | .87 | .043 | |
| ckd by dry heat | 127 | 59.9 | 4.1 | 0.8 | 54 | 120 | 1 | | .42 | 8 | 61 | 26 | 28 | .75 | .019 |
| 3 oz | 85 | 21.1 | 0.0 | 1.2 | | 36 | | | | | 389 | 207 | 1.20 | .120 | |
| **mussels, blue** | | | | | | | | | | | | | | | |
| raw | 73 | 68.5 | 1.9 | 0.5 | 24 | | | | | | 243 | 22 | 29 | 1.36 | |
| 3 oz | 85 | 10.1 | 3.1 | 0.4 | | | | | | | 272 | 168 | 3.36 | .080 | |
| ckd by moist heat | 147 | 52.0 | 3.8 | 1.0 | 48 | | | | | | 313 | 28 | 32 | 2.27 | |
| 3 oz | 85 | 20.2 | 6.3 | 0.7 | | | | | | | 228 | 242 | 5.71 | 1.270 | |
| **ocean perch, atlantic** | | | | | | | | | | | | | | | |
| raw | 80 | 66.9 | 1.4 | 0.4 | 36 | 34 | | .09 | | | 64 | 91 | 26 | .41 | .013 |
| 3 oz | 85 | 15.8 | 0.0 | 0.2 | | 10 | | 1.7 | .85 | .31 | 232 | 184 | .78 | .022 | |
| ckd by dry heat | 103 | 61.8 | 1.8 | 0.5 | 46 | 39 | | .11 | | | 82 | 117 | 33 | .52 | |
| 3 oz | 85 | 20.3 | 0.0 | 0.3 | | 12 | | 2.1 | .98 | | 298 | 235 | 1.00 | .028 | |
| **oysters, eastern** | | | | | | | | | | | | | | | |
| raw | 58 | 71.5 | 2.1 | 0.6 | 46 | | | .14 | .04 | 8 | 94 | 38 | 46 | 76.4 | .378 |
| 6 med | 84 | 5.9 | 3.3 | 0.5 | | | | 1.1 | 16.07 | .16 | 192 | 117 | 5.63 | 3.747 | |
| breaded & fried[b] | 167 | 55.0 | 10.7 | 2.8 | 69 | | | .17 | .05 | 12 | 355 | 53 | 49 | 74.06 | |
| 3 oz (about 6 med) | 85 | 7.5 | 9.9 | 2.7 | | | | 1.4 | 13.29 | | 208 | 135 | 5.91 | 3.650 | |
| cnd | 58 | 72.4 | 2.1 | 0.6 | 4.6 | | | .14 | .08 | 8 | 95 | 38 | 46 | 77.31 | |
| 3 oz | 85 | 6.0 | 3.3 | 0.5 | | | | 1.1 | 16.26 | | 195 | 118 | 5.70 | 3.792 | |
| ckd by moist heat | 117 | 59.7 | 4.2 | 1.3 | 93 | | | .28 | .08 | 15 | 190 | 76 | 92 | 154.62 | |
| 3 oz (12 med) | 85 | 12.0 | 6.7 | 1.1 | | | | 2.1 | 32.53 | | 389 | 236 | 11.39 | 7.584 | |

[a] Prepared w/ onion, sweet pickle, celery, egg, mayonnaise & tomato.    [b] Prepared w/ bread crumbs, egg, milk & salt.

| | KCAL | H$_2$O (g) | FAT (g) | PUFA (g) | CHOL (mg) | A (RE) | C (mg) | B-2 (mg) | B-6 (mg) | FOL (mcg) | Na (mg) | Ca (mg) | Mg (mg) | Zn (mg) | Mn (mg) |
| --- | --- | --- | --- | --- | --- | --- | --- | --- | --- | --- | --- | --- | --- | --- | --- |
| | WT (g) | PRO (g) | CHO (g) | SFA (g) | DFIB (g) | A (IU) | B-1 (mg) | NIA (mg) | B-12 (mcg) | PANT (mg) | K (mg) | P (mg) | Fe (mg) | Cu (mg) | |
| **oysters, pacific, raw** | 69 | 69.8 | 2.0 | 0.4 | | | | .20 | | | 90 | 7 | 19 | 14.13 | .547 |
| *3 oz* | 85 | 8.0 | 4.2 | 0.4 | | | .06 | 1.7 | | | 143 | 138 | 4.34 | 1.340 | |
| **perch** | | | | | | | | | | | | | | | |
| raw | 77 | 67.3 | 0.8 | 0.3 | 76 | | | | | | 52 | 68 | 26 | .95 | .595 |
| *3 oz* | 85 | 16.5 | 0.0 | 0.2 | | | | | | | 228 | 170 | .77 | .128 | |
| ckd by dry heat | 99 | 62.3 | 1.0 | 0.4 | 98 | | | | | | 67 | 87 | 33 | 1.21 | |
| *3 oz* | 85 | 21.0 | 0.0 | 0.2 | | | | | | | 293 | 218 | .98 | .163 | |
| frzn | | | | | | | | | | | | | | | |
| batter-dipped, Van de Kamp's | 270 | | 15.0 | | | | | | | | 510 | | | | |
| *2 pieces (4 oz)* | 113 | 10.0 | 20.0 | | | | | | | | | | | | |
| fillet, light & crispy, Van de Kamp's | 170 | | 10.0 | | | | | | | | 115 | | | | |
| *2 oz piece* | 57 | 5.0 | 10.0 | | | | | | | | | | | | |
| **pike, northern** | | | | | | | | | | | | | | | |
| raw | 75 | 67.1 | 0.6 | 0.2 | 33 | 60 | 3 | .05 | .10 | | 33 | 48 | | .57 | |
| *3 oz* | 85 | 16.4 | 0.0 | 0.1 | | 18 | .05 | | | | 220 | 187 | .47 | .043 | |
| ckd by dry heat | 96 | 62.0 | 0.8 | 0.2 | 43 | 69 | 3 | .07 | .12 | | 42 | 62 | | .73 | |
| *3 oz* | 85 | 21.0 | 0.0 | 0.1 | | 21 | .06 | | | | 282 | 239 | .60 | .055 | |
| **pike, pickerel, raw** | 84 | 79.7 | 0.5 | | | | | | | | | | | .70 | |
| *3.5 oz* | 100 | 18.7 | 0.0 | | 0.0 | | | | | | | | | | |
| **pike, walleye, raw** | 79 | 67.4 | 1.0 | 0.4 | 73 | | | | | | 43 | 94 | 26 | .53 | .680 |
| *3 oz* | 85 | 16.3 | 0.0 | 0.2 | | | | | | | 331 | 179 | 1.11 | .151 | |
| **pollock, atlantic, raw** | 78 | 66.5 | 0.8 | 0.4 | 60 | 30 | | .16 | .24 | | 73 | 51 | 57 | .40 | .013 |
| *3 oz* | 85 | 16.5 | 0.0 | 0.1 | | 9 | .04 | 2.8 | 2.71 | .30 | 302 | 188 | .39 | .043 | |
| **pollock, ckd, creamed[a]** | 128 | 74.7 | 5.9 | | | | 0 | .13 | | | 111 | | | | |
| *3.5 oz* | 100 | 13.9 | 4.0 | | 0.0 | | .03 | 0.7 | | | 238 | | | | |
| **pollock, walleye** | | | | | | | | | | | | | | | |
| raw | 68 | 69.3 | 0.7 | 0.4 | 61 | 56 | | .05 | .05 | 3 | 84 | 4 | | .37 | .013 |
| *3 oz* | 85 | 14.6 | 0.0 | 0.1 | | 17 | .06 | 1.1 | 2.64 | .12 | 277 | | .20 | .037 | |
| ckd by dry heat | 96 | 63.0 | 1.0 | 0.4 | 82 | 65 | | .07 | .06 | 3 | 98 | 5 | | .51 | |
| *3 oz* | 85 | 20.0 | 0.0 | 0.2 | | 19 | .06 | 1.4 | 3.57 | | 329 | | .24 | .047 | |
| **pompano, florida** | | | | | | | | | | | | | | | |
| raw | 140 | 60.5 | 8.1 | 1.0 | 43 | | | | | | 55 | 19 | 23 | .61 | .011 |
| *3 oz* | 85 | 15.7 | 0.0 | 3.0 | | | | | | | 324 | 166 | .51 | .032 | |
| ckd by dry heat | 179 | 53.5 | 10.3 | 1.2 | 54 | | | | | | 65 | 36 | 27 | .59 | .021 |
| *3 oz* | 85 | 20.1 | 0.0 | 3.8 | | | | | | | 541 | 290 | .57 | .066 | |
| **porgy/scup** | | | | | | | | | | | | | | | |
| raw | 112 | 76.2 | 3.4 | | | | | | | | 63 | 54 | | | |
| *3.5 oz* | 100 | 19.0 | 0.0 | | 0.0 | | | | | | 287 | 250 | | | |
| fried | 279 | | 15.5 | | | | 0 | .08 | | | 58 | 24 | | | |
| *3.3 oz* | 93 | 22.7 | 10.8 | | | 75 | .07 | 3.7 | | | 266 | 258 | 1.50 | | |
| **pout, ocean, raw** | 67 | 69.2 | 0.8 | 0.0 | 44 | | | | | | 52 | 8 | 11 | .88 | .013 |
| *3 oz* | 85 | 14.1 | 0.0 | 0.3 | | | | | | | | | .24 | .027 | |
| **rockfish, pacific** | | | | | | | | | | | | | | | |
| raw | 80 | 67.4 | 1.3 | 0.4 | 29 | 162 | | .06 | | | 51 | 8 | 22 | .35 | .014 |
| *3 oz* | 85 | 15.9 | 0.0 | 0.3 | | 48 | .03 | 2.7 | | | 344 | 151 | .35 | .025 | |
| ckd by dry heat | 103 | 62.4 | 1.7 | 0.5 | 38 | 186 | | .07 | | | 65 | 10 | 29 | .45 | |
| *3 oz* | 85 | 20.4 | 0.0 | 0.4 | | 56 | .04 | 3.3 | | | 442 | 194 | .45 | .031 | |
| **roe, mixed species, raw** | 39 | 19.0 | 1.8 | 0.7 | 105 | | | | | | | | | | |
| *1 oz* | 28 | 6.3 | 0.4 | 0.4 | | | | | | | | | | | |
| **roughy, orange, raw** | 107 | 64.5 | 6.0 | 0.1 | 17 | | | | | | 54 | | | | |
| *3 oz* | 85 | 12.5 | 0.0 | 0.1 | | | | | | | | | .15 | | |
| **sablefish** | | | | | | | | | | | | | | | |
| raw | 166 | 60.4 | 13.0 | 1.7 | 42 | | | | | | 48 | | | .28 | .013 |
| *3 oz* | 85 | 11.4 | 0.0 | 2.7 | | | | | | | 304 | | 1.09 | .019 | |

[a] Prepared w/ flour, butter & milk.

| | KCAL | H₂O (g) | FAT (g) | PUFA (g) | CHOL (mg) | A (RE) | C (mg) | B-2 (mg) | B-6 (mg) | FOL (mcg) | Na (mg) | Ca (mg) | Mg (mg) | Zn (mg) | Mn (mg) |
|---|---|---|---|---|---|---|---|---|---|---|---|---|---|---|---|
| | WT (g) | PRO (g) | CHO (g) | SFA (g) | DFIB (g) | A (IU) | B-1 (mg) | NIA (mg) | B-12 (mcg) | PANT (mg) | K (mg) | P (mg) | Fe (mg) | Cu (mg) | |
| smoked | 218 | 51.1 | 17.1 | 2.3 | 55 | | | | | | 626 | | | | .36 |
| *3 oz* | 85 | 15.0 | 0.0 | 3.6 | | | | | | | 401 | | | | .031 |
| **salmon, atlantic, raw** | 121 | 58.2 | 5.4 | 2.2 | 47 | 34 | | .32 | .70 | | 37 | 10 | | | |
| *3 oz* | 85 | 16.9 | 0.0 | 0.8 | | 10 | .19 | 6.7 | 2.70 | 1.41 | 417 | 170 | .68 | | |
| **salmon, chinook** | | | | | | | | | | | | | | | |
| raw | 153 | 62.2 | 8.9 | 1.8 | 56 | | 3 | .10 | | | 40 | 19 | | .38 | .013 |
| *3 oz* | 85 | 17.1 | 0.0 | 2.1 | | | .03 | 6.7 | | | 335 | | .60 | .035 | |
| smoked | 99 | 61.2 | 3.7 | 0.8 | 20 | 75 | | .09 | .24 | 2 | 666 | 9 | 15 | .26 | .014 |
| *3 oz* | 85 | 15.5 | 0.0 | 0.8 | | 22 | .02 | 4.0 | 2.77 | .74 | 149 | 139 | .72 | .196 | |
| **salmon, chum, raw** | | | | | | | | | | | | | | | |
| raw | 102 | 64.1 | 3.2 | 0.8 | 63 | 84 | | .15 | | | 42 | 9 | | .40 | .013 |
| *3 oz* | 85 | 17.1 | 0.0 | 0.7 | | 25 | .07 | | | | 365 | 241 | .47 | .047 | |
| cnd w/ bone | 120 | 60.2 | 4.7 | 1.3 | 33 | 51 | | | | | 414ᵃ | 212ᵇ | | | |
| *3 oz* | 85 | 18.2 | 0.0 | 1.3 | | 15 | | | | | | 301 | | | |
| **salmon, coho** | | | | | | | | | | | | | | | |
| raw | 124 | 61.7 | 5.1 | 1.5 | 33 | | 1 | | | | 39 | | | .35 | .013 |
| *3 oz* | 85 | 18.4 | 0.0 | 0.9 | | | | | | | 359 | | .60 | .043 | |
| ckd by moist heat | 157 | 55.6 | 6.4 | 1.9 | 42 | | 1 | | | | 50 | | | .44 | |
| *3 oz* | 85 | 23.3 | 0.0 | 1.2 | | | | | | | 454 | | .76 | .055 | |
| **salmon, pink** | | | | | | | | | | | | | | | |
| raw | 99 | 64.9 | 2.9 | 1.2 | 44 | 100 | | | | | 57 | | | .46 | .013 |
| *3 oz* | 85 | 17.0 | 0.0 | 0.5 | | 30 | | | | | 274 | | .65 | .065 | |
| cnd w/ bone | 118 | 58.5 | 5.1 | 1.7 | | 47 | 0 | .16 | | 13 | 471ᵃ | 181ᵇ | 29 | .78 | |
| *3 oz* | 85 | 16.8 | 0.0 | 1.3 | | 14 | .02 | 5.6 | | | 277 | 279 | .72 | .087 | |
| **salmon, sockeye** | | | | | | | | | | | | | | | |
| raw | 143 | 59.7 | 7.3 | 1.6 | 53 | 163 | | .13 | .16 | | 40 | 5 | 20 | .45 | .012 |
| *3 oz* | 85 | 18.1 | 0.0 | 1.3 | | 49 | .17 | 4.9 | .24 | .52 | 332 | 183 | .40 | .044 | |
| cnd w/ bone | 130 | 58.4 | 6.2 | 1.9 | 37 | 149 | 0 | .16 | | 8 | 458ᵃ | 203ᵇ | 25 | .86 | |
| *3 oz* | 85 | 17.4 | 0.0 | 1.4 | | 45 | .01 | 4.7 | | | 321 | 277 | .90 | .071 | |
| ckd by dry heat | 83 | 52.6 | 9.3 | 2.0 | 74 | 178 | | .15 | .19 | | 56 | 6 | 26 | .43 | |
| *3 oz* | 85 | 23.2 | 0.0 | 1.6 | | 53 | .18 | 5.7 | 4.93 | | 319 | 234 | .47 | .057 | |
| **sardines** | | | | | | | | | | | | | | | |
| atlantic, cnd in soybean oil | 50 | 14.3 | 2.8 | 1.2 | 34 | 54 | | .05 | .04 | 3 | 121 | 92ᵇ | 9 | .31 | .026 |
| *2 sardines (3"x1"x1/2")* | 24 | 5.9 | 0.0 | 0.4 | | 16 | .02 | 1.3 | 2.15 | .15 | 95 | 118 | .70 | .045 | |
| pacific, cnd in tomato sce | 68 | 26.0 | 4.6 | 1.6 | 23 | 139 | 0 | .07 | .05 | 9 | 157 | 91ᵇ | 13 | .53 | .078 |
| *1 sardine (4 3/4"x1 1/8"x5/8")* | 38 | 6.2 | 0.0 | 1.2 | | 26 | .02 | 1.6 | 3.42 | .28 | 130 | 139 | .87 | .103 | |
| **scallops** | | | | | | | | | | | | | | | |
| raw | 75 | 66.8 | 0.6 | 0.2 | 28 | | | .06 | | | 137 | 21 | 48 | .81 | .077 |
| *3 oz (6 large or 14 small)* | 85 | 14.3 | 2.0 | 0.1 | | | .01 | 1.0 | 1.30 | .12 | 274 | 186 | .25 | .045 | |
| breaded & friedᶜ | 67 | 18.1 | 3.4 | 0.9 | 19 | | | .03 | | | 144 | 13 | 18 | .33 | |
| *2 large* | 31 | 5.6 | 3.1 | 0.8 | | | .01 | 0.5 | .41 | | 103 | 73 | .25 | .024 | |
| imitation, made from surimi | 84 | 62.8 | 0.4 | | 18 | | | .01 | | | 676 | 7 | | | |
| *3 oz* | 85 | 10.9 | 9.0 | | | | .01 | 0.3 | | | 88 | | .26 | | |
| **scup, raw** | 89 | 64.1 | 2.3 | | | | | | | | 36 | 34 | 19 | .41 | .030 |
| *3 oz* | 85 | 16.0 | 0.0 | | | | | | | | 244 | | .45 | .043 | |
| **sea bass** | | | | | | | | | | | | | | | |
| raw | 82 | 66.5 | 1.7 | 0.6 | 35 | 157 | | | | | 58 | 9 | 35 | .34 | .013 |
| *3 oz* | 85 | 15.7 | 0.0 | 0.4 | | 47 | | | | | 218 | 165 | .25 | .016 | |
| ckd by dry heat | 105 | 61.3 | 2.2 | 0.8 | 45 | 181 | | | | | 74 | 11 | 45 | .44 | |
| *3 oz* | 85 | 20.1 | 0.0 | 0.6 | | 54 | | | | | 279 | 211 | .32 | .020 | |
| **seafood (crab, langostinos & gulf shrimp)** | 132 | | 3.5 | | 65 | | 1 | .11 | | | 342 | 132 | | | |
| *w/ crm sce, frzn, Am Hosp Co—6 oz* | 170 | 16.2 | 10.8 | | | 654 | .08 | 1.8 | | | 288 | | 1.20 | | |
| **sea nuggets/strips, frzn, Fishery** | 171 | | 4.6 | | 35 | | | | | | 498 | | | | |
| **Productsᵈ—4 oz** | 113 | 15.0 | 16.4 | | | | | | | | | | | | |

ᵃ Value is for product w/ salt added. If no salt is added, sodium is 64 mg.
ᵇ If bones are discarded, calcium is greatly reduced.
ᶜ Prepared w/ bread crumbs, egg, milk & salt.

ᵈ Values reflect averages for natural fillet, natural shaped & formed sea nuggets and prime sea strips.

| | KCAL / WT (g) | H₂O (g) / PRO (g) | FAT (g) / CHO (g) | PUFA (g) / SFA (g) | CHOL (mg) / DFIB (g) | A (RE) / A (IU) | C (mg) / B-1 (mg) | B-2 (mg) / NIA (mg) | B-6 (mg) / B-12 (mcg) | FOL (mcg) / PANT (mg) | Na (mg) / K (mg) | Ca (mg) / P (mg) | Mg (mg) / Fe (mg) | Zn (mg) / Cu (mg) | Mn (mg) |
|---|---|---|---|---|---|---|---|---|---|---|---|---|---|---|---|
| **seatrout, raw** | 88 | 66.4 | 3.1 | 0.6 | 71 | | | | | | 49 | 15 | 27 | .38 | .013 |
| *3 oz* | 85 | 14.2 | 0.0 | 0.9 | | | | | | | 290 | 212 | .23 | .026 | |
| **shad, american, raw** | 167 | 58.0 | 11.7 | | | | | | | | 44 | 40 | 26 | .31 | .036 |
| *3 oz* | 85 | 14.4 | 0.0 | | | | | | | | 326 | 231 | .82 | .054 | |
| **sheepshead** | | | | | | | | | | | | | | | |
| raw | 92 | 66.3 | 2.1 | 0.4 | | | | | | | 61 | 18 | 27 | .33 | .011 |
| *3 oz* | 85 | 17.2 | 0.0 | 0.5 | | | | | | | 344 | 266 | .39 | .026 | |
| ckd by dry heat | 107 | 58.7 | 1.4 | 0.3 | | | | | | | 62 | 32 | 30 | .54 | .018 |
| *3 oz* | 85 | 22.1 | 0.0 | 0.3 | | | | | | | 435 | 297 | .57 | .104 | |
| **shrimp** | | | | | | | | | | | | | | | |
| raw | 90 | 64.5 | 1.5 | 0.6 | 130 | | | .03 | .09 | 3 | 126 | 44 | 31 | .94 | .043 |
| *3 oz (12 large)* | 85 | 17.3 | 0.8 | 0.3 | | | .02 | 2.2 | .99 | .24 | 157 | 175 | 2.05 | .224 | |
| breaded & fried[a] | 206 | 44.9 | 10.4 | 4.3 | 150 | | | .12 | .08 | 7 | 292 | 57 | 34 | 1.17 | |
| *3 oz (11 large)* | 85 | 18.2 | 9.8 | 1.8 | | | .11 | 2.6 | 1.59 | | 191 | 185 | 1.07 | .233 | |
| cnd | 102 | 61.7 | 1.7 | 0.6 | 147 | | | .03 | .09 | 2 | 143 | 50 | 35 | 1.07 | |
| *3 oz* | 85 | 19.6 | 0.9 | 0.3 | | | .02 | 2.3 | .95 | | 179 | 198 | 2.32 | .255 | |
| ckd by moist heat | 84 | 65.7 | 0.9 | 0.4 | 166 | | | .03 | .11 | 3 | 190 | 33 | 29 | 1.33 | .029 |
| *3 oz (15 1/2 large)* | 85 | 17.8 | 0.0 | 0.2 | | | .03 | 2.2 | 1.27 | | 154 | 116 | 2.62 | .164 | |
| french fried[b] | 225 | 56.9 | 10.8 | | 120 | | | .08 | | | 186 | 72 | 51 | | |
| *3.5 oz* | 100 | 20.3 | 10.0 | | | | .04 | 2.7 | | | 229 | 191 | 2.00 | | |
| frzn, breaded, raw | 139 | 65.0 | 0.7 | | | | | .03 | | | | 38 | | | |
| *3.5 oz* | 100 | 12.3 | 19.9 | | 0.1 | | .03 | 2.0 | | | | 111 | 1.00 | | |
| imitation, made from surimi | 86 | 63.7 | 1.3 | | 31 | | | .03 | | | 599 | 16 | | | |
| *3 oz* | 85 | 10.5 | 7.8 | | | | .02 | 0.1 | | | 76 | | .51 | | |
| **shrimp paste** | 180 | 61.3 | 9.4 | | | | | | | | | | | | |
| *3.5 oz* | 100 | 20.8 | 1.5 | | | | | | | | | | .26 | | |
| **skate (rajah fish), raw** | 98 | 77.8 | 0.7 | | | | | | | | | | | | |
| *3.5 oz* | 100 | 21.5 | 0.0 | | 0.0 | | .02 | | | | | | | | |
| **smelt, atlantic** | | | | | | | | | | | | | | | |
| raw | 98 | 79.0 | 0.0 | | | | | .12 | | | | | | | |
| *4-5 med* | 100 | 18.6 | 2.1 | | 0.0 | | .01 | 1.4 | | | | 272 | .40 | | |
| cnd | 200 | 62.7 | 13.5 | | | | | | | | | 358 | | | |
| *4-5 med* | 100 | 18.4 | 0.0 | | | | | | | | | 370 | 1.70 | | |
| **smelt, rainbow** | | | | | | | | | | | | | | | |
| raw | 83 | 67.0 | 2.1 | 0.8 | 60 | | | .10 | | | 51 | 51 | 26 | 1.40 | .595 |
| *3 oz* | 85 | 15.0 | 0.0 | 0.4 | | | | 1.2 | 2.92 | .54 | 247 | 196 | .77 | .118 | |
| ckd by dry heat | 106 | 61.9 | 2.6 | 1.0 | 76 | | | .12 | | | 65 | 65 | 33 | 1.80 | |
| *3 oz* | 85 | 19.2 | 0.0 | 0.5 | | | | 1.5 | 3.37 | | 316 | 251 | .98 | .151 | |
| **snapper** | | | | | | | | | | | | | | | |
| raw | 85 | 65.3 | 1.1 | 0.4 | 31 | | | .00 | | | 54 | 27 | 27 | .30 | .011 |
| *3 oz* | 85 | 17.4 | 0.0 | 0.2 | | | .04 | 0.2 | | | 355 | 169 | .15 | .024 | |
| ckd by dry heat | 109 | 59.8 | 1.5 | 0.5 | 40 | | | .00 | | | 48 | 34 | 31 | .37 | .014 |
| *3 oz* | 85 | 22.4 | 0.0 | 0.3 | | | .05 | 0.3 | | | 444 | 171 | .20 | .039 | |
| **sole** | | | | | | | | | | | | | | | |
| raw | 68 | | 0.5 | | | | | .05 | | | 56 | 61 | 30 | | |
| *3.5 oz* | 100 | 14.9 | 0.0 | | 0.0 | | .06 | 1.7 | | | 366 | 195 | .80 | | |
| fillet | 80 | | 0.8 | | | | | | | | 162 | | | | |
| *1 serving* | 113 | 17.7 | 0.6 | | | | | | | | 281 | | | | |
| **frzn fillet** | | | | | | | | | | | | | | | |
| Am Hosp Co | 82 | | 0.8 | | 80 | | | .06 | | | 88 | 70 | | | |
| *4 oz* | 113 | 18.0 | 0.6 | | | | .07 | 2.0 | | | 282 | | .88 | | |
| batter-dipped, Van de Kamp's | 250 | | 15.0 | | | | | | | | 575 | | | | |
| *2 pieces (4 oz)* | 113 | 15.0 | 25.0 | | | | | | | | | | | | |
| breaded, Van de Kamp's | 300 | | 15.0 | | | | | | | | 410 | | | | |
| *5 oz piece* | 142 | 15.0 | 15.0 | | | | | | | | | | | | |

[a] Prepared w/ bread crumbs, egg, milk & salt.

[b] Dipped in egg & flour/bread crumbs or in batter.

| | KCAL | H₂O (g) | FAT (g) | PUFA (g) | CHOL (mg) | A (RE) | C (mg) | B-2 (mg) | B-6 (mg) | FOL (mcg) | Na (mg) | Ca (mg) | Mg (mg) | Zn (mg) | Mn (mg) |
|---|---|---|---|---|---|---|---|---|---|---|---|---|---|---|---|
| | WT (g) | PRO (g) | CHO (g) | SFA (g) | DFIB (g) | A (IU) | B-1 (mg) | NIA (mg) | B-12 (mcg) | PANT (mg) | K (mg) | P (mg) | Fe (mg) | Cu (mg) | |
| w/ crabmeat stuffing & herb sce, Am Hosp Co—4.44 oz | 100 | | 6.7 | | 48 | | 0 | .04 | | | 194 | 18 | | | |
| | 126 | 7.6 | 2.4 | | | 278 | .03 | 0.7 | | | 155 | | .38 | | |
| w/ herb sce, Am Hosp Co  3.5 oz | 110 | | 6.7 | | 57 | | 0 | .05 | | | 150 | 19 | | | |
| | 100 | 10.3 | 2.3 | | | 245 | .03 | 1.0 | | | 214 | | .50 | | |
| spiny lobster, raw  3 oz | 95 | 63.0 | 1.3 | 0.5 | 60 | | | .04 | | | 150 | 41 | | 4.82 | .013 |
| | 85 | 17.5 | 2.1 | 0.2 | | | .01 | 3.6 | | | | 202 | 1.04 | .324 | |
| spot, raw  3 oz | 105 | 64.6 | 4.2 | 0.9 | | | | | | | 24 | 12 | 36 | .43 | .030 |
| | 85 | 15.7 | 0.0 | 1.2 | | | | | | | 422 | 158 | .27 | .039 | |
| **sturgeon** | | | | | | | | | | | | | | | |
| raw  3 oz | 90 | 65.1 | 3.4 | 0.6 | | 595 | | | | | | | | .36 | .021 |
| | 85 | 13.7 | 0.0 | 0.8 | | 179 | | | | | 241 | | | .035 | |
| ckd by dry heat  3 oz | 115 | 59.5 | 4.4 | 0.8 | | 687 | | | | | | | | .46 | |
| | 85 | 17.6 | 0.0 | 1.0 | | 206 | | | | | 309 | | | .045 | |
| smoked  3 oz | 147 | 53.1 | 3.7 | 0.4 | | | | | | | | | | | |
| | 85 | 26.5 | 0.0 | 0.9 | | | | | | | | | | | |
| sucker, white, raw  3 oz | 79 | 67.8 | 2.0 | 0.7 | 35 | | | | | | 34 | 60 | 26 | .64 | .500 |
| | 85 | 14.2 | 0.0 | 0.4 | | | | | | | 323 | 179 | 1.11 | .166 | |
| sunfish, pumpkinseed, raw  3 oz | 76 | 67.6 | 0.6 | 0.2 | 57 | | | | | | 68 | 68 | 26 | 1.32 | .595 |
| | 85 | 16.5 | 0.0 | 0.1 | | | | | | | 298 | 153 | 1.02 | .255 | |
| surimi[a]  3 oz | 84 | 64.9 | 0.8 | | 25 | | | .02 | | | 122 | 7 | | | |
| | 85 | 12.9 | 5.8 | | | | .02 | 0.2 | | | 95 | | .22 | | |
| **swordfish** | | | | | | | | | | | | | | | |
| raw  3 oz | 103 | 64.3 | 3.4 | 0.8 | 33 | 101 | 1 | .08 | .28 | | 76 | 4 | 23 | .97 | .016 |
| | 85 | 16.8 | 0.0 | 0.9 | | 30 | .03 | 8.2 | 1.49 | .35 | 245 | 224 | .69 | .107 | |
| ckd by dry heat  3 oz | 132 | 58.4 | 4.4 | 1.0 | 43 | 117 | 1 | .10 | .32 | | 98 | 5 | 29 | 1.25 | |
| | 85 | 21.6 | 0.0 | 1.2 | | 35 | .04 | 10.0 | 1.72 | | 314 | 287 | .88 | .138 | |
| tautog (blackfish), raw  3.5 oz | 89 | 79.3 | 1.1 | | | | | | | | | | | | |
| | 100 | 18.6 | 0.0 | | 0.0 | | | | | | | 227 | | | |
| **tilefish** | | | | | | | | | | | | | | | |
| raw  3 oz | 81 | 67.1 | 2.0 | 0.5 | | | | | | | 45 | 22 | 24 | .31 | .009 |
| | 85 | 14.9 | 0.0 | 0.4 | | | | | | | 368 | 159 | .21 | .035 | |
| ckd by dry heat  3 oz | 125 | 59.7 | 4.0 | 1.1 | | | | | | | 50 | 22 | 28 | .45 | .013 |
| | 85 | 20.8 | 0.0 | 0.7 | | | | | | | 435 | 201 | .26 | .044 | |
| tomcod, atlantic, raw  3.5 oz | 77 | 81.5 | 0.4 | | | | | .17 | | | | | | | |
| | 100 | 17.2 | 0.0 | | 0.0 | | | | | | | | | | |
| trout, dolly varden  3.5 oz | 144 | 73.1 | 6.5 | | | | | .06 | | | | | | | |
| | 100 | 19.9 | 0.0 | | 0.0 | | .06 | | | | | | | | |
| trout, mixed species, raw  3 oz | 126 | 60.7 | 5.6 | 2.0 | 49 | 49 | 0 | .28 | | 11 | 44 | 36 | 19 | .56 | .723 |
| | 85 | 17.7 | 0.0 | 1.0 | | 15 | .30 | | 6.62 | 1.65 | 307 | 208 | 1.27 | .160 | |
| **trout, rainbow** | | | | | | | | | | | | | | | |
| raw  3 oz | 100 | 60.8 | 2.9 | 1.0 | 48 | 55 | 3 | .16 | | | 23 | 57 | 26 | .92 | .595 |
| | 85 | 17.5 | 0.0 | 0.6 | | 17 | .06 | | | | 421 | 213 | 1.62 | .094 | |
| ckd by dry heat  3 oz | 129 | 53.9 | 3.7 | 1.3 | 62 | 63 | 3 | .19 | | | 29 | 73 | 33 | 1.18 | |
| | 85 | 22.4 | 0.0 | 0.7 | | 19 | .07 | | | | 539 | 272 | 2.07 | .120 | |
| **tuna** | | | | | | | | | | | | | | | |
| cnd in oil | | | | | | | | | | | | | | | |
| light  3 oz | 169 | 50.9 | 7.0 | 2.5 | 15 | 66 | | | .09 | 5 | 301[b] | 11 | 26 | .77 | .013 |
| | 85 | 24.8 | 0.0 | 1.3 | | 20 | .03 | | | | 176 | 265 | 1.18 | .060 | |
| light, chunk, Star-Kist  2 oz | 170 | | 13.0 | 7.0 | 20 | | | | | | 310 | | 54 | | |
| | 58 | 13.0 | 0.0 | 1.0 | 0.0 | | | | | | 79 | 83 | | | |
| light, chunk, 60% less salt, Star-Kist  2 oz | 170 | | 13.0 | 7.0 | 20 | | | | | | 135 | | 54 | | |
| | 58 | 14.0 | 0.0 | 1.0 | 0.0 | | | | | | 79 | 83 | | | |
| light, solid, Star-Kist  2 oz | 150 | | 13.0 | 7.0 | 20 | | | | | | 310 | | 54 | | |
| | 58 | 13.0 | 0.0 | 1.0 | 0.0 | | | | | | 79 | 83 | | | |
| white  3 oz | 158 | 54.4 | 6.9 | | 26 | | | .07 | | 4 | 336[b] | 4 | 29 | .40 | |
| | 85 | 22.6 | 0.0 | | | | .01 | 9.9 | | | 283 | 227 | .56 | .111 | |

[a] Prepared from walleye pollock.

[b] Value reflects added salt. If no salt is added, sodium is 43 mg.

| Food | KCAL / WT (g) | H₂O / PRO (g) | FAT / CHO (g) | PUFA / SFA (g) | CHOL / DFIB (mg/g) | A (RE) / A (IU) | C / B-1 (mg) | B-2 / NIA (mg) | B-6 / B-12 (mg/mcg) | FOL / PANT (mcg/mg) | Na / K (mg) | Ca / P (mg) | Mg / Fe (mg) | Zn / Cu (mg) | Mn (mg) |
|---|---|---|---|---|---|---|---|---|---|---|---|---|---|---|---|
| white, chunk, Star-Kist | 140 | | 10.0 | 7.0 | 20 | | | | | | 310 | | 54 | | |
| 2 oz | 58 | 14.0 | 0.0 | 1.0 | 0.0 | | | | | | 79 | 83 | | | |
| white, solid, Star-Kist | 140 | | 10.0 | 7.0 | 20 | | | | | | 310 | | 54 | | |
| 2 oz | 58 | 14.0 | 0.0 | 1.0 | 0.0 | | | | | | 79 | 83 | | | |
| **cnd in spring water** | | | | | | | | | | | | | | | |
| light | 111 | 60.0 | 0.4 | 0.1 | | | | | .32 | 4 | 303ᵃ | 10 | 25 | .37 | |
| 3 oz | 85 | 25.1 | 0.0 | 0.1 | | | | | | | 267 | 158 | 2.72 | .009 | |
| light, chunk, Star-Kist | 60 | | 1.0 | 0.8 | 20 | | | | | | 310 | | 54 | | |
| 2 oz | 58 | 13.0 | 0.0 | 0.2 | 0.0 | | | | | | 85 | 83 | | | |
| light, chunk, 60% less salt, Star-Kist | 65 | | 1.0 | 0.8 | 20 | | | | | | 135 | | 54 | | |
| 2 oz | 58 | 14.0 | 0.0 | 0.2 | 0.0 | | | | | | 85 | 83 | | | |
| light, solid, Star-Kist | 60 | | 1.0 | 0.8 | 20 | | | | | | 310 | | 54 | | |
| 2 oz | 58 | 14.0 | 0.0 | 0.2 | 0.0 | | | | | | 85 | 83 | | | |
| white | 116 | 59.1 | 2.1 | 0.8 | 35 | | | .04 | | 4 | 333ᵃ | | | | |
| 3 oz | 85 | 22.7 | 0.0 | 0.6 | | | .00 | 4.9 | | | 241 | | .51 | .163 | |
| white, chunk, dietetic, Star-Kist | 70 | | 1.0 | 0.8 | 20 | | | | | | 30 | | 54 | | |
| 2 oz | 58 | 15.0 | 0.0 | 0.2 | 0.0 | | | | | | 85 | 83 | | | |
| white, chunk, 60% less salt, Star-Kist | 70 | | 1.0 | 0.8 | 20 | | | | | | 120 | | 54 | | |
| 2 oz | 58 | 15.0 | 0.0 | 0.2 | 0.0 | | | | | | 85 | 83 | | | |
| white, solid, import albacore, Star-Kist—2 oz | 70 | | 1.0 | 0.8 | 20 | | | | | | 310 | | 54 | | |
| | 58 | 15.0 | 0.0 | 0.2 | 0.0 | | | | | | 85 | 83 | | | |
| white, solid, local albacore, Star-Kist | 100 | | 5.0 | | 20 | | | | | | 310 | | 54 | | |
| 2 oz | 58 | 14.0 | 0.0 | | 0.0 | | | | | | 85 | 83 | | | |
| saladᵇ | 383 | 129.5 | 19.0 | 8.5 | 27 | 199 | 5 | | .17 | 15 | 824 | 35 | 40 | 1.15 | |
| 1/2 cup | 205 | 32.9 | 19.3 | 3.2 | | 55 | .06 | | | | 365 | 365 | 2.04 | .297 | |
| **tuna, bluefin** | | | | | | | | | | | | | | | |
| raw | 122 | 57.9 | 4.2 | 1.4 | 32 | 1856 | | .21 | .39 | | 33 | | | .51 | .013 |
| 3 oz | 85 | 19.8 | 0.0 | 1.1 | | 557 | .21 | 7.4 | 8.01 | .90 | 214 | | .87 | .073 | |
| ckd in dry heat | 157 | 50.2 | 5.3 | 1.6 | 42 | 2142 | | .26 | .45 | | 43 | | | .65 | |
| 3 oz | 85 | 25.4 | 0.0 | 1.4 | | 642 | .24 | 9.0 | 9.25 | | 275 | | 1.11 | .094 | |
| **tuna, skipjack, raw** | 88 | 60.0 | 0.9 | 0.3 | 40 | 44 | | | .72 | | 31 | 24 | 29 | .70 | .013 |
| 3 oz | 85 | 18.7 | 0.0 | 0.3 | | 13 | .03 | | | | 346 | 188 | 1.06 | .073 | |
| **tuna, yellowfin, raw** | 92 | 60.3 | 0.8 | 0.2 | 38 | 30 | | .04 | | | 31 | 14 | | .45 | .013 |
| 3 oz | 85 | 19.9 | 0.0 | 0.2 | | 15 | .37 | 8.3 | | | | 163 | .62 | .054 | |
| **turbot, european, raw** | 81 | 65.4 | 2.5 | | | 30 | | .07 | | | 127 | 15 | 44 | .19 | |
| 3 oz | 85 | 13.6 | 0.0 | | | 9 | .06 | 1.9 | 1.87 | .49 | 202 | 1.9 | | .031 | |
| **weakfish (sea trout)** | | | | | | | | | | | | | | | |
| raw | 121 | 76.5 | 5.6 | | | | | .06 | | | 75 | | | | |
| 3.5 oz | 100 | 16.5 | 0.0 | | 0.0 | | .09 | 2.7 | | | 317 | | | | |
| broiled | 208 | 61.4 | 11.4 | | | | | .08 | | | 560 | | | | |
| 3.5 oz | 100 | 24.6 | 0.0 | | 0.0 | | .10 | 3.5 | | | 465 | | | | |
| **whelk** | | | | | | | | | | | | | | | |
| raw | 117 | 56.1 | 0.3 | 0.0 | 55 | 72 | | .09 | .29 | 5 | 175 | 48 | 73 | 1.39 | .380 |
| 3 oz | 85 | 20.3 | 6.6 | 0.0 | | 22 | .02 | 0.9 | 7.71 | .18 | 295 | 120 | 4.28 | .876 | |
| ckd by moist heat | 233 | 27.2 | 0.7 | 0.0 | 110 | 137 | | .18 | .55 | 10 | 350 | 96 | 147 | 2.77 | |
| 3 oz | 85 | 40.5 | 13.2 | 0.1 | | 41 | .04 | 1.7 | 15.42 | | 590 | 240 | 8.55 | 1.751 | |
| **whitefish** | | | | | | | | | | | | | | | |
| raw | 114 | 61.9 | 5.0 | 1.8 | 51 | | | | | | 43 | | 28 | .84 | |
| 3 oz | 85 | 16.2 | 0.0 | 0.8 | | | | | | | 269 | | .31 | .061 | |
| baked, stuffedᶜ | 215 | 63.2 | 14.0 | | | | 0 | .11 | | | 195 | | | | |
| 3.5 oz | 100 | 15.2 | 5.8 | | | | .11 | 2.3 | | | 291 | 246 | .50 | | |
| smoked | 92 | 60.2 | 0.8 | 0.2 | 28 | 162 | | .09 | .33 | 6 | 866 | 15 | 19 | .41 | .029 |
| 3 oz | 85 | 19.9 | 0.0 | 0.2 | | 48 | .03 | 2.0 | 2.77 | .09 | 360 | 112 | .43 | .268 | |
| **white perch** | | | | | | | | | | | | | | | |
| raw | 118 | 75.7 | 4.0 | | | | | | | | | | | | |
| 3.5 oz | 100 | 19.3 | 0.0 | | 0.0 | | | | | | | 192 | | | |

ᵃ Value reflects added salt. If no salt is added, sodium is 43 mg.
ᵇ Prepared w/ light tuna cnd in oil, pickle relish, salad dressing, onion & celery.
ᶜ Stuffed w/ bacon, onion, celery & bread crumbs.

| | KCAL / WT (g) | H₂O (g) / PRO (g) | FAT (g) / CHO (g) | PUFA (g) / SFA (g) | CHOL (mg) / DFIB (g) | A (RE) / A (IU) | C (mg) / B-1 (mg) | B-2 (mg) / NIA (mg) | B-6 (mg) / B-12 (mcg) | FOL (mcg) / PANT (mg) | Na (mg) / K (mg) | Ca (mg) / P (mg) | Mg (mg) / Fe (mg) | Zn (mg) / Cu (mg) | Mn (mg) |
|---|---|---|---|---|---|---|---|---|---|---|---|---|---|---|---|
| fried fillet | 108 | | 5.3 | | | | | | 0 | .05 | | | | 9 | |
| *2.3 oz* | 65 | 12.5 | 0.0 | | 0.0 | 0 | .04 | 2.7 | | | | 113 | .70 | | |
| **whiting** | | | | | | | | | | | | | | | |
| raw | 77 | 68.2 | 1.1 | 0.4 | 57 | 84 | | .04 | .13 | 11 | 61 | 41 | 18 | .75 | .088 |
| *3 oz* | 85 | 15.6 | 0.0 | 0.2 | | 25 | .05 | 1.1 | 1.96 | .18 | 212 | 189 | .29 | .026 | |
| ckd by dry heat | 98 | 63.5 | 1.4 | 0.5 | 71 | 97 | | .05 | .15 | 13 | 113 | 53 | 23 | .45 | .034 |
| *3 oz* | 85 | 20.0 | 0.0 | 0.3 | | 29 | .06 | 1.4 | 2.21 | | 369 | 242 | .36 | .034 | |
| **wolffish, atlantic, raw** | 82 | 67.9 | 2.0 | 0.7 | 39 | 319 | | .07 | | | 72 | | | .66 | .013 |
| *3 oz* | 85 | 14.9 | 0.0 | 0.3 | | 96 | .15 | 1.8 | 1.73 | .49 | | | .08 | .025 | |
| **yellowtail, raw** | 124 | 63.3 | 4.5 | | | 81 | 2 | .03 | .14 | 3 | 33 | | | .44 | .013 |
| *3 oz* | 85 | 19.7 | | | | 24 | .12 | 5.8 | 1.11 | .50 | | 133 | .41 | .038 | |

## 14. FRUIT & VEGETABLE JUICES

| | KCAL / WT (g) | H₂O (g) / PRO (g) | FAT (g) / CHO (g) | PUFA (g) / SFA (g) | CHOL (mg) / DFIB (g) | A (RE) / A (IU) | C (mg) / B-1 (mg) | B-2 (mg) / NIA (mg) | B-6 (mg) / B-12 (mcg) | FOL (mcg) / PANT (mg) | Na (mg) / K (mg) | Ca (mg) / P (mg) | Mg (mg) / Fe (mg) | Zn (mg) / Cu (mg) | Mn (mg) |
|---|---|---|---|---|---|---|---|---|---|---|---|---|---|---|---|
| **acerola jce, fresh** | 51 | 228.2 | 0.7 | | | 123 | 3872 | .15 | .01 | | 7 | 24 | 29 | | |
| *8 fl oz* | 242 | 1.0 | 11.6 | | | 1232 | .05 | 1.0 | .00 | .50 | 235 | 22 | 1.21 | | |
| **apple jce, cnd/bottled** | 116 | 218.1 | 0.3 | 0.1 | 0 | 0 | 2 | .04 | .07 | 0 | 7 | 16 | 8 | .07 | .280 |
| *8 fl oz* | 248 | 0.2 | 29.0 | 0.0 | | 2 | .05 | 0.2 | .00 | | 296 | 18 | .92 | .055 | |
| **apple jce, from frzn conc** | 111 | 210.1 | 0.3 | 0.1 | 0 | | 1 | .04 | .08 | 1 | 17 | 14 | 12 | .09 | .151 |
| *8 fl oz* | 239 | 0.3 | 27.6 | 0.0 | | | .01 | 0.1 | .00 | .15 | 301 | 16 | .61 | .033 | |
| **apricot nectar, cnd** | 141 | 213.0 | 0.2 | 0.0 | 0 | 330 | 1 | .04 | | 3 | 9 | 17 | 13 | .23 | |
| *8 fl oz* | 251 | 0.9 | 36.1 | 0.0 | 0.8 | 3304 | .02 | 0.7 | .00 | | 286 | 23 | .96 | .183 | |
| **beef broth & tomato jce** | 61 | 151.0 | 0.2 | | | 21 | 2 | .05 | | | 220 | 19 | | | |
| *5.5 fl oz can* | 168 | 1.0 | 14.3 | 0.1 | | 215 | .00 | 0.3 | | | 162 | | .98 | | |
| **carrot jce, cnd** | 73 | 163.5 | 0.3 | 0.1 | 0 | 4738 | 16 | .10 | .40 | 7 | 54 | 44 | 26 | .33 | .239 |
| *6 fl oz* | 184 | 1.7 | 17.1 | 0.1 | | 47381 | .17 | 0.7 | .00 | .42 | 538 | 77 | .85 | .085 | |
| **clam & tomato jce, cnd** | 77 | 145.3 | 0.1 | 0.0 | | 36 | 7 | .05 | | | 664 | 21 | | | |
| *5.5 fl oz can* | 166 | 1.1 | 18.1 | 0.0 | | 357 | .07 | 0.3 | | | 149 | | 1.00 | | |
| **cranberry jce cocktail, bottled** | 147 | 215.1 | 0.1 | | 0 | | 108 | .04 | | 1 | 10 | 8 | 8 | .05 | .397 |
| *8 fl oz* | 253 | 0.1 | 37.7 | | | | .01 | 0.1 | .00 | .17 | 61 | 3 | .40 | .033 | |
| **grape jce, cnd/bottled** | 155 | 212.8 | 0.2 | 0.1 | 0 | 2 | 0 | .09 | .16 | 7 | 7 | 22 | 24 | .13 | .911 |
| *8 fl oz* | 253 | 1.4 | 37.9 | 0.1 | | 20 | .07 | 0.7 | .00 | .10 | 334 | 27 | .60 | .071 | |
| **grape jce, from frzn conc, sweetened** | 128 | 217.3 | 0.2 | 0.1 | 0 | 2 | 60 | .07 | .11 | 3 | 5 | 9 | 11 | .10 | .443 |
| *8 fl oz* | 250 | 0.5 | 31.9 | 0.1 | | 19 | .04 | 0.3 | .00 | .06 | 53 | 11 | .26 | .033 | |
| **grapefruit jce, fresh** | 96 | 222.3 | 0.3 | 0.1 | 0 | | 94 | .05 | | | 2 | 22 | 30 | .13 | .049 |
| *8 fl oz* | 247 | 1.2 | 22.7 | 0.0 | | a | .10 | 0.5 | .00 | | 400 | 37 | .49 | .082 | |
| **grapefruit jce, cnd** | 93 | 222.6 | 0.2 | 0.1 | 0 | 2 | 72 | .05 | .05 | 26 | 3 | 18 | 24 | .21 | .049 |
| *8 fl oz* | 247 | 1.3 | 22.1 | 0.0 | | 18 | .10 | 0.6 | .00 | .32 | 378 | 27 | .50 | .094 | |
| **grapefruit jce, cnd, sweetened** | 116 | 218.4 | 0.2 | 0.1 | 0 | 0 | 67 | .06 | .05 | 26 | 4 | 20 | 24 | .15 | .050 |
| *8 fl oz* | 250 | 1.5 | 27.8 | 0.0 | | 0 | .10 | 0.8 | .00 | .33 | 405 | 27 | .89 | .120 | |
| **grapefruit jce, from frzn conc** | 102 | 220.6 | 0.3 | 0.1 | 0 | 2 | 83 | .05 | .11 | 9 | 2 | 19 | 26 | .13 | .049 |
| *8 fl oz* | 247 | 1.4 | 24.0 | 0.0 | | 22 | .10 | 0.5 | .00 | .47 | 337 | 34 | .34 | .082 | |
| **lemon jce, fresh** | 4 | 13.8 | 0.0 | | 0 | 0 | 7 | .00 | .01 | 2 | 0 | 1 | 1 | .01 | .001 |
| *1 T* | 15 | 0.1 | 1.3 | | | 3 | .01 | 0.0 | .00 | .02 | 19 | 1 | .00 | .004 | |
| **lemon jce, fresh** | 60 | 221.4 | 0.0 | | 0 | 5 | 112 | .02 | .12 | 32 | 2 | 18 | 16 | .12 | .020 |
| *8 fl oz* | 244 | 0.9 | 21.1 | | | 49 | .07 | 0.2 | .00 | .25 | 303 | 14 | .08 | .071 | |
| **lemon jce, cnd/bottled** | 3 | 14.1 | 0.0 | 0.0 | 0 | 0 | 4 | .00 | .01 | 2 | 3 | 1 | 1 | .01 | .003 |
| *1 T* | 15 | 0.1 | 1.0 | 0.0 | | 2 | .01 | 0.0 | .00 | .01 | 15 | 1 | .02 | .006 | |
| **lemon jce, frzn, single-strength** | 3 | 14.0 | 0.1 | 0.0 | 0 | 0 | 5 | .00 | .01 | 1 | 0 | 1 | 1 | .01 | .005 |
| *1 T* | 15 | 0.1 | 1.0 | 0.0 | | 2 | .01 | 0.0 | .00 | .02 | 14 | 1 | .02 | | |
| **lime jce, fresh** | 4 | 13.9 | 0.0 | 0.0 | 0 | 0 | 5 | .00 | .01 | | 0 | 1 | 1 | .01 | .001 |
| *1 T* | 15 | 0.1 | 1.4 | 0.0 | | 2 | .00 | 0.0 | .00 | .02 | 17 | 1 | .00 | .005 | |
| **lime jce, fresh** | 66 | 221.9 | 0.3 | 0.1 | 0 | 2 | 72 | .03 | .11 | | 2 | 22 | 14 | .15 | .020 |
| *8 fl oz* | 246 | 1.1 | 22.2 | 0.0 | | 25 | .05 | 0.2 | .00 | .34 | 268 | 18 | .08 | .074 | |
| **lime jce, cnd/bottled** | 3 | 14.3 | 0.0 | 0.0 | 0 | 0 | 1 | .00 | .00 | 1 | 2 | 2 | 1 | .01 | .001 |
| *1 T* | 15 | 0.0 | 1.0 | .0 | | 3 | .01 | 0.0 | .00 | .01 | 12 | 1 | .03 | .005 | |
| **new breakfast jce, cnd, Dole[b]** | 90 | | 0.0 | | | | 60 | | | | 8 | | | | |
| *6 fl oz* | | 1.0 | 22.1 | | | | | | | | 59 | | | | |
| **orange jce, fresh** | 111 | 219.0 | 0.5 | 0.1 | 0 | 50 | 124 | .07 | .01 | | 2 | 27 | 27 | .13 | .035 |
| *8 fl oz* | 248 | 1.7 | 25.8 | 0.1 | | 496 | .22 | 0.1 | .00 | .47 | 496 | 42 | .50 | .109 | |

a 25 IU for white grapefruit jce: 1087 IU for pink or red grapefruit jce.    b Avg of 3 flavors - pineapple, pineapple-orange & pineapple-grapefruit.

| | KCAL / WT (g) | H₂O (g) / PRO (g) | FAT (g) / CHO (g) | PUFA (g) / SFA (g) | CHOL (mg) / DFIB (g) | A (RE) / A (IU) | C (mg) / B-1 (mg) | B-2 (mg) / NIA (mg) | B-6 (mg) / B-12 (mcg) | FOL (mcg) / PANT (mg) | Na (mg) / K (mg) | Ca (mg) / P (mg) | Mg (mg) / Fe (mg) | Zn (mg) / Cu (mg) | Mn (mg) |
|---|---|---|---|---|---|---|---|---|---|---|---|---|---|---|---|
| orange jce, cnd | 104 | 221.6 | 0.4 | 0.1 | 0 | 44 | 86 | .07 | .22 | | 6 | 21 | 27 | .17 | .035 |
| 8 fl oz | 249 | 1.5 | 24.5 | 0.0 | | 437 | .15 | 0.8 | .00 | .37 | 436 | 36 | 1.10 | .142 | |
| orange jce, from frzn conc | 112 | 219.4 | 0.1 | 0.0 | 0 | 19 | 97 | .05 | .11 | 109 | 2 | 22 | 24 | .13 | .035 |
| 8 fl oz | 249 | 1.7 | 26.8 | 0.0 | | 194 | .20 | 0.5 | .00 | .39 | 474 | 40 | .24 | .110 | |
| orange jce, unsweetened, Kraft | 83 | 158.8 | 0.2 | 0.0 | 0 | | 69 | .04 | .05 | 5 | 2 | 12 | 18 | | |
| 6 fl oz | 180 | 1.2 | 19.1 | 0.0 | | 47 | .13 | 0.4 | .00 | .28 | 335 | 30 | .20 | | |
| orange grapefruit jce, cnd | 107 | 218.9 | 0.2 | 0.0 | 0 | 29 | 72 | .07 | .06 | | 8 | 21 | 24 | .18 | .042 |
| 8 fl oz | 247 | 1.5 | 25.4 | 0.0 | | 293 | .14 | 0.8 | .00 | .35 | 390 | 34 | 1.15 | .188 | |
| papaya nectar, cnd | 142 | 212.5 | 0.4 | 0.1 | 0 | 28 | 8 | .01 | .02 | 5 | 14 | 24 | 8 | .38 | .033 |
| 8 fl oz | 250 | 0.4 | 36.3 | 0.1 | | 277 | .02 | 0.4 | .00 | .14 | 78 | 1 | .86 | .033 | |
| passion fruit jce, purple, fresh | 126 | 211.5 | 0.1 | 0 | | 177 | 74 | .32 | | | | 9 | | | |
| 8 fl oz | 247 | 1.0 | 33.6 | | | 1771 | | 3.6 | .00 | | | 31 | .59 | | |
| passion fruit jce, yellow, fresh | 149 | 208.0 | 0.4 | | 0 | 595 | 45 | .25 | | | 15 | 9 | 41 | | |
| 8 fl oz | 247 | 1.7 | 35.7 | | | 5953 | | 5.5 | .00 | | 687 | 61 | .89 | | |
| peach nectar, cnd | 134 | 213.2 | 0.1 | 0.0 | 0 | 64 | 13 | .04 | | | 17 | 13 | 11 | .20 | .047 |
| 8 fl oz | 249 | 0.7 | 34.7 | 0.0 | 0.4 | 643 | .01 | 0.7 | .00 | | 101 | 16 | .47 | .172 | |
| pear nectar, cnd | 149 | 210.0 | 0.0 | 0.0 | 0 | 0 | 3 | .03 | | | 9 | 11 | 6 | .16 | .075 |
| 8 fl oz | 250 | 0.3 | 39.4 | 0.0 | 1.6 | 1 | .01 | 0.3 | .00 | | 33 | 7 | .65 | .168 | |
| pineapple jce, cnd | 139 | 213.8 | 0.2 | 0.1 | 0 | 1 | 27 | .06 | .24 | 58 | 2 | 42 | 34 | .29 | 2.475 |
| 8 fl oz | 250 | 0.8 | 34.4 | 0.0 | | 12 | .14 | 0.6 | .00 | .25 | 334 | 20 | .65 | .225 | |
| pineapple jce, cnd, Dole | 103 | | 0.2 | | | | | .04 | | | 2 | 28 | | | |
| 6 fl oz | 188 | 0.8 | 25.4 | | | 90 | .09 | 0.4 | | | 280 | 17 | .60 | | |
| pineapple jce, from frzn conc | 129 | 216.3 | 0.1 | 0.0 | 0 | 3 | 30 | .05 | .19 | | 3 | 28 | 23 | .29 | 2.475 |
| 8 fl oz | 250 | 1.0 | 31.9 | 0.0 | | 25 | .18 | 0.5 | .00 | .31 | 340 | 20 | .75 | .225 | |
| prune jce, cnd | 181 | 208.0 | 0.1 | 0.0 | 0 | 1 | 11 | .18 | | 1 | 11 | 30 | 36 | .52 | .387 |
| 8 fl oz | 256 | 1.6 | 44.7 | 0.0 | | 9 | .04 | 2.0 | .00 | | 706 | 64 | 3.03 | .174 | |
| tangerine jce, fresh | 106 | 219.6 | 0.5 | 0.1 | 0 | 104 | 77 | .05 | | | 2 | 44 | 20 | .06 | .091 |
| 8 fl oz | 247 | 1.2 | 25.0 | 0.0 | | 1037 | .15 | 0.2 | .00 | | 440 | 35 | .49 | .062 | |
| tangerine jce, cnd, sweetened | 125 | 216.6 | 0.5 | 0.1 | 0 | 105 | 55 | .05 | .80 | | 2 | 45 | 20 | .06 | .092 |
| 8 fl oz | 249 | 1.3 | 29.9 | 0.0 | | 1046 | .15 | 0.2 | .00 | | 443 | 35 | .50 | .062 | |
| tangerine jce, from frzn conc, sweetened | 110 | 212.3 | 0.3 | 0.0 | 0 | 138 | 58 | .05 | .10 | 11 | 2 | 18 | 19 | .06 | .089 |
| 8 fl oz | 241 | 1.0 | 27.7 | 0.0 | | 1382 | .13 | 0.2 | .00 | .30 | 273 | 20 | .23 | .060 | |
| tomato jce | 32 | 170.9 | 0.1 | 0.0 | 0 | 101 | 33 | .06 | .20 | 36 | 658ª | 16 | 20 | .26 | .140 |
| 6 fl oz | 182 | 1.4 | 7.7 | 0.0 | | 1012 | .09 | 1.2 | .00 | .46 | 400 | 34 | 1.06 | .184 | |
| tomato jce cocktail, cnd | 51 | 226.0 | 0.2 | | | | 39 | .05 | | | | 486 | 24 | | |
| 8 fl oz | 243 | 1.7 | 12.2 | | | 1940 | .12 | 1.5 | | | 537 | 44 | 2.20 | | |
| tomato jce, from concentrate, Campbell's | 39 | | 0.0 | | | | 25 | .05 | | | | 589 | 20 | | |
| 6 fl oz | 182 | 1.6 | 8.0 | | | 1148 | .06 | 1.1 | | | 376 | | 2.20 | | |
| veg jce cocktail, cnd | 34 | 170.2 | 0.2 | 0.1 | 0 | 213 | 50 | .05 | .26 | | 664 | 20 | 20 | .36 | .182 |
| 6 fl oz | 182 | 1.1 | 8.3 | 0.0 | | 2130 | .08 | 1.3 | .00 | | 351 | 31 | .77 | .364 | |
| V-8 vegetable cocktail, Campbell's | 37 | | 0.1 | | | | 37 | .04 | | | | 593 | 23 | | |
| 6 fl oz | 182 | 1.3 | 7.8 | | | 2522 | .04 | 1.3 | | | 383 | | 1.00 | | |
| no salt added | 40 | | 0.0 | | | | 39 | .05 | | | | 41 | 31 | | |
| 6 fl oz | 182 | 1.6 | 8.2 | | | 3204 | .04 | 1.2 | | | 439 | | 1.20 | | |
| spicy hot | 37 | | 0.0 | | | | 38 | .04 | | | | 634 | 24 | | |
| 6 fl oz | 182 | 1.5 | 7.8 | | | 2680 | .03 | 1.2 | | | 408 | | 1.20 | | |

# 15. FRUITS

| | KCAL / WT (g) | H₂O (g) / PRO (g) | FAT (g) / CHO (g) | PUFA (g) / SFA (g) | CHOL (mg) / DFIB (g) | A (RE) / A (IU) | C (mg) / B-1 (mg) | B-2 (mg) / NIA (mg) | B-6 (mg) / B-12 (mcg) | FOL (mcg) / PANT (mg) | Na (mg) / K (mg) | Ca (mg) / P (mg) | Mg (mg) / Fe (mg) | Zn (mg) / Cu (mg) | Mn (mg) |
|---|---|---|---|---|---|---|---|---|---|---|---|---|---|---|---|
| acerola, raw | 31 | 89.6 | 0.3 | | 0 | 75 | 1644 | .06 | .01 | | 7 | 12 | 18 | | |
| 1 cup | 98 | 0.4 | 7.5 | | | 751 | .02 | 0.4 | .00 | .30 | 143 | 11 | .20 | | |
| apple | | | | | | | | | | | | | | | |
| raw, w/ skin | 81 | 115.8 | 0.5 | 0.1 | 0 | 7 | 8 | .02 | .07 | 4 | 1 | 10 | 6 | .05 | .062 |
| 1 med | 138 | 0.3 | 21.1 | 0.1 | 2.8 | 74 | .02 | 0.1 | .00 | .08 | 159 | 10 | .25 | .057 | |
| raw, w/o skin | 72 | 108.1 | 0.4 | 0.1 | 0 | 6 | 5 | .01 | .06 | 1 | 0 | 5 | 4 | .05 | .029 |
| 1 med | 128 | 0.2 | 19.0 | 0.1 | 2.9 | 56 | .02 | 0.1 | .00 | .07 | 144 | 9 | .09 | .040 | |
| boiled, w/o skin | 91 | 146.2 | 0.6 | 0.2 | 0 | 7 | 0 | .02 | .08 | 1 | 1 | 8 | 5 | .07 | .202 |
| 1 cup | 171 | 0.5 | 23.3 | 0.1 | 3.3 | 75 | .03 | 0.2 | .00 | .08 | 150 | 13 | .32 | .060 | |

ª If no salt added, Na is 18 mg.

| | KCAL | H₂O (g) | FAT (g) | PUFA (g) | CHOL (mg) | A (RE) | C (mg) | B-2 (mg) | B-6 (mg) | FOL (mcg) | Na (mg) | Ca (mg) | Mg (mg) | Zn (mg) | Mn (mg) |
|---|---|---|---|---|---|---|---|---|---|---|---|---|---|---|---|
| | WT (g) | PRO (g) | CHO (g) | SFA (g) | DFIB (g) | A (IU) | B-1 (mg) | NIA (mg) | B-12 (mcg) | PANT (mg) | K (mg) | P (mg) | Fe (mg) | Cu (mg) | |
| cnd, sliced, sweetened | 68 | 84.0 | 0.5 | 0.1 | 0 | 5 | 0 | .01 | .05 | 0 | 3 | 4 | 2 | .03 | .156 |
| *1/2 cup* | 102 | 0.2 | 17.0 | 0.1 | 1.9 | 52 | .01 | 0.1 | .00 | .03 | 69 | 6 | .23 | .054 | |
| dried, sulfured | 155 | 20.3 | 0.2 | 0.1 | 0 | 0 | 3 | .10 | .08 | | 56 | 9 | 10 | .13 | .058 |
| *10 rings* | 64 | 0.6 | 42.4 | 0.0 | | 0 | .00 | 0.6 | .00 | | 288 | 25 | .90 | .122 | |
| micro ckd w/o skin | 96 | 143.9 | 0.7 | 0.2 | 0 | 7 | 1 | .02 | .08 | 1 | 1 | 8 | 6 | .06 | .241 |
| *1 cup* | 170 | 0.5 | 24.5 | 0.1 | 4.0 | 68 | .03 | 0.1 | .00 | .08 | 159 | 14 | .28 | .078 | |
| **applesce, cnd, sweetened** | 97 | 101.9 | 0.2 | 0.1 | 0 | 1 | 2 | .04 | .03 | 1 | 4 | 5 | 4 | .05 | .096 |
| *1/2 cup* | 128 | 0.2 | 25.5 | 0.0 | 1.4 | 14 | .02 | 0.2 | .00 | .07 | 78 | 9 | .45 | .055 | |
| **applesce, cnd, unsweetened** | 53 | 107.8 | 0.1 | | | | 2 | .02 | | | 2 | 4 | 4 | .03 | .092 |
| *1/2 cup* | 122 | 0.2 | 13.8 | | 1.4 | 29 | .01 | 0.0 | | | 91 | 9 | .15 | .032 | |
| **apricots** | | | | | | | | | | | | | | | |
| raw | 51 | 91.5 | 0.4 | 0.1 | 0 | 277 | 11 | .04 | .06 | 9 | 1 | 15 | 8 | .28 | .084 |
| *3 med* | 106 | 1.5 | 11.8 | 0.0 | 1.4 | 2769 | .03 | 0.6 | .00 | .25 | 313 | 21 | .58 | .094 | |
| cnd, heavy syrup | 75 | 69.9 | 0.1 | 0.0 | 0 | 112 | 3 | .02 | .05 | 2 | 9 | 8 | 7 | .09 | .046 |
| *4 halves* | 90 | 0.5 | 19.3 | 0.0 | | 1116 | .02 | 0.4 | .00 | .08 | 120 | 12 | .38 | .059 | |
| cnd, jce pack | 40 | 72.8 | 0.0 | 0.0 | 0 | 142 | 4 | .02 | | | 3 | 10 | 8 | .09 | .044 |
| *3 halves* | 84 | 0.5 | 10.4 | 0.0 | 0.4 | 1421 | .02 | 0.3 | .00 | | 139 | 17 | .25 | .045 | |
| cnd, light syrup | 54 | 70.2 | 0.0 | 0.0 | 0 | 112 | 2 | .02 | .05 | 1 | 3 | 10 | 7 | .09 | .044 |
| *3 halves* | 85 | 0.5 | 14.0 | 0.0 | | 1124 | .01 | 0.3 | .00 | .08 | 117 | 11 | .33 | .067 | |
| cnd, water pack | 20 | 84.1 | 0.0 | 0.0 | 0 | 163 | 2 | .02 | .05 | 2 | 10 | 8 | 8 | .10 | .048 |
| *4 halves* | 90 | 0.6 | 4.9 | 0.0 | | 1629 | .02 | 0.4 | .00 | .08 | 139 | 15 | .49 | .061 | |
| dried, sulfured | 83 | 10.9 | 0.2 | 0.0 | 0 | 253 | 1 | .05 | .06 | 4 | 3 | 16 | 16 | .26 | .096 |
| *10 halves* | 35 | 1.3 | 21.6 | 0.0 | | 2534 | .00 | 1.0 | .00 | .26 | 482 | 41 | 1.65 | .150 | |
| frzn, sweetened | 119 | 88.7 | 0.1 | 0.0 | 0 | 203 | 11 | .05 | .07 | | 5 | 12 | 11 | .12 | .061 |
| *1/2 cup* | 121 | 0.9 | 30.4 | 0.0 | | 2033 | .02 | 1.0 | .00 | .24 | 277 | 23 | 1.09 | .077 | |
| **banana, raw** | 105 | 84.7 | 0.6 | 0.1 | 0 | 9 | 10 | .11 | .66 | 22 | 1 | 7 | 33 | .19 | .173 |
| *1 med* | 114 | 1.2 | 26.7 | 0.2 | 1.6 | 92 | .05 | 0.6 | .00 | .30 | 451 | 22 | .35 | .119 | |
| **blackberries** | | | | | | | | | | | | | | | |
| raw | 37 | 61.7 | 0.3 | | 0 | 12 | 15 | .03 | .04 | | 0 | 23 | 14 | .20 | .930 |
| *1/2 cup* | 72 | 0.5 | 9.2 | | 3.3 | 119 | .02 | 0.3 | .00 | .17 | 141 | 15 | .41 | .101 | |
| cnd, heavy syrup | 118 | 96.1 | 0.2 | | 0 | 28 | 4 | .05 | .05 | 34 | 3 | 27 | 22 | .23 | .892 |
| *1/2 cup* | 128 | 1.7 | 29.6 | | | 280 | .04 | 0.4 | 0 | .19 | 127 | 18 | .83 | .170 | |
| frzn, unsweetened | 97 | 124.1 | 0.7 | | 0 | 17 | 5 | .07 | .09 | 51 | 2 | 44 | 33 | .37 | 1.847 |
| *1 cup* | 151 | 1.8 | 23.7 | | | 172 | .04 | 1.8 | .00 | .23 | 211 | 46 | 1.21 | .181 | |
| **blueberries** | | | | | | | | | | | | | | | |
| raw | 82 | 122.7 | 0.6 | | 0 | 15 | 19 | .07 | .05 | 9 | 9 | 9 | 7 | .16 | .409 |
| *1 cup* | 145 | 1.0 | 20.5 | | 4.4 | 145 | .07 | 0.5 | .00 | .14 | 129 | 15 | .24 | .088 | |
| cnd, heavy syrup | 112 | 98.3 | 0.4 | | 0 | 8 | 1 | .07 | .05 | 2 | 4 | 7 | 4 | .09 | .260 |
| *1/2 cup* | 128 | 0.8 | 28.2 | | | 82 | .04 | 0.1 | 0 | .11 | 51 | 13 | .42 | .068 | |
| frzn, sweetened | 187 | 178.0 | .3 | | 0 | 10 | 2 | .12 | .14 | 16 | 3 | 13 | 6 | .14 | .603 |
| *1 cup* | 230 | 0.9 | 50.5 | | | 102 | .05 | 0.6 | .00 | .29 | 137 | 16 | .90 | .090 | |
| **boysenberries** | | | | | | | | | | | | | | | |
| cnd, heavy syrup | 113 | 97.6 | 0.2 | | 0 | 5 | 8 | .04 | .05 | 44 | 4 | 23 | 14 | .24 | .320 |
| *1/2 cup* | 128 | 1.3 | 28.6 | | | 21 | .03 | 0.3 | .00 | .17 | 115 | 13 | .55 | .090 | |
| frzn, unsweetened | 66 | 113.4 | 0.4 | | 0 | 9 | 4 | .05 | .07 | 84 | 2 | 36 | 21 | .29 | .722 |
| *1 cup* | 132 | 1.5 | 16.1 | | | 89 | .07 | 1.0 | .00 | .33 | 183 | 36 | 1.12 | .106 | |
| **breadfruit, raw** | 99 | 67.8 | 0.2 | | 0 | 4 | 28 | .03 | | | 2 | 17 | 24 | .11 | .058 |
| *1/4 small* | 96 | 1.0 | 26.0 | | | 38 | .11 | 0.9 | .00 | .44 | 470 | 29 | .52 | .081 | |
| **cantaloupe, raw** | 57 | 143.6 | 0.4 | | 0 | 516 | 68 | .03 | .18 | 27 | 14 | 17 | 17 | .25 | .075 |
| *1 cup pieces* | 160 | 1.4 | 13.4 | | 0.5 | 5158 | .06 | 0.9 | .00 | .21 | 494 | 27 | .34 | .067 | |
| **carambola, raw** | 42 | 115.5 | 0.4 | | 0 | 62 | 27 | .03 | | | 2 | 6 | 12 | .14 | .104 |
| *1 med* | 127 | 0.7 | 9.9 | | 1.5 | 626 | .04 | 0.5 | .00 | | 207 | 20 | .33 | .152 | |
| **carissa, raw** | 12 | 16.8 | 0.3 | | 0 | 1 | 8 | .01 | | | 1 | 2 | 3 | | |
| *1 med* | 20 | 0.1 | 2.7 | | | 8 | .01 | 0.0 | .00 | | 52 | 1 | .26 | .042 | |
| **casaba melon, raw** | 45 | 156.4 | 0.2 | | 0 | 5 | 27 | .03 | | | 20 | 9 | 14 | | |
| *1 cup pieces* | 170 | 1.5 | 10.5 | | | 51 | .10 | 0.7 | .00 | | 357 | 12 | .68 | | |
| **cherimoya, raw** | 515 | 402.1 | 2.2 | | 0 | 5 | 49 | .60 | | | | 126 | | | |
| *1 med* | 547 | 7.1 | 131.3 | | | 55 | .55 | 7.1 | .00 | | | 219 | 2.74 | | |

| | KCAL / WT (g) | H$_2$O (g) / PRO (g) | FAT (g) / CHO (g) | PUFA (g) / SFA (g) | CHOL (mg) / DFIB (g) | A (RE) / A (IU) | C (mg) / B-1 (mg) | B-2 (mg) / NIA (mg) | B-6 (mg) / B-12 (mcg) | FOL (mcg) / PANT (mg) | Na (mg) / K (mg) | Ca (mg) / P (mg) | Mg (mg) / Fe (mg) | Zn (mg) / Cu (mg) | Mn (mg) |
|---|---|---|---|---|---|---|---|---|---|---|---|---|---|---|---|
| **cherries** | | | | | | | | | | | | | | | |
| sour, cnd, heavy syrup | 116 | 96.8 | 0.1 | 0.0 | 0 | 91 | 3 | .05 | .06 | 10 | 9 | 13 | 7 | .08 | .092 |
| *1/2 cup* | 128 | 0.9 | 29.8 | 0.0 | | 914 | .02 | 0.2 | .00 | .13 | 119 | 12 | 1.70 | .084 | |
| sour, cnd, water pack | 43 | 109.7 | 0.1 | 0.0 | 0 | 92 | 3 | .05 | .05 | 10 | 9 | 13 | 7 | .08 | .093 |
| *1/2 cup* | 122 | 0.9 | 10.9 | 0.0 | | 920 | .02 | 0.2 | .00 | .13 | 120 | 12 | 1.67 | .085 | |
| sweet, raw | 49 | 54.9 | 0.7 | 0.2 | 0 | 15 | 5 | .04 | .02 | 3 | 0 | 10 | 8 | .04 | .063 |
| *10 cherries* | 68 | 0.8 | 11.3 | 0.1 | 1.1 | 146 | .03 | 0.3 | .00 | .09 | 152 | 13 | .26 | .065 | |
| sweet, cnd, heavy syrup | 107 | 100.1 | 0.2 | 0.1 | 0 | 20 | 5 | | .04 | | 3 | 12 | 11 | .13 | .076 |
| *1/2 cup* | 129 | 0.8 | 27.4 | 0.0 | | 199 | .03 | 0.5 | .00 | | 187 | 23 | .46 | .183 | |
| sweet, cnd, jce pack | 68 | 106.2 | 0.0 | 0.0 | 0 | 16 | 3 | | .03 | | 3 | 17 | 16 | .12 | .076 |
| *1/2 cup* | 125 | 1.1 | 17.3 | 0.0 | 0.3 | 156 | .02 | 0.5 | | | 163 | 27 | .73 | .091 | |
| sweet, cnd, water pack | 57 | 107.9 | 0.2 | 0.0 | 0 | 20 | 3 | .05 | .04 | | 2 | 13 | 11 | .09 | .077 |
| *1/2 cup* | 124 | 1.0 | 14.6 | 0.0 | | 198 | .03 | 0.5 | .00 | | 162 | 19 | .45 | .093 | |
| sweet, frzn, sweetened | 232 | 195.6 | 0.3 | 0.1 | 0 | 49 | 3 | .12 | | | 3 | 31 | 26 | .10 | .282 |
| *1 cup* | 259 | 3.0 | 57.9 | 0.1 | | 489 | .07 | 0.5 | .00 | | 514 | 41 | .90 | .062 | |
| **crabapples, raw** | 83 | 86.8 | 0.3 | 0.1 | 0 | 4 | 9 | .02 | | | 1 | 20 | 7 | | .127 |
| *1 cup slices* | 110 | 0.4 | 21.9 | 0.1 | | 44 | .03 | 0.1 | .00 | | 213 | 17 | .39 | .074 | |
| **cranberries, raw** | 46 | 82.2 | 0.2 | | 0 | 4 | 13 | .02 | .06 | 2 | 1 | 7 | 5 | .12 | .149 |
| *1 cup whole* | 95 | 0.4 | 12.1 | | | 44 | .03 | 0.1 | .00 | .21 | 67 | 8 | .19 | .055 | |
| **cranberry sce, jelled, cnd** | 209 | 83.7 | 0.2 | | 0 | 3 | 3 | .03 | .02 | | 40 | 5 | 4 | .07 | .083 |
| *1/2 cup* | 138 | 0.3 | 53.7 | | | 28 | .02 | 0.1 | .00 | | 35 | 8 | .30 | .028 | |
| **cranberry orange relish, cnd** | 246 | 73.4 | 0.1 | | | 10 | 25 | .03 | | 0 | 44 | 15 | 6 | | |
| *1/2 cup* | 138 | 0.4 | 63.8 | | | 97 | .04 | 0.1 | .00 | | 53 | 11 | .28 | .055 | |
| **currants, european black, raw** | 36 | 45.9 | 0.2 | 0.1 | 0 | 13 | 101 | .03 | .04 | | 1 | 31 | 14 | .15 | .143 |
| *1/2 cup* | 56 | 0.8 | 8.6 | 0.0 | 3.0 | 129 | .03 | 0.2 | .00 | .22 | 180 | 33 | .86 | .048 | |
| **currants, red & white, raw** | 31 | 47.0 | 0.1 | 0.0 | 0 | 7 | 23 | .03 | .04 | | 1 | 18 | 7 | .13 | .104 |
| *1/2 cup* | 56 | 0.8 | 7.7 | 0.0 | | 67 | .02 | 0.1 | .00 | .04 | 154 | 24 | .56 | .060 | |
| **currants, zante, dried[a]** | 204 | 13.8 | 0.2 | 0.1 | 0 | 5 | 3 | .10 | .21 | 7 | 6 | 62 | 30 | .47 | .338 |
| *1/2 cup* | 72 | 2.9 | 53.3 | 0.0 | | 52 | .12 | 1.2 | .00 | .03 | 642 | 90 | 2.34 | .337 | |
| **custard apple, raw** | 101 | 71.5 | 0.6 | | 0 | | 19 | .10 | .22 | | 4 | 30 | 18 | | |
| *3.5 oz* | 100 | 1.7 | 25.2 | | | | .08 | 0.5 | .00 | .14 | 382 | 21 | .71 | | |
| **dates, dried** | 228 | 18.7 | 0.4 | | 0 | 4 | 0 | .08 | .16 | 10 | 2 | 27 | 29 | .24 | .247 |
| *10 dates* | 83 | 1.6 | 61.0 | | 4.2 | 42 | .08 | 1.8 | .00 | .65 | 541 | 33 | .96 | .239 | |
| **dates, dried, chopped, Dromedary** | 130 | | 0.0 | | | | | | | | 0 | | | | |
| *1/4 cup* | | 1.0 | 31.0 | | | | | | | | 190 | | | | |
| **elderberries, raw** | 105 | 115.7 | 0.7 | | 0 | 87 | 52 | .09 | .33 | | | 55 | | | |
| *1 cup* | 145 | 1.0 | 26.7 | | | 870 | .10 | 0.7 | .00 | .20 | 406 | 57 | 2.32 | | |
| **figs, raw** | 37 | 39.6 | 0.2 | 0.1 | 0 | 7 | 1 | .03 | .06 | | 1 | 18 | 8 | .07 | .064 |
| *1 med* | 50 | 0.4 | 9.6 | 0.0 | | 71 | .03 | 0.2 | .00 | .15 | 116 | 7 | .18 | .035 | |
| **figs, cnd, heavy syrup** | 75 | 64.9 | 0.1 | 0.0 | 0 | 3 | 1 | .03 | | | 1 | 23 | 8 | .09 | .071 |
| *3 figs* | 85 | 0.3 | 19.5 | 0.0 | | 31 | .02 | 0.4 | .00 | .06 | 85 | 9 | .24 | .090 | |
| **figs, dried** | 477 | 53.2 | 2.2 | 1.0 | 0 | 25 | 2 | .17 | .42 | 14 | 20 | 269 | 111 | .94 | .726 |
| *10 figs* | 187 | 5.7 | 122.2 | 0.4 | | 248 | .13 | 1.3 | .00 | .81 | 1332 | 128 | 4.18 | .585 | |
| **fruit bars, General Mills[b]** | 90 | | 2.0 | | | | | | | | 10 | | | | |
| *1 bar* | 23 | 1.0 | 17.2 | | | | | | | | 37 | | | | |
| **fruit cocktail[c]** | | | | | | | | | | | | | | | |
| cnd, heavy syrup | 93 | 102.9 | 0.1 | 0.0 | 0 | 26 | 2 | .02 | .06 | | 7 | 8 | 7 | .11 | |
| *1/2 cup* | 128 | 0.5 | 24.2 | 0.0 | | 262 | .02 | 0.5 | .00 | .08 | 112 | 14 | .36 | .088 | |
| cnd, jce pack | 56 | 108.4 | 0.0 | 0.0 | 0 | 38 | 3 | .02 | | | 4 | 10 | 9 | .11 | |
| *1/2 cup* | 124 | 0.6 | 14.7 | 0.0 | | 376 | .02 | 0.5 | .00 | | 118 | 17 | .26 | .077 | |
| cnd, water pack | 40 | 110.7 | 0.1 | 0.0 | 0 | 30 | 3 | .01 | .06 | | 5 | 6 | 8 | .11 | |
| *1/2 cup* | 122 | 0.5 | 10.4 | 0.0 | | 305 | .02 | 0.4 | .00 | .08 | 115 | 14 | .31 | .087 | |

[a] Dried black Corinth grapes: not related to European black, red or white currants.

[b] Values are averages for cherry, grape, orange-pineapple, strawberry & tropical flavors.

[c] Peaches, pears, grapes, pineapples & cherries.

| | KCAL / WT (g) | H₂O (g) / PRO (g) | FAT (g) / CHO (g) | PUFA (g) / SFA (g) | CHOL (mg) / DFIB (g) | A (RE) / A (IU) | C (mg) / B-1 (mg) | B-2 (mg) / NIA (mg) | B-6 (mg) / B-12 (mcg) | FOL (mcg) / PANT (mg) | Na (mg) / K (mg) | Ca (mg) / P (mg) | Mg (mg) / Fe (mg) | Zn (mg) / Cu (mg) | Mn (mg) |
|---|---|---|---|---|---|---|---|---|---|---|---|---|---|---|---|
| **fruit roll-ups, General Mills[a]** | 50 | | 1.0 | | | | | | | | 7 | | | | |
| *1 roll* | 15 | 0.0 | 12.0 | | | | | | | | 43 | | | | |
| **fruit salad, cnd** | | | | | | | | | | | | | | | |
| heavy syrup[b] | 94 | 102.7 | 0.1 | 0.0 | 0 | 65 | 3 | .03 | .04 | · | 7 | 8 | 7 | .09 | |
| *1/2 cup* | 128 | 0.4 | 24.5 | 0.0 | | 646 | .02 | 0.4 | .00 | | 103 | 12 | .36 | .082 | |
| jce pack[b] | 62 | 106.8 | 0.0 | 0.0 | 0 | 74 | 4 | .02 | | | 7 | 14 | 10 | .18 | |
| *1/2 cup* | 124 | 0.6 | 16.2 | 0.0 | | 744 | .01 | 0.4 | .00 | | 144 | 18 | .31 | .062 | |
| tropical, heavy syrup[c] | 110 | 98.3 | 0.1 | | 0 | 16 | 22 | .06 | | | 3 | 17 | 17 | .14 | |
| *1/2 cup* | 128 | 0.5 | 28.6 | | | 162 | .07 | 0.7 | .00 | | 168 | 10 | .66 | .102 | |
| **fruit salad, Fresh Chef** | | | | | | | | | | | | | | | |
| fruit cooler | 67 | | 0.1 | | | | 2 | .04 | | | 121 | 22 | | | |
| *2/5 cup* | 99 | 0.8 | 15.7 | | | 78 | .02 | 0.3 | | | 66 | | .40 | | |
| tropical delight | 235 | | 10.8 | | | | 7 | .12 | | | 253 | 65 | | | |
| *4/5 cup* | 198 | 2.4 | 32.1 | | | 803 | .08 | 0.3 | | | 147 | | 1.30 | | |
| **fruit wrinkles, General Mills[d]** | 100 | | 2.0 | | | | | | | | 105 | | | | |
| *1 pouch* | 26 | 1.0 | 21.0 | | | | | | | | 38 | | | | |
| **gooseberries, raw** | 67 | 131.8 | 0.9 | 0.0 | 0 | 44 | 42 | .05 | .12 | | 1 | 38 | 15 | .18 | .216 |
| *1 cup* | 150 | 1.3 | 15.3 | 0.1 | | 435 | .06 | 0.5 | .00 | .43 | 297 | 40 | .47 | .105 | |
| **gooseberries, cnd, light syrup** | 93 | 100.9 | 0.3 | 0.1 | 0 | 17 | 13 | .07 | .02 | 4 | 3 | 20 | 8 | .14 | .223 |
| *1/2 cup* | 126 | 0.8 | 23.6 | 0.0 | | 174 | .03 | 0.2 | .00 | .17 | 97 | 9 | .42 | .273 | |
| **grapefruit** | | | | | | | | | | | | | | | |
| raw, pink & red | 37 | 112.4 | 0.1 | 0.0 | 0 | 32 | 47 | .03 | .05 | 15 | 0 | 13 | 10 | .09 | .012 |
| *1/2 med* | 123 | 0.7 | 9.5 | 0.0 | | 318 | .04 | 0.2 | .00 | .35 | 158 | 11 | .15 | .054 | |
| raw, white | 39 | 106.8 | 0.1 | 0.0 | 0 | 1 | 39 | .02 | .05 | 12 | 0 | 14 | 11 | .08 | .015 |
| *1/2 med* | 118 | 0.8 | 9.9 | 0.0 | | 12 | .04 | 0.3 | .00 | .33 | 175 | 9 | .07 | .059 | |
| cnd, jce pack | 46 | 111.2 | 0.1 | 0.0 | 0 | 0 | 42 | .02 | | | 9 | 19 | 13 | .09 | .009 |
| *1/2 cup* | 124 | 0.9 | 11.4 | 0.0 | 0.3 | 0 | .04 | 0.2 | .00 | | 209 | 15 | .26 | .046 | |
| cnd, light syrup | 76 | 106.2 | 0.1 | 0.0 | 0 | 0 | 27 | .03 | .03 | 11 | 2 | 18 | 13 | .11 | .009 |
| *1/2 cup* | 127 | 0.7 | 19.6 | 0.0 | | 0 | .05 | 0.3 | .00 | .15 | 164 | 13 | .51 | .084 | |
| **grapes** | | | | | | | | | | | | | | | |
| american (slip skin), raw | 58 | 74.8 | 0.3 | 0.1 | 0 | 9 | 4 | .05 | .10 | 4 | 2 | 13 | 5 | .04 | .661 |
| *1 cup* | 92 | 0.6 | 15.8 | 0.1 | | 92 | .09 | 0.3 | .00 | .02 | 176 | 9 | .27 | .037 | |
| european (adherent skin), raw | 114 | 128.9 | 0.9 | 0.3 | 0 | 12 | 17 | .09 | .18 | 6 | 3 | 17 | 10 | .09 | .093 |
| *1 cup* | 160 | 1.1 | 28.4 | 0.3 | 2.6 | 117 | .15 | 0.5 | .00 | .04 | 296 | 21 | .41 | .144 | |
| thompson seedless, cnd, heavy syrup | 94 | 101.8 | 0.1 | 0.0 | 0 | 8 | 1 | .03 | | | 7 | 13 | 8 | .06 | .049 |
| *1/2 cup* | 128 | 0.6 | 25.2 | 0.0 | | 81 | .04 | 0.2 | .00 | | 132 | 22 | 1.20 | .069 | |
| **groundcherries, raw[e]** | 74 | 119.6 | 1.0 | | | 101 | 15 | .06 | | 0 | | 13 | | | |
| *1 cup* | 140 | 2.7 | 15.7 | | | 1008 | .15 | 3.9 | .00 | | | 56 | 1.40 | | |
| **guava, raw** | 45 | 77.5 | 0.5 | 0.2 | 0 | 71 | 165 | .05 | .13 | | 2 | 18 | 9 | .21 | .130 |
| *1 med* | 90 | 0.7 | 10.7 | 0.2 | | 713 | .05 | 1.1 | .00 | .14 | 256 | 23 | .28 | .093 | |
| **guava, strawberry, raw** | 169 | 196.8 | 1.5 | 0.6 | 0 | 22 | 90 | .07 | | | 89 | 52 | 41 | | |
| *1 cup* | 244 | 1.4 | 42.4 | 0.4 | | 220 | .07 | 1.5 | .00 | | 713 | 67 | .53 | | |
| **honeydew melon, raw** | 33 | | 0.3 | | | | 23 | .03 | | | 12 | 14 | | | |
| *1/4 cup* | 100 | 0.8 | 7.7 | | | 40 | .04 | 0.6 | | | 251 | 16 | .40 | | |
| **jackfruit, raw** | 94 | 72.3 | 0.3 | | | 30 | 7 | | .11 | 0 | 3 | 34 | 37 | .42 | .197 |
| *3.5 oz* | 100 | 1.5 | 24.0 | | | 297 | .03 | 0.4 | .00 | | 303 | 36 | .60 | .187 | |
| **java plum, raw** | 82 | 112.2 | 0.3 | | | 0 | 19 | .02 | .05 | | 18 | 25 | 21 | | |
| *1 cup* | 135 | 1.0 | 21.0 | | | 5 | .01 | 0.4 | .00 | | 106 | 23 | .25 | | |
| **jujube** | | | | | | | | | | | | | | | |
| raw | 79 | 77.9 | 0.2 | | | 4 | 69 | .04 | .08 | 0 | 3 | 21 | 10 | .05 | .084 |
| *3.5 oz* | 100 | 1.2 | 20.2 | | | 40 | .02 | 0.9 | .00 | | 250 | 23 | .48 | .073 | |
| dried | 287 | 19.7 | 1.1 | | | | 13 | .36 | | 0 | 9 | 79 | 37 | .19 | .305 |
| *3.5 oz* | 100 | 3.7 | 73.6 | | | | .21 | 0.5 | .00 | | 531 | 100 | 1.80 | .265 | |

[a] Values are averages for apple, apricot, cherry, grape, orange, raspberry & strawberry flavors.

[b] Peaches, pears, apricots, pineapples & cherries.

[c] Pineapples, papayas, pineapple jce, bananas, guava puree, cherries & passion fruit jce.

[d] Values are averages for cherry, lemon, orange & strawberry flavors.

[e] Roundish yellow berries 3/4 inch across, sweet & slightly acid: enclosed within the laternlike, light brown calyx or husk; native to eastern & central North America.

| | KCAL / WT (g) | $H_2O$ (g) / PRO (g) | FAT (g) / CHO (g) | PUFA (g) / SFA (g) | CHOL (mg) / DFIB (g) | A (RE) / A (IU) | C (mg) / B-1 (mg) | B-2 (mg) / NIA (mg) | B-6 (mg) / B-12 (mcg) | FOL (mcg) / PANT (mg) | Na (mg) / K (mg) | Ca (mg) / P (mg) | Mg (mg) / Fe (mg) | Zn (mg) / Cu (mg) | Mn (mg) |
|---|---|---|---|---|---|---|---|---|---|---|---|---|---|---|---|
| **kiwifruit, raw** | 46 | 63.1 | 0.3 | | | 13 | 75 | .04 | | 0 | 4 | 20 | 23 | | |
| *1 med* | 76 | 0.8 | 11.3 | | | 133 | .02 | 0.4 | .00 | | 252 | 31 | .31 | | |
| **kumquats, raw** | 12 | 15.5 | 0.0 | | 0 | 6 | 7 | .02 | | | 1 | 8 | 2 | .02 | .016 |
| *1 med* | 19 | 0.2 | 3.1 | | | 57 | .02 | | .00 | | 37 | 4 | .07 | .020 | |
| **lemon peel** | [a] | 4.9 | 0.0 | 0.0 | | 0 | 8 | .01 | .01 | | 0 | 8 | 1 | | |
| *1 T* | 6 | 0.1 | 1.0 | 0.0 | | 3 | .00 | .00 | .00 | .02 | 10 | 1 | .05 | | |
| **lemon, raw** | 17 | 51.6 | 0.2 | 0.0 | 0 | 2 | 31 | .01 | .05 | 6 | 1 | 15 | | | .04 |
| *1 med* | 58 | 0.6 | 5.4 | 0.0 | | 17 | .02 | .06 | .00 | .11 | 80 | 9 | .35 | .021 | |
| **lime, raw** | 20 | 59.1 | 0.1 | 0.0 | 0 | 1 | 20 | .01 | | 6 | 1 | 22 | | | .07 |
| *1 med* | 67 | 0.5 | 7.1 | 0.0 | | 7 | .02 | 0.1 | .00 | .15 | 68 | 12 | .40 | .044 | |
| **loganberries, frzn** | 80 | 124.4 | 0.5 | | 0 | 5 | 23 | .05 | .10 | 38 | 1 | 38 | 32 | .50 | 1.833 |
| *1 cup* | 147 | 2.2 | 19.1 | | | 52 | .07 | 1.2 | .00 | .36 | 213 | 38 | .94 | .172 | |
| **longans** | | | | | | | | | | | | | | | |
| raw | 60 | 82.8 | 0.1 | | 0 | | 84 | .14 | | | 0 | 1 | 10 | .05 | .052 |
| *31 fruits* | 100 | 1.3 | 15.1 | | | | .03 | 0.3 | .00 | | 266 | 21 | .13 | .169 | |
| dried | 286 | 17.6 | 0.4 | | 0 | 0 | 28 | | | | 48 | 45 | 46 | .22 | .248 |
| *3.5 oz* | 100 | 4.9 | 74.0 | | | 0 | .04 | | .00 | | 658 | 196 | 5.40 | .807 | |
| **loquats, raw** | 47 | 86.7 | 0.2 | 0.1 | 0 | 153 | 1 | .02 | | | 1 | 16 | 13 | .05 | .148 |
| *10 med* | 100 | 0.4 | 12.1 | 0.0 | | 1528 | .02 | 0.2 | .00 | | 266 | 27 | .28 | .040 | |
| **lychees** | | | | | | | | | | | | | | | |
| raw | 66 | 81.8 | 0.4 | | 0 | 0 | 72 | .07 | | | 1 | 5 | 10 | .07 | .055 |
| *10 med* | 100 | 0.8 | 16.5 | | | 0 | .01 | 0.6 | .00 | | 171 | 31 | .31 | .148 | |
| dried | 277 | 22.3 | 1.2 | | 0 | 0 | 183 | .57 | | | 3 | 33 | 42 | .28 | .234 |
| *3.5 oz* | 100 | 3.8 | 70.7 | | | 0 | .01 | 3.1 | .00 | | 1110 | 181 | 1.70 | .631 | |
| **mammy apple, raw** | 51 | 86.2 | 0.5 | | 0 | 23 | 14 | .04 | | | 15 | 11 | | | |
| *1/8 med* | 100 | 0.5 | 12.5 | | | 230 | .02 | 0.4 | .00 | .10 | 47 | 11 | .70 | | |
| **mandarin oranges, cnd** | | | | | | | | | | | | | | | |
| jce pack | 46 | 111.0 | 0.0 | 0.0 | 0 | 106 | 43 | .04 | | | 7 | 14 | 14 | .63 | |
| *1/2 cup* | 124 | 0.8 | 11.9 | 0.0 | | 1056 | .10 | | .00 | | 165 | 13 | .33 | .041 | |
| light syrup | 76 | 104.7 | 0.1 | 0.0 | 0 | 106 | 25 | .06 | | | 8 | 9 | 10 | .30 | |
| *1/2 cup* | 126 | 0.6 | 20.4 | 0.0 | | 1058 | .07 | 0.6 | .00 | | 99 | 12 | .46 | .055 | |
| **mango, raw** | 135 | 169.1 | 0.6 | 0.1 | 0 | 806 | 57 | .12 | .28 | | 4 | 21 | 18 | .07 | .056 |
| *1 med* | 207 | 1.1 | 35.2 | 0.1 | 2.2 | 8060 | .12 | 1.2 | .00 | .33 | 322 | 22 | .26 | .228 | |
| **melon balls (cantaloupe & honeydew),** | 55 | 156.1 | 0.4 | | 0 | 307 | 11 | .04 | .18 | 45 | 53 | 17 | 24 | .29 | .069 |
| **frzn—***1 cup* | 173 | 1.5 | 13.7 | | | 3069 | .29 | 1.1 | .00 | .28 | 484 | 22 | .50 | .104 | |
| **mixed fruit** | | | | | | | | | | | | | | | |
| cnd, heavy syrup[b] | 92 | 103.1 | 0.1 | 0.0 | 0 | 25 | 88[c] | .05 | | | 5 | 1 | 6 | .09 | |
| *1/2 cup* | 128 | 0.5 | 24.0 | 0.0 | | 248 | .02 | 0.8 | .00 | | 108 | 13 | .46 | .074 | |
| dried | 243 | 31.2 | 0.5 | 0.1 | 0 | 244 | 4 | .16 | .16 | | 18 | 38 | 39 | .50 | .227 |
| *3.5 oz* | 100 | 2.5 | 64.1 | 0.0 | | 2442 | .04 | 1.9 | .00 | | 796 | 77 | 2.71 | .385 | |
| dried, diced, Del Monte | 74 | 7.0 | 0.1 | | | | 3 | .10 | | | 26 | 15 | 11 | .11 | |
| *1 oz* | 28 | 0.8 | 19.5 | | | 743 | .01 | 0.4 | | | 292 | 5 | 1.00 | .080 | |
| frzn, in syrup, Birds Eye[d] | 123 | 109.2 | 0.4 | 0.1 | 0 | | 27 | .05 | .03 | 8 | 4 | 9 | 8 | .09 | |
| *1/2 cup* | 142 | 0.8 | 31.0 | 0.1 | | 348 | .03 | 0.6 | .00 | .14 | 161 | 14 | .42 | .058 | |
| frzn, sweetened[d] | 245 | 184.3 | 0.5 | 0.2 | 0 | 81 | 188[c] | .09 | .25 | 9 | 8 | 18 | 14 | .12 | .160 |
| *1 cup* | 250 | 3.5 | 60.6 | 0.1 | | 806 | .04 | 1.0 | .00 | .41 | 327 | 30 | .70 | .085 | |
| **mulberries, raw** | 61 | 122.8 | 0.6 | | 0 | 4 | 51 | .14 | | | 14 | 55 | 25 | | |
| *1 cup* | 140 | 2.0 | 13.7 | | | 35 | .04 | 0.9 | .00 | | 271 | 53 | 2.59 | | |
| **nectarine, raw** | 67 | 117.3 | 0.6 | | 0 | 100 | 7 | .06 | .03 | 5 | 0 | 6 | 11 | .12 | .060 |
| *1 med* | 136 | 1.3 | 16.0 | | | 1001 | .02 | 1.3 | .00 | .22 | 288 | 22 | .21 | .099 | |
| **oheloberries, raw** | 39 | 129.2 | 0.3 | | 0 | 116 | 8 | .05 | | | 2 | 10 | 9 | | |
| *1 cup* | 140 | 0.5 | 9.6 | | | 1162 | .02 | 0.4 | .00 | | 54 | 14 | .13 | | |
| **orange** | | | | | | | | | | | | | | | |
| navel, raw | 65 | 121.5 | 0.1 | 0.0 | 0 | 26 | 80 | .06 | .10 | 47 | 1 | 56 | 15 | .08 | .038 |
| *1 med* | 140 | 1.4 | 16.3 | 0.0 | | 256 | .12 | 0.4 | .00 | .35 | 250 | 27 | .17 | .078 | |
| valencia, raw | 59 | 104.5 | 0.4 | 0.1 | 0 | 28 | 59 | .05 | .08 | 47 | 1 | 48 | 12 | .07 | .028 |
| *1 med* | 121 | 1.3 | 14.4 | 0.0 | | 278 | .11 | 0.3 | .00 | .30 | 217 | 21 | .11 | .045 | |

[a] Cannot be calculated; no digestibility value for peel.
[b] Peaches, pears & pineapple.
[c] Added vitamin C.
[d] Peaches, sweet cherries, red sour cherries, red raspberries, boysenberries & grapes.

|  | KCAL / WT (g) | H₂O (g) / PRO (g) | FAT (g) / CHO (g) | PUFA (g) / SFA (g) | CHOL (mg) / DFIB (g) | A (RE) / A (IU) | C (mg) / B-1 (mg) | B-2 (mg) / NIA (mg) | B-6 (mg) / B-12 (mcg) | FOL (mcg) / PANT (mg) | Na (mg) / K (mg) | Ca (mg) / P (mg) | Mg (mg) / Fe (mg) | Zn (mg) / Cu (mg) | Mn (mg) |
|---|---|---|---|---|---|---|---|---|---|---|---|---|---|---|---|
| **orange peel** | a | 4.4 | 0.0 | 0.0 | 0 | 3 | 8 | .01 | .01 |  | 0 | 10 | 1 |  |  |
| *1 T* | 6 | 0.1 | 1.5 | 0.0 |  | 25 | .01 | 0.1 | .00 | .03 | 13 | 1 | .05 |  |  |
| **papaya, raw** | 117 | 270.0 | 0.4 | 0.1 | 0 | 612 | 188 | .10 | .06 |  | 8 | 72 | 31 | .22 | .033 |
| *1 med* | 304 | 1.9 | 29.8 | 0.1 | 2.8 | 6122 | .08 | 1.0 | .00 | .66 | 780 | 16 | .30 | .049 |  |
| **passion fruit (purple grandilla), purple,** | 18 | 13.1 | 0.1 |  | 0 | 13 | 5 | .02 |  |  | 5 | 2 | 5 |  |  |
| **raw—*1 med*** | 18 | 0.4 | 4.2 |  |  | 126 |  | 0.3 | .00 |  | 63 | 12 | .29 |  |  |
| **peach** |  |  |  |  |  |  |  |  |  |  |  |  |  |  |  |
| raw | 37 | 76.3 | 0.1 | 0.0 | 0 | 47 | 6 | .04 | .02 | 3 | 0 | 5 | 6 | .12 | .041 |
| *1 med* | 87 | 0.6 | 9.7 | 0.0 | 0.5 | 465 | .02 | 0.9 | .00 | .15 | 171 | 11 | .10 | .059 |  |
| cnd, heavy syrup | 190 | 203.0 | 0.3 | 0.1 | 0 | 85 | 7 | .06 | .05 | 8 | 16 | 8 | 13 | .22 | .115 |
| *1 cup* | 256 | 1.2 | 51.0 | 0.0 |  | 849 | .03 | 1.6 | .00 | .13 | 235 | 29 | .69 | .131 |  |
| cnd, heavy syrup, spiced | 66 | 69.7 | 0.1 | 0.0 | 0 | 28 | 5 | .03 |  |  | 3 | 5 | 6 | .07 |  |
| *1 med* | 88 | 0.4 | 17.7 | 0.0 |  | 279 | .01 | 0.5 | .00 |  | 75 | 8 | .25 | .086 |  |
| cnd, jce pack | 109 | 217.0 | 0.1 | 0.0 | 0 | 95 | 9 | .04 |  |  | 11 | 15 | 18 | .26 |  |
| *1 cup* | 248 | 1.6 | 28.7 | 0.0 | 1.1 | 945 | .02 | 1.4 | .00 |  | 317 | 43 | .66 | .124 |  |
| cnd, light syrup | 136 | 212.6 | 0.1 | 0.0 | 0 | 89 | 6 | .06 | .05 | 8 | 13 | 9 | 12 | .22 | .115 |
| *1 cup* | 251 | 1.1 | 36.5 | 0.0 |  | 888 | .02 | 1.5 | .00 | .13 | 244 | 27 | .90 | .131 |  |
| cnd, water pack | 58 | 227.2 | 0.1 | 0.0 | 0 | 130 | 7 | .05 | .05 | 8 | 8 | 6 | 12 | .22 | .117 |
| *1 cup* | 244 | 1.1 | 14.9 | 0.0 |  | 1298 | .02 | 1.3 | .00 | .12 | 241 | 25 | .77 | .132 |  |
| dried, sulfured | 311 | 41.3 | 1.0 | 0.5 | 0 | 281 | 6 | .28 | .09 |  | 9 | 37 | 54 | .75 | .397 |
| *10 halves* | 130 | 4.7 | 79.7 | 0.1 |  | 2812 | .00 | 5.7 | .00 |  | 1295 | 155 | 5.28 | .473 |  |
| frzn, sweetened | 235 | 186.8 | 0.3 | 0.2 | 0 | 71 | 235[b] | .09 | .05 | 24 | 16 | 6 | 12 | .13 | .073 |
| *1 cup* | 250 | 1.6 | 59.9 | 0.0 |  | 709 | .03 | 1.6 | .00 | .33 | 325 | 28 | .93 | .060 |  |
| **pear** |  |  |  |  |  |  |  |  |  |  |  |  |  |  |  |
| raw | 98 | 139.1 | 0.7 | 0.2 | 0 | 3 | 7 | .07 | .03 | 12 | 1 | 19 | 9 | .20 | .126 |
| *1 med* | 166 | 0.7 | 25.1 | 0.0 | 4.1 | 33 | .03 | 0.2 | .00 | .12 | 208 | 18 | .41 | .188 |  |
| cnd, heavy pack | 188 | 204.9 | 0.3 | 0.1 | 0 | 0 | 3 | .06 | .04 | 3 | 13 | 12 | 11 | .21 | .082 |
| *1 cup* | 255 | 0.5 | 48.9 | 0.0 |  | 0 | .03 | 0.6 | .00 | .06 | 165 | 17 | .56 | .125 |  |
| cnd, jce pack | 123 | 214.5 | 0.2 | 0.0 | 0 | 1 | 4 | .03 |  |  | 10 | 21 | 17 | .22 |  |
| *1 cup* | 248 | 0.9 | 32.1 | 0.0 | 2.3 | 14 | .03 | 0.5 | .00 |  | 238 | 29 | .71 | .131 |  |
| cnd, light syrup | 144 | 212.0 | 0.1 | 0.0 | 0 | 0 | 2 | .04 | .04 | 3 | 13 | 13 | 11 | .21 | .083 |
| *1 cup* | 251 | 0.5 | 38.1 | 0.0 |  | 0 | .03 | 0.4 | .00 | .06 | 165 | 17 | .70 | .123 |  |
| cnd, water pack | 71 | 224.0 | 0.1 | 0.0 | 0 | 0 | 3 | .02 | .03 | 3 | 5 | 9 | 9 | .21 | .083 |
| *1 cup* | 244 | 0.5 | 19.1 | 0.0 |  | 0 | .02 | 0.1 | .00 | .05 | 130 | 17 | .52 | .124 |  |
| dried, sulfured | 459 | 46.7 | 1.1 | 0.3 | 0 | 1 | 12 | .25 |  |  | 10 | 59 | 58 | .68 | .572 |
| *10 halves* | 175 | 3.3 | 122.0 | 0.1 |  | 6 | .01 | 2.4 | .00 |  | 932 | 103 | 3.68 | .649 |  |
| **persimmon, raw** | 32 | 16.1 | 0.1 |  | 0 |  | 17 |  |  |  | 0 | 7 |  |  |  |
| *1 med* | 25 | 0.2 | 8.4 |  |  |  |  |  | .00 |  | 78 | 7 | .63 |  |  |
| **persimmon, japanese** |  |  |  |  |  |  |  |  |  |  |  |  |  |  |  |
| raw | 118 | 134.9 | 0.3 |  | 0 | 364 | 13 | .03 |  | 13 | 3 | 13 | 15 | .18 | .596 |
| *1 med* | 168 | 1.0 | 31.2 |  |  | 3640 | .05 | 0.2 | .00 |  | 270 | 28 | .26 | .190 |  |
| dried | 93 | 7.8 | 0.2 |  | 0 | 19 | 0 | .01 |  |  | 1 | 8 | 11 | .14 | .473 |
| *1 med* | 34 | 0.5 | 25.0 |  |  | 190 |  | 0.1 | .00 |  | 273 | 27 | .25 | .150 |  |
| **pineapple** |  |  |  |  |  |  |  |  |  |  |  |  |  |  |  |
| raw | 77 | 135.1 | 0.7 | 0.2 | 0 | 4 | 24 | .06 | .14 | 16 | 1 | 11 | 21 | .12 | 2.556 |
| *1 cup pieces* | 155 | 0.6 | 19.2 | 0.0 | 2.4 | 35 | .14 | 0.7 | .00 | .25 | 175 | 11 | .57 | .171 |  |
| cnd, heavy syrup | 199 | 201.4 | 0.3 | 0.1 | 0 | 4 | 19 | .06 | .19 | 12 | 3 | 35 | 40 | .29 | 2.754 |
| *1 cup pieces* | 255 | 0.9 | 51.5 | 0.0 |  | 37 | .23 | 0.7 | .00 | .26 | 264 | 17 | .98 | .258 |  |
| cnd, jce pack | 150 | 208.8 | 0.2 | 0.1 | 0 | 9 | 24 | .05 |  |  | 4 | 34 | 35 | .24 |  |
| *1 cup pieces* | 250 | 1.0 | 39.2 | 0.0 | 1.9 | 95 | .24 | 0.7 | .00 |  | 304 | 16 | .70 | .215 |  |
| **pitanga, raw** | 57 | 157.1 | 0.7 |  | 0 | 260 | 46 | .07 |  |  | 5 | 16 | 21 |  |  |
| *1 cup* | 173 | 1.4 | 13.0 |  |  | 2595 | .05 | 0.5 | .00 |  | 178 | 19 | .35 |  |  |
| **plantain, ckd** | 179 | 103.6 | 0.3 |  | 0 | 140 | 17 | .08 | .37 | 40 | 8 | 3 | 49 | .20 |  |
| *1 cup slices* | 154 | 1.2 | 48.0 |  |  | 1400 | .07 | 1.2 | .00 | .36 | 716 | 43 | .89 | .102 |  |
| **plum** |  |  |  |  |  |  |  |  |  |  |  |  |  |  |  |
| raw | 36 | 56.2 | 0.4 | 0.1 | 0 | 21 | 6 | .06 | .05 | 1 | 0 | 2 | 4 | .06 | .032 |
| *1 med* | 66 | 0.5 | 8.6 | 0.0 |  | 213 | .03 | 0.3 | .00 | .12 | 113 | 7 | .07 | .028 |  |

[a] Cannot be calculated; no digestibility value for peel.　　[b] Contains added ascorbic acid.

| | KCAL | H₂O (g) | FAT (g) | PUFA (g) | CHOL (mg) | A (RE) | C (mg) | B-2 (mg) | B-6 (mg) | FOL (mcg) | Na (mg) | Ca (mg) | Mg (mg) | Zn (mg) | Mn (mg) |
|---|---|---|---|---|---|---|---|---|---|---|---|---|---|---|---|
| | WT (g) | PRO (g) | CHO (g) | SFA (g) | DFIB (g) | A (IU) | B-1 (mg) | NIA (mg) | B-12 (mcg) | PANT (mg) | K (mg) | P (mg) | Fe (mg) | Cu (mg) | |
| heavy syrup | 119 | 101.2 | 0.1 | 0.0 | 0 | 34 | 1 | .05 | .04 | 3 | 26 | 12 | 7 | .10 | .041 |
| *3 plums* | 133 | 0.5 | 30.9 | 0.0 | | 344 | .02 | 0.4 | .00 | .10 | 121 | 17 | 1.12 | .049 | |
| cnd, jce pack | 55 | 79.8 | 0.0 | 0.0 | 0 | 96 | 3 | .06 | | | 1 | 9 | 8 | .10 | |
| *3 plums* | 95 | 0.5 | 14.4 | 0.0 | 0.4 | 958 | .02 | 0.5 | .00 | | 147 | 15 | .32 | .051 | |
| **pomegranate, raw** | 104 | 124.7 | 0.5 | | 0 | | 9 | .05 | .16 | | 5 | 5 | | | |
| *1 med* | 154 | 1.5 | 26.4 | | | | .05 | 0.5 | .00 | .92 | 399 | 12 | .46 | | |
| **pricklypear, raw** | 42 | 90.2 | 0.5 | | 0 | 5 | 14 | .06 | | | 6 | 58 | 88 | | |
| *1 med* | 103 | 0.8 | 9.9 | | | 53 | .01 | 0.5 | .00 | | 226 | 25 | .31 | | |
| **prunes** | | | | | | | | | | | | | | | |
| cnd, heavy syrup | 90 | 60.8 | 0.2 | 0.0 | 0 | 69 | 2 | .11 | | | 2 | 15 | 13 | .16 | .084 |
| *5 prunes* | 86 | 0.8 | 23.9 | 0.0 | | 686 | .03 | 0.7 | .00 | | 194 | 22 | .35 | .101 | |
| dried | 201 | 27.2 | 0.4 | 0.1 | 0 | 167 | 3 | .14 | .22 | 3 | 3 | 43 | 38 | .45 | .185 |
| *10 prunes* | 84 | 2.2 | 52.7 | 0.0 | | 1669 | .07 | 1.6 | .00 | .39 | 626 | 66 | 2.08 | .361 | |
| dried, ckd | 113 | 73.9 | 0.2 | 0.0 | 0 | 32 | 3 | .11 | .23 | 0 | 2 | 24 | 21 | .25 | .104 |
| *1/2 cup* | 106 | 1.2 | 29.8 | 0.0 | | 324 | .03 | 0.8 | .00 | .11 | 354 | 37 | 1.18 | .205 | |
| **pummelo, raw** | 71 | 169.3 | 0.1 | | 0 | 0 | 116 | .05 | .07 | | 2 | 7 | 12 | .15 | .032 |
| *1 cup pieces* | 190 | 1.4 | 18.3 | | | 0 | .07 | 0.4 | .00 | | 411 | 32 | .22 | .091 | |
| **quince, raw** | 53 | 77.1 | 0.1 | 0.0 | 0 | 4 | 14 | .03 | .04 | | 4 | 10 | 7 | | |
| *1 med* | 92 | 0.4 | 14.1 | 0.0 | | 38 | .02 | 0.2 | .00 | .08 | 181 | 16 | .64 | .120 | |
| **raisins** | | | | | | | | | | | | | | | |
| golden seedless | 302 | 14.9 | 0.5 | 0.1 | 0 | 4 | 3 | .19 | .32 | 3 | 12 | 53 | 35 | .32 | .308 |
| *2/3 cup* | 100 | 3.4 | 79.5 | 0.2 | | 44 | .01 | 1.1 | .00 | .14 | 746 | 115 | 1.79 | .363 | |
| seeded | 296 | 16.6 | 0.5 | 0.2 | 0 | 0 | 5 | .18 | .19 | 3 | 28 | 28 | 30 | .18 | .267 |
| *2/3 cup* | 100 | 2.5 | 78.5 | 0.2 | | 0 | .11 | 1.1 | .00 | | 825 | 75 | 2.59 | .302 | |
| seedless | 300 | 15.4 | 0.5 | 0.1 | 0 | 1 | 3 | .09 | .25 | 3 | 12 | 49 | 33 | .27 | .308 |
| *2/3 cup* | 100 | 3.2 | 79.1 | 0.2 | | 8 | .16 | 0.8 | .00 | .05 | 751 | 97 | 2.08 | .309 | |
| w/ van yogurt coating, Del Monte | 134 | 0.8 | 5.5 | | | | 1 | .02 | | | 27 | 51 | 10 | .15 | |
| *1 oz* | 28 | 1.6 | 19.5 | | | 3 | .03 | 0.0 | | | 239 | 38 | .15 | .032 | |
| **raspberries** | | | | | | | | | | | | | | | |
| raw | 61 | 106.5 | 0.7 | 0.4 | 0 | 16 | 31 | .11 | .07 | | 0 | 27 | 22 | .57 | 1.246 |
| *1 cup* | 123 | 1.1 | 14.2 | 0.0 | 5.8 | 160 | .04 | 1.1 | .00 | .30 | 187 | 15 | .70 | .091 | |
| cnd, heavy syrup | 117 | 96.4 | 0.2 | 0.1 | 0 | 4 | 11 | .04 | .05 | 13 | 4 | 14 | 16 | .20 | .298 |
| *1/2 cup* | 128 | 1.1 | 29.9 | 0.0 | | 43 | .03 | 0.6 | .00 | .31 | 120 | 12 | .54 | .073 | |
| frzn, in lite syrup, Birds Eye | 99 | 115.7 | 0.5 | 0.3 | 0 | | 23 | .08 | .05 | 24 | 0 | 20 | 17 | .43 | |
| *1/2 cup* | 142 | 0.8 | 24.6 | 0.0 | 4.3 | 120 | .03 | 0.8 | .00 | .22 | 141 | 11 | .54 | .071 | |
| frzn, sweetened | 103 | 72.8 | 0.2 | 0.1 | 0 | 6 | 17 | .05 | .03 | 26 | 1 | 15 | 13 | .18 | .650 |
| *2/5 cup* | 100 | 0.7 | 26.2 | 0.0 | | 60 | .02 | 0.2 | .00 | .15 | 114 | 17 | .65 | .110 | |
| **rose apple, raw** | 25 | 93.0 | 0.3 | | 0 | 34 | 22 | .03 | | | 0 | 29 | 5 | .06 | .029 |
| *3.5 oz* | 100 | 0.6 | 5.7 | | | 339 | .02 | 0.8 | .00 | | 123 | 8 | .07 | .016 | |
| **roselle, raw** | 28 | 49.4 | 0.4 | | 0 | 16 | 7 | .02 | | | 3 | 123 | 29 | | |
| *1 cup* | 57 | 0.6 | 6.5 | | | 163 | .01 | 0.2 | .00 | | 118 | 21 | .84 | | |
| **sapodilla, raw** | 140 | 132.6 | 1.9 | | 0 | 10 | 25 | .03 | .06 | | 20 | 36 | | | |
| *1 med* | 170 | 0.7 | 33.9 | | 9.0 | 102 | | 0.3 | .00 | .43 | 328 | 20 | 1.36 | | |
| **sapote, raw** | 301 | 140.5 | 1.4 | | 0 | 92 | 45 | .05 | | | 21 | 88 | 68 | | |
| *1 med* | 225 | 4.8 | 76.0 | | | 923 | .02 | 4.1 | .00 | | 773 | 63 | 2.25 | | |
| **soursop, raw** | 150 | 182.6 | 0.7 | | 0 | 1 | 46 | .11 | .13 | | 31 | 32 | 46 | | |
| *1 cup* | 225 | 2.3 | 37.9 | | | 5 | .16 | 2.0 | .00 | .57 | 626 | 61 | 1.35 | | |
| **strawberries** | | | | | | | | | | | | | | | |
| raw | 45 | 136.4 | 0.6 | 0.3 | 0 | 4 | 85 | .10 | .09 | 26 | 2 | 21 | 16 | .19 | .432 |
| *1 cup* | 149 | 0.9 | 10.5 | 0.0 | 2.8 | 41 | .03 | 0.3 | .00 | .51 | 247 | 28 | .57 | .073 | |
| frzn, in lite syrup, Birds Eye | 87 | 118.8 | 0.4 | 0.2 | 0 | | 64 | .07 | .07 | 20 | 1 | 16 | 11 | .15 | |
| *1/2 cup* | 142 | 0.7 | 21.6 | 0.2 | 2.2 | 31 | .02 | 0.3 | .00 | .39 | 189 | 22 | .44 | .058 | |
| frzn, sweetened | 245 | 186.6 | 0.3 | 0.2 | 0 | 6 | 106 | .13 | .08 | 38 | 8 | 28 | 18 | .14 | .638 |
| *1 cup* | 255 | 1.4 | 66.1 | 0.0 | | 61 | .04 | 1.02 | .00 | .28 | 249 | 32 | 1.49 | .051 | |
| frzn, unsweetened | 52 | 134.1 | 0.2 | 0.1 | 0 | 7 | 61 | .06 | .04 | 25 | 3 | 23 | 16 | .19 | .432 |
| *1 cup* | 149 | 0.6 | 13.6 | 0.0 | | 66 | .03 | 0.7 | .00 | .16 | 220 | 20 | 1.12 | .073 | |
| **sugar apple, raw** | 146 | 113.5 | 0.5 | | 0 | 1 | 56 | .18 | .31 | | 15 | 37 | 33 | | |
| *1 med* | 155 | 3.2 | 36.6 | | | 9 | .17 | 1.4 | .00 | .35 | 384 | 50 | .93 | | |

| | KCAL | H₂O (g) | FAT (g) | PUFA (g) | CHOL (mg) | A (RE) | C (mg) | B-2 (mg) | B-6 (mg) | FOL (mcg) | Na (mg) | Ca (mg) | Mg (mg) | Zn (mg) | Mn (mg) |
|---|---|---|---|---|---|---|---|---|---|---|---|---|---|---|---|
| | WT (g) | PRO (g) | CHO (g) | SFA (g) | DFIB (g) | A (IU) | B-1 (mg) | NIA (mg) | B-12 (mcg) | PANT (mg) | K (mg) | P (mg) | Fe (mg) | Cu (mg) | |
| tamarind, raw | 287 | 37.7 | 0.7 | 0.1 | 0 | 4 | 4 | .18 | .08 | | 33 | 89 | 110 | | |
| *1 cup* | 120 | 3.4 | 75.0 | 0.3 | | 36 | .51 | 2.3 | .00 | .17 | 753 | 136 | 3.36 | | |
| tangerine, raw | 37 | 73.6 | 0.2 | 0.0 | 0 | 77 | 26 | .02 | .06 | 17 | 1 | 12 | 10 | | .027 |
| *1 med* | 84 | 0.5 | 9.4 | 0.0 | | 773 | .09 | 0.1 | .00 | .17 | 132 | 8 | .09 | .024 | |
| watermelon, raw | 50 | 146.4 | 0.7 | | 0 | 58 | 15 | .03 | .23 | 3 | 3 | 13 | 17 | .11 | .059 |
| *1 cup* | 160 | 1.0 | 11.5 | | 0.3 | 585 | .13 | 0.3 | .00 | .34 | 186 | 14 | .28 | .051 | |

# 16. GRAIN FRACTIONS

| | KCAL | H₂O | FAT | PUFA | CHOL | A | C | B-2 | B-6 | FOL | Na | Ca | Mg | Zn | Mn |
|---|---|---|---|---|---|---|---|---|---|---|---|---|---|---|---|
| **barley, pearled** | | | | | | | | | | | | | | | |
| light | 698 | 22.2 | 2.0 | | | | 0 | .10 | | | 6 | 32 | | | |
| *1 cup* | 200 | 16.4 | 157.6 | | | 0 | .24 | 6.2 | | | 320 | 378 | 4.00 | | |
| med, Scotch Brand | 172 | 5.0 | 0.5 | | | | | .06 | .13 | 32 | 5 | 11 | 34 | .00 | .000 |
| *1/4 cup* | 48 | 5.5 | 36.3 | | | 11 | .11 | 2.2 | .00 | .00 | 130 | 113 | 1.24 | .210 | |
| pot/scotch | 696 | 21.6 | 2.2 | | | | 0 | .14 | | | | 68 | | | |
| *1 cup* | 200 | 19.2 | 154.4 | | | 0 | .42 | 7.4 | | | 592 | 580 | 5.40 | | |
| quick, Scotch Brand | 172 | 5.0 | 0.5 | | | | | .06 | .13 | 32 | 5 | 11 | 34 | .00 | .000 |
| *1/4 cup* | 48 | 5.5 | 36.3 | | | 11 | .11 | 2.2 | .00 | .00 | 130 | 113 | 1.24 | .210 | |
| **bisquick, General Mills** | 240 | | 8.0 | | | | | | | | 700 | | | | |
| *2 oz* | 57 | 4.0 | 37.0 | | | | | | | | 80 | | | | |
| **buckwheat flour** | | | | | | | | | | | | | | | |
| dark | 326 | 11.8 | 2.5 | | | | 0 | .15 | | | | 32 | | | |
| *1 cup* | 98 | 11.5 | 70.6 | | | 0 | .57 | 2.8 | | | | 340 | 2.70 | | |
| light | 340 | 11.8 | 1.2 | | | | 0 | .04 | | | | 11 | | | |
| *1 cup* | 98 | 6.3 | 77.9 | | | 0 | .08 | 0.4 | | | 314 | 86 | 1.00 | | |
| **carob (St. Johnsbread) flour** | 185 | 3.7 | 0.7 | 0.2 | 0 | 1 | 0 | .48 | .38 | 30 | 36 | 359 | 56 | .94 | .523 |
| *1 cup* | 103 | 4.8 | 91.6 | 0.1 | 10.9 | 15 | .06 | 2.0 | .00 | .05 | 852 | 81 | 3.03 | .588 | |
| **corn flour** | 431 | 14.0 | 3.0 | | | | 0 | .07 | | | 1 | 7 | | | |
| *1 cup* | 117 | 9.1 | 89.9 | 0.3 | | 400ᵃ | .23 | 1.6 | | | | 92 | 2.10 | | |
| **corn germ, Ener-G Foods** | 490 | | 25.0 | | | | 4 | .75 | 1.41 | 90 | 31 | 0 | 672 | 10.60 | |
| *1 cup* | 100 | 17.0 | 42.0 | | 20.8 | 60 | 1.70 | 2.2 | | | 1420 | 1587 | 7.80 | .500 | |
| **corn meal mix** | | | | | | | | | | | | | | | |
| white, bolted, Aunt Jemima | 99 | 2.9 | 0.7 | | | | | .14 | .14 | 19 | 337 | 60 | 21 | .00 | .000 |
| *1/6 cup (1 oz)* | 28 | 2.4 | 20.8 | | | 0 | .22 | 1.6 | .00 | .00 | 68 | 181 | 1.08 | .040 | |
| white, buttermilk, self-rising, Aunt Jemima—*3 T (1 oz)* | 101 | 2.6 | 1.1 | | | | | .14 | .12 | 10 | 439 | 60 | 25 | 1.00 | .000 |
| | 28 | 2.5 | 20.2 | | | 0 | .22 | 1.6 | .00 | PANT .00 | 87 | 207 | 1.08 | .080 | |
| yellow, bolted, Aunt Jemima | 97 | 2.9 | 0.4 | | | | | .14 | .07 | 14 | 369 | 60 | 10 | .00 | .000 |
| *1/6 cup (1 oz)* | 28 | 2.4 | 20.9 | | | 81 | .22 | 1.6 | .00 | .00 | 40 | 156 | 1.08 | .020 | |
| **corn meal, white, bolted** | 442 | 14.6 | 4.1 | | | | 0 | .10 | | | 1 | 21 | | | |
| *1 cupᵇ* | 122 | 11.0 | 90.9 | 0.5 | | 0 | .37 | 2.3 | | | 303 | 272 | 2.20 | | |
| enr, self-rising, Aunt Jemima | 99 | 3.0 | 0.9 | | | | | .07 | .15 | 16 | 382 | 109 | 24 | 1.00 | .000 |
| *1/6 cup (1 oz)* | 28 | 2.3 | 20.4 | | | 0 | .12 | 1.0 | .00 | .00 | 78 | 207 | .81 | .040 | |
| **corn meal, white, degermed** | | | | | | | | | | | | | | | |
| enr | 502 | 16.6 | 1.7 | | | | 0 | .36 | | | 1 | 8 | | | |
| *1 cup* | 138 | 10.9 | 108.2 | | | 0 | .61 | 4.8 | | | 166 | 137 | 4.00 | | |
| enr, ckd | 120 | 210.5 | 0.5 | | | | 0 | .10 | | | 264 | 2 | | | |
| *1 cup* | 240 | 2.6 | 25.7 | | | 0 | .14 | 1.2 | | | 38 | 34 | 1.00 | | |
| enr, Quaker/Aunt Jemima | 102 | 3.0 | 0.5 | | | | | .07 | .10 | 15 | 1 | 1 | 12 | .00 | .000 |
| *3 T (1 oz)* | 28 | 2.4 | 22.2 | | | 0 | .12 | 1.0 | .00 | .00 | 51 | 37 | .81 | .020 | |
| enr, self-rising, Aunt Jemima | 98 | 3.0 | 0.5 | | | | | .07 | .11 | 9 | 381 | 109 | 14 | .00 | .000 |
| *1/6 cup (1 oz)* | 28 | 2.3 | 21.1 | | | 0 | .12 | 1.0 | .00 | .00 | 45 | 179 | .81 | .040 | |
| unenr | 502 | 16.6 | 1.7 | | | | 0 | .07 | | | 1 | 8 | | | |
| *1 cup* | 138 | 10.9 | 108.2 | | | 0 | .19 | 1.4 | | | 166 | 137 | 1.50 | | |

ᵃ For yellow varieties; white varieties have only a trace of Vit A activity.    ᵇ Nearly whole grain.

| | KCAL / WT (g) | H₂O (g) / PRO (g) | FAT (g) / CHO (g) | PUFA (g) / SFA (g) | CHOL (mg) / DFIB (g) | A (RE) / A (IU) | C (mg) / B-1 (mg) | B-2 (mg) / NIA (mg) | B-6 (mg) / B-12 (mcg) | FOL (mcg) / PANT (mg) | Na (mg) / K (mg) | Ca (mg) / P (mg) | Mg (mg) / Fe (mg) | Zn (mg) / Cu (mg) | Mn (mg) |
|---|---|---|---|---|---|---|---|---|---|---|---|---|---|---|---|
| unenr, ckd | 120 | 210.5 | 0.5 | | | | 0 | .02 | | | 264 | 2 | | | |
| *1 cup* | 240 | 2.6 | 25.7 | | | 0 | .05 | 0.2 | | | 38 | 34 | .50 | | |
| unenr, self-rising | 491 | 15.9 | 1.6 | | | | 0 | .07 | | | 1946 | 409 | | | |
| *1 cup* | 141 | 10.6 | 106.2 | | | 0 | .18 | 1.3 | | | 159 | 739 | 1.40 | | |
| **corn meal, white, whole ground** | 433 | 14.6 | 4.8 | | | | 0 | .13 | | | 1 | 24 | | | |
| *1 cup* | 122 | 11.2 | 89.9 | 0.5 | | 0 | .46 | 2.4 | | | 346 | 312 | 2.90 | | |
| self-rising | 465 | 15.1 | 4.3 | | | | 0 | .11 | | | 1849 | 402 | | | |
| *1 cup* | 134 | 11.4 | 95.9 | 0.5 | | 0 | .38 | 2.4 | | | 314 | 859 | 2.30 | | |
| **corn meal, yellow, bolted**[a] | 442 | 14.6 | 4.1 | | | | 0 | .10 | | | 1 | 21 | | | |
| *1 cup* | 122 | 11.0 | 90.0 | 0.5 | | 590 | .37 | 2.3 | | | 303 | 272 | 2.20 | | |
| **corn meal, yellow, degermed** | | | | | | | | | | | | | | | |
| enr | 502 | 16.6 | 1.7 | | | | 0 | .36 | | | 1 | 8 | | | |
| *1 cup* | 138 | 10.9 | 108.2 | | | 610 | .61 | 4.8 | | | 166 | 137 | 4.00 | | |
| enr, ckd | 120 | 210.5 | 0.5 | | | | 0 | .10 | | | 264 | 2 | | | |
| *1 cup* | 240 | 2.6 | 25.7 | | | 140 | .14 | 1.2 | | | 38 | 34 | 1.00 | | |
| enr, Quaker/Aunt Jemima | 102 | 3.0 | 0.5 | | | | | .07 | .10 | 15 | 1 | 1 | 12 | .00 | .000 |
| *3 T (1 oz)* | 28 | 2.4 | 22.2 | | | 115 | .12 | 1.0 | .00 | .00 | 51 | 37 | .81 | .020 | |
| unenr | 502 | 16.6 | 1.7 | | | | 0 | .07 | | | 1 | 8 | | | |
| *1 cup* | 138 | 10.9 | 108.2 | | | 610 | .19 | 1.4 | | | 166 | 137 | 1.50 | | |
| unenr, ckd | 120 | 210.5 | 0.5 | | | | 0 | .02 | | | 264 | 2 | | | |
| *1 cup* | 240 | 2.6 | 25.7 | | | 140 | .05 | 0.2 | | | 38 | 34 | .50 | | |
| unenr, self-rising | 491 | 15.9 | 1.6 | | | | 0 | .07 | | | 1946 | 409 | | | |
| *1 cup* | 141 | 10.6 | 106.2 | | | 590 | .18 | 1.3 | | | 159 | 739 | 1.40 | | |
| **corn meal, yellow, whole ground** | 433 | 14.6 | 4.8 | | | | 0 | .13 | | | 1 | 24 | | | |
| *1 cup* | 122 | 11.2 | 89.9 | 0.5 | | 620 | .46 | 2.4 | | | 346 | 312 | 2.90 | | |
| self-rising | 465 | 15.1 | 4.3 | | | | 0 | .11 | | | 1849 | 402 | | | |
| *1 cup* | 134 | 11.4 | 95.9 | 0.5 | | 600 | .38 | 2.4 | | | 314 | 859 | 2.30 | | |
| **masa harina de maiz, Quaker** | 137 | 3.2 | 1.5 | | | | | .29 | .19 | 17 | 2 | 77 | 41 | 1.00 | .000 |
| *1/3 cup* | 37 | 3.5 | 27.4 | | | 0 | .52 | 3.5 | .00 | .00 | 115 | 86 | 2.93 | .080 | |
| **masa trigo, Quaker** | 149 | 3.7 | 4.0 | | | | | .24 | .01 | 29 | 794 | 66 | 8 | .00 | .000 |
| *1/3 cup* | 37 | 3.5 | 24.7 | | | 0 | .39 | 3.1 | .00 | .00 | 36 | 77 | 2.60 | .040 | |
| **millet, proso (broomcorn/hogmillet),** | 327 | 11.8 | 2.9 | | | | 0 | .38 | | | | 20 | 162 | | |
| **whole grain**—*3.5 oz* | 100 | 9.9 | 72.9 | | | 0 | .73 | 2.3 | | | 430 | 311 | 6.80 | | |
| **oat bran, Quaker** | 110 | 2.6 | 2.5 | | | | | .12 | .04 | 20 | 1 | 20 | 67 | 1.00 | 2.000 |
| *1/3 cup (1 oz)* | 28 | 5.7 | 16.2 | | | 0 | .33 | .23 | .00 | .00 | 170 | 200 | 1.63 | .080 | |
| **potato flour** | 316 | 6.8 | 0.7 | 0.3 | 0 | | 17 | .13 | | | 31 | 30 | | | |
| *1/2 cup* | 90 | 7.2 | 71.9 | 0.2 | | 0 | .38 | 3.1 | .00 | | 1429 | 160 | 15.48 | | |
| **rice bran, Ener-G Foods** | 438 | 5.2 | 21.7 | | | | 0 | .26 | | | 6 | 355 | | 5.98 | |
| *3.5 oz* | 100 | 11.9 | 45.6 | | | 0 | 2.21 | 31.2 | | | 1370 | | 7.88 | .750 | |
| **rice flour, Ener-G Foods** | 398 | 13.6 | 0.9 | | | | 0 | .59 | | | 45 | 13 | 60 | | |
| *1 cup* | 113 | 7.1 | 91.0 | | | 0 | .52 | 2.9 | | | 168 | 249 | 3.28 | | |
| **rice polish, Ener-G Foods** | 220 | 5.5 | 7.0 | | | | 0 | .22 | | | 21 | 34 | | | |
| *1/2 cup* | 56 | 7.0 | 33.0 | | | 0 | 1.79 | 0.2 | | | 829 | | .08 | | |
| **rye & wheat flour, bohemian style,** | 400 | 12.9 | 1.5 | | | | 0 | .29 | | | 2 | 24 | | | |
| **Pillsbury**—*1 cup* | 112 | 12.3 | 84.4 | | | 0 | .56 | 4.4 | | | 167 | 196 | 4.03 | | |
| **rye flour** | | | | | | | | | | | | | | | |
| dark | 419 | 14.1 | 3.3 | | | | 0 | .28 | | | 1 | 69 | | | |
| *1 cup* | 128 | 20.9 | 87.2 | | | 0 | .78 | 3.5 | | | 1101 | 686 | 5.80 | | |
| light | 364 | 11.2 | 1.0 | | | | 0 | .07 | | | 1 | 22 | | | |
| *1 cup* | 102 | 9.6 | 79.5 | | | 0 | .15 | 0.6 | | | 159 | 189 | 1.10 | | |
| med, Pillsbury's Best | 400 | 11.1 | 2.2 | | | | 0 | .11 | | | 5 | 22 | | | |
| *1 cup* | 111 | 12.2 | 81.0 | | | 0 | .33 | 1.3 | | | 322 | 152 | 2.78 | | |
| **sorghum grain** | 332 | 11.0 | 3.3 | | | | 0 | .15 | | | | 28 | | | |
| *3.5 oz* | 100 | 11.0 | 73.0 | 0.0 | | 0 | .38 | 3.9 | | | 350 | 287 | 4.40 | | |

[a] Nearly whole grain.

| | KCAL | H₂O (g) | FAT (g) | PUFA (g) | CHOL (mg) | A (RE) | C (mg) | B-2 (mg) | B-6 (mg) | FOL (mcg) | Na (mg) | Ca (mg) | Mg (mg) | Zn (mg) | Mn (mg) |
| --- | --- | --- | --- | --- | --- | --- | --- | --- | --- | --- | --- | --- | --- | --- | --- |
| | WT (g) | PRO (g) | CHO (g) | SFA (g) | DFIB (g) | A (IU) | B-1 (mg) | NIA (mg) | B-12 (mcg) | PANT (mg) | K (mg) | P (mg) | Fe (mg) | Cu (mg) | |
| **soybean flour** | | | | | | | | | | | | | | | |
| defatted | 327 | 7.3 | 1.2 | 0.5 | 0 | 4 | 0 | .25 | .57 | 305 | 20 | 241 | 290 | 2.46 | 3.018 |
| *1 cup* | 100 | 51.5 | 33.9 | 0.1 | | 40 | .70 | 2.6 | .00 | 2.00 | 2384 | 674 | 9.24 | 4.065 | |
| full fat | 368 | 4.4 | 17.6 | 9.9 | 0 | 10 | 0 | .99 | .39 | 293 | 11 | 175 | 364 | 3.33 | 1.934 |
| *1 cup* | 85 | 32.1 | 27.1 | 2.5 | | 102 | .49 | 3.7 | .00 | 1.35 | 2138 | 420 | 5.42 | 2.482 | |
| full fat, roasted | 373 | 3.2 | 18.6 | 10.5 | 0 | 9 | 0 | .80 | .30 | 193 | 11 | 160 | 314 | 3.04 | 1.765 |
| *1 cup* | 85 | 32.4 | 25.8 | 2.7 | | 93 | .35 | 2.8 | .00 | 1.03 | 1734 | 405 | 4.94 | 1.888 | |
| low fat | 326 | 2.4 | 5.9 | 3.3 | 0 | 3 | 0 | .25 | .46 | 361 | 16 | 165 | 202 | 1.04 | 2.710 |
| *1 cup* | 88 | 44.8 | 29.6 | 0.9 | | 35 | .33 | 1.9 | .00 | 1.60 | 2262 | 522 | 5.27 | 4.470 | |
| **soy meal, defatted** | 411 | 8.5 | 2.9 | 1.3 | 0 | 5 | 0 | .31 | .69 | 369 | 3 | 297 | 373 | 6.17 | 4.636 |
| *1 cup* | 122 | 60.0 | 43.8 | 0.3 | 14.0 | 48 | .84 | 3.2 | .00 | 2.41 | 3038 | 855 | 16.71 | 2.440 | |
| **wheat bran** | | | | | | | | | | | | | | | |
| toasted, Kretschmer | 60 | | 1.0 | | 0 | | | | | | | 0 | | | |
| *1 oz* | 28 | 5.0 | 18.0 | | 12.0 | | | | | | 410 | | | | |
| unprocessed, Quaker | 21 | 0.8 | 0.2 | | | | | .03 | .04 | 11 | 0 | 6 | 46 | 1.00 | 1.000 |
| *2 T* | 7 | 1.1 | 3.6 | | | 0 | .04 | 1.5 | .00 | .00 | 106 | 115 | 1.02 | .080 | |
| **wheat flour** | | | | | | | | | | | | | | | |
| all purpose, enr | 499 | 16.4 | 1.4 | | | | 0 | .36 | | | 3 | 22 | | | |
| *1 cup* | 137 | 14.4 | 104.3 | | | 0 | .60 | 4.8 | | | 130 | 119 | 4.00 | | |
| all purpose, enr, Ballard | 399 | 10.1 | 1.0 | | | | 0 | .44 | | | 7 | 230 | | | |
| *1 cup* | 109 | 10.7 | 86.1 | | | 0 | .76 | 4.8 | | | 132 | 110 | 4.91 | | |
| all purpose, enr, Pillsbury's Best | 401 | 13.3 | 0.9 | | | | 0 | .34 | | | 2 | 238 | | | |
| *1 cup* | 113 | 10.8 | 87.0 | | | 0 | .79 | 6.2 | | | 148 | 113 | 5.09 | | |
| all purpose, enr, unbleached, Pillsbury's Best—*1 cup* | 401 | 10.9 | 2.2 | | | | 0 | .37 | | | 3 | 230 | | | |
| | 109 | 12.3 | 82.8 | | | 0 | .76 | 5.5 | | | 136 | 518 | 4.91 | | |
| bread, enr | 500 | 16.4 | 1.5 | | | | 0 | .36 | | | 3 | 22 | | | |
| *1 cup* | 137 | 16.2 | 102.3 | | | 0 | .60 | 4.8 | | | 130 | 130 | 4.00 | | |
| bread, Pillsbury's Best | 401 | 14.6 | 3.0 | | | | 0 | .56 | | | 9 | 236 | | | |
| *1 cup* | 112 | 13.4 | 79.5 | | | 0 | 1.01 | 2.7 | | | 91 | 115 | 5.04 | | |
| cake/pastry | 430 | 14.2 | 0.9 | | | | 0 | .04 | | | 2 | 20 | | | |
| *1 cup* | 118 | 8.9 | 93.7 | | | 0 | .04 | 0.8 | | | 112 | 86 | .60 | | |
| gluten (45% gluten & 55% all-purpose) | 529 | 11.9 | 2.7 | | | | 0 | | | | 3 | 56 | | | |
| *1 cup* | 140 | 58.0 | 66.1 | | | 0 | | | | | 84 | 196 | | | |
| sauce 'n gravy, Pillsbury's Best | 50 | 1.5 | 0.1 | | | | 0 | .05 | | | 1 | 30 | | | |
| *2 T* | 14 | 1.5 | 10.8 | | | 0 | .08 | 0.7 | | | 12 | 14 | .41 | | |
| self-rising, enr | 440 | 14.4 | 1.3 | | | | 0 | .33 | | | 1349 | 331 | | | |
| *1 cup* | 125 | 11.6 | 92.8 | | | 0 | .55 | 4.4 | | | | 583 | 3.60 | | |
| self-rising, enr, Aunt Jemima | 109 | 3.1 | 0.3 | | | | | .11 | .01 | 12 | 368 | 60 | 6 | .00 | .000 |
| *1/4 cup (1 oz)* | 28 | 3.0 | 23.6 | | | 0 | .18 | 1.5 | .00 | .00 | 32 | 153 | 1.25 | .020 | |
| self-rising, enr, bleached/unbleached, Pillsbury's Best/Ballard—*1 cup* | 380 | 15.0 | 1.2 | | | | 0 | .39 | | | 1309 | 243 | | | |
| | 115 | 8.7 | 84.0 | | | 0 | .74 | 5.8 | | | 104 | 546 | 5.18 | | |
| whole wheat | 400 | 14.4 | 2.4 | | | | 0 | .14 | | | 4 | 49 | | | |
| *1 cup* | 120 | 16.0 | 85.2 | | | 0 | .66 | 5.2 | | | 444 | 446 | 4.00 | | |
| whole wheat, Pillsbury's Best | 398 | 12.2 | 2.1 | | | | 0 | .20 | | | 9 | 30 | | | |
| *1 cup* | 111 | 16.7 | 77.7 | | | 0 | .43 | 7.3 | | | 487 | 382 | 4.33 | | |
| **wheat germ** | | | | | | | | | | | | | | | |
| toasted | 108 | 1.6 | 3.0 | 1.8 | | | 2 | .23 | .28 | 100 | 1 | 13 | 91 | 4.73 | 5.658 |
| *1/4 cup (1 oz)* | 28 | 8.3 | 14.1 | 0.5 | 3.0 | | .47 | 1.6 | | .39 | 268 | 325 | 2.58 | .176 | |
| toasted w/ brown sugar & honey | 107 | 1.6 | 2.3 | 1.4 | | | | .18 | .21 | 75 | 1 | 9 | 68 | 3.54 | 4.243 |
| *1/4 cup (1 oz)* | 28 | 6.2 | 17.2 | 0.4 | 2.0 | | .35 | 1.2 | | .30 | 201 | 244 | 1.93 | .132 | |

| | KCAL | H₂O (g) | FAT (g) | PUFA (g) | CHOL (mg) | A (RE) | C (mg) | B-2 (mg) | B-6 (mg) | FOL (mcg) | Na (mg) | Ca (mg) | Mg (mg) | Zn (mg) | Mn (mg) |
|---|---|---|---|---|---|---|---|---|---|---|---|---|---|---|---|
| | WT (g) | PRO (g) | CHO (g) | SFA (g) | DFIB (g) | A (IU) | B-1 (mg) | NIA (mg) | B-12 (mcg) | PANT (mg) | K (mg) | P (mg) | Fe (mg) | Cu (mg) | |

# 17. GRAIN PRODUCTS
## 17.1. BISCUITS

| | KCAL / WT | H₂O / PRO | FAT / CHO | PUFA / SFA | CHOL / DFIB | A(RE) / A(IU) | C / B-1 | B-2 / NIA | B-6 / B-12 | FOL / PANT | Na / K | Ca / P | Mg / Fe | Zn / Cu | Mn |
|---|---|---|---|---|---|---|---|---|---|---|---|---|---|---|---|
| **from mix** | 93 | 8.0 | 3.3 | | | | 0 | .11 | .01 | 2 | 262 | 58 | 7 | .18 | |
| *1 biscuit* | 28 | 2.1 | 13.6 | | | 16 | .12 | 0.8 | .05 | .10 | 56 | 128 | .57 | .031 | |
| **from refrig dough** | 91 | 8.4 | 3.1 | | | | 0 | .07 | .01 | | 349 | 6 | 4 | .12 | |
| *1 biscuit* | 28 | 2.0 | 13.6 | | | 0 | .11 | 0.9 | .00 | .07 | 25 | 110 | .66 | .020 | |
| **homemade, enr** | 103 | 7.7 | 4.8 | | | | 0 | .06 | | | 175 | 34 | | | |
| *1 biscuit* | 28 | 2.1 | 12.8 | 1.2ᵃ | | 0 | .06 | 0.5 | | | 23 | 49 | .40 | | |
| **homemade, unenr** | 102 | 7.7 | 4.8 | | | | 0 | .03 | | | 175 | 34 | | | |
| *1 biscuit* | 28 | 2.1 | 12.8 | 1.2ᵃ | | 0 | .01 | 0.1 | | | 33 | 49 | .10 | | |
| **refrig dough** | | | | | | | | | | | | | | | |
| baking powder, 1869 Brand | 207 | 21.4 | 10.1 | | | | 0 | .20 | | | 616 | 24 | | | |
| *2 biscuits* | 63 | 3.8 | 25.2 | | | 2 | .20 | 1.9 | | | 60 | 265 | 1.51 | | |
| baking powder/buttermilk, tenderflake, Pillsbury—2 biscuits | 110 | 12.6 | 5.3 | | | | 0 | .07 | | | 333 | 5 | | | |
| | 35 | 1.9 | 14.0 | | | 0 | .10 | 0.9 | | | 19 | 139 | .77 | | |
| butter/buttermilk/country, Pillsbury | 101 | 17.2 | 1.5 | | | | 0 | .11 | | | 361 | 10 | | | |
| *2 biscuits* | 43 | 2.7 | 19.8 | | | 0 | .15 | 1.4 | | | 209 | 196 | 1.18 | | |
| buttermilk/buttertastin', 1869 Brand | 209 | 21.4 | 10.1 | | | | 0 | .17 | | | 278 | 23 | | | |
| *2 biscuits* | 63 | 3.8 | 25.8 | | | 3 | .18 | 1.7 | | | 57 | 260 | 1.39 | | |
| butter flavored, Continental | 190 | | 8.0 | | | | | | | | 520 | | | | |
| *2 biscuits* | 57 | 3.0 | 25.0 | | | | | | | | 45 | | | | |
| butter-me-not, Continental | 190 | | 9.0 | | | | | | | | 530 | | | | |
| *2 biscuits* | 57 | 3.0 | 22.0 | | | | | | | | 40 | | | | |
| buttermilk, big country, Pillsbury | 201 | 24.1 | 7.6 | | | | 0 | .11 | | | 633 | 15 | | | |
| *2 biscuits* | 67 | 4.3 | 28.8 | | | 0 | .32 | 1.2 | | | 176 | 304 | 2.01 | | |
| buttermilk, deluxe heat 'n eat, Pillsbury | 281 | 17.3 | 14.8 | | | | 0 | .32 | | | 614 | 37 | | | |
| *2 biscuits* | 72 | 4.7 | 32.4 | | | 5 | .19 | 1.8 | | | 78 | 228 | 1.44 | | |
| buttermilk, extra rich, Hungry Jack | 110 | 17.6 | 2.6 | | | | 0 | .11 | | | 360 | 11 | | | |
| *2 biscuits* | 44 | 2.6 | 19.4 | | | 0 | .15 | 1.4 | | | 209 | 194 | 1.14 | | |
| buttermilk, flaky, extra lights, Pillsbury | 109 | 16.0 | 3.4 | | | | 0 | .09 | | | 323 | 9 | | | |
| *2 biscuits* | 41 | 2.4 | 17.2 | | | 0 | .15 | 1.2 | | | 186 | 175 | .78 | | |
| buttermilk, flaky, Hungry Jack | 171 | 19.6 | 6.5 | | | | 0 | .12 | | | 582 | 8 | | | |
| *2 biscuits* | 56 | 3.4 | 24.6 | | | 0 | .17 | 1.8 | | | 41 | 230 | 1.06 | | |
| buttermilk, fluffy, Hungry Jack | 179 | 20.3 | 8.1 | | | | 0 | .13 | | | 571 | 9 | | | |
| *2 biscuits* | 58 | 3.5 | 24.1 | | | 0 | .19 | 1.7 | | | 34 | 238 | 1.39 | | |
| buttermilk, heat 'n eat, Pillsbury | 170 | 14.6 | 5.2 | | | | 0 | .14 | | | 532 | 24 | | | |
| *2 biscuits* | 52 | 3.9 | 26.5 | | | 3 | .19 | 1.6 | | | 55 | 237 | 1.04 | | |
| buttermilk/plain, Ballard Ovenready | 99 | 17.2 | 1.3 | | | | 0 | .11 | | | 361 | 10 | | | |
| *2 biscuits* | 43 | 2.7 | 19.8 | | | 0 | .15 | 1.4 | | | 209 | 196 | 1.12 | | |
| buttermilk, Weight Watchers | 90 | | 1.0 | | | | | | | | 420 | | | | |
| *2 biscuits* | 40 | 2.0 | 18.0 | | | | | | | | 30 | | | | |
| buttertastin', big country, Pillsbury | 191 | 26.9 | 7.9 | | | | 0 | .16 | | | 658 | 13 | | | |
| *2 biscuits* | 69 | 3.7 | 27.6 | | | 0 | .26 | 2.0 | | | 184 | 295 | 1.24 | | |
| buttertastin', flaky, Hungry Jack | 180 | 20.0 | 7.4 | | | | 0 | .32 | | | 307 | 11 | | | |
| *2 biscuits* | 57 | 3.4 | 24.5 | | | 0 | .23 | 1.5 | | | 25 | 250 | 1.60 | | |
| flaky, Hungry Jack | 169 | 20.2 | 7.3 | | | | 0 | .13 | | | 580 | 9 | | | |
| *2 biscuits* | 56 | 3.1 | 23.5 | | | 0 | .18 | 1.6 | | | 32 | 240 | 1.34 | | |
| good 'n buttery, fluffy, Pillsbury | 179 | 19.8 | 9.5 | | | | 0 | .13 | | | 727 | 12 | | | |
| *2 biscuits* | 56 | 2.7 | 21.0 | | | 0 | .18 | 1.6 | | | 143 | 238 | 1.34 | | |
| homestyle, Continental | 100 | | 2.0 | | | | | | | | 340 | | | | |
| *2 biscuits* | 43 | 3.0 | 18.0 | | | | | | | | 115 | | | | |
| mountain man, Continental | 190 | | 8.0 | | | | | | | | 630 | | | | |
| *2 biscuits* | 57 | 3.0 | 25.0 | | | | | | | | 75 | | | | |
| southern style, Big Country | 201 | 24.1 | 8.0 | | | | 0 | .16 | | | 624 | 16 | | | |
| *2 biscuits* | 67 | 3.7 | 28.8 | | | 0 | .23 | 2.0 | | | 40 | 291 | 1.74 | | |
| texas style, butter flavored, Continental | 210 | | 9.0 | | | | | | | | 660 | | | | |
| *2 biscuits* | 68 | 4.0 | 28.0 | | | | | | | | 70 | | | | |
| texas style, Continental | 190 | | 5.0 | | | | | | | | 760 | | | | |
| *2 biscuits* | 68 | 4.0 | 32.0 | | | | | | | | 65 | | | | |

ᵃ Made w/ veg shortening; 1.8 g if made w/ lard.

| | KCAL / WT (g) | H₂O (g) / PRO (g) | FAT (g) / CHO (g) | PUFA (g) / SFA (g) | CHOL (mg) / DFIB (g) | A (RE) / A (IU) | C (mg) / B-1 (mg) | B-2 (mg) / NIA (mg) | B-6 (mg) / B-12 (mcg) | FOL (mcg) / PANT (mg) | Na (mg) / K (mg) | Ca (mg) / P (mg) | Mg (mg) / Fe (mg) | Zn (mg) / Cu (mg) | Mn (mg) |
|---|---|---|---|---|---|---|---|---|---|---|---|---|---|---|---|
| texas style, flaky, Continental | 220 | | 9.0 | | | | | | | | 640 | | | | |
| *2 biscuits* | 68 | 4.0 | 30.0 | | | | | | | | 50 | | | | |
| wheat, Weight Watchers | 90 | | 1.0 | | | | | | | | 440 | | | | |
| *2 biscuits* | 40 | 2.0 | 18.0 | | | | | | | | 50 | | | | |

## 17.2. BREADS & BREAD PRODUCTS

| | KCAL / WT (g) | H₂O (g) / PRO (g) | FAT (g) / CHO (g) | PUFA (g) / SFA (g) | CHOL (mg) / DFIB (g) | A (RE) / A (IU) | C (mg) / B-1 (mg) | B-2 (mg) / NIA (mg) | B-6 (mg) / B-12 (mcg) | FOL (mcg) / PANT (mg) | Na (mg) / K (mg) | Ca (mg) / P (mg) | Mg (mg) / Fe (mg) | Zn (mg) / Cu (mg) | Mn (mg) |
|---|---|---|---|---|---|---|---|---|---|---|---|---|---|---|---|
| **bagel** | 163 | 16.0 | 1.4 | | | | 0 | .16 | .02 | 13 | 198 | 23 | 11 | .29 | |
| *1 bagel* | 55 | 6.0 | 30.9 | | 0.6 | 0 | .21 | 1.9 | .00 | .20 | 41 | 37 | 1.46 | .046 | |
| **boston brown** | | | | | | | | | | | | | | | |
| cnd | 95 | 20.3 | 0.6 | | | | 0 | .03 | | | 113 | 41 | | | |
| *1 piece* | 45 | 2.5 | 20.5 | | | 0 | .05 | 0.5 | | | 131 | 72 | .90 | | |
| plain/raisin, cnd, B&M/Friends | 80 | | 0.0 | | | | | | | | 220 | | | | |
| *1/2" slice* | 45 | 2.0 | 18.0 | | | | | | | | | | | | |
| **bran 'n honey, Country Hearth** | 70 | | 1.0 | | | | | | | | 160 | | | | |
| *1 slice* | 28 | 3.0 | 13.0 | | | | | | | | 50 | | | | |
| **bread crumbs** | | | | | | | | | | | | | | | |
| dry, grated, enr | 392 | 6.5 | 4.6 | | | | 0 | .30 | | | 736 | 122 | | | |
| *1 cup* | 100 | 12.6 | 73.4 | 1.1 | | 0 | .22 | 3.5 | | | 152 | 141 | 3.60 | | |
| seasoned, Contadina | 35 | 0.6 | 0.3 | 0.0 | 1 | | 0 | .04 | | | 250 | 9 | 3 | .14 | |
| *1 rd T* | 10 | 1.4 | 6.8 | 0.1 | | 9 | .04 | 0.5 | | | 14 | 14 | .42 | | |
| **bread sticks** | 77 | 1.0 | 0.6 | | | | 0 | .01 | | | 140 | 6 | | | |
| *2 sticks* | 20 | 2.4 | 15.1 | 0.1 | | 0 | .01 | 0.2 | | | 18 | 20 | .18 | | |
| **bread sticks, soft, refrig dough, Pillsbury** | 100 | 14.4 | 2.5 | | | | 1 | .73 | | | 238 | 4 | | | |
| *1 stick* | 37 | 3.1 | 16.2 | | | 0 | | 1.2 | | | 297 | 35 | 1.04 | | |
| **buttermilk, Grant's Farm** | 80 | | 1.0 | | 0 | | | | | | 190 | | | | |
| *1 slice* | 28 | 3.0 | 14.0 | | | | | | | | 50 | | | | |
| **buttermilk, old fashioned, Country Hearth** | 70 | | 1.0 | | | | | | | | 190 | | | | |
| *1 slice* | 28 | 3.0 | 13.0 | | | | | | | | 35 | | | | |
| **cinnamon raisin** | 80 | | 1.0 | | 5 | | | | | | 140 | | | | |
| *1 slice* | 28 | 2.0 | 15.0 | | | | | | | | | | | | |
| **corn bread** | | | | | | | | | | | | | | | |
| from mix | 178 | 16.7 | 5.8 | | | | 0 | .10 | | | 263 | 133 | | | |
| *1 piece* | 55 | 3.8 | 27.5 | 1.7 | | 130 | .10 | 0.8 | | | 61 | 209 | .80 | | |
| from mix, Dromedary | 130 | | 3.0 | | | | | | | | 480 | | | | |
| *2" square* | | 3.0 | 20.0 | | | | | | | | 65 | | | | |
| mix, Aunt Jemima | 205 | 2.5 | 6.1 | | | | | .20 | .08 | 46 | 519 | 15 | 13 | .00 | .000 |
| *1.7 oz dry mix* | 48 | 3.6 | 33.9 | | | 39 | .26 | 2.1 | .00 | .00 | 55 | 270 | 1.48 | .040 | |
| w/ enr corn meal, homemade | 198 | 41.7 | 7.3 | | | | 0 | .15 | .06 | 8 | 232 | 90 | 15 | .39 | |
| *1 piece* | 83 | 4.1 | 28.7 | | | 114 | .15 | 1.2 | .14 | .32 | 78 | 81 | 1.24 | .033 | |
| w/ whole ground corn meal, homemade—*1 piece* | 172 | 42.0 | 6.9 | | | | 0 | .11 | .08 | 6 | 209 | 83 | 20 | .46 | |
| | 78 | 3.7 | 24.1 | | | 104 | .11 | 0.8 | .13 | .28 | 88 | 90 | .83 | .047 | |
| **corn pone w/ white whole ground corn meal**[a]—*1 piece* | 122 | 31.1 | 3.2 | | | | 0 | .03 | | | 238 | 37 | | | |
| | 60 | 2.7 | 21.7 | 0.6 | | 0 | .09 | 0.5 | | | 37 | 98 | .70 | | |
| **country meal, Continental** | 80 | | 1.0 | | 0 | | | | | | 135 | | | | |
| *1 slice* | 28 | 3.0 | 14.0 | | 1.3 | | | | | | 60 | | | | |
| **cracked wheat** | 66 | 8.8 | 0.9 | | | | 0 | .10 | .02 | | 108 | 16 | 9 | | |
| *1 slice* | 25 | 2.3 | 12.5 | | 1.1 | 0 | .10 | 0.8 | .00 | .15 | 33 | 32 | .67 | | |
| mini loaf, Earth Grains | 70 | | 1.0 | | | | | | | | 170 | | | | |
| *1 oz* | 28 | 2.0 | 14.0 | | | | | | | | 55 | | | | |
| toasted | 63 | 5.5 | 0.8 | | | | 0 | .09 | .02 | | 104 | 16 | 8 | .39 | .403 |
| *1 slice* | 21 | 2.2 | 12.0 | | 1.1 | 0 | .07 | 0.8 | .00 | .14 | 32 | 30 | .64 | .067 | |
| Wonder | 70 | | 1.0 | | 5 | | | | | | 180 | | | | |
| *1 slice* | 28 | 3.0 | 13.0 | | | | | | | | | | | | |
| **d'italia, Country Hearth** | 70 | | 1.0 | | | | | | | | 200 | | | | |
| *1 slice* | 28 | 3.0 | 13.0 | | | | | | | | 25 | | | | |

[a] Cornbread often made w/o milk or eggs, shaped in irregular ovals by the palm of the hand & baked or fried on a griddle.

| | KCAL<br>WT (g) | H₂O (g)<br>PRO (g) | FAT (g)<br>CHO (g) | PUFA (g)<br>SFA (g) | CHOL (mg)<br>DFIB (g) | A (RE)<br>A (IU) | C (mg)<br>B-1 (mg) | B-2 (mg)<br>NIA (mg) | B-6 (mg)<br>B-12 (mcg) | FOL (mcg)<br>PANT (mg) | Na (mg)<br>K (mg) | Ca (mg)<br>P (mg) | Mg (mg)<br>Fe (mg) | Zn (mg)<br>Cu (mg) | Mn (mg) |
|---|---|---|---|---|---|---|---|---|---|---|---|---|---|---|---|
| **european, butter sesame, Country Hearth** | 70 | | 1.0 | | | | | | | | 190 | | | | |
| *1 slice* | 28 | 3.0 | 12.0 | | | | | | | | 25 | | | | |
| **french** | 81 | 8.3 | 1.1 | | | | | .07 | .01 | 9 | 163 | 22 | 6 | .24 | .154 |
| *1 slice* | 28 | 2.7 | 14.8 | 0.6 | | | .11 | 1.2 | | .12 | 32 | 30 | .92 | .056 | |
|   DiCarlo Parisian | 70 | | 1.0 | | 5 | | | | | | 180 | | | | |
|   *1 slice* | 28 | 3.0 | 13.0 | | | | | | | | | | | | |
|   from mix, Home Hearth | 170 | | 3.0 | | | | | | | | 320 | | | | |
|   *two 3/8″ slices* | | 6.0 | 29.0 | | | | | | | | 70 | | | | |
|   refrig dough, Pillsbury | 61 | 10.7 | 0.3 | | | | | 0 | .07 | | 129 | 5 | | | |
|   *1″ slice* | 26 | 2.6 | 11.4 | | | 0 | .12 | 1.0 | | | 16 | 15 | .86 | | |
|   vienna | 70 | 8.5 | 1.0 | | 0 | | 0 | .09 | .01 | 9 | 138 | 28 | 5 | .16 | |
|   *1 slice* | 25 | 2.4 | 12.6 | | | 0 | .12 | 1.0 | .00 | .09 | 22 | 20 | .77 | .036 | |
|   Wonder | 70 | | 1.0 | | 0 | | | | | | 180 | | | | |
|   *1 slice* | 28 | 3.0 | 13.0 | | | | | | | | | | | | |
| **fruit quick bread, from mix** | 118 | 13.0 | 2.4 | | | | | .09 | | | 126 | 12 | 6 | .16 | |
| *1 slice* | 40 | 1.8 | 22.3 | | | | .10 | 1.1 | | | 40 | 48 | .69 | .041 | |
| **fruit/nut quick bread, from mix,** | 161 | | 4.4 | | | | | | | | 162 | | | | |
|   Pillsbury[a]—*1/12 loaf* | | 2.4 | 28.0 | | | | | | | | 51 | | | | |
| **grainola, Country Hearth** | 70 | | 1.0 | | | | | | | | 240 | | | | |
| *1 slice* | 28 | 3.0 | 12.0 | | | | | | | | 60 | | | | |
| **hillbilly, Continental** | 70 | | 1.0 | | 5 | | | | | | 140 | | | | |
| *1 slice* | 28 | 3.0 | 14.0 | | | | | | | | | | | | |
| **hollywood, Continental** | | | | | | | | | | | | | | | |
|   dark | 70 | | 1.0 | | 5 | | | | | | 160 | | | | |
|   *1 slice* | 28 | 3.0 | 13.0 | | | | | | | | | | | | |
|   light | 70 | | 1.0 | | 5 | | | | | | 150 | | | | |
|   *1 slice* | 28 | 3.0 | 13.0 | | | | | | | | | | | | |
| **honey & oat, Country Hearth** | 70 | | 1.0 | | | | | | | | 180 | | | | |
| *1 slice* | 28 | 3.0 | 13.0 | | | | | | | | 40 | | | | |
| **honey grain, Continental** | 70 | | 1.0 | | 0 | | | | | | 170 | | | | |
| *1 slice* | 28 | 3.0 | 13.0 | 1.0 | | | | | | | 45 | | | | |
| **italian** | 78 | 8.9 | 0.6 | | | | | .06 | .01 | 9 | 151 | 14 | 7 | .24 | .134 |
| *1 slice* | 28 | 2.8 | 14.9 | 0.3 | | | .10 | 1.2 | | .11 | 31 | 26 | .74 | .056 | |
|   Wonder Family | 70 | | 1.0 | | 5 | | | | | | 160 | | | | |
|   *1 slice* | 28 | 2.0 | 13.0 | | | | | | | | | | | | |
| **mixed grain** | 64 | 9.4 | 0.9 | | | | 0 | .10 | .03 | 16 | 103 | 26 | 12 | .30 | .350 |
| *1 slice* | 25 | 2.5 | 11.7 | 1.0 | | 0 | .10 | 1.0 | .00 | .16 | 55 | 53 | .82 | .071 | |
|   toasted | 63 | 5.8 | 0.9 | | | | 0 | .09 | .03 | 16 | 100 | 25 | 12 | .29 | |
|   *1 slice* | 21 | 2.4 | 11.4 | | | 0 | .08 | 1.0 | .00 | .15 | 53 | 52 | .79 | .069 | |
| **nature's wheat, Country Hearth** | 70 | | 1.0 | | | | | | | | 150 | | | | |
| *1 slice* | 28 | 3.0 | 13.0 | | | | | | | | 50 | | | | |
| **oatmeal** | 71 | 10.3 | 1.2 | | | | | .06 | .01 | 9 | 138 | 17 | 10 | .27 | .241 |
| *1 slice* | 28 | 2.4 | 13.0 | 0.6 | | | .10 | 0.9 | | .10 | 44 | 35 | .74 | .062 | |
| **pita pocket** | 106 | 11.9 | 0.6 | | | | 0 | .10 | .01 | 8 | 215 | 31 | 10 | .30 | .186 |
| *1 pocket* | 38 | 4.0 | 20.6 | 0.3 | | 0 | .18 | 1.6 | | .16 | 45 | 38 | .92 | .068 | |
| **raisin** | 70 | 8.3 | 1.0 | | | | 0 | .16 | .01 | 9 | 94 | 26 | 4 | .16 | .126 |
| *1 slice* | 25 | 2.1 | 13.2 | 0.6 | | 0 | .08 | 1.0 | .00 | .11 | 60 | 22 | .78 | .035 | |
|   toasted | 66 | 5.1 | 0.9 | | | | 0 | .15 | .01 | 8 | 90 | 24 | 6 | .15 | |
|   *1 slice* | 21 | 1.9 | 12.6 | | | 0 | .06 | 1.0 | .00 | .10 | 57 | 21 | .74 | .033 | |
| **roman meal** | 70 | | 1.0 | | 5 | | | | | | 140 | | | | |
| *1 slice* | 28 | 3.0 | 13.0 | | | | | | | | | | | | |

[a] Values are averages for applesce spice, apricot nut, banana, blueberry nut, carrot nut, cherry nut, cranberry, date, honey granola & nut.

|  | KCAL | H₂O (g) | FAT (g) | PUFA (g) | CHOL (mg) | A (RE) | C (mg) | B-2 (mg) | B-6 (mg) | FOL (mcg) | Na (mg) | Ca (mg) | Mg (mg) | Zn (mg) | Mn (mg) |
|---|---|---|---|---|---|---|---|---|---|---|---|---|---|---|---|
|  | WT (g) | PRO (g) | CHO (g) | SFA (g) | DFIB (g) | A (IU) | B-1 (mg) | NIA (mg) | B-12 (mcg) | PANT (mg) | K (mg) | P (mg) | Fe (mg) | Cu (mg) |  |
| **rye** |  |  |  |  |  |  |  |  |  |  |  |  |  |  |  |
| am | 66 | 9.4 | 0.9 |  |  |  | 0 | .08 | .02 | 10 | 174 | 20 | 6 | .32 |  |
| *1 slice* | 25 | 2.1 | 12.0 |  |  | 0 | .10 | 0.8 | .00 | .11 | 51 | 36 | .68 | .026 |  |
| am, toasted | 66 | 6.3 | 0.9 |  |  |  | 0 | .08 | .02 | 10 | 175 | 20 | 6 | .32 |  |
| *1 slice* | 22 | 2.1 | 12.0 |  |  | 0 | .08 | 0.8 | .00 | .11 | 51 | 37 | .68 | .026 |  |
| deli, Country Hearth | 70 |  | 1.0 |  |  |  |  |  |  |  | 160 |  |  |  |  |
| *1 slice* | 28 | 3.0 | 14.0 |  |  |  |  |  |  |  | 40 |  |  |  |  |
| from mix, Home Hearth | 150 |  | 1.0 |  |  |  |  |  |  |  | 360 |  |  |  |  |
| *two 3/8″ slices* |  | 6.0 | 28.0 |  |  |  |  |  |  |  | 90 |  |  |  |  |
| hearty/mild | 70 |  | 1.0 |  | 5 |  |  |  |  |  | 180 |  |  |  |  |
| *1 slice* | 28 | 3.0 | 13.0 |  |  |  |  |  |  |  |  |  |  |  |  |
| honey cracked, Grant's Farm | 70 |  | 1.0 |  | 0 |  |  |  |  |  | 190 |  |  |  |  |
| *1 slice* | 28 | 3.0 | 13.0 |  |  |  |  |  |  |  | 55 |  |  |  |  |
| pumpernickel | 82 | 11.9 | 0.8 |  |  |  | 0 | .17 | .05 |  | 173 | 23 | 22 | .36 |  |
| *1 slice* | 32 | 2.9 | 15.4 |  |  | 0 | .11 | 1.1 | .00 | .15 | 139 | 70 | .88 |  |  |
| pumpernickel, toasted | 82 | 7.9 | 1.1 |  |  |  | 0 | .17 | .05 |  | 174 | 23 | 22 | .36 |  |
| *1 slice* | 28 | 2.9 | 15.4 |  |  | 0 | .09 | 1.1 | .00 | .15 | 139 | 70 | .88 |  |  |
| **seven grain, Grant's Farm** | 70 |  | 1.0 |  | 0 |  |  |  |  |  | 140 |  |  |  |  |
| *1 slice* | 28 | 3.0 | 13.0 |  |  |  |  |  |  |  | 60 |  |  |  |  |
| **seven grain, Home Pride** | 70 |  | 1.0 |  | 5 |  |  |  |  |  | 140 |  |  |  |  |
| *1 slice* | 28 | 3.0 | 13.0 |  |  |  |  |  |  |  |  |  |  |  |  |
| **seven whole grain, Country Hearth** | 80 |  | 1.0 |  |  |  |  |  |  |  | 190 |  |  |  |  |
| *1 slice* | 28 | 3.0 | 14.0 |  |  |  |  |  |  |  | 45 |  |  |  |  |
| **sourdough** |  |  |  |  |  |  |  |  |  |  |  |  |  |  |  |
| DiCarlo | 70 |  | 1.0 |  | 0 |  |  |  |  |  | 140 |  |  |  |  |
| *1 slice* | 28 | 3.0 | 12.0 |  |  |  |  |  |  |  |  |  |  |  |  |
| mini loaf, Earth Grains | 80 |  | 1.0 |  |  |  |  |  |  |  | 210 |  |  |  |  |
| *1 oz* | 28 | 2.0 | 14.0 |  |  |  |  |  |  |  | 40 |  |  |  |  |
| **spoon bread w/ white whole ground cornmeal**[a]—*1 cup* | 468 | 151.2 | 27.4 |  |  |  | 1 | .43 |  |  | 1157 | 230 |  |  |  |
|  | 240 | 16.1 | 40.6 | 8.7 |  | 700 | .22 | 1.0 |  |  | 317 | 394 | 2.40 |  |  |
| **wheat** | 61 | 8.9 | 1.0 |  | 0 |  | 0 | .08 | .03 | 11 | 129 | 30 | 11 | .25 |  |
| *1 slice*[b] | 24 | 2.3 | 11.3 |  |  | 0 | .11 | 1.1 | 1.1 | .10 | 33 | 44 | .84 | .058 |  |
| toasted[b] | 61 | 5.9 | 1.0 |  |  |  | 0 | .08 | .03 | 11 | 129 | 30 | 11 | .25 |  |
| *1 slice* | 21 | 2.3 | 11.3 |  |  | 0 | .09 | 1.1 | .00 | .10 | 33 | 44 | .84 | .058 |  |
| butter split top, Country Hearth | 70 |  | 1.0 |  |  |  |  |  |  |  | 160 |  |  |  |  |
| *1 slice* | 28 | 3.0 | 13.0 |  |  |  |  |  |  |  | 45 |  |  |  |  |
| butter top, Home Pride | 70 |  | 1.0 |  | 5 |  |  |  |  |  | 140 |  |  |  |  |
| *1 slice* | 28 | 3.0 | 13.0 |  |  |  |  |  |  |  |  |  |  |  |  |
| Fresh & Natural | 70 |  | 1.0 |  | 0 |  |  |  |  |  | 140 |  |  |  |  |
| *1 slice* | 28 | 3.0 | 13.0 |  |  |  |  |  |  |  |  |  |  |  |  |
| Fresh Horizons | 50 |  | 1.0 |  | 0 |  |  |  |  |  | 140 |  |  |  |  |
| *1 slice* | 28 | 3.0 | 10.0 |  |  |  |  |  |  |  |  |  |  |  |  |
| honey buttered, split top, Family Recipe—*1 slice* | 70 |  | 1.0 |  | 0 |  |  |  |  |  | 150 |  |  |  |  |
|  | 28 | 3.0 | 14.0 |  | 1.2 |  |  |  |  |  | 55 |  |  |  |  |
| refrig dough, pipin' hot, Pillsbury | 81 | 12.1 | 1.9 |  |  |  | 0 | .07 |  |  | 185 | 5 |  |  |  |
| *1″ slice* | 31 | 2.9 | 13.0 |  |  | 0 | .65 | 1.0 |  |  | 21 | 26 | .90 |  |  |
| sandwich, Country Hearth | 70 |  | 1.0 |  |  |  |  |  |  |  | 150 |  |  |  |  |
| *1 slice* | 28 | 3.0 | 13.0 |  |  |  |  |  |  |  | 50 |  |  |  |  |
| sandwich, Family Recipe | 70 |  | 1.0 |  | 0 |  |  |  |  |  | 150 |  |  |  |  |
| *1 slice* | 28 | 3.0 | 14.0 |  | 1.0 |  |  |  |  |  | 45 |  |  |  |  |
| stone ground, Grant's Farm | 70 |  | 1.0 |  | 0 |  |  |  |  |  | 150 |  |  |  |  |
| *1 slice* | 28 | 3.0 | 12.0 |  |  |  |  |  |  |  | 60 |  |  |  |  |
| wheat berry, Country Hearth | 70 |  | 1.0 |  |  |  |  |  |  |  | 160 |  |  |  |  |
| *1 slice* | 28 | 3.0 | 13.0 |  |  |  |  |  |  |  | 50 |  |  |  |  |
| wheat berry, Grant's Farm | 70 |  | 1.0 |  | 0 |  |  |  |  |  | 170 |  |  |  |  |
| *1 slice* | 28 | 3.0 | 13.0 |  |  |  |  |  |  |  | 45 |  |  |  |  |
| wheat berry, Home Pride | 70 |  | 1.0 |  | 5 |  |  |  |  |  | 160 |  |  |  |  |
| *1 slice* | 28 | 3.0 | 12.0 |  |  |  |  |  |  |  |  |  |  |  |  |

[a] Bread made of cornmeal w/ or w/o added rice & hominy & mixed w/ milk, eggs, shortening & leavening to a consistency that is served w/ a spoon.

[b] Made w/ white enr flour & colored brown; not the same as whole wheat bread.

| | KCAL / WT (g) | H₂O (g) / PRO (g) | FAT (g) / CHO (g) | PUFA (g) / SFA (g) | CHOL (mg) / DFIB (g) | A (RE) / A (IU) | C (mg) / B-1 (mg) | B-2 (mg) / NIA (mg) | B-6 (mg) / B-12 (mcg) | FOL (mcg) / PANT (mg) | Na (mg) / K (mg) | Ca (mg) / P (mg) | Mg (mg) / Fe (mg) | Zn (mg) / Cu (mg) | Mn (mg) |
|---|---|---|---|---|---|---|---|---|---|---|---|---|---|---|---|
| Wonder Family | 70 | | 1.0 | | 5 | | | | | | 140 | | | | |
| *1 slice* | 28 | 3.0 | 13.0 | | | | | | | | | | | | |
| white | 64 | 8.9 | 0.9 | | | | 0 | .07 | .01 | 8 | 123 | 30 | 5 | .15 | |
| *1 slice* | 24 | 2.0 | 11.7 | | | 0 | .11 | 0.9 | .00 | .10 | 27 | 26 | .68 | .033 | |
| toasted | 64 | 5.9 | 0.9 | | | | 0 | .08 | .01 | 8 | 123 | 30 | 5 | .15 | |
| *1 slice* | 21 | 2.0 | 11.7 | | | 0 | .03 | 0.9 | .00 | .10 | 27 | 26 | .68 | .033 | |
| homemade | 72 | 9.0 | 1.7 | | | | 0 | .08 | .01 | 9 | 102 | 16 | 6 | .16 | |
| *1 slice* | 25 | 1.9 | 12.0 | | | 13 | .08 | 0.7 | .03 | .12 | 33 | 25 | .54 | .019 | |
| homemade, toasted | 70 | 5.5 | 1.6 | | | | 0 | .08 | .01 | 9 | 98 | 16 | 5 | .16 | |
| *1 slice* | 21 | 1.8 | 11.7 | | | 12 | .06 | 0.7 | .03 | .11 | 32 | 24 | .52 | .018 | |
| butter split, Country Hearth | 70 | | 1.0 | | | | | | | | 160 | | | | |
| *1 slice* | 28 | 3.0 | 13.0 | | | | | | | | 30 | | | | |
| butter top, Home Pride | 70 | | 1.0 | | 5 | | | | | | 160 | | | | |
| *1 slice* | 28 | 3.0 | 13.0 | | | | | | | | 30 | | | | |
| country mini loaf, Earth Grains | 70 | | 1.0 | | | | | | | | 150 | | | | |
| *1 oz* | 28 | 2.0 | 14.0 | | | | | | | | 40 | | | | |
| Fresh Horizons | 50 | | 1.0 | | 0 | | | | | | 140 | | | | |
| *1 slice* | 28 | 3.0 | 10.0 | | | | | | | | | | | | |
| from mix, Home Hearth | 150 | | 1.0 | | | | | | | | 260 | | | | |
| *two 3/8″ slices* | | 6.0 | 29.0 | | | | | | | | 70 | | | | |
| honey-buttered split top, Family Recipe | 80 | | 1.0 | | 0 | | | | | | 150 | | | | |
| *1 slice* | 28 | 2.0 | 14.0 | | | | | | | | 40 | | | | |
| old fashioned, Country Hearth | 70 | | 1.0 | | | | | | | | 160 | | | | |
| *1 slice* | 28 | 3.0 | 13.0 | | | | | | | | 30 | | | | |
| refrig dough, pipin' hot, Pillsbury | 81 | 12.0 | 1.7 | | | | 0 | .08 | | | 179 | 5 | | | |
| *1″ slice* | 30 | 2.8 | 12.9 | | | 0 | .62 | 1.0 | | | 18 | 23 | .84 | | |
| Rich's dough, baked | 116 | 16.5 | 1.1 | | 0 | | | .14 | | | 300 | 110 | 11 | .30 | |
| *2 slices* | 46 | 3.9 | 22.7 | | | | .18 | 1.7 | | | 51 | 55 | 2.10 | .070 | |
| w/ buttermilk, Wonder | 70 | | 1.0 | | 5 | | | | | | 160 | | | | |
| *1 slice* | 28 | 2.0 | 13.0 | | | | | | | | | | | | |
| Wonder | 70 | | 1.0 | | 5 | | | | | | 140 | | | | |
| *1 slice* | 28 | 3.0 | 13.0 | | | | | | | | | | | | |
| whole wheat | 61 | 9.6 | 1.1 | | | | 0 | .05 | .05 | 14 | 159 | 18 | 23 | .42 | .594 |
| *1 slice* | 25 | 2.4 | 11.4 | | 1.6 | 0 | .09 | 1.0 | .00 | .18 | 44 | 65 | .86 | .086 | |
| toasted | 59 | 6.1 | 1.1 | | | | 0 | .05 | .04 | 13 | 153 | 17 | 23 | .40 | |
| *1 slice* | 21 | 2.3 | 10.9 | | | 0 | .07 | 0.9 | .00 | .18 | 42 | 63 | .82 | .082 | |
| homemade | 67 | 9.0 | 1.6 | | | | 0 | .04 | .05 | 12 | 89 | 20 | 23 | .56 | |
| *1 slice* | 25 | 2.2 | 11.6 | | | 11 | .07 | 0.8 | .03 | .20 | 85 | 63 | .67 | .064 | |
| homemade, toasted | 65 | 5.5 | 1.6 | | | | 0 | .04 | .05 | 12 | 87 | 19 | 23 | .55 | |
| *1 slice* | 21 | 2.2 | 11.3 | | | 11 | .05 | 0.8 | .03 | .20 | 83 | 61 | .65 | .062 | |
| stone ground, 100%, Country Hearth | 70 | | 1.0 | | | | | | | | 160 | | | | |
| *1 slice* | 28 | 3.0 | 12.0 | | | | | | | | 75 | | | | |
| Wonder | 70 | | 1.0 | | 5 | | | | | | 160 | | | | |
| *1 slice* | 28 | 3.0 | 12.0 | | | | | | | | | | | | |
| Wonder, soft | 70 | | 1.0 | | 0 | | | | | | 140 | | | | |
| *1 slice* | 28 | 4.0 | 10.0 | | | | | | | | | | | | |

## 17.3. CRACKERS

| | KCAL / WT (g) | H₂O (g) / PRO (g) | FAT (g) / CHO (g) | PUFA (g) / SFA (g) | CHOL (mg) / DFIB (g) | A (RE) / A (IU) | C (mg) / B-1 (mg) | B-2 (mg) / NIA (mg) | B-6 (mg) / B-12 (mcg) | FOL (mcg) / PANT (mg) | Na (mg) / K (mg) | Ca (mg) / P (mg) | Mg (mg) / Fe (mg) | Zn (mg) / Cu (mg) | Mn (mg) |
|---|---|---|---|---|---|---|---|---|---|---|---|---|---|---|---|
| **bacon flavored thins, Nabisco** | 70 | | 4.0 | | | | | | | | 210 | | | | |
| *7 crackers* | 14 | 1.0 | 8.0 | | | | | | | | 20 | | | | |
| **bacon, Great Crisps** | 70 | | 4.0 | | | | | | | | 230 | | | | |
| *9 crackers* | 14 | 2.0 | 8.0 | | | | | | | | 20 | | | | |
| **blue cheese/cheddar/nacho/swiss thins, Nabisco**—*10 crackers* | 70 | | 4.0 | | | | | | | | 233 | | | | |
| | 14 | 1.3 | 8.0 | | | | | | | | 15 | | | | |
| **cheddar cheese, Safari** | 130 | | 10.0 | | | | | | | | 450 | | | | |
| *1 oz* | 28 | 3.0 | 14.0 | | | | | | | | | | | | |
| **cheese** | 81 | 0.6 | 4.9 | | | | 0 | .06 | | | 180 | 16 | 3 | .15 | |
| *5 pieces* | 15 | 1.4 | 7.8 | | | | .06 | 1.2 | | | 28 | 32 | .53 | .070 | |

| | KCAL | H₂O (g) | FAT (g) | PUFA (g) | CHOL (mg) | Vitamins A (RE) | C (mg) | B-2 (mg) | B-6 (mg) | FOL (mcg) | Minerals Na (mg) | Ca (mg) | Mg (mg) | Zn (mg) | Mn (mg) |
|---|---|---|---|---|---|---|---|---|---|---|---|---|---|---|---|
| | WT (g) | PRO (g) | CHO (g) | SFA (g) | DFIB (g) | A (IU) | B-1 (mg) | NIA (mg) | B-12 (mcg) | PANT (mg) | K (mg) | P (mg) | Fe (mg) | Cu (mg) | |
| cheese 'n chives, Dip in a Chip | 70 | | 4.0 | | | | | | | | 130 | | | | |
| 8 crackers | 14 | 1.0 | 8.0 | | | | | | | | 40 | | | | |
| cheese 'n chives, Great Crisps | 70 | | 4.0 | | | | | | | | 170 | | | | |
| 9 crackers | 14 | 2.0 | 8.0 | | | | | | | | 20 | | | | |
| cheese nips, Nabisco | 70 | | 3.0 | | | | | | | | 130 | | | | |
| 13 crackers | 14 | 1.0 | 9.0 | | | | | | | | 25 | | | | |
| cheese, Ritz | 70 | | 3.0 | | | | | | | | 120 | | | | |
| 5 crackers | 14 | 1.0 | 8.0 | | | | | | | | 15 | | | | |
| cheese tidbits | 70 | | 4.0 | | | | | | | | 200 | | | | |
| 16 crackers | 14 | 1.0 | 8.0 | | | | | | | | 20 | | | | |
| cheese wheat thins | 70 | | 3.0 | | | | | | | | 220 | | | | |
| 9 crackers | 14 | 2.0 | 9.0 | | | | | | | | 35 | | | | |
| cheese w/ peanut butter filling | 209 | 1.0 | 10.2 | | | | 0 | .03 | | | 422 | 24 | | | |
| 6 sandwiches | 42 | 6.5 | 23.8 | 2.7 | | 20 | .01 | 1.5 | | | 96 | 76 | .30 | | |
| cheese w/ peanut butter filling, Nabisco | 70 | | 3.0 | | | | | | | | 150 | | | | |
| 2 sandwiches | 14 | 2.0 | 8.0 | | | | | | | | 25 | | | | |
| chicken in a biskit | 70 | | 4.0 | | | | | | | | 115 | | | | |
| 7 crackers | 14 | 1.0 | 8.0 | | | | | | | | 20 | | | | |
| cinnamon treats, Nabisco | 60 | | 1.0 | | | | | | | | 80 | | | | |
| 2 crackers | 14 | 1.0 | 11.0 | | | | | | | | 20 | | | | |
| cracker meal, Nabisco | 50 | | 0.0 | | | | | | | | 0 | | | | |
| 2 T | 14 | 1.0 | 12.0 | | | | | | | | 20 | | | | |
| escort, Nabisco | 80 | | 4.0 | | | | | | | | 110 | | | | |
| 3 crackers | 14 | 1.0 | 9.0 | | | | | | | | 20 | | | | |
| french onion, Great Crisps | 70 | | 4.0 | | | | | | | | 90 | | | | |
| 7 crackers | 14 | 1.0 | 8.0 | | | | | | | | 20 | | | | |
| garlic butter n' cheese, Safari | 150 | | 9.0 | | | | | | | | 690 | | | | |
| 1 oz | 28 | 2.0 | 15.0 | | | | | | | | | | | | |
| garlic, Great Crisps | 70 | | 3.0 | | | | | | | | 190 | | | | |
| 8 crackers | 14 | 1.0 | 9.0 | | | | | | | | 20 | | | | |
| graham | 60 | 0.5 | 1.5 | | | | 0 | .04 | .01 | 2 | 66 | 5 | 5 | .11 | |
| 2 squares | 14 | 1.0 | 10.8 | | | 0 | .05 | 0.4 | .00 | .07 | 23 | 17 | .37 | .017 | |
| graham crumbs, Nabisco | 60 | | 1.0 | | | | | | | | 90 | | | | |
| 2 T | 14 | 1.0 | 11.0 | | | | | | | | 15 | | | | |
| graham, Nabisco | 60 | | 1.0 | | | | | | | | 115 | | | | |
| 2 crackers | 14 | 1.0 | 11.0 | | | | | | | | 20 | | | | |
| holland rusk | 60 | | 1.0 | | | | | | | | 35 | | | | |
| 1 cracker | 14 | 2.0 | 10.0 | | | | | | | | 35 | | | | |
| meal mates sesame wafers | 70 | | 3.0 | | | | | | | | 140 | | | | |
| 3 crackers | 14 | 1.0 | 9.0 | | | | | | | | 30 | | | | |
| nacho, Great Crisps | 70 | | 4.0 | | | | | | | | 250 | | | | |
| 8 crackers | 14 | 1.0 | 8.0 | | | | | | | | 30 | | | | |
| nutty wheat thins, Nabisco | 80 | | 5.0 | | | | | | | | 250 | | | | |
| 7 crackers | 14 | 1.0 | 8.0 | | | | | | | | 35 | | | | |
| onion 'n cheese, Safari | 150 | | 9.0 | | | | | | | | 750 | | | | |
| 1 oz | 28 | 2.0 | 15.0 | | | | | | | | | | | | |
| oyster | 33 | 0.3 | 1.0 | | | | 0 | .00 | | | 83 | 2 | | | |
| 10 crackers | 8 | 0.7 | 5.3 | 0.2 | | 0 | .00 | 0.1 | | | 9 | 7 | .10 | | |
| oyster, Dandy | 60 | | 1.0 | | | | | | | | 220 | | | | |
| 20 crackers | 14 | 1.0 | 10.0 | | | | | | | | 20 | | | | |
| pizza, Safari | 150 | | 9.0 | | | | | | | | 480 | | | | |
| 1 oz | 28 | 3.0 | 15.0 | | | | | | | | | | | | |
| premium unsalted tops | 60 | | 2.0 | | | | | | | | 115 | | | | |
| 5 crackers | 14 | 1.0 | 10.0 | | | | | | | | 20 | | | | |
| rice cakes, Chico San | 35 | | 0.2 | | | | 0 | .01 | | | a | 0 | | | |
| 1 cake | | 0.4 | 8.0 | | 0.4 | 14 | .00 | 0.6 | | | 25 | | .10 | | |
| ritz | 70 | | 4.0 | | | | | | | | 120[b] | | | | |
| 4 crackers | 14 | 1.0 | 9.0 | | | | | | | | 15 | | | | |
| round toast, Planters | 140 | | 7.0 | | | | | | | | 270 | | | | |
| 1 oz | 28 | 4.0 | 15.0 | | | | | | | | 85 | | | | |
| royal lunch, Nabisco | 60 | | 2.0 | | | | | | | | 80 | | | | |
| 1 cracker | 14 | 1.0 | 10.0 | | | | | | | | 15 | | | | |

[a] 0 mg in sodium free varieties; 10 mg in very low sodium varieties.  [b] Low sodium Ritz crackers contain 60 mg sodium.

| Food | KCAL / WT (g) | H₂O (g) / PRO (g) | FAT (g) / CHO (g) | PUFA (g) / SFA (g) | CHOL (mg) / DFIB (g) | A (RE) / A (IU) | C (mg) / B-1 (mg) | B-2 (mg) / NIA (mg) | B-6 (mg) / B-12 (mcg) | FOL (mcg) / PANT (mg) | Na (mg) / K (mg) | Ca (mg) / P (mg) | Mg (mg) / Fe (mg) | Zn (mg) / Cu (mg) | Mn (mg) |
|---|---|---|---|---|---|---|---|---|---|---|---|---|---|---|---|
| **rusk** | 38 | 0.4 | 0.8 |  |  |  | 0 | .02 |  |  | 22 | 2 |  |  |  |
| *1 rusk* | 9 | 1.2 | 6.4 | 0.2 |  | 20 | .01 | 0.1 |  |  | 14 | 11 | .10 |  |  |
| **rye, whole grain** | 45 | 0.8 | 0.2 |  |  |  | 0 | .03 |  |  | 115 | 7 |  |  |  |
| *2 wafers* | 13 | 1.7 | 9.9 |  |  | 0 | .04 | 0.2 |  |  | 78 | 50 | .50 |  |  |
| **ry-krisp** | 40 |  | 0.2 |  |  |  |  | .07 | .06 | 7 | 112 | 12 | 34 | .79 |  |
| *1/4 large square* | 14 | 1.5 | 13.0 |  | 2.5 |  | .04 | 0.3 |  | .16 | 63 | 93 | .44 | .135 |  |
| **seasoned** | 50 |  | 1.1 |  |  |  |  | .11 | .05 | 27 | 147 | 11 | 32 | .75 |  |
| *1/4 large square* | 14 | 1.5 | 10.0 |  | 2.4 |  | .03 | 0.6 |  | .12 | 61 | 47 | .45 | .120 |  |
| **sesame** | 60 |  | 1.4 |  |  |  |  | .06 | .05 | 9 | 148 | 5 | 36 | .80 |  |
| *2 triple crackers* | 14 | 1.6 | 12.0 |  | 2.1 |  | .04 | 0.4 |  | .12 | 61 | 88 | .45 | .140 |  |
| **saltines** | 26 | 0.2 | 0.6 |  |  |  | 0 | .03 | .00 | 1 | 80 | 4 | 2 | .04 |  |
| *2 crackers* | 6 | 0.6 | 4.4 |  |  | 0 | .02 | 0.4 | .00 | .02 | 8 | 6 | .16 | .010 |  |
| **saltines, Premium** | 60 |  | 2.0 |  |  |  |  |  |  |  | 180 |  |  |  |  |
| *5 crackers* | 14 | 1.0 | 10.0 |  |  |  |  |  |  |  | 20 |  |  |  |  |
| **sea round, Nabisco** | 60 |  | 2.0 |  |  |  |  |  |  |  | 140 |  |  |  |  |
| *1 cracker* | 14 | 1.0 | 10.0 |  |  |  |  |  |  |  | 20 |  |  |  |  |
| **sesame, Great Crisps** | 70 |  | 4.0 |  |  |  |  |  |  |  | 190 |  |  |  |  |
| *9 crackers* | 14 | 2.0 | 8.0 |  |  |  |  |  |  |  | 25 |  |  |  |  |
| **sociables, Nabisco** | 70 |  | 3.0 |  |  |  |  |  |  |  | 130 |  |  |  |  |
| *6 crackers* | 14 | 1.0 | 9.0 |  |  |  |  |  |  |  | 30 |  |  |  |  |
| **soda** | 125 | 1.1 | 3.7 |  |  |  | 0 | .01 |  |  | 312 | 6 |  |  |  |
| *10 crackers* | 28 | 2.6 | 20.1 | 0.9 |  | 0 | .00 | 0.3 |  |  | 34 | 25 | .40 |  |  |
| **soda, Sultana** | 60 |  | 1.0 |  |  |  |  |  |  |  | 115 |  |  |  |  |
| *4 crackers* | 14 | 1.0 | 11.0 |  |  |  |  |  |  |  | 20 |  |  |  |  |
| **square cheese, Planters** | 140 |  | 7.0 |  |  |  |  |  |  |  | 270 |  |  |  |  |
| *1 oz* | 28 | 4.0 | 15.0 |  |  |  |  |  |  |  | 85 |  |  |  |  |
| **tomato & celery, Great Crisps** | 70 |  | 4.0 |  |  |  |  |  |  |  | 160 |  |  |  |  |
| *9 crackers* | 14 | 1.0 | 8.0 |  |  |  |  |  |  |  | 35 |  |  |  |  |
| **triscuit** | 60 |  | 2.0 |  |  |  |  |  |  |  | 90[a] |  |  |  |  |
| *3 crackers* | 14 | 1.0 | 10.0 |  |  |  |  |  |  |  | 40 |  |  |  |  |
| **twigs, sesame & cheese, Nabisco** | 70 |  | 4.0 |  |  |  |  |  |  |  | 200 |  |  |  |  |
| *7 crackers* | 14 | 1.0 | 8.0 |  |  |  |  |  |  |  | 25 |  |  |  |  |
| **uneeda unsalted tops, Nabisco** | 60 |  | 2.0 |  |  |  |  |  |  |  | 100 |  |  |  |  |
| *3 crackers* | 14 | 1.0 | 10.0 |  |  |  |  |  |  |  | 20 |  |  |  |  |
| **vegetable thins, Nabisco** | 70 |  | 4.0 |  |  |  |  |  |  |  | 100 |  |  |  |  |
| *7 crackers* | 14 | 1.0 | 8.0 |  |  |  |  |  |  |  | 30 |  |  |  |  |
| **waverly, Nabisco** | 70 |  | 3.0 |  |  |  |  |  |  |  | 160 |  |  |  |  |
| *4 crackers* | 14 | 1.0 | 10.0 |  |  |  |  |  |  |  | 15 |  |  |  |  |
| **wheatsworth stone ground wheat** | 70 |  | 3.0 |  |  |  |  |  |  |  | 135 |  |  |  |  |
| *5 crackers* | 14 | 1.0 | 9.0 |  |  |  |  |  |  |  | 35 |  |  |  |  |
| **wheat thins, Nabisco** | 70 |  | 3.0 |  |  |  |  |  |  |  | 120[b] |  |  |  |  |
| *8 crackers* | 14 | 1.0 | 9.0 |  |  |  |  |  |  |  | 25 |  |  |  |  |
| **zwieback** | 30 | 0.4 | 0.6 |  |  |  | 0 | .00 |  |  | 18 | 1 |  |  |  |
| *1 piece* | 7 | 0.7 | 5.2 | 0.2 |  | 0 | .00 | 0.1 |  |  | 11 | 5 | .00 |  |  |
| **zwieback, Nabisco** | 60 |  | 1.0 |  |  |  |  |  |  |  | 20 |  |  |  |  |
| *2 pieces* | 14 | 2.0 | 10.0 |  |  |  |  |  |  |  | 20 |  |  |  |  |

## 17.4. FRENCH TOAST

| Food | KCAL / WT (g) | H₂O (g) / PRO (g) | FAT (g) / CHO (g) | PUFA (g) / SFA (g) | CHOL (mg) / DFIB (g) | A (RE) / A (IU) | C (mg) / B-1 (mg) | B-2 (mg) / NIA (mg) | B-6 (mg) / B-12 (mcg) | FOL (mcg) / PANT (mg) | Na (mg) / K (mg) | Ca (mg) / P (mg) | Mg (mg) / Fe (mg) | Zn (mg) / Cu (mg) | Mn (mg) |
|---|---|---|---|---|---|---|---|---|---|---|---|---|---|---|---|
| **frzn** |  |  |  |  |  |  |  |  |  |  |  |  |  |  |  |
| Am Hosp Co | 71 |  | 0.8 |  | 7 |  | 0 | .02 |  |  | 33 | 24 |  |  |  |
| *1.3 oz* | 37 | 4.3 | 11.6 |  |  | 436 | .03 |  |  |  | 48 |  | .55 |  |  |
| Aunt Jemima | 168 | 46.2 | 3.9 |  |  |  |  | .17 | .30 | 37 | 430 | 94 | 12 | 1.00 | .000 |
| *2 slices* | 85 | 6.4 | 26.8 |  |  | 173 | .15 | 1.6 | .90 | 1.00 | 97 | 120 | 1.44 | .080 |  |
| cinn swirl, Aunt Jemima | 190 | 43.4 | 6.0 |  |  |  |  | .17 | .30 | 48 | 359 | 94 | 16 | 1.00 | .000 |
| *2 slices* | 85 | 6.4 | 27.6 |  |  | 183 | .15 | 1.6 | .90 | 1.00 | 126 | 126 | 1.44 | .060 |  |
| raisin, Aunt Jemima | 185 | 42.3 | 4.2 |  |  |  |  | .17 | .20 | 18 | 423 | 96 | 17 | 1.00 | .000 |
| *2 slices* | 85 | 7.3 | 29.4 |  |  | 120 | .15 | 1.2 | .60 | 1.00 | 160 | 99 | 1.44 | .100 |  |

[a] Low salt triscuits contain 35 mg sodium.

[b] Low salt wheat thins contain 35 mg sodium.

|  | KCAL | H₂O (g) | FAT (g) | PUFA (g) | CHOL (mg) | A (RE) | C (mg) | B-2 (mg) | B-6 (mg) | FOL (mcg) | Na (mg) | Ca (mg) | Mg (mg) | Zn (mg) | Mn (mg) |
|---|---|---|---|---|---|---|---|---|---|---|---|---|---|---|---|
|  | WT (g) | PRO (g) | CHO (g) | SFA (g) | DFIB (g) | A (IU) | B-1 (mg) | NIA (mg) | B-12 (mcg) | PANT (mg) | K (mg) | P (mg) | Fe (mg) | Cu (mg) |  |
| **homemade** | 153 | 34.3 | 6.7 |  |  |  | 0 | .16 | .04 | 18 | 257 | 72 | 12 | .55 |  |
| *1 slice* | 65 | 5.7 | 17.2 |  |  | 111 | .12 | 1.0 | .29 | .53 | 86 | 87 | 1.34 | .059 |  |

## 17.5. MUFFINS

|  | KCAL | H₂O (g) | FAT (g) | PUFA (g) | CHOL (mg) | A (RE) | C (mg) | B-2 (mg) | B-6 (mg) | FOL (mcg) | Na (mg) | Ca (mg) | Mg (mg) | Zn (mg) | Mn (mg) |
|---|---|---|---|---|---|---|---|---|---|---|---|---|---|---|---|
|  | WT (g) | PRO (g) | CHO (g) | SFA (g) | DFIB (g) | A (IU) | B-1 (mg) | NIA (mg) | B-12 (mcg) | PANT (mg) | K (mg) | P (mg) | Fe (mg) | Cu (mg) |  |
| **apple steusel, frzn, Am Hosp Co** | 225 |  | 10.6 |  | 37 |  | 0 | .03 |  |  | 517 | 20 |  |  |  |
| *3 oz* | 85 | 3.0 | 29.4 |  |  | 269 | .03 | 0.1 |  |  | 243 |  | 2.00 |  |  |
| **banana, frzn, Am Hosp Co** | 242 |  | 10.3 |  | 51 |  |  | .12 |  |  | 251 | 65 |  |  |  |
| *3 oz* | 85 | 5.8 | 27.2 |  |  | 178 | .01 | 1.2 |  |  | 90 |  | .60 |  |  |
| **banana nut, frzn, Am Hosp Co** | 371 |  | 15.8 |  | 64 |  | 0 | .13 |  |  | 676 | 21 |  |  |  |
| *4 oz* | 113 | 6.4 | 52.2 |  |  | 90 | .14 | 0.0 |  |  | 219 |  | 1.60 |  |  |
| **blueberry** |  |  |  |  |  |  |  |  |  |  |  |  |  |  |  |
| from mix | 126 | 13.0 | 4.3 |  |  |  | 0 | .07 |  |  | 200 | 14 | 4 | .20 |  |
| *1 muffin* | 40 | 2.4 | 19.5 |  |  | 40 | .10 | 1.0 |  |  | 48 | 80 | .48 | .032 |  |
| homemade, enr | 112 | 15.6 | 3.7 |  |  |  | 0 | .08 |  |  | 253 | 34 |  |  |  |
| *1 muffin* | 40 | 2.9 | 16.8 | 1.1 |  | 90 | .06 | 0.5 |  |  | 46 | 53 | .60 |  |  |
| muffin mix, Duncan Hines | 99 | 5.1 | 2.7 |  | 0 |  |  | .06 |  |  | 147 | 9 | 3 | .11 |  |
| *1/12 pkg (1 muffin)* | 27 | 1.5 | 17.0 |  |  |  | .07 | 1.0 |  |  | 30 | 57 | .35 | .022 |  |
| **bran & honey muffin mix, Duncan Hines** | 98 | 1.1 | 2.8 |  | 0 |  |  | .06 |  |  | 161 | 8 | 20 | .35 |  |
| *1/12 pkg (1 muffin)* | 23 | 1.7 | 16.3 |  |  |  | .08 | 1.2 |  |  | 46 | 110 | .83 | .048 |  |
| **bran, homemade** | 112 | 14.2 | 5.1 |  |  |  | 2 | .11 | .11 | 17 | 168 | 54 | 35 | 1.08 |  |
| *1 muffin* | 40 | 3.0 | 16.7 |  |  | 206 | .10 | 1.3 | .09 | .24 | 99 | 111 | 1.26 | .085 |  |
| **carrot, frzn, Am Hosp Co** | 260 |  | 13.7 |  | 53 |  | 0 | .09 |  |  | 248 | 22 |  |  |  |
| *3 oz* | 85 | 5.1 | 25.5 |  |  | 26 | .04 |  |  |  | 109 |  | .34 |  |  |
| **corn** |  |  |  |  |  |  |  |  |  |  |  |  |  |  |  |
| from mix | 130 | 12.2 | 4.2 |  |  |  | 0 | .08 |  |  | 192 | 96 |  |  |  |
| *1 muffin* | 40 | 2.8 | 20.0 | 1.2 |  | 100 | .07 | 0.6 |  |  | 44 | 152 | .60 |  |  |
| from mix, Dromedary | 120 |  | 4.0 |  |  |  |  |  |  |  | 270 |  |  |  |  |
| *1 muffin* |  | 3.0 | 20.0 |  |  |  |  |  |  |  | 50 |  |  |  |  |
| homemade w/ enr degermed corn meal | 126 | 13.1 | 4.0 |  |  |  | 0 | .09 |  |  | 192 | 42 |  |  |  |
| *1 muffin* | 40 | 2.8 | 19.2 | 1.2 |  | 120 | .08 | 0.6 |  |  | 54 | 68 | .70 |  |  |
| homemade w/ whole ground corn meal | 115 | 15.1 | 4.1 |  |  |  | 0 | .07 |  |  | 198 | 45 |  |  |  |
| *1 muffin* | 40 | 2.9 | 17.0 | 1.2 |  | 120 | .07 | 0.4 |  |  | 53 | 86 | .60 |  |  |
| muffin mix, Flako | 116 | 2.2 | 2.2 |  |  |  |  | .03 | .02 | 3 | 317 | 18 | 5 | .00 | .000 |
| *1 oz dry mix* | 28 | 1.9 | 19.5 |  |  | 32 | .05 | 0.6 | .00 | .00 | 26 | 25 | .38 | .020 |  |
| **date nut, frzn, Am Hosp Co** | 427 |  | 16.7 |  | 73 |  | 9 | .02 |  |  | 612 | 45 |  |  |  |
| *4 oz* | 113 | 5.7 | 63.5 |  |  | 124 | .01 | 1.1 |  |  | 256 |  | 2.72 |  |  |
| **english muffin** |  |  |  |  |  |  |  |  |  |  |  |  |  |  |  |
| cinn raisin, refrig dough | 140 |  | 1.0 |  |  |  |  |  |  |  | 250 |  |  |  |  |
| *1 muffin* | 57 | 4.0 | 30.0 |  |  |  |  |  |  |  | 105 |  |  |  |  |
| multi grain, refrig dough | 130 |  | 1.0 |  |  |  |  |  |  |  | 270 |  |  |  |  |
| *1 muffin* | 57 | 4.0 | 26.0 |  |  |  |  |  |  |  | 80 |  |  |  |  |
| plain | 135 | 23.9 | 1.1 |  | 0 |  | 0 | .18 | .02 | 18 | 364 | 92 | 11 | .41 |  |
| *1 muffin* | 57 | 4.5 | 26.2 |  |  | 0 | .26 | 2.1 | .00 | .29 | 319 | 64 | 1.61 | .177 |  |
| plain, Earth Grains | 150 |  | 1.0 |  |  |  |  |  |  |  | 450 |  |  |  |  |
| *1 muffin* | 65 | 5.0 | 30.0 |  |  |  |  |  |  |  | 70 |  |  |  |  |
| plain, refrig dough | 120 |  | 1.0 |  |  |  |  |  |  |  | 280 |  |  |  |  |
| *1 muffin* | 57 | 4.0 | 24.0 |  |  |  |  |  |  |  | 45 |  |  |  |  |
| plain, toasted | 145 | 14.5 | 1.2 |  | 0 |  | 0 | .19 | .02 | 19 | 391 | 99 | 12 | .44 |  |
| *1 muffin* | 50 | 4.8 | 28.1 |  |  | 0 | .22 | 2.3 | .00 | .31 | 343 | 68 | 1.73 | .190 |  |
| plain, Wonder | 130 |  | 1.0 |  | 0 |  |  |  |  |  | 280 |  |  |  |  |
| *1 muffin* | 56 | 4.0 | 26.0 |  |  |  |  |  |  |  |  |  |  |  |  |
| sour dough, Wonder | 130 |  | 1.0 |  | 0 |  |  |  |  |  | 250 |  |  |  |  |
| *1 muffin* | 56 | 4.0 | 27.0 |  |  |  |  |  |  |  |  |  |  |  |  |
| wheatberry, Earth Grains | 150 |  | 1.0 |  |  |  |  |  |  |  | 460 |  |  |  |  |
| *1 muffin* | 65 | 6.0 | 28.0 |  |  |  |  |  |  |  | 110 |  |  |  |  |
| whole wheat, Earth Grains | 170 |  | 2.0 |  |  |  |  |  |  |  | 540 |  |  |  |  |
| *1 muffin* | 82 | 7.0 | 33.0 |  |  |  |  |  |  |  | 190 |  |  |  |  |
| w/ raisins, Earth Grains | 150 |  | 1.0 |  |  |  |  |  |  |  | 390 |  |  |  |  |
| *1 muffin* | 65 | 5.0 | 31.0 |  |  |  |  |  |  |  | 135 |  |  |  |  |

|  | KCAL | H₂O (g) | FAT (g) | PUFA (g) | CHOL (mg) | A (RE) | C (mg) | B-2 (mg) | B-6 (mg) | FOL (mcg) | Na (mg) | Ca (mg) | Mg (mg) | Zn (mg) | Mn (mg) |
|---|---|---|---|---|---|---|---|---|---|---|---|---|---|---|---|
|  | WT (g) | PRO (g) | CHO (g) | SFA (g) | DFIB (g) | A (IU) | B-1 (mg) | NIA (mg) | B-12 (mcg) | PANT (mg) | K (mg) | P (mg) | Fe (mg) | Cu (mg) | |
| w/ raisins, Wonder | 140 |  | 2.0 |  | 0 |  |  |  |  |  | 280 |  |  |  |  |
| *1 muffin* | 56 | 4.0 | 27.0 |  |  |  |  |  |  |  |  |  |  |  | |
| **plain, homemade, enr** | 118 | 15.2 | 4.0 |  |  |  | 0 | .09 |  |  | 176 | 42 |  |  |  |
| *1 muffin* | 40 | 3.1 | 16.9 | 1.0 |  | 40 | .07 | 0.6 |  |  | 50 | 60 | .60 |  | |
| **toaster muffin, Pillsbury** |  |  |  |  |  |  |  |  |  |  |  |  |  |  |  |
| apple spice | 138 |  | 4.5 |  |  |  | 0 | .05 |  |  | 123 | 16 |  |  |  |
| *1 muffin* | 39 | 1.9 | 24.1 |  |  | 12 | .07 | 0.6 |  |  | 50 | 75 | .62 |  | |
| banana nut | 141 |  | 6.2 |  |  |  | 1 | .06 |  |  | 83 | 10 |  |  |  |
| *1 muffin* | 39 | 2.1 | 19.7 |  |  | 28 | .08 | 0.7 |  |  | 69 | 35 | .66 |  | |
| blueberry | 131 |  | 4.1 |  |  |  | 0 | .05 |  |  | 122 | 9 |  |  |  |
| *1 muffin* | 39 | 1.6 | 23.0 |  |  | 10 | .07 | 0.7 |  |  | 26 | 55 | .53 |  | |
| corn, old fashioned | 141 |  | 5.1 |  |  |  | 0 | .08 |  |  | 253 | 20 |  |  |  |
| *1 muffin* | 38 | 2.7 | 20.9 |  |  | 42 | .09 | 0.7 |  |  | 52 | 130 | .49 |  | |
| raisin bran | 121 |  | 4.1 |  |  |  | 0 | .07 |  |  | 222 | 27 |  |  |  |
| *1 muffin* | 39 | 2.4 | 19.9 |  |  | 15 | .07 | 0.9 |  |  | 118 | 108 | 1.01 |  | |

## 17.6. PANCAKES

|  | KCAL | H₂O (g) | FAT (g) | PUFA (g) | CHOL (mg) | A (RE) | C (mg) | B-2 (mg) | B-6 (mg) | FOL (mcg) | Na (mg) | Ca (mg) | Mg (mg) | Zn (mg) | Mn (mg) |
|---|---|---|---|---|---|---|---|---|---|---|---|---|---|---|---|
|  | WT (g) | PRO (g) | CHO (g) | SFA (g) | DFIB (g) | A (IU) | B-1 (mg) | NIA (mg) | B-12 (mcg) | PANT (mg) | K (mg) | P (mg) | Fe (mg) | Cu (mg) | |
| **from frzn batter** |  |  |  |  |  |  |  |  |  |  |  |  |  |  |  |
| blueberry, Aunt Jemima | 205 | 61.2 | 1.6 |  |  |  |  | .23 | .11 | 9 | 698 | 68 | 17 | .00 | .000 |
| *three 4″ pancakes* | 113 | 6.2 | 41.5 |  |  | 54 | .32 | 2.0 | .89 | .00 | 93 | 329 | 1.44 | .090 | |
| buttermilk, Aunt Jemima | 212 | 59.2 | 1.5 |  |  |  |  | .28 | .06 | 14 | 733 | 91 | 18 | .00 | .000 |
| *three 4″ pancakes* | 113 | 7.1 | 42.6 |  |  | 56 | .34 | 2.2 | .28 | .00 | 129 | 340 | 1.70 | .090 | |
| plain, Aunt Jemima | 210 | 60.2 | 1.6 |  |  |  |  | .24 | .05 | 19 | 857 | 68 | 16 | .00 | .000 |
| *three 4″ pancakes* | 113 | 6.6 | 42.2 |  |  | 53 | .35 | 2.1 | .37 | .00 | 92 | 329 | 1.51 | .090 | |
| **from mix** |  |  |  |  |  |  |  |  |  |  |  |  |  |  |  |
| buttermilk complete, Hungry Jack | 180 |  | 1.0 |  |  |  | 0 | .20 |  |  | 710 | 154 |  |  |  |
| *three 4″ pancakes* |  | 4.2 | 38.2 |  |  | 51 | .24 | 2.1 |  |  | 80 | 368 | 2.65 |  | |
| extra lights complete, Hungry Jack | 190 |  | 2.5 |  |  |  | 0 | .18 |  |  | 698 | 133 |  |  |  |
| *three 4″ pancakes* |  | 4.2 | 37.1 |  |  | 42 | .28 | 2.1 |  |  | 32 | 357 | 2.86 |  | |
| plain | 159 | 39.1 | 5.9 |  |  |  | 0 | .16 | .15 | 8 | 431 | 96 | 14 | .52 |  |
| *1 large (7 T batter)* | 73 | 5.0 | 21.3 |  |  | 104 | .10 | 0.7 | .96 | .26 | 117 | 191 | .72 | .044 | |
| **frzn** |  |  |  |  |  |  |  |  |  |  |  |  |  |  |  |
| apple, Am Hosp Co | 90 |  | 0.4 |  | 0 |  | 2 | .07 |  |  | 262 | 11 |  |  |  |
| *2 oz* | 57 | 1.6 | 20.3 |  |  | 6 | .08 | 0.6 |  |  | 48 |  |  |  | |
| blueberry, Am Hosp Co | 93 |  | 0.4 |  | 0 |  | 2 | .06 |  |  | 256 | 11 |  |  |  |
| *2 oz* | 57 | 1.6 | 20.8 |  |  | 11 | .08 | 0.5 |  |  | 44 |  | .70 |  | |
| blueberry, Aunt Jemima | 249 | 45.8 | 4.0 |  |  |  |  | .34 | .05 | 55 | 789 | 67 | 20 | 1.00 | .000 |
| *three 4″ pancakes* | 106 | 6.8 | 46.4 |  |  | 131 | .24 | 2.1 | .64 | 1.00 | 136 | 380 | 1.95 | .100 | |
| buttermilk, Aunt Jemima | 240 | 47.6 | 3.7 |  |  |  |  | .33 | .04 | 29 | 778 | 76 | 20 | 1.00 | .000 |
| *three 4″ pancakes* | 106 | 7.0 | 44.7 |  |  | 0 | .26 | 2.1 | .59 | 1.00 | 103 | 309 | 2.06 | .080 | |
| buttermilk, Pillsbury Microwave | 260 | 44.3 | 3.6 |  |  |  | 0 | .22 |  |  | 592 | 90 |  |  |  |
| *3 pancakes* | 108 | 5.6 | 50.8 |  |  | 26 | .32 | 2.4 |  |  | 85 | 162 | 1.30 |  | |
| plain, Aunt Jemima | 246 | 46.0 | 3.7 |  |  |  |  | .41 | .05 | 26 | 777 | 66 | 19 | 1.00 | .000 |
| *three 4″ pancakes* | 106 | 6.7 | 46.6 |  |  | 83 | .25 | 2.2 | .32 | 1.00 | 133 | 367 | 1.17 | .070 | |
| plain, Pillsbury Microwave | 241 | 47.7 | 3.5 |  |  |  | 0 | .21 |  |  | 542 | 85 |  |  |  |
| *3 pancakes* | 106 | 5.3 | 46.6 |  |  | 3 | .21 | 2.1 |  |  | 85 | 153 | 1.17 |  | |
| **homemade, enr, plain** | 62 | 13.5 | 1.9 |  |  |  | 0 | .06 |  |  | 115 | 27 |  |  |  |
| *one 4″ pancake* | 27 | 1.9 | 9.2 | 0.5 |  | 30 | .05 | 0.4 |  |  | 33 | 38 | .40 |  | |
| **pancake batter, panshakes, Hungry Jack** | 197 | 5.0 | 3.2 |  |  |  | 0 | .27 |  |  | 834 | 45 |  |  |  |
| *amt for three 4″ pancakes* | 54 | 4.2 | 38.8 |  |  | 0 | .41 | 3.4 |  |  | 38 | 400 | 2.16 |  | |
| **pancake/waffle mix** |  |  |  |  |  |  |  |  |  |  |  |  |  |  |  |
| blueberry, Hungry Jack | 171 | 22.4 | 1.0 |  |  |  | 1 | .14 |  |  | 772 | 52 |  |  |  |
| *amt for three 4″ pancakes* | 68 | 3.2 | 37.4 |  |  | 33 | .20 | 1.8 |  |  | 51 | 116 | 1.63 |  | |
| buckwheat, Aunt Jemima | 107 | 2.9 | 0.8 |  |  |  |  | .12 | .05 | 11 | 432 | 150 | 42 | .00 | .000 |
| *1/4 cup dry mix* | 31 | 3.4 | 21.3 |  |  | 0 | .17 | 1.4 | .00 | .00 | 99 | 273 | 1.66 | .110 | |

| | KCAL / WT (g) | H₂O (g) / PRO (g) | FAT (g) / CHO (g) | PUFA (g) / SFA (g) | CHOL (mg) / DFIB (g) | A (RE) / A (IU) | C (mg) / B-1 (mg) | B-2 (mg) / NIA (mg) | B-6 (mg) / B-12 (mcg) | FOL (mcg) / PANT (mg) | Na (mg) / K (mg) | Ca (mg) / P (mg) | Mg (mg) / Fe (mg) | Zn (mg) / Cu (mg) | Mn (mg) |
|---|---|---|---|---|---|---|---|---|---|---|---|---|---|---|---|
| buttermilk, Aunt Jemima | 175 | 5.1 | 0.7 | | | | | .28 | .05 | 12 | 832 | 230 | 28 | .00 | .000 |
| *1/3 cup dry mix* | 51 | 5.7 | 36.5 | | | 0 | .34 | 2.4 | .00 | | 114 | 342 | 1.85 | .100 | |
| buttermilk, complete, Aunt Jemima | 264 | 5.8 | 3.0 | | | | | .42 | .09 | 19 | 858 | 403 | 37 | 1.00 | .000 |
| *1/2 cup dry mix* | 71 | 8.1 | 51.2 | | | 0 | .39 | 2.8 | .00 | 1.00 | 236 | 514 | 2.40 | .140 | |
| buttermilk, Hungry Jack | 131 | 3.0 | 0.4 | | | | 0 | .15 | | | 514 | 26 | | | |
| *amt for three 4″ pancakes* | 37 | 3.0 | 28.5 | | | 0 | .19 | 1.1 | | | 61 | 226 | 1.52 | | |
| extra lights, Hungry Jack | 119 | 3.1 | 0.3 | | | | 0 | .09 | | | 429 | 99 | | | |
| *amt for three 4″ pancakes* | 34 | 2.6 | 26.2 | | | 0 | .26 | 1.1 | | | 102 | 228 | 1.22 | | |
| plain, Aunt Jemima | 108 | 2.9 | 0.6 | | | | | .06 | .06 | 4 | 450 | 140 | 19 | .00 | .000 |
| *1/4 cup dry mix* | 31 | 3.0 | 22.5 | | | 0 | .15 | 0.9 | .00 | .00 | 61 | 242 | 1.17 | .060 | |
| plain, complete, Aunt Jemima | 272 | 7.0 | 3.6 | | | | | .36 | .16 | 86 | 881 | 155 | 33 | 1.00 | .000 |
| *1/2 cup dry mix* | 74 | 7.5 | 52.3 | | | 50 | .39 | 2.5 | .00 | 1.00 | 182 | 503 | 2.43 | .100 | |
| whole wheat, Aunt Jemima | 142 | 4.0 | 0.5 | | | | | .17 | .06 | 21 | 587 | 181 | 51 | 1.00 | 1.000 |
| *1/3 cup dry mix* | 43 | 5.9 | 28.5 | | | 0 | .15 | 2.0 | .00 | .00 | 184 | 311 | 1.78 | .210 | |

## 17.7. PASTA

| | KCAL / WT (g) | H₂O (g) / PRO (g) | FAT (g) / CHO (g) | PUFA (g) / SFA (g) | CHOL (mg) / DFIB (g) | A (RE) / A (IU) | C (mg) / B-1 (mg) | B-2 (mg) / NIA (mg) | B-6 (mg) / B-12 (mcg) | FOL (mcg) / PANT (mg) | Na (mg) / K (mg) | Ca (mg) / P (mg) | Mg (mg) / Fe (mg) | Zn (mg) / Cu (mg) | Mn (mg) |
|---|---|---|---|---|---|---|---|---|---|---|---|---|---|---|---|
| **macaroni, enr, ckd** | 159 | 100.1 | 0.7 | 0 | | | 0 | .11 | .01 | 3 | 1 | 11 | 25 | .70 | .280 |
| *1 cup* | 140 | 5.2 | 33.7 | 0.6 | | 0 | .20 | 1.5 | .00 | .15 | 85 | 70 | 2.25 | .028 | |
| **macaroni salad, cnd, Joan of Arc** | 200 | 75.0 | 12.8 | | | | | .09 | | | 830 | 13 | | | |
| *1/2 cup* | 112 | 2.9 | 18.5 | | | 22 | .09 | 0.9 | | | | 47 | .90 | | |
| **noodles, chow mein, cnd** | 220 | 0.5 | 10.6 | | | | | | | | | | | | |
| *1 cup* | 45 | 5.9 | 26.1 | | | | | | | | | | | | |
| **noodles** | | | | | | | | | | | | | | | |
| enr, ckd | 200 | 112.6 | 2.4 | 50 | | | 0 | .19 | .01 | 7 | 3 | 16 | 28 | .20 | .320 |
| *1 cup* | 160 | 6.6 | 37.3 | 0.2 | | 110 | .26 | 1.9 | .50 | .25 | 70 | 94 | 2.40 | .136 | |
| Mueller's | 220 | 5.5 | 2.9 | 55 | | | | .30 | | | 9 | | | | |
| *2 oz dry* | 57 | 8.0 | 39.8 | | | | .60 | 4.2 | | | | | 2.00 | | |
| Mueller's golden rich | 220 | 6.2 | 3.2 | 70 | | | | .30 | | | 5 | | | | |
| *2 oz dry* | 57 | 8.0 | 38.8 | | | | .60 | 4.2 | | | | | 2.00 | | |
| lasagne, Mueller's | 210 | 5.5 | 1.4 | 0 | | | | .30 | | | 3 | | | | |
| *2 oz dry* | 57 | 7.8 | 41.6 | | | | .60 | 4.2 | | | | | 2.00 | | |
| parsleyed, frzn, Banquet | 186 | | 10.0 | 35 | | | 0 | .07 | | | 568 | 40 | | | |
| *4 oz* | 113 | 5.0 | 19.0 | | | 270 | .07 | 0.4 | | | 21 | | .60 | | |
| romanoff w/ cheese sce, frzn, Am Hosp | 198 | | 5.6 | 9 | | | 0 | .15 | | | 124 | 199 | | | |
| Co—*4 oz* | 113 | 16.8 | 20.4 | | | 264 | .09 | | | | 256 | | .60 | | |
| **pasta salad, italian, Fresh Chef** | 111 | | 5.3 | | | | 1 | .06 | | | 334 | 25 | | | |
| *3.2 oz* | 92 | 2.4 | 13.4 | | | 234 | .06 | 0.7 | | | 47 | | 1.60 | | |
| **pasta salad, seafood, Fresh Chef** | 229 | | 16.2 | | | | 1 | .12 | | | 426 | 41 | | | |
| *4.3 oz* | 123 | 6.0 | 14.7 | | | 176 | .09 | 1.1 | | | 117 | | 1.80 | | |
| **spaghetti, enr, ckd** | 159 | 100.1 | 0.7 | 0 | | | 0 | .11 | .01 | 3 | 1 | 11 | 25 | .70 | .322 |
| *1 cup* | 140 | 5.2 | 33.7 | 0.6 | | 0 | .20 | 1.5 | .00 | .15 | 85 | 70 | 2.25 | .028 | |
| **spaghetti/macaroni, Mueller's** | 210 | 5.8 | 1.1 | 0 | | | | .30 | | | 2 | 8 | | | |
| *2 oz dry* | 57 | 7.3 | 42.1 | | | | .60 | 4.2 | | | | | 2.00 | | |

## 17.8. ROLLS

| | KCAL / WT (g) | H₂O (g) / PRO (g) | FAT (g) / CHO (g) | PUFA (g) / SFA (g) | CHOL (mg) / DFIB (g) | A (RE) / A (IU) | C (mg) / B-1 (mg) | B-2 (mg) / NIA (mg) | B-6 (mg) / B-12 (mcg) | FOL (mcg) / PANT (mg) | Na (mg) / K (mg) | Ca (mg) / P (mg) | Mg (mg) / Fe (mg) | Zn (mg) / Cu (mg) | Mn (mg) |
|---|---|---|---|---|---|---|---|---|---|---|---|---|---|---|---|
| **brown 'n serve, Wonder** | | | | | | | | | | | | | | | |
| gem style | 80 | | 2.0 | 5 | | | | | | | 140 | | | | |
| *1 roll* | 28 | 2.0 | 13.0 | | | | | | | | | | | | |
| half & half | 80 | | 2.0 | 5 | | | | | | | 140 | | | | |
| *1 roll* | 28 | 2.0 | 13.0 | | | | | | | | | | | | |
| home bake | 80 | | 2.0 | 5 | | | | | | | 130 | | | | |
| *1 roll* | 28 | 2.0 | 13.0 | | | | | | | | | | | | |
| w/ buttermilk | 80 | | 2.0 | 5 | | | | | | | 140 | | | | |
| *1 roll* | 28 | 2.0 | 13.0 | | | | | | | | | | | | |
| **dinner, Home Pride** | 80 | | 2.0 | 5 | | | | | | | 170 | | | | |
| *1 roll* | 28 | 2.0 | 14.0 | | | | | | | | | | | | |
| **dinner/pan** | 85 | 9.0 | 2.1 | | | | 0 | .09 | .02 | 11 | 155 | 33 | 6 | .20 | |
| *1 roll* | 28 | 2.4 | 14.0 | | | 0 | .14 | 1.1 | | .15 | 36 | 44 | .83 | .023 | |

| | KCAL / WT (g) | H₂O (g) / PRO (g) | FAT (g) / CHO (g) | PUFA (g) / SFA (g) | CHOL (mg) / DFIB (g) | A (RE) / A (IU) | C (mg) / B-1 (mg) | B-2 (mg) / NIA (mg) | B-6 (mg) / B-12 (mcg) | FOL (mcg) / PANT (mg) | Na (mg) / K (mg) | Ca (mg) / P (mg) | Mg (mg) / Fe (mg) | Zn (mg) / Cu (mg) | Mn (mg) |
|---|---|---|---|---|---|---|---|---|---|---|---|---|---|---|---|
| **french** | | | | | | | | | | | | | | | |
| Earth Grains | 100 | | 1.0 | | | | | | | | 270 | | | | |
| *1 roll* | 34 | 4.0 | 19.0 | | | | | | | | 45 | | | | |
| enr | 137 | 16.0 | 0.4 | | | | 0 | .18 | .03 | 29 | 287 | 8 | 12 | .30 | |
| *1 roll* | 50 | 4.3 | 28.3 | | | 0 | .20 | 2.0 | .00 | .24 | 50 | 41 | 1.48 | .050 | |
| sourdough, Earth Grains | 100 | | 1.0 | | | | | | | | 160 | | | | |
| *1 roll* | 34 | 3.0 | 19.0 | | | | | | | | 40 | | | | |
| unenr | 137 | 16.0 | 0.4 | | | | 0 | .06 | .03 | 29 | 287 | 8 | 12 | .30 | |
| *1 roll* | 50 | 4.3 | 28.3 | | | 0 | .05 | 0.6 | .00 | .25 | 50 | 41 | .63 | .050 | |
| from mix, Pillsbury | 240 | | 4.0 | | | | | | | | 430 | | | | |
| *2 rolls* | | 7.0 | 42.0 | | | | | | | | 90 | | | | |
| hamburger | 114 | 13.6 | 2.1 | | | | 0 | .13 | .01 | 15 | 241 | 54 | 8 | .25 | |
| *1 roll* | 40 | 3.4 | 20.1 | | | 0 | .20 | 1.6 | .00 | .21 | 37 | 33 | 1.19 | .066 | |
| hamburger, Wonder | 80 | | 1.0 | | 5 | | | | | | 150 | | | | |
| *1 roll* | 28 | 2.0 | 14.0 | | | | | | | | | | | | |
| hoagie | 400 | | 7.0 | | 5 | | | | | | 840 | | | | |
| *1 roll* | 142 | 13.0 | 73.0 | | | | | | | | | | | | |
| home style, Rich's dough, baked | 152 | 20.8 | 2.4 | | | | | .20 | | | 335 | 27 | 12 | .34 | |
| *2 rolls* | 50 | 4.5 | 28.1 | | | | .32 | 2.1 | | | 68 | 76 | 2.04 | .180 | |
| hot dog | 114 | 13.6 | 2.1 | | | | 0 | .13 | .01 | 15 | 241 | 54 | 8 | .25 | |
| *1 roll* | 40 | 3.4 | 20.1 | | | 0 | .20 | 1.6 | .00 | .21 | 37 | 33 | 1.19 | .070 | |
| hot dog, Wonder | 80 | | 1.0 | | 5 | | | | | | 150 | | | | |
| *1 roll* | 28 | 2.0 | 14.0 | | | | | | | | | | | | |
| kaiser, Earth Grains | 190 | | 2.0 | | | | | | | | 520 | | | | |
| *1 roll* | 65 | 7.0 | 37.0 | | | | | | | | 85 | | | | |
| onion, Earth Grains | 190 | | 2.0 | | | | | | | | 530 | | | | |
| *1 roll* | 65 | 7.0 | 35.0 | | | | | | | | 100 | | | | |
| pan, Wonder | 80 | | 1.0 | | 5 | | | | | | 140 | | | | |
| *1 roll* | 28 | 2.0 | 14.0 | | | | | | | | | | | | |
| popover, enr, homemade | 90 | 22.0 | 3.7 | | | | 0 | .10 | | | 88 | 38 | | | |
| *1 popover* | 40 | 3.5 | 10.3 | 1.3 | | 130 | .06 | 0.4 | | | 60 | 56 | .60 | | |
| popover mix, Flako | 102 | 3.3 | 1.2 | | | | | .02 | .02 | 6 | 273 | 9 | 8 | .00 | .000 |
| *1 oz dry mix* | 28 | 3.2 | 19.6 | | | 0 | .07 | 0.5 | .00 | .00 | 31 | 28 | .45 | .040 | |
| **refrig dough** | | | | | | | | | | | | | | | |
| butterflake, Pillsbury | 110 | 14.1 | 3.8 | | | | 0 | .08 | | | 415 | 5 | | | |
| *1 roll* | 38 | 2.5 | 16.3 | | | 0 | .13 | 1.0 | | | 20 | 165 | .66 | | |
| crescent, Continental | 190 | | 8.0 | | | | | | | | 600 | | | | |
| *2 rolls* | 57 | 3.0 | 25.0 | | | | | | | | 40 | | | | |
| crescent, Pillsbury | 200 | 17.7 | 11.2 | | | | 0 | .12 | | | 463 | 11 | | | |
| *2 rolls* | 57 | 3.4 | 22.2 | | | 0 | .17 | 1.5 | | | 127 | 215 | 1.31 | | |
| submarine, Earth Grains | 180 | | 1.0 | | | | | | | | 500 | | | | |
| *1/2 roll* | 64 | 7.0 | 36.0 | | | | | | | | 85 | | | | |
| wheat, Earth Grains | 110 | | 1.0 | | | | | | | | 260 | | | | |
| *1 roll* | 40 | 4.0 | 22.0 | | | | | | | | 65 | | | | |
| whole wheat | 72 | 9.0 | 0.8 | | | | 0 | .04 | | | 158 | 30 | | | |
| *1 roll* | 28 | 2.8 | 14.6 | | | 0 | .10 | 0.8 | | | 82 | 79 | .67 | | |
| weiner wrap, Pillsbury | 60 | 7.9 | 1.4 | | | | 0 | .05 | | | 373 | 4 | | | |
| *1 wrap* | 22 | 1.5 | 10.5 | | | 0 | .18 | 0.8 | | | 23 | 112 | .75 | | |

## 17.9. STUFFING

| | KCAL / WT (g) | H₂O (g) / PRO (g) | FAT (g) / CHO (g) | PUFA (g) / SFA (g) | CHOL (mg) / DFIB (g) | A (RE) / A (IU) | C (mg) / B-1 (mg) | B-2 (mg) / NIA (mg) | B-6 (mg) / B-12 (mcg) | FOL (mcg) / PANT (mg) | Na (mg) / K (mg) | Ca (mg) / P (mg) | Mg (mg) / Fe (mg) | Zn (mg) / Cu (mg) | Mn (mg) |
|---|---|---|---|---|---|---|---|---|---|---|---|---|---|---|---|
| **from mix** | | | | | | | | | | | | | | | |
| americana san francisco style, Stove Top—*1/2 cup* | 173 | 72.0 | 8.7 | 0.6 | 21 | | 0 | .11 | .04 | 29 | 638 | 34 | 15 | .27 | |
| | 107 | 4.1 | 19.9 | 5.0 | | 293 | .15 | 1.4 | .02 | .22 | 77 | 47 | 1.17 | .079 | |
| bread | 416 | 122.8 | 25.6 | | | | 0 | .18 | | | 1008 | 80 | | | |
| *1 cup* | 200 | 8.8 | 39.4 | 13.1 | | 840 | .10 | 1.6 | | | 116 | 132 | 2.00 | | |
| chicken flavored, Stove Top | 176 | 72.0 | 8.8 | 0.6 | 21 | | 1 | .10 | .04 | 24 | 560 | 33 | 12 | .25 | |
| *1/2 cup* | 107 | 3.9 | 20.5 | 5.0 | | 319 | .15 | 1.3 | .02 | .20 | 86 | 41 | 1.23 | .081 | |
| chicken flavored w/ rice, Stove Top | 182 | 72.3 | 8.8 | 0.6 | 22 | | 1 | .09 | .04 | 23 | 557 | 32 | 12 | .28 | |
| *1/2 cup* | 109 | 4.0 | 22.0 | 5.0 | | 324 | .16 | 1.3 | .02 | .17 | 84 | 42 | 1.27 | .082 | |

| | KCAL | H₂O (g) | FAT (g) | PUFA (g) | CHOL (mg) | A (RE) | C (mg) | B-2 (mg) | B-6 (mg) | FOL (mcg) | Na (mg) | Ca (mg) | Mg (mg) | Zn (mg) | Mn (mg) |
|---|---|---|---|---|---|---|---|---|---|---|---|---|---|---|---|
| | WT (g) | PRO (g) | CHO (g) | SFA (g) | DFIB (g) | A (IU) | B-1 (mg) | NIA (mg) | B-12 (mcg) | PANT (mg) | K (mg) | P (mg) | Fe (mg) | Cu (mg) | |
| chicken florentine, Stove Top | 207 | 62.9 | 12.7 | 0.7 | 32 | | 4 | .10 | .06 | 37 | 670 | 56 | 26 | .32 | |
| *1/2 cup* | 102 | 4.2 | 19.7 | 7.4 | | 1119 | .11 | 1.1 | .03 | .12 | 178 | 66 | 1.33 | .097 | |
| cornbread, Stove Top | 175 | 72.0 | 8.5 | 0.5 | 21 | | 1 | .07 | .04 | 12 | 568 | 24 | 13 | .21 | |
| *1/2 cup* | 107 | 3.2 | 21.5 | 5.0 | | 334 | .10 | 0.8 | .01 | .09 | 84 | 34 | .94 | .066 | |
| for beef, Stove Top | 178 | 71.9 | 8.6 | 0.6 | 21 | | 1 | .10 | .05 | 25 | 581 | 33 | 11 | .26 | |
| *1/2 cup* | 108 | 4.1 | 21.4 | 5.0 | | 815 | .16 | 1.3 | .02 | .18 | 82 | 42 | 1.30 | .085 | |
| for pork, Stove Top | 174 | 72.0 | 8.7 | 0.6 | 21 | | 1 | .11 | .05 | 27 | 620 | 36 | 13 | .24 | |
| *1/2 cup* | 107 | 3.8 | 20.4 | 5.0 | | 353 | .23 | 1.4 | .02 | .19 | 91 | 45 | 1.40 | .100 | |
| garden herb, Stove Top | 208 | 56.3 | 12.6 | 0.7 | 32 | | 2 | .09 | .05 | 19 | 416 | 41 | 16 | .30 | |
| *1/2 cup* | 95 | 3.7 | 20.8 | 7.4 | | 576 | .13 | 1.2 | .03 | .13 | 151 | 48 | 1.28 | .099 | |
| homestyle herb, Stove Top | 173 | 61.7 | 8.6 | 1.2 | 16 | | 1 | .09 | .03 | 19 | 530 | 37 | 11 | .25 | |
| *1/2 cup* | 96 | 3.8 | 20.1 | 4.1 | | 314 | .11 | 1.2 | .02 | .11 | 74 | 39 | 1.28 | .081 | |
| long grain & wild rice flavor, Stove Top | 183 | 72.3 | 8.7 | 0.6 | 21 | | 0 | .10 | .03 | 22 | 552 | 32 | 12 | .28 | |
| *1/2 cup* | 109 | 3.9 | 22.2 | 5.0 | | 325 | .16 | 1.3 | .02 | .15 | 70 | 41 | 1.33 | .079 | |
| savory herbs flavor, Stove Top | 175 | 72.0 | 8.8 | 0.6 | 22 | | 1 | .10 | .04 | 24 | 579 | 36 | 13 | .26 | |
| *1/2 cup* | 107 | 4.0 | 20.3 | 5.0 | | 345 | .15 | 1.3 | .02 | .16 | 89 | 41 | 1.45 | .082 | |
| turkey flavor, Stove Top | 174 | 72.0 | 8.7 | 0.6 | 21 | | 1 | .09 | .04 | 24 | 628 | 33 | 13 | .24 | |
| *1/2 cup* | 107 | 3.7 | 20.6 | 5.0 | | 318 | .15 | 1.2 | .02 | .16 | 83 | 41 | 1.21 | .080 | |
| veg & almond, Stove Top | 215 | 56.2 | 14.2 | 1.2 | 32 | | 9 | .12 | .06 | 22 | 439 | 47 | 23 | .40 | |
| *1/2 cup* | 95 | 4.0 | 18.8 | 7.6 | | 1376 | .11 | 1.2 | .03 | .15 | 142 | 59 | 1.44 | .122 | |
| wild rice & mushroom, Stove Top | 205 | 56.2 | 12.4 | 0.7 | 31 | | 17 | .12 | .05 | 17 | 582 | 31 | 15 | .33 | |
| *1/2 cup* | 95 | 3.7 | 20.6 | 7.3 | | 857 | .12 | 1.5 | .03 | .36 | 140 | 57 | 1.20 | .135 | |
| **frzn** | | | | | | | | | | | | | | | |
| apple, Am Hosp Co | 84 | | 2.1 | | 9 | | 1 | .02 | | | 38 | 11 | | | |
| *1 oz* | 28 | 1.4 | 12.8 | | | 11 | .06 | 0.2 | | | 20 | | | .27 | |
| chicken flavored, Banquet | 281 | | 8.0 | | 15 | | 0 | .27 | | | 693 | 65 | | | |
| *4 oz* | 113 | 8.0 | 44.0 | | | 127 | .55 | 3.3 | | | 99 | | 3.50 | | |
| chicken, Stuffing Originals | 170 | 61.1 | 7.5 | | | | 0 | .12 | | | 686 | 27 | | | |
| *1/2 cup* | 96 | 3.6 | 21.8 | | | 127 | .32 | 1.7 | | | 93 | 42 | 1.44 | | |
| cornbread, Stuffing Originals | 170 | 58.9 | 6.4 | | | | 0 | .10 | | | 662 | 20 | | | |
| *1/2 cup* | 95 | 3.3 | 24.7 | | | 125 | .28 | 1.5 | | | 100 | 40 | 1.02 | | |
| mushroom, Stuffing Originals | 150 | 60.7 | 6.4 | | | | 0 | .12 | | | 763 | 25 | | | |
| *1/2 cup* | 92 | 4.0 | 18.7 | | | 98 | .18 | 1.7 | | | 100 | 46 | 1.29 | | |

## 17.10.  TORTILLAS

| | KCAL | H₂O | FAT | PUFA | CHOL | A (RE) | C | B-2 | B-6 | FOL | Na | Ca | Mg | Zn | Mn |
|---|---|---|---|---|---|---|---|---|---|---|---|---|---|---|---|
| **corn** | | | | | | | | | | | | | | | |
| enr | 67 | 13.6 | 1.1 | | | | 0 | .14 | .09 | 6 | 53 | 42 | 20 | .43 | .123 |
| *1 tortilla* | 30 | 2.1 | 12.8 | | 1.0 | | .20 | 1.5 | .00 | .06 | 52 | 55 | 1.42 | .090 | |
| taco/tostada shell | 50 | 0.4 | 2.2 | | | | | .02 | | | 72 | 16 | 11 | .14 | |
| *1 shell* | 11 | 1.0 | 7.2 | | | | .03 | 0.2 | .00 | | 25 | 25 | .29 | .035 | |
| unenr | 67 | 13.6 | 1.1 | | | | 0 | .03 | .09 | 6 | 53 | 42 | 20 | .43 | |
| *1 tortilla* | 30 | 2.1 | 12.8 | | | | .05 | 0.4 | .00 | .06 | 52 | 55 | .57 | .090 | |
| **flour, El Charrito** | 170 | | 4.0 | | | | | | | | 310 | | | | |
| *2 tortillas* | | 5.0 | 30.0 | | | | | | | | 60 | | | | |

## 17.11.  WAFFLES

| | KCAL | H₂O | FAT | PUFA | CHOL | A (RE) | C | B-2 | B-6 | FOL | Na | Ca | Mg | Zn | Mn |
|---|---|---|---|---|---|---|---|---|---|---|---|---|---|---|---|
| **homemade, plain** | 245 | 27.6 | 12.6 | | | | 0 | .24 | .05 | 14 | 445 | 154 | 17 | .65 | |
| *1 large waffle* | 75 | 6.9 | 25.7 | | | 140 | .18 | 1.5 | .36 | .60 | 129 | 135 | 1.48 | .050 | |
| **from mix, plain, enr** | 206 | 31.2 | 8.0 | | | | 0 | .17 | | | 515 | 179 | | | |
| *1 waffle (7″ diameter)* | 75 | 6.6 | 27.2 | 2.7 | | 170 | .11 | 0.7 | | | 146 | 257 | 1.00 | | |
| **frzn** | | | | | | | | | | | | | | | |
| apple & cinn, Aunt Jemima | 173 | 31.0 | 4.3 | | | | | .34 | .40 | 30 | 503 | 100 | 14 | 1.00 | .000 |
| *2 waffles* | 71 | 4.6 | 29.0 | | | 0 | .30 | 3.0 | 1.50 | .00 | 87 | 270 | 3.60 | .050 | |
| blueberry, Aunt Jemima | 173 | 31.0 | 4.3 | | | | | .34 | .40 | 30 | 503 | 100 | 14 | 1.00 | .000 |
| *2 waffles* | 71 | 4.6 | 29.0 | | | 0 | .30 | 3.0 | 1.50 | .00 | 87 | 270 | 3.60 | .050 | |
| blueberry/raisin & bran, nutri-grain, Eggo—*1 rd waffle* | 130 | | 5.0 | | | | 0 | .17 | | | 300 | 20 | | | |
| | 39 | 3.0 | 18.0 | | | 500 | .15 | 2.0 | | | | | 1.80 | | |
| buttermilk, Aunt Jemima | 175 | 31.0 | 4.3 | | | | | .34 | .40 | 30 | 550 | 100 | 14 | 1.00 | .000 |
| *2 waffles* | 71 | 4.6 | 29.0 | | | 0 | .30 | 3.0 | 1.50 | .00 | 79 | 270 | 3.60 | .050 | |

| | KCAL | H$_2$O (g) | FAT (g) | PUFA (g) | CHOL (mg) | A (RE) | C (mg) | Vitamins B-2 (mg) | B-6 (mg) | FOL (mcg) | Na (mg) | Ca (mg) | Minerals Mg (mg) | Zn (mg) | Mn (mg) |
|---|---|---|---|---|---|---|---|---|---|---|---|---|---|---|---|
| | WT (g) | PRO (g) | CHO (g) | SFA (g) | DFIB (g) | A (IU) | B-1 (mg) | NIA (mg) | B-12 (mcg) | PANT (mg) | K (mg) | P (mg) | Fe (mg) | Cu (mg) | |
| buttermilk/homestyle, Eggo | 120 | | 5.0 | | | | 0 | .17 | | | 300 | 20 | | | |
| *1 rd waffle* | 39 | 3.0 | 16.0 | | | 500 | .15 | 2.0 | | | | | 1.80 | | |
| plain | 95 | 13.7 | 3.2 | | | | 0 | .18 | .09 | 1 | 235 | 28 | 7 | .28 | |
| *1 waffle* | 34 | 2.0 | 14.2 | | | 436 | .15 | 1.8 | | .12 | 71 | 130 | 1.65 | .021 | |
| plain, Aunt Jemima | 173 | 31.0 | 4.3 | | | | | .34 | .40 | 30 | 539 | 100 | 14 | 1.00 | .000 |
| *2 waffles* | 71 | 4.6 | 29.0 | | | 0 | .30 | 3.0 | 1.50 | .00 | 86 | 270 | 3.60 | .050 | |
| raisin, Aunt Jemima | 200 | 34.6 | 3.9 | | | | | .34 | .40 | 11 | 526 | 100 | 19 | .00 | .000 |
| *2 waffles* | 82 | 4.7 | 36.4 | | | 0 | .30 | 3.0 | 1.50 | .00 | 163 | 257 | 3.60 | .110 | |

| | KCAL | H₂O (g) | FAT (g) | PUFA (g) | CHOL (mg) | A (RE) | C (mg) | B-2 (mg) | B-6 (mg) | FOL (mcg) | Na (mg) | Ca (mg) | Mg (mg) | Zn (mg) | Mn (mg) |
|---|---|---|---|---|---|---|---|---|---|---|---|---|---|---|---|
| | WT (g) | PRO (g) | CHO (g) | SFA (g) | DFIB (g) | A (IU) | B-1 (mg) | NIA (mg) | B-12 (mcg) | PANT (mg) | K (mg) | P (mg) | Fe (mg) | Cu (mg) | |
| | | | | | INOS (mg) | D (IU) | E (IU) | K (mcg) | BIO (mcg) | CHLN (mg) | Cl (mg) | I (mcg) | Mo (mg) | | |
| | TRY (mg) | THR (mg) | ISO (mg) | LEU (mg) | LYS (mg) | MET (mg) | CYS (mg) | PHE (mg) | TYR (mg) | VAL (mg) | ARG (mg) | HIS (mg) | | | |

## 18. INFANT FORMULA

**enfamil, Mead Johnson** — *1 fl oz* (whey, nonfat milk, coconut oil, corn oil & lactose)

| | KCAL/WT/INOS/TRY | | | | | | | | | | | | | | |
|---|---|---|---|---|---|---|---|---|---|---|---|---|---|---|---|
| | 20 | 26.8 | 1.1 | | | | 2 | .03 | .01 | 3 | 5 | 14 | 2 | .16 | .003 |
| | 30 | 0.4 | 2.1 | | | 62 | .02 | 0.3 | .05 | .09 | 22 | 9 | .03ᵃ | .019 | |
| | | | | | 0.9 | 12 | 0.6 | 2 | 0.5 | 3.1 | 12 | 2 | | | |
| | 7 | 23 | 27 | 46 | 31 | 9 | 5 | 17 | 20 | 27 | | 9 | | | |

**enfamil human milk fortifier, Mead Johnson**ᵇ — *4 packets* (corn syrup solids, whey protein concentrate & casein)

| | | | | | | | | | | | | | | | |
|---|---|---|---|---|---|---|---|---|---|---|---|---|---|---|---|
| | 14 | 0.2 | 0.0 | | | | | | | | 7 | 60 | 4 | .80 | |
| | 3.8 | 0.7 | 2.7 | | | | | | | | 16 | 33 | | .040 | |
| | | | | | | | | | | | 18 | | | | |

**enfamil premature formula, 20 cal/fl oz, Mead Johnson** — *1 fl oz* (corn syrup solids, whey protein concentrate, nonfat milk, soy oil, MCTs & coconut oil)

| | | | | | | | | | | | | | | | |
|---|---|---|---|---|---|---|---|---|---|---|---|---|---|---|---|
| | 20 | 26.6 | 1.0 | | | | 7 | .07 | .05 | 7 | 8 | 23 | 1 | .20 | .003 |
| | 30 | 0.6 | 2.2 | | | 240 | .05 | 0.8 | .06 | .24 | 22 | 12 | .05 | .032 | |
| | | | | | 0.9 | 66 | 0.9 | 3 | 0.4 | 1.5 | 17 | 2 | | | |
| | 9 | 33 | 35 | 58 | 46 | 14 | 6 | 23 | 27 | 36 | | 12 | | | |

**enfamil premature formula, 24 cal/fl oz, Mead Johnson** — *1 fl oz* (corn syrup solids, whey protein concentrate, nonfat milk, soy oil, MCTs & coconut oil)

| | | | | | | | | | | | | | | | |
|---|---|---|---|---|---|---|---|---|---|---|---|---|---|---|---|
| | 24 | 25.7 | 1.2 | | | | 8 | .08 | .06 | 8 | 9 | 28 | 1 | .24 | .003 |
| | 30 | 0.7 | 2.6 | | | 286 | .06 | 1.0 | .07 | .29 | 26 | 14 | .06 | .038 | |
| | | | | | 1.1 | 79 | 1.1 | 3 | 0.5 | 1.8 | 20 | 2 | | | |
| | 11 | 40 | 42 | 70 | 55 | 16 | 8 | 28 | 32 | 44 | | 12 | | | |

**isomil, 20 cal/fl oz, Ross Labs** — *1 fl oz* (soy protein isolate, corn syrup, sucrose, soy & coconut oils)

| | | | | | | | | | | | | | | | |
|---|---|---|---|---|---|---|---|---|---|---|---|---|---|---|---|
| | 20 | 27.0 | 1.1 | 0.4 | 0 | 18 | 2 | .02 | .01 | 3 | 9 | 21 | 2 | .15 | .006 |
| | 30 | 0.5 | 2.0 | 0.5 | 0.0 | 60 | .01 | 0.3 | .09 | .15 | 28 | 15 | .36 | .015 | |
| | | | | | 1.0 | 12 | 0.6ᶜ | 3.0 | 0.9 | 1.6 | 13 | 3 | | | |
| | 6 | 20 | 23 | 42 | 32 | 12 | 6 | 27 | 19 | 23 | 38 | 13 | | | |

**isomil, SF, 20 cal/fl oz, Ross Labs** — *1 fl oz* (soy protein isolate, corn syrup solids, soy & coconut oils)

| | | | | | | | | | | | | | | | |
|---|---|---|---|---|---|---|---|---|---|---|---|---|---|---|---|
| | 20 | 27.0 | 1.1 | 0.4 | 0 | 18 | 2 | .02 | .01 | 3 | 9 | 21 | 2 | .15 | .006 |
| | 30 | 0.6 | 2.0 | 0.5 | 0.0 | 60 | .01 | 0.3 | .09 | .15 | 23 | 15 | .36 | .015 | |
| | | | | | 1.0 | 12 | 0.6ᶜ | 3.0 | 0.9 | 1.6 | 18 | 3 | | | |
| | 6 | 23 | 26 | 47 | 36 | 13 | 7 | 30 | 21 | 25 | 43 | 14 | | | |

**lofenalac, Mead Johnson**ᵈ — *1 fl oz* (corn syrup solids, enzymatic digest of casein processed to remove phe, corn oil & modified tapioca starch)

| | | | | | | | | | | | | | | | |
|---|---|---|---|---|---|---|---|---|---|---|---|---|---|---|---|
| | 20 | | 0.8 | | | | 2 | .02 | .01 | 3 | 9 | 19 | 2 | .12 | .032 |
| | 30 | 0.7 | 2.7 | | | 50 | .02 | 0.3 | .06 | .09 | 20 | 14 | .38 | | |
| | | | | | 0.9 | 12 | 0.3 | 3 | 1.6 | 2.7 | 14 | 1 | .018 | | |
| | 9 | 34 | 38 | 74 | 72 | 24 | 3 | 3 | 35 | 60 | | 21 | | | |

**low met diet, Mead Johnson**ᵉ — *1 fl oz* (corn syrup solids, soy protein isolate, coconut oil & corn oil)

| | | | | | | | | | | | | | | | |
|---|---|---|---|---|---|---|---|---|---|---|---|---|---|---|---|
| | 20 | 27.0 | 1.1 | | | | 2 | .02 | .01 | 3 | 9 | 19 | 2 | .16 | .006 |
| | 30 | 0.6 | 2.0 | | | 50 | .02 | 0.2 | .06 | .09 | 23 | 15 | .38 | .019 | |
| | | | | | 0.9 | 12 | 0.3 | 3 | 1.6 | 1.6 | 16 | 2 | | | |
| | 7 | 19 | 28 | 46 | 36 | 6 | 6 | 29 | 20 | 28 | | 14 | | | |

**low phe/try diet, Mead Johnson**ᶠ — *5 fl oz* (corn syrup solids, specially processed casein hydrolysate, corn oil, modified tapioca starch)

| | | | | | | | | | | | | | | | |
|---|---|---|---|---|---|---|---|---|---|---|---|---|---|---|---|
| | 100 | 134.0 | 3.9 | | | | 8 | .09 | .07 | 16 | 47 | 94 | 11 | .63 | .152 |
| | 150 | 3.3 | 13.0 | | | 250 | .08 | 1.3 | .30 | .48 | 102 | 70 | 1.87 | .087 | |
| | | | | | 4.8 | 63 | 1.5 | 16 | 7.8 | 13.3 | 70 | 7 | | | |
| | 43 | 172 | 191 | 370 | 360 | 119 | 13 | 16 | <8 | 300 | | 99 | | | |

**mono- and disaccharide-free diet, Mead Johnson**ᵍ — *5 fl oz* (modified tapioca starch, MCTs, casein enzymically hydrolyzed & charcoal treated & corn oil)

| | | | | | | | | | | | | | | | |
|---|---|---|---|---|---|---|---|---|---|---|---|---|---|---|---|
| | 100 | 127.0 | 4.2 | | | | 12 | .09 | .06 | 16 | 43 | 94 | 11 | .62 | .031 |
| | 150 | 2.8 | 13.4 | | | 380 | .08 | 1.3 | .31 | .47 | 109 | 62 | 1.88 | .094 | |
| | | | | | 4.7 | 75 | 3.8 | 19 | 7.8 | 13.3 | 86 | 7 | | | |
| | 70 | 220 | 260 | 450 | 380 | 136 | 70 | 210 | 101 | 330 | | 132 | | | |

**msud diet, Mead Johnson**ʰ — *5 fl oz* (corn syrup solids, casein enzymically hydrolyzed, corn oil & modified tapioca starch)

| | | | | | | | | | | | | | | | |
|---|---|---|---|---|---|---|---|---|---|---|---|---|---|---|---|
| | 100 | 134.0 | 3.9 | | | | 8 | .09 | .06 | 16 | 47 | 94 | 11 | .78 | .031 |
| | 150 | 3.3 | 13.0 | | | 310 | .08 | 1.3 | .31 | .47 | 102 | 70 | 1.88 | .094 | |
| | | | | | 4.7 | 62 | 3.1 | 16 | 7.8 | 13.3 | 70 | 7 | | | |
| | 41 | 114 | | | 105 | 51 | 51 | 114 | 134 | | | 51 | | | |

**nursoy, 20 cal/fl oz, Wyeth** — *1 fl oz*

| | | | | | | | | | | | | | | | |
|---|---|---|---|---|---|---|---|---|---|---|---|---|---|---|---|
| | 20 | 26.4 | 1.1 | 0.1 | 0 | 18 | 2 | .03 | .01 | 1 | 6 | 18 | 2 | .15 | .006 |
| | 30 | 0.6 | 2.0 | 0.4 | 0.0 | 59 | .02 | 0.1 | .06 | .09 | 21 | 12 | .34 | .014 | |
| | | | | | 0.8 | 12 | 0.2 | 3 | 0.4 | 3 | | 2 | | | |
| | 7 | 21 | 34 | 52 | 39 | 16 | 6 | 36 | 26 | 34 | 49 | 17 | | | |

ᵃ Enfamil w/ iron contains .38 mg.
ᵇ Nutritional supplement to be added to mother's milk for premature infants.
ᶜ Alpha-tocopherol is 0.4 mg.
ᵈ Low phenylalanine formula for infants & children w/ phenylketonuria.
ᵉ Formula w/o added methionine for management of infants w/ homocystinuria.
ᶠ Formula low in phenylalanine & tyrosine for use in tyrosinemia.
ᵍ Protein hydrolysate formula base for use w/ added carbohydrate.
ʰ Free of branched chain amino acids for use w/ maple syrup urine disease.

| | | | | | Vitamins | | | | | Minerals | | | | |
|---|---|---|---|---|---|---|---|---|---|---|---|---|---|---|
| KCAL | H₂O (g) | FAT (g) | PUFA (g) | CHOL (mg) | A (RE) | C (mg) | B-2 (mg) | B-6 (mg) | FOL (mcg) | Na (mg) | Ca (mg) | Mg (mg) | Zn (mg) | Mn (mg) |
| WT (g) | PRO (g) | CHO (g) | SFA (g) | DFIB (g) | A (IU) | B-1 (mg) | NIA (mg) | B-12 (mcg) | PANT (mg) | K (mg) | P (mg) | Fe (mg) | Cu (mg) | |
| | | | | INOS (mg) | D (IU) | E (IU) | K (mcg) | BIO (mcg) | CHLN (mg) | Cl (mg) | I (mcg) | Mo (mg) | | |
| TRY (mg) | THR (mg) | ISO (mg) | LEU (mg) | LYS (mg) | MET (mg) | CYS (mg) | PHE (mg) | TYR (mg) | VAL (mg) | ARG (mg) | HIS (mg) | | | |

**nutramigen, Mead Johnson[a] — 1 fl oz**
(corn syrup solids, corn oil, casein enzymically hydrolyzed & charcoal-treated & modified corn starch)

| 20 | 26.6 | 0.8 | | | | 2 | .02 | .01 | 3 | 9 | 19 | 2 | .16 | .006 |
|---|---|---|---|---|---|---|---|---|---|---|---|---|---|---|
| 30 | 0.6 | 2.7 | | | 62 | .02 | 0.3 | .06 | .09 | 22 | 12 | .38 | .019 | |
| | | | | 0.9 | 12 | 0.6 | 3 | 1.6 | 2.7 | 17 | 1 | | | |
| 7 | 32 | 40 | 68 | 56 | 20 | 3 | 32 | 7 | 50 | | 20 | | | |

**portagen, 20 cal/fl oz, Mead Johnson[b] 1 fl oz**
(corn syrup solids, MCTs, sodium caseinate, sucrose & corn oil)

| 20 | 26.8 | 1.0 | | | | 2 | .04 | .04 | 3 | 10 | 19 | 4 | .19 | .025 |
|---|---|---|---|---|---|---|---|---|---|---|---|---|---|---|
| 30 | 0.7 | 2.3 | | | 156 | .03 | 0.4 | .12 | .21 | 25 | 14 | .38 | .031 | |
| | | | | | 16 | 0.6 | 3 | 1.6 | 2.7 | 17 | 1 | | | |
| 9 | 29 | 40 | 70 | 60 | 20 | 2 | 38 | 40 | 50 | | 22 | | | |

**pregestimil, Mead Johnson[c] — 1 fl oz**
(corn syrup solids, casein enzymically hydrolyzed & charcoal-treated, corn oil, modified tapioca starch & MCTs)

| 20 | 25.4 | 0.8 | | | | 2 | .02 | .01 | 3 | 9 | 19 | 2 | .12 | .006 |
|---|---|---|---|---|---|---|---|---|---|---|---|---|---|---|
| 30 | 0.6 | 2.7 | | | 62 | .02 | 0.3 | .06 | .09 | 22 | 12 | .38 | .019 | |
| | | | | 0.9 | 12 | 0.5 | 3 | 1.6 | 2.7 | 17 | 1 | | | |
| 9 | 27 | 34 | 58 | 48 | 17 | 9 | 27 | 13 | 42 | | 17 | | | |

**prosobee, Mead Johnson[d] 1 fl oz**
(corn syrup solids, soy protein isolate, coconut oil & corn/soy oil)

| 20 | 26.8 | 1.1 | | | | 2 | .02 | .01 | 3 | 7 | 19 | 2 | .16 | .005 |
|---|---|---|---|---|---|---|---|---|---|---|---|---|---|---|
| 30 | 0.6 | 2.0 | | | 62 | .02 | 0.3 | .06 | .09 | 24 | 15 | .38 | .019 | |
| | | | | 0.9 | 12 | 0.6 | 3 | 1.6 | 1.6 | 17 | 2 | | | |
| 7 | 19 | 28 | 46 | 36 | 11 | 5 | 29 | 20 | 27 | | 14 | | | |

**protein-free diet powder, Mead Johnson[e] — 100 g dry powder**
(corn syrup solids, corn oil & modified tapioca starch)

| 490 | 3.0 | 22.5 | | | | 45 | .54 | .36 | 90 | 540 | | | | |
|---|---|---|---|---|---|---|---|---|---|---|---|---|---|---|
| 100 | 0.0 | 71.8 | | | 1440 | .45 | 7.2 | 1.80 | 2.70 | | | | | |
| | | | | 27.0 | 360 | 9.0 | 90 | 45.0 | 76 | | | | | |

**RCF (Ross carbohydrate free), Ross Labs[f] — 1 fl oz**
(soy protein isolate, soy & coconut oils)

| 12 | 26.0 | 1.1 | 0.4 | 0 | | 2 | .02 | .01 | 3 | 9 | 21 | 2 | .15 | .006 |
|---|---|---|---|---|---|---|---|---|---|---|---|---|---|---|
| 30 | 0.6 | 0.0 | 0.4 | 0.0 | 60 | .01 | 0.3 | .09 | .15 | 23 | 15 | .05 | .015 | |
| | | | | 1.0 | 12 | 0.6[f] | 3.0 | 0.9 | 1.6 | 13 | 3 | | | |
| 6 | 23 | 26 | 47 | 36 | 13 | 7 | 30 | 21 | 25 | 43 | 14 | | | |

**Similac, 13 cal/fl oz, Ross Labs 1 fl oz**
(cow milk, lactose, soy & coconut oils)

| 13 | 28.0 | 0.7 | 0.3 | 0 | | 1 | .02 | .01 | 2 | 6 | 12 | 1 | .10 | .001 |
|---|---|---|---|---|---|---|---|---|---|---|---|---|---|---|
| 30 | 0.4 | 1.4 | 0.3 | 0.0 | 39 | .01 | 0.1 | .03 | .06 | 18 | 9 | [g] | .012 | |
| | | | | 0.6 | 8 | 0.4[h] | 1.0 | 0.6 | 2.1 | 12 | 2 | | | |
| 5 | 15 | 17 | 34 | 26 | 10 | 3 | 17 | 15 | 20 | 11 | 8 | | | |

**Similac, 20 cal/fl oz, Ross Labs 1 fl oz**
(cow milk, lactose, soy & coconut oils)

| 20 | 27.0 | 1.1 | 0.4 | 0 | | 2 | .03 | .01 | 3 | 6 | 15 | 1 | .15 | .001 |
|---|---|---|---|---|---|---|---|---|---|---|---|---|---|---|
| 30 | 0.4 | 2.1 | 0.5 | 0.0 | 60 | .02 | 0.2 | .05 | .09 | 24 | 12 | [i] | .018 | |
| | | | | 0.9 | 12 | 0.6[f] | 1.6 | 0.9 | 3.2 | 15 | 3 | | | |
| 6 | 19 | 22 | 42 | 32 | 13 | 4 | 22 | 20 | 24 | 15 | 9 | | | |

**Similac, 24 cal/fl oz, Ross Labs 1 fl oz**
(cow milk, lactose, soy & coconut oils)

| 24 | 26.0 | 1.3 | 0.5 | 1 | | 2 | .04 | .01 | 4 | 10 | 21 | 2 | .18 | .001 |
|---|---|---|---|---|---|---|---|---|---|---|---|---|---|---|
| 30 | 0.7 | 2.5 | 0.5 | 0.0 | 72 | .02 | 0.3 | .06 | .11 | 32 | 17 | [j] | .021 | |
| | | | | 1.1 | 14 | 0.7[k] | 1.9 | 1.0 | 3.8 | 21 | 4 | | | |
| 8 | 28 | 32 | 62 | 47 | 18 | 6 | 32 | 29 | 36 | 22 | 14 | | | |

**Similac, 27 cal/fl oz, Ross Labs 1 fl oz**
(cow milk, lactose, soy & coconut oils)

| 27 | 26.0 | 1.4 | 0.5 | 1 | | 2 | .04 | .02 | 4 | 12 | 24 | 2 | .20 | .001 |
|---|---|---|---|---|---|---|---|---|---|---|---|---|---|---|
| 30 | 0.7 | 2.8 | 0.6 | 0.0 | 81 | .03 | 0.3 | .07 | .12 | 36 | 19 | .06 | .024 | |
| | | | | 1.3 | 16 | 0.8[k] | 2.2 | 1.2 | 4.3 | 24 | 4 | | | |
| 10 | 32 | 36 | 70 | 53 | 20 | 6 | 36 | 34 | 40 | 25 | 15 | | | |

**Similac LBW (low birth weight), 24 cal/fl oz, Ross Labs — 1 fl oz**
(cow milk, lactose, corn syrup solids, MCT, soy & coconut oils)

| 24 | 26.6 | 1.3 | 0.2 | 0 | | 3 | .04 | .01 | 4 | 10 | 21 | 2 | .24 | .001 |
|---|---|---|---|---|---|---|---|---|---|---|---|---|---|---|
| 30 | 0.7 | 2.5 | 0.9 | 0.0 | 72 | .03 | 0.3 | .06 | .11 | 36 | 17 | .09 | .024 | |
| | | | | 1.1 | 14 | 0.7[k] | 1.9 | 1.0 | 3.8 | 26 | 4 | | | |
| 8 | 28 | 32 | 62 | 47 | 18 | 6 | 32 | 29 | 36 | 22 | 14 | | | |

**Similac Natural Care, 24 cal/fl oz, Ross Labs — 1 fl oz**
(cow milk, whey, lactose, corn syrup solids, MCT, soy & coconut oils)

| 24 | 26.0 | 1.3 | 0.2 | 1 | 49 | 9 | .15 | .06 | 9 | 12 | 50 | 3 | .36 | .003 |
|---|---|---|---|---|---|---|---|---|---|---|---|---|---|---|
| 30 | 0.7 | 2.5 | 0.8 | 0.0 | 162 | .06 | 1.2 | .13 | .45 | 33 | 25 | .09 | .060 | |
| | | | | 1.3 | 36 | 1.0[l] | 2.9 | 8.8 | 2.4 | 21 | 5 | | | |
| 8 | 38 | 35 | 65 | 52 | 16 | 11 | 22 | 22 | 36 | 18 | 13 | | | |

**Similac PM 60/40, 20 cal/fl oz, Ross Labs — 1 fl oz**
(whey, caseinate, lactose, soy & coconut oils)

| 20 | 27.0 | 1.1 | 0.4 | 1 | | 2 | .03 | .01 | 3 | 5 | 11 | 1 | .15 | .001 |
|---|---|---|---|---|---|---|---|---|---|---|---|---|---|---|
| 30 | 0.5 | 2.0 | 0.5 | 0.0 | 60 | .02 | 0.2 | .05 | .09 | 17 | 6 | .04 | .018 | |
| | | | | 0.9 | 12 | 0.6[f] | 1.6 | 1.8 | 3.2 | 12 | 1 | | | |
| 7 | 28 | 29 | 49 | 41 | 12 | 8 | 18 | 17 | 30 | 14 | 11 | | | |

[a] Hypoallergenic formula supplying protein nutrients in hydrolyzed form for infants & children sensitive to intact proteins of milk & other foods.

[b] Nutritionally complete formula for infants, children & adults who do not efficiently digest conventional food fat or absorb the resulting long chain fatty acids.

[c] Formula w/ readily digestible sources of protein, fat & carbohydrate in hypoallergenic, low osmolality form.

[d] Milk-free, lactose-free & sucrose-free formula w/ soy protein for infants w/ milk sensitivity.

[e] Formula base for use in making diets for infants requiring specific mixtures of amino acids.

[f] Alpha-tocopherol is 0.4 mg.

[g] .03 mg iron for Similac 13 and .23 mg iron for Similac 13 w/ iron.

[h] Alpha-tocopherol is 0.3 mg.

[i] .04 mg iron for Similac 20 and .36 mg iron for Similac 20 w/ iron.

[j] .05 mg iron for Similac 24 and .43 mg iron for Similac 24 w/ iron.

[k] Alpha-tocopherol is 0.5 mg.

[l] Alpha-tocopherol is 0.7 mg.

| | KCAL | H₂O (g) | FAT (g) | PUFA (g) | CHOL (mg) | A (RE) | C (mg) | Vitamins B-2 (mg) | B-6 (mg) | FOL (mcg) | Na (mg) | Ca (mg) | Minerals Mg (mg) | Zn (mg) | Mn (mg) |
|---|---|---|---|---|---|---|---|---|---|---|---|---|---|---|---|
| | WT (g) | PRO (g) | CHO (g) | SFA (g) | DFIB (g) | A (IU) | B-1 (mg) | NIA (mg) | B-12 (mcg) | PANT (mg) | K (mg) | P (mg) | Fe (mg) | Cu (mg) | |
| | | | | | INOS (mg) | D (IU) | E (IU) | K (mcg) | BIO (mcg) | CHLN (mg) | Cl (mg) | I (mcg) | Mo (mg) | | |
| | TRY (mg) | THR (mg) | ISO (mg) | LEU (mg) | LYS (mg) | MET (mg) | CYS (mg) | PHE (mg) | TYR (mg) | VAL (mg) | ARG (mg) | HIS (mg) | | | |
| **Similac Special Care, 20 cal/fl oz, Ross** Labs—*1 fl oz* (cow milk, whey, lactose, corn syrup solids, MCT, soy & coconut oils) | 20 | 27.0 | 1.1 | 0.2 | 1 | 41 | 7 | .12 | .05 | 7 | 10 | 36 | 2 | .30 | .002 |
| | 30 | 0.5 | 2.1 | 0.6 | 0.0 | 136 | .05 | 1.0 | .11 | .38 | 28 | 18 | .07 | .050 | |
| | | | | | 0.9 | 8 | 0.8ᵃ | 2.4 | 0.9 | 3.2 | 18 | 4 | | | |
| | 6 | 32 | 29 | 54 | 44 | 14 | 9 | 18 | 19 | 30 | 15 | 11 | | | |
| **Similac Special Care, 24 cal/fl oz, Ross** Labs—*1 fl oz* (cow milk, whey, lactose, corn syrup solids, MCT, soy & coconut oils) | 24 | 26.0 | 1.3 | 0.2 | | 41 | 9 | .15 | .06 | 9 | 10 | 36 | 2 | .30 | .002 |
| | 30 | 0.7 | 2.1 | 0.8 | | 136 | .06 | 1.2 | .13 | .45 | 28 | 18 | .07 | .050 | |
| | | | | | 1.1 | 30 | 1.0ᵃ | 2.9 | 1.0 | 3.8 | 21 | 4 | | | |
| | 8 | 38 | 35 | 65 | 52 | 16 | 11 | 22 | 22 | 36 | 18 | 13 | | | |
| **Similac w/ whey & iron, 20 cal/fl oz, Ross** Labs—*1 fl oz* (cow milk, whey, lactose, soy & coconut oils) | 20 | | 1.1 | | | 18 | 2 | .03 | .01 | 3 | 7 | 12 | 2 | .15 | .001 |
| | 30 | 0.4 | 2.1 | | | 60 | .02 | 0.2 | .05 | .09 | 22 | 9 | .36 | .018 | |
| | | | | | 0.9 | 12 | 0.6ᵇ | 1.6 | 0.9 | 3.2 | 13 | 3 | | | |
| | 6 | 28 | 27 | 48 | 38 | 14 | 7 | 20 | 18 | 29 | 14 | 11 | | | |
| **SMA preemie, 24 cal/fl oz, Wyeth** *1 fl oz* | 24 | 25.9 | 1.3 | 0.2 | | 21 | 2 | .04 | .01 | 3 | 9 | 22 | 2 | .24 | .006 |
| | 30 | 0.6 | 2.5 | 0.6 | | 71 | .02 | 0.2 | .06 | .11 | 22 | 12 | .09 | .021 | |
| | | | | | 0.9 | 14 | 0.3 | 2 | 1.0 | 4 | | 2 | | | |
| | 10 | 41 | 40 | 73 | 61 | 14 | 11 | 32 | 32 | 43 | 21 | 15 | | | |
| **SMA w/ iron, 20 cal/fl oz, Wyeth** *1 fl oz* | 20 | 26.6 | 1.1 | 0.1 | 1 | 18 | 2 | .03 | .01 | 1 | 4 | 12 | 1 | .15 | .004 |
| | 30 | 0.4 | 2.1 | 0.4 | 0.0 | 59 | .02 | 0.1 | .04 | .06 | 16 | 8 | .35 | .014 | |
| | | | | | 0.9 | 12 | 0.2 | 2 | 0.5 | 3 | | 2 | | | |
| | 8 | 31 | 30 | 54 | 46 | 10 | 8 | 24 | 24 | 32 | 16 | 11 | | | |

ᵃ Alpha-tocopherol is 0.5 mg.

ᵇ Alpha-tocopherol is 0.4 mg.

| | KCAL / WT (g) | H₂O (g) / PRO (g) | FAT (g) / CHO (g) | PUFA (g) / SFA (g) | CHOL (mg) / DFIB (g) | A (RE) / A (IU) | C (mg) / B-1 (mg) | B-2 (mg) / NIA (mg) | B-6 (mg) / B-12 (mcg) | FOL (mcg) / PANT (mg) | Na (mg) / K (mg) | Ca (mg) / P (mg) | Mg (mg) / Fe (mg) | Zn (mg) / Cu (mg) | Mn (mg) |
|---|---|---|---|---|---|---|---|---|---|---|---|---|---|---|---|

# 19. INFANT, JUNIOR & TODDLER FOODS

## 19.1. BAKED PRODUCTS

| Food / serving | KCAL/WT | H₂O/PRO | FAT/CHO | PUFA/SFA | CHOL/DFIB | A(RE)/A(IU) | C/B-1 | B-2/NIA | B-6/B-12 | FOL/PANT | Na/K | Ca/P | Mg/Fe | Zn/Cu | Mn |
|---|---|---|---|---|---|---|---|---|---|---|---|---|---|---|---|
| **arrowroot cookie** | 24 | 0.3 | 0.9 | 0.0 | 0.1 | | 0 | .03 | .00 | | 22 | 2 | 1 | .03 | |
| *1 cookie* | 6 | 0.4 | 4.3 | 0.2 | 0.0 | | .03 | 0.3 | .00 | | 9 | 7 | .18 | | |
| **baby cookie** | 28 | 0.4 | 0.9 | 0.0 | | 0 | 1 | .21 | .38 | | 12 | 7 | 3 | .07 | |
| *1 cookie* | 7 | 0.8 | 4.4 | 0.2 | 0.1 | 2 | .10 | 1.0 | .30 | | 33 | 12 | .27 | | |
| **baby pretzel** | 24 | 0.2 | 0.1 | | | | | .03 | .00 | | 16 | 1 | 2 | .05 | |
| *1 pretzel* | 6 | 0.7 | 4.9 | | 0.1 | | .04 | 0.4 | | | 8 | 7 | .23 | | |
| **teething biscuit** | 43 | 0.7 | 0.5 | | | 1 | 1 | .06 | .01 | | 40 | 29 | 4 | .10 | |
| *1 biscuit* | 11 | 1.2 | 8.4 | | 0.1 | 13 | .03 | 0.5 | .01 | | 35 | 18 | .39 | | |
| **zwieback** | 30 | 0.3 | 0.7 | 0.1 | 1 | 0 | 0 | .02 | .01 | | 16 | 1 | 1 | .04 | |
| *1 piece* | 7 | 0.7 | 5.2 | 0.3 | 0.0 | 4 | .02 | 0.1 | | | 21 | 4 | .04 | | |

## 19.2. CEREALS

| Food / serving | KCAL/WT | H₂O/PRO | FAT/CHO | PUFA/SFA | CHOL/DFIB | A(RE)/A(IU) | C/B-1 | B-2/NIA | B-6/B-12 | FOL/PANT | Na/K | Ca/P | Mg/Fe | Zn/Cu | Mn |
|---|---|---|---|---|---|---|---|---|---|---|---|---|---|---|---|
| **barley** | | | | | | | | | | | | | | | |
| dry | 9 | 0.2 | 0.1 | | | | 0 | .07 | .01 | 1 | 1 | 19 | 3 | .08 | |
| *1 T* | 2.4 | 0.3 | 1.8 | | 0.1 | | .07 | 0.9 | | | 9 | 11 | 1.80 | .011 | |
| prep w/ whole milk | 31 | 21.2 | 0.9 | | | | 0 | .16 | .03 | 3 | 14 | 65 | 8 | .24 | |
| *1 oz* | 28 | 1.3 | 4.6 | | | 30 | .14 | 1.7 | | | 54 | 43 | 3.50 | | |
| **cereal & egg yolks** | | | | | | | | | | | | | | | |
| jr | 110 | 189.0 | 3.8 | 0.3 | | 88 | 2 | .10 | .04 | 7 | 70 | 51 | 6 | .62 | |
| *1 jar* | 213 | 4.1 | 15.1 | 1.3 | | 306 | .02 | 0.1 | .13 | | 75 | 84 | 1.09 | .047 | |
| str | 66 | 113.7 | 2.3 | 0.2 | 81 | 52 | 1 | .06 | .03 | 4 | 42 | 30 | 4 | .37 | |
| *1 jar* | 128 | 2.5 | 9.0 | 0.8 | | 181 | .01 | 0.1 | .09 | | 50 | 51 | .60 | .028 | |
| **cereal, egg yolks & bacon** | | | | | | | | | | | | | | | |
| jr | 178 | 180.9 | 11.0 | | | | 3 | .11 | | 9 | 97 | 54 | 10 | .61 | |
| *1 jar* | 213 | 5.4 | 15.1 | | | 142 | .04 | 0.3 | | | 79 | | 1.06 | .045 | |
| str | 101 | 109.9 | 6.4 | | | | 1 | .10 | | 5 | 62 | 36 | 6 | .35 | |
| *1 jar* | 128 | 3.2 | 8.0 | | | 121 | .06 | 0.3 | | | 44 | | .60 | .026 | |
| **grits & egg yolks, str** | 76 | 112.7 | 2.9 | | | 39 | 1 | .09 | .03 | 4 | | 36 | 6 | .29 | |
| *1 jar* | 128 | 2.3 | 10.1 | | | 156 | .04 | 0.4 | .05 | | 71 | 46 | .64 | | |
| **high protein** | | | | | | | | | | | | | | | |
| dry | 9 | 0.1 | 0.1 | | | | 0 | .07 | .01 | 5 | 1 | 17 | 5 | .11 | |
| *1 T* | 2.4 | 0.9 | 1.1 | | 0.1 | | .06 | 0.8 | | | 32 | 15 | 1.77 | .031 | |
| prep w/ whole milk | 31 | 21.1 | 1.1 | | | | 0 | .16 | .03 | 10 | 14 | 62 | 14 | .30 | |
| *1 oz* | 28 | 2.5 | 3.3 | | | 30 | .13 | 1.6 | | | 99 | 50 | 3.44 | | |
| w/ apple & orange, dry | 9 | 0.1 | 0.2 | | | | 0 | .10 | .01 | | 2 | 18 | 4 | .07 | |
| *1 T* | 2.4 | 0.6 | 1.4 | | | 1 | .09 | 0.6 | .01 | | 32 | 13 | 2.10 | | |
| w/ apple & orange, prep w/ whole milk | 32 | 21.1 | 1.1 | | | 8 | 0 | .24 | .03 | | 16 | 63 | 10 | .22 | |
| *1 oz* | 28 | 2.0 | 3.8 | | | 27 | .19 | 1.1 | .10 | | 98 | 47 | 4.09 | | |
| **mixed** | | | | | | | | | | | | | | | |
| dry | 9 | 0.2 | 0.1 | | | | 0 | .07 | .01 | 1 | 1 | 18 | 2 | .06 | |
| *1 T* | 2.4 | 0.3 | 1.8 | | 0.1 | | .06 | 0.8 | | | 10 | 9 | 1.52 | .013 | |
| prep w/ whole milk | 32 | 21.2 | 1.0 | | | | 0 | .17 | .02 | 3 | 13 | 62 | 8 | .20 | |
| *1 oz* | 28 | 1.3 | 4.5 | | | 30 | .12 | 1.6 | | | 56 | 40 | 2.96 | | |
| w/ applesce & bananas, jr | 183 | 175.1 | 0.9 | | | 4 | 20 | .78 | .31 | 8 | 78 | 9 | 16 | .48 | |
| *1 jar* | 220 | 2.6 | 40.5 | | 1.3 | 41 | .63 | 8.9 | | | 70 | 63 | 12.33 | | |
| w/ applesce & bananas, str | 111 | 108.0 | 0.7 | | | 2 | 35 | .47 | .19 | 5 | 3 | 9 | 11 | .26 | |
| *1 jar* | 135 | 1.6 | 24.2 | | 0.8 | 24 | .38 | 5.4 | | | 55 | 32 | 8.94 | | |
| w/ bananas, dry | 9 | 0.1 | 0.1 | | | | 0 | .09 | .10 | | 3 | 17 | 2 | .03 | |
| *1 T* | 2.4 | 0.3 | 1.9 | | 0.1 | 3 | .09 | 0.5 | .01 | | 16 | 9 | 1.62 | | |
| w/ bananas, prep w/ whole milk | 33 | 21.1 | 1.0 | | | 8 | 0 | .20 | .03 | | 17 | 61 | 7 | .16 | |
| *1 oz* | 28 | 1.3 | 4.7 | | | 31 | .19 | 1.0 | .10 | | 67 | 39 | 3.16 | | |
| w/ bananas & apple jce, inst, Heinz | 50 | | 0.0 | | | | 17 | .28 | .06 | | 2 | 6 | | .18 | |
| *4 T dry* | 14 | 1.0 | 12.0 | | | 10 | .24 | 3.6 | | | 80 | 26 | 7.00 | .040 | |

| | KCAL / WT (g) | H₂O / PRO (g) | FAT / CHO (g) | PUFA / SFA (g) | CHOL / DFIB (mg)(g) | A (RE) / A (IU) | C / B-1 (mg) | B-2 / NIA (mg) | B-6 / B-12 | FOL / PANT | Na / K (mg) | Ca / P (mg) | Mg / Fe (mg) | Zn / Cu (mg) | Mn (mg) |
|---|---|---|---|---|---|---|---|---|---|---|---|---|---|---|---|
| w/ honey, dry | 9 | 0.1 | 0.1 | | | 0 | 0 | .07 | | | 1 | 28 | | | |
| *1 T* | 2.4 | 0.3 | 1.8 | | | 1 | .06 | 0.9 | | | 6 | 16 | 1.64 | | |
| w/ honey, prep w/ whole milk | 33 | 21.0 | 1.0 | | | 7 | 0 | .17 | | | 14 | 83 | | | |
| *1 oz* | 28 | 1.4 | 4.5 | | | 26 | .13 | 1.8 | | | 49 | 52 | 3.20 | | |
| **oatmeal** | | | | | | | | | | | | | | | |
| dry | 10 | 0.1 | 0.2 | | | | 0 | .06 | .00 | 1 | 1 | 18 | 3 | .09 | |
| *1 T* | 2.4 | 0.3 | 1.7 | | 0.1 | | .07 | 0.9 | | | 11 | 12 | 1.77 | .013 | |
| prep w/ whole milk | 33 | 21.1 | 1.2 | | | | 0 | .16 | .02 | 3 | 13 | 62 | 10 | .26 | |
| *1 oz* | 28 | 1.4 | 4.3 | | | 30 | .14 | 1.7 | | | 58 | 45 | 3.44 | | |
| w/ applesce & bananas, jr | 165 | 179.9 | 1.6 | | | | 42 | .11 | .53 | 8 | 69 | 12 | 24 | .73 | |
| *1 jar* | 220 | 2.9 | 34.6 | | 1.5 | | .53 | 7.4 | | | 106 | 89 | 12.13 | .165 | |
| w/ applesce & bananas, str | 99 | 110.9 | 0.9 | | | 4 | 29 | .49 | .27 | 5 | 2 | 11 | 15 | .47 | |
| *1 jar* | 135 | 1.8 | 20.8 | | 1.1 | 40 | .57 | 6.8 | | | 63 | 56 | 7.63 | .099 | |
| w/ bananas, dry | 9 | 0.1 | 0.1 | | | 0 | 0 | .09 | .01 | | 3 | 16 | 3 | .05 | |
| *1 T* | 2.4 | 0.3 | 1.8 | | 0.1 | 2 | .09 | 0.5 | .01 | | 18 | 11 | 1.63 | | |
| w/ bananas, prep w/ whole milk | 33 | 21.1 | 1.1 | | | 8 | 0 | .21 | .03 | | 17 | 59 | 9 | .18 | |
| *1 oz* | 28 | 1.3 | 4.5 | | | 28 | .18 | 1.0 | .09 | | 70 | 43 | 3.18 | | |
| w/ bananas & apple jce, inst, Heinz | 60 | | 0.0 | | | | 17 | .28 | .07 | | 1 | 12 | | .25 | |
| *4 T dry* | 14 | 1.0 | 12.0 | | | 4 | .24 | 3.6 | | | 112 | 38 | 7.00 | .050 | |
| w/ honey, dry | 9 | 0.1 | 0.2 | | | 0 | 0 | .07 | | | 1 | 28 | | | |
| *1 T* | 2.4 | 0.3 | 1.7 | | | 1 | .07 | 0.9 | | | 6 | 18 | 1.61 | | |
| w/ honey, prep w/ whole milk | 33 | 21.1 | 1.1 | | | 7 | 0 | .17 | | | 14 | 82 | | | |
| *1 oz* | 28 | 1.4 | 4.3 | | | 26 | .14 | 1.7 | | | 48 | 56 | 3.14 | | |
| **rice** | | | | | | | | | | | | | | | |
| dry | 9 | 0.2 | 0.1 | | | | 0 | .05 | .01 | 1 | 1 | 20 | 5 | .05 | |
| *1 T* | 2.4 | 0.2 | 1.9 | | 0.0 | | .06 | 0.8 | | | 9 | 14 | 1.77 | .008 | |
| prep w/ whole milk | 33 | 21.2 | 1.0 | | | | 0 | .14 | .03 | 2 | 13 | 68 | 13 | .18 | |
| *1 oz* | 28 | 1.1 | 4.7 | | | 30 | .13 | 1.5 | | | 54 | 50 | 3.46 | | |
| w/ applesce & bananas, str | 107 | 109.4 | 0.5 | | | 3 | 43 | .57 | .32 | 3 | 38 | 23 | 4 | .11 | |
| *1 jar* | 135 | 1.6 | 23.1 | | 0.4 | 28 | .35 | 5.4 | | | 38 | 16 | 9.09 | | |
| w/ bananas, dry | 10 | 0.1 | 0.1 | | | 0 | 0 | .09 | .02 | | 2 | 17 | 3 | .04 | |
| *1 T* | 2.4 | 0.2 | 1.9 | | 0.0 | 1 | .10 | 0.6 | .01 | | 18 | 10 | 1.61 | | |
| w/ bananas, prep w/ whole milk | 33 | 21.1 | 1.0 | | | 7 | 0 | .22 | .04 | | 16 | 60 | 10 | .16 | |
| *1 oz* | 28 | 1.2 | 4.8 | | | 26 | .19 | 1.1 | .09 | | 72 | 41 | 3.13 | | |
| w/ bananas & apple jce, inst, Heinz | 50 | | 0.0 | | | | 17 | .28 | .07 | | 1 | 5 | | .16 | |
| *4 T dry* | 14 | 1.0 | 12.0 | | | 10 | .24 | 3.6 | | | 70 | 20 | 7.00 | .040 | |
| w/ honey, dry | 9 | 0.1 | 0.1 | | | 0 | 0 | .07 | | | 1 | 28 | | | |
| *1 T* | 2.4 | 0.2 | 1.9 | | | 1 | .07 | 0.9 | | | 2 | 15 | 1.57 | | |
| w/ honey, prep w/ whole milk | 33 | 21.1 | 0.9 | | | 7 | 0 | .17 | | | 14 | 83 | | | |
| *1 oz* | 28 | 1.1 | 4.9 | | | 26 | .14 | 1.7 | | | 40 | 51 | 3.07 | | |
| w/ mixed fruit, jr | 186 | 175.2 | 0.5 | | | 3 | 45 | 1.31 | .54 | | 24 | 43 | 10 | .40 | |
| *1 jar* | 220 | 2.3 | 41.0 | | 0.7 | 33 | .55 | 6.0 | | | 72 | 51 | 10.36 | | |
| w/ pears & apple jce, inst, Heinz | 50 | | 0.0 | | | | 17 | .28 | .02 | | 8 | 8 | | .17 | |
| *4 T dry* | 14 | 1.0 | 13.0 | | | 12 | .24 | 3.6 | | | 43 | 22 | 7.00 | .060 | |

## 19.3. DESSERTS

| | KCAL / WT (g) | H₂O / PRO (g) | FAT / CHO (g) | PUFA / SFA (g) | CHOL / DFIB (mg)(g) | A (RE) / A (IU) | C / B-1 (mg) | B-2 / NIA (mg) | B-6 / B-12 | FOL / PANT | Na / K (mg) | Ca / P (mg) | Mg / Fe (mg) | Zn / Cu (mg) | Mn (mg) |
|---|---|---|---|---|---|---|---|---|---|---|---|---|---|---|---|
| **apple betty** | | | | | | | | | | | | | | | |
| jr | 153 | 177.1 | 0.0 | | | 3 | 60 | .11 | | 1 | 19 | 36 | | | |
| *1 jar* | 220 | 0.8 | 41.7 | | | 35 | .02 | 0.1 | | | 117 | | .44 | | |
| str | 97 | 107.9 | 0.0 | | | 2 | 47 | .05 | | 1 | 14 | 25 | | | |
| *1 jar* | 135 | 0.5 | 26.5 | | | 23 | .02 | 0.1 | | | 68 | | .24 | | |
| **banana apple** | | | | | | | | | | | | | | | |
| jr, Gerber | 143 | | 0.4 | | | 6 | 16 | .04 | .15 | | 11 | 6 | | | |
| *1 jar* | 213 | 0.6 | 33.9 | | 0.6 | | .02 | 0.3 | | | 153 | 13 | .21 | | |
| str, Gerber | 86 | | 0.3 | | | 4 | 16 | .03 | .09 | | 9 | 4 | | | |
| *1 jar* | 128 | 0.4 | 21.0 | | 0.4 | | .01 | 0.2 | | | 91 | 12 | .13 | | |
| **banana pudding, str, Heinz** | 96 | | 0.6 | | | | 15 | .04 | .14 | | 15 | 13 | | .15 | |
| *1 jar* | 128 | 1.0 | 21.6 | | | 59 | .01 | 0.2 | | | 99 | 40 | .51 | .051 | |

| | KCAL | H₂O (g) | FAT (g) | PUFA (g) | CHOL (mg) | A (RE) | C (mg) | B-2 (mg) | B-6 (mg) | FOL (mcg) | Na (mg) | Ca (mg) | Mg (mg) | Zn (mg) | Mn (mg) |
|---|---|---|---|---|---|---|---|---|---|---|---|---|---|---|---|
| | WT (g) | PRO (g) | CHO (g) | SFA (g) | DFIB (g) | A (IU) | B-1 (mg) | NIA (mg) | B-12 (mcg) | PANT (mg) | K (mg) | P (mg) | Fe (mg) | Cu (mg) | |
| **caramel pudding** | | | | | | | | | | | | | | | |
| jr | 167 | 171.2 | 1.9 | | | 7 | 5 | .15 | | 2 | 60 | 116 | | | |
| 1 jar | 213 | 2.9 | 36.2 | | | 69 | .02 | 0.1 | | | 124 | | | .34 | |
| str | 104 | 108.5 | 0.9 | | | 5 | 3 | .11 | | 1 | 37 | 60 | | | |
| 1 jar | 135 | 1.8 | 23.2 | | | 49 | .01 | .05 | | | 70 | | | .23 | |
| **cherry van pudding** | | | | | | | | | | | | | | | |
| jr | 152 | 178.2 | 0.4 | | | 44 | 2 | .02 | .03 | 1 | 32 | 11 | 5 | .07 | |
| 1 jar | 220 | 0.4 | 40.5 | | 0.2 | 440 | .02 | 0.1 | | | 73 | 15 | .38 | | |
| str | 91 | 110.0 | 0.4 | | | 27 | 2 | .02 | .02 | 0 | 22 | 7 | 3 | .05 | |
| 1 jar | 135 | 0.3 | 24.1 | | 0.1 | 270 | .01 | 0.1 | | | 46 | 10 | .26 | | |
| **choc custard pudding** | | | | | | | | | | | | | | | |
| jr | 195 | 172.7 | 3.5 | | | 10 | 2 | .24 | .03 | 11 | 55 | 134 | 23 | .73 | |
| 1 jar | 220 | 4.2 | 38.3 | | | 101 | .03 | 0.2 | | | 196 | 112 | .88 | | |
| str | 107 | 102.2 | 2.1 | | | 6 | 2 | .13 | .02 | 6 | 30 | 78 | 13 | .41 | |
| 1 jar | 135 | 2.4 | 20.6 | | 0.1 | 58 | .02 | 0.1 | | | 110 | 63 | .48 | | |
| **cottage cheese w/ pineapple** | | | | | | | | | | | | | | | |
| jr | 172 | 176.5 | 1.5 | | | 3 | 52 | .11 | .02 | 11 | 113 | 68 | 8 | .39 | |
| 1 jar | 220 | 6.5 | 35.1 | | | 35 | .03 | 0.1 | .16 | | 92 | 86 | .28 | | |
| str | 94 | 111.5 | 1.1 | | | 4 | 31 | .07 | .02 | 6 | 70 | 35 | 5 | .21 | |
| 1 jar | 135 | 4.0 | 17.8 | | | 39 | .02 | 0.1 | .10 | | 58 | 51 | .14 | | |
| **dutch apple** | | | | | | | | | | | | | | | |
| jr | 151 | 180.6 | 2.1 | 0.0 | | 11 | 47 | .03 | .03 | 2 | 36 | 10 | 4 | .06 | |
| 1 jar | 220 | 0.0 | 37.0 | 1.4 | 0.9 | 110 | .03 | 0.1 | | | 82 | 8 | .44 | | |
| str | 92 | 111.0 | 1.2 | 0.0 | | 7 | 29 | .02 | .02 | 1 | 21 | 6 | 2 | .01 | |
| 1 jar | 135 | 0.0 | 22.6 | 0.8 | 0.5 | 66 | .02 | 0.1 | | | 44 | 5 | .27 | | |
| **fruit dessert** | | | | | | | | | | | | | | | |
| jr | 138 | 180.9 | 0.0 | | | 53 | 66 | .03 | .07 | 8 | 29 | 19 | 11 | .11 | |
| 1 jar | 220 | 0.6 | 37.9 | | | 525 | .05 | 0.3 | | | 208 | 17 | .46 | .066 | |
| str | 79 | 112.6 | 0.0 | | | 34 | 3 | .01 | .05 | 4 | 18 | 11 | 7 | .05 | |
| 1 jar | 135 | 0.4 | 21.6 | | 0.3 | 338 | .02 | 0.2 | | | 127 | 9 | .29 | .041 | |
| **hawaiian delight** | | | | | | | | | | | | | | | |
| jr, Gerber | 190 | | 0.6 | | | 4 | 16 | .11 | .09 | | 40 | 81 | | | |
| 1 jar | 213 | 3.0 | 42.2 | | 0.2 | | .09 | 0.3 | | | 181 | 72 | .21 | | |
| str, Gerber | 113 | | 0.5 | | | 1 | 16 | .06 | .05 | | 23 | 49 | | | |
| 1 jar | 128 | 1.9 | 24.8 | | | | .04 | 0.2 | | | 104 | 44 | .13 | | |
| **orange pudding, str** | 108 | 107.7 | 1.2 | | | 16 | 12 | .08 | .04 | 11 | | 43 | 7 | .23 | |
| 1 jar | 135 | 1.5 | 23.8 | | 0.1 | 155 | .05 | .02 | | | 117 | 38 | .14 | | |
| **peach cobbler** | | | | | | | | | | | | | | | |
| jr | 147 | 178.6 | 0.0 | | | 31 | 45 | .03 | .02 | 3 | 20 | 9 | | | .07 |
| 1 jar | 220 | 0.7 | 40.3 | | 0.7 | 312 | .02 | 0.6 | | | 123 | 13 | .22 | | |
| str | 88 | 110.4 | 0.0 | | | 19 | 28 | .02 | .01 | 2 | 10 | 6 | | | .41 |
| 1 jar | 135 | 0.4 | 24.0 | | 0.4 | 192 | .01 | 0.4 | | | 73 | 7 | | .256 | |
| **peach melba** | | | | | | | | | | | | | | | |
| jr | 132 | 182.5 | 0.0 | | | 43 | 57 | .07 | | 4 | 19 | 23 | | | |
| 1 jar | 220 | 0.6 | 36.1 | | | 430 | .02 | 0.6 | | | 205 | | .66 | | |
| str | 81 | 111.9 | 0.0 | | | 25 | 42 | .05 | | 3 | 12 | 13 | | | |
| 1 jar | 135 | 0.3 | 22.3 | | | 249 | .01 | 0.5 | | | 112 | | .45 | | |
| **pineapple orange dessert, str** | 89 | 103.0 | 0.0 | | | 7 | 18 | .03 | | 3 | 13 | 14 | 5 | | |
| 1 jar | 128 | 0.3 | 24.4 | | | 73 | .02 | 0.1 | | | 61 | 5 | .23 | .026 | |
| **pineapple pudding** | | | | | | | | | | | | | | | |
| jr | 192 | 167.4 | 0.9 | | | 8 | 59 | .11 | .09 | 12 | 48 | 75 | 20 | .42 | |
| 1 jar | 220 | 3.1 | 47.4 | | | 80 | .09 | 0.3 | .14 | | 198 | 67 | .41 | | |

| | KCAL / WT (g) | $H_2O$ / PRO (g) | FAT / CHO (g) | PUFA / SFA (g) | CHOL / DFIB (mg/g) | A-RE / A-IU | C / B-1 (mg) | B-2 / NIA (mg) | B-6 / B-12 (mg/mcg) | FOL / PANT (mcg/mg) | Na / K (mg) | Ca / P (mg) | Mg / Fe (mg) | Zn / Cu (mg) | Mn (mg) |
|---|---|---|---|---|---|---|---|---|---|---|---|---|---|---|---|
| str | 104 | 99.3 | 0.4 | | | 5 | 35 | .06 | .05 | 7 | 24 | 40 | 11 | | .26 |
| *1 jar* | 128 | 1.6 | 26.0 | | | 52 | .05 | 0.1 | .08 | | 104 | 39 | .23 | | |
| **tropical fruit dessert, jr** | 131 | 183.1 | 0.0 | | | 4 | 41 | .07 | | | 16 | 22 | | | |
| *1 jar* | 220 | 0.4 | 36.1 | | | 43 | .02 | 0.2 | | | 128 | | .57 | | |
| **tutti frutti** | | | | | | | | | | | | | | | |
| jr, Heinz | 149 | | 0.9 | | | | 15 | .04 | .04 | | 36 | 32 | | | .40 |
| *1 jar* | 213 | 0.9 | 34.3 | | | 430 | .06 | 0.2 | | | 92 | 34 | .64 | .426 | |
| str, Heinz | 88 | | 0.4 | | | | 16 | .03 | .03 | | 19 | 15 | | | .10 |
| *1 jar* | 128 | 0.5 | 20.6 | | | 166 | .03 | 0.1 | | | 51 | 15 | .26 | .026 | |
| **van custard pudding** | | | | | | | | | | | | | | | |
| jr | 196 | 174.7 | 5.0 | 0.2 | | 8 | 2 | .17 | .04 | 14 | 64 | 123 | 11 | | .61 |
| *1 jar* | 220 | 3.5 | 35.7 | 2.6 | | 79 | .03 | 0.1 | | .56 | 136 | 99 | .57 | .112 | |
| str | 109 | 102.2 | 2.5 | 0.1 | | 8 | 1 | .10 | .03 | 8 | 36 | 71 | 7 | | .36 |
| *1 jar* | 128 | 2.0 | 20.6 | 1.3 | | 82 | .02 | 0.1 | | .32 | 85 | 57 | .31 | .064 | |

## 19.4. DINNERS

| | KCAL / WT (g) | $H_2O$ / PRO (g) | FAT / CHO (g) | PUFA / SFA (g) | CHOL / DFIB (mg/g) | A-RE / A-IU | C / B-1 (mg) | B-2 / NIA (mg) | B-6 / B-12 (mg/mcg) | FOL / PANT (mcg/mg) | Na / K (mg) | Ca / P (mg) | Mg / Fe (mg) | Zn / Cu (mg) | Mn (mg) |
|---|---|---|---|---|---|---|---|---|---|---|---|---|---|---|---|
| **beef & egg noodles** | | | | | | | | | | | | | | | |
| jr | 122 | 186.9 | 4.0 | | | 187 | 3 | .08 | .07 | 12 | 37 | 18 | 16 | | .85 |
| *1 jar* | 213 | 5.4 | 15.7 | | 0.9 | 1397 | .06 | 1.2 | .20 | .49 | 99 | 64 | .92 | .068 | |
| str | 68 | 113.4 | 2.2 | | | 141 | 2 | .05 | .06 | 7 | 37 | 12 | 9 | | .48 |
| *1 jar* | 128 | 2.9 | 9.0 | | | 1053 | .05 | 0.9 | .12 | .27 | 61 | 37 | .53 | .038 | |
| **beef & egg noodles w/ veg, toddler, Gerber—1 jar** | 119 | | 3.9 | | | 303 | 3 | .09 | .09 | | 374 | 20 | | | |
| *1 jar* | 170 | 6.8 | 15.8 | | 1.0 | | .09 | 1.5 | | | 236 | 75 | 1.02 | | |
| **beef & egg rice, toddler** | 146 | 144.9 | 5.1 | | | | 7 | .12 | .25 | | 632 | 20 | 15 | 1.62 | |
| *1 jar* | 177 | 8.9 | 15.5 | | | 889 | .03 | 2.4 | | | 212 | 62 | 1.23 | .096 | |
| **beef lasagna, toddler** | 137 | 145.7 | 3.8 | | | | 3 | .16 | .13 | | 804 | 32 | 20 | 1.24 | |
| *1 jar* | 177 | 7.4 | 17.7 | | | 2058 | .13 | 2.4 | | | 216 | 70 | 1.55 | | |
| **beef stew, toddler** | 90 | 153.8 | 2.1 | 0.0 | 22 | | 5 | .12 | .13 | | 611 | 16 | 20 | 1.54 | |
| *1 jar* | 177 | 9.1 | 9.6 | 1.0 | | 2918 | .03 | 2.3 | | | 251 | 78 | 1.27 | | |
| **chicken & noodles** | | | | | | | | | | | | | | | |
| inst, Heinz | 60 | | 2.0 | | | | 0 | .06 | .07 | | 35 | 24 | | | .40 |
| *6 T dry* | 14 | 4.0 | 7.0 | | | 150 | .08 | 1.1 | | | 161 | 70 | .90 | .080 | |
| jr | 109 | 189.0 | 3.0 | | | 229 | 3 | .07 | .06 | 11 | 36 | 36 | 19 | | .63 |
| *1 jar* | 213 | 4.1 | 16.1 | | 0.4 | 1907 | .06 | 1.1 | | | 75 | 51 | .84 | .083 | |
| str | 67 | 113.3 | 1.9 | | | 144 | 1 | .07 | .04 | 7 | 20 | 29 | 11 | | .38 |
| *1 jar* | 128 | 2.7 | 9.6 | | | 1158 | .04 | 0.6 | | | 50 | 31 | .58 | .051 | |
| **chicken soup, crm of, str** | 74 | 111.5 | 2.0 | | | 149 | 2 | .06 | .06 | | 24 | 44 | 7 | | .33 |
| *1 jar* | 128 | 3.2 | 10.8 | | | 929 | .01 | 0.5 | .07 | | 100 | 38 | .38 | | |
| **chicken soup, str** | 64 | 114.1 | 2.2 | | | | 1 | .04 | | 7 | 20 | 47 | | | |
| *1 jar* | 128 | 2.0 | 9.2 | | | 1772 | .02 | 0.4 | | | | | .35 | | |
| **chicken stew, toddler** | 132 | 141.5 | 6.4 | 0.1 | 49 | | 3 | .13 | .08 | | 683 | 60 | 18 | .70 | |
| *1 jar* | 170 | 8.9 | 10.9 | 1.9 | | 1718 | .05 | 2.0 | | | 156 | 87 | 1.13 | .034 | |
| **lamb & noodles, jr** | 138 | 184.3 | 4.7 | | | | 4 | .14 | | | 39 | 39 | | | |
| *1 jar* | 213 | 4.8 | 18.6 | | | 1667 | .08 | 1.4 | | | 165 | | .78 | | |
| **macaroni alphabets** | | | | | | | | | | | | | | | |
| w/ beef & tomato sce, toddler, Gerber | 140 | | 3.4 | | | 11 | 3 | .11 | .16 | | 356 | 21 | | | |
| *1 jar* | 177 | 7.1 | 20.4 | | 0.9 | | .11 | 2.4 | | | 262 | 87 | 1.42 | | |
| w/ tomato sce & cheese, toddler, Gerber—1 jar | 120 | | 1.8 | | | 175 | 5 | .12 | .11 | | 550 | 51 | | | |
| *1 jar* | 177 | 3.7 | 22.5 | | 0.7 | | .09 | 1.5 | | | 250 | 81 | .71 | | |
| **macaroni & bacon, jr** | 160 | 181.2 | 7.1 | | | | 5 | .18 | | | 166 | 152 | | | |
| *1 jar* | 213 | 5.4 | 18.2 | | | 2471 | .10 | 1.3 | | | 180 | | .80 | | |
| **macaroni & cheese** | | | | | | | | | | | | | | | |
| jr | 130 | 184.2 | 4.3 | | | 6 | 3 | .14 | .03 | 3 | 163 | 108 | 14 | | .68 |
| *1 jar* | 213 | 5.5 | 17.5 | | 0.4 | 28 | .12 | 1.2 | .06 | | 94 | 125 | .64 | .045 | |

| | KCAL / WT (g) | H₂O / PRO (g) | FAT / CHO (g) | PUFA / SFA (g) | CHOL / DFIB (mg/g) | A (RE) / A (IU) | C / B-1 (mg) | B-2 / NIA (mg) | B-6 / B-12 (mg/mcg) | FOL / PANT (mcg/mg) | Na / K (mg) | Ca / P (mg) | Mg / Fe (mg) | Zn / Cu (mg) | Mn (mg) |
|---|---|---|---|---|---|---|---|---|---|---|---|---|---|---|---|
| str | 76 | 111.5 | 2.7 | | | 7 | 2 | .09 | .02 | 2 | 93 | 69 | 11 | | .44 |
| *1 jar* | 128 | 3.3 | 9.6 | | | 35 | .07 | 0.6 | .04 | | 59 | 73 | | .40 | .026 |
| macaroni & ham, jr | 127 | 184.2 | 2.9 | | | | 5 | .21 | | | 101 | 159 | | | |
| *1 jar* | 213 | 6.8 | 18.0 | | | 1120 | .12 | 1.7 | | | 225 | | | .81 | |
| **macaroni, tomato & beef** | | | | | | | | | | | | | | | |
| jr | 125 | 184.6 | 2.4 | | | 233 | 3 | .12 | .10 | | 35 | 30 | 15 | | .77 |
| *1 jar* | 213 | 5.3 | 20.1 | | 1.1 | 1471 | .10 | 1.6 | .51 | | 153 | 94 | .76 | .083 | |
| str | 71 | 111.7 | 1.4 | | | 116 | 2 | .08 | .06 | 26 | 21 | 21 | 12 | | .40 |
| *1 jar* | 128 | 2.9 | 11.3 | | | 679 | .09 | 1.1 | .29 | | 123 | 54 | .63 | .051 | |
| **mixed veg dinner** | | | | | | | | | | | | | | | |
| jr | 71 | 193.0 | 0.1 | | | 520 | 7 | .05 | | 14 | 19 | 37 | | | |
| *1 jar* | 213 | 2.1 | 16.8 | | | 5205 | .03 | 0.9 | | | 240 | | | .65 | |
| str | 52 | 113.6 | 0.1 | | | 349 | 4 | .04 | | 10 | 10 | 29 | | | |
| *1 jar* | 128 | 1.5 | 12.2 | | | 3492 | .02 | 0.6 | | | 155 | | | .42 | |
| noodles & beef, homestyle, toddler, Gerber—*1 jar* | 143 | | 5.1 | | | 119 | 2 | .12 | .09 | | 369 | 37 | | | |
| | 170 | 6.5 | 17.7 | 0.7 | | | .09 | 1.8 | | | 167 | 97 | 1.19 | | |
| noodles & chicken w/ carrots & peas, toddler, Gerber—*1 jar* | 109 | | 2.9 | | | 332 | 3 | .09 | .10 | | 316 | 19 | | | |
| | 170 | 6.5 | 14.1 | 1.0 | | | .07 | 2.1 | | | 162 | 71 | .68 | | |
| potatoes & ham, toddler, Gerber | 111 | | 4.3 | | | 10 | 4 | .05 | .12 | | 272 | 27 | | | |
| *1 jar* | 170 | 3.9 | 14.6 | 0.5 | | | .09 | 1.1 | | | 216 | 60 | .34 | | |
| rice w/ beef & tomato sce, toddler, Gerber | 135 | | 3.7 | | | 117 | 3 | .11 | .16 | | 372 | 23 | | | |
| *1 jar* | 177 | 5.7 | 19.5 | 0.9 | | | .04 | 1.5 | | | 285 | 67 | 1.42 | | |
| saucy rice w/ chicken, toddler, Gerber | 109 | | 2.2 | | | 320 | 3 | .07 | .12 | | 391 | 29 | | | |
| *1 jar* | 170 | 5.4 | 16.8 | 0.7 | | | .03 | 1.6 | | | 170 | 85 | .68 | | |
| **spaghetti, tomato & meat** | | | | | | | | | | | | | | | |
| jr | 135 | 182.1 | 2.7 | | | 284 | 5 | .15 | .13 | | 42 | 39 | | | .90 |
| *1 jar* | 213 | 5.4 | 21.6 | | 1.1 | 1477 | .14 | 2.3 | | .38 | 230 | 79 | 1.16 | | |
| toddler | 133 | 144.4 | 1.8 | | | | 7 | .18 | .15 | | 634 | 39 | 26 | | .85 |
| *1 jar* | 177 | 9.4 | 19.1 | | | 784 | .11 | 2.8 | | | 289 | 79 | 1.59 | .035 | |
| spaghetti, tomato sce & beef, toddler, Gerber—*1 jar* | 129 | | 2.8 | | | 195 | 4 | .12 | .12 | | 358 | 37 | | | |
| | 177 | 6.4 | 19.6 | | 1.1 | | .12 | 2.0 | | | 281 | 74 | 1.06 | | |
| split peas & ham, jr | 152 | 177.8 | 2.8 | | | 170 | 4 | .10 | .09 | | 30 | 49 | | | |
| *1 jar* | 213 | 7.0 | 24.1 | | 1.7 | 1284 | .10 | 1.0 | | | 291 | 104 | 1.06 | | |
| **turkey & rice** | | | | | | | | | | | | | | | |
| jr | 104 | 190.2 | 2.9 | 0.4 | | 316 | 3 | .06 | .06 | 7 | 33 | 50 | | | |
| *1 jar* | 213 | 3.8 | 15.3 | 0.9 | 0.9 | 2256 | .02 | 0.6 | | | 71 | 36 | .62 | | |
| str | 63 | 114.0 | 1.7 | 0.2 | 13 | 122 | 2 | .03 | .04 | 4 | 21 | 27 | | | |
| *1 jar* | 128 | 2.4 | 9.4 | 0.5 | | 783 | .01 | 0.4 | | | 53 | 26 | .33 | | |
| **veg & bacon** | | | | | | | | | | | | | | | |
| jr | 150 | 183.5 | 8.2 | 0.1 | | 463 | 2 | .06 | .14 | 19 | 96 | 23 | | | |
| *1 jar* | 213 | 3.9 | 16.1 | 3.0 | 1.5 | 3356 | .11 | 1.2 | | | 184 | 81 | .88 | | |
| str | 88 | 110.0 | 4.2 | 0.1 | 4 | 382 | 2 | .04 | .10 | 12 | 55 | 17 | | | |
| *1 jar* | 128 | 2.0 | 11.0 | 1.5 | | 3409 | .04 | 0.7 | .13 | | 115 | 40 | .45 | | |
| **veg & beef** | | | | | | | | | | | | | | | |
| inst, Heinz | 60 | | 2.0 | | | | 0 | .04 | .05 | | 25 | 12 | | | .51 |
| *5 T dry* | 14 | 3.0 | 7.0 | | | 354 | .04 | 0.8 | | | 142 | 47 | .90 | .070 | |
| jr | 113 | 187.3 | 3.6 | | | 410 | 3 | .07 | .14 | 10 | 52 | 22 | 13 | | .88 |
| *1 jar* | 213 | 5.0 | 15.8 | | 1.1 | 3011 | .07 | 1.4 | .56 | .27 | 224 | 91 | 1.01 | .083 | |
| str | 67 | 113.3 | 2.6 | | | 219 | 2 | .04 | .07 | 6 | 27 | 16 | 7 | | .42 |
| *1 jar* | 128 | 2.5 | 9.0 | | | 1520 | .03 | 0.7 | .32 | .15 | 129 | 52 | .49 | .013 | |
| toddler, Gerber | 120 | | 3.7 | | | 250 | 4 | .07 | .12 | | 317 | 19 | | | |
| *1 jar* | 177 | 6.2 | 15.2 | 0.9 | | | .04 | 1.3 | | | 297 | 65 | .89 | | |
| **veg & chicken** | | | | | | | | | | | | | | | |
| inst, Heinz | 60 | | 2.0 | | | | 0 | .02 | .06 | | 30 | 24 | | | .36 |
| *6 T dry* | 14 | 3.0 | 8.0 | | | 424 | .05 | 1.1 | | | 130 | 58 | .90 | .060 | |

| | KCAL / WT (g) | H₂O (g) / PRO (g) | FAT (g) / CHO (g) | PUFA (g) / SFA (g) | CHOL (mg) / DFIB (g) | A (RE) / A (IU) | C (mg) / B-1 (mg) | B-2 (mg) / NIA (mg) | B-6 (mg) / B-12 (mcg) | FOL (mcg) / PANT (mg) | Na (mg) / K (mg) | Ca (mg) / P (mg) | Mg (mg) / Fe (mg) | Zn (mg) / Cu (mg) | Mn (mg) |
|---|---|---|---|---|---|---|---|---|---|---|---|---|---|---|---|
| jr | 106 | 187.9 | 2.3 | | | 316 | 3 | .04 | .08 | 8 | 18 | 30 | | | |
| *1 jar* | 213 | 4.0 | 18.0 | | 0.6 | 2546 | .03 | 0.7 | | .50 | 54 | 55 | .64 | | |
| str | 55 | 115.2 | 1.4 | | | 176 | 1 | .02 | .03 | 4 | 14 | 18 | | | |
| *1 jar* | 128 | 2.5 | 8.5 | | | 1416 | .02 | 0.2 | | .26 | 38 | 32 | .35 | | |
| toddler, Gerber | 119 | | 2.8 | | | 276 | 3 | .05 | .09 | | 324 | 19 | | | |
| *1 jar* | 177 | 6.5 | 16.6 | | 1.1 | | .05 | 1.5 | | | 211 | 78 | .71 | | |
| **veg & ham** | | | | | | | | | | | | | | | |
| inst, Heinz | 60 | | 2.0 | | | | 1 | .04 | .05 | | 30 | 12 | | | .47 |
| *6 T dry* | 14 | 4.0 | 7.0 | | | 300 | .08 | 0.6 | | | 86 | 47 | .60 | .060 | |
| jr | 110 | 188.2 | 3.6 | | | 173 | 3 | .05 | .07 | 11 | 37 | 16 | 15 | .48 | |
| *1 jar* | 213 | 5.2 | 14.9 | | 0.9 | 1310 | .08 | 0.7 | | | 197 | 55 | .47 | .066 | |
| str | 62 | 114.2 | 2.2 | | | 122 | 2 | .04 | .04 | 6 | 15 | 11 | 6 | .25 | |
| *1 jar* | 128 | 2.2 | 8.8 | | | 872 | .04 | 0.5 | | | 109 | 29 | .38 | .037 | |
| toddler | 128 | 148.0 | 5.2 | 0.3 | 14 | | 7 | .10 | .15 | | 531 | 41 | 30 | .83 | |
| *1 jar* | 177 | 7.4 | 13.9 | 1.9 | 0.9 | 629 | .08 | 1.2 | | | 271 | 71 | 1.23 | .071 | |
| **veg & lamb** | | | | | | | | | | | | | | | |
| jr | 108 | 188.8 | 3.7 | | | 423 | 4 | .07 | .09 | 8 | 28 | 27 | 16 | .47 | |
| *1 jar* | 213 | 4.4 | 15.1 | | 0.9 | 3158 | .05 | 1.2 | .34 | .34 | 202 | 104 | .72 | .062 | |
| str | 67 | 113.4 | 2.6 | | | 363 | 2 | .04 | .06 | 5 | 26 | 15 | 9 | .28 | |
| *1 jar* | 128 | 2.5 | 8.9 | | | 2554 | .02 | 0.7 | .20 | .21 | 120 | 63 | .44 | .037 | |
| **veg & liver** | | | | | | | | | | | | | | | |
| jr | 93 | 189.4 | 1.2 | | | 1524 | 4 | .48 | .21 | 68 | 27 | 20 | | | |
| *1 jar* | 213 | 3.9 | 17.5 | | | 8368 | .05 | 2.5 | | | 189 | 81 | 3.86 | | |
| str | 50 | 115.2 | 0.6 | | | 940 | 2 | .34 | .11 | 37 | 24 | 9 | | | |
| *1 jar* | 128 | 2.8 | 8.8 | | | 3981 | .02 | 1.5 | | | 120 | 51 | 2.83 | | |
| **veg & turkey** | | | | | | | | | | | | | | | |
| inst, Heinz | 60 | | 2.0 | | | | 0 | .02 | .03 | | 25 | 12 | | | .42 |
| *6 T dry* | 14 | 4.0 | 8.0 | | | 450 | .05 | 1.1 | | | 140 | 57 | .90 | .070 | |
| jr | 101 | 189.5 | 2.7 | | | 244 | 2 | .04 | .05 | 6 | 36 | 27 | | | .54 |
| *1 jar* | 213 | 3.6 | 16.4 | | 0.9 | 1909 | .03 | 0.5 | | .45 | 53 | 40 | .68 | .055 | |
| str | 54 | 115.4 | 1.5 | | | 143 | 1 | .02 | .04 | 3 | 17 | 21 | | | .29 |
| *1 jar* | 128 | 2.1 | 8.4 | | | 1068 | .01 | 0.4 | | .24 | 56 | 24 | .34 | .029 | |
| toddler | 141 | 145.7 | 6.1 | | | | 6 | .16 | .11 | | 591 | 82 | 29 | .55 | |
| *1 jar* | 177 | 8.5 | 14.2 | | 0.9 | 3715 | .04 | 1.0 | | | 294 | 102 | 1.07 | | |
| **veg, dumplings & beef** | | | | | | | | | | | | | | | |
| jr | 103 | 188.7 | 1.7 | | | | 2 | .08 | | 16 | 110 | 30 | 14 | .70 | |
| *1 jar* | 213 | 4.4 | 17.0 | | | 1407 | .08 | 1.0 | | | | | 1.00 | | |
| str | 61 | 113.8 | 1.2 | | | | 1 | .05 | | 9 | 62 | 18 | 8 | .51 | |
| *1 jar* | 128 | 2.6 | 9.8 | | | 533 | .06 | 0.7 | | | | | .49 | | |
| **veg, noodles & chicken** | | | | | | | | | | | | | | | |
| jr | 137 | 183.7 | 4.8 | | | | 2 | .08 | .05 | 7 | 54 | 54 | | | .68 |
| *1 jar* | 213 | 3.7 | 19.4 | | | 2238 | .09 | 1.4 | .19 | .44 | 126 | 70 | 1.04 | .124 | |
| str | 81 | 111.6 | 3.3 | | | | 1 | .06 | .03 | 4 | 26 | 35 | | | .32 |
| *1 jar* | 128 | 2.6 | 10.1 | | | 1813 | .04 | 0.5 | .10 | .24 | 70 | 39 | .45 | .069 | |
| **veg, noodles & turkey** | | | | | | | | | | | | | | | |
| jr | 110 | 189.0 | 3.2 | | | | 2 | .09 | .04 | 6 | 37 | 67 | 20 | .64 | |
| *1 jar* | 213 | 3.9 | 16.1 | | | 2118 | .05 | 0.6 | .25 | | 156 | 62 | .55 | | |
| str | 56 | 115.6 | 1.6 | | | | 1 | .06 | .02 | 3 | 27 | 41 | 10 | .35 | |
| *1 jar* | 128 | 1.5 | 8.7 | | | 1268 | .02 | 0.3 | .13 | | 81 | 32 | .25 | | |

| | KCAL | H₂O (g) | FAT (g) | PUFA (g) | CHOL (mg) | A (RE) | C (mg) | B-2 (mg) | B-6 (mg) | FOL (mcg) | Na (mg) | Ca (mg) | Mg (mg) | Zn (mg) | Mn (mg) |
|---|---|---|---|---|---|---|---|---|---|---|---|---|---|---|---|
| | WT (g) | PRO (g) | CHO (g) | SFA (g) | DFIB (g) | A (IU) | B-1 (mg) | NIA (mg) | B-12 (mcg) | PANT (mg) | K (mg) | P (mg) | Fe (mg) | Cu (mg) | |

## 19.5. DINNERS, HIGH MEAT/CHEESE

**beef w/ veg**

| | KCAL | H₂O | FAT | PUFA | CHOL | A(RE) | C | B-2 | B-6 | FOL | Na | Ca | Mg | Zn | Mn |
|---|---|---|---|---|---|---|---|---|---|---|---|---|---|---|---|
| jr | 108 | 106.5 | 5.9 | | | 126 | 2 | .10 | .11 | 8 | 42 | 15 | 10 | 1.79 | |
| *1 jar* | 128 | 8.1 | 6.7 | | 0.5 | 1014 | .05 | 1.8 | .75 | .35 | 191 | 66 | 1.01 | .118 | |
| str | 96 | 109.3 | 5.3 | | | 141 | 3 | .08 | .11 | 7 | 46 | 15 | 10 | 1.66 | |
| *1 jar* | 128 | 7.3 | 5.3 | | 0.4 | 1003 | .04 | 1.7 | .65 | .31 | 179 | 62 | .93 | .102 | |

**chicken w/ veg**

| | KCAL | H₂O | FAT | PUFA | CHOL | A(RE) | C | B-2 | B-6 | FOL | Na | Ca | Mg | Zn | Mn |
|---|---|---|---|---|---|---|---|---|---|---|---|---|---|---|---|
| jr | 117 | 105.8 | 7.0 | | | 167 | 1 | .09 | .05 | 2 | 33 | 56 | 9 | 1.28 | |
| *1 jar* | 128 | 9.0 | 5.4 | | 0.5 | 1071 | .04 | 1.3 | .20 | .44 | 79 | 68 | .95 | | |
| str | 100 | 107.2 | 4.6 | | | 106 | 1 | .09 | .08 | 1 | 35 | 66 | 9 | 1.21 | |
| *1 jar* | 128 | 8.0 | 7.6 | | 0.5 | 737 | .04 | 1.3 | .18 | .41 | 76 | 69 | 1.27 | | |
| **cottage cheese w/ pineapple, str** | 157 | 97.2 | 3.0 | | | 10 | 2 | .19 | .06 | | 201 | 88 | 9 | .39 | |
| *1 jar* | 135 | 8.5 | 25.4 | | | 104 | .05 | 0.1 | .30 | | 128 | 98 | .14 | | |

**ham w/ veg**

| | KCAL | H₂O | FAT | PUFA | CHOL | A(RE) | C | B-2 | B-6 | FOL | Na | Ca | Mg | Zn | Mn |
|---|---|---|---|---|---|---|---|---|---|---|---|---|---|---|---|
| jr | 98 | 107.0 | 4.2 | 0.3 | 23 | 85 | 2 | .11 | .12 | 8 | 28 | 12 | 12 | 1.39 | |
| *1 jar* | 128 | 8.2 | 7.9 | 1.4 | 0.5 | 332 | .14 | 1.5 | .36 | .52 | 208 | 71 | .76 | | |
| str | 97 | 107.6 | 4.4 | 0.3 | | 52 | 2 | .11 | .14 | 8 | 29 | 14 | 11 | 1.28 | |
| *1 jar* | 128 | 8.0 | 7.1 | 1.5 | 0.4 | 214 | .13 | 1.8 | .34 | .50 | 198 | 72 | .75 | | |

**turkey w/ veg**

| | KCAL | H₂O | FAT | PUFA | CHOL | A(RE) | C | B-2 | B-6 | FOL | Na | Ca | Mg | Zn | Mn |
|---|---|---|---|---|---|---|---|---|---|---|---|---|---|---|---|
| jr | 115 | 105.6 | 6.4 | | | 143 | 2 | .09 | .05 | 13 | 56 | 91 | 10 | 1.16 | |
| *1 jar* | 128 | 7.6 | 7.5 | | 0.4 | 810 | .01 | 1.0 | .58 | | 137 | 81 | 1.00 | .054 | |
| str | 111 | 106.3 | 6.1 | | | 119 | 2 | .09 | .05 | 12 | 38 | 80 | 10 | 1.28 | |
| *1 jar* | 128 | 7.2 | 7.7 | | 0.3 | 419 | .01 | 1.3 | .56 | | 153 | 90 | .88 | .052 | |

**veal w/ veg**

| | KCAL | H₂O | FAT | PUFA | CHOL | A(RE) | C | B-2 | B-6 | FOL | Na | Ca | Mg | Zn | Mn |
|---|---|---|---|---|---|---|---|---|---|---|---|---|---|---|---|
| jr | 93 | 107.9 | 4.0 | | | 101 | 2 | .11 | .09 | | 32 | 14 | 12 | 1.41 | |
| *1 jar* | 128 | 7.8 | 7.4 | | 0.5 | 545 | .03 | 2.0 | .59 | .32 | 201 | 69 | 1.13 | .131 | |
| str | 89 | 108.2 | 3.4 | | | 96 | 2 | .10 | .11 | | 30 | 12 | 10 | 1.28 | |
| *1 jar* | 128 | 7.6 | 7.8 | | 0.3 | 349 | .03 | 2.1 | .58 | .32 | 196 | 69 | .76 | .128 | |

## 19.6. FRUIT JUICES

**apple**

| | KCAL | H₂O | FAT | PUFA | CHOL | A(RE) | C | B-2 | B-6 | FOL | Na | Ca | Mg | Zn | Mn |
|---|---|---|---|---|---|---|---|---|---|---|---|---|---|---|---|
| str | 61 | 114.3 | 0.1 | | | 2 | 75 | .02 | .04 | 0 | 4 | 6 | 4 | .04 | |
| *1 jar* | 130 | 0.0 | 15.2 | | 0.1 | 24 | .01 | 0.1 | | | 118 | 7 | .73 | | |
| toddler, Gerber | 116 | | 0.2 | | | 2 | 76 | .02 | .07 | | 5 | 7 | | | |
| *1 jar* | 236 | 0.5 | 27.6 | | 0.2 | | .02 | 0.2 | | | 212 | 17 | .47 | | |

**apple-apricot**

| | KCAL | H₂O | FAT | PUFA | CHOL | A(RE) | C | B-2 | B-6 | FOL | Na | Ca | Mg | Zn | Mn |
|---|---|---|---|---|---|---|---|---|---|---|---|---|---|---|---|
| str, Gerber | 61 | | 0.1 | | | 56 | 40 | .02 | .02 | | 4 | 7 | | | |
| *1 jar* | 124 | 0.2 | 14.5 | | 0.2 | | .01 | 0.2 | | | 140 | 10 | .25 | | |
| str, Heinz | 61 | | 0.3 | | | | 42 | .01 | .04 | | 8 | 14 | | .09 | |
| *1 jar* | 130 | 0.1 | 14.7 | | | 553 | .03 | 0.2 | | | 148 | 14 | .65 | .039 | |
| **apple-banana, str, Gerber** | 62 | | 0.2 | | | 2 | 40 | .02 | .07 | | 4 | 5 | | | |
| *1 jar* | 124 | 0.2 | 14.8 | | 0.2 | | .01 | 0.2 | | | 143 | 9 | .12 | | |
| **apple-berry, toddler, Gerber** | 109 | | 0.2 | | | | 76 | .05 | .07 | | 14 | 24 | | | |
| *1 jar* | 236 | 0.2 | 26.4 | | 0.2 | | .02 | 0.3 | | | 264 | 19 | .71 | | |

**apple-cherry**

| | KCAL | H₂O | FAT | PUFA | CHOL | A(RE) | C | B-2 | B-6 | FOL | Na | Ca | Mg | Zn | Mn |
|---|---|---|---|---|---|---|---|---|---|---|---|---|---|---|---|
| str | 53 | 116.3 | 0.3 | | | 1 | 76 | .02 | .04 | 0 | 4 | 7 | 4 | .04 | |
| *1 jar* | 130 | 0.2 | 12.9 | | 0.1 | 7 | .01 | 0.1 | | | 127 | 7 | .86 | | |
| toddler, Gerber | 113 | | 0.2 | | | 2 | 76 | .05 | .05 | | 12 | 14 | | | |
| *1 jar* | 236 | 0.5 | 27.1 | | 0.2 | | .02 | 0.2 | | | 241 | 19 | .71 | | |

| | KCAL / WT (g) | H2O (g) / PRO (g) | FAT (g) / CHO (g) | PUFA (g) / SFA (g) | CHOL (mg) / DFIB (g) | A (RE) / A (IU) | C (mg) / B-1 (mg) | B-2 (mg) / NIA (mg) | B-6 (mg) / B-12 (mcg) | FOL (mcg) / PANT (mg) | Na (mg) / K (mg) | Ca (mg) / P (mg) | Mg (mg) / Fe (mg) | Zn (mg) / Cu (mg) | Mn (mg) |
|---|---|---|---|---|---|---|---|---|---|---|---|---|---|---|---|
| **apple-grape** | | | | | | | | | | | | | | | |
| str | 60 | 114.5 | 0.2 | | | 1 | 70 | .03 | .04 | 0 | 4 | 7 | 4 | .05 | |
| *1 jar* | 130 | 0.1 | 14.8 | | 0.1 | 7 | .01 | 0.1 | | | 118 | 7 | .51 | | |
| toddler, Gerber | 116 | | 0.2 | | | 2 | 76 | .05 | .07 | | 9 | 14 | | | |
| *1 jar* | 236 | 0.5 | 27.6 | | 0.2 | | .02 | 0.2 | | | 212 | 17 | .24 | | |
| **apple-peach, str** | 55 | 115.7 | 0.1 | | | 8 | 76 | .01 | .03 | 2 | | 4 | 4 | .03 | |
| *1 jar* | 130 | 0.2 | 13.6 | | 0.1 | 82 | .01 | 0.3 | | | 126 | 6 | .73 | | |
| **apple-pear, toddler, Gerber** | 111 | | 0.2 | | | 2 | 76 | .02 | .05 | | 7 | 14 | | | |
| *1 jar* | 236 | 0.5 | 26.7 | | 0.7 | | .02 | 0.2 | | | 222 | 14 | .47 | | |
| **apple-pineapple** | | | | | | | | | | | | | | | |
| str, Gerber | 60 | | 0.2 | | | 1 | 40 | .01 | .04 | | 2 | 10 | | | |
| *1 jar* | 124 | 0.2 | 14.5 | | 0.1 | | .04 | 0.1 | | | 130 | 7 | .12 | | |
| str, Heinz | 61 | | 0.3 | | | | 42 | .01 | .06 | | 7 | 16 | | | .07 |
| *1 jar* | 130 | 0.3 | 14.6 | | | 21 | .03 | 0.1 | | | 108 | 10 | .39 | .026 | |
| **apple-plum** | 63 | 113.5 | 0.0 | | | 6 | 76 | .02 | .04 | 0 | | 6 | 4 | .04 | |
| *1 jar* | 130 | 0.1 | 16.0 | | | 55 | .03 | 0.3 | | | 131 | 4 | .81 | | |
| **apple-prune** | 94 | 105.7 | 0.2 | | | | 88 | .00 | .05 | 0 | 7 | 12 | | | |
| *1 jar* | 130 | 0.3 | 23.4 | | 0.1 | | .01 | 0.4 | | | 192 | 20 | 1.24 | | |
| **fruit-a-plenty, toddler, Gerber** | 113 | | 0.2 | | | | 76 | .02 | .07 | | 31 | 21 | | | |
| *1 jar* | 236 | 0.2 | 27.6 | | 0.2 | | .02 | 0.3 | | | 243 | 17 | .71 | | |
| **fruits of the sun, toddler, Gerber** | 113 | | 0.2 | | | | 76 | .05 | .09 | | 26 | 26 | | | |
| *1 jar* | 236 | 0.5 | 26.9 | | 0.2 | | .05 | 0.3 | | | 413 | 24 | .24 | | |
| **mixed fruit** | | | | | | | | | | | | | | | |
| str | 61 | 114.3 | 0.1 | | | 5 | 83 | .02 | .06 | 9 | 5 | 10 | 7 | .04 | |
| *1 jar* | 130 | 0.2 | 15.1 | | 0.1 | 54 | .03 | 0.2 | | | 131 | 7 | .44 | | |
| toddler, Gerber | 113 | | 0.2 | | | 7 | 76 | .02 | .07 | | 9 | 21 | | | |
| *1 jar* | 236 | 0.7 | 26.4 | | 0.2 | | .07 | 0.3 | | | 262 | 19 | .47 | | |
| **orange** | 58 | 115.0 | 0.3 | | | 7 | 81 | .04 | .07 | 34 | 2 | 16 | 11 | .07 | |
| *1 jar* | 130 | 0.8 | 13.3 | | 0.1 | 72 | .06 | 0.3 | | | 240 | 14 | .22 | | |
| **orange-apple** | 56 | 115.5 | 0.3 | | | 9 | 100 | .04 | .05 | 16 | 4 | 13 | 6 | .03 | |
| *1 jar* | 130 | 0.5 | 13.2 | | 0.1 | 95 | .05 | 0.2 | | | 179 | 9 | .26 | | |
| **orange-apple-banana** | 61 | 113.9 | 0.1 | | | 4 | 42 | .04 | .08 | 13 | 6 | 6 | 7 | .03 | |
| *1 jar* | 130 | 0.5 | 15.0 | | | 35 | .06 | 0.3 | | | 174 | 10 | .45 | | |
| **orange-apricot** | 60 | 114.1 | 0.1 | | | 28 | 112 | .04 | .07 | 26 | 7 | 8 | 9 | .05 | |
| *1 jar* | 130 | 1.0 | 14.2 | | | 281 | .08 | 0.3 | | | 259 | 15 | .49 | | |
| **orange-banana** | 65 | 113.0 | 0.1 | | | 6 | 44 | .06 | | 32 | 4 | 22 | | | |
| *1 jar* | 130 | 0.9 | 15.4 | | | 60 | .07 | 0.2 | | | 261 | | .14 | | |
| **orange-pineapple** | 63 | 113.5 | 0.1 | | | 4 | 69 | .03 | .08 | 24 | 2 | 10 | 12 | .05 | |
| *1 jar* | 130 | 0.7 | 15.2 | | | 40 | .07 | 0.3 | | | 183 | 11 | .55 | | |
| **prune-orange** | 91 | 106.5 | 0.4 | | | 17 | 83 | .16 | .08 | 17 | 2 | 16 | 10 | .05 | |
| *1 jar* | 130 | 0.8 | 21.8 | | | 170 | .06 | 0.5 | | | 236 | 14 | 1.13 | | |

## 19.7. FRUITS

| | KCAL / WT (g) | H2O (g) / PRO (g) | FAT (g) / CHO (g) | PUFA (g) / SFA (g) | CHOL (mg) / DFIB (g) | A (RE) / A (IU) | C (mg) / B-1 (mg) | B-2 (mg) / NIA (mg) | B-6 (mg) / B-12 (mcg) | FOL (mcg) / PANT (mg) | Na (mg) / K (mg) | Ca (mg) / P (mg) | Mg (mg) / Fe (mg) | Zn (mg) / Cu (mg) | Mn (mg) |
|---|---|---|---|---|---|---|---|---|---|---|---|---|---|---|---|
| **apple-blueberry** | | | | | | | | | | | | | | | |
| jr | 137 | 182.2 | 0.4 | | | 9 | 31 | .10 | .09 | 8 | 28 | 10 | | | |
| *1 jar* | 220 | 0.4 | 36.5 | | 2.2 | 92 | .04 | 0.2 | | | 143 | 15 | .88 | | |
| str | 82 | 112.2 | 0.3 | | | 3 | 38 | .05 | .05 | 5 | 2 | 5 | | | |
| *1 jar* | 135 | 0.3 | 22.0 | | 1.4 | 27 | .02 | 0.2 | | | 93 | 11 | .27 | | |
| **apple-raspberry** | | | | | | | | | | | | | | | |
| jr | 127 | 184.7 | 0.4 | | | 7 | 64 | .06 | .08 | 7 | 4 | 11 | | | |
| *1 jar* | 220 | 0.4 | 34.1 | | | 66 | .03 | 0.2 | | .19 | 158 | 17 | .48 | | |
| str | 79 | 113.1 | 0.2 | | | 3 | 36 | .04 | .05 | 5 | 3 | 7 | | | |
| *1 jar* | 135 | 0.3 | 21.2 | | | 29 | .02 | 0.1 | | .12 | 108 | 11 | .30 | | |
| **apples, inst, Heinz** | 50 | | 0.0 | | | | 16 | .01 | .03 | | 4 | 8 | | .04 | |
| *4 T dry* | 14 | 0.0 | 13.0 | | | 28 | .02 | 0.1 | | | 104 | 9 | .20 | .040 | |

Each food item has two data lines. The upper line values correspond to the first label in each column header; the lower line (serving size) values correspond to the second label.

| Food / Serving | KCAL / WT (g) | H₂O (g) / PRO (g) | FAT (g) / CHO (g) | PUFA (g) / SFA (g) | CHOL (mg) / DFIB (g) | A (RE) / A (IU) | C (mg) / B-1 (mg) | B-2 (mg) / NIA (mg) | B-6 (mg) / B-12 (mcg) | FOL (mcg) / PANT (mg) | Na (mg) / K (mg) | Ca (mg) / P (mg) | Mg (mg) / Fe (mg) | Zn (mg) / Cu (mg) | Mn (mg) |
|---|---|---|---|---|---|---|---|---|---|---|---|---|---|---|---|
| **apples & apricots, inst, Heinz** | 50 | | 1.0 | | | | 17 | .02 | .04 | | 2 | 11 | | .06 | |
| *3 T dry* | 14 | 0.0 | 13.0 | | | 566 | .02 | 0.2 | | | 160 | 10 | | .040 | |
| **apples & apricots** | | | | | | | | | | | | | | | |
| jr, Heinz | 115 | | 0.6 | | | | 15 | .04 | .11 | | 4 | 17 | | .15 | |
| *1 jar* | 213 | 0.9 | 26.6 | | | 694 | .09 | 0.3 | | | 217 | 34 | .43 | .192 | |
| str, Heinz | 69 | | 0.4 | | | | 16 | .03 | .06 | | 3 | 19 | | .09 | |
| *1 jar* | 128 | 0.5 | 16.0 | | | 417 | .05 | 0.2 | | | 131 | 20 | .26 | .115 | |
| **apples & bananas, inst, Heinz** | 50 | | 0.0 | | | | 17 | .01 | .04 | | 3 | 0 | | .04 | |
| *4 T dry* | 14 | 0.0 | 13.0 | | | 28 | .02 | 0.1 | | | 143 | 7 | .20 | .010 | |
| **apples & cranberries w/ tapioca** | | | | | | | | | | | | | | | |
| jr, Heinz | 179 | | 0.6 | | | | 6 | .02 | .04 | | 19 | 13 | | .06 | |
| *1 jar* | 213 | 0.2 | 43.0 | | | 60 | .02 | 0.2 | | | 38 | 13 | .43 | .085 | |
| str, Heinz | 108 | | 0.4 | | | | 4 | .01 | .03 | | 7 | 8 | | .04 | |
| *1 jar* | 128 | 0.1 | 25.9 | | | 36 | .01 | 0.1 | | | 23 | 8 | .26 | .051 | |
| **apples & peaches, inst, Heinz** | 50 | | 0.0 | | | | 17 | .02 | .04 | | 7 | 8 | | .06 | |
| *3 T dry* | 14 | 0.0 | 13.0 | | | 212 | .02 | 0.2 | | | 128 | 10 | .30 | .030 | |
| **apples & pears** | | | | | | | | | | | | | | | |
| inst, Heinz | 50 | | 1.0 | | | | 17 | .01 | .02 | | 2 | 9 | | .05 | |
| *3 T dry* | 14 | 0.0 | 13.0 | | | 28 | .01 | 0.1 | | | 107 | 8 | .20 | .050 | |
| jr, Heinz | 121 | | 0.4 | | | | 15 | .04 | .06 | | 4 | 17 | | .13 | |
| *1 jar* | 213 | 0.4 | 28.8 | | | 87 | .04 | 0.3 | | | 222 | 19 | .43 | .128 | |
| str, Heinz | 73 | | 0.3 | | | | 16 | .03 | .04 | | 3 | 10 | | .08 | |
| *1 jar* | 128 | 0.3 | 17.3 | | | 52 | .03 | 0.2 | | | 133 | 12 | .26 | .077 | |
| **applesce** | | | | | | | | | | | | | | | |
| jr | 79 | 190.7 | 0.0 | | | 2 | 81 | .06 | .06 | 4 | 5 | 10 | 6 | .09 | |
| *1 jar* | 213 | 0.1 | 21.9 | | 1.7 | 20 | .03 | 0.1 | | .21 | 164 | 13 | .46 | .075 | |
| str | 53 | 113.4 | 0.2 | | | 2 | 49 | .04 | .04 | 2 | 3 | 5 | 4 | .03 | |
| *1 jar* | 128 | 0.2 | 14.0 | | 1.0 | 22 | .02 | 0.1 | | .14 | 91 | 9 | .28 | .049 | |
| **applesce & apricots** | | | | | | | | | | | | | | | |
| jr | 104 | 191.1 | 0.5 | | | 74 | 39 | .07 | .07 | 3 | 6 | 13 | 8 | .07 | |
| *1 jar* | 220 | 0.5 | 27.3 | | 2.0 | 745 | .03 | 0.3 | | | 240 | 23 | .57 | | |
| str | 60 | 118.3 | 0.3 | | | 52 | 26 | .04 | .04 | 2 | 4 | 8 | 5 | .06 | |
| *1 jar* | 135 | 0.3 | 15.7 | | 1.4 | 523 | .02 | 0.2 | | | 162 | 13 | .34 | | |
| **applesce & cherries** | | | | | | | | | | | | | | | |
| jr | 106 | 189.9 | 0.0 | | | 9 | 51 | .10 | | 1 | 6 | 20 | | | |
| *1 jar* | 220 | 0.6 | 28.9 | | | 91 | .03 | 0.2 | | | 214 | | .89 | | |
| str | 65 | 116.6 | 0.0 | | | 5 | 45 | .06 | | 1 | 3 | 14 | | | |
| *1 jar* | 135 | 0.4 | 17.7 | | | 53 | .02 | 0.1 | | | 130 | | .52 | | |
| **applesce & pineapple** | | | | | | | | | | | | | | | |
| jr | 83 | 189.8 | 0.2 | | | 4 | 57 | .06 | .08 | 4 | 4 | 8 | 7 | .64 | |
| *1 jar* | 213 | 0.2 | 22.3 | | | 45 | .05 | 0.2 | | | 162 | 13 | .21 | | |
| str | 48 | 114.6 | 0.1 | | | 3 | 36 | .03 | .05 | 3 | 3 | 5 | 4 | .02 | |
| *1 jar* | 128 | 0.1 | 12.9 | | 1.2 | 26 | .03 | 0.1 | | | 100 | 8 | .13 | | |
| **apricots w/ tapioca** | | | | | | | | | | | | | | | |
| jr | 139 | 180.5 | 0.0 | | | 159 | 39 | .03 | .06 | 4 | 14 | 18 | 9 | .09 | |
| *1 jar* | 220 | 0.6 | 38.0 | | 0.7 | 1590 | .02 | 0.4 | | .30 | 274 | 22 | .58 | | |
| str | 80 | 112.2 | 0.0 | | | 98 | 29 | .02 | .04 | 2 | 11 | 12 | 5 | .06 | |
| *1 jar* | 135 | 0.4 | 22.0 | | 0.4 | 979 | .01 | 0.3 | | .18 | 163 | 14 | .40 | .046 | |
| **bananas, inst, Heinz** | 50 | | 0.0 | | | | 16 | .04 | .24 | | 4 | 4 | | .10 | |
| *3 T dry* | 14 | 1.0 | 13.0 | | | 60 | .01 | 0.2 | | | 236 | 16 | .20 | .050 | |
| **bananas & pineapple w/ tapioca** | | | | | | | | | | | | | | | |
| jr | 143 | 179.8 | 0.0 | | | 9 | 42 | .04 | .18 | 12 | 13 | 15 | 14 | .09 | |
| *1 jar* | 220 | 0.5 | 39.3 | | 0.9 | 90 | .04 | 0.4 | | | 149 | 11 | .51 | .086 | |

| | KCAL / WT (g) | H₂O (g) / PRO (g) | FAT (g) / CHO (g) | PUFA (g) / SFA (g) | CHOL (mg) / DFIB (g) | A (RE) / A (IU) | C (mg) / B-1 (mg) | B-2 (mg) / NIA (mg) | B-6 (mg) / B-12 (mcg) | FOL (mcg) / PANT (mg) | Na (mg) / K (mg) | Ca (mg) / P (mg) | Mg (mg) / Fe (mg) | Zn (mg) / Cu (mg) | Mn (mg) |
|---|---|---|---|---|---|---|---|---|---|---|---|---|---|---|---|
| str | 91 | 109.5 | 0.1 | | | 5 | 29 | .03 | .12 | 7 | 10 | 9 | 8 | .04 | |
| 1 jar | 135 | 0.3 | 24.8 | | 0.4 | 55 | .02 | 0.2 | | | 105 | 7 | .18 | .054 | |
| **bananas w/ tapioca** | | | | | | | | | | | | | | | |
| jr | 147 | 179.3 | 0.4 | | | 10 | 57 | .04 | .31 | 14 | 21 | 17 | 25 | .15 | |
| 1 jar | 220 | 0.8 | 39.1 | | 0.7 | 97 | .03 | 0.5 | | .38 | 237 | 20 | .66 | .101 | |
| str | 77 | 113.4 | 0.1 | | | 6 | 23 | .04 | .16 | 7 | 12 | 6 | 14 | .08 | |
| 1 jar | 135 | 0.5 | 20.6 | | 0.5 | 58 | .02 | 0.2 | | .20 | 118 | 9 | .26 | .054 | |
| guava, str, Gerber | 79 | | 0.1 | | | 32 | 16 | .03 | .05 | | 3 | 8 | | | |
| 1 jar | 128 | 0.3 | 19.2 | | 0.9 | | .01 | 0.5 | | | 114 | 6 | .26 | | |
| guava & papaya w/ tapioca, str | 80 | 105.6 | 0.1 | | | 24 | 104 | .03 | .02 | | 5 | 9 | 6 | .08 | |
| 1 jar | 128 | 0.3 | 21.8 | | | 236 | .01 | 0.3 | | | 95 | 7 | .26 | | |
| guava w/ tapioca, str | 86 | 103.9 | 0.0 | | | 38 | 97 | .09 | .05 | | 2 | 9 | 3 | .10 | |
| 1 jar | 128 | 0.4 | 23.4 | | | 383 | .02 | 0.5 | | | 94 | 6 | .26 | | |
| mango, str, Gerber | 86 | | 0.3 | | | 110 | 16 | .01 | | | 4 | 8 | | | |
| 1 jar | 128 | 0.3 | 20.6 | | 0.4 | | .03 | 0.3 | | | 81 | 6 | .13 | | |
| mango w/ tapioca, str | 109 | 104.9 | 0.3 | | | 90 | 168 | .04 | .16 | | 6 | 5 | 5 | .08 | |
| 1 jar | 135 | 0.4 | 29.2 | | | 898 | .03 | 0.3 | | | 80 | 8 | .14 | | |
| mixed fruit, inst, Heinz | 50 | | 0.0 | | | | 17 | .02 | .04 | | 2 | 9 | | .08 | |
| 4 T dry | 14 | 1.0 | 13.0 | | | 212 | .01 | 0.5 | | | 167 | 9 | .20 | .060 | |
| papaya, str, Gerber | 74 | | 0.5 | | | 12 | 16 | .01 | .01 | | 9 | 8 | | | |
| 1 jar | 128 | 0.3 | 17.0 | | 0.4 | | .01 | 0.1 | | | 81 | 5 | .13 | | |
| papaya & applesce w/ tapioca, str | 89 | 103.2 | 0.1 | | | 10 | 145 | .04 | .03 | | 6 | 9 | 7 | .04 | |
| 1 jar | 128 | 0.3 | 24.2 | | | 97 | .01 | 0.1 | | | 101 | 7 | | | |
| **peaches** | | | | | | | | | | | | | | | |
| inst, Heinz | 50 | | 1.0 | | | | 16 | .01 | .04 | | 2 | 12 | | .14 | |
| 3 T dry | 14 | 1.0 | 13.0 | | | 224 | .01 | 0.5 | | | 202 | 20 | .40 | .070 | |
| jr | 157 | 176.1 | 0.4 | | | 39 | 42 | .07 | .04 | 9 | 10 | 11 | 12 | .13 | |
| 1 jar | 220 | 1.3 | 41.6 | | 1.3 | 392 | .03 | 1.4 | | .29 | 342 | 24 | .59 | .110 | |
| str | 96 | 108.1 | 0.2 | | | 22 | 42 | .05 | .02 | 5 | 8 | 8 | 8 | .12 | |
| 1 jar | 135 | 0.7 | 25.5 | | 0.8 | 217 | .02 | 0.8 | | .18 | 219 | 16 | .32 | .072 | |
| **pears** | | | | | | | | | | | | | | | |
| jr | 93 | 187.0 | 0.2 | | | 7 | 47 | .06 | .02 | 8 | 4 | 18 | 19 | .17 | |
| 1 jar | 213 | 0.6 | 24.7 | | 4.0 | 72 | .03 | 0.4 | | .20 | 246 | 26 | .54 | .170 | |
| str | 53 | 113.2 | 0.2 | | | 4 | 31 | .04 | .01 | 5 | 3 | 11 | 10 | .10 | |
| 1 jar | 128 | 0.4 | 13.9 | | 2.3 | 43 | .02 | 0.2 | | .12 | 166 | 15 | .30 | .083 | |
| **pears & pineapple** | | | | | | | | | | | | | | | |
| jr | 93 | 187.0 | 0.4 | | | 7 | 36 | .05 | .03 | 6 | 2 | 21 | 16 | .27 | |
| 1 jar | 213 | 0.6 | 24.4 | | 3.8 | 68 | .05 | 0.4 | | | 251 | 21 | .44 | .224 | |
| str | 52 | 113.3 | 0.1 | | | 4 | 35 | .04 | .02 | 4 | 5 | 13 | 9 | .08 | |
| 1 jar | 128 | 0.4 | 13.9 | | 1.5 | 37 | .03 | 0.3 | | | 148 | 11 | .32 | .179 | |
| **plums w/ tapioca** | | | | | | | | | | | | | | | |
| jr | 163 | 174.3 | 0.0 | | | 21 | 2 | .07 | .06 | 2 | 18 | 12 | 9 | .18 | |
| 1 jar | 220 | 0.3 | 45.0 | | 0.9 | 207 | .01 | 0.5 | | .25 | 182 | 14 | .48 | .084 | |
| str | 96 | 108.0 | 0.0 | | | 13 | 1 | .04 | .03 | 1 | 8 | 8 | 5 | .11 | |
| 1 jar | 135 | 0.2 | 26.6 | | 0.5 | 128 | .01 | 0.3 | | .15 | 115 | 8 | .27 | .050 | |
| **prunes w/ tapioca** | | | | | | | | | | | | | | | |
| jr | 155 | 176.1 | 0.2 | | | 90 | 2 | .18 | .19 | 1 | 5 | 33 | 21 | .22 | |
| 1 jar | 220 | 1.3 | 41.2 | | | 895 | .05 | 1.2 | | .31 | 357 | 32 | .72 | | |
| str | 94 | 108.4 | 0.1 | | | 61 | 1 | .10 | .11 | 0 | 6 | 20 | 14 | .12 | |
| 1 jar | 135 | 0.8 | 25.0 | | 0.9 | 612 | .03 | 0.7 | | .19 | 238 | 21 | .47 | .082 | |
| tropical fruit medley, str, Gerber | 86 | | 0.9 | | | 37 | 16 | .01 | .03 | | 6 | 6 | | | |
| 1 jar | 128 | 0.3 | 19.1 | | 0.3 | | .03 | 0.1 | | | 50 | 5 | .13 | | |

| | KCAL / WT (g) | H₂O (g) / PRO (g) | FAT (g) / CHO (g) | PUFA (g) / SFA (g) | CHOL (mg) / DFIB (g) | A (RE) / A (IU) | C (mg) / B-1 (mg) | B-2 (mg) / NIA (mg) | B-6 (mg) / B-12 (mcg) | FOL (mcg) / PANT (mg) | Na (mg) / K (mg) | Ca (mg) / P (mg) | Mg (mg) / Fe (mg) | Zn (mg) / Cu (mg) | Mn (mg) |
|---|---|---|---|---|---|---|---|---|---|---|---|---|---|---|---|

## 19.8. MEAT/EGG YOLKS

**beef**

| | KCAL/WT | H₂O/PRO | FAT/CHO | PUFA/SFA | CHOL/DFIB | A(RE)/A(IU) | C/B-1 | B-2/NIA | B-6/B-12 | FOL/PANT | Na/K | Ca/P | Mg/Fe | Zn/Cu | Mn |
|---|---|---|---|---|---|---|---|---|---|---|---|---|---|---|---|
| jr | 105 | 79.1 | 4.9 | 0.2 | | 31 | 2 | .16 | .12 | 6 | 65 | 8 | 9 | 1.98 | |
| *1 jar* | 99 | 14.3 | 0.0 | 2.6 | 0.1 | 102 | .01 | 3.3 | .146 | .35 | 189 | 71 | 1.63 | .091 | |
| str | 106 | 79.8 | 5.3 | 0.2 | | 55 | 2 | .14 | .14 | 6 | 80 | 7 | 17 | 2.43 | |
| *1 jar* | 99 | 13.5 | 0.0 | 2.6 | | 183 | .01 | 2.8 | 1.41 | .34 | 218 | 83 | 1.46 | .043 | |
| beef w/ beef heart, str | 93 | 81.7 | 4.4 | 0.2 | | 37 | 2 | .35 | .12 | 5 | 62 | 4 | 12 | 1.82 | |
| *1 jar* | 99 | 12.6 | 0.0 | 2.1 | | 124 | .02 | 3.8 | | | 198 | 93 | 1.97 | .128 | |
| **chicken** | | | | | | | | | | | | | | | |
| jr | 148 | 75.2 | 9.5 | 2.3 | | 55 | 2 | .16 | .19 | 11 | 50 | 54 | 11 | 1.00 | |
| *1 jar* | 99 | 14.6 | 0.0 | 2.4 | | 184 | .01 | 3.4 | | .72 | 121 | 89 | .98 | .045 | |
| str | 128 | 76.7 | 7.8 | 1.9 | | 40 | 2 | .15 | .20 | 10 | 47 | 63 | 13 | 1.20 | |
| *1 jar* | 99 | 13.6 | 0.1 | 2.0 | | 133 | .01 | 3.2 | | .67 | 139 | 96 | 1.39 | .045 | |
| chicken sticks, jr | 134 | 48.5 | 10.2 | | | 678 | 1 | .14 | .07 | | 340 | 52 | | | |
| *1 jar* | 71 | 10.4 | 1.0 | | 0.1 | 2257 | .01 | 1.4 | | | 75 | 86 | 1.11 | | |
| egg yolks, str | 191 | 66.3 | 16.3 | 1.8 | 739 | 353 | 1 | .25 | .15 | .87 | 37 | 72 | 6 | 1.80 | |
| *1 jar* | 94 | 9.4 | 0.9 | 4.9 | | 1176 | .07 | 0.0 | 1.45 | 2.01 | 73 | 270 | 2.60 | .066 | |
| **ham** | | | | | | | | | | | | | | | |
| jr | 123 | 77.8 | 6.6 | 0.9 | | 9 | 2 | .19 | .20 | 2 | 66 | 5 | 11 | 1.68 | |
| *1 jar* | 99 | 14.9 | 0.0 | 2.2 | 0.1 | 31 | .14 | 2.8 | | .53 | 208 | 88 | 1.00 | | |
| str | 110 | 78.6 | 5.7 | 0.8 | | 11 | 2 | .15 | .25 | 2 | 40 | 6 | 13 | 2.22 | |
| *1 jar* | 99 | 13.7 | 0.0 | 1.9 | | 38 | .14 | 2.6 | | .51 | 202 | 80 | 1.02 | .064 | |
| **lamb** | | | | | | | | | | | | | | | |
| jr | 111 | 78.8 | 5.2 | 0.2 | | 8 | 2 | .20 | .18 | 2 | 73 | 7 | 10 | 2.57 | |
| *1 jar* | 99 | 15.0 | 0.0 | 2.5 | | 27 | .02 | 3.2 | 2.25 | .42 | 209 | 90 | 1.65 | .056 | |
| str | 102 | 79.5 | 4.7 | 0.2 | | 25 | 1 | .20 | .15 | 2 | 62 | 7 | 13 | 2.73 | |
| *1 jar* | 99 | 13.9 | 0.1 | 2.3 | | 85 | .02 | 2.9 | 2.17 | .41 | 203 | 96 | 1.48 | .054 | |
| liver, beef, str | 100 | 78.5 | 3.7 | 0.1 | 182 | 11337 | 19 | 1.8 | .34 | 334 | 73 | 3 | 13 | 2.95 | |
| *1 jar* | 99 | 14.2 | 1.4 | 1.4 | | 37754 | .05 | 8.2 | 2.14 | | 224 | 201 | 5.23 | 1.965 | |
| meat sticks, jr | 130 | 49.3 | 10.4 | 1.1 | | 15 | 2 | .12 | .06 | | 388 | 24 | | | |
| *1 jar* | 71 | 9.5 | 0.8 | 4.1 | 0.1 | 49 | .04 | 1.1 | | | 81 | 73 | .98 | | |
| pork, str | 123 | 77.6 | 7.1 | 0.8 | | 11 | 2 | .20 | .20 | 2 | 42 | 5 | 10 | 2.25 | |
| *1 jar* | 99 | 13.8 | 0.0 | 2.4 | | 38 | .15 | 2.2 | 98 | | 221 | 93 | .99 | .071 | |
| **turkey** | | | | | | | | | | | | | | | |
| jr | 128 | 76.7 | 7.0 | 1.7 | | 169 | 2 | .25 | .16 | 12 | 72 | 28 | 11 | 1.78 | |
| *1 jar* | 99 | 15.2 | 0.0 | 2.3 | | 563 | .02 | 3.4 | 1.06 | .60 | 178 | 94 | 1.34 | | |
| str | 113 | 78.1 | 5.8 | 1.4 | | 166 | 2 | .21 | .18 | 11 | 54 | 23 | 14 | 1.81 | |
| *1 jar* | 99 | 14.1 | 0.1 | 1.9 | | 554 | .02 | 3.6 | .99 | .56 | 229 | 125 | 1.19 | .040 | |
| turkey sticks, jr | 129 | 49.6 | 10.1 | | | 49 | 1 | .11 | .05 | | 343 | 51 | | | |
| *1 jar* | 71 | 9.7 | 1.0 | | 0.2 | 162 | .01 | 1.2 | | | 65 | 73 | .88 | | |
| **veal** | | | | | | | | | | | | | | | |
| jr | 109 | 79.0 | 4.9 | 0.2 | | 15 | 2 | .18 | .12 | 7 | 68 | 6 | 11 | 2.49 | |
| *1 jar* | 99 | 15.1 | 0.0 | 2.4 | 0.1 | 50 | .02 | 3.8 | | .45 | 234 | 97 | 1.24 | .074 | |
| str | 100 | 80.0 | 4.7 | 0.2 | | 14 | 2 | .16 | .15 | 6 | 64 | 7 | 12 | 1.98 | |
| *1 jar* | 99 | 13.4 | 0.0 | 2.3 | | 45 | .02 | 3.5 | | .43 | 214 | 97 | 1.26 | .040 | |

## 19.9. VEGETABLES

**beans, green**

| | KCAL/WT | H₂O/PRO | FAT/CHO | PUFA/SFA | CHOL/DFIB | A(RE)/A(IU) | C/B-1 | B-2/NIA | B-6/B-12 | FOL/PANT | Na/K | Ca/P | Mg/Fe | Zn/Cu | Mn |
|---|---|---|---|---|---|---|---|---|---|---|---|---|---|---|---|
| jr | 51 | 190.5 | 0.3 | | | 89 | 17 | .21 | .07 | 67 | 3 | 133 | 46 | .40 | |
| *1 jar* | 206 | 2.5 | 11.8 | | | 892 | .04 | 0.7 | | .31 | 263 | 39 | 2.23 | .101 | |
| str | 32 | 117.8 | 0.1 | | | 57 | 7 | .11 | .05 | 44 | 2 | 49 | 30 | .26 | |
| *1 jar* | 128 | 1.7 | 7.6 | | 1.4 | 574 | .03 | 0.4 | | .21 | 202 | 26 | .96 | .065 | |

| | KCAL | H₂O (g) | FAT (g) | PUFA (g) | CHOL (mg) | A (RE) | C (mg) | B-2 (mg) | B-6 (mg) | FOL (mcg) | Na (mg) | Ca (mg) | Mg (mg) | Zn (mg) | Mn (mg) |
|---|---|---|---|---|---|---|---|---|---|---|---|---|---|---|---|
| | WT (g) | PRO (g) | CHO (g) | SFA (g) | DFIB (g) | A (IU) | B-1 (mg) | NIA (mg) | B-12 (mcg) | PANT (mg) | K (mg) | P (mg) | Fe (mg) | Cu (mg) | |
| **beans, green, buttered** | | | | | | | | | | | | | | | |
| jr | 67 | 187.9 | 1.8 | | | 79 | 18 | .23 | | 56 | 4 | 143 | | | |
| *1 jar* | 206 | 2.7 | 12.5 | | | 787 | .03 | 0.7 | | | 351 | | 2.38 | | |
| str | 42 | 116.3 | 1.0 | | | 58 | 11 | .14 | | 36 | 4 | 82 | | | |
| *1 jar* | 128 | 1.6 | 8.5 | | | 584 | .02 | 0.4 | | | 205 | | 1.64 | | |
| **beans, green, creamed** | 68 | 193.6 | 0.9 | | | 32 | 6 | .12 | .03 | | 26 | 68 | 16 | | .34 |
| *1 jar* | 213 | 2.1 | 15.3 | | 1.5 | 320 | .05 | 0.5 | | | 139 | 39 | .56 | | |
| **beets, str** | 43 | 115.3 | 0.1 | | | 4 | 3 | .06 | .03 | 39 | 106 | 18 | 18 | | .15 |
| *1 jar* | 128 | 1.7 | 9.8 | | 0.8 | 43 | .01 | 0.2 | | | 233 | 17 | .41 | .090 | |
| **carrots** | | | | | | | | | | | | | | | |
| inst, Heinz | 60 | | 2.0 | | | | 1 | .05 | .03 | | 30 | 45 | | | .22 |
| *4 T dry* | 14 | 1.0 | 11.0 | | | 9056 | .04 | 0.3 | | | 225 | 38 | .60 | .080 | |
| jr | 67 | 193.9 | 0.4 | | | 2516 | 12 | .09 | .17 | 37 | 104 | 49 | 23 | | .38 |
| *1 jar* | 213 | 1.7 | 15.4 | | 1.7 | 25156 | .05 | 1.1 | | .59 | 429 | 43 | .82 | .100 | |
| str | 34 | 118.1 | 0.2 | | | 1467 | 7 | .05 | .09 | 19 | 48 | 29 | 12 | | .20 |
| *1 jar* | 128 | 1.0 | 7.7 | | 0.9 | 14670 | .03 | 0.6 | | .31 | 251 | 25 | .47 | .052 | |
| **carrots, buttered** | | | | | | | | | | | | | | | |
| jr | 70 | 194.6 | 1.2 | | | 2096 | 16 | .12 | | 18 | 34 | 76 | | | |
| *1 jar* | 213 | 1.7 | 14.3 | | | 20960 | .04 | 1.1 | | | 310 | | .66 | | |
| str | 46 | 116.0 | 0.8 | | | 1386 | 12 | .07 | | 12 | 24 | 45 | | | |
| *1 jar* | 128 | 1.1 | 9.4 | | | 13860 | .02 | 0.8 | | | 292 | | .36 | | |
| **corn, creamed** | | | | | | | | | | | | | | | |
| inst, Heinz | 60 | | 1.0 | | | | 0 | .01 | .04 | | 1 | 4 | | | .24 |
| *6 T dry* | 14 | 2.0 | 10.0 | | | 23 | .02 | 0.3 | | | 91 | 30 | .30 | .020 | |
| jr | 138 | 173.5 | 0.8 | | | 16 | 5 | .10 | .09 | 27 | 111 | 39 | 17 | | .49 |
| *1 jar* | 213 | 3.1 | 34.7 | | 0.9 | 165 | .03 | 1.1 | .05 | .70 | 172 | 71 | .58 | .081 | |
| str | 73 | 107.0 | 0.5 | | | 10 | 3 | .06 | .05 | 14 | 55 | 25 | 11 | | .24 |
| *1 jar* | 128 | 1.8 | 18.1 | | 0.5 | 96 | .02 | 0.7 | .02 | .37 | 115 | 43 | .36 | .044 | |
| **garden veg, str** | 48 | 115.2 | 0.3 | | | 777 | 7 | .09 | .13 | 52 | 45 | 36 | 27 | | .33 |
| *1 jar* | 128 | 2.9 | 8.7 | | 1.7 | 7766 | .08 | 1.0 | | | 215 | 35 | 1.06 | .090 | |
| **mixed veg** | | | | | | | | | | | | | | | |
| inst, Heinz | 60 | | 2.0 | | | | 0 | .04 | .05 | | 3 | 12 | | | .25 |
| *5 T dry* | 14 | 2.0 | 9.0 | | | 1556 | .05 | 0.6 | | | 116 | 31 | .30 | .060 | |
| jr | 88 | 190.4 | 0.8 | | | 894 | 5 | .07 | .17 | 9 | 77 | 24 | 23 | | .58 |
| *1 jar* | 213 | 3.1 | 17.4 | | 1.7 | 8935 | .06 | 1.4 | | .55 | 362 | 53 | .87 | .087 | |
| str | 52 | 114.9 | 0.6 | | | 511 | 2 | .03 | .07 | 5 | 6 | 17 | 13 | | .19 |
| *1 jar* | 128 | 1.6 | 10.2 | | 0.8 | 5109 | .03 | 0.4 | | .32 | 163 | 29 | .41 | .051 | |
| **peas** | | | | | | | | | | | | | | | |
| jr, Gerber | 113 | | 1.1 | | | 75 | 9 | .13 | .09 | | 15 | 34 | | | |
| *1 jar* | 213 | 7.0 | 19.0 | | 4.0 | | .15 | 2.0 | | | 198 | 104 | 1.91 | | |
| str | 52 | 112.0 | 0.4 | | | 72 | 9 | .08 | .09 | 33 | 5 | 26 | 19 | | .45 |
| *1 jar* | 128 | 4.5 | 10.4 | | 2.3 | 723 | .10 | 1.3 | | .36 | 144 | 55 | 1.23 | .082 | |
| **peas, buttered** | | | | | | | | | | | | | | | |
| jr | 123 | 172.0 | 2.6 | | | 84 | 26 | .16 | | 75 | 11 | 93 | | | |
| *1 jar* | 206 | 7.3 | 23.3 | | | 845 | .15 | 2.8 | | | 240 | | 2.14 | | |
| str | 72 | 107.8 | 1.4 | | | 42 | 15 | .09 | | 44 | 10 | 49 | | | |
| *1 jar* | 128 | 4.7 | 13.6 | | | 422 | .10 | 1.8 | | | 124 | | 1.41 | | |
| **peas, creamed** | | | | | | | | | | | | | | | |
| inst, Heinz | 60 | | 2.0 | | | | 0 | .05 | .06 | | 2 | 12 | | | .46 |
| *5 T dry* | 14 | 3.0 | 8.0 | | | 142 | .08 | 0.5 | | | 91 | 49 | .60 | .070 | |
| str | 68 | 110.7 | 2.4 | | | 11 | 2 | .07 | .06 | 29 | 18 | 16 | | | .50 |
| *1 jar* | 128 | 2.8 | 11.4 | | | 110 | .11 | 1.0 | .10 | | 113 | 40 | .72 | .065 | |

| | KCAL | H₂O (g) | FAT (g) | PUFA (g) | CHOL (mg) | A (RE) | C (mg) | Vitamins B-2 (mg) | B-6 (mg) | FOL (mcg) | Na (mg) | Ca (mg) | Minerals Mg (mg) | Zn (mg) | Mn (mg) |
|---|---|---|---|---|---|---|---|---|---|---|---|---|---|---|---|
| | WT (g) | PRO (g) | CHO (g) | SFA (g) | DFIB (g) | A (IU) | B-1 (mg) | NIA (mg) | B-12 (mcg) | PANT (mg) | K (mg) | P (mg) | Fe (mg) | Cu (mg) | |
| **spinach, creamed** | | | | | | | | | | | | | | | |
| jr | 90 | 187.9 | 3.0 | | | 783 | 8 | .18 | .12 | 147 | 117 | 240 | 134 | .85 | |
| *1 jar* | 213 | 6.4 | 13.7 | | | 7830 | .05 | 0.6 | | | 471 | 104 | 2.98 | .145 | |
| str | 48 | 114.7 | 1.7 | | | 534 | 11 | .13 | .10 | 78 | 62 | 113 | 71 | .40 | |
| *1 jar* | 128 | 3.2 | 7.3 | | 1.0 | 5338 | .02 | 0.3 | | | 244 | 70 | .80 | .077 | |
| **squash** | | | | | | | | | | | | | | | |
| inst, Heinz | 60 | | 0.0 | | | | 1 | .05 | .05 | | 1 | 12 | | .25 | |
| *5 T dry* | 14 | 1.0 | 10.0 | | | 2830 | .04 | 0.6 | | | 330 | 32 | .30 | .050 | |
| jr | 51 | 197.6 | 0.4 | | | 429 | 17 | .14 | .15 | 33 | 3 | 50 | 25 | .17 | |
| *1 jar* | 213 | 1.8 | 12.0 | | 1.7 | 4291 | .02 | 0.8 | | .47 | 393 | 34 | .74 | .115 | |
| str | 30 | 118.7 | 0.2 | | | 259 | 10 | .07 | .08 | 20 | 3 | 30 | 16 | .18 | |
| *1 jar* | 128 | 1.1 | 7.2 | | 1.3 | 2590 | .01 | 0.5 | | .28 | 229 | 20 | .38 | .069 | |
| **squash, buttered** | | | | | | | | | | | | | | | |
| jr | 63 | 195.5 | 1.3 | | | 326 | 16 | .14 | | 25 | 3 | 65 | | | |
| *1 jar* | 213 | 1.5 | 13.7 | | | 3259 | .02 | 0.7 | | | 288 | | .89 | | |
| str | 37 | 117.4 | 0.4 | | | 212 | 10 | .09 | | 15 | 2 | 42 | | | |
| *1 jar* | 128 | 0.8 | 8.8 | | | 2123 | .01 | 0.5 | | | 163 | | .53 | | |
| **sweet potatoes** | | | | | | | | | | | | | | | |
| inst, Heinz | 50 | | 0.0 | | | | 1 | .01 | .05 | | 15 | 21 | | .16 | |
| *4 T dry* | 14 | 1.0 | 11.0 | | | 6940 | .03 | 0.2 | | | 246 | 24 | .30 | .100 | |
| jr | 133 | 185.0 | 0.3 | | | 1460 | 21 | .08 | .25 | 23 | 49 | 35 | 26 | .24 | |
| *1 jar* | 220 | 2.4 | 30.7 | | 1.8 | 14600 | .06 | 0.8 | | .90 | 535 | 52 | .85 | .220 | |
| str | 77 | 114.5 | 0.2 | | | 869 | 13 | .05 | .13 | 13 | 27 | 21 | 18 | .28 | |
| *1 jar* | 135 | 1.5 | 17.8 | | 0.9 | 8691 | .04 | 0.5 | | .53 | 355 | 32 | .50 | .109 | |
| **sweet potatoes, buttered** | | | | | | | | | | | | | | | |
| jr | 126 | 188.3 | 1.6 | | | 1330 | 21 | .10 | | 29 | 17 | 61 | | | |
| *1 jar* | 220 | 1.8 | 26.8 | | | 13295 | .04 | 0.7 | | | 474 | | .87 | | |
| str | 76 | 115.9 | 1.0 | | | 920 | 12 | .05 | | 18 | 11 | 28 | | | |
| *1 jar* | 135 | 1.3 | 15.9 | | | 9199 | .02 | 0.4 | | | 281 | | .60 | | |

# 20. MEAT ANALOGUES & MEAT ANALOGUE ENTREES

| | KCAL | H₂O (g) | FAT (g) | PUFA (g) | CHOL (mg) | A (RE) | C (mg) | B-2 (mg) | B-6 (mg) | FOL (mcg) | Na (mg) | Ca (mg) | Mg (mg) | Zn (mg) | Mn (mg) |
|---|---|---|---|---|---|---|---|---|---|---|---|---|---|---|---|
| **bacon, simulated meat product** | 25 | 3.9 | 2.4 | 1.2 | 0 | 1 | 0 | .04 | .04 | 3 | 117 | 2 | 2 | .03 | .016 |
| *1 strip* | 8 | 0.9 | 0.5 | 0.4 | 0.1 | 7 | .35 | 0.6 | .00 | .01 | 14 | 6 | .19 | .008 | |
| **big franks, cnd, Loma Linda** | 100 | 30.0 | 5.0 | | 0 | | | .61 | .50 | | 220 | 17 | | .61 | |
| *1 frank* | 51 | 10.0 | 4.0 | | | | .56 | 8.2 | 1.20 | .82 | 75 | | .92 | | |
| **bologna, frzn, Loma Linda** | 150 | 26.0 | 9.0 | | 0 | | | .31 | .64 | | 490 | 23 | | .91 | |
| *2 slices* | 57 | 14.0 | 5.0 | | | | .54 | 6.4 | 2.00 | 2.00 | 160 | | 1.30 | | |
| **burger-like, Millstone** | 90 | 89.0 | 0.2 | | 0 | | | .03 | | | 440 | 38 | | 1.10 | |
| *4 oz* | 113 | 13.0 | 8.0 | | | | .03 | 1.8 | | | 430 | | .57 | | |
| **burger mix, Millstone** | 90 | 2.9 | 0.7 | | 0 | | | .17 | | | 368 | 66 | | .55 | |
| *1 oz* | 28 | 10.0 | 12.0 | | | | .23 | 0.3 | | 1.70 | 34 | | 2.30 | | |
| **chicken, fried, Loma Linda** | 180 | 26.0 | 14.0 | | 0 | | | .51 | .63 | | 510 | 26 | | .30 | |
| *1 piece* | 57 | 13.0 | 2.0 | | | | .63 | 9.1 | 2.00 | 2.50 | 80 | | 1.10 | | |
| **chicken, fried w/ gravy, cnd, Loma Linda** | 140 | 60.0 | 10.0 | | 0 | | | .41 | .43 | | 340 | 20 | | .55 | |
| *2 pieces* | 85 | 9.0 | 4.0 | | | | .60 | 4.0 | 2.00 | 1.50 | 250 | | 1.40 | | |
| **chicken, frzn, Loma Linda** | 160 | 31.0 | 13.0 | | 0 | | | .41 | .51 | | 330 | 25 | | .63 | |
| *2 slices* | 57 | 10.0 | 1.0 | | | | .46 | 5.1 | 2.00 | 1.40 | 120 | | 1.10 | | |
| **chicken supreme dry mix, Loma Linda** | 50 | 1.0 | 0.0 | | 0 | | | .26 | .40 | | 450 | 20 | | .40 | |
| *1/4 cup* | 16 | 9.0 | 4.0 | | | | .61 | 3.0 | 1.00 | 1.50 | 190 | | .72 | | |
| **chicken nuggets, frzn, Loma Linda** | 230 | 41.0 | 13.0 | | 0 | | | .40 | .51 | | 640 | 41 | | .72 | |
| *5 pieces* | 85 | 14.0 | 15.0 | | | | .49 | 6.6 | 3.00 | 1.90 | 180 | | 1.90 | | |
| **chik-patties, frzn, Loma Linda** | 230 | 41.0 | 13.0 | | 0 | | | .40 | .51 | | 640 | 41 | | .72 | |
| *1 patty* | 85 | 14.0 | 15.0 | | | | .49 | 6.6 | 3.00 | 1.90 | 180 | | 1.90 | | |

| | KCAL | H₂O (g) | FAT (g) | PUFA (g) | CHOL (mg) | A (RE) | C (mg) | Vitamins B-2 (mg) | B-6 (mg) | FOL (mcg) | Na (mg) | Minerals Ca (mg) | Mg (mg) | Zn (mg) | Mn (mg) |
|---|---|---|---|---|---|---|---|---|---|---|---|---|---|---|---|
| | WT (g) | PRO (g) | CHO (g) | SFA (g) | DFIB (g) | A (IU) | B-1 (mg) | NIA (mg) | B-12 (mcg) | PANT (mg) | K (mg) | P (mg) | Fe (mg) | Cu (mg) | |
| chik stiks, Worthington | 112 | 25.5 | 6.3 | 3.4 | 0 | | | .22 | .29 | | 325 | 22 | | | |
| 1 piece | 47 | 9.8 | 3.9 | 1.0 | | | .60 | 5.4 | 4.30 | | 90 | | 2.24 | | |
| choplets, Worthington | 105 | 66.3 | 1.4 | | | | | | | | 317 | 11 | | | |
| 2 slices | 92 | 19.1 | 4.0 | | | | | | | | 33 | | 1.86 | | |
| corn dogs, frzn, Loma Linda | 200 | 32.0 | 10.0 | | 0 | | | .62 | .80 | | 620 | 20 | | .44 | |
| 1 corn dog | 71 | 7.0 | 21.0 | | | | .58 | 6.2 | 3.00 | 2.60 | 150 | | .73 | | |
| dinner cuts, cnd, Loma Linda | 110 | 71.0 | 1.0 | | 0 | | | .27 | .46 | | 550ª | 20 | | 1.30 | |
| 2 cuts | 100 | 21.0 | 4.0 | | | | .20 | 1.0 | 1.00 | .21 | 180ª | | 2.00 | | |
| dinner loaf, dry pack, Loma Linda | 50 | 1.0 | 1.0 | | 0 | | | .24 | .58 | | 380 | 26 | | .30 | |
| 1/4 cup | 16 | 9.0 | 4.0 | | | | .61 | 4.0 | 1.00 | 1.90 | 140 | | .64 | | |
| frichik, Worthington | 155 | 61.8 | 9.8 | 7.7 | | | | .21 | .18 | | 487 | 18 | | | |
| 2 pieces | 90 | 12.1 | 4.5 | 1.5 | | | .21 | 3.1 | 3.92 | | 41 | | 1.72 | | |
| fripats, Worthington | 193 | 29.5 | 12.3 | 6.2 | | | | .32 | .44 | | 304 | 77 | | | |
| 1 piece | 64 | 15.5 | 5.0 | 2.1 | | | | 8.8 | 7.04 | | 135 | | 3.72 | | |
| griddle steaks, frzn, Loma Linda | 160 | 19.0 | 11.0 | | 0 | | | .33 | .56 | | 385 | 33 | | .52 | |
| 1 steak | 47 | 11.0 | 4.0 | | | | .52 | 4.1 | 2.00 | 1.70 | 250 | | .61 | | |
| grillers, Morningstar Farms | 190 | 29.9 | 11.9 | 6.2 | 1 | | | .38 | .44 | | 285 | 66 | | | |
| 1 patty | 64 | 15.6 | 5.1 | 2.1 | | | | 7.5 | 6.70 | | 140 | | 3.48 | | |
| leanies, Worthington | 93 | 21.5 | 5.0 | 3.8 | | | | .18 | .19 | | 385 | 41 | | | |
| 1 link | 40 | 8.0 | 4.0 | 0.7 | | | .31 | 3.3 | 3.10 | | 39 | | 1.89 | | |
| linketts, cnd, Loma Linda | 150 | 44.0 | 8.0 | | 0 | | | .44 | .37 | | 340 | 20 | | .89 | |
| 2 links | 74 | 15.0 | 5.0 | | | | .37 | 6.0 | 2.00 | .81 | 75 | | 1.80 | | |
| link, Morningstar Farms | 178 | 35.5 | 11.0 | 7.4 | 1 | | | .34 | .39 | | 406 | 22 | | | |
| 3 links | 68 | 14.5 | 5.2 | 1.9 | | | | 7.5 | 6.75 | | 85 | | 3.90 | | |
| little links, cnd, Loma Linda | 80 | 29.0 | 5.0 | | 0 | | | .41 | .16 | | 210 | 12 | | .60 | |
| 2 links | 46 | 8.0 | 2.0 | | | | .55 | 6.0 | 2.00 | 1.50 | 40 | | 1.10 | | |
| meat extender, simulated meat product | 88 | 2.1 | 0.8 | 0.5 | 0 | 1 | | .25 | .37 | | 3 | 57 | 61 | | |
| 1 oz | 28 | 10.7 | 10.7 | 0.1 | | 9 | .20 | 6.2 | 1.76 | | | | 3.36 | | |
| meatless loaf, Millstone | 90 | 2.9 | 0.8 | | 0 | | | .16 | | | 380 | 67 | | .46 | |
| 1 oz | 28 | 9.9 | 12.0 | | | | .29 | 0.6 | | 1.20 | 290 | | 2.20 | | |
| nuteena, cnd, Loma Linda | 160 | 39.0 | 12.0 | | 0 | | | .58 | .45 | | 120 | 21 | | .87 | |
| 1/2" slice | 67 | 8.0 | 5.0 | | | | .47 | 14.0 | 1.00 | 2.80 | 200 | | 1.20 | | |
| nut meat, Millstone | 150 | 44.0 | 10.0 | | 0 | | | .03 | | | 280 | 21 | | .61 | |
| 2.5 oz | 71 | 7.2 | 6.6 | | | | .01 | 2.0 | | .92 | 260 | | .36 | | |
| ocean fillet, frzn, Loma Linda | 130 | 21.0 | 8.0 | | 0 | | | .42 | .71 | | 230 | 45 | | .66 | |
| 1 fillet | 47 | 11.0 | 4.0 | | | | .52 | 5.6 | 2.00 | 2.10 | 280 | | .94 | | |
| ocean platter, dry pack, Loma Linda | 50 | 1.0 | 1.0 | | 0 | | | .26 | .40 | | 260 | 26 | | .35 | |
| 1/4 cup | 16 | 8.0 | 5.0 | | | | .61 | 3.0 | 2.00 | 1.50 | 170 | | .72 | | |
| patties, Morningstar Farms | 203 | 37.1 | 11.4 | 6.0 | 1 | | | .38 | .50 | | 640 | 38 | | | |
| 2 patties | 76 | 18.2 | 6.8 | 2.3 | | | | 9.2 | 7.14 | | 149 | | 4.27 | | |
| patty mix, dry pack, Loma Linda | 50 | 1.0 | 1.0 | | 0 | | | .34 | .58 | | 320 | 30 | | .29 | |
| 1/4 cup | 16 | 9.0 | 4.0 | | | | .61 | 3.7 | 2.00 | 1.50 | 150 | | .72 | | |
| proteena, cnd, Loma Linda | 140 | 40.0 | 6.0 | | 0 | | | .50 | .50 | | 460 | 22 | | 1.20 | |
| 1/2" slice | 71 | 17.0 | 5.0 | | | | .64 | 7.8 | 2.00 | 2.50 | 280 | | 1.60 | | |
| redi-burger, cnd, Loma Linda | 130 | 39.0 | 6.0 | | 0 | | | .40 | .80 | | 370 | 19 | | 1.20 | |
| 1/2" slice | 68 | 14.0 | 5.0 | | | | .60 | 6.7 | 2.00 | 1.50 | 120 | | 1.40 | | |
| roast beef, frzn, Loma Linda | 150 | 31.0 | 11.0 | | 0 | | | .29 | .32 | | 670 | 24 | | .80 | |
| 2 slices | 57 | 11.0 | 2.0 | | | | .17 | 1.4 | 1.00 | 1.80 | 120 | | 1.50 | | |
| salami, frzn, Loma Linda | 130 | 33.0 | 7.0 | | 0 | | | .34 | .63 | | 640 | 13 | | .91 | |
| 2 slices | 57 | 13.0 | 2.0 | | | | .38 | 3.0 | 2.00 | 2.10 | 70 | | 1.10 | | |
| sandwich spread, cnd, Loma Linda | 70 | 34.0 | 4.0 | | 0 | | | .34 | .53 | | 300 | 21 | | .62 | |
| 3 T | 48 | 4.0 | 4.0 | | | | .29 | 6.2 | 2.00 | 1.20 | 160 | | .72 | | |
| sausage, simulated meat product | 64 | 12.6 | 4.5 | 2.3 | 0 | 16 | 0 | .10 | .21 | 7 | 222 | 16 | 9 | .37 | .181 |
| 1 link | 25 | 4.6 | 2.5 | 0.7 | 0.1 | 160 | .59 | 2.8 | .00 | .08 | 58 | 56 | .93 | .063 | |
| sausage, simulated meat product | 97 | 19.2 | 6.9 | 3.5 | 0 | 24 | 0 | .15 | .32 | 10 | 337 | 24 | 14 | .55 | .276 |
| 1 patty | 38 | 7.0 | 3.7 | 1.1 | | 243 | .89 | 4.3 | .00 | .12 | 88 | 85 | 1.41 | .095 | |
| sizzle burger, frzn, Loma Linda | 210 | 28.0 | 11.0 | | 0 | | | .51 | .78 | | 320 | 49 | | .78 | |
| 1 burger | 71 | 15.0 | 13.0 | | | | .64 | 8.5 | 2.00 | 1.50 | 180 | | 1.60 | | |
| sizzle franks, cnd, Loma Linda | 170 | 43.0 | 13.0 | | 0 | | | .35 | .35 | | 340 | 20 | | .63 | |
| 2 franks | 70 | 10.0 | 3.0 | | | | .35 | 4.1 | 2.00 | 2.30 | 100 | | 1.40 | | |
| stakelets, Worthington | 143 | 41.4 | 6.5 | 3.4 | | | | .29 | .32 | | 431 | 63 | | | |
| 1 piece | 71 | 14.4 | 6.5 | 1.2 | | | | 5.8 | 5.16 | | 143 | | 3.28 | | |

ª Product w/ no added salt contains 30 mg Na and 75 mg K.

| | KCAL | H₂O (g) | FAT (g) | PUFA (g) | CHOL (mg) | A (RE) | C (mg) | B-2 (mg) | B-6 (mg) | FOL (mcg) | Na (mg) | Ca (mg) | Mg (mg) | Zn (mg) | Mn (mg) |
|---|---|---|---|---|---|---|---|---|---|---|---|---|---|---|---|
| | WT (g) | PRO (g) | CHO (g) | SFA (g) | DFIB (g) | A (IU) | B-1 (mg) | NIA (mg) | B-12 (mcg) | PANT (mg) | K (mg) | P (mg) | Fe (mg) | Cu (mg) | |
| **stew pac, cnd, Loma Linda** | 70 | 39.0 | 2.0 | | 0 | | | .34 | .62 | | 220 | 17 | | .62 | |
| *2 oz* | 57 | 10.0 | 4.0 | | | | .39 | 6.7 | 1.00 | 1.60 | 60 | | .73 | | |
| **stripples, Worthington** | 110 | 14.5 | 8.6 | 5.8 | | | | .15 | .16 | | 362 | 17 | | | |
| *4 strips* | 33 | 4.2 | 3.9 | 1.1 | | | | 2.7 | 1.78 | | 35 | | .95 | | |
| **strips, Morningstar Farms** | 83 | 11.0 | 6.5 | 4.1 | 0 | | | .11 | .12 | | 274 | 13 | | | |
| *3 strips* | 25 | 3.2 | 2.9 | 0.8 | | | | 2.0 | 1.35 | | 26 | | .72 | | |
| **swedish meatballs, frzn, Loma Linda** | 190 | 30.0 | 8.0 | | 0 | | | .42 | .70 | | 420 | 32 | | .65 | |
| *8 meatballs* | 70 | 22.0 | 7.0 | | | | .49 | 4.9 | 2.00 | 1.50 | 170 | | 1.80 | | |
| **swiss steak w/ gravy, cnd, Loma Linda** | 140 | 45.0 | 8.0 | | 0 | | | .44 | .37 | | 350 | 34 | | .59 | |
| *1 steak* | 74 | 9.0 | 8.0 | | | | .52 | 4.0 | 1.00 | 1.50 | 180 | | 1.50 | | |
| **tastee cuts, cnd, Loma Linda** | 70 | 54.0 | 1.0 | | 0 | | | .18 | .04 | | 230 | 13 | | 1.40 | |
| *2 cuts* | 71 | 12.0 | 2.0 | | | | .37 | 1.3 | .20 | .16 | 40 | | 1.10 | | |
| **tender bits, cnd, Loma Linda** | 80 | 40.0 | 3.0 | | 0 | | | .29 | .63 | | 340 | 17 | | .63 | |
| *4 pieces* | 57 | 8.0 | 4.0 | | | | .51 | 5.6 | 1.00 | 2.00 | 45 | | .91 | | |
| **tender cuts, Millstone** | 80 | 82.0 | 1.2 | | 0 | | | | | | 410 | 13 | | 3.00 | |
| *3.6 oz* | 102 | 14.0 | 3.3 | | | | .10 | 4.4 | | 2.30 | 50 | | 1.30 | | |
| **tender rounds w/ gravy, cnd, Loma Linda** | 120 | 46.0 | 4.0 | | 0 | | | .44 | .88 | | 310 | 29 | | .66 | |
| *6 rounds* | 75 | 15.0 | 7.0 | | | | .66 | 5.0 | 2.00 | .80 | 115 | | 1.80 | | |
| **turkey, frzn, Loma Linda** | 160 | 31.0 | 12.0 | | 0 | | | .23 | .59 | | 1350 | 19 | | .86 | |
| *2 slices* | 57 | 10.0 | 3.0 | | | | .46 | 1.9 | 2.00 | 2.50 | 110 | | 1.10 | | |
| **vege-burger, cnd, Loma Linda** | 110 | 79.0 | 1.0 | | 0 | | | .68 | .56 | | 190 | 32 | | 1.10 | |
| *1/2 cup* | 108 | 22.0 | 4.0 | | | | .53 | 5.0 | 2.00 | 2.90 | 110 | | 2.70 | | |
| **vege-burger, Millstone** | 110 | 76.0 | 1.7 | | 0 | | | .14 | | | 450 | 12 | | 2.70 | |
| *1/2 cup* | 108 | 20.0 | 3.0 | | | | .03 | | | 1.80 | 75 | | 1.10 | | |
| **vege-burger, no salt added, cnd, Loma Linda**—*1/2 cup* | 140 | 72.0 | 2.0 | | 0 | | | .51 | .93 | | 55 | 43 | | 1.70 | |
| | 108 | 27.0 | 4.0 | | | | .53 | 6.5 | 2.00 | 1.30 | 200 | | 1.80 | | |
| **vegelona, cnd, Loma Linda** | 100 | 41.0 | 1.0 | | 0 | | | .50 | .50 | | 210 | 15 | | 1.20 | |
| *1/2" slice* | 67 | 18.0 | 6.0 | | | | .54 | 8.7 | .90 | 1.50 | 100 | | 1.50 | | |
| **vege-scallops, cnd, Loma Linda** | 70 | 60.0 | 1.0 | | 0 | | | .08 | .02 | | 180 | 17 | | 1.10 | |
| *6 pieces* | 78 | 14.0 | 2.0 | | | | .34 | 0.7 | 2.00 | .18 | 30 | | 1.10 | | |
| **vegetarian burger, Worthington** | 140 | 79.8 | 3.0 | | | | | .25 | .44 | | 520 | 8 | | | |
| *1/2 cup* | 113 | 21.8 | 6.5 | | | | .63 | 12.1 | 8.45 | | 57 | | 4.48 | | |
| **veg skallops, Worthington** | 92 | 62.2 | 1.1 | | | | | | | | 347 | 9 | | | |
| *1/2 cup* | 85 | 16.9 | 3.4 | | | | | | | | 12 | | 1.51 | | |
| **veja-links, Worthington** | 114 | 40.6 | 6.6 | 2.8 | | | | .22 | .16 | | 297 | 7 | | | |
| *2 links* | 62 | 8.2 | 5.4 | 1.1 | | | .29 | 3.1 | 4.04 | | 35 | | 1.46 | | |
| **vita-burger granules, dry pack, Loma Linda**[a]—*3 T* | 70 | 2.0 | 0.0 | | 0 | | | .13 | .29 | | 150 | 42 | | 1.20 | |
| | 21 | 10.0 | 7.0 | | | | .13 | 3.4 | 1.00 | .42 | 460 | | 1.80 | | |
| **wheat fries, Millstone** | 60 | 56.0 | 0.9 | | 0 | | | .12 | | | 180 | 5 | | .90 | |
| *2.5 oz* | 71 | 12.0 | 2.4 | | | | | .80 | | 1.20 | 20 | | 1.40 | | |

# 21. MEATS
## 21.1. BEEF

| | KCAL | H₂O (g) | FAT (g) | PUFA (g) | CHOL (mg) | A (RE) | C (mg) | B-2 (mg) | B-6 (mg) | FOL (mcg) | Na (mg) | Ca (mg) | Mg (mg) | Zn (mg) | Mn (mg) |
|---|---|---|---|---|---|---|---|---|---|---|---|---|---|---|---|
| | WT (g) | PRO (g) | CHO (g) | SFA (g) | DFIB (g) | A (IU) | B-1 (mg) | NIA (mg) | B-12 (mcg) | PANT (mg) | K (mg) | P (mg) | Fe (mg) | Cu (mg) | |
| **breakfast strips** | | | | | | | | | | | | | | | |
| ckd | 153 | 8.9 | 11.7 | 0.5 | 40 | 12[b] | | .09 | .11 | | 766 | | 9 | 2.17 | |
| *3 slices* | 34 | 10.6 | 0.5 | 4.9 | | | .03 | 2.2 | 1.17 | | 140 | 80 | 1.07 | | |
| ckd, Lean 'n Tasty | 46 | 4.6 | 3.8 | | 13 | | | | | | 190 | 1 | 2 | .48 | |
| *1 slice* | 12 | 2.9 | 0.2 | | | | | | | | 36 | 20 | .23 | .040 | |
| **brisket** | | | | | | | | | | | | | | | |
| sep lean & fat, braised | 391 | 43.0 | 32.4 | 1.2 | 93 | 0 | | .17 | .25 | 6 | 61 | 9 | 18 | 5.01 | .014 |
| *3.5 oz* | 100 | 23.0 | 0.0 | 13.2 | 0.0 | | .06 | 3.0 | 2.23 | .29 | 229 | 184 | 2.19 | .094 | |
| sep lean, braised | 241 | 55.7 | 12.8 | 0.4 | 93 | 0 | | .22 | .30 | 8 | 72 | 6 | 23 | 6.88 | .017 |
| *3.5 oz* | 100 | 29.4 | 0.0 | 4.6 | 0.0 | | .07 | 3.8 | 2.55 | .36 | 287 | 239 | 2.77 | .120 | |
| **brisket, flat half** | | | | | | | | | | | | | | | |
| sep lean & fat, braised | 408 | 41.5 | 34.9 | 1.2 | 92 | 0 | | .18 | .23 | 6 | 65 | 9 | 16 | 5.30 | .013 |
| *3.5 oz* | 100 | 22.0 | 0.0 | 14.5 | 0.0 | | .06 | 2.9 | 2.24 | .27 | 219 | 173 | 2.18 | .090 | |
| sep lean, braised | 263 | 53.8 | 15.9 | 0.4 | 91 | 0 | | .23 | .28 | 8 | 77 | 6 | 22 | 7.39 | .017 |
| *3.5 oz* | 100 | 28.1 | 0.0 | 6.3 | 0.0 | | .07 | 3.6 | 2.58 | .34 | 273 | 226 | 2.79 | .115 | |

[a] Values correspond to 1/4 cup of vita-burger chunks.

[b] Contains added sodium ascorbate.

| | KCAL | H₂O (g) | FAT (g) | PUFA (g) | CHOL (mg) | A (RE) | C (mg) | B-2 (mg) | B-6 (mg) | FOL (mcg) | Na (mg) | Ca (mg) | Mg (mg) | Zn (mg) | Mn (mg) |
|---|---|---|---|---|---|---|---|---|---|---|---|---|---|---|---|
| | WT (g) | PRO (g) | CHO (g) | SFA (g) | DFIB (g) | A (IU) | B-1 (mg) | NIA (mg) | B-12 (mcg) | PANT (mg) | K (mg) | P (mg) | Fe (mg) | Cu (mg) | |
| **brisket, point half** | | | | | | | | | | | | | | | |
| sep lean & fat, braised | 366 | 44.9 | 28.9 | 1.1 | 95 | | 0 | .17 | .25 | 6 | 56 | 8 | 19 | 4.72 | .014 |
| *3.5 oz* | 100 | 24.7 | 0.0 | 11.8 | 0.0 | | .06 | 3.1 | 2.29 | .30 | 239 | 197 | 2.25 | .098 | |
| sep lean, braised | 212 | 57.8 | 8.6 | 0.3 | 95 | | 0 | .22 | .31 | 8 | 63 | 5 | 25 | 6.36 | .017 |
| *3.5 oz* | 100 | 31.5 | 0.0 | 3.1 | 0.0 | | .07 | 3.9 | 2.63 | .37 | 298 | 257 | 2.84 | .124 | |
| **chuck arm pot roast** | | | | | | | | | | | | | | | |
| sep lean & fat, braised | 350 | 45.5 | 26.0 | 1.0 | 99 | | 0 | .24 | .28 | 9 | 60 | 10 | 19 | 6.74 | .016 |
| *3.5 oz* | 100 | 27.1 | 0.0 | 10.7 | 0.0 | | .07 | 3.1 | 2.93 | .32 | 244 | 217 | 3.07 | .132 | |
| sep lean, braised | 231 | 55.2 | 10.0 | 0.4 | 101 | | 0 | .29 | .33 | 11 | 66 | 9 | 24 | 8.66 | .019 |
| *3.5 oz* | 100 | 33.0 | 0.0 | 3.8 | 0.0 | | .08 | 3.7 | 3.40 | .38 | 289 | 268 | 3.79 | .164 | |
| **chuck blade roast** | | | | | | | | | | | | | | | |
| sep lean & fat, braised | 383 | 43.3 | 30.4 | 1.1 | 103 | | 0 | .23 | .25 | 5 | 63 | 13 | 18 | 7.83 | .015 |
| *3.5 oz* | 100 | 25.4 | 0.0 | 12.7 | 0.0 | | .07 | 2.4 | 2.23 | .30 | 223 | 191 | 2.96 | .119 | |
| sep lean, braised | 270 | 52.7 | 15.3 | 0.5 | 106 | | 0 | .28 | .29 | 6 | 71 | 13 | 23 | 10.27 | .018 |
| *3.5 oz* | 100 | 31.1 | 0.0 | 6.2 | 0.0 | | .08 | 2.7 | 2.47 | .35 | 263 | 235 | 3.68 | .148 | |
| **corned beef** | | | | | | | | | | | | | | | |
| cured brisket, ckd | 251 | 59.8 | 19.0 | 0.7 | 98 | | 16[a] | .17 | .23 | | 1134 | 8 | 12 | 4.58 | .022 |
| *3.5 oz* | 100 | 18.2 | 0.5 | 6.3 | | | .03 | 3.0 | 1.63 | .42 | 145 | 125 | 1.86 | .154 | |
| cured, cnd | 250 | 57.7 | 14.9 | 0.6 | 86 | 0 | 2 | .15 | .13 | | 1006 | | 14 | 3.57 | .014 |
| *3.5 oz* | 100 | 27.1 | 0.0 | 6.2 | 0.0 | 0 | .02 | 2.4 | 1.62 | | 136 | 111 | 2.08 | .064 | |
| **dried (chipped)** | 47 | 16.0 | 1.1 | 0.1 | | | | | | | 984 | 2 | 9 | 1.49 | |
| *1 oz* | 28 | 8.3 | 0.4 | 0.5 | | | | | | | 126 | 49 | 1.28 | .045 | |
| **flank** | | | | | | | | | | | | | | | |
| sep lean & fat, braised | 257 | 56.2 | 15.5 | 0.5 | 72 | | 0 | .18 | .35 | 9 | 71 | 7 | 23 | 5.92 | .019 |
| *3.5 oz* | 100 | 27.5 | 0.0 | 6.6 | 0.0 | | .14 | 4.5 | 3.36 | .38 | 344 | 261 | 3.40 | .123 | |
| sep lean & fat, broiled | 254 | 56.9 | 16.3 | 0.5 | 71 | | 0 | .19 | .42 | 8 | 82 | 6 | 24 | 4.71 | .020 |
| *3.5 oz* | 100 | 25.1 | 0.0 | 7.0 | 0.0 | | .11 | 4.8 | 3.02 | .44 | 398 | 215 | 2.50 | .098 | |
| sep lean, braised | 244 | 57.3 | 13.8 | 0.4 | 71 | | 0 | .19 | .36 | 9 | 72 | 6 | 24 | 6.05 | .019 |
| *3.5 oz* | 100 | 28.0 | 0.0 | 5.9 | 0.0 | | .14 | 4.6 | 3.41 | .38 | 351 | 267 | 3.47 | .124 | |
| sep lean, broiled | 243 | 57.8 | 15.0 | 0.5 | 70 | | 0 | .19 | .42 | 8 | 83 | 6 | 25 | 4.79 | .020 |
| *3.5 oz* | 100 | 25.4 | 0.0 | 6.4 | 0.0 | | .11 | 4.9 | 3.05 | .44 | 405 | 218 | 2.53 | .098 | |
| **ground, extra lean** | | | | | | | | | | | | | | | |
| baked, med | 250 | 58.6 | 16.1 | 0.6 | 82 | | 0 | .24 | .22 | 9 | 49 | 7 | 17 | 5.34 | .015 |
| *3.5 oz* | 100 | 24.5 | 0.0 | 6.3 | 0.0 | | .04 | 4.2 | 1.73 | .27 | 224 | 124 | 2.28 | .075 | |
| baked, well done | 274 | 52.7 | 16.0 | 0.6 | 107 | | 0 | .31 | .29 | 11 | 64 | 9 | 22 | 6.94 | .020 |
| *3.5 oz* | 100 | 30.3 | 0.0 | 6.3 | 0.0 | | .05 | 5.4 | 1.86 | .35 | 291 | 162 | 2.96 | .097 | |
| broiled, med | 256 | 57.3 | 16.3 | 0.6 | 84 | | 0 | .27 | .27 | 9 | 70 | 7 | 21 | 5.45 | .016 |
| *3.5 oz* | 100 | 25.4 | 0.0 | 6.4 | 0.0 | | .06 | 5.0 | 2.17 | .35 | 313 | 161 | 2.35 | .070 | |
| broiled, well done | 265 | 53.9 | 15.8 | 0.6 | 99 | | 0 | .32 | .32 | 11 | 82 | 9 | 25 | 6.43 | .019 |
| *3.5 oz* | 100 | 28.6 | 0.0 | 6.2 | 0.0 | | .07 | 5.9 | 2.56 | .42 | 369 | 190 | 2.77 | .083 | |
| pan fried, med | 255 | 57.6 | 16.4 | 0.6 | 81 | | 0 | .26 | .27 | 9 | 70 | 7 | 21 | 5.42 | .016 |
| *3.5 oz* | 100 | 25.0 | 0.0 | 6.5 | 0.0 | | .06 | 4.7 | 2.00 | .25 | 312 | 160 | 2.36 | .087 | |
| pan fried, well done | 263 | 53.9 | 16.0 | 0.6 | 93 | | 0 | .30 | .31 | 10 | 81 | 8 | 24 | 6.27 | .018 |
| *3.5 oz* | 100 | 28.0 | 0.0 | 6.3 | 0.0 | | .07 | 5.4 | 2.32 | .29 | 360 | 185 | 2.73 | .101 | |
| **ground, lean** | | | | | | | | | | | | | | | |
| baked, med | 268 | 56.9 | 18.3 | 0.7 | 78 | | 0 | .19 | .20 | 9 | 56 | 9 | 17 | 5.10 | .014 |
| *3.5 oz* | 100 | 23.9 | 0.0 | 7.2 | 0.0 | | .05 | 4.3 | 1.77 | .27 | 224 | 128 | 2.09 | .072 | |
| baked, well done | 292 | 51.3 | 18.4 | 0.7 | 99 | | 0 | .24 | .26 | 12 | 71 | 12 | 21 | 6.51 | .018 |
| *3.5 oz* | 100 | 29.6 | 0.0 | 7.2 | 0.0 | | .07 | 5.5 | 2.26 | .34 | 286 | 164 | 2.66 | .092 | |
| broiled, med | 272 | 55.7 | 18.5 | 0.7 | 87 | | 0 | .21 | .26 | 9 | 77 | 11 | 21 | 5.36 | .014 |
| *3.5 oz* | 100 | 24.7 | 0.0 | 7.3 | 0.0 | | .05 | 5.2 | 2.35 | .38 | 301 | 158 | 2.11 | .066 | |
| broiled, well done | 280 | 52.9 | 17.6 | 0.7 | 101 | | 0 | .24 | .30 | 11 | 89 | 12 | 24 | 6.20 | .017 |
| *3.5 oz* | 100 | 28.2 | 0.0 | 6.9 | 0.0 | | .06 | 6.0 | 2.72 | .44 | 349 | 182 | 2.45 | .077 | |
| pan fried, med | 275 | 55.6 | 19.1 | 0.7 | 84 | | 0 | .22 | .28 | 9 | 77 | 10 | 20 | 5.20 | .014 |
| *3.5 oz* | 100 | 24.2 | 0.0 | 7.5 | 0.0 | | .05 | 4.8 | 2.27 | .32 | 299 | 159 | 2.18 | .077 | |

[a] Contains added sodium ascorbate.

| | KCAL | H₂O (g) | FAT (g) | PUFA (g) | CHOL (mg) | A (RE) | C (mg) | B-2 (mg) | B-6 (mg) | FOL (mcg) | Na (mg) | Ca (mg) | Mg (mg) | Zn (mg) | Mn (mg) |
|---|---|---|---|---|---|---|---|---|---|---|---|---|---|---|---|
| | WT (g) | PRO (g) | CHO (g) | SFA (g) | DFIB (g) | A (IU) | B-1 (mg) | NIA (mg) | B-12 (mcg) | PANT (mg) | K (mg) | P (mg) | Fe (mg) | Cu (mg) | |
| pan fried, well done | 277 | 53.7 | 17.7 | 0.7 | 95 | | 0 | .24 | .32 | 10 | 87 | 11 | 23 | 5.91 | .016 |
| 3.5 oz | 100 | 27.6 | 0.0 | 6.9 | 0.0 | | .06 | 5.5 | 2.58 | .36 | 340 | 181 | 2.48 | .088 | |
| **ground, regular** | | | | | | | | | | | | | | | |
| baked, med | 287 | 55.1 | 20.9 | 0.8 | 87 | | 0 | .16 | .23 | 9 | 60 | 10 | 15 | 4.89 | .017 |
| 3.5 oz | 100 | 23.0 | 0.0 | 8.2 | 0.0 | | .03 | 4.8 | 2.34 | .22 | 221 | 137 | 2.41 | .070 | |
| baked, well done | 317 | 48.9 | 21.5 | 0.8 | 108 | | 0 | .20 | .29 | 11 | 75 | 12 | 19 | 6.07 | .021 |
| 3.5 oz | 100 | 28.8 | 0.0 | 8.4 | 0.0 | | .04 | 5.9 | 2.90 | .27 | 274 | 170 | 2.99 | .086 | |
| broiled, med | 289 | 54.2 | 20.7 | 0.8 | 90 | | 0 | .19 | .27 | 9 | 83 | 11 | 20 | 5.18 | .017 |
| 3.5 oz | 100 | 24.1 | 0.0 | 8.1 | 0.0 | | .03 | 5.8 | 2.93 | .33 | 292 | 170 | 2.44 | .082 | |
| broiled, well done | 292 | 52.0 | 19.5 | 0.7 | 101 | | 0 | .21 | .30 | 10 | 93 | 12 | 22 | 5.81 | .020 |
| 3.5 oz | 100 | 27.2 | 0.0 | 7.7 | 0.0 | | .04 | 6.5 | 3.28 | .37 | 327 | 191 | 2.74 | .092 | |
| pan fried, med | 306 | 52.3 | 22.6 | 0.8 | 89 | | 0 | .20 | .24 | 9 | 84 | 11 | 20 | 5.07 | .017 |
| 3.5 oz | 100 | 23.9 | 0.0 | 8.9 | 0.0 | | .03 | 5.8 | 2.71 | .34 | 300 | 171 | 2.45 | .081 | |
| pan fried, well done | 286 | 52.7 | 18.9 | 0.7 | 98 | | 0 | .21 | .27 | 10 | 93 | 13 | 22 | 5.62 | .019 |
| 3.5 oz | 100 | 27.0 | 0.0 | 7.4 | 0.0 | | .04 | 6.5 | 3.00 | .38 | 332 | 189 | 2.71 | .090 | |
| **rib eye, small end (rib 10-12)** | | | | | | | | | | | | | | | |
| sep lean & fat, broiled | 295 | 52.3 | 20.6 | 0.7 | 83 | | 0 | .20 | .36 | 7 | 64 | 13 | 24 | 6.13 | .014 |
| 3.5 oz | 100 | 25.4 | 0.0 | 8.7 | 0.0 | | .09 | 4.3 | 3.06 | .31 | 352 | 188 | 2.34 | .098 | |
| sep lean, broiled | 225 | 58.4 | 11.6 | 0.4 | 80 | | 0 | .22 | .40 | 8 | 69 | 13 | 27 | 6.99 | .016 |
| 3.5 oz | 100 | 28.0 | 0.0 | 4.9 | 0.0 | | .11 | 4.8 | 3.32 | .34 | 394 | 208 | 2.57 | .100 | |
| **rib, large end (rib 6-9)** | | | | | | | | | | | | | | | |
| sep lean & fat, broiled | 378 | 46.7 | 32.3 | 1.2 | 87 | | 0 | .16 | .26 | 6 | 60 | 10 | 18 | 4.68 | .013 |
| 3.5 oz | 100 | 20.1 | 0.0 | 13.7 | 0.0 | | .07 | 2.6 | 2.73 | .32 | 288 | 159 | 2.02 | .089 | |
| sep lean & fat, roasted | 368 | 46.1 | 30.0 | 1.1 | 85 | | 0 | .18 | .22 | 7 | 64 | 10 | 19 | 5.73 | .013 |
| 3.5 oz | 100 | 22.7 | 0.0 | 12.7 | 0.0 | | .07 | 3.6 | 2.33 | .36 | 289 | 171 | 2.32 | .100 | |
| sep lean, broiled | 233 | 60.1 | 14.2 | 0.4 | 82 | | 0 | .20 | .32 | 7 | 70 | 8 | 24 | 6.25 | .016 |
| 3.5 oz | 100 | 24.6 | 0.0 | 6.1 | | | .09 | 3.1 | 3.26 | .41 | 369 | 199 | 2.48 | .089 | |
| sep lean, roasted | 244 | 57.0 | 14.0 | 0.4 | 81 | | 0 | .22 | .26 | 9 | 73 | 8 | 25 | 7.46 | .016 |
| 3.5 oz | 100 | 27.5 | 0.0 | 5.9 | 0.0 | | .09 | 4.4 | 2.61 | .45 | 357 | 209 | 2.82 | .105 | |
| **rib, shortribs** | | | | | | | | | | | | | | | |
| sep lean & fat, braised | 471 | 35.7 | 42.0 | 1.5 | 94 | | 0 | .15 | .22 | 5 | 50 | 12 | 15 | 4.88 | .013 |
| 3.5 oz | 100 | 21.6 | 0.0 | 17.8 | 0.0 | | .05 | 2.5 | 2.62 | .25 | 224 | 162 | 2.31 | .099 | |
| sep lean, braised | 295 | 50.2 | 18.1 | 0.6 | 93 | | 0 | .20 | .28 | 7 | 58 | 11 | 22 | 7.80 | .018 |
| 3.5 oz | 100 | 30.8 | 0.0 | 7.7 | 0.0 | | .07 | 3.2 | 3.46 | .34 | 313 | 235 | 3.36 | .107 | |
| **rib, small end (ribs 10-12)** | | | | | | | | | | | | | | | |
| sep lean & fat, broiled | 326 | 49.5 | 24.8 | 0.9 | 84 | | 0 | .19 | .34 | 7 | 62 | 13 | 22 | 5.70 | .013 |
| 3.5 oz | 100 | 24.0 | 0.0 | 10.5 | DFIB | | .09 | 4.1 | 2.93 | .30 | 331 | 177 | 2.22 | .097 | |
| sep lean & fat, roasted | 359 | 47.5 | 29.3 | 1.0 | 85 | | 0 | .17 | .31 | 7 | 65 | 13 | 20 | 4.86 | .013 |
| 3.5 oz | 100 | 22.3 | 0.0 | 12.4 | 0.0 | | .07 | 3.1 | 2.88 | .36 | 325 | 179 | 1.95 | .089 | |
| sep lean, broiled | 221 | 58.7 | 11.2 | 0.3 | 80 | | 0 | .22 | .40 | 8 | 69 | 13 | 27 | 6.99 | .016 |
| 3.5 oz | 100 | 28.0 | 0.0 | 4.8 | 0.0 | | .11 | 4.8 | 3.32 | .34 | 394 | 208 | 2.57 | .100 | |
| sep lean, roasted | 236 | 58.7 | 13.5 | 0.4 | 80 | | 0 | .20 | .37 | 8 | 75 | 13 | 25 | 6.19 | .016 |
| 3.5 oz | 100 | 26.7 | 0.0 | 5.7 | 0.0 | | .08 | 3.6 | 3.37 | .44 | 404 | 219 | 2.30 | .089 | |
| **rib, whole (ribs 6-12)** | | | | | | | | | | | | | | | |
| sep lean & fat, broiled | 362 | 47.4 | 30.0 | 1.0 | 86 | | 0 | .17 | .29 | 6 | 61 | 11 | 20 | 5.03 | .013 |
| 3.5 oz | 100 | 21.5 | 0.0 | 12.7 | 0.0 | | .08 | 3.1 | 2.79 | .31 | 302 | 165 | 2.08 | .092 | |
| sep lean & fat, roasted | 381 | 45.2 | 31.8 | 1.1 | 85 | | 0 | .17 | .25 | 7 | 63 | 11 | 19 | 5.17 | .013 |
| 3.5 oz | 100 | 21.9 | 0.0 | 13.4 | 0.0 | | .07 | 3.3 | 2.51 | .35 | 294 | 169 | 2.11 | .095 | |
| sep lean, broiled | 228 | 59.5 | 13.0 | 0.4 | 82 | | 0 | .21 | .35 | 8 | 69 | 10 | 25 | 6.55 | .016 |
| 3.5 oz | 100 | 26.0 | 0.0 | 5.5 | 0.0 | | .09 | 3.8 | 3.28 | .38 | 379 | 202 | 2.52 | .094 | |
| sep lean, roasted | 240 | 57.7 | 13.8 | 0.4 | 81 | | 0 | .21 | .30 | 8 | 74 | 10 | 25 | 6.94 | .016 |
| 3.5 oz | 100 | 27.2 | 0.0 | 5.8 | 0.0 | | .08 | 4.1 | 2.92 | .44 | 376 | 213 | 2.61 | .098 | |
| **round, bottom** | | | | | | | | | | | | | | | |
| sep lean & fat, braised | 261 | 53.9 | 14.8 | 0.6 | 96 | | 0 | .25 | .34 | 11 | 51 | 6 | 23 | 5.13 | .017 |
| 3.5 oz | 100 | 29.8 | 0.0 | 5.7 | 0.0 | | .07 | 3.9 | 2.40 | .40 | 292 | 255 | 3.25 | .130 | |

| | KCAL | H₂O (g) | FAT (g) | PUFA (g) | CHOL (mg) | A (RE) | C (mg) | B-2 (mg) | B-6 (mg) | FOL (mcg) | Na (mg) | Ca (mg) | Mg (mg) | Zn (mg) | Mn (mg) |
|---|---|---|---|---|---|---|---|---|---|---|---|---|---|---|---|
| | WT (g) | PRO (g) | CHO (g) | SFA (g) | DFIB (g) | A (IU) | B-1 (mg) | NIA (mg) | B-12 (mcg) | PANT (mg) | K (mg) | P (mg) | Fe (mg) | Cu (mg) | |
| sep lean, braised | 222 | 57.2 | 9.7 | 0.4 | 96 | 0 | | .26 | .36 | 11 | 51 | 5 | 25 | 5.48 | .018 |
| 3.5 oz | 100 | 31.6 | 0.0 | 3.4 | 0.0 | | .08 | 4.1 | 2.47 | .42 | 308 | 272 | 3.46 | .134 | |
| **round, eye of** | | | | | | | | | | | | | | | |
| sep lean & fat, roasted | 243 | 57.5 | 14.2 | 0.5 | 73 | 0 | | .16 | .35 | 7 | 59 | 6 | 25 | 4.33 | .015 |
| 3.5 oz | 100 | 26.8 | 0.0 | 5.8 | 0.0 | | .08 | 3.5 | 2.10 | .42 | 362 | 208 | 1.84 | .099 | |
| sep lean, roasted | 183 | 62.8 | 6.5 | 0.2 | 69 | 0 | | .17 | .38 | 7 | 62 | 5 | 27 | 4.74 | .016 |
| 3.5 oz | 100 | 29.0 | 0.0 | 2.5 | 0.0 | | .09 | 3.8 | 2.17 | .46 | 395 | 226 | 1.95 | .100 | |
| **round, full cut** | | | | | | | | | | | | | | | |
| sep lean & fat, broiled | 274 | 55.1 | 18.2 | 0.8 | 84 | 0 | | .21 | .44 | 9 | 60 | 7 | 24 | 4.13 | .015 |
| 3.5 oz | 100 | 25.5 | 0.0 | 7.3 | 0.0 | | .09 | 3.7 | 2.75 | .36 | 366 | 211 | 2.42 | .097 | |
| sep lean, broiled | 184 | 63.4 | 7.0 | 0.3 | 82 | 0 | | .23 | .50 | 10 | 64 | 5 | 28 | 4.68 | .016 |
| 3.5 oz | 100 | 28.5 | 0.0 | 2.5 | 0.0 | | .10 | 4.2 | 2.98 | .41 | 415 | 237 | 2.69 | .107 | |
| **round, tip** | | | | | | | | | | | | | | | |
| sep lean & fat, roasted | 251 | 57.3 | 15.3 | 0.6 | 83 | 0 | | .25 | .37 | 7 | 62 | 6 | 25 | 6.37 | .015 |
| 3.5 oz | 100 | 26.5 | 0.0 | 6.1 | 0.0 | | .09 | 3.5 | 2.74 | .43 | 353 | 221 | 2.71 | .121 | |
| sep lean, roasted | 190 | 62.8 | 7.5 | 0.2 | 81 | 0 | | .27 | .40 | 8 | 65 | 5 | 27 | 7.07 | .017 |
| 3.5 oz | 100 | 28.7 | 0.0 | 2.8 | 0.0 | | .10 | 3.7 | 2.89 | .47 | 386 | 242 | 2.94 | .125 | |
| **round, top** | | | | | | | | | | | | | | | |
| sep lean & fat, broiled | 211 | 59.2 | 8.8 | 0.4 | 85 | 0 | | .26 | .54 | 12 | 60 | 6 | 30 | 5.40 | .016 |
| 3.5 oz | 100 | 30.8 | 0.0 | 3.3 | 0.0 | | .11 | 5.9 | 2.44 | .48 | 429 | 239 | 2.81 | .121 | |
| sep lean & fat, pan fried | 290 | 50.4 | 17.1 | 1.1 | 97 | 0 | | .25 | .55 | 11 | 67 | 6 | 31 | 4.18 | .018 |
| 3.5 oz | 100 | 31.7 | 0.0 | 6.5 | 0.0 | | .10 | 4.9 | 3.18 | .42 | 459 | 262 | 2.86 | .125 | |
| sep lean, broiled | 191 | 60.9 | 6.2 | 0.2 | 84 | 0 | | .27 | .56 | 12 | 61 | 6 | 31 | 5.57 | .017 |
| 3.5 oz | 100 | 31.7 | 0.0 | 2.2 | 0.0 | | .12 | 6.0 | 2.48 | .49 | 442 | 246 | 2.88 | .123 | |
| sep lean, pan fried | 227 | 55.5 | 8.6 | 0.9 | 97 | 0 | | .28 | .61 | 13 | 71 | 5 | 35 | 4.62 | .020 |
| 3.5 oz | 100 | 35.1 | 0.0 | 2.8 | 0.0 | | .11 | 5.5 | 3.43 | .46 | 513 | 392 | 3.15 | .131 | |
| sausage, smoked, cnd | 89 | 15.2 | 7.6 | 0.3 | 19 | 3[a] | .04 | .03 | | | 321 | 2 | 4 | .79 | |
| 1 oz | 28 | 4.0 | 0.7 | 3.2 | | | .01 | 0.9 | .53 | | 50 | 30 | .50 | | |
| | 134 | 23.0 | 11.6 | 0.5 | 29 | 5[a] | .06 | .05 | | | 486 | 4 | 6 | 1.20 | |
| 1 sausage (8 per 12 oz pkg) | 43 | 6.1 | 1.0 | 4.9 | | | .02 | 1.4 | .80 | | 76 | 45 | .76 | | |
| **shank, crosscuts** | | | | | | | | | | | | | | | |
| sep lean & fat, simmered | 244 | 54.6 | 12.1 | 0.5 | 79 | 0 | | .20 | .34 | 9 | 62 | 30 | 28 | 9.67 | .018 |
| 3.5 oz | 100 | 31.6 | 0.0 | 4.8 | 0.0 | | .13 | 5.5 | 3.59 | .38 | 417 | 246 | 3.61 | .161 | |
| sep lean, simmered | 201 | 58.2 | 6.4 | 0.2 | 78 | 0 | | .21 | .37 | 10 | 64 | 32 | 30 | 10.49 | .020 |
| 3.5 oz | 100 | 33.7 | 0.0 | 2.3 | 0.0 | | .14 | 5.9 | 3.79 | .41 | 447 | 263 | 3.86 | .172 | |
| **short loin porterhouse steak** | | | | | | | | | | | | | | | |
| sep lean & fat, broiled | 299 | 52.4 | 21.2 | 0.8 | 83 | 0 | | .22 | .35 | 7 | 61 | 8 | 25 | 4.70 | .014 |
| 3.5 oz | 100 | 25.1 | 0.0 | 8.8 | 0.0 | | .10 | 4.1 | 2.16 | .31 | 356 | 189 | 2.66 | .133 | |
| sep lean, broiled | 218 | 59.5 | 10.8 | 0.4 | 80 | 0 | | .25 | .40 | 8 | 66 | 7 | 29 | 5.40 | .015 |
| 3.5 oz | 100 | 28.2 | 0.0 | 4.3 | 0.0 | | .11 | 4.6 | 2.27 | .34 | 407 | 213 | 3.08 | .143 | |
| **short loin T-bone steak** | | | | | | | | | | | | | | | |
| sep lean & fat, broiled | 324 | 50.4 | 24.6 | 0.9 | 84 | 0 | | .21 | .33 | 7 | 60 | 9 | 24 | 4.46 | .013 |
| 3.5 oz | 100 | 24.0 | 0.0 | 10.2 | 0.0 | | .09 | 3.9 | 2.12 | .29 | 339 | 177 | 2.54 | .130 | |
| sep lean, broiled | 214 | 60.3 | 10.4 | 0.4 | 80 | 0 | | .25 | .39 | 8 | 66 | 7 | 29 | 5.40 | .015 |
| 3.5 oz | 100 | 28.1 | 0.0 | 4.2 | 0.0 | | .11 | 4.6 | 2.27 | .33 | 407 | 208 | 3.00 | .143 | |
| **short loin tenderloin** | | | | | | | | | | | | | | | |
| sep lean & fat, broiled | 266 | 55.0 | 17.2 | 0.7 | 86 | 0 | | .27 | .40 | 7 | 61 | 8 | 27 | 5.04 | .015 |
| 3.5 oz | 100 | 26.0 | 0.0 | 7.0 | 0.0 | | .12 | 3.6 | 2.45 | .35 | 380 | 217 | 3.25 | .167 | |
| sep lean & fat, roasted | 303 | 52.5 | 22.0 | 0.9 | 87 | 0 | | .28 | .34 | 7 | 56 | 8 | 23 | 4.48 | .014 |
| 3.5 oz | 100 | 24.5 | 0.0 | 9.0 | 0.0 | | .09 | 3.1 | 2.56 | .40 | 343 | 207 | 3.19 | .152 | |
| sep lean, broiled | 204 | 60.4 | 9.3 | 0.4 | 84 | 0 | | .30 | .44 | 7 | 63 | 7 | 30 | 5.59 | .017 |
| 3.5 oz | 100 | 28.3 | 0.0 | 3.6 | 0.0 | | .13 | 3.9 | 2.57 | .38 | 419 | 238 | 3.58 | .179 | |

[a] Contains added sodium ascorbate.

| | KCAL | H₂O (g) | FAT (g) | PUFA (g) | CHOL (mg) | A (RE) | C (mg) | B-2 (mg) | B-6 (mg) | FOL (mcg) | Na (mg) | Ca (mg) | Mg (mg) | Zn (mg) | Mn (mg) |
|---|---|---|---|---|---|---|---|---|---|---|---|---|---|---|---|
| | WT (g) | PRO (g) | CHO (g) | SFA (g) | DFIB (g) | A (IU) | B-1 (mg) | NIA (mg) | B-12 (mcg) | PANT (mg) | K (mg) | P (mg) | Fe (mg) | Cu (mg) | |
| sep lean, roasted | 219 | 60.0 | 11.3 | 0.4 | 86 | | 0 | .32 | .38 | 8 | 59 | 7 | 27 | 5.17 | .016 |
| *3.5 oz* | 100 | 27.5 | 0.0 | 4.4 | 0.0 | | .11 | 3.4 | 2.77 | .45 | 393 | 236 | 3.66 | .167 | |
| **short loin, top loin** | | | | | | | | | | | | | | | |
| sep lean & fat, broiled | 280 | 53.5 | 18.8 | 0.7 | 79 | | 0 | .18 | .37 | 7 | 63 | 9 | 24 | 4.60 | .014 |
| *3.5 oz* | 100 | 25.7 | 0.0 | 7.8 | 0.0 | | .08 | 4.7 | 1.94 | .33 | 351 | 195 | 2.24 | .104 | |
| sep lean, broiled | 203 | 60.2 | 8.9 | 0.3 | 76 | | 0 | .20 | .42 | 8 | 68 | 8 | 27 | 5.22 | .016 |
| *3.5 oz* | 100 | 28.6 | 0.0 | 3.6 | 0.0 | | .09 | 5.3 | 2.00 | .37 | 396 | 218 | 2.47 | .107 | |
| **wedge-bone sirloin** | | | | | | | | | | | | | | | |
| sep lean & fat, broiled | 280 | 52.6 | 18.0 | 0.7 | 90 | | 0 | .26 | .40 | 9 | 63 | 11 | 28 | 5.75 | .015 |
| *3.5 oz* | 100 | 27.4 | 0.0 | 7.5 | 0.0 | | .11 | 3.9 | 2.66 | .35 | 360 | 218 | 3.01 | .137 | |
| sep lean & fat, pan fried | 339 | 47.3 | 24.6 | 1.3 | 98 | | 0 | .27 | .42 | 9 | 68 | 11 | 27 | 5.25 | .016 |
| *3.5 oz* | 100 | 27.5 | 0.0 | 10.1 | 0.0 | | .12 | 3.7 | 3.21 | .37 | 385 | 223 | 3.25 | .135 | |
| sep lean, broiled | 208 | 58.6 | 8.7 | 0.4 | 89 | | 0 | .30 | .45 | 10 | 66 | 11 | 32 | 6.52 | .017 |
| *3.5 oz* | 100 | 30.4 | 0.0 | 3.6 | 0.0 | | .13 | 4.3 | 2.85 | .39 | 403 | 244 | 3.36 | .146 | |
| sep lean, pan fried | 238 | 55.9 | 11.0 | 0.9 | 99 | | 0 | .33 | .50 | 10 | 77 | 11 | 33 | 6.40 | .019 |
| *3.5 oz* | 100 | 32.5 | 0.0 | 4.2 | 0.0 | | .14 | 4.3 | 3.69 | .43 | 465 | 267 | 3.90 | .149 | |

## 21.2. LAMB

| | KCAL | H₂O (g) | FAT (g) | PUFA (g) | CHOL (mg) | A (RE) | C (mg) | B-2 (mg) | B-6 (mg) | FOL (mcg) | Na (mg) | Ca (mg) | Mg (mg) | Zn (mg) | Mn (mg) |
|---|---|---|---|---|---|---|---|---|---|---|---|---|---|---|---|
| **leg** | | | | | | | | | | | | | | | |
| sep lean & fat, roasted | 237 | 45.9 | 16.1 | | | | | .23 | | | 52 | 9 | | | |
| *3 oz* | 85 | 21.5 | 0.0 | 9.0 | | | .13 | 4.7 | | | 241 | 177 | 1.40 | | |
| sep lean, roasted | 158 | 52.9 | 6.0 | | | | | .26 | | | 60 | 11 | | | |
| *3 oz* | 85 | 24.4 | 0.0 | 3.4 | | | .14 | 5.3 | | | 273 | 202 | 1.90 | | |
| **loin chop** | | | | | | | | | | | | | | | |
| sep lean & fat, broiled | 255 | 33.4 | 20.9 | | 58 | | | .16 | | | 38 | 6 | | | |
| *1 chop* | 71 | 15.6 | 0.0 | 11.7 | | | .09 | 3.6 | | | 175 | 122 | .90 | | |
| sep lean, broiled | 92 | 30.4 | 3.7 | | 39 | | | .14 | | | 34 | 6 | | | |
| *1 chop* | 49 | 13.8 | 0.0 | 2.1 | | | .07 | 3.0 | | | 155 | 107 | 1.00 | | |
| **rib chop** | | | | | | | | | | | | | | | |
| sep lean & fat, broiled | 273 | 28.7 | 23.9 | | | | | .14 | | | 33 | 6 | | | |
| *1 chop* | 67 | 13.5 | 0.0 | 13.4 | | | .08 | 3.1 | | | 151 | 105 | .70 | | |
| sep lean, broiled | 91 | 25.9 | 4.5 | | | | | .12 | | | 29 | 5 | | | |
| *1 chop* | 43 | 11.7 | 0.0 | 2.5 | | | .06 | 2.5 | | | 131 | 91 | .80 | | |
| **shoulder** | | | | | | | | | | | | | | | |
| sep lean & fat, roasted | 287 | 42.2 | 23.1 | | | | | .20 | | | 45 | 9 | | | |
| *3 oz* | 85 | 18.4 | 0.0 | 12.9 | | | .11 | 4.0 | | | 206 | 146 | 1.00 | | |
| sep lean, roasted | 174 | 52.2 | 8.5 | | | | | .24 | | | 56 | 10 | | | |
| *3 oz* | 85 | 22.8 | 0.0 | 4.8 | | | .13 | 4.8 | | | 255 | 186 | 1.60 | | |

## 21.3. PORK

| | KCAL | H₂O (g) | FAT (g) | PUFA (g) | CHOL (mg) | A (RE) | C (mg) | B-2 (mg) | B-6 (mg) | FOL (mcg) | Na (mg) | Ca (mg) | Mg (mg) | Zn (mg) | Mn (mg) |
|---|---|---|---|---|---|---|---|---|---|---|---|---|---|---|---|
| **arm picnic** | | | | | | | | | | | | | | | |
| sep lean & fat, braised | 345 | 46.6 | 25.5 | 2.9 | 109 | 3 | 0 | .31 | .27 | 4 | 88 | 7 | 18 | 4.04 | .014 |
| *3.5 oz* | 100 | 26.8 | 0.0 | 9.3 | 0.0 | 9 | .54 | 5.2 | .69 | .56 | 336 | 191 | 1.61 | .138 | |
| sep lean & fat, roasted | 331 | 51.1 | 26.1 | 2.9 | 94 | 2 | 0 | .30 | .28 | 4 | 70 | 8 | 17 | 3.31 | .033 |
| *3.5 oz* | 100 | 22.3 | 0.0 | 9.5 | 0.0 | 8 | .52 | 3.9 | .74 | .49 | 293 | 206 | 1.19 | .112 | |
| sep lean, braised | 248 | 54.3 | 12.2 | 1.5 | 114 | 2 | 0 | .36 | .41 | 5 | 102 | 8 | 22 | 4.97 | .017 |
| *3.5 oz* | 100 | 32.3 | 0.0 | 4.2 | 0.0 | 8 | .60 | 5.9 | .71 | .67 | 405 | 226 | 1.95 | .161 | |
| sep lean, roasted | 228 | 60.3 | 12.6 | 1.5 | 95 | 2 | 0 | .36 | .41 | 5 | 80 | 9 | 20 | 4.07 | .041 |
| *3.5 oz* | 100 | 26.7 | 0.0 | 4.4 | 0.0 | 7 | .58 | 4.3 | .78 | .59 | 351 | 247 | 1.42 | .128 | |
| **arm picnic, cured** | | | | | | | | | | | | | | | |
| sep lean & fat, roasted | 280 | 54.7 | 21.4 | 2.3 | 58 | 0 | | .19 | .28 | 3 | 1072 | 10 | 14 | 2.51 | .024 |
| *3.5 oz* | 100 | 20.4 | 0.0 | 7.7 | 0.0 | 0 | .61 | 4.1 | .93 | .56 | 258 | 221 | .95 | .113 | |

| | KCAL | H₂O (g) | FAT (g) | PUFA (g) | CHOL (mg) | A (RE) | C (mg) | B-2 (mg) | B-6 (mg) | FOL (mcg) | Na (mg) | Ca (mg) | Mg (mg) | Zn (mg) | Mn (mg) |
|---|---|---|---|---|---|---|---|---|---|---|---|---|---|---|---|
| | WT (g) | PRO (g) | CHO (g) | SFA (g) | DFIB (g) | A (IU) | B-1 (mg) | NIA (mg) | B-12 (mcg) | PANT (mg) | K (mg) | P (mg) | Fe (mg) | Cu (mg) | |
| sep lean, roasted | 170 | 63.9 | 7.0 | 0.8 | 48 | 0 | | .23 | .37 | 4 | 1231 | 11 | 16 | 2.94 | .030 |
| *3.5 oz* | 100 | 24.9 | 0.0 | 2.4 | 0.0 | 0 | .73 | 4.8 | 1.11 | .65 | 292 | 243 | 1.00 | .128 | |
| **bacon, canadian style** | | | | | | | | | | | | | | | |
| unheated[a] | 89 | 38.0 | 4.0 | 0.4 | 28 | 0 | 12[b] | .10 | .22 | 2 | 799 | 5 | 10 | .79 | .013 |
| *2 slices* | 57 | 11.7 | 1.0 | 1.3 | 0.0 | 0 | .43 | 3.5 | .38 | .30 | 195 | 138 | .38 | .026 | |
| grilled[a] | 86 | 28.7 | 3.9 | 0.4 | 27 | 0 | 10[b] | .09 | .21 | 2 | 719 | 5 | 10 | .79 | .013 |
| *2 slices* | 47 | 11.3 | 0.6 | 1.3 | 0.0 | 0 | .38 | 3.2 | .36 | .24 | 181 | 138 | .38 | .025 | |
| **bacon, cured** | | | | | | | | | | | | | | | |
| broiled/pan fried | 109 | 2.5 | 9.4 | 1.1 | 16 | 0 | 6[b] | .05 | .05 | 1 | 303 | 2 | 5 | .62 | .008 |
| *3 med pieces* | 19 | 5.8 | 0.1 | 3.3 | 0.0 | 0 | .13 | 1.4 | .33 | .20 | 92 | 64 | .31 | .032 | |
| broiled/pan fried | 732 | 16.4 | 62.5 | 7.4 | 107 | 0 | 43[b] | .36 | .35 | 6 | 2026 | 15 | 30 | 4.14 | .052 |
| *4.48 oz[c]* | 127 | 38.7 | 0.8 | 22.1 | 0.0 | 0 | .88 | 9.3 | 2.23 | 1.34 | 617 | 426 | 2.05 | .216 | |
| raw | 378 | 21.5 | 39.1 | 4.6 | 46 | 0 | 15[b] | .07 | .10 | 1 | 466 | 5 | 6 | .78 | .005 |
| *3 med slices* | 68 | 5.9 | 0.1 | 14.5 | 0.0 | 0 | .25 | 1.9 | .63 | .24 | 95 | 97 | .41 | .044 | |
| **bacon pieces** | | | | | | | | | | | | | | | |
| bacon bits, Oscar Mayer | 21 | 2.6 | 1.0 | | 6 | | 1 | .03 | .02 | | 181 | 1 | 2 | .33 | |
| *1/4 cup* | 7 | 2.6 | 0.2 | | | | .05 | 0.7 | .15 | .08 | 38 | 40 | .14 | .020 | |
| bacOs, General Mills | 30 | | 1.0 | | | | | | | | 130 | | | | |
| *1 T* | | 3.0 | 2.0 | | | | | | | | 210 | | | | |
| **blade roll, cured, sep lean & fat, roasted** | 287 | 56.2 | 23.5 | 2.5 | 67 | 0 | 3 | .29 | .21 | 3 | 973 | 7 | 13 | 2.45 | .023 |
| *3.5 oz* | 100 | 17.3 | 0.4 | 8.4 | 0.0 | 0 | .46 | 2.4 | 1.05 | .77 | 194 | 156 | .89 | .076 | |
| **boston blade** | | | | | | | | | | | | | | | |
| sep lean & fat, braised | 371 | 43.3 | 28.7 | 3.3 | 111 | 3 | 0 | .33 | .23 | 1 | 67 | 7 | 19 | 4.61 | .013 |
| *3.5 oz* | 100 | 26.4 | 0.0 | 10.3 | 0.0 | 10 | .51 | 4.0 | .84 | .13 | 348 | 184 | 1.72 | .143 | |
| sep lean & fat, broiled | 350 | 48.5 | 28.5 | 3.3 | 103 | 3 | 0 | .38 | .27 | 4 | 75 | 5 | 24 | 3.62 | .008 |
| *3.5 oz* | 100 | 21.9 | 0.0 | 10.2 | 0.0 | 9 | .67 | 4.0 | 1.04 | .69 | 351 | 211 | 1.17 | .117 | |
| sep lean & fat, roasted | 321 | 52.0 | 25.3 | 2.9 | 97 | 2 | 0 | .33 | .27 | 4 | 67 | 6 | 18 | 3.82 | .012 |
| *3.5 oz* | 100 | 21.8 | 0.0 | 9.1 | 0.0 | 8 | .55 | 4.0 | .91 | .51 | 313 | 195 | 1.42 | .118 | |
| sep lean, braised | 294 | 49.4 | 17.6 | 2.1 | 116 | 3 | 0 | .39 | .27 | 5 | 75 | 8 | 22 | 5.57 | .016 |
| *3.5 oz* | 100 | 31.2 | 0.0 | 6.1 | 0.0 | 9 | .55 | 4.3 | .90 | .64 | 412 | 214 | 2.05 | .165 | |
| sep lean, broiled | 274 | 55.1 | 18.4 | 2.2 | 105 | 2 | 0 | .44 | .31 | 5 | 84 | 6 | 28 | 4.27 | .009 |
| *3.5 oz* | 100 | 25.2 | 0.0 | 6.4 | 0.0 | 8 | .75 | 4.3 | 1.13 | .82 | 409 | 244 | 1.35 | .131 | |
| sep lean, roasted | 256 | 57.7 | 16.8 | 2.0 | 98 | 2 | 0 | .37 | .30 | 5 | 73 | 7 | 20 | 4.37 | .014 |
| *3.5 oz* | 100 | 24.4 | 0.0 | 5.8 | 0.0 | 7 | .59 | 4.3 | .96 | .57 | 353 | 219 | 1.60 | .129 | |
| **breakfast strips** | | | | | | | | | | | | | | | |
| ckd | 156 | 9.2 | 12.5 | 1.9 | 36 | 0 | 15[b] | .13 | .12 | 1 | 714 | 5 | 9 | 1.25 | .015 |
| *3 slices* | 34 | 9.8 | 0.4 | 4.3 | 0.0 | 0 | .25 | 2.6 | .60 | .31 | 158 | 90 | .67 | .052 | |
| ckd, Lean 'n Tasty | 50 | 4.9 | 4.3 | | 13 | | | | | | 191 | 1 | 2 | .33 | |
| *1 slice* | 12 | 2.8 | 0.1 | | | | | | | | 40 | 23 | .14 | .040 | |
| **center loin** | | | | | | | | | | | | | | | |
| sep lean & fat, braised | 354 | 44.1 | 25.4 | 2.9 | 107 | 3 | 0 | .24 | .38 | 4 | 51 | 6 | 19 | 2.47 | .027 |
| *3.5 oz* | 100 | 29.4 | 0.0 | 9.2 | 0.0 | 9 | .77 | 6.0 | .61 | .62 | 317 | 215 | .83 | .094 | |
| sep lean & fat, broiled | 316 | 49.8 | 22.1 | 2.5 | 97 | 3 | 0 | .27 | .40 | 5 | 70 | 4 | 25 | 1.93 | .009 |
| *3.5 oz* | 100 | 27.4 | 0.0 | 8.0 | 0.0 | 9 | 1.00 | 5.0 | .71 | .59 | 359 | 211 | .81 | .076 | |
| sep lean & fat, pan fried | 375 | 45.4 | 30.5 | 3.5 | 103 | 3 | 0 | .28 | .39 | 5 | 72 | 5 | 26 | 1.96 | .009 |
| *3.5 oz* | 100 | 23.3 | 0.0 | 11.0 | 0.0 | 9 | 1.02 | 5.2 | .77 | 1.01 | 363 | 214 | .84 | .080 | |
| sep lean & fat, roasted | 305 | 51.8 | 21.8 | 2.5 | 91 | 2 | 0 | .24 | .40 | 1 | 64 | 5 | 19 | 2.04 | .014 |
| *3.5 oz* | 100 | 25.4 | 0.0 | 7.9 | 0.0 | 8 | .83 | 5.0 | .60 | .77 | 322 | 196 | .99 | .077 | |
| sep lean, braised | 272 | 50.2 | 13.7 | 1.7 | 111 | 3 | 0 | .27 | .45 | 5 | 55 | 6 | 22 | 2.91 | .032 |
| *3.5 oz* | 100 | 34.8 | 0.0 | 4.7 | 0.0 | 9 | .88 | 6.8 | .61 | .74 | 372 | 251 | .95 | .104 | |
| sep lean, broiled | 231 | 56.8 | 10.5 | 1.3 | 98 | 2 | 0 | .31 | .47 | 6 | 78 | 5 | 30 | 2.23 | .011 |
| *3.5 oz* | 100 | 32.0 | 0.0 | 3.6 | 0.0 | 8 | 1.15 | 5.5 | .74 | .69 | 420 | 244 | .92 | .082 | |
| sep lean, pan fried | 266 | 54.4 | 15.9 | 2.0 | 107 | 2 | 0 | .33 | .50 | 6 | 85 | 5 | 32 | 2.41 | .012 |
| *3.5 oz* | 100 | 28.8 | 0.0 | 5.5 | 0.0 | 8 | 1.25 | 6.0 | .73 | .79 | 455 | 265 | 1.00 | .089 | |
| sep lean, roasted | 240 | 57.3 | 13.1 | 1.6 | 91 | 2 | 0 | .26 | .45 | 1 | 69 | 6 | 21 | 2.28 | .016 |
| *3.5 oz* | 100 | 28.5 | 0.0 | 4.5 | 0.0 | 8 | .91 | 5.5 | .60 | .65 | 362 | 219 | 1.09 | .081 | |

[a] Bacon is fully cooked as purchased.
[b] Contains added ascorbic acid or sodium ascorbate.
[c] Yield from 1 lb raw bacon.

| | KCAL / WT (g) | H₂O (g) / PRO (g) | FAT (g) / CHO (g) | PUFA (g) / SFA (g) | CHOL (mg) / DFIB (g) | A (RE) / A (IU) | C (mg) / B-1 (mg) | B-2 (mg) / NIA (mg) | B-6 (mg) / B-12 (mcg) | FOL (mcg) / PANT (mg) | Na (mg) / K (mg) | Ca (mg) / P (mg) | Mg (mg) / Fe (mg) | Zn (mg) / Cu (mg) | Mn (mg) |
|---|---|---|---|---|---|---|---|---|---|---|---|---|---|---|---|
| **center rib** | | | | | | | | | | | | | | | |
| sep lean & fat, braised | 367 | 43.2 | 27.2 | 3.1 | 95 | 3 | 0 | .27 | .32 | 6 | 48 | 10 | 20 | 2.35 | .010 |
| *3.5 oz* | 100 | 28.6 | 0.0 | 9.8 | 0.0 | 10 | .53 | 5.6 | .54 | .55 | 413 | 210 | 1.07 | .090 | |
| sep lean & fat, broiled | 343 | 47.5 | 26.4 | 3.0 | 93 | 2 | 0 | .28 | .34 | 7 | 61 | 13 | 25 | 2.03 | .017 |
| *3.5 oz* | 100 | 24.6 | 0.0 | 9.5 | 0.0 | 7 | .79 | 4.7 | .68 | .63 | 371 | 227 | .72 | .075 | |
| sep lean & fat, pan fried | 390 | 44.1 | 33.0 | 3.7 | 84 | 3 | 0 | .28 | .33 | 6 | 45 | 7 | 21 | 1.62 | .006 |
| *3.5 oz* | 100 | 21.6 | 0.0 | 11.9 | 0.0 | 9 | .64 | 4.4 | .62 | .60 | 352 | 208 | .66 | .068 | |
| sep lean & fat, roasted | 318 | 50.7 | 23.6 | 2.7 | 81 | 3 | 0 | .28 | .35 | 8 | 44 | 10 | 19 | 1.96 | .009 |
| *3.5 oz* | 100 | 24.7 | 0.0 | 8.5 | 0.0 | 8 | .59 | 4.9 | .56 | .68 | 368 | 224 | .89 | .074 | |
| sep lean, braised | 277 | 49.9 | 14.4 | 1.8 | 97 | 3 | 0 | .32 | .39 | 8 | 52 | 12 | 23 | 2.82 | .012 |
| *3.5 oz* | 100 | 34.4 | 0.0 | 5.0 | 0.0 | 9 | .59 | 6.5 | .52 | .66 | 501 | 250 | 1.26 | .100 | |
| sep lean, broiled | 258 | 54.5 | 14.9 | 1.8 | 94 | 2 | 0 | .32 | .40 | 9 | 67 | 15 | 30 | 2.38 | .020 |
| *3.5 oz* | 100 | 28.8 | 0.0 | 5.2 | 0.0 | 6 | .89 | 5.2 | .70 | .75 | 439 | 266 | .81 | .080 | |
| sep lean, pan fried | 257 | 55.1 | 15.3 | 1.9 | 81 | 2 | 0 | .35 | .44 | 8 | 50 | 9 | 28 | 2.06 | .007 |
| *3.5 oz* | 100 | 28.0 | 0.0 | 5.3 | 0.0 | 8 | .77 | 5.2 | .62 | .79 | 465 | 271 | .80 | .075 | |
| sep lean, roasted | 245 | 57.0 | 13.8 | 1.7 | 79 | 3 | 0 | .31 | .40 | 9 | 46 | 11 | 21 | 2.22 | .011 |
| *3.5 oz* | 100 | 28.2 | 0.0 | 4.8 | 0.0 | 8 | .64 | 5.4 | .55 | .58 | 423 | 256 | 1.00 | .078 | |
| **ham, cured, lean** | | | | | | | | | | | | | | | |
| cnd | 120 | 73.5 | 4.6 | 0.4 | 38 | 0 | 27[a] | .23 | .45 | 6 | 1255 | 6 | 17 | 1.93 | .025 |
| *3.5 oz* | 100 | 18.5 | 0.0 | 1.5 | 0.0 | 0 | .84 | 5.3 | .82 | .49 | 364 | 224 | .94 | .084 | |
| cnd, roasted | 136 | 69.5 | 4.9 | 0.4 | 30 | 0 | 28[a] | .25 | .45 | 5 | 1135 | 6 | 21 | 2.23 | .024 |
| *3.5 oz* | 100 | 21.2 | 0.5 | 1.6 | 0.0 | 0 | 1.04 | 4.9 | .71 | .57 | 348 | 209 | .92 | .050 | |
| roasted[b] | 145 | 67.7 | 5.5 | 0.5 | 53 | 0 | 21[a] | .20 | .40 | 3 | 1203 | 8 | 14 | 2.88 | .054 |
| *3.5 oz* | 100 | 20.9 | 1.5 | 1.8 | 0.0 | 0 | .75 | 4.0 | .65 | .40 | 287 | 196 | 1.48 | .079 | |
| unheated[b] | 131 | 70.5 | 5.0 | 0.5 | 47 | 0 | 26[a] | .22 | .46 | 4 | 1429 | 7 | 17 | 1.93 | .033 |
| *3.5 oz* | 100 | 19.4 | 1.0 | 1.6 | 0.0 | 0 | .93 | 4.8 | .75 | .47 | 350 | 218 | .76 | .074 | |
| **ham, cured, regular** | | | | | | | | | | | | | | | |
| center slice, sep lean & fat, unheated[b] | 203 | 63.5 | 12.9 | 1.4 | 54 | 0 | | .21 | .47 | 4 | 1386 | 7 | 16 | 1.88 | .031 |
| *3.5 oz* | 100 | 20.2 | 0.1 | 4.6 | 0.0 | 0 | .85 | 4.8 | .80 | .50 | 337 | 215 | .75 | .074 | |
| cnd | 190 | 66.5 | 13.0 | 1.5 | 39 | 0 | 22[a] | .23 | .48 | 5 | 1240 | 6 | 14 | 1.66 | .023 |
| *3.5 oz* | 100 | 17.0 | 0.0 | 4.3 | 0.0 | 0 | .96 | 3.2 | .78 | .39 | 316 | 175 | .83 | .067 | |
| cnd, roasted | 226 | 60.9 | 15.2 | 1.8 | 62 | 0 | 14[a] | .26 | .30 | 5 | 941 | 8 | 17 | 2.50 | .029 |
| *3.5 oz* | 100 | 20.5 | 0.4 | 5.0 | 0.0 | 0 | .82 | 5.3 | 1.06 | .73 | 357 | 243 | 1.37 | .130 | |
| roasted[b] | 178 | 64.5 | 9.0 | 1.4 | 59 | 0 | 23[a] | .33 | .31 | | 1500 | 8 | 22 | 2.47 | .041 |
| *3.5 oz* | 100 | 22.6 | 0.0 | 3.1 | 0.0 | 0 | .73 | 6.2 | .70 | .72 | 409 | 281 | 1.34 | .145 | |
| unheated[b] | 182 | 64.6 | 10.6 | 1.2 | 57 | 0 | 28[a] | .25 | .34 | 3 | 1317 | 7 | 19 | 2.14 | .031 |
| *3.5 oz* | 100 | 17.6 | 3.1 | 3.4 | 0.0 | 0 | .86 | 5.3 | .83 | .45 | 332 | 247 | .99 | .099 | |
| **ham patties** | | | | | | | | | | | | | | | |
| grilled[c] | 203 | 30.6 | 18.4 | 2.0 | 43 | 0 | 0 | .11 | .10 | | 632 | 5 | 6 | 1.13 | |
| *1 patty* | 60 | 7.9 | 1.0 | 6.6 | | 0 | .21 | 1.9 | .42 | .16 | 145 | 60 | .96 | .060 | |
| unheated[c] | 206 | 35.5 | 18.4 | 2.0 | 46 | 0 | 0 | .10 | .10 | | 709 | 5 | 6 | 1.02 | |
| *1 patty* | 65 | 8.3 | 1.1 | 6.6 | | 0 | .30 | 2.0 | .71 | .20 | 156 | 97 | .69 | .046 | |
| **leg** | | | | | | | | | | | | | | | |
| sep lean & fat, roasted | 294 | 52.4 | 20.7 | 2.3 | 93 | 2 | 0 | .31 | .39 | 10 | 59 | 6 | 22 | 2.86 | .032 |
| *3.5 oz* | 100 | 25.0 | 0.0 | 7.5 | 0.0 | 8 | .63 | 4.6 | .70 | .59 | 329 | 247 | 1.00 | .100 | |
| sep lean, roasted | 220 | 59.7 | 11.0 | 1.3 | 94 | 2 | 0 | .35 | .45 | 12 | 64 | 7 | 25 | 3.26 | .037 |
| *3.5 oz* | 100 | 28.3 | 0.0 | 3.8 | 0.0 | 7 | .69 | 4.9 | .72 | .67 | 373 | 281 | 1.12 | .108 | |
| **loin** | | | | | | | | | | | | | | | |
| sep lean & fat, braised | 368 | 43.8 | 27.9 | 3.2 | 102 | 3 | 0 | .30 | .36 | 4 | 65 | 8 | 20 | 3.03 | .015 |
| *3.5 oz* | 100 | 27.2 | 0.0 | 10.1 | 0.0 | 9 | .61 | 6.0 | .79 | .57 | 345 | 199 | 1.16 | .109 | |
| sep lean & fat, broiled | 346 | 48.0 | 27.2 | 3.1 | 94 | 3 | 0 | .36 | .38 | 5 | 66 | 7 | 25 | 2.45 | .009 |
| *3.5 oz* | 100 | 23.6 | 0.0 | 9.8 | 0.0 | 9 | .84 | 5.3 | .98 | .75 | 351 | 235 | .81 | .089 | |
| sep lean & fat, roasted | 319 | 51.3 | 24.3 | 2.8 | 90 | 2 | 0 | .32 | .38 | 5 | 63 | 8 | 19 | 2.62 | .014 |
| *3.5 oz* | 100 | 23.4 | 0.0 | 8.8 | 0.0 | 8 | .72 | 5.4 | .87 | .55 | 318 | 221 | 1.01 | .093 | |
| sep lean, braised | 273 | 51.1 | 14.6 | 1.8 | 105 | 2 | 0 | .36 | .45 | 5 | 75 | 10 | 24 | 3.72 | .018 |
| *3.5 oz* | 100 | 33.0 | 0.0 | 5.0 | 0.0 | 8 | .69 | 6.9 | .84 | .70 | 419 | 239 | 1.40 | .125 | |

[a] Contains added ascorbic acid or sodium ascorbate.
[b] Ham is fully cooked as purchased.
[c] Fully cooked as purchased.

| | KCAL | H₂O (g) | FAT (g) | PUFA (g) | CHOL (mg) | A (RE) | C (mg) | B-2 (mg) | B-6 (mg) | FOL (mcg) | Na (mg) | Ca (mg) | Mg (mg) | Zn (mg) | Mn (mg) |
|---|---|---|---|---|---|---|---|---|---|---|---|---|---|---|---|
| | WT (g) | PRO (g) | CHO (g) | SFA (g) | DFIB (g) | A (IU) | B-1 (mg) | NIA (mg) | B-12 (mcg) | PANT (mg) | K (mg) | P (mg) | Fe (mg) | Cu (mg) | |
| sep lean, broiled | 257 | 55.5 | 15.3 | 1.9 | 95 | 2 | 0 | .42 | .46 | 5 | 75 | 7 | 29 | 2.92 | .010 |
| *3.5 oz* | 100 | 27.8 | 0.0 | 5.3 | 0.0 | 8 | .97 | 6.0 | 1.08 | .91 | 418 | 279 | .93 | .098 | |
| sep lean, roasted | 240 | 58.1 | 13.9 | 1.7 | 90 | 2 | 0 | .36 | .45 | 6 | 69 | 9 | 22 | 3.04 | .016 |
| *3.5 oz* | 100 | 26.9 | 0.0 | 4.8 | 0.0 | 7 | .80 | 6.0 | .93 | .64 | 367 | 254 | 1.15 | .101 | |
| **loin blade** | | | | | | | | | | | | | | | |
| sep lean & fat, braised | 410 | 41.0 | 34.1 | 3.9 | 108 | 2 | 0 | .28 | .32 | 4 | 69 | 14 | 17 | 3.85 | .013 |
| *3.5 oz* | 100 | 24.0 | 0.0 | 12.3 | 0.0 | 7 | .49 | 4.8 | .76 | .52 | 334 | 176 | 1.30 | .109 | |
| sep lean & fat, broiled | 393 | 44.4 | 33.8 | 3.9 | 98 | 3 | 0 | .32 | .34 | 4 | 67 | 11 | 21 | 3.05 | .008 |
| *3.5 oz* | 100 | 20.7 | 0.0 | 12.2 | 0.0 | 9 | .66 | 4.2 | .94 | .66 | 332 | 202 | .91 | .090 | |
| sep lean & fat, pan fried | 414 | 42.5 | 36.9 | 4.2 | 95 | 3 | 0 | .29 | .29 | 1 | 61 | 10 | 19 | 2.71 | .007 |
| *3.5 oz* | 100 | 18.8 | 0.0 | 13.3 | 0.0 | 10 | .61 | 3.9 | .87 | .59 | 297 | 182 | .82 | .083 | |
| sep lean & fat, roasted | 364 | 48.2 | 30.5 | 3.5 | 90 | 3 | 0 | .30 | .36 | 4 | 61 | 12 | 15 | 2.99 | .011 |
| *3.5 oz* | 100 | 21.1 | 0.0 | 10.9 | 0.0 | 0 | .52 | 4.2 | .76 | .60 | 293 | 173 | 1.07 | .090 | |
| sep lean, braised | 313 | 48.6 | 20.6 | 2.5 | 113 | 2 | 0 | .33 | .41 | 5 | 81 | 17 | 20 | 4.93 | .016 |
| *3.5 oz* | 100 | 29.7 | 0.0 | 7.1 | 0.0 | 5 | .55 | 5.6 | .82 | .65 | 417 | 214 | 1.62 | .128 | |
| sep lean, broiled | 300 | 52.4 | 21.5 | 2.6 | 100 | 3 | 0 | .38 | .43 | 5 | 77 | 13 | 25 | 3.79 | .009 |
| *3.5 oz* | 100 | 24.9 | 0.0 | 7.4 | 0.0 | 8 | .76 | 4.7 | 1.04 | .82 | 408 | 245 | 1.08 | .101 | |
| sep lean, pan fried | 283 | 53.5 | 19.8 | 2.5 | 97 | 2 | 0 | .37 | .40 | 0 | 74 | 13 | 24 | 3.67 | .009 |
| *3.5 oz* | 100 | 24.3 | 0.0 | 6.8 | 0.0 | 8 | .74 | 4.5 | 1.00 | .80 | 394 | 237 | 1.04 | .098 | |
| sep lean, roasted | 279 | 55.8 | 19.3 | 2.3 | 89 | 2 | 0 | .34 | .44 | 5 | 68 | 14 | 17 | 3.59 | .013 |
| *3.5 oz* | 100 | 24.7 | 0.0 | 6.7 | 0.0 | 8 | .57 | 4.7 | .80 | .53 | 346 | 201 | 1.25 | .099 | |
| **rump** | | | | | | | | | | | | | | | |
| sep lean & fat, roasted | 274 | 54.7 | 17.8 | 2.0 | 95 | 3 | 0 | .33 | .27 | 6 | 61 | 7 | 26 | 2.74 | .024 |
| *3.5 oz* | 100 | 26.6 | 0.0 | 6.5 | 0.0 | 10 | .71 | 4.7 | .71 | .68 | 356 | 260 | 1.05 | .103 | |
| sep lean, roasted | 221 | 59.3 | 10.7 | 1.3 | 96 | 3 | 0 | .36 | .30 | 6 | 65 | 7 | 29 | 3.01 | .026 |
| *3.5 oz* | 100 | 29.1 | 0.0 | 3.7 | 0.0 | 9 | .76 | 5.0 | .73 | .75 | 391 | 285 | 1.14 | .109 | |
| **sausage, fresh** | | | | | | | | | | | | | | | |
| ckd | 48 | 5.8 | 4.1 | 0.5 | 11 | | 0 | .03 | .04 | | 168 | 4 | 2 | .33 | .009 |
| *1 link* | 13 | 2.6 | 0.1 | 1.4 | 0.0 | | .10 | 0.6 | .22 | .09 | 47 | 24 | .16 | .018 | |
| ckd | 100 | 12.0 | 8.4 | 1.0 | 22 | | 1 | .07 | .09 | | 349 | 9 | 5 | .68 | .019 |
| *1 patty* | 27 | 5.3 | 0.3 | 2.9 | 0.0 | | .20 | 1.2 | .47 | .20 | 97 | 50 | .34 | .038 | |
| w/ beef, ckd | 52 | 5.8 | 4.7 | 0.5 | | | | .02 | .01 | | 105 | | 1 | .24 | |
| *1 link* | 13 | 1.8 | 0.4 | 1.7 | | | | .05 | 0.4 | .06 | .06 | | 14 | .15 | .000 |
| **shank** | | | | | | | | | | | | | | | |
| sep lean & fat, roasted | 303 | 52.8 | 22.1 | 2.5 | 92 | 2 | 0 | .30 | .39 | 5 | 58 | 6 | 21 | 2.93 | .028 |
| *3.5 oz* | 100 | 24.3 | 0.0 | 8.0 | 0.0 | 8 | .58 | 4.5 | .69 | .59 | 310 | 239 | .97 | .098 | |
| sep lean, roasted | 215 | 60.4 | 10.5 | 1.3 | 92 | 2 | 0 | .34 | .46 | 6 | 64 | 7 | 25 | 3.45 | .034 |
| *3.5 oz* | 100 | 28.2 | 0.0 | 3.6 | 0.0 | 7 | .63 | 4.9 | .71 | .69 | 360 | 278 | 1.11 | .108 | |
| **shoulder** | | | | | | | | | | | | | | | |
| sep lean & fat, roasted | 326 | 51.6 | 25.7 | 2.9 | 96 | 2 | 0 | .32 | .33 | 4 | 68 | 7 | 18 | 3.59 | .022 |
| *3.5 oz* | 100 | 22.0 | 0.0 | 9.3 | 0.0 | 8 | .54 | 4.0 | .83 | .50 | 304 | 200 | 1.31 | .115 | |
| sep lean, roasted | 244 | 58.8 | 15.0 | 1.8 | 97 | 2 | 0 | .36 | .40 | 5 | 76 | 8 | 20 | 4.24 | .026 |
| *3.5 oz* | 100 | 25.4 | 0.0 | 5.2 | 0.0 | 7 | .58 | 4.3 | .88 | .58 | 352 | 231 | 1.52 | .129 | |
| **sirloin** | | | | | | | | | | | | | | | |
| sep lean & fat, braised | 352 | 45.1 | 25.7 | 2.9 | 106 | 3 | 0 | .30 | .36 | 4 | 54 | 6 | 23 | 2.56 | .014 |
| *3.5 oz* | 100 | 28.0 | 0.0 | 9.3 | 0.0 | 0 | .66 | 5.0 | .66 | .59 | 369 | 196 | 1.13 | .116 | |
| sep lean & fat, broiled | 331 | 49.3 | 25.3 | 2.9 | 97 | 3 | 0 | .35 | .44 | 5 | 55 | 5 | 29 | 2.03 | .009 |
| *3.5 oz* | 100 | 24.2 | 0.0 | 9.1 | 0.0 | 9 | .90 | 4.3 | .80 | .76 | 367 | 226 | .78 | .095 | |
| sep lean & fat, roasted | 291 | 54.0 | 20.4 | 2.3 | 91 | 2 | 0 | .31 | .38 | 5 | 59 | 9 | 22 | 2.27 | .025 |
| *3.5 oz* | 100 | 25.0 | 0.0 | 7.4 | 0.0 | 8 | .74 | 5.2 | .76 | .57 | 337 | 229 | 1.00 | .099 | |
| sep lean, braised | 261 | 52.1 | 13.0 | 1.6 | 110 | 3 | 0 | .35 | .53 | 5 | 59 | 7 | 28 | 3.07 | .017 |
| *3.5 oz* | 100 | 33.5 | 0.0 | 4.5 | 0.0 | 8 | .74 | 5.7 | .67 | .71 | 443 | 232 | 1.33 | .133 | |
| sep lean, broiled | 243 | 56.7 | 13.6 | 1.7 | 98 | 2 | 0 | .40 | .54 | 6 | 60 | 5 | 34 | 2.36 | .010 |
| *3.5 oz* | 100 | 28.3 | 0.0 | 4.7 | 0.0 | 8 | 1.03 | 4.8 | .84 | .91 | 434 | 265 | .89 | .105 | |
| sep lean, roasted | 236 | 58.7 | 13.2 | 1.6 | 90 | 2 | 0 | .33 | .42 | 6 | 62 | 10 | 24 | 2.49 | .028 |
| *3.5 oz* | 100 | 27.5 | 0.0 | 4.5 | 0.0 | 7 | .80 | 5.6 | .78 | .63 | 370 | 252 | 1.09 | .107 | |

| | KCAL / WT (g) | H₂O(g) / PRO(g) | FAT(g) / CHO(g) | PUFA(g) / SFA(g) | CHOL(mg) / DFIB(g) | A(RE) / A(IU) | C(mg) / B-1(mg) | B-2(mg) / NIA(mg) | B-6(mg) / B-12(mcg) | FOL(mcg) / PANT(mg) | Na(mg) / K(mg) | Ca(mg) / P(mg) | Mg(mg) / Fe(mg) | Zn(mg) / Cu(mg) | Mn(mg) |
|---|---|---|---|---|---|---|---|---|---|---|---|---|---|---|---|
| spareribs, sep lean & fat, braised | 397 | 40.4 | 30.3 | 3.5 | 121 | 3 | | .38 | .35 | 4 | 93 | 47 | 24 | 4.60 | .014 |
| *3.5 oz* | 100 | 29.1 | 0.0 | 11.8 | 0.0 | 10 | .41 | 5.5 | 1.08 | .75 | 320 | 261 | 1.85 | .142 | |
| tenderloin, sep lean, roasted | 166 | 65.2 | 4.8 | 0.6 | 93 | 2 | 0 | .39 | .42 | 6 | 67 | 9 | 25 | 3.00 | .039 |
| *3.5 oz* | 100 | 28.8 | 0.0 | 1.7 | 0.0 | 7 | .94 | 4.7 | .55 | .69 | 538 | 288 | 1.54 | .160 | |
| **top loin** | | | | | | | | | | | | | | | |
| sep lean & fat, braised | 381 | 42.1 | 29.2 | 3.3 | 95 | 3 | 0 | .27 | .31 | 6 | 47 | 10 | 19 | 2.28 | .010 |
| *3.5 oz* | 100 | 27.7 | 0.0 | 10.6 | 0.0 | 10 | .52 | 5.5 | .54 | .53 | 399 | 204 | 1.03 | .088 | |
| sep lean & fat, broiled | 360 | 46.1 | 28.6 | 3.2 | 93 | 2 | 0 | .27 | .34 | 7 | 59 | 12 | 24 | 1.97 | .016 |
| *3.5 oz* | 100 | 23.7 | 0.0 | 10.4 | 0.0 | 8 | .76 | 4.6 | .67 | .61 | 357 | 219 | .70 | .074 | |
| sep lean & fat, pan fried | 392 | 44.0 | 33.2 | 3.7 | 84 | 3 | 0 | .28 | .33 | 6 | 45 | 7 | 21 | 1.62 | .006 |
| *3.5 oz* | 100 | 21.5 | 0.0 | 12.0 | 0.0 | 9 | .63 | 4.4 | .61 | .59 | 350 | 207 | .66 | .068 | |
| sep lean & fat, roasted | 330 | 49.7 | 25.1 | 2.8 | 82 | 3 | 0 | .27 | .34 | 7 | 44 | 10 | 18 | 1.92 | .009 |
| *3.5 oz* | 100 | 24.2 | 0.0 | 9.1 | 0.0 | 8 | .58 | 4.8 | .56 | .50 | 359 | 219 | .88 | .073 | |
| sep lean, braised | 277 | 49.9 | 14.4 | 1.8 | 97 | 3 | 0 | .32 | .39 | 8 | 52 | 12 | 23 | 2.82 | .012 |
| *3.5 oz* | 100 | 34.4 | 0.0 | 5.0 | 0.0 | 9 | .59 | 6.5 | .52 | .66 | 501 | 250 | 1.26 | .100 | |
| sep lean, broiled | 258 | 54.5 | 14.9 | 1.8 | 94 | 2 | 0 | .32 | .40 | 9 | 67 | 15 | 30 | 2.38 | .020 |
| *3.5 oz* | 100 | 28.8 | 0.0 | 5.2 | 0.0 | 6 | .89 | 5.2 | .70 | .75 | 439 | 266 | .81 | .080 | |
| sep lean, pan fried | 257 | 55.1 | 15.3 | 1.9 | 81 | 2 | 0 | .35 | .44 | 8 | 50 | 9 | 28 | 2.06 | .007 |
| *3.5 oz* | 100 | 28.0 | 0.0 | 5.3 | 0.0 | 8 | .77 | 5.2 | .62 | .79 | 465 | 271 | .80 | .075 | |
| sep lean, roasted | 245 | 57.0 | 13.8 | 1.7 | 79 | 3 | 0 | .31 | .40 | 9 | 46 | 11 | 21 | 2.22 | .011 |
| *3.5 oz* | 100 | 28.2 | 0.0 | 4.8 | 0.0 | 8 | .64 | 5.4 | .55 | .58 | 423 | 256 | 1.00 | .078 | |

## 21.4. VEAL

| | KCAL / WT (g) | H₂O(g) / PRO(g) | FAT(g) / CHO(g) | PUFA(g) / SFA(g) | CHOL(mg) / DFIB(g) | A(RE) / A(IU) | C(mg) / B-1(mg) | B-2(mg) / NIA(mg) | B-6(mg) / B-12(mcg) | FOL(mcg) / PANT(mg) | Na(mg) / K(mg) | Ca(mg) / P(mg) | Mg(mg) / Fe(mg) | Zn(mg) / Cu(mg) | Mn(mg) |
|---|---|---|---|---|---|---|---|---|---|---|---|---|---|---|---|
| **chuck, braised/pot roastd/stewed** | 200 | 49.7 | 10.9 | | | | | .25 | | | 41 | 10 | | | |
| *3 oz* | 85 | 23.7 | 0.0 | 5.2 | | | .08 | 5.4 | | | 190 | 128 | 3.00 | | |
| **leg, sliced, frzn, Am Hosp Co** | 135 | | 3.9 | | 75 | | | .20 | | | 42 | 6 | | | |
| *3 oz* | 85 | 24.9 | 0.1 | | | | .14 | 6.9 | | | 261 | | 2.40 | | |
| **loin, braised/broiled** | 199 | 50.1 | 11.4 | | | | | .21 | | | 55 | 9 | | | |
| *3 oz* | 85 | 22.4 | 0.0 | 5.5 | | | .06 | 4.6 | | | 251 | 191 | 2.70 | | |
| **plate (breast), braised/stewed** | 258 | 44.3 | 18.0 | | | | | .20 | | | 39 | 10 | | | |
| *3 oz* | 85 | 22.2 | 0.0 | 8.7 | | | .04 | 3.9 | | | 178 | 117 | 2.81 | | |
| **rib roast, roasted** | 229 | 46.4 | 14.4 | | | | | .26 | | | 57 | 10 | | | |
| *3 oz* | 85 | 23.1 | 0.0 | 6.9 | | | .11 | 6.6 | | | 259 | 211 | 2.90 | | |
| **round w/ rump, braised/broiled** | 184 | 51.3 | 9.4 | | | | | .21 | | | 56 | 9 | | | |
| *3 oz* | 85 | 23.0 | 0.0 | 4.5 | | | .06 | 4.6 | | | 258 | 196 | 2.70 | | |

## 21.5. VARIETY CUTS

| | KCAL / WT (g) | H₂O(g) / PRO(g) | FAT(g) / CHO(g) | PUFA(g) / SFA(g) | CHOL(mg) / DFIB(g) | A(RE) / A(IU) | C(mg) / B-1(mg) | B-2(mg) / NIA(mg) | B-6(mg) / B-12(mcg) | FOL(mcg) / PANT(mg) | Na(mg) / K(mg) | Ca(mg) / P(mg) | Mg(mg) / Fe(mg) | Zn(mg) / Cu(mg) | Mn(mg) |
|---|---|---|---|---|---|---|---|---|---|---|---|---|---|---|---|
| **brains** | | | | | | | | | | | | | | | |
| beef, pan fried | 196 | 70.8 | 15.8 | 2.3 | 1995 | 0 | 3 | .26 | .39 | 6 | 158 | 9 | 15 | 1.35 | .032 |
| *3.5 oz* | 100 | 12.6 | 0.0 | 3.7 | 0.0 | 0 | .13 | 3.8 | 15.2 | .57 | 354 | 386 | 2.22 | .220 | |
| beef, simmered | 160 | 73.3 | 12.5 | 1.4 | 2054 | 0 | 1 | .17 | .24 | 7 | 120 | 9 | 14 | 1.25 | .035 |
| *3.5 oz* | 100 | 11.1 | 0.0 | 2.9 | 0.0 | 0 | .08 | 2.2 | 8.60 | .57 | 240 | 352 | 2.21 | .240 | |
| pork, braised | 138 | 75.9 | 9.5 | 1.5 | 2552 | 0 | 14 | .22 | .14 | | 91 | 9 | 12 | 1.48 | .085 |
| *3.5 oz* | 100 | 12.1 | 0.0 | 2.2 | 0.0 | 0 | .08 | 3.3 | 1.42 | 1.82 | 195 | 220 | 1.82 | .263 | |
| **chitterlings, pork, simmered** | 303 | 62.4 | 28.8 | 7.2 | 143 | 0 | 0 | .08 | | | 39 | 27 | 10 | 5.06 | |
| *3.5 oz* | 100 | 10.3 | 0.0 | 10.1 | 0.0 | 0 | .00 | 0.1 | | | 8 | 47 | 3.70 | .233 | |
| **ears, pork, simmered** | 183 | 79.9 | 11.9 | | 99 | 0 | 0 | .08 | | | 183 | 20 | 8 | | |
| *1 ear* | 111 | 17.6 | 0.0 | | 0.0 | 0 | .02 | 0.6 | | | 44 | 27 | 1.65 | | |
| **feet, pork** | | | | | | | | | | | | | | | |
| cured, pickled | 203 | 68.6 | 16.1 | 1.8 | 92 | 0 | 0 | .04 | | | | 32 | 4 | | |
| *3.5 oz* | 100 | 13.5 | 0.0 | 5.6 | 0.0 | 0 | .01 | 0.4 | | | | 34 | | | |
| simmered | 194 | 66.0 | 12.4 | 1.4 | 100 | 0 | 0 | .06 | | | | 45 | 5 | | |
| *3.5 oz* | 100 | 19.2 | 0.0 | 4.3 | 0.0 | 0 | .01 | 0.5 | | | | 48 | | | |
| **heart** | | | | | | | | | | | | | | | |
| beef, simmered | 175 | 64.1 | 5.6 | 1.4 | 193 | 0 | 2 | 1.54 | .21 | 2 | 63 | 6 | 25 | 3.13 | .059 |
| *3.5 oz* | 100 | 28.8 | 0.4 | 1.7 | 0.0 | 0 | .14 | 4.1 | 14.30 | .87 | 233 | 250 | 7.51 | .740 | |

| | KCAL | H₂O (g) | FAT (g) | PUFA (g) | CHOL (mg) | A (RE) | C (mg) | B-2 (mg) | B-6 (mg) | FOL (mcg) | Na (mg) | Ca (mg) | Mg (mg) | Zn (mg) | Mn (mg) |
|---|---|---|---|---|---|---|---|---|---|---|---|---|---|---|---|
| | WT (g) | PRO (g) | CHO (g) | SFA (g) | DFIB (g) | A (IU) | B-1 (mg) | NIA (mg) | B-12 (mcg) | PANT (mg) | K (mg) | P (mg) | Fe (mg) | Cu (mg) | |
| lamb, braised | 377 | 78.4 | 20.9 | | | | 0 | 1.49 | | | | 20 | | | |
| *1 cup* | 145 | 42.8 | 1.5 | | | 150 | .30 | 9.3 | | | | 335 | | | |
| pork, braised | 191 | 87.8 | 6.5 | 1.7 | 285 | 9 | 3 | 2.20 | .50 | 5 | 46 | 9 | 32 | 3.99 | .094 |
| *1 heart* | 129 | 30.4 | 0.5 | 1.7 | 0.0 | 29 | .72 | 7.8 | 4.89 | 3.19 | 266 | 230 | 7.52 | .655 | |
| **jowl, pork, raw** | 655 | 22.2 | 69.6 | 8.1 | 90 | 3 | | .24 | .09 | 1 | 25 | 4 | 3 | | .005 |
| *3.5 oz* | 100 | 6.4 | 0.0 | 25.3 | 0.0 | 9 | .39 | 4.5 | .82 | .25 | 148 | 86 | .42 | .040 | |
| **kidneys** | | | | | | | | | | | | | | | |
| beef, simmered | 144 | 68.8 | 3.4 | 0.7 | 387 | 373 | 1 | 4.06 | .52 | 98 | 134 | 17 | 18 | 4.22 | .185 |
| *3.5 oz* | 100 | 25.5 | 1.0 | 1.1 | 0.0 | 1241 | .19 | 6.0 | 51.30 | 1.69 | 179 | 306 | 7.31 | .680 | |
| pork, braised | 151 | 68.7 | 4.7 | 0.4 | 480 | 78 | 11 | 1.59 | .46 | 41 | 80 | 13 | 18 | 4.15 | .149 |
| *3.5 oz* | 100 | 25.4 | 0.0 | 1.5 | 0.0 | 260 | .40 | 5.8 | 7.79 | 2.87 | 143 | 240 | 5.29 | .683 | |
| **liver** | | | | | | | | | | | | | | | |
| beef, braised | 161 | 65.9 | 4.9 | 1.1 | 389 | 10602 | 23 | 4.10 | .91 | 217 | 70 | 7 | 20 | 6.07 | .413 |
| *3.5 oz* | 100 | 24.4 | 3.4 | 1.9 | 0.0 | 35679 | .20 | 10.7 | 71.00 | 4.57 | 235 | 404 | 6.77 | 2.789 | |
| beef, pan fried | 217 | 55.7 | 8.0 | 1.8 | 482 | 10728 | 23 | 4.14 | 1.43 | 220 | 106 | 11 | 23 | 5.45 | .423 |
| *3.5 oz* | 100 | 26.7 | 7.9 | 2.8 | 0.0 | 36105 | .21 | 14.4 | 111.80 | 5.92 | 364 | 461 | 6.28 | 2.822 | |
| lamb, broiled | 117 | 22.7 | 5.6 | | | | 16 | 2.30 | | | 38 | 7 | | | |
| *1 slice* | 45 | 14.5 | 1.3 | | | 33530 | .22 | 11.2 | | | 149 | 257 | 8.10 | | |
| pork, braised | 165 | 64.3 | 4.4 | 1.1 | 355 | 5399 | 24 | 2.20 | .57 | 163 | 49 | 10 | 14 | 6.72 | .300 |
| *3.5 oz* | 100 | 26.0 | 3.8 | 1.4 | 0.0 | 17997 | .26 | 8.4 | 18.67 | 4.77 | 150 | 241 | 17.92 | .634 | |
| **lungs** | | | | | | | | | | | | | | | |
| beef, braised | 120 | 76.4 | 3.7 | 0.5 | 277 | 12 | 33 | .14 | .02 | 8 | 101 | 11 | 10 | 1.64 | .015 |
| *3.5 oz* | 100 | 20.4 | 0.0 | 1.3 | 0.0 | 39 | .04 | 2.5 | 2.59 | .62 | 173 | 178 | 5.40 | .221 | |
| lamb, raw | 103 | 76.7 | 2.3 | | | | | | | | | | | | |
| *3.5 oz* | 100 | 19.3 | 0.0 | | 0.0 | | | | | | | 180 | | | |
| pork, braised | 99 | 80.0 | 3.1 | 0.4 | 387 | 0 | 8 | .32 | .08 | | 81 | 8 | 12 | 2.45 | |
| *3.5 oz* | 100 | 16.6 | 0.0 | 1.1 | 0.0 | 0 | .08 | 1.9 | 2.03 | .66 | 151 | 186 | 16.41 | | |
| **pancreas** | | | | | | | | | | | | | | | |
| beef, braised | 271 | 55.6 | 17.2 | | | 0 | 20 | .49 | .18 | | 60 | 16 | 21 | 4.60 | .208 |
| *3.5 oz* | 100 | 27.1 | 0.0 | | 0.0 | 0 | .18 | 4.0 | 16.60 | 4.25 | 246 | 453 | 2.61 | .089 | |
| pork, braised | 219 | 60.3 | 10.8 | | 315 | 0 | 6 | .66 | | | 42 | 16 | 23 | 4.29 | .198 |
| *3.5 oz* | 100 | 28.5 | 0.0 | | 0.0 | 0 | .09 | 3.2 | 17.07 | 4.74 | 168 | 291 | 2.69 | .110 | |
| **spleen** | | | | | | | | | | | | | | | |
| beef, braised | 145 | 70.0 | 4.2 | | 347 | 0 | 50 | .30 | .04 | | 57 | 12 | 19 | 2.79 | .075 |
| *3.5 oz* | 100 | 25.1 | 0.0 | | 0.0 | 0 | .05 | 5.6 | 5.02 | | 284 | 305 | 39.36 | .924 | |
| lamb, raw | 115 | 74.4 | 3.9 | | | | | | | | | | | | |
| *3.5 oz* | 100 | 18.8 | 0.0 | | 0.0 | | | | | | | | | | |
| pork, braised | 149 | 66.7 | 3.2 | 0.2 | 504 | 0 | 12 | .26 | .06 | | | 13 | | 3.54 | .045 |
| *3.5 oz* | 100 | 28.2 | 0.0 | 1.1 | 0.0 | 0 | .14 | 5.9 | 2.76 | .89 | 227 | 283 | 22.2 | .133 | |
| **stomach, pork, raw** | 157 | 73.6 | 9.6 | | 193 | | | .12 | .04 | | 52 | 10 | | 2.01 | |
| *3.5 oz* | 100 | 16.5 | 0.0 | | 0.0 | | .09 | 4.5 | .99 | | 201 | 155 | 2.18 | .365 | |
| **sweetbreads** | | | | | | | | | | | | | | | |
| beef (yearlings), ckd | 272 | 42.2 | 19.7 | | | | | | | | 99 | | | | |
| *3 oz* | 85 | 22.0 | 0.0 | | | | | | | | 368 | 309 | | | |
| calf, ckd | 143 | 53.3 | 2.7 | | | | | .14 | | | | | | | |
| *3 oz* | 85 | 27.7 | 0.0 | | | | .05 | 2.5 | | | | | | | |
| lamb, ckd | 149 | 54.9 | 5.2 | | | | | | | | | | | | |
| *3 oz* | 85 | 23.9 | 0.0 | | | | | | | | | 173 | | | |
| **tail, pork, simmered** | 396 | 46.7 | 35.8 | 3.9 | 129 | 0 | 0 | .07 | | | | 14 | 7 | | |
| *3.5 oz* | 100 | 17.0 | 0.0 | 12.5 | 0.0 | 0 | .07 | 1.1 | | | | 47 | | | |
| **thymus, beef, braised** | 319 | 52.8 | 25.0 | | 294 | 0 | 30 | | | | 116 | | | | |
| *3.5 oz* | 100 | 21.9 | 0.0 | | 0.0 | 0 | | | 1.51 | | 423 | 364 | 1.49 | | |
| **tongue** | | | | | | | | | | | | | | | |
| beef, simmered | 283 | 56.1 | 20.7 | 0.8 | 107 | | 1 | .35 | .16 | 5 | 60 | 7 | 17 | 4.80 | .026 |
| *3.5 oz* | 100 | 22.1 | 0.3 | 8.9 | 0.0 | | .03 | 2.2 | 5.90 | .52 | 180 | 142 | 3.39 | .220 | |

| | KCAL / WT (g) | H₂O (g) / PRO (g) | FAT (g) / CHO (g) | PUFA (g) / SFA (g) | CHOL (mg) / DFIB (g) | A (RE) / A (IU) | C (mg) / B-1 (mg) | B-2 (mg) / NIA (mg) | B-6 (mg) / B-12 (mcg) | FOL (mcg) / PANT (mg) | Na (mg) / K (mg) | Ca (mg) / P (mg) | Mg (mg) / Fe (mg) | Zn (mg) / Cu (mg) | Mn (mg) |
|---|---|---|---|---|---|---|---|---|---|---|---|---|---|---|---|
| calf, braised | 32 | 13.7 | 1.2 | | | | | | | | | | | | |
| *1 slice* | 20 | 4.8 | 0.2 | | | | | | | | | | | | |
| lamb, braised | 51 | 12.0 | 3.6 | | | | | | | | | | | | |
| *1 slice* | 20 | 4.1 | 0.1 | | | | | | | | | 20 | | | |
| pork, braised | 271 | 56.9 | 18.6 | 1.9 | 146 | 0 | 2 | .51 | .23 | | 109 | 19 | 20 | 4.53 | |
| *3.5 oz* | 100 | 24.1 | 0.0 | 6.5 | 0.0 | 0 | .32 | 5.3 | 2.39 | | 237 | 174 | 4.99 | | |
| sheep, braised | 65 | 10.3 | 5.1 | | | | | | | | | | | | |
| *1 slice* | 20 | 4.0 | 0.5 | | | | | | | | | | .70 | | |
| **tripe, beef, raw** | 98 | 81.4 | 4.0 | 0.1 | 95 | 0 | 3 | .17 | | 2 | 46 | | 8 | 2.47 | |
| *3.5 oz* | 100 | 14.6 | 0.0 | 2.0 | 0.0 | 0 | .01 | 0.1 | 1.54 | | 270 | 79 | 1.95 | .090 | |

## 21.6. OTHER MEATS

| | KCAL / WT (g) | H₂O (g) / PRO (g) | FAT (g) / CHO (g) | PUFA (g) / SFA (g) | CHOL (mg) / DFIB (g) | A (RE) / A (IU) | C (mg) / B-1 (mg) | B-2 (mg) / NIA (mg) | B-6 (mg) / B-12 (mcg) | FOL (mcg) / PANT (mg) | Na (mg) / K (mg) | Ca (mg) / P (mg) | Mg (mg) / Fe (mg) | Zn (mg) / Cu (mg) | Mn (mg) |
|---|---|---|---|---|---|---|---|---|---|---|---|---|---|---|---|
| **beaver, roasted** | 211 | 47.8 | 11.6 | | | | | .32 | | | | | | | |
| *3 oz* | 85 | 24.8 | 0.0 | | | | .07 | | | | | | | | |
| **eel** | | | | | | | | | | | | | | | |
| raw | 156 | 58.0 | 9.9 | 0.8 | 107 | 2954 | | .03 | .06 | | 43 | 17 | | 1.38 | .030 |
| *3 oz* | 85 | 15.7 | 0.0 | 2.0 | | 886 | .13 | 3.0 | 2.55 | .20 | 232 | 183 | .43 | .020 | |
| ckd by dry heat | 200 | 50.4 | 12.7 | 1.0 | 137 | 3219 | | .04 | .07 | | 55 | 22 | | 1.76 | |
| *3 oz* | 85 | 20.1 | 0.0 | 2.6 | | 966 | .16 | 3.8 | 2.45 | | 297 | 235 | .54 | .025 | |
| smoked | 330 | 50.2 | 27.8 | | | | | | | | | | | | |
| *3.5 oz* | 100 | 18.6 | 0.0 | 6.0 | | | | | | | | | | | |
| **frog legs, raw** | 73 | 81.9 | 0.3 | | | | | .25 | | | | 18 | | | |
| *3.5 oz* | 100 | 16.4 | 0.0 | | | 0 | .14 | 1.2 | | | 147 | | 1.50 | | |
| **muskrat, roasted** | 153 | 67.3 | 4.1 | | | | | .21 | | | | | | | |
| *3.5 oz* | 100 | 27.2 | 0.0 | | | | .16 | | | | | | | | |
| **octopus, raw** | 70 | 68.2 | 0.9 | 0.2 | 41 | | | .03 | | | | 45 | | 1.43 | .021 |
| *3 oz* | 85 | 12.7 | 1.9 | 0.2 | | | .03 | 1.8 | | | | 158 | 4.51 | .370 | |
| **opossum, roasted** | 221 | 57.3 | 10.2 | | | | | .38 | | | | | | | |
| *3.5 oz* | 100 | 30.2 | 0.0 | | | | .12 | | | | | | | | |
| **rabbit, stewed** | 302 | 83.7 | 14.1 | | | | | .10 | | | 57 | 29 | | | |
| *1 cup diced* | 140 | 41.0 | 0.0 | | | | .07 | 15.8 | | | 515 | 363 | 2.10 | | |
| **racoon, roasted** | 255 | 54.8 | 14.5 | | | | | .52 | | | | | | | |
| *3.5 oz* | 100 | 29.2 | 0.0 | | | | .59 | | | | | | | | |
| **reindeer, lean, raw** | 127 | 73.3 | 3.8 | | | | | .68 | | | | | | | |
| *3.5 oz* | 100 | 21.8 | 0.0 | | | | .33 | 5.5 | | | | | 5.30 | | |
| **shark** | | | | | | | | | | | | | | | |
| raw | 111 | 62.5 | 3.8 | 1.3 | 43 | 198 | | .05 | | | 67 | 29 | 42 | .36 | .013 |
| *3 oz* | 85 | 17.8 | 0.0 | 0.8 | | 60 | .04 | 2.5 | 1.27 | .59 | 136 | 179 | .71 | .028 | |
| batter-dipped & fried[a] | 194 | 51.1 | 11.8 | 3.1 | 50 | 153 | | .08 | | | 103 | 42 | 37 | .41 | |
| *3 oz* | 85 | 15.8 | 5.4 | 2.7 | | 46 | .06 | 2.4 | 1.03 | | 132 | 165 | .94 | .036 | |
| **snail, raw** | 90 | 79.2 | 1.4 | | | | | | | | | | | | |
| *3.5 oz* | 100 | 16.1 | 2.0 | | | | | | | | | | 3.50 | | |
| **snail, giant african, raw** | 73 | 82.2 | 1.4 | | | | | | | | | | | | |
| *3.5 oz* | 100 | 9.9 | 4.4 | | | | | | | | | | | | |
| **squid** | | | | | | | | | | | | | | | |
| raw | 78 | 66.8 | 1.2 | 0.4 | 198 | | 4 | .35 | .05 | | 37 | 27 | 28 | 1.30 | .030 |
| *3 oz* | 85 | 13.2 | 2.6 | 0.3 | | | .02 | 1.8 | 1.10 | | 209 | 188 | .58 | 1.607 | |
| fried[b] | 149 | 54.9 | 6.4 | 1.8 | 221 | | 4 | .39 | .05 | | 260 | 33 | 33 | 1.48 | |
| *3 oz* | 85 | 15.3 | 6.6 | 1.6 | | | .05 | 2.2 | 1.04 | | 237 | 213 | .86 | 1.797 | |
| **turtle, green** | | | | | | | | | | | | | | | |
| cnd | 106 | 75.0 | 0.7 | | | | | | | | | | | | |
| *3.5 oz* | 100 | 23.4 | 0.0 | | | | | | | | | | | | |
| raw | 89 | 78.5 | 0.5 | | | | | | | | | | | | |
| *3.5 oz* | 100 | 19.8 | 0.0 | | | | | | | | | | | | |
| **turtle, terrapin (diamond back), raw** | 111 | 77.0 | 3.5 | | | | | | | | | | | | |
| *3.5 oz* | 100 | 18.6 | 0.0 | | 0.0 | | | | | | | | 3.20 | | |
| **venison, lean, raw** | 107 | 62.9 | 3.4 | | | | | .41 | | | | 9 | | | |
| *3 oz* | 85 | 17.9 | 0.0 | 2.1 | | | .20 | 5.4 | | | | 212 | | | |

[a] Prepared w/ flour, oil, egg, milk, baking powder & salt.   [b] Dipped in flour & salt before frying.

| KCAL | H₂O (g) | FAT (g) | PUFA (g) | CHOL (mg) | A (RE) | C (mg) | B-2 (mg) | B-6 (mg) | FOL (mcg) | Na (mg) | Ca (mg) | Mg (mg) | Zn (mg) | Mn (mg) |
|---|---|---|---|---|---|---|---|---|---|---|---|---|---|---|
| WT (g) | PRO (g) | CHO (g) | SFA (g) | DFIB (g) | A (IU) | B-1 (mg) | NIA (mg) | B-12 (mcg) | PANT (mg) | K (mg) | P (mg) | Fe (mg) | Cu (mg) | |
| **whale meat, raw** | | | | | | | | | | | | | | |
| 156 | 70.9 | 7.5 | | | | 6 | .08 | | | | 78 | 12 | | |
| *3.5 oz* | | | | | | | | | | | | | | |
| 100 | 20.6 | 0.0 | 1.0 | | 1860 | .09 | | | | 22 | 144 | | | |

## 22. MEATS, LUNCHEON[a]

| KCAL | H₂O (g) | FAT (g) | PUFA (g) | CHOL (mg) | A (RE) | C (mg) | B-2 (mg) | B-6 (mg) | FOL (mcg) | Na (mg) | Ca (mg) | Mg (mg) | Zn (mg) | Mn (mg) |
|---|---|---|---|---|---|---|---|---|---|---|---|---|---|---|
| WT (g) | PRO (g) | CHO (g) | SFA (g) | DFIB (g) | A (IU) | B-1 (mg) | NIA (mg) | B-12 (mcg) | PANT (mg) | K (mg) | P (mg) | Fe (mg) | Cu (mg) | |
| **bbq loaf (pork & beef)** | | | | | | | | | | | | | | |
| 40 | 14.9 | 2.1 | 0.2 | 9 | | 4 | .06 | .06 | | 307 | 13 | 4 | .60 | .009 |
| *1 slice* | | | | | | | | | | | | | | |
| 23 | 3.6 | 1.5 | 0.7 | | | .08 | 0.5 | .39 | .36 | 76 | 30 | .27 | .020 | |
| **bbq loaf (pork & beef), Oscar Mayer** | | | | | | | | | | | | | | |
| 48 | 18.0 | 2.5 | | 13 | | 5 | .07 | .07 | | 346 | 16 | 5 | .70 | .012 |
| *1 oz slice* | | | | | | | | | | | | | | |
| 28 | 4.5 | 1.9 | | | 28 | .11 | 0.6 | .45 | .44 | 94 | 42 | .35 | .020 | |
| **beef** | | | | | | | | | | | | | | |
| chopped, smoked | | | | | | | | | | | | | | |
| 38 | 19.5 | 1.3 | 0.1 | 13 | | 6 | .05 | .10 | | 357 | | 6 | 1.11 | |
| *1 oz* | | | | | | | | | | | | | | |
| 28 | 5.7 | 0.5 | 0.5 | | | .02 | 1.3 | .49 | .17 | 107 | 51 | .81 | | |
| italian style, Oscar Mayer | | | | | | | | | | | | | | |
| 18 | 12.5 | 0.5 | | 6 | | | | | | 209 | 2 | 3 | .52 | |
| *1 slice* | | | | | | | | | | | | | | |
| 17 | 3.2 | 0.2 | | | | | | | | 54 | 35 | .47 | .050 | |
| jellied lunch meat | | | | | | | | | | | | | | |
| 31 | 21.2 | 0.9 | 0.1 | | | | | | | 375 | 3 | 5 | 1.01 | |
| *1 oz* | | | | | | | | | | | | | | |
| 28 | 5.4 | 0.0 | 0.4 | | | | | | | 114 | | .98 | .034 | |
| loaved lunch meat | | | | | | | | | | | | | | |
| 87 | 14.9 | 7.4 | 0.3 | 18 | | 4 | .06 | .05 | | 377 | 3 | 4 | .72 | .013 |
| *1 slice* | | | | | | | | | | | | | | |
| 28 | 4.1 | 0.8 | 3.2 | 0.0 | | .03 | 1.0 | 1.10 | .15 | 59 | 34 | .66 | .030 | |
| summer sausage | | | | | | | | | | | | | | |
| 77 | 11.7 | 6.8 | 0.3 | 17 | | 5 | .08 | .06 | | 286 | 3 | 3 | .59 | |
| *1 slice* | | | | | | | | | | | | | | |
| 23 | 3.6 | 0.1 | 2.8 | | | .04 | 1.0 | 1.27 | | 62 | 26 | .58 | .035 | |
| thin sliced lunch meat | | | | | | | | | | | | | | |
| 37 | 12.2 | 0.8 | 0.0 | 9 | | 3 | .04 | .07 | | 302 | 2 | 4 | .84 | .008 |
| *5 slices* | | | | | | | | | | | | | | |
| 21 | 5.9 | 1.2 | 0.4 | | | .02 | 1.1 | .54 | .12 | 90 | 35 | .57 | .007 | |
| **berliner (pork & beef)** | | | | | | | | | | | | | | |
| 53 | 14.0 | 4.0 | 0.4 | 11 | | 2 | .05 | .05 | | 298 | 3 | 3 | .57 | .009 |
| *1 slice* | | | | | | | | | | | | | | |
| 23 | 3.5 | 0.6 | 1.4 | 0.0 | | .09 | 0.7 | .61 | | 65 | 30 | .27 | .020 | |
| **blood sausage (blood pudding)[b]** | | | | | | | | | | | | | | |
| 95 | 11.8 | 8.6 | 0.9 | 30 | | | | | | | | | | |
| *1 slice* | | | | | | | | | | | | | | |
| 25 | 3.7 | 0.3 | 3.3 | | | | | | | | | | | |
| **bockwurst (pork, veal, milk, etc.), raw** | | | | | | | | | | | | | | |
| 200 | 36.5 | 17.9 | 1.9 | | | | | | | | | | | |
| *1 link* | | | | | | | | | | | | | | |
| 65 | 8.7 | 0.3 | 6.6 | | | | | | | | | | | |
| **bologna** | | | | | | | | | | | | | | |
| beef | | | | | | | | | | | | | | |
| 72 | 12.7 | 6.6 | 0.3 | 13 | | 5 | .03 | .03 | 1 | 226 | 3 | 3 | .50 | .006 |
| *1 slice* | | | | | | | | | | | | | | |
| 23 | 2.8 | 0.2 | 2.8 | 0.0 | | .01 | 0.6 | .33 | .06 | 36 | 20 | .38 | .010 | |
| beef & pork | | | | | | | | | | | | | | |
| 73 | 12.5 | 6.5 | 0.6 | 13 | | 5 | .03 | .04 | 1 | 234 | 3 | 3 | .45 | .01 |
| *1 slice* | | | | | | | | | | | | | | |
| 23 | 2.7 | 0.6 | 2.5 | 0.0 | | .04 | 0.6 | .31 | .06 | 41 | 21 | .35 | .020 | |
| beef garlic, Oscar Mayer | | | | | | | | | | | | | | |
| 73 | 12.5 | 6.8 | | 13 | | 4 | .02 | .03 | | 241 | 3 | 3 | .51 | |
| *1 slice* | | | | | | | | | | | | | | |
| 23 | 2.5 | 0.5 | | | | .01 | 0.5 | .25 | | 44 | 22 | .31 | .010 | |
| pork | | | | | | | | | | | | | | |
| 57 | 13.9 | 4.6 | 0.5 | 14 | | 8 | .04 | .06 | 1 | 272 | 3 | 3 | .47 | .008 |
| *1 slice* | | | | | | | | | | | | | | |
| 23 | 3.5 | 0.2 | 1.6 | 0.0 | | .12 | 0.9 | .21 | .17 | 65 | 32 | .18 | .017 | |
| turkey | | | | | | | | | | | | | | |
| 60 | 18.5 | 4.5 | 1.1 | 20 | | | .05 | .05 | | 222 | 26 | 4 | .64 | |
| *1 slice* | | | | | | | | | | | | | | |
| 28 | 3.9 | 0.6 | 1.4 | | | .01 | 1.1 | .44 | | 53 | 44 | .36 | .010 | |
| turkey, Louis Rich | | | | | | | | | | | | | | |
| 58 | 18.5 | 4.6 | 1.3 | 19 | | | | | | 225 | 31 | 5 | .59 | |
| *1 oz slice* | | | | | | | | | | | | | | |
| 28 | 3.6 | 0.5 | 1.5 | | | | | | | 48 | 45 | .41 | | |
| turkey, Oscar Mayer | | | | | | | | | | | | | | |
| 58 | 18.5 | 4.7 | | 19 | | 0 | .05 | | | 225 | 31 | 5 | .59 | .008 |
| *1 oz slice* | | | | | | | | | | | | | | |
| 28 | 3.6 | 0.5 | | | | .01 | 1.1 | .42 | | 48 | 45 | .41 | .020 | |
| w/ cheese, Oscar Mayer | | | | | | | | | | | | | | |
| 74 | 12.2 | 6.7 | | 14 | | 4 | .03 | .04 | 1 | 242 | 13 | 3 | .39 | |
| *1 slice* | | | | | | | | | | | | | | |
| 23 | 2.7 | 0.6 | | | | .05 | 0.6 | .29 | .08 | 40 | 41 | .28 | .020 | |
| **bratwurst, pork, ckd** | | | | | | | | | | | | | | |
| 256 | 47.7 | 22.0 | 2.3 | 51 | | 1 | .16 | .18 | | 473 | 38 | 12 | 1.96 | .039 |
| *1 link* | | | | | | | | | | | | | | |
| 85 | 12.0 | 1.8 | 7.9 | | | .43 | 2.7 | .81 | .27 | 180 | 126 | 1.09 | .079 | |
| **braunschweiger (pork liver sausage)** | | | | | | | | | | | | | | |
| 65 | 8.6 | 5.8 | 0.7 | 28 | 760 | 2 | .28 | .06 | | 206 | 2 | 2 | .51 | .028 |
| *1 slice* | | | | | | | | | | | | | | |
| 18 | 2.4 | 0.6 | 2.0 | 0.0 | 2529 | .05 | 1.5 | 3.62 | .61 | 36 | 30 | 1.68 | .043 | |
| german brand, Oscar Mayer | | | | | | | | | | | | | | |
| 94 | 14.2 | 8.4 | | 46 | | 10 | .47 | .09 | 26 | 341 | 3 | 4 | .86 | |
| *1 oz* | | | | | | | | | | | | | | |
| 28 | 3.9 | 0.5 | | | 5113 | .06 | 2.4 | 4.97 | .83 | 60 | 57 | 2.79 | .120 | |
| in tube, Oscar Mayer | | | | | | | | | | | | | | |
| 96 | 13.8 | 8.7 | | 41 | | 2 | .43 | .09 | 17 | 319 | 2 | 3 | .83 | |
| *1 oz* | | | | | | | | | | | | | | |
| 28 | 3.8 | 0.8 | | | 4668 | .06 | 2.3 | 5.19 | .81 | 50 | 52 | 2.68 | .080 | |
| **brotwurst (pork & beef w/ nfdm)** | | | | | | | | | | | | | | |
| 226 | 35.9 | 19.5 | 2.0 | 44 | | 20 | .16 | .09 | | 778 | 34 | 11 | 1.47 | .027 |
| *1 link* | | | | | | | | | | | | | | |
| 70 | 10.0 | 2.1 | 7.0 | | | .18 | 2.3 | 1.44 | .04 | 197 | 94 | .72 | .050 | |

[a] Some luncheon meats contain added ascorbic acid or sodium ascorbate.   [b] Sausage contains a large proportion of blood so that it is very dark in color.

| | KCAL | $H_2O$ (g) | FAT (g) | PUFA (g) | CHOL (mg) | A (RE) | C (mg) | B-2 (mg) | B-6 (mg) | FOL (mcg) | Na (mg) | Ca (mg) | Mg (mg) | Zn (mg) | Mn (mg) |
|---|---|---|---|---|---|---|---|---|---|---|---|---|---|---|---|
| | WT (g) | PRO (g) | CHO (g) | SFA (g) | DFIB (g) | A (IU) | B-1 (mg) | NIA (mg) | B-12 (mcg) | PANT (mg) | K (mg) | P (mg) | Fe (mg) | Cu (mg) | |
| **chicken roll, light meat** | 90 | 38.9 | 4.2 | 0.9 | 28 | | | .07 | | | 331 | 24 | 10 | .41 | |
| *2 slices* | 57 | 11.1 | 1.4 | 1.2 | | | .04 | 3.0 | | | 129 | 89 | .55 | .020 | |
| **chorizo (pork & beef)** | 265 | 19.1 | 23.0 | 2.1 | | | | | | | | | | | |
| *1 link* | 60 | 14.5 | 0.0 | 8.6 | | | | | | | | | | | |
| **corned beef loaf, jellied** | 43 | 19.6 | 1.7 | 0.1 | 13 | 2 | | .03 | .03 | 1 | 270 | 3 | 3 | 1.16 | .009 |
| *1 oz slice* | 28 | 6.5 | 0.0 | 0.7 | | | .00 | 0.5 | .36 | .05 | 29 | 21 | .58 | .017 | |
| **corned beef, sliced, Oscar Mayer** | 16 | 12.7 | 0.3 | | 5 | | | | | | 201 | 1 | 3 | .50 | |
| *1 thin slice* | 17 | 3.3 | 0.0 | | | | | | | | 53 | 34 | .48 | .050 | |
| **frankfurter** | | | | | | | | | | | | | | | |
| beef | 180 | 31.2 | 16.3 | 0.8 | 35 | 14 | | .06 | .07 | 2 | 585 | 11 | 2 | 1.24 | .019 |
| *1 frank (8 per 1 lb pkg)* | 57 | 6.9 | 1.0 | 6.9 | | | .03 | 1.4 | .87 | .17 | 94 | 50 | .81 | .030 | |
| beef | 142 | 24.6 | 12.8 | 0.6 | 27 | 11 | | .05 | .05 | 2 | 462 | 9 | 2 | .98 | .015 |
| *1 frank (10 per 1 lb pkg)* | 45 | 5.4 | 0.8 | 5.4 | | | .02 | 1.1 | .69 | .13 | 75 | 39 | .64 | .030 | |
| beef & pork | 144 | 24.2 | 13.1 | 1.2 | 22 | 12 | | .05 | .06 | 2 | 504 | 5 | 5 | .83 | .01 |
| *1 frank* | 45 | 5.1 | 1.2 | 4.8 | 0.0 | | .09 | 1.2 | .58 | .16 | 75 | 38 | .52 | .040 | |
| beef & pork, small, Oscar Mayer | 28 | 4.9 | 2.6 | | 5 | 2 | | .01 | .01 | 0 | 92 | 1 | 1 | .17 | |
| *1 frank* | 9 | 1.0 | 0.2 | | | | .02 | 0.2 | .11 | .04 | 15 | 8 | .10 | .010 | |
| chicken | 116 | 25.9 | 8.8 | 1.8 | 45 | | | .05 | | | 617 | 43 | | | |
| *1 frank* | 45 | 5.8 | 3.1 | 2.5 | | | .03 | 1.4 | | | | | .90 | | |
| nacho style w/ cheese, Oscar Mayer | 138 | 24.4 | 12.5 | | 30 | | | | | | 550 | 23 | 5 | .66 | |
| *1 frank* | 45 | 5.4 | 1.1 | | | | | | | | 75 | 77 | .34 | .070 | |
| w/ bacon & cheddar cheese, Oscar Mayer—1 frank | 143 | 23.5 | 12.7 | | 30 | | | | | | 509 | 17 | 5 | .75 | |
| | 45 | 6.1 | 1.1 | | | | | | | | 85 | 86 | .42 | .100 | |
| turkey | 100 | 28.8 | 8.1 | 2.1 | 39 | | | .08 | .09 | | 472 | 58 | 8 | 1.00 | |
| *1 frank* | 45 | 5.8 | 0.6 | 2.7 | | | .03 | 1.7 | .58 | | 72 | 83 | .71 | .020 | |
| turkey, Louis Rich | 103 | 28.3 | 8.5 | 2.2 | 39 | | | | | | 482 | 61 | 7 | .98 | |
| *1 frank* | 45 | 5.6 | 1.1 | 2.7 | | | | | | | 88 | 83 | .75 | | |
| turkey, Oscar Mayer | 103 | 28.3 | 8.5 | | 40 | 0 | | .08 | .09 | | 484 | 61 | 7 | .98 | .017 |
| *1 frank* | 45 | 5.6 | 1.1 | | | | .03 | 1.7 | .58 | | 88 | 83 | .75 | .030 | |
| turkey w/ cheese, Louis Rich | 108 | 27.1 | 8.6 | 2.2 | 40 | | | | | | 514 | 46 | 8 | .83 | |
| *1 frank* | 45 | 6.0 | 1.6 | 3.1 | | | | | | | 73 | 95 | .65 | | |
| turkey w/ cheese, Oscar Mayer | 103 | 25.9 | 8.3 | | 37 | | | | | | 487 | 55 | 7 | .85 | |
| *1 frank* | 43 | 5.8 | 1.5 | | | | | | | | 76 | 92 | .67 | .030 | |
| **ham, cured** | | | | | | | | | | | | | | | |
| chopped, cnd | 50 | 12.8 | 4.0 | 0.4 | 10 | 0 | 0 | .04 | .07 | | 287 | 1 | 3 | .38 | .005 |
| *1 slice* | 21 | 3.4 | 0.1 | 1.3 | 0.0 | 0 | .11 | 0.7 | .15 | | 60 | 29 | .20 | .010 | |
| chopped, packaged | 48 | 13.4 | 3.6 | 0.4 | 11 | 0 | 4 | .04 | .07 | 0 | 288 | 1 | 3 | .41 | .009 |
| *1 slice* | 21 | 3.6 | 0.0 | 1.2 | 0.0 | 0 | .13 | 0.8 | .19 | .06 | 67 | 33 | .17 | .013 | |
| minced | 55 | 12.0 | 4.3 | 0.5 | 15 | 0 | 6 | .04 | .06 | | 261 | 2 | 3 | .40 | .007 |
| *1 slice* | 21 | 3.4 | 0.4 | 1.5 | 0.0 | 0 | .15 | 0.9 | .20 | PANT | 65 | 33 | .16 | .016 | |
| sliced, lean (5% fat) | 37 | 20.0 | 1.4 | 0.1 | 13 | | 7 | .06 | .13 | 1 | 405 | 2 | 5 | .55 | .009 |
| *1 slice* | 28 | 5.5 | 0.3 | 0.5 | 0.0 | | .26 | 1.4 | .21 | .13 | 99 | 62 | .22 | .020 | |
| sliced, reg (11% fat) | 52 | 18.3 | 3.0 | 0.3 | | | 8 | .07 | .10 | 1 | 373 | 2 | 5 | .61 | .009 |
| *1 slice* | 28 | 5.5 | 0.9 | 1.0 | 0.0 | | .24 | 1.5 | .24 | .13 | 94 | 70 | .28 | .030 | |
| w/ black cracked pepper, Oscar Mayer | 24 | 15.4 | 0.9 | | 1 | | | | | | 269 | 1 | 4 | .41 | |
| *1 slice* | 21 | 3.9 | 0.1 | | | | | | | | 61 | 58 | .23 | .060 | |
| **ham & cheese loaf/roll** | 73 | 16.4 | 5.7 | 0.6 | 16 | | 7 | .05 | .07 | | 381 | 16 | 5 | .57 | .008 |
| *1 slice* | 28 | 4.7 | 0.4 | 2.1 | 0.0 | | .17 | 1.0 | .23 | .15 | 83 | 72 | .26 | .021 | |
| **headcheese (pork)** | 60 | 18.4 | 4.5 | 0.5 | 23 | | 6 | .05 | .05 | 1 | 356 | 4 | 3 | .37 | .005 |
| *1 slice* | 28 | 4.5 | 0.1 | 1.4 | 0.0 | | .01 | 0.3 | .30 | .06 | 9 | 17 | .33 | .035 | |
| **honey loaf (pork & beef)** | 36 | 20.0 | 1.3 | 0.1 | 10 | | 6 | .07 | .09 | | 374 | 5 | 5 | .69 | .009 |
| *1 slice* | 28 | 4.5 | 1.5 | 0.4 | | | .14 | 0.9 | .31 | .19 | 97 | 41 | .38 | .020 | |
| **honey roll sausage (beef)** | 42 | 14.9 | 2.4 | 0.1 | 12 | | 4 | .04 | .06 | | 304 | 2 | 4 | .75 | .008 |
| *1 slice* | 23 | 4.3 | 0.5 | 0.9 | 0.0 | | .02 | 1.0 | .54 | .11 | 67 | 31 | .51 | .020 | |
| **italian sausage, pork, ckd** | 217 | 33.5 | 17.2 | 2.2 | 52 | | 1 | .16 | .22 | | 618 | 16 | 12 | 1.59 | .055 |
| *1 link* | 67 | 13.4 | 1.0 | 6.1 | | | .42 | 2.8 | .87 | .30 | 204 | 114 | 1.01 | .054 | |
| **kielbasa/kolbassy (pork & beef w/ nfdm)** | 81 | 14.0 | 7.1 | 0.8 | 17 | | 6 | .06 | .05 | | 280 | 11 | 4 | .53 | .010 |
| *1 slice* | 26 | 3.5 | 0.6 | 2.6 | 0.0 | | .06 | 0.7 | .42 | .21 | 70 | 38 | .38 | .030 | |
| **knackwurst/knockwurst (pork & beef)** | 209 | 37.7 | 18.9 | 2.0 | 39 | | 18 | .10 | .11 | | 687 | 7 | 8 | 1.13 | |
| *1 slice* | 68 | 8.1 | 1.2 | 6.9 | 0.0 | | .23 | 1.9 | .80 | .22 | 136 | 67 | .62 | .040 | |

| | KCAL / WT (g) | H₂O (g) / PRO (g) | FAT (g) / CHO (g) | PUFA (g) / SFA (g) | CHOL (mg) / DFIB (g) | A (RE) / A (IU) | C (mg) / B-1 (mg) | B-2 (mg) / NIA (mg) | B-6 (mg) / B-12 (mcg) | FOL (mcg) / PANT (mg) | Na (mg) / K (mg) | Ca (mg) / P (mg) | Mg (mg) / Fe (mg) | Zn (mg) / Cu (mg) | Mn (mg) |
|---|---|---|---|---|---|---|---|---|---|---|---|---|---|---|---|
| **lebanon bologna (beef)** | 49 | 14.0 | 3.0 | 0.1 | 16 | 5 | | .04 | .06 | 1 | 308 | 3 | 4 | .92 | .013 |
| *1 slice* | 23 | 4.5 | 0.6 | 1.3 | | | .01 | 1.0 | .59 | .12 | 69 | 35 | .57 | .020 | |
| **livercheese, pork fat wrapped, Oscar Mayer—1 slice** | 116 | 20.2 | 10.0 | | 76 | | 1 | .84 | .17 | 43 | 433 | 3 | 5 | 1.43 | |
| | 38 | 5.8 | 0.7 | | | | .08 | 4.6 | 9.23 | 1.42 | 83 | 83 | 4.31 | .160 | |
| **livercheese (pork liver)** | 115 | 20.4 | 9.7 | 1.3 | 66 | 1996 | 1 | .85 | .18 | | 465 | 3 | 4 | 1.41 | .076 |
| *1 slice* | 38 | 5.8 | 0.8 | 3.4 | | 6646 | .08 | 4.5 | 9.33 | 1.34 | 86 | 79 | 4.11 | .146 | |
| **liver pate** | | | | | | | | | | | | | | | |
| chicken, cnd | 57 | | 3.7 | | | | 3 | .40 | | | | 3 | | | |
| *1 oz* | 28 | 3.8 | 1.9 | | | 205 | .02 | 2.1 | | | | | 2.60 | | |
| goose (pate de fois gras), cnd | 60 | 4.8 | 5.7 | | | | | .04 | | | | | | | |
| *1 T* | 13 | 1.5 | 0.6 | | | | .01 | 0.3 | | | | | | | |
| goose, smoked, cnd | 131 | 10.5 | 12.4 | | 43 | | | .09 | | | | | | | |
| *1 oz* | 28 | 3.2 | 1.3 | | 0.0 | | .03 | 0.7 | 2.66 | | | | | | |
| unspecified, cnd | 90 | 15.3 | 7.9 | | | | 0 | .17 | .02 | 17 | 198 | 20 | 4 | | .034 |
| *1 oz* | 28 | 4.0 | 0.4 | | | 936 | .01 | 0.9 | .91 | .34 | 39 | 57 | 1.56 | .110 | |
| **liver sausage/liverwurst (pork)** | 59 | 9.4 | 5.1 | 0.5 | 28 | | | .19 | .03 | 5 | | 5 | | | |
| *1 slice* | 18 | 2.5 | 0.4 | 1.9 | | | .05 | | 2.42 | .53 | | 41 | 1.15 | | |
| **luxury loaf (pork)** | 40 | 19.4 | 1.4 | 0.1 | 10 | | 6 | .08 | .09 | 1 | 347 | 10 | 6 | .86 | .012 |
| *1 slice* | 28 | 5.2 | 1.4 | 0.5 | | | .20 | 1.0 | .39 | .15 | 107 | 52 | .30 | .028 | |
| **meat spread** | | | | | | | | | | | | | | | |
| chicken, Carnation | 100 | 34.1 | 6.0 | 4.0 | 16 | | 0 | .03 | .12 | 3 | 200 | 6 | 7 | .28 | |
| *1.9 oz* | 53 | 6.0 | 2.0 | 1.2 | | 9 | .02 | 2.4 | .07 | .19 | 72 | 47 | .30 | .020 | |
| chicken, cnd | 55 | | 3.3 | | | | | .03 | | | | 35 | | | |
| *1 oz* | 28 | 4.4 | 1.5 | | | | .00 | 0.8 | | | | | .66 | | |
| chicken, cnd, Swanson | 60 | | 3.9 | | | | 0 | .03 | | | 136 | 68 | | | |
| *1.02 oz* | 29 | 4.4 | 1.8 | | | 0 | .00 | 0.9 | | | 37 | | .60 | | |
| ham & cheese | 69 | 16.8 | 5.3 | 0.4 | 17 | | 2 | .06 | .04 | | 339 | 62 | 5 | .64 | .010 |
| *1 oz* | 28 | 4.6 | 0.6 | 2.4 | | | .09 | 0.6 | .21 | .17 | 46 | 140 | .22 | .026 | |
| ham & cheese, Oscar Mayer | 66 | 16.7 | 5.1 | | 16 | | 2 | .07 | .04 | | 329 | 51 | 5 | .60 | |
| *1 oz* | 28 | 4.5 | 0.6 | | | | .09 | 0.6 | .19 | | 47 | 134 | .18 | .030 | |
| ham, Carnation | 100 | 34.2 | 6.0 | 2.3 | 24 | | 0 | .05 | .00 | 3 | 350 | 6 | 2 | .05 | |
| *1.9 oz* | 53 | 5.0 | 4.0 | 1.8 | | 4 | .15 | 1.0 | .00 | .01 | 104 | 47 | .82 | .010 | |
| ham salad | 61 | 17.8 | 4.4 | 0.8 | 10 | | 2 | .03 | .04 | | 259 | 2 | 3 | .31 | |
| *1 oz* | 28 | 2.5 | 3.0 | 1.4 | | | .12 | 0.6 | .22 | .09 | 42 | 34 | .17 | .021 | |
| ham salad, Oscar Mayer | 62 | 17.1 | 4.2 | | 11 | | 2 | .03 | .04 | 0 | 265 | 2 | 3 | .30 | |
| *1 oz* | 28 | 2.5 | 3.5 | | | | .13 | 0.7 | .20 | .09 | 39 | 34 | .17 | .020 | |
| Oscar Mayer | 67 | 16.7 | 4.9 | | 10 | | 0 | .04 | .03 | 1 | 261 | 3 | 3 | .27 | |
| *1 oz* | 28 | 2.1 | 3.6 | | | | .05 | 0.5 | .30 | .12 | 29 | 17 | .25 | .030 | |
| pork & beef | 67 | 17.1 | 4.9 | 0.7 | 11 | | 0 | .04 | .03 | | 287 | 3 | 2 | .29 | .01 |
| *1 oz* | 28 | 2.2 | 3.4 | 1.7 | | | .05 | 0.5 | .32 | .12 | 31 | 17 | .22 | .040 | |
| poultry (chicken/turkey) salad | 57 | | 3.8 | 1.8 | 9 | | 0 | .02 | .03 | 1 | 107 | 3 | | | |
| *1 oz* | 28 | 3.3 | 2.1 | 1.0 | | 39 | .01 | 0.5 | .11 | .08 | 52 | 9 | .17 | | |
| tuna, Carnation | 90 | 34.9 | 6.0 | 3.7 | 13 | | 0 | .02 | .00 | 3 | 370 | 6 | 2 | .05 | |
| *1.9 oz* | 53 | 6.0 | 2.0 | 0.9 | | 22 | .01 | 2.8 | .00 | .01 | 82 | 45 | .43 | .010 | |
| turkey, Carnation | 100 | 34.9 | 6.0 | 3.9 | 20 | | 0 | .04 | .10 | 4 | 190 | 7 | 8 | .67 | |
| *1.9 oz* | 53 | 6.0 | 2.0 | 1.1 | | 3 | .02 | 1.1 | .08 | .21 | 76 | 48 | .50 | .040 | |
| **mortadella (beef & pork)** | 47 | 7.9 | 3.8 | 0.5 | 8 | | 4 | .02 | .02 | | 187 | 3 | 2 | .32 | .004 |
| *1 slice* | 15 | 2.5 | 0.5 | 1.4 | | | .02 | 0.4 | .22 | | 24 | 15 | .21 | .010 | |
| **mothers loaf (pork)** | 59 | 11.5 | 4.7 | 0.5 | 9 | | 0 | .04 | .04 | | 237 | 9 | 3 | .30 | .014 |
| *1 slice* | 21 | 2.5 | 1.6 | 1.7 | | | .12 | 0.7 | .22 | .10 | 47 | 27 | .28 | .020 | |
| **new england brand sausage (pork & beef)** | 37 | 15.4 | 1.7 | 0.2 | 11 | | 5 | .06 | .08 | 2 | 281 | 2 | 4 | .62 | .008 |
| *1 slice* | 23 | 4.0 | 1.1 | 1.6 | 0.0 | | .15 | 0.8 | .31 | .16 | 74 | 31 | .22 | .020 | |
| **old fashioned loaf (pork & beef)** | 68 | 16.8 | 5.1 | 0.5 | 13 | | 5 | .08 | .06 | 1 | 354 | 24 | 6 | .49 | .009 |
| *1 slice* | 28 | 3.8 | 1.6 | 1.8 | | | .09 | 0.7 | .37 | .17 | 107 | 46 | .35 | .020 | |
| **olive loaf (pork)** | 67 | 16.5 | 4.7 | 0.6 | 11 | | 3 | .07 | .07 | 1 | 421 | 31 | 5 | .39 | .010 |
| *1 slice* | 28 | 3.4 | 2.6 | 1.7 | | | .08 | 0.5 | .36 | .22 | 84 | 36 | .15 | .014 | |
| **pastrami** | | | | | | | | | | | | | | | |
| beef | 99 | 13.3 | 8.3 | 0.3 | 26 | | 1 | .05 | .05 | | 348 | 2 | 5 | 1.21 | |
| *1 oz* | 28 | 4.9 | 0.9 | 3.0 | | | .03 | 1.4 | .50 | | 65 | 43 | .54 | | |

| | KCAL | H₂O (g) | FAT (g) | PUFA (g) | CHOL (mg) | Vitamins | | | | | Minerals | | | | |
|---|---|---|---|---|---|---|---|---|---|---|---|---|---|---|---|
| | | | | | | A (RE) | C (mg) | B-2 (mg) | B-6 (mg) | FOL (mcg) | Na (mg) | Ca (mg) | Mg (mg) | Zn (mg) | Mn (mg) |
| | WT (g) | PRO (g) | CHO (g) | SFA (g) | DFIB (g) | A (IU) | B-1 (mg) | NIA (mg) | B-12 (mcg) | PANT (mg) | K (mg) | P (mg) | Fe (mg) | Cu (mg) | |
| sliced, Oscar Mayer | 17 | 12.6 | 0.4 | | 5 | | | | | | 216 | 1 | 3 | .49 | |
| *1 slice* | 17 | 3.2 | 0.1 | | | | | | | | 52 | 35 | .43 | .060 | |
| peppered loaf (pork & beef) | 42 | 19.1 | 1.8 | 0.1 | 13 | | 7 | .09 | .08 | 1 | 432 | 15 | 6 | .92 | .018 |
| *1 slice* | 28 | 4.9 | 1.3 | 0.7 | | | .11 | 0.9 | .56 | .15 | 112 | 48 | .30 | .030 | |
| pepperoni (pork & beef) | 27 | 1.5 | 2.4 | 0.2 | | | | .01 | .01 | | 112 | 1 | 1 | .14 | |
| *1 slice* | 6 | 1.2 | 0.2 | 0.9 | 0.0 | | .02 | 0.3 | .14 | .10 | 19 | 7 | .08 | .000 | |
| pickle & pimento loaf (pork) | 74 | 16.2 | 6.0 | 0.7 | 10 | | 4 | .07 | .05 | 1 | 394 | 27 | 5 | .40 | .008 |
| *1 slice* | 28 | 3.3 | 1.7 | 2.2 | | 28 | .08 | 0.6 | .33 | .23 | 96 | 40 | .29 | .035 | |
| picnic loaf (pork & beef) | 66 | 17.1 | 4.7 | 0.5 | 11 | | 5 | .07 | .09 | 1 | 330 | 13 | 4 | .62 | .008 |
| *1 slice* | 28 | 4.2 | 1.4 | 1.7 | | | .11 | 0.7 | .42 | .19 | 76 | 36 | .29 | .020 | |
| polish sausage (pork) | 92 | 15.1 | 8.1 | 0.9 | 20 | 0 | | .04 | .05 | | 248 | 3 | 4 | .55 | .014 |
| *1 oz* | 28 | 4.0 | 0.5 | 2.9 | 0.0 | | .14 | 1.0 | .28 | .13 | 67 | 39 | .41 | .026 | |
| pork & beef lunch meat | 100 | 14.0 | 9.1 | 1.1 | 15 | | 4 | .04 | .06 | 2 | 367 | 3 | 4 | .47 | .008 |
| *1 slice* | 28 | 3.6 | 0.7 | 3.3 | 0.0 | | .09 | 0.8 | .36 | .18 | 57 | 24 | .24 | .010 | |
| pork & beef luncheon sausage | 60 | 13.5 | 4.8 | 0.5 | 15 | | 4 | .05 | .05 | | 272 | 3 | 3 | .56 | .01 |
| *1 slice* | 23 | 3.5 | 0.4 | 1.8 | 0.0 | | .05 | 0.8 | .45 | .09 | 56 | 28 | .33 | .020 | |
| pork lunch meat, cnd | 70 | 10.8 | 6.4 | 0.8 | 13 | 0 | | .04 | .04 | 1 | 271 | 1 | 2 | .31 | .005 |
| *1 slice* | 21 | 2.6 | 0.4 | 2.3 | 0.0 | | .08 | 0.7 | .19 | .10 | 45 | 17 | .15 | .008 | |
| **salami** | | | | | | | | | | | | | | | |
| beerwurst, beef | 76 | 12.2 | 6.9 | 0.3 | 14 | | 4 | .03 | .04 | 1 | 236 | 2 | 3 | .56 | |
| *1 slice* | 23 | 2.9 | 0.4 | 3.0 | 0.0 | | .02 | 0.8 | .45 | .08 | 40 | 22 | .35 | .009 | |
| beerwurst, pork | 55 | 14.1 | 4.3 | 0.5 | 14 | | 7 | .04 | .08 | 1 | 285 | 2 | 3 | .40 | .007 |
| *1 slice* | 23 | 3.3 | 0.5 | 1.4 | 0.0 | | .13 | 0.7 | .20 | .11 | 58 | 24 | .17 | .012 | |
| ckd, beef | 60 | 13.4 | 4.8 | 0.2 | 15 | | 4 | .04 | .04 | 0 | 271 | 2 | 3 | .50 | .011 |
| *1 slice* | 23 | 3.5 | 0.7 | 2.1 | | | .02 | 0.7 | .70 | .22 | 51 | 26 | .50 | .028 | |
| ckd, beef & pork | 57 | 13.9 | 4.6 | 0.5 | 15 | | 3 | .09 | .05 | 0 | 245 | 3 | 3 | .49 | .013 |
| *1 slice* | 23 | 3.2 | 0.5 | 1.9 | 0.0 | | .06 | 0.8 | 0.8 | .20 | 46 | 27 | .61 | .050 | |
| dry/hard pork | 41 | 3.6 | 3.4 | 0.4 | | | | .03 | .06 | | 226 | 1 | 2 | .42 | .007 |
| *1 slice* | 10 | 2.3 | 0.2 | 1.2 | 0.0 | | .09 | 0.6 | .28 | | | 23 | .13 | .016 | |
| dry/hard pork & beef | 42 | 3.5 | 3.4 | 0.3 | 8 | | 3 | .03 | .05 | | 186 | 1 | 2 | .32 | .000 |
| *1 slice* | 10 | 2.3 | 0.3 | 1.2 | | | .06 | 0.5 | .19 | .11 | 38 | 14 | .15 | .010 | |
| **smoked link sausage** | | | | | | | | | | | | | | | |
| pork | 265 | 26.7 | 21.6 | 2.6 | 46 | | 1 | .18 | .24 | | 1020 | 20 | 13 | 1.92 | |
| *1 link* | 68 | 15.1 | 1.4 | 7.7 | 0.0 | | .48 | 3.1 | 1.11 | .53 | 228 | 110 | .79 | .049 | |
| pork & beef | 229 | 35.5 | 20.6 | 2.2 | 48 | | 13 | .12 | .12 | | 642 | 7 | 8 | 1.44 | .03 |
| *1 link* | 68 | 9.1 | 1.0 | 9.2 | 0.0 | | .18 | 2.2 | 1.03 | .30 | 129 | 73 | .99 | .040 | |
| pork & beef, Oscar Mayer | 28 | 4.8 | 2.5 | | 5 | | | | | | 92 | 1 | 2 | .19 | |
| *1 small link* | 9 | 1.2 | 0.2 | | | | | | | | 17 | 20 | .11 | .020 | |
| pork & beef w/ american cheese | 141 | 22.6 | 12.5 | 1.3 | 29 | | 8 | .07 | .05 | | 465 | 25 | 5 | .97 | .01 |
| *1 link* | 43 | 6.0 | 0.6 | 4.5 | | | .11 | 1.2 | .74 | .33 | 89 | 76 | .46 | .030 | |
| pork & beef w/ flour & nfdm | 182 | 39.0 | 14.6 | 1.5 | 59 | | 2 | .12 | .09 | | 741 | 12 | 9 | 1.36 | .035 |
| *1 link* | 68 | 9.5 | 2.7 | 5.3 | | | .16 | 1.8 | .89 | | 105 | 74 | 1.05 | .060 | |
| pork & beef w/ nfdm | 213 | 36.7 | 18.8 | 2.1 | 44 | | 14 | .15 | .12 | | 798 | 28 | 11 | 1.33 | .026 |
| *1 link* | 68 | 9.0 | 1.3 | 6.6 | 0.0 | | .13 | 1.9 | 1.07 | .41 | 194 | 92 | 1.00 | .060 | |
| **thuringer (cervelat/summer sausage)** | | | | | | | | | | | | | | | |
| beef | 70 | 11.7 | 6.2 | 0.3 | 17 | | 5 | .07 | .06 | 1 | 317 | 2 | 3 | .48 | |
| *1 slice* | 23 | 3.4 | 0.7 | 2.8 | | | .03 | 1.0 | 1.29 | | 53 | 24 | .52 | .020 | |
| beef & pork | 80 | 11.0 | 6.9 | 0.4 | 16 | | 5 | .07 | .07 | 1 | 334 | 2 | 3 | .47 | .007 |
| *1 slice* | 23 | 3.7 | 0.5 | 2.8 | 0.0 | | .04 | 0.9 | 1.06 | .13 | 53 | 23 | .47 | .020 | |
| turkey breast meat | 23 | 15.1 | 0.3 | 0.1 | 9 | 0 | | .02 | .07 | | 301 | 1 | 4 | .24 | |
| *1 slice* | 21 | 4.7 | 0.0 | 0.1 | | | .01 | 1.7 | .42 | .12 | 58 | 48 | .08 | .010 | |
| **turkey cotto salami** | | | | | | | | | | | | | | | |
| Louis Rich | 52 | 18.8 | 3.7 | 0.9 | 22 | | | | | | 257 | 5 | 5 | .71 | |
| *1 oz slice* | 28 | 4.4 | 0.3 | 1.1 | | | | | | | 60 | 43 | .49 | | |
| Oscar Mayer | 52 | 18.8 | 3.7 | | 22 | 0 | | .09 | .07 | | 256 | 5 | 5 | .71 | .014 |
| *1 oz slice* | 28 | 4.4 | 0.3 | | | | .03 | 1.2 | .99 | | 62 | 43 | .49 | .050 | |
| turkey ham (cured thigh meat) | 73 | 40.5 | 2.9 | 0.9 | 34 | | | .14 | .14 | | 565 | 5 | 10 | 1.50 | |
| *2 slices* | 57 | 10.7 | 0.2 | 1.0 | | | .03 | 2.0 | 1.02 | | 184 | 108 | 1.57 | .060 | |

| | KCAL / WT (g) | H₂O (g) / PRO (g) | FAT (g) / CHO (g) | PUFA (g) / SFA (g) | CHOL (mg) / DFIB (g) | A (RE) / A (IU) | C (mg) / B-1 (mg) | B-2 (mg) / NIA (mg) | B-6 (mg) / B-12 (mcg) | FOL (mcg) / PANT (mg) | Na (mg) / K (mg) | Ca (mg) / P (mg) | Mg (mg) / Fe (mg) | Zn (mg) / Cu (mg) | Mn (mg) |
|---|---|---|---|---|---|---|---|---|---|---|---|---|---|---|---|
| turkey luncheon loaf, Louis Rich | 43 | 19.5 | 2.6 | 0.7 | 14 | | | | | | 278 | 2 | 5 | .45 | |
| *1 oz slice* | 28 | 4.6 | 0.4 | 0.8 | | | | | | | 59 | 65 | .15 | | |
| turkey luncheon loaf, Oscar Mayer | 43 | 19.6 | 2.6 | | 14 | | 0 | .03 | .07 | | 278 | 2 | 5 | .45 | .005 |
| *1 oz slice* | 28 | 4.6 | 0.4 | | | | .01 | 1.6 | .19 | | 60 | 65 | .15 | .010 | |
| turkey pastrami | 80 | 40.1 | 3.5 | 0.9 | 30 | | | .14 | .16 | | 593 | 5 | 8 | 1.22 | |
| *2 slices* | 57 | 10.4 | 0.9 | 1.0 | | | .03 | 2.0 | 1.14 | | 147 | 113 | .94 | .030 | |
| Louis Rich | 33 | 20.3 | 1.2 | 0.4 | 17 | | | | | | 276 | 2 | 6 | .82 | |
| *1 oz slice* | 28 | 5.4 | 0.1 | 0.4 | | | | | | | 75 | 85 | .40 | | |
| Oscar Mayer | 33 | 20.3 | 1.2 | | 17 | | 0 | .08 | .08 | | 275 | 2 | 6 | .82 | .017 |
| *1 oz slice* | 28 | 5.4 | 0.1 | | | | .03 | 1.5 | .57 | | 76 | 85 | .40 | .040 | |
| turkey roll | | | | | | | | | | | | | | | |
| light & dark meat | 84 | 39.8 | 4.0 | 1.0 | 31 | | | .16 | | | 332 | 18 | 10 | 1.13 | |
| *2 slices* | 57 | 10.3 | 1.2 | 1.2 | | | .05 | 2.7 | | | 153 | 95 | .76 | .040 | |
| light meat | 83 | 40.6 | 4.1 | 1.0 | 24 | | | .13 | | | 277 | 23 | 9 | .88 | |
| *2 slices* | 57 | 10.6 | 0.3 | 1.1 | | | .05 | 4.0 | | | 142 | 104 | .72 | .020 | |
| turkey salami | 111 | 37.3 | 7.8 | | 46 | | 0 | .10 | | | 569 | 11 | 8 | 1.03 | |
| *2 slices* | 57 | 9.3 | 0.3 | | | | .04 | 2.0 | | | 138 | 60 | .91 | .031 | |
| ckd | 50 | 19.0 | 3.4 | 1.1 | 20 | | | .08 | .07 | | 251 | 7 | 5 | .72 | |
| *1 slice* | 28 | 4.5 | 0.3 | 1.0 | | | .02 | 1.2 | .60 | | 63 | 45 | .38 | .030 | |
| Louis Rich | 52 | 18.9 | 3.7 | 1.0 | 19 | | | | | | 245 | 6 | 5 | .69 | |
| *1 oz slice* | 28 | 4.5 | 0.1 | 1.1 | | | | | | | 61 | 42 | .35 | | |
| Oscar Mayer | 52 | 18.9 | 3.7 | | 19 | | 0 | .07 | .07 | | 244 | 6 | 5 | .69 | .007 |
| *1 oz slice* | 28 | 4.5 | 0.1 | | | | .02 | 1.3 | .43 | | 63 | 42 | .35 | .030 | |
| turkey summer sausage | | | | | | | | | | | | | | | |
| Louis Rich | 52 | 18.3 | 3.5 | 0.9 | 22 | | | | | | 311 | 4 | 5 | .68 | |
| *1 oz slice* | 28 | 4.7 | 0.4 | 1.2 | | | | | | | 68 | 71 | .56 | | |
| Oscar Mayer | 52 | 18.3 | 3.5 | | 23 | | 0 | .12 | .07 | | 312 | 4 | 5 | .68 | .035 |
| *1 oz slice* | 28 | 4.7 | 0.4 | | | | .03 | 1.4 | 1.15 | | 69 | 71 | .56 | .040 | |
| vienna sausage, cnd (beef & pork) | 45 | 9.6 | 4.0 | 0.3 | 8 | | 0 | .02 | .02 | | 152 | 2 | 1 | .26 | .005 |
| *1 sausage* | 16 | 1.7 | 0.3 | 1.5 | 0.0 | | .01 | 0.3 | .16 | | 16 | 8 | .14 | .000 | |

# 23. MILK, YOGURT, MILK BEVERAGES & MILK BEVERAGE MIXES
23.1. COW MILK

| | KCAL / WT (g) | H₂O (g) / PRO (g) | FAT (g) / CHO (g) | PUFA (g) / SFA (g) | CHOL (mg) / DFIB (g) | A (RE) / A (IU) | C (mg) / B-1 (mg) | B-2 (mg) / NIA (mg) | B-6 (mg) / B-12 (mcg) | FOL (mcg) / PANT (mg) | Na (mg) / K (mg) | Ca (mg) / P (mg) | Mg (mg) / Fe (mg) | Zn (mg) / Cu (mg) | Mn (mg) |
|---|---|---|---|---|---|---|---|---|---|---|---|---|---|---|---|
| buttermilk, cultured | 99 | 220.8 | 2.2 | 0.0 | 9 | 20 | 2 | .38 | .08 | | 257 | 285 | 27 | 1.03 | |
| *8 fl oz* | 245 | 8.1 | 11.7 | 1.3 | 0.0 | 81 | .08 | 0.1 | .54 | .67 | 371 | 219 | .12 | | |
| buttermilk, dry | 25 | 0.2 | 0.4 | 0.0 | 5 | 4 | 0 | .10 | .02 | 3 | 34 | 77 | 7 | .26 | |
| *1 T* | 7 | 2.2 | 3.2 | 0.2 | 0.0 | 14 | .03 | 0.1 | .25 | .21 | 103 | 61 | .02 | | |
| calcimilk (lactose reduced lowfat milk w/ added Ca)ᵃ—8 fl oz | 102 | | 3.0 | | 10 | | 2 | .41 | | | 123 | 500 | | | |
| | | 8.0 | 12.0 | | | 500 | .10 | 0.2 | | | 381 | 340 | .12 | | |
| condensed, sweetened, cnd | 123 | 10.4 | 3.3 | 0.1 | 13 | 31 | 1 | .16 | .02 | 4 | 49 | 108 | 10 | .49 | |
| *1 fl oz* | 38 | 3.0 | 20.8 | 2.1 | 0.0 | 125 | .03 | 0.1 | .17 | .29 | 142 | 97 | .07 | | |
| evaporated, lowfat, cnd, Carnation | 110 | 97.3 | 3.0 | | | | 1 | .34 | .06 | 10 | 138 | 318 | 32 | | |
| *4 fl oz* | 127 | 9.0 | 12.0 | | | 630 | .04 | 0.2 | .27 | | 416 | 267 | .29 | | |
| evaporated, skim, cnd | 25 | 25.3 | 0.1 | 0.0 | 1 | 37 | 0 | .10 | .02 | 3 | 37 | 92 | 9 | .29 | |
| *1 fl oz* | 32 | 2.4 | 3.6 | 0.0 | 0.0 | 125 | .01 | 0.1 | .08 | .24 | 106 | 62 | .09 | | |
| evaporated, whole, cnd | 42 | 23.3 | 2.4 | 0.1 | 9 | 17 | 1 | .10 | .02 | 2 | 33 | 82 | 8 | .24 | |
| *1 fl oz* | 32 | 2.1 | 3.2 | 1.5 | 0.0 | 77 | .02 | 0.1 | .05 | .20 | 95 | 64 | .06 | | |
| evaporated, whole, cnd | 169 | 93.3 | 9.5 | 0.3 | 37 | 68 | 2 | .40 | .06 | 10 | 133 | 329 | 30 | .97 | |
| *4 fl oz* | 126 | 8.6 | 12.7 | 5.8 | 0.0 | 306 | .06 | 0.2 | .21 | .80 | 382 | 255 | .24 | | |
| lactaid (lactose reduced lowfat milk)ᵃ | 102 | | 3.0 | | 10 | | 2 | .41 | | | 123 | 300 | | | |
| *8 fl oz* | | 8.0 | 12.0 | | | 500 | .10 | 0.2 | | | 381 | 235 | .12 | | |
| lowfat 1% fat | 102 | 219.8 | 2.6 | 0.1 | 10 | 145 | 2 | .41 | .11 | 12 | 123 | 300 | 34 | .95 | |
| *8 fl oz* | 244 | 8.0 | 11.7 | 1.6 | 0.0 | 500 | .10 | 0.2 | .90 | .79 | 381 | 235 | .12 | | |
| lowfat 1% fat, pro fortified | 119 | 218.3 | 2.9 | 0.1 | 10 | 145 | 3 | .47 | .12 | 15 | 143 | 349 | 39 | 1.11 | |
| *8 fl oz* | 246 | 9.7 | 13.6 | 1.8 | 0.0 | 500 | .11 | 0.3 | 1.05 | .92 | 444 | 273 | .15 | | |

ᵃ Lactose content is 3 g/cup.

| | KCAL | H₂O (g) | FAT (g) | PUFA (g) | CHOL (mg) | A (RE) | C (mg) | B-2 (mg) | B-6 (mg) | FOL (mcg) | Na (mg) | Ca (mg) | Mg (mg) | Zn (mg) | Mn (mg) |
|---|---|---|---|---|---|---|---|---|---|---|---|---|---|---|---|
| | WT (g) | PRO (g) | CHO (g) | SFA (g) | DFIB (g) | A (IU) | B-1 (mg) | NIA (mg) | B-12 (mcg) | PANT (mg) | K (mg) | P (mg) | Fe (mg) | Cu (mg) | |
| lowfat 1% fat w/ nfdm | 104 | 220.0 | 2.4 | 0.1 | 10 | 145 | 2 | .42 | .11 | 13 | 128 | 313 | 35 | .98 | |
| 8 fl oz | 245 | 8.5 | 12.2 | 1.5 | 0.0 | 500 | .10 | 0.2 | .94 | .82 | 397 | 245 | .12 | | |
| lowfat 2% fat | 121 | 217.7 | 4.7 | 0.2 | 18 | 140 | 2 | .40 | .11 | 12 | 122 | 297 | 33 | .95 | |
| 8 fl oz | 244 | 8.1 | 11.7 | 2.9 | 0.0 | 500 | .10 | 0.2 | .89 | .78 | 377 | 232 | .12 | | |
| lowfat 2% fat, pro fortified | 137 | 215.8 | 4.9 | 0.2 | 19 | 140 | 3 | .48 | .13 | 15 | 145 | 352 | 40 | 1.11 | |
| 8 fl oz | 246 | 9.7 | 13.5 | 3.0 | 0.0 | 500 | .11 | 0.3 | 1.05 | .93 | 447 | 276 | .15 | | |
| lowfat 2% fat w/ nfdm | 125 | 217.7 | 4.7 | 0.2 | 18 | 140 | 2 | .42 | .11 | 13 | 128 | 313 | 35 | .98 | |
| 8 fl oz | 245 | 8.5 | 12.2 | 2.9 | 0.0 | 500 | .10 | 0.2 | .94 | .82 | 397 | 245 | .12 | | |
| skim | 86 | 222.5 | 0.4 | 0.0 | 4 | 149 | 2 | .34 | .10 | 13 | 126 | 302 | 28 | .98 | |
| 8 fl oz | 245 | 8.4 | 11.9 | 0.3 | 0.0 | 500 | .09 | 0.2 | .93 | .81 | 406 | 247 | .10 | | |
| skim, dry | 109 | 1.0 | 0.0 | 0.0 | 6 | 2 | 2 | .47 | .11 | 15 | 161 | 377 | 33 | 1.22 | |
| 1/4 cup | 30 | 10.9 | 15.6 | 0.2 | 0.0 | 11 | .12 | .29 | 1.21 | 1.07 | 538 | 290 | .10 | | |
| skim, dry, Ca reduced | 100 | 1.4 | 0.1 | 0.0 | 1 | 1 | | .47 | .08 | | 646 | 79 | 17 | | |
| 1 oz | 28 | 10.1 | 14.7 | 0.0 | 0.0 | 2 | .05 | 0.2 | 1.13 | .94 | 193 | 287 | | | |
| skim, dry, inst | 326 | 3.6 | 0.7 | 0.0 | 17 | 646 | 5 | 1.59 | .31 | 45 | 499 | 1120 | 107 | 4.01 | |
| 1 1/3 cups (3.2 oz envelope)[a] | 91 | 31.9 | 47.5 | 0.4 | 0.0 | 2157 | .38 | 0.8 | 3.63 | 2.94 | 1552 | 896 | .28 | | |
| skim pro fortified | 100 | 219.8 | 0.6 | 0.0 | 5 | 149 | 3 | .48 | .12 | 15 | 144 | 352 | 40 | 1.11 | |
| 8 fl oz | 246 | 9.7 | 13.7 | 0.4 | 0.0 | 500 | .11 | 0.3 | 1.05 | .93 | 446 | 275 | .15 | | |
| skim w/ nfdm | 90 | 221.4 | 0.6 | 0.0 | 5 | 149 | 2 | .43 | .11 | 13 | 130 | 316 | 36 | 1.00 | |
| 8 fl oz | 245 | 8.8 | 12.3 | 0.4 | 0.0 | 500 | .10 | 0.2 | .95 | .83 | 418 | 255 | .12 | | |
| whole, 3.3% fat | 150 | 214.7 | 8.2 | 0.3 | 33 | 76 | 2 | .40 | .10 | 12 | 120 | 291 | 33 | .93 | |
| 8 fl oz | 244 | 8.0 | 11.4 | 5.1 | 0.0 | 307 | .09 | 0.2 | .87 | .77 | 370 | 228 | .12 | | |
| whole, 3.5% fat | 150 | 213.3 | 8.0 | 0.2 | 34 | | 5 | .42 | .02 | 37 | 122 | 288 | 24 | 1.00 | |
| 8 fl oz | 244 | 8.0 | 11.0 | 4.9 | 0.0 | | .10 | 0.2 | 1.34 | .85 | 351 | 227 | | | |
| whole, 3.7% fat | 157 | 214.0 | 8.9 | 0.3 | 35 | 83 | 4 | .39 | .10 | 12 | 119 | 290 | 33 | .93 | |
| 8 fl oz | 244 | 8.0 | 11.4 | 5.6 | 0.0 | 337 | .09 | 0.2 | .87 | .76 | 368 | 227 | .12 | | |
| whole, dry | 159 | 0.8 | 8.6 | 0.2 | 31 | 90 | 3 | .39 | .10 | 12 | 119 | 292 | 27 | 1.07 | |
| 1/4 cup | 32 | 8.4 | 12.3 | 5.4 | 0.0 | 295 | .09 | 0.2 | 1.04 | .73 | 426 | 248 | .15 | | |
| whole, low Na | 149 | 215.2 | 8.4 | 0.3 | 33 | 78 | | .26 | .08 | | 6 | 246 | 12 | | |
| 8 fl oz | 244 | 7.6 | 10.9 | 5.3 | 0.0 | 317 | .05 | 0.1 | .88 | .74 | 617 | 209 | | | |

## 23.2. OTHER MILK

| | KCAL | H₂O (g) | FAT (g) | PUFA (g) | CHOL (mg) | A (RE) | C (mg) | B-2 (mg) | B-6 (mg) | FOL (mcg) | Na (mg) | Ca (mg) | Mg (mg) | Zn (mg) | Mn (mg) |
|---|---|---|---|---|---|---|---|---|---|---|---|---|---|---|---|
| | WT (g) | PRO (g) | CHO (g) | SFA (g) | DFIB (g) | A (IU) | B-1 (mg) | NIA (mg) | B-12 (mcg) | PANT (mg) | K (mg) | P (mg) | Fe (mg) | Cu (mg) | |
| filled[b,c] | 154 | 213.9 | 8.4 | 1.8 | 4 | 5 | 2 | .30 | .10 | 12 | 138 | 312 | 32 | .88 | |
| 8 fl oz | 244 | 8.1 | 11.6 | 1.9 | 0.0 | 17 | .07 | 0.2 | .83 | .73 | 339 | 236 | .12 | | |
| filled[b,d] | 153 | 214.4 | 8.3 | 0.0 | 4 | 5 | 2 | .30 | .10 | 12 | 138 | 312 | 31 | .88 | |
| 8 fl oz | 244 | 8.1 | 11.6 | 7.6 | 0.0 | 17 | .07 | 0.2 | .83 | .73 | 339 | 236 | .12 | | |
| goat | 168 | 212.4 | 10.1 | 0.4 | 28 | 137 | 3 | .34 | .11 | 1 | 122 | 326 | 34 | .73 | |
| 8 fl oz | 244 | 8.7 | 10.9 | 6.5 | 0.0 | 451 | .12 | 0.7 | .16 | .76 | 499 | 270 | .12 | | |
| human | 21 | 27.0 | 1.4 | 0.2 | 4 | 20 | 1 | .01 | .00 | 2 | 5 | 10 | 1 | .05 | |
| 1 fl oz | 31 | 0.3 | 2.1 | 0.6 | 0.0 | 74 | .00 | 0.1 | .01 | .07 | 16 | 4 | .07 | | |
| imitation[c,e] | 150 | 215.3 | 8.3 | 1.2 | 0 | 0 | 0 | .22 | .00 | 0 | 191 | 79 | 16 | 2.88 | |
| 8 fl oz | 244 | 4.3 | 15.0 | 1.9 | 0.0 | 0 | .03 | 0.0 | .00 | .00 | 279 | 181 | .95 | | |
| imitation[d,e] | 150 | 215.2 | 8.3 | 0.0 | 0 | 0 | 0 | .22 | .00 | 0 | 191 | 79 | 16 | 2.88 | |
| 8 fl oz | 244 | 4.3 | 15.0 | 7.4 | 0.0 | 0 | .03 | 0.0 | .00 | .00 | 279 | 181 | .95 | | |
| indian buffalo | 236 | 203.5 | 16.8 | 0.4 | 46 | 129 | 6 | .33 | .06 | 14 | 127 | 412 | 76 | .54 | |
| 8 fl oz | 244 | 9.2 | 12.6 | 11.2 | 0.0 | 434 | .13 | 0.2 | .89 | .47 | 434 | 286 | .29 | | |
| sheep | 264 | 197.7 | 17.2 | 0.8 | | 103 | 10 | .87 | | | 108 | 474 | 45 | | |
| 8 fl oz | 245 | 14.7 | 13.1 | 11.3 | 0.0 | 360 | .16 | 1.0 | 1.74 | 1.00 | 334 | 387 | .24 | | |
| soy | 79 | 223.9 | 4.6 | 2.0 | 0 | 8 | 0 | .17 | .10 | 4 | 30 | 10 | 45 | .54 | .408 |
| 1 cup | 240 | 6.6 | 4.3 | 0.5 | 2.6 | 77 | .39 | 0.4 | .00 | .12 | 338 | 117 | 1.38 | .288 | |

[a] Reconstitutes to 1 qt fluid skim milk.
[b] Filled milk contains fats or oils other than milk fat; contains milk solids (milk, cream, or skim milk).
[c] Contains blend of hydrogenated soybean, cottonseed &/or safflower oils.
[d] Contains lauric acid oils which include modified coconut oil, hydrogenated coconut oil &/or palm kernel oil.
[e] Imitation milk contains fats or oils other than milk fat; contains food solids, excluding milk solids.

| | KCAL | H₂O (g) | FAT (g) | PUFA (g) | CHOL (mg) | A (RE) | C (mg) | B-2 (mg) | B-6 (mg) | FOL (mcg) | Na (mg) | Ca (mg) | Mg (mg) | Zn (mg) | Mn (mg) |
|---|---|---|---|---|---|---|---|---|---|---|---|---|---|---|---|
| | WT (g) | PRO (g) | CHO (g) | SFA (g) | DFIB (g) | A (IU) | B-1 (mg) | NIA (mg) | B-12 (mcg) | PANT (mg) | K (mg) | P (mg) | Fe (mg) | Cu (mg) | |

## 23.3. YOGURT (FROM COW MILK)

| | KCAL | H₂O | FAT | PUFA | CHOL | A(RE) | C | B-2 | B-6 | FOL | Na | Ca | Mg | Zn | Mn |
|---|---|---|---|---|---|---|---|---|---|---|---|---|---|---|---|
| **custard style** | 160 | | 4.0 | | | | | | | | 140 | | | | |
| *8 fl oz* | 227 | 12.0 | 18.0 | | | | | | | | 560 | | | | |
| **flavored[a]** | 187 | | 4.0 | | | | | | | | 97 | | | | |
| *6 fl oz* | 170 | 7.0 | 31.4 | | | | | | | | 291 | | | | |
| **lowfat, breakfast, Yoplait[b]** | 228 | | 3.7 | | | | | | | | 91 | | | | |
| *6 fl oz* | 170 | 8.0 | 40.6 | | | | | | | | 354 | | | | |
| **lowfat w/ nfdm** | 144 | 193.1 | 3.5 | 0.1 | 14 | 36 | 2 | .49 | .11 | 25 | 159 | 415 | 40 | 2.02 | |
| *8 fl oz* | 227 | 11.9 | 16.0 | 2.3 | 0.0 | 150 | .10 | 0.3 | 1.28 | 1.34 | 531 | 326 | .18 | | |
| coffee/van flavor | 194 | 179.3 | 2.8 | 0.0 | 11 | 30 | 2 | .46 | .10 | 24 | 149 | 389 | 37 | 1.88 | |
| *8 fl oz* | 227 | 11.2 | 31.3 | 1.8 | 0.0 | 123 | .10 | 0.2 | 1.20 | 1.25 | 498 | 306 | .16 | | |
| fruit flavor | 225 | 170.9 | 2.6 | 0.1 | 10 | 27 | 1 | .37 | .08 | 19 | 121 | 314 | 30 | 1.52 | |
| *8 fl oz* | 227 | 9.0 | 42.3 | 1.7 | | 111 | .08 | 0.2 | .97 | 1.01 | 402 | 247 | .14 | | |
| **skim w/ nfdm** | 127 | 193.5 | 0.4 | 0.0 | 4 | 5 | 2 | .53 | .12 | 28 | 174 | 452 | 43 | 2.20 | |
| *8 fl oz* | 227 | 13.0 | 17.4 | 0.3 | 0.0 | 16 | .11 | 0.3 | 1.39 | 1.46 | 579 | 355 | .20 | | |
| **whole** | 139 | 199.5 | 7.4 | 0.2 | 29 | 68 | 1 | .32 | .07 | 17 | 105 | 274 | 26 | 1.34 | |
| *8 fl oz* | 227 | 7.9 | 10.6 | 4.8 | 0.0 | 279 | .07 | 0.2 | .84 | .88 | 351 | 215 | .11 | | |
| fruit flavor, Yoplait[b] | 190 | | 4.0 | | | | | | | | 105 | | | | |
| *6 fl oz* | 170 | 7.0 | 32.0 | | | | | | | | 350 | | | | |
| **yo creme, Yoplait[c]** | 236 | | 9.2 | | | | | | | | 83 | | | | |
| *5 fl oz* | | 6.4 | 31.6 | | | | | | | | 320 | | | | |

## 23.4. MILK BEVERAGES

| | KCAL | H₂O | FAT | PUFA | CHOL | A(RE) | C | B-2 | B-6 | FOL | Na | Ca | Mg | Zn | Mn |
|---|---|---|---|---|---|---|---|---|---|---|---|---|---|---|---|
| **Alba choc flavor nonfat dry milk in water** | 80 | | 1.0 | | | | 1 | .29 | .06 | | 120 | 310 | | | |
| *8 fl oz* | | 6.0 | 13.0 | | | 378 | .07 | 0.2 | | | 169 | | .24 | | |
| **carob flavor mix in whole milk** | 195 | 215.0 | 8.2 | 0.3 | 33 | 76 | 2 | .39 | .12 | 12 | 132 | 291 | 33 | .93 | .005 |
| *3 t powder in 8 fl oz milk* | 256 | 8.2 | 22.6 | 5.1 | | 307 | .10 | 0.3 | .87 | .77 | 370 | 228 | .67 | .023 | |
| **choc flavor mix in whole milk** | 226 | 215.2 | 8.8 | 0.3 | 33 | 76 | 3 | .43 | .10 | 12 | 165 | 300 | 54 | 1.26 | .157 |
| *2-3 hp t powder in 8 fl oz milk* | 266 | 8.8 | 30.9 | 5.5 | | 312 | .10 | 0.3 | .87 | .77 | 498 | 256 | .80 | .176 | |
| **choc malted milk flavor mix** | | | | | | | | | | | | | | | |
| in whole milk | 229 | 215.0 | 8.9 | 0.4 | 34 | 80 | 3 | .44 | .14 | 16 | 172 | 304 | 47 | 1.09 | .005 |
| *3 hp t powder in 8 fl oz milk* | 265 | 9.1 | 29.8 | 5.5 | | 326 | .13 | 0.6 | .91 | .77 | 499 | 265 | .60 | .066 | |
| w/ added nutrients in whole milk | 225 | 215.2 | 8.9 | 0.4 | 33 | 900 | 34 | 1.26 | 1.02 | 32 | 244 | 384 | 53 | 1.15 | .135 |
| *4-5 hp t powder in 8 fl oz milk* | 265 | 9.1 | 29.1 | 5.5 | | 3058 | .73 | 10.9 | .87 | .91 | 620 | 312 | 3.77 | .156 | |
| **choc milk** | | | | | | | | | | | | | | | |
| 1% fat milk | 158 | 211.3 | 2.5 | 0.1 | 7 | 148 | 2 | .42 | .10 | 12 | 152 | 287 | 33 | 1.02 | |
| *8 fl oz* | 250 | 8.1 | 26.1 | 1.5 | | 500 | .10 | 0.3 | .86 | .76 | 426 | 256 | .60 | | |
| 2% fat milk | 179 | 209.0 | 5.0 | 0.2 | 17 | 142 | 2 | .41 | .10 | 12 | 150 | 284 | 33 | 1.02 | |
| *8 fl oz* | 250 | 8.0 | 26.0 | 3.1 | | 500 | .09 | 0.3 | .85 | .75 | 422 | 254 | .60 | | |
| whole milk | 208 | 205.8 | 8.5 | 0.3 | 30 | 72 | 2 | .41 | .10 | 12 | 149 | 280 | 33 | 1.02 | .120 |
| *8 fl oz* | 250 | 7.9 | 25.9 | 5.3 | | 302 | .09 | 0.3 | .84 | .74 | 417 | 251 | .60 | .146 | |
| whole milk w/ malt | 233 | 215.1 | 9.1 | 0.4 | 34 | 80 | 2 | .43 | .13 | 17 | 168 | 304 | 48 | 1.11 | .095 |
| *8 fl oz* | 265 | 9.4 | 29.2 | 5.5 | | 326 | .14 | 0.7 | .92 | .77 | 500 | 265 | .50 | .066 | |
| **choc syrup in whole milk** | 232 | 229.0 | 8.5 | 0.3 | 33 | 77 | 2 | .42 | .10 | 14 | 156 | 297 | 57 | 1.20 | .149 |
| *2 T syrup in 8 fl oz milk* | 282 | 8.8 | 33.5 | 5.3 | | 319 | .10 | 0.3 | .87 | .77 | 455 | 277 | .91 | .217 | |
| **choc syrup w/ added nutrients in whole** | 196 | 220.4 | 8.4 | 0.3 | 33 | 320 | 3 | .55 | .11 | 12 | 148 | 292 | 33 | .93 | .005 |
| **milk**—*1 T syrup in 8 fl oz milk* | 263 | 8.4 | 23.8 | 5.2 | | 1125 | .10 | 6.5 | .87 | .77 | 460 | 228 | 2.67 | .024 | |
| **cocoa/hot chocolate** | | | | | | | | | | | | | | | |
| prep w/ whole milk | 218 | 204.0 | 9.1 | 0.3 | 33 | 85 | 2 | .44 | .11 | 12 | 123 | 298 | 56 | 1.22 | |
| *8 fl oz* | 250 | 9.1 | 25.8 | 5.6 | | 318 | .10 | 0.4 | .87 | .81 | 480 | 270 | .78 | | |

[a] Values are averages for 7 flavors.
[b] Values are averages for 9 flavors.
[c] Values are averages for 5 flavors.

| | KCAL / WT (g) | H₂O (g) / PRO (g) | FAT (g) / CHO (g) | PUFA (g) / SFA (g) | CHOL (mg) / DFIB (g) | A (RE) / A (IU) | C (mg) / B-1 (mg) | B-2 (mg) / NIA (mg) | B-6 (mg) / B-12 (mcg) | FOL (mcg) / PANT (mg) | Na (mg) / K (mg) | Ca (mg) / P (mg) | Mg (mg) / Fe (mg) | Zn (mg) / Cu (mg) | Mn (mg) |
|---|---|---|---|---|---|---|---|---|---|---|---|---|---|---|---|
| prep w/ milk, sugar & high-fat plain | 218 | 204.1 | 9.1 | 0.3 | 33 | 85 | 2 | .44 | .11 | 12 | 123 | 298 | 56 | 1.22 | |
| cocoa—8 fl oz | 250 | 9.1 | 25.8 | 5.6 | | 318 | .10 | 0.4 | .87 | .81 | 480 | 270 | .78 | | |
| prep w/ water from mix | 103 | 177.9 | 1.1 | 0.0 | | 1 | 1 | .16 | .03 | 0 | 149 | 96 | 25 | .46 | .078 |
| *3/4 hp t powder in 6 fl oz water* | 206 | 3.1 | 22.5 | 0.7 | | 4 | .03 | 0.2 | .37 | .25 | 203 | 89 | .35 | .093 | |
| sweetened w/ aspartame | 48 | 177.5 | 0.4 | 0.0 | | | 0 | .21 | .05 | 2 | 173 | 90 | 33 | .56 | .100 |
| *.53 oz pkt in 6 fl oz water* | 192 | 3.8 | 8.5 | 0.3 | | | .04 | 0.2 | | .57 | 405 | 134 | .75 | .121 | |
| w/ added nutrients | 120 | 178.1 | 3.0 | 0.1 | | 150 | 6 | .17 | | | 207 | 104 | 24 | .27 | .092 |
| *1 pkt in 6 fl oz water* | 209 | 1.9 | 24.1 | 1.8 | | 501 | .15 | 2.0 | | | 405 | 111 | 1.81 | .111 | |
| **dairy drink mix w/ aspartame,** | 64 | 185.3 | 0.5 | 0.0 | | 73 | 0 | .41 | 0.2 | 9 | 172 | 192 | 47 | .81 | .157 |
| **choc, in water**—*3/4 oz pkt in water*[a] | 204 | 5.3 | 10.7 | 0.4 | 0.2 | 245 | .02 | 0.3 | .51 | .46 | 479 | | 1.65 | .182 | |
| **eggnog, nonalcoholic** | 342 | 188.9 | 19.0 | 0.9 | 149 | 203 | 4 | .48 | .13 | 2 | 138 | 330 | 47 | 1.17 | |
| *8 fl oz* | 254 | 9.7 | 34.4 | 11.3 | 0.0 | 894 | .09 | 0.3 | 1.14 | 1.06 | 420 | 278 | .51 | | |
| mix in whole milk | 260 | 214.5 | 8.4 | 0.3 | 33 | 76 | 2 | .39 | .10 | 12 | 163 | 291 | 33 | .92 | .005 |
| *2 hp t in 8 fl oz milk* | 272 | 8.1 | 39.0 | 5.1 | | 307 | .09 | 0.2 | .87 | .76 | 369 | 228 | .38 | .024 | |
| mix in whole milk, Delmark | 290 | | 9.0 | | 35 | | 11 | .65 | .16 | 0 | 220 | 470 | 59 | 1.14 | .010 |
| *1.23 oz mix in 8 fl oz milk* | 257 | 15.0 | 37.0 | 5.7 | 0.0 | 1090 | .29 | 4.2 | 1.90 | 1.30 | 600 | 370 | 3.70 | .070 | |
| **instant breakfast in whole milk** | 280 | | 8.5 | | | | 29 | .60 | .50 | 112 | 280 | 431 | 113 | 3.93 | |
| *1 pkt in 8 fl oz milk*[b] | 265 | 15.0 | 34.5 | | | 2000 | .39 | 5.2 | 1.47 | 2.70 | 670 | 376 | 4.60 | .530 | |
| choc, Delmark | 290 | | 9.0 | | 40 | | 20 | .71 | .66 | 130 | 270 | 470 | 132 | 4.90 | .010 |
| *1.23 oz mix in 8 fl oz milk* | 279 | 15.0 | 37.0 | | 0.0 | 1650 | .50 | 6.6 | 2.00 | 3.30 | 720 | 420 | 5.90 | .660 | |
| van/strawberry, Delmark | 290 | | 9.0 | | 40 | | 20 | .71 | .66 | 130 | 220 | 470 | 132 | 4.90 | .010 |
| *1.23 oz mix in 8 fl oz milk* | 279 | 15.0 | 37.0 | | 0.0 | 1650 | .50 | 6.6 | 2.00 | 3.30 | 630 | 420 | 5.90 | .660 | |
| **instant breakfast, van/strawberry, liquid** | 250 | | 8.0 | | 20 | | 15 | .42 | .50 | 100 | 190 | 300 | 60 | 3.70 | 1.000 |
| **pack, Delmark**—*8 fl oz* | 279 | 12.0 | 33.0 | | | 1250 | .37 | 5.0 | 1.50 | 2.50 | 480 | 300 | 4.50 | .500 | |
| **malted milk** | 236 | 215.2 | 9.9 | 0.6 | 37 | 93 | 2 | .54 | .18 | 22 | 215 | 347 | 52 | 1.14 | .095 |
| *8 fl oz* | 265 | 10.8 | 26.6 | 6.0 | | 376 | .20 | 1.3 | 1.04 | .77 | 529 | 307 | .29 | .066 | |
| **malted milk flavor mix** | | | | | | | | | | | | | | | |
| in whole milk | 237 | 215.1 | 9.8 | 0.6 | 37 | 94 | 3 | .59 | .19 | 22 | 223 | 354 | 52 | 1.13 | .005 |
| *3 hp t in 8 fl oz milk* | 265 | 10.4 | 27.3 | 6.0 | | 369 | .20 | 1.3 | 1.03 | .77 | 529 | 303 | .27 | .066 | |
| w/ added nutrients in whole milk | 230 | 215.3 | 8.7 | 0.4 | 33 | 743 | 29 | 1.15 | .87 | | 205 | 370 | 47 | 1.08 | .093 |
| *4-5 hp t in 8 fl oz milk* | 265 | 9.9 | 28.4 | 5.4 | | 2530 | .71 | 10.4 | | .77 | 573 | 307 | 3.61 | .082 | |
| **milk shake** | | | | | | | | | | | | | | | |
| mix in whole milk, Delmark | | | | | | | | | | | | | | | |
| choc | 230 | | 9.0 | | 35 | | 2 | .41 | .10 | 0 | 240 | 300 | 49 | .93 | .120 |
| *.667 oz mix in 8 fl oz milk* | 263 | 9.0 | 28.0 | | | 340 | .08 | 0.3 | 1.30 | .83 | 450 | 270 | .47 | .034 | |
| strawberry | 230 | | 9.0 | | 35 | | 2 | .40 | .10 | 0 | 160 | 290 | 39 | .93 | |
| *.667 oz mix in 8 fl oz milk* | 263 | 8.0 | 29.0 | | | 340 | .07 | 0.2 | 1.30 | .80 | 360 | 230 | .18 | .040 | |
| van | 230 | | 9.0 | | 35 | | 2 | .40 | .10 | 0 | 160 | 290 | 39 | .93 | |
| *.667 oz mix in 8 fl oz milk* | 263 | 8.0 | 30.0 | | | 340 | .07 | 0.2 | 1.30 | .80 | 360 | 230 | .17 | .039 | |
| thick | | | | | | | | | | | | | | | |
| choc | 356 | 216.6 | 8.1 | 0.3 | 32 | | 0 | .67 | .08 | 15 | 333 | 396 | 48 | 1.44 | |
| *1 avg* | 300 | 9.2 | 63.5 | 5.0 | | 258 | .14 | 0.4 | .95 | 1.09 | 672 | 378 | .93 | | |
| van | 350 | 233.0 | 9.5 | 0.4 | 37 | | 0 | .61 | .13 | 21 | 299 | 457 | 37 | 1.22 | |
| *1 avg* | 313 | 12.1 | 55.6 | 5.9 | | 357 | .09 | 0.5 | 1.63 | | 572 | 361 | .31 | | |
| **strawberry flavored mix in whole milk** | 234 | 215.1 | 8.2 | 0.3 | 33 | 76 | 2 | .42 | .10 | 12 | 128 | 292 | 33 | .93 | .005 |
| *2-3 hp t powder in 8 fl oz milk* | 266 | 8.1 | 32.8 | 5.1 | | 308 | .09 | 0.2 | .87 | .77 | 370 | 228 | .22 | .024 | |

## 23.5. MILK BEVERAGE MIXES

| | KCAL / WT (g) | H₂O (g) / PRO (g) | FAT (g) / CHO (g) | PUFA (g) / SFA (g) | CHOL (mg) / DFIB (g) | A (RE) / A (IU) | C (mg) / B-1 (mg) | B-2 (mg) / NIA (mg) | B-6 (mg) / B-12 (mcg) | FOL (mcg) / PANT (mg) | Na (mg) / K (mg) | Ca (mg) / P (mg) | Mg (mg) / Fe (mg) | Zn (mg) / Cu (mg) | Mn (mg) |
|---|---|---|---|---|---|---|---|---|---|---|---|---|---|---|---|
| **carob flavor mix, powder** | 45 | 0.3 | 0.0 | 0.0 | 0 | | 0 | | .02 | | | | | | |
| *3 t* | 12 | 0.2 | 11.2 | 0.0 | | | .00 | 0.1 | | | | 12 | .55 | | |
| **choc flavor mix, powder** | 75 | 0.2 | 0.7 | 0.0 | 0 | 0 | 0 | .03 | .00 | | 45 | 8 | 21 | .33 | .153 |
| *2-3 hp t* | 22 | 0.7 | 19.5 | 0.4 | | 4 | .01 | 0.1 | .00 | | 128 | 28 | .68 | .152 | |
| **choc malted milk flavor mix, powder** | 79 | 0.3 | 0.8 | 0.1 | 1 | 4 | 0 | .04 | .03 | 4 | 53 | 13 | 15 | .17 | |
| *3/4 oz (3 hp t)* | 21 | 1.1 | 18.4 | 0.5 | | 19 | .04 | 0.4 | .04 | | 130 | 37 | .48 | .042 | |
| **choc malted milk flavor mix w/ added** | 75 | 0.5 | 0.7 | 0.1 | | 824 | 32 | .86 | .92 | 20 | 125 | 93 | 20 | .22 | .132 |
| **nutrients, powder**—*3/4 oz (4-5 hp t)* | 21 | 1.0 | 17.7 | 0.4 | | 2751 | .64 | 10.7 | | .14 | 251 | 84 | 3.65 | .133 | |
| **choc syrup** | 82 | 13.9 | 0.3 | 0.0 | 0 | 1 | 0 | .02 | .00 | 2 | 36 | 5 | 24 | .27 | .143 |
| *2 T (1 fl oz)* | 38 | 0.7 | 22.1 | 0.2 | | 1 | .00 | 0.1 | .00 | .01 | 84 | 48 | .79 | .192 | |

[a] 4 fl oz water w/ 3 ice cubes.   [b] Averages for various flavors of instant breakfast.

| | KCAL | H₂O (g) | FAT (g) | PUFA (g) | CHOL (mg) | A (RE) | C (mg) | B-2 (mg) | B-6 (mg) | FOL (mcg) | Na (mg) | Ca (mg) | Mg (mg) | Zn (mg) | Mn (mg) |
|---|---|---|---|---|---|---|---|---|---|---|---|---|---|---|---|
| | WT (g) | PRO (g) | CHO (g) | SFA (g) | DFIB (g) | A (IU) | B-1 (mg) | NIA (mg) | B-12 (mcg) | PANT (mg) | K (mg) | P (mg) | Fe (mg) | Cu (mg) | |
| **choc syrup w/ added nutrients** | 46 | 5.5 | 0.2 | 0.0 | 0 | 245 | 0 | .16 | .00 | | 29 | | | | |
| *1 T* | 19 | 0.3 | 12.4 | 0.1 | | 817 | .00 | 6.3 | | | 90 | | 2.55 | | |
| **cocoa mix, powder** | 102 | 0.4 | 1.1 | 0.0 | | 1 | 1 | .16 | .03 | 0 | 143 | 93 | 24 | .41 | .076 |
| *1 oz pkt (3-4 hp t)* | 28 | 3.1 | 22.5 | 0.7 | | 4 | .03 | 0.2 | .38 | .25 | 202 | 89 | .34 | .081 | |
| **Alba** | 62 | | 0.5 | | 4 | | 1 | .29 | | | 134 | 323 | | | |
| *19.14 g pkt* | 19 | 5.4 | 10.2 | | | 283 | .06 | 0.2 | | | 425 | 238 | .07 | | |
| **aspartame sweetened** | 48 | 0.5 | 0.4 | 0.0 | | 0 | 1 | .21 | .05 | 2 | 168 | 86 | 31 | .52 | .100 |
| *.53 oz pkt* | 15 | 3.8 | 8.5 | 0.3 | | | .04 | 0.2 | | .57 | 405 | 134 | .74 | .110 | |
| **choc & marshmallow** | 110 | 0.5 | 1.0 | | | | 1 | .15 | .01 | 1 | 120 | 49 | 1 | .12 | .000 |
| *1 oz* | 28 | 2.0 | 23.0 | | | 1 | .02 | 0.1 | .05 | .04 | 179 | 76 | .23 | .003 | |
| **milk choc** | 110 | 0.7 | 1.0 | | | | 0 | .17 | .03 | 4 | 120 | 89 | 7 | .25 | .001 |
| *1 oz* | 28 | 3.0 | 23.0 | | | 3 | .03 | 0.1 | .30 | .20 | 174 | 96 | .21 | .020 | |
| **rich choc** | 110 | 0.5 | 1.0 | | | | 0 | .15 | .01 | 1 | 120 | 49 | 1 | .12 | .002 |
| *1 oz* | 28 | 2.0 | 23.0 | | | 1 | .02 | 0.1 | .06 | .04 | 179 | 76 | .21 | .003 | |
| **rich choc, 70 cal** | 70 | 0.4 | 0.0 | | | | 1 | .16 | .04 | 5 | 125 | 89 | 16 | .40 | .07 |
| *1 pkt (3 hp t)* | 21 | 3.0 | 15.0 | | | 3 | .01 | 0.1 | .37 | .30 | 196 | 85 | .46 | .100 | |
| **sugar-free** | 50 | 0.6 | 0.0 | | | | 1 | .23 | .04 | 6 | 160 | 123 | 20 | .50 | .09 |
| *1 pkt (4 hp t)* | 15 | 4.0 | 8.2 | | | 4 | .03 | 0.2 | .46 | .34 | 290 | 131 | .87 | .120 | |
| **Hershey** | 76 | | 0.4 | | | | | .01 | | | 50 | 6 | 23 | .38 | .168 |
| *3 t (3/4 oz)* | 21 | 1.0 | 16.8 | | | 4 | .01 | 0.1 | | | 89 | 17 | .69 | .168 | |
| **w/ added nutrients** | 120 | 0.5 | 3.0 | 0.1 | | 150 | 6 | .17 | | | 201 | 100 | 22 | .22 | .090 |
| *1.1 oz pkt* | 31 | 1.9 | 24.0 | 1.8 | | 500 | .15 | 2.0 | | | 404 | 111 | 1.80 | .100 | |
| **dairy drink mix, choc powder, aspartame sweetened**—*3/4 oz pkt* | 63 | 2.7 | 0.5 | 0.0 | | 73 | 0 | .41 | .02 | 9 | 166 | 187 | 45 | .77 | .155 |
| | 21 | 5.3 | 10.7 | 0.4 | 0.3 | 245 | .02 | 0.3 | .51 | .46 | 477 | | 1.64 | .170 | |
| **dairy light, Alba** | 10 | | 0.0 | | | | 0 | .06 | | | 15 | 40 | | | |
| *2.8 g pkt* | 2.8 | 1.0 | 1.0 | | | 0 | .01 | 0.0 | | | | | .08 | | |
| **eggnog mix, powder, nonalcoholic** | 111 | 0.1 | 0.3 | 0.0 | | 0 | | | .00 | | 44 | | | | |
| *2 hp t* | 28 | 0.1 | 27.7 | 0.1 | | | .00 | 0.0 | | | | | .26 | | |
| **fit 'n frosty, Alba** | | | | | | | | | | | | | | | |
| **choc** | 70 | | 1.0 | | | | 1 | .30 | | | 210 | 310 | | | |
| *21.26 g pkt* | 21 | 6.0 | 11.0 | | | 304 | .07 | 0.4 | | | | 176 | .43 | | |
| **choc marshmallow** | 70 | | 1.0 | | | | 1 | .29 | | | 250 | 310 | | | |
| *21.26 g pkt* | 21 | 6.0 | 11.0 | | | 305 | .07 | 0.5 | | | | 177 | .39 | | |
| **double fudge** | 70 | | 1.0 | | | | 1 | .28 | | | 170 | 310 | | | |
| *21.26 g pkt* | 21 | 6.0 | 11.0 | | | 305 | .07 | 0.5 | | | | 173 | .42 | | |
| **strawberry** | 70 | | 0.0 | | | | 1 | .36 | | | 150 | 310 | | | |
| *21.26 g pkt* | 21 | 5.0 | 12.0 | | | 265 | .09 | 0.6 | | | | 187 | .10 | | |
| **van** | 70 | | 0.0 | | | | 1 | .30 | | | 150 | 310 | | | |
| *21.26 g pkt* | 21 | 5.0 | 12.0 | | | 218 | .08 | 1.9 | | | | 182 | .10 | | |
| **instant breakfast** | | | | | | | | | | | | | | | |
| **choc, Carnation** | 130 | 1.0 | 0.0 | | | | 27 | .24 | .40 | 100 | 135 | 165 | 80 | 3.00 | |
| *1.25 oz pkt* | 35 | 7.0 | 24.0 | | | 1750 | .30 | 5.0 | .60 | 2.00 | 290 | 160 | 4.50 | .500 | |
| **choc, Pillsbury** | 137 | 1.0 | 0.5 | | | | 24 | .37 | | | 149 | 97 | | | |
| *1 pouch* | 37 | 5.9 | 27.0 | | | 1777 | .48 | 6.1 | | | 270 | 94 | 5.92 | | |
| **choc malt, Carnation** | 130 | 1.0 | 1.0 | | | | 27 | .12 | .40 | 100 | 170 | 80 | 80 | 3.00 | |
| *1.24 oz pkt* | 35 | 7.0 | 23.0 | | | 1750 | .30 | 5.0 | .60 | 2.00 | 200 | 115 | 4.50 | .500 | |
| **choc malt, Pillsbury** | 134 | 1.1 | 0.5 | | | | 24 | .44 | | | 126 | 124 | | | |
| *1 pouch* | 37 | 5.9 | 26.6 | | | 1780 | .48 | 6.1 | | | 278 | 132 | 5.92 | | |
| **coffee, Carnation** | 130 | 1.0 | 0.0 | | | | 27 | .30 | .40 | 100 | 130 | 200 | 80 | 3.00 | |
| *1.26 oz pkt* | 36 | 7.0 | 24.0 | | | 1750 | .30 | 5.0 | .60 | 2.00 | 400 | 180 | 4.50 | .500 | |
| **eggnog, Carnation** | 130 | 1.0 | 0.0 | | | | 27 | .18 | .40 | 100 | 180 | 135 | 80 | 3.00 | |
| *1.20 oz pkt* | 34 | 7.0 | 24.0 | | | 1750 | .30 | 5.0 | .60 | 2.00 | 220 | 125 | 4.50 | .500 | |
| **strawberry, Carnation** | 130 | 1.0 | 0.0 | .01 | 3 | | 27 | .30 | .40 | 100 | 190 | 200 | 80 | 3.00 | |
| *1.25 oz pkt* | 35 | 7.0 | 24.0 | .08 | | 1750 | .30 | 5.0 | .60 | 2.00 | 360 | 180 | 4.50 | .500 | |
| **strawberry, Pillsbury** | 137 | 0.9 | 0.3 | | | | 24 | .33 | | | 138 | 96 | | | |
| *1 pouch* | 37 | 5.7 | 27.9 | | | 1777 | .48 | 6.1 | | | 265 | 81 | 5.70 | | |
| **van, Carnation** | 130 | 1.0 | 0.0 | | | | 27 | .30 | .40 | 100 | 135 | 200 | 80 | 3.00 | |
| *1.23 oz pkt* | 35 | 7.0 | 24.0 | | | 1750 | .30 | 5.0 | .60 | 2.00 | 360 | 180 | 4.50 | .500 | |

| | KCAL / WT (g) | H₂O (g) / PRO (g) | FAT (g) / CHO (g) | PUFA (g) / SFA (g) | CHOL (mg) / DFIB (g) | A (RE) / A (IU) | C (mg) / B-1 (mg) | B-2 (mg) / NIA (mg) | B-6 (mg) / B-12 (mcg) | FOL (mcg) / PANT (mg) | Na (mg) / K (mg) | Ca (mg) / P (mg) | Mg (mg) / Fe (mg) | Zn (mg) / Cu (mg) | Mn (mg) |
|---|---|---|---|---|---|---|---|---|---|---|---|---|---|---|---|
| van, Pillsbury | 140 | 0.9 | 0.2 | | | | 24 | .26 | | | 210 | 84 | | | |
| *1 pouch* | 37 | 5.6 | 28.9 | | | 2073 | .33 | 5.0 | | | 242 | 117 | 5.40 | | |
| **instant breakfast, no sugar added, Carnation** | | | | | | | | | | | | | | | |
| choc | 70 | 0.9 | 1.0 | | | | 27 | .17 | .40 | 100 | 140 | 100 | 80 | 3.00 | |
| *.69 oz pkt* | 20 | 7.0 | 8.0 | | | 1750 | .30 | 5.0 | .60 | 2.00 | 268 | 100 | 4.50 | .500 | |
| choc malted | 70 | 0.9 | 1.0 | | | | 27 | .14 | .40 | 100 | 150 | 60 | 80 | 3.00 | |
| *.71 oz pkt* | 20 | 7.0 | 9.0 | | | 1750 | .30 | 5.0 | .60 | 2.00 | 181 | 80 | 4.50 | .500 | |
| strawberry | 70 | 0.8 | 0.0 | | | | 27 | .26 | .40 | 100 | 120 | 150 | 80 | 3.00 | |
| *.68 oz pkt* | 19 | 7.0 | 9.0 | | | 1750 | .30 | 5.0 | .60 | 2.00 | 296 | 100 | 4.50 | .500 | |
| van | 70 | 0.8 | 0.0 | | | | 27 | .26 | .40 | 100 | 120 | 150 | 80 | 3.00 | |
| *.67 oz pkt* | 19 | 7.0 | 9.0 | | | 1750 | .30 | 5.0 | .60 | 2.00 | 296 | 100 | 4.50 | .500 | |
| **malted milk flavor mix, powder** | 87 | 0.4 | 1.7 | 0.3 | 4 | 19 | 1 | .19 | .09 | 10 | 103 | 63 | 20 | .21 | |
| *3/4 oz (3 hp t)* | 21 | 2.3 | 15.9 | 0.9 | | 61 | .11 | 1.1 | .16 | | 159 | 75 | .15 | .042 | |
| **malted milk flavor mix w/ added nutrients, powder**—*3/4 oz (4-5 hp t)* | 80 | 0.6 | 0.6 | 0.1 | | 668 | 27 | .75 | .76 | | 85 | 79 | 14 | .15 | .089 |
| | 21 | 1.8 | 17.1 | 0.3 | | 222 | .62 | 10.2 | | | 203 | 79 | 3.49 | .059 | |
| **strawberry flavor mix, powder** | 84 | 0.1 | 0.0 | | 0 | | 0 | .02 | .00 | | 8 | | | | |
| *2-3 hp t* | 22 | 0.0 | 21.4 | | | | .00 | 0.0 | .00 | | | | | .09 | |

## 24. NUTS, NUT PRODUCTS & SEEDS

| | KCAL / WT (g) | H₂O (g) / PRO (g) | FAT (g) / CHO (g) | PUFA (g) / SFA (g) | CHOL (mg) / DFIB (g) | A (RE) / A (IU) | C (mg) / B-1 (mg) | B-2 (mg) / NIA (mg) | B-6 (mg) / B-12 (mcg) | FOL (mcg) / PANT (mg) | Na (mg) / K (mg) | Ca (mg) / P (mg) | Mg (mg) / Fe (mg) | Zn (mg) / Cu (mg) | Mn (mg) |
|---|---|---|---|---|---|---|---|---|---|---|---|---|---|---|---|
| **acorn flour, full-fat** | 142 | 1.7 | 8.6 | 1.7 | 0 | | | | | | | 12 | 31 | .18 | |
| *1 oz* | 28 | 2.1 | 15.5 | 1.1 | | | | .00 | | | 202 | 29 | .34 | .174 | |
| **acorns** | | | | | | | | | | | | | | | |
| raw | 105 | 7.9 | 6.8 | 1.3 | 0 | | 0 | .03 | | | 0 | 12 | 18 | .14 | |
| *1 oz* | 28 | 1.8 | 11.6 | 0.9 | | | .03 | 0.5 | .00 | | 153 | 12 | .22 | .176 | |
| dried | 145 | 1.4 | 8.9 | 1.7 | 0 | | 0 | .04 | | | 0 | 15 | 23 | .19 | |
| *1 oz* | 28 | 2.3 | 15.2 | 1.2 | | | .04 | 0.7 | .00 | | 201 | 29 | .30 | .232 | |
| **almond butter** | 101 | 0.2 | 9.5 | 2.0 | 0 | 0 | 0 | .10 | .01 | 10 | 2[a] | 43 | 48 | .49 | .377 |
| *1 T* | 16 | 2.4 | 3.4 | 0.9 | | 0 | .02 | 0.5 | .00 | .04 | 121 | 84 | .59 | .144 | |
| **almond butter w/ honey & cinn** | 96 | 0.3 | 8.4 | 1.8 | 0 | 0 | 0 | .10 | .01 | 10 | 2[b] | 43 | 48 | .48 | .373 |
| *1 T* | 16 | 2.5 | 4.3 | 0.8 | | 0 | .02 | 0.5 | .00 | .04 | 120 | 83 | .59 | .155 | |
| **almond meal, partially defatted** | 116 | 2.0 | 5.2 | 1.1 | 0 | 0 | | .48 | | | 2[c] | 120 | | | |
| *1 oz* | 28 | 11.2 | 8.2 | 0.5 | | 0 | .09 | 1.8 | .00 | | 398 | 260 | 2.41 | | |
| **almond paste** | 127 | 4.4 | 7.7 | 1.6 | 0 | 0 | 0 | .21 | .03 | 16 | 3 | 65 | 73 | .73 | .571 |
| *1 oz* | 28 | 3.4 | 12.4 | 0.7 | | 0 | .06 | 0.8 | .00 | .12 | 184 | 127 | .90 | .237 | |
| **almonds** | | | | | | | | | | | | | | | |
| barbeque, Blue Diamond | 166 | 0.4 | 14.9 | | | | | .33 | | | 172 | 92 | | | |
| *1 oz* | 28 | 6.1 | 4.8 | | | | .03 | 1.0 | | | 116 | | 1.07 | | |
| blanched, Blue Diamond | 174 | 1.4 | 14.4 | 3.3 | 0 | | | .20 | .03 | 10 | 1 | 73 | 86 | .94 | |
| *1 oz* | 28 | 6.0 | 5.2 | 1.2 | | | .04 | 0.9 | | | 173 | 150 | 1.09 | .310 | |
| blanched, slivered, Blue Diamond | 176 | 1.3 | 14.6 | 3.3 | 0 | | | .19 | .03 | 10 | 0 | 72 | 87 | .98 | |
| *1 oz* | 28 | 6.0 | 5.1 | 1.2 | | | .05 | 0.9 | | | 179 | 151 | 1.04 | .330 | |
| cheese, Blue Diamond | 156 | 0.4 | 12.5 | | | | | .34 | | | 95 | 102 | | | |
| *1 oz* | 28 | 6.1 | 7.4 | | | | .03 | 0.8 | | | 126 | | 1.04 | | |
| chopped, Blue Diamond | 175 | 1.3 | 14.6 | 3.3 | 0 | | | .20 | .03 | 10 | 0 | 77 | 85 | .92 | |
| *1 oz* | 28 | 6.0 | 5.0 | 1.2 | | | .06 | 0.9 | | | 174 | 151 | 1.15 | .300 | |
| dried | 167 | 1.3 | 14.8 | 3.1 | 0 | 0 | 0 | .22 | .03 | 17 | 3 | 75 | 84 | .83 | .646 |
| *1 oz (24 nuts)* | 28 | 5.7 | 5.8 | 1.4 | 1.3 | 0 | .06 | 1.0 | .00 | .13 | 208 | 148 | 1.04 | .268 | |
| dry roasted | 167 | 0.9 | 14.7 | 3.1 | 0 | 0 | 0 | .17 | .02 | 18 | 3[d] | 80 | 86 | 1.39 | .561 |
| *1 oz* | 28 | 4.6 | 6.9 | 1.4 | | 0 | .04 | 0.8 | .00 | .07 | 219 | 156 | 1.08 | .348 | |
| dry roasted, hickory smoke, Blue Diamond—*1 oz* | 166 | 0.7 | 15.0 | | | | | .42 | | | 121 | 117 | | | |
| | 28 | 5.9 | 4.9 | | | | .08 | 1.4 | | | 109 | | 1.31 | | |
| dry roasted, unsalted, Blue Diamond | 168 | 0.5 | 15.1 | | | | | .41 | | | 1 | 92 | | | |
| *1 oz* | 28 | 6.0 | 5.1 | | | | .01 | 0.6 | | | 175 | | 1.35 | | |
| oil roasted | 176 | 0.9 | 16.4 | 3.4 | 0 | 0 | 0 | .28 | .02 | 18 | 3[d] | 66 | 86 | 1.39 | .561 |
| *1 oz (22 nuts)* | 28 | 5.8 | 4.5 | 1.6 | | 0 | .04 | 1.0 | .00 | .07 | 194 | 155 | 1.09 | .348 | |

[a] If salt is added, Na is 126 mg.
[b] If salt is added, Na is 48 mg.
[c] If salt is added, Na is 209 mg.
[d] If salt is added, Na is 218 mg.

| | KCAL / WT (g) | H₂O (g) / PRO (g) | FAT (g) / CHO (g) | PUFA (g) / SFA (g) | CHOL (mg) / DFIB (g) | A (RE) / A (IU) | C (mg) / B-1 (mg) | B-2 (mg) / NIA (mg) | B-6 (mg) / B-12 (mcg) | FOL (mcg) / PANT (mg) | Na (mg) / K (mg) | Ca (mg) / P (mg) | Mg (mg) / Fe (mg) | Zn (mg) / Cu (mg) | Mn (mg) |
|---|---|---|---|---|---|---|---|---|---|---|---|---|---|---|---|
| oil roasted, blanched, salted, Blue Diamond—1 oz | 174 | 0.7 | 16.3 | | | | | .40 | | | 70 | 65 | | | |
|  | 28 | 5.9 | 4.0 | | | | .02 | 1.2 | | | 165 | | 1.40 | | |
| oil roasted, salted, Blue Diamond | 174 | 0.4 | 16.4 | | | | | .31 | | | 95 | 87 | | | |
| 1 oz | 28 | 6.3 | 3.4 | | | | .03 | 1.0 | | | 132 | | 1.07 | | |
| onion garlic, Blue Diamond | 160 | 0.5 | 13.6 | | | | | .32 | | | 168 | 125 | | | |
| 1 oz | 28 | 6.1 | 6.3 | | | | .02 | 0.9 | | | 112 | | 1.12 | | |
| sliced, Blue Diamond | 175 | 1.3 | 14.6 | 3.3 | 0 | | | .20 | .03 | 10 | 0 | 77 | 85 | .92 | |
| 1 oz | 28 | 6.0 | 5.0 | 1.2 | | | .06 | 0.9 | | | 174 | 151 | 1.15 | .300 | |
| smokehouse, Blue Diamond | 171 | 0.4 | 15.8 | | | | | .34 | | | 123 | 101 | | | |
| 1 oz | 28 | 5.9 | 4.3 | | | | .03 | 1.0 | | | 129 | | 1.11 | | |
| toasted | 167 | 0.7 | 14.4 | 3.0 | 0 | 0 | 0 | .17 | .02 | 18 | 3 | 80 | 87 | 1.40 | .569 |
| 1 oz | 28 | 5.8 | 6.5 | 1.4 | | 0 | .04 | 0.8 | .00 | .07 | 220 | 156 | 1.40 | .349 | |
| whole, Blue Diamond | 173 | 1.4 | 14.2 | 3.3 | 0 | | 0 | .30 | .03 | 10 | 0 | 79 | 86 | .95 | .510 |
| 1 oz | 28 | 5.9 | 5.4 | 1.2 | 3.5 | 0 | .05 | 0.9 | .00 | .00 | 179 | 149 | 1.30 | .300 | |
| **beechnuts, dried** | 164 | 1.9 | 14.2 | 5.7 | 0 | | | | | | | 0 | | | |
| 1 oz | 28 | 1.8 | 9.5 | 1.6 | | | | .00 | | | | 0 | | | |
| **brazilnuts, dried** | 186 | 1.0 | 18.8 | 6.9 | 0 | | 0 | .04 | .07 | 1 | 0 | 50 | 64 | 1.30 | .220 |
| 1 oz (8 med nuts) | 28 | 4.1 | 3.6 | 4.6 | | | .28 | 0.5 | .00 | .07 | 170 | 170 | 1.0 | .503 | |
| **butternuts, dried** | 174 | 1.0 | 16.2 | 12.1 | 0 | | | | | | 0 | 15 | 67 | .89 | 1.863 |
| 1 oz | 28 | 7.1 | 3.4 | 0.4 | | | | .00 | | | 119 | 127 | 1.14 | .128 | |
| **cashew butter** | 167 | 0.8 | 14.0 | 2.4 | 0 | 0 | 0 | .05 | .07 | 19 | 4[a] | 12 | 73 | 1.47 | |
| 1 oz | 28 | 5.0 | 7.8 | 2.8 | | 0 | .09 | 0.5 | .00 | .34 | 155 | 130 | 1.43 | .622 | |
| **cashews** | | | | | | | | | | | | | | | |
| dry roasted | 163 | 0.5 | 13.2 | 2.2 | 0 | 0 | 0 | .06 | .07 | 20 | 4[b] | 13 | 74 | 1.59 | |
| 1 oz | 28 | 4.4 | 9.3 | 2.6 | | 0 | .06 | 0.4 | .00 | .35 | 160 | 139 | 1.70 | .630 | |
| honey roast, Planters | 170 | | 12.0 | 2 | | | | | | | 170 | | | | |
| 1 oz | 28 | 4.0 | 11.0 | 2 | | | | | | | 135 | | | | |
| oil roasted | 163 | 1.1 | 13.7 | 2.3 | 0 | 0 | 0 | .05 | .07 | 19 | 5[c] | 12 | 72 | 1.35 | .229 |
| 1 oz (18 med nuts) | 28 | 4.6 | 8.1 | 2.7 | | 0 | .12 | 0.5 | .00 | .34 | 151 | 121 | 1.16 | .616 | |
| **cashew & peanuts, honey roast, Planters** | 170 | | 12.0 | 3 | | | | | | | 170 | | | | |
| 1 oz | 28 | 5.0 | 9.0 | 2 | | | | | | | 150 | | | | |
| **chestnuts, chinese** | | | | | | | | | | | | | | | |
| raw | 64 | 12.5 | 0.3 | 0.1 | 0 | 6 | 10 | .05 | | | 1 | 5 | 24 | .25 | .455 |
| 1 oz | 28 | 1.2 | 13.9 | 0.0 | | 57 | .05 | 0.2 | .00 | | 127 | 27 | .40 | .103 | |
| boiled & steamed | 44 | 17.5 | 0.2 | 0.1 | 0 | | | | | | 1 | 3 | 16 | .17 | .312 |
| 1 oz | 28 | 0.8 | 9.6 | 0.0 | | | | .00 | | | 87 | 19 | .27 | .071 | |
| dried | 103 | 2.5 | 0.5 | 0.1 | 0 | | | | | | 2 | 8 | 39 | .40 | .739 |
| 1 oz | 28 | 1.9 | 22.7 | 0.1 | | | | .00 | | | 206 | 44 | .65 | .168 | |
| roasted | 68 | 11.4 | 0.3 | 0.1 | 0 | 0 | | .03 | | | 1 | 5 | 26 | .26 | |
| 1 oz | 28 | 1.3 | 14.9 | 0.1 | | 1 | .04 | 0.4 | .00 | | 135 | 29 | .43 | .110 | |
| **chestnuts, european** | | | | | | | | | | | | | | | |
| raw | 60 | 13.8 | 0.6 | 0.3 | 0 | 1 | 12 | .05 | .11 | 18 | 1 | 8 | 9 | .15 | .270 |
| 1 oz (2 1/2 nuts) | 28 | 0.7 | 12.9 | 0.1 | 2.8 | 8 | .07 | 0.3 | .00 | .15 | 147 | 26 | .29 | .127 | |
| boiled & steamed | 37 | 19.4 | 0.4 | 0.2 | 0 | | | | | | 8 | 13 | 15 | .07 | .243 |
| 1 oz | 28 | 0.6 | 7.9 | 0.1 | | | | .00 | | | 203 | 28 | .49 | .134 | |
| dried | 106 | 2.7 | 1.3 | 0.5 | 0 | 0 | 4 | .10 | .19 | 31 | 11 | 19 | 21 | .10 | .369 |
| 1 oz | 28 | 1.8 | 22.0 | 0.2 | | 0 | .08 | 0.2 | .00 | .26 | 280 | 50 | .68 | .185 | |
| roasted | 70 | 11.5 | 0.6 | 0.2 | 0 | 1 | 7 | .05 | .14 | 20 | 1 | 8 | 9 | .16 | .335 |
| 1 oz (3 1/2 nuts) | 28 | 0.9 | 15.0 | 0.1 | 3.3 | 7 | .07 | 0.4 | .00 | .16 | 168 | 30 | .26 | .144 | |
| **chestnuts, japanese** | | | | | | | | | | | | | | | |
| raw | 44 | 17.4 | 0.2 | 0.0 | 0 | 1 | 8 | .05 | | | 4 | 9 | 14 | .31 | .452 |
| 1 oz | 28 | 0.6 | 9.9 | 0.0 | | 10 | .10 | 0.4 | .00 | .06 | 94 | 21 | .41 | .160 | |
| boiled & steamed | 16 | 24.4 | 0.1 | 0.0 | 0 | 0 | 3 | .02 | | | 1 | 3 | 5 | .11 | .164 |
| 1 oz | 28 | 0.2 | 3.6 | 0.0 | | 4 | .04 | 0.2 | .00 | .02 | 34 | 7 | .15 | .058 | |
| dried | 102 | 2.8 | 0.4 | 0.1 | 0 | 2 | 17 | .11 | | | 10 | 20 | 33 | .73 | 1.054 |
| 1 oz | 28 | 1.5 | 23.1 | 0.1 | | 24 | .23 | 1.0 | .00 | .14 | 218 | 48 | .96 | .373 | |
| roasted | 57 | 14.2 | 0.2 | 0.1 | 0 | 2 | 8 | .07 | | | | 10 | 18 | .41 | .586 |
| 1 oz | 28 | 0.8 | 12.8 | 0.0 | | 21 | .13 | 0.2 | .00 | | | 26 | .60 | .207 | |

[a] If salt is added, Na is 172 mg.
[b] If salt is added, Na is 179 mg.
[c] If salt is added, Na is 175 mg.

| | | | | | | Vitamins | | | | | Minerals | | | | |
|---|---|---|---|---|---|---|---|---|---|---|---|---|---|---|---|
| | KCAL | H₂O (g) | FAT (g) | PUFA (g) | CHOL (mg) | A (RE) | C (mg) | B-2 (mg) | B-6 (mg) | FOL (mcg) | Na (mg) | Ca (mg) | Mg (mg) | Zn (mg) | Mn (mg) |
| | WT (g) | PRO (g) | CHO (g) | SFA (g) | DFIB (g) | A (IU) | B-1 (mg) | NIA (mg) | B-12 (mcg) | PANT (mg) | K (mg) | P (mg) | Fe (mg) | Cu (mg) | |
| **coconut** | | | | | | | | | | | | | | | |
| raw | 159 | 21.2 | 15.1 | 0.2 | 0 | 0 | 2 | .01 | .02 | 12 | 9 | 6 | 14 | .50 | .675 |
| *1 piece (2"x2"x1/2")* | 45 | 1.5 | 6.9 | 13.4 | | 0 | .03 | 0.2 | .00 | .14 | 160 | 51 | 1.1 | .196 | |
| dried | 187 | 0.9 | 18.3 | 0.2 | 0 | 0 | 0 | .03 | .09 | 3 | 11 | 7 | 26 | .57 | .780 |
| *1 oz* | 28 | 2.0 | 6.7 | 16.3 | | 0 | .02 | 0.2 | .00 | .23 | 154 | 59 | .94 | .226 | |
| dried, sweetened, flaked, cnd | 505 | 26.5 | 36.1 | 0.4 | 0 | 0 | 0 | .02 | | | 23 | 16 | 56 | 1.81 | 2.475 |
| *4 oz* | 114 | 3.8 | 46.6 | 32.0 | | 0 | .03 | 0.3 | .00 | | 369 | 117 | 2.10 | .351 | |
| dried, sweetened, flaked, cnd, Angel Flake—*1/3 cup loosely packed* | 114 | 5.5 | 8.7 | 0.1 | 0 | 0 | 0 | .01 | .04 | 1 | 6 | 3 | 11 | .25 | |
| | 25 | 0.8 | 9.8 | 7.7 | | 0 | .01 | 0.1 | .00 | .10 | 67 | 25 | .42 | .099 | |
| dried, sweetened, flaked, packaged | 351 | 11.6 | 23.8 | 0.3 | 0 | 0 | 0 | .02 | | | 189 | 10 | 36 | 1.30 | 1.767 |
| *1 cup* | 74 | 2.4 | 35.2 | 21.1 | | 0 | .02 | 0.2 | .00 | | 234 | 74 | 1.33 | .223 | |
| dried, sweetened, flaked, packaged, Angel Flake—*1/3 cup loosely pckd* | 116 | 4.5 | 8.1 | 0.1 | 0 | 0 | 0 | .01 | .04 | 1 | 74 | 3 | 10 | .24 | |
| | 25 | 0.8 | 10.4 | 7.2 | | 0 | .01 | 0.1 | .00 | .10 | 63 | 24 | .39 | .093 | |
| dried, sweetened, shredded | 466 | 11.7 | 33.0 | 0.4 | 0 | 0 | 1 | .02 | | | 244 | 14 | 47 | 1.69 | 2.302 |
| *1 cup* | 93 | 2.7 | 44.3 | 29.3 | | 0 | .03 | 0.4 | .00 | | 313 | 99 | 1.78 | .291 | |
| dried, sweetened, shredded, Bakers *1/3 cup loosely packed* | 133 | 4.5 | 9.3 | 0.1 | 0 | 0 | 0 | .01 | .04 | 1 | 83 | 3 | 12 | .27 | |
| | 28 | 0.9 | 12.1 | 8.3 | | 0 | .01 | 0.1 | .00 | .11 | 72 | 27 | .45 | .107 | |
| dried, toasted | 168 | 0.3 | 13.4 | 0.1 | 0 | | | | | | 11 | 8 | 26 | .58 | .795 |
| *1 oz* | 28 | 1.5 | 12.6 | 11.8 | | | | | .00 | | 157 | 60 | .96 | .231 | |
| coconut cream, raw[a] | 792 | 129.4 | 83.2 | 0.9 | 0 | 0 | 7 | .00 | | | 10 | 26 | | 2.30 | 3.130 |
| *1 cup* | 240 | 8.7 | 16.0 | 73.8 | | 0 | .07 | 2.1 | .00 | | 781 | 293 | 5.5 | .907 | |
| coconut cream, sweetened, cnd[a] | 568 | 210.7 | 52.4 | 0.6 | 0 | | | .12 | | | 149 | 4 | | 1.77 | 2.412 |
| *1 cup* | 296 | 8.0 | 24.7 | 46.5 | | | .07 | .11 | .00 | | 299 | 66 | 1.50 | .699 | |
| coconut milk, raw[b] | 552 | 162.3 | 57.2 | 0.6 | 0 | 0 | 7 | .00 | | | 37 | 39 | 89 | 1.61 | 2.198 |
| *1 cup* | 240 | 5.5 | 13.3 | 50.7 | | 0 | .06 | 1.8 | .00 | | 630 | 240 | 3.94 | .638 | |
| coconut milk, cnd[b] | 445 | 164.7 | 48.2 | 0.5 | 0 | | 2 | | | | 29 | 40 | 104 | 1.27 | 1.736 |
| *1 cup* | 226 | 4.6 | 6.3 | 42.7 | | | | | .00 | | 497 | 217 | 7.46 | .504 | |
| coconut water[c] | 46 | 228.0 | 0.5 | 0.0 | 0 | 0 | 6 | .14 | .08 | | 252 | 58 | 60 | .25 | |
| *1 cup* | 240 | 1.7 | 8.9 | 0.4 | | 0 | .07 | 0.2 | .00 | .10 | 600 | 49 | .69 | .096 | |
| **filberts (hazelnuts)** | | | | | | | | | | | | | | | |
| chopped/sliced, Blue Diamond | 161 | 1.6 | 14.4 | | | | 1 | .07 | | | 0 | 38 | | | |
| *1 oz* | 28 | 5.5 | 5.1 | | | 0 | .22 | 0.5 | | | 211 | | 1.17 | | |
| dried | 179 | 1.5 | 17.8 | 1.7 | 0 | 2 | 0 | .03 | .17 | 20 | 1 | 53 | 81 | .68 | .573 |
| *1 oz* | 28 | 3.7 | 4.4 | 1.3 | | 19 | .14 | 0.3 | .00 | .33 | 126 | 89 | .93 | .429 | |
| dry roasted | 188 | 0.5 | 18.8 | 1.8 | 0 | | | | | | 1[d] | 55 | 84 | .71 | .594 |
| *1 oz* | 28 | 2.8 | 5.1 | 1.4 | | | | | .00 | | 131 | 92 | .96 | .444 | |
| oil roasted | 187 | 0.3 | 18.1 | 1.7 | 0 | | | | | | 1[e] | 56 | 85 | .71 | .598 |
| *1 oz* | 28 | 4.1 | 5.4 | 1.3 | | | | | .00 | | 132 | 92 | .97 | .448 | |
| roasted, salted, Blue Diamond | 180 | 0.6 | 17.7 | | | | 1 | .06 | .08 | 70 | 39 | 51 | 46 | .65 | |
| *1 oz* | 28 | 4.6 | 3.9 | | | 0 | .08 | 0.3 | .00 | .19 | 157 | 79 | 1.09 | .350 | |
| whole, Blue Diamond | 166 | 1.7 | 15.4 | 2.8 | 0 | | 0 | .06 | | | 1 | 40 | | | |
| *1 oz* | 28 | 4.9 | 5.0 | 1.1 | | 0 | .17 | 0.3 | | | 167 | | 1.18 | | |
| **fruit 'n nut mix, Planters** | 150 | | 9.0 | 2.0 | | | | | | | 90 | | | | |
| *1 oz* | 28 | 5.0 | 13.0 | 2.0 | | | | | | | 200 | | | | |
| **ginko nuts** | | | | | | | | | | | | | | | |
| raw | 52 | 15.7 | 0.5 | 0.2 | 0 | 16 | 4 | .03 | | | 2 | 1 | 8 | .10 | .032 |
| *1 oz* | 28 | 1.2 | 10.7 | 0.1 | | 158 | .06 | 1.7 | .00 | .05 | 145 | 35 | .28 | .078 | |
| cnd | 32 | 20.7 | 0.5 | 0.2 | 0 | | | | | | 87 | 1 | 5 | .06 | .019 |
| *1 oz (14 med nuts)* | 28 | 0.7 | 6.3 | 0.1 | | | | | .00 | | 51 | 15 | .08 | .047 | |
| dried | 99 | 3.5 | 0.6 | 0.2 | 0 | 31 | 8 | .05 | | | 4 | 6 | 15 | .19 | .062 |
| *1 oz* | 28 | 2.9 | 20.6 | 0.1 | | 310 | .12 | 3.3 | .00 | .38 | 283 | 76 | .45 | .152 | |
| **hickorynuts, dried** | 187 | 0.8 | 18.3 | 6.2 | 0 | | | | | | 0 | 17 | 49 | 1.22 | |
| *1 oz* | 28 | 3.6 | 5.2 | 2.0 | | | | | .00 | | 124 | 95 | .60 | .210 | |
| **macadamia nuts** | | | | | | | | | | | | | | | |
| dried | 199 | 0.8 | 20.9 | 0.4 | 0 | 0 | | .03 | | | 1 | 20 | 33 | .49 | |
| *1 oz* | 28 | 2.4 | 3.9 | 3.1 | | 0 | .10 | 0.6 | .00 | | 104 | 39 | .68 | .084 | |
| dry roasted, Blue Diamond | 193 | 0.4 | 21.2 | 1.0 | 0 | | 0 | .03 | .05 | 70 | 117 | 21 | 28 | .60 | |
| *1 oz* | 28 | 2.4 | 2.5 | 3.1 | | 79 | .09 | 0.7 | .00 | .08 | 76 | 122 | .70 | .400 | |

[a] Liquid expressed from grated coconut.
[b] Liquid expressed from grated coconut & water.
[c] Liquid from coconuts.
[d] If salt is added, Na is 218 mg.
[e] If salt is added, Na is 220 mg.

| | KCAL | H₂O (g) | FAT (g) | PUFA (g) | CHOL (mg) | A (RE) | C (mg) | B-2 (mg) | B-6 (mg) | FOL (mcg) | Na (mg) | Ca (mg) | Mg (mg) | Zn (mg) | Mn (mg) |
|---|---|---|---|---|---|---|---|---|---|---|---|---|---|---|---|
| | WT (g) | PRO (g) | CHO (g) | SFA (g) | DFIB (g) | A (IU) | B-1 (mg) | NIA (mg) | B-12 (mcg) | PANT (mg) | K (mg) | P (mg) | Fe (mg) | Cu (mg) | |
| oil roasted | 204 | 0.5 | 21.7 | 0.4 | 0 | 0 | 0 | .03 | | | 2[a] | 13 | 33 | .31 | |
| *1 oz (10-12 nuts)* | 28 | 2.1 | 3.7 | 3.3 | | 3 | .06 | 0.6 | .00 | | 94 | 57 | .51 | .085 | |
| **mixed nuts** | | | | | | | | | | | | | | | |
| dry roasted[b] | 169 | 0.5 | 14.6 | 3.1 | 0 | 0 | 0 | .06 | .08 | 14 | 3[c] | 20 | 64 | 1.08 | .550 |
| *1 oz* | 28 | 4.9 | 7.2 | 2.0 | | 4 | .06 | 1.3 | .00 | .34 | 169 | 124 | 1.05 | .363 | |
| oil roasted[d] | 175 | 0.6 | 16.0 | 3.8 | 0 | 1 | 0 | .06 | .07 | 24 | 3[e] | 31 | 67 | 1.44 | .537 |
| *1 oz* | 28 | 4.8 | 6.1 | 2.5 | | 6 | .14 | 1.4 | .00 | .35 | 165 | 132 | .91 | .472 | |
| w/o peanuts, oil roasted[f] | 175 | 0.9 | 16.0 | 3.3 | 0 | 1 | 0 | .14 | .05 | 16 | 3[g] | 30 | 71 | 1.32 | .439 |
| *1 oz* | 28 | 4.4 | 6.3 | 2.6 | | 6 | .14 | 0.6 | .00 | .27 | 154 | 127 | .73 | .510 | |
| **nuts, wheat-base formulated** | | | | | | | | | | | | | | | |
| flavored[h] | 184 | 0.6 | 17.7 | 6.9 | 0 | | | .09 | | | 26 | 6 | | | |
| *1 oz* | 28 | 3.7 | 5.9 | 2.7 | | | .11 | 0.4 | .00 | | 91 | 104 | .74 | | |
| macadamia flavored[i] | 176 | 0.9 | 16.1 | 6.2 | 0 | | | .06 | | | 13 | 6 | | | |
| *1 oz* | 28 | 3.2 | 7.9 | 2.4 | | | .06 | 0.3 | .00 | | 74 | 85 | .57 | | |
| unflavored[j] | 177 | 0.7 | 16.4 | 6.5 | 0 | | | .09 | | | 143 | 7 | | | |
| *1 oz* | 28 | 3.9 | 6.7 | 2.5 | | | .09 | 0.4 | .00 | | 90 | 105 | .68 | | |
| **nut topping, Planters** | 180 | | 16.0 | 5.0 | 0 | | | | | | 0 | | | | |
| *1 oz* | 28 | 5.0 | 9.0 | 2.0 | | | | | | | 170 | | | | |
| **peanut butter, creamy/smooth** | 95 | 0.2 | 8.2 | 2.5 | 0 | 0 | 0 | .02 | .06 | 13 | 3[k] | 5 | 28 | .47 | .257 |
| *1 T* | 16 | 4.6 | 2.5 | 1.4 | | 0 | .02 | 2.2 | .00 | .15 | 110 | 60 | .29 | .094 | |
| Jif | 186 | 0.4 | 15.7 | 4.8 | | | | .03 | | | 157 | 13 | 48 | .74 | |
| *2 T* | 32 | 9.0 | 5.4 | 2.3 | | | .02 | 3.8 | | | 234 | 99 | .58 | .192 | |
| Skippy | 95 | 0.2 | 8.2 | 2.5 | | | | .01 | | | 75 | 5 | 30 | .50 | |
| *1 T* | 16 | 4.6 | 2.2 | 1.7 | | | .01 | 1.9 | | .20 | 105 | 60 | .30 | | |
| **peanut butter, chunk style/crunchy** | 188 | 0.4 | 16.0 | 4.6 | 0 | 0 | 0 | .04 | .14 | 29 | 156[l] | 13 | 51 | .89 | .597 |
| *2 T* | 32 | 7.7 | 6.9 | 3.1 | 0.9 | 0 | .04 | 4.4 | .00 | .31 | 239 | 101 | .61 | .165 | |
| Jif | 186 | 0.3 | 15.7 | | | | | .03 | | | 131 | 12 | | | |
| *2 T* | 32 | 9.0 | 5.4 | | | | .02 | 3.8 | | | | | .58 | | |
| Skippy | 95 | 0.2 | 8.4 | 2.5 | 0 | | | .01 | | | 65 | 5 | 25 | .50 | |
| *1 T* | 16 | 4.5 | 2.1 | 1.7 | | | .01 | 1.9 | | .20 | 100 | 60 | .30 | | |
| **peanut flour** | | | | | | | | | | | | | | | |
| defatted | 13 | 0.3 | 0.0 | 0.0 | 0 | | | .02 | | | 1[m] | 6 | 15 | .20 | .196 |
| *1 T* | 4 | 2.1 | 1.4 | 0.0 | | | .03 | 1.1 | | | 52 | 30 | .08 | .072 | |
| low-fat | 120 | 2.2 | 6.1 | 1.9 | | | | | | | 0 | 36 | 13 | 1.68 | 1.185 |
| *1 oz* | 28 | 9.5 | 8.8 | 0.9 | | | | | | | 380 | | 1.33 | .571 | |
| **peanuts** | | | | | | | | | | | | | | | |
| boiled | 102 | 13.4 | 7.0 | 2.2 | 0 | 0 | 0 | .02 | .05 | 24 | 240 | 18 | 33 | .59 | .327 |
| *1/2 cup* | 32 | 4.3 | 6.8 | 1.0 | | 0 | .08 | 1.7 | .00 | .26 | 58 | 63 | .32 | .160 | |
| dried | 161 | 1.9 | 14.0 | 4.4 | 0 | 0 | 0 | .04 | .08 | 29 | 5 | 17 | 51 | .93 | .316 |
| *1 oz* | 28 | 7.3 | 4.6 | 1.9 | | 0 | .19 | 4.0 | .00 | .79 | 204 | 109 | .92 | .285 | |
| dry roasted | 164 | 0.4 | 13.9 | 4.4 | 0 | 0 | 0 | .03 | .07 | 41 | 228[n] | 15 | 49 | .93 | .583 |
| *1 oz* | 28 | 6.6 | 6.0 | 1.9 | | 0 | .12 | 3.8 | .00 | .39 | 184 | 100 | .63 | .188 | |
| dry roasted, lite, Planters | 90 | | 6.0 | 2.0 | 0 | | | | | | 180 | | | | |
| *2/3 oz* | 19 | 6.0 | 5.0 | 1.0 | | | | | | | 160 | | | | |
| honey roast, Planters | 170 | | 13.0 | 4.0 | | | | | | | 180 | | | | |
| *1 oz* | 28 | 6.0 | 8.0 | 2.0 | | | | | | | 160 | | | | |

[a] If salt is added, Na is 73 mg.
[b] Cashews, almonds, peanuts, filberts & pecans.
[c] If salt is added, Na is 187 mg.
[d] Cashews, peanuts, brazilnuts, filberts, almonds & pecans.
[e] If salt is added, Na is 183 mg.
[f] Cashews, almonds, brazilnuts, pecans & filberts.
[g] If salt is added, Na is 196 mg.
[h] Hydrogenated soybean oil, wheat germ, sugar, sodium caseinate, soy protein, natural & artificial flavors, & artificial color.
[i] Hydrogenated soybean oil, wheat germ, sugar, wheat starch, sodium caseinate, soy protein, natural & artificial flavor.
[j] Hydrogenated soybean oil, wheat germ, fructose, wheat starch, sodium caseinate, soy protein, & salt.
[k] If salt is added, Na is 131 mg.
[l] If no salt is added, sodium is 5 mg.
[m] If salt is added, Na is 50 mg.
[n] If no salt is added, sodium is 2 mg.

|  | KCAL | H₂O (g) | FAT (g) | PUFA (g) | CHOL (mg) | A (RE) | C (mg) | B-2 (mg) | B-6 (mg) | FOL (mcg) | Na (mg) | Ca (mg) | Mg (mg) | Zn (mg) | Mn (mg) |
|---|---|---|---|---|---|---|---|---|---|---|---|---|---|---|---|
|  | WT (g) | PRO (g) | CHO (g) | SFA (g) | DFIB (g) | A (IU) | B-1 (mg) | NIA (mg) | B-12 (mcg) | PANT (mg) | K (mg) | P (mg) | Fe (mg) | Cu (mg) |  |
| oil roasted | 165 | 0.6 | 14.0 | 4.4 | 0 | 0 | 0 | .03 | .11 | 30 | 4[a] | 24 | 53 | 1.88 | .351 |
| *1 oz* | 28 | 7.6 | 5.3 | 1.9 |  | 0 | .08 | 4.2 | .00 | .59 | 200 | 144 | .54 | .362 |  |
| peanuts, spanish, oil-roasted | 162 | 0.5 | 13.7 | 4.7 | 0 | 0 | 0 | .02 | .07 | 35 | 121[b] | 28 | 47 | .56 | .659 |
| *1 oz* | 28 | 7.8 | 4.9 | 2.1 |  | 0 | .09 | 4.2 | .00 | .39 | 217 | 108 | .64 | .185 |  |
| peanuts, valencia, oil-roasted | 165 | 0.6 | 14.4 | 5.0 | 0 | 0 | 0 | .04 | .07 | 35 | 216[b] | 15 | 45 | .86 | .482 |
| *1 oz* | 28 | 7.6 | 4.6 | 2.2 |  | 0 | .03 | 4.0 | .00 | .39 | 171 | 89 | .46 | .235 |  |
| peanuts, virginia, oil-roasted | 161 | 0.6 | 13.6 | 4.1 | 0 | 0 | 0 | .03 | .07 | 35 | 121[b] | 24 | 53 | 1.85 | .562 |
| *1 oz* | 28 | 8.3 | 4.5 | 1.8 |  | 0 | .08 | 4.1 | .00 | .39 | 183 | 142 | .47 | .356 |  |
| **pecans** |  |  |  |  |  |  |  |  |  |  |  |  |  |  |  |
| dried | 190 | 1.4 | 19.2 | 4.8 | 0 | 4 | 1 | .04 | .05 | 11 | 0 | 10 | 36 | 1.55 | 1.280 |
| *1 oz (31 large nuts)* | 28 | 2.2 | 5.2 | 1.5 |  | 36 | .24 | 0.3 | .00 | .49 | 111 | 83 | .60 | .336 |  |
| dry roasted | 187 | 0.3 | 18.4 | 4.5 | 0 |  |  | .03 |  | 12 | 0[c] | 10 | 38 | 1.61 | 1.337 |
| *1 oz* | 28 | 2.3 | 6.3 | 1.5 |  |  | .09 |  | .00 |  | 105 | 86 | .62 | .351 |  |
| oil roasted | 195 | 1.2 | 20.2 | 5.0 | 0 |  |  |  |  |  | 0[d] | 10 | 37 | 1.56 | 1.294 |
| *1 oz (15 halves)* | 28 | 2.0 | 4.6 | 1.6 |  |  |  |  | .00 |  | 102 | 84 | .60 | .340 |  |
| **pilinuts, dried** | 204 | 0.8 | 22.6 | 2.2 | 0 | 1 |  | .03 |  |  | 1 | 41 |  |  |  |
| *1 oz (15 nuts)* | 28 | 3.1 | 1.1 | 8.9 |  | 12 | .26 | 0.1 | .00 |  | 144 | 163 | 1.00 |  |  |
| **pine nuts, pignolia, dried** | 146 | 1.9 | 14.4 | 6.1 | 0 |  |  | .05 |  |  | 1 | 7 |  | 1.21 |  |
| *1 oz* | 28 | 6.8 | 4.0 | 2.2 |  |  | .23 | 1.0 | .00 |  | 170 | 144 | 2.61 | .291 |  |
| **pine nuts, pinyon, dried** | 161 | 1.7 | 17.3 | 7.3 | 0 | 1 | 1 | .06 |  |  | 20 | 2 | 67 | 1.22 |  |
| *1 oz* | 28 | 3.3 | 5.5 | 2.7 |  | 8 | .35 | 1.2 | .00 |  | 178 | 10 | .87 | .294 |  |
| **pistachio nuts** |  |  |  |  |  |  |  |  |  |  |  |  |  |  |  |
| dried | 164 | 1.1 | 13.7 | 2.1 | 0 | 7 |  | .05 |  | 17 | 2 | 38 | 45 | .38 | .093 |
| *1 oz (47 nuts)* | 28 | 5.8 | 7.1 | 1.7 |  | 66 | .23 | 0.3 | .00 |  | 310 | 143 | 1.92 | .338 |  |
| dry roasted | 172 | 0.6 | 15.0 | 2.3 | 0 |  |  | .07 |  |  | 2[c] | 20 | 37 | .39 | .095 |
| *1 oz* | 28 | 4.2 | 7.8 | 1.9 |  |  | .12 | 0.4 | .00 |  | 275 | 135 | .90 | .344 |  |
| dry roasted, Blue Diamond | 162 | 0.8 | 13.9 | 4.5 | 0 |  | 1 | .09 | .04 | 120 | 173 | 41 | 33 | .31 |  |
| *1 oz* | 28 | 5.8 | 6.0 | 2.3 |  | 0 | .16 | 0.3 | .00 | .06 | 230 | 51 | 1.20 | .100 |  |
| dry roasted, red | 158 | 0.7 | 13.4 |  | 0 |  | 0 | .09 |  |  | 254 | 29 |  |  |  |
| *1 oz* | 28 | 5.7 | 6.5 |  |  | 0 | .16 | 0.3 |  |  | 254 |  | 1.20 |  |  |
| **pumpkin & squash seeds** |  |  |  |  |  |  |  |  |  |  |  |  |  |  |  |
| dried | 154 | 2.0 | 13.0 | 5.9 | 0 | 11 |  | .09 |  |  | 5 | 12 | 152 | 2.12 |  |
| *1 oz (142 seeds)* | 28 | 7.0 | 5.1 | 2.5 |  | 108 | .06 | 0.5 | .00 |  | 229 | 333 | 4.25 | .394 |  |
| roasted | 148 | 2.0 | 12.0 | 5.5 | 0 |  |  |  | .03 |  | 5[e] | 12 | 152 | 2.11 |  |
| *1 oz* | 28 | 9.4 | 3.8 | 2.3 |  |  |  |  | .00 |  | 229 | 333 | 4.24 | .393 |  |
| **sesame butter (tahini)** | 89 | 0.5 | 8.1 | 3.5 | 0 |  | 0 | .07 |  |  | 17 | 64 | 14 | .69 |  |
| *1 T* | 15 | 2.6 | 3.2 | 1.1 |  |  | .18 | 0.8 | .00 |  | 62 | 110 | 1.34 | .242 |  |
| **sesame nut mix** |  |  |  |  |  |  |  |  |  |  |  |  |  |  |  |
| dry roasted, Planters | 160 |  | 12.0 | 4.0 |  |  |  |  |  |  | 330 |  |  |  |  |
| *1 oz* | 28 | 5.0 | 8.0 | 3.0 |  |  |  |  |  |  | 140 |  |  |  |  |
| oil roasted, Planters | 160 |  | 13.0 | 2.0 |  |  |  |  |  |  | 220 |  |  |  |  |
| *1 oz* | 28 | 5.0 | 8.0 | 2.0 |  |  |  |  |  |  | 110 |  |  |  |  |
| **sesame seeds** |  |  |  |  |  |  |  |  |  |  |  |  |  |  |  |
| kernels, dried[f] | 47 | 0.4 | 4.4 | 1.9 | 0 | 1 |  | .01 |  |  | 3 | 10 | 28 | .82 |  |
| *1 T* | 8 | 2.1 | 0.8 | 0.6 |  | 5 | .06 | 0.4 | .00 | .05 | 33 | 62 | .62 |  |  |
| kernels, toasted[f] | 161 | 1.4 | 13.6 | 6.0 | 0 |  |  | .13 |  |  | 11 | 37 | 98 | 2.90 |  |
| *1 oz* | 28 | 4.8 | 7.4 | 1.9 |  |  | .34 | 1.5 | .00 |  | 115 | 220 | 2.21 |  |  |
| whole, dried | 52 | 0.4 | 4.5 | 2.0 | 0 | 0 | 0 | .02 | .07 | 9 | 1 | 88 | 32 | .70 | .221 |
| *1 T* | 9 | 1.6 | 2.1 | 0.6 |  | 1 | .07 | 0.4 | .00 | .01 | 42 | 57 | 1.31 | .367 |  |
| whole, toasted & roasted | 161 | 0.9 | 13.6 | 6.0 | 0 |  |  |  |  |  | 3 | 281 | 101 | 2.03 | .709 |
| *1 oz* | 28 | 4.8 | 7.3 | 1.9 |  |  |  |  | .00 |  | 135 | 181 | 4.19 | .701 |  |
| **soybean nuts** |  |  |  |  |  |  |  |  |  |  |  |  |  |  |  |
| dry roasted | 387 | 0.7 | 18.6 | 10.5 | 0 | 2 | 4 | .65 | .19 | 176 | 2 | 232 | 196 | 4.10 | 1.878 |
| *1/2 cup* | 86 | 34.0 | 28.1 | 2.7 |  | 20 | .37 | 0.9 | .00 | .41 | 1173 | 558 | 3.40 | .928 |  |
| roasted | 405 | 1.7 | 21.8 | 12.3 | 0 | 17 | 2 | .13 | .18 | 182 | 140 | 119 | 125 | 2.70 | 1.856 |
| *1/2 cup* | 86 | 30.3 | 28.9 | 3.2 |  | 172 | .09 | 1.2 | .00 | .39 | 1264 | 312 | 3.35 | .712 |  |

[a] If salt is added, Na is 121 mg.
[b] If no salt is added, sodium is 2 mg.
[c] If salt is added, Na is 218 mg.
[d] If salt is added, Na is 212 mg.
[e] If salt is added, Na is 161 mg.
[f] Decorticated seeds.

| | | | | | Vitamins | | | | | Minerals | | | | |
|---|---|---|---|---|---|---|---|---|---|---|---|---|---|---|
| KCAL | H₂O (g) | FAT (g) | PUFA (g) | CHOL (mg) | A (RE) | C (mg) | B-2 (mg) | B-6 (mg) | FOL (mcg) | Na (mg) | Ca (mg) | Mg (mg) | Zn (mg) | Mn (mg) |
| WT (g) | PRO (g) | CHO (g) | SFA (g) | DFIB (g) | A (IU) | B-1 (mg) | NIA (mg) | B-12 (mcg) | PANT (mg) | K (mg) | P (mg) | Fe (mg) | Cu (mg) | |

**roasted & toasted**
| 129 | 1.2 | 6.8 | 3.6 | 0 | 6 | 1 | .04 | .09 | 64 | 1ᵃ | 39 | 49 | 1.03 | |
*1 oz (95 nuts)*
| 28 | 10.5 | 8.7 | 0.9 | | 57 | .03 | 0.5 | .00 | .13 | 417 | 103 | 1.26 | .302 | |

**sunflower seeds**
dried
| 162 | 1.5 | 14.1 | 9.3 | 0 | 1 | | .07 | | | 1 | 33 | 100 | 1.44 | .574 |
*1 oz*
| 28 | 6.5 | 5.3 | 1.5 | | 14 | .65 | 1.3 | .00 | | 196 | 200 | 1.92 | .498 | |
dry roasted
| 165 | 0.3 | 14.1 | 9.3 | 0 | | | .07 | | | 1ᵇ | 20 | 37 | 1.50 | .599 |
*1 oz*
| 28 | 5.5 | 6.8 | 1.5 | | | .03 | 2.0 | .00 | | 241 | 328 | 1.1 | .520 | |
oil roasted
| 175 | 0.7 | 16.3 | 10.8 | 0 | | 0 | .08 | | 67 | 1ᶜ | 16 | 36 | 1.48 | .591 |
*1 oz*
| 28 | 6.1 | 4.2 | 1.7 | | | .09 | 1.2 | .00 | | 137 | 323 | 1.90 | .512 | |
**tavern nuts, Planters**
| 170 | | 15.0 | 4.0 | | | | | | | 65 | | | | |
*1 oz*
| 28 | 7.0 | 6.0 | 2.0 | | | | | | | 190 | | | | |
**walnuts, black, dried**
| 172 | 1.2 | 16.1 | 10.6 | 0 | 8 | | .03 | | | 0 | 16 | 57 | .97 | 1.213 |
*1 oz*
| 28 | 6.9 | 3.4 | 1.0 | | 84 | .06 | 0.2 | .00 | | 149 | 132 | .87 | .290 | |
**walnuts, english/persian, dried**
| 182 | 1.0 | 17.6 | 11.1 | 0 | 4 | 1 | .04 | .16 | 19 | 3 | 27 | 48 | .78 | .823 |
*1 oz (14 halves)*
| 28 | 4.1 | 5.2 | 1.6 | | 35 | .11 | 0.3 | .00 | .18 | 142 | 90 | .69 | .394 | |
**watermelon seeds, dried**
| 158 | 1.4 | 13.5 | 8.0 | 0 | 0 | 0 | .04 | | 16 | 28 | 15 | 146 | | |
*1 oz (95 large seeds)*
| 28 | 8.1 | 4.4 | 2.8 | | 0 | .05 | 1.0 | .00 | | 184 | 215 | 2.1 | | |

# 25. POULTRYᵈ
## 25.1. CHICKEN
### 25.1.1. BROILER/FRYER MEAT

**dark meat w/ skin, fried**
| 285 | 50.8 | 16.9 | 3.9 | 92 | 31 | 0 | .24 | .32 | 8 | 89 | 17 | 24 | 2.60 | .039 |
*3.5 oz*
| 100 | 27.2 | 4.1 | 4.6 | | 104 | .10 | 6.8 | .30 | 1.16 | 230 | 176 | 1.50 | .088 | |
**dark meat w/ skin, roasted**
| 253 | 58.6 | 15.8 | 3.5 | 91 | 58 | 0 | .21 | .31 | 7 | 87 | 15 | 22 | 2.49 | .021 |
*3.5 oz*
| 100 | 26.0 | 0.0 | 4.4 | 0.0 | 201 | .07 | 6.4 | .29 | 1.11 | 220 | 168 | 1.36 | .077 | |
**dark meat w/ skin, stewed**
| 233 | 63.0 | 14.7 | 3.2 | 82 | 54 | 0 | .18 | .17 | 6 | 70 | 14 | 18 | 2.26 | .019 |
*3.5 oz*
| 100 | 23.5 | 0.0 | 4.1 | 0.0 | 186 | .05 | 4.5 | .20 | .77 | 166 | 133 | 1.31 | .068 | |
**dark meat w/o skin, fried**
| 239 | 55.7 | 11.6 | 2.8 | 96 | 24 | 0 | .25 | .37 | 9 | 97 | 18 | 25 | 2.91 | .033 |
*3.5 oz*
| 100 | 29.0 | 2.6 | 3.1 | | 79 | .09 | 7.1 | .33 | 1.26 | 253 | 187 | 1.49 | .089 | |
**dark meat w/o skin, roasted**
| 205 | 63.1 | 9.7 | 2.3 | 93 | 22 | 0 | .23 | .36 | 8 | 93 | 15 | 23 | 2.80 | .017 |
*3.5 oz*
| 100 | 27.4 | 0.0 | 2.7 | 0.0 | 72 | .07 | 6.6 | .32 | 1.21 | 240 | 179 | 1.33 | .080 | |
**dark meat w/o skin, stewed**
| 192 | 65.8 | 9.0 | 2.1 | 88 | 21 | 0 | .20 | .21 | 7 | 74 | 14 | 20 | 2.66 | .021 |
*3.5 oz*
| 100 | 26.0 | 0.0 | 2.5 | 0.0 | 69 | .06 | 4.7 | .22 | .89 | 181 | 143 | 1.36 | .075 | |
**light & dark meat w/ skin, fried, batter dipped—3.5 oz**
| 289 | 49.4 | 17.4 | 4.1 | 87 | 28 | 0 | .19 | .31 | 8 | 292 | 21 | 21 | 1.67 | .057 |
| 100 | 22.5 | 9.4 | 4.6 | | 93 | .12 | 7.0 | .28 | .89 | 185 | 155 | 1.37 | .072 | |
**light & dark meat w/ skin, fried, flour coated—3.5 oz**
| 269 | 52.4 | 14.9 | 3.4 | 90 | 27 | 0 | .19 | .41 | 6 | 84 | 17 | 25 | 2.04 | .034 |
| 100 | 28.6 | 3.2 | 4.1 | | 89 | .09 | 9.0 | .31 | 1.08 | 234 | 191 | 1.38 | .075 | |
**light & dark meat w/ skin, roasted**
| 239 | 59.5 | 13.6 | 3.0 | 88 | 47 | 0 | .17 | .40 | 5 | 82 | 15 | 23 | 1.94 | .020 |
*3.5 oz*
| 100 | 27.3 | 0.0 | 3.8 | 0.0 | 161 | .06 | 8.5 | .30 | 1.03 | 223 | 182 | 1.26 | .066 | |
**light & dark meat w/ skin, stewed**
| 219 | 63.9 | 12.6 | 2.7 | 78 | 42 | 0 | .15 | .22 | 5 | 67 | 13 | 19 | 1.76 | .019 |
*3.5 oz*
| 100 | 24.7 | 0.0 | 3.5 | 0.0 | 146 | .05 | 5.6 | .20 | .67 | 166 | 139 | 1.16 | .057 | |
**light & dark meat w/o skin, fried**
| 219 | 57.3 | 9.1 | 2.2 | 94 | 18 | 0 | .20 | .48 | 7 | 91 | 17 | 27 | 2.24 | .028 |
*3.5 oz*
| 100 | 30.6 | 1.7 | 2.5 | | 59 | .09 | 9.7 | .34 | 1.17 | 257 | 205 | 1.35 | .075 | |
**light & dark meat w/o skin, roasted**
| 190 | 63.8 | 7.4 | 1.7 | 89 | 16 | 0 | .18 | .47 | 6 | 86 | 15 | 25 | 2.10 | .019 |
*3.5 oz*
| 100 | 28.9 | 0.0 | 2.0 | 0.0 | 53 | .07 | 9.2 | .33 | 1.10 | 243 | 195 | 1.21 | .067 | |
**light & dark meat w/o skin, stewed**
| 177 | 66.8 | 6.7 | 1.5 | 83 | 15 | 0 | .16 | .26 | 6 | 70 | 14 | 21 | 1.99 | .019 |
*3.5 oz*
| 100 | 27.3 | 0.0 | 1.8 | 0.0 | 50 | .05 | 6.1 | .22 | .75 | 180 | 150 | 1.17 | .061 | |
**light meat w/ skin, fried**
| 246 | 54.7 | 12.1 | 2.7 | 87 | 20 | 0 | .13 | .54 | 4 | 77 | 16 | 27 | 1.26 | .026 |
*3.5 oz*
| 100 | 30.5 | 1.8 | 3.3 | | 68 | .08 | 12.0 | .33 | .97 | 239 | 213 | 1.21 | .058 | |
**light meat w/ skin, roasted**
| 222 | 60.5 | 10.9 | 2.3 | 84 | 32 | 0 | .12 | .52 | 3 | 75 | 15 | 25 | 1.23 | .021 |
*3.5 oz*
| 100 | 29.0 | 0.0 | 3.1 | 0.0 | 110 | .06 | 11.1 | .32 | .93 | 227 | 200 | 1.14 | .053 | |
**light meat w/ skin, stewed**
| 201 | 65.1 | 10.0 | 2.1 | 74 | 28 | 0 | .11 | .27 | 3 | 63 | 13 | 20 | 1.14 | .018 |
*3.5 oz*
| 100 | 26.1 | 0.0 | 2.8 | 0.0 | 96 | .04 | 6.9 | .20 | .54 | 167 | 146 | .98 | .044 | |
**light meat w/o skin, fried**
| 192 | 60.1 | 5.5 | 1.3 | 90 | 9 | 0 | .13 | .63 | 4 | 81 | 16 | 29 | 1.27 | .020 |
*3.5 oz*
| 100 | 32.8 | 0.4 | 1.5 | | 30 | .07 | 13.4 | .36 | 1.03 | 263 | 231 | 1.14 | .054 | |
**light meat w/o skin, roasted**
| 173 | 64.8 | 4.5 | 1.0 | 85 | 9 | 0 | .12 | .60 | 4 | 77 | 15 | 27 | 1.23 | .017 |
*3.5 oz*
| 100 | 30.9 | 0.0 | 1.3 | 0.0 | 29 | .07 | 12.4 | 34 | .97 | 247 | 216 | 1.06 | .050 | |
**light meat w/o skin, stewed**
| 159 | 68.0 | 4.0 | 0.9 | 77 | 8 | 0 | .12 | .33 | 3 | 65 | 13 | 22 | 1.19 | .018 |
*3.5 oz*
| 100 | 28.9 | 0.0 | 1.1 | 0.0 | 27 | .04 | 7.8 | .23 | .57 | 180 | 159 | .93 | .044 | |

ᵃ If salt is added, Na is 46 mg.
ᵇ If salt is added, Na is 218 mg.
ᶜ If salt is added, Na is 169 mg.
ᵈ Gram weights are edible portions.

| | KCAL / WT (g) | H₂O (g) / PRO (g) | FAT (g) / CHO (g) | PUFA (g) / SFA (g) | CHOL (mg) / DFIB (g) | A (RE) / A (IU) | C (mg) / B-1 (mg) | B-2 (mg) / NIA (mg) | B-6 (mg) / B-12 (mcg) | FOL (mcg) / PANT (mg) | Na (mg) / K (mg) | Ca (mg) / P (mg) | Mg (mg) / Fe (mg) | Zn (mg) / Cu (mg) | Mn (mg) |
|---|---|---|---|---|---|---|---|---|---|---|---|---|---|---|---|

## 25.1.2. BROILER/FRYER PARTS

**back w/ skin, fried** — *1/2 back*

| | KCAL/WT | H₂O/PRO | FAT/CHO | PUFA/SFA | CHOL/DFIB | A(RE)/A(IU) | C/B-1 | B-2/NIA | B-6/B-12 | FOL/PANT | Na/K | Ca/P | Mg/Fe | Zn/Cu | Mn |
|---|---|---|---|---|---|---|---|---|---|---|---|---|---|---|---|
| back w/ skin, fried | 238 | 31.7 | 14.9 | 3.5 | 64 | 27 | 0 | .17 | .22 | 6 | 65 | 17 | 17 | 1.78 | .036 |
| *1/2 back* | 72 | 20.0 | 6.7 | 4.0 | | 88 | .08 | 5.3 | .20 | .79 | 163 | 119 | 1.17 | .066 | |
| breast w/ skin, fried | 218 | 55.5 | 8.7 | 1.9 | 88 | 15 | 0 | .13 | .57 | 4 | 75 | 16 | 29 | 1.07 | .015 |
| *1/2 breast* | 98 | 31.2 | 1.6 | 2.4 | | 49 | .08 | 13.5 | .34 | .98 | 253 | 228 | 1.17 | .056 | |
| breast w/ skin, roasted | 193 | 61.2 | 7.6 | 1.6 | 83 | 26 | 0 | .12 | .54 | 3 | 69 | 14 | 27 | 1.00 | .018 |
| *1/2 breast* | 98 | 29.2 | 0.0 | 2.2 | 0.0 | 91 | .07 | 12.5 | .32 | .92 | 240 | 210 | 1.04 | .049 | |
| breast w/ skin, stewed | 202 | 72.8 | 8.2 | 1.7 | 83 | 26 | 0 | .13 | .32 | 3 | 68 | 14 | 24 | 1.06 | .020 |
| *1/2 breast* | 110 | 30.1 | 0.0 | 2.3 | 0.0 | 90 | .05 | 8.6 | .23 | .60 | 195 | 172 | 1.01 | .048 | |
| breast w/o skin, fried | 161 | 51.8 | 4.1 | 0.9 | 78 | 6 | 0 | .11 | .55 | 4 | 68 | 14 | 27 | .93 | .018 |
| *1/2 breast* | 86 | 28.8 | 0.4 | 1.1 | | 20 | .07 | 12.7 | .31 | .89 | 237 | 212 | .98 | .046 | |
| breast w/o skin, roasted | 142 | 56.1 | 3.1 | 0.7 | 73 | 5 | 0 | .10 | .51 | 3 | 63 | 13 | 25 | .86 | .015 |
| *1/2 breast* | 86 | 26.7 | 0.0 | 0.9 | 0.0 | 18 | .06 | 11.8 | .29 | .83 | 220 | 196 | .89 | .042 | |
| breast w/o skin, stewed | 144 | 64.9 | 2.9 | 0.6 | 73 | 6 | 0 | .11 | .32 | 3 | 59 | 12 | 22 | .92 | .017 |
| *1/2 breast* | 95 | 27.5 | 0.0 | 0.8 | 0.0 | 18 | .04 | 8.0 | .22 | .54 | 178 | 157 | .84 | .041 | |
| drumstick w/ skin, fried | 120 | 27.8 | 6.7 | 1.6 | 44 | 12 | 0 | .11 | .17 | 4 | 44 | 6 | 11 | 1.42 | .014 |
| *1 drumstick* | 49 | 13.2 | 0.8 | 1.8 | | 41 | .04 | 3.0 | .16 | .60 | 112 | 86 | .66 | .039 | |
| drumstick w/ skin, roasted | 112 | 32.6 | 5.8 | 1.3 | 48 | 15 | 0 | .11 | .18 | 4 | 47 | 6 | 12 | 1.49 | .011 |
| *1 drumstick* | 52 | 14.1 | 0.0 | 1.6 | 0.0 | 52 | .04 | 3.1 | .17 | .63 | 119 | 91 | .69 | .040 | |
| drumstick w/ skin, stewed | 116 | 37.1 | 6.1 | 1.4 | 48 | 15 | 0 | .11 | .11 | 4 | 43 | 7 | 11 | 1.51 | .011 |
| *1 drumstick* | 57 | 14.4 | 0.0 | 1.7 | 0.0 | 52 | .03 | 2.4 | .12 | .49 | 105 | 80 | .76 | .040 | |
| drumstick w/o skin, stewed | 76 | 29.4 | 2.5 | 0.6 | 41 | 8 | 0 | .10 | .17 | 4 | 42 | 5 | 11 | 1.40 | .009 |
| *1 drumstick* | 44 | 12.5 | 0.0 | 0.7 | 0.0 | 26 | .03 | 2.7 | .15 | .57 | 108 | 81 | .57 | .035 | |
| leg w/ skin, fried | 285 | 61.9 | 16.2 | 3.7 | 105 | 31 | 0 | .26 | .38 | 9 | 99 | 15 | 27 | 3.00 | .036 |
| *1 leg* | 112 | 30.1 | 2.8 | 4.4 | | 103 | .10 | 7.3 | .35 | 1.34 | 261 | 204 | 1.60 | .095 | |
| leg w/ skin, roasted | 265 | 69.5 | 15.4 | 3.4 | 105 | 45 | 0 | .24 | .37 | 8 | 99 | 14 | 26 | 2.96 | .024 |
| *1 leg* | 114 | 29.6 | 0.0 | 4.2 | 0.0 | 154 | .08 | 7.1 | .35 | 1.32 | 256 | 199 | 1.52 | .088 | |
| leg w/ skin, stewed | 275 | 80.0 | 16.2 | 3.6 | 105 | 46 | 0 | .24 | .23 | 8 | 92 | 14 | 24 | 3.04 | .024 |
| *1 leg* | 125 | 30.2 | 0.0 | 4.5 | 0.0 | 156 | .07 | 5.7 | .25 | 1.02 | 220 | 174 | 1.69 | .089 | |
| leg w/o skin, stewed | 187 | 67.1 | 8.1 | 1.9 | 90 | 18 | 0 | .22 | .22 | 8 | 78 | 11 | 21 | 2.81 | .019 |
| *1 leg* | 101 | 26.5 | 0.0 | 2.2 | 0.0 | 60 | .06 | 4.8 | .23 | .92 | 192 | 151 | 1.41 | .078 | |
| neck w/ skin, fried | 119 | 17.1 | 8.5 | 2.0 | 34 | 21 | 0 | .09 | .09 | 2 | 29 | 11 | 7 | 1.11 | .019 |
| *1 neck* | 36 | 8.6 | 1.5 | 2.3 | | 69 | .03 | 1.9 | .09 | .35 | 65 | 48 | .87 | .047 | |
| neck w/ skin, simmered | 94 | 23.5 | 6.9 | 1.5 | 27 | 18 | 0 | .09 | .04 | 1 | 20 | 10 | 5 | 1.03 | .017 |
| *1 neck* | 38 | 7.5 | 0.0 | 1.9 | 0.0 | 61 | .02 | 1.3 | .05 | .20 | 41 | 46 | .87 | .037 | |
| neck w/o skin, simmered | 32 | 12.1 | 1.5 | 0.4 | 14 | 7 | 0 | .05 | .03 | 1 | 12 | 8 | 3 | .68 | .009 |
| *1 neck* | 18 | 4.4 | 0.0 | 0.4 | 0.0 | 22 | .01 | 0.7 | .03 | .12 | 25 | 23 | .47 | .023 | |
| thigh w/ skin, fried | 162 | 33.6 | 9.3 | 2.1 | 60 | 18 | 0 | .15 | .21 | 5 | 55 | 8 | 5 | 1.56 | .022 |
| *1 thigh* | 62 | 16.6 | 2.0 | 2.5 | | 61 | .06 | 4.3 | .19 | .74 | 147 | 116 | .93 | .055 | |
| thigh w/ skin, roasted | 153 | 36.8 | 9.6 | 2.1 | 58 | 30 | 0 | .13 | .19 | 4 | 52 | 8 | 14 | 1.46 | .013 |
| *1 thigh* | 62 | 15.5 | 0.0 | 2.7 | 0.0 | 102 | .04 | 3.9 | .18 | .69 | 137 | 108 | .83 | .048 | |
| thigh w/ skin, stewed | 158 | 42.9 | 10.0 | 2.2 | 57 | 30 | 0 | .13 | .12 | 4 | 49 | 8 | 13 | 1.53 | .013 |
| *1 thigh* | 68 | 15.8 | 0.0 | 2.8 | 0.0 | 103 | .04 | 3.3 | .13 | .53 | 115 | 94 | .93 | .048 | |
| thigh w/o skin, roasted | 109 | 32.7 | 5.7 | 1.3 | 49 | 10 | 0 | .12 | .18 | 4 | 46 | 6 | 12 | 1.34 | .010 |
| *1 thigh* | 52 | 13.5 | 0.0 | 1.6 | 0.0 | 34 | .04 | 3.4 | .16 | .62 | 124 | 95 | .68 | .042 | |
| wing w/ skin, fried | 103 | 15.6 | 7.1 | 1.6 | 26 | 12 | 0 | .04 | .13 | 1 | 25 | 5 | 6 | .56 | .009 |
| *1 wing* | 32 | 8.4 | 0.8 | 1.9 | | 40 | .02 | 2.1 | .09 | .28 | 57 | 48 | .40 | .020 | |
| wing w/ skin, roasted | 99 | 18.7 | 6.6 | 1.4 | 29 | 16 | 0 | .04 | .14 | 1 | 28 | 5 | 7 | .62 | .006 |
| *1 wing* | 34 | 9.1 | 0.0 | 1.9 | 0.0 | 54 | .01 | 2.3 | .10 | .31 | 62 | 51 | .43 | .019 | |
| wing w/ skin, stewed | 100 | 24.9 | 6.7 | 1.4 | 28 | 16 | 0 | .04 | .09 | 1 | 27 | 5 | 6 | .65 | .007 |
| *1 wing* | 40 | 9.1 | 0.0 | 1.9 | 0.0 | 53 | .02 | 1.8 | .07 | .20 | 56 | 48 | .45 | .018 | |

## 25.1.3. CAPON

| | KCAL/WT | H₂O/PRO | FAT/CHO | PUFA/SFA | CHOL/DFIB | A(RE)/A(IU) | C/B-1 | B-2/NIA | B-6/B-12 | FOL/PANT | Na/K | Ca/P | Mg/Fe | Zn/Cu | Mn |
|---|---|---|---|---|---|---|---|---|---|---|---|---|---|---|---|
| meat w/ skin, roasted | 229 | 58.7 | 11.7 | 2.5 | 86 | 20 | 0 | .17 | .43 | 6 | 49 | 14 | 24 | 1.74 | .021 |
| *3.5 oz* | 100 | 29.0 | 0.0 | 3.3 | 0.0 | 68 | .07 | 8.9 | .33 | 1.10 | 255 | 246 | 1.49 | .069 | |

## 25.1.4. ROASTER

| | KCAL/WT | H₂O/PRO | FAT/CHO | PUFA/SFA | CHOL/DFIB | A(RE)/A(IU) | C/B-1 | B-2/NIA | B-6/B-12 | FOL/PANT | Na/K | Ca/P | Mg/Fe | Zn/Cu | Mn |
|---|---|---|---|---|---|---|---|---|---|---|---|---|---|---|---|
| dark meat w/o skin, roasted | 178 | 67.1 | 8.8 | 2.0 | 75 | 16 | 0 | .19 | .31 | 7 | 95 | 11 | 20 | 2.13 | .019 |
| *3.5 oz* | 100 | 23.3 | 0.0 | 2.4 | 0.0 | 54 | .06 | 5.7 | .27 | 1.03 | 224 | 171 | 1.33 | .070 | |

| | KCAL | H₂O (g) | FAT (g) | PUFA (g) | CHOL (mg) | A (RE) | C (mg) | B-2 (mg) | B-6 (mg) | FOL (mcg) | Na (mg) | Ca (mg) | Mg (mg) | Zn (mg) | Mn (mg) |
|---|---|---|---|---|---|---|---|---|---|---|---|---|---|---|---|
| | WT (g) | PRO (g) | CHO (g) | SFA (g) | DFIB (g) | A (IU) | B-1 (mg) | NIA (mg) | B-12 (mcg) | PANT (mg) | K (mg) | P (mg) | Fe (mg) | Cu (mg) | |
| **light & dark meat w/ skin, roasted** | 223 | 62.1 | 13.4 | 2.9 | 76 | 25 | 0 | .14 | .35 | 5 | 73 | 12 | 20 | 1.45 | .018 |
| *3.5 oz* | 100 | 24.0 | 0.0 | 3.7 | 0.0 | 83 | .06 | 7.4 | .27 | .92 | 211 | 179 | 1.26 | .058 | |
| **light & dark meat w/o skin, roasted** | 167 | 67.4 | 6.6 | 1.5 | 75 | 12 | 0 | .15 | .41 | 5 | 75 | 12 | 21 | 1.52 | .017 |
| *3.5 oz* | 100 | 25.0 | 0.0 | 1.8 | 0.0 | 41 | .06 | 7.9 | .29 | .97 | 229 | 192 | 1.21 | .057 | |
| **light meat w/o skin, roasted** | 153 | 67.9 | 4.1 | 0.9 | 75 | 8 | 0 | .09 | .54 | 3 | 51 | 13 | 23 | .78 | .015 |
| *3.5 oz* | 100 | 27.1 | 0.0 | 1.1 | 0.0 | 25 | .06 | 10.5 | .31 | .91 | 236 | 217 | 1.08 | .042 | |

## 25.1.5. STEWER

| | KCAL | H₂O (g) | FAT (g) | PUFA (g) | CHOL (mg) | A (RE) | C (mg) | B-2 (mg) | B-6 (mg) | FOL (mcg) | Na (mg) | Ca (mg) | Mg (mg) | Zn (mg) | Mn (mg) |
|---|---|---|---|---|---|---|---|---|---|---|---|---|---|---|---|
| | WT (g) | PRO (g) | CHO (g) | SFA (g) | DFIB (g) | A (IU) | B-1 (mg) | NIA (mg) | B-12 (mcg) | PANT (mg) | K (mg) | P (mg) | Fe (mg) | Cu (mg) | |
| **dark meat w/o skin, stewed** | 258 | 55.1 | 15.3 | 3.7 | 95 | 43 | 0 | .35 | .24 | 8 | 95 | 12 | 22 | 3.12 | .023 |
| *3.5 oz* | 100 | 28.1 | 0.0 | 4.1 | 0.0 | 145 | .13 | 4.6 | .25 | 1.01 | 204 | 187 | 1.64 | .144 | |
| **light & dark meat w/ skin, stewed** | 285 | 53.1 | 18.9 | 4.2 | 79 | 39 | 0 | .24 | .25 | 5 | 73 | 13 | 20 | 1.77 | .021 |
| *3.5 oz* | 100 | 26.9 | 0.0 | 5.1 | 0.0 | 191 | .09 | 5.8 | .23 | .75 | 182 | 180 | 1.37 | .100 | |
| **light & dark meat w/o skin, stewed** | 237 | 56.4 | 11.9 | 2.8 | 83 | 33 | 0 | .28 | .31 | 6 | 78 | 13 | 22 | 2.06 | .022 |
| *3.5 oz* | 100 | 30.4 | 0.0 | 3.1 | 0.0 | 112 | .11 | 6.4 | .26 | .86 | 202 | 204 | 1.43 | .116 | |
| **light meat w/o skin, stewed** | 213 | 57.8 | 8.0 | 1.9 | 70 | 22 | 0 | .20 | .39 | 4 | 58 | 14 | 23 | .83 | .020 |
| *3.5 oz* | 100 | 33.0 | 0.0 | 2.0 | 0.0 | 73 | .09 | 8.5 | .27 | .69 | 199 | 225 | 1.19 | .085 | |

## 25.1.6. UNSPECIFIED TYPE

| | KCAL | H₂O (g) | FAT (g) | PUFA (g) | CHOL (mg) | A (RE) | C (mg) | B-2 (mg) | B-6 (mg) | FOL (mcg) | Na (mg) | Ca (mg) | Mg (mg) | Zn (mg) | Mn (mg) |
|---|---|---|---|---|---|---|---|---|---|---|---|---|---|---|---|
| | WT (g) | PRO (g) | CHO (g) | SFA (g) | DFIB (g) | A (IU) | B-1 (mg) | NIA (mg) | B-12 (mcg) | PANT (mg) | K (mg) | P (mg) | Fe (mg) | Cu (mg) | |
| **breast cutlets, breaded & fried, Perdue** | 240 | | 11.0 | | 45 | | | | | | 513 | | | | |
| *4 oz cutlet* | 119 | 19.0 | 17.0 | | | | | | | | | | | | |
| **breast, fried, frzn, Am Hosp Co** | 241 | | 14.7 | | 85 | | | .15 | | | 525 | 20 | | | |
| *3.5 oz* | 100 | 16.5 | 10.8 | | | 67 | .12 | 10.5 | | | 201 | | 1.23 | | |
| **breast, fried, frzn, Banquet** | 238 | | 12.0 | | | | 0 | .07 | | | 772 | 16 | | | |
| *1/5 of 22 oz pkg* | 125 | 17.0 | 14.0 | | | 46 | .06 | 6.6 | | | 141 | | 1.00 | | |
| **breast, oven roasted, Louis Rich** | 39 | 20.0 | 1.8 | 0.4 | 14 | | | | | | 165 | 10 | 6 | .17 | |
| *1 oz slice* | 28 | 5.4 | 0.2 | 0.7 | | | | | | | 59 | 70 | .13 | | |
| **cnd** | 309 | 101.7 | 18.3 | | | | 6 | .19 | | | | 33 | | | |
| *5.5 oz can* | 156 | 33.9 | 0.0 | 5.8 | | 360 | .06 | 6.9 | | | 215 | 385 | 2.30 | | |
| **cnd, chunks o' chicken, Swanson** | 104 | | 3.0 | | | | 0 | .12 | | | 230 | 7 | | | |
| *2.5 oz* | 71 | 19.2 | 0.0 | | | 0 | .02 | 4.9 | | | 132 | | .90 | | |
| **cnd, chunk, white & dark, Swanson** | 108 | | 5.6 | | | | 0 | .09 | | | 263 | 9 | | | |
| *2.5 oz* | 71 | 14.5 | 0.1 | | | 0 | .01 | 3.5 | | | 108 | | .90 | | |
| **cnd, chunk white, Swanson** | 97 | | 3.7 | | | | 0 | .07 | | | 236 | 7 | | | |
| *2.5 oz* | 71 | 15.7 | 0.2 | | | 0 | .01 | 4.7 | | | 124 | | .60 | | |
| **cnd, chunk white in water, Swanson** | 82 | | 1.3 | | | | 0 | .04 | | | 239 | 5 | | | |
| *2.5 oz* | 71 | 16.8 | 0.7 | | | 0 | .01 | 5.0 | | | 89 | | .50 | | |
| **cnd, mixin chicken, Swanson** | 124 | | 7.6 | | | | 0 | .08 | | | 225 | 38 | | | |
| *2.5 oz* | 71 | 13.9 | 0.1 | | | 0 | .01 | 2.9 | | | 105 | | 1.10 | | |
| **drum snackers, breaded & fried, frzn, Banquet**—*3 oz* | 202 | | 10.0 | | | | 1 | .08 | | | 532 | 23 | | | |
| | 85 | 14.0 | 14.0 | | | 46 | .05 | 4.9 | | | 157 | | .90 | | |
| **fried, frzn, Banquet** | 325 | | 19.0 | | | | 0 | .10 | | | 1201 | 21 | | | |
| *1/5 of 32 oz pkg* | 181 | 18.0 | 20.0 | | | 85 | .08 | 4.8 | | | 144 | | 1.00 | | |
| **fried, hot & spicy, frzn, Banquet** | 325 | | 19.0 | | | | 0 | .10 | | | 1201 | 21 | | | |
| *1/5 of 32 oz pkg* | 181 | 18.0 | 20.0 | | | 85 | .08 | 4.8 | | | 144 | | 1.00 | | |
| **nuggets** | | | | | | | | | | | | | | | |
| breaded & fried, frzn, Banquet | 233 | | 14.0 | | | | 0 | .04 | | | 573 | 9 | | | |
| *3 oz* | 85 | 14.0 | 14.0 | | | 0 | .08 | 3.0 | | | 150 | | .90 | | |
| breaded & fried, Perdue | 160 | | 8.0 | | 40 | | | | | | 312 | | | | |
| *4 nuggets* | 74 | 12.0 | 8.0 | | | | | | | | | | | | |
| hot & spicy, fried, frzn, Banquet | 235 | | 14.0 | | | | | | | | | | | | |
| *3 oz* | 85 | 13.0 | 13.0 | | | | | | | | | | | | |
| w/ cheddar, fried, frzn, Banquet | 275 | | 19.0 | | | | | | | | | | | | |
| *3 oz* | 85 | 14.0 | 11.0 | | | | | | | | | | | | |
| **patties, breaded & fried, frzn, Banquet** | 225 | | 14.0 | | | | 0 | .05 | | | 513 | 8 | | | |
| *3 oz* | 85 | 13.0 | 13.0 | | | 0 | .08 | 3.2 | | | 150 | | .90 | | |
| **roasted, Perdue** | 220 | | 16.0 | | 88 | | | | | | 396 | | | | |
| *4 oz* | 113 | 24.0 | 0.0 | | | | | | | | | | | | |
| **roll, light meat** | 159 | 68.6 | 7.4 | 1.6 | 50 | | | .13 | | | 584 | 43 | 19 | .72 | |
| *3.5 oz* | 100 | 19.5 | 2.5 | 2.0 | | | .07 | 5.3 | | | 228 | 157 | .97 | .041 | |

| | KCAL | H₂O (g) | FAT (g) | PUFA (g) | CHOL (mg) | A (RE) | C (mg) | B-2 (mg) | B-6 (mg) | FOL (mcg) | Na (mg) | Ca (mg) | Mg (mg) | Zn (mg) | Mn (mg) |
|---|---|---|---|---|---|---|---|---|---|---|---|---|---|---|---|
| | WT (g) | PRO (g) | CHO (g) | SFA (g) | DFIB (g) | A (IU) | B-1 (mg) | NIA (mg) | B-12 (mcg) | PANT (mg) | K (mg) | P (mg) | Fe (mg) | Cu (mg) | |
| sticks, breaded & fried, frzn, Banquet | 228 | | 13.0 | | | | 0 | .04 | | | 566 | 8 | | | |
| *3 oz* | 85 | 14.0 | 15.0 | | | 0 | .08 | 3.3 | | | 150 | | .90 | | |
| tenders, breaded & fried, Perdue | 212 | | 12.0 | | 68 | | | | | | 192 | | | | |
| *4 oz* | 113 | 20.0 | 8.0 | | | | | | | | | | | | |
| thighs & drumsticks, fried, frzn, Am Hosp | 190 | | 9.3 | | 74 | | | .18 | | | 360 | 15 | | | |
| Co—*3 oz* | 85 | 13.6 | 12.9 | | | 74 | .10 | 4.4 | | | 159 | | 1.15 | | |
| thighs & drumsticks, fried, frzn, Banquet | 277 | | 16.0 | | | | 0 | .13 | | | 892 | 16 | | | |
| *5 oz* | 142 | 16.0 | 16.0 | | | 69 | .06 | 6.5 | | | 136 | | 1.00 | | |
| winglets, breaded & fried, frzn, Banquet | 202 | | 10.0 | | | | 1 | .08 | | | 532 | 23 | | | |
| *3 oz* | 85 | 14.0 | 14.0 | | | 46 | .05 | 4.9 | | | 157 | | .90 | | |

## 25.2. TURKEY

| | KCAL | H₂O (g) | FAT (g) | PUFA (g) | CHOL (mg) | A (RE) | C (mg) | B-2 (mg) | B-6 (mg) | FOL (mcg) | Na (mg) | Ca (mg) | Mg (mg) | Zn (mg) | Mn (mg) |
|---|---|---|---|---|---|---|---|---|---|---|---|---|---|---|---|
| | WT (g) | PRO (g) | CHO (g) | SFA (g) | DFIB (g) | A (IU) | B-1 (mg) | NIA (mg) | B-12 (mcg) | PANT (mg) | K (mg) | P (mg) | Fe (mg) | Cu (mg) | |
| **breast** | | | | | | | | | | | | | | | |
| barbequed, Louis Rich | 39 | 19.1 | 1.3 | | | | | | | | 316 | 2 | 5 | .31 | |
| *1 oz* | 28 | 6.2 | 0.5 | | | | | | | | 82 | 76 | .23 | | |
| ckd, Louis Rich | 51 | 17.6 | 1.9 | 0.4 | 12 | | | | | | 21 | 2 | 7 | .63 | |
| *1 oz* | 28 | 8.5 | 0.0 | 0.6 | | | | | | | 87 | 61 | .33 | | |
| fillet w/ cheese, Land O' Lakes | 304 | | 15.6 | 3.7 | 34 | | | .31 | | | 834 | 125 | | | |
| *5 oz* | 142 | 25.3 | 15.6 | 4.5 | | | .10 | 8.7 | | | 315 | 392 | 1.36 | | |
| hickory smoked, Louis Rich | 35 | 19.8 | 1.1 | 0.3 | 13 | | | | | | 227 | 1 | 7 | .30 | |
| *1 oz* | 28 | 6.2 | 0.2 | 0.3 | | | | | | | 69 | 80 | .20 | | |
| oven roasted, Louis Rich | 30 | 20.8 | 0.7 | 0.1 | 10 | | | | | | 222 | 1 | 7 | .31 | |
| *1 oz* | 28 | 5.8 | 0.1 | 0.3 | | | | | | | 63 | 76 | .13 | | |
| sliced, ckd, Louis Rich | 44 | 18.1 | 0.9 | 0.1 | 13 | | | | | | 29 | 1 | 8 | .46 | |
| *1 oz* | 28 | 8.9 | 0.0 | 0.2 | | | | | | | 115 | 72 | .29 | | |
| smoked, Louis Rich | 34 | 20.0 | 1.0 | 0.3 | 11 | | | | | | 260 | 2 | 7 | .32 | |
| *1 oz* | 28 | 5.8 | 0.3 | 0.4 | | | | | | | 69 | 82 | .25 | | |
| smoked, sliced, Louis Rich | 21 | 15.4 | 0.3 | 0.1 | 7 | | | | | | 194 | 1 | 5 | .24 | |
| *1 slice* | 21 | 4.5 | 0.1 | 0.1 | | | | | | | 58 | 61 | .10 | | |
| tenderloins, ckd, Louis Rich | 41 | 18.5 | 0.5 | 0.1 | 9 | | | | | | 22 | 1 | 8 | .46 | |
| *1 oz* | 28 | 9.0 | 0.0 | 0.2 | | | | | | | 115 | 75 | .33 | | |
| ckd, Louis Rich | 57 | 17.5 | 2.9 | 0.6 | 18 | | | | | | 20 | 3 | 6 | .61 | |
| *1 oz slice* | 28 | 7.7 | 0.0 | 0.7 | | | | | | | 81 | 55 | .29 | | |
| cnd | 315 | 101.2 | 19.5 | | | | | .22 | | | | 16 | | | |
| *5.5 oz can* | 156 | 32.6 | 0.0 | 5.7 | | 200 | .03 | 7.3 | | | | | 2.20 | | |
| dark meat w/ skin, roasted | 221 | 60.2 | 11.5 | 3.1 | 89 | 0 | 0 | .24 | .32 | 9 | 76 | 33 | 23 | 4.16 | .023 |
| *3.5 oz* | 100 | 27.5 | 0.0 | 3.5 | 0.0 | 0 | .06 | 3.5 | .36 | 1.16 | 274 | 196 | 2.27 | .150 | |
| dark meat w/o skin, roasted | 187 | 63.1 | 7.2 | 2.2 | 85 | 0 | 0 | .25 | .36 | 9 | 79 | 32 | 24 | 4.46 | .023 |
| *3.5 oz* | 100 | 28.6 | 0.0 | 2.4 | 0.0 | 0 | .06 | 3.6 | .37 | 1.29 | 290 | 204 | 2.33 | .160 | |
| drumstick, ckd, Louis Rich | 55 | 17.4 | 2.4 | 0.6 | 33 | | | | | | 21 | 3 | 6 | 1.49 | |
| *1 oz* | 28 | 8.2 | 0.0 | 0.9 | | | | | | | 49 | 43 | .67 | | |
| ground, ckd, Louis Rich | 61 | 17.1 | 3.5 | 0.9 | 24 | | | | | | 30 | 7 | 6 | .97 | |
| *1 oz* | 28 | 7.3 | 0.0 | 1.2 | | | | | | | 76 | 56 | .48 | | |
| ham, cured thigh meat | 128 | 71.4 | 5.1 | 1.5 | 62 | | | .25 | .28 | | 996 | 10 | 21 | 3.06 | |
| *3.5 oz* | 100 | 18.9 | 0.4 | 1.7 | | | .05 | 3.5 | 2.27 | | 325 | 191 | 2.76 | .100 | |
| chopped, Louis Rich | 42 | 19.5 | 2.3 | 0.6 | 17 | | | | | | 254 | 2 | 5 | .73 | |
| *1 oz* | 28 | 5.1 | 0.2 | 0.7 | | | | | | | 70 | 56 | .34 | | |
| Louis Rich | 34 | 20.1 | 1.2 | 0.3 | 18 | | | | | | 278 | 2 | 6 | .76 | |
| *1 oz* | 28 | 5.5 | 0.3 | 0.5 | | | | | | | 78 | 81 | .36 | | |
| w/ added water, Louis Rich | 34 | 20.5 | 1.4 | 0.4 | 21 | | | | | | 281 | 1 | 5 | .68 | |
| *1 oz* | 28 | 5.0 | 0.2 | 0.5 | | | | | | | 76 | 83 | .34 | | |
| light & dark meat, w/ skin, roasted | 208 | 61.7 | 9.7 | 2.5 | 82 | 0 | 0 | .18 | .41 | 7 | 68 | 26 | 25 | 2.96 | .021 |
| *3.5 oz* | 100 | 28.1 | 0.0 | 2.8 | 0.0 | 0 | .06 | 5.1 | .35 | .86 | 280 | 203 | 1.79 | .093 | |
| light & dark meat, w/o skin, roasted | 170 | 64.9 | 5.0 | 1.4 | 76 | 0 | 0 | .18 | .46 | 7 | 70 | 25 | 26 | 3.10 | .021 |
| *3.5 oz* | 100 | 29.3 | 0.0 | 1.6 | 0.0 | 0 | .06 | 5.4 | .37 | .94 | 298 | 213 | 1.78 | .094 | |
| light meat, w/ skin, roasted | 197 | 62.8 | 8.3 | 2.0 | 76 | 0 | 0 | .13 | .47 | 6 | 63 | 21 | 26 | 2.04 | .020 |
| *3.5 oz* | 100 | 28.6 | 0.0 | 2.3 | 0.0 | 0 | .06 | 6.3 | .35 | .63 | 285 | 208 | 1.41 | .048 | |
| light meat, w/o skin, roasted | 157 | 66.3 | 3.2 | 0.9 | 69 | 0 | 0 | .13 | .54 | 6 | 64 | 19 | 28 | 2.04 | .020 |
| *3.5 oz* | 100 | 29.9 | 0.0 | 1.0 | 0.0 | 0 | .06 | 6.8 | .37 | .68 | 305 | 219 | 1.35 | .042 | |

| | KCAL / WT (g) | H₂O (g) / PRO (g) | FAT (g) / CHO (g) | PUFA (g) / SFA (g) | CHOL (mg) / DFIB (g) | A (RE) / A (IU) | C (mg) / B-1 (mg) | B-2 (mg) / NIA (mg) | B-6 (mg) / B-12 (mcg) | FOL (mcg) / PANT (mg) | Na (mg) / K (mg) | Ca (mg) / P (mg) | Mg (mg) / Fe (mg) | Zn (mg) / Cu (mg) | Mn (mg) |
|---|---|---|---|---|---|---|---|---|---|---|---|---|---|---|---|
| **loaf, breast meat** | 110 | 71.9 | 1.6 | 0.3 | 41 | 0 | 0 | .11 | .36 | | 1431 | 7 | 20 | 1.13 | |
| *3.5 oz* | 100 | 22.5 | 0.0 | 0.5 | | 0 | .04 | 8.3 | 2.02 | .59 | 278 | 229 | .40 | .053 | |
| **patties, breaded & fried** | 266 | 46.7 | 16.9 | | | | | .18 | | | 752 | 13 | | | |
| *1 patty* | 94 | 13.2 | 14.8 | | | | .09 | 2.2 | | | 259 | 254 | 2.07 | | |
| **roll** | | | | | | | | | | | | | | | |
| light & dark meat | 149 | 70.2 | 7.0 | 1.8 | 55 | | | .28 | | | 586 | 32 | 18 | 2.00 | |
| *3.5 oz* | 100 | 18.1 | 2.1 | 2.0 | | | .09 | 4.8 | | | 270 | 168 | 1.35 | .077 | |
| light meat | 147 | 71.6 | 7.2 | 1.7 | 43 | | | .23 | | | 489 | 40 | 16 | 1.56 | |
| *3.5 oz* | 100 | 18.7 | 0.5 | 2.0 | | | .09 | 7.0 | | | 251 | 183 | 1.28 | .044 | |
| **sausage** | | | | | | | | | | | | | | | |
| breakfast, ckd, Louis Rich | 60 | 17.2 | 3.9 | 1.2 | 23 | | | | | | 200 | 6 | 6 | .93 | |
| *1 oz* | 28 | 6.2 | 0.0 | 1.5 | | | | | | | 80 | 53 | .53 | | |
| smoked, Louis Rich | 55 | 18.3 | 3.8 | 1.1 | 19 | | | | | | 230 | 5 | 5 | .71 | |
| *1 oz* | 28 | 4.6 | 0.4 | 1.4 | | | | | | | 60 | 37 | .40 | | |
| **smoked, Louis Rich** | 33 | 20.3 | 1.1 | 0.3 | 12 | | | | | | 279 | 2 | 6 | .52 | |
| *1 oz* | 28 | 5.5 | 0.2 | 0.4 | | | | | | | 76 | 73 | .14 | | |
| **sticks, breaded & fried** | 357 | 63.2 | 21.6 | | | | | .23 | | | 1073 | 18 | | | |
| *2 sticks* | 128 | 18.2 | 21.8 | | | | .13 | 2.7 | | | 333 | 300 | 2.82 | | |
| **thigh, ckd, Louis Rich** | 64 | 16.6 | 3.7 | 0.6 | 28 | | | | | | 21 | 3 | 6 | 1.22 | |
| *1 oz* | 28 | 7.7 | 0.0 | 0.9 | | | | | | | 55 | 52 | .52 | | |
| **wing drumettes, ckd, Louis Rich** | 52 | 17.8 | 2.2 | 0.4 | 20 | | | | | | 20 | 3 | 5 | .85 | |
| *1 oz* | 28 | 8.1 | 0.0 | 0.7 | | | | | | | 43 | 40 | .27 | | |
| **wings, ckd, Louis Rich** | 54 | 18.0 | 2.6 | 0.6 | 26 | | | | | | 18 | 3 | 6 | .93 | |
| *1 oz* | 28 | 7.5 | 0.0 | 0.8 | | | | | | | 38 | 34 | .28 | | |

## 25.3. OTHER POULTRY

| | KCAL / WT (g) | H₂O (g) / PRO (g) | FAT (g) / CHO (g) | PUFA (g) / SFA (g) | CHOL (mg) / DFIB (g) | A (RE) / A (IU) | C (mg) / B-1 (mg) | B-2 (mg) / NIA (mg) | B-6 (mg) / B-12 (mcg) | FOL (mcg) / PANT (mg) | Na (mg) / K (mg) | Ca (mg) / P (mg) | Mg (mg) / Fe (mg) | Zn (mg) / Cu (mg) | Mn (mg) |
|---|---|---|---|---|---|---|---|---|---|---|---|---|---|---|---|
| **duck w/ skin, roasted** | 337 | 51.8 | 28.4 | 3.7 | 84 | 63 | 0 | .27 | .18 | 6 | 59 | 11 | 16 | 1.86 | |
| *3.5 oz* | 100 | 19.0 | 0.0 | 9.7 | 0.0 | 210 | .17 | 4.8 | .30 | 1.10 | 204 | 156 | 2.70 | .227 | |
| **duck w/o skin, roasted** | 201 | 64.2 | 11.2 | 1.4 | 89 | 23 | 0 | .47 | .25 | 10 | 65 | 12 | 20 | 2.60 | |
| *3.5 oz* | 100 | 23.5 | 0.0 | 4.2 | 0.0 | 77 | .26 | 5.1 | .40 | 1.50 | 252 | 203 | 2.70 | .231 | |
| **goose w/ skin, roasted** | 305 | 52.0 | 21.9 | 2.5 | 91 | 21 | 0 | .32 | .37 | 2 | 70 | 13 | 22 | | |
| *3.5 oz* | 100 | 25.2 | 0.0 | 6.9 | 0.0 | 70 | .08 | 4.2 | | | 329 | 270 | 2.83 | .264 | |
| **goose w/o skin, roasted** | 238 | 57.2 | 12.7 | 1.5 | 96 | | 0 | .39 | .47 | | 76 | 14 | 25 | | |
| *3.5 oz* | 100 | 29.0 | 0.0 | 4.6 | 0.0 | | .09 | 4.1 | | | 388 | 309 | 2.87 | .276 | |
| **guinea hen w/o skin, raw** | 110 | 74.4 | 2.5 | | 63 | | | | | | | | | | |
| *3.5 oz* | 100 | 20.6 | 0.0 | | 0.0 | | | | | | | | | | |
| **pheasant w/ skin, raw** | 152 | 68.9 | 5.2 | | | | | | | | | | | | |
| *3.5 oz* | 100 | 24.7 | 0.0 | | | | | | | | | | | | |
| **pheasant w/o skin, raw** | 133 | 72.8 | 3.6 | 0.6 | | 49 | 6 | .15 | .74 | | 37 | 13 | 20 | .97 | .017 |
| *3.5 oz* | 100 | 23.6 | 0.0 | 1.2 | 0.0 | 165 | .08 | 6.8 | .84 | .96 | 262 | 230 | 1.15 | .069 | |
| **quail w/o skin, raw** | 134 | 70.0 | 4.5 | 1.2 | | 17 | 7 | .29 | | | 51 | 13 | | | |
| *3.5 oz* | 100 | 21.8 | 0.0 | 1.3 | 0.0 | 57 | .28 | 8.2 | | | 237 | 307 | 4.50 | .594 | |
| **squab (pigeon) w/o skin, raw** | 142 | 72.8 | 7.5 | 1.6 | 90 | | | | | | | | | | |
| *3.5 oz* | 100 | 17.5 | 0.0 | 2.0 | 0.0 | | | 6.9 | | | | | | | |

## 25.4. INTERNAL ORGANS

### 25.4.1. GIBLETS

| | KCAL / WT (g) | H₂O (g) / PRO (g) | FAT (g) / CHO (g) | PUFA (g) / SFA (g) | CHOL (mg) / DFIB (g) | A (RE) / A (IU) | C (mg) / B-1 (mg) | B-2 (mg) / NIA (mg) | B-6 (mg) / B-12 (mcg) | FOL (mcg) / PANT (mg) | Na (mg) / K (mg) | Ca (mg) / P (mg) | Mg (mg) / Fe (mg) | Zn (mg) / Cu (mg) | Mn (mg) |
|---|---|---|---|---|---|---|---|---|---|---|---|---|---|---|---|
| **chicken, fried** | 277 | 47.9 | 13.5 | 3.4 | 446 | 3579 | 9 | 1.52 | .61 | 379 | 113 | 18 | 25 | 6.27 | .222 |
| *3.5 oz* | 100 | 32.5 | 4.4 | 3.8 | | 11929 | .10 | 11.0 | 13.31 | 4.45 | 330 | 286 | 10.32 | .422 | |
| **chicken, simmered** | 157 | 67.6 | 4.8 | 1.1 | 393 | 2229 | 8 | .95 | .34 | 376 | 58 | 12 | 20 | 4.57 | .170 |
| *3.5 oz* | 100 | 25.9 | 1.0 | 1.5 | 0.0 | 7431 | .09 | 4.1 | 10.14 | 2.96 | 158 | 229 | 6.44 | .255 | |
| **pheasant, raw** | 139 | 71.4 | 4.9 | | | | | | | | | | | | |
| *3.5 oz* | 100 | 20.8 | 1.6 | | | | | | | | | | | | |
| **squab (pigeon), raw** | 154 | 69.8 | 7.2 | | | | | | | | | | | | |
| *3.5 oz* | 100 | 19.8 | 1.2 | | | | | | | | | | | | |
| **turkey, simmered** | 167 | 65.4 | 5.1 | 1.1 | 418 | 1795 | 2 | .90 | .33 | 345 | 59 | 13 | 17 | 3.68 | .175 |
| *3.5 oz* | 100 | 26.6 | 2.1 | 1.5 | 0.0 | 6036 | .05 | 4.5 | 24.03 | 3.46 | 200 | 204 | 6.71 | .391 | |

| | KCAL | H₂O (g) | FAT (g) | PUFA (g) | CHOL (mg) | A (RE) | C (mg) | B-2 (mg) | B-6 (mg) | FOL (mcg) | Na (mg) | Ca (mg) | Mg (mg) | Zn (mg) | Mn (mg) |
|---|---|---|---|---|---|---|---|---|---|---|---|---|---|---|---|
| | WT (g) | PRO (g) | CHO (g) | SFA (g) | DFIB (g) | A (IU) | B-1 (mg) | NIA (mg) | B-12 (mcg) | PANT (mg) | K (mg) | P (mg) | Fe (mg) | Cu (mg) | |

### 25.4.2. GIZZARD

| | KCAL/WT | H₂O/PRO | FAT/CHO | PUFA/SFA | CHOL/DFIB | A(RE)/A(IU) | C/B-1 | B-2/NIA | B-6/B-12 | FOL/PANT | Na/K | Ca/P | Mg/Fe | Zn/Cu | Mn |
|---|---|---|---|---|---|---|---|---|---|---|---|---|---|---|---|
| chicken, simmered | 153 | 67.3 | 3.7 | 1.1 | 194 | 56 | 2 | .24 | .12 | 53 | 67 | 10 | 20 | 4.38 | .062 |
| 3.5 oz | 100 | 27.2 | 1.1 | 1.0 | 0.0 | 188 | .03 | 4.0 | 1.94 | .71 | 179 | 155 | 4.15 | .110 | |
| goose, raw | 139 | 73.0 | 5.3 | | | | | | | | | | | | |
| 3.5 oz | 100 | 21.4 | 0.0 | | | | | | | | | | | | |
| turkey, simmered | 163 | 65.4 | 3.9 | 1.1 | 232 | 55 | 2 | .33 | .12 | 52 | 54 | 15 | 19 | 4.16 | .098 |
| 3.5 oz | 100 | 29.4 | 0.6 | 1.1 | 0.0 | 185 | .03 | 3.1 | 1.90 | .85 | 211 | 128 | 5.44 | .173 | |

### 25.4.3. HEART

| | KCAL/WT | H₂O/PRO | FAT/CHO | PUFA/SFA | CHOL/DFIB | A(RE)/A(IU) | C/B-1 | B-2/NIA | B-6/B-12 | FOL/PANT | Na/K | Ca/P | Mg/Fe | Zn/Cu | Mn |
|---|---|---|---|---|---|---|---|---|---|---|---|---|---|---|---|
| chicken, simmered | 185 | 64.9 | 7.9 | 2.3 | 242 | 9 | 2 | .74 | .32 | 80 | 48 | 19 | 20 | 7.30 | .107 |
| 3.5 oz | 100 | 26.5 | 0.1 | 2.3 | 0.0 | 28 | .07 | 2.8 | 7.29 | 2.65 | 132 | 199 | 9.03 | .502 | |
| turkey, simmered | 177 | 64.2 | 6.1 | 1.8 | 226 | 8 | 2 | .88 | .32 | 79 | 55 | 13 | 22 | 5.27 | .092 |
| 3.5 oz | 100 | 26.8 | 2.1 | 1.8 | 0.0 | 28 | .07 | 3.3 | 7.15 | 2.72 | 183 | 205 | 6.89 | .627 | |

### 25.4.4. LIVER

| | KCAL/WT | H₂O/PRO | FAT/CHO | PUFA/SFA | CHOL/DFIB | A(RE)/A(IU) | C/B-1 | B-2/NIA | B-6/B-12 | FOL/PANT | Na/K | Ca/P | Mg/Fe | Zn/Cu | Mn |
|---|---|---|---|---|---|---|---|---|---|---|---|---|---|---|---|
| chicken, simmered | 157 | 68.3 | 5.5 | 0.9 | 631 | 4913 | 16 | 1.75 | .58 | 770 | 51 | 14 | 21 | 4.34 | .297 |
| 3.5 oz | 100 | 24.4 | 0.9 | 1.8 | 0.0 | 16375 | .15 | 4.5 | 19.39 | 5.41 | 140 | 312 | 8.47 | .370 | |
| duck, raw | 136 | 71.8 | 4.6 | 0.6 | | 11946 | | | | | | 11 | | | |
| 3.5 oz | 100 | 18.7 | 3.5 | 1.4 | 0.0 | 39907 | | 54.00 | | | | 269 | 30.53 | 5.962 | |
| goose, raw | 125 | 67.5 | 4.0 | 0.2 | | 8728 | | .84 | .72 | | 132 | 40 | 23 | | |
| 3.3 oz | 94 | 15.4 | 5.9 | 1.5 | 0.0 | 29138 | .53 | 6.1 | | | 216 | 245 | | 7.701 | |
| turkey, simmered | 169 | 65.6 | 6.0 | 1.1 | 626 | 3741 | 2 | 1.42 | .52 | 666 | 64 | 11 | 15 | 3.09 | .250 |
| 3.5 oz | 100 | 24.0 | 3.4 | 1.9 | 0.0 | 12581 | .05 | 5.9 | 47.50 | 5.96 | 194 | 272 | 7.80 | .560 | |

## 26. SALAD DRESSINGS
### 26.1. LOW CALORIE SALAD DRESSINGS

| | KCAL/WT | H₂O/PRO | FAT/CHO | PUFA/SFA | CHOL/DFIB | A(RE)/A(IU) | C/B-1 | B-2/NIA | B-6/B-12 | FOL/PANT | Na/K | Ca/P | Mg/Fe | Zn/Cu | Mn |
|---|---|---|---|---|---|---|---|---|---|---|---|---|---|---|---|
| french | 22 | 11.3 | 0.9 | 0.5 | 1 | | | | | | 128 | 2 | | .03 | |
| 1 T | 16 | 0.0 | 3.5 | 0.1 | | | | | | | 13 | 2 | .10 | | |
| italian | 16 | 12.3 | 1.5 | 0.9 | 1 | | | | | | 118 | 0 | | | |
| 1 T | 15 | 0.0 | 0.7 | 0.2 | | | | | | | 2 | 1 | .00 | | |
| italian, lite, from mix, Good Seasons | 26 | 10.9 | 2.5 | 1.0 | 0 | | 0 | .00 | .00 | | 175 | 1 | 0 | .01 | |
| 1 T | 15 | 0.1 | 0.8 | 0.4 | | 7 | .00 | 0.0 | .00 | .00 | 6 | 1 | .03 | .001 | |
| italian, lite, zesty, from mix, Good Seasons—1 T | 26 | 11.1 | 2.6 | 1.0 | 0 | | 0 | .00 | .00 | | 132 | 2 | 0 | .01 | |
| | 15 | 0.1 | 0.8 | 0.4 | | 8 | .00 | 0.0 | .00 | .00 | 7 | 2 | .03 | .002 | |
| italian, no oil, from mix, Good Seasons | 7 | 15.1 | 0.0 | 0.0 | 0 | | 0 | .00 | .00 | | 31 | 1 | 0 | .01 | |
| 1 T | 17 | 0.1 | 1.8 | 0.0 | | 11 | .00 | 0.0 | .00 | .00 | 6 | 1 | .02 | .002 | |
| russian | 23 | 10.6 | 0.7 | 0.4 | 1 | | | | | | 141 | 3 | | | |
| 1 T | 16 | 0.1 | 4.5 | 0.1 | | | | | | | 26 | 6 | .10 | | |
| thousand island | 24 | 10.6 | 1.6 | 1.0 | 2 | 49 | | | | | 153 | 2 | | | |
| 1 T | 15 | 0.1 | 2.5 | 0.2 | | | | | | | 17 | 3 | .10 | | |

### 26.2. REGULAR SALAD DRESSINGS

| | KCAL/WT | H₂O/PRO | FAT/CHO | PUFA/SFA | CHOL/DFIB | A(RE)/A(IU) | C/B-1 | B-2/NIA | B-6/B-12 | FOL/PANT | Na/K | Ca/P | Mg/Fe | Zn/Cu | Mn |
|---|---|---|---|---|---|---|---|---|---|---|---|---|---|---|---|
| bleu cheese & herbs, from mix, Good Seasons—1 T | 85 | 5.5 | 9.2 | 3.4 | 0 | | 0 | .00 | .00 | 0 | 156 | 3 | 0 | .02 | |
| | 16 | 0.1 | 0.7 | 1.4 | | 9 | .00 | 0.0 | .01 | .01 | 4 | 3 | .02 | .002 | |
| blue (bleu) cheese | 77 | 4.9 | 8.0 | 4.3 | | 32 | 0 | .00 | | | | 12 | | | |
| 1 T | 15 | 0.7 | 1.1 | 1.5 | | | .00 | .00 | | | | 11 | .00 | | |
| buttermilk farm style, from mix, Good Seasons—1 T | 58 | 7.9 | 5.8 | 2.9 | 5 | | 0 | .02 | .01 | 1 | 138 | 16 | 2 | .05 | |
| | 16 | 0.5 | 1.2 | 1.0 | | 31 | .01 | 0.0 | .04 | .05 | 24 | 14 | .05 | .001 | |
| cheese garlic, from mix, Good Seasons | 85 | 5.5 | 9.2 | 3.4 | 0 | | 0 | .00 | .00 | 0 | 173 | 4 | 0 | .02 | |
| 1 T | 16 | 0.2 | 0.5 | 1.4 | | 3 | .00 | 0.0 | .01 | .01 | 5 | 3 | .03 | .002 | |
| cheese italian, from mix, Good Seasons | 84 | 5.5 | 9.1 | 3.4 | 0 | | 0 | .00 | .00 | | 134 | 6 | 0 | .01 | |
| 1 T | 16 | 0.1 | 0.6 | 1.4 | | 2 | .00 | 0.0 | .00 | .01 | 7 | 4 | .02 | .001 | |
| ckd, homemade | 25 | 11.1 | 1.5 | 0.3 | | 66 | 0 | .02 | | | 117 | 13 | | | |
| 1 T | 16 | 0.7 | 2.4 | 0.5 | | | .01 | 0.0 | | | 19 | 14 | .10 | | |
| classic herb, from mix, Good Seasons | 85 | 5.7 | 9.3 | 3.5 | 0 | | 0 | .00 | .00 | | 150 | 2 | 1 | .01 | |
| 1 T | 16 | 0.1 | 0.3 | 1.4 | | 2 | .00 | 0.0 | .00 | | 6 | 2 | .05 | .000 | |
| french | 67 | 5.9 | 6.4 | 3.4 | | | | | | | 214 | 2 | | .01 | |
| 1 T | 16 | 0.1 | 2.7 | 1.5 | | | | | | | 12 | 2 | .10 | | |
| french, Catalina, Kraft | 65 | 5.2 | 5.5 | 3.3 | 0 | | 1 | .00 | .01 | 5 | 185 | 2 | 0 | .05 | |
| 1 T | 15 | 0.1 | 3.7 | 0.8 | | 53 | .00 | 0.1 | .00 | .01 | 15 | 1 | .10 | .010 | |

| | KCAL / WT (g) | H₂O (g) / PRO (g) | FAT (g) / CHO (g) | PUFA (g) / SFA (g) | CHOL (mg) / DFIB (g) | A (RE) / A (IU) | C (mg) / B-1 (mg) | B-2 (mg) / NIA (mg) | B-6 (mg) / B-12 (mcg) | FOL (mcg) / PANT (mg) | Na (mg) / K (mg) | Ca (mg) / P (mg) | Mg (mg) / Fe (mg) | Zn (mg) / Cu (mg) | Mn (mg) |
|---|---|---|---|---|---|---|---|---|---|---|---|---|---|---|---|
| **french, homemade** | 88 | 3.4 | 9.8 | 4.7 | | 72 | 0 | .00 | | | 92 | 1 | | | |
| *1 T* | 14 | 0.0 | 0.5 | 1.8 | | | .00 | 0.0 | | | 3 | 0 | .00 | | |
| **garlic & herbs, from mix, Good Seasons** | 84 | 5.5 | 9.1 | 3.4 | 0 | | 8 | .00 | | | 186 | 2 | 0 | .01 | |
| *1 T* | 16 | 0.1 | 0.7 | 1.3 | | 0 | .00 | 0.0 | .00 | | 5 | 2 | .03 | .000 | |
| **italian** | 69 | 5.6 | 7.1 | 4.1 | | | | | | | 116 | 1 | | .02 | |
| *1 T* | 15 | 0.1 | 1.5 | 1.0 | | | | | | | 2 | 1 | .00 | | |
| **italian, from mix, Good Seasons** | 84 | 5.6 | 9.2 | 3.5 | 0 | | | .00 | .00 | | 150 | 1 | 0 | .01 | |
| *1 T* | 16 | 0.1 | 0.5 | 1.4 | | 6 | .00 | 0.0 | .00 | | 5 | 1 | .03 | .001 | |
| **italian, mild, from mix, Good Seasons** | 88 | 5.7 | 9.4 | 3.5 | 0 | | | .00 | | | 198 | 2 | 0 | .01 | |
| *1 T* | 17 | 0.0 | 1.2 | 1.4 | | 10 | .00 | 0.0 | .00 | | 5 | 1 | .03 | .001 | |
| **italian, zesty, from mix, Good Seasons** | 85 | 5.6 | 9.2 | 3.5 | 0 | | 0 | .00 | .00 | | 123 | 1 | 0 | .01 | |
| *1 T* | 16 | 0.1 | 0.6 | 1.4 | | 0 | .00 | 0.0 | .00 | .00 | 6 | 2 | .03 | .002 | |
| **lemon & herbs, from mix, Good Seasons** | 85 | 5.6 | 9.2 | 3.5 | 0 | | 0 | .00 | | 0 | 145 | 2 | 0 | .00 | |
| *1 T* | 16 | 0.0 | 0.6 | 1.4 | | 7 | .00 | 0.0 | .00 | .00 | 3 | 1 | .04 | .000 | |
| **mayonnaise type** | 57 | 5.9 | 4.9 | 2.6 | 4 | 32 | | | | | 105 | 2 | 0 | | |
| *1 T* | 15 | 0.1 | 3.5 | 0.7 | 0.0 | | | | | | 1 | 4 | .00 | | |
| **russian** | 76 | 5.3 | 7.8 | 4.5 | | 106 | 1 | .01 | | | 133 | 3 | | .07 | |
| *1 T* | 15 | 0.2 | 1.6 | 1.1 | | | .01 | 0.1 | | | 24 | 6 | .10 | | |
| **sesame seed** | 68 | 6.0 | 6.9 | 3.8 | 0 | | | | | | 153 | | | | |
| *1 T* | 15 | 0.5 | 1.3 | 0.9 | | | | | | | | | | | |
| **thousand island** | 59 | 7.2 | 5.6 | 3.1 | | 50 | | | | | 109 | 2 | | .02 | |
| *1 T* | 16 | 0.1 | 2.4 | 0.9 | | | | | | | 18 | 3 | .10 | | |
| **vinegar & oil, homemade** | 72 | 7.6 | 8.0 | 3.9 | | | | | | | 0 | | | | |
| *1 T* | 16 | 0.0 | 0.4 | 1.5 | | | | | | | 1 | | | | |

# 27. SAUCES, CONDIMENTS & GRAVIES
## 27.1. SAUCES & CONDIMENTS

| | KCAL / WT (g) | H₂O (g) / PRO (g) | FAT (g) / CHO (g) | PUFA (g) / SFA (g) | CHOL (mg) / DFIB (g) | A (RE) / A (IU) | C (mg) / B-1 (mg) | B-2 (mg) / NIA (mg) | B-6 (mg) / B-12 (mcg) | FOL (mcg) / PANT (mg) | Na (mg) / K (mg) | Ca (mg) / P (mg) | Mg (mg) / Fe (mg) | Zn (mg) / Cu (mg) | Mn (mg) |
|---|---|---|---|---|---|---|---|---|---|---|---|---|---|---|---|
| **alfredo fetticini sce, cnd, Prego** | 251 | | 12.6 | | | | 1 | .17 | | | 369 | 79 | | | |
| *5 oz* | 142 | 7.7 | 26.6 | | | 244 | .21 | 1.3 | | | 39 | | 1.90 | | |
| **alfredo sce, refrig, Fresh Chef** | 298 | | 26.8 | | | | 1 | .20 | | | 731 | 202 | | | |
| *4 oz* | 113 | 11.2 | 3.0 | | | 147 | .02 | 0.1 | | | 32 | | 1.30 | | |
| **barbeque sce** | 12 | 12.6 | 0.3 | 0.1 | 0 | 14 | 1 | .00 | .01 | 0 | 127 | 3 | 1 | .012 | |
| *1 T* | 16 | 0.3 | 2.0 | 0.0 | | 136 | .01 | 0.1 | 0 | .00 | 27 | 3 | .14 | .006 | |
|   Am Hosp Co | 18 | | 0.6 | | | | 4 | .01 | | | 22 | 3 | | | |
|   *1 oz* | 28 | 0.3 | 2.9 | | | 265 | .02 | 0.3 | | | 73 | | .30 | | |
|   Heinz chunky/reg | 20 | | 0.0 | | | | | | | | 230 | | | | |
|   *1 T* | | 0.0 | 5.0 | | | | | | | | | | | | |
|   Heinz hickory smoke/hot/mushroom | 20 | | 0.0 | | | | | | | | 220 | | | | |
|   *1 T* | | 0.0 | 5.0 | | | | | | | | | | | | |
|   Heinz onion | 20 | | 0.0 | | | | | | | | 200 | | | | |
|   *1 T* | | 0.0 | 5.0 | | | | | | | | | | | | |
|   Kraft | 42 | 21.5 | 0.6 | 0.3 | 0 | | 0 | .01 | .01 | 0 | 508 | 8 | 3 | .07 | |
|   *2 T* | 33 | 0.3 | 9.2 | 0.1 | | 323 | .01 | 0.2 | .00 | .01 | 49 | 6 | .30 | .018 | |
|   Open Pit | 22 | 11.5 | 0.2 | 0.1 | 0 | | 0 | .00 | .00 | | 249 | 1 | 1 | .01 | |
|   *1 T* | 18 | 0.1 | 5.4 | 0.0 | | 12 | .00 | 0.0 | .00 | .00 | 5 | 1 | .03 | .007 | |
|   Open Pit hickory smoke flavor | 22 | 11.5 | 0.2 | 0.1 | 0 | | 0 | .00 | .00 | | 230 | 1 | 1 | .01 | |
|   *1 T* | 18 | 0.1 | 5.4 | 0.0 | | 12 | .00 | 0.0 | .00 | .00 | 5 | 1 | .03 | .007 | |
|   Open Pit hickory thick & tangy | 23 | 11.3 | 0.2 | 0.1 | 0 | | 0 | .00 | .00 | | 231 | 1 | 1 | .02 | |
|   *1 T* | 18 | 0.1 | 5.6 | 0.0 | | 23 | .00 | 0.0 | .00 | .00 | 8 | 1 | .05 | .012 | |
|   Open Pit hot 'n tangy flavor | 22 | 11.6 | 0.2 | 0.1 | 0 | | 0 | .00 | .00 | | 208 | 2 | 1 | .02 | |
|   *1 T* | 18 | 0.1 | 5.4 | 0.0 | | 17 | .00 | 0.0 | .00 | .00 | 7 | 2 | .10 | .006 | |
|   Open Pit mesquite 'n tangy | 23 | 11.2 | 0.2 | 0.1 | 0 | | 0 | .00 | .00 | | 250 | 1 | 1 | .02 | |
|   *1 T* | 18 | 0.1 | 5.5 | 0.0 | | 19 | .00 | 0.0 | .00 | .00 | 7 | 1 | .04 | .010 | |
|   Open Pit sweet 'n tangy flavor | 24 | 10.9 | 0.2 | 0.1 | 0 | | 0 | .00 | .01 | | 188 | 3 | 1 | .01 | |
|   *1 T* | 18 | 0.1 | 6.0 | 0.0 | | 27 | .00 | 0.0 | .00 | .01 | 18 | 2 | .11 | .026 | |
|   Open Pit w/ onions | 23 | 11.3 | 0.2 | 0.1 | 0 | | 0 | .00 | .00 | | 249 | 1 | 1 | .01 | |
|   *1 T* | 18 | 0.1 | 5.6 | 0.0 | | 12 | .00 | 0.0 | .00 | .00 | 9 | 2 | .04 | .007 | |
| **bearnaise sce, from mix** | 263 | 58.5 | 25.6 | 1.1 | 71 | | | | | | 474 | | | | |
| *1/4 pkt prep* | 96 | 3.1 | 6.6 | 15.7 | | | | | | | | | | | |

| | KCAL | H₂O (g) | FAT (g) | PUFA (g) | CHOL (mg) | A (RE) | C (mg) | B-2 (mg) | B-6 (mg) | FOL (mcg) | Na (mg) | Ca (mg) | Mg (mg) | Zn (mg) | Mn (mg) |
|---|---|---|---|---|---|---|---|---|---|---|---|---|---|---|---|
| | WT (g) | PRO (g) | CHO (g) | SFA (g) | DFIB (g) | A (IU) | B-1 (mg) | NIA (mg) | B-12 (mcg) | PANT (mg) | K (mg) | P (mg) | Fe (mg) | Cu (mg) | |
| **bolognese sce, refrig, Fresh Chef** | 127 | | 6.2 | | | | 10 | .13 | | | 585 | 44 | | | |
| *4 oz* | 113 | 5.6 | 12.2 | | | 591 | .08 | 1.6 | | | 444 | | 1.10 | | |
| **brown sce, frzn, Am Hosp Co** | 14 | | 0.1 | | 0 | | 0 | .00 | | | 28 | 0 | | | |
| *1 oz* | 28 | 1.1 | 2.2 | | | 0 | .00 | 1.1 | | | 82 | | .00 | | |
| **burgundy wine sce, frzn, Am Hosp Co** | 10 | | 0.3 | | 0 | | 1 | .00 | | | 5 | 1 | | | |
| *1 oz* | 28 | 0.3 | 1.4 | | | 53 | .01 | | | | 5 | | .10 | | |
| **catsup (ketchup), tomato** | 16 | 10.3 | 0.1 | | | | 2 | .01 | | | 156 | 3 | | | |
| *1 T* | 15 | 0.3 | 3.8 | | | 210 | .01 | 0.2 | | | 54 | 8 | .10 | | |
| Campbell's | 17 | | 0.0 | | | | 2 | .01 | | | 172 | 3 | | | |
| *1 T* | 14 | 0.2 | 4.0 | | | 129 | .01 | 0.2 | | | 56 | | .10 | | |
| Heinz | 18 | | 0.0 | | | | | | | | 180 | 7 | | | |
| *1 T* | | 0.2 | 4.0 | | | | | | | | | | .10 | | |
| Heinz lite | 8 | | 0.0 | | | | | | | | 110ᵃ | 7 | | | |
| *1 T* | | 0.2 | 2.0 | | | | | | | | | | .10 | | |
| **chili hot dog sce, Wolf Brand** | 44 | 25.6 | 2.3 | | | | | .10 | .05 | 9 | 199 | 16 | 15 | .00 | .000 |
| *1/6 cup* | 35 | 1.5 | 4.4 | | | 410 | .06 | 0.4 | .00 | .00 | 102 | 41 | .57 | .070 | |
| **chili sce, Heinz** | 17 | | 0.0 | | | | | | | | 191 | | | | |
| *1 T* | | 0.2 | 3.8 | | | | | | | | | | | | |
| **clam sce, red, refrig, Fresh Chef** | 81 | | 3.2 | | | | 9 | .07 | | | 556 | 32 | | | |
| *4 oz* | 113 | 3.6 | 9.3 | | | 641 | .06 | 0.9 | | | 274 | | 1.20 | | |
| **clam sce, white, refrig, Fresh Chef** | 121 | | 9.6 | | | | 2 | .03 | | | 639 | 28 | | | |
| *4 oz* | 113 | 4.5 | 4.2 | | | 112 | .02 | 0.4 | | | 139 | | 1.30 | | |
| **curry sce, from mix** | 84 | 67.5 | 4.6 | 0.9 | 11 | | | | | | 399 | 152 | | | |
| *1/4 pkt prep* | 85 | 3.4 | 8.1 | 1.9 | | | | | | | | 88 | | | |
| **Heinz 57 sce** | 15 | | 0.2 | | | | | | | | 265 | | | | |
| *1 T* | | 0.4 | 2.7 | | | | | | | | | | | | |
| **hollandaise sce** | | | | | | | | | | | | | | | |
| w/ butterfat, from mix | 47 | 42.7 | 3.9 | 0.2 | 10 | | | .04 | | | 308 | 24 | | | |
| *1/4 pkt prep* | 51 | 0.9 | 2.7 | 2.3 | | | | 0.0 | | | 25 | | .18 | | |
| w/ veg oil, from mix | 264 | 58.5 | 25.6 | 1.1 | 71 | | | | | | 425 | | | | |
| *1/4 pkt prep* | 96 | 3.1 | 6.7 | 15.7 | | | | | | | | | | | |
| **horseradish, prep** | 6 | 13.1 | 0.0 | 0.0 | | | | | | | 14 | 9 | | | |
| *1 T* | 15 | 0.2 | 1.4 | 0.0 | | | | | | | 44 | 5 | .10 | | |
| **horseradish sce, Sauceworks** | 54 | 6.4 | 4.9 | 2.9 | 7 | | 0 | .00 | .00 | 1 | 108 | 1 | 0 | .02 | |
| *1 T* | 14 | 0.1 | 2.3 | 0.8 | | 9 | .00 | 0.0 | .02 | .02 | 1 | 2 | .03 | .002 | |
| **madeira sce, frzn, Am Hosp Co** | 10 | | 0.2 | | 0 | | 1 | .01 | | | 14 | 2 | | | |
| *1 oz* | 28 | 0.2 | 2.0 | | | 52 | .01 | 0.0 | | | 21 | | .11 | | |
| **marinara (tomato based) sce** | 171 | 206.3 | 8.4 | 2.3 | 0 | 240 | 32 | .15 | | | 1572 | 44 | 59 | .67 | |
| *1 cup* | 250 | 4.0 | 25.4 | 1.2 | | 2403 | .11 | 4.0 | .00 | | 1061 | 88 | 2.00 | .353 | |
| **marinara (tomato based) sce, Prego** | 91 | | 4.4 | | | | 18 | .05 | | | 623 | 32 | | | |
| *4 oz* | 113 | 1.8 | 11.1 | | | 848 | .08 | 1.3 | | | 435 | | .80 | | |
| **mushroom sce, from mix** | 71 | 67.4 | 3.2 | 0.4 | 11 | | | | | | 479 | | | | |
| *1/4 pkt prep* | 83 | 3.5 | 7.4 | 1.7 | | | | | | | | | | | |
| **mustard** | | | | | | | | | | | | | | | |
| brown | 5 | 3.9 | 0.3 | | | | | | | | 65 | 6 | | | |
| *1 t* | 5 | 0.3 | 0.3 | | | | | | | | 7 | 7 | .10 | | |
| mild, Heinz | 5 | | 0.2 | | | | | | | | 71 | 4 | | | |
| *1 t* | | 0.3 | 0.5 | | | | | | | | | | .10 | | |
| pourable, Heinz | 5 | | 0.2 | | | | | | | | 71 | 4 | | | |
| *1 t* | | 0.3 | 0.5 | | | | | | | | | | .10 | | |
| yellow | 4 | 4.0 | 0.2 | | | | | | | | 63 | 4 | | | |
| *1 t* | 5 | 0.2 | 0.3 | | | | | | | | 7 | 4 | .10 | | |
| **pesto sce, refrig, Fresh Chef** | 155 | | 14.6 | | | | 0 | .07 | | | 244 | 98 | | | |
| *1 oz* | 28 | 2.8 | 3.0 | | | 494 | .01 | 0.2 | | | 27 | | .30 | | |
| **pizza sce, cnd** | | | | | | | | | | | | | | | |
| Contadina | 40 | 50.0 | 2.0 | 0.7 | 0 | | 2 | .03 | | | 350 | 12 | | | |
| *1/4 cup* | 60 | 0.0 | 5.0 | 0.2 | | 363 | .01 | 0.7 | | | 230 | | .43 | | |

ᵃ Low sodium lite ketchup contains 90 mg sodium per tablespoon.

| | KCAL / WT (g) | H₂O (g) / PRO (g) | FAT (g) / CHO (g) | PUFA (g) / SFA (g) | CHOL (mg) / DFIB (g) | A (RE) / A (IU) | C (mg) / B-1 (mg) | B-2 (mg) / NIA (mg) | B-6 (mg) / B-12 (mcg) | FOL (mcg) / PANT (mg) | Na (mg) / K (mg) | Ca (mg) / P (mg) | Mg (mg) / Fe (mg) | Zn (mg) / Cu (mg) | Mn (mg) |
|---|---|---|---|---|---|---|---|---|---|---|---|---|---|---|---|
| w/ cheese, Contadina | 40 | 48.4 | 2.0 | 0.7 | 0 | | 2 | .03 | | | 350 | 19 | | | |
| *1/4 cup* | 60 | 1.0 | 6.0 | 0.7 | | 458 | .01 | 0.7 | | | 302 | | .37 | | |
| w/ pepperoni, Contadina | 45 | 48.2 | 2.0 | 0.7 | 0 | | 2 | .05 | | | 340 | 12 | | | |
| *1/4 cup* | 60 | 1.0 | 6.0 | 0.4 | | 301 | .01 | 0.8 | | | 300 | | .43 | | |
| w/ tomato chunks, Contadina | 25 | 52.3 | 1.0 | | | | 2 | .01 | | | 280 | 19 | | | |
| *1/4 cup* | 60 | 0.0 | 5.0 | | | 292 | .01 | 0.6 | | | 176 | | .38 | | |
| **seafood cocktail sce, Heinz** | 20 | | | | | | | | | | 160 | | | | |
| *1 T* | | | | | | | | | | | | | | | |
| **sour cream sce, from mix** | 64 | 27.0 | 3.8 | 0.4 | 12 | | | .09 | | | 126 | 68 | | .17 | |
| *1/4 pkt prep* | 39 | 2.4 | 5.7 | 2.0 | | | | 0.1 | | | 92 | | .08 | .010 | |
| **soy sce** | | | | | | | | | | | | | | | |
| made w/ hydrolyzed veg protein | 24 | 43.9 | 0.1 | 0.0 | 0 | 0 | 0 | .06 | .08 | 8 | 3300 | 3 | 3 | .18 | |
| *1/4 cup* | 58 | 1.4 | 4.5 | 0.0 | | 0 | .02 | 1.6 | .00 | .16 | 88 | 54 | .86 | .056 | |
| made w/ soy & wheat (shoyu) | 30 | 41.2 | 0.1 | 0.0 | 0 | 0 | 0 | .08 | .10 | 9 | 3314ᵃ | 10 | 20 | .21 | |
| *1/4 cup* | 58 | 3.0 | 4.9 | 0.0 | | 0 | .03 | 1.9 | .00 | .19 | 104 | 64 | 1.17 | .067 | |
| made w/ soy (tamari) | 35 | 38.3 | 0.1 | 0.0 | 0 | 0 | 0 | .09 | .12 | 11 | 3240 | 12 | 23 | .25 | |
| *1/4 cup* | 58 | 6.1 | 3.2 | 0.0 | | 0 | .03 | 2.3 | .00 | .22 | 123 | 75 | 1.38 | .078 | |
| **spaghetti sce, cnd** | 272 | 187.7 | 11.9 | 3.3 | 0 | 306 | 28 | .15 | | | 1236 | 70 | 60 | .53 | |
| *1 cup* | 249 | 4.5 | 39.7 | 1.7 | | 3055 | .14 | 3.7 | .00 | | 957 | 90 | 1.62 | .284 | |
| no salt added, Prego | 100 | | 5.7 | | | | 19 | .06 | | | 21 | 43 | | | |
| *4 oz* | 113 | 2.0 | 10.3 | | | 1642 | .07 | 1.7 | | | 528 | | 1.10 | | |
| Prego | 136 | | 5.6 | | | | 18 | .05 | | | 623 | 36 | | | |
| *4 oz* | 113 | 1.9 | 19.6 | | | 1085 | .04 | 1.2 | | | 386 | 52 | 1.20 | | |
| w/ meat flavor, Prego | 142 | | 5.8 | | | | 16 | .06 | | | 625 | 34 | | | |
| *4 oz* | 113 | 2.4 | 20.2 | | | 1059 | .04 | 1.5 | | | 419 | 51 | 1.20 | | |
| w/ mushrooms & chunk tomatoes, Prego—4 oz | 121 | | 4.7 | | | | 15 | .07 | | | 406 | 41 | | | |
| | 113 | 2.1 | 17.4 | | | 916 | .04 | 0.9 | | | 325 | | 1.20 | | |
| w/ mushrooms, Prego | 133 | | 5.2 | | | | 17 | .07 | | | 632 | 40 | | | |
| *4 oz* | 113 | 1.8 | 19.8 | | | 1002 | .05 | 1.5 | | | 410 | 54 | 1.20 | | |
| **spaghetti sce, frzn, w/ ground beef, Am Hosp Co—3 oz** | 116 | | 4.6 | | 15 | | 18 | .08 | | | 489 | 23 | | | |
| | 85 | 5.3 | 13.3 | | | 1061 | .09 | 1.9 | | | 393 | | 2.01 | | |
| **stroganoff sce, from mix** | 73 | 62.4 | 2.9 | 0.1 | 10 | | | .21 | | | 493 | 141 | | .30 | |
| *1/4 pkt prep* | 80 | 3.2 | 9.1 | 1.8 | | | .23 | 0.2 | | | 181 | 81 | .36 | .023 | |
| **sweet & sour sce, from mix** | 55 | 44.7 | 0.0 | 0.0 | 0 | | | .02 | | | 146 | 8 | | .02 | |
| *1/4 pkt prep* | 59 | 0.2 | 13.6 | 0.0 | | | | 0 | | | 12 | | .30 | .005 | |
| **sweet & sour sce, frzn, Am Hosp Co** | 19 | | 0.0 | | 0 | 0 | 0 | .00 | | | 6 | 1 | | | |
| *1 oz* | 28 | 0.1 | 4.5 | | | 75 | .00 | 0.1 | | | 27 | | .04 | | |
| **tartar sce, Best Foods/Hellmann's** | 70 | 5.1 | 8.1 | 4.5 | 5 | | | | | | 220 | | | | |
| *1 T* | 14 | 0.2 | 0.1 | 1.2 | | | | | | | | | | | |
| **teriyaki sce** | | | | | | | | | | | | | | | |
| bottled | 15 | 12.2 | 0.0 | 0.0 | 0 | 0 | 0 | .01 | .02 | 4 | 690 | 4 | 11 | .02 | .000 |
| *1 T* | 18 | 1.1 | 2.9 | 0.0 | | 0 | .01 | 0.2 | 0 | .04 | 41 | 28 | .31 | .018 | |
| from mix | 8 | 14.8 | 0.1 | 0.0 | 0 | | | | | | 299 | 7 | | | |
| *1 T* | 18 | 0.3 | 1.7 | 0.0 | | | | 0.1 | 0 | | 14 | | .17 | | |
| **tomato chili sce** | 16 | 10.2 | 0.0 | | | | 2 | .01 | | | 201 | 3 | | | |
| *1 T* | 15 | 0.4 | 3.7 | | | 210 | .01 | 0.2 | | | 56 | 8 | .10 | | |
| **tomato sce, cnd** | 37 | 108.7 | 0.2 | 0.1 | 0 | 119 | 16 | .07 | | | 738 | 17 | 23 | .30 | |
| *1/2 cup* | 122 | 1.6 | 8.8 | 0.0 | | 1195 | .08 | 1.4 | .00 | .377 | 452 | 39 | .94 | .239 | |
| al fresco, Prego | 94 | | 5.1 | | | | 19 | .05 | | | 610 | 36 | | | |
| *4 oz* | 113 | 1.7 | 10.3 | | | 1106 | .07 | 1.4 | | | 426 | | .90 | | |
| Contadina | 45 | 112.0 | 1.0 | 0.0 | 0 | | 15 | .05 | | | 520 | 15 | 19 | | |
| *1/2 cup* | 124 | 2.0 | 9.0 | 0.0 | | 750 | .05 | 1.2 | | | 467 | 35 | .92 | | |
| italian style, Contadina | 40 | 113.0 | 1.0 | 0.0 | 0 | | 1 | .04 | | | 760 | 16 | | | |
| *1/2 cup* | 124 | 1.0 | 8.0 | 0.0 | | 688 | .02 | 1.3 | | | | 468 | .57 | | |
| no salt added, Heinz | 32 | 91.3 | 0.1 | | | | 5 | .04 | | | 17 | 14 | 14 | .17 | |
| *3.5 oz* | 100 | 1.0 | 6.9 | | | 618 | .05 | 0.9 | | | 299 | 20 | .50 | .150 | |

ᵃ Low sodium types contain 1933 mg sodium.

| | KCAL / WT (g) | H₂O (g) / PRO (g) | FAT (g) / CHO (g) | PUFA (g) / SFA (g) | CHOL (mg) / DFIB (g) | A (RE) / A (IU) | C (mg) / B-1 (mg) | B-2 (mg) / NIA (mg) | B-6 (mg) / B-12 (mcg) | FOL (mcg) / PANT (mg) | Na (mg) / K (mg) | Ca (mg) / P (mg) | Mg (mg) / Fe (mg) | Zn (mg) / Cu (mg) | Mn (mg) |
|---|---|---|---|---|---|---|---|---|---|---|---|---|---|---|---|
| refrig, Fresh Chef | 151 | | 10.3 | | | | 17 | .09 | | | 686 | 73 | | | |
| *4 oz* | 113 | 3.1 | 11.6 | | | 681 | .08 | 1.1 | | | 468 | | 1.10 | | |
| spanish style | 40 | 108.7 | 0.3 | 0.1 | 0 | 120 | 11 | .08 | | | 576 | 20 | | | |
| *1/2 cup* | 122 | 1.8 | 8.8 | 0.0 | | 1202 | .09 | 1.6 | .00 | | | | 4.25 | | |
| w/ herbs & cheese | 72 | 101.8 | 2.4 | 1.0 | | 120 | 12 | .15 | | | | 45 | | | |
| *1/2 cup* | 122 | 2.6 | 12.5 | 0.8 | | 1205 | .09 | 1.5 | .00 | | | | 1.06 | | |
| w/ mushrooms | 42 | 107.3 | 0.2 | 0.1 | 0 | 116 | 15 | .13 | | | 552 | 16 | 23 | .25 | |
| *1/2 cup* | 122 | 1.8 | 10.3 | 0.0 | | 1165 | .09 | 1.5 | .00 | | 464 | 39 | 1.1 | .243 | |
| w/ mushrooms al fresco, Prego | 95 | | 4.9 | | | | 18 | .06 | | | 545 | 25 | | | |
| *4 oz* | 113 | 1.6 | 11.2 | | | 802 | .06 | 1.1 | | | 438 | | .50 | | |
| w/ red peppers, al fresco, Prego | 92 | | 5.0 | | | | 21 | .06 | | | 531 | 22 | | | |
| *4 oz* | 113 | 1.5 | 10.2 | | | 968 | .07 | 1.1 | | | 423 | | .80 | | |
| w/ onions | 52 | 105.0 | 0.2 | 0.1 | 0 | 104 | 16 | .16 | | | 672 | 20 | 23 | .28 | |
| *1/2 cup* | 122 | 1.9 | 12.1 | 0.0 | | 1038 | .09 | 1.5 | .00 | | 504 | 48 | 1.13 | .221 | |
| w/ onions, green peppers & celery | 50 | 107.7 | 0.9 | 0.4 | 0 | 99 | 16 | .15 | | | | 16 | | | |
| *1/2 cup* | 122 | 1.2 | 10.7 | 0.2 | | 988 | .08 | 1.3 | .00 | | | | .92 | | |
| w/ tomato tidbits | 39 | 108.7 | 0.5 | 0.2 | 0 | 98 | 26 | .12 | | | 18 | 13 | 24 | .23 | .268 |
| *1/2 cup* | 122 | 1.6 | 8.7 | 0.1 | | 977 | .09 | 1.4 | .00 | | 455 | 51 | .83 | .017 | |
| **tomato sce, frzn, Am Hosp Co** | 14 | | 0.4 | | 1 | | 4 | .01 | | | 19 | 2 | | | |
| *1 oz* | 28 | 0.6 | 1.9 | | | 248 | .02 | 1.1 | | | 90 | | .20 | | |
| **veloutee sce, frzn, Am Hosp Co**[a] | 19 | | 0.5 | | 1 | | 0 | .01 | | | 23 | 32 | | | |
| *1 oz* | 28 | 1.0 | 2.8 | | | 15 | .01 | 0.0 | | | 11 | | .05 | | |
| **white cream (bechamel) sce, cnd,** | 59 | | 4.5 | | | | 0 | .02 | | | 265 | 14 | | | |
| **Campbell's**—*2 oz* | 57 | 0.7 | 3.8 | | | 0 | .01 | 0.1 | | | 32 | | .20 | | |
| **white sce, from mix** | 151 | 134.4 | 8.4 | 1.1 | 22 | | | .28 | .04 | | 498 | 265 | 165 | .34 | |
| *1/4 pkt prep* | 165 | 6.4 | 13.4 | 4.0 | | | .05 | 0.3 | | | 277 | 160 | .17 | .028 | |
| **worcestershire sce, Heinz** | 11 | | | | | | | | | | 234 | | | | |
| *1 T* | | | | | | | | | | | | | | | |

## 27.2. GRAVIES

| | KCAL / WT (g) | H₂O (g) / PRO (g) | FAT (g) / CHO (g) | PUFA (g) / SFA (g) | CHOL (mg) / DFIB (g) | A (RE) / A (IU) | C (mg) / B-1 (mg) | B-2 (mg) / NIA (mg) | B-6 (mg) / B-12 (mcg) | FOL (mcg) / PANT (mg) | Na (mg) / K (mg) | Ca (mg) / P (mg) | Mg (mg) / Fe (mg) | Zn (mg) / Cu (mg) | Mn (mg) |
|---|---|---|---|---|---|---|---|---|---|---|---|---|---|---|---|
| **au jus** | | | | | | | | | | | | | | | |
| cnd | 24 | | 0.3 | 0.0 | 0 | 0 | 1 | .09 | | | 839 | 6 | | | |
| *1/2 can* | 149 | 1.8 | 3.7 | 0.1 | | 0 | .03 | 1.3 | | | 115 | 47 | .89 | | |
| cnd, Franco-American | 9 | | 0.1 | | | | 0 | .01 | | | 325 | 3 | | | |
| *2 oz* | 57 | 0.6 | 1.5 | | | 0 | .00 | 0.6 | | | 42 | | .20 | | |
| from mix | 9 | 120.0 | 0.4 | 0.0 | 0.4 | | | | | | 289 | 5 | | .02 | |
| *1/2 cup* | 123 | 0.3 | 1.2 | 0.2 | | | | | | | | | | .005 | |
| **beef** | | | | | | | | | | | | | | | |
| cnd | 77 | 127.3 | 3.4 | 0.1 | 4 | 0 | 0 | .05 | .01 | 0 | 73 | 8 | | 1.45 | .291 |
| *1/2 can* | 145 | 5.4 | 7.0 | 1.7 | | 0 | .04 | 0.9 | | | 118 | 43 | 1.02 | .145 | |
| cnd, Franco-American | 25 | | 1.0 | | | | 0 | .02 | | | 303 | 3 | | | |
| *2 oz* | 57 | 1.2 | 2.8 | | | 2 | .01 | 0.5 | | | 37 | | .20 | | |
| **brown** | | | | | | | | | | | | | | | |
| cnd, Campbell's | 47 | | 3.2 | | | | 0 | .01 | | | 302 | 3 | | | |
| *2 oz* | 57 | 1.2 | 3.3 | | | 0 | .00 | 0.2 | | | 26 | | .20 | | |
| cnd, homestyle, Heinz | 29 | | 2.3 | | | | 1 | .02 | | | 130 | 0 | | | |
| *2 oz* | 57 | 0.7 | 1.4 | | | 0 | .00 | 0.1 | | | 80 | | .05 | | |
| from mix | 4 | 136.8 | 0.1 | 0.0 | 0 | | | .00 | | | 66 | 4 | 0 | .01 | .005 |
| *1/2 cup* | 138 | 0.1 | 0.8 | 0.0 | | | .00 | 0.0 | | | 3 | 2 | .01 | .000 | |
| from mix, Pillsbury | 16 | | 0.2 | | | | 0 | .00 | | | 328 | 4 | | | |
| *1/4 cup* | | 0.4 | 3.2 | | | 0 | .01 | 0.0 | | | 5 | 3 | .04 | | |
| w/ onions, cnd, Franco-American | 25 | | 0.9 | | | | 0 | .00 | | | 332 | 6 | | | |
| *2 oz* | 57 | 0.4 | 3.7 | | | 0 | .01 | 0.1 | | | 25 | | .20 | | |
| **chicken** | | | | | | | | | | | | | | | |
| cnd | 118 | 127.1 | 8.5 | 2.2 | 3 | | 0 | .06 | .01 | | 859 | 30 | | 1.19 | .300 |
| *1/2 can* | 149 | 2.8 | 8.1 | 2.1 | | 550 | .02 | 0.6 | | | 162 | 43 | .70 | .149 | |

[a] Chicken-based sauce.

| | KCAL | $H_2O$ (g) | FAT (g) | PUFA (g) | CHOL (mg) | A (RE) | C (mg) | B-2 (mg) | B-6 (mg) | FOL (mcg) | Na (mg) | Ca (mg) | Mg (mg) | Zn (mg) | Mn (mg) |
|---|---|---|---|---|---|---|---|---|---|---|---|---|---|---|---|
| | WT (g) | PRO (g) | CHO (g) | SFA (g) | DFIB (g) | A (IU) | B-1 (mg) | NIA (mg) | B-12 (mcg) | PANT (mg) | K (mg) | P (mg) | Fe (mg) | Cu (mg) | |
| cnd, Campbell's | 41 | | 2.4 | | | | 0 | .02 | | | 245 | 18 | | | |
| 2 oz | 57 | 1.3 | 3.5 | | | 149 | .01 | 0.3 | | | 31 | | .20 | | |
| cnd, Franco-American | 42 | | 3.2 | | | | 0 | .01 | | | 305 | 11 | | | |
| 2 oz | 57 | 0.8 | 2.6 | | | 217 | .01 | 0.2 | | | 26 | | .20 | | |
| cnd, homestyle, Heinz | 35 | | 2.3 | | | | 1 | .02 | | | 110 | 0 | | | |
| 2 oz | 57 | 0.7 | 2.9 | | | 0 | .00 | 0.1 | | | 50 | | .04 | | |
| from mix | 41 | 118.7 | 0.9 | 0.2 | 1 | | | .07 | | | 566 | 19 | | .16 | |
| 1/2 cup | 130 | 1.3 | 7.1 | 0.2 | | | | | | | | | | .013 | |
| from mix, Pillsbury | 25 | | 1.0 | | | | | | | | 230 | | | | |
| 1/4 cup | | 1.0 | 4.0 | | | | | | | | 20 | | | | |
| **chicken giblet, cnd, Franco-American** | 29 | | 1.5 | | | | 0 | .02 | | | 301 | 4 | | | |
| 2 oz | 57 | 1.1 | 2.7 | | | 0 | .00 | 0.2 | | | 15 | | .30 | | |
| **homestyle, from mix, Pillsbury** | 16 | | 0.1 | | | | 0 | .00 | | | 339 | 3 | | | |
| 1/4 cup | | 0.5 | 3.1 | | | 0 | .01 | 0.0 | | | 5 | 3 | .03 | | |
| **mushroom** | | | | | | | | | | | | | | | |
| cnd | 75 | 132.6 | 4.0 | 1.5 | 0 | 0 | 0 | .09 | .03 | 0 | 849 | 11 | | 1.04 | .445 |
| 1/2 can | 149 | 1.9 | 8.1 | 0.6 | | 0 | .05 | 1.0 | | | 158 | 22 | .98 | .149 | |
| cnd, Franco-American | 21 | | 0.8 | | | | 0 | .03 | | | 287 | 3 | | | |
| 2 oz | 57 | 0.6 | 2.7 | | | 0 | .01 | 0.3 | | | 31 | | .20 | | |
| cnd, homestyle, Heinz | 21 | | 0.9 | | | | 1 | .02 | | | 200 | 0 | | | |
| 2 oz | 57 | 0.4 | 2.7 | | | 0 | .00 | 0.1 | | | 70 | | .10 | | |
| from mix | 35 | 118.6 | 0.4 | 0.0 | 0 | | | | | | 701 | 24 | | .16 | |
| 1/2 cup | 129 | 1.0 | 6.9 | 0.2 | | | | | | | | | | .057 | |
| **onion** | | | | | | | | | | | | | | | |
| cnd, homestyle, Heinz | 24 | | 0.8 | | | | 1 | .02 | | | 150 | 0 | | | |
| 2 oz | 57 | 0.4 | 3.6 | | | 0 | .00 | 0.1 | | | 80 | | .11 | | |
| from mix | 40 | 118.8 | 0.3 | 0.0 | 0 | | | | | | 518 | 34 | | .10 | |
| 1/2 cup | 130 | 1.1 | 8.4 | 0.2 | | | | | | | | | | .021 | |
| **pork** | | | | | | | | | | | | | | | |
| cnd, Franco-American | 38 | | 2.7 | | | | 0 | .01 | | | 346 | 3 | | | |
| 2 oz | 57 | 0.7 | 2.8 | | | 17 | .01 | 0.2 | | | 28 | | .20 | | |
| cnd, homestyle, Heinz | 31 | | 1.7 | | | | 1 | .02 | | | 130 | 0 | | | |
| 2 oz | 57 | 1.8 | 2.1 | | | 0 | .00 | 0.1 | | | 80 | | .06 | | |
| from mix | 38 | 118.7 | 0.9 | 0.1 | 1 | | | .03 | | | 617 | 16 | | | |
| 1/2 cup | 129 | 0.9 | 6.7 | 0.4 | | | | | | | | | | | |
| **turkey** | | | | | | | | | | | | | | | |
| cnd | 76 | 132.0 | 3.1 | 0.7 | 3 | 0 | 0 | .12 | | | 868 | 6 | | | |
| 1/2 can | 149 | 3.9 | 7.6 | 0.9 | | 0 | .03 | 1.9 | | | 154 | 60 | 1.04 | | |
| cnd, Franco-American | 26 | | 1.2 | | | | 0 | .02 | | | 280 | 4 | | | |
| 2 oz | 57 | 1.0 | 3.0 | | | 8 | .01 | 0.5 | | | 36 | | .20 | | |
| cnd, homestyle, Heinz | 29 | | 2.0 | | | | 1 | .02 | | | 140 | 0 | | | |
| 2 oz | 57 | 0.8 | 2.1 | | | 0 | .00 | 0.0 | | | 90 | | .07 | | |
| from mix | 43 | 118.8 | 0.9 | 0.2 | 1 | | | .05 | | | 749 | 25 | | | |
| 1/2 cup | 130 | 1.4 | 7.5 | 0.3 | | | | | | | | | | | |

# 28. SOUPS
## 28.1. CANNED, CONDENSED

| | KCAL | $H_2O$ (g) | FAT (g) | PUFA (g) | CHOL (mg) | A (RE) | C (mg) | B-2 (mg) | B-6 (mg) | FOL (mcg) | Na (mg) | Ca (mg) | Mg (mg) | Zn (mg) | Mn (mg) |
|---|---|---|---|---|---|---|---|---|---|---|---|---|---|---|---|
| | WT (g) | PRO (g) | CHO (g) | SFA (g) | DFIB (g) | A (IU) | B-1 (mg) | NIA (mg) | B-12 (mcg) | PANT (mg) | K (mg) | P (mg) | Fe (mg) | Cu (mg) | |
| **celery, crm of** | 219 | 259.1 | 13.6 | 6.1 | 34 | 75 | 1 | .12 | .03 | 6 | 2308 | 98 | 16 | .37 | .610 |
| 1 can | 305 | 4.0 | 21.5 | 3.4 | | 745 | .07 | 0.8 | | | 299 | 91 | 1.52 | .345 | |
| **cheese** | 311 | 198.3 | 21.0 | 0.6 | 59 | 218 | 0 | .27 | .05 | | 1920 | 284 | 8 | 1.29 | .514 |
| 1 can | 257 | 10.9 | 21.1 | 13.3 | | 2177 | .03 | 0.8 | 0 | | 308 | 272 | 1.49 | .257 | |
| **chicken, crm of** | 283 | 249.3 | 17.9 | 3.6 | 24 | 136 | 0 | .15 | .04 | 4 | 2397 | 83 | 6 | 1.53 | .915 |
| 1 can | 305 | 8.3 | 22.5 | 5.1 | | 1362 | .07 | 2.0 | | | 212 | 92 | 1.47 | .305 | |
| **mushroom, crm of** | 313 | 247.7 | 23.1 | 10.8 | 3 | 0 | 3 | .20 | .03 | | 2469 | 78 | 11 | 1.44 | .610 |
| 1 can | 305 | 4.9 | 22.6 | 6.3 | | 0 | .07 | 2.0 | | | 203 | 102 | 1.28 | .305 | |
| **tomato** | 208 | 247.8 | 4.7 | 2.3 | 0 | 169 | 162 | .12 | .28 | 36 | 2120 | 32 | 18 | .59 | .610 |
| 1 can | 305 | 5.0 | 40.3 | 0.9 | | 1693 | .21 | 3.4 | .00 | | 641 | 82 | 4.27 | .610 | |

| | KCAL | H₂O (g) | FAT (g) | PUFA (g) | CHOL (mg) | A (RE) | C (mg) | B-2 (mg) | B-6 (mg) | FOL (mcg) | Na (mg) | Ca (mg) | Mg (mg) | Zn (mg) | Mn (mg) |
|---|---|---|---|---|---|---|---|---|---|---|---|---|---|---|---|
| | WT (g) | PRO (g) | CHO (g) | SFA (g) | DFIB (g) | A (IU) | B-1 (mg) | NIA (mg) | B-12 (mcg) | PANT (mg) | K (mg) | P (mg) | Fe (mg) | Cu (mg) | |

## 28.2. CANNED, CONDENSED, PREPARED WITH MILK

| | KCAL/WT | H₂O/PRO | FAT/CHO | PUFA/SFA | CHOL/DFIB | A(RE)/A(IU) | C/B-1 | B-2/NIA | B-6/B-12 | FOL/PANT | Na/K | Ca/P | Mg/Fe | Zn/Cu | Mn |
|---|---|---|---|---|---|---|---|---|---|---|---|---|---|---|---|
| **asparagus, crm of** | 161 | 213.3 | 8.2 | 2.2 | 22 | 83 | 4 | .28 | .06 | | 1041 | 175 | 20 | .92 | .379 |
| *1 cup* | 248 | 6.3 | 16.4 | 3.3 | | 599 | .10 | 0.9 | | | 359 | 153 | .87 | .139 | |
| **celery, crm of** | 165 | 214.4 | 9.7 | 2.7 | 32 | 68 | 1 | .25 | .06 | 9 | 1010 | 186 | 22 | .20 | .253 |
| *1 cup* | 248 | 5.7 | 14.5 | 4.0 | | 461 | .07 | 0.4 | | | 309 | 151 | .69 | .154 | |
| **cheese** | 230 | 206.9 | 14.6 | 0.4 | 48 | 147 | 1 | .33 | .08 | | 1020 | 288 | 20 | .69 | .259 |
| *1 cup* | 251 | 9.5 | 16.2 | 9.1 | | 1243 | .06 | 0.5 | .44 | | 340 | 250 | .81 | .141 | |
| **chicken, crm of** | 191 | 210.4 | 11.5 | 1.6 | 27 | 94 | 1 | .26 | .07 | 8 | 1046 | 180 | 18 | .68 | .379 |
| *1 cup* | 248 | 7.5 | 15.0 | 4.6 | | 715 | .07 | 0.9 | | | 273 | 152 | .67 | .139 | |
| **clam chowder, new england** | 163 | 211.4 | 6.6 | 1.1 | 22 | 40 | 4 | .24 | .13 | 10 | 992 | 187 | 23 | .80 | .253 |
| *1 cup* | 248 | 9.5 | 16.6 | 3.0 | | 164 | .07 | 1.0 | 10.25 | | 300 | 157 | 1.48 | 1.39 | |
| **mushroom, crm of** | 203 | 209.7 | 13.6 | 4.6 | 20 | 38 | 2 | .28 | .06 | | 1076 | 178 | 20 | .64 | .253 |
| *1 cup* | 248 | 6.1 | 15.0 | 5.1 | | 154 | .08 | 0.9 | | | 270 | 156 | .59 | .139 | |
| **onion, crm of** | a | | 9.4 | 1.6 | 32 | 68 | 2 | .27 | | | | | 180 | | |
| *1 cup* | 248 | 6.8 | a | 4.0 | | 451 | .10 | 0.6 | | | | | .69 | | |
| **oyster stew** | 134 | 217.9 | 7.9 | 0.3 | 32 | 45 | 4 | .23 | .06 | | 1040 | 167 | 21 | 10.33 | .370 |
| *1 cup* | 245 | 6.1 | 9.8 | 5.1 | | 225 | .07 | 0.3 | 2.63 | | 235 | 162 | 1.04 | 1.605 | |
| **pea, green** | 239 | 197.9 | 7.0 | 0.5 | 18 | 58 | 3 | .27 | .10 | 8 | 1048 | 173 | 55 | 1.76 | .660 |
| *1 cup* | 254 | 12.6 | 32.2 | 4.0 | | 356 | .16 | 1.3 | .44 | | 377 | 238 | 2.01 | .391 | |
| **potato, crm of[b]** | 148 | 215.0 | 6.5 | 0.6 | 22 | 67 | 1 | .24 | .09 | 9 | 1060 | 166 | 17 | .68 | .379 |
| *1 cup* | 248 | 5.8 | 17.2 | 3.8 | | 443 | .08 | 0.6 | | | 323 | 160 | .54 | .263 | |
| **shrimp, crm of** | 165 | 214.3 | 9.3 | 0.4 | 35 | 54 | 1 | .23 | | | 1036 | 164 | | .80 | |
| *1 cup* | 248 | 6.8 | 13.9 | 5.8 | | 313 | .06 | 0.5 | | | | | .59 | | |
| **tomato** | 160 | 210.0 | 6.0 | 1.1 | 17 | 108 | 68 | .25 | .16 | 21 | 932 | 159 | 23 | .29 | .251 |
| *1 cup* | 248 | 6.1 | 22.3 | 2.9 | | 849 | .13 | 1.5 | .44 | | 450 | 148 | 1.82 | .263 | |
| **tomato bisque** | 198 | 204.6 | 6.6 | 1.2 | 22 | 110 | 7 | .27 | .14 | | 1108 | 186 | 25 | .63 | .259 |
| *1 cup* | 251 | 6.3 | 29.4 | 3.1 | | 879 | .11 | 1.3 | .44 | | 604 | 174 | .88 | .141 | |

## 28.3. CANNED, CONDENSED, PREPARED WITH WATER

| | KCAL/WT | H₂O/PRO | FAT/CHO | PUFA/SFA | CHOL/DFIB | A(RE)/A(IU) | C/B-1 | B-2/NIA | B-6/B-12 | FOL/PANT | Na/K | Ca/P | Mg/Fe | Zn/Cu | Mn |
|---|---|---|---|---|---|---|---|---|---|---|---|---|---|---|---|
| **asparagus, crm of** | 87 | 224.0 | 4.1 | 1.8 | 5 | 44 | 3 | .08 | .01 | | 981 | 29 | 4 | .88 | .376 |
| *1 cup* | 244 | 2.3 | 10.7 | 1.0 | | 445 | .05 | 0.8 | | | 173 | 39 | .80 | .124 | |
| **bean w/ bacon** | 173 | 212.9 | 5.9 | 1.8 | 3 | 89 | 2 | .03 | .04 | 32 | 952 | 81 | 44 | 1.03 | .670 |
| *1 cup* | 253 | 7.9 | 22.8 | 1.5 | | 889 | .09 | 0.6 | | | 403 | 132 | 2.05 | .402 | |
| **bean w/ franks** | 187 | 207.6 | 7.0 | 1.6 | 12 | 87 | 1 | .07 | .13 | | 1092 | 86 | 49 | 1.18 | .788 |
| *1 cup* | 250 | 10.0 | 22.0 | 2.1 | | 869 | .11 | 1.0 | | | 477 | 166 | 2.34 | .395 | |
| **beef broth & barley, Campbell's** | 59 | | 1.0 | | | | 0 | .01 | | | 871 | 12 | | | |
| *1 cup* | 233 | 2.5 | 10.0 | | | 1568 | .02 | 0.5 | | | 87 | | .60 | | |
| **beef, Campbell's** | 71 | | 1.5 | | | | 2 | .05 | | | 837 | 13 | | | |
| *1 cup* | 233 | 4.9 | 9.6 | | | 1443 | .03 | 1.0 | | | 123 | | .80 | | |
| **beef mushroom** | a | | 3.0 | 0.1 | 7 | 0 | 5 | .06 | | | | 5 | | | |
| *1 cup* | 244 | 5.8 | a | 1.5 | | 0 | .04 | 0.9 | | | | | .88 | | |
| **beef noodle** | 84 | 224.5 | 3.1 | 0.5 | 5 | 63 | 0 | .06 | .04 | 4 | 952 | 15 | 6 | 1.54 | .273 |
| *1 cup* | 244 | 4.8 | 9.0 | 1.2 | | 629 | .07 | 1.1 | .20 | | 99 | 46 | 1.10 | .139 | |
| **beef noodle homestyle, Campbell's** | 80 | | 2.9 | | | | 2 | .10 | | | 798 | 9 | | | |
| *1 cup* | 233 | 6.1 | 7.3 | | | 104 | .08 | 1.7 | | | 138 | | 1.00 | | |
| **black bean** | 116 | 215.6 | 1.5 | 0.5 | 0 | 49 | 1 | .05 | .09 | 25 | 1198 | 45 | 42 | 1.41 | .642 |
| *1 cup* | 247 | 5.6 | 19.8 | 0.4 | | 506 | .08 | 0.5 | .02 | .20 | 273 | 107 | 2.16 | .385 | |
| **broccoli, creamy, Campbell's** | 69 | | 2.7 | | | | 11 | .05 | | | 667 | 25 | | | |
| *1 cup* | 233 | 1.5 | 9.5 | | | 493 | .02 | 0.5 | | | 45 | | .40 | | |
| **cauliflower, creamy, Campbell's** | 97 | | 5.9 | | | | 6 | .06 | | | 825 | 19 | | | |
| *1 cup* | 233 | 1.5 | 9.6 | | | 0 | .03 | 0.6 | | | 63 | | .50 | | |
| **celery, crm of** | 90 | 225.1 | 5.6 | 2.5 | 15 | 31 | 0 | .05 | .01 | 2 | 949 | 40 | 6 | .15 | .251 |
| *1 cup* | 244 | 1.7 | 8.8 | 1.4 | | 306 | .03 | 0.3 | | | 123 | 37 | .62 | .142 | |
| **cheese** | 155 | 217.7 | 10.5 | 0.3 | 30 | 109 | 0 | .14 | .03 | | 959 | 142 | 4 | .64 | .257 |
| *1 cup* | 247 | 5.4 | 10.5 | 6.7 | | 1088 | .02 | 0.4 | .00 | | 154 | 136 | .75 | .128 | |
| **chicken alphabet, Campbell's** | 71 | | 2.0 | | | | 1 | .08 | | | 802 | 13 | | | |
| *1 cup* | 233 | 3.6 | 9.6 | | | 1109 | .06 | 1.4 | | | 89 | | .80 | | |
| **chicken & dumplings** | 97 | 221.2 | 5.5 | 1.3 | 34 | 52 | 0 | .07 | .04 | | 861 | 15 | 4 | .37 | .489 |
| *1 cup* | 241 | 5.6 | 6.0 | 1.3 | | 518 | .02 | 1.8 | .16 | | 116 | 61 | .62 | .123 | |

[a] Kcal & cho not available.  [b] Includes vichyssoise.

| | KCAL / WT (g) | H₂O (g) / PRO (g) | FAT (g) / CHO (g) | PUFA (g) / SFA (g) | CHOL (mg) / DFIB (g) | A (RE) / A (IU) | C (mg) / B-1 (mg) | B-2 (mg) / NIA (mg) | B-6 (mg) / B-12 (mcg) | FOL (mcg) / PANT (mg) | Na (mg) / K (mg) | Ca (mg) / P (mg) | Mg (mg) / Fe (mg) | Zn (mg) / Cu (mg) | Mn (mg) |
|---|---|---|---|---|---|---|---|---|---|---|---|---|---|---|---|
| chicken & stars, Campbell's | 55 | | 1.8 | | | | 0 | .06 | | | 875 | 13 | | | |
| 1 cup | 233 | 3.1 | 6.5 | | | 409 | .06 | 1.1 | | | 64 | | .60 | | |
| chicken & wild rice, Golden Classic, Campbell's—1 cup | 76 | | 2.3 | | | | 2 | .08 | | | 738 | 19 | | | |
|  | 233 | 3.5 | 10.3 | | | 921 | .04 | 1.2 | | | 119 | | .40 | | |
| chicken barley, Campbell's | 70 | | 1.8 | | | | 0 | .03 | | | 846 | 12 | | | |
| 1 cup | 233 | 3.6 | 9.8 | | | 1170 | .01 | 1.0 | | | 86 | | .70 | | |
| chicken broth | 39 | 234.1 | 1.4 | 0.3 | 1 | 0 | 0 | .07 | .02 | | 776 | 9 | 2 | .25 | .249 |
| 1 cup | 244 | 4.9 | 0.9 | 0.4 | | 0 | .01 | 3.3 | .24 | | 210 | 73 | .51 | .124 | |
| chicken broth & noodles, Campbell's | 58 | | 1.8 | | | | 0 | .08 | | | 864 | 11 | | | |
| 1 cup | 233 | 2.4 | 7.9 | | | 903 | .10 | 1.4 | | | 72 | | .80 | | |
| chicken broth & rice, Campbell's | 44 | | 1.0 | | | | 0 | .02 | | | 857 | 7 | | | |
| 1 cup | 233 | 1.4 | 7.4 | | | 482 | .01 | 0.7 | | | 50 | | .30 | | |
| chicken, crm of | 116 | 221.1 | 7.4 | 1.5 | 10 | 56 | 0 | .06 | .02 | 2 | 986 | 34 | 3 | .63 | .376 |
| 1 cup | 244 | 3.4 | 9.3 | 2.1 | | 560 | .03 | 0.8 | | | 87 | 38 | .61 | .124 | |
| chicken, crm of, Special Request (1/3 less salt)—1 cup | 106 | | 6.6 | | | | 0 | .04 | | | 519 | 25 | | | |
|  | 233 | 2.9 | 8.7 | | | 667 | .02 | 0.6 | | | 69 | | .40 | | |
| chicken creamy mushroom, Campbell's | 111 | | 7.2 | | | | 0 | .07 | | | 925 | 21 | | | |
| 1 cup | 233 | 3.4 | 8.2 | | | 790 | .01 | 1.0 | | | 92 | | .50 | | |
| chicken gumbo | 56 | 229.0 | 1.4 | 0.4 | 5 | 14 | 5 | .05 | .06 | | 955 | 24 | 4 | .38 | .251 |
| 1 cup | 244 | 2.6 | 8.4 | 0.3 | | 136 | .02 | 0.7 | | | 75 | 25 | .89 | .124 | |
| chicken mushroom | ᵃ | | 9.2 | 2.3 | 10 | 112 | 0 | .11 | | | | 29 | | | |
| 1 cup | 244 | 4.4 | ᵃ | 2.4 | | 1135 | .02 | 1.6 | | | | | .88 | | |
| chicken noodle | 75 | 221.7 | 2.5 | 0.6 | 7 | 72 | 0 | .06 | .03 | 2 | 1107 | 17 | 5 | .40 | .289 |
| 1 cup | 241 | 4.0 | 9.4 | 0.7 | | 711 | .05 | 1.4 | | | 55 | 36 | .78 | .195 | |
| chicken noodle, Special Request, (1/3 less salt)—1 cup | 61 | | 2.0 | | | | 0 | .07 | | | 578 | 11 | | | |
|  | 233 | 3.1 | 7.6 | | | 332 | .09 | 1.2 | | | 54 | | .80 | | |
| chicken noodle-o's, Campbell's | 66 | | 2.0 | | | | 0 | .07 | | | 816 | 13 | | | |
| 1 cup | 233 | 3.3 | 8.6 | | | 458 | .07 | 1.2 | | | 61 | | .80 | | |
| chicken rice | 60 | 226.1 | 1.9 | 0.4 | 7 | 66 | 0 | .02 | .02 | 1 | 814 | 17 | 1 | .26 | .366 |
| 1 cup | 241 | 3.5 | 7.2 | 0.5 | | 660 | .02 | 1.1 | | | 100 | 21 | .75 | .118 | |
| chicken veg | 74 | 223.3 | 2.8 | 0.6 | 10 | 266 | 1 | .06 | .05 | | 944 | 18 | 6 | .40 | .366 |
| 1 cup | 241 | 3.6 | 8.6 | 0.9 | | 2656 | .04 | 1.2 | | | 154 | 41 | .87 | .123 | |
| chili beef | 169 | 211.7 | 6.6 | 0.3 | 12 | 151 | 4 | .08 | .16 | | 1035 | 43 | 30 | 1.40 | 1.050 |
| 1 cup | 250 | 6.7 | 21.5 | 3.3 | | 1510 | .06 | 1.1 | .32 | | 525 | 148 | 2.13 | .395 | |
| clam chowder, manhattan | 78 | 218.4 | 2.3 | 1.3 | 2 | 93 | 3 | .05 | .08 | 10 | 1808 | 34 | 10 | .93 | .376 |
| 1 cup | 244 | 4.2 | 12.2 | 0.4 | | 920 | .06 | 1.3 | 2.19 | .12 | 262 | 57 | 1.89 | .148 | |
| clam chowder, new england | 95 | 220.9 | 2.9 | 1.1 | 5 | 1 | 2 | .04 | .08 | 4 | 914 | 43 | 7 | .75 | .251 |
| 1 cup | 244 | 4.8 | 12.4 | 0.4 | | 8 | .02 | 1.0 | 8.01 | .32 | 146 | 54 | 1.48 | .124 | |
| consomme w/ gelatin | 29 | 231.9 | 0.0 | 0.0 | 0 | 0 | 1 | .03 | .02 | 3 | 637 | 8 | 0 | .37 | .366 |
| 1 cup | 241 | 5.4 | 1.8 | 0.0 | | 0 | .02 | 0.7 | .00 | | 153 | 32 | .53 | .246 | |
| corn potage, Campbell's | 93 | | 2.4 | | | | 0 | .05 | | | 898 | 27 | | | |
| 1 cup | 233 | 1.8 | 16.1 | | | 584 | .01 | 0.5 | | | 95 | | .30 | | |
| curly noodle w/ chicken, Campbell's | 67 | | 2.3 | | | | 0 | .07 | | | 955 | 13 | | | |
| 1 cup | 233 | 3.2 | 8.3 | | | 1406 | .07 | 1.2 | | | 72 | | .80 | | |
| garden veg, Campbell's | 63 | | 1.8 | | | | 3 | .04 | | | 801 | 18 | | | |
| 1 cup | 233 | 2.2 | 9.7 | | | 3465 | .03 | 0.8 | | | 167 | | .60 | | |
| gazpacho, Campbell's | 41 | | 0.2 | | | | 6 | .03 | | | 585 | 27 | | | |
| 1 cup | 233 | 0.9 | 9.0 | | | 2089 | .03 | 0.5 | | | 219 | | .70 | | |
| meatball alphabet, Campbell's | 98 | | 3.8 | | | | 2 | .07 | | | 909 | 16 | | | |
| 1 cup | 233 | 4.8 | 11.0 | | | 1856 | .06 | 1.4 | | | 163 | | 1.00 | | |
| minestrone | 83 | 220.1 | 2.5 | 1.1 | | 234 | 1 | .04 | .10 | 16 | 911 | 34 | 7 | .74 | .366 |
| 1 cup | 241 | 4.3 | 11.2 | 0.5 | | 2337 | .05 | 0.9 | .00 | | 312 | 56 | .92 | .123 | |
| mushroom barley | ᵃ | | 2.3 | 0.7 | 0 | 20 | 0 | .09 | | 0 | | 13 | | | |
| 1 cup | 244 | 1.9 | ᵃ | 0.4 | | 198 | .02 | 0.9 | | | | | .50 | | |
| mushroom, crm of | 129 | 220.4 | 9.0 | 4.2 | 2 | 0 | 1 | .09 | .06 | | 1031 | 46 | 5 | .59 | .251 |
| 1 cup | 244 | 2.3 | 9.3 | 2.4 | | 0 | .05 | 0.7 | .05 | .29 | 101 | 50 | .51 | .124 | |
| mushroom, golden, Campbell's | 73 | | 3.0 | | | | 1 | .09 | | | 865 | 8 | | | |
| 1 cup | 233 | 2.6 | 9.3 | | | 832 | .03 | 1.1 | | | 128 | | .50 | | |
| mushroom w/ beef stock | 85 | 224.7 | 4.0 | 0.8 | 7 | 126 | 1 | .10 | .04 | 9 | 970 | 10 | 9 | 1.38 | .376 |
| 1 cup | 244 | 3.2 | 9.3 | 1.6 | | 1255 | .03 | 1.2 | .00 | | 158 | 36 | .84 | .251 | |
| nacho cheese, Campbell's | 105 | | 7.2 | | | | 5 | .06 | | | 754 | 78 | | | |
| 1 cup | 233 | 3.8 | 6.4 | | | 1354 | .01 | 0.3 | | | 56 | | .60 | | |

ᵃ Kcal & cho not available.

| | KCAL | H2O (g) | FAT (g) | PUFA (g) | CHOL (mg) | A (RE) | C (mg) | B-2 (mg) | B-6 (mg) | FOL (mcg) | Na (mg) | Ca (mg) | Mg (mg) | Zn (mg) | Mn (mg) |
|---|---|---|---|---|---|---|---|---|---|---|---|---|---|---|---|
| | WT (g) | PRO (g) | CHO (g) | SFA (g) | DFIB (g) | A (IU) | B-1 (mg) | NIA (mg) | B-12 (mcg) | PANT (mg) | K (mg) | P (mg) | Fe (mg) | Cu (mg) | |
| noodles & ground beef, Campbell's | 90 | | 3.5 | | | | 0 | .10 | | | 825 | 18 | | | |
| *1 cup* | 233 | 4.7 | 9.9 | | | 1242 | .10 | 1.6 | | | 115 | | 1.10 | | |
| onion | 57 | 224.3 | 1.7 | 0.7 | 0 | 0 | 1 | .02 | .05 | 15 | 1053 | 26 | 2 | .61 | .246 |
| *1 cup* | 241 | 3.8 | 8.2 | 0.3 | | 0 | .03 | 0.6 | .00 | | 69 | 11 | .67 | .123 | |
| onion, crm of | ᵃ | | 5.3 | 1.5 | 15 | 30 | 1 | .08 | | | | 34 | | | |
| *1 cup* | 244 | 2.8 | ᵃ | 1.5 | | 296 | .05 | 0.5 | | | | | .63 | | |
| oyster stew | 59 | 228.6 | 3.8 | 0.2 | 14 | 7 | 3 | .04 | .01 | | 980 | 22 | 5 | 10.29 | .366 |
| *1 cup* | 241 | 2.1 | 4.1 | 2.5 | | 71 | .02 | 0.2 | 2.19 | | 49 | 48 | .98 | 1.593 | |
| pea, green | 164 | 208.7 | 2.9 | 0.4 | 0 | 20 | 2 | .07 | .05 | 2 | 987 | 27 | 39 | 1.71 | .658 |
| *1 cup* | 250 | 8.6 | 26.5 | 1.4 | | 202 | .11 | 1.2 | .00 | | 190 | 124 | 1.95 | .378 | |
| pea, split w/ ham | 189 | 206.9 | 4.4 | 0.6 | 8 | 44 | 1 | .08 | .07 | 3 | 1008 | 22 | 48 | 1.32 | .670 |
| *1 cup* | 253 | 10.3 | 28.0 | 1.8 | | 444 | .15 | 1.5 | | | 399 | 213 | 2.28 | .369 | |
| pea, split w/ ham & bacon, Campbell's | 159 | | 3.2 | | | | 1 | .06 | | | 793 | 18 | | | |
| *1 cup* | 233 | 8.8 | 24.0 | | | 491 | .13 | 1.2 | | | 319 | | 1.80 | | |
| pepperpot | 103 | 217.3 | 4.6 | 0.4 | 10 | 87 | 1 | .05 | .06 | | 970 | 23 | 5 | 1.22 | .612 |
| *1 cup* | 241 | 6.4 | 9.4 | 2.1 | | 865 | .05 | 1.2 | .17 | | 152 | 42 | .89 | .123 | |
| potato, crm ofᵇ | 73 | 225.7 | 2.4 | 0.4 | 5 | 29 | 0 | .04 | .04 | 3 | 1000 | 20 | 1 | .63 | .379 |
| *1 cup* | 244 | 1.7 | 11.5 | 1.2 | | 288 | .03 | 0.5 | | | 137 | 46 | .48 | .251 | |
| scotch broth | 80 | 221.1 | 2.6 | 0.6 | 5 | 218 | 1 | .05 | .07 | | 1012 | 15 | 4 | 1.59 | .366 |
| *1 cup* | 241 | 5.0 | 9.5 | 1.1 | | 2180 | .02 | 1.2 | .27 | | 159 | 55 | .83 | .246 | |
| shrimp, crm of | 90 | 225.0 | 5.2 | 0.2 | 17 | 16 | 0 | .03 | | | 976 | 18 | | .75 | |
| *1 cup* | 244 | 2.8 | 8.2 | 3.2 | | 158 | .02 | 0.4 | | | | | .53 | | |
| spinach, creamy, Campbell's | 88 | | 5.5 | | | | 2 | .07 | | | 679 | 33 | | | |
| *1 cup* | 233 | 1.4 | 8.3 | | | 1639 | .01 | 0.3 | | | 61 | | .60 | | |
| stockpot | 100 | 223.7 | 3.9 | 1.8 | 5 | 398 | 2 | .05 | .09 | | 1048 | 22 | 4 | 1.16 | .257 |
| *1 cup* | 247 | 4.9 | 11.5 | 0.9 | | 3980 | .04 | 1.2 | .00 | | 238 | 54 | .87 | .128 | |
| tomato | 86 | 220.5 | 1.9 | 1.0 | 0 | 69 | 67 | .05 | .11 | 15 | 872 | 13 | 8 | .24 | .253 |
| *1 cup* | 244 | 2.1 | 16.6 | 0.4 | | 688 | .09 | 1.4 | .00 | | 263 | 34 | 1.76 | .251 | |
| tomato beef w/ noodle | 140 | 211.5 | 4.3 | 0.7 | 5 | 53 | 0 | .09 | .09 | | 917 | 18 | 8 | .75 | .251 |
| *1 cup* | 244 | 4.5 | 21.2 | 1.6 | | 533 | .08 | 1.9 | .19 | | 221 | 56 | 1.12 | .124 | |
| tomato bisque | 123 | 215.3 | 2.5 | 1.1 | 4 | 72 | 6 | .07 | .09 | | 1048 | 40 | 9 | .59 | .257 |
| *1 cup* | 247 | 2.3 | 23.7 | 0.5 | | 721 | .07 | 1.1 | .00 | | 417 | 60 | .82 | .128 | |
| tomato, crm of, Campbell's | 104 | | 2.2 | | | | 25 | .04 | | | 823 | 14 | | | |
| *1 cup* | 233 | 1.3 | 19.9 | | | 596 | .04 | .09 | | | 249 | | 1.10 | | |
| tomato garden, crispy, Campbell's | 78 | | 0.3 | | | | 12 | .05 | | | 492 | 34 | | | |
| *1 cup* | 233 | 1.4 | 17.4 | | | 3431 | .05 | 1.2 | | | 406 | | .90 | | |
| tomato rice | 120 | 217.6 | 2.7 | 1.4 | 2 | 76 | 15 | .05 | .08 | | 815 | 23 | 5 | .51 | .385 |
| *1 cup* | 247 | 2.1 | 21.9 | 0.5 | | 755 | .06 | 1.1 | .00 | | 330 | 33 | .79 | .128 | |
| tomato zesty, Campbell's | 89 | | 0.4 | | | | 23 | .06 | | | 769 | 36 | | | |
| *1 cup* | 233 | 2.4 | 19.0 | | | 1353 | .04 | 1.2 | | | 269 | | .90 | | |
| tortellini & veg, Golden Classic, Campbell's—*1 cup* | 79 | | 2.1 | | | | 4 | .05 | | | 861 | 41 | | | |
| | 233 | 2.8 | 12.0 | | | 1736 | .42 | 2.2 | | | 152 | | 1.80 | | |
| turkey noodle | 69 | 226.9 | 2.0 | 0.5 | 5 | 29 | 0 | .06 | .04 | | 815 | 12 | 5 | .58 | .251 |
| *1 cup* | 244 | 3.9 | 8.6 | 0.6 | | 292 | .07 | 1.4 | | | 75 | 48 | .94 | .124 | |
| turkey veg | 74 | 223.9 | 3.0 | 0.7 | 2 | 244 | 0 | .04 | .05 | | 905 | 17 | 4 | .61 | .246 |
| *1 cup* | 241 | 3.1 | 8.6 | 0.9 | | 2445 | .03 | 1.0 | .17 | | 175 | 40 | .76 | .123 | |
| veg, Campbell's | 79 | | 1.5 | | | | 5 | .04 | | | 796 | 16 | | | |
| *1 cup* | 233 | 3.1 | 13.3 | | | 3186 | .06 | 1.0 | | | 130 | | .70 | | |
| veg, Special Request (1/3 less salt) | 79 | | 1.5 | | | | 4 | .04 | | | 523 | 16 | | | |
| *1 cup* | 233 | 3.1 | 13.2 | | | 3091 | .06 | 1.0 | | | 132 | | .70 | | |
| veg, old fashioned, Campbell's | 60 | | 1.6 | | | | 3 | .04 | | | 887 | 19 | | | |
| *1 cup* | 233 | 2.4 | 9.0 | | | 3094 | .03 | 0.8 | | | 150 | | .60 | | |
| veg vegetarian | 72 | 222.5 | 1.9 | 0.7 | 0 | 300 | 1 | .05 | .06 | 11 | 823 | 21 | 7 | .46 | .460 |
| *1 cup* | 241 | 2.1 | 12.0 | 0.3 | | 3005 | .05 | 0.9 | .00 | | 209 | 35 | 1.08 | .123 | |
| veg w/ beefᶜ | 79 | 223.5 | 1.9 | 0.1 | 5 | 189 | 2 | .05 | .08 | 11 | 957 | 17 | 6 | 1.55 | .315 |
| *1 cup* | 244 | 5.6 | 10.2 | 0.9 | | 1891 | .04 | 1.0 | .31 | | 173 | 40 | 1.11 | .183 | |
| veg w/ beef broth | 81 | 220.5 | 1.9 | 0.8 | 2 | 209 | 2 | .05 | .06 | | 810 | 18 | 7 | .80 | .337 |
| *1 cup* | 241 | 3.0 | 13.1 | 0.4 | | 2091 | .05 | 1.0 | .00 | | 192 | 39 | .97 | .154 | |
| won ton, Campbell's | 41 | | 1.0 | | | | 0 | .06 | | | 878 | 10 | | | |
| *1 cup* | 233 | 3.4 | 4.5 | | | 25 | .04 | 1.4 | | | 76 | | .60 | | |

ᵃ Kcal & cho not available.
ᵇ Includes vichyssoise.
ᶜ Includes beef; beef veg; barley & veg beef.

| | KCAL | H₂O (g) | FAT (g) | PUFA (g) | CHOL (mg) | A (RE) | C (mg) | Vitamins B-2 (mg) | B-6 (mg) | FOL (mcg) | Na (mg) | Ca (mg) | Minerals Mg (mg) | Zn (mg) | Mn (mg) |
|---|---|---|---|---|---|---|---|---|---|---|---|---|---|---|---|
| | WT (g) | PRO (g) | CHO (g) | SFA (g) | DFIB (g) | A (IU) | B-1 (mg) | NIA (mg) | B-12 (mcg) | PANT (mg) | K (mg) | P (mg) | Fe (mg) | Cu (mg) | |

**28.4. CANNED, READY-TO-SERVE**

| | KCAL | H₂O / PRO | FAT / CHO | PUFA / SFA | CHOL / DFIB | A(RE) / A(IU) | C / B-1 | B-2 / NIA | B-6 / B-12 | FOL / PANT | Na / K | Ca / P | Mg / Fe | Zn / Cu | Mn |
|---|---|---|---|---|---|---|---|---|---|---|---|---|---|---|---|
| bean, Campbell's | 143 | | 3.9 | | | | 0 | .02 | | | 822 | 72 | | | |
| 7.5 oz | 213 | 6.3 | 20.7 | | | 830 | .10 | 0.6 | | | 274 | | 2.20 | | |
| bean w/ ham, chunky | 231 | 191.1 | 8.5 | 1.0 | 22 | 395 | 4 | .15 | | | 972 | 79 | | | |
| 1 cup | 243 | 12.6 | 27.1 | 3.3 | | 3950 | .15 | 1.7 | | | | | 3.23 | | |
| beef barley, Progresso | 200 | | 9.0 | | | | | | | | 1420 | | | | |
| 10.5 oz | 298 | 8.0 | 16.0 | | | | | | | | 230 | | | | |
| beef broth/ bouillon | 16 | 234.1 | 0.5 | 0.0 | 0 | 0 | 0 | .05 | | | 782 | 15 | | | |
| 1 cup | 240 | 2.7 | 0.1 | 0.3 | | 0 | .01 | 1.9 | | | 130 | 31 | .41 | | |
| beef, chunky | 171 | 200.0 | 5.1 | 0.2 | 14 | 261 | 7 | .15 | .13 | 13 | 867 | 31 | | 2.64 | 2.40 |
| 1 cup | 240 | 11.7 | 19.6 | 2.6 | | 2611 | .06 | 2.7 | .61 | | 336 | 120 | 2.32 | .240 | |
| beef minestrone, Progresso | 150 | | 4.0 | | | | | | | | 1040 | | | | |
| 9 oz | 269 | 11.0 | 19.0 | | | | | | | | 440 | | | | |
| beef noodle, Campbell's | 73 | | 2.6 | | | | 0 | .08 | | | 806 | 13 | | | |
| 7.27 oz | 206 | 4.5 | 7.9 | | | 350 | .10 | 1.3 | | | 79 | | 1.10 | | |
| beef noodle, Home Cookin, Campbell's | 144 | | 3.8 | | | | 8 | .19 | | | 1129 | 34 | | | |
| 10.76 oz | 305 | 16.9 | 10.4 | | | 2076 | .07 | 4.0 | | | 351 | | 3.00 | | |
| beef ravioli romano, chunky, Campbell's | 231 | | 8.3 | | | | 13 | .14 | | | 1047 | 64 | | | |
| 9.49 oz | 269 | 8.1 | 30.9 | | | 6470 | .11 | 3.1 | | | 412 | | 3.10 | | |
| beef, Progresso | 160 | | 4.0 | | | | | | | | 1390 | | | | |
| 9.5 oz | 269 | 12.0 | 19.0 | | | | | | | | 416 | | | | |
| beef veg, Progresso | 150 | | 2.0 | | | | | | | | 1140 | | | | |
| 9.5 oz | 269 | 12.0 | 19.0 | | | | | | | | 450 | | | | |
| beef w/ mushroom, chunky, low Na, Campbell's—10.76 oz | 204 | | 6.6 | | | | 11 | .35 | | | 65 | 41 | | | |
| | 305 | 13.4 | 22.9 | | | 5949 | .13 | 4.3 | | | 480 | | 2.50 | | |
| beef w/ noodles, stroganoff style, chunky, Campbell's—10.76 oz | 300 | | 14.1 | | | | 0 | .31 | | | 1222 | 76 | | | |
| | 305 | 15.4 | 27.9 | | | 2985 | .14 | 3.2 | | | 330 | | 2.90 | | |
| chickarina w/ tiny meatballs, Progresso | 90 | | 6.0 | | | | | | | | 1060 | | | | |
| 9.5 oz | 269 | 8.0 | 8.0 | | | | | | | | 190 | | | | |
| chicken broth, low Na, Campbell's | 19 | | 0.6 | | | | 1 | .08 | | | 49 | 10 | | | |
| 7.27 oz | 206 | 2.4 | 1.1 | | | 0 | .02 | 2.3 | | | 99 | | .80 | | |
| chicken broth, Swanson | 25 | | 1.2 | | | | 0 | .07 | | | 895 | 9 | | | |
| 7.27 oz | 206 | 2.6 | 0.8 | | | 0 | .01 | 3.0 | | | 145 | | .60 | | |
| chicken, chunky | 178 | 211.1 | 6.6 | 1.4 | 30 | 130 | 1 | .17 | .05 | 5 | 887 | 24 | | 1.00 | .251 |
| 1 cup | 251 | 12.7 | 17.3 | 2.0 | | 1299 | .09 | 4.4 | .25 | | 176 | 113 | 1.73 | .251 | |
| chicken, crm of, Campbell's | 85 | | 5.5 | | | | 0 | .03 | | | 833 | 29 | | | |
| 7.27 oz | 206 | 2.3 | 6.5 | | | 484 | .02 | 0.5 | | | 65 | | .60 | | |
| chicken, hearty, Progresso | 170 | | 8.0 | | | | | | | | 1010 | | | | |
| 9.5 oz | 269 | 10.0 | 12.0 | | | | | | | | 180 | | | | |
| chicken, homestyle, Progresso | 90 | | 2.0 | | | | | | | | 1190 | | | | |
| 9.5 oz | 269 | 9.0 | 8.0 | | | | | | | | | | | | |
| chicken minestrone, Progresso | 150 | | 6.0 | | | | | | | | 1220 | | | | |
| 9.5 oz | 269 | 11.0 | 14.0 | | | | | | | | 290 | | | | |
| chicken mushroom, creamy, chunky, Campbell's—9.38 oz | 272 | | 21.5 | | | | 1 | .22 | | | 1259 | 23 | | | |
| | 266 | 10.4 | 9.3 | | | 1212 | .07 | 2.6 | | | 84 | | 1.80 | | |
| chicken noodle, Campbell's | 60 | | 2.0 | | | | 0 | .07 | | | 870 | 14 | | | |
| 7.27 oz | 206 | 3.3 | 7.1 | | | 340 | .10 | 1.3 | | | 65 | | 1.00 | | |
| chicken noodle, chunky | ᵃ | | 6.0 | 1.5 | 18 | 122 | 0 | .17 | | | | 24 | | | |
| 1 cup | 240 | 12.7 | ᵃ | 1.4 | | 1222 | .07 | 4.3 | | | | | 1.44 | | |
| chicken noodle, Progresso | 130 | | 4.0 | | | | | | | | 990 | | | | |
| 9.5 oz | 269 | 11.0 | 10.0 | | | | | | | | 202 | | | | |
| chicken noodle w/ meatballs | 99 | 225.0 | 3.6 | 0.8 | 10 | 233 | 8 | .12 | | | 1039 | 30 | | | |
| 1 cup | 248 | 8.1 | 8.4 | 1.1 | | 2326 | .12 | 2.15 | | | | | 1.74 | | |
| chicken rice, chunky | 127 | 208.3 | 3.2 | 0.7 | 12 | 586 | 4 | .10 | | 4 | 888 | 35 | | | |
| 1 cup | 240 | 12.3 | 13.0 | 1.0 | | 5858 | .02 | 4.1 | | | | | 1.87 | | |
| chicken rice, Campbell's | 52 | | 2.1 | | | | 0 | .01 | | | 810 | 12 | | | |
| 7.27 oz | 206 | 2.9 | 5.5 | | | 556 | .01 | 0.8 | | | 52 | | .50 | | |
| chicken rice w/ veg, Progresso | 140 | | 3.0 | | | | | | | | 940 | | | | |
| 9.5 oz | 269 | 8.0 | 20.0 | | | | | | | | 240 | | | | |

ᵃ Kcal & cho not available.

| | KCAL / WT (g) | H₂O (g) / PRO (g) | FAT (g) / CHO (g) | PUFA (g) / SFA (g) | CHOL (mg) / DFIB (g) | A (RE) / A (IU) | C (mg) / B-1 (mg) | B-2 (mg) / NIA (mg) | B-6 (mg) / B-12 (mcg) | FOL (mcg) / PANT (mg) | Na (mg) / K (mg) | Ca (mg) / P (mg) | Mg (mg) / Fe (mg) | Zn (mg) / Cu (mg) | Mn (mg) |
|---|---|---|---|---|---|---|---|---|---|---|---|---|---|---|---|
| chicken veg, chunky | 167 | 200.3 | 4.8 | 1.0 | 17 | 599 | 6 | .17 | | | 1068 | 25 | | | |
| *1 cup* | 240 | 12.3 | 18.9 | 1.4 | | 5991 | .04 | 3.3 | | | | | 1.47 | | |
| chicken veg, chunky, low Na, Campbell's | 236 | | 10.9 | | | | 12 | .41 | | | 91 | 44 | | | |
| *10.76 oz* | 305 | 15.4 | 19.0 | | | 7930 | .20 | 5.6 | | | 449 | | 1.70 | | |
| chicken veg, Progresso | 130 | | 5.0 | | | | | | | | 760 | | | | |
| *9.5 oz* | 269 | 9.0 | 20.0 | | | | | | | | 450 | | | | |
| chicken veg w/ rice, Home Cookin, Campbell's—*10.76 oz* | 131 | | 2.7 | | | | 9 | .07 | | | 991 | 46 | | | |
| | 305 | 13.0 | 13.7 | | | 3752 | .09 | 3.3 | | | 280 | | 2.20 | | |
| chicken w/ noodles & mushrooms, chunky, Campbell's—*10.76 oz* | 195 | | 6.6 | | | | 0 | .24 | | | 1142 | 34 | | | |
| | 305 | 13.9 | 20.1 | | | 1406 | .12 | 4.7 | | | 238 | | 2.10 | | |
| chicken w/ noodles, Home Cookin, Campbell's—*10.76 oz* | 129 | | 3.4 | | | | 4 | .15 | | | 1126 | 38 | | | |
| | 305 | 13.8 | 10.9 | | | 3846 | .08 | 4.2 | | | 183 | | 2.00 | | |
| chicken w/ noodles, low Na, Campbell's | 160 | | 5.0 | | | | 4 | .35 | | | 82 | 32 | | | |
| *10.76 oz* | 305 | 13.7 | 15.1 | | | 2274 | .17 | 5.5 | | | 254 | | 2.10 | | |
| chicken w/ rice, chunky, Campbell's | 142 | | 4.3 | | | | 5 | .10 | | | 1072 | 37 | | | |
| *9.49 oz* | 269 | 11.1 | 14.8 | | | 6111 | .01 | 3.2 | | | 229 | | 1.30 | | |
| chili beef, chunky, Campbell's | 256 | | 5.7 | | | | 6 | .13 | | | 984 | 61 | | | |
| *9.74 oz* | 276 | 18.8 | 32.4 | | | 1433 | .11 | 2.3 | | | 553 | | 4.10 | | |
| **clam chowder** | | | | | | | | | | | | | | | |
| manhattan, Campbell's | 67 | | 1.8 | | | | 4 | .02 | | | 800 | 25 | | | |
| *7.27 oz* | 206 | 2.0 | 10.7 | | | 1756 | .02 | 0.7 | | | 221 | | 1.00 | | |
| manhattan, chunky | 133 | 206.5 | 3.4 | 0.1 | 14 | 329 | 12 | .06 | .26 | 9 | 1000 | 67 | | 1.68 | .240 |
| *1 cup* | 240 | 7.3 | 18.8 | 2.1 | | 3292 | .06 | 1.8 | 7.92 | | 384 | 84 | 2.64 | .240 | |
| manhattan, Progresso | 140 | | 3.0 | | | | | | | | 1240 | | | | |
| *9.5 oz* | 269 | 7.0 | 19.0 | | | | | | | | 430 | | | | |
| new england, chunky, Campbell's | 162 | | 4.0 | | | | 11 | .11 | | | 1102 | 63 | | | |
| *10.76 oz* | 305 | 7.3 | 24.1 | | | 7084 | .03 | 1.7 | | | 494 | | 2.40 | | |
| crab | 76 | 223.3 | 1.5 | 0.4 | 10 | 50 | 0 | .07 | .12 | | 1234 | 65 | | | |
| *1 cup* | 244 | 5.5 | 10.3 | 0.4 | | 505 | .20 | 1.3 | .20 | .29 | 326 | 88 | 1.22 | | |
| escarole | 27 | 240.3 | 1.8 | 0.4 | 2 | 217 | 5 | .05 | | | 3865 | 32 | | | |
| *1 cup* | 248 | 1.5 | 1.8 | 0.5 | | 2170 | .08 | 2.3 | | | | | .74 | | |
| escarole in chicken broth, Progresso | 40 | | 2.0 | | | | | | | | 1050 | | | | |
| *9.5 oz* | 269 | 2.0 | 3.0 | | | | | | | | 250 | | | | |
| fisherman chowder, chunky, Campbell's | 229 | | 12.2 | | | | 3 | .04 | | | 1130 | 67 | | | |
| *9.49 oz* | 269 | 9.9 | 19.8 | | | 0 | .02 | 1.3 | | | 240 | | 1.60 | | |
| french onion, Progresso | 120 | | 8.0 | | | | | | | | 1270 | | | | |
| *9.5 oz* | 269 | 5.0 | 8.0 | | | | | | | | 180 | | | | |
| gazpacho | 57 | 228.8 | 2.2 | 1.3 | 0 | 20 | 3 | .02 | .15 | | 1183 | 24 | | | |
| *1 cup* | 244 | 8.7 | 0.8 | 0.3 | | 200 | .05 | 0.9 | .00 | .17 | 224 | 37 | .98 | | |
| ham & beans, Progresso | 180 | | 2.0 | | | | | | | | 1050 | | | | |
| *9.5 oz* | 269 | 11.0 | 30.0 | | | | | | | | 590 | | | | |
| ham n' butter bean, chunky, Campbell's | 273 | | 9.8 | | | | 6 | .11 | | | 1180 | 41 | | | |
| *10.76 oz* | 305 | 12.7 | 33.6 | | | 3031 | .14 | 2.1 | | | 617 | | 2.80 | | |
| lentil, Home Cookin, Campbell's | 164 | | 1.0 | | | | 5 | .10 | | | 938 | 54 | | | |
| *10.76 oz* | 305 | 10.3 | 28.5 | | | 3900 | .18 | 1.4 | | | 305 | | 4.00 | | |
| lentil, Prego | 165 | | 1.5 | | | | 6 | .10 | | | 935 | 41 | | | |
| *9.49 oz* | 269 | 10.5 | 27.4 | | | 713 | .08 | 1.4 | | | 386 | | 4.20 | | |
| lentil, Progresso | 170 | | 2.0 | | | | | | | | 1020 | | | | |
| *9.5 oz* | 269 | 10.0 | 25.0 | | | | | | | | 450 | | | | |
| lentil w/ ham | 140 | 212.7 | 2.8 | 0.3 | 7 | 36 | 4 | .11 | .22 | 50 | 1318 | 42 | | | |
| *1 cup* | 248 | 9.3 | 20.2 | 1.1 | | 360 | .17 | 1.4 | .30 | .35 | 356 | 184 | 2.64 | | |
| macaroni & bean, Progresso | 180 | | 3.0 | | | | | | | | 1290 | | | | |
| *9.5 oz* | 269 | 6.0 | 30.0 | | | | | | | | 536 | | | | |
| mediterranean veg, chunky, Campbell's | 150 | | 4.3 | | | | 9 | .13 | | | 1007 | 71 | | | |
| *9.49 oz* | 269 | 4.5 | 23.3 | | | 6019 | .08 | 1.8 | | | 367 | | 2.10 | | |
| minestrone, Campbell's | 70 | | 2.1 | | | | 2 | .04 | | | 724 | 25 | | | |
| *7.27 oz* | 206 | 2.9 | 9.8 | | | 3171 | .06 | 0.9 | | | 165 | | 1.00 | | |
| minestrone, chunky | 127 | 208.1 | 2.8 | 0.3 | 5 | 435 | 5 | .12 | | | 864 | 61 | | | |
| *1 cup* | 240 | 5.1 | 20.7 | 1.5 | | 4352 | .06 | 1.2 | | | | | 1.77 | | |
| minestrone, Progresso | 150 | | 3.0 | | | | | | | | 850 | | | | |
| *9.5 oz* | 269 | 6.0 | 22.0 | | | | | | | | 410 | | | | |

| Food | KCAL / WT (g) | H₂O (g) / PRO (g) | FAT (g) / CHO (g) | PUFA (g) / SFA (g) | CHOL (mg) / DFIB (g) | A (RE) / A (IU) | C (mg) / B-1 (mg) | B-2 (mg) / NIA (mg) | B-6 (mg) / B-12 (mcg) | FOL (mcg) / PANT (mg) | Na (mg) / K (mg) | Ca (mg) / P (mg) | Mg (mg) / Fe (mg) | Zn (mg) / Cu (mg) | Mn (mg) |
|---|---|---|---|---|---|---|---|---|---|---|---|---|---|---|---|
| minestrone w/ italian sausage, Prego | 169 | | 8.4 | | | | 6 | .25 | | | 1170 | 48 | | | |
| 9.49 oz | 269 | 6.5 | 16.9 | | | 5452 | .14 | 1.7 | | | 322 | | 1.50 | | |
| mushroom, crm of, Campbell's | 99 | | 6.7 | | | | 0 | .06 | | | 909 | 34 | | | |
| 7.27 oz | 206 | 1.9 | 7.8 | | | 0 | .02 | 0.5 | | | 85 | | .70 | | |
| mushroom, crm of, low Na, Campbell's | 141 | | 9.9 | | | | 1 | .18 | | | 33 | 50 | | | |
| 7.27 oz | 206 | 2.3 | 10.8 | | | 0 | .02 | 0.9 | | | 93 | | .80 | | |
| mushroom, creamy, chunky, Campbell's | 226 | | 18.5 | | | | 2 | .30 | | | 1134 | 26 | | | |
| 9.38 oz | 266 | 4.4 | 10.6 | | | 0 | .07 | 2.8 | | | 90 | | | | |
| onion, low Na, Campbell's | 48 | | 2.2 | | | | 7 | .14 | | | 32 | 22 | | | |
| 7.27 oz | 206 | 1.5 | 5.3 | | | 0 | .07 | 1.9 | | | 126 | | 1.20 | | |
| pea, green, Campbell's | 136 | | 2.6 | | | | 0 | .03 | | | 782 | 19 | | | |
| 7.5 oz | 213 | 6.8 | 21.3 | | | 46 | .13 | 0.9 | | | 272 | | 1.60 | | |
| **pea, split** | | | | | | | | | | | | | | | |
|   low Na, Campbell's | 159 | | 2.9 | | | | 4 | .11 | | | 16 | 28 | | | |
|   7.27 oz | 206 | 7.9 | 25.2 | | | 956 | .13 | 1.6 | | | 322 | | 1.90 | | |
|   Progresso | 190 | | 2.0 | | | | | | | | 1050 | | | | |
|   9.5 oz | 269 | 11.0 | 30.0 | | | | | | | | 430 | | | | |
|   w/ ham, chunky | 184 | 194.3 | 4.0 | 0.6 | 7 | 487 | 7 | .09 | | 5 | 965 | 33 | | | |
|   1 cup | 240 | 11.1 | 26.8 | 1.6 | | 4871 | .12 | 2.5 | | | | | 2.14 | | |
|   w/ ham, Home Cookin, Campbell's | 201 | | 3.4 | | | | 9 | .13 | | | 1233 | 45 | | | |
|   10.76 oz | 305 | 13.8 | 28.6 | | | 2332 | .16 | 2.1 | | | 321 | | 2.20 | | |
|   w/ ham, Progresso | 170 | | 4.0 | | | | | | | | 1030 | | | | |
|   9.5 oz | 269 | 10.0 | 26.0 | | | | | | | | 380 | | | | |
| sirloin burger, chunky, Campbell's | 191 | | 7.3 | | | | 9 | .16 | | | 1105 | 34 | | | |
| 9.49 oz | 269 | 11.0 | 20.3 | | | 5566 | .05 | 3.0 | | | 412 | | 2.30 | | |
| steak & potato, chunky, Campbell's | 169 | | 3.8 | | | | 7 | .19 | | | 990 | 15 | | | |
| 9.49 oz | 269 | 12.7 | 21.0 | | | 57 | .05 | 2.9 | | | 414 | | 2.20 | | |
| tomato, Campbell's | 106 | | 1.7 | | | | 30 | .05 | | | 786 | 33 | | | |
| 7.27 oz | 206 | 2.2 | 20.5 | | | 684 | .05 | 1.0 | | | 283 | | .90 | | |
| tomato w/ macaroni shells, Progresso | 130 | | 2.0 | | | | | | | | 1270 | | | | |
| 10.5 oz | 298 | 4.0 | 24.0 | | | | | | | | | | | | |
| tomato w/ tomato pieces, low Na, Campbell's—7.27 oz | 124 | | 3.5 | | | | 30 | .11 | | | 23 | 32 | | | |
| | 206 | 2.6 | 20.5 | | | 942 | .10 | 2.1 | | | 429 | | 1.20 | | |
| tomato w/ veg & macaroni, Progresso | 120 | | 2.0 | | | | | | | | 1260 | | | | |
| 9.5 oz | 269 | 3.0 | 24.0 | | | | | | | | 380 | | | | |
| tortellini, Progresso | 80 | | 3.0 | | | | | | | | 1080 | | | | |
| 9.5 oz | 269 | 4.0 | 11.0 | | | | | | | | 280 | | | | |
| tortilla, chunky, Campbell's | 293 | | 9.6 | | | | 12 | .11 | | | 1034 | 101 | | | |
| 10.76 oz | 305 | 17.1 | 34.4 | | | 669 | .05 | 2.6 | | | 390 | | 3.50 | | |
| turkey, chunky | 136 | 203.8 | 4.4 | 1.1 | 9 | 716 | 6 | .11 | .31 | 11 | 923 | 50 | | 2.12 | .236 |
| 1 cup | 236 | 10.2 | 14.1 | 1.2 | | 7156 | .04 | 3.6 | 2.12 | | 361 | 104 | 1.91 | .236 | |
| **veg** | | | | | | | | | | | | | | | |
|   Campbell's | 68 | | 1.4 | | | | 3 | .04 | | | 724 | 19 | | | |
|   7.27 oz | 206 | 2.4 | 11.3 | | | 3053 | .04 | 0.9 | | | 141 | | 1.00 | | |
|   chunky | 122 | 210.2 | 3.7 | 1.4 | 0 | 588 | 6 | .07 | .19 | 17 | 1010 | 56 | | 3.12 | .480 |
|   1 cup | 240 | 3.5 | 19.0 | 0.6 | | 5877 | .07 | 1.2 | .00 | | 396 | 72 | 1.63 | .240 | |
|   Progresso | 130 | | 5.0 | | | | | | | | 1150 | | | | |
|   9.5 oz | 269 | 4.0 | 15.0 | | | | | | | | 260 | | | | |
| **veg w/ beef** | | | | | | | | | | | | | | | |
|   Campbell's | 138 | | 2.6 | | | | 10 | .13 | | | 1139 | 49 | | | |
|   10.76 oz | 305 | 13.5 | 15.2 | | | 5113 | .09 | 2.5 | | | 337 | | 2.90 | | |
|   chunky, Campbell's | 153 | | 4.1 | | | | 8 | .15 | | | 972 | 50 | | | |
|   9.49 oz | 269 | 11.6 | 17.4 | | | 5705 | .06 | 2.5 | | | 414 | | 2.40 | | |
|   chunky, low Na, Campbell's | 156 | | 4.8 | | | | 13 | .28 | | | 60 | 55 | | | |
|   10.76 oz | 305 | 13.2 | 15.0 | | | 5603 | .18 | 4.0 | | | 390 | | 2.40 | | |
| won ton, imperial, chunky, Campbell's | 121 | | 3.1 | | | | 9 | .11 | | | 1062 | 39 | | | |
| 9.49 oz | 269 | 7.3 | 15.7 | | | 633 | .07 | 3.1 | | | 245 | | 2.70 | | |

| | KCAL / WT (g) | H₂O (g) / PRO (g) | FAT (g) / CHO (g) | PUFA (g) / SFA (g) | CHOL (mg) / DFIB (g) | A (RE) / A (IU) | C (mg) / B-1 (mg) | B-2 (mg) / NIA (mg) | B-6 (mg) / B-12 (mcg) | FOL (mcg) / PANT (mg) | Na (mg) / K (mg) | Ca (mg) / P (mg) | Mg (mg) / Fe (mg) | Zn (mg) / Cu (mg) | Mn (mg) |
|---|---|---|---|---|---|---|---|---|---|---|---|---|---|---|---|

## 28.5. DEHYDRATED

| | KCAL/WT | H₂O/PRO | FAT/CHO | PUFA/SFA | CHOL/DFIB | A(RE)/A(IU) | C/B-1 | B-2/NIA | B-6/B-12 | FOL/PANT | Na/K | Ca/P | Mg/Fe | Zn/Cu | Mn |
|---|---|---|---|---|---|---|---|---|---|---|---|---|---|---|---|
| **beef broth cube** | 6 | 0.1 | 0.1 | 0.0 | 0 | | | .01 | | | 864 | | 2 | .01 | .014 |
| *1 cube* | 4 | 0.6 | 0.6 | 0.1 | | | .01 | 0.1 | | | 15 | 8 | .08 | | |
| **chicken broth cube** | 9 | 0.1 | 0.2 | 0.1 | 1 | | | .02 | | | 1152 | | 3 | .01 | .018 |
| *1 cube* | 5 | 0.7 | 1.1 | 0.1 | | | .01 | 0.2 | | | 18 | 9 | .09 | | |
| **chicken noodle w/ meat, Campbell's** | 99 | | 1.7 | | | | 0 | .12 | | | 805 | 9 | | | |
| *0.92 oz* | 26 | 5.7 | 15.0 | | | 0 | .15 | 3.2 | | | 89 | | .90 | | |
| **chicken rice, Campbell's** | 90 | | 1.3 | | | | 0 | .18 | | | 800 | 7 | | | |
| *0.85 oz* | 24 | 3.7 | 15.8 | | | 0 | .04 | 1.4 | | | 77 | | .10 | | |
| **onion soup mix** | 115 | 1.43 | 2.3 | 0.3 | 2 | 1 | 1 | .24 | | 6 | 3493 | 55 | 25 | .23 | .248 |
| *1 pkt* | 39 | 4.5 | 20.9 | 0.5 | | 8 | .11 | 2.0 | | | 260 | 126 | .58 | .064 | |

## 28.6. DEHYDRATED, RECONSTITUTED SOUPS

| | KCAL/WT | H₂O/PRO | FAT/CHO | PUFA/SFA | CHOL/DFIB | A(RE)/A(IU) | C/B-1 | B-2/NIA | B-6/B-12 | FOL/PANT | Na/K | Ca/P | Mg/Fe | Zn/Cu | Mn |
|---|---|---|---|---|---|---|---|---|---|---|---|---|---|---|---|
| **asparagus, crm of** | 59 | 235.5 | 1.7 | 0.7 | 0 | | | | | | 801 | | | | |
| *1 cup* | 251 | 2.2 | 9.0 | 0.3 | | | | | | | | | | | |
| **bean w/ bacon** | 105 | 237.7 | 2.2 | 0.2 | 3 | | | | | | 928 | | | | |
| *1 cup* | 265 | 5.5 | 16.4 | 1.0 | | | | | | | 326 | | | | |
| **beef broth/ bouillon** | 19 | 236.3 | 0.7 | 0.0 | 1 | | | .02 | | | 1358 | 5 | 4 | | .037 |
| *1 cup* | 244 | 1.3 | 1.9 | 0.3 | | 4 | .01 | 0.4 | | | 36 | 26 | | | |
| **beef noodle[a]** | 41 | 239.2 | 0.8 | 0.2 | 2 | 1 | 1 | .06 | .04 | 2 | 1041 | 5 | 9 | .10 | |
| *1 cup* | 251 | 2.2 | 6.0 | 0.3 | | 9 | .12 | 0.7 | | | 81 | 40 | .33 | | |
| **cauliflower** | 68 | 238.0 | 1.7 | 0.7 | 0 | | | | | | 843 | | | | |
| *1 cup* | 256 | 2.9 | 10.7 | 0.3 | | | | | | | | | | | |
| **celery, crm of** | 63 | 237.4 | 1.6 | 0.6 | 1 | | | | | | 839 | | | | |
| *1 cup* | 254 | 2.6 | 9.8 | 0.2 | | | | | | | | | | | |
| **chicken broth/bouillon[b]** | 21 | 236.2 | 1.1 | 0.4 | 1 | | 0 | .03 | | | 1484 | 15 | 4 | .01 | |
| *1 cup* | 244 | 1.3 | 1.4 | 0.3 | | 40 | .01 | 0.2 | | | 25 | 13 | .08 | | |
| **chicken, crm of** | 107 | 237.5 | 5.3 | 0.4 | 3 | | | .20 | | | 1184 | 76 | | | |
| *1 cup* | 261 | 1.8 | 13.4 | 3.4 | | | | | | | 215 | 96 | | | |
| **chicken noodle[c]** | 53 | 237.6 | 1.2 | 0.3 | 3 | 6 | 0 | .06 | .01 | 1 | 1284 | 32 | 7 | .20 | .024 |
| *1 cup* | 252 | 2.9 | 7.4 | 0.3 | | 63 | .07 | 0.9 | | | 31 | 32 | .50 | .035 | |
| **chicken rice** | 60 | 237.2 | 1.4 | 0.4 | 3 | | | | | | 980 | 8 | | | |
| *1 cup* | 253 | 2.4 | 9.3 | 0.3 | | | | 0.4 | | | 10 | 10 | | | |
| **chicken veg** | 49 | 237.2 | 0.8 | 0.2 | 3 | 1 | 1 | .05 | .09 | | 808 | | 21 | .21 | |
| *1 cup* | 251 | 2.7 | 7.8 | 0.2 | | 14 | .07 | 0.7 | | | 68 | 32 | .59 | .025 | |
| **clam chowder** | | | | | | | | | | | | | | | |
|   manhattan | 65 | | 1.6 | 0.5 | 0 | | | | | | 1336 | | | | |
|   *1 cup* | 250 | 2.1 | 10.9 | 0.3 | | | | | | | | | | | |
|   new england | 95 | | 3.7 | 1.2 | 1 | | | .16 | | | 745 | 76 | | | |
|   *1 cup* | 250 | 2.8 | 12.9 | 0.6 | | | | | | | 205 | 100 | | | |
| **consomme w/ gelatin** | 17 | 236.5 | 0.0 | 0.0 | 0 | | | | | | 3299 | | | | |
| *1 cup* | 249 | 2.2 | 2.1 | 0.0 | | | | | | | | | | | |
| **leek** | 71 | 235.6 | 2.1 | 0.1 | 3 | | | | | | 966 | | | .24 | |
| *1 cup* | 254 | 2.1 | 11.4 | 1.0 | | | | | | | | | | .036 | |
| **minestrone** | 79 | 232.8 | 1.7 | 0.1 | 3 | | | | | | 1026 | | | | |
| *1 cup* | 254 | 4.4 | 11.9 | 0.8 | | | | | | | | | | | |
| **mushroom** | 96 | 231.9 | 4.9 | 1.5 | 1 | 1 | | .11 | | | 1019 | 67 | | .09 | |
| *1 cup* | 253 | 2.2 | 11.1 | 0.8 | | 7 | .28 | 0.5 | | .24 | 199 | 77 | | .030 | |
| **onion[d]** | 28 | 236.9 | 0.6 | 0.1 | 0 | 0 | 0 | .06 | | 2 | 848 | 13 | 6 | .06 | .060 |
| *1 cup* | 246 | 1.1 | 5.1 | 0.1 | | 2 | .03 | 0.5 | | | 63 | 31 | .14 | .015 | |
| **oxtail** | 71 | 235.3 | 2.6 | 0.1 | 3 | | | | | | 1210 | | | | |
| *1 cup* | 253 | 2.8 | 9.0 | 1.3 | | | | | | | | | | | |
| **pea, green/split[e]** | 133 | 235.2 | 1.6 | 0.3 | 3 | 5 | 0 | .15 | .05 | 15 | 1220 | 22 | 46 | .59 | .268 |
| *1 cup* | 271 | 7.7 | 22.7 | 0.4 | | 49 | .22 | 1.3 | | .26 | 238 | 134 | 1.01 | .192 | |
| **tomato[f]** | 102 | 237.7 | 2.4 | 0.2 | 1 | 82 | 5 | .05 | .10 | 7 | 943 | 54 | 15 | .21 | |
| *1 cup* | 265 | 2.5 | 19.4 | 1.1 | | 832 | .06 | 0.8 | | | 295 | 66 | .42 | .093 | |
| **tomato veg[g]** | 55 | 236.6 | 0.9 | 0.1 | 0 | 20 | 6 | .05 | | | 1146 | 8 | 20 | .17 | |
| *1 cup* | 253 | 2.0 | 10.2 | 0.4 | | 190 | .06 | 0.8 | | .14 | 103 | 29 | .63 | .033 | |

[a] Includes beef & macaroni & beef-flavored noodle.
[b] Includes chicken consomme.
[c] Includes chicken broth w/ noodles.
[d] Includes french onion.
[e] Includes pea w/ ham.
[f] Includes crm of tomato.
[g] Includes italian veg & spring veg.

| | KCAL | H₂O (g) | FAT (g) | PUFA (g) | CHOL (mg) | A (RE) | C (mg) | B-2 (mg) | B-6 (mg) | FOL (mcg) | Na (mg) | Ca (mg) | Mg (mg) | Zn (mg) | Mn (mg) |
|---|---|---|---|---|---|---|---|---|---|---|---|---|---|---|---|
| | WT (g) | PRO (g) | CHO (g) | SFA (g) | DFIB (g) | A (IU) | B-1 (mg) | NIA (mg) | B-12 (mcg) | PANT (mg) | K (mg) | P (mg) | Fe (mg) | Cu (mg) | |
| **veg beef** | 53 | 237.5 | 1.1 | 0.1 | 1 | 24 | | .04 | .05 | | 1000 | | | | .27 |
| *1 cup* | 253 | 2.9 | 8.0 | 0.6 | | 238 | .03 | 0.5 | | | | 37 | .85 | .030 | |
| **veg, crm of** | 105 | 237.2 | 5.7 | 1.5 | 0 | 4 | 4 | .11 | | | 1171 | | | | |
| *1 cup* | 260 | 1.9 | 12.3 | 1.4 | | 35 | 1.22 | 0.5 | | | 96 | 54 | | | |

# 29. SPECIAL DIETARY FOODS

| | KCAL | H₂O (g) | FAT (g) | PUFA (g) | CHOL (mg) | A (RE) | C (mg) | B-2 (mg) | B-6 (mg) | FOL (mcg) | Na (mg) | Ca (mg) | Mg (mg) | Zn (mg) | Mn (mg) |
|---|---|---|---|---|---|---|---|---|---|---|---|---|---|---|---|
| | WT (g) | PRO (g) | CHO (g) | SFA (g) | DFIB (g) | A (IU) | B-1 (mg) | NIA (mg) | B-12 (mcg) | PANT (mg) | K (mg) | P (mg) | Fe (mg) | Cu (mg) | |
| **breakfast bar, Carnation** | | | | | | | | | | | | | | | |
| choc chip | 200 | 1.9 | 11.0 | | | | 28 | .03 | .40 | 100 | 180 | 20 | 60 | 3.00 | |
| *1.44 oz bar* | 41 | 6.0 | 20.0 | | | 1750 | .30 | 5.0 | .63 | 2.00 | 80 | 60 | 4.50 | .500 | |
| choc crunch | 190 | 1.7 | 10.0 | | | | 28 | .03 | .40 | 100 | 140 | 20 | 60 | 3.00 | |
| *1.34 oz bar* | 38 | 6.0 | 20.0 | | | 1750 | .30 | 5.0 | .63 | 2.00 | 103 | 60 | 4.50 | .500 | |
| peanut butter crunch | 190 | 1.5 | 11.0 | | | | 28 | .03 | .40 | 100 | 170 | 20 | 60 | 3.00 | |
| *1.35 oz bar* | 38 | 7.0 | 20.0 | | | 1750 | .30 | 5.0 | .63 | 2.00 | 85 | 60 | 4.50 | .500 | |
| peanut butter w/ choc chips | 200 | 1.3 | 11.0 | | | | 28 | .03 | .40 | 100 | 160 | 20 | 60 | 3.00 | |
| *1.39 oz bar* | 39 | 7.0 | 20.0 | | | 1750 | .30 | 5.0 | .63 | 2.00 | 87 | 60 | 4.50 | .500 | |
| **figurine diet bar, Pillsbury** | | | | | | | | | | | | | | | |
| choc | 98 | 0.7 | 5.2 | | | | 10 | .13 | .23 | 63 | 46 | 55 | 36 | 1.47 | |
| *1 bar* | 21 | 2.2 | 10.9 | | | 584 | .23 | 2.6 | .46 | | 105 | 59 | 2.37 | .252 | |
| choc caramel | 98 | 0.7 | 5.5 | | | | 10 | .13 | .23 | 63 | 55 | 58 | 36 | 1.47 | |
| *1 bar* | 21 | 2.2 | 10.4 | | | 584 | .23 | 2.6 | .46 | | 88 | 55 | 2.25 | .252 | |
| choc peanut butter | 98 | 0.7 | 5.5 | | | | 10 | .13 | .25 | 63 | 46 | 56 | 38 | 1.47 | |
| *1 bar* | 21 | 2.9 | 9.7 | | | 584 | .23 | 3.0 | .46 | | 102 | 59 | 2.31 | .256 | |
| s'mores | 99 | 0.7 | 5.3 | | | | 10 | .13 | .25 | 63 | 45 | 55 | 36 | 1.47 | |
| *1 bar* | 21 | 2.1 | 11.0 | | | 584 | .23 | 2.6 | .46 | | 83 | 50 | 2.31 | .252 | |
| van | 99 | 0.7 | 5.2 | | | | 10 | .08 | .25 | 63 | 46 | 58 | 36 | 1.47 | |
| *1 bar* | 21 | 2.1 | 11.1 | | | 584 | .18 | 2.6 | .46 | | 86 | 54 | 2.25 | .252 | |
| **fortified pudding, from mix, Delmark** | | | | | | | | | | | | | | | |
| choc | 250 | | 8.0 | | 20 | | 11 | .37 | .36 | 70 | 140 | 270 | 72 | 2.70 | .010 |
| *1/2 cup* | 164 | 9.0 | 35.0 | | | 900 | .27 | 3.6 | 1.10 | 1.80 | 755 | 270 | 3.20 | .360 | |
| van/lemon | 250 | | 8.0 | | 20 | | 11 | .37 | .36 | 70 | 140 | 270 | 72 | 2.70 | .010 |
| *1/2 cup* | 164 | 9.0 | 35.0 | | | 900 | .27 | 3.6 | 1.10 | 1.80 | 675 | 270 | 3.20 | .360 | |
| **gluten-free, wheat-free foods, Ener-G Foods** | | | | | | | | | | | | | | | |
| baking mix | | | | | | | | | | | | | | | |
| rice, brown | 653 | | 23.0 | | | | 0 | .25 | | | 34 | 122 | 119 | | |
| *1 cup* | 153 | 13.0 | 98.8 | | | 199 | .29 | 6.0 | | | 252 | | 3.52 | .459 | |
| rice, white | 111 | 3.1 | 2.9 | | | | 0 | .01 | | | 93 | 8 | | | |
| *1 oz* | 28 | 1.7 | 19.5 | | | 0 | .02 | 1.3 | | | 38 | | .72 | | |
| bread | | | | | | | | | | | | | | | |
| rice, brown | 175 | 30.7 | 1.5 | | | | 4 | .11 | | | 16 | 66 | | | |
| *2 slices* | 73 | 4.2 | 36.1 | | | 0 | .01 | 5.0 | | | 99 | | 3.80 | | |
| rice, white | 121 | 21.1 | 0.8 | | | | 0 | .03 | | | 230 | 45 | | | |
| *2 slices* | 51 | 2.8 | 25.8 | | | 0 | .23 | 0.9 | | | | | 2.04 | | |
| rice, white, yeast-free | 384 | 12.5 | 3.6 | | | | 0 | | | | 48 | 5 | | | |
| *2 slices* | 105 | 3.9 | 84.2 | | | 0 | .81 | 1.2 | | | | | 1.05 | | |
| cookies | | | | | | | | | | | | | | | |
| almond butter | 239 | 2.7 | 12.2 | | | | 1 | .25 | | | 118 | 5 | | | |
| *3 cookies* | 48 | 4.1 | 28.2 | | | 0 | .08 | 0.2 | | | 66 | | .24 | | |
| choc | 199 | 6.0 | 4.5 | | | | 0 | .04 | | | 167 | 88 | | | |
| *3 cookies* | 51 | 2.9 | 36.6 | | | 17 | .04 | 1.7 | | | | | 2.04 | | |
| choc chip potato | 243 | 8.5 | 10.1 | | | | 1 | .06 | | | 80 | 28 | 27 | 2.32 | |
| *3 cookies* | 57 | 3.1 | 34.6 | | | 57 | .06 | 0.2 | | | 116 | 80 | 1.48 | .274 | |
| peanut butter | 255 | 10.0 | 7.2 | | | | 0 | .05 | | | 211 | 104 | | | |
| *3 cookies* | 66 | 5.9 | 41.7 | | | 0 | .06 | 2.3 | | | | | 2.64 | | |

| | KCAL | H₂O (g) | FAT (g) | PUFA (g) | CHOL (mg) | A (RE) | C (mg) | B-2 (mg) | B-6 (mg) | FOL (mcg) | Na (mg) | Ca (mg) | Mg (mg) | Zn (mg) | Mn (mg) |
|---|---|---|---|---|---|---|---|---|---|---|---|---|---|---|---|
| | WT (g) | PRO (g) | CHO (g) | SFA (g) | DFIB (g) | A (IU) | B-1 (mg) | NIA (mg) | B-12 (mcg) | PANT (mg) | K (mg) | P (mg) | Fe (mg) | Cu (mg) | |
| doughnut, rice, plain | 186 | 19.6 | 10.7 | | | | 0 | .13 | | | 285 | 143 | | | |
| *1 doughnut* | 54 | 3.3 | 19.1 | | | 0 | .04 | 0.5 | | | | | .92 | | |
| granola | 204 | 1.0 | 5.1 | | | | 1 | .14 | | | 1 | 35 | | | |
| *1/2 cup* | 50 | 5.0 | 34.5 | | | 0 | .02 | 1.4 | | | 598 | | 2.00 | | |
| nutquik milk powder | 164 | 1.5 | 14.7 | | | | 0 | .29 | .04 | 0 | 4 | 67 | 80 | 1.09 | |
| *1 oz* | 28 | 6.9 | 4.2 | | | 1 | .06 | 1.1 | .00 | | 193 | 123 | 1.34 | .336 | |
| pizza shell, rice, low protein | 191 | 20.4 | 6.8 | | | | 0 | .02 | | | 88 | 85 | 5 | 1.80 | |
| *2 oz* | 60 | 0.2 | 32.2 | | | 0 | .16 | 0.1 | | | 14 | 25 | .60 | | |
| rice mix | 98 | | 0.6 | | | | 0 | .01 | | | | 90 | | | |
| *1 oz* | 28 | 1.8 | 21.4 | | | 0 | .11 | 1.4 | | | | | .36 | | |
| soup, mushroom, dry mix | 66 | 2.4 | 0.0 | | | | 0 | .20 | | | 160 | 17 | | | |
| *2 3/4 T* | 20 | 2.4 | 13.9 | | | 0 | .07 | 1.0 | | | 273 | | .66 | | |
| soup, tomato, dry mix | 51 | 1.9 | 0.0 | | | | 8 | .06 | | | 23 | 13 | | | |
| *1 2/3 T* | 15 | 0.7 | 11.9 | | | 240 | .06 | 0.8 | | | 35 | | .60 | | |
| soyquix milk powder | 50 | 0.9 | 0.1 | | | | 1 | .06 | | | 39 | 36 | 43 | .28 | |
| *2 T* | 14 | 7.3 | 4.9 | | | 0 | .14 | 0.8 | | | 294 | 91 | 1.82 | .140 | |
| **high protein foods, Delmark** | | | | | | | | | | | | | | | |
| broth, beef, from mix | 120 | | 0.4 | | 1 | 0 | 0 | .02 | .01 | 2 | 370 | 10 | 3 | .07 | .030 |
| *6 fl oz* | 183 | 7.0 | 22.0 | | | 0 | .07 | 0.1 | .11 | .02 | 125 | 110 | .08 | .020 | |
| broth, chicken, from mix | 120 | | 0.4 | | 0 | 0 | 0 | .02 | .01 | 2 | 370 | 10 | 3 | .07 | .030 |
| *6 fl oz* | 183 | 7.0 | 22.0 | | | 0 | .03 | 0.1 | .11 | .02 | 125 | 110 | .08 | .020 | |
| gelatin dessert, all flavors, from mix | 140 | | 0.2 | | 0 | 0 | 0 | .44 | | 15 | 250 | 10 | 17 | .12 | .009 |
| *5 fl oz* | 175 | 17.0 | 18.0 | | | 0 | .02 | 0.2 | .04 | .12 | 210 | 20 | .21 | .090 | |
| **sego lite, liquid diet meal, cnd, Pet** | | | | | | | | | | | | | | | |
| choc/dutch choc | 150 | | 3.0 | | | | | | | | 475 | | | | |
| *10 fl oz* | ᵃ | 11.0 | 20.0 | | | | | | | | 690 | | | | |
| choc malt/double choc/choc jamocha | 150 | | 3.0 | | | | | | | | 475 | | | | |
| *almond—10 fl oz* | ᵃ | 11.0 | 20.0 | | | | | | | | 690 | | | | |
| french van/strawberry | 150 | | 4.0 | | | | | | | | 390 | | | | |
| *10 fl oz* | ᵃ | 11.0 | 17.0 | | | | | | | | 600 | | | | |
| van | 150 | | 4.0 | | | | | | | | 490 | | | | |
| *10 fl oz* | ᵃ | 11.0 | 17.0 | | | | | | | | 600 | | | | |
| **sego, liquid diet meal, cnd, Pet** | | | | | | | | | | | | | | | |
| very choc/choc malt/dutch choc | 225 | | 1.0 | | | | | | | | 445 | | | | |
| *10 fl oz* | ᵃ | 11.0 | 43.0 | | | | | | | | 690 | | | | |
| very van/strawberry | 225 | | 5.0 | | | | | | | | 360 | | | | |
| *10 fl oz* | ᵃ | 11.0 | 34.0 | | | | | | | | 600 | | | | |
| **slender bars, Carnation** | | | | | | | | | | | | | | | |
| choc | 270 | 1.8 | 14.0 | | | | 15 | .43 | .42 | 100 | 285 | 250 | 100 | 3.75 | |
| *2 bars* | 55 | 11.0 | 26.0 | | | 1250 | .38 | 5.0 | 1.50 | 2.50 | 345 | 250 | 4.50 | .500 | |
| choc chip | 270 | 1.6 | 14.0 | | | | 15 | .43 | .42 | 100 | 315 | 250 | 100 | 3.75 | |
| *2 bars* | 55 | 11.0 | 26.0 | | | 1250 | .38 | 5.0 | 1.50 | 2.50 | 355 | 250 | 4.50 | .500 | |
| choc peanut butter | 270 | 1.5 | 15.0 | | | | 15 | .43 | .42 | 100 | 285 | 250 | 100 | 3.75 | |
| *2 bars* | 55 | 11.0 | 24.0 | | | 1250 | .38 | 5.0 | 1.50 | 2.50 | 369 | 250 | 4.50 | .500 | |
| van | 270 | 1.6 | 15.0 | | | | 15 | .43 | .42 | 100 | 320 | 250 | 100 | 3.75 | |
| *2 bars* | 55 | 11.0 | 24.0 | | | 1250 | .38 | 5.0 | 1.50 | 2.50 | 349 | 250 | 4.50 | .500 | |
| **slender, liquid diet meal, cnd, Carnation** | | | | | | | | | | | | | | | |
| banana | 220 | 258.0 | 4.0 | | | | 15 | .43 | .50 | 100 | 430 | 250 | 100 | 3.75 | |
| *10 fl oz* | 313 | 11.0 | 34.0 | | | 1250 | .38 | 5.0 | 1.50 | 2.50 | 448 | 250 | 4.50 | .500 | |
| choc | 220 | 257.0 | 4.0 | | | | 15 | .43 | .50 | 100 | 515 | 250 | 100 | 3.75 | |
| *10 fl oz* | 313 | 11.0 | 34.0 | | | 1250 | .38 | 5.0 | 1.50 | 2.50 | 555 | 250 | 4.50 | .500 | |
| choc fudge | 220 | 255.0 | 4.0 | | | | 15 | .43 | .50 | 100 | 550 | 250 | 100 | 3.75 | |
| *10 fl oz* | 313 | 11.0 | 34.0 | | | 1250 | .38 | 5.0 | 1.50 | 2.50 | 585 | 250 | 4.50 | .500 | |
| choc malt | 220 | 257.0 | 4.0 | | | | 15 | .43 | .50 | 100 | 530 | 250 | 100 | 3.75 | |
| *10 fl oz* | 313 | 11.0 | 34.0 | | | 1250 | .38 | 5.0 | 1.50 | 2.50 | 495 | 250 | 4.50 | .500 | |
| milk choc | 220 | 257.0 | 4.0 | | | | 15 | .43 | .50 | 100 | 520 | 250 | 100 | 3.75 | |
| *10 fl oz* | 313 | 11.0 | 34.0 | | | 1250 | .38 | 5.0 | 1.50 | 2.50 | 560 | 250 | 4.50 | .500 | |

ᵃ Gram wt not available.

| | KCAL | H$_2$O (g) | FAT (g) | PUFA (g) | CHOL (mg) | A (RE) | C (mg) | B-2 (mg) | B-6 (mg) | FOL (mcg) | Na (mg) | Ca (mg) | Mg (mg) | Zn (mg) | Mn (mg) |
|---|---|---|---|---|---|---|---|---|---|---|---|---|---|---|---|
| | WT (g) | PRO (g) | CHO (g) | SFA (g) | DFIB (g) | A (IU) | B-1 (mg) | NIA (mg) | B-12 (mcg) | PANT (mg) | K (mg) | P (mg) | Fe (mg) | Cu (mg) | |
| peach | 220 | 258.0 | 4.0 | | | | 15 | .43 | | | 430 | 250 | | | |
| *10 fl oz* | 313 | 11.0 | 34.0 | | | 1250 | .38 | 5.0 | | | 448 | | | | |
| strawberry | 220 | 258.0 | 4.0 | | | | 15 | .43 | .50 | 100 | 430 | 250 | 100 | 3.75 | |
| *10 fl oz* | 313 | 11.0 | 34.0 | | | 1250 | .38 | 5.0 | 1.50 | 2.50 | 448 | 250 | 4.50 | .500 | |
| van | 220 | 258.0 | 4.0 | | | | | .43 | .50 | 100 | 550 | 250 | 100 | 3.75 | |
| *10 fl oz* | 313 | 11.0 | 34.0 | | | 1250 | .38 | 5.0 | 1.50 | 2.50 | 585 | 250 | 4.50 | .500 | |

**Column legend**

| | KCAL | $H_2O$ (g) | FAT (g) | PUFA (g) | CHOL (mg) | A (RE) | C (mg) | B-2 (mg) | B-6 (mg) | FOL (mcg) | Na (mg) | Ca (mg) | Mg (mg) | Zn (mg) | Mn (mg) |
|---|---|---|---|---|---|---|---|---|---|---|---|---|---|---|---|
| | WT (g) | PRO (g) | CHO (g) | SFA (g) | DFIB (g) | A (IU) | B-1 (mg) | NIA (mg) | B-12 (mcg) | PANT (mg) | K (mg) | P (mg) | Fe (mg) | Cu (mg) | |
| | | | | | INOS (mg) | D (IU) | E (IU) | K (mcg) | BIO (mcg) | CHLN (mg) | Cl (mg) | I (mcg) | Mo (mg) | | |
| | TRY (mg) | THR (mg) | ISO (mg) | LEU (mg) | LYS (mg) | MET (mg) | CYS (mg) | PHE (mg) | TYR (mg) | VAL (mg) | ARG (mg) | HIS (mg) | | | |

*(The "Vitamins" columns span A–FOL / A–PANT / D–CHLN / MET–VAL; the "Minerals" columns span Na–Mn / K–Cu / Cl–Mo / ARG–HIS.)*

# 30. SPECIAL DIETARY FORMULAS, COMMERCIAL & HOSPITAL

Each food item is given as four stacked rows corresponding to the four legend rows above.

| Item | C1 | C2 | C3 | C4 | C5 | C6 | C7 | C8 | C9 | C10 | C11 | C12 | C13 | C14 | C15 |
|---|---|---|---|---|---|---|---|---|---|---|---|---|---|---|---|
| amin-acid inst drink powder, Am McGaw[a] — 5.2 oz pkt | 665 | | 15.7 | | | | | | | | | | | | |
| | 147 | 6.6 | 124.3 | | | | | | | | | | | | |
| | | | | | | | | | | | | | | | |
| | | | | | | | | | | | | | | | |
| casec protein supplement, Mead Johnson[b] — 100 g dry powder | 370 | 5.5 | 2.0 | | | | | | | | 150 | 1600 | | | |
| | 100 | 88.0 | 0.0 | | | | | | | | 10 | 800 | | | |
| | | | | | | | | | 10 | | | | | | |
| | 1120 | 3600 | 5000 | 8800 | 7500 | 2500 | 260 | 4800 | 5000 | 6300 | 3500 | 2800 | | | |
| compleat, modified formula, Sandoznutrition[c] — 250 ml can | 267 | | 9.2 | | | 250 | 15 | .43 | .50 | 70 | 170 | 170 | 67 | 2.50 | .670 |
| | | 10.7 | 35.0 | | | 833 | .37 | 3.3 | 1.00 | 1.70 | 350 | 230 | 3.00 | .330 | |
| | | | | | | 67 | d | 17 | 50 | 50 | 120 | 25 | .050 | .017 | |
| | 134 | 475 | 640 | 984 | 901 | 296 | 90 | 518 | 496 | 699 | 599 | 345 | | | |
| compleat, regular formula, Sandoznutrition[e] — 150 ml can/bottle | 267 | | 10.7 | | | 250 | 15 | .43 | .50 | 70 | 320 | 170 | 67 | 2.50 | .670 |
| | | 10.7 | 32.0 | | | 833 | .37 | 3.3 | 1.00 | 1.70 | 350 | 330 | 3.00 | .330 | |
| | | | | | | 67 | d | 17 | 50 | 50 | 220 | 25 | .050 | .017 | |
| | 139 | 484 | 622 | 965 | 885 | 262 | 116 | 479 | 455 | 663 | 538 | 326 | | | |
| criticare HN, Mead Johnson[f] 8 fl oz | 250 | | 0.8 | 0.6 | 0 | | 38 | .54 | .62 | 50 | 150 | 125 | 50 | 2.50 | .620 |
| | 260 | 9.0 | 52.5 | 0.1 | | 625 | .48 | 6.2 | 1.88 | 3.10 | 310 | 125 | 2.20 | .250 | |
| | | | | | | 50 | 9.4 | 31 | 38 | 62 | 250 | 19 | | | |
| | 145 | 440 | 550 | 925 | 775 | 405 | 35 | 433 | 198 | 675 | 360 | 270 | | | |
| enrich, Ross Labs[g] 8 fl oz | 260 | 196 | 8.8 | 4.8 | 5 | | 51 | .44 | .51 | 102 | 200 | 170 | 68 | 3.83 | .850 |
| | 255 | 9.4 | 38.3 | 1.3 | 3.4 | 850 | .39 | 5.1 | 1.60 | 2.55 | 370 | 170 | 3.06 | .340 | |
| | | | | | | 68 | 7.7 | 12 | 77 | 102 | 340 | 26 | | | |
| | 103 | 385 | 442 | 837 | 677 | 226 | 56 | 470 | 414 | 555 | 395 | 254 | | | |
| ensure HN, Ross Labs[h] 8 fl oz | 250 | 199 | 8.4 | 4.6 | 4 | 268 | 54 | .46 | .54 | 108 | 220 | 179 | 72 | 4.02 | .890 |
| | 253 | 10.5 | 33.4 | 1.2 | 0.0 | 893 | .41 | 5.4 | 1.70 | 2.68 | 370 | 179 | 3.22 | .360 | |
| | | | 8.2 | | | 72 | 8.1 | 13 | 81 | 107 | 340 | 27 | | | |
| | 126 | 431 | 473 | 914 | 725 | 273 | 53 | 504 | 515 | 525 | 389 | 252 | | | |
| ensure plus, Ross Labs[i] 8 fl oz | 355 | 182 | 12.6 | 6.9 | 5 | | 50 | .57 | .67 | 134 | 270 | 167 | 67 | 3.75 | .830 |
| | 259 | 13.0 | 47.3 | 1.9 | 0.0 | 834 | .50 | 6.7 | 2.00 | 3.34 | 500 | 167 | 3.00 | .340 | |
| | | | 10.2 | | | 67 | 7.5 | 12 | 100 | 100 | 470 | 25 | | | |
| | 156 | 533 | 585 | 1131 | 897 | 338 | 65 | 624 | 637 | 650 | 481 | 312 | | | |
| ensure plus HN, Ross Labs[j] 8 fl oz | 355 | 181 | 11.8 | 6.5 | 5 | | 75 | .85 | 1.00 | 200 | 280 | 250 | 100 | 5.63 | 1.250 |
| | 260 | 14.8 | 47.3 | 1.7 | 0.0 | 1250 | .75 | 10.0 | 3.00 | 5.00 | 430 | 250 | 4.50 | .500 | |
| | | | | | | 100 | 11.3 | 18 | 150 | 150 | 380 | 38 | | | |
| | 178 | 607 | 666 | 1288 | 1021 | 385 | 74 | 710 | 725 | 740 | 548 | 355 | | | |
| ensure pudding, van, Ross Labs[k] 5 oz | 250 | 91.0 | 9.7 | 0.8 | 5 | | 15 | .29 | .34 | 68 | 240 | 200 | 68 | 3.83 | .850 |
| | 142 | 6.8 | 34.0 | 2.3 | | 850 | .26 | 3.4 | 1.10 | 1.70 | 330 | 200 | 3.06 | .340 | |
| | | | | | | 68 | 7.7 | 12 | 51 | 25 | 220 | 60 | | | |
| | 102 | 299 | 340 | 673 | 530 | 184 | 54 | 320 | 306 | 435 | 224 | 163 | | | |

[a] Oral or tube feeding for uremic patients; available in orange, lemon-lime, strawberry and berry flavors; requires 250 g water to reconstitute.

[b] Used to increase the protein content of the diets of children & adults.

[c] Ready-to-use liquid tube feeding formulated from natural foods providing complete, balanced nutrition in a lactose-free, low sodium, isotonic formula; for short and long term tube-fed patients with normal gastrointestinal tracts.

[d] Alpha-tocopherol is 5.0 mg.

[e] Ready-to-use liquid tube feeding formulated from natural foods for short and long term tube-fed patients with normal gastrointestinal tracts; complete, balanced nutrition.

[f] Ready-to-use high nitrogen elemental diet.

[g] Fiber-containing, nutritionally complete liquid formula suitable for patients who do not require a low-residue diet; may be fed orally or by tube.

[h] Nutrient-dense, high-nitrogen, low-residue liquid food for patients w/ energy requirements less than 2000 kcal/day (elderly, comatose) or those with elevated nitrogen requirements; may be fed orally or by tube.

[i] Nutritionally complete, high-calorie liquid food providing 1.5 kcal/ml; useful when extra energy and nutrients, but normal protein concentration are needed in a limited volume; oral or tube feeding.

[j] Nutritionally complete, high-calorie, high-nitrogen liquid food, designed to meet the needs of stressed patients w/ higher energy and protein needs or for those with limited volume tolerance.

[k] Calorically dense supplement for patients in need of increased nutrient intake.

| | | | | | | Vitamins | | | | | Minerals | | | | |
|---|---|---|---|---|---|---|---|---|---|---|---|---|---|---|---|
| | KCAL | H2O (g) | FAT (g) | PUFA (g) | CHOL (mg) | A (RE) | C (mg) | B-2 (mg) | B-6 (mg) | FOL (mcg) | Na (mg) | Ca (mg) | Mg (mg) | Zn (mg) | Mn (mg) |
| | WT (g) | PRO (g) | CHO (g) | SFA (g) | DFIB (g) | A (IU) | B-1 (mg) | NIA (mg) | B-12 (mcg) | PANT (mg) | K (mg) | P (mg) | Fe (mg) | Cu (mg) | |
| | | | | | INOS (mg) | D (IU) | E (IU) | K (mcg) | BIO (mcg) | CHLN (mg) | Cl (mg) | I (mcg) | Mo (mg) | | |
| | TRY (mg) | THR (mg) | ISO (mg) | LEU (mg) | LYS (mg) | MET (mg) | CYS (mg) | PHE (mg) | TYR (mg) | VAL (mg) | ARG (mg) | HIS (mg) | | | |
| ensure, Ross Labs[a] | 250 | 200 | 8.8 | 4.8 | 4 | 188 | 38 | .43 | .50 | 100 | 200 | 125 | 50 | 2.82 | .620 |
| *8 fl oz* | 253 | 8.8 | 34.3 | 1.3 | 0.0 | 625 | .38 | 5.0 | 1.50 | 2.50 | 370 | 125 | 2.25 | .250 | |
| | | | | | | 50 | 5.63 | 9 | 75 | 75 | 340 | 19 | | | |
| | 106 | 361 | 396 | 766 | 607 | 229 | 44 | 422 | 431 | 440 | 326 | 211 | | | |
| hepatic-aid II inst drink powder, Am McGaw[b]—*3.1 oz pkt* | 400 | | 12.3 | | | | | | | | | | | | |
| | 88 | 15.0 | 57.3 | | | | | | | | | | | | |
| isocal HCN, Mead Johnson[c] | 473 | | 24.2 | 9.9 | 7 | | 71 | 1.02 | 1.18 | 95 | 190 | 240 | 95 | 7.10 | .780 |
| *8 fl oz* | 260 | 17.7 | 47.3 | 2.5 | | 1180 | .90 | 11.8 | 3.50 | 5.90 | 400 | 240 | 4.30 | .710 | |
| | | | | | | 95 | 17.7 | 59 | 71.0 | 118.0 | 280 | 35 | | | |
| | 227 | 738 | 1041 | 1797 | 1514 | 511 | 52 | 993 | 1041 | 1277 | 724 | 563 | | | |
| isocal, Mead Johnson[d] | 250 | | 10.5 | 5.3 | 0 | | 38 | .54 | .62 | 50 | 125 | 150 | 50 | 2.50 | .620 |
| *8 fl oz* | 250 | 8.1 | 31.5 | 1.3 | | 625 | .48 | 6.2 | 1.88 | 3.10 | 310 | 125 | 2.20 | .250 | |
| | | | | | | 50 | 9.4 | 31 | 38.0 | 62.0 | 250 | 19 | | | |
| | 145 | 320 | 425 | 775 | 575 | 193 | 40 | 400 | 375 | 550 | 305 | 215 | | | |
| lonalac, Mead Johnson[e]—*8 fl oz (47 g powder in 6.25 fl oz water)* | 240 | 203.4 | 13.2 | 0.2 | | | | .65 | | | 10 | 423 | 34 | | |
| | 250 | 12.7 | 17.9 | 9.6 | | 360 | .15 | 0.3 | | | 470 | 375 | | | |
| | | | | | | | | | | | 188 | | | | |
| | 163 | 528 | 720 | 1272 | 1080 | 362 | 38 | 696 | 720 | 912 | 504 | 398 | | | |
| lytren, Mead Johnson[f] | 10 | | 0.0 | | | | | | | | 177 | | | | |
| *100 ml* | | 0.0 | 2.5 | | | | | | | | 58 | | | | |
| | | | | | | | | | | | 173 | | | | |
| MCT oil (medium chain triglycerides), Mead Johnson[g]—*1 T* | 115 | 0.0 | 13.9 | | | | | | | | | | | | |
| | 14 | 0.0 | 0.0 | | | | | | | | | | | | |
| moducal, Mead Johnson[h] | 380 | 5.0 | 0.0 | 0.0 | | | | | | | 70 | | | | |
| *100 g powder* | 100 | 0.0 | 95.0 | 0.0 | | | | | | | 5 | | | | |
| | | | | | | | | | | | 170 | | | | |
| osmolite HN, Ross Labs[i] | 250 | 199 | 8.7 | 2.8 | 5 | 268 | 54 | .46 | .54 | 108 | 220 | 179 | 72 | 4.02 | .890 |
| *8 fl oz* | 253 | 10.5 | 33.4 | 5.4 | 0.0 | 893 | .41 | 5.4 | 1.70 | 2.68 | 370 | 179 | 3.22 | .360 | |
| | | | | | 0 | 72 | 8.1 | 13 | 81 | 42 | 340 | 27 | | | |
| | 126 | 431 | 473 | 914 | 725 | 273 | 53 | 504 | 515 | 525 | 389 | 252 | | | |
| osmolite, Ross Labs[j] | 250 | 199 | 9.1 | 3.0 | 5 | 188 | 38 | .43 | .50 | 100 | 150 | 125 | 50 | 2.82 | .620 |
| *8 fl oz* | 253 | 8.8 | 34.3 | 4.4 | 0.0 | 625 | .38 | 5.0 | 1.50 | 2.50 | 240 | 125 | 2.25 | .250 | |
| | | | | | 0 | 50 | 5.6 | 9 | 75 | 75 | 200 | 19 | | | |
| | 106 | 361 | 396 | 766 | 607 | 229 | 44 | 422 | 431 | 440 | 326 | 211 | | | |
| phenyl-free, Mead Johnson[k] | 100 | 95.0 | 1.7 | | | | 13 | .25 | .22 | 31 | 100 | 125 | 38 | 1.75 | .250 |
| *4 fl oz* | 120 | 5.0 | 16.2 | | | 300 | .15 | 2.0 | .62 | .75 | 338 | 125 | 3.00 | .150 | |
| | | | | | 7.5 | 38 | 2.5 | 25 | 7.5 | 21.0 | 230 | 11 | | | |
| | 70 | 230 | 270 | 420 | 460 | 155 | 85 | 5 | 230 | 310 | 115 | | | | |

[a] Oral/tube, liquid, low-residue feeding; complete, balanced formula.

[b] Oral or tube feeding for patients with chronic liver disease; available in choc, eggnog & custard flavors; requires 280 g water to reconstitute.

[c] For tube feedings that are hypermetabolic, fluid-restricted or volume-limited.

[d] Nutritionally complete formula to meet the dietary needs of most tube-fed patients.

[e] Low sodium, high protein beverage mix.

[f] Electrolytes plus carbohydrate for oral administration; contains dextrose, potassium citrate, sodium chloride, sodium citrate & citric acid.

[g] Substitute or supplemental source of fat calories for patients with poor digestion, absorption or utilization of conventional food fats. Lipid fraction of coconut oil contains < 6% fatty acids shorter than C8, 67% fatty acids with C8 (caprylic), 23% fatty acids with C10 (capric) & < 4% fatty acids longer than C10.

[h] Refined readily digestible carbohydrate which can be added to foods to increase caloric content for patients with increased caloric requirements; 100% maltodextrin from hydrolysis of corn starch.

[i] Nutrient-dense, high nitrogen, isotonic, low-residue liquid food for patients with energy requirements less than 2000 kcal/day or for patients with elevated nitrogen requirements who require tube feeding; may also be used for oral feeding.

[j] Isotonic, low-residue, liquid, complete, balanced formula for hospitalized patients who require tube feeding (nasogastric, nasoduodenal, jejunal); may also be used for oral feeding.

[k] Phenylalanine-free food used in the management of phenylketonuria.

Each food item is listed with four data rows corresponding to the four header tiers shown below.

| Tier | Col1 | Col2 | Col3 | Col4 | Col5 | Col6 | Col7 | Col8 | Col9 | Col10 | Col11 | Col12 | Col13 | Col14 | Col15 |
|---|---|---|---|---|---|---|---|---|---|---|---|---|---|---|---|
| 1 | KCAL | H2O (g) | FAT (g) | PUFA (g) | CHOL (mg) | A (RE) | C (mg) | B-2 (mg) | B-6 (mg) | FOL (mcg) | Na (mg) | Ca (mg) | Mg (mg) | Zn (mg) | Mn (mg) |
| 2 | WT (g) | PRO (g) | CHO (g) | SFA (g) | DFIB (g) | A (IU) | B-1 (mg) | NIA (mg) | B-12 (mcg) | PANT (mg) | K (mg) | P (mg) | Fe (mg) | Cu (mg) | |
| 3 | | | | | INOS (mg) | D (IU) | E (IU) | K (mcg) | BIO (mcg) | CHLN (mg) | Cl (mg) | I (mcg) | Mo (mg) | | |
| 4 | TRY (mg) | THR (mg) | ISO (mg) | LEU (mg) | LYS (mg) | MET (mg) | CYS (mg) | PHE (mg) | TYR (mg) | VAL (mg) | ARG (mg) | HIS (mg) | | | |

**polycose, Ross Labs[a]** — *100 ml*

| Tier | | | | | | | | | | | | | | | |
|---|---|---|---|---|---|---|---|---|---|---|---|---|---|---|---|
| 1 | 200 | 70.0 | 0.0 | 0.0 | 0 | | | | | | 70 | 20 | | | |
| 2 | 120 | 0.0 | 50.0 | 0.0 | 0.0 | | | | | | 6 | 3 | | | |
| 3 | | | | | | | | | | | 140 | | | | |
| 4 | 0 | 0 | 0 | 0 | 0 | 0 | 0 | 0 | 0 | 0 | 0 | 0 | | | |

**portagen, 30 cal/fl oz, Mead Johnson[b]** — *8 fl oz*

| Tier | | | | | | | | | | | | | | | |
|---|---|---|---|---|---|---|---|---|---|---|---|---|---|---|---|
| 1 | 240 | | 11.5 | 0.9 | 2 | | 20 | .45 | .50 | 38 | 113 | 225 | 50 | 2.25 | .300 |
| 2 | 240 | 8.5 | 27.5 | 0.3 | | 1875 | .38 | 5.0 | 1.50 | 2.50 | 300 | 169 | 4.50 | .375 | |
| 3 | | | | | 11.3 | 188 | 7.5 | 38 | 18.8 | 31.3 | 206 | 18 | | | |
| 4 | 108 | 346 | 480 | 840 | 720 | 240 | 24 | 461 | 480 | 600 | 338 | 264 | | | |

**portagen, 60 cal/fl oz, Mead Johnson[b]** — *8 fl oz*

| Tier | | | | | | | | | | | | | | | |
|---|---|---|---|---|---|---|---|---|---|---|---|---|---|---|---|
| 1 | 480 | | 22.9 | 1.9 | 4 | | 39 | .90 | 1.00 | 75 | 225 | 450 | 100 | 4.50 | .600 |
| 2 | 240 | 16.8 | 55.3 | 0.7 | | 3750 | .75 | 10.0 | 3.00 | 5.00 | 600 | 338 | 9.00 | .750 | |
| 3 | | | | | 22.5 | 375 | 15 | 75 | 37.5 | 62.5 | 413 | 35 | | | |
| 4 | 216 | 692 | 960 | 1680 | 1440 | 480 | 48 | 922 | 960 | 1200 | 676 | 528 | | | |

**pro mod, Ross Labs[c]** — *1 scoop*

| Tier | | | | | | | | | | | | | | | |
|---|---|---|---|---|---|---|---|---|---|---|---|---|---|---|---|
| 1 | 28 | 0.6 | 0.6 | | | | | | | | 13 | 23 | | | |
| 2 | 5 | 5.0 | 0.7 | | | | | | | | 65 | 22 | | | |
| 4 | 95 | 365 | 310 | 540 | 465 | 110 | 130 | 180 | 170 | 300 | 130 | 95 | | | |

**pulmocare, Ross Labs[d]** — *8 fl oz*

| Tier | | | | | | | | | | | | | | | |
|---|---|---|---|---|---|---|---|---|---|---|---|---|---|---|---|
| 1 | 355 | 186 | 21.8 | 12.0 | 6 | | 75 | .85 | 1.00 | 200 | 310 | 250 | 100 | 5.63 | 1.250 |
| 2 | 250 | 14.8 | 25.0 | 3.2 | 0.0 | 1250 | .75 | 10.0 | 3.00 | 5.00 | 450 | 250 | 4.50 | .500 | |
| 3 | | | | | | 100 | 11.3 | 18 | 150 | 150 | 400 | 38 | | | |
| 4 | 163 | 592 | 755 | 1362 | 1110 | 444 | 59 | 710 | 710 | 947 | 533 | 414 | | | |

**ross SLD (surgical liquid diet), Ross Labs[e]** — *200 ml (1.3 oz pkt in water)*

| Tier | | | | | | | | | | | | | | | |
|---|---|---|---|---|---|---|---|---|---|---|---|---|---|---|---|
| 1 | 140 | 164.0 | 0.1 | 0.0 | 0 | | 15 | .43 | .50 | 100 | 167 | 167 | 67 | 3.80 | .840 |
| 2 | 214 | 7.5 | 27.3 | 0.0 | | 834 | .39 | 5.0 | 1.50 | 2.50 | 167 | 167 | 3.00 | .330 | |
| 3 | | | | | | 67 | 7.5 | 6 | 75 | 75 | 200 | 25 | | | |
| 4 | 83 | 383 | 413 | 690 | 563 | 248 | 188 | 533 | 338 | 570 | 525 | 203 | | | |

**sustacal HC, Mead Johnson[f]** — *8 fl oz*

| Tier | | | | | | | | | | | | | | | |
|---|---|---|---|---|---|---|---|---|---|---|---|---|---|---|---|
| 1 | 360 | | 13.6 | 5.4 | 4 | | 18 | .51 | .60 | 120 | 200 | 200 | 80 | 3.00 | .600 |
| 2 | 260 | 14.4 | 45.0 | 2.1 | | 1000 | .45 | 6.0 | 1.80 | 3.00 | 350 | 200 | 3.60 | .400 | |
| 3 | | | | | 50 | 80 | 6 | 50 | 90 | 50 | 300 | 30 | | | |
| 4 | 184 | 594 | 828 | 1440 | 1224 | 410 | 43 | 792 | 828 | 1044 | 580 | 450 | | | |

**sustacal, Mead Johnson[g]** — *8 fl oz*

| Tier | | | | | | | | | | | | | | | |
|---|---|---|---|---|---|---|---|---|---|---|---|---|---|---|---|
| 1 | 240 | | 5.5 | 2.1 | 4 | | 13 | .40 | .47 | 89 | 220 | 240 | 90 | 3.30 | .670 |
| 2 | 260 | 14.5 | 33.1 | 0.9 | | 1110 | .33 | 4.7 | 1.33 | 2.30 | 490 | 220 | 4.00 | .470 | |
| 3 | | | | | 89 | 89 | 6.7 | 56 | 67 | 56 | 370 | 33 | | | |
| 4 | 158 | 552 | 768 | 1320 | 1056 | 346 | 58 | 744 | 696 | 912 | 624 | 389 | | | |

**sustacal powder, vanilla, Mead Johnson** — *1 pkt*

| Tier | | | | | | | | | | | | | | | |
|---|---|---|---|---|---|---|---|---|---|---|---|---|---|---|---|
| 1 | 200 | | 0.3 | | | | 20 | .20 | .55 | 133 | 190 | 290 | 105 | 4.00 | 1.000 |
| 2 | 54 | 12.5 | 36.0 | | | 1290 | .40 | 6.8 | 1.00 | 2.70 | 560 | 250 | 6.00 | .700 | |
| 3 | | | | | 33 | | 10 | | 93 | | 220 | 40 | | | |

**sustacal powder, vanilla w/ 8 fl oz whole milk, Mead Johnson** — *8 fl oz*

| Tier | | | | | | | | | | | | | | | |
|---|---|---|---|---|---|---|---|---|---|---|---|---|---|---|---|
| 1 | 360 | | 9.2 | | | | 20 | .60 | .70 | 133 | 330 | 580 | 135 | 5.00 | 1.000 |
| 2 | 290 | 20.5 | 48.0 | | | 1670 | .50 | 7.0 | 2.00 | 3.50 | 910 | 480 | 6.00 | .700 | |
| 3 | | | | | 133 | | 10 | | 100 | | 480 | 50 | | | |

**sustacal pudding, Mead Johnson[h]** — *5 fl oz*

| Tier | | | | | | | | | | | | | | | |
|---|---|---|---|---|---|---|---|---|---|---|---|---|---|---|---|
| 1 | 240 | 92.0 | 9.5 | 3.7 | 5 | | 9 | .26 | .30 | 60 | 120 | 220 | 60 | 2.20 | .670 |
| 2 | 142 | 6.8 | 32.0 | 1.5 | | 750 | .23 | 3.0 | .90 | 1.50 | 320 | 220 | 2.70 | .300 | |
| 3 | | | | | | 60 | 4.5 | | 50 | | 200 | 22 | | | |
| 4 | 94 | 271 | 362 | 672 | 442 | 151 | 34 | 310 | 355 | 408 | 158 | 144 | | | |

[a] Glucose polymers for energy support to be mixed with food or beverage; may be used as enteral carbohydrate supplement.

[b] Nutritionally complete formula for children & adults who do not efficiently digest conventional fat or absorb the resulting long chain fatty acids.

[c] Protein supplement to be used enterally or orally.

[d] High-fat, low-carbohydrate enteral formula designed to reduce carbon dioxide production, thereby minimizing carbon dioxide retention resulting from chronic obstructive pulmonary disease or acute respiratory failure. Can be used for enteral tube feeding or oral supplementation and is appropriate for ambulatory or ventilation-dependent patients.

[e] Highly fortified, low-residue, low-fat formula for patients restricted to clear liquid diets.

[f] Complete or supplemental oral formula for patients who are fluid restricted and volume sensitive.

[g] Complete or supplemental oral formula for patients who have difficulty meeting nutritional requirements through normal diets.

[h] Nutritionally complete dietary supplement.

|  | KCAL | H₂O (g) | FAT (g) | PUFA (g) | CHOL (mg) | A (RE) | C (mg) | B-2 (mg) | B-6 (mg) | FOL (mcg) | Na (mg) | Ca (mg) | Mg (mg) | Zn (mg) | Mn (mg) |
|---|---|---|---|---|---|---|---|---|---|---|---|---|---|---|---|
|  | WT (g) | PRO (g) | CHO (g) | SFA (g) | DFIB (g) | A (IU) | B-1 (mg) | NIA (mg) | B-12 (mcg) | PANT (mg) | K (mg) | P (mg) | Fe (mg) | Cu (mg) |  |
|  |  |  |  |  | INOS (mg) | D (IU) | E (IU) | K (mcg) | BIO (mcg) | CHLN (mg) | Cl (mg) | I (mcg) | Mo (mg) |  |  |
|  | TRY (mg) | THR (mg) | ISO (mg) | LEU (mg) | LYS (mg) | MET (mg) | CYS (mg) | PHE (mg) | TYR (mg) | VAL (mg) | ARG (mg) | HIS (mg) |  |  |  |
| **sustagen, Mead Johnson[a]** 8 fl oz | 438 |  | 4.0 |  | 14 |  | 75 | 1.08 | 1.25 | 100 | 250 | 800 | 100 | 5.00 | 1.250 |
|  | 260 | 26.8 | 75.0 |  |  |  | .95 | 12.5 | 3.75 | 6.25 | 800 | 600 | 4.50 | .500 |  |
|  |  |  |  |  | 210 | 100 | 11 | 63 | 75 | 125 | 675 | 38 |  |  |  |
|  | 447 | 1051 | 1402 | 2540 |  | 657 | 184 | 1270 | 1270 | 1752 | 837 | 731 |  |  |  |
| **traum-aid HBC powder, Am McGaw[b]** 4.2 oz pkt | 500 |  | 6.2 |  |  |  | 14 | .24 | .28 | 56 | 265 |  | 56 | 2.81 | .546 |
|  | 119 | 28.0 | 83.0 |  |  |  | .21 | 2.8 | .84 | 1.39 | 585 | 168 | 2.52 | .281 |  |
|  |  |  |  |  |  | 56 | 8.4 | 21 | 42 | 59 | 344 | 21 | .021 | .021 | .007 |
| **traumaCal, Mead Johnson[c]** 8 fl oz | 355 | 184.9 | 16.2 | 7.5 | 1 |  | 35 | .51 | .59 | 47 | 280 | 177 | 47 | 3.50 | .590 |
|  | 260 | 19.5 | 33.7 | 1.9 |  | 590 | .45 | 5.9 | 1.77 | 3.00 | 330 | 117 | 2.10 | .350 |  |
|  |  |  |  |  |  | 47 | 8.9 | 30 | 35 | 59 | 380 | 18 |  |  |  |
|  | 249 | 817 | 1101 | 1953 | 1669 | 554 | 57 | 1065 | 1101 | 1385 | 781 | 614 |  |  |  |
| **two cal HN, Ross Labs** 8 fl oz | 478 |  | 21.5 |  |  |  | 75 | .68 | .80 | 160 | 250 | 250 | 100 | 5.63 | 1.250 |
|  |  | 19.8 | 51.4 |  |  |  | .60 | 8.0 | 2.40 | 4.00 | 550 | 250 | 4.50 | .500 |  |
|  |  |  |  |  |  | 100 | 11.3 | 18 | 120 | 150 | 370 | 38 |  |  |  |
|  | 218 | 792 | 1010 | 1822 | 1485 | 594 | 79 | 950 | 950 | 1267 | 713 | 554 |  |  |  |
| **vital high nitrogen, Ross Labs[d]** 300 ml (79 g pkt w/ 255 ml water) | 300 | 255 | 3.3 | 1.2 | 6 |  | 60 | .68 | .80 | 160 | 140 | 200 | 80 | 4.50 | 1.000 |
|  | 326 | 12.5 | 55.4 | 1.4 | 0.0 | 1000 | .60 | 8.0 | 2.40 | 4.00 | 400 | 200 | 3.60 | .400 |  |
|  |  |  |  |  | 0 | 80 | 9 | 14 | 120 | 120 | 270 | 30 | .025 | .006 | .026 |
|  | 138 | 475 | 575 | 1000 | 663 | 275 | 113 | 563 | 475 | 700 | 688 | 325 |  |  |  |
| **vivonex flavor packets, Norwich Eaton Pharmaceuticals[e]** — 1 pkt | [f] |  | 0.0 |  |  |  |  |  |  |  |  |  |  |  |  |
|  | 2.5 | 0.0 | [g] |  |  |  |  |  |  |  |  |  |  |  |  |
| **vivonex high nitrogen, Norwich Eaton Pharmaceuticals[h]** — 1000 ml | 1000 | 6.7 | 0.9 | 0.8 | 0 |  | 20 | .57 | .67 | 133 | 529 | 333 | 133 | 5.00 | .940 |
|  | 267 | 44.3 | 203.7 | 0.1 | 0.0 | 1667 | .50 | 6.7 | 2.00 | 3.30 | 1173 | 333 | 6.00 | .670 |  |
|  |  |  |  |  | 0 | 133 | [i] | 22 | 100 | 25 |  | 150 | .050 | .050 | .017 |
|  | 567 | 1833 | 1838 | 2900 | 2200 | 2029 | 0 | 3133 | 372 | 2029 | 186 | 50 |  |  |  |
| **vivonex, standard, Norwich Eaton Pharmaceuticals[h]** — 1000 ml | 1000 | 6.7 | 1.5 | 1.3 | 0 |  | 33 | .94 | 1.11 | 220 | 468 | 556 | 222 | 8.33 | 1.560 |
|  | 267 | 20.6 | 226.3 | 0.1 | 0.0 | 2778 | .83 | 11.1 | 3.33 | 5.55 | 1172 | 556 | 10.00 | 1.110 |  |
|  |  |  |  |  | 0 | 222 | [j] | 37 | 170 | 41 |  | 83 | .083 | .083 | .028 |
|  | 290 | 937 | 937 | 1483 | 1114 | 960 | 0 | 1067 | 194 | 1034 | 1827 | 455 |  |  |  |
| **vivonex, TEN, Norwich Eaton Pharmaceuticals[h]** — 1000 ml | 1000 | 6.7 | 2.8 | 2.6 | 0 |  | 60 | 1.70 | 2.00 | 400 | 460 | 500 | 200 | 10.00 | .940 |
|  | 268 | 38.2 | 205.6 | 0.3 | 0.0 | 2500 | 1.50 | 20.0 | 6.00 | 10.00 | 782 | 500 | 9.00 | 1.000 |  |
|  |  |  |  |  | 0 | 200 | [k] | 22 | 300 | 74 |  | 75 | .050 | .050 | .017 |
|  | 489 | 1528 | 3159 | 6326 | 1948 | 1398 | 0 | 1971 | 321 | 3159 | 2918 | 901 |  |  |  |

[a] High calorie, high protein nutritional supplement.

[b] Oral or tube feeding for catabolic patients; available in lemon-creme flavor; requires 420 g water to reconstitute.

[c] Oral or tube nutritionally complete feeding for patients with multiple trauma and major burns having elevated caloric requirements, exceptional nitrogen needs and volume restrictions.

[d] Nutritionally complete elemental diet for patients with impaired gastrointestinal function.

[e] Used to enhance the flavor of orally administered vivonex diets. They contain 20 mg of saccharin per pkt. Available in lemon-lime, orange-pineapple, strawberry & vanilla.

[f] 6 kcal/pkt for lemon-lime & orange-pineapple; 8 kcal/pkt for strawberry; 9 kcal/pkt for vanilla.

[g] Cho/pkt is 0.8 for lemon-lime, 0.9 for orange-pineapple, 1.3 for strawberry & 2.2 for vanilla.

[h] Elemental chemically defined diet.

[i] Alpha-tocopherol is 6.7 mg.

[j] Alpha-tocopherol is 11.19 mg.

[k] Alpha-tocopherol is 10.0 mg.

|  | KCAL | H$_2$O (g) | FAT (g) | PUFA (g) | CHOL (mg) | A (RE) | C (mg) | B-2 (mg) | B-6 (mg) | FOL (mcg) | Na (mg) | Ca (mg) | Mg (mg) | Zn (mg) | Mn (mg) |
|---|---|---|---|---|---|---|---|---|---|---|---|---|---|---|---|
|  | WT (g) | PRO (g) | CHO (g) | SFA (g) | DFIB (g) | A (IU) | B-1 (mg) | NIA (mg) | B-12 (mcg) | PANT (mg) | K (mg) | P (mg) | Fe (mg) | Cu (mg) |  |

## 31. SPICES, HERBS, & FLAVORINGS

| | | | | | | | | | | | | | | | |
|---|---|---|---|---|---|---|---|---|---|---|---|---|---|---|---|
| **allspice, ground** | 5 | 0.2 | 0.2 | 0.0 | 0 | 1 | 1 | .00 | | | 1 | 13 | 3 | .02 | |
| *1 t* | 2 | 0.1 | 1.4 | 0.1 | | 10 | .00 | 0.0 | | .00 | 20 | 2 | .13 | | |
| **anise seed** | 7 | 0.2 | 0.3 | 0.1 | 0 | | | | | | 0 | 14 | 4 | .11 | |
| *1 t* | 2 | 0.4 | 1.1 | | | | | | | .00 | 30 | 9 | .78 | | |
| **basil, ground** | 4 | 0.1 | 0.1 | | 0 | 13 | 1 | .00 | | | 0 | 30 | 6 | .08 | |
| *1 t* | 1 | 0.2 | 0.9 | | | 131 | .00 | 0.1 | | .00 | 48 | 7 | .59 | | |
| **bay leaf, crumbled** | 2 | 0.0 | 0.1 | 0.0 | 0 | 4 | 0 | .00 | | | 0 | 5 | 1 | .02 | |
| *1 t* | 1 | 0.1 | 0.5 | 0.0 | | 37 | .00 | 0.0 | | .00 | 3 | 1 | .26 | | |
| **caraway seed** | 7 | 0.2 | 0.3 | 0.1 | 0 | 1 | | .01 | | | 0 | 14 | 5 | .12 | |
| *1 t* | 2 | 0.4 | 1.1 | 0.0 | | 8 | .01 | 0.1 | | .00 | 28 | 12 | .34 | | |
| **cardamom, ground** | 6 | 0.2 | 0.1 | 0.0 | 0 | | | .00 | | | 0 | 8 | 5 | .15 | |
| *1 t* | 2 | 0.2 | 1.4 | 0.0 | | | .00 | 0.0 | | .00 | 22 | 4 | .28 | | |
| **celery seed** | 8 | 0.1 | 0.5 | 0.1 | 0 | 0 | 0 | | | | 3 | 35 | 9 | .14 | |
| *1 t* | 2 | 0.4 | 0.8 | 0.0 | | 1 | | 0.0 | | | 28 | 11 | .90 | | |
| **chervil, dried** | 1 | 0.0 | 0.0 | | 0 | | | | .01 | | 0 | 8 | 1 | .05 | |
| *1 t* | 1 | 0.1 | 0.3 | | | | | | .00 | | 28 | 3 | .19 | | |
| **chili powder**[a] | 8 | 0.2 | 0.4 | | 0 | 91 | 2 | .02 | | | 26 | 7 | 4 | .07 | |
| *1 t* | 3 | 0.3 | 1.4 | | | 908 | .01 | 0.2 | | .00 | 50 | 8 | .37 | | |
| **cinn, ground** | 6 | 0.2 | 0.1 | 0.0 | 0 | 1 | 1 | .00 | | | 1 | 28 | 1 | .05 | |
| *1 t* | 2 | 0.1 | 1.8 | 0.0 | | 6 | .00 | 0.0 | | .00 | 11 | 1 | .88 | | |
| **cloves, ground** | 7 | 0.1 | 0.4 | | 0 | 1 | 2 | .01 | | | 5 | 14 | 6 | .02 | |
| *1 t* | 2 | 0.1 | 1.3 | 0.1 | | 11 | .00 | 0.0 | | .00 | 23 | 2 | .18 | | |
| **coriander leaf, dried** | 2 | 0.0 | 0.0 | | 0 | | 3 | .01 | | | 1 | 7 | 4 | | |
| *1 t* | 1 | 0.1 | 0.3 | | | | .01 | 0.1 | | .00 | 27 | 3 | .25 | | |
| **coriander seed** | 5 | 0.2 | 0.3 | 0.0 | 0 | | | .01 | | | 1 | 13 | 6 | .08 | |
| *1 t* | 2 | 0.2 | 1.0 | 0.0 | | | .00 | 0.0 | | .00 | 23 | 7 | .29 | | |
| **cumin seed** | 8 | 0.2 | 0.5 | | 0 | 3 | 0 | .01 | | | 4 | 20 | 8 | .10 | |
| *1 t* | 2 | 0.4 | 0.9 | | | 27 | .01 | 0.1 | | .00 | 38 | 10 | 1.39 | | |
| **curry powder** | 6 | 0.2 | 0.3 | | 0 | 2 | 0 | .01 | | | 1 | 10 | 5 | .08 | |
| *1 t* | 2 | 0.3 | 1.2 | | | 20 | .01 | 0.1 | | .00 | 31 | 7 | .59 | | |
| **dill seed** | 6 | 0.2 | 0.3 | 0.0 | 0 | 0 | | .01 | | | 0 | 32 | 5 | .11 | |
| *1 t* | 2 | 0.3 | 1.2 | 0.0 | | 1 | .01 | 0.1 | | .00 | 25 | 6 | .34 | | |
| **dill weed, dried** | 3 | 0.1 | 0.0 | | 0 | | | .00 | .02 | | 2 | 18 | 5 | .03 | |
| *1 t* | 1 | 0.2 | 0.6 | | | | .00 | 0.0 | .00 | | 33 | 5 | .49 | | |
| **fennel seed** | 7 | 0.2 | 0.2 | 0.0 | 0 | 0 | | .01 | | | 2 | 24 | 8 | .07 | |
| *1 t* | 2 | 0.3 | 1.1 | 0.0 | | 3 | .01 | 0.1 | | .00 | 34 | 10 | .37 | | |
| **fenugreek seed** | 12 | 0.3 | 0.2 | | 0 | 0 | | .01 | | 2 | 2 | 6 | 7 | .09 | |
| *1 t* | 4 | 0.9 | 2.2 | | | | .01 | 0.1 | | .00 | 28 | 11 | 1.24 | | |
| **garlic powder** | 9 | 0.2 | 0.0 | | 0 | | | .00 | | | 1 | 2 | 2 | .07 | |
| *1 t* | 3 | 0.5 | 2.0 | | | | .01 | 0.0 | | .00 | 31 | 12 | .08 | | |
| **ginger, ground** | 6 | 0.2 | 0.1 | 0.0 | 0 | 0 | | .00 | | | 1 | 2 | 3 | .08 | |
| *1 t* | 2 | 0.2 | 1.3 | 0.0 | | 3 | .00 | 0.1 | | .00 | 24 | 3 | .21 | | |
| **mace, ground** | 8 | 0.1 | 0.6 | 0.1 | 0 | 1 | | .01 | | | 1 | 4 | 3 | .04 | |
| *1 t* | 2 | 0.1 | 0.9 | 0.2 | | 14 | .01 | 0.0 | | .00 | 8 | 2 | .24 | | |
| **marjoram, dried** | 2 | 0.0 | | | 0 | 5 | 0 | .00 | | | 0 | 12 | 2 | .02 | |
| *1 t* | 1 | 0.4 | | | | 48 | .00 | 0.0 | | .00 | 9 | 2 | .50 | | |
| **mustard seed, yellow** | 15 | 0.2 | 1.0 | 0.2 | 0 | 0 | | .01 | | | 0 | 17 | 10 | .19 | |
| *1 t* | 3 | 0.8 | 1.2 | 0.1 | | 2 | .02 | 0.3 | | .00 | 23 | 28 | .33 | | |
| **nutmeg, ground** | 12 | 0.1 | 0.8 | 0.0 | 0 | 0 | | .00 | | | 0 | 4 | 4 | .05 | |
| *1 t* | 2 | 0.1 | 1.1 | 0.6 | | 2 | .01 | 0.0 | | .00 | 8 | 5 | .07 | | |
| **onion powder** | 7 | 0.1 | 0.0 | | 0 | | | .00 | .00 | | 1 | 8 | 3 | .05 | |
| *1 t* | 2 | 0.2 | 1.7 | | | | .01 | 0.0 | .00 | | 20 | 7 | .05 | | |
| **oregano, ground** | 5 | 0.1 | 0.2 | 0.1 | 0 | 10 | | | | | 0 | 24 | 4 | .07 | |
| *1 t* | 2 | 0.2 | 1.0 | 0.0 | | 104 | .01 | 0.1 | | .00 | 25 | 3 | .66 | | |
| **paprika** | 6 | 0.2 | 0.3 | 0.2 | 0 | 127 | 1 | .04 | | | 1 | 4 | 4 | .08 | |
| *1 t* | 2 | 0.3 | 1.2 | 0.0 | | 1273 | .01 | 0.3 | | .00 | 49 | 7 | .50 | | |
| **parsley, dried** | 4 | 0.1 | 0.1 | | 0 | 30 | 2 | .02 | .01 | | 6 | 19 | 3 | .06 | |
| *1 t* | 1 | 0.3 | 0.7 | | | 303 | .00 | 0.1 | | .00 | 49 | 5 | 1.27 | | |

[a] Contains red pepper, cumin, oregano, salt & garlic powder.

| | KCAL | H₂O (g) | FAT (g) | PUFA (g) | CHOL (mg) | A (RE) | C (mg) | B-2 (mg) | B-6 (mg) | FOL (mcg) | Na (mg) | Ca (mg) | Mg (mg) | Zn (mg) | Mn (mg) |
|---|---|---|---|---|---|---|---|---|---|---|---|---|---|---|---|
| | WT (g) | PRO (g) | CHO (g) | SFA (g) | DFIB (g) | A (IU) | B-1 (mg) | NIA (mg) | B-12 (mcg) | PANT (mg) | K (mg) | P (mg) | Fe (mg) | Cu (mg) | |
| **pepper, black** | 5 | 0.2 | 0.1 | 0.0 | 0 | 0 | | .01 | | | 1 | 9 | 4 | .03 | |
| *1 t* | 2 | 0.2 | 1.4 | 0.0 | | 4 | .00 | 0.0 | .00 | | 26 | 4 | .61 | | |
| **pepper, red/cayenne** | 6 | 0.1 | 0.3 | 0.2 | 0 | 75 | 1 | .02 | | | 1 | 3 | 3 | .05 | |
| *1 t* | 2 | 0.2 | 1.0 | 0.1 | | 749 | .01 | 0.2 | .00 | | 36 | 5 | .14 | | |
| **pepper, white** | 7 | 0.3 | 0.1 | | 0 | | | .00 | | | 0 | 6 | 2 | .03 | |
| *1 t* | 2 | 0.3 | 1.7 | | | | .00 | 0.0 | .00 | | 2 | 4 | .34 | | |
| **poppy seed** | 15 | 0.2 | 1.3 | 0.9 | 0 | | | .01 | .01 | | 1 | 41 | 9 | .29 | |
| *1 t* | 3 | 0.5 | 0.7 | 0.1 | | | .02 | 0.0 | .00 | | 20 | 24 | .26 | | |
| **poultry seasoning**[a] | 5 | 0.1 | 0.1 | | 0 | 4 | 0 | .00 | | | 0 | 15 | 3 | .05 | |
| *1 t* | 2 | 0.1 | 1.0 | | | 39 | .00 | 0.0 | .00 | | 10 | 3 | .53 | | |
| **pumpkin pie spice**[b] | 6 | 0.1 | 0.2 | | 0 | 0 | 0 | .00 | | | 1 | 12 | 2 | .04 | |
| *1 t* | 2 | 0.1 | 1.2 | | | 4 | .00 | 0.0 | .00 | | 11 | 2 | .34 | | |
| **rosemary, dried** | 4 | 0.1 | 0.2 | | 0 | 4 | 1 | | | | 1 | 15 | 3 | .04 | |
| *1 t* | 2 | 0.1 | 0.8 | | | 38 | .01 | 0.0 | .00 | | 11 | 1 | .35 | | |
| **saffron** | 2 | 0.1 | 0.0 | | 0 | | | | | | 1 | 1 | | | |
| *1 t* | 1 | 0.1 | 0.5 | | | | | | .00 | | 12 | 2 | .08 | | |
| **sage, ground** | 2 | 0.1 | 0.1 | 0.0 | 0 | 4 | 0 | .00 | | | 0 | 12 | 3 | .03 | |
| *1 t* | 1 | 0.1 | 0.4 | 0.1 | | 41 | .01 | 0.0 | .00 | | 7 | 1 | .20 | | |
| **salt**[c] | 0 | | 0.0 | 0.0 | | | | | | | 2300 | | 0 | | |
| *1 t* | 6 | 0.0 | 0.0 | 0.0 | | | | | | | 0 | | | | |
| **salt, kosher, Morton** | 0 | | 0.0 | | | | | | | | 1880 | | | | |
| *1 t* | 5 | 0.0 | 0.0 | | | | | | | | | | | | |
| | | | | | | | | | | | | | | | |
| **salt substitutes** | | | | | | | | | | | | | | | |
|   Morton lite salt[d] | 0 | | 0.0 | 0.0 | 0 | | | | | | 1100 | 0 | 4 | | |
| *1 t* | 6 | 0.0 | 0.0 | 0.0 | 0.0 | | | | | | 1500 | | | | |
|   Morton salt substitute | 0 | | 0.0 | 0.0 | 0 | | | | | | 0 | 30 | 0 | | |
| *1 t* | 6 | 0.0 | 0.1 | 0.0 | 0.0 | | | | | | 2800 | 28 | | | |
|   Morton seasoned salt substitute | 2 | | 0.0 | | | | | | | | 0 | | | | |
| *1 t* | 5 | 0.0 | 0.5 | | | | | | | | 2100 | | | | |
|   No Salt salt alternative | | | | | 0 | | | | | | 5 | | | | |
| *1 t* | | 0.0 | | | | | | | | | 2500 | | | | |
|   No Salt salt alternative, seasoned | 4 | | 0.0 | | 0 | | | | | | 2 | | | | |
| *1 t* | 4.5 | 0.0 | 0.9 | | | | | | | | 1330 | | | | |
|   Nu-Salt | | | | | | | | | | | 0 | 0 | 0 | | |
| *1 t* | 1 | | | | | | | | | | 1 | | | | |
| **savorex, Loma Linda**[e] | 16 | 2.0 | 1.0 | | 0 | | | .42 | .25 | 90 | 320 | 4 | 14 | .35 | |
| *1 t* | 7 | 3.0 | 1.0 | | | | .14 | 3.5 | | .42 | 210 | | .35 | | |
| **savory, ground** | 4 | 0.1 | 0.1 | | 0 | 7 | | | | | 0 | 30 | 5 | .06 | |
| *1 t* | 1 | 0.1 | 1.0 | | | 72 | .01 | 0.1 | .00 | | 15 | 2 | .53 | | |
| **seasoning blend, Nature's Seasons, Morton**—*1 t* | 3 | | 0.5 | | | | | | | | 1300 | | | | |
| | 4 | 0.0 | 0.0 | | | | | | | | 10 | | | | |
| **tarragon, ground** | 5 | 0.1 | 0.1 | | 0 | 7 | | .00 | | | 1 | 18 | 6 | .06 | |
| *1 t* | 2 | 0.4 | 0.8 | | | 67 | .00 | 0.1 | .00 | | 48 | 5 | .52 | | |
| **tumeric, ground** | 8 | 0.3 | 0.2 | | 0 | | 1 | .01 | | | 1 | 4 | 4 | .10 | |
| *1 t* | 2 | 0.2 | 1.4 | | | | .00 | 0.1 | .00 | | 56 | 6 | .91 | | |

## 32. SPREADS (BUTTER, MARGARINE, MAYONNAISE, ETC.)

| | KCAL | H₂O (g) | FAT (g) | PUFA (g) | CHOL (mg) | A (RE) | C (mg) | B-2 (mg) | B-6 (mg) | FOL (mcg) | Na (mg) | Ca (mg) | Mg (mg) | Zn (mg) | Mn (mg) |
|---|---|---|---|---|---|---|---|---|---|---|---|---|---|---|---|
| **butter** | 36 | 0.8 | 4.1 | 0.2 | 11 | 38 | 0 | .00 | .00 | 0 | 41 | 1 | 0 | .00 | |
| *1 t* | 5 | 0.0 | 0.0 | 2.5 | 0.0 | 153 | .00 | 0.0 | | | 1 | 1 | .01 | | |
| | 108 | 2.4 | 12.2 | 0.5 | 33 | 114 | 0 | .01 | .00 | 0 | 123 | 3 | 0 | .00 | |
| *1 T* | 15 | 0.1 | 0.0 | 7.6 | 0.0 | 459 | .00 | 0.0 | | | 3 | 3 | .03 | | |
|   sweet (unsalted) | 36 | 0.8 | 4.1 | 0.2 | 11 | 38 | 0 | .00 | .00 | 0 | 1 | 1 | 0 | .00 | |
| *1 t* | 5 | 0.0 | 0.0 | 2.5 | 0.0 | 165 | .00 | 0.0 | | | 1 | 1 | .01 | | |
|   sweet (unsalted) | 108 | 2.4 | 12.2 | 0.5 | 33 | 114 | 0 | .01 | .00 | 0 | 2 | 3 | 0 | .00 | |
| *1 T* | 15 | 0.1 | 0.0 | 7.6 | 0.0 | 495 | .00 | 0.0 | | | 3 | 3 | .03 | | |

[a] Contains white pepper, sage, thyme, marjoram, savory, ginger, allspice & nutmeg.

[b] Contains cinn, ginger, nutmeg, allspice & cloves.

[c] Contains 3.6 g Cl & 400 mcg I if iodized; contains less than 100 mcg if not iodized.

[d] Contains 400 mcg I.

[e] Contains yeast extract, veg flavors & salt.

| | KCAL / WT (g) | H₂O (g) / PRO (g) | FAT (g) / CHO (g) | PUFA (g) / SFA (g) | CHOL (mg) / DFIB (g) | A (RE) / A (IU) | C (mg) / B-1 (mg) | B-2 (mg) / NIA (mg) | B-6 (mg) / B-12 (mcg) | FOL (mcg) / PANT (mg) | Na (mg) / K (mg) | Ca (mg) / P (mg) | Mg (mg) / Fe (mg) | Zn (mg) / Cu (mg) | Mn (mg) |
|---|---|---|---|---|---|---|---|---|---|---|---|---|---|---|---|
| whipped | 27 | 0.6 | 3.1 | 0.1 | 8 | 29 | 0 | .00 | .00 | 0 | 31 | 1 | 0 | .00 | |
| *1 t* | 4 | 0.0 | 0.0 | 1.9 | 0.0 | 116 | .00 | 0.0 | | | 1 | 1 | .01 | | |
| whipped | 81 | 1.8 | 9.2 | 0.3 | 24 | 87 | 0 | .00 | .00 | 0 | 93 | 3 | 0 | .00 | |
| *1 T* | 11 | 0.1 | 0.0 | 5.7 | 0.0 | 319 | .00 | 0.0 | | | 3 | 3 | .03 | | |
| **butter blend, stick/soft, Blue Bonnet** | 90 | | 11.0 | 5.0 | 5 | | | | | | 95[a] | | | | |
| *1 T* | | 0.0 | 0.0 | 2.0 | | | | | | | 10[a] | | | | |
| **butter buds** | 12 | | 0.1 | | 0 | | | | | | 170 | | | | |
| *2 t dry*[b] | 4 | 0.0 | 2.9 | | | 7 | | | | | 3 | | | | |
| **buttermatch blend, Shedd's** | 90 | | 10.0 | | | | | | | | | | | | |
| *1 T* | 14 | 0.0 | 0.0 | | | | | | | | | | | | |
| **buttermatch blend, whipped, Shedd's** | 60 | | 7.0 | | | | | | | | | | | | |
| *1 T* | 10 | 0.0 | 0.0 | | | | | | | | | | | | |
| **buttery blend, liquid, Mrs. Filberts** | 120 | | 14.0 | 4.0 | 0 | | | | | | 60 | | | | |
| *1 T* | 14 | 0.0 | 0.0 | 3.0 | | | | | | | | | | | |
| | | | | | | | | | | | | | | | |
| **margarine by brand** | | | | | | | | | | | | | | | |
| Blue Bonnet soft | 100 | | 11.0 | 4.0 | 0 | | | | | | 95 | | | | |
| *1 T* | | 0.0 | 0.0 | 2.0 | | | | | | | 5 | | | | |
| Blue Bonnet soft, whipped | 70 | | 7.0 | 2.0 | 0 | | | | | | 70 | | | | |
| *1 T* | | 0.0 | 0.0 | 2.0 | | | | | | | 5 | | | | |
| Blue Bonnet, stick | 100 | | 11.0 | 3.0 | 0 | | | | | | 95 | | | | |
| *1 T* | | 0.0 | 0.0 | 2.0 | | | | | | | 5 | | | | |
| Blue Bonnet, stick, whipped | 70 | | 7.0 | 2.0 | 0 | | | | | | 70 | | | | |
| *1 T* | | 0.0 | 0.0 | 2.0 | | | | | | | 5 | | | | |
| Fleischmann's soft | 100 | | 11.0 | 5.0 | 0 | | | | | | 95[c] | | | | |
| *1 T* | | 0.0 | 0.0 | 2.0 | | | | | | | 5 | | | | |
| Fleischmann's squeeze | 100 | | 11.0 | 6.0 | 0 | | | | | | 85 | | | | |
| *1 T* | | 0.0 | 0.0 | 2.0 | | | | | | | 5 | | | | |
| Fleischmann's stick | 100 | | 11.0 | 4.0 | 0 | | | | | | 95[d] | | | | |
| *1 T* | | 0.0 | 0.0 | 2.0 | | | | | | | 5 | | | | |
| Fleischmann's whipped, lightly salted | 70 | | 7.0 | 3.0 | 0 | | | | | | 60[e] | | | | |
| *1 T* | | 0.0 | 0.0 | 2.0 | | | | | | | 5 | | | | |
| Mazola | 100 | 2.2 | 11.3 | 4.0 | 0 | | | | | | 100 | | | | |
| *1 T* | 14 | 0.0 | 0.2 | 1.9 | | 500 | | | | | | | | | |
| Mazola unsalted | 100 | 2.7 | 11.3 | 4.0 | 0 | | | | | | 0 | | | | |
| *1 T* | 14 | 0.0 | 0.0 | 1.9 | | 500 | | | | | | | | | |
| Nucoa | 100 | 2.3 | 11.3 | 3.3 | 0 | | | | | | 160 | | | | |
| *1 T* | 14 | 0.0 | 0.0 | 2.4 | | 500 | | | | | | | | | |
| Nucoa soft | 90 | 2.0 | 10.5 | 4.2 | 0 | | | | | | 150 | | | | |
| *1 T* | 13 | 0.0 | 0.1 | 2.0 | | 520 | | | | | | | | | |
| Shedd's liquid | 100 | | 11.0 | 6.0 | 0 | | | | | | 100 | | | | |
| *1 T* | 14 | 0.0 | 0.0 | 2.0 | | | | | | | | | | | |
| | | | | | | | | | | | | | | | |
| **margarine by form & type of oil** | | | | | | | | | | | | | | | |
| liquid, soybean & cottonseed | 34 | 0.7 | 3.8 | 1.7 | | 47 | 0 | .00 | .00 | 0 | 37 | 3 | 0 | | |
| *1 t* | 5 | 0.1 | 0.0 | 0.6 | | 155 | .00 | 0.0 | .01 | .01 | 4 | 2 | | | |
| stick, corn | 34 | 0.7 | 3.8 | 0.8 | | 47 | 0 | .00 | .00 | 0 | 44[f] | 1 | 0 | | |
| *1 t* | 5 | 0.0 | 0.0 | 0.6 | | 155 | .00 | 0.0 | .00 | .00 | 2 | 1 | | | |
| stick, safflower & soybean | 34 | 0.7 | 3.8 | 1.5 | | 47 | 0 | .00 | .00 | 0 | 44[f] | 1 | 0 | | |
| *1 t* | 5 | 0.0 | 0.0 | 0.6 | | 155 | .00 | 0.0 | .00 | .00 | 2 | 1 | | | |
| stick, soybean | 34 | 0.7 | 3.8 | 1.0 | | 47 | 0 | .00 | .00 | 0 | 44[f] | 1 | 0 | | |
| *1 t* | 5 | 0.0 | 0.0 | 0.8 | | 155 | .00 | 0.0 | .00 | .00 | 2 | 1 | | | |
| stick, soybean & cottonseed | 34 | 0.7 | 3.8 | 0.9 | | 47 | 0 | .00 | .00 | 0 | 44[f] | 1 | 0 | | |
| *1 t* | 5 | 0.0 | 0.0 | 0.8 | | 155 | .00 | 0.0 | .00 | .00 | 2 | 1 | | | |
| tub, corn | 34 | 0.8 | 3.8 | 1.5 | | 47 | 0 | .00 | .00 | 0 | 51[g] | 1 | 0 | | |
| *1 t* | 5 | 0.0 | 0.0 | 0.7 | | 158 | .00 | 0.0 | .00 | .00 | 2 | 1 | | | |
| tub, safflower | 34 | 0.8 | 3.8 | 2.1 | | 47 | 0 | .00 | .00 | 0 | 51[g] | 1 | 0 | | |
| *1 t* | 5 | 0.0 | 0.0 | 0.4 | | 155 | .00 | 0.0 | .00 | .00 | 2 | 1 | | | |
| tub, soybean | 34 | 0.8 | 3.8 | 1.3 | | 47 | 0 | .00 | .00 | 0 | 51[g] | 1 | 0 | | |
| *1 t* | 5 | 0.0 | 0.0 | 0.6 | | 155 | .00 | 0.0 | .00 | .00 | 2 | 1 | | | |
| tub, soybean & cottonseed | 34 | 0.8 | 3.8 | 1.4 | | 47 | 0 | .00 | .00 | 0 | 51[g] | 1 | 0 | | |
| *1 t* | 5 | 0.0 | 0.0 | 0.8 | | 155 | .00 | 0.0 | .00 | .00 | 2 | 1 | | | |

[a] Unsalted butter blend contains 0 mg sodium & 0 mg potassium.
[b] Corresponds to 2 T liquid (28 g).
[c] Unsalted soft margarine contains 0 mg sodium.
[d] Unsalted stick margarine contains 0 mg sodium.
[e] Unsalted whipped margarine contains 0 mg sodium.
[f] Unsalted stick margaring contains 1 mg sodium.
[g] Unsalted tub margarine contains 2 mg sodium.

| | KCAL | H₂O (g) | FAT (g) | PUFA (g) | CHOL (mg) | A (RE) | C (mg) | B-2 (mg) | B-6 (mg) | FOL (mcg) | Na (mg) | Ca (mg) | Mg (mg) | Zn (mg) | Mn (mg) |
|---|---|---|---|---|---|---|---|---|---|---|---|---|---|---|---|
| | WT (g) | PRO (g) | CHO (g) | SFA (g) | DFIB (g) | A (IU) | B-1 (mg) | NIA (mg) | B-12 (mcg) | PANT (mg) | K (mg) | P (mg) | Fe (mg) | Cu (mg) | |
| **margarine, imitation (diet) by brand** | | | | | | | | | | | | | | | |
| Blue Bonnet | 50 | | 6.0 | 2.0 | 0 | | | | | | 100 | | | | |
| *1 T* | | 0.0 | 0.0 | 1.0 | | | | | | | 5 | | | | |
| Fleischmann's | 50 | | 6.0 | 2.0 | 0 | | | | | | 100 | | | | |
| *1 T* | | 0.0 | 0.0 | 1.0 | | | | | | | 5 | | | | |
| Fleischmann's w/ lite salt | 50 | | 6.0 | 3.0 | 0 | | | | | | 50 | | | | |
| *1 T* | | 0.0 | 0.0 | 2.0 | | | | | | | 5 | | | | |
| Mazola diet | 50 | 8.1 | 5.5 | 2.4 | 0 | | | | | | 130 | | | | |
| *1 T* | 14 | 0.0 | 0.0 | 0.9 | | 500 | | | | | | | | | |
| Parkay, diet soft | 50 | 8.0 | 5.6 | 1.8 | 0 | | 0 | .00 | .00 | 0 | 90 | 1 | 0 | .00 | |
| *1 T* | 14 | 0.0 | 0.0 | 1.0 | | 526 | .00 | 0.0 | .00 | .00 | 4 | 1 | .00 | .007 | |
| **margarine, imitation (diet) by form & type of oil** | | | | | | | | | | | | | | | |
| tub, corn | 17 | 2.8 | 1.9 | 0.8 | | 48 | 0 | .00 | .00 | 0 | 46 | 1 | 0 | | |
| *1 t* | 5 | 0.0 | 0.0 | 0.3 | | 159 | .00 | 0.0 | .00 | .00 | 1 | 1 | | | |
| tub, soybean & cottonseed | 17 | 2.8 | 1.9 | 0.5 | | 48 | 0 | .00 | .00 | 0 | 46 | 1 | 0 | | |
| *1 t* | 5 | 0.0 | 0.0 | 0.3 | | 159 | .00 | 0.0 | .00 | .00 | 1 | 1 | | | |
| **mayonnaise** | | | | | | | | | | | | | | | |
| Best Foods/Hellmann's | 100 | 2.3 | 11.2 | 6.1 | 7 | | | | | | 80 | | | | |
| *1 T* | 14 | 0.2 | 0.1 | 1.7 | | | | | | | | | | | |
| safflower & soybean | 99 | 2.1 | 11.0 | 7.6 | | 39 | 0 | | | | 78 | 2 | | .02 | |
| *1 T* | 14 | 0.2 | 0.4 | 1.2 | 0.0 | | .00 | | | | 5 | 4 | .10 | | |
| soybean | 99 | 2.1 | 11.0 | 5.7 | 8 | 39 | 1 | | | | 78 | 2 | | .02 | |
| *1 T* | 14 | 0.2 | 0.4 | 1.6 | 0.0 | | .00 | | | | 5 | 4 | .10 | | |
| **mayonnaise, imitation, soybean** | 35 | 9.4 | 2.9 | 1.6 | 4 | | | | | | 75 | | | .02 | |
| *1 T* | 15 | 0.0 | 2.4 | 0.5 | 0.0 | | | | | | | | | | |
| **miracle whip, Kraft** | 69 | 5.1 | 6.9 | 4.1 | 6 | | 0 | .00 | .00 | 5 | 84 | 1 | 0 | .05 | |
| *1 T* | 14 | 0.1 | 1.7 | 1.1 | | 14 | .00 | 0.0 | .02 | .02 | 2 | 2 | .05 | .005 | |
| **miracle whip, light, Kraft** | 44 | 7.6 | 3.9 | 2.2 | 3 | | 0 | .00 | .00 | 5 | 96 | 1 | 0 | .05 | |
| *1 T* | 14 | 0.1 | 2.2 | 0.6 | | 14 | .00 | 0.0 | .04 | .01 | 1 | 3 | .05 | .005 | |
| **sandwich spread** | 60 | 6.2 | 5.2 | 3.1 | 12 | | | | | | | | | | |
| *1 T* | 15 | 0.1 | 3.4 | 0.8 | | | | | | | | | | | |
| **sandwich spread, Best Foods/Hellmann's** | 55 | 7.1 | 4.9 | 2.6 | 5 | | | | | | 175 | | | | |
| *1 T* | 15 | 0.1 | 2.4 | 0.8 | | | | | | | | | | | |
| **shedd's spread, Country Crock** | | | | | | | | | | | | | | | |
| corn oil | 50 | | 6.0 | | | | | | | | | | | | |
| *1 T* | 10 | 0.0 | 0.0 | | | | | | | | | | | | |
| soybean oil | 50 | | 5.0 | 2.0 | 0 | | | | | | 70 | | | | |
| *1 T* | 10 | 0.0 | 0.0 | 1.0 | | | | | | | | | | | |
| **vegetable oil spread by brand** | | | | | | | | | | | | | | | |
| Blue Bonnet, 52% veg oil | 80 | | 8.0 | 3.0 | 0 | | | | | | 110 | | | | |
| *1 T* | | 0.0 | 0.0 | 2.0 | | | | | | | 15 | | | | |
| Blue Bonnet, light tasty, 52% veg oil | 60 | | 7.0 | 2.0 | 0 | | | | | | 100 | | | | |
| *1 T* | | 0.0 | 0.0 | 1.0 | | | | | | | 10 | | | | |
| Blue Bonnet, stick, 60% fat | 50 | | 6.0 | 2.0 | 0 | | | | | | 55 | | | | |
| *1 T* | | 0.0 | 0.0 | 1.0 | | | | | | | 5 | | | | |
| Blue Bonnet, stick, 70% fat | 90 | | 10.0 | 3.0 | 0 | | | | | | 95 | | | | |
| *1 T* | | 0.0 | 0.0 | 2.0 | | | | | | | 10 | | | | |
| Blue Bonnet, stick, 75% fat | 90 | | 11.0 | 3.0 | 0 | | | | | | 95 | | | | |
| *1 T* | | 0.0 | 0.0 | 2.0 | | | | | | | 10 | | | | |
| Fleischmann's soft/stick, light corn oil | 80 | | 8.0 | 3.0 | 0 | | | | | | 70 | | | | |
| *1 T* | | 0.0 | 0.0 | 2.0 | | | | | | | 10 | | | | |
| **vegetable oil spread by form & type of oil** | | | | | | | | | | | | | | | |
| stick, soybean & palm | 26 | 1.8 | 2.9 | 0.9 | | 48 | 0 | .00 | .00 | 0 | 48 | 1 | 0 | | |
| *1 t* | 5 | 0.0 | 0.0 | 0.7 | | 159 | .00 | 0.0 | .00 | .00 | 1 | 1 | | | |
| stick, soybean & cottonseed | 26 | 1.8 | 2.9 | 0.3 | | 48 | 0 | .00 | .00 | 0 | 48 | 1 | 0 | | |
| *1 t* | 5 | 0.0 | 0.0 | 0.6 | | 159 | .00 | 0.0 | .00 | .00 | 1 | 1 | | | |

| | KCAL | H₂O (g) | FAT (g) | PUFA (g) | CHOL (mg) | A (RE) | C (mg) | B-2 (mg) | B-6 (mg) | FOL (mcg) | Na (mg) | Ca (mg) | Mg (mg) | Zn (mg) | Mn (mg) |
|---|---|---|---|---|---|---|---|---|---|---|---|---|---|---|---|
| | WT (g) | PRO (g) | CHO (g) | SFA (g) | DFIB (g) | A (IU) | B-1 (mg) | NIA (mg) | B-12 (mcg) | PANT (mg) | K (mg) | P (mg) | Fe (mg) | Cu (mg) | |

## 33. SUGARS, SYRUPS & OTHER SWEETENERS

| | KCAL / WT | H₂O / PRO | FAT / CHO | PUFA / SFA | CHOL / DFIB | A(RE) / A(IU) | C / B-1 | B-2 / NIA | B-6 / B-12 | FOL / PANT | Na / K | Ca / P | Mg / Fe | Zn / Cu | Mn |
|---|---|---|---|---|---|---|---|---|---|---|---|---|---|---|---|
| **honey** | 64 | 3.6 | 0.0 | | | | 0 | .01 | | | 1 | 1 | | | |
| *1 T* | 21 | 0.1 | 17.3 | | | 0 | .00 | 0.0 | | | 11 | 1 | .10 | | |
| **jams/preserves** | 54 | 5.8 | 0.0 | | | | 0ª | .01 | | | 2 | 4 | | | |
| *1 T* | 20 | 0.1 | 14.0 | | | 0 | .00 | 0.0 | | | 18 | 2 | .20 | | |
| **jelly** | 49 | 5.2 | 0.0 | | | | 1ᵇ | .01 | | | 3 | 4 | | | |
| *1 T* | 18 | 0.0 | 12.7 | | | 0 | .00 | 0.0 | | | 14 | 1 | .30 | | |
| **jelly, all flavors, Kraft** | 16 | 2.3 | 0.0 | 0.0 | 0 | | 0 | .00 | .00 | 5 | 2 | 1 | 0 | | |
| *1 t* | 7 | 0.0 | 4.2 | 0.0 | | 0 | .00 | 0.0 | .00 | .00 | 4 | 0 | .05 | | |
| **jelly, imitation, sweetened w/ saccharin,** | 4 | | 0.0 | | 0 | | | | | | 4 | | | | |
| **all flavors, Estee**—*1/2 oz* | 14 | 0.0 | 1.0 | | | | | | | | 20 | | | | |
| **marmalade, citrus** | 51 | 5.8 | 0.0 | 0.0 | | | 1 | .00 | | | 3 | 7 | | | |
| *1 T* | 20 | 0.1 | 14.0 | 0.0 | | | .00 | 0.0 | | | 7 | 12 | .10 | | |
| **molasses** | | | | | | | | | | | | | | | |
| barbados | 54 | 4.8 | 0.0 | | | | | .04 | | | | 49 | | | |
| *1 T* | 20 | 0.0 | 14.0 | | | | .01 | | | | | 10 | | | |
| blackstrap | 43 | 4.8 | 0.0 | 0.0 | | | | .04 | | | 19 | 137 | | | |
| *1 T* | 20 | 0.0 | 11.0 | 0.0 | | | .02 | 0.4 | | | 585 | 17 | 3.20 | | |
| light | 50 | 4.8 | 0.0 | 0.0 | | | | .01 | | | 3 | 33 | | | |
| *1 T* | 20 | 0.0 | 13.0 | 0.0 | | | .01 | 0.0 | | | 183 | 9 | .90 | | |
| med | 46 | 4.8 | 0.0 | 0.0 | | | | .02 | | | 7 | 58 | | | |
| *1 T* | 20 | 0.0 | 12.0 | 0.0 | | | | 0.2 | | | 213 | 14 | 1.20 | | |
| **preserves, strawberry, reduced calorie,** | 6 | 3.8 | 0.0 | 0.0 | 0 | | 0 | .00 | .00 | 1 | 7 | 1 | 0 | .00 | .010 |
| **Kraft**—*1 t* | 6 | 0.0 | 1.7 | 0.0 | | 0 | .00 | 0.0 | .00 | .00 | 9 | 8 | .02 | .001 | |
| **sugar** | | | | | | | | | | | | | | | |
| brown | 541 | 3.0 | 0.0 | 0.0 | | | 0 | .04 | | | 44 | 123 | | | |
| *1 cup not packed* | 145 | 0.0 | 139.8 | 0.0 | | 0 | .01 | 0.3 | | | 499 | 28 | 4.90 | | |
| powdered | 462 | 0.6 | 0.0 | 0.0 | | | 0 | .00 | | | 1 | 0 | | | |
| *1 cup* | 120 | 0.0 | 119.4 | 0.0 | | 0 | .00 | 0.0 | | | 4 | 0 | .10 | | |
| white, granulated | 15 | 0.0 | 0.0 | 0.0 | | | 0 | .00 | | | 0 | 0 | | | |
| *1 t* | 4 | 0.0 | 4.0 | 0.0 | | 0 | .00 | 0.0 | | | 0 | 0 | .00 | | |
| white, granulated | 46 | 0.1 | 0.0 | 0.0 | | | 0 | .00 | | | 0 | 0 | | | |
| *1 T* | 12 | 0.0 | 11.9 | 0.0 | | 0 | .00 | 0.0 | | | 0 | 0 | .00 | | |
| white, granulated | 770 | 1.0 | 0.0 | 0.0 | | | 0 | .00 | | | 2 | 0 | | | |
| *1 cup* | 200 | 0.0 | 199.0 | 0.0 | | 0 | .00 | 0.0 | | | 6 | 0 | .20 | | |
| **sugar substitute** | | | | | | | | | | | | | | | |
| equal powderᶜ | 4 | | 0.0 | | | | | | | | 0 | | | | |
| *1 g pkt* | 1 | 0.0 | 1.0 | | | | | | | | | | | | |
| equal tabletᵈ | 0 | | 0.0 | | | | | | | | 0 | | | | |
| *1 tablet* | | 0.0 | 0.7 | | | | | | | | | | | | |
| sprinkle sweet | 2 | 0.2 | 0.0 | | | | 0 | .00 | | | 1 | 0 | | | |
| *1 t* | 0.7 | 0.0 | 0.5 | | | 0 | .00 | 0.0 | | | 0 | 0 | .00 | | |
| sweet 'n low | 4 | | 0.0 | | 0 | | | | | | 4 | | | | |
| *1 pkt* | 1 | 0.0 | 0.9 | | | | | | | | 3 | | | | |
| sweet 10 | 0 | | 0.0 | | | | | | | | 0 | | | | |
| *1/8 t* | 0.8 | 0.0 | 0.0 | | | 0 | .00 | 0.0 | | | 0 | 0 | .00 | | |
| **syrup** | | | | | | | | | | | | | | | |
| cane & maple | 50 | 6.5 | 0.0 | | | | 0 | .00 | | | 0 | 3 | | | |
| *1 T* | 20 | 0.0 | 12.8 | | | 0 | .00 | 0.0 | | | 5 | 0 | .00 | | |
| corn | 59 | 4.9 | 0.0 | | | | 0 | .00 | | | 14 | 9 | | | |
| *1 T* | 21 | 0.0 | 15.4 | | | 0 | .00 | 0.0 | | | 1 | 3 | .80 | | |

ᵃ For cherry/strawberry jams/preserves Vit C = 3 mg.
ᵇ For guava jelly, Vit C = 7 mg.
ᶜ Contains dextrose w/ dried corn syrup, aspartame, silicon dioxide, cellulose, tribasic calcium phosphate & cellulose derivatives.
ᵈ Contains lactose, aspartame, maltodextrin, leucine, cellulose & cellulose derivatives.

| | KCAL | H₂O (g) | FAT (g) | PUFA (g) | CHOL (mg) | A (RE) | C (mg) | B-2 (mg) | B-6 (mg) | FOL (mcg) | Na (mg) | Ca (mg) | Mg (mg) | Zn (mg) | Mn (mg) |
|---|---|---|---|---|---|---|---|---|---|---|---|---|---|---|---|
| | WT (g) | PRO (g) | CHO (g) | SFA (g) | DFIB (g) | A (IU) | B-1 (mg) | NIA (mg) | B-12 (mcg) | PANT (mg) | K (mg) | P (mg) | Fe (mg) | Cu (mg) | |
| corn, dark, Karo | 60 | 5.4 | 0.0 | | | | | | | | | 40 | | | |
| *1 T* | 21 | 0.0 | 15.0ᵃ | | | | | | | | | | | | |
| corn, light, Karo | 60 | 5.4 | 0.0 | | | | | | | | | 30 | | | |
| *1 T* | 21 | 0.0 | 14.9ᵇ | | | | | | | | | | | | |
| maple | 50 | 6.5 | 0.0 | | | | 0 | | | | 2 | 20 | | | |
| *1 T* | 20 | 0.0 | 12.8 | | | | | | | | 35 | 2 | .20 | | |
| maple honey, Log Cabin | 106 | 10.7 | 0.0 | 0.0 | 0 | | 0 | .00 | .00 | | 7 | 7 | | | |
| *1 fl oz* | 39 | 0.0 | 28.1 | 0.0 | 0.0 | 0 | .00 | 0.0 | .00 | .00 | 6 | 2 | .43 | .047 | |
| **pancake & waffle** | | | | | | | | | | | | | | | |
| Aunt Jemima | 103 | | 0.0 | | | | | .00 | .00 | 0 | 21 | 0 | 0 | .00 | .000 |
| *1 fl oz* | 40 | 0.0 | 25.8 | | | 0 | .00 | 0.0 | .00 | .00 | 3 | 0 | .00 | .000 | |
| Aunt Jemima butter lite | 52 | | 0.0 | | | | | .00 | .00 | 0 | 67 | 0 | 0 | .00 | .000 |
| *1 fl oz* | 34 | 0.0 | 12.9 | | | 0 | .00 | 0.0 | .00 | .00 | 0 | 0 | .00 | .000 | |
| Aunt Jemima lite | 60 | | 0.0 | | | | | .00 | .00 | 0 | 66 | 0 | 0 | .00 | .000 |
| *1 fl oz* | 34 | 0.0 | 15.1 | | | 0 | .00 | 0.0 | .00 | .00 | 1 | 0 | .00 | .000 | |
| Golden Griddle | 57 | 5.7 | 0.0 | | | | | | | | | 15 | | | |
| *1 T* | 20 | 0.0 | 14.2ᶜ | | | | | | | | | | | | |
| Karo | 60 | 5.5 | 0.0 | | | | | | | | | 35 | | | |
| *1 T* | 21 | 0.0 | 14.9ᵈ | | | | | | | | | | | | |
| Log Cabin | 99 | 12.7 | 0.0 | 0.0 | 0 | | 0 | .00 | .00 | 0 | 38 | 2 | 1 | .04 | |
| *1 fl oz* | 39 | 0.0 | 26.1 | 0.0 | 0.0 | 0 | .00 | 0.0 | .00 | .00 | 3 | 1 | .06 | .003 | |
| Log Cabin buttered | 105 | 11.9 | 0.6 | 0.0 | 2 | | 0 | .00 | .00 | 0 | 74 | 5 | 0 | .00 | |
| *1 fl oz* | 39 | 0.0 | 26.1 | 0.4 | 0.0 | 24 | .00 | 0.0 | .00 | .00 | 1 | 2 | .41 | .036 | |
| Log Cabin country kitchen | 101 | 12.7 | 0.0 | 0.0 | 0 | | 0 | .00 | .00 | 0 | 19 | 11 | | | |
| *1 fl oz* | 39 | 0.0 | 26.0 | 0.0 | 0.0 | 0 | .00 | 0.0 | .00 | .00 | 1 | 4 | .95 | .083 | |
| Log Cabin lite | 61 | 19.8 | 0.0 | 0.0 | 0 | | 0 | .00 | .00 | 0 | 84 | 0 | 0 | .00 | |
| *1 fl oz* | 36 | 0.0 | 15.8 | 0.0 | 0.0 | 0 | .00 | 0.0 | .00 | .00 | 1 | 15 | .01 | .001 | |
| sorghum | 53 | 4.7 | 0.0 | | | | | .02 | | | | 35 | | | |
| *1 T* | 21 | 0.0 | 14.0 | | | | | 0.0 | | | | 5 | 2.60 | | |

## 34. VEGETABLES, VEGETABLE PRODUCTS & VEGETABLE SALADSᵉ

| | KCAL | H₂O (g) | FAT (g) | PUFA (g) | CHOL (mg) | A (RE) | C (mg) | B-2 (mg) | B-6 (mg) | FOL (mcg) | Na (mg) | Ca (mg) | Mg (mg) | Zn (mg) | Mn (mg) |
|---|---|---|---|---|---|---|---|---|---|---|---|---|---|---|---|
| **adzuki beans** | | | | | | | | | | | | | | | |
| boiled | 294 | 152.5 | 0.2 | | 0 | 1 | 0 | .15 | | | 18 | 63 | 120 | 4.06 | 1.318 |
| *1 cup* | 230 | 17.3 | 57.0 | | | 13 | .27 | 1.6 | .00 | | 1224 | 385 | 4.60 | .685 | |
| cnd, sweetened | 702 | 120.1 | 0.1 | | 0 | | | | | | 646 | 66 | 91 | | |
| *1 cup* | 296 | 11.3 | 162.8 | | | | | | .00 | | 353 | 220 | 3.34 | | |
| w/ sugar (yokan) | 112 | 15.2 | 0.1 | | 0 | | | | | | 36 | 12 | 8 | | |
| *three 1/4" thick slices* | 43 | 1.4 | 26.1 | | | | | | .00 | | 19 | 17 | .50 | | |
| **alfalfa seeds, sprouted, raw** | 10 | 30.1 | 0.2 | 0.1 | 0 | 5 | 3 | .04 | .01 | 12 | 2 | 10 | 9 | .30 | .062 |
| *1 cup* | 33 | 1.3 | 1.3 | 0.0 | 0.7 | 51 | .03 | 0.2 | .00 | .19 | 26 | 23 | .32 | .052 | |
| **amaranth, boiled** | 14 | 60.4 | 0.1 | 0.1 | 0 | 183 | 27 | .09 | | | 14 | 138 | 36 | | |
| *1/2 cup* | 66 | 1.4 | 2.7 | 0.0 | | 1828 | .01 | 0.4 | .00 | | 423 | 47 | 1.49 | | |
| **arrowhead, boiled** | 9 | 9.3 | 0.0 | | | 0 | 0 | .01 | | | 2 | 1 | 6 | | |
| *1 med corm (1" diameter)* | 12 | 0.5 | 1.9 | | | 0 | .02 | 0.1 | .00 | | 106 | 24 | .15 | | |
| **artichoke** | | | | | | | | | | | | | | | |
| boiled | 53 | 103.8 | 0.2 | 0.1 | 0 | 17 | 9 | .06 | .10 | 54 | 79 | 47 | 47 | .43 | .328 |
| *1 med* | 300ᶠ | 2.8 | 12.4 | 0.0 | | 172 | .07 | 0.7 | .00 | .24 | 316 | 72 | 1.62 | .083 | |
| frzn, boiled | 36 | 69.2 | 0.4 | 0.2 | 0 | 13 | 4 | .13 | .07 | 95 | 42 | 17 | 25 | .29 | .218 |
| *2.8 oz* | 80 | 2.5 | 7.3 | 0.1 | | 131 | .05 | 0.7 | .00 | .16 | 211 | 49 | .45 | .049 | |
| **artichoke hearts, boiled** | 37 | 72.7 | 0.1 | 0.1 | 0 | 12 | 6 | .04 | .07 | 37 | 55 | 33 | 33 | .30 | .229 |
| *1/2 cup* | 84 | 1.9 | 8.7 | 0.0 | | 121 | .05 | 0.5 | .00 | .17 | 221 | 50 | 1.13 | .051 | |
| **asparagus** | | | | | | | | | | | | | | | |
| boiled | 22 | 82.8 | 0.3 | 0.1 | 0 | 75 | 18 | .11 | .13 | 88 | 4 | 22 | 17 | .43 | .187 |
| *1/2 cup (6 spears)* | 90 | 2.3 | 4.0 | 0.1 | | 746 | .09 | 0.9 | .00 | .15 | 279 | 54 | .59 | .090 | |

ᵃ 0.3 g fructose, 3.1 g glucose, 0.6 g sucrose, 2.0 g maltose, 1.6 g trisaccharides & 7.4 g other polysaccharides.

ᵇ 0.4 g fructose, 3.9 g glucose, 1.9 g maltose, 1.6 g trisaccharides & 7.1 g other polysaccharides.

ᶜ 0.9 g fructose, 3.2 g glucose, 2.2 g disaccharides, 1.6 g trisaccharides & 6.3 g other polysaccharides.

ᵈ 0.8 g fructose, 3.6 g glucose, 1.9 g maltose, 1.5 g trisaccharides & 7.1 g other polysaccharides.

ᵉ Beans are listed by type unless the product is specified simply as "beans".

ᶠ Weight w/ refuse.

| | KCAL / WT (g) | H2O (g) / PRO (g) | FAT (g) / CHO (g) | PUFA (g) / SFA (g) | CHOL (mg) / DFIB (g) | A (RE) / A (IU) | C (mg) / B-1 (mg) | B-2 (mg) / NIA (mg) | B-6 (mg) / B-12 (mcg) | FOL (mcg) / PANT (mg) | Na (mg) / K (mg) | Ca (mg) / P (mg) | Mg (mg) / Fe (mg) | Zn (mg) / Cu (mg) | Mn (mg) |
|---|---|---|---|---|---|---|---|---|---|---|---|---|---|---|---|
| cnd | 24 | 113.7 | 0.8 | 0.3 | 0 | | | | | 116 | | | | .49 | |
| 1/2 cup | 121 | 2.6 | 3.0 | 0.2 | | | | | .00 | | | | 2.22 | .116 | |
| frzn, boiled | 17 | 54.7 | 0.3 | 0.1 | 0 | 49 | 15 | .06 | .01 | 81 | 2 | 14 | 8 | .33 | .111 |
| 4 spears | 60 | 1.8 | 2.9 | 0.1 | | 491 | .04 | 0.6 | .00 | .10 | 131 | 33 | .38 | .103 | |
| **avocado, raw** | | | | | | | | | | | | | | | |
| calif | 306 | 125.5 | 30.0 | 3.5 | 0 | 106 | 14 | .21 | .48 | 113 | 21 | 19 | 70 | .73 | .422 |
| 1 med | 173 | 3.6 | 12.0 | 4.5 | 4.7 | 1059 | .19 | 3.3 | .00 | 1.68 | 1097 | 73 | 2.04 | .460 | |
| florida | 339 | 242.4 | 27.0 | 4.5 | 0 | 186 | 24 | .37 | .85 | 162 | 14 | 33 | 104 | 1.28 | .517 |
| 1 med | 304 | 4.8 | 27.1 | 5.3 | | 1860 | .33 | 5.8 | .00 | 2.95 | 1484 | 119 | 1.60 | .763 | |
| **bamboo shoots** | | | | | | | | | | | | | | | |
| raw | 21 | 69.2 | 0.2 | 0.1 | 0 | 2 | 3 | .05 | | | 3 | 10 | 2 | | |
| 1/2 cup | 76 | 2.0 | 4.0 | 0.1 | 2.0 | 15 | .11 | 0.5 | .00 | | 405 | 45 | .38 | | |
| boiled | 15 | 115.1 | 0.3 | 0.1 | 0 | 0 | 0 | .06 | | | 5 | 14 | 3 | | |
| 1 cup | 120 | 1.8 | 2.3 | 0.1 | | 0 | .02 | 0.4 | .00 | | 640 | 24 | .29 | | |
| cnd | 25 | 123.6 | 0.5 | 0.2 | 0 | 1 | 1 | .03 | | | 9 | 10 | 6 | | |
| 1 cup | 131 | 2.3 | 4.2 | 0.1 | | 11 | .03 | .18 | .00 | | 104 | 33 | .42 | | |
| **bean salad, cnd** | | | | | | | | | | | | | | | |
| 3 bean, Joan of Arc | 90 | | 0.3 | | | | 2 | .05 | | | 920 | 44 | | | |
| 1/2 cup | 127 | 2.2 | 19.8 | | | 239 | .05 | 0.9 | | | 188 | 39 | 1.02 | | |
| 3 bean, Pillsbury | 80 | 91.5 | 0.2 | | | | 3 | .06 | | | 522 | 31 | | | |
| 1/2 cup | 113 | 2.3 | 17.4 | | | 305 | .03 | 0.4 | | | 116 | 42 | .34 | | |
| 4 bean, Joan of Arc | 120 | | 0.2 | | | | 3 | .04 | | | 894 | 46 | | | |
| 1/2 cup | 138 | 2.8 | 26.9 | | | 282 | .06 | 0.7 | | | 185 | 48 | 1.10 | | |
| **beans, cnd** | | | | | | | | | | | | | | | |
| baked | | | | | | | | | | | | | | | |
| B&M | 330 | | 8.0 | | | | | | | | 770 | | | | |
| 7/8 cup | 227 | 16.0 | 49.0 | | | | | | | | 840 | | | | |
| Friend's | 360 | | 5.0 | | | | | | | | 1270 | | | | |
| 1 cup | 255 | 17.0 | 62.0 | | | | | | | | | | | | |
| B&M | 290 | | 4.0 | | | | | | | | 1050 | | | | |
| 7/8 cup | 227 | 15.0 | 49.0 | | | | | | | | 1010 | | | | |
| Campbell's | 248 | | 4.0 | | | | 5 | .07 | | | 1037 | 95 | | | |
| 7.9 oz | 223 | 10.8 | 42.3 | | | 501 | .10 | 1.1 | | | 632 | | 3.00 | | |
| Special Recipe | 217 | | 3.5 | | | | 5 | .06 | | | 907 | 83 | | | |
| 6.9 oz | 195 | 9.4 | 37.0 | | | 438 | .09 | 1.0 | | | 552 | | 2.60 | | |
| Joan of Arc | 100 | | 1.1 | | | | 0 | .10 | | | 691 | 35 | | | |
| 1/2 cup | 119 | 6.1 | 16.7 | | | 495 | .12 | 0.8 | | | 224 | 113 | 2.14 | | |
| mexican, Van Camp's | 210 | 171.2 | 2.4 | | | | | .14 | | | 718 | 75 | | | |
| 1 cup | 227 | 11.4 | 35.8 | | | 1595 | .12 | 0.9 | | | 640 | | 4.42 | | |
| baked, garden style, Special Recipe | 191 | | 1.5 | | | | 3 | .08 | | | 807 | 128 | | | |
| 6.9 oz | 195 | 7.2 | 37.2 | | | 638 | .09 | 0.5 | | | 421 | | 2.90 | | |
| baked, homestyle, Campbell's | 265 | | 3.1 | | | | 6 | .07 | | | 1105 | 133 | | | |
| 8 oz | 227 | 11.5 | 47.8 | | | 343 | .09 | 1.1 | | | 584 | | 4.00 | | |
| baked, honey, B&M | 280 | | 2.0 | | | | | | | | 940 | | | | |
| 7/8 cup | 227 | 15.0 | 50.0 | | | | | | | | 930 | | | | |
| baked, maple, Friend's | 280 | | 2.0 | | | | | | | | 1000 | | | | |
| 7/8 cup | 227 | 15.0 | 50.0 | | | | | | | | | | | | |
| baked, new england style, Special Recipe—6.9 oz | 256 | | 4.4 | | | | 5 | .11 | | | 755 | 172 | | | |
| | 195 | 10.3 | 43.9 | | | 0 | .06 | 0.4 | | | 350 | | 4.20 | | |
| baked, old fashioned, Special Recipe 6.9 oz | 225 | | 3.8 | | | | 5 | .08 | | | 817 | 126 | | | |
| | 195 | 7.7 | 39.9 | | | 0 | .09 | 0.6 | | | 307 | | 2.90 | | |
| baked, ranchero, Campbell's | 216 | | 4.6 | | | | 6 | .08 | | | 841 | 90 | | | |
| 7.7 oz | 219 | 10.3 | 33.4 | | | 601 | .10 | 0.9 | | | 668 | | 3.80 | | |
| baked, tomato, B&M | 270 | | 3.0 | | | | | | | | 1010 | | | | |
| 7/8 cup | 227 | 12.0 | 48.0 | | | | | | | | 920 | | | | |
| baked, vegetarian | 235 | 184.5 | 1.1 | 0.5 | 0 | 43 | | .15 | .34 | 61 | 1008 | 128 | 82 | 3.55 | .879 |
| 1 cup | 254 | 12.2 | 52.1 | 0.3 | 6.6 | 434 | .39 | 1.1 | .00 | .24 | 752 | 264 | .74 | .523 | |

| Food | KCAL / WT (g) | H₂O (g) / PRO (g) | FAT (g) / CHO (g) | PUFA (g) / SFA (g) | CHOL (mg) / DFIB (g) | A (RE) / A (IU) | C (mg) / B-1 (mg) | B-2 (mg) / NIA (mg) | B-6 (mg) / B-12 (mcg) | FOL (mcg) / PANT (mg) | Na (mg) / K (mg) | Ca (mg) / P (mg) | Mg (mg) / Fe (mg) | Zn (mg) / Cu (mg) | Mn (mg) |
|---|---|---|---|---|---|---|---|---|---|---|---|---|---|---|---|
| baked, western, Van Camp's | 207 | 173.7 | 3.8 | | | | | .14 | | | 1006 | 73 | | | |
| 1 cup | 227 | 11.1 | 32.0 | | | 1962 | .11 | 0.9 | | | 589 | | 2.71 | | |
| baked w/ brown sugar, Van Camp's | 284 | 155.9 | 5.1 | | | | | .12 | | | 692 | 121 | | | |
| 1 cup | 227 | 11.6 | 47.8 | | | 0 | .09 | 0.9 | | | 535 | | 3.83 | | |
| baked w/ molasses & brown sugar, Campbell's—8 oz | 265 | | 2.9 | | | | 9 | .06 | | | 1017 | 128 | | | |
| | 227 | 11.3 | 48.5 | | | 116 | .06 | 0.8 | | | 600 | | | | |
| baked w/ pork & sweet sce | 282 | 178.9 | 3.7 | 0.5 | 17 | 29 | 8 | .15 | .22 | 95 | 849 | 155 | 87 | 3.80 | .939 |
| 1 cup | 253 | 13.4 | 53.1 | 1.4 | | 289 | .12 | 0.9 | .06 | .26 | 673 | 266 | 4.20 | .253 | |
| baked w/ pork & tomato sce | 247 | 183.9 | 2.6 | 0.3 | 17 | 31 | 8 | .12 | .18 | 57 | 1113 | 141 | 88 | 14.83 | 1.240 |
| 1 cup | 253 | 13.1 | 49.1 | 1.0 | 5.6 | 313 | .13 | 1.3 | .03 | 1.34 | 759 | 297 | 8.30 | .643 | |
| Campbell's | 237 | | 2.9 | | | | 5 | .05 | | | 730 | 102 | | | |
| 8 oz | 227 | 9.9 | 42.9 | | | 330 | .13 | 0.6 | | | 400 | | 3.60 | | |
| Joan of Arc | 130 | | 0.7 | | | | 1 | .07 | | | 688 | 60 | | | |
| 1/2 cup | 133 | 6.5 | 23.9 | | | 86 | .07 | 1.0 | | | 245 | 82 | 3.86 | | |
| Van Camp's | 216 | 168.9 | 1.9 | | | | | .12 | | | 1011 | 97 | | | |
| 1 cup | 227 | 10.9 | 38.8 | | | 164 | .12 | 1.0 | | | 563 | | 4.29 | | |
| **beans, baked, homemade**[a] | 382 | 164.9 | 13.0 | 1.9 | 13 | 0 | 3 | .12 | .23 | 122 | 1068 | 155 | 110 | 1.84 | .645 |
| 1 cup | 253 | 14.0 | 54.1 | 4.9 | | 1 | .34 | 1.0 | .03 | .39 | 907 | 275 | 5.04 | .402 | |
| **beans, refried, cnd** | 270 | 182.9 | 2.7 | 0.3 | | | 15 | .14 | | | 1071 | 118 | 99 | 3.45 | |
| 1 cup | 253 | 15.8 | 46.8 | 1.0 | | | .12 | 1.2 | | | 994 | 214 | 4.47 | 1.040 | |
| **beet greens, boiled** | 20 | 64.2 | 0.1 | 0.1 | 0 | 367 | 18 | .21 | .10 | | 173 | 82 | 49 | .36 | |
| 1/2 cup | 72 | 1.9 | 3.9 | 0.0 | | 3672 | .08 | .36 | .00 | .24 | 654 | 29 | 1.37 | .181 | |
| **beets** | | | | | | | | | | | | | | | |
| boiled | 26 | 77.3 | 0.0 | 0.0 | 0 | 1 | 5 | .01 | .03 | 45 | 42 | 9 | 31 | .21 | .204 |
| 1/2 cup slices | 85 | 0.9 | 5.7 | 0.0 | | 11 | .03 | 0.2 | .00 | .08 | 266 | 26 | .53 | .048 | |
| cnd | 27 | 77.3 | 0.1 | 0.0 | 0 | | | | | | | 2 | | .18 | .244 |
| 1/2 cup slices | 85 | 0.8 | 6.1 | 0.0 | | | | .00 | | | | | 1.55 | .050 | |
| cnd, harvard | 89 | 98.6 | 0.1 | 0.0 | 0 | | 3 | .06 | | | 199 | 13 | 24 | | |
| 1/2 cup slices | 123 | 1.0 | 22.4 | 0.0 | | | | 0.1 | .00 | | 201 | 21 | .44 | | |
| cnd, pickled | 75 | 93.3 | 0.1 | 0.0 | 0 | 1 | 3 | .06 | | | 301 | 13 | 18 | .30 | |
| 1/2 cup slices | 114 | 0.9 | 18.6 | 0.0 | | 7 | .03 | 0.3 | .00 | | 169 | 20 | .47 | .132 | |
| **black beans, boiled** | 227 | 113.1 | 0.9 | 0.4 | 0 | 1 | 0 | .10 | .12 | 256 | 1 | 47 | 121 | 1.92 | .764 |
| 1 cup | 172 | 15.2 | 40.8 | 0.2 | 7.2 | 10 | .42 | 0.9 | .00 | .42 | 611 | 241 | 3.60 | .359 | |
| **black turtle beans** | | | | | | | | | | | | | | | |
| boiled | 241 | 121.6 | 0.6 | 0.3 | 0 | 1 | 0 | .10 | .14 | 158 | 6 | 103 | 91 | 1.41 | .605 |
| 1 cup | 185 | 15.1 | 45.1 | 0.2 | | 11 | .42 | 1.0 | .00 | .48 | 801 | 282 | 5.27 | .498 | |
| cnd | 218 | 181.5 | 0.7 | 0.3 | 0 | 1 | 6 | .29 | .13 | 146 | 922 | 84 | 84 | 1.30 | .559 |
| 1 cup | 240 | 14.5 | 39.7 | 0.2 | | 10 | .34 | 1.5 | .00 | .44 | 739 | 260 | 4.56 | .461 | |
| **broadbeans** | | | | | | | | | | | | | | | |
| boiled | 186 | 121.6 | 0.7 | 0.3 | 0 | 3 | 1 | .15 | .12 | 177 | 8 | 62 | 73 | 1.72 | .716 |
| 1 cup | 170 | 12.9 | 33.4 | 0.1 | 8.7 | 26 | .17 | 1.2 | .00 | .27 | 456 | 212 | 2.54 | .440 | |
| cnd | 183 | 205.6 | 0.6 | 0.2 | 0 | 3 | 5 | .13 | .12 | 84 | 1161 | 67 | 82 | 1.60 | .737 |
| 1 cup | 256 | 14.0 | 31.8 | 0.1 | | 26 | .05 | 2.5 | .00 | .31 | 620 | 202 | 2.56 | .279 | |
| falafel[b] | 170 | 17.7 | 9.1 | 2.1 | 0 | 1 | 1 | .09 | .06 | 40 | 150 | 27 | 42 | .77 | .352 |
| 3 patties w/ 2 1/4" diameter | 51 | 6.8 | 16.2 | 1.2 | | 7 | .07 | 0.5 | .00 | .15 | 298 | 98 | 1.74 | .132 | |
| **broccoli** | | | | | | | | | | | | | | | |
| raw | 12 | 39.9 | 0.2 | 0.1 | 0 | 68 | 41 | .05 | .07 | 31 | 12 | 21 | 11 | .18 | .101 |
| 1/2 cup chopped | 44 | 1.3 | 2.3 | 0.0 | 0.6 | 678 | .03 | 0.3 | .00 | .24 | 143 | 29 | .39 | .020 | |
| boiled | 23 | 70.4 | 0.2 | 0.1 | 0 | 110 | 49 | .16 | .15 | 54 | 8 | 89 | 47 | .12 | .191 |
| 1/2 cup | 78 | 2.3 | 4.3 | 0.0 | | 1099 | .06 | 0.6 | .00 | .23 | 127 | 37 | .89 | .054 | |
| **frzn** | | | | | | | | | | | | | | | |
| chopped, boiled | 25 | 83.5 | 0.1 | 0.1 | 0 | 174 | 37 | .08 | .12 | 52 | 22 | 47 | 19 | .28 | .299 |
| 1/2 cup | 92 | 2.9 | 4.9 | 0.0 | 2.0 | 1741 | .05 | 0.4 | .00 | .25 | 166 | 51 | .56 | .040 | |
| spears, boiled | 25 | 83.5 | 0.1 | 0.1 | 0 | 174 | 37 | .08 | .12 | 79 | 22 | 47 | 19 | .28 | .299 |
| 1/2 cup | 92 | 2.9 | 4.9 | 0.0 | 2.0 | 1741 | .05 | 0.4 | .00 | .25 | 166 | 51 | .56 | .040 | |
| spears w/ butter sce, Pillsbury | 51 | 94.3 | 2.0 | | | | 31 | .07 | | | 387 | 38 | | | |
| 1/2 cup | 106 | 2.1 | 5.9 | | | 245 | .02 | 0.4 | | | 166 | 47 | .39 | | |

[a] White beans, onions, salt pork, molasses, brown sugar, vinegar, salt, pepper & dry mustard.   [b] Broadbeans, soybean oil, onions, flour, salt, garlic, coriander & cumin.

| | KCAL / WT (g) | H₂O (g) / PRO (g) | FAT (g) / CHO (g) | PUFA (g) / SFA (g) | CHOL (mg) / DFIB (g) | A (RE) / A (IU) | C (mg) / B-1 (mg) | B-2 (mg) / NIA (mg) | B-6 (mg) / B-12 (mcg) | FOL (mcg) / PANT (mg) | Na (mg) / K (mg) | Ca (mg) / P (mg) | Mg (mg) / Fe (mg) | Zn (mg) / Cu (mg) | Mn (mg) |
|---|---|---|---|---|---|---|---|---|---|---|---|---|---|---|---|
| w/ cheddar cheese sce, Pillsbury | 60 | 95.9 | 2.5 | | | | 38 | .10 | | | 436 | 70 | | | |
| *1/2 cup* | 109 | 3.1 | 6.2 | | | 308 | .03 | 0.7 | | | 158 | 71 | .33 | | |
| w/ cheese sce, Birds Eye | 116 | 117.4 | 6.2 | 0.9 | 6 | | 43 | .19 | .13 | 68 | 488 | 109 | 20 | .47 | |
| *1/2 cup* | 142 | 4.8 | 11.6 | 1.9 | | 3490 | .06 | 0.5 | .30 | .42 | 249 | 103 | .76 | .040 | |
| w/ creamy italian cheese sce, | 90 | 109.1 | 5.6 | 0.4 | 14 | | 47 | .15 | .13 | 74 | 391 | 93 | 17 | .43 | |
| Birds Eye—*1/2 cup* | 128 | 5.0 | 6.6 | 3.0 | | 1941 | .06 | 0.5 | .25 | .32 | 225 | 86 | .91 | .036 | |
| **brussels sprouts** | | | | | | | | | | | | | | | |
| boiled | 30 | 68.1 | 0.4 | 0.2 | 0 | 56 | 48 | .06 | .14 | 47 | 17 | 28 | 16 | .25 | .177 |
| *1/2 cup (4 sprouts)* | 78 | 2.0 | 6.8 | 0.1 | 1.1 | 561 | .08 | 0.5 | .00 | .20 | 247 | 44 | .94 | .065 | |
| frzn | | | | | | | | | | | | | | | |
| boiled | 33 | 67.7 | 0.3 | 0.2 | 0 | 46 | 36 | .09 | .23 | 79 | 18 | 19 | 19 | .28 | .250 |
| *1/2 cup* | 78 | 2.8 | 6.5 | 0.1 | 1.4 | 459 | .08 | 0.4 | .00 | .27 | 254 | 42 | .58 | .065 | |
| w/ butter sce, Pillsbury | 60 | 81.9 | 1.0 | | | | 59 | .08 | | | 296 | 28 | | | |
| *1/2 cup* | 102 | 2.9 | 9.8 | | | 785 | .09 | 0.7 | | | 298 | 49 | .45 | | |
| w/ cheese sce, Birds Eye | 113 | 103.0 | 5.6 | 0.9 | 5 | | 56 | .19 | .13 | 90 | 417 | 77 | 21 | .40 | |
| *1/2 cup* | 128 | 5.0 | 12.5 | 1.7 | | 2622 | .09 | 0.6 | .26 | .38 | 359 | 96 | .84 | .028 | |
| w/ cheese sce, Pillsbury | 79 | 97.9 | 1.5 | | | | 59 | .18 | | | 493 | 67 | | | |
| *1/2 cup* | 118 | 3.1 | 13.0 | | | 610 | .06 | 1.2 | | | 325 | 185 | .52 | | |
| **burdock root, boiled** | 110 | 94.6 | 0.2 | | 0 | 0 | | .07 | | | 5 | 62 | 49 | | |
| *1 cup* | 125 | 2.6 | 26.4 | | | 0 | .05 | 0.4 | .00 | | 450 | 116 | .96 | | |
| **butter beans** | | | | | | | | | | | | | | | |
| cnd, Joan of Arc | 100 | | 0.4 | | | | 0 | .05 | | | 434 | 40 | | | |
| *1/2 cup* | 122 | 5.7 | 18.3 | | | 59 | .06 | 0.6 | | | 254 | 93 | 1.83 | | |
| cnd, Van Camp's | 162 | 180.9 | 0.5 | | | | | .08 | | | 752 | 41 | | | |
| *1 cup* | 227 | 11.0 | 28.4 | | | 0 | .09 | 0.5 | | | 639 | | 3.78 | | |
| **butterbur (fuki), boiled** | 8 | 96.7 | 0.0 | | 0 | 3 | 19 | .01 | | | 4 | 59 | 8 | | |
| *3.5 oz* | 100 | 0.2 | 2.2 | | | 27 | .01 | 0.1 | .00 | | 354 | 7 | .10 | | |
| **cabbage, chinese (pak-choi)** | | | | | | | | | | | | | | | |
| raw | 5 | 33.4 | 0.1 | 0.0 | 0 | 105 | 16 | .03 | | | 23 | 37 | 7 | | |
| *1/2 cup shredded* | 35 | 0.5 | 0.8 | 0.0 | | 1050 | .01 | 0.2 | .00 | | 83 | 13 | .28 | | |
| boiled | 10 | 81.2 | 0.1 | 0.1 | 0 | 218 | 22 | .05 | | | 29 | 79 | 9 | | |
| *1/2 cup shredded* | 85 | 1.3 | 1.5 | 0.0 | | 2183 | .03 | 0.4 | .00 | | 315 | 25 | .88 | | |
| **cabbage, green** | | | | | | | | | | | | | | | |
| raw | 8 | 32.4 | 0.1 | 0.0 | 0 | 4 | 17 | .01 | .03 | 20 | 6 | 16 | 5 | .06 | .056 |
| *1/2 cup shredded* | 35 | 0.4 | 1.9 | 0.0 | 0.4 | 44 | .02 | 0.1 | .00 | .05 | 86 | 8 | .20 | .008 | |
| boiled | 16 | 70.2 | 0.1 | 0.1 | 0 | 6 | 18 | .04 | .05 | 15 | 14 | 25 | 11 | .12 | .097 |
| *1/2 cup shredded* | 75 | 0.7 | 3.6 | 0.0 | | 64 | .04 | 0.2 | .00 | .05 | 154 | 18 | .29 | .021 | |
| **cabbage, red** | | | | | | | | | | | | | | | |
| raw | 10 | 32.0 | 0.1 | 0.0 | 0 | 1 | 20 | .01 | .07 | 7 | 4 | 18 | 5 | .07 | .063 |
| *1/2 cup shredded* | 35 | 0.5 | 2.1 | 0.0 | 0.4 | 14 | .02 | 0.1 | .00 | .11 | 72 | 15 | .17 | .034 | |
| boiled | 16 | 70.2 | 0.2 | 0.1 | 0 | 2 | 26 | .02 | .11 | 9 | 6 | 28 | 8 | .11 | .097 |
| *1/2 cup shredded* | 75 | 0.8 | 3.5 | 0.0 | | 20 | .03 | 0.2 | .00 | .17 | 105 | 21 | .27 | .052 | |
| **cabbage, savoy** | | | | | | | | | | | | | | | |
| raw | 10 | 31.9 | 0.0 | 0.0 | 0 | 35 | 11 | .01 | .07 | | 10 | 12 | 10 | | |
| *1/2 cup shredded* | 35 | 0.7 | 2.1 | 0.0 | | 350 | .03 | 0.1 | .00 | | 81 | 15 | .14 | | |
| boiled | 18 | 67.2 | 0.1 | 0.0 | 0 | 65 | 12 | .02 | .11 | | 17 | 22 | 17 | | |
| *1/2 cup shredded* | 73 | 1.3 | 4.0 | 0.0 | | 649 | .04 | 0.0 | .00 | | 134 | 24 | .28 | | |
| **cannellini beans (white kidney beans),** | 180 | | 1.0 | | | | | | | | 717 | | | | |
| cnd, Progresso—*8 oz* | 227 | 12.0 | 30.0 | | | | | | | | | | | | |
| **cardoon, boiled** | 22 | 93.5 | 0.1 | 0.0 | 0 | 12 | 2 | .03 | | | 176 | 72 | 43 | | |
| *3.5 oz* | 100 | 0.8 | 5.3 | 0.0 | | 118 | .02 | 0.3 | .00 | | 392 | 23 | .73 | | |
| **carrots** | | | | | | | | | | | | | | | |
| raw | 31 | 63.2 | 0.1 | 0.1 | 0 | 2025 | 7 | .04 | .11 | 10 | 25 | 19 | 11 | .14 | .102 |
| *1 med* | 72 | 0.7 | 7.3 | 0.0 | 1.1 | 20253 | .07 | 0.7 | .00 | .14 | 233 | 32 | .36 | .034 | |

| | KCAL / WT (g) | $H_2O$ (g) / PRO (g) | FAT (g) / CHO (g) | PUFA (g) / SFA (g) | CHOL (mg) / DFIB (g) | A (RE) / A (IU) | C (mg) / B-1 (mg) | B-2 (mg) / NIA (mg) | B-6 (mg) / B-12 (mcg) | FOL (mcg) / PANT (mg) | Na (mg) / K (mg) | Ca (mg) / P (mg) | Mg (mg) / Fe (mg) | Zn (mg) / Cu (mg) | Mn (mg) |
|---|---|---|---|---|---|---|---|---|---|---|---|---|---|---|---|
| boiled | 35 | 68.2 | 0.1 | 0.1 | 0 | 1915 | 2 | .04 | .19 | 11 | 52 | 24 | 10 | .23 | .587 |
| *1/2 cup slices* | 78 | 0.9 | 8.2 | 0.0 | 1.5 | 19152 | .03 | 0.4 | .00 | .24 | 177 | 24 | .48 | .105 | |
| cnd | 17 | 67.9 | 0.1 | 0.1 | 0 | 1006 | 2 | .02 | .08 | 7 | 176ᵃ | 19 | 6 | .19 | .329 |
| *1/2 cup slices* | 73 | 0.5 | 4.0 | 0.0 | 0.9 | 10050 | .01 | 0.4 | .00 | .10 | 131 | 17 | .47 | .076 | |
| frzn, boiled | 26 | 65.6 | 0.1 | 0.1 | 0 | 1292 | 2 | .03 | .09 | 8 | 43 | 21 | 7 | .18 | .296 |
| *1/2 cup slices* | 73 | 0.9 | 6.0 | 0.0 | 1.3 | 12922 | .02 | 0.3 | .00 | .12 | 115 | 19 | .35 | .053 | |
| **cassava, raw** | 120 | 68.5 | 0.4 | 0.1 | 0 | 1 | 48 | .10 | | | 8 | 91 | 66 | | |
| *3.5 oz* | 100 | 3.1 | 26.9 | 0.1 | | 10 | .23 | 1.4 | .00 | | 764 | 70 | 3.60 | | |
| **cauliflower** | | | | | | | | | | | | | | | |
| raw | 12 | 46.1 | 0.1 | 0.0 | 0 | 1 | 36 | .03 | .12 | 33 | 7 | 14 | 7 | .09 | .102 |
| *1/2 cup pieces* | 50 | 1.0 | 2.5 | 0.0 | | 8 | .04 | 0.3 | .00 | .07 | 178 | 23 | .29 | .016 | |
| boiled | 15 | 57.4 | 0.1 | 0.1 | 0 | 1 | 34 | .03 | .13 | 32 | 4 | 17 | 7 | .15 | .110 |
| *1/2 cup pieces* | 62 | 1.2 | 2.9 | 0.0 | 1.0 | 9 | .04 | 0.3 | .00 | .08 | 200 | 22 | .26 | .056 | |
| frzn | | | | | | | | | | | | | | | |
| boiled | 17 | 84.6 | 0.2 | 0.1 | 0 | 2 | 28 | .05 | .08 | 37 | 16 | 15 | 8 | .12 | .135 |
| *1/2 cup pieces* | 90 | 1.5 | 3.4 | 0.0 | 1.5 | 20 | .03 | 0.3 | .00 | .09 | 125 | 22 | .37 | .022 | |
| w/ butter sce, Pillsbury | 30 | 80.1 | 1.2 | | | | 24 | .04 | | | 319 | 21 | | | |
| *1/2 cup* | 88 | 1.1 | 3.5 | | | 64 | .02 | 0.4 | | | 123 | 24 | .35 | | |
| w/ cheddar cheese sce, Pillsbury | 70 | 104.1 | 3.5 | | | | 52 | .12 | | | 446 | 69 | | | |
| *1/2 cup* | 121 | 3.4 | 7.1 | | | 70 | .08 | 0.5 | | | 247 | 75 | .79 | | |
| w/ cheese sce, Birds Eye | 114 | 118.2 | 6.1 | 0.9 | 6 | | 39 | .16 | .12 | 42 | 483 | 83 | 17 | .35 | |
| *1/2 cup* | 142 | 4.0 | 11.7 | 1.9 | | 2298 | .06 | 0.4 | .30 | .33 | 240 | 88 | .50 | .026 | |
| w/ cheese sce, Pillsbury | 60 | 92.4 | 1.7 | | | | 30 | .13 | | | 427 | 56 | | | |
| *1/2 cup* | 107 | 1.5 | 9.2 | | | 703 | .03 | 0.1 | | | 229 | 156 | .37 | | |
| **celeriac, raw** | 25 | 92.0 | 0.2 | | 0 | 0 | 4 | .04 | .01 | | 61 | 26 | 12 | | |
| *3.5 oz* | 100 | 1.0 | 5.9 | | | 0 | .03 | 0.4 | .00 | | 173 | 66 | .43 | | |
| **celery** | | | | | | | | | | | | | | | |
| raw | 6 | 37.9 | 0.1 | 0.0 | 0 | 5 | 3 | .01 | .01 | 4 | 35 | 14 | 5 | .07 | .054 |
| *1 stalk (7.5" long)* | 40 | 0.3 | 1.5 | 0.0 | 0.4 | 51 | .01 | 0.1 | .00 | .07 | 114 | 10 | .19 | .014 | |
| boiled | 11 | 71.3 | 0.1 | 0.0 | 0 | 8 | 4 | .02 | .02 | 5 | 48 | 27 | 9 | .12 | .092 |
| *1/2 cup diced* | 75 | 0.4 | 2.6 | 0.0 | | 81 | .02 | 0.2 | .00 | .11 | 266 | 18 | .10 | .023 | |
| **celtuce, raw** | 22 | 94.5 | 0.3 | | 0 | 350 | 20 | .07 | | | 1 | 39 | 28 | | |
| *12 leaves* | 100 | 0.9 | 3.7 | | | 3500 | .06 | 0.6 | .00 | | 330 | 39 | .55 | | |
| **chard, swiss, boiled** | 18 | 81.5 | 0.1 | | 0 | 276 | 16 | .08 | | | 158 | 51 | 76 | | |
| *1/2 cup chopped* | 88 | 1.7 | 3.6 | | | 2762 | .03 | 0.3 | .00 | .14 | 483 | 29 | 1.99 | | |
| **chayote, boiled** | 19 | 74.7 | 0.4 | | 0 | 4 | 6 | .03 | | | 1 | 10 | 9 | | |
| *1/2 cup pieces* | 80 | 0.5 | 4.1 | | | 37 | .02 | 0.3 | .00 | .33 | 138 | 23 | .18 | | |
| **chickpeas (garbanzo beans)** | | | | | | | | | | | | | | | |
| boiled | 269 | 98.8 | 4.3 | 1.9 | 0 | 4 | 2 | .10 | .23 | 282 | 11 | 80 | 78 | 2.51 | 1.689 |
| *1 cup* | 164 | 14.5 | 45.0 | 0.4 | 5.7 | 44 | .19 | 0.9 | .00 | .47 | 477 | 275 | 4.74 | .577 | |
| cnd | 285 | 167.3 | 2.7 | 1.2 | 0 | 6 | 9 | .08 | 1.14 | 160 | 718 | 78 | 70 | 2.53 | 1.450 |
| *1 cup* | 240 | 11.9 | 54.3 | 0.3 | | 58 | .07 | 0.3 | .00 | .72 | 413 | 216 | 3.23 | .418 | |
| hummusᵇ | 420 | 159.7 | 20.8 | 7.8 | 0 | 6 | 19 | .13 | .98 | 146 | 599 | 124 | 71 | 2.70 | 1.400 |
| *1 cup* | 246 | 12.1 | 49.6 | 3.1 | | 61 | .23 | 1.0 | .00 | .71 | 427 | 275 | 3.87 | .561 | |
| **chickory greens, raw** | 21 | 82.8 | 0.3 | 0.1 | 0 | 360 | 22 | .09 | | | 41 | 90 | 27 | | |
| *1/2 cup chopped* | 90 | 1.5 | 4.2 | 0.1 | | 3600 | .05 | 0.5 | .00 | | 378 | 42 | .81 | | |
| **chickory witloof, raw** | 7 | 42.8 | 0.1 | 0.0 | 0 | 0 | 5 | .06 | .02 | | 3 | | 6 | | |
| *1/2 cup* | 45 | 0.5 | 1.4 | 0.0 | | 0 | .03 | 0.2 | .00 | | 82 | 9 | .23 | | |
| **chives** | | | | | | | | | | | | | | | |
| raw | 1 | 2.8 | 0.0 | 0.0 | 0 | 19 | 2 | .01 | .01 | | 0 | 2 | 2 | | |
| *1 T chopped* | 3 | 0.1 | 0.1 | 0.0 | | 192 | .00 | 0.0 | .00 | .01 | 8 | 2 | .05 | | |
| freeze-dried | 2 | 0.0 | 0.0 | 0.0 | 0 | 55 | 5 | .01 | | | | 7 | | | |
| *1/4 cup* | 0.8 | 0.2 | 0.5 | 0.0 | | 546 | .01 | 0.0 | .00 | | 24 | 4 | .16 | | |
| **coleslaw** | | | | | | | | | | | | | | | |
| Fresh Chef | 199 | | 14.6 | | | | 77 | .03 | | | 214 | 38 | | | |
| *4 oz* | 113 | 0.9 | 16.0 | | | 337 | .05 | 0.2 | | | 122 | | 1.40 | | |

ᵃ The special dietary pack contains 31 mg Na.  ᵇ Chickpeas, lemon jce, tahini, olive oil & garlic.

| | KCAL / WT (g) | H₂O (g) / PRO (g) | FAT (g) / CHO (g) | PUFA (g) / SFA (g) | CHOL (mg) / DFIB (g) | A (RE) / A (IU) | C (mg) / B-1 (mg) | B-2 (mg) / NIA (mg) | B-6 (mg) / B-12 (mcg) | FOL (mcg) / PANT (mg) | Na (mg) / K (mg) | Ca (mg) / P (mg) | Mg (mg) / Fe (mg) | Zn (mg) / Cu (mg) | Mn (mg) |
|---|---|---|---|---|---|---|---|---|---|---|---|---|---|---|---|
| homemade[a] | 42 / 60 | 48.9 / 0.8 | 1.6 / 7.5 | 0.8 / 0.2 | 5 / | 49 / 381 | 20 / .04 | .04 / 0.2 | .08 / .02 | 16 / .08 | 14 / 109 | 27 / 19 | 6 / .35 | .12 / .014 | .058 |
| **collards** | | | | | | | | | | | | | | | |
| boiled | 27 / 190 | 181.9 / 2.1 | 0.3 / 5.0 | | 0 / | 422 / 4218 | 19 / .03 | .08 / 0.4 | .08 / .00 | 12 / .08 | 36 / 177 | 148 / 19 | 21 / .78 | 1.22 / .285 | .467 |
| frzn, boiled | 31 / 85 | 75.2 / 2.5 | 0.4 / 6.1 | | 0 / | 508 / 5084 | 23 / .04 | .10 / 0.5 | .10 / .00 | 65 / .10 | 42 / 214 | 179 / 23 | 26 / .95 | .23 / .047 | .564 |
| **coriander, raw** | 1 / 4 | 3.7 / 0.1 | 0.0 / 0.1 | | 0 / | 11 / 111 | 0 / .00 | .01 / 0.0 | / .00 | | 1 / 22 | 4 / 1 | 1 / .08 | | |
| **corn, white** | | | | | | | | | | | | | | | |
| cnd, Pillsbury | 90 / 94 | 70.5 / 2.2 | 0.4 / 19.5 | | | / 300 | 9 / .06 | .07 / 1.4 | | | 259 / 198 | 5 / 60 | / .32 | | |
| frzn, Pillsbury | 80 / 70 | 50.8 / 2.0 | 0.8 / 16.0 | | | / 13 | 5 / .03 | .04 / 0.8 | | | 2 / 159 | 6 / 51 | / .25 | | |
| frzn w/ butter sce, Pillsbury | 110 / 111 | 84.4 / 2.6 | 2.0 / 20.5 | | | / 31 | 7 / .03 | .06 / 1.0 | | | 301 / 202 | 7 / 63 | / .26 | | |
| **corn, yellow** | | | | | | | | | | | | | | | |
| boiled | 89 / 82 | 57.0 / 2.7 | 1.1 / 20.6 | 0.5 / 0.2 | 0 / | 18[b] / 178[b] | 5 / .18 | .06 / 1.3 | .05 / .00 | 38 / .72 | 14 / 204 | 2 / 84 | 26 / .50 | .39 / .043 | .159 |
| cnd | 66 / 82 | 63.1 / 2.2 | 0.8 / 15.2 | 0.4 / 0.1 | 0 / 1.1 | 13[b] / 128[b] | | / | .00 | | | | / .70 | .32 / .048 | .142 |
| cream style | 93 / 128 | 100.8 / 2.2 | 0.5 / 23.2 | 0.3 / 0.1 | 0 / | 12[b] / 124[b] | 6 / .03 | .07 / 1.2 | .08 / .00 | 57 / .23 | 365[c] / 172 | 4 / 65 | 22 / .49 | .68 / .067 | .050 |
| vacuum pack | 83 / 105 | 80.4 / 2.5 | 0.5 / 20.4 | 0.2 / 0.1 | 0 / | 25[b] / 253[b] | 9 / .04 | .08 / 1.2 | .06 / .00 | 52 / .71 | 286[d] / 195 | 5 / 67 | 24 / .44 | .48 / .050 | .070 |
| w/ red & green peppers | 86 / 114 | 88.4 / 2.7 | 0.6 / 20.7 | 0.3 / 0.1 | 0 / | 26 / 265 | 10 / .03 | .09 / 1.1 | / .00 | | 396 / 174 | 5 / 71 | 29 / .90 | .42 / .068 | |
| frzn | | | | | | | | | | | | | | | |
| boiled | 67 / 82 | 62.1 / 2.5 | 0.1 / 16.8 | 0.0 / 0.0 | 0 / 1.7 | 20[b] / 204[b] | 2 / .06 | .06 / 1.1 | .08 / .00 | 19 / .18 | 4 / 114 | 2 / 39 | 15 / .25 | .28 / .027 | .148 |
| cream style, Pillsbury | 120 / 128 | 97.5 / 2.9 | 0.6 / 25.6 | | | / 166 | 5 / .09 | .05 / 0.6 | | | 320 / 183 | 9 / 65 | / .26 | | |
| on-the-cob, Birds Eye | 120 / 125 | 90.5 / 4.1 | 1.0 / 28.7 | 0.5 / 0.1 | 0 / | / 261 | 8 / .15 | .11 / 2.1 | .22 / .00 | 49 / .37 | 4 / 378 | 5 / 113 | 40 / .86 | .87 / .063 | |
| on-the-cob, Pillsbury | 150 / 133 | 95.8 / 3.9 | 1.2 / 31.0 | | | / 258 | 12 / .12 | .20 / 2.4 | | | 20 / 358 | 4 / 109 | / .65 | | |
| w/ butter sce, Niblets | 100 / 111 | 87.7 / 2.4 | 2.1 / 17.9 | | | / 78 | 6 / .08 | .06 / 1.5 | | | 275 / 176 | 8 / 57 | / .36 | | |
| w/ peppers, Mexicorn | 80 / 92 | 70.8 / 1.8 | 0.3 / 17.3 | | | / 513 | 6 / .05 | .07 / 1.0 | | | 316 / 151 | 6 / 51 | / .37 | | |
| **corn pudding**[e] | 271 / 250 | 190.8 / 11.0 | 13.3 / 31.9 | 1.7 / 6.3 | 230 / | 89 / 616 | 7 / 1.03 | .32 / 2.5 | .30 / .23 | 63 / .62 | 138 / 402 | 100 / 143 | 37 / 1.39 | 1.26 / .108 | |
| **cornsalad, raw**[f] | 6 / 28 | 26.0 / 0.6 | 0.1 / 1.0 | | 0 / | | | / | / .00 | | | | | | |
| **cowpeas, (blackeye peas)** | | | | | | | | | | | | | | | |
| boiled | 198 / 171 | 119.8 / 13.2 | 0.9 / 35.5 | 0.4 / 0.2 | 0 / 4.4 | 3 / 26 | 1 / .35 | .09 / 0.8 | .17 / .00 | 356 / .70 | 6 / 476 | 42 / 266 | 91 / 4.29 | 2.20 / .458 | .812 |
| cnd | 184 / 240 | 191.1 / 11.4 | 1.3 / 32.7 | 0.6 / 0.3 | 0 / | 3 / 32 | 7 / .18 | .18 / 0.9 | .11 / .00 | 123 / .46 | 718 / 413 | 48 / 167 | 66 / 2.34 | 1.68 / .281 | .679 |
| frzn, boiled | 112 / 85 | 56.2 / 7.2 | 0.6 / 20.2 | 0.1 / 0.2 | 0 / | 6 / 64 | 2 / .22 | .05 / 0.6 | .08 / .00 | 120 / .18 | 5 / 319 | 20 / 104 | 42 / 1.80 | 1.21 / .156 | .672 |
| young pods w/ seeds, boiled | 16 / 47 | 42.1 / 1.2 | 0.1 / 3.3 | 0.0 / 0.0 | 0 / | 66 / 658 | 8 / .04 | .04 / 0.4 | / .00 | | 1 / 92 | 26 / 23 | / .33 | | |
| **cowpeas, catjang, boiled** | 200 / 171 | 119.2 / 13.9 | 1.2 / 34.7 | 0.5 / 0.3 | 0 / | 2 / 17 | 1 / .28 | .08 / 1.2 | .16 / .00 | 242 / .66 | 32 / 641 | 44 / 242 | 165 / 5.22 | 3.20 / .463 | .809 |

[a] Cabbage, celery, table cream, sugar, green pepper, lemon jce, onion, pimiento, vinegar, salt, dry mustard & white pepper.
[b] For yellow varieties: white varieties contain only a trace of vitamin A.
[c] Special dietary pack contains 4 mg Na.
[d] Special dietary pack contains 3 mg Na.
[e] Yellow corn, whole milk, egg, sugar, butter, salt & pepper.
[f] European herb widely cultivated as a salad plant & potherb.

| | KCAL / WT (g) | H₂O (g) / PRO (g) | FAT (g) / CHO (g) | PUFA (g) / SFA (g) | CHOL (mg) / DFIB (g) | A (RE) / A (IU) | C (mg) / B-1 (mg) | B-2 (mg) / NIA (mg) | B-6 (mg) / B-12 (mcg) | FOL (mcg) / PANT (mg) | Na (mg) / K (mg) | Ca (mg) / P (mg) | Mg (mg) / Fe (mg) | Zn (mg) / Cu (mg) | Mn (mg) |
|---|---|---|---|---|---|---|---|---|---|---|---|---|---|---|---|
| **cranberry beans** | | | | | | | | | | | | | | | |
| boiled | 240 | 114.4 | 0.8 | 0.4 | 0 | 0 | 0 | .12 | .14 | 366 | 1 | 89 | 89 | 2.01 | .655 |
| *1 cup* | 177 | 16.5 | 43.3 | 0.2 | 6.0 | 0 | .37 | 0.9 | .00 | .43 | 685 | 240 | 3.70 | .409 | |
| cnd | 216 | 201.6 | 0.7 | 0.3 | 0 | 0 | 2 | .10 | .14 | 201 | 863 | 87 | 83 | 2.18 | .520 |
| *1 cup* | 260 | 14.4 | 39.3 | 0.2 | | 0 | .10 | 1.3 | .00 | .37 | 675 | 223 | 4.02 | .369 | |
| **cucumber, raw** | 7 | 49.9 | 0.1 | 0.0 | 0 | 2 | 2 | .01 | .03 | 7 | 1 | 7 | 6 | .12 | .032 |
| *1/2 cup slices (1/6 cucumber)* | 52 | 0.3 | 1.5 | 0.0 | 0.3 | 23 | .02 | 0.2 | .00 | .13 | 78 | 9 | .14 | .021 | |
| **dandelion greens** | | | | | | | | | | | | | | | |
| raw | 13 | 24.0 | 0.2 | | 0 | 392 | 10 | .07 | | | 21 | 52 | 10 | | |
| *1/2 cup chopped* | 28 | 0.8 | 2.6 | | | 3920 | .05 | | .00 | | 111 | 18 | .87 | | |
| boiled | 17 | 46.7 | 0.3 | | 0 | 608 | 9 | .09 | | | 23 | 73 | | | |
| *1/2 cup* | 52 | 1.0 | 3.3 | | | 6084 | .07 | | .00 | | 121 | 22 | .94 | | |
| **dock** | | | | | | | | | | | | | | | |
| raw | 15 | 62.3 | 0.5 | | 0 | 268 | 32 | .07 | | | 3 | 29 | 69 | | |
| *1/2 cup chopped* | 67 | 1.3 | 2.1 | | | 2680 | .03 | 0.3 | .00 | | 261 | 42 | 1.61 | | |
| boiled | 20 | 93.6 | 0.6 | | 0 | 347 | 26 | .09 | | | 3 | 38 | 89 | | |
| *3.5 oz* | 100 | 1.8 | 2.9 | | | 3474 | .03 | 0.4 | .00 | | 321 | 52 | 2.08 | | |
| **eggplant** | | | | | | | | | | | | | | | |
| raw | 11 | 37.7 | 0.0 | 0.0 | 0 | 3 | 1 | .01 | .04 | 7 | 1 | 15 | 5 | .06 | .057 |
| *1/2 cup pieces* | 41 | 0.5 | 2.6 | 0.0 | 0.6 | 29 | .04 | 0.2 | .00 | .03 | 90 | 13 | .22 | .046 | |
| boiled | 13 | 44.1 | 0.1 | 0.0 | 0 | 3 | 1 | .01 | .04 | 7 | 2 | 3 | 6 | .07 | .065 |
| *1/2 cup* | 48 | 0.4 | 3.2 | 0.0 | | 31 | .04 | 0.3 | .00 | .04 | 119 | 11 | .17 | .052 | |
| **endive, raw** | 4 | 23.5 | 0.1 | 0.0 | 0 | 51 | 2 | .02 | .01 | 36 | 6 | 13 | 4 | .20 | .105 |
| *1/2 cup chopped* | 25 | 0.3 | 0.8 | 0.0 | | 513 | .02 | 0.1 | .00 | .23 | 79 | 7 | .21 | .025 | |
| **fava beans, cnd, Progresso** | 180 | | 1.0 | | | | | | | | | | | | |
| *8 oz* | 227 | 14.0 | 31.0 | | | | | | | | | | | | |
| **french beans, boiled** | 228 | 117.8 | 1.3 | 0.8 | 0 | 0 | 2 | .11 | .19 | 132 | 11 | 111 | 99 | 1.13 | .676 |
| *1 cup* | 177 | 12.5 | 42.5 | 0.1 | | 5 | .23 | 1.0 | .00 | .39 | 655 | 181 | 1.92 | .204 | |
| **garden cress** | | | | | | | | | | | | | | | |
| raw | 8 | 22.4 | 0.2 | 0.1 | 0 | 23 | 17 | .07 | .06 | | | 20 | | | |
| *1/2 cup* | 25 | 0.7 | 1.4 | 0.0 | | 2325 | .02 | 0.3 | .00 | | | | .33 | | |
| boiled | 16 | 62.9 | 0.4 | 0.1 | 0 | 524 | 16 | .11 | | | 5 | 41 | | | |
| *1/2 cup* | 68 | 1.3 | 2.6 | 0.0 | | 5236 | .04 | .54 | .00 | | 240 | 33 | .54 | | |
| **garden salad, cnd, Joan of Arc** | 80 | | 0.3 | | | 3 | | .04 | | | 636 | 48 | | | |
| *1/2 cup* | 136 | 1.5 | 18.1 | | | 392 | .08 | 0.5 | | | 194 | 45 | .82 | | |
| **garlic, raw** | 13 | 5.3 | 0.1 | 0.0 | 0 | 0 | 3 | .01 | | 0 | 2 | 16 | 2 | | |
| *3 cloves* | 9 | 0.6 | 3.0 | 0.0 | | 0 | .02 | 0.1 | .00 | | 36 | 14 | .15 | | |
| **ginger root, raw** | 17 | 19.6 | 0.2 | 0.0 | 0 | 0 | 1 | .01 | .04 | | 3 | 4 | 10 | | |
| *1/4 cup slices* | 24 | 0.4 | 3.6 | 0.0 | | 0 | .01 | 0.2 | .00 | .05 | 100 | 7 | .12 | | |
| **gourd, calabash (white-flowered), boiled** | 11 | 69.6 | 0.0 | 0.0 | 0 | 0 | 6 | .02 | | | 1 | 18 | 8 | | |
| *1/2 cup cubes* | 73 | 0.4 | 2.7 | 0.0 | | 0 | .02 | 0.3 | .00 | | 124 | 9 | .18 | | |
| **gourd, dishcloth (towelgourd), boiled** | 50 | 75.0 | 0.3 | 0.1 | 0 | 23 | 5 | .04 | | | 18 | 8 | 18 | | |
| *1/2 cup slices* | 89 | 0.6 | 12.8 | 0.0 | 0.4 | 231 | .04 | 0.2 | .00 | | 403 | 28 | .32 | | |
| **great northern beans** | | | | | | | | | | | | | | | |
| boiled | 210 | 122.1 | 0.8 | 0.3 | 0 | 0 | 2 | .10 | .21 | 181 | 4 | 121 | 88 | 1.55 | .917 |
| *1 cup* | 177 | 14.8 | 37.3 | 0.2 | 6.0 | 2 | .28 | 1.2 | .00 | .47 | 692 | 293 | 3.77 | .437 | |
| cnd | 300 | 183.1 | 1.0 | 0.4 | 0 | 0 | 3 | .16 | .28 | 213 | 11 | 139 | 134 | 1.70 | 1.069 |
| *1 cup* | 262 | 19.3 | 55.1 | 0.3 | | 3 | .38 | 1.2 | .00 | .73 | 919 | 355 | 4.11 | .419 | |
| cnd, Joan of Arc | 90 | | 0.1 | | | 0 | | .06 | | | 421 | 65 | | | |
| *1/2 cup* | 118 | 5.3 | 16.9 | | | 71 | .08 | 0.4 | | | 168 | 99 | 1.42 | | |
| **green beans (snap beans)** | | | | | | | | | | | | | | | |
| boiled[a] | 22 | 55.3 | 0.2 | 0.1 | 0 | 41 | 6 | .06 | .04 | 21 | 2 | 29 | 16 | .23 | .182 |
| *1/2 cup* | 62 | 1.2 | 4.9 | 0.0 | 1.1 | 413[b] | .05 | 0.4 | .00 | .05 | 185 | 24 | .79 | .064 | |

[a] Includes Italian, green & yellow varieties.

[b] For green varieties; yellow varieties contain 50 IU.

| | KCAL / WT (g) | H₂O (g) / PRO (g) | FAT (g) / CHO (g) | PUFA (g) / SFA (g) | CHOL (mg) / DFIB (g) | A (RE) / A (IU) | C (mg) / B-1 (mg) | B-2 (mg) / NIA (mg) | B-6 (mg) / B-12 (mcg) | FOL (mcg) / PANT (mg) | Na (mg) / K (mg) | Ca (mg) / P (mg) | Mg (mg) / Fe (mg) | Zn (mg) / Cu (mg) | Mn (mg) |
|---|---|---|---|---|---|---|---|---|---|---|---|---|---|---|---|
| cnd | 13 | 63.4 | 0.1 | 0.0 | 0 | 24 | 3 | .04 | | 22 | 170[b] | 18 | 9 | .20 | .136 |
| *1/2 cup[a]* | 68 | 0.8 | 3.1 | 0.0 | 0.9 | 237[c] | .01 | 0.1 | .00 | | 74 | 13 | .61 | .026 | |
| cut, no salt added, Heinz | 16 | 95.7 | 0.1 | | | 4 | .01 | | | | 1 | 25 | 16 | .20 | |
| *3.5 oz* | 100 | 0.9 | 3.1 | | | 471 | .02 | 0.3 | | | 78 | 19 | .60 | .060 | |
| cut, Pillsbury | 18 | 90.3 | 0.4 | | | 3 | .05 | | | | 259 | 22 | | | |
| *1/2 cup* | 95 | 0.8 | 2.7 | | | 202 | .03 | 0.4 | | | 92 | 14 | .67 | | |
| french style, no salt added, Heinz | 16 | 95.8 | 0.1 | | | 4 | .00 | | | | 1 | 25 | 15 | .19 | |
| *3.5 oz* | 100 | 0.7 | 3.2 | | | 500 | .02 | 0.2 | | | 64 | 14 | .60 | .070 | |
| french style, Pillsbury | 18 | 103.6 | 0.1 | | | 3 | .03 | | | | 261 | 21 | | | |
| *1/2 cup* | 109 | 0.9 | 3.3 | | | 238 | .02 | 0.1 | | | 106 | 12 | .76 | | |
| w/ onions, red peppers & garlic | 18 | 107.5 | 0.2 | 0.1 | 0 | 60 | 4 | .06 | | | 425 | 25 | 15 | .16 | |
| *1/2 cup* | 114 | 1.0 | 4.0 | 0.1 | | 599 | .03 | 0.3 | .00 | | 106 | 18 | .54 | .068 | |
| **frzn** | | | | | | | | | | | | | | | |
| boiled[a] | 18 | 62.5 | 0.1 | 0.0 | 0 | 36 | 6 | .05 | .04 | | 9 | 31 | 15 | .42 | .252 |
| *1/2 cup* | 68 | 0.9 | 4.2 | 0.0 | 1.1 | 359[d] | .03 | 0.3 | .00 | .04 | 76 | 16 | .56 | .046 | |
| cut, Birds Eye | 25 | 77.4 | 0.1 | 0.1 | 0 | | 9 | .07 | .05 | 11 | 3 | 35 | 17 | .17 | |
| *1/2 cup* | 85 | 1.4 | 5.8 | 0.0 | 2.2 | 455 | .05 | 0.3 | .00 | .06 | 131 | 23 | .73 | .039 | |
| cut w/ butter sce, Pillsbury | 35 | 80.0 | 1.4 | | | | 2 | .05 | | | 243 | 0 | | | |
| *1/2 cup* | 88 | 0.8 | 4.8 | | | 111 | .03 | 0.0 | | | 108 | 17 | .53 | | |
| french style, Birds Eye | 26 | 77.1 | 0.2 | 0.1 | 0 | | 8 | .07 | .04 | 11 | 3 | 39 | 18 | .22 | |
| *1/2 cup* | 85 | 1.4 | 5.9 | 0.0 | 2.2 | 390 | .05 | 0.3 | .00 | .09 | 145 | 21 | .80 | .044 | |
| french style w/ butter sce, Pillsbury | 40 | 90.7 | 1.4 | | | | 7 | .07 | | | 349 | 31 | | | |
| *1/2 cup* | 100 | 1.3 | 5.6 | | | 450 | .04 | 0.3 | | | 120 | 24 | .48 | | |
| french style w/ toasted almonds, | 52 | 71.2 | 1.6 | 0.5 | 0 | | 8 | .06 | .05 | 11 | 335 | 36 | 25 | .28 | |
| Birds Eye—*1/2 cup* | 85 | 2.5 | 8.4 | 0.2 | | 372 | .05 | 0.4 | .00 | .11 | 167 | 32 | .52 | .070 | |
| italian, Birds Eye | 31 | 75.2 | 0.1 | 0.1 | 0 | | 14 | .10 | .04 | 14 | 3 | 35 | 19 | .25 | |
| *1/2 cup* | 85 | 1.8 | 7.2 | 0.0 | 2.7 | 374 | .07 | 0.5 | .00 | .22 | 184 | 31 | .74 | .050 | |
| whole, Birds Eye | 30 | 103.9 | 0.2 | 0.1 | 0 | | 12 | .10 | .05 | 13 | 2 | 44 | 23 | .27 | |
| *4 oz* | 113 | 1.7 | 6.7 | 0.1 | 2.5 | 776 | .07 | 0.3 | .00 | .18 | 200 | 28 | .87 | .047 | |
| **green bean salad, german style, cnd, Joan** | 90 | | 2.0 | | | | 3 | .04 | | | 770 | 44 | | | |
| **of Arc**—*1/2 cup* | 132 | 1.8 | 14.9 | | | 384 | .04 | 0.5 | | | 152 | 48 | 1.60 | | |
| **hominy, cnd** | | | | | | | | | | | | | | | |
| white, Van Camp's | 138 | 213.4 | 0.7 | | | | | .06 | | | 708 | 10 | | | |
| *1 cup* | 246 | 2.0 | 30.0 | | | 0 | .02 | 0.1 | | | 37 | | 1.44 | | |
| yellow, Van Camp's | 128 | 211.0 | 0.6 | | | | | .06 | | | 701 | 9 | | | |
| *1 cup* | 242 | 2.7 | 27.9 | | | 277 | .01 | 0.1 | | | 33 | | 2.27 | | |
| yellow w/ red & green peppers, Van | 129 | 210.6 | 0.5 | | | | | .07 | | | 685 | 10 | | | |
| Camp's—*1 cup* | 242 | 2.6 | 28.5 | | | 408 | .01 | 0.2 | | | 46 | | 1.46 | | |
| **hyacinth beans, boiled** | 228 | 134.1 | 1.1 | | 0 | | 0 | .07 | | | 13 | 77 | 159 | 5.53 | |
| *1 cup* | 194 | 15.8 | 40.2 | | | | .52 | 0.8 | .00 | | 653 | 233 | 8.88 | .662 | |
| **jerusalem artichoke, raw** | 57 | 58.5 | 0.0 | 0.0 | 0 | 2 | 3 | .05 | | | | 10 | 13 | | .045 |
| *1/2 cup slices* | 75 | 1.5 | 13.1 | 0.0 | | 15 | .15 | 1.0 | | | | 58 | 2.55 | | |
| **jew's ear (pepeao)** | | | | | | | | | | | | | | | |
| raw | 25 | 91.7 | 0.0 | | 0 | 0 | 1 | .20 | | | 9 | 16 | 25 | | |
| *1 cup slices* | 99 | 0.5 | 6.7 | | | 0 | .08 | 0.1 | .00 | | 42 | 14 | .55 | | |
| dried | 36 | 1.3 | 0.1 | | | 0 | 0 | .04 | | | 8 | 14 | 17 | | |
| *1/2 cup* | 12 | 0.6 | 9.7 | | | 0 | | 0.4 | .00 | | 85 | 14 | .74 | | |
| **jute, potherb, boiled** | 16 | 37.5 | 0.1 | 0.0 | 0 | 223 | 14 | .08 | | | 5 | 91 | 27 | | |
| *1/2 cup* | 43 | 1.6 | 3.1 | 0.0 | | 2230 | .04 | 0.4 | .00 | | 237 | 31 | 1.35 | | |
| **kale** | | | | | | | | | | | | | | | |
| boiled | 21 | 59.3 | 0.3 | 0.1 | 0 | 481 | 27 | .05 | .09 | 9 | 15 | 47 | 12 | .15 | .270 |
| *1/2 cup chopped* | 65 | 1.2 | 3.7 | 0.0 | | 4810 | .03 | 0.3 | .00 | .03 | 148 | 18 | .59 | .101 | |
| frzn, boiled | 20 | 58.8 | 0.3 | 0.2 | 0 | 413 | 16 | .07 | .06 | 9 | 10 | 90 | 12 | .12 | .292 |
| *1/2 cup chopped* | 65 | 1.9 | 3.4 | 0.0 | | 4130 | .03 | 0.4 | .00 | .03 | 209 | 18 | .61 | .031 | |
| **kale, scotch, boiled** | 18 | 59.3 | 0.3 | 0.1 | 0 | 130 | 34 | .03 | .09 | 9 | 29 | 86 | 37 | .15 | .271 |
| *1/2 cup chopped* | 65 | 1.2 | 3.7 | 0.0 | | 1296 | .03 | 0.5 | .00 | .03 | 178 | 25 | 1.25 | .101 | |

[a] Includes Italian, green & yellow varieties.
[b] Special dietary pack contains 1 mg Na.
[c] For green varieties; yellow varieties contain 71 IU.
[d] For green varieties; yellow varieties contain 76 IU.

| | KCAL / WT (g) | H₂O (g) / PRO (g) | FAT (g) / CHO (g) | PUFA (g) / SFA (g) | CHOL (mg) / DFIB (g) | A (RE) / A (IU) | C (mg) / B-1 (mg) | B-2 (mg) / NIA (mg) | B-6 (mg) / B-12 (mcg) | FOL (mcg) / PANT (mg) | Na (mg) / K (mg) | Ca (mg) / P (mg) | Mg (mg) / Fe (mg) | Zn (mg) / Cu (mg) | Mn (mg) |
|---|---|---|---|---|---|---|---|---|---|---|---|---|---|---|---|
| **kidney beans** | | | | | | | | | | | | | | | |
| boiled | 225 | 118.5 | 0.9 | 0.5 | 0 | 0 | 2 | .10 | .21 | 229 | 4 | 50 | 80 | 1.89 | .844 |
| *1 cup* | 177 | 15.4 | 40.4 | 0.1 | 6.4 | 0 | .28 | 1.0 | .00 | .39 | 713 | 252 | 5.20 | .428 | |
| cnd | 208 | 199.6 | 0.8 | 0.4 | 0 | 0 | 3 | .18 | .18 | 126 | 889 | 69 | 79 | 1.41 | .556 |
| *1 cup* | 256 | 13.3 | 38.1 | 0.1 | | 0 | .28 | 1.3 | .00 | .37 | 658 | 269 | 3.14 | .384 | |
| **kidney beans, red** | | | | | | | | | | | | | | | |
| boiled | 225 | 118.5 | 0.9 | 0.5 | 0 | 0 | 2 | .10 | .21 | 229 | 4 | 50 | 80 | 1.89 | .844 |
| *1 cup* | 177 | 15.4 | 40.4 | 0.1 | 6.4 | 0 | .28 | 1.0 | .00 | .39 | 713 | 252 | 5.20 | .428 | |
| cnd | 216 | 198.0 | 0.9 | 0.5 | 0 | 0 | 3 | .23 | .06 | 129 | 873 | 62 | 73 | 1.41 | .620 |
| *1 cup* | 256 | 13.4 | 39.9 | 0.1 | | 0 | .27 | 1.2 | .00 | .38 | 658 | 240 | 3.22 | .384 | |
| **kidney beans, red, california, boiled** | 219 | 118.5 | 0.2 | 0.1 | 0 | 0 | 2 | .11 | .18 | 131 | 7 | 116 | 85 | 1.52 | .563 |
| *1 cup* | 177 | 16.2 | 39.7 | 0.0 | | 5 | .23 | 1.0 | .00 | .39 | 741 | 242 | 5.27 | .512 | |
| **kidney beans, royal, red, boiled** | 218 | 118.6 | 0.3 | 0.2 | 0 | 0 | 2 | .12 | .18 | 130 | 8 | 78 | 74 | 1.58 | .451 |
| *1 cup* | 177 | 16.8 | 38.7 | 0.0 | | 5 | .17 | 1.0 | .00 | .39 | 669 | 251 | 4.90 | .464 | |
| **kohlrabi, boiled** | 24 | 74.1 | 0.1 | 0.0 | 0 | 2 | 44 | .02 | | | 17 | 20 | 16 | | |
| *1/2 cup slices* | 82 | 1.5 | 5.5 | 0.0 | | 29 | .03 | 0.3 | .00 | | 279 | 37 | .33 | | |
| **lambsquarters, boiled** | 29 | 80.0 | 0.6 | 0.3 | 0 | 873 | 33 | .23 | | | | 232 | | | |
| *1/2 cup chopped* | 90 | 2.9 | 4.5 | 0.0 | | 8730 | .09 | 0.8 | .00 | | | 41 | .63 | | |
| **leeks** | | | | | | | | | | | | | | | |
| raw | 16 | 21.6 | 0.1 | 0.0 | 0 | 2 | 3 | .01 | | 17 | 5 | 15 | 7 | | |
| *1/4 cup chopped* | 26 | 0.4 | 3.7 | 0.0 | 0.3 | 25 | .02 | 0.1 | .00 | | 47 | 9 | .55 | | |
| boiled | 8 | 23.6 | 0.1 | 0.0 | 0 | 1 | 1 | .01 | | 6 | 3 | 8 | 4 | | |
| *1/4 cup chopped* | 26 | 0.2 | 2.0 | 0.0 | | 12 | .01 | 0.1 | .00 | | 23 | 4 | .29 | | |
| freeze-dried | 3 | 0.0 | 0.0 | 0.0 | 0 | 0 | 1 | .00 | | 3 | 0 | 3 | 1 | | |
| *1/4 cup* | 0.8 | 0.1 | 0.6 | 0.0 | | 2 | .01 | 0.0 | .00 | | 19 | 3 | .06 | | |
| **lentils, boiled** | 231 | 137.9 | 0.7 | 0.3 | 0 | 2 | 3 | .15 | .35 | 358 | 4 | 37 | 71 | 2.50 | .978 |
| *1 cup* | 198 | 17.9 | 39.9 | 0.1 | 7.9 | 15 | .34 | 2.1 | .00 | 1.26 | 731 | 356 | 6.59 | .497 | |
| **lentils, sprouted, stir-fried** | 101 | 68.7 | 0.5 | 0.2 | 0 | 4 | 13 | .09 | | | | 14 | 35 | 1.60 | .502 |
| *3.5 oz* | 100 | 8.8 | 21.3 | 0.1 | | 41 | .22 | 1.2 | .00 | .57 | 284 | 153 | 3.10 | .337 | |
| **lettuce** | | | | | | | | | | | | | | | |
| butterhead, raw[a] | 2 | 14.3 | 0.0 | 0.0 | 0 | 15 | 1 | .01 | | 11 | 1 | | | .03 | .020 |
| *2 leaves* | 15 | 0.2 | 0.4 | 0.0 | 0.1 | 146 | .01 | 0.0 | .00 | | 39 | | .04 | .003 | |
| cos/romaine, raw | 4 | 26.6 | 0.1 | 0.0 | 0 | 73 | 7 | .03 | | 38 | 2 | 10 | 2 | | |
| *1/2 cup shredded* | 28 | 0.5 | 0.7 | 0.0 | | 728 | .03 | 0.1 | .00 | | 81 | 13 | .31 | | |
| iceberg, raw[b] | 3 | 19.2 | 0.0 | 0.0 | 0 | 7 | 1 | .01 | .01 | 11 | 2 | 4 | 2 | .04 | .030 |
| *1 leaf* | 20 | 0.2 | 0.4 | 0.1 | 0.2 | 66 | .01 | 0.0 | .00 | .01 | 32 | 4 | .10 | .006 | |
| looseleaf, raw | 5 | 26.3 | 0.1 | 0.0 | 0 | 53 | 5 | .02 | .02 | | 3 | 19 | 3 | | |
| *1/2 cup shredded* | 28 | 0.4 | 1.0 | 0.0 | | 532 | .01 | 0.1 | .00 | .06 | 74 | 7 | .39 | | |
| **lima beans** | | | | | | | | | | | | | | | |
| boiled | 217 | 131.2 | 0.7 | 0.3 | 0 | 0 | 0 | .10 | .30 | 156 | 4 | 32 | 82 | 1.79 | .970 |
| *1 cup* | 188 | 14.7 | 39.3 | 0.2 | 6.2 | 0 | .30 | 0.8 | .00 | .79 | 955 | 208 | 4.50 | .442 | |
| cnd | 191 | 185.8 | 0.4 | 0.2 | 0 | 0 | 0 | .08 | .22 | 121 | 809 | 50 | 94 | 1.57 | .875 |
| *1 cup* | 241 | 11.9 | 35.9 | 0.1 | | 0 | .13 | 0.6 | .00 | .62 | 531 | 178 | 4.35 | .434 | |
| **lima beans, baby** | | | | | | | | | | | | | | | |
| boiled | 229 | 122.2 | 0.7 | 0.3 | 0 | 0 | 0 | .10 | .14 | 273 | 5 | 52 | 97 | 1.87 | 1.065 |
| *1 cup* | 182 | 14.6 | 42.4 | 0.2 | 7.8 | 0 | .29 | 1.2 | .00 | .86 | 729 | 231 | 4.36 | .391 | |
| frzn, boiled | 94 | 65.1 | 0.3 | 0.1 | 0 | 15 | 5 | .05 | .10 | 80 | 26 | 25 | 50 | .50 | .732 |
| *1/2 cup* | 90 | 6.0 | 17.5 | 0.1 | | 150 | .06 | 0.7 | .00 | .16 | 370 | 101 | 1.76 | .177 | |
| frzn w/ butter sce, Pillsbury | 110 | 73.7 | 1.7 | | | | 14 | .04 | | | 399 | 32 | | | |
| *1/2 cup* | 101 | 5.4 | 18.4 | | | 222 | .06 | 1.0 | | | 340 | 77 | 1.31 | | |
| **lima beans, fordhook, frzn, boiled** | 85 | 62.5 | 0.3 | 0.1 | 0 | 16 | 11 | .05 | .10 | 74 | 45 | 19 | 29 | .37 | .264 |
| *1/2 cup* | 85 | 5.2 | 16.0 | 0.1 | | 162 | .06 | 0.9 | .0 | .14 | 347 | 54 | 1.16 | .047 | |
| **lotus root** | | | | | | | | | | | | | | | |
| raw | 45 | 64.1 | 0.1 | 0.0 | 0 | 0 | 36 | .18 | | | 33 | 36 | 18 | | |
| *10 slices* | 81 | 2.1 | 14.0 | 0.0 | | 0 | .13 | 0.3 | .00 | | 450 | 81 | .94 | | |

[a] Includes Boston & Bibb types.

[b] Includes crisphead types.

| | KCAL / WT (g) | H₂O (g) / PRO (g) | FAT (g) / CHO (g) | PUFA (g) / SFA (g) | CHOL (mg) / DFIB (g) | A (RE) / A (IU) | C (mg) / B-1 (mg) | B-2 (mg) / NIA (mg) | B-6 (mg) / B-12 (mcg) | FOL (mcg) / PANT (mg) | Na (mg) / K (mg) | Ca (mg) / P (mg) | Mg (mg) / Fe (mg) | Zn (mg) / Cu (mg) | Mn (mg) |
|---|---|---|---|---|---|---|---|---|---|---|---|---|---|---|---|
| boiled | 59 | 72.5 | 0.1 | 0.0 | 0 | 0 | 24 | .01 | | | 40 | 23 | 20 | | |
| *10 slices* | 89 | 1.4 | 14.3 | 0.0 | | 0 | .11 | 0.3 | .00 | | 323 | 69 | .80 | | |
| **lupins, boiled** | 197 | 118.0 | 4.8 | 1.2 | 0 | | | .09 | | | 7 | 85 | 90 | 2.29 | |
| *1 cup* | 166 | 25.8 | 16.4 | 0.6 | | | .22 | 0.8 | .00 | | 407 | 212 | 1.99 | .383 | |
| **mixed veg** | | | | | | | | | | | | | | | |
| cnd[a] | 39 | 71.4 | 0.2 | 0.1 | 0 | 995 | 4 | .04 | .07 | 19 | 122 | 22 | 13 | .34 | |
| *1/2 cup* | 82 | 2.1 | 7.6 | 0.0 | 2.0 | 9551 | .04 | 0.5 | .00 | .12 | 239 | 34 | .86 | .060 | |
| frzn[b] | 54 | 75.7 | 0.1 | 0.1 | 0 | 389 | 3 | .11 | .07 | 17 | 32 | 22 | 20 | .45 | .345 |
| *1/2 cup* | 91 | 2.6 | 11.9 | 0.0 | 2.1 | 3892 | .07 | 0.8 | .00 | .14 | 154 | 46 | .75 | .076 | |
| Birds Eye[c] | 59 | 78.5 | 0.4 | 0.2 | 0 | | 9 | .07 | .13 | 27 | 41 | 22 | 18 | .40 | |
| *1/2 cup* | 95 | 2.6 | 12.9 | 0.1 | 2.5 | 6507 | .10 | 1.2 | .00 | .15 | 187 | 52 | .81 | .063 | |
| Pillsbury | 50 | 54.3 | 0.3 | | | | 5 | .05 | | | 27 | 16 | | | |
| *1/2 cup* | 67 | 2.1 | 9.6 | | | 1627 | .05 | 0.3 | | | 155 | 41 | .54 | | |
| w/ butter sce, Pillsbury | 80 | 94.6 | 1.7 | | | | 9 | .07 | | | 374 | 23 | | | |
| *1/2 cup* | 114 | 2.9 | 13.3 | | | 2453 | .06 | 0.9 | | | 190 | 56 | .68 | | |
| w/ onion sce, Birds Eye[d] | 97 | 55.6 | 5.2 | 1.0 | 1 | | 5 | .11 | .10 | 15 | 340 | 43 | 15 | .26 | |
| *1/3 cup* | 76 | 2.2 | 11.6 | 1.1 | | 4155 | .06 | 0.6 | .19 | .24 | 182 | 59 | .53 | .041 | |
| **mothbeans, boiled** | 207 | 122.5 | 1.0 | 0.5 | 0 | 2 | 2 | .04 | | | 17 | 6 | 184 | 1.04 | .933 |
| *1 cup* | 177 | 13.8 | 37.1 | 0.2 | | 17 | .22 | 1.2 | .00 | | 538 | 265 | 5.56 | .290 | |
| **mountain yam, hawaii, steamed** | 59 | 55.5 | 0.1 | 0.0 | 0 | 0 | 0 | .01 | | | 9 | 5 | 7 | | |
| *1/2 cup cubes* | 72 | 1.2 | 14.4 | 0.0 | | 0 | .06 | 0.1 | .00 | | 356 | 29 | .31 | | |
| **mung beans, boiled** | 213 | 146.8 | 0.8 | 0.3 | 0 | 5 | 2 | .12 | .14 | 321 | 4 | 55 | 97 | 1.70 | .602 |
| *1 cup* | 202 | 14.2 | 38.7 | 0.2 | 5.1 | 48 | .33 | 1.2 | .00 | .83 | 536 | 201 | 2.83 | .315 | |
| **mung beans, sprouted[e]** | | | | | | | | | | | | | | | |
| raw | 16 | 47.0 | 0.1 | 0.0 | 0 | 1 | 7 | .06 | .05 | 32 | 3 | 7 | 11 | .21 | .098 |
| *1/2 cup* | 52 | 1.6 | 3.1 | 0.0 | 0.6 | 11 | .04 | 0.4 | .00 | .20 | 77 | 28 | .47 | .085 | |
| cnd | 8 | 59.6 | 0.0 | 0.0 | 0 | 1 | 0 | .04 | | 6 | | 9 | 5 | | .045 |
| *1/2 cup* | 62 | 0.9 | 1.3 | 0.0 | | 14 | .02 | 0.1 | .00 | | 17 | 20 | .27 | .097 | |
| ckd | 13 | 57.9 | 0.1 | 0.0 | 0 | 1 | 7 | .06 | | 14 | 6 | 7 | 9 | .29 | .087 |
| *1/2 cup* | 62 | 1.3 | 2.6 | 0.0 | | 8 | .03 | 0.5 | .00 | .15 | 63 | 17 | .40 | .076 | |
| stir-fried | 31 | 52.3 | 0.1 | 0.0 | 0 | | 10 | .11 | | | | 8 | | .56 | |
| *1/2 cup* | 62 | 2.7 | 6.6 | 0.0 | | | .09 | 0.7 | .00 | | | | 1.18 | | |
| **mungo beans, boiled** | 190 | 130.5 | 1.0 | 0.6 | 0 | 6 | 2 | .14 | .10 | 170 | 13 | 95 | 113 | 1.50 | .742 |
| *1 cup* | 180 | 13.6 | 33.0 | 0.1 | | 56 | .27 | 2.7 | .00 | .78 | 416 | 280 | 3.14 | .250 | |
| **mushroom marinara salad, Fresh Chef** | 75 | | 5.8 | | | | 1 | .10 | | | 392 | 35 | | | |
| *3.2 oz* | 92 | 1.7 | 4.1 | | | 210 | .03 | 1.0 | | | 153 | | .50 | | |
| **mushrooms** | | | | | | | | | | | | | | | |
| raw[f] | 9 | 32.1 | 0.2 | 0.1 | 0 | 0 | 1 | .16 | .03 | 7 | 1 | 2 | 4 | .17 | .000 |
| *1/2 cup pieces* | 35 | 0.7 | 1.6 | 0.0 | | 0 | .04 | 1.4 | .00 | .77 | 130 | 36 | .43 | .039 | |
| boiled | 21 | 71.0 | 0.4 | 0.1 | 0 | 0 | 3 | .23 | .07 | 14 | 2 | 4 | 10 | .68 | .090 |
| *1/2 cup pieces* | 78 | 1.7 | 4.0 | 0.0 | | 0 | .06 | 3.5 | .00 | 1.69 | 277 | 68 | 1.36 | .393 | |
| cnd | 19 | 71.0 | 0.2 | 0.1 | 0 | 0 | | | | 10 | | | | .56 | .067 |
| *1/2 cup pieces* | 78 | 1.5 | 3.9 | 0.0 | | 0 | | | .00 | | | | .62 | .183 | |
| cnd w/ butter sce, Pillsbury | 25 | 98.6 | 0.4 | | | | 5 | .17 | | | 559 | 8 | | | |
| *2 oz* | 106 | 2.3 | 3.0 | | | 0 | .00 | 1.6 | | | 162 | 47 | .64 | | |
| **mushrooms, shitake** | | | | | | | | | | | | | | | |
| ckd | 40 | 60.1 | 0.2 | 0.0 | 0 | 0 | 0 | .12 | | | 3 | 2 | 10 | | |
| *4 mushrooms* | 72 | 1.1 | 10.3 | 0.0 | | 0 | .03 | 1.1 | .00 | | 85 | 21 | .32 | | |
| cnd, Campbell's | 45 | | 0.3 | | | | 0 | .11 | | | 74 | 10 | | | |
| *4 oz* | 113 | 3.1 | 7.4 | | | 0 | .02 | 2.9 | | | 146 | | 1.20 | | |
| dried | 44 | 1.4 | 0.2 | 0.0 | 0 | 0 | 1 | .19 | | | 2 | 2 | 20 | | |
| *4 mushrooms* | 15 | 1.4 | 11.3 | 0.0 | | 0 | .05 | 2.1 | .00 | | 230 | 44 | .26 | | |
| **mushrooms, sovereign, cnd, Campbell's** | 39 | | 0.4 | | | | 2 | .41 | | | 73 | 6 | | | |
| *4 oz* | 113 | 3.7 | 5.1 | | | 0 | .08 | 1.9 | | | 220 | | 1.50 | | |

[a] Carrots, green peas, snap beans & lima beans.
[b] Corn, lima beans, snapp beans, green peas & carrots.
[c] Corn, carrots, peas & green beans.
[d] Carrots, corn, green beans, peas & pearl onions.
[e] Seeds attached to sprouts.
[f] Agaricus bisporus.

| | KCAL | H₂O (g) | FAT (g) | PUFA (g) | CHOL (mg) | A (RE) | C (mg) | B-2 (mg) | B-6 (mg) | FOL (mcg) | Na (mg) | Ca (mg) | Mg (mg) | Zn (mg) | Mn (mg) |
|---|---|---|---|---|---|---|---|---|---|---|---|---|---|---|---|
| | WT (g) | PRO (g) | CHO (g) | SFA (g) | DFIB (g) | A (IU) | B-1 (mg) | NIA (mg) | B-12 (mcg) | PANT (mg) | K (mg) | P (mg) | Fe (mg) | Cu (mg) | |
| **mustard greens** | | | | | | | | | | | | | | | |
| boiled | 11 | 66.1 | 0.2 | 0.0 | 0 | 212 | 18 | .04 | | | 11 | 52 | 10 | | |
| *1/2 cup chopped* | 70 | 1.6 | 1.5 | 0.0 | | 2122 | .03 | 0.3 | .00 | .08 | 141 | 29 | .49 | | |
| frzn, boiled | 14 | 70.4 | 0.2 | 0.0 | 0 | 335 | 10 | .04 | .08 | | 19 | 75 | 10 | .15 | .221 |
| *1/2 cup chopped* | 75 | 1.7 | 2.3 | 0.0 | | 3352 | .03 | 0.2 | .00 | .01 | 104 | 18 | .84 | .044 | |
| **mustard spinach (tendergreen)** | | | | | | | | | | | | | | | |
| raw | 17 | 69.2 | 0.2 | | 0 | 743 | 98 | | | | | 158 | | | |
| *1/2 cup chopped* | 75 | 1.7 | 2.9 | | | 7425 | | .00 | | | | 21 | 1.13 | | |
| boiled | 14 | 85.1 | 0.2 | | 0 | 738 | 59 | | | | | 142 | | | |
| *1/2 cup chopped* | 90 | 1.5 | 2.5 | | | 7380 | | .00 | | | | 16 | .72 | | |
| **navy beans** | | | | | | | | | | | | | | | |
| boiled | 259 | 115.0 | 1.0 | 0.4 | 0 | 0 | 2 | .11 | .30 | 255 | 2 | 128 | 107 | 1.93 | 1.012 |
| *1 cup* | 182 | 15.8 | 47.9 | 0.3 | 6.6 | 3 | .37 | 1.0 | .00 | .46 | 669 | 285 | 4.51 | .537 | |
| cnd | 296 | 184.6 | 1.1 | 0.5 | 0 | 0 | 2 | .14 | .27 | 163 | 1173 | 123 | 122 | 2.02 | .983 |
| *1 cup* | 262 | 19.7 | 53.6 | 0.3 | | 4 | .37 | 1.3 | .00 | .45 | 755 | 352 | 4.84 | .545 | |
| **new zealand spinach** | | | | | | | | | | | | | | | |
| raw | 4 | 26.3 | 0.1 | 0.0 | 0 | 123 | 8 | .04 | | | 36 | 16 | 11 | | |
| *1/2 cup chopped* | 28 | 0.4 | 0.7 | 0.0 | | 1232 | .01 | 0.1 | .00 | .09 | 36 | 8 | .22 | | |
| boiled | 11 | 85.3 | 0.2 | 0.1 | 0 | 326 | 14 | .10 | | | 97 | 43 | 29 | | |
| *1/2 cup chopped* | 90 | 1.2 | 2.0 | 0.0 | | 3260 | .03 | 0.4 | .00 | .23 | 92 | 20 | .59 | | |
| **okra** | | | | | | | | | | | | | | | |
| boiled | 25 | 71.9 | 0.1 | 0.0 | 0 | 46 | 13 | .04 | .15 | 37 | 4 | 50 | 46 | .44 | .729 |
| *1/2 cup slices* | 80 | 1.5 | 5.8 | 0.0 | | 460 | .11 | 0.7 | .00 | .17 | 257 | 45 | .36 | .069 | |
| frzn, boiled | 34 | 83.8 | 0.3 | 0.1 | 0 | 47 | 11 | .11 | .04 | 134 | 3 | 88 | 47 | .57 | .939 |
| *1/2 cup slices* | 92 | 1.9 | 7.5 | 0.1 | | 473 | .09 | 0.7 | .00 | .22 | 215 | 42 | .62 | .089 | |
| **onion rings, frzn, heated[a]** | 285 | 20.0 | 18.7 | 3.6 | 0 | 16 | 1 | .10 | .05 | 9 | 263 | 21 | 14 | .29 | .294 |
| *7 rings* | 70 | 3.7 | 26.7 | 6.0 | | 158 | .20 | 2.5 | .00 | .16 | 90 | 57 | 1.18 | .056 | |
| **onions** | | | | | | | | | | | | | | | |
| raw | 27 | 72.7 | 0.2 | 0.1 | 0 | 0 | 7 | .01 | .13 | 16 | 2 | 20 | 8 | .14 | .106 |
| *1/2 cup chopped* | 80 | 0.9 | 5.9 | 0.0 | 0.6 | 0 | .05 | 0.1 | .00 | .11 | 124 | 23 | .29 | .032 | |
| boiled | 29 | 96.9 | 0.2 | 0.1 | 0 | 0 | 6 | .01 | .19 | 13 | 8 | 29 | 11 | .19 | .118 |
| *1/2 cup chopped* | 105 | 1.0 | 6.6 | 0.0 | | 0 | .04 | 0.1 | .00 | .13 | 159 | 24 | .21 | .042 | |
| cnd | 21 | 105.4 | 0.1 | 0.0 | 0 | | | | | | 416 | 51 | 6 | .32 | .114 |
| *1/2 cup chopped* | 112 | 1.0 | 4.5 | 0.0 | 1.2 | | | | .00 | | 124 | 31 | .15 | .062 | |
| dehydrated flakes | 45 | 0.6 | 0.1 | 0.0 | 0 | 0 | 11 | .01 | .22 | 23 | 3 | 36 | 13 | .26 | .194 |
| *1/4 cup* | 14 | 1.3 | 11.7 | 0.0 | | 0 | .07 | 0.1 | .00 | .19 | 227 | 42 | .22 | .058 | |
| frzn | | | | | | | | | | | | | | | |
| boiled | 28 | 92.2 | 0.1 | 0.0 | 0 | 2 | 5 | .02 | .07 | 13 | 8 | 27 | 8 | .09 | .040 |
| *3.5 oz* | 100 | 0.7 | 6.7 | 0.0 | | 21 | .02 | 0.1 | .00 | .08 | 101 | 2 | .34 | .024 | |
| small, whole, Birds Eye | 40 | 101.9 | 0.1 | 0.0 | 0 | | 9 | .03 | .10 | 24 | 10 | 40 | 12 | .13 | |
| *1/2 cup* | 113 | 1.0 | 9.6 | 0.0 | | 19 | .03 | 0.2 | .00 | .11 | 156 | 26 | .52 | .057 | |
| small w/ cream sce, Birds Eye | 100 | 65.4 | 5.9 | 1.1 | 1 | | 6 | .10 | .08 | 15 | 345 | 55 | 12 | .12 | |
| *1/2 cup* | 85 | 1.6 | 10.8 | 1.2 | | 251 | .03 | 0.2 | .22 | .24 | 168 | 55 | .36 | .038 | |
| **onions, spring, raw[b]** | 13 | 46.0 | 0.1 | 0.0 | 0 | 250 | 23 | .07 | | 7 | 2 | 30 | 10 | .22 | |
| *1/2 cup chopped* | 50 | 0.9 | 2.8 | 0.0 | | 2500 | .04 | 0.1 | .00 | .07 | 128 | 16 | .94 | .030 | |
| **onions, welsh, raw** | 34 | 90.5 | 0.4 | 0.2 | 0 | | 27 | .09 | | | | 18 | | | |
| *3.5 oz* | 100 | 1.9 | 6.5 | 0.1 | | | .05 | 0.4 | .00 | | | 49 | | | |
| **parsley** | | | | | | | | | | | | | | | |
| raw | 10 | 26.5 | 0.1 | | 0 | 156 | 27 | .03 | .05 | 55 | 12 | 39 | 13 | .22 | .048 |
| *1/2 cup chopped* | 30 | 0.7 | 2.1 | | | 1560 | .02 | 0.2 | .00 | .09 | 161 | 12 | 1.86 | .017 | |
| freeze-dried | 4 | 0.0 | 0.1 | | 0 | 89 | 2 | .03 | .02 | 22 | 5 | 2 | 5 | .09 | .019 |
| *1/4 cup* | 1.4 | 0.4 | 0.6 | | | 885 | .02 | 0.1 | .00 | .04 | 88 | 8 | .75 | .006 | |
| **parsnips, boiled** | 63 | 60.6 | 0.2 | 0.0 | 0 | 0 | 10 | .04 | .07 | 45 | 8 | 29 | 23 | .20 | .229 |
| *1/2 cup slices* | 78 | 1.0 | 15.2 | 0.0 | 2.1 | 0 | .07 | .6 | .00 | .46 | 287 | 54 | .45 | .108 | |

[a] Breaded & parboiled in veg oil.  [b] Includes tops & bulbs.

| | KCAL / WT (g) | H₂O (g) / PRO (g) | FAT (g) / CHO (g) | PUFA (g) / SFA (g) | CHOL (mg) / DFIB (g) | A (RE) / A (IU) | C (mg) / B-1 (mg) | B-2 (mg) / NIA (mg) | B-6 (mg) / B-12 (mcg) | FOL (mcg) / PANT (mg) | Na (mg) / K (mg) | Ca (mg) / P (mg) | Mg (mg) / Fe (mg) | Zn (mg) / Cu (mg) | Mn (mg) |
|---|---|---|---|---|---|---|---|---|---|---|---|---|---|---|---|
| **peas, green** | | | | | | | | | | | | | | | |
| raw | 63 | 61.5 | 0.3 | 0.1 | 0 | 50 | 31 | .10 | .13 | 51 | 4 | 19 | 26 | .97 | .320 |
| *1/2 cup* | 78 | 4.2 | 11.3 | 0.1 | 2.7 | 499 | .21 | 1.6 | .00 | .08 | 190 | 84 | 1.15 | .137 | |
| boiled | 67 | 62.3 | 0.2 | 0.1 | 0 | 48 | 11 | .12 | .17 | 51 | 2 | 22 | 31 | .95 | .420 |
| *1/2 cup* | 80 | 4.3 | 12.5 | 0.0 | 3.0 | 478 | .21 | 1.6 | .00 | .12 | 217 | 94 | 1.24 | .138 | |
| cnd | 59 | 69.4 | 0.3 | 0.1 | 0 | 65 | 8 | .07 | .05 | 38 | 186ᵃ | 17 | 15 | .60 | .258 |
| *1/2 cup* | 85 | 3.8 | 10.7 | 0.1 | 3.5 | 653 | .10 | 0.6 | .00 | .11 | 147 | 57 | .81 | .070 | |
| w/ onions, red peppers & garlic | 57 | 98.6 | 0.3 | 0.1 | | 49 | 13 | .08 | | | 290 | 18 | 17 | .74 | |
| *1/2 cup* | 114 | 3.5 | 10.6 | 0.1 | | 494 | .11 | 0.8 | .00 | | 139 | 61 | 1.37 | .113 | |
| frzn | | | | | | | | | | | | | | | |
| boiled | 63 | 63.6 | 0.2 | 0.1 | 0 | 53 | 8 | .08 | .09 | 47 | 70 | 19 | 23 | .75 | .331 |
| *1/2 cup* | 80 | 4.1 | 11.4 | 0.0 | 3.0 | 534 | .23 | 1.2 | .00 | .11 | 134 | 72 | 1.26 | .111 | |
| w/ butter sce, Le Sueur | 90 | 93.2 | 2.0 | | | | 17 | .09 | | | 542 | 19 | | | |
| *1/2 cup* | 115 | 4.9 | 13.6 | | | 626 | .30 | 1.8 | | | 138 | 83 | 1.84 | | |
| w/ cream sce, Birds Eye | 118 | 51.5 | 5.6 | 1.0 | 1 | | 6 | .13 | .08 | 37 | 368 | 42 | 23 | .63 | |
| *1/2 cup* | 76 | 4.1 | 13.4 | 1.1 | 2.7 | 637 | .19 | 1.0 | .20 | .24 | 171 | 91 | 1.02 | .089 | |
| w/ cream sce, Pillsbury | 100 | 92.9 | 4.2 | | | | 11 | .11 | | | 317 | 57 | | | |
| *1/2 cup* | 114 | 3.8 | 11.5 | | | 412 | .46 | 2.1 | | | 164 | 25 | 1.03 | | |
| **peas, green, early june** | | | | | | | | | | | | | | | |
| cnd, Pillsbury | 60 | 101.5 | 0.2 | | | | 8 | .08 | | | 367 | 21 | | | |
| *1/2 cup* | 118 | 3.4 | 11.1 | | | 485 | .13 | 0.4 | | | 100 | 63 | 1.18 | | |
| frzn, Le Sueur | 60 | 60.8 | 0.2 | | | | 11 | .30 | | | 169 | 21 | | | |
| *1/2 cup* | 76 | 4.7 | 9.1 | | | 406 | .18 | 1.4 | | | 116 | 74 | 1.14 | | |
| **peas, mature seeds, sprouted, boiled**ᵇ | 118 | 74.4 | 0.5 | 0.2 | 0 | 11 | 7 | .29 | .13 | 36 | 3 | 26 | 41 | .78 | .325 |
| *3.5 oz* | 100 | 7.1 | 21.9 | 0.1 | 3.3 | 107 | .22 | 1.1 | .00 | .68 | 268 | 24 | 1.67 | .020 | |
| **peas, split, boiled** | 231 | 136.2 | 0.8 | 0.3 | 0 | 1 | 1 | .11 | .09 | 127 | 4 | 26 | 71 | 1.96 | .776 |
| *1 cup* | 196 | 16.4 | 41.4 | 0.1 | | 14 | .37 | 1.7 | .00 | 1.17 | 710 | 195 | 2.52 | .355 | |
| **peppers, hot chili** | | | | | | | | | | | | | | | |
| rawᶜ | 18 | 39.5 | 0.1 | 0.0 | 0 | 35 | 109 | .04 | .13 | 11 | 3 | 8 | 11 | .14 | .107 |
| *1 pepper* | 45 | 0.9 | 4.3 | 0.0 | | 346ᵈ | .04 | 0.4 | .00 | .03 | 153 | 20 | .54 | .078 | |
| cndᶜ | 17 | 62.9 | 0.1 | 0.0 | 0 | 42 | 46 | .03 | | | | 5 | | | |
| *1/2 cup chopped* | 68 | 0.6 | 4.2 | 0.0 | | 415ᵉ | .01 | 0.5 | .00 | | | 12 | .34 | | |
| cnd, Del Monte | 28 | 86.8 | 0.1 | | | | 10 | .06 | | | 1882 | 49 | 17 | .16 | |
| *3.5 oz* | 100 | 1.1 | 6.9 | | | 272 | .03 | 0.5 | | | 138 | 26 | .70 | .180 | |
| **peppers, jalapeno, cnd** | 17 | 61.1 | 0.4 | 0.2 | 0 | 116 | 9 | .03 | | | 995 | 18 | 8 | .13 | |
| *1/2 cup chopped* | 68 | 0.5 | 3.3 | 0.0 | | 1156 | .02 | 0.3 | .00 | .73 | 92 | 12 | 1.90 | .095 | |
| **peppers, sweet** | | | | | | | | | | | | | | | |
| rawᶜ | 12 | 46.4 | 0.2 | 0.1 | 0 | 26 | 64ᶠ | .03 | .08 | 8 | 2 | 3 | 7 | .09 | .070 |
| *1/2 cup chopped* | 50 | 0.4 | 2.7 | 0.0 | 0.6 | 265ᵍ | .04 | 0.3 | .00 | .02 | 98 | 11 | .63 | .052 | |
| boiledᶜ | 12 | 64.4 | 0.2 | 0.1 | 0 | 26 | 76 | .02 | .07 | 7 | 1 | 3 | 7 | .08 | .066 |
| *1/2 cup chopped* | 68 | 0.4 | 2.7 | 0.0 | | 264ʰ | .04 | 0.2 | .00 | .02 | 88 | 10 | .60 | .048 | |
| cndᶜ | 13 | 63.9 | 0.2 | 0.1 | 0 | 11 | 33 | .02 | | | 958 | 28ⁱ | 8 | .12 | |
| *1/2 cup halves* | 70 | 0.6 | 2.7 | 0.0 | | 109ʲ | .02 | 0.4 | .00 | | 102 | 14 | .56 | .091 | |
| cherry, cnd, Del Monte | 42 | 82.4 | 0.1 | | | | 69 | .12 | | | 1970 | 18 | 20 | .24 | |
| *3.5 oz* | 100 | 1.8 | 10.4 | | | 2977 | .05 | 1.2 | | | 217 | 39 | .80 | .180 | |
| freeze-driedᶜ | 5 | 0.0 | 0.1 | 0.0 | 0 | 10 | 30 | .02 | .04 | 4 | 3 | 2 | 3 | .04 | .030 |
| *1/4 cup* | 1.6 | 0.3 | 1.1 | 0.0 | | 100ᵏ | .02 | 0.1 | .00 | .01 | 51 | 5 | .17 | .022 | |
| frzn, boiledᶜ | 18 | 94.7 | 0.2 | 0.1 | 0 | 29 | 41 | .03 | .11 | 10 | 4 | 8 | 7 | .05 | .097 |
| *3.5 oz* | 100 | 1.0 | 3.9 | 0.0 | | 290ˡ | .05 | 1.1 | .00 | .02 | 72 | 13 | .52 | .044 | |
| **pigeonpeas, boiled** | 204 | 115.2 | 0.6 | 0.3 | 0 | 0 | 0 | .10 | .08 | 186 | 9 | 72 | 77 | 1.51 | .842 |
| *1 cup* | 168 | 11.4 | 39.1 | 0.1 | 7.9 | 4 | .25 | 1.3 | .00 | .54 | 644 | 201 | 1.86 | .452 | |

ᵃ Special dietary pack contains 2 mg Na.
ᵇ Seeds attached to sprouts.
ᶜ Includes green & red varieties.
ᵈ For green varieties; red varieties contain 484 IU.
ᵉ For green varieties; red varieties contain 8087 IU.
ᶠ For green varieties; red varieties contain 95 mg.
ᵍ For green varieties; red varieties contain 2850 IU.
ʰ For green varieties; red varieties contain 2557 IU.
ⁱ Ca added as firming agent.
ʲ For green varieties; red varieties contain 364 IU.
ᵏ For green varieties; red varieties contain 1236 IU.
ˡ For green varieties; red varieties contain 3343 IU.

| | KCAL | H2O (g) | FAT (g) | PUFA (g) | CHOL (mg) | A (RE) | C (mg) | B-2 (mg) | B-6 (mg) | FOL (mcg) | Na (mg) | Ca (mg) | Mg (mg) | Zn (mg) | Mn (mg) |
| --- | --- | --- | --- | --- | --- | --- | --- | --- | --- | --- | --- | --- | --- | --- | --- |
| | WT (g) | PRO (g) | CHO (g) | SFA (g) | DFIB (g) | A (IU) | B-1 (mg) | NIA (mg) | B-12 (mcg) | PANT (mg) | K (mg) | P (mg) | Fe (mg) | Cu (mg) | |
| **pimientos, cnd, Dromedary** | 10 | | 0.0 | | | | | | | | 5 | | | | |
| *1 oz* | 28 | 0.0 | 2.0 | | | | | | | | 45 | | | | |
| **pink beans, boiled** | 252 | 103.4 | 0.8 | 0.4 | 0 | 0 | 0 | .11 | .30 | 284 | 3 | 88 | 110 | 1.63 | .926 |
| *1 cup* | 169 | 15.3 | 47.2 | 0.2 | 7.4 | 0 | .43 | 1.0 | .00 | .51 | 858 | 279 | 3.89 | .458 | |
| **pinto beans** | | | | | | | | | | | | | | | |
| boiled | 235 | 109.9 | 0.9 | 0.3 | 0 | 0 | 4 | .16 | .27 | 294 | 3 | 82 | 95 | 1.85 | .951 |
| *1 cup* | 171 | 14.0 | 43.9 | 0.2 | 6.8 | 3 | .32 | 0.7 | .00 | .49 | 800 | 273 | 4.47 | .439 | |
| cnd | 186 | 189.1 | 0.8 | 0.3 | 0 | 0 | 2 | .15 | .18 | 145 | 998 | 89 | 64 | 1.66 | .550 |
| *1 cup* | 240 | 11.0 | 34.9 | 0.2 | | 3 | .24 | 0.7 | .00 | .33 | 723 | 220 | 3.85 | .336 | |
| poi | 134 | 86.0 | 0.2 | 0.1 | 0 | 2 | 5 | .05 | | | 14 | 19 | 29 | | |
| *1/2 cup* | 120 | 0.5 | 32.7 | | | 24 | .16 | 1.3 | .00 | | 220 | 47 | 1.06 | | |
| **pokeberry shoots, boiled** | 16 | 76.2 | 0.3 | | 0 | 713 | 67 | .21 | | | | 43 | | | |
| *1/2 cup* | 82 | 1.9 | 2.5 | | | 7134 | .06 | 0.9 | .00 | | | 27 | .98 | | |
| **potato** | | | | | | | | | | | | | | | |
| raw w/o skin | 88 | 88.4 | 0.1 | 0.0 | 0 | | 22 | .04 | .29 | 14 | 7 | 8 | 24 | .44 | .295 |
| *1 potato* | 112 | 2.3 | 20.1 | 0.0 | | | .10 | 1.7 | .00 | .43 | 608 | 52 | .85 | .290 | |
| baked w/ skin | 220 | 143.8 | 0.2 | 0.1 | 0 | | 26 | .07 | .70 | 22 | 16 | 20 | 55 | .65 | .463 |
| *1 potato* | 202 | 4.7 | 51.0 | 0.1 | | | .22 | 3.3 | .00 | 1.12 | 844 | 115 | 2.75 | .616 | |
| baked w/o skin | 145 | 117.7 | 0.2 | 0.1 | 0 | | 20 | .03 | .47 | 14 | 8 | 8 | 39 | .45 | .251 |
| *1 potato* | 156 | 3.1 | 33.6 | 0.0 | | | .16 | 2.2 | .00 | .87 | 610 | 78 | .55 | .335 | |
| baked w/ cheese topping, frzn, Pillsbury | 200 | 96.6 | 5.5 | | | | 7 | .07 | | | | 521 | 42 | | |
| *5 oz* | 142 | 4.5 | 32.9 | | | 339 | .06 | 2.4 | | | 625 | 112 | .85 | | |
| baked w/ sour cream & chives, frzn, Pillsbury—*5 oz* | 231 | 93.7 | 9.9 | | | | 5 | .09 | | | | 579 | 50 | | |
| | 142 | 4.7 | 30.7 | | | 439 | .07 | 2.4 | | | 575 | 111 | .99 | | |
| boiled w/o skin | 116 | 104.6 | 0.1 | 0.1 | 0 | | 10 | .03 | .36 | 12 | 7 | 10 | 26 | .37 | .189 |
| *1 potato* | 135 | 2.3 | 27.0 | 0.0 | | | .13 | 1.8 | .00 | .69 | 443 | 54 | .42 | .225 | |
| cnd w/o skin | 54 | 75.9 | 0.2 | 0.1 | 0 | | 5 | .01 | .17 | 6 | | 5 | 12 | .25 | .087 |
| *1/2 cup* | 90 | 1.3 | 12.3 | 0.0 | | | .06 | 0.8 | .00 | .32 | 206 | 25 | 1.13 | .051 | |
| cottage fries, frzn, heated[a] | 109 | 26.5 | 4.1 | 1.7 | 0 | | 5 | .02 | .12 | 8 | 23 | 5 | 11 | .21 | .152 |
| *10 strips* | 50 | 1.7 | 17.0 | 1.9 | | | .06 | 1.2 | .00 | .35 | 240 | 33 | .75 | .100 | |
| french fried, from restaurant[b] | 158 | 19.0 | 8.3 | 3.8 | 0 | | 5 | .01 | .12 | 15 | 108 | 10 | 17 | .19 | .096 |
| *10 pieces* | 50 | 2.0 | 20.0 | 2.5 | | | .09 | 1.6 | .00 | .33 | 366 | 47 | .38 | .069 | |
| french fried, frzn, heated[a] | 111 | 26.5 | 4.4 | 0.3 | 0 | | 6 | .02 | .12 | 8 | 15 | 4 | 11 | .21 | .148 |
| *10 pieces* | 50 | 1.7 | 17.0 | 2.1 | | | .06 | 1.2 | .00 | .33 | 229 | 43 | .67 | .082 | |
| frzn, boiled w/o skin | 65 | 82.8 | 0.1 | 0.1 | 0 | | 9 | .03 | .20 | 8 | 20 | 7 | 11 | .25 | .185 |
| *3.5 oz* | 100 | 2.0 | 14.5 | 0.0 | | | .10 | 1.3 | .00 | .28 | 287 | 26 | .84 | .078 | |
| hash brown, frzn, prep[c] | 170 | 43.8 | 9.0 | 1.0 | | | 5 | .02 | .10 | | 27 | 12 | 13 | .25 | .174 |
| *1/2 cup* | 78 | 2.5 | 21.9 | 3.5 | | | .09 | 1.9 | .00 | .35 | 340 | 56 | 1.17 | .119 | |
| hash brown, homemade[c] | 163 | 48.0 | 10.9 | 1.3 | | | 5 | .02 | .22 | 6 | 19 | 6 | 16 | .23 | .119 |
| *1/2 cup* | 78 | 1.9 | 16.6 | 4.2 | | | .06 | 1.6 | .00 | .39 | 251 | 32 | .63 | .140 | |
| hash brown w/ butter sce, frzn, prep | 178 | 63.7 | 8.9 | 1.8 | 23 | 16 | 4 | .03 | | | 101 | 33 | | | |
| *3.5 oz* | 100 | 2.5 | 24.1 | 3.4 | | 111 | .05 | 1.4 | | | 327 | | .99 | | |
| mashed, from flakes[d] | 118 | 80.1 | 5.9 | 0.3 | 15 | 22 | 10 | .05 | .01 | 8 | 349 | 52 | 19 | .18 | |
| *1/2 cup* | 105 | 2.0 | 15.8 | 3.6 | | 189 | .12 | 0.7 | .08 | .13 | 245 | 59 | .23 | .017 | |
| mashed, from granules[d] | 137 | 77.7 | 6.5 | 1.4 | 18 | 192 | 1 | .06 | .44 | 7 | 358 | 57 | 19 | .09 | |
| *1/2 cup* | 105 | 2.0 | 17.6 | 1.2 | | 778 | .04 | 0.7 | .46 | 1.57 | 223 | 50 | 4.27 | | |
| mashed, from mix, French's | 130 | | 6.0 | | | | | | | | 340 | | | | |
| *1/2 cup* | 105 | 2.0 | 16.0 | | | | | | | | 270 | | | | |
| mashed, from mix, Hungry Jack | 140 | | 7.0 | | | | | | | | 270 | | | | |
| *1/2 cup* | 105 | 3.0 | 17.0 | | | | | | | | 380 | | | | |
| mashed, homemade[e] | 111 | 80.1 | 4.4 | 1.3 | 2[f] | 21 | 6 | .04 | .24 | 8 | 309 | 27 | 19 | .29 | .120 |
| *1/2 cup* | 105 | 2.0 | 17.5 | 1.1 | | 177 | .09 | 1.1 | .05 | .60 | 303 | 49 | .28 | .144 | |
| microwaved w/ skin | 212 | 145.5 | 0.2 | 0.1 | 0 | | 31 | .07 | .70 | 24 | 16 | 22 | 54 | .73 | .590 |
| *1 potato* | 202 | 4.9 | 48.7 | 0.1 | | | .24 | 3.5 | .00 | | 903 | 212 | 2.50 | .675 | |
| microwaved w/o skin | 156 | 114.7 | 0.2 | 0.1 | 0 | | 24 | .04 | .50 | 19 | 11 | 8 | 39 | .51 | .265 |
| *1 potato* | 156 | 3.3 | 36.3 | 0.0 | | | .20 | 2.5 | .00 | .93 | 641 | 170 | .64 | .370 | |

[a] Pan-fried in veg oil.
[b] Fried in veg oil; french fries fried in animal fat & veg oil contain 0.5 g PUFA, 3.4 g SFA & 6 mg cholestrol.
[c] Prepared w/ veg oil.
[d] Whole milk & butter added.
[e] Whole milk, margarine & salt added.
[f] If butter is used in place of margarine, cholestrol is 13 mg.

| | KCAL / WT (g) | H₂O (g) / PRO (g) | FAT (g) / CHO (g) | PUFA (g) / SFA (g) | CHOL (mg) / DFIB (g) | A (RE) / A (IU) | C (mg) / B-1 (mg) | B-2 (mg) / NIA (mg) | B-6 (mg) / B-12 (mcg) | FOL (mcg) / PANT (mg) | Na (mg) / K (mg) | Ca (mg) / P (mg) | Mg (mg) / Fe (mg) | Zn (mg) / Cu (mg) | Mn (mg) |
|---|---|---|---|---|---|---|---|---|---|---|---|---|---|---|---|
| **potato pancakes** | | | | | | | | | | | | | | | |
| from mix, French's | 80 | | 1.0 | | | | | | | | 410 | | | | |
| *1/2 cup* | | 3.0 | 16.0 | | | | | | | | 140 | | | | |
| homemade[a] | 495 | 30.3 | 12.6 | 2.5 | 93 | 27 | 0 | .10 | .29 | 22 | 388 | 21 | 24 | .68 | .296 |
| *1 pancake* | 76 | 4.6 | 26.4 | 3.4 | | 89 | .10 | 1.6 | .22 | .71 | 538 | 78 | 1.21 | .273 | |
| **potato puffs, frzn, prep[b]** | 138 | 32.8 | 6.7 | 0.5 | 0 | 1 | 4 | .05 | .14 | 10 | 462 | 19 | 12 | .19 | .168 |
| *1/2 cup* | 62 | 2.1 | 18.9 | 3.2 | | 10 | .12 | 1.3 | .00 | .41 | 236 | 30 | .97 | .037 | |
| **potato salad, commercial** | | | | | | | | | | | | | | | |
| Fresh Chef | 210 | | 14.0 | | | | 3 | .11 | | | 320 | 21 | | | |
| *4 oz* | 113 | 2.1 | 18.9 | | | 0 | .04 | 0.8 | | | 244 | | 1.30 | | |
| german style, cnd, Joan of Arc | 120 | | 1.3 | | | | 13 | .07 | | | 854 | 6 | | | |
| *1/2 cup* | 130 | 2.0 | 24.6 | | | 172 | .04 | 0.9 | | | 216 | 27 | .65 | | |
| home style, cnd, Joan of Arc | 160 | | 8.6 | | | | 5 | .08 | | | 728 | 16 | | | |
| *1/2 cup* | 120 | 2.0 | 18.2 | | | 187 | .10 | 1.4 | | | 281 | 54 | .72 | | |
| **potato salad, homemade[c]** | 179 | 95.0 | 10.3 | 4.7 | 86 | 41 | 13 | .08 | .18 | 8 | 661 | 24 | 19 | .39 | .126 |
| *1/2 cup* | 125 | 3.4 | 14.0 | 1.8 | | 261 | .10 | 1.1 | .19 | .67 | 317 | 65 | .81 | .148 | |
| **potatoes, au gratin** | | | | | | | | | | | | | | | |
| from mix[d] | 127 | 108.2 | 5.6 | 0.2 | | 4 | | .11 | .06 | | 601 | 114 | 21 | .33 | |
| *1/6 of 5.5 oz pkg* | 137 | 3.2 | 17.6 | 3.5 | | | .03 | 1.3 | | .33 | 300 | 130 | .44 | .063 | |
| from mix, French's | 140 | | 6.0 | | | | | | | | 470 | | | | |
| *1/2 cup* | | 4.0 | 19.0 | | | | | | | | 220 | | | | |
| frzn, Am Hosp Co | 164 | | 8.8 | | 8 | | 8 | .10 | | | 147 | 94 | | | |
| *4 oz* | 113 | 5.6 | 15.6 | | | 133 | .07 | | .08 | | 456 | | .32 | | |
| frzn, Banquet | 98 | | 2.0 | | 15 | | 0 | | .08 | | 472 | 41 | | | |
| *4 oz* | 113 | 2.0 | 17.0 | | | 19 | .04 | 0.3 | | | 127 | | .40 | | |
| homemade[e] | 160 | 90.3 | 9.3 | 0.3 | 29[f] | 47 | 12 | .14 | .21 | 10 | 528 | 146 | 24 | .84 | .196 |
| *1/2 cup* | 122 | 6.2 | 13.7 | 5.8 | | 322 | .08 | 1.2 | .25 | .47 | 483 | 138 | .78 | .195 | |
| **potatoes, creamy ital style w/ parmesan sce, from mix, French's—*1/2 cup*** | 130 | | 4.0 | | | | | | | | 430 | | | | |
| | | 3.0 | 21.0 | | | | | | | | 190 | | | | |
| **potatoes, creamy stroganoff, from mix, French's—*1/2 cup*** | 130 | | 4.0 | | | | | | | | 520 | | | | |
| | | 3.0 | 20.0 | | | | | | | | 210 | | | | |
| **potatoes, o'brien** | | | | | | | | | | | | | | | |
| frzn, prep | 204 | 62.0 | 13.2 | 3.5 | | 19 | 10 | .14 | | | 43 | 20 | | | |
| *3.5 oz* | 100 | 2.2 | 21.9 | 3.3 | | 188 | .05 | 1.4 | | | | | .96 | | |
| homemade[g] | 157 | 154.4 | 2.5 | 0.1 | 7 | 111 | 32 | .11 | .41 | 16 | 421 | 70 | 35 | .59 | .235 |
| *1 cup* | 194 | 4.6 | 30.0 | 1.5 | | 934 | .15 | 2.0 | .16 | .85 | 516 | 97 | .91 | .250 | |
| **potatoes, scalloped** | | | | | | | | | | | | | | | |
| from mix[h] | 127 | 108.5 | 5.9 | 0.3 | | | 5 | .08 | .06 | 2 | 467 | 49 | 19 | .34 | |
| *1/6 of 5.5 oz pkg* | 137 | 2.9 | 17.5 | 3.6 | | | .03 | 1.4 | | .45 | 278 | 77 | .52 | .067 | |
| from mix, crispy top w/ savory onion, French's—*1/2 cup* | 140 | | 5.0 | | | | | | | | 420 | | | | |
| | | 3.0 | 20.0 | | | | | | | | 200 | | | | |
| from mix w/ cheese, French's | 140 | | 5.0 | | | | | | | | 370 | | | | |
| *1/2 cup* | | 3.0 | 20.0 | | | | | | | | 200 | | | | |
| homemade[i] | 105 | 98.8 | 4.5 | 0.2 | 14[j] | 23 | 13 | .11 | .22 | 11 | 409 | 70 | 23 | .49 | .203 |
| *1/2 cup* | 122 | 3.5 | 13.2 | 2.8 | | 165 | .08 | 1.3 | .17 | .63 | 461 | 77 | .70 | .199 | |
| **potatoes w/ sour cream & chives, from mix, French's—*1/2 cup*** | 150 | | 6.0 | | | | | | | | 560 | | | | |
| | | 3.0 | 20.0 | | | | | | | | 220 | | | | |
| **pumpkin** | | | | | | | | | | | | | | | |
| boiled | 24 | 114.3 | 0.1 | 0.0 | 0 | 132 | 6 | .10 | | | 2 | 18 | 11 | | |
| *1/2 cup mashed* | 122 | 0.9 | 6.0 | 0.0 | | 1320 | .04 | 0.5 | .00 | | 281 | 37 | .70 | | |
| cnd | 41 | 109.8 | 0.3 | 0.0 | 0 | 2691 | 5 | .07 | .07 | 15 | 6 | 32 | 28 | .21 | |
| *1/2 cup* | 122 | 1.3 | 9.9 | 0.2 | | 26908 | .03 | 0.4 | .00 | .49 | 251 | 42 | 1.70 | .131 | |

[a] Potatoes, eggs, onion, margarine, flour & salt.
[b] Pan-fried in veg oil.
[c] Potatoes, egg, mayonnaise, celery, sweet pickle relish, onion, green pepper, pimiento, salt & dry mustard.
[d] Water, whole milk & margarine added.
[e] Potatoes, whole milk, cheddar cheese, butter, flour & salt.
[f] If margarine is used in place of butter, cholesterol is 18 mg.
[g] Potatoes, whole milk, onions, green pepper, bread crumbs, salt, butter & black pepper.
[h] Water, whole milk & butter added.
[i] Potatoes, whole milk, butter, flour & salt.
[j] If margarine is used in place of butter, cholesterol is 7 mg.

| | KCAL / WT (g) | H₂O (g) / PRO (g) | FAT (g) / CHO (g) | PUFA (g) / SFA (g) | CHOL (mg) / DFIB (g) | A (RE) / A (IU) | C (mg) / B-1 (mg) | B-2 (mg) / NIA (mg) | B-6 (mg) / B-12 (mcg) | FOL (mcg) / PANT (mg) | Na (mg) / K (mg) | Ca (mg) / P (mg) | Mg (mg) / Fe (mg) | Zn (mg) / Cu (mg) | Mn (mg) |
|---|---|---|---|---|---|---|---|---|---|---|---|---|---|---|---|
| **pumpkin pie mix, cnd** | 141 | 96.5 | 0.2 | 0.0 | 0 | 1120 | 5 | .16 | | | 280 | 49 | 22 | .36 | |
| *1/2 cup* | 135 | 1.5 | 35.6 | 0.1 | | 11203 | .02 | 0.5 | .00 | | 186 | 60 | 1.43 | .092 | |
| **purslane, boiled** | 10 | 54.2 | 0.1 | | 0 | 107 | 6 | .05 | | | 26 | 45 | 39 | | |
| *1/2 cup* | 58 | 0.9 | 2.1 | | | 1074 | .02 | 0.3 | .00 | | 283 | 22 | .45 | | |
| **radish, raw** | 7 | 42.7 | 0.2 | 0.0 | 0 | 0 | 10 | .02 | .03 | 12 | 11 | 9 | 4 | .13 | .032 |
| *10 radishes* | 45 | 0.3 | 1.6 | 0.0 | | 3 | .00 | 0.1 | .00 | .04 | 104 | 8 | .13 | .018 | |
| **radish, oriental[a]** | | | | | | | | | | | | | | | |
| raw | 8 | 41.6 | 0.0 | 0.0 | 0 | 0 | 10 | .01 | | 0 | 9 | 12 | 7 | | |
| *1/2 cup slices* | 44 | 0.3 | 1.8 | 0.0 | | 0 | .01 | 0.1 | | | 100 | 10 | .18 | | |
| boiled | 13 | 70.3 | 0.2 | 0.1 | 0 | 0 | 11 | .02 | | | 10 | 12 | 7 | | |
| *1/2 cup slices* | 74 | 0.5 | 2.5 | 0.1 | | 0 | .00 | 0.1 | .00 | | 211 | 18 | .11 | | |
| dried | 157 | 11.4 | 0.4 | 0.2 | 0 | 0 | 0 | .39 | | | 161 | 365 | 99 | | |
| *1/2 cup* | 58 | 4.6 | 36.8 | 0.1 | | 0 | .16 | 2.0 | .00 | | 2027 | 118 | 3.90 | | |
| **red beans** | | | | | | | | | | | | | | | |
| Joan of Arc | 100 | | 0.4 | | | | 0 | .11 | | | 445 | 39 | | | |
| *1/2 cup* | 118 | 5.3 | 18.9 | | | 28 | .08 | 1.0 | | | 152 | 94 | 1.77 | | |
| Van Camp's | 194 | 173.0 | 0.6 | | | | | .10 | | | 928 | 84 | | | |
| *1 cup* | 227 | 11.5 | 35.6 | | | 0 | .10 | 0.6 | | | 546 | | 3.65 | | |
| **rhubarb** | | | | | | | | | | | | | | | |
| frzn, raw | 29 | 128.1 | 0.2 | | 0 | 15 | 7 | .04 | .03 | 11 | 2 | 266 | 25 | .14 | .133 |
| *1 cup* | 137 | 0.8 | 7.0 | | | 147 | .04 | 0.3 | .00 | .09 | 148 | 17 | .39 | .032 | |
| frzn, ckd, sweetened | 139 | 81.4 | 0.1 | | | 8 | 4 | .03 | .02 | 6 | 2 | 174 | 15 | .10 | .088 |
| *1/2 cup* | 120 | 0.5 | 37.4 | | | 83 | .02 | 0.2 | .00 | .06 | 115 | 10 | .25 | .032 | |
| **rice, brown, ckd** | 232 | 137.1 | 1.2 | | 0 | 0 | 0 | .04 | | | 550[b] | 23 | | | |
| *1 cup* | 195 | 4.9 | 49.7 | | | 0 | .18 | 2.7 | .00 | | 137 | 142 | 1.00 | | |
| **rice, white** | | | | | | | | | | | | | | | |
| enr, ckd | 223 | 148.8 | 0.2 | | | | 0 | .02 | | | 767[b] | 21 | | | |
| *1 cup* | 205 | 4.1 | 49.6 | | | 0 | .23 | 2.1 | | | 57 | 57 | 1.80 | | |
| enr, inst, ckd | 180 | 120.3 | 0.0 | | | | 0 | | | | 450[b] | 5 | | | |
| *1 cup* | 165 | 3.6 | 39.9 | | | 0 | .21 | 1.7 | | | | 31 | 1.30 | | |
| enr, parboiled, ckd | 186 | 128.5 | 0.2 | | | | 0 | .02 | | | 627[b] | 33 | | | |
| *1 cup* | 175 | 3.7 | 40.8 | | | 0 | .19 | 2.1 | | | 75 | 100 | 1.40 | | |
| extra long grain, enr, ckd | 85 | 57.0 | 0.0 | 0.0 | 0 | 0 | 0 | .00 | .00 | 0 | 0[c] | 22 | | | |
| *1/2 cup* | 80 | 2.0 | 19.0 | 0.0 | 0.1 | 0 | .00 | 1.0 | .00 | | 22 | 8 | .70 | | |
| extra long grain, enr, parboiled, ckd, Chef-Way—*1/2 cup* | 83 | 57.0 | 0.1 | 0.0 | 0 | 0 | 0 | .00 | | 0 | 0[c] | 15 | | | |
| | 80 | 2.0 | 18.0 | 0.0 | 0.0 | 0 | .00 | 0.9 | .00 | | 34 | 45 | .60 | | |
| from mix, Minute | 141 | 92.0 | 2.0 | 0.1 | 5 | | 0 | .01 | .01 | 1 | 21 | 5 | 6 | .37 | |
| *2/3 cup* | 124 | 2.6 | 27.4 | 1.2 | | 72 | .15 | 1.2 | .00 | .10 | 1 | 34 | 1.08 | .041 | |
| for rib roast | 152 | 82.6 | 4.1 | 0.2 | 10 | | 0 | .02 | .02 | 2 | 724 | 10 | 10 | .36 | |
| *1/2 cup* | 117 | 3.0 | 25.2 | 2.4 | | 146 | .16 | 1.4 | .01 | .08 | 25 | 38 | 1.21 | .041 | |
| fried | 159 | 62.1 | 4.8 | 1.8 | 0 | | 0 | .01 | .02 | 2 | 551 | 10 | 9 | .37 | |
| *1/2 cup* | 97 | 3.2 | 25.2 | 0.7 | | 1 | .16 | 1.4 | .00 | .08 | 47 | 37 | 1.30 | .043 | |
| w/ chicken flavor | 153 | 72.7 | 4.2 | 0.3 | 10 | | 0 | .01 | .01 | 2 | 688 | 11 | 12 | .39 | |
| *1/2 cup* | 107 | 3.1 | 25.1 | 2.5 | | 148 | .17 | 1.4 | .01 | .07 | 22 | 40 | 1.25 | .039 | |
| frzn, w/ herb butter sce, Rice Originals | 150 | 86.5 | 5.0 | | | | 0 | .04 | | | 406 | 18 | | | |
| *1/2 cup* | 119 | 2.9 | 23.3 | | | 206 | .24 | 2.5 | | | 49 | 40 | 1.79 | | |
| **rice, long grain & wild** | | | | | | | | | | | | | | | |
| from mix, Minute | 148 | 81.9 | 4.1 | 0.2 | 10 | | 1 | .02 | .02 | 3 | 571 | 14 | 10 | .29 | |
| *1/2 cup* | 115 | 2.8 | 24.7 | 2.4 | | 153 | .20 | 2.4 | .01 | .13 | 40 | 25 | 1.45 | .046 | |
| frzn, Rice Originals | 120 | 80.7 | 2.1 | | | | 3 | .03 | | | 530 | 14 | | | |
| *1/2 cup* | 109 | 2.6 | 22.5 | | | 89 | .21 | 1.3 | | | 39 | 40 | 1.42 | | |
| **rice pilaf, frzn, Rice Originals** | 121 | 87.8 | 1.6 | | | | 1 | .04 | | | 537 | 12 | | | |
| *1/2 cup* | 117 | 2.8 | 23.4 | | | 35 | .26 | 2.6 | | | 88 | 35 | 1.52 | | |
| **rutabaga, boiled** | 29 | 76.7 | 0.2 | 0.1 | 0 | 0 | 19 | .03 | .08 | 13 | 15 | 36 | 18 | .26 | .130 |
| *1/2 cup cubes* | 85 | 0.9 | 6.6 | 0.0 | | 0 | .06 | 0.5 | .00 | .12 | 244 | 42 | .40 | .031 | |

[a] Includes daikon (Japanese) & Chinese.
[b] Salt added as specified on pkg; if no salt is added, Na is negligible.
[c] No salt added during cooking.

| | KCAL | H2O (g) | FAT (g) | PUFA (g) | CHOL (mg) | A (RE) | C (mg) | B-2 (mg) | B-6 (mg) | FOL (mcg) | Na (mg) | Ca (mg) | Mg (mg) | Zn (mg) | Mn (mg) |
|---|---|---|---|---|---|---|---|---|---|---|---|---|---|---|---|
| | WT (g) | PRO (g) | CHO (g) | SFA (g) | DFIB (g) | A (IU) | B-1 (mg) | NIA (mg) | B-12 (mcg) | PANT (mg) | K (mg) | P (mg) | Fe (mg) | Cu (mg) | |
| **salad, Fresh Chef** | | | | | | | | | | | | | | | |
| chicken w/ pineapple tidbits | 346 | | 29.7 | | | | 3 | .07 | | | 622 | 29 | | | |
| 4.66 oz | 132 | 13.2 | 6.7 | | | 82 | .05 | 1.1 | | | 201 | | .90 | | |
| ham & cheddar cheese | 322 | | 28.1 | | | | 4 | .16 | | | 1061 | 79 | | | |
| 4.65 oz | 132 | 11.6 | 5.5 | | | 149 | .32 | 1.5 | | | 256 | | 1.10 | | |
| **salsify, boiled** | 46 | 55.1 | 0.1 | | 0 | 0 | 3 | .12 | | | 11 | 32 | 12 | | |
| 1/2 cup slices | 68 | 1.9 | 10.5 | | | 0 | .04 | 0.3 | .00 | | 192 | 38 | .37 | | |
| **sauerkraut** | | | | | | | | | | | | | | | |
| bottled, Claussen | 6 | 25.9 | 0.1 | | | | 3 | .00 | .03 | 1 | 189 | 9 | 3 | | .04 |
| 1 oz | 28 | 0.2 | 1.2 | | | | .01 | 0.0 | | .03 | 43 | 5 | .16 | .010 | |
| cnd | 22 | 109.2 | 0.2 | 0.1 | 0 | 2 | 17 | .03 | .15 | | 780 | 36 | 15 | .22 | |
| 1/2 cup | 118 | 1.1 | 5.1 | 0.0 | | 21 | .03 | 0.2 | .00 | .11 | 201 | 23 | 1.73 | .113 | |
| **seaweed** | | | | | | | | | | | | | | | |
| agar, raw | 26 | 91.3 | 0.0 | 0.0 | 0 | 0 | 0 | .02 | | | 9 | 54 | 67 | | .373 |
| 3.5 oz | 100 | 0.5 | 6.8 | 0.0 | | 0 | .01 | 0.1 | .00 | | 226 | 5 | 1.86 | | |
| agar, dried | 306 | 8.7 | 0.3 | 0.1 | 0 | 0 | 0 | .22 | | | 102 | 625 | 770 | | 4.300 |
| 3.5 oz | 100 | 6.2 | 80.9 | 0.1 | | 0 | .01 | 0.2 | .00 | | 1125 | 52 | 21.40 | | |
| irishmoss, raw | 49 | 81.3 | 0.2 | 0.1 | 0 | | 0 | .59 | | | 67 | 72 | | 1.95 | .370 |
| 3.5 oz | 100 | 1.5 | 12.3 | 0.0 | | | .47 | 0.2 | .00 | | 63 | 157 | 8.90 | .149 | |
| kelp (kombu/tangle), raw | 43 | 81.6 | 0.6 | 0.0 | 0 | 12 | | .15 | | 180 | 233 | 168 | 121 | 1.23 | .200 |
| 3.5 oz | 100 | 1.7 | 9.6 | 0.2 | | 116 | .05 | 0.5 | .00 | | 89 | 42 | 2.85 | .130 | |
| laver (nori), raw | 35 | 85.0 | 0.3 | 0.1 | 0 | 520 | 39 | .45 | .16 | | 48 | 70 | 2 | 1.05 | .988 |
| 3.5 oz | 100 | 5.8 | 5.1 | 0.1 | | 5202 | .10 | 1.5 | .00 | | 356 | 58 | 1.80 | .264 | |
| spirulina, raw | 26 | 90.7 | 0.4 | 0.1 | 0 | 1 | | .34 | .03 | | 98 | | | | |
| 3.5 oz | 100 | 5.9 | 2.4 | 0.1 | | | .22 | 1.2 | .00 | .33 | 127 | 11 | | | |
| spirulina, dried | 290 | 4.7 | 7.7 | 2.1 | 0 | 10 | | 3.67 | .36 | | 1048 | | 195 | | |
| 3.5 oz | 100 | 57.5 | 23.9 | 2.7 | | | 2.38 | 12.8 | .00 | 3.48 | 1363 | 118 | 28.50 | | |
| wakame, raw | 45 | 80.0 | 0.6 | 0.2 | 0 | 36 | 3 | .23 | | | 872 | 150 | 107 | .38 | 1.400 |
| 3.5 oz | 100 | 3.0 | 9.1 | 0.1 | | 360 | .06 | 1.6 | .00 | | 50 | 80 | 2.18 | .284 | |
| **shallots** | | | | | | | | | | | | | | | |
| raw | 7 | 8.0 | 0.0 | 0.0 | 0 | 1 | | .00 | | | 1 | 4 | | | |
| 1 T chopped | 10 | 0.3 | 1.7 | 0.0 | | | .01 | 0.0 | .00 | | 33 | 6 | .12 | | |
| freeze-dried | 13 | 0.1 | 0.0 | 0.0 | 0 | 1 | | .00 | .06 | 4 | 2 | 7 | 4 | .07 | .051 |
| 1/4 cup | 4 | 0.4 | 2.9 | 0.0 | | | .01 | 0.0 | .00 | .05 | 59 | 11 | .22 | .015 | |
| **shellie beans, cnd** | 37 | 110.6 | 0.2 | 0.1 | 0 | 28 | 4 | .07 | | | 408 | 36 | | | |
| 1/2 cup | 122 | 2.1 | 7.6 | 0.0 | | 278 | .04 | 0.3 | .00 | | 133 | | 1.21 | | |
| **soybean products** | | | | | | | | | | | | | | | |
| miso | 284 | 57.2 | 8.4 | 4.7 | 0 | 12 | 0 | .35 | .30 | 46 | 5032 | 92 | 58 | 4.58 | 1.185 |
| 1/2 cup | 138 | 16.3 | 38.6 | 1.2 | 3.9 | 120 | .13 | 1.2 | .29 | .36 | 226 | 211 | 3.78 | .603 | |
| natto | 187 | 48.4 | 9.7 | 5.5 | 0 | 0 | 11 | .17 | | | 6 | 191 | 101 | 2.67 | 1.345 |
| 1/2 cup | 88 | 15.6 | 12.6 | 1.4 | | 0 | .14 | 0.0 | | | 642 | 153 | 7.57 | .587 | |
| tempeh | 165 | 45.6 | 6.4 | 3.6 | 0 | 57 | 0 | .09 | .25 | 43 | 5 | 77 | 58 | 1.50 | 1.187 |
| 1/2 cup | 83 | 15.7 | 14.1 | 0.9 | | 569 | .11 | 3.8 | .70 | .30 | 305 | 171 | 1.88 | .556 | |
| tofu, dried-frozen (koyadufu) | 82 | 1.0 | 5.2 | 2.9 | 0 | 9 | 0 | .05 | .05 | 16 | 1 | 62 | 10 | .83 | .627 |
| 1 piece | 17 | 8.2 | 2.5 | 0.7 | | 88 | .08 | 0.2 | .00 | .07 | 3 | 82 | 1.65 | .200 | |
| tofu, fried | 35 | 6.6 | 2.6 | 1.5 | 0 | 0 | 0 | .01 | .01 | 4 | 2 | 48 | 8 | .26 | .194 |
| 1 piece | 13 | 2.2 | 1.4 | 0.4 | | | .02 | 0.0 | .00 | .02 | 19 | 37 | .63 | .052 | |
| tofu, okara | 47 | 49.8 | 1.1 | 0.5 | 0 | 0 | 0 | .01 | | | 6 | 49 | 16 | | |
| 1/2 cup | 61 | 2.0 | 7.7 | 0.1 | | 0 | .01 | 0.1 | .00 | | 130 | 37 | .79 | | |
| tofu, raw | 94 | 104.8 | 5.9 | 3.3 | 0 | 11 | 0 | .06 | .06 | 19 | 9 | 130 | 127 | 1.00 | .750 |
| 1/2 cup | 124 | 10.0 | 2.3 | 0.9 | 0.6 | 105 | .10 | 0.2 | .00 | .08 | 150 | 120 | 6.65 | .239 | |
| tofu, raw, firm | 183 | 88.0 | 11.0 | 6.2 | 0 | 21 | 0 | .13 | .12 | 37 | 17 | 258 | 118 | 1.98 | 1.488 |
| 1/2 cup | 126 | 19.9 | 5.4 | 1.6 | | 209 | .20 | 0.5 | .00 | .17 | 298 | 239 | 13.19 | .476 | |
| tofu, salted & fermented (fuyu) | 13 | 7.7 | 0.9 | 0.5 | 0 | | | | | | 316 | 5 | 6 | | |
| 1 block | 11 | 0.9 | 0.6 | 0.1 | | | | | .00 | | 8 | 8 | .22 | | |
| **soybeans, green, boiled** | 127 | 61.7 | 5.8 | 3.2 | 0 | 14 | 15 | .14 | | | | 131 | | | |
| 1/2 cup | 90 | 11.1 | 10.0 | 0.6 | | 140 | .23 | 1.1 | .00 | | | 142 | 2.25 | | |

| | KCAL / WT (g) | H2O (g) / PRO (g) | FAT (g) / CHO (g) | PUFA (g) / SFA (g) | CHOL (mg) / DFIB (g) | A (RE) / A (IU) | C (mg) / B-1 (mg) | B-2 (mg) / NIA (mg) | B-6 (mg) / B-12 (mcg) | FOL (mcg) / PANT (mg) | Na (mg) / K (mg) | Ca (mg) / P (mg) | Mg (mg) / Fe (mg) | Zn (mg) / Cu (mg) | Mn (mg) |
|---|---|---|---|---|---|---|---|---|---|---|---|---|---|---|---|
| **soybeans, mature, boiled** | 298 | 107.6 | 15.4 | 8.7 | 0 | 2 | 3 | .49 | .40 | 93 | 1 | 175 | 148 | 1.98 | 1.417 |
| *1 cup* | 172 | 28.6 | 17.1 | 2.2 | | 15 | .27 | 0.7 | .00 | .31 | 886 | 421 | 8.84 | .700 | |
| **soybeans, mature, sprouted[a]** | | | | | | | | | | | | | | | |
| steamed | 38 | 37.3 | 2.1 | 1.2 | 0 | 1 | 4 | .03 | | | 5 | 28 | 28 | .49 | .334 |
| *1/2 cup* | 47 | 4.0 | 3.1 | 0.2 | | 5 | .10 | 0.5 | .00 | .35 | 167 | 64 | .62 | .155 | |
| stir-fried[b] | 125 | 67.2 | 7.1 | | 0 | 2 | 12 | .19 | | | | 82 | 96 | 2.10 | 1.133 |
| *3.5 oz* | 100 | 13.1 | 9.4 | | | 17 | .42 | 1.1 | .00 | 1.19 | 567 | 216 | .40 | .527 | |
| **spinach** | | | | | | | | | | | | | | | |
| raw | 6 | 25.6 | 0.1 | 0.0 | 0 | 188 | 8 | .05 | .06 | 54 | 22 | 28 | 22 | .15 | .251 |
| *1/2 cup chopped* | 28 | 0.8 | 1.0 | 0.0 | 0.9 | 1880 | .02 | 0.2 | .00 | .02 | 156 | 14 | .76 | .036 | |
| boiled | 21 | 82.1 | 0.2 | 0.1 | 0 | 737 | 9 | .21 | .22 | 131 | 63 | 122 | 79 | .69 | .842 |
| *1/2 cup* | 90 | 2.7 | 3.4 | 0.0 | 1.7 | 7371 | .09 | .44 | .00 | .13 | 419 | 50 | 3.21 | .157 | |
| cnd | 25 | 98.2 | 0.5 | 0.2 | 0 | 939 | 15 | .15 | .11 | 105 | 29c | 135 | 81 | .49 | .639 |
| *1/2 cup* | 107 | 3.0 | 3.6 | 0.1 | 3.0 | 9391 | .02 | 0.4 | .00 | .05 | 370 | 47 | 2.46 | .193 | |
| **frzn** | | | | | | | | | | | | | | | |
| boiled | 27 | 85.5 | 0.2 | 0.1 | 0 | 739 | 12 | .16 | .14 | 102 | 82 | 139 | 65 | .66 | .895 |
| *1/2 cup* | 95 | 3.0 | 5.1 | 0.0 | 2.0 | 7395 | .06 | 0.4 | .00 | .08 | 283 | 46 | 1.44 | .134 | |
| creamed, Birds Eye | 59 | 72.7 | 3.8 | 0.7 | 1 | | 11 | .12 | .06 | 16 | 312 | 72 | 27 | .16 | |
| *1/3 cup* | 85 | 2.1 | 5.1 | 0.8 | 1.5 | 4231 | .05 | 0.2 | .13 | .14 | 199 | 43 | 1.08 | .042 | |
| creamed, Pillsbury | 80 | 93.0 | 2.9 | | | | 3 | .22 | | | 475 | 130 | | | |
| *1/2 cup* | 112 | 3.6 | 9.7 | | | 1848 | .67 | 0.1 | | | 385 | 84 | .90 | | |
| w/ butter sce, Pillsbury | 60 | 130.5 | 1.5 | | | | 26 | .26 | | | 579 | 207 | | | |
| *1/2 cup* | 150 | 4.5 | 6.6 | | | 2907 | .06 | 1.1 | | | 530 | 36 | 2.25 | | |
| **squash, summer** | | | | | | | | | | | | | | | |
| all varieties, raw | 13 | 60.9 | 0.1 | 0.1 | 0 | 13 | 10 | .02 | .07 | 17 | 1 | 13 | 15 | .17 | .102 |
| *1/2 cup slices* | 65 | 0.8 | 2.8 | 0.0 | 0.7 | 127 | .04 | 0.4 | .00 | .07 | 126 | 23 | .30 | .049 | |
| all varieties, boiled | 18 | 84.3 | 0.3 | 0.1 | 0 | 26 | 5 | .04 | .06 | 18 | 1 | 24 | 22 | .35 | .192 |
| *1/2 cup slices* | 90 | 0.8 | 3.9 | 0.1 | 1.0 | 259 | .04 | 0.5 | .00 | .12 | 173 | 35 | .32 | .093 | |
| crookneck, raw[d] | 12 | 61.2 | 0.2 | 0.1 | 0 | 22 | 5 | .03 | .07 | 15 | 1 | 14 | 14 | .19 | .102 |
| *1/2 cup slices* | 65 | 0.6 | 2.6 | 0.0 | 0.7 | 220 | .03 | 0.3 | .00 | .07 | 138 | 21 | .31 | .066 | |
| crookneck, boiled[d] | 18 | 84.3 | 0.3 | 0.1 | 0 | 26 | 5 | .04 | .09 | 18 | 1 | 24 | 22 | .35 | .192 |
| *1/2 cup slices* | 90 | 0.8 | 3.9 | 0.1 | 1.0 | 259 | .04 | 0.5 | .00 | .12 | 173 | 35 | .32 | .093 | |
| crookneck, cnd[d] | 14 | 103.7 | 0.1 | 0.0 | 0 | 13 | 3 | .03 | .05 | 11 | 5c | 13 | 14 | .32 | .105 |
| *1/2 cup slices* | 108 | 0.7 | 3.2 | 0.0 | 1.1 | 130 | .02 | 0.5 | .00 | .05 | 104 | 22 | .77 | .086 | |
| crookneck, frzn, boiled[d] | 24 | 88.6 | 0.2 | 0.1 | 0 | 19 | 7 | .05 | .10 | 12 | 6 | 19 | 26 | .32 | .252 |
| *1/2 cup slices* | 96 | 1.2 | 5.3 | 0.0 | 1.2 | 187 | .04 | 0.4 | .00 | .10 | 243 | 40 | .49 | .070 | |
| scallop, raw | 12 | 61.2 | 0.1 | 0.1 | 0 | 7 | 12 | .02 | .07 | 20 | 1 | 12 | 15 | .19 | .102 |
| *1/2 cup slices* | 65 | 0.8 | 2.5 | 0.0 | | 72 | .05 | 0.4 | .00 | .07 | 118 | 23 | .26 | .066 | |
| scallop, boiled | 14 | 85.5 | 0.2 | 0.1 | 0 | 8 | 10 | .02 | .08 | 19 | 1 | 14 | 17 | .22 | .115 |
| *1/2 cup slices* | 90 | 0.9 | 3.0 | 0.0 | | 77 | .05 | 0.4 | .00 | .07 | 126 | 25 | .29 | .075 | |
| zucchini, raw | 9 | 61.9 | 0.1 | 0.0 | 0 | 22 | 6 | .02 | .06 | 14 | 2 | 10 | 14 | .13 | .083 |
| *1/2 cup slices* | 65 | 0.8 | 1.9 | 0.0 | 0.3 | 221 | .05 | 0.3 | .00 | .05 | 161 | 21 | .28 | .037 | |
| zucchini, boiled | 14 | 85.3 | 0.1 | 0.0 | 0 | 22 | 4 | .04 | .07 | 15 | 2 | 12 | 19 | .16 | .160 |
| *1/2 cup slices* | 90 | 0.6 | 3.5 | 0.0 | | 216 | .04 | 0.4 | .00 | .10 | 228 | 36 | .32 | .077 | |
| zucchini, frzn, boiled | 19 | 106.1 | 0.2 | 0.1 | 0 | 48 | 4 | .05 | .05 | 9 | 2 | 19 | 14 | .22 | .258 |
| *1/2 cup slices* | 112 | 1.3 | 4.0 | 0.0 | | 483 | .05 | 0.4 | .00 | .30 | 218 | 28 | .54 | .053 | |
| zucchini, italian style, cnd[e] | 33 | 103.3 | 0.1 | 0.1 | 0 | 61 | 3 | .05 | | | 427 | 19 | 16 | .29 | |
| *1/2 cup slices* | 114 | 1.2 | 7.8 | 0.0 | | 615 | .05 | 0.6 | .00 | | 312 | 33 | .78 | .112 | |
| **squash, winter** | | | | | | | | | | | | | | | |
| all varieties, baked | 39 | 90.8 | 0.6 | 0.3 | 0 | 363 | 10 | .02 | .07 | 29 | 1 | 14 | 8 | .27 | .215 |
| *1/2 cup cubes* | 102 | 0.9 | 8.9 | 0.1 | 1.2 | 3628 | .09 | 0.7 | .00 | .36 | 445 | 20 | .33 | .097 | |
| acorn, baked | 57 | 84.6 | 0.1 | 0.1 | 0 | 44 | 11 | .01 | .20 | 19 | 4 | 45 | 43 | .18 | |
| *1/2 cup cubes* | 102 | 1.1 | 14.9 | 0.0 | | 437 | .17 | 0.9 | .00 | .51 | 446 | 46 | .95 | .088 | |
| acorn, boiled, mashed | 41 | 109.4 | 0.1 | 0.0 | 0 | 31 | 8 | .01 | .14 | 14 | 3 | 32 | 31 | .13 | |
| *1/2 cup* | 122 | 0.8 | 10.7 | 0.0 | | 315 | .12 | 0.6 | .00 | .37 | 321 | 33 | .68 | .063 | |
| butternut, boiled | 41 | 89.6 | 0.1 | 0.0 | 0 | 714 | 15 | .02 | .13 | 20 | 4 | 42 | 30 | .13 | |
| *1/2 cup cubes* | 102 | 0.9 | 10.7 | 0.0 | | 7141 | .07 | 1.0 | .00 | .37 | 290 | 27 | .61 | .066 | |

[a] Seeds attached to sprouts.
[b] Stir-fried in veg oil.
[c] No salt used in processing.
[d] Includes straightneck varieties.
[e] Packed in tomato jce.

| | KCAL / WT (g) | H₂O (g) / PRO (g) | FAT (g) / CHO (g) | PUFA (g) / SFA (g) | CHOL (mg) / DFIB (g) | A (RE) / A (IU) | C (mg) / B-1 (mg) | B-2 (mg) / NIA (mg) | B-6 (mg) / B-12 (mcg) | FOL (mcg) / PANT (mg) | Na (mg) / K (mg) | Ca (mg) / P (mg) | Mg (mg) / Fe (mg) | Zn (mg) / Cu (mg) | Mn (mg) |
|---|---|---|---|---|---|---|---|---|---|---|---|---|---|---|---|
| butternut, frzn, boiled | 47 | 105.4 | 0.1 | 0.0 | 0 | 401 | 4 | .05 | .08 | | 2 | 23 | 11 | .14 | |
| *1/2 cup mashed* | 120 | 1.5 | 12.1 | 0.0 | | 4007 | .06 | 0.6 | .00 | .19 | 160 | 17 | .70 | .043 | |
| hubbard, baked | 51 | 86.8 | 0.6 | 0.3 | 0 | 616 | 10 | .05 | .18 | 17 | 8 | 17 | 22 | .15 | |
| *1/2 cup cubes* | 102 | 2.5 | 11.0 | 0.1 | | 6156 | .08 | 0.6 | .00 | .46 | 365 | 23 | .48 | .046 | |
| hubbard, boiled, mashed | 35 | 107.5 | 0.4 | 0.2 | 0 | 473 | 8 | .03 | .12 | 12 | 6 | 12 | 16 | .11 | |
| *1/2 cup* | 118 | 1.8 | 7.6 | 0.1 | | 4726 | .05 | 0.4 | .00 | .35 | 252 | 17 | .33 | .055 | |
| spaghetti, boiled/baked | 23 | 72.0 | 0.2 | 0.1 | 0 | 9 | 3 | .02 | .08 | 6 | 14 | 17 | 8 | .16 | |
| *1/2 cup* | 78 | 0.5 | 5.0 | 0.0 | | 86 | .03 | 0.6 | .00 | .28 | 91 | 11 | .26 | .027 | |
| **succotash** | | | | | | | | | | | | | | | |
| boiled | 111 | 65.6 | 0.8 | 0.4 | 0 | 28 | 8 | .09 | .11 | | 16 | 16 | 51 | .61 | |
| *1/2 cup* | 96 | 4.9 | 23.4 | 0.1 | | 282 | .16 | 1.3 | .00 | .54 | 393 | 112 | 1.46 | .172 | |
| cnd | 81 | 104.9 | 0.6 | 0.3 | 0 | 19 | 6 | .07 | .06 | 41 | 283 | 14 | 24 | .64 | .468 |
| *1/2 cup* | 128 | 3.3 | 17.9 | 0.1 | | 187 | .04 | 0.8 | .00 | .40 | 209 | 71 | .68 | .140 | |
| cnd w/ cream style corn | 102 | 104.0 | 0.7 | 0.3 | 0 | 19 | 9 | .09 | .17 | 59 | 325 | 15 | 1 | | .858 |
| *1/2 cup* | 133 | 3.5 | 23.4 | 0.1 | | 187 | .04 | 0.8 | .00 | .29 | 243 | 78 | .83 | .237 | |
| frzn, boiled | 79 | 63.0 | 0.8 | 0.4 | 0 | 20 | 5 | .06 | .08 | 28 | 38 | 13 | 19 | .38 | .238 |
| *1/2 cup* | 85 | 3.7 | 17.0 | 0.1 | | 196 | .06 | 1.1 | .00 | .20 | 225 | 57 | .76 | .051 | |
| **swamp cabbage** | | | | | | | | | | | | | | | |
| raw | 11 | 51.8 | 0.1 | | 0 | 353 | 31 | .06 | | | 63 | 43 | 40 | | |
| *1 cup chopped* | 56 | 1.5 | 1.8 | | | 3528 | .02 | 0.5 | .00 | | 174 | 22 | .94 | | |
| boiled | 10 | 45.5 | 0.1 | | 0 | 255 | 8 | .04 | | | 60 | 26 | 15 | | |
| *1/2 cup chopped* | 49 | 1.0 | 1.8 | | | 2548 | .01 | 0.2 | .00 | | 139 | 21 | .65 | | |
| **sweet potato** | | | | | | | | | | | | | | | |
| baked | 118 | 83.0 | 0.1 | 0.1 | 0 | 2488 | 28 | .15 | .28 | 26 | 12 | 32 | 23 | .33 | .638 |
| *1 sweet potato* | 114 | 2.0 | 27.7 | 0.0 | 2.1 | 24877 | .08 | 0.7 | .00 | .74 | 397 | 62 | .52 | .237 | |
| boiled | 172 | 119.5 | 0.5 | 0.2 | 0 | 2797 | 28 | .23 | .40 | 18 | 21 | 35 | 16 | .43 | .553 |
| *1/2 cup mashed* | 164 | 2.7 | 39.8 | 0.1 | | 27968 | .09 | 1.1 | .00 | .87 | 301 | 44 | .92 | .264 | |
| candied[a] | 144 | 70.3 | 3.4 | 0.2 | 8[b] | 440 | 7 | .04 | .04 | 12 | 73 | 27 | 12 | .16 | |
| *1 piece 2 1/2" long & 2" diameter* | 105 | 0.9 | 29.3 | 1.4 | | 4399 | .02 | 0.4 | .03 | | 198 | 27 | 1.19 | .107 | |
| cnd | 183 | 152.1 | 0.4 | 0.2 | 0 | 1597 | 53 | .11 | .38 | 33 | 107 | 44 | 45 | .36 | .910 |
| *1 cup pieces* | 200 | 3.3 | 42.3 | 0.1 | | 15965 | .07 | 1.5 | .00 | 1.05 | 625 | 98 | 1.77 | .278 | |
| mashed, Joan of Arc | 130 | | 0.2 | | | | 3 | .09 | | | 59 | 24 | | | |
| *1/2 cup* | 118 | 1.9 | 29.5 | | | 24411 | .07 | 1.3 | | | 312 | 54 | .83 | | |
| syrup pack | 106 | 71.0 | 0.3 | 0.1 | 0 | 701 | 11 | .04 | .06 | | 38 | 16 | 12 | .16 | .603 |
| *1/2 cup* | 98 | 1.3 | 24.9 | 0.1 | | 7014 | .03 | 0.3 | .00 | .39 | 189 | 25 | .93 | .164 | |
| w/ orange pineapple sce, Joan of Arc | 180 | | 0.2 | | | | 6 | .03 | | | 57 | 23 | | | |
| *1/2 cup* | 114 | 1.3 | 43.3 | | | 16509 | .06 | 0.6 | | | 302 | 29 | .80 | | |
| frzn, baked | 88 | 64.9 | 0.1 | 0.0 | 0 | 1444 | 8 | .05 | .16 | 20 | 7 | 31 | 18 | .26 | .585 |
| *1/2 cup cubes* | 88 | 1.5 | 20.6 | 0.0 | 1.3 | 14441 | .06 | 0.5 | .00 | .49 | 332 | 39 | .47 | .161 | |
| **taro, ckd** | 94 | 42.1 | 0.1 | 0.0 | 0 | 0 | 3 | .02 | | | 10 | 12 | 20 | | |
| *1/2 cup slices* | 66 | 0.3 | 22.8 | 0.0 | | 0 | .07 | 0.3 | .00 | | 319 | 50 | .48 | | |
| **taro, tahitian, ckd** | 30 | 58.8 | 0.5 | 0.2 | 0 | 120 | 26 | .14 | | | 37 | 101 | 34 | | |
| *1/2 cup slices* | 68 | 2.8 | 4.7 | 0.1 | | 1200 | .03 | 0.3 | .00 | | 423 | 45 | 1.06 | | |
| **tomato, green, raw** | 30 | 114.4 | 0.3 | 0.1 | 0 | 79 | 29 | .05 | | | 16 | 16 | 13 | .09 | .123 |
| *1 tomato* | 123 | 1.5 | 6.3 | 0.0 | | 789 | .07 | 0.6 | .00 | .62 | 251 | 35 | .63 | .111 | |
| **tomato, red** | | | | | | | | | | | | | | | |
| raw | 24 | 115.6 | 0.3 | 0.1 | 0 | 139 | 22 | .06 | .06 | 12 | 10 | 8 | 14 | .13 | .150 |
| *1 tomato* | 123 | 1.1 | 5.3 | 0.0 | 1.0 | 1394 | .07 | 0.7 | .00 | .30 | 254 | 29 | .59 | .095 | |
| boiled | 30 | 110.9 | 0.3 | 0.1 | 0 | 162 | 25 | .07 | .04 | 11 | 13 | 10 | 17 | .16 | .184 |
| *1/2 cup* | 120 | 1.3 | 6.8 | 0.0 | | 1623 | .09 | 0.9 | .00 | .35 | 312 | 35 | .72 | .116 | |
| bottled, kosher, Claussen | 5 | 25.8 | 0.0 | | 0 | | 0 | .00 | .02 | 1 | 324 | 4 | 2 | .02 | |
| *1 oz* | 28 | 0.2 | 1.0 | | | | .01 | 0.1 | | .03 | 41 | 3 | .08 | .020 | |
| **cnd** | | | | | | | | | | | | | | | |
| crushed in tomato puree, Contadina | 35 | 108.0 | 1.0 | 0.0 | 0 | | 8 | .04 | | | 340 | 33 | | | |
| *1/2 cup* | 119 | 1.0 | 6.0 | 0.0 | | 615 | .02 | 1.3 | | | 352 | | .51 | | |

[a] Canned sweet potato & syrup, brown sugar, butter & salt.    [b] If margarine is used in place of butter, cholesterol is 0 mg.

| | KCAL | $H_2O$ (g) | FAT (g) | PUFA (g) | CHOL (mg) | A (RE) | C (mg) | B-2 (mg) | B-6 (mg) | FOL (mcg) | Na (mg) | Ca (mg) | Mg (mg) | Zn (mg) | Mn (mg) |
|---|---|---|---|---|---|---|---|---|---|---|---|---|---|---|---|
| | WT (g) | PRO (g) | CHO (g) | SFA (g) | DFIB (g) | A (IU) | B-1 (mg) | NIA (mg) | B-12 (mcg) | PANT (mg) | K (mg) | P (mg) | Fe (mg) | Cu (mg) | |
| italian style (pear), Contadina | 25 | 111.9 | 1.0 | 0.1 | 0 | | 12 | .03 | | | 320 | 20 | 12 | | |
| 1/2 cup | 120 | 1.0 | 5.0 | 0.0 | | 500 | .03 | 0.8 | | | 247 | 20 | .36 | | |
| sliced, Contadina | 35 | | 1.0 | | | | 5 | .03 | | | 370 | 17 | | | |
| 1/2 cup | 120 | 1.0 | 9.0 | | | 239 | .02 | 0.8 | | | 374 | | .48 | | |
| stewed | 34 | 116.9 | 0.2 | 0.1 | 0 | 71 | 17 | .05 | | | 325 | 42[a] | 15 | .21 | |
| 1/2 cup | 128 | 1.2 | 8.3 | 0.0 | | 710 | .06 | 0.9 | .00 | | 307 | 25 | .93 | .143 | |
| stewed, Contadina | 35 | | 1.0 | 0.0 | | | 15 | .34 | | | 330 | 40 | 16 | | |
| 1/2 cup | 123 | 1.0 | 9.0 | 0.0 | | 500 | .06 | 0.8 | | | 265 | 20 | .36 | | |
| wedges in tomato jce | 34 | 120.2 | 0.2 | 0.1 | 0 | 76 | 19 | .04 | | | 285 | 34[a] | 15 | .21 | |
| 1/2 cup | 131 | 1.0 | 8.3 | 0.0 | | 757 | .07 | 0.9 | .00 | | 329 | 31 | .61 | .136 | |
| whole, peeled | 24 | 112.4 | 0.3 | 0.1 | 0 | 72 | 18 | .04 | .11 | | 195[b] | 32[a] | 14 | .19 | |
| 1/2 cup | 120 | 1.1 | 5.2 | 0.0 | 0.8 | 725 | .05 | 0.9 | .00 | .20 | 265 | 23 | .73 | .132 | |
| whole, peeled, Contadina | 25 | 111.9 | 1.0 | 0.1 | 0 | | 18 | .03 | | | 360 | 40 | 16 | | |
| 1/2 cup | 120 | 1.0 | 6.0 | 0.0 | | 500 | .06 | 0.8 | | | 256 | 20 | .36 | | |
| w/ green chili | 18 | 113.1 | 0.1 | 0.0 | 0 | 47 | 8 | .02 | | | 481 | 24[a] | 13 | .16 | |
| 1/2 cup | 120 | 0.8 | 4.3 | 0.0 | | 468 | .04 | 0.7 | .00 | | 129 | 17 | .31 | .108 | |
| stewed[c] | 59 | 85.0 | 2.2 | 0.4 | 0 | 102 | 15 | .06 | .03 | 10 | 374 | 19 | 13 | .17 | .109 |
| 1 cup | 101 | 1.8 | 10.4 | 0.4 | | 1017 | .07 | 0.8 | .00 | .21 | 170 | 32 | .78 | .069 | |
| **tomato paste, cnd** | 110 | 97.0 | 1.2 | 0.5 | 0 | 323 | 55 | .25 | .50 | | 86[d] | 46 | 67 | 1.05 | |
| 1/2 cup | 131 | 5.0 | 24.7 | 0.2 | | 3234 | .20 | 4.2 | .00 | .99 | 1221 | 104 | 3.91 | .776 | |
| Contadina | 38 | 31.5 | 0.3 | | | | 13 | .04 | | | 10 | 12 | 21 | | |
| 1/4 cup | 43 | 1.5 | 8.8 | | | 875 | .05 | 1.4 | | | 497 | 33 | .72 | | |
| italian, Contadina | 70 | 37.9 | 1.0 | 0.6 | 0 | | 1 | .08 | | | 710 | 24 | | | |
| 1/4 cup | 57 | 2.0 | 13.0 | 0.2 | | 855 | .03 | 1.6 | | | 474 | | .81 | | |
| no salt added, Heinz | 87 | 73.3 | 0.1 | | | | 27 | .18 | | | 65 | 47 | 55 | .56 | |
| 3.5 oz | 100 | 3.6 | 20.4 | | | 2108 | .18 | 3.0 | | | 967 | 75 | 1.30 | .570 | |
| **tomato puree** | 102 | 218.2 | 0.3 | 0.1 | 0 | 340 | 88 | .14 | .38 | | 49[e] | 37 | 60 | .54 | |
| 1 cup | 250 | 4.2 | 25.1 | 0.0 | | 3402 | .18 | 4.3 | .00 | 1.10 | 1051 | 99 | 2.32 | .408 | |
| Contadina | 50 | 107.0 | 1.0 | | | | 15 | .34 | | | 80 | 16 | 16 | | |
| 1/2 cup | 119 | 2.0 | 11.0 | | | 1250 | .60 | 1.2 | | | 577 | 40 | .72 | | |
| **turnip** | | | | | | | | | | | | | | | |
| boiled | 14 | 73.0 | 0.1 | 0.0 | 0 | 0 | 9 | .02 | .05 | 7 | 39 | 18 | 6 | | |
| 1/2 cup cubes | 78 | 0.6 | 3.8 | 0.0 | | 0 | .02 | 0.2 | .00 | .11 | 106 | 15 | .17 | | |
| frzn, boiled | 23 | 93.6 | 0.2 | 0.1 | 0 | 2 | 4 | .03 | | | 36 | 32 | 14 | | |
| 3.5 oz | 100 | 1.5 | 4.4 | 0.0 | | 25 | .04 | 0.6 | .00 | | 182 | 26 | .98 | | |
| **turnip greens** | | | | | | | | | | | | | | | |
| raw | 7 | 25.5 | 0.1 | 0.0 | 0 | 213 | 17 | .03 | .07 | 54 | 11 | 53 | 9 | .05 | .130 |
| 1/2 cup chopped | 28 | 0.4 | 1.6 | 0.0 | | 2128 | .02 | 0.2 | .00 | .11 | 83 | 12 | .31 | .098 | |
| boiled | 15 | 67.1 | 0.2 | 0.1 | 0 | 396 | 20 | .05 | .13 | 85 | 21 | 99 | 16 | .10 | .243 |
| 1/2 cup chopped | 72 | 0.8 | 3.1 | 0.0 | | 3959 | .03 | 0.3 | .00 | .20 | 146 | 21 | .57 | .182 | |
| cnd | 17 | 110.8 | 0.4 | 0.1 | 0 | 420 | 18 | .07 | .04 | 48 | 325 | 138 | 24 | .27 | .324 |
| 1/2 cup | 117 | 1.6 | 2.8 | 0.1 | | 4196 | .01 | 0.4 | .00 | .05 | 165 | 24 | 1.77 | .097 | |
| frzn, boiled | 24 | 74.1 | 0.4 | 0.1 | 0 | 654 | 18 | .06 | .06 | 32 | 12 | 125 | 21 | .34 | .390 |
| 1/2 cup | 82 | 2.8 | 4.1 | 0.1 | | 6540 | .04 | 0.4 | .00 | .06 | 184 | 27 | 1.59 | .123 | |
| **turnip greens & turnips, frzn, boiled** | 17 | 94.2 | 0.2 | 0.1 | 0 | 516 | 9 | .07 | | | 15 | 91 | 12 | | |
| 3.5 oz | 100 | 2.1 | 2.9 | 0.0 | | 5161 | .03 | 0.3 | .00 | | 62 | 17 | 1.33 | | |
| **vegetable combinations, cnd** | | | | | | | | | | | | | | | |
| peas & carrots | 48 | 112.8 | 0.4 | 0.2 | 0 | 739 | 8 | .07 | .11 | 24 | 332[f] | 29 | 18 | .74 | .457 |
| 1/2 cup | 128 | 2.8 | 10.9 | 0.1 | | 7386 | .10 | 0.7 | .00 | .15 | 128 | 58 | .97 | .132 | |
| peas & onions | 30 | 51.8 | 0.2 | 0.1 | 0 | 10 | 2 | .04 | | | 265 | 10 | 10 | .35 | |
| 1/2 cup | 60 | 2.0 | 5.1 | 0.0 | | 96 | .06 | 0.8 | .00 | | 57 | 30 | .52 | .060 | |
| peas & onions, Pillsbury | 60 | 103.2 | 0.3 | | | | 10 | .08 | | | 530 | 20 | | | |
| 1/2 cup | 120 | 3.5 | 10.8 | | | 558 | .11 | 1.7 | | | 115 | 62 | .96 | | |

[a] Ca added as firming agent.
[b] Special dietary pack contains 16 mg Na.
[c] Tomatoes, bread crumbs, margarine, sugar, onions, salt & pepper.
[d] If salt is added, Na is 1035 mg.
[e] If salt is added, Na is 998 mg.
[f] Special dietary pack contains 5 mg Na.

| | KCAL | H₂O (g) | FAT (g) | PUFA (g) | CHOL (mg) | A (RE) | C (mg) | B-2 (mg) | B-6 (mg) | FOL (mcg) | Na (mg) | Ca (mg) | Mg (mg) | Zn (mg) | Mn (mg) |
|---|---|---|---|---|---|---|---|---|---|---|---|---|---|---|---|
| | WT (g) | PRO (g) | CHO (g) | SFA (g) | DFIB (g) | A (IU) | B-1 (mg) | NIA (mg) | B-12 (mcg) | PANT (mg) | K (mg) | P (mg) | Fe (mg) | Cu (mg) | |

**vegetable combinations, frzn**

am style, Pillsbury — 1/2 cup
| | KCAL | H₂O | FAT | PUFA | CHOL | A(RE) | C | B-2 | B-6 | FOL | Na | Ca | Mg | Zn | Mn |
|---|---|---|---|---|---|---|---|---|---|---|---|---|---|---|---|
| | 90 | 87.5 | 2.1 | | | | 23 | .04 | | | 322 | 17 | | | |
| | 108 | 2.4 | 15.1 | | | 819 | .06 | 1.1 | | | 164 | 52 | .43 | | |

broccoli & carrots, Pillsbury — 1/2 cup
| | 20 | 66.6 | 0.1 | | | | 23 | .01 | | | 27 | 21 | | | |
| | 74 | 1.3 | 3.1 | | | 1654 | .03 | 0.5 | | | 158 | 25 | .37 | | |

**broccoli & cauliflower**

Pillsbury — 1/2 cup
| | 60 | 96.0 | 1.2 | | | | 84 | .06 | | | 460 | 23 | | | |
| | 111 | 2.2 | 9.9 | | | 1995 | .06 | 0.9 | | | 248 | 42 | .47 | | |

w/ creamy italian cheese sce, Birds Eye—1/2 cup
| | 89 | 109.6 | 5.5 | 0.4 | 14 | | 45 | .14 | .12 | 60 | 388 | 79 | 15 | .36 | |
| | 128 | 4.6 | 6.7 | 3.0 | | 1084 | .05 | 0.4 | .25 | .28 | 220 | 78 | .77 | .029 | |

broccoli, carrots & pasta w/ lightly seasoned sce, Birds Eye—2/3 cup
| | 87 | 76.6 | 4.4 | 0.9 | 0 | | 22 | .07 | .12 | 35 | 269 | 35 | 13 | .27 | |
| | 95 | 2.2 | 10.6 | 0.8 | | 8850 | .06 | 0.6 | .00 | .16 | 164 | 40 | .76 | .053 | |

broccoli, carrots & water chestnuts, Birds Eye—3/4 cup
| | 45 | 99.8 | 0.3 | 0.1 | 0 | | 42 | .11 | .20 | 67 | 34 | 49 | 18 | .37 | |
| | 113 | 2.7 | 9.4 | 0.0 | 3.5 | 6032 | .06 | 0.7 | .00 | .30 | 278 | 54 | .83 | .087 | |

**broccoli, cauliflower & carrots**

Birds Eye — 3/4 cup
| | 33 | 102.8 | 0.3 | 0.1 | 0 | | 45 | .08 | .17 | 60 | 33 | 42 | 15 | .30 | |
| | 113 | 2.4 | 6.8 | 0.0 | 2.7 | 7821 | .06 | 0.6 | .00 | .22 | 234 | 48 | .82 | .048 | |

w/ butter sce, Pillsbury — 1/2 cup
| | 30 | 72.1 | 1.2 | | | | 21 | .05 | | | 318 | 24 | | | |
| | 81 | 1.2 | 3.6 | | | 1750 | .02 | 0.6 | | | 132 | 26 | .41 | | |

w/ cheese sce, Birds Eye — 1/2 cup
| | 99 | 119.9 | 4.7 | 0.7 | 4 | | 39 | .15 | .15 | 53 | 381 | 86 | 18 | .40 | |
| | 142 | 4.0 | 11.6 | 1.5 | | 6158 | .06 | 0.6 | .23 | .35 | 257 | 84 | .73 | .042 | |

w/ cheese sce, Pillsbury — 1/2 cup
| | 70 | 101.9 | 2.1 | | | | 12 | .18 | | | 516 | 68 | | | |
| | 119 | 2.9 | 10.0 | | | 1587 | .04 | 0.4 | | | 255 | 174 | .36 | | |

broccoli, corn & red peppers, Birds Eye — 2/3 cup
| | 59 | 95.2 | 0.5 | 0.2 | 0 | | 39 | .09 | .16 | 66 | 16 | 33 | 20 | .40 | |
| | 113 | 3.2 | 13.3 | 0.1 | 2.9 | 1682 | .07 | 1.2 | .00 | .23 | 225 | 66 | .77 | .047 | |

broccoli fanfare, Pillsbury — 3/4 cup
| | 80 | 91.8 | 1.8 | | | | 35 | .06 | | | 417 | 32 | | | |
| | 111 | 3.0 | 12.8 | | | 1254 | .10 | 0.8 | | | 141 | 51 | .78 | | |

broccoli, green beans, pearl onions & red peppers, Birds Eye—3/4 cup
| | 32 | 103.1 | 0.2 | 0.1 | 0 | | 42 | .09 | .12 | 58 | 18 | 51 | 18 | .29 | |
| | 113 | 2.4 | 6.6 | 0.0 | 2.9 | 1848 | .06 | 0.6 | .00 | .19 | 199 | 44 | .91 | .052 | |

broccoli, red peppers, bamboo shoots & straw mushrm, Birds Eye—3/4 cup
| | 29 | 103.6 | 0.3 | 0.1 | 0 | | 51 | .10 | .12 | 66 | 21 | 43 | 14 | .25 | |
| | 113 | 2.8 | 5.6 | 0.0 | 3.0 | 2233 | .07 | 0.8 | .00 | .19 | 253 | 54 | .81 | .037 | |

brussel sprouts, cauliflower & carrots, Birds Eye—3/4 cup
| | 40 | 100.6 | 0.3 | 0.2 | 0 | | 58 | .09 | .21 | 87 | 26 | 31 | 18 | .28 | |
| | 113 | 3.0 | 8.2 | 0.1 | 3.7 | 4047 | .08 | 0.7 | .00 | .29 | 308 | 53 | .81 | .039 | |

carrots, peas & pearl onions, Birds Eye — 1/2 cup
| | 48 | 81.8 | 0.2 | 0.1 | 0 | | 9 | .05 | .16 | 22 | 61 | 29 | 14 | .35 | |
| | 95 | 2.1 | 10.1 | 0.0 | 2.0 | 9344 | .10 | 1.0 | .00 | .17 | 181 | 37 | .86 | .067 | |

cauliflower & carrots, Pillsbury — 1/2 cup
| | 60 | 97.7 | 2.9 | | | | 27 | .07 | | | 287 | 16 | | | |
| | 111 | 2.2 | 7.0 | | | 1485 | .11 | 0.7 | | | 161 | 39 | .67 | | |

cauliflower, carrots & snow peas, Birds Eye—2/3 cup
| | 38 | 101.9 | 0.2 | 0.1 | 0 | | 33 | .07 | .18 | 33 | 33 | 33 | 15 | .26 | |
| | 113 | 2.0 | 8.1 | 0.0 | 2.9 | 7670 | .05 | 0.7 | .00 | .26 | 228 | 36 | .88 | .039 | |

**chinese style**

Birds Eye[a] — 1/2 cup
| | 68 | 80.3 | 3.9 | 0.7 | 0 | | 16 | .05 | .08 | 32 | 299 | 32 | 24 | .20 | |
| | 95 | 2.2 | 7.7 | 0.7 | | 1669 | .04 | 0.4 | .00 | .15 | 148 | 32 | .77 | .038 | |

stir fry, Birds Eye[b] — 1/2 cup
| | 36 | 82.8 | 0.2 | 0.1 | 0 | | 16 | .11 | .08 | 23 | 540 | 44 | 24 | .27 | |
| | 95 | 2.0 | 7.9 | 0.0 | 1.9 | 2153 | .07 | 0.6 | .00 | .20 | 234 | 36 | .98 | .087 | |

chow mein style, Birds Eye[c] — 1/2 cup
| | 89 | 75.5 | 4.2 | 0.8 | 0 | | 6 | .09 | .09 | 20 | 368 | 25 | 16 | .26 | |
| | 95 | 1.6 | 12.4 | 0.8 | | 2745 | .06 | 0.6 | .00 | .20 | 202 | 36 | .63 | .097 | |

corn & broccoli, Pillsbury — 1/2 cup
| | 45 | 68.9 | 0.6 | | | | 24 | .02 | | | 14 | 17 | | | |
| | 82 | 2.1 | 7.9 | | | 284 | .02 | 1.0 | | | 188 | 44 | .49 | | |

corn, green beans & pasta curls w/ light cream sce, Birds Eye—1/2 cup
| | 108 | 71.1 | 4.9 | 0.9 | 1 | | 8 | .07 | .07 | 17 | 283 | 53 | 18 | .37 | |
| | 95 | 3.0 | 14.9 | 1.1 | | 630 | .07 | 0.9 | .01 | .10 | 141 | 68 | .63 | .040 | |

green beans, bavarian style & spaetzle (noodles), Birds Eye—1/2 cup
| | 98 | 74.8 | 5.3 | 1.0 | 14 | | 4 | .06 | .05 | 13 | 357 | 40 | 14 | .25 | |
| | 95 | 2.4 | 11.5 | 1.0 | | 572 | .04 | 0.3 | .10 | .10 | 73 | 36 | .72 | .046 | |

**italian style**

Birds Eye[d] — 1/2 cup
| | 102 | 74.7 | 5.5 | 1.0 | 0 | | 27 | .08 | .08 | 16 | 489 | 38 | 15 | .17 | |
| | 95 | 2.1 | 11.1 | 1.0 | | 736 | .04 | 0.4 | .01 | .11 | 102 | 33 | .62 | .057 | |

Pillsbury — 1/2 cup
| | 50 | 97.9 | 2.0 | | | | 32 | .08 | | | 301 | 52 | | | |
| | 110 | 2.9 | 5.0 | | | 1415 | .03 | 0.4 | | | 134 | 51 | .55 | | |

[a] Bean sprouts, cabbage, pea pods, spinach, red peppers & water chestnuts.
[b] Snow peas, spinach, bean sprouts, celery, water chestnuts & red peppers.
[c] Bean sprouts, french green beans, water chestnuts, carrots, celery, straw mushrooms & sce.
[d] Italian green beans, chickpeas, red peppers, onions & ripe olives.

| Item | KCAL / WT (g) | H₂O / PRO (g) | FAT / CHO (g) | PUFA / SFA (g) | CHOL / DFIB (mg/g) | A (RE) / A (IU) | C / B-1 (mg) | B-2 / NIA (mg) | B-6 / B-12 | FOL / PANT | Na / K (mg) | Ca / P (mg) | Mg / Fe (mg) | Zn / Cu (mg) | Mn (mg) |
|---|---|---|---|---|---|---|---|---|---|---|---|---|---|---|---|
| **japanese style** | | | | | | | | | | | | | | | |
| Birds Eye[a] 1/2 cup | 89 | 76.6 | 5.0 | 1.0 | 0 | | 18 | .06 | .08 | 26 | 426 | 31 | 16 | .23 | |
| | 95 | 2.0 | 10.0 | 0.9 | | 774 | .04 | 0.2 | .01 | .11 | 134 | 37 | .57 | .048 | |
| Pillsbury 1/2 cup | 45 | | 0.9 | | | | 23 | .06 | | | 405 | 33 | | | |
| | 110 | 2.0 | 7.2 | | | 1235 | .03 | 0.4 | | | 173 | 34 | .77 | | |
| stir fry, Birds Eye[b] 1/2 cup | 30 | 84.9 | 0.2 | 0.1 | 0 | | 24 | .09 | .09 | 29 | 516 | 28 | 12 | .20 | |
| | 95 | 1.6 | 6.6 | 0.0 | | 917 | .05 | 0.7 | .00 | .28 | 157 | 35 | .70 | .074 | |
| le sueur style, Pillsbury 1/2 cup | 90 | 93.2 | 2.3 | | | | 11 | .07 | | | 346 | 26 | | | |
| | 115 | 4.5 | 12.8 | | | 461 | .28 | 0.9 | | | 89 | 63 | 1.73 | | |
| mandarin style, Birds Eye[c] 1/2 cup | 87 | 76.0 | 4.1 | 0.8 | 0 | | 20 | .07 | .13 | 25 | 390 | 41 | 15 | .21 | |
| | 95 | 1.4 | 11.9 | 0.8 | | 4053 | .04 | 0.6 | .00 | .20 | 223 | 32 | .64 | .052 | |
| mexican style, Pillsbury 1/2 cup | 151 | 105.7 | 5.2 | | | | 24 | .11 | | | 529 | 74 | | | |
| | 140 | 4.6 | 22.4 | | | 1812 | .08 | 1.5 | | | 256 | 136 | .50 | | |
| new england style, Birds Eye[d] 1/2 cup | 125 | 70.4 | 6.2 | 1.6 | 0 | | 10 | .08 | .11 | 29 | 357 | 26 | 21 | .24 | |
| | 95 | 3.1 | 14.2 | 1.2 | | 885 | .09 | 0.6 | .01 | .25 | 157 | 42 | .61 | .048 | |
| pasta primavera style, Birds Eye[e] 1/2 cup | 122 | 69.0 | 5.2 | 0.9 | 3 | | 17 | .13 | .10 | 29 | 338 | 95 | 20 | .53 | |
| | 95 | 5.0 | 14.3 | 1.4 | | 4279 | .14 | 1.1 | .13 | .23 | 172 | 97 | .95 | .067 | |
| peas & carrots 1/2 cup | 38 | 68.6 | 0.3 | 0.2 | 0 | 621 | 7 | .05 | .07 | 21 | 55 | 18 | 13 | .36 | .162 |
| | 80 | 2.5 | 8.1 | 0.1 | | 6209 | .18 | 0.9 | .00 | .13 | 127 | 39 | .75 | .061 | |
| peas & onions, boiled 1/2 cup | 40 | 79.4 | 0.2 | 0.1 | 0 | 31 | 6 | .06 | | | | 13 | | | |
| | 90 | 2.3 | 7.8 | 0.0 | | 313 | .14 | 0.9 | .00 | | | | .84 | | |
| **peas & pearl onions** | | | | | | | | | | | | | | | |
| Birds Eye 1/2 cup | 71 | 75.6 | 0.2 | 0.1 | 0 | | 19 | .08 | .13 | 44 | 442 | 15 | 18 | .48 | |
| | 95 | 4.6 | 13.5 | 0.0 | 3.5 | 636 | .24 | 1.8 | .00 | .17 | 172 | 59 | .85 | .083 | |
| w/ cheese sce, Birds Eye 1/2 cup | 137 | 111.6 | 4.9 | 0.8 | 4 | | 15 | .16 | .13 | 43 | 446 | 76 | 25 | .72 | |
| | 142 | 5.7 | 18.1 | 1.5 | | 2145 | .22 | 1.5 | .23 | .29 | 217 | 109 | 1.22 | .094 | |
| peas & potatoes w/ cream sce, Birds Eye—1/2 cup | 127 | 50.0 | 6.2 | 1.1 | 1 | | 6 | .13 | .12 | 26 | 390 | 42 | 21 | .48 | |
| | 76 | 3.4 | 14.8 | 1.3 | | 520 | .15 | 0.9 | .23 | .33 | 208 | 84 | .74 | .093 | |
| peas, onions & carrots w/ butter sce, Le Sueur—1/2 cup | 80 | | 3.0 | | | | | | | | 470 | | | | |
| | | 4.0 | 11.0 | | | | | | | | 115 | | | | |
| peas, pea pods & water chestnuts w/ butter sce, Le Sueur—1/2 cup | 80 | 99.1 | 2.5 | | | | 192 | .07 | | | 426 | 31 | | | |
| | 118 | 4.1 | 10.4 | | | 861 | .25 | 1.1 | | | 124 | 68 | 1.32 | | |
| rice & broccoli w/ cheese sce, Rice Originals—1/2 cup | 120 | 82.6 | 4.1 | | | | 6 | .04 | | | 487 | 47 | | | |
| | 109 | 3.4 | 17.3 | | | 952 | .22 | 1.5 | | | 69 | 72 | 1.42 | | |
| rice & peas w/ mushrooms, Birds Eye 2/3 cup | 108 | 38.0 | 0.2 | 0.1 | 0 | | 10 | .14 | .07 | 18 | 321 | 8 | 8 | .33 | |
| | 66 | 3.5 | 23.0 | 0.0 | | 424 | .16 | 1.8 | .00 | .04 | 68 | 39 | .84 | .049 | |
| rice & spinach w/ cheese sce, Rice Originals—1/2 cup | 170 | 79.4 | 6.6 | | | | 0 | .08 | | | 406 | 67 | | | |
| | 115 | 4.1 | 23.5 | | | 601 | .22 | 2.0 | | | 101 | 60 | 2.19 | | |
| rice, french style, Birds Eye[f] 1/2 cup | 107 | 67.3 | 0.4 | 0.1 | 0 | | 1 | .02 | .03 | 6 | 615 | 11 | 8 | .37 | |
| | 95 | 2.7 | 22.9 | 0.1 | | 48 | .05 | 0.5 | .00 | .07 | 33 | 41 | .95 | .109 | |
| rice, italian style, Birds Eye[g] 1/2 cup | 120 | 64.4 | 0.7 | 0.1 | 0 | | 8 | .02 | .05 | 8 | 349 | 13 | 8 | .35 | |
| | 95 | 2.9 | 26.0 | 0.1 | | 319 | .06 | 0.7 | .00 | .11 | 51 | 41 | 1.02 | .100 | |
| rice jubilee, Rice Originals 1/2 cup | 150 | 80.6 | 5.7 | | | | 0 | .03 | | | 333 | 15 | | | |
| | 112 | 2.4 | 22.2 | | | 1025 | .19 | 2.4 | | | 54 | 34 | 1.57 | | |
| rice medley, Rice Originals 1/2 cup | 150 | 105.6 | 3.4 | | | | 0 | .04 | | | 326 | 17 | | | |
| | 140 | 3.6 | 26.3 | | | 545 | .41 | 2.9 | | | 66 | 53 | 2.24 | | |
| rice, spanish style, Birds Eye[h] 1/2 cup | 111 | 66.5 | 0.5 | 0.2 | 0 | | 33 | .02 | .07 | 11 | 547 | 8 | 8 | .32 | |
| | 95 | 2.5 | 23.8 | 0.1 | | 422 | .08 | 0.8 | .00 | .09 | 57 | 38 | .71 | .081 | |
| san francisco style, Birds Eye[i] 1/2 cup | 90 | 77.0 | 4.5 | 0.9 | 0 | | 10 | .07 | .07 | 25 | 334 | 21 | 15 | .25 | |
| | 95 | 2.2 | 10.4 | 0.9 | | 489 | .06 | 0.5 | .00 | .15 | 154 | 38 | .53 | .077 | |
| sweet peas & cauliflower, Pillsbury 1/2 cup | 30 | 62.8 | 0.2 | | | | 21 | .05 | | | 60 | 19 | | | |
| | 73 | 2.5 | 4.5 | | | 968 | .10 | 0.9 | | | 131 | 42 | .66 | | |
| veg & rice w/ butter, Banquet 4 oz | 183 | | 9.0 | | 25 | | 0 | .04 | | | 650 | 20 | | | |
| | 113 | 3.0 | 23.0 | | | 227 | .04 | 0.4 | | | 30 | | .60 | | |
| **vinespinach, raw** 3.5 oz | 19 | 93.1 | 0.3 | | 0 | 800 | 102 | | | | 30 | 109 | | | |
| | 100 | 1.8 | 3.4 | | | 8000 | .05 | 0.5 | .00 | | | 52 | 1.20 | | |

[a] French green beans, broccoli, pearl onions, mushrooms & red peppers.
[b] Green beans, broccoli, green peppers, mushrooms & red peppers.
[c] Cabbage, carrots, bok choy, water chestnuts, snow pea pods, straw mushrooms & sce.
[d] French style green beans, corn, broccoli & red peppers.
[e] Peas, broccoli, carrots, red peppers, macaroni & sce.
[f] W/ french style green beans, onions, wild rice & mushrooms.
[g] W/ italian green beans, ripe olives & red peppers.
[h] W/ onions, peas, green peppers & red peppers.
[i] French style green beans, bean sprouts, celery, mushrooms & red peppers.

| | KCAL / WT (g) | H₂O (g) / PRO (g) | FAT (g) / CHO (g) | PUFA (g) / SFA (g) | CHOL (mg) / DFIB (g) | A (RE) / A (IU) | C (mg) / B-1 (mg) | B-2 (mg) / NIA (mg) | B-6 (mg) / B-12 (mcg) | FOL (mcg) / PANT (mg) | Na (mg) / K (mg) | Ca (mg) / P (mg) | Mg (mg) / Fe (mg) | Zn (mg) / Cu (mg) | Mn (mg) |
|---|---|---|---|---|---|---|---|---|---|---|---|---|---|---|---|
| **water chestnuts, chinese** | | | | | | | | | | | | | | | |
| raw | 66 | 45.5 | 0.1 | | 0 | 0 | 3 | .12 | | | 9 | 7 | 14 | | |
| *1/2 cup slices* | 62 | 0.9 | 14.8 | | | 0 | .09 | 0.6 | .00 | | 362 | 39 | .37 | | |
| cnd | 35 | 60.5 | 0.0 | | 0 | 0 | 1 | .02 | | | 6 | 3 | 3 | .27 | |
| *1/2 cup slices* | 70 | 0.6 | 8.7 | | | 3 | .01 | 0.3 | .00 | | 82 | 14 | .61 | .070 | |
| **watercress, raw** | 2 | 16.2 | 0.0 | 0.0 | 0 | 80 | 7 | .02 | .02 | | 7 | 20 | 4 | | |
| *1/2 cup chopped* | 17 | 0.4 | 0.2 | 0.0 | | 799 | .02 | 0.0 | .00 | .05 | 56 | 10 | .03 | | |
| **wax beans, cut, cnd, Joan of Arc** | 25 | | 0.2 | | | | 6 | .04 | | | 321 | 87 | | | |
| *1/2 cup* | 119 | 1.3 | 4.5 | | | 81 | .04 | 0.3 | | | 261 | 17 | 3.09 | | |
| **waxgourd, boiled[a]** | 11 | 83.6 | 0.2 | 0.1 | 0 | 0 | 9 | .00 | | | 93 | 16 | | | |
| *1/2 cup cubes* | 87 | 0.4 | 2.6 | | | 0 | .03 | 0.3 | .00 | | 5 | 15 | .33 | | |
| **white beans** | | | | | | | | | | | | | | | |
| boiled | 249 | 112.9 | 0.6 | 0.3 | 0 | 0 | 0 | .08 | .17 | 145 | 11 | 161 | 113 | 2.46 | 1.138 |
| *1 cup* | 179 | 17.4 | 44.9 | 0.2 | | 0 | .21 | 0.3 | .00 | .41 | 1003 | 202 | 6.61 | .514 | |
| cnd | 306 | 183.7 | 0.8 | 0.3 | 0 | 0 | 0 | .10 | .20 | 171 | 13 | 191 | 134 | 2.92 | 1.349 |
| *1 cup* | 262 | 19.0 | 57.5 | 0.2 | | 0 | .25 | 0.3 | .00 | .49 | 1189 | 239 | 7.84 | .608 | |
| **white beans, small, boiled** | 253 | 113.2 | 1.2 | 0.5 | 0 | 0 | 0 | .11 | .23 | 245 | 4 | 131 | 122 | 1.96 | .913 |
| *1 cup* | 179 | 16.1 | 46.2 | 0.3 | 7.9 | 0 | .42 | 0.5 | .00 | .45 | 828 | 302 | 5.09 | .267 | |
| **wild rice, raw** | 565 | 13.6 | 1.1 | | | 0 | 0 | 1.01 | | | 11 | 30 | | | |
| *1 cup* | 160 | 22.6 | 120.5 | | | 0 | .72 | 9.9 | | | 352 | 542 | 6.70 | | |
| **winged beans, boiled** | 252 | 115.6 | 10.1 | 2.7 | 0 | 0 | 0 | .22 | .08 | 18 | 22 | 244 | 94 | 2.48 | 2.062 |
| *1 cup* | 172 | 18.3 | 25.7 | 1.4 | | 0 | .51 | 1.4 | .00 | | 481 | 264 | 7.45 | 1.330 | |
| **yam, boiled/baked[b]** | 79 | 47.7 | 0.1 | 0.0 | 0 | 0 | 8 | .02 | .16 | 11 | 6 | 9 | 12 | .13 | |
| *1/2 cup cubes* | 68 | 1.0 | 18.8 | 0.0 | | 0 | .07 | 0.4 | .00 | .21 | 455 | 33 | .35 | .103 | |
| **yambean, boiled** | 46 | 87.9 | 0.1 | | 0 | 0 | 16 | .03 | | | 6 | 16 | 17 | | |
| *3.5 oz* | 100 | 1.2 | 10.4 | | | 0 | .04 | 0.3 | .00 | | 181 | 23 | .29 | | |
| **yardlong bean, boiled** | 202 | 117.7 | 0.8 | 0.3 | 0 | 3 | 1 | .11 | .16 | 249 | 9 | 72 | 167 | 1.84 | .833 |
| *1 cup* | 171 | 14.2 | 36.1 | 0.2 | | 27 | .36 | 0.9 | .00 | .68 | 539 | 309 | 4.51 | .385 | |
| **yellow beans** | | | | | | | | | | | | | | | |
| baked, cnd, B&M | 326 | | 7.0 | | | | | | | | 770 | | | | |
| *7/8 cup* | 227 | 15.0 | 50.0 | | | | | | | | 760 | | | | |
| baked, cnd, Friend's | 360 | | 6.0 | | | | | | | | 1040 | | | | |
| *1 cup* | 255 | 18.0 | 60.0 | | | | | | | | | | | | |
| boiled | 254 | 111.5 | 1.9 | 0.8 | 0 | 0 | 3 | .18 | .23 | 143 | 8 | 110 | 131 | 1.87 | .805 |
| *1 cup* | 177 | 16.2 | 44.7 | 0.5 | | 4 | .33 | 1.3 | .00 | .41 | 576 | 324 | 4.39 | .329 | |

## 35. MISCELLANEOUS

| | KCAL / WT (g) | H₂O (g) / PRO (g) | FAT (g) / CHO (g) | PUFA (g) / SFA (g) | CHOL (mg) / DFIB (g) | A (RE) / A (IU) | C (mg) / B-1 (mg) | B-2 (mg) / NIA (mg) | B-6 (mg) / B-12 (mcg) | FOL (mcg) / PANT (mg) | Na (mg) / K (mg) | Ca (mg) / P (mg) | Mg (mg) / Fe (mg) | Zn (mg) / Cu (mg) | Mn (mg) |
|---|---|---|---|---|---|---|---|---|---|---|---|---|---|---|---|
| **baking choc, unsweetened, Bakers** | 139 | 0.4 | 14.6 | 0.4 | 0 | | 0 | .07 | .01 | 3 | 1 | 23 | 85 | | |
| *1 oz* | 28 | 3.1 | 8.4 | 8.7 | | 17 | .01 | 0.4 | .00 | .05 | 242 | 112 | 1.96 | .779 | |
| **baking choc, unsweetened, Hershey** | 185 | | 15.8 | | | | | .13 | | | 3 | 20 | 84 | 1.12 | .560 |
| *1 oz* | 28 | 4.0 | 6.7 | | | 6 | .02 | 0.3 | | | 224 | 123 | 2.04 | .560 | |
| **baking powder** | | | | | | | | | | | | | | | |
| Calumet | 3 | 0.2 | 0.0 | 0.0 | 0 | | 0 | .00 | .00 | 0 | 426 | 241 | 0 | .00 | |
| *1 t* | 4 | 0.0 | 0.7 | 0.0 | | 0 | .00 | 0.0 | .00 | .00 | 0 | 83 | .00 | .000 | |
| cream of tartar | 7 | 1.0 | 0.0 | | | | 0 | .00 | | | 694 | 0 | | | |
| *1 T* | 10 | 0.0 | 1.8 | | | 0 | .00 | 0.0 | | | 361 | 0 | .00 | | |
| sodium aluminum silicate | 14 | 0.2 | 0.0 | | | | 0 | .00 | | | 1205 | 213 | | | |
| *1 T* | 11 | 0.0 | 3.4 | | | 0 | .00 | 0.0 | | | 17 | 319 | | | |
| **bubble gum** | | | | | | | | | | | | | | | |
| blueberry/grape/raspberry/strawberry, Hubba Bubba—*1 piece* | 23 | | 0.0 | 0.0 | 0 | 0 | 0 | .00 | .00 | 0 | 0 | 0 | 0 | .00 | .000 |
| | 8 | 0.0 | 5.8 | 0.0 | | 0 | .00 | 0.0 | .00 | .00 | 0 | 0 | .00 | .000 | |
| Bubble Yum[c] | 25 | | 0.0 | | | | | | | | 0 | | | | |
| *1 piece* | | | 0.0 | 7.0 | | | | | | | | | | | |

[c] Values are for 9 flavors.

[a] Chinese preserving melon.
[b] This is the true yam of tropical areas (Dioscorea species), not the american yam which is really a sweet potato.

| | KCAL / WT (g) | H₂O (g) / PRO (g) | FAT (g) / CHO (g) | PUFA (g) / SFA (g) | CHOL (mg) / DFIB (g) | A (RE) / A (IU) | C (mg) / B-1 (mg) | B-2 (mg) / NIA (mg) | B-6 (mg) / B-12 (mcg) | FOL (mcg) / PANT (mg) | Na (mg) / K (mg) | Ca (mg) / P (mg) | Mg (mg) / Fe (mg) | Zn (mg) / Cu (mg) | Mn (mg) |
|---|---|---|---|---|---|---|---|---|---|---|---|---|---|---|---|
| Bubble Yum, sugarless[a] | 20 | | 0.0 | | | | | | | | 0 | | | | |
| *1 piece* | | 0.0 | 5.0 | | | | | | | | 0 | | | | |
| Carefree, sugarless[b] | 10 | | 0.0 | | | | | | | | 0 | | | | |
| *1 piece* | | 0.0 | 2.0 | | | | | | | | 0 | | | | |
| fruit/original, Hubba Bubba | 23 | | 0.0 | 0.0 | 0 | 0 | 0 | .00 | .00 | 0 | 0 | 30 | 0 | .00 | .000 |
| *1 piece* | 8 | 0.0 | 5.8 | 0.0 | | 0 | .00 | 0.0 | .00 | .00 | 0 | 0 | | .00 | .000 |
| fruit stripe, cherry/fruit/grape/lemon | 10 | | 0.0 | | | | | | | | 0 | | | | |
| *1 piece* | | 0.0 | 2.0 | | | | | | | | 0 | | | | |

### chewing gum

| | KCAL / WT (g) | H₂O (g) / PRO (g) | FAT (g) / CHO (g) | PUFA (g) / SFA (g) | CHOL (mg) / DFIB (g) | A (RE) / A (IU) | C (mg) / B-1 (mg) | B-2 (mg) / NIA (mg) | B-6 (mg) / B-12 (mcg) | FOL (mcg) / PANT (mg) | Na (mg) / K (mg) | Ca (mg) / P (mg) | Mg (mg) / Fe (mg) | Zn (mg) / Cu (mg) | Mn (mg) |
|---|---|---|---|---|---|---|---|---|---|---|---|---|---|---|---|
| big red/doublemint/freedent/juicy fruit/ spearmint, Wrigley's—1 piece | 10 | | 0.0 | 0.0 | 0 | 0 | 0 | .00 | .00 | 0 | 0 | 3 | 0 | .00 | .000 |
| | 3.2 | 0.0 | 2.3 | 0.0 | | 0 | .00 | 0.0 | .00 | .00 | 0 | 0 | | .00 | .000 |
| candy coated Beechies, fruit/pepper-mint/pepsin/spearmint—1 piece | 6 | | 0.0 | | | | | | | | 0 | | | | |
| | | 0.0 | 2.0 | | | | | | | | 0 | | | | |
| Carefree, sugarless[a] | 8 | | 0.0 | | | | | | | | 0 | | | | |
| *1 piece* | | 0.0 | 2.0 | | | | | | | | 0 | | | | |
| cinn/fruit/peppermint/spearmint, Beech-Nut—1 piece | 10 | | 0.0 | | | | | | | | 0 | | | | |
| | | 0.0 | 2.0 | | | | | | | | 0 | | | | |
| fruit stripe, cherry/lemon/lime/orange | 9 | | 0.0 | | | | | | | | 0 | | | | |
| *1 piece* | | 0.0 | 2.0 | | | | | | | | 0 | | | | |
| peppermint/spearmint, extra sugarfree, Wrigley's[c]—1 piece | 8 | | 0.0 | 0.0 | 0 | 0 | 0 | .00 | .00 | 0 | 0 | 5 | 0 | .00 | .000 |
| | 2.7 | 0.0 | 0.0 | 0.0 | | 0 | .00 | 0.0 | .00 | .00 | 0 | 0 | | .00 | .000 |

### cocoa

| | KCAL / WT (g) | H₂O (g) / PRO (g) | FAT (g) / CHO (g) | PUFA (g) / SFA (g) | CHOL (mg) / DFIB (g) | A (RE) / A (IU) | C (mg) / B-1 (mg) | B-2 (mg) / NIA (mg) | B-6 (mg) / B-12 (mcg) | FOL (mcg) / PANT (mg) | Na (mg) / K (mg) | Ca (mg) / P (mg) | Mg (mg) / Fe (mg) | Zn (mg) / Cu (mg) | Mn (mg) |
|---|---|---|---|---|---|---|---|---|---|---|---|---|---|---|---|
| dry powder | 14 | 0.2 | 1.0 | | | | 0 | .02 | | | 0 | 7 | 21 | | |
| *1 T* | 5 | 0.9 | 2.8 | 0.6 | | 0 | .01 | 0.1 | | | 82 | 35 | .60 | | |
| dry powder, processed w/ alkali | 14 | 0.2 | 1.0 | | | | 0 | .02 | | | 39 | 7 | 21 | | |
| *1 T* | 5 | 0.9 | 2.6 | 0.6 | | 0 | .01 | 0.1 | | | 35 | 35 | .60 | | |
| Hershey | 115 | | 3.6 | | | | | .15 | | | 11 | 41 | 154 | 2.13 | 1.064 |
| *1/3 cup (1 oz)* | 28 | 7.6 | 12.8 | | | 22 | .02 | 0.6 | | | 476 | 221 | 4.54 | 1.008 | |
| cornstarch | 30 | 0.8 | 0.0 | | | | 0 | .00 | | | 0 | 0 | | | |
| *1 T* | 8 | 0.0 | 7.2 | | | 0 | .00 | 0.0 | | | 0 | 0 | .00 | | |

### fruit pectin

| | KCAL / WT (g) | H₂O (g) / PRO (g) | FAT (g) / CHO (g) | PUFA (g) / SFA (g) | CHOL (mg) / DFIB (g) | A (RE) / A (IU) | C (mg) / B-1 (mg) | B-2 (mg) / NIA (mg) | B-6 (mg) / B-12 (mcg) | FOL (mcg) / PANT (mg) | Na (mg) / K (mg) | Ca (mg) / P (mg) | Mg (mg) / Fe (mg) | Zn (mg) / Cu (mg) | Mn (mg) |
|---|---|---|---|---|---|---|---|---|---|---|---|---|---|---|---|
| Certo | 2 | 13.1 | 0.0 | 0.0 | 0 | | 0 | .00 | .00 | 0 | 1 | 0 | 0 | .00 | |
| *1 T* | 14 | 0.0 | 0.4 | 0.0 | | 0 | .00 | 0.0 | .00 | .00 | 33 | | .00 | | |
| light, sweetened, Sure-Jell | 32 | 0.9 | 0.0 | 0.0 | 0 | | 0 | .00 | .00 | 0 | 1 | 0 | 0 | .00 | |
| *1/4 pkt* | 12 | 0.0 | 9.6 | 0.0 | | 0 | .00 | 0.0 | .00 | .00 | 0 | 0 | .00 | .000 | |
| sweetened, Sure-Jell | 37 | 1.0 | 0.0 | 0.0 | 0 | | 0 | .00 | .00 | 0 | 1 | 0 | 0 | .00 | |
| *1/4 pkt* | 12 | 0.0 | 10.3 | 0.0 | | 0 | .00 | 0.0 | .00 | .00 | 0 | 0 | .00 | .000 | |

### gelatin, dry

| | KCAL / WT (g) | H₂O (g) / PRO (g) | FAT (g) / CHO (g) |
|---|---|---|---|
| **gelatin, dry** | 23 | 0.9 | 0.0 |
| *1 pkt* | 7 | 6.0 | 0.0 |

### meat/poultry coatings
#### oven fry

| | KCAL / WT (g) | H₂O (g) / PRO (g) | FAT (g) / CHO (g) | PUFA (g) / SFA (g) | CHOL (mg) / DFIB (g) | A (RE) / A (IU) | C (mg) / B-1 (mg) | B-2 (mg) / NIA (mg) | B-6 (mg) / B-12 (mcg) | FOL (mcg) / PANT (mg) | Na (mg) / K (mg) | Ca (mg) / P (mg) | Mg (mg) / Fe (mg) | Zn (mg) / Cu (mg) | Mn (mg) |
|---|---|---|---|---|---|---|---|---|---|---|---|---|---|---|---|
| extra crispy recipe for chicken | 112 | 1.3 | 2.0 | 0.8 | 0 | | 0 | .03 | .02 | 15 | 804 | 31 | 9 | .20 | |
| *1/4 pouch* | 29 | 3.3 | 20.1 | 0.3 | | 190 | .02 | 0.4 | .00 | .14 | 49 | 30 | 1.08 | .068 | |
| extra crispy recipe for pork | 116 | 1.2 | 2.5 | 1.0 | 0 | | 0 | .03 | .01 | 11 | 689 | 10 | 11 | .22 | |
| *1/4 pouch* | 29 | 2.7 | 20.6 | 0.4 | | 372 | .02 | 0.3 | .00 | .09 | 49 | 34 | .59 | .052 | |
| light crispy homestyle recipe | 82 | 1.3 | 2.0 | 0.3 | 0 | | 0 | .04 | .02 | 2 | 942 | 14 | 12 | .11 | |
| *1/4 pouch* | 22 | 1.3 | 14.7 | 1.0 | | 250 | .05 | 0.5 | .00 | .03 | 27 | 27 | .43 | .022 | |

#### shake & bake

| | KCAL / WT (g) | H₂O (g) / PRO (g) | FAT (g) / CHO (g) | PUFA (g) / SFA (g) | CHOL (mg) / DFIB (g) | A (RE) / A (IU) | C (mg) / B-1 (mg) | B-2 (mg) / NIA (mg) | B-6 (mg) / B-12 (mcg) | FOL (mcg) / PANT (mg) | Na (mg) / K (mg) | Ca (mg) / P (mg) | Mg (mg) / Fe (mg) | Zn (mg) / Cu (mg) | Mn (mg) |
|---|---|---|---|---|---|---|---|---|---|---|---|---|---|---|---|
| barbeque for chicken | 93 | 0.7 | 2.1 | 0.1 | 0 | | 1 | .01 | .00 | 2 | 848 | 17 | 7 | .09 | |
| *1/4 pouch* | 25 | 0.8 | 18.5 | 0.9 | | 239 | .01 | 0.1 | .00 | .03 | 88 | 16 | .38 | .027 | |
| barbeque for pork | 75 | 0.6 | 1.7 | 0.1 | 0 | | 2 | .02 | .01 | 4 | 690 | 15 | 6 | .09 | |
| *1/4 pouch* | 20 | 0.9 | 14.5 | 0.8 | | 313 | .02 | 0.2 | .00 | .05 | 75 | 15 | .33 | .027 | |
| country mild recipe | 77 | 1.0 | 3.8 | 0.2 | 0 | | 1 | .02 | .01 | 4 | 506 | 5 | 3 | .08 | |
| *1/4 pouch* | 17 | 0.8 | 10.0 | 2.1 | | 450 | .01 | 0.2 | .00 | .04 | 26 | 11 | .27 | .017 | |
| for chicken | 75 | 1.1 | 1.7 | 0.3 | 0 | | 0 | .07 | .07 | 18 | 440 | 6 | 6 | .16 | |
| *1/4 pouch* | 19 | 1.6 | 13.3 | 0.6 | | 307 | .06 | 0.8 | .19 | .05 | 38 | 22 | .33 | .041 | |

[a] Values are for 4 flavors.
[b] Values are for 3 flavors.
[c] Contains 2.0 g polyols which are metabolized as carbohydrates, but more slowly.

| | KCAL | H₂O (g) | FAT (g) | PUFA (g) | CHOL (mg) | A (RE) | C (mg) | B-2 (mg) | B-6 (mg) | FOL (mcg) | Na (mg) | Ca (mg) | Mg (mg) | Zn (mg) | Mn (mg) |
|---|---|---|---|---|---|---|---|---|---|---|---|---|---|---|---|
| | WT (g) | PRO (g) | CHO (g) | SFA (g) | DFIB (g) | A (IU) | B-1 (mg) | NIA (mg) | B-12 (mcg) | PANT (mg) | K (mg) | P (mg) | Fe (mg) | Cu (mg) | |
| for fish | 74 | 1.0 | 1.3 | 0.5 | 0 | | 0 | .01 | .01 | 1 | 414 | 4 | 4 | .14 | |
| *1/4 pouch* | 19 | 1.3 | 14.2 | 0.2 | | 149 | .01 | 0.1 | .00 | | 25 | 12 | .39 | .018 | |
| for pork | 81 | 0.7 | 1.1 | 0.4 | 0 | | 0 | .00 | | | 595 | 9 | 4 | .20 | |
| *1/4 pouch* | 21 | 1.3 | 16.2 | 0.3 | | 162 | .00 | 0.0 | .00 | | 34 | 16 | .72 | .015 | |
| italian herb recipe | 75 | 1.1 | 1.1 | 0.4 | 0 | | 0 | .01 | .01 | 6 | 626 | 14 | 5 | .15 | |
| *1/4 pouch* | 20 | 1.6 | 14.4 | 0.2 | | 107 | .01 | 0.2 | .01 | .05 | 30 | 18 | .50 | .036 | |
| **olives, pickled, green** | 45 | 36.0 | 4.9 | | | | | | | | 926 | 24 | | | |
| *10 large* | 46 | 0.5 | 0.5 | 0.5 | | 120 | | | | | 21 | 7 | .60 | | |
| **olives, pickled, ripe, greek style (salt cured, oil coated)—10 med** | 65 | 10.5 | 6.9 | | | | | | | | 631 | 6 | | | |
| | 24 | 0.4 | 1.7 | 0.8 | | | | | | | 29 | 3 | | | |
| **olives, pickled, ripe, manzanillo/mission** | 4 | 2.6 | 0.4 | 0.0 | | | 0 | .00 | .00 | | | | | | |
| *1 small* | 3.3 | 0.0 | 0.2 | 0.0 | 0.1 | 13 | .00 | 0.0 | | | 0 | | .11 | .008 | |
| | 5 | 3.2 | 0.4 | 0.0 | | | 0 | .00 | .00 | | 35 | 4 | | | |
| *1 med* | 4.0 | 0.0 | 0.3 | 0.1 | 0.1 | 16 | .00 | 0.0 | | | 0 | | .13 | .010 | |
| | 5 | 3.7 | 0.5 | 0.0 | | | 0 | .00 | .00 | | 40 | 4 | | | |
| *1 large* | 4.6 | 0.0 | 0.3 | 0.1 | 0.1 | 19 | .00 | 0.0 | | | 0 | | .15 | .012 | |
| | 7 | 4.8 | 0.6 | 0.0 | | | 0 | .00 | .00 | | 52 | 5 | | | |
| *1 extra large* | 6.0 | 0.1 | 0.4 | 0.1 | 0.2 | 24 | .00 | 0.0 | | | 0 | | .20 | .015 | |
| **olives, pickled, ripe, sevillano/ascolano** | 7 | 7.7 | 0.6 | 0.1 | | | 0 | .00 | .00 | | 82 | 9 | | | |
| *1 jumbo* | 9.1 | 0.1 | 0.5 | 0.1 | 0.3 | 31 | .00 | 0.0 | | | 1 | | .30 | .021 | |
| | 9 | 9.5 | 0.8 | 0.1 | | | 0 | .00 | .00 | | 101 | 11 | | | |
| *1 colossal* | 11.3 | 0.1 | 0.6 | 0.1 | 0.3 | 39 | .00 | 0.0 | | | 1 | | .38 | .026 | |
| | 13 | 13.7 | 1.1 | 0.1 | | | 0 | .00 | .00 | | 145 | 15 | | | |
| *1 super colossal* | 16.2 | 0.2 | 0.9 | 0.2 | 0.4 | 56 | .00 | 0.0 | | | 1 | | .54 | .037 | |
| **pickle relish** | | | | | | | | | | | | | | | |
| hamburger, Del Monte | 38 | 17.0 | 0.2 | | | | 1 | .01 | | | 308 | 2 | 2 | .03 | |
| *1 oz* | 28 | 0.2 | 10.2 | | | 76 | .01 | 0.2 | | | 22 | 5 | .34 | .023 | |
| hot dog, Del Monte | 25 | 20.5 | 0.1 | | | | 0 | .01 | | | 328 | 5 | 5 | .06 | |
| *1 oz* | 28 | 0.5 | 6.4 | | | 47 | .01 | 0.1 | | | 22 | 11 | .40 | .023 | |
| picalilli, Heinz | 30 | | 0.0 | | | | | | | | 140 | | | | |
| *1 oz* | 28 | 0.0 | 7.0 | | | | | | | | | | | | |
| sweet | 21 | 9.5 | 0.1 | | | | | | | | 107 | 3 | | | |
| *1 T* | 15 | 0.1 | 5.1 | | | | | | | | | 2 | .10 | | |
| sweet, Del Monte | 38 | 17.4 | 0.1 | | | | 0 | .01 | | | 235 | 0 | 1 | .04 | |
| *1 oz* | 28 | 0.1 | 10.1 | | | 44 | | 0.1 | | | 7 | 4 | .28 | .023 | |
| **pickles** | | | | | | | | | | | | | | | |
| bread & butter | 11 | 11.8 | 0.0 | | | | 1 | .00 | | | 101 | 5 | | | |
| *2 slices* | 15 | 0.1 | 2.7 | | | 20 | .00 | 0.0 | | | | 4 | .30 | | |
| Claussen | 20 | 22.5 | 0.1 | | 0 | | 1 | .00 | .01 | | 170 | 22 | 3 | .11 | |
| *1 oz* | 28 | 0.2 | 4.7 | | | | .00 | 0.0 | | | 33 | 9 | .11 | .030 | |
| Heinz | 25 | | 0.0 | | | | | | | | 170 | | | | |
| *1 oz* | 28 | 0.0 | 6.0 | | | | | | | | | | | | |
| **chow chow** | | | | | | | | | | | | | | | |
| sour[a] | 35 | 105.1 | 1.5 | | | | | | | | 1605 | 38 | | | |
| *1/2 cup* | 120 | 1.7 | 4.9 | | | | | | | | | 63 | 3.10 | | |
| sweet[a] | 142 | 84.1 | 1.1 | | | | | | | | 645 | 28 | | | |
| *1/2 cup* | 122 | 1.8 | 33.1 | | | | | | | | | 27 | 1.80 | | |
| dill | 1 | 12.1 | 0.0 | | | | 1 | .00 | | | 186 | 3 | | | |
| *2 slices* | 13 | 0.1 | 0.3 | | | 10 | .00 | 0.0 | | | 26 | 3 | .10 | | |
| *1 med (3 3/4" long, 1 1/4" diameter)* | 7 | 60.6 | 0.1 | | | | 4 | .01 | | | 928 | 17 | | | |
| | 65 | 0.5 | 1.4 | | | 70 | .00 | 0.0 | | | 130 | 14 | .70 | | |
| halves, del Monte | 3 | 26.6 | 0.1 | | | | 0 | .00 | | | 440 | 4 | 3 | .04 | |
| *1 oz* | 28 | 0.1 | 0.5 | | | 62 | | 0.0 | | | 26 | 4 | .23 | .020 | |

[a] Pickled cucumber w/ cauliflower, onions & mustard.

| | KCAL | $H_2O$ (g) | FAT (g) | PUFA (g) | CHOL (mg) | A (RE) | C (mg) | B-2 (mg) | B-6 (mg) | FOL (mcg) | Na (mg) | Ca (mg) | Mg (mg) | Zn (mg) | Mn (mg) |
|---|---|---|---|---|---|---|---|---|---|---|---|---|---|---|---|
| | WT (g) | PRO (g) | CHO (g) | SFA (g) | DFIB (g) | A (IU) | B-1 (mg) | NIA (mg) | B-12 (mcg) | PANT (mg) | K (mg) | P (mg) | Fe (mg) | Cu (mg) | |
| hamburger chips, Del Monte | 2 | 26.4 | 0.1 | | | | 0 | .00 | | | 494 | 1 | 1 | .02 | |
| *1 oz* | 28 | 0.1 | 0.5 | | | 15 | | | | | 10 | 3 | .28 | .028 | |
| hot garlic, Del Monte | 6 | 25.7 | 0.1 | | | | 0 | .01 | | | 383 | 5 | 5 | .08 | |
| *1 oz* | 28 | 0.2 | 1.2 | | | 73 | .01 | 0.0 | | | 49 | 7 | .34 | .037 | |
| kosher, halves, Claussen | 4 | 26.3 | 0.1 | | 0 | | 1 | .00 | .01 | 1 | 325 | 4 | 2 | .03 | |
| *1 oz* | 28 | 0.1 | 0.6 | | | | .00 | 0.0 | | .05 | 28 | 4 | .07 | .010 | |
| kosher, slices, Claussen | 3 | 26.4 | 0.1 | | | | 0 | .01 | .01 | | 315 | 5 | 2 | .03 | |
| *1 oz* | 28 | 0.1 | 0.4 | | | | .00 | 0.0 | | | 30 | 4 | .08 | .010 | |
| kosher, whole, Claussen | 3 | 26.3 | 0.1 | | | | 1 | .01 | .01 | 1 | 323 | 4 | 2 | .03 | .017 |
| *1 oz* | 28 | 0.2 | 0.5 | | | | .00 | 0.1 | | .06 | 33 | 5 | .09 | .030 | |
| kosher, whole, Del Monte | 2 | 26.5 | 0.1 | | | | 0 | .00 | | | 464 | 1 | 1 | .01 | |
| *1 oz* | 28 | 0.1 | 0.5 | | | 50 | | | | | 11 | 3 | .14 | .017 | |
| no garlic, Claussen | 6 | 25.8 | 0.1 | | | | | | | | 297 | 10 | 2 | .03 | |
| *1 oz* | 28 | 0.2 | 1.0 | | | | | | | | 54 | 5 | .08 | .010 | |
| polish style, Heinz | 4 | | 0.0 | | | | | | | | 285 | | | | |
| *1 oz* | 28 | 0.0 | 1.0 | | | | | | | | | | | | |
| sweet halves, Del Monte | 29 | 19.2 | 0.1 | | | | 0 | .01 | | | 430 | 1 | 1 | .03 | |
| *1 oz* | 28 | 0.1 | 8.0 | | | 72 | .01 | 0.1 | | | 8 | 3 | .17 | .028 | |
| whole genuine, Del Monte | 2 | 26.6 | 0.1 | | | | 0 | .00 | | | 418 | 4 | 3 | .05 | |
| *1 oz* | 28 | 0.1 | 0.5 | | | 59 | | 0.0 | | | 27 | 5 | .23 | .014 | |
| polskie ogorki, Del Monte | 6 | 26.1 | 0.1 | | | | 1 | .01 | | | 273 | 4 | 4 | .04 | |
| *1 oz* | 28 | 0.2 | 1.3 | | | 133 | .01 | | | | 42 | 7 | .11 | .023 | |
| **sour** | | | | | | | | | | | | | | | |
| *1 med (3 3/4" long, 1 1/2" diameter)* | 7 | 61.6 | 0.1 | | | | 5 | .01 | | | 879 | 11 | | | |
| | 65 | 0.3 | 1.3 | | | 70 | .00 | 0.0 | | | | 10 | 2.10 | | |
| whole, Del Monte | 3 | 26.7 | 0.1 | | | | 0 | .00 | | | 342 | 1 | 1 | .01 | |
| *1 oz* | 28 | 0.1 | 0.6 | | | 41 | | | | | 6 | 4 | .11 | .023 | |
| **sweet** | | | | | | | | | | | | | | | |
| *1 small (2 1/3" long, 3/4" diameter)* | 22 | 9.1 | 0.1 | | | | 1 | .00 | | | | 2 | | | |
| | 15 | 0.1 | 5.5 | | | 10 | .00 | 0.0 | | | | 2 | .20 | | |
| chips, Del Monte | 30 | 19.4 | 0.1 | | | | 0 | .01 | | | 322 | 0 | 1 | .01 | |
| *1 oz* | 28 | 0.1 | 8.2 | | | 33 | .00 | 0.0 | | | 5 | 3 | .11 | .028 | |
| Claussen | 50 | 15.5 | 0.4 | | | | | | | | 167 | 13 | 1 | .05 | |
| *1 oz* | 28 | 0.1 | 11.6 | | | | | | | | 34 | 3 | .10 | .020 | |
| Del Monte | 38 | 17.1 | 0.1 | | | | 0 | .01 | | | 268 | 0 | 1 | .02 | |
| *1 oz* | 28 | 0.1 | 10.4 | | | 30 | | 0.1 | | | 5 | 3 | .23 | .028 | |
| mild, Del Monte | 31 | 19.0 | 0.1 | | | | 0 | .01 | | | 262 | 0 | 1 | .01 | |
| *1 oz* | 28 | 0.1 | 8.6 | | | 48 | .00 | 0.0 | | | 3 | 3 | .11 | .026 | |
| **sweet mixed** | | | | | | | | | | | | | | | |
| Del Monte | 37 | 17.3 | 0.1 | | | | 0 | .01 | | | 345 | 1 | 1 | .02 | |
| *1 oz* | 28 | 0.1 | 10.1 | | | 43 | .00 | 0.1 | | | 6 | 3 | .23 | .026 | |
| Heinz | 40 | | 0.0 | | | | | | | | 200 | | | | |
| *1 oz* | 28 | 0.0 | 9.0 | | | | | | | | | | | | |
| sweet salad cubes, Heinz | 30 | | 0.0 | | | | | | | | 270 | | | | |
| *1 oz* | 28 | 0.0 | 7.0 | | | | | | | | | | | | |
| **rennin (salt, starch, rennin enzyme)** | 12 | 1.0 | 0.1 | | | | 0 | .00 | | | 2453 | 386 | | | |
| *1 pkt* | 11 | 0.0 | 2.7 | | | 0 | .00 | 0.0 | | | | 22 | | | |
| **soybean protein concentrate** | 92 | 1.6 | 0.1 | 0.1 | 0 | 0 | 0 | .04 | .04 | 95 | 1 | 102 | 88 | 1.23 | 1.173 |
| *1 oz* | 28 | 17.8 | 7.1 | 0.0 | | 0 | .09 | 0.2 | .00 | .02 | 617 | 235 | 3.02 | .273 | |
| **soybean protein isolate** | 94 | 1.4 | 1.0 | 0.5 | 0 | 0 | 0 | .03 | | 49 | 281 | 50 | 11 | 1.13 | .418 |
| *1 oz* | 28 | 24.7 | 0.0 | 0.1 | | 0 | .05 | 0.4 | .00 | .02 | 23 | 217 | 4.06 | .448 | |
| **tapioca, Minute** | 32 | 1.1 | 0.0 | 0.0 | 0 | 0 | 0 | .00 | .00 | 0 | 0 | 1 | 0 | | |
| *1 T* | 9 | 0.1 | 7.8 | 0.0 | | 0 | .00 | 0.0 | .00 | .00 | 2 | 1 | .04 | .005 | |
| **tapioca, quick cooking, pearl/granulated** | 30 | 1.1 | 0.0 | 0.0 | | | 0 | .00 | | | 0 | 1 | | | |
| *1 T* | 8 | 0.1 | 7.3 | 0.0 | | 0 | .00 | 0.0 | | | 2 | 2 | .00 | | |
| **tomato powder** | 302 | 3.1 | 0.4 | 0.2 | 0 | 1725 | 117 | .76 | .46 | 120 | 134 | 166 | 178 | 1.71 | 1.951 |
| *3 1/2 oz* | 100 | 12.9 | 74.7 | 0.1 | | 17247 | .91 | 9.1 | .00 | 3.76 | 1927 | 295 | 4.56 | 1.241 | |

| | KCAL | H₂O (g) | FAT (g) | PUFA (g) | CHOL (mg) | A (RE) | C (mg) | B-2 (mg) | B-6 (mg) | FOL (mcg) | Na (mg) | Ca (mg) | Mg (mg) | Zn (mg) | Mn (mg) |
|---|---|---|---|---|---|---|---|---|---|---|---|---|---|---|---|
| | WT (g) | PRO (g) | CHO (g) | SFA (g) | DFIB (g) | A (IU) | B-1 (mg) | NIA (mg) | B-12 (mcg) | PANT (mg) | K (mg) | P (mg) | Fe (mg) | Cu (mg) | |
| **vinegar** | | | | | | | | | | | | | | | |
| cider | 2 | 14.1 | 0.0 | | | | | | | | 0 | 1 | | | |
| 1 T | 15 | 0.0 | 0.9 | | | | | | | | 15 | 1 | .10 | | |
| distilled | 2 | 14.3 | 0.0 | | | | | | | | 0 | | | | |
| 1 T | 15 | 0.0 | 0.8 | | | | | | | | 2 | | | | |
| **whey** | | | | | | | | | | | | | | | |
| acid, dry | 10 | 0.1 | 0.0 | 0.0 | | 0 | 0 | .06 | .02 | 1 | 28 | 59 | 6 | .18 | |
| 1 T | 3 | 0.3 | 2.1 | 0.0 | 0.0 | 2 | .02 | 0.0 | .07 | .16 | 66 | 39 | .04 | | |
| acid, fluid | 59 | 229.8 | 0.2 | 0.0 | | 2 | 0 | .34 | .10 | 5 | 118 | 253 | 24 | 1.06 | |
| 1 cup | 246 | 1.9 | 12.6 | 0.1 | 0.0 | 17 | .10 | 1.2 | .44 | .94 | 352 | 191 | .20 | | |
| sweet, dry | 26 | 0.2 | 0.1 | 0.0 | 0 | 1 | 0 | .17 | .04 | 1 | 80 | 59 | 13 | .15 | |
| 1 T | 8 | 1.0 | 5.6 | 0.1 | 0.0 | 3 | .04 | 0.1 | .18 | .42 | 155 | 70 | .07 | | |
| sweet, fluid | 66 | 229.1 | 0.9 | 0.0 | 5 | 10 | 0 | .39 | .08 | 2 | 132 | 115 | 20 | .32 | |
| 1 cup | 246 | 2.1 | 12.6 | 0.6 | 0.0 | 39 | .09 | 0.2 | .68 | .94 | 396 | 112 | .15 | | |
| **yeast** | | | | | | | | | | | | | | | |
| active dry, Fleischmann's | 20 | | 0.0 | | | | | | | | 10 | | | | |
| 1 pkt | | 3.0 | 3.0 | | | | | | | | 150 | | | | |
| bakers, compressed | 24 | 19.9 | 1.0 | | | | 0 | .47 | | | 5 | 4 | | | |
| 1 oz | 28 | 3.4 | 3.1 | | | 0 | .20 | 3.2 | | | 173 | 112 | 1.40 | | |
| bakers, dry | 80 | 1.4 | 0.5 | | | | 0 | 1.53 | | | 15 | 12 | | | |
| 1 oz | 28 | 10.5 | 11.0 | | | 0 | .66 | 10.4 | | | 566 | 366 | 4.6 | | |
| brewers | 80 | 1.4 | 0.3 | | | | 0 | 1.21 | | | 34 | 60 | | | |
| 1 oz | 28 | 11.0 | 10.9 | | | 0 | 4.43 | 10.7 | | | 537 | 497 | 4.90 | | |
| compressed, Fleischmann's | 15 | | 0.0 | | | | | | | | 5 | | | | |
| 1 cube | | 2.0 | 2.0 | | | | | | | | 100 | | | | |
| rapid rise, Fleischmann's | 20 | | 0.0 | | | | | | | | 10 | | | | |
| 1 pkt | | 3.0 | 3.0 | | | | | | | | 150 | | | | |
| torula | 79 | 1.7 | 0.3 | | | | 0 | 1.43 | | | 4 | 120 | | | |
| 1 oz | 28 | 10.9 | 10.5 | | | 0 | 3.97 | 12.6 | | | 580 | 486 | 5.50 | | |
| torula, dried, Lake States | 348 | 4.8 | 4.4 | | | | | | 4.45 | 225 | 33 | 350 | 175 | 12.90 | 2.500 |
| 3.5 oz | 100 | 47.5 | 29.0 | | | | | | .59 | 7.75 | 2100 | 1375 | 22.50 | .295 | |

# Supplementary Tables

|  | TRY | THR | ISO | LEU | LYS | MET | CYS | PHE | TYR | VAL | ARG | HIS |
|---|---|---|---|---|---|---|---|---|---|---|---|---|
| **1. Beverages** | | | | | | | | | | | | |
| **1.1. Alcoholic Beverages** | | | | | | | | | | | | |
| **1.1.1. Ales, Beers & Malt Liquors** | | | | | | | | | | | | |
| beer—*12 fl oz (356 g)* | 11 | 18 | 18 | 21 | 25 | 4 | 11 | 21 | 53 | 32 | 32 | 18 |
| beer, light—*12 fl oz (354 g)* | 11 | 14 | 14 | 18 | 18 | 4 | 7 | 18 | 42 | 25 | 25 | 14 |
| **1.1.2. Cocktails & Cocktail Mixes** | | | | | | | | | | | | |
| bourbon & soda—*4 fl oz cocktail (116 g)* | 0 | 0 | 0 | 0 | 0 | 0 | 0 | 0 | 0 | 0 | 0 | 0 |
| screwdriver (orange jce & vodka)—*7 fl oz cocktail (213 g)* | 2 | 13 | 13 | 21 | 15 | 6 | 9 | 15 | 6 | 19 | 79 | 4 |
| **1.1.3. Distilled Spirits** | | | | | | | | | | | | |
| gin, 90 proof—*1.5 fl oz jigger (42 g)* | 0 | 0 | 0 | 0 | 0 | 0 | 0 | 0 | 0 | 0 | 0 | 0 |
| gin/rum/vodka/whiskey, 94 proof—*1.5 fl oz jigger (42 g)* | 0 | 0 | 0 | 0 | 0 | 0 | 0 | 0 | 0 | 0 | 0 | 0 |
| rum, 80 proof—*1.5 fl oz jigger (42 g)* | 0 | 0 | 0 | 0 | 0 | 0 | 0 | 0 | 0 | 0 | 0 | 0 |
| vodka, 80 proof—*1.5 fl oz jigger (42 g)* | 0 | 0 | 0 | 0 | 0 | 0 | 0 | 0 | 0 | 0 | 0 | 0 |
| whiskey, 86 proof—*1.5 fl oz jigger (42 g)* | 0 | 0 | 0 | 0 | 0 | 0 | 0 | 0 | 0 | 0 | 0 | 0 |
| **1.1.4. Liqueurs** | | | | | | | | | | | | |
| coffee w/ cream, 34 proof—*1.5 fl oz (47 g)* | 19 | 60 | 80 | 129 | 105 | 33 | 12 | 64 | 64 | 88 | 48 | 36 |
| creme de menthe—*1.5 fl oz (50 g)* | 0 | 0 | 0 | 0 | 0 | 0 | 0 | 0 | 0 | 0 | 0 | 0 |
| **1.2. Carbonated Beverages** | | | | | | | | | | | | |
| cream soda—*12 fl oz (371 g)* | 0 | 0 | 0 | 0 | 0 | 0 | 0 | 0 | 0 | 0 | 0 | 0 |
| grape soda—*12 fl oz (372 g)* | 0 | 0 | 0 | 0 | 0 | 0 | 0 | 0 | 0 | 0 | 0 | 0 |
| lemon-lime soda—*12 fl oz (368 g)* | 0 | 0 | 0 | 0 | 0 | 0 | 0 | 0 | 0 | 0 | 0 | 0 |
| orange soda—*12 fl oz (372 g)* | 0 | 0 | 0 | 0 | 0 | 0 | 0 | 0 | 0 | 0 | 0 | 0 |
| pepper type soda—*12 fl oz (368 g)* | 0 | 0 | 0 | 0 | 0 | 0 | 0 | 0 | 0 | 0 | 0 | 0 |
| tonic water/quinine water—*12 fl oz (366 g)* | 0 | 0 | 0 | 0 | 0 | 0 | 0 | 0 | 0 | 0 | 0 | 0 |
| **1.3. Carbonated Beverages, Low Calorie** | | | | | | | | | | | | |
| club soda—*12 fl oz (355 g)* | 0 | 0 | 0 | 0 | 0 | 0 | 0 | 0 | 0 | 0 | 0 | 0 |
| diet cherry coke, Coca-Cola—*12 fl oz (354 g)* | | | | | | | | 104[b] | | | | |
| diet coke, Coca-Cola—*12 fl oz (354 g)* | | | | | | | | 104[b] | | | | |
| diet Sprite—*12 fl oz (354 g)* | | | | | | | | 96[b] | | | | |
| Fresca—*12 fl oz (354 g)* | | | | | | | | 98[b] | | | | |
| Tab—*12 fl oz (354 g)* | | | | | | | | 16[b] | | | | |
| **1.4. Cereal Grain Beverages** | | | | | | | | | | | | |
| powder—*1 t (2.3 g)* | 2 | 4 | 5 | 9 | 5 | 2 | 3 | 6 | 4 | 6 | 6 | 3 |
| prep from powder | | | | | | | | | | | | |
| w/ water—*6 fl oz water & 1 t powder (180 g)* | 2 | 4 | 5 | 9 | 5 | 2 | 2 | 5 | 4 | 7 | 7 | 2 |
| w/ whole milk—*6 fl oz milk & 1 t powder (185 g)* | 85 | 278 | 368 | 598 | 481 | 154 | 57 | 296 | 294 | 409 | 224 | 165 |
| **1.5. Coffee** | | | | | | | | | | | | |
| brewed—*6 fl oz (177 g)* | 0 | 2 | 4 | 9 | 2 | 0 | 4 | 5 | 4 | 5 | 2 | 4 |
| inst powder—*1 rd t (1.8 g)* | 1 | 3 | 3 | 9 | 2 | 0 | 4 | 5 | 3 | 5 | 1 | 3 |
| cappuccino flavor, sugar sweetened—*2 rd t (14 g)* | 1 | 5 | 6 | 16 | 3 | 1 | 7 | 9 | 5 | 9 | 2 | 5 |
| decaffeinated—*1 rd t (1.8 g)* | 1 | 2 | 3 | 8 | 2 | 0 | 3 | 5 | 3 | 5 | 1 | 3 |
| french flavor, sugar sweetened—*2 rd t (11.5 g)* | 1 | 6 | 7 | 19 | 4 | 1 | 8 | 10 | 6 | 11 | 2 | 6 |
| mocha flavor, sugar sweetened—*2 rd t (11.5 g)* | 5 | 14 | 14 | 24 | 17 | 3 | 6 | 18 | 14 | 21 | 18 | 7 |

[a] Amino acids for infant formulas and special dietary formulas are in the main table.

[b] Phenylalanine is from aspartame.

219

| | TRY | THR | ISO | LEU | LYS | MET | CYS | PHE | TYR | VAL | ARG | HIS |
|---|---|---|---|---|---|---|---|---|---|---|---|---|
| w/ chicory—*1 rd t (1.8 g)* | 0 | 2 | 2 | 6 | 1 | 0 | 3 | 3 | 2 | 4 | 1 | 2 |
| prep from inst powder—*6 fl oz water & 1 rd t powder (179 g)* | 0 | 2 | 4 | 9 | 2 | 0 | 4 | 5 | 4 | 5 | 2 | 4 |
| cappuccino flavor, sugar sweetened—*6 fl oz water & 2 rd t powder (192 g)* | 2 | 4 | 6 | 15 | 4 | 0 | 6 | 8 | 6 | 10 | 2 | 6 |
| decaffeinated—*6 fl oz water & 1 rd t powder (179 g)* | 0 | 2 | 4 | 9 | 2 | 0 | 4 | 5 | 4 | 5 | 2 | 4 |
| french flavor, sugar sweetened—*6 fl oz water & 2 rd t powder (189 g)* | 2 | 6 | 8 | 19 | 4 | 0 | 8 | 9 | 6 | 11 | 2 | 6 |
| mocha flavor, sugar sweetened—*6 fl oz water & 2 rd t powder (188 g)* | 6 | 13 | 13 | 24 | 17 | 4 | 6 | 17 | 13 | 21 | 19 | 8 |
| w/ chicory—*6 fl oz water & 1 rd t powder (179 g)* | 0 | 2 | 2 | 5 | 2 | 0 | 2 | 4 | 2 | 4 | 0 | 2 |
| **1.6. Fruit Juice Drinks & Fruit Flavored Beverages** | | | | | | | | | | | | |
| lemonade, from powder—*8 fl oz (240 g)* | 0 | 0 | 0 | 0 | 0 | 0 | 0 | 0 | 0 | 0 | 0 | 0 |
| orange breakfast drink, from frozn conc—*6 fl oz (188 g)* | 0 | 2 | 2 | 4 | 4 | 2 | 2 | 4 | 2 | 4 | 13 | 2 |
| orange flavor gelatin drink, prep from powder—*1 pkt in 4 fl oz water (136 g)* | 0 | 122 | 94 | 201 | 261 | 48 | | 144 | 26 | 169 | 521 | 54 |
| thirst quencher, bottled—*8 fl oz (241 g)* | 0 | 0 | 0 | 0 | 0 | 0 | 0 | 0 | 0 | 0 | 0 | 0 |
| **1.8. Tea, hot/iced** | | | | | | | | | | | | |
| brewed 3 min—*6 fl oz (178 g)* | 0 | 0 | 0 | 0 | 0 | 0 | 0 | 0 | 0 | 0 | 0 | 0 |
| inst powder—*1 t (0.7 g)* | 1 | 0 | 0 | 0 | 0 | 0 | 0 | 0 | 0 | 0 | 0 | 0 |
| w/ lemon flavor—*1 rd t (1.4 g)* | 1 | 0 | 0 | 0 | 0 | 0 | 1 | 0 | 0 | 0 | 1 | 0 |
| w/ sugar & lemon flavor—*3 rd t (23 g)* | 1 | 1 | 1 | 1 | 1 | 0 | 1 | 0 | 1 | 1 | 1 | 0 |
| w/ sodium saccharin & lemon flavor—*2 t (1.6 g)* | 1 | 0 | 0 | 0 | 0 | 0 | 0 | 0 | 0 | 0 | 0 | 0 |
| prep from inst powder—*1 t powder in 8 fl oz water (237 g)* | 0 | 0 | 0 | 0 | 0 | 0 | 0 | 0 | 0 | 0 | 0 | 0 |
| w/ lemon flavor—*1 rd t powder in 8 fl oz water (238 g)* | 0 | 0 | 0 | 0 | 0 | 0 | 0 | 0 | 0 | 0 | 0 | 0 |
| w/ sugar & lemon flavor—*3 rd t powder in 8 fl oz water (259 g)* | 0 | 0 | 0 | 0 | 0 | 0 | 0 | 0 | 0 | 0 | 0 | 0 |
| w/ sodium saccharin & lemon flavor—*2 t powder in 8 fl oz water (238 g)* | 0 | 0 | 0 | 0 | 0 | 0 | 0 | 0 | 0 | 0 | 0 | 0 |
| **1.9. Water** | | | | | | | | | | | | |
| bottled, Perrier—*6.5 fl oz bottled (192 g)* | 0 | 0 | 0 | 0 | 0 | 0 | 0 | 0 | 0 | 0 | 0 | 0 |
| bottled, Poland Spring—*8 fl oz (237 g)* | 0 | 0 | 0 | 0 | 0 | 0 | 0 | 0 | 0 | 0 | 0 | 0 |
| municipal—*8 fl oz (237 g)* | 0 | 0 | 0 | 0 | 0 | 0 | 0 | 0 | 0 | 0 | 0 | 0 |
| **2. Candy** | | | | | | | | | | | | |
| milk choc, Cadbury—*1 oz (28 g)* | 120 | 300 | 400 | 680 | 480 | 160 | 80 | 410 | 200 | 440 | 270 | 220 |
| **3. Cereals, Cooked or to-be-Cooked** | | | | | | | | | | | | |
| corn grits, reg/quick, enr, ckd—*1 cup (242 g)* | 19 | 121 | 136 | 520 | 68 | 82 | 77 | 177 | 148 | 177 | 114 | 94 |
| cream of rice, ckd—*¾ cup (183 g)* | 24 | 81 | 27 | 134 | 68 | 48 | 27 | 68 | 90 | 104 | 132 | 48 |
| cream of wheat, inst ckd—*¾ cup (181 g)* | 45 | 105 | 145 | 252 | 85 | 62 | 74 | 179 | 105 | 161 | 143 | 76 |
| mix & eat—*1 pkt prep (142 g)* | 38 | 86 | 120 | 208 | 72 | 51 | 62 | 149 | 88 | 135 | 122 | 62 |
| mix & eat, flavored[a]—*1 pkt prep (150 g)* | 34 | 78 | 106 | 186 | 64 | 46 | 55 | 132 | 78 | 118 | 109 | 57 |
| cream of wheat, quick, ckd—*¾ cup (179 g)* | 38 | 86 | 120 | 206 | 70 | 50 | 61 | 147 | 86 | 132 | 118 | 63 |
| cream of wheat, reg, ckd—*¾ cup (188 g)* | 39 | 90 | 126 | 216 | 73 | 53 | 64 | 154 | 90 | 137 | 124 | 66 |
| farina, ckd, enr—*¾ cup (175 g)* | 35 | 77 | 110 | 191 | 58 | 46 | 56 | 137 | 79 | 121 | 102 | 56 |

[a] Apple w/cinn, banana & spice, or maple & brown sugar.

| | TRY | THR | ISO | LEU | LYS | MET | CYS | PHE | TYR | VAL | ARG | HIS |
|---|---|---|---|---|---|---|---|---|---|---|---|---|
| oatmeal, quick/reg, ckd—¾ cup (from ⅓ cup or 1 oz dry) (175 g) | 61 | 158 | 207 | 345 | 184 | 75 | 112 | 247 | 161 | 264 | 338 | 102 |
| **4. Cereals, Ready-to-Eat** | | | | | | | | | | | | |
| alpha-bits, Post—1 cup (1 oz) (28 g) | 26 | 76 | 97 | 200 | 79 | 39 | 53 | 117 | 81 | 124 | 143 | 51 |
| bran, 100%—½ cup (1 oz) (28 g) | 55 | 115 | 113 | 210 | 137 | 50 | 69 | 136 | 101 | 166 | 248 | 97 |
| bran flakes—⅔ cup (1 oz) (28 g) | 56 | 103 | 120 | 214 | 107 | 50 | 65 | 147 | 96 | 156 | 190 | 82 |
| cap'n crunch, Quaker—¾ cup (1 oz) (28 g) | 12 | 51 | 61 | 184 | 39 | 31 | 34 | 76 | 59 | 78 | 67 | 37 |
| cap'n crunch's crunchberries, Quaker—¾ cup (1 oz) (28 g) | 13 | 52 | 63 | 183 | 42 | 32 | 33 | 77 | 60 | 79 | 67 | 38 |
| peanut butter, Quaker—¾ cup (1 oz) (28 g) | 20 | 68 | 85 | 210 | 65 | 35 | 39 | 108 | 86 | 105 | 164 | 54 |
| cheerios, General Mills—1¼ cups (1 oz) (28 g) | 58 | 149 | 196 | 327 | 175 | 71 | 107 | 233 | 153 | 251 | 320 | 97 |
| cocoa pebbles, Post—⅞ cup (1 oz) (28 g) | 18 | 65 | 69 | 108 | 56 | 38 | 22 | 58 | 73 | 86 | 106 | 39 |
| corn flakes, Post Toasties, Post—1 cup (1 oz) (28 g) | 14 | 80 | 89 | 343 | 45 | 54 | 51 | 117 | 97 | 117 | 75 | 62 |
| crispy wheats & raisins, General Mills—¾ cup (1 oz) (28 g) | 33 | 58 | 75 | 129 | 53 | 31 | 38 | 92 | 55 | 90 | 90 | 43 |
| C.W. Post—¼ cup (1 oz) (28 g) | 37 | 95 | 120 | 199 | 103 | 48 | 60 | 135 | 98 | 151 | 187 | 62 |
| C.W. Post w/ raisins—¼ cup (1 oz) (28 g) | 34 | 89 | 112 | 185 | 96 | 45 | 56 | 125 | 91 | 140 | 173 | 57 |
| fortified oat flakes, Post—⅔ cup (1 oz) (28 g) | 92 | 252 | 295 | 490 | 344 | 99 | 131 | 278 | 200 | 318 | 342 | 130 |
| frosted rice krinkles—⅞ cup (1 oz) (28 g) | 20 | 69 | 73 | 114 | 58 | 41 | 24 | 59 | 77 | 89 | 113 | 41 |
| fruity pebbles, Post—⅞ cup (1 oz) (28 g) | 17 | 57 | 60 | 95 | 48 | 34 | 20 | 48 | 64 | 74 | 93 | 34 |
| golden grahams, General Mills—¾ cup (1 oz) (28 g) | 18 | 56 | 67 | 193 | 46 | 35 | 33 | 82 | 64 | 84 | 63 | 42 |
| granola homemade—¼ cup (1 oz) (28 g) | 42 | 127 | 153 | 249 | 151 | 60 | 71 | 168 | 110 | 189 | 311 | 87 |
| Nature Valley[a]—⅓ cup (1 oz) (28 g) | 39 | 101 | 134 | 222 | 118 | 49 | 72 | 158 | 103 | 170 | 218 | 66 |
| grape-nut flakes, Post—⅞ cup (1 oz) (28 g) | 55 | 97 | 124 | 215 | 93 | 51 | 60 | 154 | 93 | 152 | 155 | 73 |
| grape-nuts, Post—¼ cup (1 oz) (28 g) | 60 | 106 | 136 | 235 | 101 | 56 | 66 | 168 | 102 | 166 | 169 | 80 |
| honeycomb, Post—1⅓ cups (1 oz) (28 g) | 14 | 57 | 67 | 207 | 43 | 35 | 38 | 85 | 66 | 87 | 75 | 42 |
| honey nut cheerios, General Mills—¾ cup (1 oz) (28 g) | 79 | 114 | 136 | 367 | 145 | 54 | 75 | 160 | 108 | 177 | 240 | 76 |
| king vitamin, Quaker—1¼ cups (1 oz) (28 g) | 12 | 52 | 62 | 191 | 39 | 33 | 34 | 77 | 61 | 79 | 67 | 38 |
| kix, General Mills—1½ cups (1 oz) (28 g) | 20 | 88 | 103 | 325 | 65 | 55 | 58 | 131 | 102 | 134 | 112 | 65 |
| life, cinn, Quaker—⅔ cup (1 oz) (28 g) | 75 | 210 | 277 | 446 | 297 | 96 | 107 | 284 | 206 | 313 | 368 | 133 |
| life, Quaker—⅔ cup (1 oz) (28 g) | 75 | 210 | 277 | 446 | 297 | 96 | 107 | 284 | 206 | 313 | 368 | 133 |
| lucky charms, General Mills—1 cup (1 oz) (28 g) | 35 | 90 | 119 | 198 | 105 | 43 | 64 | 141 | 92 | 151 | 193 | 58 |
| puffed rice—1 cup (½ oz) (14 g) | 13 | 45 | 48 | 75 | 38 | 27 | 15 | 38 | 50 | 58 | 74 | 27 |
| puffed wheat—1 cup (½ oz) (14 g) | 32 | 64 | 89 | 151 | 58 | 36 | 41 | 108 | 63 | 100 | 101 | 54 |
| Quaker 100% natural ¼ cup (1 oz) (28 g) | 46 | 123 | 167 | 273 | 160 | 62 | 63 | 174 | 125 | 197 | 227 | 82 |
| w/ apples & cinn—¼ cup (1 oz) (28 g) | 42 | 111 | 150 | 244 | 149 | 58 | 57 | 154 | 113 | 177 | 182 | 72 |
| w/ raisins & dates—¼ cup (1 oz) (28 g) | 40 | 106 | 143 | 234 | 138 | 53 | 53 | 149 | 106 | 169 | 192 | 71 |
| quisp, Quaker—1 cup (1 oz) (28 g) | 12 | 50 | 60 | 179 | 38 | 31 | 33 | 75 | 57 | 76 | 66 | 36 |
| raisin bran, Post—½ cup (1 oz) (28 g) | 39 | 74 | 86 | 153 | 77 | 37 | 46 | 105 | 68 | 112 | 133 | 58 |
| shredded wheat 1 oz (28 g) | 60 | 104 | 123 | 215 | 96 | 54 | 60 | 150 | 91 | 154 | 162 | 72 |
| 1 biscuit (24 g) | 49 | 86 | 101 | 177 | 79 | 45 | 49 | 124 | 75 | 127 | 133 | 60 |
| sugar sparkled flakes, Post—¾ cup (1 oz) (28 g) | 9 | 52 | 58 | 223 | 29 | 35 | 33 | 76 | 63 | 76 | 48 | 40 |

[a] Cinn & raisin, coconut & honey, fruit & nut or toasted oat.

| | TRY | THR | ISO | LEU | LYS | MET | CYS | PHE | TYR | VAL | ARG | HIS |
|---|---|---|---|---|---|---|---|---|---|---|---|---|
| super sugar crisp—⅞ cup (1 oz) (28 g) | 28 | 56 | 78 | 133 | 50 | 32 | 36 | 95 | 56 | 88 | 89 | 47 |
| team flakes—1 cup (1 oz) (28 g) | 26 | 77 | 87 | 156 | 69 | 44 | 36 | 87 | 84 | 109 | 127 | 50 |
| total, General Mills—1 cup (1 oz) (28 g) | 54 | 94 | 111 | 195 | 87 | 49 | 54 | 136 | 83 | 139 | 147 | 66 |
| trix, General Mills—1 cup (1 oz) (28 g) | 11 | 55 | 63 | 214 | 37 | 35 | 36 | 82 | 65 | 82 | 65 | 41 |
| wheaties, General Mills—1 cup (1 oz) (28 g) | 51 | 90 | 106 | 186 | 83 | 47 | 51 | 130 | 79 | 133 | 140 | 62 |

## 5. Cheese & Cheese Products
### 5.1. Cheese

| | TRY | THR | ISO | LEU | LYS | MET | CYS | PHE | TYR | VAL | ARG | HIS |
|---|---|---|---|---|---|---|---|---|---|---|---|---|
| american, processed—1 oz (28 g) | 92 | 204 | 290 | 555 | 623 | 162 | 40 | 319 | 344 | 376 | 263 | 256 |
| blue—1 oz (28 g) | 89 | 223 | 319 | 545 | 526 | 166 | 30 | 309 | 368 | 442 | 202 | 215 |
| brick—1 oz (28 g) | 92 | 250 | 322 | 636 | 602 | 160 | 37 | 349 | 316 | 417 | 248 | 233 |
| brie—1 oz (28 g) | 91 | 213 | 288 | 547 | 525 | 168 | 32 | 328 | 340 | 380 | 208 | 203 |
| camembert—1 oz (28 g) | 87 | 203 | 275 | 522 | 501 | 160 | 31 | 313 | 325 | 362 | 199 | 194 |
| cheddar—1 oz (28 g) | 91 | 251 | 438 | 676 | 588 | 185 | 35 | 372 | 341 | 471 | 267 | 248 |
| cheddar—3.5 oz (100 g) | 320 | 886 | 1546 | 2385 | 2072 | 652 | 125 | 1311 | 1202 | 1663 | 941 | 874 |
| cheddar, grated—1 cup, not packed (113 g) | 362 | 1001 | 1746 | 2695 | 2342 | 737 | 141 | 1482 | 1358 | 1879 | 1063 | 988 |
| cheshire—1 oz (28 g) | 85 | 236 | 411 | 635 | 551 | 173 | 33 | 349 | 320 | 442 | 250 | 233 |
| colby—1 oz (28 g) | 87 | 240 | 418 | 645 | 561 | 176 | 34 | 355 | 325 | 450 | 254 | 236 |
| cottage cheese, creamed—1 rd T (28 g) | 39 | 155 | 206 | 360 | 283 | 105 | 32 | 188 | 186 | 216 | 160 | 116 |
| cottage cheese, creamed—4 oz (113 g) | 157 | 626 | 830 | 1451 | 1141 | 425 | 131 | 761 | 752 | 874 | 644 | 469 |
| cottage cheese, creamed—1 cup, not packed (210 g) | 292 | 1163 | 1542 | 2697 | 2121 | 789 | 243 | 1414 | 1398 | 1624 | 1196 | 872 |
| cottage cheese, creamed w/ fruit—1 cup (226 g) | 249 | 992 | 1315 | 2301 | 1810 | 673 | 207 | 1206 | 1192 | 1385 | 1021 | 743 |
| cottage cheese, dry curd—1 cup, not packed (145 g) | 279 | 1111 | 1472 | 2575 | 2025 | 754 | 232 | 1350 | 1334 | 1550 | 1142 | 832 |
| cottage cheese, low fat, 1% fat—1 cup (226 g) | 312 | 1242 | 1646 | 2879 | 2265 | 843 | 259 | 1510 | 1492 | 1734 | 1277 | 930 |
| cottage cheese, low fat, 2% fat—1 cup (226 g) | 346 | 1377 | 1825 | 3193 | 2511 | 934 | 287 | 1674 | 1655 | 1923 | 1416 | 1032 |
| cream cheese—1 oz (2T) (28 g) | 19 | 91 | 113 | 207 | 192 | 51 | 19 | 119 | 102 | 125 | 81 | 77 |
| edam—1 oz (28 g) | | 264 | 371 | 728 | 754 | 204 | | 406 | 413 | 513 | 273 | 293 |
| gjetost—1 oz (28 g) | 38 | 111 | 147 | 281 | 231 | 90 | 16 | 153 | 154 | 217 | 93 | 83 |
| gouda—1 oz (28 g) | | 264 | 370 | 727 | 752 | 204 | | 406 | 412 | 512 | 273 | 293 |
| gruyere—1 oz (28 g) | 119 | 309 | 457 | 880 | 768 | 233 | 86 | 494 | 503 | 636 | 276 | 317 |
| limburger—1 oz (28 g) | 82 | 209 | 346 | 593 | 475 | 176 | | 316 | 339 | 408 | 198 | 164 |
| monterey—1 oz (28 g) | 89 | 247 | 431 | 665 | 578 | 182 | 35 | 365 | 335 | 463 | 262 | 244 |
| mozzarella—1 oz (28 g) | | 210 | 264 | 537 | 559 | 154 | 33 | 287 | 318 | 344 | 236 | 207 |
| mozzarella, low moisture—1 oz (28 g) | | 233 | 294 | 597 | 622 | 171 | 36 | 320 | 354 | 383 | 263 | 230 |
| mozzarella, part skim—1 oz (28 g) | | 262 | 330 | 671 | 699 | 192 | 41 | 359 | 398 | 430 | 295 | 259 |
| mozzarella, part skim, low moisture—1 oz (28 g) | | 184 | 232 | 471 | 491 | 135 | 29 | 252 | 280 | 302 | 208 | 182 |
| muenster—1 oz (28 g) | 93 | 252 | 325 | 641 | 606 | 161 | 37 | 352 | 318 | 420 | 250 | 235 |
| neufchatel—1 oz (28 g) | 25 | 120 | 149 | 274 | 253 | 68 | 25 | 157 | 135 | 166 | 107 | 101 |
| parmesan, grated—1 T (5 g) | 28 | 77 | 110 | 201 | 192 | 56 | 14 | 112 | 116 | 143 | 77 | 80 |
| parmesan, hard—1 oz (28 g) | 137 | 373 | 537 | 979 | 937 | 272 | 67 | 545 | 566 | 696 | 373 | 392 |
| pimento, processed—1 oz (28 g) | 91 | 204 | 290 | 555 | 622 | 162 | 40 | 319 | 343 | 376 | 263 | 256 |
| port du salut—1 oz (28 g) | 97 | 248 | 410 | 704 | 563 | 208 | | 375 | 403 | 484 | 235 | 194 |
| provolone—1 oz (28 g) | | 278 | 309 | 651 | 750 | 194 | 33 | 365 | 431 | 465 | 290 | 316 |
| ricotta, part skim—½ cup (124 g) | | 649 | 739 | 1532 | 1678 | 352 | 124 | 697 | 739 | 868 | 793 | 576 |
| ricotta, whole milk—½ cup (124 g) | | 641 | 731 | 1514 | 1659 | 348 | 123 | 689 | 731 | 858 | 783 | 569 |
| swiss—1 oz (28 g) | 114 | 294 | 436 | 839 | 733 | 222 | 82 | 471 | 480 | 606 | 263 | 302 |
| swiss, processed—1 oz (28 g) | 102 | 227 | 324 | 620 | 696 | 181 | 45 | 356 | 384 | 420 | 293 | 286 |
| tilsit, whole milk—1 oz (28 g) | 100 | 255 | 421 | 722 | 578 | 214 | | 385 | 413 | 497 | 241 | 200 |

### 5.2. Cheese Products
cheese spread

| | TRY | THR | ISO | LEU | LYS | MET | CYS | PHE | TYR | VAL | ARG | HIS |
|---|---|---|---|---|---|---|---|---|---|---|---|---|
| american—1 T (16 g) | | 101 | 135 | 288 | 243 | 87 | | 150 | 144 | 221 | 88 | 82 |
| american—1 oz (28 g) | | 178 | 236 | 505 | 427 | 152 | | 264 | 252 | 387 | 155 | 144 |

| | TRY | THR | ISO | LEU | LYS | MET | CYS | PHE | TYR | VAL | ARG | HIS |
|---|---|---|---|---|---|---|---|---|---|---|---|---|
| **7. Creams & Cream Substitutes** | | | | | | | | | | | | |
| creamers | | | | | | | | | | | | |
| liquid/frzn[a]—*½ fl oz (15 g)* | 2 | 7 | 8 | 13 | 10 | 2 | 3 | 8 | 6 | 8 | 12 | 4 |
| liquid/frzn[b]—*½ fl oz (15 g)* | 2 | 6 | 9 | 15 | 12 | 5 | 1 | 8 | 9 | 11 | 6 | 4 |
| powdered[b]—*1 t (2 g)* | 1 | 4 | 6 | 9 | 8 | 3 | 0 | 5 | 5 | 7 | 4 | 3 |
| half & half cream—*1 T (15 g)* | 6 | 20 | 27 | 43 | 35 | 11 | 4 | 21 | 21 | 30 | 16 | 12 |
| light (coffee/table) cream—*1 T (15 g)* | 6 | 18 | 25 | 40 | 32 | 10 | 4 | 20 | 20 | 27 | 15 | 11 |
| medium (25% fat) cream—*1 T (15 g)* | 5 | 17 | 22 | 36 | 29 | 9 | 3 | 18 | 18 | 25 | 13 | 10 |
| sour cream, cultured—*1 T (12 g)* | 4 | 15 | 20 | 32 | 25 | 8 | | 15 | | 22 | | |
| whipped cream, pressurized—*1 T (3 g)* | 1 | 4 | 6 | 9 | 8 | 2 | 1 | 5 | 5 | 6 | 3 | 3 |
| whipping cream | | | | | | | | | | | | |
| heavy, fluid—*1 T (15 g)* | 4 | 14 | 19 | 30 | 24 | 8 | 3 | 15 | 15 | 21 | 11 | 8 |
| light, fluid—*1 T (15 g)* | 5 | 15 | 20 | 32 | 26 | 8 | 3 | 16 | 16 | 22 | 12 | 9 |
| whipped topping | | | | | | | | | | | | |
| from mix, prep w/ whole milk—*1 T (4 g)* | 2 | 6 | 9 | 14 | 11 | 4 | 1 | 7 | 7 | 10 | 5 | 4 |
| frzn—*1 T (4 g)* | 1 | 2 | 3 | 5 | 4 | 2 | 0 | 3 | 3 | 4 | 2 | 1 |
| pressurized—*1 T (4 g)* | 1 | 2 | 2 | 4 | 3 | 1 | 0 | 2 | 2 | 3 | 2 | 1 |
| **8. Desserts** | | | | | | | | | | | | |
| **8.7. Frozen Desserts** | | | | | | | | | | | | |
| ice cream | | | | | | | | | | | | |
| french van, soft serve—*1 cup (173 g)* | 100 | 325 | 423 | 680 | 549 | 177 | 72 | 337 | 335 | 466 | 281 | 188 |
| van, reg (10% fat)—*1 cup (133 g)* | 68 | 217 | 290 | 470 | 381 | 120 | 44 | 232 | 232 | 321 | 174 | 130 |
| van, rich (16% fat)—*1 cup (148 g)* | 58 | 186 | 250 | 405 | 327 | 104 | 38 | 199 | 199 | 276 | 150 | 112 |
| ice milk | | | | | | | | | | | | |
| van—*1 cup (131 g)* | 73 | 233 | 312 | 506 | 409 | 129 | 48 | 249 | 249 | 345 | 187 | 140 |
| van, soft serve—*1 cup (175 g)* | 113 | 363 | 486 | 787 | 637 | 201 | 74 | 388 | 388 | 538 | 291 | 218 |
| sherbet, orange—*1 cup (193 g)* | 30 | 98 | 131 | 212 | 171 | 54 | 20 | 104 | 104 | 145 | 78 | 59 |
| sorbet, Dole | | | | | | | | | | | | |
| mandarin orange—*½ cup (104 g)* | | | | | | | | 3 | | | | |
| peach—*½ cup (104 g)* | | | | | | | | 3 | | | | |
| pineapple—*½ cup (104 g)* | | | | | | | | 3 | | | | |
| raspberry—*½ cup (104 g)* | | | | | | | | 3 | | | | |
| strawberry—*½ cup (104 g)* | | | | | | | | 3 | | | | |
| **9. Eggs, Egg Dishes & Egg Substitutes** | | | | | | | | | | | | |
| **9.1. Eggs, Chicken** | | | | | | | | | | | | |
| boiled, hard/soft—*1 large (50 g)* | 97 | 298 | 380 | 533 | 410 | 196 | 145 | 343 | 253 | 437 | 388 | 147 |
| fried—*1 large (46 g)* | 86 | 264 | 336 | 472 | 363 | 174 | 128 | 303 | 224 | 387 | 344 | 130 |
| omelet, plain—*1 large egg (64 g)* | 94 | 290 | 372 | 565 | 410 | 188 | 133 | 332 | 252 | 426 | 364 | 146 |
| poached—*1 large (50 g)* | 97 | 297 | 378 | 531 | 408 | 195 | 144 | 341 | 251 | 435 | 387 | 146 |
| scrambled w/ milk & fat—*1 large egg (64 g)* | 94 | 290 | 372 | 565 | 410 | 188 | 133 | 332 | 252 | 426 | 364 | 146 |
| white, fresh/frzn—*white of 1 large egg (33 g)* | 51 | 149 | 204 | 291 | 206 | 130 | 83 | 210 | 134 | 251 | 195 | 76 |
| whole, dried, stabilized (glucose reduced)—*1 T (5 g)* | 39 | 118 | 151 | 212 | 163 | 78 | 57 | 136 | 100 | 173 | 154 | 58 |
| whole, fresh/frzn—*1 large (50 g)* | 97 | 298 | 380 | 533 | 410 | 196 | 145 | 343 | 253 | 437 | 388 | 147 |
| yolk, fresh—*yolk of 1 large egg (17 g)* | 41 | 151 | 160 | 237 | 189 | 71 | 50 | 121 | 120 | 170 | 193 | 67 |
| **9.2. Eggs, Other** | | | | | | | | | | | | |
| duck, whole—*1 egg (70 g)* | 182 | 515 | 419 | 768 | 666 | 403 | 199 | 588 | 429 | 620 | 535 | 224 |
| **9.3. Egg (Chicken) Dishes** | | | | | | | | | | | | |
| souffle, spinach[c]—*1 cup (136 g)* | 166 | 458 | 650 | 994 | 782 | 298 | 143 | 574 | 487 | 719 | 533 | 313 |
| **10. Entrees & Meals** | | | | | | | | | | | | |
| **10.2. Canned Entrees** | | | | | | | | | | | | |
| beans, baked | | | | | | | | | | | | |
| w/ beef—*1 cup (266 g)* | 205 | 713 | 742 | 1357 | 1202 | 277 | 181 | 875 | 484 | 878 | 1067 | 484 |

[a] Contains hydrogenated veg oil & soy protein; veg oils are usually soybean, cottonseed, safflower, or blends thereof.
[b] Contains lauric acid oils and Na caseinate; lauric oils include modified coconut oil, hydrogenated coconut oil, and/or palm kernel oil.
[c] Contains whole milk, spinach, egg white, cheddar cheese, egg yolk, butter, flour, salt & pepper.

| | TRY | THR | ISO | LEU | LYS | MET | CYS | PHE | TYR | VAL | ARG | HIS |
|---|---|---|---|---|---|---|---|---|---|---|---|---|
| w/ franks—*1 cup (257 g)* | 198 | 717 | 763 | 1372 | 1213 | 270 | 190 | 897 | 488 | 887 | 1097 | 488 |
| w/ pork—*1 cup (253 g)* | 157 | 559 | 587 | 1063 | 913 | 202 | 144 | 721 | 374 | 696 | 825 | 372 |
| chili w/ beans—*1 cup (255 g)* | 176 | 612 | 638 | 1163 | 1043 | 242 | 156 | 745 | 418 | 750 | 918 | 418 |
| cowpeas, common w/ pork—*1 cup (240 g)* | 82 | 250 | 269 | 504 | 446 | 94 | 72 | 384 | 214 | 314 | 456 | 204 |
| **11. Fast Foods** | | | | | | | | | | | | |
| shake | | | | | | | | | | | | |
| choc—*10 fl oz (283 g)* | 136 | 436 | 583 | 945 | 764 | 241 | 88 | 464 | 464 | 645 | 348 | 263 |
| strawberry—*10 fl oz (283 g)* | 133 | 430 | 577 | 931 | 753 | 238 | 88 | 458 | 458 | 637 | 342 | 260 |
| van—*10 fl oz (283 g)* | 139 | 447 | 597 | 965 | 781 | 246 | 91 | 475 | 475 | 659 | 354 | 269 |
| **12. Fats** | | | | | | | | | | | | |
| beef suet, raw—*1 oz (28 g)* | | 12 | 8 | 24 | 21 | 5 | | 14 | 9 | 15 | 27 | 6 |
| pork separable fat—*1 oz (28 g)* | 6 | 61 | 49 | 130 | 153 | 27 | 16 | 69 | 30 | 88 | 191 | 21 |
| salt pork, raw—*1 oz (28 g)* | 5 | 47 | 38 | 100 | 119 | 21 | 12 | 54 | 23 | 69 | 148 | 16 |
| **13. Fish, Shellfish & Crustacea** | | | | | | | | | | | | |
| abalone | | | | | | | | | | | | |
| raw—*3 oz (85 g)* | 163 | 626 | 632 | 1023 | 1086 | 328 | 190 | 521 | 465 | 635 | 1061 | 279 |
| fried[a]—*3 oz (85 g)* | 190 | 712 | 726 | 1178 | 1218 | 375 | 222 | 608 | 533 | 731 | 1199 | 321 |
| alewife | | | | | | | | | | | | |
| raw—*3.5 oz (100 g)* | 194 | 834 | 989 | 1474 | 1707 | 563 | | 718 | | 1028 | | |
| cnd—*3.5 oz (100 g)* | 162 | 697 | 826 | 1231 | 1426 | 470 | | 599 | | 859 | | |
| anchovy | | | | | | | | | | | | |
| raw—*3 oz (85 g)* | 194 | 758 | 797 | 1406 | 1589 | 512 | 185 | 675 | 584 | 891 | 1034 | 509 |
| cnd in olive oil—*5 anchovies (20 g)* | 65 | 253 | 266 | 470 | 531 | 171 | 62 | 226 | 195 | 298 | 346 | 170 |
| paste—*1 t (7 g)* | 14 | 60 | 71 | 106 | 123 | 41 | | 52 | | 74 | | |
| pickled—*1 oz (28 g)* | 59 | 252 | 299 | 445 | 515 | 170 | | 216 | | 311 | | |
| bass, black | | | | | | | | | | | | |
| raw—*3.5 oz (100 g)* | 192 | 826 | 979 | 1459 | 1690 | 557 | | 710 | | 1018 | | |
| baked—*4 oz (113 g)* | 212 | 1062 | 1227 | 1864 | 2384 | 661 | | 897 | | 1298 | | |
| stuffed, baked[b]—*3.5 oz (100 g)* | 162 | 687 | 826 | 1231 | 1426 | 470 | | 599 | | 859 | | |
| bass, freshwater, raw—*3 oz (85 g)* | 179 | 703 | 739 | 1303 | 1472 | 474 | 172 | 626 | 541 | 825 | 959 | 472 |
| bass, striped, raw—*3 oz (85 g)* | 169 | 660 | 694 | 1225 | 1384 | 446 | 162 | 588 | 509 | 777 | 902 | 444 |
| bluefish, raw—*3 oz (85 g)* | 190 | 746 | 785 | 1385 | 1564 | 504 | 183 | 665 | 575 | 877 | 1019 | 502 |
| bullhead, black, raw—*3.5 oz (100 g)* | 163 | 701 | 831 | 1239 | 1435 | 473 | | 603 | | 864 | | |
| burbot, raw—*3 oz (85 g)* | 184 | 720 | 757 | 1335 | 1508 | 486 | 176 | 641 | 554 | 846 | 983 | 484 |
| butterfish, raw—*3 oz (85 g)* | 165 | 644 | 677 | 1194 | 1349 | 435 | 157 | 574 | 496 | 757 | 879 | 433 |
| carp | | | | | | | | | | | | |
| raw—*3 oz (85 g)* | 170 | 665 | 699 | 1232 | 1392 | 449 | 162 | 592 | 512 | 781 | 907 | 446 |
| ckd by dry heat—*3 oz (85 g)* | 218 | 852 | 896 | 1579 | 1785 | 575 | 208 | 759 | 656 | 1001 | 1163 | 572 |
| catfish, channel | | | | | | | | | | | | |
| raw—*3 oz (85 g)* | 173 | 677 | 712 | 1255 | 1419 | 457 | 166 | 604 | 522 | 796 | 925 | 455 |
| breaded & fried[c]—*3 oz (85 g)* | 170 | 672 | 711 | 1282 | 1357 | 448 | 174 | 617 | 529 | 802 | 915 | 451 |
| caviar, black & red, granular—*1 T (16 g)* | 52 | 202 | 166 | 341 | 293 | 103 | 72 | 171 | 155 | 202 | 254 | 104 |
| cisco | | | | | | | | | | | | |
| raw—*3 oz (85 g)* | 181 | 707 | 744 | 1312 | 1482 | 478 | 173 | 630 | 545 | 831 | 966 | 475 |
| smoked—*3 oz (85 g)* | 156 | 609 | 641 | 1131 | 1278 | 411 | 149 | 543 | 469 | 717 | 832 | 410 |
| clam liquid, cnd—*1 cup (240 g)* | 0 | 0 | 0 | 0 | | | | 0 | 0 | 0 | 0 | 0 |
| clams | | | | | | | | | | | | |
| raw—*3 oz (4 large or 9 small) (85 g)* | 122 | 468 | 473 | 764 | 811 | 245 | 143 | 389 | 348 | 474 | 792 | 208 |
| breaded & fried[d]—*3 oz (9 small) (85 g)* | 143 | 512 | 541 | 870 | 843 | 275 | 173 | 467 | 394 | 553 | 837 | 238 |
| cnd—*3 oz (85 g)* | 243 | 934 | 945 | 1528 | 1623 | 490 | 285 | 778 | 694 | 949 | 1584 | 417 |
| ckd by moist heat—*3 oz (9 small) (85 g)* | 243 | 934 | 945 | 1528 | 1623 | 490 | 285 | 778 | 694 | 949 | 1584 | 417 |
| cod, atlantic | | | | | | | | | | | | |
| raw—*3 oz (85 g)* | 169 | 664 | 698 | 1230 | 1390 | 448 | 162 | 591 | 511 | 779 | 906 | 445 |

[a] Dipped in flour & salt before frying.
[b] Stuffed w/ bacon, butter, celery, onion & bread cubes.
[c] Breading consists of cornmeal, egg, milk & salt.
[d] Prepared w/ bread crumbs, egg, milk & salt.

| | TRY | THR | ISO | LEU | LYS | MET | CYS | PHE | TYR | VAL | ARG | HIS |
|---|---|---|---|---|---|---|---|---|---|---|---|---|
| cnd—*3 oz (85 g)* | 217 | 848 | 892 | 1573 | 1777 | 573 | 207 | 756 | 653 | 997 | 1158 | 570 |
| ckd by dry heat—*3 oz (85 g)* | 218 | 851 | 894 | 1578 | 1782 | 575 | 208 | 757 | 655 | 1000 | 1161 | 571 |
| dried & salted—*3 oz (85 g)* | 598 | 2341 | 2461 | 4340 | 4904 | 1580 | 572 | 2084 | 1803 | 2751 | 3195 | 1572 |
| cod, pacific, raw—*3 oz (85 g)* | 170 | 667 | 701 | 1237 | 1397 | 451 | 163 | 594 | 513 | 784 | 910 | 448 |
| crab, alaska king | | | | | | | | | | | | |
| raw—*3 oz (85 g)* | 217 | 630 | 754 | 1234 | 1353 | 438 | 174 | 657 | 518 | 732 | 1358 | 316 |
| ckd by moist heat—*3 oz (85 g)* | 229 | 666 | 797 | 1306 | 1431 | 463 | 184 | 694 | 547 | 774 | 1437 | 334 |
| imitation, made from surimi—*3 oz (85 g)* | 62 | 494 | 478 | 809 | 933 | 347 | 110 | 400 | 412 | 519 | 678 | 235 |
| crab, blue | | | | | | | | | | | | |
| raw—*3 oz (85 g)* | 213 | 621 | 744 | 1218 | 1336 | 432 | 172 | 649 | 511 | 722 | 1340 | 312 |
| cnd—*3 oz (85 g)* | 243 | 706 | 846 | 1384 | 1518 | 491 | 196 | 737 | 581 | 820 | 1524 | 354 |
| ckd by moist heat—*3 oz (85 g)* | 239 | 695 | 832 | 1363 | 1494 | 484 | 192 | 725 | 571 | 808 | 1500 | 349 |
| crab cakes[a]—*1 cake (60 g)* | 169 | 497 | 598 | 970 | 1040 | 341 | 143 | 522 | 409 | 588 | 1038 | 248 |
| crab, dungeness, raw—*3 oz (85 g)* | 206 | 599 | 717 | 1174 | 1288 | 417 | 166 | 625 | 492 | 696 | 1293 | 301 |
| crab, queen, raw—*3 oz (85 g)* | 219 | 637 | 762 | 1248 | 1369 | 443 | 176 | 664 | 524 | 740 | 1374 | 320 |
| crayfish | | | | | | | | | | | | |
| raw—*3 oz (85 g)* | 221 | 642 | 768 | 1259 | 1380 | 446 | 178 | 670 | 528 | 746 | 1386 | 322 |
| ckd by moist heat—*3 oz (85 g)* | 283 | 823 | 986 | 1613 | 1770 | 573 | 228 | 859 | 677 | 956 | 1777 | 413 |
| croaker, atlantic | | | | | | | | | | | | |
| raw—*3 oz (85 g)* | 169 | 663 | 696 | 1228 | 1388 | 447 | 162 | 590 | 510 | 779 | 904 | 445 |
| breaded & fried[b]—*3 oz (85 g)* | 177 | 670 | 720 | 1258 | 1335 | 446 | 184 | 631 | 528 | 805 | 902 | 446 |
| cusk, raw—*3 oz (85 g)* | 181 | 708 | 744 | 1312 | 1482 | 478 | 173 | 631 | 545 | 832 | 966 | 475 |
| cuttlefish, raw—*3 oz (85 g)* | 155 | 594 | 601 | 972 | 1031 | 311 | 181 | 495 | 442 | 603 | 1007 | 265 |
| dolphinfish, raw—*3 oz (85 g)* | 176 | 689 | 724 | 1278 | 1444 | 466 | 168 | 614 | 531 | 810 | 941 | 463 |
| drum, freshwater, raw—*3 oz (85 g)* | 167 | 654 | 687 | 1211 | 1309 | 441 | 160 | 582 | 503 | 768 | 892 | 439 |
| fish pieces, frzn, reheated[c]—*1 piece (4"x2"x½") (57 g)* | 111 | 368 | 425 | 722 | 640 | 242 | 129 | 398 | 307 | 476 | 483 | 239 |
| fish sticks, frzn[c]—*1 stick (4"x2"x½") (28 g)* | 54 | 181 | 209 | 354 | 314 | 119 | 64 | 196 | 151 | 234 | 237 | 117 |
| flatfish | | | | | | | | | | | | |
| raw—*3 oz (85 g)* | 179 | 702 | 738 | 1302 | 1471 | 474 | 172 | 626 | 541 | 825 | 959 | 472 |
| ckd by dry heat—*3 oz (85 g)* | 230 | 900 | 946 | 1669 | 1886 | 608 | 220 | 802 | 694 | 1058 | 1229 | 604 |
| flounder/sole | | | | | | | | | | | | |
| raw—*3.5 oz (100 g)* | 148 | 646 | 756 | 1125 | 1306 | 434 | | 553 | | 794 | | |
| baked—*3.5 oz (100 g)* | 300 | 1290 | 1530 | 2250 | 2640 | 870 | | 1110 | | 1590 | | |
| gefiltefish w/ broth, sweet—*1 piece (42 g)* | 36 | 205 | 204 | 340 | 354 | 107 | 47 | 207 | 160 | 230 | 250 | 110 |
| grouper | | | | | | | | | | | | |
| raw—*3 oz (85 g)* | 184 | 722 | 759 | 1339 | 1512 | 488 | 177 | 643 | 556 | 848 | 985 | 485 |
| ckd by dry heat—*3 oz (85 g)* | 236 | 926 | 973 | 1716 | 1940 | 625 | 226 | 825 | 713 | 1088 | 1264 | 621 |
| haddock | | | | | | | | | | | | |
| raw—*3 oz (85 g)* | 180 | 705 | 740 | 1306 | 1476 | 476 | 173 | 627 | 542 | 828 | 961 | 473 |
| ckd by dry heat—*3 oz (85 g)* | 231 | 904 | 949 | 1675 | 1893 | 610 | 221 | 804 | 695 | 1062 | 1233 | 607 |
| smoked—*3 oz (85 g)* | 241 | 940 | 988 | 1743 | 1969 | 635 | 230 | 836 | 724 | 1105 | 1283 | 632 |
| halibut, atlantic & pacific | | | | | | | | | | | | |
| raw—*3 oz (85 g)* | 198 | 775 | 815 | 1438 | 1624 | 524 | 190 | 691 | 598 | 911 | 1058 | 521 |
| ckd by dry heat—*3 oz (85 g)* | 254 | 995 | 1046 | 1844 | 2083 | 672 | 243 | 886 | 766 | 1169 | 1357 | 668 |
| halibut, greenland, raw—*3 oz (85 g)* | 137 | 536 | 563 | 993 | 1122 | 361 | 131 | 477 | 412 | 629 | 731 | 360 |
| herring, atlantic | | | | | | | | | | | | |
| raw—*3 oz (85 g)* | 171 | 669 | 704 | 1241 | 1403 | 452 | 164 | 596 | 515 | 786 | 914 | 450 |
| ckd by dry heat—*3 oz (85 g)* | 219 | 859 | 902 | 1591 | 1798 | 580 | 210 | 764 | 661 | 1009 | 1171 | 576 |
| kippered—*1 piece (4⅜"x1¾"x ¼") (40 g)* | 110 | 431 | 453 | 799 | 903 | 291 | 106 | 384 | 332 | 506 | 588 | 290 |
| pickled—*1 piece (1¾"x⅞"x½") (15 g)* | 24 | 93 | 98 | 173 | 195 | 63 | 23 | 83 | 72 | 110 | 127 | 63 |
| herring, pacific, raw—*3 oz (85 g)* | 156 | 611 | 642 | 1132 | 1280 | 412 | 150 | 544 | 470 | 718 | 834 | 411 |
| ling, raw—*3 oz (85 g)* | 181 | 707 | 744 | 1312 | 1482 | 478 | 173 | 630 | 545 | 831 | 966 | 475 |
| lingcod, raw—*3 oz (85 g)* | 168 | 658 | 692 | 1220 | 1379 | 445 | 161 | 586 | 507 | 774 | 898 | 442 |

[a] Prepared w/ crab meat, egg, onion & margarine.
[b] Breading consists of bread crumbs, egg, milk & salt.
[c] Prepared from walleye pollock, bread crumbs, egg, milk & salt.

| | TRY | THR | ISO | LEU | LYS | MET | CYS | PHE | TYR | VAL | ARG | HIS |
|---|---|---|---|---|---|---|---|---|---|---|---|---|
| lobster, northern | | | | | | | | | | | | |
| raw—*3 oz (85 g)* | 223 | 647 | 774 | 1268 | 1391 | 450 | 179 | 675 | 532 | 751 | 1396 | 325 |
| ckd by moist heat—*3 oz (85 g)* | 242 | 706 | 845 | 1383 | 1516 | 490 | 196 | 736 | 580 | 819 | 1522 | 354 |
| mackerel, atlantic | | | | | | | | | | | | |
| raw—*3 oz (85 g)* | 177 | 693 | 728 | 1285 | 1452 | 468 | 169 | 617 | 534 | 814 | 946 | 466 |
| ckd by dry heat—*3 oz (85 g)* | 227 | 888 | 934 | 1647 | 1822 | 600 | 218 | 791 | 684 | 1044 | 1213 | 597 |
| mackerel, jack, cnd—*1 cup (190 g)* | 494 | 1932 | 2029 | 3582 | 4047 | 1303 | 473 | 1720 | 1488 | 2271 | 2637 | 1298 |
| mackerel, king, raw—*3 oz (85 g)* | 193 | 756 | 795 | 1401 | 1584 | 510 | 184 | 673 | 582 | 888 | 1032 | 507 |
| mackerel, pacific & jack, raw—*3 oz (85 g)* | 191 | 748 | 785 | 1386 | 1567 | 505 | 183 | 666 | 575 | 879 | 1021 | 502 |
| mackerel, spanish | | | | | | | | | | | | |
| raw—*3 oz (85 g)* | 184 | 719 | 756 | 1333 | 1505 | 485 | 176 | 640 | 553 | 845 | 981 | 483 |
| ckd by dry heat—*3 oz (85 g)* | 224 | 879 | 924 | 1629 | 1841 | 593 | 215 | 783 | 677 | 1033 | 1199 | 590 |
| milkfish, raw—*3 oz (85 g)* | 196 | 765 | 804 | 1419 | 1603 | 517 | 187 | 682 | 589 | 899 | 1045 | 513 |
| monkfish, raw—*3 oz (85 g)* | 138 | 540 | 567 | 1000 | 1131 | 365 | 132 | 480 | 416 | 634 | 737 | 362 |
| mullet, striped | | | | | | | | | | | | |
| raw—*3 oz (85 g)* | 184 | 721 | 758 | 1337 | 1510 | 487 | 176 | 642 | 555 | 847 | 984 | 485 |
| ckd by dry heat—*3 oz (85 g)* | 236 | 925 | 972 | 1714 | 1936 | 624 | 226 | 823 | 711 | 1086 | 1261 | 621 |
| mussels, blue | | | | | | | | | | | | |
| raw—*3 oz (85 g)* | 113 | 435 | 440 | 712 | 756 | 228 | 133 | 362 | 324 | 442 | 738 | 194 |
| ckd by moist heat—*3 oz (85 g)* | 227 | 871 | 881 | 1425 | 1512 | 456 | 265 | 725 | 648 | 884 | 1476 | 388 |
| ocean perch, atlantic | | | | | | | | | | | | |
| raw—*3 oz (85 g)* | 178 | 694 | 729 | 1287 | 1454 | 468 | 170 | 618 | 535 | 816 | 948 | 466 |
| ckd by dry heat—*3 oz (85 g)* | 227 | 890 | 935 | 1650 | 1864 | 601 | 218 | 792 | 685 | 1046 | 1215 | 598 |
| oysters, eastern | | | | | | | | | | | | |
| raw—*6 med (84 g)* | 66 | 255 | 258 | 417 | 444 | 134 | 78 | 213 | 190 | 259 | 433 | 114 |
| breaded & fried[a]—*3 oz (about 6 med) (85 g)* | 89 | 310 | 337 | 542 | 495 | 169 | 111 | 299 | 247 | 348 | 497 | 149 |
| cnd—*3 oz (85 g)* | 67 | 258 | 261 | 422 | 449 | 135 | 79 | 215 | 192 | 262 | 438 | 116 |
| ckd by moist heat—*3 oz (12 med) (85 g)* | 134 | 517 | 522 | 845 | 897 | 271 | 157 | 430 | 384 | 524 | 876 | 230 |
| oysters, pacific, raw—*3 oz (85 g)* | 53 | 204 | 206 | 333 | 353 | 107 | 62 | 170 | 151 | 207 | 345 | 91 |
| perch | | | | | | | | | | | | |
| raw—*3 oz (85 g)* | 184 | 723 | 759 | 1340 | 1514 | 488 | 177 | 643 | 557 | 849 | 986 | 485 |
| ckd by dry heat—*3 oz (85 g)* | 236 | 927 | 973 | 1717 | 1941 | 626 | 226 | 825 | 713 | 1089 | 1264 | 622 |
| pike, northern | | | | | | | | | | | | |
| raw—*3 oz (85 g)* | 184 | 717 | 754 | 1330 | 1503 | 485 | 175 | 639 | 553 | 843 | 979 | 482 |
| ckd by dry heat—*3 oz (85 g)* | 235 | 920 | 967 | 1706 | 1927 | 621 | 225 | 819 | 708 | 1081 | 1255 | 618 |
| pike, pickerel, raw—*3.5 oz (100 g)* | 187 | 804 | 954 | 1402 | 1646 | 542 | | 692 | | 991 | | |
| pike, walleye, raw—*3 oz (85 g)* | 182 | 713 | 750 | 1322 | 1494 | 481 | 174 | 635 | 549 | 838 | 973 | 479 |
| pollock, atlantic, raw—*3 oz (85 g)* | 185 | 724 | 762 | 1343 | 1518 | 490 | 177 | 645 | 558 | 852 | 989 | 486 |
| pollock, walleye | | | | | | | | | | | | |
| raw—*3 oz (85 g)* | 163 | 640 | 673 | 1187 | 1341 | 433 | 156 | 570 | 493 | 752 | 874 | 430 |
| ckd by dry heat—*3 oz (85 g)* | 224 | 876 | 921 | 1624 | 1835 | 592 | 214 | 780 | 675 | 1029 | 1196 | 588 |
| pompano, florida | | | | | | | | | | | | |
| raw—*3 oz (85 g)* | 176 | 689 | 723 | 1277 | 1442 | 465 | 168 | 613 | 530 | 809 | 940 | 462 |
| ckd by dry heat—*3 oz (85 g)* | 225 | 882 | 928 | 1636 | 1849 | 596 | 216 | 786 | 680 | 1037 | 1204 | 592 |
| porgy/scup | | | | | | | | | | | | |
| raw—*3.5 oz (100 g)* | 190 | 817 | 969 | 1425 | 1672 | 551 | | 703 | | 1007 | | |
| fried—*3.3 oz (93 g)* | 227 | 976 | 1158 | 1702 | 1998 | 658 | | 840 | | 1203 | | |
| pout, ocean, raw—*3 oz (85 g)* | 158 | 620 | 652 | 1149 | 1299 | 418 | 151 | 553 | 478 | 728 | 847 | 417 |
| rockfish, pacific | | | | | | | | | | | | |
| raw—*3 oz (85 g)* | 179 | 699 | 734 | 1295 | 1464 | 472 | 171 | 622 | 538 | 821 | 954 | 469 |
| ckd by dry heat—*3 oz (85 g)* | 229 | 896 | 942 | 1661 | 1877 | 605 | 219 | 797 | 690 | 1052 | 1222 | 602 |
| roe, mixed species, raw—*1 oz (28 g)* | 82 | 285 | 320 | 548 | 476 | 155 | 109 | 306 | 314 | 366 | 358 | 170 |
| roughy, orange, raw—*3 oz (85 g)* | 140 | 547 | 575 | 1016 | 1148 | 370 | 134 | 488 | 422 | 643 | 748 | 368 |
| sablefish | | | | | | | | | | | | |
| raw—*3 oz (85 g)* | 128 | 500 | 525 | 927 | 1047 | 337 | 122 | 445 | 385 | 587 | 683 | 336 |
| smoked—*3 oz (85 g)* | 168 | 658 | 692 | 1220 | 1379 | 445 | 161 | 586 | 507 | 774 | 898 | 442 |
| salmon, atlantic, raw—*3 oz (85 g)* | 189 | 740 | 777 | 1371 | 1549 | 499 | 181 | 659 | 570 | 869 | 1009 | 496 |

[a] Prepared w/ bread crumbs, egg, milk & salt.

| | TRY | THR | ISO | LEU | LYS | MET | CYS | PHE | TYR | VAL | ARG | HIS |
|---|---|---|---|---|---|---|---|---|---|---|---|---|
| salmon, chinook | | | | | | | | | | | | |
| raw—*3 oz (85 g)* | 191 | 747 | 785 | 1386 | 1566 | 505 | 183 | 666 | 575 | 878 | 1020 | 502 |
| smoked—*3 oz (85 g)* | 174 | 681 | 716 | 1263 | 1427 | 460 | 167 | 607 | 524 | 801 | 930 | 457 |
| salmon, chum, raw | | | | | | | | | | | | |
| raw—*3 oz (85 g)* | 192 | 751 | 789 | 1391 | 1572 | 507 | 184 | 668 | 578 | 881 | 1024 | 504 |
| cnd w/ bone—*3 oz (85 g)* | 204 | 799 | 840 | 1481 | 1673 | 539 | 196 | 711 | 615 | 938 | 1090 | 536 |
| salmon, coho | | | | | | | | | | | | |
| raw—*3 oz (85 g)* | 206 | 805 | 847 | 1493 | 1687 | 544 | 197 | 717 | 621 | 946 | 1090 | 541 |
| ckd by moist heat—*3 oz (85 g)* | 260 | 1020 | 1072 | 1890 | 2136 | 689 | 249 | 908 | 785 | 1199 | 1391 | 685 |
| salmon, pink | | | | | | | | | | | | |
| raw—*3 oz (85 g)* | 190 | 743 | 781 | 1378 | 1556 | 502 | 182 | 661 | 572 | 873 | 1014 | 499 |
| cnd w/ bone—*3 oz (85 g)* | 189 | 737 | 775 | 1367 | 1544 | 498 | 180 | 656 | 568 | 866 | 1006 | 495 |
| salmon, sockeye | | | | | | | | | | | | |
| raw—*3 oz (85 g)* | 203 | 794 | 835 | 1471 | 1663 | 536 | 194 | 707 | 611 | 932 | 1084 | 533 |
| cnd w/ bone—*3 oz (85 g)* | 195 | 762 | 802 | 1414 | 1598 | 515 | 186 | 679 | 587 | 897 | 1041 | 513 |
| ckd by dry heat—*3 oz (85 g)* | 260 | 1017 | 1069 | 1886 | 2132 | 687 | 249 | 906 | 784 | 1196 | 1389 | 683 |
| sardines | | | | | | | | | | | | |
| atlantic, cnd in soybean oil—*2 sardines (3"x1"x½") (24 g)* | 66 | 259 | 272 | 480 | 542 | 175 | 63 | 231 | 199 | 304 | 354 | 174 |
| pacific, cnd in tomato sce—*1 sardine (4¾"x1⅛"x⅝") (38 g)* | 60 | 302 | 302 | 516 | 532 | 181 | 53 | 301 | 238 | 352 | 399 | 258 |
| scallops | | | | | | | | | | | | |
| raw—*3 oz (6 large or 14 small) (85 g)* | 160 | 614 | 621 | 1004 | 1066 | 322 | 187 | 511 | 456 | 623 | 1040 | 274 |
| breaded & fried[a]—*2 large (31 g)* | 65 | 238 | 248 | 401 | 397 | 126 | 78 | 213 | 182 | 254 | 392 | 110 |
| imitation, made from surimi—*3 oz (85 g)* | 66 | 524 | 507 | 859 | 992 | 368 | 116 | 426 | 438 | 551 | 721 | 250 |
| scup, raw—*3 oz (85 g)* | 179 | 703 | 740 | 1304 | 1473 | 475 | 172 | 626 | 541 | 826 | 960 | 473 |
| sea bass | | | | | | | | | | | | |
| raw—*3 oz (85 g)* | 175 | 687 | 722 | 1273 | 1439 | 464 | 168 | 612 | 529 | 808 | 938 | 462 |
| ckd by dry heat—*3 oz (85 g)* | 225 | 881 | 926 | 1633 | 1845 | 594 | 215 | 785 | 678 | 1034 | 1202 | 592 |
| seatrout, raw—*3 oz (85 g)* | 160 | 624 | 656 | 1157 | 1307 | 422 | 152 | 556 | 480 | 734 | 851 | 419 |
| shad, american, raw—*3 oz (85 g)* | 162 | 631 | 663 | 1170 | 1322 | 426 | 155 | 562 | 486 | 741 | 861 | 423 |
| sheepshead | | | | | | | | | | | | |
| raw—*3 oz (85 g)* | 192 | 753 | 791 | 1397 | 1578 | 508 | 184 | 671 | 580 | 885 | 1029 | 506 |
| ckd by dry heat—*3 oz (85 g)* | 247 | 970 | 1019 | 1798 | 2032 | 655 | 237 | 864 | 746 | 1139 | 1323 | 651 |
| shrimp | | | | | | | | | | | | |
| raw—*3 oz (12 large) (85 g)* | 241 | 699 | 837 | 1370 | 1503 | 486 | 194 | 729 | 575 | 813 | 1509 | 351 |
| breaded & fried[a]—*3 oz (11 large) (85 g)* | 254 | 731 | 886 | 1443 | 1499 | 502 | 219 | 789 | 611 | 871 | 1516 | 371 |
| cnd—*3 oz (85 g)* | 273 | 794 | 951 | 1557 | 1708 | 553 | 220 | 829 | 653 | 923 | 1714 | 399 |
| ckd by moist heat—*3 oz (15½ large) (85 g)* | 247 | 719 | 862 | 1410 | 1547 | 501 | 199 | 751 | 592 | 836 | 1552 | 361 |
| imitation, made from surimi—*3 oz (85 g)* | 64 | 509 | 492 | 834 | 962 | 357 | 113 | 413 | 424 | 534 | 700 | 242 |
| smelt, atlantic | | | | | | | | | | | | |
| raw—*4-5 med (100 g)* | 186 | 800 | 949 | 1395 | 1637 | 539 | | 688 | | 986 | | |
| cnd—*4-5 med (100 g)* | 184 | 791 | 938 | 1380 | 1619 | 534 | | 681 | | 975 | | |
| smelt, rainbow | | | | | | | | | | | | |
| raw—*3 oz (85 g)* | 167 | 657 | 690 | 1218 | 1376 | 444 | 161 | 585 | 506 | 772 | 897 | 441 |
| ckd by dry heat—*3 oz (85 g)* | 215 | 842 | 885 | 1561 | 1765 | 569 | 206 | 750 | 649 | 989 | 1149 | 565 |
| snapper | | | | | | | | | | | | |
| raw—*3 oz (85 g)* | 196 | 764 | 803 | 1417 | 1601 | 516 | 187 | 681 | 588 | 898 | 1043 | 513 |
| ckd by dry heat—*3 oz (85 g)* | 250 | 980 | 1030 | 1816 | 2053 | 661 | 240 | 873 | 755 | 1152 | 1337 | 658 |
| sole | | | | | | | | | | | | |
| raw—*3.5 oz (100 g)* | 148 | 646 | 756 | 1125 | 1306 | 434 | | 553 | | 794 | | |
| spiny lobster, raw—*3 oz (85 g)* | 244 | 709 | 848 | 1389 | 1523 | 493 | 196 | 740 | 582 | 824 | 1529 | 355 |
| spot, raw—*3 oz (85 g)* | 176 | 690 | 725 | 1279 | 1445 | 466 | 168 | 615 | 531 | 811 | 942 | 463 |
| sturgeon | | | | | | | | | | | | |
| raw—*3 oz (85 g)* | 154 | 602 | 632 | 1115 | 1261 | 406 | 147 | 536 | 463 | 707 | 821 | 404 |
| ckd by dry heat—*3 oz (85 g)* | 197 | 771 | 811 | 1430 | 1616 | 521 | 189 | 687 | 594 | 906 | 1052 | 518 |
| smoked—*3 oz (85 g)* | 297 | 1163 | 1222 | 2156 | 2439 | 785 | 284 | 1035 | 895 | 1366 | 1387 | 781 |

[a] Prepared w/ bread crumbs, egg, milk & salt.

| | TRY | THR | ISO | LEU | LYS | MET | CYS | PHE | TYR | VAL | ARG | HIS |
|---|---|---|---|---|---|---|---|---|---|---|---|---|
| sucker, white, raw—*3 oz (85 g)* | 160 | 625 | 656 | 1158 | 1308 | 422 | 153 | 556 | 481 | 734 | 853 | 419 |
| sunfish, pumpkinseed, raw—*3 oz (85 g)* | 184 | 723 | 760 | 1340 | 1515 | 488 | 177 | 643 | 557 | 849 | 987 | 485 |
| surimi[a]—*3 oz (85 g)* | 78 | 624 | 603 | 1022 | 1179 | 438 | 139 | 506 | 520 | 655 | 857 | 298 |
| swordfish | | | | | | | | | | | | |
| raw—*3 oz (85 g)* | 189 | 738 | 775 | 1368 | 1545 | 498 | 180 | 657 | 568 | 867 | 1007 | 496 |
| ckd by dry heat—*3 oz (85 g)* | 241 | 946 | 995 | 1754 | 1982 | 638 | 231 | 842 | 728 | 1112 | 1291 | 635 |
| tilefish | | | | | | | | | | | | |
| raw—*3 oz (85 g)* | 167 | 652 | 685 | 1209 | 1366 | 440 | 160 | 581 | 502 | 767 | 890 | 438 |
| ckd by dry heat—*3 oz (85 g)* | 233 | 913 | 959 | 1692 | 1912 | 616 | 224 | 813 | 703 | 1073 | 1245 | 613 |
| tomcod, atlantic, raw—*3.5 oz (100 g)* | 172 | 740 | 877 | 1290 | 1514 | 499 | | 636 | | 912 | | |
| trout, dolly varden—*3.5 oz (100 g)* | 199 | 856 | 1015 | 1512 | 1751 | 577 | | 736 | | 1055 | | |
| trout, mixed species, raw—*3 oz (85 g)* | 198 | 774 | 813 | 1435 | 1621 | 523 | 190 | 689 | 596 | 910 | 1056 | 519 |
| trout, rainbow | | | | | | | | | | | | |
| raw—*3 oz (85 g)* | 196 | 766 | 805 | 1420 | 1604 | 517 | 187 | 682 | 590 | 899 | 1045 | 514 |
| ckd by dry heat—*3 oz (85 g)* | 251 | 982 | 1032 | 1820 | 2056 | 663 | 240 | 874 | 756 | 1153 | 1340 | 659 |
| tuna | | | | | | | | | | | | |
| cnd in oil | | | | | | | | | | | | |
| light—*3 oz (85 g)* | 277 | 1085 | 1141 | 2013 | 2274 | 733 | 265 | 966 | 836 | 1276 | 1482 | 729 |
| white—*3 oz (85 g)* | 252 | 989 | 1040 | 1833 | 2071 | 667 | 241 | 881 | 762 | 1162 | 1350 | 664 |
| cnd in spring water | | | | | | | | | | | | |
| light—*3 oz (85 g)* | 281 | 1102 | 1159 | 2043 | 2309 | 745 | 269 | 982 | 849 | 1295 | 1505 | 740 |
| white—*3 oz (85 g)* | 254 | 994 | 1045 | 1842 | 2082 | 671 | 243 | 885 | 765 | 1168 | 1356 | 667 |
| salad[b]—*½ cup (205 g)* | 369 | 1437 | 1515 | 2651 | 2987 | 964 | 353 | 1283 | 1105 | 1689 | 1982 | 957 |
| tuna, bluefin | | | | | | | | | | | | |
| raw—*3 oz (85 g)* | 222 | 870 | 914 | 1612 | 1821 | 587 | 213 | 774 | 669 | 1022 | 1187 | 584 |
| ckd in dry heat—*3 oz (85 g)* | 285 | 1114 | 1171 | 2066 | 2335 | 752 | 273 | 993 | 859 | 1310 | 1522 | 748 |
| tuna, skipjack, raw—*3 oz (85 g)* | 209 | 819 | 862 | 1520 | 1717 | 553 | 201 | 730 | 632 | 963 | 119 | 551 |
| tuna, yellowfin, raw—*3 oz (85 g)* | 223 | 871 | 915 | 1615 | 1825 | 588 | 213 | 776 | 671 | 1023 | 1189 | 585 |
| turbot, european, raw—*3 oz (85 g)* | 153 | 598 | 629 | 1109 | 1253 | 404 | 146 | 533 | 461 | 703 | 816 | 402 |
| weakfish (sea trout) | | | | | | | | | | | | |
| raw—*3.5 oz (100 g)* | 165 | 710 | 842 | 1238 | 1452 | 478 | | 610 | | 874 | | |
| broiled—*3.5 oz (100 g)* | 246 | 1058 | 1255 | 1845 | 2165 | 713 | | 910 | | 1304 | | |
| whelk | | | | | | | | | | | | |
| raw—*3 oz (85 g)* | 263 | 908 | 704 | 1618 | 1245 | 513 | 159 | 700 | 645 | 881 | 2098 | 415 |
| ckd by moist heat—*3 oz (85 g)* | 525 | 1816 | 1407 | 3236 | 2491 | 1024 | 318 | 1401 | 1290 | 1764 | 4196 | 830 |
| whitefish | | | | | | | | | | | | |
| raw—*3 oz (85 g)* | 182 | 711 | 748 | 1318 | 1490 | 480 | 174 | 633 | 547 | 836 | 971 | 478 |
| baked, stuffed[c]—*3.5 oz (100 g)* | 152 | 654 | 775 | 1140 | 1338 | 441 | | 562 | | 806 | | |
| smoked—*3 oz (85 g)* | 223 | 872 | 916 | 1617 | 1827 | 589 | 213 | 777 | 672 | 1025 | 1190 | 586 |
| whiting | | | | | | | | | | | | |
| raw—*3 oz (85 g)* | 174 | 683 | 717 | 1265 | 1430 | 461 | 167 | 608 | 525 | 802 | 932 | 458 |
| ckd by dry heat—*3 oz (85 g)* | 224 | 875 | 920 | 1623 | 1833 | 591 | 214 | 779 | 674 | 1029 | 1194 | 587 |
| wolffish, atlantic, raw—*3 oz (85 g)* | 167 | 652 | 685 | 1209 | 1366 | 440 | 160 | 581 | 502 | 767 | 890 | 438 |
| yellowtail, raw—*3 oz (85 g)* | 220 | 863 | 906 | 1599 | 1807 | 582 | 211 | 768 | 664 | 1013 | 1177 | 579 |
| **14. Fruit & Vegetable Juices** | | | | | | | | | | | | |
| beef broth & tomato jce—*5.5 fl oz can (168 g)* | 2 | 18 | 15 | 30 | 37 | 7 | 2 | 22 | 5 | 25 | 69 | 10 |
| clam & tomato jce, cnd—*5.5 fl oz can (166 g)* | 7 | 25 | 20 | 30 | 30 | 5 | 7 | 22 | 15 | 22 | 22 | 17 |
| grape jce, cnd/bottled—*8 fl oz (253 g)* | | 40 | 18 | 30 | 25 | 3 | | 30 | 8 | 25 | 119 | 18 |
| grape jce, from frzn conc, sweetened—*8 fl oz (250 g)* | | 13 | 5 | 10 | 8 | | | 10 | 3 | 8 | 40 | 5 |
| orange jce, fresh—*8 fl oz (248 g)* | 5 | 20 | 20 | 32 | 22 | 7 | 12 | 22 | 10 | 27 | 117 | 7 |
| orange jce, cnd—*8 fl oz (249 g)* | 5 | 17 | 15 | 27 | 20 | 7 | 10 | 17 | 7 | 22 | 100 | 7 |
| orange jce, from frzn conc—*8 fl oz (249 g)* | 5 | 20 | 17 | 32 | 22 | 7 | 12 | 20 | 10 | 27 | 112 | 7 |
| tangerine jce, fresh—*8 fl oz (247 g)* | 2 | 15 | 12 | 25 | 17 | 5 | 10 | 15 | 7 | 20 | 84 | 5 |

[a] Prepared from walleye pollock.
[b] Prepared w/ light tuna cnd in oil, pickle relish, salad dressing, onions & celery

[c] Stuffed w/ bacon, onion, celery & bread crumbs.

|  | TRY | THR | ISO | LEU | LYS | MET | CYS | PHE | TYR | VAL | ARG | HIS |
|---|---|---|---|---|---|---|---|---|---|---|---|---|
| tangerine jce, cnd, sweetened—*8 fl oz (249 g)* | 2 | 15 | 12 | 25 | 17 | 5 | 10 | 15 | 7 | 20 | 85 | 5 |
| tangerine jce, from frzn conc, sweetened—*8 fl oz (241 g)* | 2 | 12 | 12 | 19 | 14 | 5 | 7 | 12 | 5 | 17 | 70 | 5 |
| tomato jce—*6 fl oz (182 g)* | 9 | 31 | 27 | 38 | 40 | 7 | 7 | 29 | 18 | 27 | 27 | 22 |

**15. Fruits**

|  | TRY | THR | ISO | LEU | LYS | MET | CYS | PHE | TYR | VAL | ARG | HIS |
|---|---|---|---|---|---|---|---|---|---|---|---|---|
| apple |  |  |  |  |  |  |  |  |  |  |  |  |
| raw, w/ skin—*1 med (138 g)* | 3 | 10 | 11 | 17 | 17 | 3 | 4 | 7 | 6 | 12 | 8 | 4 |
| raw, w/o skin—*1 med (128 g)* | 1 | 6 | 8 | 12 | 12 | 3 | 3 | 5 | 4 | 9 | 6 | 3 |
| boiled, w/o skin—*1 cup (171 g)* | 3 | 15 | 17 | 27 | 27 | 5 | 7 | 12 | 9 | 21 | 14 | 7 |
| cnd, sliced, sweetened—*½ cup (102 g)* | 2 | 6 | 7 | 11 | 11 | 2 | 2 | 5 | 3 | 8 | 6 | 3 |
| dried, sulfured—*10 rings (64 g)* | 6 | 21 | 24 | 36 | 37 | 6 | 8 | 17 | 11 | 28 | 19 | 10 |
| micro ckd w/o skin—*1 cup (170 g)* | 5 | 17 | 19 | 29 | 31 | 5 | 7 | 14 | 9 | 22 | 15 | 7 |
| applesce, cnd, sweetened—*½ cup (128 g)* | 3 | 9 | 9 | 14 | 14 | 3 | 3 | 6 | 4 | 10 | 8 | 4 |
| applesce, cnd, unsweetened—*½ cup (122 g)* | 2 | 7 | 7 | 12 | 12 | 2 | 2 | 6 | 4 | 10 | 6 | 4 |
| apricots |  |  |  |  |  |  |  |  |  |  |  |  |
| raw—*3 med (106 g)* | 16 | 50 | 43 | 82 | 103 | 6 | 3 | 55 | 31 | 50 | 48 | 29 |
| cnd, heavy syrup—*4 halves (90 g)* | 8 | 16 | 14 | 27 | 32 | 3 | 2 | 19 | 11 | 17 | 18 | 7 |
| cnd, jce pack—*3 halves (84 g)* | 9 | 19 | 16 | 31 | 37 | 3 | 2 | 22 | 13 | 19 | 20 | 8 |
| cnd, light syrup—*3 halves (85 g)* | 8 | 16 | 14 | 26 | 31 | 3 | 2 | 19 | 10 | 16 | 18 | 8 |
| cnd, water pack—*4 halves (90 g)* | 11 | 23 | 19 | 36 | 43 | 3 | 2 | 25 | 14 | 23 | 24 | 10 |
| dried, sulfured—*10 halves (35 g)* | 23 | 46 | 39 | 75 | 89 | 6 | 4 | 53 | 30 | 47 | 49 | 21 |
| frzn, sweetened—*½ cup (121 g)* | 10 | 29 | 24 | 47 | 59 | 4 | 2 | 31 | 18 | 29 | 27 | 16 |
| banana, raw—*1 med (114 g)* | 14 | 39 | 38 | 81 | 55 | 13 | 19 | 43 | 27 | 54 | 54 | 92 |
| blueberries |  |  |  |  |  |  |  |  |  |  |  |  |
| raw—*1 cup (145 g)* | 4 | 26 | 30 | 58 | 17 | 16 | 10 | 35 | 12 | 41 | 49 | 15 |
| cnd, heavy syrup—*½ cup (128 g)* | 4 | 23 | 26 | 50 | 15 | 13 | 9 | 29 | 10 | 35 | 42 | 13 |
| frzn, sweetened—*1 cup (230 g)* | 5 | 25 | 28 | 53 | 16 | 14 | 9 | 32 | 12 | 39 | 46 | 14 |
| breadfruit, raw—*¼ small (96 g)* |  | 50 | 61 | 62 | 36 | 10 | 9 | 25 | 18 | 45 |  |  |
| carambola, raw—*1 med (127 g)* | 5 | 29 | 29 | 51 | 51 | 14 |  | 24 | 29 | 33 | 14 | 5 |
| crabapples, raw—*1 cup slices (110 g)* | 4 | 15 | 18 | 28 | 28 | 4 | 6 | 12 | 9 | 21 | 14 | 7 |
| custard apple, raw—*3.5 oz (100 g)* | 7 |  |  |  | 37 | 4 |  |  |  |  |  |  |
| dates, dried—*10 dates (83 g)* | 42 | 43 | 39 | 73 | 50 | 18 | 37 | 46 | 25 | 55 | 55 | 25 |
| elderberries, raw—*1 cup (145 g)* | 19 | 39 | 39 | 87 | 38 | 20 | 22 | 58 | 74 | 48 | 68 | 22 |
| figs, raw—*1 med (50 g)* | 3 | 12 | 12 | 17 | 15 | 3 | 6 | 9 | 16 | 14 | 9 | 6 |
| figs, cnd, heavy syrup—*3 figs (85 g)* | 3 | 10 | 10 | 14 | 13 | 3 | 5 | 8 | 14 | 12 | 8 | 4 |
| figs, dried—*10 figs (187 g)* | 49 | 187 | 174 | 249 | 228 | 47 | 94 | 138 | 247 | 215 | 131 | 80 |
| grapefruit |  |  |  |  |  |  |  |  |  |  |  |  |
| raw, pink & red—*½ med (123 g)* | 2 |  |  |  | 17 | 2 |  |  |  |  |  |  |
| raw, white—*½ med (118 g)* | 2 |  |  |  | 21 | 2 |  |  |  |  |  |  |
| cnd, jce pack—*½ cup (124 g)* | 2 |  |  |  | 22 | 2 |  |  |  |  |  |  |
| cnd, light syrup—*½ cup (127 g)* | 3 |  |  |  | 18 | 3 |  |  |  |  |  |  |
| grapes |  |  |  |  |  |  |  |  |  |  |  |  |
| american (slip skin), raw—*1 cup (92 g)* | 3 | 16 | 5 | 12 | 13 | 19 | 9 | 12 | 10 | 16 | 42 | 21 |
| european (adherent skin), raw—*1 cup (160 g)* | 5 | 29 | 8 | 22 | 24 | 35 | 18 | 22 | 19 | 29 | 78 | 38 |
| thompson seedless, cnd, heavy syrup—*½ cup (128 g)* | 3 | 17 | 5 | 13 | 14 | 20 | 10 | 13 | 10 | 17 | 45 | 23 |
| guava, raw—*1 med (90 g)* | 6 | 28 | 27 | 50 | 21 | 5 |  | 2 | 9 | 25 | 19 | 6 |
| guava, strawberry, raw—*1 cup (244 g)* | 12 | 54 | 51 | 95 | 39 | 10 |  | 2 | 17 | 49 | 37 | 12 |
| lime, raw—*1 med (67 g)* | 2 |  |  |  | 9 | 1 |  |  |  |  |  |  |
| longans |  |  |  |  |  |  |  |  |  |  |  |  |
| raw—*31 fruits (100 g)* |  | 34 | 26 | 54 | 46 | 13 |  | 30 | 25 | 58 | 35 | 12 |
| dried—*3.5 oz (100 g)* |  | 128 | 97 | 202 | 172 | 49 |  | 112 | 94 | 217 | 131 | 45 |
| loquats, raw—*10 med (100 g)* | 5 | 15 | 15 | 26 | 23 | 4 | 6 | 14 | 13 | 21 | 14 | 7 |
| lychees |  |  |  |  |  |  |  |  |  |  |  |  |
| raw—*10 med (100 g)* | 7 |  |  |  | 41 | 9 |  |  |  |  |  |  |
| dried—*3.5 oz (100 g)* | 33 |  |  |  | 187 | 42 |  |  |  |  |  |  |

| | TRY | THR | ISO | LEU | LYS | MET | CYS | PHE | TYR | VAL | ARG | HIS |
|---|---|---|---|---|---|---|---|---|---|---|---|---|
| mammy apple, raw—⅛ med (100 g) | 5 | | | | 37 | 6 | | | | | | |
| mandarin oranges, cnd | | | | | | | | | | | | |
|   jce pack—½ cup (124 g) | 7 | 12 | 21 | 19 | 38 | 16 | 7 | 25 | 12 | 32 | 53 | 14 |
|   light syrup—½ cup (126 g) | 5 | 9 | 15 | 14 | 29 | 13 | 6 | 19 | 10 | 24 | 39 | 10 |
| mango, raw—1 med (207 g) | 17 | 39 | 37 | 64 | 85 | 10 | | 35 | 21 | 54 | 39 | 25 |
| orange | | | | | | | | | | | | |
|   navel, raw—1 med (140 g) | 14 | 24 | 39 | 36 | 73 | 31 | 15 | 48 | 24 | 62 | 101 | 27 |
|   valencia, raw—1 med (121 g) | 12 | 21 | 34 | 31 | 64 | 27 | 13 | 41 | 22 | 53 | 88 | 24 |
| papaya, raw—1 med (304 g) | 24 | 33 | 24 | 49 | 76 | 6 | | 27 | 15 | 30 | 30 | 15 |
| peach | | | | | | | | | | | | |
|   raw—1 med (87 g) | 2 | 23 | 17 | 35 | 20 | 15 | 5 | 19 | 16 | 33 | 16 | 11 |
|   cnd, heavy syrup—1 cup (256 g) | 3 | 46 | 33 | 67 | 38 | 28 | 10 | 36 | 31 | 64 | 31 | 20 |
|   cnd, heavy syrup, spiced—1 med (88 g) | 1 | 14 | 11 | 20 | 11 | 9 | 3 | 11 | 10 | 20 | 9 | 7 |
|   cnd, jce pack—1 cup (248 g) | 5 | 62 | 45 | 89 | 50 | 37 | 12 | 50 | 40 | 84 | 40 | 30 |
|   cnd, light syrup—1 cup (251 g) | 3 | 45 | 33 | 63 | 35 | 28 | 10 | 35 | 30 | 63 | 28 | 20 |
|   cnd, water pack—1 cup (244 g) | 2 | 41 | 32 | 61 | 34 | 27 | 10 | 34 | 27 | 59 | 27 | 20 |
|   dried, sulfured—10 halves (130 g) | 13 | 183 | 135 | 265 | 151 | 113 | 38 | 148 | 122 | 256 | 120 | 87 |
|   frzn, sweetened—1 cup (250 g) | 5 | 60 | 45 | 88 | 50 | 38 | 13 | 50 | 40 | 85 | 40 | 30 |
| pear | | | | | | | | | | | | |
|   raw—1 med (166 g) | 17 | 18 | 33 | 23 | 8 | 7 | 17 | 5 | 23 | 12 | 7 | 22 |
|   cnd, heavy pack—1 cup (255 g) | 13 | 15 | 26 | 18 | 5 | 5 | 13 | 5 | 18 | 8 | 5 | 18 |
|   cnd, jce pack—1 cup (248 g) | 22 | 25 | 42 | 30 | 10 | 7 | 22 | 7 | 30 | 15 | 10 | 27 |
|   cnd, light syrup—1 cup (251 g) | 13 | 15 | 25 | 18 | 5 | 5 | 13 | 5 | 18 | 8 | 5 | 15 |
|   cnd, water pack—1 cup (244 g) | 12 | 12 | 22 | 17 | 5 | 5 | 12 | 5 | 17 | 7 | 5 | 15 |
|   dried, sulfured—10 halves (175 g) | 86 | 95 | 165 | 116 | 39 | 32 | 86 | 28 | 116 | 56 | 35 | 109 |
| persimmon, raw—1 med (25 g) | 4 | 10 | 9 | 15 | 11 | 2 | 5 | 9 | 6 | 11 | 9 | 4 |
| persimmon, japanese | | | | | | | | | | | | |
|   raw—1 med (168 g) | 17 | 50 | 42 | 71 | 55 | 8 | 22 | 44 | 27 | 50 | 42 | 20 |
|   dried—1 med (34 g) | 8 | 24 | 20 | 34 | 27 | 4 | 10 | 21 | 13 | 24 | 20 | 9 |
| pineapple | | | | | | | | | | | | |
|   raw—1 cup pieces (155 g) | 8 | 19 | 20 | 29 | 39 | 17 | 3 | 19 | 19 | 25 | 28 | 14 |
|   cnd, heavy syrup—1 cup pieces (255 g) | 13 | 23 | 23 | 33 | 41 | 23 | 3 | 23 | 20 | 28 | 31 | 10 |
|   cnd, jce pack—1 cup pieces (250 g) | 13 | 25 | 25 | 40 | 48 | 28 | 3 | 25 | 25 | 33 | 35 | 23 |
| plantain, ckd—1 cup slices (154 g) | 14 | 32 | 34 | 55 | 57 | 15 | 18 | 42 | 31 | 43 | 102 | 60 |
| plum | | | | | | | | | | | | |
|   raw—1 med (66 g) | | 11 | 11 | 14 | 11 | 4 | 3 | 11 | 4 | 13 | 9 | 9 |
|   heavy syrup—3 plums (133 g) | | 11 | 9 | 13 | 11 | 4 | 3 | 11 | 4 | 12 | 8 | 8 |
|   cnd, jce pack—3 plums (95 g) | | 10 | 10 | 13 | 10 | 4 | 3 | 10 | 4 | 11 | 9 | 8 |
| sapodilla, raw—1 med (170 g) | 9 | 20 | 26 | 41 | 66 | 5 | | 22 | 24 | 27 | 29 | 27 |
| sapote, raw—1 med (225 g) | 52 | 131 | 104 | 189 | 216 | 36 | | 119 | 124 | 173 | 124 | 95 |
| soursop, raw—1 cup (225 g) | 25 | | | | 135 | 16 | | | | | | |
| strawberries | | | | | | | | | | | | |
|   raw—1 cup (149 g) | 10 | 28 | 21 | 46 | 37 | 1 | 7 | 27 | 31 | 27 | 39 | 18 |
|   frzn, sweetened—1 cup (255 g) | 15 | 41 | 31 | 69 | 56 | 3 | 13 | 38 | 46 | 38 | 59 | 26 |
|   frzn, unsweetened—1 cup (149 g) | 7 | 19 | 15 | 33 | 25 | 1 | 6 | 18 | 21 | 18 | 27 | 12 |
| sugar apple, raw—1 med (155 g) | 16 | | | | 85 | 11 | | | | | | |
| tamarind, raw—1 cup (120 g) | 22 | | | | 167 | 17 | | | | | | |
| tangerine, raw—1 med (84 g) | 5 | 8 | 14 | 13 | 27 | 11 | 6 | 18 | 9 | 23 | 37 | 10 |
| watermelon, raw—1 cup (160 g) | 11 | 43 | 30 | 29 | 99 | '10 | 3 | 24 | 19 | 26 | 94 | 10 |
| | | | | | | | | | | | | |
| **16. Grain Fractions** | | | | | | | | | | | | |
| corn germ, Ener-G Foods—1 cup (100 g) | | 675 | 597 | 1849 | 1076 | 269 | | 527 | 354 | 974 | 1565 | 604 |
| potato flour—½ cup (90 g) | 120 | 292 | 311 | 443 | 431 | 112 | 73 | 329 | 234 | 372 | 390 | 173 |
| rice polish, Ener-G Foods—½ cup (56 g) | | 16 | 14 | 27 | 2 | 8 | | 17 | 16 | 20 | 38 | 13 |
| soybean flour | | | | | | | | | | | | |
|   defatted—1 cup (100 g) | 683 | 2042 | 2281 | 3828 | 3129 | 634 | 757 | 2453 | 1778 | 2346 | 3647 | 1268 |
|   full fat—1 cup (85 g) | 427 | 1275 | 1424 | 2390 | 1953 | 396 | 473 | 1532 | 1110 | 1465 | 2277 | 791 |

| | TRY | THR | ISO | LEU | LYS | MET | CYS | PHE | TYR | VAL | ARG | HIS |
|---|---|---|---|---|---|---|---|---|---|---|---|---|
| full fat, roasted—*1 cup (85 g)* | 430 | 1284 | 1435 | 2409 | 1969 | 399 | 477 | 1544 | 1119 | 1476 | 2295 | 797 |
| low fat—*1 cup (88 g)* | 595 | 1778 | 1986 | 3334 | 2725 | 552 | 660 | 2137 | 1549 | 2043 | 3177 | 1104 |
| soy meal, defatted—*1 cup (122 g)* | 797 | 2381 | 2660 | 4465 | 3649 | 739 | 883 | 2862 | 2074 | 2736 | 4254 | 1479 |

**17. Grain Products**
**17.7. Pasta**

| | TRY | THR | ISO | LEU | LYS | MET | CYS | PHE | TYR | VAL | ARG | HIS |
|---|---|---|---|---|---|---|---|---|---|---|---|---|
| macaroni, enr, ckd—*1 cup (140 g)* | 58 | 186 | 238 | 308 | 152 | 72 | 90 | 248 | 158 | | 272 | 112 |
| noodles, enr, ckd—*1 cup (160 g)* | 74 | 276 | 324 | 436 | 220 | 112 | 128 | 316 | 164 | 388 | | 156 |
| spaghetti, enr, ckd—*1 cup (140 g)* | 58 | 186 | 238 | 308 | 152 | 72 | 90 | 248 | 158 | | 272 | 112 |

**19. Infant, Junior & Toddler Foods**
**19.1. Baked Products**

| | TRY | THR | ISO | LEU | LYS | MET | CYS | PHE | TYR | VAL | ARG | HIS |
|---|---|---|---|---|---|---|---|---|---|---|---|---|
| teething biscuit—*1 biscuit (11 g)* | 21 | 62 | 93 | 161 | 39 | 30 | 17 | 58 | 73 | 97 | 66 | 44 |

**19.2. Cereals**

| | TRY | THR | ISO | LEU | LYS | MET | CYS | PHE | TYR | VAL | ARG | HIS |
|---|---|---|---|---|---|---|---|---|---|---|---|---|
| barley | | | | | | | | | | | | |
| dry—*1 T (2.4 g)* | 3 | 9 | 10 | 19 | 9 | 5 | 6 | 16 | 10 | 14 | 14 | 6 |
| prep w/ whole milk—*1 oz (28 g)* | 17 | 53 | 67 | 114 | 79 | 29 | 19 | 68 | 57 | 80 | 54 | 33 |
| cereal & egg yolks | | | | | | | | | | | | |
| jr—*1 jar (213 g)* | 58 | 175 | 213 | 366 | 271 | 109 | 60 | 196 | 179 | 260 | 222 | 96 |
| str—*1 jar (128 g)* | 35 | 105 | 128 | 220 | 163 | 65 | 36 | 118 | 108 | 156 | 133 | 58 |
| cereal, egg yolks & bacon, str—*1 jar (128 g)* | 29 | 120 | 127 | 241 | 173 | 46 | | 125 | 123 | 145 | 175 | 76 |
| grits & egg yolks, str—*1 jar (128 g)* | 28 | 92 | 111 | 234 | 142 | 69 | 35 | 125 | 114 | 136 | 108 | 72 |
| high protein | | | | | | | | | | | | |
| dry—*1 T (2.4 g)* | 13 | 35 | 42 | 71 | 57 | 15 | 17 | 45 | 34 | 45 | 67 | 24 |
| prep w/ whole milk—*1 oz (28 g)* | 37 | 103 | 129 | 213 | 172 | 48 | 41 | 126 | 103 | 138 | 158 | 68 |
| w/ apple & orange, dry—*1 T (2.4 g)* | 8 | 28 | 3 | 50 | 32 | 15 | | 32 | 26 | 36 | 45 | 15 |
| mixed | | | | | | | | | | | | |
| dry—*1 T (2.4 g)* | 4 | 10 | 11 | 25 | 10 | 6 | 8 | 16 | 12 | 16 | 17 | 7 |
| prep w/ whole milk—*1 oz (28 g)* | 18 | 54 | 69 | 125 | 81 | 31 | 23 | 69 | 60 | 82 | 61 | 34 |
| w/ applesce & bananas, jr—*1 jar (220 g)* | 29 | 75 | 95 | 189 | 77 | 53 | 57 | 136 | 95 | 128 | 143 | 59 |
| w/ applesce & bananas, str—*1 jar (135 g)* | 18 | 47 | 59 | 119 | 49 | 34 | 36 | 85 | 59 | 80 | 90 | 38 |
| w/ bananas, dry—*1 T (2.4 g)* | 3 | 9 | 10 | 23 | 11 | 5 | 5 | 13 | 11 | 14 | 12 | 8 |
| w/ bananas, prep w/ whole milk—*1 oz (28 g)* | 17 | 52 | 67 | 121 | 83 | 30 | 16 | 63 | 58 | 80 | 52 | 36 |
| oatmeal | | | | | | | | | | | | |
| dry—*1 T (2.4 g)* | 4 | 11 | 13 | 26 | 14 | 6 | 12 | 13 | 13 | 19 | 25 | 6 |
| prep w/ whole milk—*1 oz (28 g)* | 19 | 57 | 73 | 126 | 88 | 32 | 29 | 63 | 63 | 88 | 76 | 32 |
| w/ applesce & bananas, jr—*1 jar (220 g)* | 37 | 101 | 108 | 220 | 119 | 68 | 66 | 147 | 114 | 152 | 207 | 75 |
| w/ applesce & bananas, str—*1 jar (135 g)* | 23 | 62 | 66 | 134 | 72 | 41 | 39 | 89 | 70 | 92 | 126 | 46 |
| w/ bananas, dry—*1 T (2.4 g)* | 4 | 10 | 12 | 23 | 13 | 6 | 7 | 15 | 12 | 17 | 17 | 9 |
| w/ bananas, prep w/ whole milk—*1 oz (28 g)* | 18 | 55 | 70 | 122 | 88 | 32 | 20 | 67 | 61 | 84 | 61 | 38 |
| rice | | | | | | | | | | | | |
| dry—*1 T (2.4 g)* | 2 | 8 | 7 | 13 | 7 | 4 | 4 | 9 | 8 | 11 | 16 | 5 |
| prep w/ whole milk—*1 oz (28 g)* | 15 | 50 | 60 | 102 | 76 | 28 | 15 | 54 | 53 | 73 | 58 | 30 |
| w/ applesce & bananas, str—*1 jar (135 g)* | 16 | 54 | 65 | 157 | 92 | 27 | 19 | 78 | 76 | 92 | 54 | 43 |
| w/ bananas, dry—*1 T (2.4 g)* | 4 | 11 | 11 | 20 | 11 | 5 | 4 | 10 | 9 | 13 | 14 | 7 |
| w/ bananas, prep w/ whole milk—*1 oz (28 g)* | 18 | 56 | 69 | 115 | 83 | 30 | 16 | 56 | 55 | 77 | 56 | 34 |
| w/ mixed fruit, jr—*1 jar (220 g)* | 24 | 81 | 110 | 213 | 139 | 42 | 35 | 119 | 108 | 139 | 143 | 64 |

**19.3. Desserts**

| | TRY | THR | ISO | LEU | LYS | MET | CYS | PHE | TYR | VAL | ARG | HIS |
|---|---|---|---|---|---|---|---|---|---|---|---|---|
| banana pudding, str, Heinz—*1 jar (128 g)* | | | | | | | | | 38 | | | |
| choc custard pudding | | | | | | | | | | | | |
| jr—*1 jar (220 g)* | | 196 | 229 | 411 | 304 | 103 | | 191 | 154 | 268 | 185 | 106 |
| str—*1 jar (135 g)* | | 111 | 129 | 233 | 173 | 59 | | 109 | 88 | 152 | 105 | 60 |

| | TRY | THR | ISO | LEU | LYS | MET | CYS | PHE | TYR | VAL | ARG | HIS |
|---|---|---|---|---|---|---|---|---|---|---|---|---|
| cottage cheese w/ pineapple | | | | | | | | | | | | |
| jr—*1 jar (220 g)* | | 163 | 216 | 398 | 312 | 57 | | 233 | 178 | 262 | 132 | 117 |
| str—*1 jar (135 g)* | | 99 | 132 | 244 | 190 | 35 | | 143 | 109 | 159 | 81 | 72 |
| orange pudding, str—*1 jar (135 g)* | | 61 | 77 | 153 | 122 | 20 | | 57 | 61 | 95 | 115 | 42 |
| tutti frutti | | | | | | | | | | | | |
| jr, Heinz—*1 jar (213 g)* | | | | | | | | 34 | | | | |
| str, Heinz—*1 jar (128 g)* | | | | | | | | 8 | | | | |
| van custard pudding | | | | | | | | | | | | |
| jr—*1 jar (220 g)* | | 130 | 167 | 130 | 251 | 101 | | 163 | 130 | 196 | 139 | 90 |
| str—*1 jar (128 g)* | | 76 | 96 | 76 | 146 | 59 | | 93 | 76 | 13 | 79 | 52 |
| **19.4. Dinners** | | | | | | | | | | | | |
| beef & egg noodles | | | | | | | | | | | | |
| jr—*1 jar (213 g)* | 58 | 211 | 294 | 443 | 394 | 113 | 62 | 249 | 198 | 281 | 334 | 158 |
| str—*1 jar (128 g)* | 32 | 114 | 159 | 238 | 212 | 60 | 33 | 134 | 106 | 151 | 180 | 84 |
| beef & egg noodles w/ veg, toddler, Gerber—*1 jar (170 g)* | 68 | 308 | 265 | 529 | 517 | 68 | | 292 | 187 | 403 | 541 | 226 |
| beef & egg rice, toddler—*1 jar (177 g)* | 81 | 354 | 434 | 694 | 666 | 218 | 96 | 349 | 285 | 487 | 598 | 227 |
| beef lasagna, toddler—*1 jar (177 g)* | 83 | 289 | 365 | 573 | 526 | 145 | 85 | 322 | 234 | 409 | 448 | 181 |
| beef stew, toddler—*1 jar (177 g)* | 94 | 372 | 435 | 687 | 697 | 251 | 94 | 356 | 281 | 481 | 625 | 227 |
| chicken & noodles | | | | | | | | | | | | |
| jr—*1 jar (213 g)* | 47 | 173 | 213 | 351 | 300 | 83 | 51 | 190 | 153 | 243 | 266 | 100 |
| str—*1 jar (128 g)* | 31 | 113 | 141 | 230 | 198 | 54 | 35 | 125 | 101 | 160 | 175 | 67 |
| chicken soup, crm of, str—*1 jar (128 g)* | 38 | 136 | 156 | 264 | 236 | 65 | 35 | 137 | 119 | 183 | 197 | 76 |
| chicken stew, toddler—*1 jar (170 g)* | 97 | 376 | 437 | 689 | 697 | 190 | 88 | 362 | 292 | 496 | 563 | 218 |
| macaroni alphabets w/ tomato sce & cheese, toddler, Gerber—*1 jar (177 g)* | 35 | 106 | 142 | 258 | 133 | 48 | | 156 | 104 | 159 | 122 | 80 |
| macaroni & cheese | | | | | | | | | | | | |
| jr—*1 jar (213 g)* | 68 | 166 | 277 | 498 | 315 | 192 | 68 | 281 | 262 | 313 | 217 | 132 |
| str—*1 jar (128 g)* | 41 | 100 | 166 | 300 | 189 | 115 | 41 | 169 | 157 | 188 | 131 | 79 |
| macaroni, tomato & beef | | | | | | | | | | | | |
| jr—*1 jar (213 g)* | 60 | 192 | 251 | 422 | 317 | 83 | 72 | 239 | 175 | 271 | 283 | 136 |
| str—*1 jar (128 g)* | 32 | 104 | 137 | 229 | 173 | 46 | 40 | 129 | 95 | 147 | 154 | 74 |
| noodles & chicken w/ carrots & peas, toddler, Gerber—*1 jar (170 g)* | 75 | 313 | 323 | 575 | 525 | 138 | | 303 | 216 | 388 | 551 | 235 |
| potatoes & ham, toddler, Gerber—*1 jar (170 g)* | 56 | 213 | 223 | 398 | 386 | 92 | | 204 | 173 | 264 | 337 | 162 |
| spaghetti, tomato & meat, toddler—*1 jar (177 g)* | 115 | 349 | 474 | 731 | 554 | 184 | 117 | 427 | 326 | 506 | 503 | 250 |
| spaghetti, tomato sce & beef, toddler, Gerber—*1 jar (177 g)* | 58 | 237 | 276 | 490 | 365 | 106 | | 193 | 193 | 304 | 370 | 173 |
| split peas & ham, jr—*1 jar (213 g)* | 72 | 262 | 285 | 515 | 479 | 115 | 60 | 326 | 245 | 328 | 624 | 192 |
| turkey & rice | | | | | | | | | | | | |
| jr—*1 jar (213 g)* | 40 | 158 | 192 | 307 | 309 | 104 | 40 | 162 | 138 | 217 | 281 | 92 |
| str—*1 jar (128 g)* | 26 | 100 | 122 | 195 | 196 | 67 | 26 | 102 | 87 | 137 | 178 | 58 |
| veg & bacon | | | | | | | | | | | | |
| jr—*1 jar (213 g)* | 36 | 130 | 175 | 273 | 232 | 79 | 55 | 164 | 121 | 207 | 258 | 85 |
| str—*1 jar (128 g)* | 19 | 69 | 84 | 133 | 109 | 41 | 29 | 79 | 70 | 109 | 142 | 44 |
| veg & beef | | | | | | | | | | | | |
| jr—*1 jar (213 g)* | 49 | 181 | 213 | 345 | 358 | 81 | 49 | 175 | 130 | 256 | 302 | 113 |
| str—*1 jar (128 g)* | 26 | 91 | 106 | 173 | 179 | 41 | 24 | 87 | 65 | 128 | 151 | 56 |
| toddler, Gerber—*1 jar (177 g)* | 57 | 303 | 219 | 474 | 522 | 41 | | 235 | 161 | 359 | 520 | 214 |
| veg & chicken | | | | | | | | | | | | |
| jr—*1 jar (213 g)* | 43 | 143 | 187 | 283 | 251 | 75 | 58 | 162 | 124 | 215 | 245 | 79 |
| str—*1 jar (128 g)* | 27 | 88 | 116 | 174 | 155 | 46 | 35 | 100 | 76 | 133 | 151 | 49 |
| toddler, Gerber—*1 jar (177 g)* | 46 | 253 | 198 | 418 | 480 | 35 | | 289 | 235 | 310 | 462 | 234 |
| veg & ham | | | | | | | | | | | | |
| jr—*1 jar (213 g)* | 55 | 194 | 232 | 381 | 354 | 109 | 55 | 194 | 158 | 271 | 343 | 141 |
| str—*1 jar (128 g)* | 23 | 84 | 100 | 165 | 152 | 47 | 23 | 84 | 68 | 118 | 148 | 60 |
| toddler—*1 jar (177 g)* | 101 | 301 | 370 | 575 | 540 | 143 | 83 | 320 | 251 | 405 | 471 | 202 |
| veg & lamb | | | | | | | | | | | | |
| jr—*1 jar (213 g)* | 51 | 164 | 202 | 330 | 328 | 66 | 38 | 177 | 141 | 217 | 300 | 102 |
| str—*1 jar (128 g)* | 29 | 93 | 115 | 188 | 187 | 38 | 22 | 101 | 79 | 124 | 170 | 59 |

| | TRY | THR | ISO | LEU | LYS | MET | CYS | PHE | TYR | VAL | ARG | HIS |
|---|---|---|---|---|---|---|---|---|---|---|---|---|
| veg & liver | | | | | | | | | | | | |
| jr—*1 jar (213 g)* | 58 | 158 | 183 | 339 | 290 | 89 | 51 | 183 | 134 | 243 | 232 | 94 |
| str—*1 jar (128 g)* | 41 | 114 | 133 | 244 | 209 | 64 | 37 | 133 | 97 | 175 | 168 | 68 |
| veg & turkey | | | | | | | | | | | | |
| jr—*1 jar (213 g)* | 38 | 145 | 175 | 281 | 266 | 81 | 38 | 136 | 124 | 204 | 228 | 77 |
| str—*1 jar (128 g)* | 23 | 84 | 102 | 165 | 156 | 47 | 23 | 79 | 73 | 120 | 134 | 45 |
| toddler—*1 jar (177 g)* | 106 | 329 | 441 | 689 | 586 | 156 | 92 | 354 | 308 | 492 | 522 | 202 |

**19.5. Dinners, High Meat/Cheese**

| | TRY | THR | ISO | LEU | LYS | MET | CYS | PHE | TYR | VAL | ARG | HIS |
|---|---|---|---|---|---|---|---|---|---|---|---|---|
| beef w/ veg | | | | | | | | | | | | |
| jr—*1 jar (128 g)* | 64 | 307 | 338 | 599 | 594 | 225 | 87 | 303 | 230 | 398 | 495 | 242 |
| str—*1 jar (128 g)* | 59 | 279 | 307 | 544 | 539 | 204 | 78 | 275 | 209 | 361 | 449 | 219 |
| chicken w/ veg | | | | | | | | | | | | |
| jr—*1 jar (128 g)* | 93 | 375 | 417 | 705 | 694 | 237 | 78 | 348 | 261 | 442 | 588 | 261 |
| str—*1 jar (128 g)* | 83 | 332 | 370 | 625 | 614 | 209 | 69 | 308 | 230 | 392 | 520 | 230 |
| cottage cheese w/ pineapple, str—*1 jar (135 g)* | 128 | 293 | 374 | 752 | 585 | 267 | 61 | 394 | 405 | 474 | 288 | 238 |
| ham w/ veg | | | | | | | | | | | | |
| jr—*1 jar (128 g)* | 79 | 317 | 360 | 608 | 636 | 201 | 93 | 288 | 227 | 378 | 502 | 291 |
| str—*1 jar (128 g)* | 78 | 312 | 353 | 599 | 626 | 198 | 92 | 284 | 224 | 371 | 494 | 287 |
| turkey w/ veg | | | | | | | | | | | | |
| jr—*1 jar (128 g)* | 82 | 320 | 371 | 604 | 599 | 197 | 78 | 311 | 243 | 385 | 499 | 261 |
| str—*1 jar (128 g)* | 77 | 303 | 352 | 571 | 567 | 187 | 74 | 294 | 230 | 364 | 472 | 247 |
| veal w/ veg | | | | | | | | | | | | |
| jr—*1 jar (128 g)* | 79 | 312 | 351 | 608 | 620 | 178 | 93 | 301 | 227 | 385 | 529 | 250 |
| str—*1 jar (128 g)* | 78 | 307 | 343 | 596 | 608 | 174 | 91 | 294 | 221 | 378 | 520 | 224 |

**19.6. Fruit Juices**

| | TRY | THR | ISO | LEU | LYS | MET | CYS | PHE | TYR | VAL | ARG | HIS |
|---|---|---|---|---|---|---|---|---|---|---|---|---|
| apple-apricot, str, Heinz—*1 jar (130 g)* | | | | | | | | 4 | | | | |
| apple-pineapple, str, Heinz—*1 jar (130 g)* | | | | | | | | 7 | | | | |

**19.7. Fruits**

| | TRY | THR | ISO | LEU | LYS | MET | CYS | PHE | TYR | VAL | ARG | HIS |
|---|---|---|---|---|---|---|---|---|---|---|---|---|
| apples & apricots | | | | | | | | | | | | |
| jr, Heinz—*1 jar (213 g)* | | | | | | | | 26 | | | | |
| str, Heinz—*1 jar (128 g)* | | | | | | | | 15 | | | | |
| apples & cranberries w/ tapioca | | | | | | | | | | | | |
| jr, Heinz—*1 jar (213 g)* | | | | | | | | 4 | | | | |
| str, Heinz—*1 jar (128 g)* | | | | | | | | 3 | | | | |
| apples & pears | | | | | | | | | | | | |
| jr, Heinz—*1 jar (213 g)* | | | | | | | | 11 | | | | |
| str, Heinz—*1 jar (128 g)* | | | | | | | | 6 | | | | |

**19.8. Meat/Egg Yolks**

| | TRY | THR | ISO | LEU | LYS | MET | CYS | PHE | TYR | VAL | ARG | HIS |
|---|---|---|---|---|---|---|---|---|---|---|---|---|
| beef | | | | | | | | | | | | |
| jr—*1 jar (99 g)* | 145 | 629 | 652 | 1150 | 1194 | 441 | 167 | 555 | 477 | 726 | 978 | 487 |
| str—*1 jar (99 g)* | 136 | 591 | 613 | 1080 | 1122 | 414 | 157 | 522 | 448 | 681 | 919 | 457 |
| beef w/ beef heart, str—*1 jar (99 g)* | 125 | 506 | 613 | 1000 | 1040 | 326 | 129 | 518 | 361 | 683 | 824 | 336 |
| chicken | | | | | | | | | | | | |
| jr—*1 jar (99 g)* | 165 | 653 | 686 | 1125 | 1216 | 390 | 191 | 593 | 466 | 733 | 1018 | 441 |
| str—*1 jar (99 g)* | 154 | 609 | 639 | 1047 | 1133 | 363 | 178 | 552 | 435 | 682 | 947 | 411 |
| chicken sticks, jr—*1 jar (71 g)* | 83 | 406 | 518 | 811 | 824 | 229 | 90 | 478 | 353 | 542 | 712 | 328 |
| egg yolks, str—*1 jar (94 g)* | 101 | 433 | 532 | 795 | 737 | 255 | 161 | 389 | 389 | 603 | 658 | 199 |
| ham | | | | | | | | | | | | |
| jr—*1 jar (99 g)* | 148 | 649 | 711 | 1196 | 1270 | 382 | 184 | 570 | 501 | 771 | 1012 | 509 |
| str—*1 jar (99 g)* | 137 | 597 | 654 | 1100 | 1168 | 351 | 169 | 525 | 461 | 709 | 931 | 467 |
| lamb | | | | | | | | | | | | |
| jr—*1 jar (99 g)* | 149 | 686 | 707 | 1188 | 1336 | 471 | 207 | 592 | 527 | 762 | 986 | 380 |
| str—*1 jar (99 g)* | 139 | 636 | 655 | 1101 | 1237 | 437 | 192 | 548 | 488 | 707 | 914 | 352 |
| liver, beef, str—*1 jar (99 g)* | 220 | 676 | 694 | 1307 | 926 | 372 | 213 | 678 | 569 | 898 | 831 | 363 |
| meat sticks, jr—*1 jar (71 g)* | 65 | 413 | 474 | 740 | 734 | 219 | 52 | 431 | 370 | 491 | 618 | 327 |
| pork, str—*1 jar (99 g)* | 135 | 611 | 673 | 1116 | 1146 | 394 | 152 | 564 | 505 | 695 | 939 | 443 |
| turkey | | | | | | | | | | | | |
| jr—*1 jar (99 g)* | 158 | 674 | 764 | 1213 | 1261 | 472 | 185 | 628 | 536 | 774 | 969 | 389 |
| str—*1 jar (99 g)* | 148 | 627 | 710 | 1127 | 1172 | 439 | 172 | 584 | 498 | 720 | 900 | 362 |

| | TRY | THR | ISO | LEU | LYS | MET | CYS | PHE | TYR | VAL | ARG | HIS |
|---|---|---|---|---|---|---|---|---|---|---|---|---|
| turkey sticks, jr—*1 jar (71 g)* | 72 | 388 | 447 | 760 | 835 | 216 | 87 | 433 | 343 | 462 | 627 | 261 |
| veal | | | | | | | | | | | | |
|   jr—*1 jar (99 g)* | 174 | 632 | 682 | 1168 | 1215 | 334 | 196 | 585 | 484 | 736 | 1004 | 464 |
|   str—*1 jar (99 g)* | 145 | 558 | 604 | 1034 | 1074 | 295 | 173 | 518 | 428 | 650 | 888 | 411 |
| **19.9. Vegetables** | | | | | | | | | | | | |
| beans, green | | | | | | | | | | | | |
|   jr—*1 jar (206 g)* | 29 | 105 | 111 | 161 | 122 | 37 | 21 | 101 | 87 | 134 | 136 | 68 |
|   str—*1 jar (128 g)* | 19 | 70 | 74 | 109 | 83 | 24 | 14 | 68 | 59 | 91 | 92 | 46 |
| beans, green, buttered | | | | | | | | | | | | |
|   jr—*1 jar (206 g)* | 31 | 113 | 119 | 175 | 132 | 39 | 23 | 109 | 95 | 144 | 146 | 74 |
|   str—*1 jar (128 g)* | 18 | 65 | 69 | 100 | 76 | 23 | 13 | 63 | 54 | 83 | 84 | 42 |
| beans, green, creamed—*1 jar (213 g)* | 32 | 81 | 102 | 166 | 92 | 47 | 23 | 96 | 92 | 124 | 102 | 49 |
| beets, str—*1 jar (128 g)* | 15 | 41 | 49 | 59 | 44 | 13 | 9 | 23 | 45 | 58 | 38 | 27 |
| carrots | | | | | | | | | | | | |
|   jr—*1 jar (213 g)* | 23 | 49 | 51 | 70 | 45 | 19 | 13 | 53 | 43 | 66 | 111 | 28 |
|   str—*1 jar (128 g)* | 14 | 28 | 31 | 41 | 26 | 12 | 8 | 31 | 24 | 38 | 64 | 15 |
| carrots, buttered | | | | | | | | | | | | |
|   jr—*1 jar (213 g)* | 23 | 49 | 51 | 70 | 45 | 19 | 13 | 53 | 43 | 66 | 111 | 28 |
|   str—*1 jar (128 g)* | 15 | 31 | 32 | 44 | 27 | 12 | 8 | 33 | 26 | 41 | 68 | 17 |
| corn, creamed | | | | | | | | | | | | |
|   jr—*1 jar (213 g)* | 32 | 111 | 138 | 300 | 175 | 85 | 38 | 104 | 145 | 166 | 128 | 98 |
|   str—*1 jar (128 g)* | 19 | 67 | 83 | 179 | 104 | 51 | 23 | 63 | 86 | 99 | 77 | 59 |
| garden veg, str—*1 jar (128 g)* | 35 | 93 | 110 | 183 | 148 | 55 | 26 | 113 | 122 | 127 | 251 | 58 |
| mixed veg | | | | | | | | | | | | |
|   jr—*1 jar (213 g)* | 32 | 96 | 119 | 194 | 100 | 45 | 60 | 117 | 111 | 147 | 198 | 66 |
|   str—*1 jar (128 g)* | 17 | 49 | 60 | 99 | 51 | 23 | 31 | 60 | 56 | 74 | 101 | 33 |
| peas, str—*1 jar (128 g)* | 44 | 174 | 193 | 301 | 300 | 51 | 33 | 183 | 152 | 216 | 498 | 96 |
| peas, buttered | | | | | | | | | | | | |
|   jr—*1 jar (206 g)* | 70 | 284 | 315 | 490 | 488 | 84 | 56 | 299 | 249 | 352 | 814 | 157 |
|   str—*1 jar (128 g)* | 46 | 183 | 204 | 316 | 315 | 54 | 36 | 192 | 160 | 228 | 525 | 101 |
| spinach, creamed | | | | | | | | | | | | |
|   jr—*1 jar (213 g)* | 94 | 258 | 288 | 564 | 379 | 141 | 79 | 247 | 294 | 386 | 388 | 162 |
|   str—*1 jar (128 g)* | 46 | 129 | 143 | 283 | 189 | 70 | 40 | 123 | 147 | 193 | 195 | 82 |
| squash | | | | | | | | | | | | |
|   jr—*1 jar (213 g)* | 26 | 53 | 70 | 102 | 66 | 23 | 15 | 62 | 60 | 77 | 100 | 34 |
|   str—*1 jar (128 g)* | 15 | 32 | 42 | 60 | 40 | 13 | 9 | 37 | 36 | 46 | 59 | 20 |
| squash, buttered | | | | | | | | | | | | |
|   jr—*1 jar (213 g)* | 21 | 45 | 60 | 87 | 55 | 19 | 13 | 53 | 51 | 66 | 85 | 28 |
|   str—*1 jar (128 g)* | 12 | 24 | 32 | 46 | 29 | 10 | 8 | 28 | 28 | 36 | 45 | 15 |
| sweet potatoes | | | | | | | | | | | | |
|   jr—*1 jar (220 g)* | 46 | 117 | 110 | 167 | 95 | 51 | 33 | 134 | 88 | 156 | 117 | 55 |
|   str—*1 jar (135 g)* | 30 | 73 | 69 | 105 | 59 | 32 | 20 | 84 | 55 | 99 | 73 | 35 |
| sweet potatoes, buttered | | | | | | | | | | | | |
|   jr—*1 jar (220 g)* | 33 | 84 | 79 | 121 | 68 | 37 | 24 | 97 | 64 | 114 | 84 | 40 |
|   str—*1 jar (135 g)* | 24 | 61 | 57 | 86 | 49 | 27 | 18 | 70 | 46 | 82 | 61 | 28 |
| **20. Meat Analogues & Meat Analogue Entrees** | | | | | | | | | | | | |
| bacon, simulated meat product—*1 strip (8 g)* | 13 | 36 | 45 | 73 | 58 | 12 | 14 | 49 | 32 | 47 | 70 | 24 |
| meat extender, simulated meat product—*1 oz (28 g)* | 161 | 452 | 559 | 914 | 727 | 146 | 176 | 611 | 400 | 592 | 874 | 299 |
| sausage, simulated meat product—*1 link (25 g)* | 70 | 196 | 243 | 397 | 316 | 63 | 76 | 265 | 174 | 257 | 380 | 130 |
| sausage, simulated meat product—*1 patty (38 g)* | 106 | 298 | 369 | 603 | 480 | 96 | 116 | 403 | 264 | 391 | 577 | 197 |
| **21. Meats** | | | | | | | | | | | | |
| **21.1. Beef** | | | | | | | | | | | | |
| breakfast strips, ckd—*3 slices (34 g)* | 97 | 402 | 460 | 782 | 816 | 247 | 136 | 383 | 347 | 468 | 657 | 339 |
| brisket | | | | | | | | | | | | |
|   sep lean & fat, braised—*3.5 oz (100 g)* | 258 | 1004 | 1034 | 1817 | 1913 | 589 | 258 | 898 | 773 | 1118 | 1453 | 787 |
|   sep lean, braised—*3.5 oz (100 g)* | 329 | 1283 | 1321 | 2322 | 2445 | 752 | 329 | 1147 | 987 | 1429 | 1857 | 1006 |

| | TRY | THR | ISO | LEU | LYS | MET | CYS | PHE | TYR | VAL | ARG | HIS |
|---|---|---|---|---|---|---|---|---|---|---|---|---|
| **brisket, flat half** | | | | | | | | | | | | |
| sep lean & fat, braised—*3.5 oz (100 g)* | 246 | 960 | 988 | 1736 | 1828 | 562 | 246 | 858 | 738 | 1069 | 1388 | 752 |
| sep lean, braised—*3.5 oz (100 g)* | 312 | 1225 | 1261 | 2217 | 2333 | 718 | 314 | 1095 | 942 | 1364 | 1772 | 960 |
| **brisket, point half** | | | | | | | | | | | | |
| sep lean & fat, braised—*3.5 oz (100 g)* | 276 | 1077 | 1109 | 1949 | 2051 | 631 | 276 | 963 | 828 | 1199 | 1558 | 844 |
| sep lean, braised—*3.5 oz (100 g)* | 353 | 1377 | 1417 | 2492 | 2623 | 807 | 353 | 1231 | 1059 | 1533 | 1992 | 1079 |
| **chuck arm pot roast** | | | | | | | | | | | | |
| sep lean & fat, braised—*3.5 oz (100 g)* | 303 | 1183 | 1218 | 2141 | 2254 | 693 | 303 | 1057 | 910 | 1318 | 1712 | 927 |
| sep lean, braised—*3.5 oz (100 g)* | 370 | 1442 | 1485 | 2610 | 2747 | 845 | 370 | 1289 | 1109 | 1606 | 2087 | 1131 |
| **chuck blade roast** | | | | | | | | | | | | |
| sep lean & fat, braised—*3.5 oz (100 g)* | 285 | 1111 | 1144 | 2011 | 2117 | 651 | 285 | 993 | 855 | 1238 | 1608 | 871 |
| sep lean, braised—*3.5 oz (100 g)* | 348 | 1357 | 1396 | 2455 | 2584 | 795 | 348 | 1212 | 1043 | 1511 | 1963 | 1063 |
| **corned beef** | | | | | | | | | | | | |
| cured brisket, ckd—*3.5 oz (100 g)* | 166 | 686 | 785 | 1334 | 1392 | 421 | 232 | 654 | 593 | 799 | 1122 | 578 |
| cured, cnd—*3.5 oz (100 g)* | 247 | 1023 | 1170 | 1990 | 2076 | 629 | 347 | 975 | 884 | 1192 | 1673 | 863 |
| dried (chipped)—*1 oz (28 g)* | 67 | 346 | 338 | 616 | 673 | 199 | 98 | 309 | 249 | 379 | 557 | 239 |
| **flank** | | | | | | | | | | | | |
| sep lean & fat, braised—*3.5 oz (100 g)* | 308 | 1202 | 1237 | 2175 | 2289 | 704 | 308 | 1074 | 924 | 1338 | 1739 | 942 |
| sep lean & fat, broiled—*3.5 oz (100 g)* | 280 | 1094 | 1126 | 1979 | 2084 | 641 | 280 | 978 | 841 | 1218 | 1583 | 857 |
| sep lean, braised—*3.5 oz (100 g)* | 314 | 1224 | 1260 | 2215 | 2331 | 717 | 314 | 1094 | 941 | 1363 | 1771 | 959 |
| sep lean, broiled—*3.5 oz (100 g)* | 284 | 1109 | 1142 | 2008 | 2113 | 650 | 284 | 992 | 852 | 1235 | 1605 | 870 |
| **ground, extra lean** | | | | | | | | | | | | |
| baked, med—*3.5 oz (100 g)* | 301 | 1026 | 1049 | 1961 | 2044 | 572 | 235 | 928 | 763 | 1186 | 1652 | 779 |
| baked, well done—*3.5 oz (100 g)* | 373 | 1270 | 1299 | 2429 | 2531 | 708 | 291 | 1149 | 945 | 1469 | 2046 | 965 |
| broiled, med—*3.5 oz (100 g)* | 313 | 1065 | 1089 | 2036 | 2121 | 593 | 244 | 963 | 792 | 1231 | 1715 | 809 |
| broiled, well done—*3.5 oz (100 g)* | 352 | 1198 | 1226 | 2291 | 2387 | 668 | 274 | 1084 | 892 | 1386 | 1930 | 910 |
| pan fried, med—*3.5 oz (100 g)* | 308 | 1046 | 1070 | 2001 | 2085 | 583 | 240 | 947 | 779 | 1210 | 1685 | 795 |
| pan fried, well done—*3.5 oz (100 g)* | 345 | 1173 | 1200 | 2243 | 2338 | 654 | 269 | 1061 | 873 | 1357 | 1890 | 891 |
| **ground, lean** | | | | | | | | | | | | |
| baked, med—*3.5 oz (100 g)* | 295 | 1003 | 1026 | 1918 | 1999 | 559 | 230 | 907 | 747 | 1160 | 1616 | 762 |
| baked, well done—*3.5 oz (100 g)* | 365 | 1241 | 1269 | 2373 | 2472 | 691 | 284 | 1122 | 924 | 1435 | 1999 | 942 |
| broiled, med—*3.5 oz (100 g)* | 305 | 1036 | 1060 | 1981 | 2065 | 577 | 237 | 937 | 771 | 1198 | 1669 | 787 |
| broiled, well done—*3.5 oz (100 g)* | 347 | 1182 | 1209 | 2261 | 2355 | 659 | 271 | 1069 | 880 | 1367 | 1904 | 898 |
| pan fried, med—*3.5 oz (100 g)* | 299 | 1016 | 1039 | 1942 | 2024 | 566 | 233 | 919 | 756 | 1175 | 1636 | 772 |
| pan fried, well done—*3.5 oz (100 g)* | 340 | 1157 | 1183 | 2212 | 2305 | 645 | 265 | 1047 | 861 | 1338 | 1864 | 879 |
| **ground, regular** | | | | | | | | | | | | |
| baked, med—*3.5 oz (100 g)* | 284 | 965 | 987 | 1845 | 1923 | 538 | 221 | 873 | 718 | 1116 | 1554 | 733 |
| baked, well done—*3.5 oz (100 g)* | 355 | 1207 | 1235 | 2309 | 2405 | 673 | 276 | 1092 | 899 | 1396 | 1945 | 917 |
| broiled, med—*3.5 oz (100 g)* | 297 | 1009 | 1032 | 1929 | 2010 | 562 | 231 | 913 | 751 | 1167 | 1625 | 766 |
| broiled, well done—*3.5 oz (100 g)* | 335 | 1140 | 1166 | 2180 | 2272 | 635 | 261 | 1031 | 849 | 1319 | 1837 | 866 |
| pan fried, med—*3.5 oz (100 g)* | 295 | 1003 | 1026 | 1917 | 1998 | 559 | 230 | 907 | 746 | 1160 | 1615 | 762 |
| pan fried, well done—*3.5 oz (100 g)* | 333 | 1132 | 1158 | 2164 | 2255 | 631 | 259 | 1024 | 842 | 1309 | 1823 | 860 |
| **rib eye, small end (rib 10-12)** | | | | | | | | | | | | |
| sep lean & fat, broiled—*3.5 oz (100 g)* | 284 | 1108 | 1141 | 2006 | 2111 | 650 | 284 | 991 | 853 | 1234 | 1604 | 869 |
| sep lean, broiled—*3.5 oz (100 g)* | 314 | 1225 | 1261 | 2216 | 2333 | 718 | 314 | 1095 | 942 | 1364 | 1772 | 960 |
| **rib, large end (rib 6-9)** | | | | | | | | | | | | |
| sep lean & fat, broiled—*3.5 oz (100 g)* | 225 | 879 | 905 | 1590 | 1674 | 515 | 225 | 785 | 676 | 979 | 1272 | 689 |
| sep lean & fat, roasted—*3.5 oz (100 g)* | 254 | 992 | 1021 | 1795 | 1890 | 581 | 254 | 887 | 763 | 1105 | 1435 | 778 |
| sep lean, broiled—*3.5 oz (100 g)* | 276 | 1076 | 1108 | 1947 | 2050 | 631 | 276 | 962 | 828 | 1198 | 1557 | 844 |
| sep lean, roasted—*3.5 oz (100 g)* | 308 | 1202 | 1238 | 2176 | 2290 | 705 | 308 | 1075 | 925 | 1339 | 1740 | 942 |
| **rib, shortribs** | | | | | | | | | | | | |
| sep lean & fat, braised—*3.5 oz (100 g)* | 242 | 942 | 969 | 1704 | 1794 | 552 | 242 | 842 | 725 | 1049 | 1363 | 738 |
| sep lean, braised—*3.5 oz (100 g)* | 344 | 1343 | 1383 | 2431 | 2559 | 787 | 344 | 1201 | 1033 | 1496 | 1944 | 1053 |
| **rib, small end (ribs 10-12)** | | | | | | | | | | | | |
| sep lean & fat, broiled—*3.5 oz (100 g)* | 269 | 1050 | 1081 | 1900 | 2000 | 615 | 269 | 938 | 808 | 1169 | 1519 | 823 |
| sep lean & fat, roasted—*3.5 oz (100 g)* | 249 | 972 | 1001 | 1760 | 1852 | 570 | 249 | 869 | 748 | 1083 | 1407 | 762 |
| sep lean, broiled—*3.5 oz (100 g)* | 314 | 1225 | 1261 | 2216 | 2333 | 718 | 314 | 1095 | 942 | 1364 | 1772 | 960 |
| sep lean, roasted—*3.5 oz (100 g)* | 299 | 1168 | 1202 | 2113 | 2225 | 684 | 299 | 1044 | 898 | 1301 | 1690 | 915 |
| **rib, whole (ribs 6-12)** | | | | | | | | | | | | |
| sep lean & fat, broiled—*3.5 oz (100 g)* | 240 | 885 | 884 | 1625 | 1678 | 510 | 240 | 823 | 678 | 1005 | 1356 | 672 |

| | TRY | THR | ISO | LEU | LYS | MET | CYS | PHE | TYR | VAL | ARG | HIS |
|---|---|---|---|---|---|---|---|---|---|---|---|---|
| sep lean & fat, roasted—*3.5 oz (100 g)* | 245 | 957 | 985 | 1732 | 1824 | 561 | 245 | 856 | 736 | 1066 | 1385 | 750 |
| sep lean, broiled—*3.5 oz (100 g)* | 291 | 1136 | 1170 | 2057 | 2165 | 666 | 291 | 1016 | 874 | 1266 | 1644 | 891 |
| sep lean, roasted—*3.5 oz (100 g)* | 305 | 1188 | 1223 | 2150 | 2263 | 696 | 305 | 1062 | 914 | 1323 | 1719 | 931 |
| round, bottom | | | | | | | | | | | | |
| sep lean & fat, braised—*3.5 oz (100 g)* | 334 | 1302 | 1340 | 2356 | 2480 | 763 | 334 | 1164 | 1001 | 1450 | 1884 | 1021 |
| sep lean, braised—*3.5 oz (100 g)* | 354 | 1380 | 1420 | 2497 | 2628 | 809 | 354 | 1233 | 1061 | 1536 | 1996 | 1082 |
| round, eye of | | | | | | | | | | | | |
| sep lean & fat, roasted—*3.5 oz (100 g)* | 300 | 1169 | 1203 | 2115 | 2227 | 685 | 300 | 1045 | 899 | 1302 | 1691 | 916 |
| sep lean, roasted—*3.5 oz (100 g)* | 325 | 1266 | 1303 | 2291 | 2412 | 742 | 325 | 1132 | 974 | 1410 | 1832 | 993 |
| round, full cut | | | | | | | | | | | | |
| sep lean & fat, broiled—*3.5 oz (100 g)* | 286 | 1115 | 1148 | 2018 | 2125 | 654 | 286 | 997 | 858 | 1242 | 1614 | 874 |
| sep lean, broiled—*3.5 oz (100 g)* | 319 | 1243 | 1279 | 2249 | 2367 | 728 | 319 | 1111 | 956 | 1384 | 1798 | 974 |
| round, tip | | | | | | | | | | | | |
| sep lean & fat, roasted—*3.5 oz (100 g)* | 296 | 1156 | 1190 | 2092 | 2202 | 678 | 296 | 1033 | 889 | 1287 | 1673 | 906 |
| sep lean, roasted—*3.5 oz (100 g)* | 322 | 1254 | 1291 | 2269 | 2389 | 735 | 322 | 1121 | 965 | 1397 | 1815 | 983 |
| round, top | | | | | | | | | | | | |
| sep lean & fat, broiled—*3.5 oz (100 g)* | 345 | 1346 | 1386 | 2436 | 2565 | 789 | 345 | 1203 | 1036 | 1499 | 1948 | 1055 |
| sep lean & fat, pan fried—*3.5 oz (100 g)* | 355 | 1384 | 1425 | 2505 | 2636 | 811 | 355 | 1237 | 1065 | 1541 | 2003 | 1085 |
| sep lean, broiled—*3.5 oz (100 g)* | 355 | 1384 | 1425 | 2505 | 2637 | 811 | 355 | 1237 | 1065 | 1542 | 2003 | 1085 |
| sep lean, pan fried—*3.5 oz (100 g)* | 393 | 1532 | 1576 | 2771 | 2917 | 898 | 393 | 1369 | 1178 | 1705 | 2216 | 1201 |
| sausage, smoked, cnd | | | | | | | | | | | | |
| —*1 oz (28 g)* | 37 | 151 | 173 | 294 | 306 | 93 | 51 | 144 | 130 | 176 | 247 | 127 |
| —*1 sausage (8 per 12 oz pkg) (43 g)* | 55 | 229 | 262 | 445 | 465 | 141 | 78 | 218 | 198 | 267 | 375 | 193 |
| shank, crosscuts | | | | | | | | | | | | |
| sep lean & fat, simmered—*3.5 oz (100 g)* | 354 | 1381 | 1421 | 2498 | 2630 | 809 | 354 | 1234 | 1062 | 1537 | 1998 | 1082 |
| sep lean, simmered—*3.5 oz (100 g)* | 377 | 1471 | 1514 | 2662 | 2802 | 862 | 377 | 1315 | 1132 | 1638 | 2129 | 1153 |
| short loin porterhouse steak | | | | | | | | | | | | |
| sep lean & fat, broiled—*3.5 oz (100 g)* | 281 | 1096 | 1128 | 1983 | 2088 | 642 | 281 | 980 | 843 | 1221 | 1586 | 859 |
| sep lean, broiled—*3.5 oz (100 g)* | 315 | 1230 | 1266 | 2226 | 2343 | 721 | 315 | 1099 | 946 | 1370 | 1780 | 964 |
| short loin T-bone steak | | | | | | | | | | | | |
| sep lean & fat, broiled—*3.5 oz (100 g)* | 269 | 1048 | 1078 | 1896 | 1996 | 614 | 269 | 936 | 806 | 1167 | 1516 | 821 |
| sep lean, broiled—*3.5 oz (100 g)* | 315 | 1229 | 1265 | 2223 | 2341 | 720 | 315 | 1098 | 945 | 1368 | 1778 | 963 |
| short loin tenderloin | | | | | | | | | | | | |
| sep lean & fat, broiled—*3.5 oz (100 g)* | 291 | 1134 | 1167 | 2052 | 2160 | 665 | 291 | 1013 | 872 | 1263 | 1641 | 889 |
| sep lean & fat, roasted—*3.5 oz (100 g)* | 274 | 1069 | 1100 | 1934 | 2035 | 626 | 274 | 955 | 822 | 1190 | 1546 | 838 |
| sep lean, broiled—*3.5 oz (100 g)* | 316 | 1234 | 1270 | 2233 | 2350 | 723 | 316 | 1103 | 949 | 1374 | 1785 | 967 |
| sep lean, roasted—*3.5 oz (100 g)* | 308 | 1203 | 1238 | 2177 | 2291 | 705 | 308 | 1075 | 925 | 1339 | 1740 | 943 |
| short loin, top loin | | | | | | | | | | | | |
| sep lean & fat, broiled—*3.5 oz (100 g)* | 288 | 1124 | 1157 | 2033 | 2140 | 659 | 288 | 1004 | 864 | 1251 | 1626 | 881 |
| sep lean, broiled—*3.5 oz (100 g)* | 321 | 1250 | 1287 | 2262 | 2381 | 733 | 321 | 1117 | 962 | 1392 | 1809 | 980 |
| wedge-bone sirloin | | | | | | | | | | | | |
| sep lean & fat, broiled—*3.5 oz (100 g)* | 307 | 1196 | 1231 | 2165 | 2279 | 701 | 307 | 1069 | 920 | 1332 | 1731 | 938 |
| sep lean & fat, pan fried—*3.5 oz (100 g)* | 308 | 1199 | 1234 | 2170 | 2284 | 703 | 308 | 1072 | 923 | 1335 | 1735 | 940 |
| sep lean, broiled—*3.5 oz (100 g)* | 340 | 1327 | 1365 | 2400 | 2527 | 777 | 340 | 1186 | 1020 | 1477 | 1919 | 1040 |
| sep lean, pan fried—*3.5 oz (100 g)* | 364 | 1419 | 1460 | 2567 | 2702 | 832 | 364 | 1268 | 1091 | 1580 | 2053 | 1112 |

**21.3. Pork**
arm picnic

| | TRY | THR | ISO | LEU | LYS | MET | CYS | PHE | TYR | VAL | ARG | HIS |
|---|---|---|---|---|---|---|---|---|---|---|---|---|
| sep lean & fat, braised—*3.5 oz (100 g)* | 346 | 1241 | 1264 | 2163 | 2620 | 647 | 341 | 1069 | 929 | 1428 | 1908 | 1304 |
| sep lean & fat, roasted—*3.5 oz (100 g)* | 286 | 1030 | 1047 | 1799 | 2178 | 536 | 283 | 889 | 769 | 1188 | 1598 | 1076 |
| sep lean, braised—*3.5 oz (100 g)* | 434 | 1518 | 1559 | 2622 | 3180 | 795 | 418 | 1291 | 1151 | 1729 | 2240 | 1636 |
| sep lean, roasted—*3.5 oz (100 g)* | 359 | 1255 | 1289 | 2169 | 2630 | 657 | 346 | 1067 | 952 | 1430 | 1853 | 1353 |
| arm picnic, cured | | | | | | | | | | | | |
| sep lean & fat, roasted—*3.5 oz (100 g)* | 227 | 885 | 861 | 1602 | 1728 | 516 | 294 | 871 | 637 | 894 | 1403 | 683 |
| sep lean, roasted—*3.5 oz (100 g)* | 299 | 1109 | 1094 | 1980 | 2115 | 659 | 375 | 1078 | 818 | 1082 | 1620 | 894 |

| | TRY | THR | ISO | LEU | LYS | MET | CYS | PHE | TYR | VAL | ARG | HIS |
|---|---|---|---|---|---|---|---|---|---|---|---|---|
| bacon, canadian style[a] | | | | | | | | | | | | |
| unheated—*2 slices (57 g)* | 116 | 470 | 442 | 824 | 921 | 318 | 146 | 380 | 354 | 466 | 638 | 425 |
| grilled—*2 slices (47 g)* | 112 | 452 | 425 | 793 | 887 | 306 | 140 | 366 | 341 | 449 | 615 | 409 |
| bacon, cured | | | | | | | | | | | | |
| broiled/pan fried—*3 med pieces (19 g)* | 55 | 222 | 235 | 403 | 430 | 128 | 59 | 223 | 169 | 279 | 354 | 167 |
| broiled/pan fried—*4.48 oz*[b] *(127 g)* | 371 | 1485 | 1571 | 2691 | 2871 | 853 | 396 | 1491 | 1126 | 1862 | 2363 | 1114 |
| raw—*3 med slices (68 g)* | 56 | 226 | 239 | 409 | 437 | 130 | 61 | 227 | 171 | 284 | 360 | 169 |
| blade roll, cured, sep lean & fat, roasted—*3.5 oz (100 g)* | 207 | 768 | 757 | 1371 | 1465 | 456 | 260 | 746 | 567 | 749 | 1122 | 619 |
| boston blade | | | | | | | | | | | | |
| sep lean & fat, braised—*3.5 oz (100 g)* | 342 | 1224 | 1247 | 2131 | 2582 | 638 | 337 | 1052 | 918 | 1407 | 1875 | 1289 |
| sep lean & fat, broiled—*3.5 oz (100 g)* | 282 | 1012 | 1031 | 1764 | 2137 | 527 | 278 | 872 | 757 | 1165 | 1558 | 1064 |
| sep lean & fat, roasted—*3.5 oz (100 g)* | 282 | 1011 | 1031 | 1759 | 2131 | 527 | 278 | 869 | 758 | 1161 | 1544 | 1067 |
| sep lean, braised—*3.5 oz (100 g)* | 419 | 1466 | 1505 | 2532 | 3071 | 768 | 404 | 1246 | 1112 | 1670 | 2163 | 1580 |
| sep lean, broiled—*3.5 oz (100 g)* | 338 | 1184 | 1216 | 2046 | 2481 | 620 | 326 | 1007 | 898 | 1349 | 1748 | 1277 |
| sep lean, roasted—*3.5 oz (100 g)* | 327 | 1146 | 1177 | 1980 | 2401 | 600 | 316 | 975 | 869 | 1306 | 1692 | 1236 |
| breakfast strips, ckd—*3 slices (34 g)* | 95 | 378 | 400 | 685 | 731 | 217 | 101 | 379 | 287 | 474 | 601 | 284 |
| center loin | | | | | | | | | | | | |
| sep lean & fat, braised—*3.5 oz (100 g)* | 382 | 1366 | 1393 | 2375 | 2878 | 712 | 376 | 1173 | 1025 | 1569 | 2083 | 1442 |
| sep lean & fat, broiled—*3.5 oz (100 g)* | 357 | 1272 | 1299 | 2215 | 2683 | 663 | 350 | 1093 | 954 | 1462 | 1943 | 1344 |
| sep lean & fat, pan fried—*3.5 oz (100 g)* | 296 | 1071 | 1089 | 1873 | 2268 | 557 | 294 | 927 | 799 | 1238 | 1670 | 1116 |
| sep lean & fat, roasted—*3.5 oz (100 g)* | 332 | 1182 | 1208 | 2054 | 2490 | 617 | 325 | 1014 | 888 | 1356 | 1795 | 1253 |
| sep lean, braised—*3.5 oz (100 g)* | 467 | 1636 | 1680 | 2826 | 3427 | 857 | 451 | 1391 | 1241 | 1864 | 2414 | 1763 |
| sep lean, broiled—*3.5 oz (100 g)* | 431 | 1505 | 1547 | 2601 | 3154 | 788 | 415 | 1280 | 1141 | 1715 | 2222 | 1623 |
| sep lean, pan fried—*3.5 oz (100 g)* | 387 | 1353 | 1390 | 2338 | 2835 | 709 | 373 | 1151 | 1026 | 1542 | 1997 | 1459 |
| sep lean, roasted—*3.5 oz (100 g)* | 383 | 1340 | 1377 | 2315 | 2808 | 702 | 369 | 1140 | 1016 | 1527 | 1978 | 1445 |
| center rib | | | | | | | | | | | | |
| sep lean & fat, braised—*3.5 oz (100 g)* | 370 | 1324 | 1350 | 2307 | 2794 | 691 | 364 | 1140 | 993 | 1523 | 2030 | 1395 |
| sep lean & fat, broiled—*3.5 oz (100 g)* | 317 | 1139 | 1161 | 1983 | 2403 | 593 | 312 | 980 | 853 | 1310 | 1749 | 1198 |
| sep lean & fat, pan fried—*3.5 oz (100 g)* | 271 | 989 | 1002 | 1735 | 2100 | 513 | 271 | 860 | 734 | 1147 | 1566 | 1020 |
| sep lean & fat, roasted—*3.5 oz (100 g)* | 321 | 1149 | 1172 | 1999 | 2422 | 599 | 316 | 987 | 863 | 1320 | 1753 | 1213 |
| sep lean, braised—*3.5 oz (100 g)* | 463 | 1620 | 1664 | 2799 | 3394 | 849 | 446 | 1378 | 1229 | 1846 | 2391 | 1747 |
| sep lean, broiled—*3.5 oz (100 g)* | 387 | 1356 | 1393 | 2342 | 2840 | 710 | 373 | 1153 | 1028 | 1545 | 2001 | 1462 |
| sep lean, pan fried—*3.5 oz (100 g)* | 376 | 1315 | 1351 | 2273 | 2756 | 689 | 362 | 1119 | 998 | 1499 | 1942 | 1418 |
| sep lean, roasted—*3.5 oz (100 g)* | 379 | 1327 | 1363 | 2293 | 2781 | 695 | 366 | 1129 | 1007 | 1512 | 1959 | 1431 |
| ham, cured, lean | | | | | | | | | | | | |
| cnd—*3.5 oz (100 g)* | 210 | 826 | 796 | 1438 | 1589 | 482 | 219 | 713 | 607 | 829 | 1145 | 731 |
| cnd, roasted—*3.5 oz (100 g)* | 240 | 944 | 911 | 1645 | 1818 | 552 | 250 | 816 | 694 | 948 | 1310 | 836 |
| roasted[c]—*3.5 oz (100 g)* | 251 | 931 | 918 | 1661 | 1775 | 553 | 315 | 904 | 687 | 908 | 1360 | 750 |
| unheated[c]—*3.5 oz (100 g)* | 232 | 860 | 848 | 1535 | 1640 | 511 | 291 | 836 | 634 | 839 | 1257 | 693 |
| ham, cured, regular | | | | | | | | | | | | |
| center slice, sep lean & fat, unheated[c]—*3.5 oz (100 g)* | 235 | 888 | 871 | 1593 | 1708 | 523 | 299 | 867 | 649 | 877 | 1337 | 705 |
| cnd—*3.5 oz (100 g)* | 193 | 758 | 731 | 1320 | 1458 | 443 | 201 | 655 | 557 | 760 | 1051 | 671 |
| cnd, roasted—*3.5 oz (100 g)* | 233 | 916 | 883 | 1596 | 1764 | 535 | 243 | 791 | 673 | 920 | 1271 | 811 |
| roasted[c]—*3.5 oz (100 g)* | 238 | 882 | 870 | 1574 | 1682 | 524 | 298 | 857 | 651 | 860 | 1289 | 711 |
| unheated[c]—*3.5 oz (100 g)* | 211 | 781 | 770 | 1394 | 1489 | 464 | 264 | 759 | 576 | 762 | 1141 | 629 |
| ham patties[d] | | | | | | | | | | | | |
| grilled—*1 patty (60 g)* | 92 | 352 | 346 | 625 | 672 | 209 | 107 | 336 | 259 | 345 | 511 | 289 |
| unheated—*1 patty (65 g)* | 97 | 371 | 364 | 659 | 708 | 220 | 112 | 353 | 273 | 363 | 537 | 304 |
| leg | | | | | | | | | | | | |
| sep lean & fat, roasted—*3.5 oz (100 g)* | 326 | 1163 | 1187 | 2023 | 2451 | 607 | 320 | 998 | 873 | 1335 | 1771 | 1230 |
| sep lean, roasted—*3.5 oz (100 g)* | 381 | 1332 | 1368 | 2302 | 2791 | 698 | 367 | 1133 | 1010 | 1518 | 1966 | 1436 |

[a] Bacon is fully cooked as purchased.
[b] Yield from 1 lb raw bacon.

[c] Ham is fully cooked as purchased.
[d] Fully cooked as purchased.

| | TRY | THR | ISO | LEU | LYS | MET | CYS | PHE | TYR | VAL | ARG | HIS |
|---|---|---|---|---|---|---|---|---|---|---|---|---|
| loin | | | | | | | | | | | | |
| sep lean & fat, braised—*3.5 oz (100 g)* | 350 | 1257 | 1281 | 2191 | 2654 | 655 | 345 | 1082 | 941 | 1447 | 1934 | 1321 |
| sep lean & fat, broiled—*3.5 oz (100 g)* | 303 | 1090 | 1110 | 1901 | 2303 | 568 | 300 | 940 | 815 | 1256 | 1681 | 1144 |
| sep lean & fat, roasted—*3.5 oz (100 g)* | 304 | 1086 | 1108 | 1892 | 2292 | 566 | 299 | 934 | 814 | 1249 | 1665 | 1144 |
| sep lean, braised—*3.5 oz (100 g)* | 443 | 1551 | 1594 | 2681 | 3251 | 813 | 427 | 1319 | 1177 | 1768 | 2290 | 1673 |
| sep lean, broiled—*3.5 oz (100 g)* | 374 | 1309 | 1345 | 2263 | 2744 | 686 | 361 | 1114 | 993 | 1492 | 1933 | 1412 |
| sep lean, roasted—*3.5 oz (100 g)* | 362 | 1265 | 1300 | 2186 | 2651 | 663 | 349 | 1076 | 960 | 1442 | 1868 | 1364 |
| loin blade | | | | | | | | | | | | |
| sep lean & fat, braised—*3.5 oz (100 g)* | 305 | 1103 | 1121 | 1928 | 2335 | 574 | 303 | 954 | 823 | 1274 | 1718 | 1150 |
| sep lean & fat, broiled—*3.5 oz (100 g)* | 262 | 950 | 965 | 1662 | 2012 | 494 | 261 | 823 | 708 | 1098 | 1486 | 989 |
| sep lean & fat, pan fried—*3.5 oz (100 g)* | 232 | 856 | 864 | 1505 | 1821 | 443 | 235 | 747 | 623 | 995 | 1374 | 873 |
| sep lean & fat, roasted—*3.5 oz (100 g)* | 270 | 971 | 988 | 1696 | 2053 | 505 | 267 | 838 | 725 | 1120 | 1505 | 1016 |
| sep lean, braised—*3.5 oz (100 g)* | 399 | 1397 | 1435 | 2414 | 2927 | 732 | 385 | 1188 | 1060 | 1592 | 2062 | 1506 |
| sep lean, broiled—*3.5 oz (100 g)* | 335 | 1172 | 1204 | 2025 | 2455 | 614 | 323 | 997 | 889 | 1335 | 1730 | 1264 |
| sep lean, pan fried—*3.5 oz (100 g)* | 327 | 1144 | 1175 | 1977 | 2397 | 599 | 315 | 973 | 868 | 1303 | 1689 | 1233 |
| sep lean, roasted—*3.5 oz (100 g)* | 332 | 1161 | 1192 | 2006 | 2432 | 608 | 320 | 987 | 880 | 1323 | 1713 | 1252 |
| rump | | | | | | | | | | | | |
| sep lean & fat, roasted—*3.5 oz (100 g)* | 350 | 1242 | 1270 | 2155 | 2613 | 649 | 342 | 1063 | 936 | 1423 | 1873 | 1322 |
| sep lean, roasted—*3.5 oz (100 g)* | 392 | 1371 | 1408 | 2368 | 2872 | 718 | 378 | 1166 | 1040 | 1562 | 2023 | 1478 |
| sausage, fresh | | | | | | | | | | | | |
| ckd—*1 link (13 g)* | 20 | 101 | 93 | 171 | 194 | 62 | 26 | 85 | 74 | 103 | 151 | 74 |
| ckd—*1 patty (27 g)* | 42 | 210 | 194 | 356 | 403 | 129 | 53 | 177 | 153 | 213 | 313 | 153 |
| w/ beef, ckd—*1 link (13 g)* | 17 | 72 | 69 | 127 | 141 | 43 | 18 | 62 | 53 | 77 | 111 | 54 |
| shank | | | | | | | | | | | | |
| sep lean & fat, roasted—*3.5 oz (100 g)* | 314 | 1126 | 1148 | 1962 | 2376 | 587 | 310 | 969 | 844 | 1296 | 1727 | 1186 |
| sep lean, roasted—*3.5 oz (100 g)* | 379 | 1327 | 1363 | 2293 | 2780 | 695 | 366 | 1128 | 1006 | 1512 | 1959 | 1431 |
| shoulder | | | | | | | | | | | | |
| sep lean & fat, roasted—*3.5 oz (100 g)* | 284 | 1019 | 1038 | 1776 | 2152 | 530 | 280 | 878 | 763 | 1173 | 1568 | 1071 |
| sep lean, roasted—*3.5 oz (100 g)* | 341 | 1193 | 1226 | 2062 | 2501 | 624 | 329 | 1015 | 905 | 1360 | 1762 | 1287 |
| sirloin | | | | | | | | | | | | |
| sep lean & fat, braised—*3.5 oz (100 g)* | 362 | 1296 | 1322 | 2258 | 2735 | 675 | 356 | 1115 | 971 | 1491 | 1987 | 1365 |
| sep lean & fat, broiled—*3.5 oz (100 g)* | 311 | 1117 | 1138 | 1946 | 2357 | 582 | 307 | 961 | 836 | 1285 | 1717 | 1174 |
| sep lean & fat, roasted—*3.5 oz (100 g)* | 329 | 1166 | 1192 | 2026 | 2456 | 609 | 321 | 999 | 878 | 1338 | 1764 | 1239 |
| sep lean, braised—*3.5 oz (100 g)* | 450 | 1576 | 1619 | 2723 | 3302 | 825 | 434 | 1340 | 1195 | 1796 | 2326 | 1699 |
| sep lean, broiled—*3.5 oz (100 g)* | 380 | 1329 | 1365 | 2296 | 2784 | 696 | 366 | 1130 | 1008 | 1514 | 1962 | 1433 |
| sep lean, roasted—*3.5 oz (100 g)* | 370 | 1293 | 1328 | 2235 | 2710 | 677 | 356 | 1100 | 981 | 1474 | 1909 | 1394 |
| spareribs, sep lean & fat, braised—*3.5 oz (100 g)* | 391 | 1367 | 1404 | 2362 | 2864 | 716 | 377 | 1162 | 1037 | 1557 | 2018 | 1474 |
| tenderloin, sep lean, roasted—*3.5 oz (100 g)* | 387 | 1354 | 1391 | 2340 | 2837 | 709 | 373 | 1152 | 1027 | 1543 | 1999 | 1460 |
| top loin | | | | | | | | | | | | |
| sep lean & fat, braised—*3.5 oz (100 g)* | 355 | 1278 | 1301 | 2229 | 2700 | 666 | 351 | 1102 | 956 | 1473 | 1974 | 1340 |
| sep lean & fat, broiled—*3.5 oz (100 g)* | 303 | 1095 | 1114 | 1912 | 2315 | 570 | 300 | 945 | 818 | 1263 | 1698 | 1145 |
| sep lean & fat, pan fried—*3.5 oz (100 g)* | 269 | 985 | 997 | 1728 | 2091 | 511 | 270 | 856 | 730 | 1142 | 1561 | 1014 |
| sep lean & fat, roasted—*3.5 oz (100 g)* | 312 | 1121 | 1142 | 1953 | 2366 | 584 | 308 | 965 | 840 | 1290 | 1721 | 1179 |
| sep lean, braised—*3.5 oz (100 g)* | 463 | 1620 | 1664 | 2799 | 3394 | 849 | 446 | 1378 | 1229 | 1846 | 2391 | 1747 |
| sep lean, broiled—*3.5 oz (100 g)* | 387 | 1356 | 1393 | 2342 | 2840 | 710 | 373 | 1153 | 1028 | 1545 | 2001 | 1462 |
| sep lean, pan fried—*3.5 oz (100 g)* | 376 | 1315 | 1351 | 2273 | 2756 | 689 | 362 | 1119 | 998 | 1499 | 1942 | 1418 |
| sep lean, roasted—*3.5 oz (100 g)* | 379 | 1327 | 1363 | 2293 | 2781 | 695 | 366 | 1129 | 1007 | 1512 | 1959 | 1431 |

## 21.5. Variety Cuts

| | TRY | THR | ISO | LEU | LYS | MET | CYS | PHE | TYR | VAL | ARG | HIS |
|---|---|---|---|---|---|---|---|---|---|---|---|---|
| brains | | | | | | | | | | | | |
| beef, pan fried—*3.5 oz (100 g)* | 103 | 597 | 487 | 943 | 752 | 261 | 223 | 635 | 446 | 617 | 686 | 320 |
| beef, simmered—*3.5 oz (100 g)* | 90 | 526 | 429 | 831 | 662 | 230 | 197 | 560 | 393 | 544 | 604 | 282 |
| pork, braised—*3.5 oz (100 g)* | 155 | 567 | 561 | 1058 | 954 | 241 | | 618 | 509 | 691 | 635 | 326 |

| | TRY | THR | ISO | LEU | LYS | MET | CYS | PHE | TYR | VAL | ARG | HIS |
|---|---|---|---|---|---|---|---|---|---|---|---|---|
| chitterlings, pork, simmered—*3.5 oz (100 g)* | 61 | 451 | 420 | 809 | 656 | 194 | | 410 | 379 | 502 | 840 | 215 |
| ears, pork, simmered—*1 ear (111 g)* | 34 | 525 | 402 | 963 | 805 | 141 | | 561 | 351 | 702 | 1404 | 210 |
| feet, pork | | | | | | | | | | | | |
|   cured, pickled—*3.5 oz (100 g)* | 27 | 365 | 230 | 595 | 582 | 149 | | 392 | 216 | 338 | 1014 | 149 |
|   simmered—*3.5 oz (100 g)* | 38 | 518 | 326 | 845 | 826 | 211 | | 557 | 307 | 480 | 1440 | 211 |
| heart | | | | | | | | | | | | |
|   beef, simmered—*3.5 oz (100 g)* | 322 | 1359 | 1262 | 2547 | 2372 | 737 | 378 | 1303 | 1046 | 1502 | 1925 | 792 |
|   pork, braised—*1 heart (129 g)* | 351 | 1335 | 1467 | 2748 | 2518 | 779 | 546 | 1344 | 1042 | 1613 | 2046 | 774 |
| jowl, pork, raw—*3.5 oz (100 g)* | 21 | 210 | 168 | 446 | 528 | 95 | 56 | 239 | 104 | 305 | 659 | 72 |
| kidneys | | | | | | | | | | | | |
|   beef, simmered—*3.5 oz (100 g)* | 347 | 1231 | 1040 | 2043 | 1696 | 530 | 200 | 1223 | 958 | 1590 | 1496 | 665 |
|   pork, braised—*3.5 oz (100 g)* | 329 | 1053 | 1357 | 2280 | 1829 | 545 | 557 | 1199 | 914 | 1463 | 1561 | 610 |
| liver | | | | | | | | | | | | |
|   beef, braised—*3.5 oz (100 g)* | 351 | 1116 | 1116 | 2294 | 1693 | 616 | 374 | 1299 | 967 | 1506 | 1533 | 667 |
|   beef, pan fried—*3.5 oz (100 g)* | 385 | 1222 | 1222 | 2513 | 1855 | 675 | 410 | 1423 | 1060 | 1650 | 1680 | 731 |
|   pork, braised—*3.5 oz (100 g)* | 366 | 1107 | 1320 | 2319 | 2007 | 645 | 491 | 1274 | 887 | 1607 | 1603 | 708 |
| lungs | | | | | | | | | | | | |
|   beef, braised—*3.5 oz (100 g)* | 186 | 761 | 973 | 1498 | 1446 | 408 | 313 | 829 | 460 | 1005 | 1234 | 620 |
|   pork, braised—*3.5 oz (100 g)* | 146 | 584 | 664 | 1288 | 1211 | 268 | | 691 | | 988 | 863 | 420 |
| pancreas | | | | | | | | | | | | |
|   beef, braised—*3.5 oz (100 g)* | 351 | 1257 | 1370 | 2116 | 1999 | 490 | | 1127 | 1184 | 1453 | 1548 | 533 |
|   pork, braised—*3.5 oz (100 g)* | 625 | 1281 | 1496 | 2130 | 1965 | 470 | | 1222 | 1195 | 1537 | 1642 | 552 |
| spleen | | | | | | | | | | | | |
|   beef, braised—*3.5 oz (100 g)* | 261 | 988 | 968 | 2217 | 1815 | 462 | 727 | 1008 | 715 | 1510 | 1454 | 900 |
|   pork, braised—*3.5 oz (100 g)* | 289 | 1128 | 1259 | 2306 | 2107 | 523 | | 1205 | 790 | 1534 | 1539 | 672 |
| stomach, pork, raw—*3.5 oz (100 g)* | 98 | 510 | 560 | 990 | 874 | 288 | | 525 | 412 | 692 | 924 | 246 |
| tail, pork, simmered—*3.5 oz (100 g)* | 102 | 595 | 391 | 952 | 1020 | 306 | | 510 | 1173 | 510 | 1173 | 306 |
| thymus, beef, braised—*3.5 oz (100 g)* | 168 | 790 | 745 | 1458 | 1818 | 304 | | 626 | | 1947 | 1440 | 385 |
| tongue | | | | | | | | | | | | |
|   beef, simmered—*3.5 oz (100 g)* | 170 | 962 | 952 | 1652 | 1705 | 467 | 290 | 913 | 715 | 1058 | 1408 | 573 |
|   pork, braised—*3.5 oz (100 g)* | 278 | 1018 | 1099 | 1932 | 1970 | 540 | | 999 | | 1253 | 1488 | 605 |
| tripe, beef, raw—*3.5 oz (100 g)* | 114 | 503 | 589 | 948 | 1044 | 315 | 168 | 471 | 396 | 613 | 995 | 363 |
| **21.6. Other Meats** | | | | | | | | | | | | |
| eel | | | | | | | | | | | | |
|   raw—*3 oz (85 g)* | 176 | 688 | 723 | 1274 | 1440 | 464 | 168 | 612 | 530 | 808 | 938 | 462 |
|   ckd by dry heat—*3 oz (85 g)* | 225 | 881 | 927 | 1634 | 1845 | 595 | 215 | 785 | 678 | 1035 | 1203 | 592 |
| octopus, raw—*3 oz (85 g)* | 142 | 546 | 552 | 892 | 947 | 286 | 167 | 454 | 405 | 553 | 925 | 243 |
| shark | | | | | | | | | | | | |
|   raw—*3 oz (85 g)* | 200 | 782 | 822 | 1449 | 1637 | 528 | 191 | 696 | 602 | 919 | 1067 | 525 |
|   batter-dipped & fried[a]—*3 oz (85 g)* | 180 | 717 | 737 | 1288 | 1389 | 460 | 180 | 638 | 538 | 820 | 930 | 457 |
| squid | | | | | | | | | | | | |
|   raw—*3 oz (85 g)* | 148 | 570 | 576 | 932 | 989 | 298 | 173 | 474 | 423 | 578 | 966 | 254 |
|   fried[b]—*3 oz (85 g)* | 172 | 649 | 663 | 1077 | 1114 | 343 | 206 | 558 | 490 | 668 | 1097 | 296 |
| **22. Meats, Luncheon** | | | | | | | | | | | | |
| beef | | | | | | | | | | | | |
|   chopped, smoked—*1 oz (28 g)* | 47 | 240 | 234 | 428 | 467 | 138 | 68 | 214 | 173 | 263 | 386 | 166 |
|   jellied lunch meat—*1 oz (28 g)* | 39 | 210 | 202 | 372 | 414 | 119 | 56 | 191 | 145 | 234 | 373 | 141 |
|   summer sausage—*1 slice (23 g)* | 33 | 137 | 157 | 267 | 278 | 84 | 46 | 131 | 118 | 160 | 224 | 115 |
|   thin sliced lunch meat—*5 slices (21 g)* | 48 | 247 | 242 | 441 | 482 | 143 | 70 | 221 | 179 | 271 | 399 | 171 |
| berliner (pork & beef)—*1 slice (23 g)* | 40 | 150 | 157 | 276 | 303 | 90 | 51 | 138 | 110 | 162 | 239 | 135 |
| bockwurst (pork, veal, milk, etc.), raw—*1 link (65 g)* | 88 | 358 | 378 | 610 | 681 | 208 | 96 | 320 | 278 | 396 | 528 | 259 |
| bologna | | | | | | | | | | | | |
|   beef—*1 slice (23 g)* | 26 | 106 | 122 | 207 | 216 | 65 | 36 | 101 | 92 | 124 | 174 | 90 |
|   beef & pork—*1 slice (23 g)* | 24 | 118 | 117 | 207 | 203 | 64 | 31 | 106 | 83 | 143 | 161 | 73 |
|   pork—*1 slice (23 g)* | 34 | 147 | 152 | 269 | 277 | 95 | 39 | 135 | 111 | 170 | 231 | 111 |
| bratwurst, pork, ckd—*1 link (85 g)* | 96 | 473 | 437 | 802 | 910 | 291 | 121 | 400 | 345 | 481 | 706 | 345 |
| braunschweiger (pork liver sausage)—*1 slice (18 g)* | 26 | 96 | 87 | 186 | 164 | 56 | 45 | 100 | 77 | 111 | 138 | 58 |

[a] Prepared w/ flour, oil, egg, milk, baking powder & salt.  [b] Dipped in flour & salt before frying.

| | TRY | THR | ISO | LEU | LYS | MET | CYS | PHE | TYR | VAL | ARG | HIS |
|---|---|---|---|---|---|---|---|---|---|---|---|---|
| brotwurst (pork & beef w/ nfdm)—*1 link (70 g)* | 92 | 419 | 424 | 756 | 797 | 258 | 114 | 379 | 310 | 473 | 662 | 305 |
| chorizo (pork & beef)—*1 link (60 g)* | 167 | 884 | 1324 | 1025 | 1448 | 282 | | 689 | | 548 | 1016 | 433 |
| corned beef loaf, jellied—*1 oz slice (28 g)* | 47 | 253 | 244 | 449 | 499 | 143 | 67 | 230 | 175 | 282 | 450 | 170 |
| frankfurter | | | | | | | | | | | | |
|   beef—*1 frank (8 per 1 lb pkg) (57 g)* | 63 | 259 | 296 | 504 | 526 | 159 | 88 | 247 | 224 | 302 | 424 | 218 |
|   beef—*1 frank (10 per 1 lb pkg) (45 g)* | 50 | 204 | 234 | 398 | 415 | 126 | 69 | 195 | 177 | 238 | 334 | 172 |
|   beef & pork—*1 frank (45 g)* | 37 | 183 | 218 | 369 | 407 | 103 | 58 | 162 | 141 | 212 | 382 | 158 |
| ham, cured | | | | | | | | | | | | |
|   chopped, cnd—*1 slice (21 g)* | 38 | 151 | 145 | 262 | 290 | 88 | 40 | 131 | 111 | 151 | 209 | 134 |
|   chopped, packaged—*1 slice (21 g)* | 44 | 160 | 162 | 289 | 322 | 95 | 54 | 145 | 112 | 168 | 252 | 146 |
|   minced—*1 slice (21 g)* | 33 | 154 | 147 | 264 | 286 | 96 | 40 | 135 | 113 | 157 | 215 | 127 |
|   sliced, lean (5% fat)—*1 slice (28 g)* | 67 | 244 | 247 | 441 | 490 | 145 | 82 | 221 | 170 | 256 | 385 | 223 |
|   sliced, reg (11% fat)—*1 slice (28 g)* | 61 | 221 | 225 | 400 | 445 | 132 | 75 | 201 | 155 | 233 | 350 | 202 |
| ham & cheese loaf/roll—*1 slice (28 g)* | 59 | 204 | 214 | 384 | 428 | 124 | 67 | 196 | 159 | 227 | 317 | 192 |
| headcheese (pork)—*1 slice (28 g)* | 24 | 126 | 154 | 286 | 274 | 75 | 63 | 172 | 132 | 187 | 325 | 84 |
| honey loaf (pork & beef)—*1 slice (28 g)* | 52 | 223 | 206 | 389 | 420 | 135 | 44 | 190 | 164 | 220 | 305 | 173 |
| italian sausage, pork, ckd—*1 link (67 g)* | 108 | 531 | 490 | 900 | 1020 | 326 | 135 | 449 | 387 | 539 | 793 | 387 |
| kielbasa/kolbassy (pork & beef w/ nfdm)—*1 slice (26 g)* | 36 | 112 | 166 | 227 | 263 | 72 | 59 | 130 | 127 | 166 | 245 | 82 |
| knackwurst/knockwurst (pork & beef)—*1 slice (68 g)* | 73 | 326 | 317 | 558 | 634 | 195 | 100 | 277 | 245 | 350 | 482 | 245 |
| lebanon bologna (beef)—*1 slice (23 g)* | 36 | 186 | 182 | 332 | 363 | 107 | 53 | 167 | 135 | 204 | 300 | 129 |
| livercheese (pork liver)—*1 slice (38 g)* | 78 | 247 | 240 | 506 | 448 | 130 | 125 | 272 | 177 | 306 | 318 | 149 |
| liver pate, unspecified, cnd—*1 oz (28 g)* | 45 | 161 | 157 | 298 | 238 | 81 | 48 | 165 | 129 | 218 | 254 | 84 |
| liver sausage/liverwurst (pork)—*1 slice (18 g)* | 28 | 122 | 119 | 207 | 210 | 52 | 27 | 112 | 66 | 156 | 147 | 81 |
| luxury loaf (pork)—*1 slice (28 g)* | 61 | 249 | 231 | 430 | 468 | 133 | 43 | 204 | 183 | 253 | 332 | 186 |
| meat spread, ham salad—*1 oz (28 g)* | 25 | 116 | 114 | 206 | 219 | 65 | 14 | 100 | 79 | 127 | 168 | 99 |
| mortadella (beef & pork)—*1 slice (15 g)* | 23 | 95 | 106 | 182 | 189 | 59 | 31 | 90 | 80 | 110 | 154 | 78 |
| new england brand sausage (pork & beef)—*1 slice (23 g)* | 44 | 174 | 175 | 313 | 348 | 103 | 57 | 157 | 123 | 185 | 276 | 150 |
| old fashioned loaf (pork & beef)—*1 slice (28 g)* | 42 | 175 | 158 | 305 | 305 | 91 | 30 | 145 | 126 | 175 | 227 | 117 |
| olive loaf (pork)—*1 slice (28 g)* | 29 | 134 | 119 | 246 | 229 | 85 | 41 | 119 | 109 | 144 | 165 | 83 |
| pastrami, beef—*1 oz (28 g)* | 45 | 185 | 211 | 359 | 375 | 113 | 63 | 176 | 160 | 215 | 302 | 156 |
| peppered loaf (pork & beef)—*1 slice (28 g)* | 56 | 216 | 222 | 393 | 428 | 127 | 69 | 197 | 156 | 234 | 332 | 184 |
| pepperoni (pork & beef)—*1 slice (6 g)* | 11 | 47 | 50 | 87 | 90 | 29 | 14 | 43 | 37 | 54 | 74 | 37 |
| pickle & pimento loaf (pork)—*1 slice (28 g)* | 33 | 148 | 139 | 269 | 254 | 72 | 33 | 124 | 111 | 158 | 189 | 97 |
| picnic loaf (pork & beef)—*1 slice (28 g)* | 41 | 186 | 165 | 325 | 338 | 107 | 46 | 152 | 130 | 182 | 252 | 124 |
| polish sausage (pork)—*1 oz (28 g)* | 39 | 168 | 173 | 305 | 315 | 107 | 45 | 153 | 126 | 192 | 262 | 126 |
| pork & beef lunch meat—*1 slice (28 g)* | 38 | 154 | 182 | 297 | 336 | 82 | 65 | 145 | 142 | 202 | 262 | 115 |
| pork & beef luncheon sausage—*1 slice (23 g)* | 37 | 153 | 181 | 294 | 333 | 81 | 65 | 143 | 141 | 200 | 260 | 114 |
| pork lunch meat, cnd—*1 slice (21 g)* | 26 | 104 | 121 | 203 | 198 | 71 | 45 | 104 | 81 | 139 | 184 | 76 |
| salami | | | | | | | | | | | | |
|   beerwurst, beef—*1 slice (23 g)* | 26 | 108 | 123 | 210 | 219 | 66 | 37 | 103 | 93 | 126 | 176 | 91 |
|   beerwurst, pork—*1 slice (23 g)* | 26 | 130 | 112 | 217 | 237 | 82 | 25 | 104 | 93 | 117 | 186 | 96 |
|   ckd, beef—*1 slice (23 g)* | 32 | 131 | 150 | 254 | 265 | 80 | 44 | 124 | 113 | 152 | 214 | 110 |
|   ckd, beef & pork—*1 slice (23 g)* | 26 | 120 | 155 | 214 | 255 | 69 | 45 | 111 | 127 | 154 | 197 | 83 |
|   dry/hard pork—*1 slice (10 g)* | 25 | 101 | 108 | 163 | 188 | 47 | 29 | 94 | 69 | 112 | 137 | 61 |
|   dry/hard pork & beef—*1 slice (10 g)* | 21 | 96 | 97 | 173 | 182 | 59 | 26 | 87 | 71 | 108 | 152 | 70 |
| smoked link sausage | | | | | | | | | | | | |
|   pork—*1 link (68 g)* | 147 | 632 | 647 | 1151 | 1187 | 405 | 169 | 577 | 475 | 726 | 989 | 475 |
|   pork & beef—*1 link (68 g)* | 73 | 316 | 330 | 551 | 614 | 248 | 71 | 275 | 262 | 316 | 520 | 269 |
|   pork & beef w/ american cheese—*1 link (43 g)* | 64 | 233 | 266 | 472 | 498 | 154 | 65 | 243 | 222 | 298 | 360 | 203 |
|   pork & beef w/ flour & nfdm—*1 link (68 g)* | 95 | 389 | 422 | 732 | 734 | 244 | 110 | 367 | 312 | 460 | 591 | 295 |
|   pork & beef w/ nfdm—*1 link (68 g)* | 92 | 375 | 411 | 710 | 709 | 234 | 103 | 354 | 307 | 119 | 553 | 282 |

| | TRY | THR | ISO | LEU | LYS | MET | CYS | PHE | TYR | VAL | ARG | HIS |
|---|---|---|---|---|---|---|---|---|---|---|---|---|
| thuringer (cervelat/summer sausage) beef—*1 slice (23 g)* | 35 | 158 | 177 | 241 | 318 | 81 | 45 | 133 | 125 | 185 | 228 | 108 |
| turkey breast meat—*1 slice (21 g)* | 54 | 210 | 246 | 377 | 445 | 137 | 49 | 188 | 187 | 251 | 330 | 147 |
| turkey ham (cured thigh meat)—*2 slices (57 g)* | 122 | 477 | 558 | 855 | 1012 | 311 | 112 | 426 | 424 | 570 | 749 | 335 |
| turkey pastrami—*2 slices (57 g)* | 115 | 452 | 521 | 806 | 942 | 290 | 117 | 405 | 393 | 540 | 731 | 311 |
| vienna sausage, cnd (beef & pork)— *1 sausage (16 g)* | 17 | 57 | 89 | 128 | 127 | 42 | 28 | 68 | 55 | 92 | 113 | 44 |

### 23. Milk, Yogurt, Milk Beverages & Milk Beverage Mixes
#### 23.1. Cow Milk

| | TRY | THR | ISO | LEU | LYS | MET | CYS | PHE | TYR | VAL | ARG | HIS |
|---|---|---|---|---|---|---|---|---|---|---|---|---|
| buttermilk, cultured—*8 fl oz (245 g)* | 88 | 386 | 500 | 807 | 679 | 198 | 76 | 427 | 339 | 596 | 309 | 233 |
| buttermilk, dry—*1 T (7 g)* | 31 | 101 | 135 | 218 | 177 | 56 | 21 | 108 | 108 | 149 | 81 | 60 |
| condensed, sweetened, cnd—*1 fl oz (38 g)* | 43 | 136 | 186 | 296 | 240 | 76 | 28 | 146 | 146 | 202 | 109 | 82 |
| evaporated, lowfat, cnd, Carnation— *4 fl oz (127 g)* | 117 | 323 | 447 | 687 | 644 | 201 | 74 | 402 | 421 | 481 | | 185 |
| evaporated, skim, cnd—*1 fl oz (32 g)* | 34 | 109 | 146 | 236 | 191 | 60 | 22 | 116 | 116 | 161 | 87 | 65 |
| evaporated, whole, cnd—*1 fl oz (32 g)* | 30 | 97 | 130 | 210 | 170 | 54 | 20 | 104 | 104 | 144 | 78 | 58 |
| evaporated, whole, cnd—*4 fl oz (126 g)* | 121 | 387 | 519 | 841 | 681 | 215 | 79 | 414 | 414 | 574 | 311 | 233 |
| lowfat 1% fat—*8 fl oz (244 g)* | 113 | 362 | 486 | 786 | 637 | 201 | 74 | 388 | 388 | 537 | 291 | 218 |
| lowfat 1% fat, pro fortified—*8 fl oz (246 g)* | 136 | 436 | 585 | 947 | 767 | 242 | 89 | 467 | 467 | 647 | 350 | 262 |
| lowfat 1% fat w/ nfdm—*8 fl oz (245 g)* | 120 | 385 | 516 | 835 | 676 | 214 | 79 | 412 | 412 | 571 | 309 | 231 |
| lowfat 2% fat—*8 fl oz (244 g)* | 115 | 367 | 492 | 796 | 644 | 204 | 75 | 392 | 392 | 544 | 294 | 220 |
| lowfat 2% fat, pro fortified—*8 fl oz (246 g)* | 137 | 439 | 588 | 952 | 771 | 244 | 90 | 469 | 469 | 650 | 352 | 263 |
| lowfat 2% fat w/ nfdm—*8 fl oz (245 g)* | 120 | 385 | 516 | 835 | 676 | 214 | 79 | 412 | 412 | 571 | 309 | 231 |
| skim—*8 fl oz (245 g)* | 118 | 377 | 505 | 818 | 663 | 210 | 77 | 403 | 403 | 559 | 302 | 227 |
| skim, dry—*¼ cup (30 g)* | 153 | 490 | 656 | 1063 | 860 | 272 | 100 | 524 | 524 | 726 | 393 | 294 |
| skim, dry, Ca reduced—*1 oz (28 g)* | 142 | 454 | 609 | 986 | 798 | 252 | 93 | 486 | 486 | 674 | 364 | 273 |
| skim, dry, inst—*1⅓ cups (3.2 oz envelope)[a] (91 g)* | 451 | 1442 | 1932 | 3129 | 2533 | 801 | 295 | 1542 | 1542 | 2138 | 1156 | 866 |
| skim pro fortified—*8 fl oz (246 g)* | 137 | 440 | 589 | 954 | 773 | 244 | 93 | 470 | 470 | 652 | 353 | 264 |
| skim w/ nfdm—*8 fl oz (245 g)* | 123 | 395 | 529 | 857 | 694 | 219 | 81 | 422 | 422 | 585 | 317 | 237 |
| whole, 3.3% fat—*8 fl oz (244 g)* | 113 | 362 | 486 | 786 | 637 | 201 | 74 | 388 | 388 | 537 | 291 | 218 |
| whole, 3.5% fat—*8 fl oz (244 g)* | 119 | 391 | 544 | 842 | 663 | 204 | | 408 | | 586 | | 176 |
| whole, 3.7% fat—*8 fl oz (244 g)* | 113 | 361 | 484 | 784 | 635 | 201 | 74 | 386 | 386 | 536 | 290 | 217 |
| whole, dry—*¼ cup (32 g)* | 119 | 380 | 510 | 825 | 668 | 211 | 78 | 407 | 407 | 564 | 305 | 228 |
| whole, low Na—*8 fl oz (244 g)* | 107 | 341 | 458 | 741 | 600 | 190 | 70 | 365 | 365 | 506 | 274 | 205 |

#### 23.2. Other Milk

| | TRY | THR | ISO | LEU | LYS | MET | CYS | PHE | TYR | VAL | ARG | HIS |
|---|---|---|---|---|---|---|---|---|---|---|---|---|
| filled[b,c]—*8 fl oz (244 g)* | 115 | 367 | 492 | 796 | 644 | 204 | 75 | 392 | 392 | 544 | 294 | 220 |
| filled[c,d]—*8 fl oz (244 g)* | 115 | 367 | 492 | 796 | 644 | 204 | 75 | 392 | 392 | 544 | 294 | 220 |
| goat—*8 fl oz (244 g)* | 106 | 398 | 505 | 765 | 708 | 196 | 113 | 377 | 437 | 585 | 291 | 218 |
| human—*1 fl oz (31 g)* | 5 | 14 | 17 | 29 | 21 | 6 | 6 | 14 | 16 | 19 | 13 | 7 |
| imitation[b,e]—*8 fl oz (244 g)* | 59 | 181 | 262 | 422 | 344 | 130 | 18 | 229 | 244 | 305 | 169 | 126 |
| imitation[d,e]—*8 fl oz (244 g)* | 59 | 181 | 262 | 422 | 344 | 130 | 18 | 229 | 244 | 305 | 169 | 126 |
| indian buffalo—*8 fl oz (244 g)* | 131 | 445 | 496 | 892 | 683 | 237 | 116 | 394 | 447 | 534 | 278 | 189 |
| sheep—*8 fl oz (245 g)* | 207 | 657 | 829 | 1438 | 1256 | 379 | 85 | 696 | 689 | 1098 | 485 | 409 |
| soy—*1 cup (240 g)* | 103 | 271 | 346 | 578 | 430 | 96 | 113 | 362 | 269 | 338 | 514 | 170 |

#### 23.3. Yogurt (From Cow Milk)
lowfat w/ nfdm

| | TRY | THR | ISO | LEU | LYS | MET | CYS | PHE | TYR | VAL | ARG | HIS |
|---|---|---|---|---|---|---|---|---|---|---|---|---|
| —*8 fl oz (227 g)* | 67 | 489 | 650 | 1201 | 1068 | 351 | | 650 | 601 | 986 | 359 | 295 |
| coffee/van flavor—*8 fl oz (227 g)* | 63 | 460 | 610 | 1128 | 1003 | 330 | | 610 | 565 | 926 | 337 | 277 |
| fruit flavor—*8 fl oz (227 g)* | 51 | 371 | 493 | 911 | 810 | 266 | | 493 | 456 | 748 | 272 | 224 |

[a] Reconstitutes to 1 qt fluid skim milk.
[b] Contains blend of hydrogenated soybean, cottonseed &/or safflower oils.
[c] Filled milk contains fats or oils other than milk fat; contains milk solids (milk, cream, or skim milk).
[d] Contains lauric acid oils which include modified coconut oil, hydrogenated coconut oil &/or palm kernel oil.
[e] Imitation milk contains fats or oils other than milk fat; contains food solids, excluding milk solids.

| | TRY | THR | ISO | LEU | LYS | MET | CYS | PHE | TYR | VAL | ARG | HIS |
|---|---|---|---|---|---|---|---|---|---|---|---|---|
| skim w/ nfdm—*8 fl oz (227 g)* | 73 | 534 | 709 | 1311 | 1166 | 383 | | 709 | 656 | 1076 | 391 | 322 |
| whole—*8 fl oz (227 g)* | 44 | 323 | 430 | 794 | 706 | 232 | | 430 | 398 | 652 | 237 | 195 |

**23.4. Milk Beverages**

| | TRY | THR | ISO | LEU | LYS | MET | CYS | PHE | TYR | VAL | ARG | HIS |
|---|---|---|---|---|---|---|---|---|---|---|---|---|
| carob flavor mix in whole milk—*3 t powder in 8 fl oz milk (256 g)* | 113 | 364 | 486 | 786 | 637 | 202 | 74 | 389 | 389 | 538 | 289 | 218 |
| choc flavor mix in whole milk—*2-3 hp t powder in 8 fl oz milk (266 g)* | 122 | 388 | 511 | 825 | 668 | 207 | 80 | 418 | 412 | 575 | 325 | 229 |
| choc malted milk flavor mix in whole milk—*3 hp t powder in 8 fl oz milk (265 g)* | 125 | 395 | 519 | 848 | 670 | 215 | 93 | 427 | 419 | 578 | 334 | 239 |
| w/ added nutrients in whole milk—*4-5 hp t powder in 8 fl oz milk (265 g)* | 111 | 363 | 485 | 784 | 636 | 201 | 74 | 387 | 387 | 538 | 292 | 217 |
| choc milk | | | | | | | | | | | | |
| 1% fat milk—*8 fl oz (250 g)* | 114 | 366 | 490 | 793 | 642 | 203 | 75 | 391 | 391 | 542 | 293 | 220 |
| 2% fat milk—*8 fl oz (250 g)* | 113 | 362 | 486 | 786 | 636 | 201 | 74 | 387 | 387 | 537 | 291 | 218 |
| whole milk—*8 fl oz (250 g)* | 112 | 358 | 479 | 776 | 629 | 199 | 73 | 383 | 383 | 530 | 287 | 215 |
| whole milk w/ malt—*8 fl oz (265 g)* | 38 | 124 | 162 | 265 | 209 | 68 | 28 | 136 | 131 | 187 | | 75 |
| choc syrup in whole milk—*2 T syrup in 8 fl oz milk (282 g)* | 121 | 389 | 510 | 823 | 668 | 209 | 82 | 417 | 412 | 572 | 324 | 228 |
| choc syrup w/ added nutrients in whole milk—*1 T syrup in 8 fl oz milk (263 g)* | 116 | 376 | 497 | 805 | 652 | 205 | 76 | 402 | 400 | 555 | 308 | 224 |
| cocoa/hot chocolate | | | | | | | | | | | | |
| prep w/ whole milk—*8 fl oz (250 g)* | 128 | 411 | 551 | 891 | 722 | 228 | 84 | 439 | 439 | 609 | 329 | 247 |
| prep w/ milk, sugar & high-fat plain cocoa—*8 fl oz (250 g)* | 128 | 411 | 551 | 891 | 722 | 228 | 84 | 439 | 439 | 609 | 329 | 247 |
| prep w/ water from mix—*¾ hp t powder in 6 fl oz water (206 g)* | 43 | 130 | 163 | 262 | 212 | 62 | 29 | 142 | 134 | 192 | 119 | 72 |
| prep w/ water from mix w/ added nutrients—*1 pkt in 6 fl oz water (209 g)* | 27 | 79 | 100 | 161 | 132 | 38 | 19 | 88 | 84 | 117 | 73 | 46 |
| eggnog, nonalcoholic—*8 fl oz (254 g)* | 137 | 444 | 583 | 937 | 758 | 222 | 97 | 463 | 462 | 643 | 378 | 240 |
| mix in whole milk—*2 hp t in 8 fl oz milk (272 g)* | 114 | 370 | 492 | 794 | 645 | 204 | 76 | 392 | 392 | 544 | 299 | 220 |
| mix in whole milk, Delmark—*1.23 oz mix in 8 fl oz milk (257 g)* | 210 | 700 | 970 | 1480 | 1160 | 390 | 150 | 750 | 760 | 1050 | 580 | 390 |
| instant breakfast in whole milk—*1 pkt in 8 fl oz milk*[a] *(265 g)* | 196 | 703 | 927 | 1490 | 1210 | 387 | 142 | 746 | 757 | 1030 | | 424 |
| choc, Delmark—*1.23 oz mix in 8 fl oz milk (279 g)* | 260 | 850 | 1150 | 1790 | 1400 | 440 | 190 | 920 | 930 | 1260 | 710 | 480 |
| van/strawberry, Delmark—*1.23 oz mix in 8 fl oz milk (279 g)* | 380 | 1250 | 1730 | 2670 | 2110 | 660 | 240 | 1310 | 1380 | 1870 | 990 | 710 |
| malted milk—*8 fl oz (265 g)* | 143 | 433 | 567 | 944 | 712 | 239 | 129 | 479 | 464 | 630 | | 272 |
| malted milk flavor mix in whole milk—*3 hp t in 8 fl oz milk (265 g)* | 138 | 427 | 559 | 925 | 702 | 236 | 122 | 469 | 456 | 620 | 382 | 265 |
| milk shake, thick | | | | | | | | | | | | |
| choc—*1 avg (300 g)* | 129 | 413 | 554 | 896 | 726 | 229 | 85 | 442 | 442 | 612 | 331 | 248 |
| van—*1 avg (313 g)* | 170 | 545 | 731 | 1184 | 958 | 303 | 112 | 583 | 583 | 809 | 437 | 328 |
| strawberry flavored mix in whole milk—*2-3 hp t powder in 8 fl oz milk (266 g)* | 112 | 364 | 487 | 787 | 638 | 202 | 74 | 388 | 388 | 537 | 290 | 218 |

**23.5. Milk Beverage Mixes**

| | TRY | THR | ISO | LEU | LYS | MET | CYS | PHE | TYR | VAL | ARG | HIS |
|---|---|---|---|---|---|---|---|---|---|---|---|---|
| choc flavor mix, powder—*2-3 hp t (22 g)* | 10 | 24 | 23 | 37 | 31 | 5 | 8 | 30 | 23 | 36 | 34 | 10 |
| choc malted milk flavor mix, powder—*¾ oz (3 hp t) (21 g)* | 12 | 30 | 34 | 61 | 34 | 13 | 20 | 39 | 32 | 41 | 43 | 21 |
| choc syrup—*2 T (1 fl oz) (38 g)* | 10 | 24 | 24 | 37 | 31 | 6 | 8 | 30 | 24 | 36 | 34 | 11 |
| choc syrup w/ added nutrients—*1 T (19 g)* | 5 | 11 | 11 | 18 | 15 | 3 | 4 | 14 | 11 | 17 | 16 | 5 |
| cocoa mix, powder—*1 oz pkt (3-4 hp t) (28 g)* | 43 | 129 | 162 | 262 | 213 | 62 | 29 | 142 | 135 | 191 | 119 | 73 |

[a] Averages for various flavors of instant breakfast.

| | TRY | THR | ISO | LEU | LYS | MET | CYS | PHE | TYR | VAL | ARG | HIS |
|---|---|---|---|---|---|---|---|---|---|---|---|---|
| **Carnation** | | | | | | | | | | | | |
| choc & marshmallow—*1 oz (28 g)* | 32 | 97 | 110 | 175 | 140 | 43 | 26 | 81 | 77 | 117 | | 42 |
| milk choc—*1 oz (28 g)* | 31 | 100 | 138 | 212 | 168 | 53 | 19 | 105 | 108 | 149 | | 57 |
| rich choc—*1 oz (28 g)* | 32 | 98 | 110 | 174 | 140 | 43 | 26 | 81 | 77 | 117 | | 43 |
| rich choc, 70 cal—*1 pkt (3 hp t) (21 g)* | 40 | 130 | 170 | 260 | 210 | 70 | 20 | 130 | 140 | 180 | | 70 |
| sugar-free—*1 pkt (4 hp t) (15 g)* | 59 | 191 | 252 | 384 | 307 | 97 | 39 | 236 | 196 | 264 | | 104 |
| w/ added nutrients—*1.1 oz pkt (31 g)* | 26 | 79 | 100 | 161 | 131 | 38 | 18 | 87 | 83 | 117 | 73 | 45 |
| **eggnog mix, powder, nonalcoholic—***2 hp t (28 g)* | 2 | 6 | 7 | 10 | 8 | 3 | 2 | 5 | 5 | 7 | 8 | 3 |
| **instant breakfast** | | | | | | | | | | | | |
| choc, Carnation—*1.25 oz pkt (35 g)* | 80 | 331 | 418 | 673 | 545 | 173 | 70 | 347 | 351 | 471 | | 194 |
| choc malt, Carnation—*1.24 oz pkt (35 g)* | 86 | 289 | 381 | 612 | 469 | 160 | 71 | 337 | 331 | 424 | | 182 |
| coffee, Carnation—*1.26 oz pkt (36 g)* | 83 | 367 | 468 | 752 | 621 | 196 | 70 | 369 | 385 | 522 | | 218 |
| eggnog, Carnation—*1.20 oz pkt (34 g)* | 85 | 330 | 447 | 705 | 573 | 176 | 55 | 356 | 578 | 498 | | 206 |
| strawberry, Carnation—*1.25 oz pkt (35 g)* | 83 | 367 | 468 | 752 | 621 | 196 | 70 | 369 | 385 | 522 | | 218 |
| van, Carnation—*1.23 oz pkt (35 g)* | 83 | 367 | 467 | 751 | 621 | 195 | 70 | 369 | 385 | 521 | | 218 |
| **instant breakfast, no sugar added, Carnation** | | | | | | | | | | | | |
| choc—*.69 oz pkt (20 g)* | 102 | 320 | 423 | 659 | 503 | 205 | 102 | 410 | 302 | 491 | | 167 |
| choc malted—*.71 oz pkt (20 g)* | 96 | 288 | 394 | 611 | 447 | 203 | 102 | 399 | 312 | 462 | | 171 |
| strawberry—*.68 oz pkt (19 g)* | 111 | 346 | 470 | 730 | 571 | 224 | 99 | 434 | 320 | 534 | | 180 |
| van—*.67 oz pkt (19 g)* | 111 | 346 | 470 | 730 | 571 | 224 | 99 | 434 | 320 | 534 | | 180 |
| **malted milk flavor mix, powder—***¾ oz (3 hp t) (21 g)* | 26 | 63 | 73 | 140 | 67 | 34 | 49 | 82 | 68 | 83 | 90 | 49 |
| **24. Nuts, Nut Products & Seeds** | | | | | | | | | | | | |
| acorn flour, full-fat—*1 oz (28 g)* | 26 | 82 | 99 | 169 | 133 | 36 | 38 | 93 | 64 | 120 | 164 | 59 |
| **acorns** | | | | | | | | | | | | |
| raw—*1 oz (28 g)* | 21 | 67 | 81 | 139 | 109 | 29 | 31 | 76 | 53 | 98 | 134 | 48 |
| dried—*1 oz (28 g)* | 28 | 89 | 107 | 183 | 143 | 39 | 41 | 101 | 70 | 129 | 177 | 64 |
| almond butter—*1 T (16 g)* | 43 | 89 | 105 | 188 | 81 | 28 | 43 | 135 | 85 | 124 | 302 | 68 |
| almond butter w/ honey & cinn—*1 T (16 g)* | 45 | 94 | 110 | 197 | 85 | 29 | 45 | 141 | 89 | 131 | 317 | 71 |
| almond meal, partially defatted—*1 oz (28 g)* | 201 | 416 | 487 | 873 | 375 | 128 | 201 | 626 | 396 | 578 | 1403 | 314 |
| almond paste—*1 oz (28 g)* | 60 | 125 | 146 | 262 | 112 | 38 | 60 | 188 | 119 | 174 | 421 | 94 |
| **almonds** | | | | | | | | | | | | |
| blanched, Blue Diamond—*1 oz (28 g)* | 48 | 184 | 223 | 416 | 192 | 45 | 133 | 320 | 164 | 266 | 708 | 144 |
| blanched, slivered, Blue Diamond—*1 oz (28 g)* | 51 | 204 | 238 | 447 | 229 | 34 | 133 | 374 | 192 | 283 | 822 | 164 |
| chopped, Blue Diamond—*1 oz (28 g)* | 48 | 187 | 227 | 419 | 192 | 39 | 138 | 326 | 167 | 266 | 722 | 144 |
| dried—*1 oz (24 nuts) (28 g)* | 102 | 210 | 246 | 441 | 189 | 64 | 102 | 316 | 200 | 282 | 709 | 158 |
| dry roasted—*1 oz (28 g)* | 83 | 172 | 201 | 361 | 155 | 53 | 83 | 259 | 164 | 239 | 580 | 130 |
| oil roasted—*1 oz (22 nuts) (28 g)* | 104 | 215 | 252 | 450 | 193 | 66 | 104 | 323 | 204 | 298 | 724 | 162 |
| sliced, Blue Diamond—*1 oz (28 g)* | 48 | 187 | 227 | 419 | 192 | 39 | 138 | 326 | 167 | 266 | 722 | 144 |
| toasted—*1 oz (28 g)* | 104 | 215 | 251 | 450 | 193 | 66 | 104 | 323 | 204 | 298 | 724 | 162 |
| whole, Blue Diamond—*1 oz (28 g)* | 48 | 184 | 227 | 416 | 192 | 36 | 124 | 326 | 167 | 269 | 720 | 144 |
| brazilnuts, dried—*1 oz (8 med nuts) (28 g)* | 74 | 131 | 171 | 337 | 154 | 288 | 99 | 212 | 130 | 259 | 679 | 114 |
| butternuts, dried—*1 oz (28 g)* | 104 | 267 | 335 | 625 | 219 | 174 | 137 | 410 | 277 | 438 | 1381 | 229 |
| cashew butter—*1 oz (28 g)* | 77 | 193 | 238 | 419 | 266 | 89 | 92 | 258 | 160 | 339 | 567 | 130 |
| **cashews** | | | | | | | | | | | | |
| dry roasted—*1 oz (28 g)* | 67 | 168 | 208 | 365 | 232 | 78 | 80 | 225 | 139 | 295 | 494 | 113 |
| oil roasted—*1 oz (18 med nuts) (28 g)* | 71 | 178 | 219 | 385 | 245 | 82 | 85 | 237 | 147 | 312 | 522 | 119 |
| **chestnuts, chinese** | | | | | | | | | | | | |
| raw—*1 oz (28 g)* | 14 | 47 | 45 | 74 | 65 | 29 | 31 | 54 | 36 | 62 | 122 | 34 |
| boiled & steamed—*1 oz (28 g)* | 10 | 33 | 31 | 51 | 44 | 20 | 21 | 37 | 24 | 43 | 84 | 24 |
| dried—*1 oz (28 g)* | 23 | 77 | 72 | 120 | 105 | 47 | 51 | 88 | 58 | 102 | 199 | 56 |
| roasted—*1 oz (28 g)* | 15 | 51 | 47 | 78 | 69 | 31 | 33 | 58 | 38 | 67 | 130 | 37 |

| | TRY | THR | ISO | LEU | LYS | MET | CYS | PHE | TYR | VAL | ARG | HIS |
|---|---|---|---|---|---|---|---|---|---|---|---|---|
| chestnuts, european | | | | | | | | | | | | |
| raw—*1 oz (2½ nuts) (28 g)* | 8 | 24 | 27 | 41 | 41 | 16 | 22 | 29 | 19 | 38 | 49 | 19 |
| boiled & steamed—*1 oz (28 g)* | 6 | 20 | 22 | 34 | 34 | 13 | 18 | 24 | 16 | 32 | 41 | 16 |
| dried—*1 oz (28 g)* | 20 | 65 | 72 | 107 | 107 | 43 | 57 | 77 | 50 | 101 | 130 | 50 |
| roasted—*1 oz (3½ nuts) (28 g)* | 10 | 32 | 36 | 53 | 53 | 21 | 29 | 38 | 25 | 51 | 64 | 25 |
| chestnuts, japanese | | | | | | | | | | | | |
| raw—*1 oz (28 g)* | 9 | 26 | 32 | 39 | 42 | 15 | 18 | 25 | 18 | 38 | 42 | 16 |
| boiled & steamed—*1 oz (28 g)* | 3 | 9 | 11 | 14 | 15 | 6 | 7 | 9 | 7 | 14 | 16 | 6 |
| dried—*1 oz (28 g)* | 21 | 60 | 73 | 92 | 97 | 36 | 43 | 58 | 43 | 89 | 98 | 37 |
| roasted—*1 oz (28 g)* | 12 | 34 | 41 | 52 | 55 | 20 | 24 | 33 | 24 | 50 | 55 | 21 |
| coconut | | | | | | | | | | | | |
| raw—*1 piece (2"x2"x½") (45 g)* | 18 | 54 | 59 | 111 | 66 | 28 | 30 | 76 | 46 | 91 | 246 | 35 |
| dried—*1 oz (28 g)* | 23 | 71 | 77 | 145 | 86 | 37 | 39 | 99 | 60 | 118 | 321 | 45 |
| dried, sweetened, flaked, cnd—*4 oz (114 g)* | 44 | 139 | 150 | 284 | 169 | 72 | 75 | 194 | 119 | 231 | 628 | 88 |
| dried, sweetened, flaked, packaged—*1 cup (74 g)* | 28 | 88 | 95 | 180 | 107 | 45 | 48 | 123 | 75 | 147 | 398 | 56 |
| dried, sweetened, shredded—*1 cup (93 g)* | 32 | 98 | 105 | 199 | 118 | 50 | 53 | 136 | 83 | 163 | 440 | 61 |
| dried, toasted—*1 oz (28 g)* | 18 | 55 | 59 | 112 | 66 | 28 | 30 | 76 | 47 | 91 | 247 | 35 |
| coconut cream, raw[a]—*1 cup (240 g)* | 101 | 317 | 341 | 646 | 384 | 163 | 173 | 442 | 269 | 528 | 1428 | 199 |
| coconut cream, sweetened, cnd[a]—*1 cup (296 g)* | 92 | 290 | 314 | 592 | 352 | 148 | 157 | 406 | 246 | 482 | 1308 | 184 |
| coconut milk, raw[b]—*1 cup (240 g)* | 65 | 199 | 216 | 408 | 242 | 103 | 108 | 278 | 170 | 334 | 902 | 127 |
| coconut milk, cnd[b]—*1 cup (226 g)* | 54 | 167 | 179 | 339 | 201 | 86 | 90 | 231 | 140 | 276 | 748 | 104 |
| coconut water[c]—*1 cup (240 g)* | 19 | 62 | 67 | 127 | 77 | 31 | 34 | 89 | 53 | 106 | 283 | 41 |
| filberts (hazelnuts) | | | | | | | | | | | | |
| dried—*1 oz (28 g)* | 61 | 127 | 161 | 312 | 113 | 46 | 65 | 195 | 129 | 188 | 612 | 93 |
| dry roasted—*1 oz (28 g)* | 47 | 98 | 124 | 240 | 87 | 36 | 50 | 150 | 99 | 144 | 470 | 71 |
| oil roasted—*1 oz (28 g)* | 67 | 139 | 176 | 341 | 124 | 50 | 71 | 213 | 141 | 205 | 669 | 102 |
| roasted, salted, Blue Diamond—*1 oz (28 g)* | 36 | 164 | 184 | 345 | 121 | 90 | 85 | 176 | 130 | 263 | 710 | 124 |
| whole, Blue Diamond—*1 oz (28 g)* | 167 | 147 | 181 | 320 | 136 | 51 | 65 | 218 | 138 | 223 | 691 | 104 |
| ginko nuts | | | | | | | | | | | | |
| raw—*1 oz (28 g)* | 20 | 76 | 59 | 90 | 59 | 16 | 7 | 49 | 17 | 80 | 119 | 29 |
| cnd—*1 oz (14 med nuts) (28 g)* | 11 | 40 | 32 | 48 | 31 | 8 | 3 | 26 | 9 | 43 | 63 | 15 |
| dried—*1 oz (28 g)* | 48 | 182 | 142 | 214 | 140 | 38 | 16 | 116 | 41 | 192 | 285 | 69 |
| hickorynuts, dried—*1 oz (28 g)* | 39 | 120 | 164 | 292 | 141 | 85 | 77 | 202 | 129 | 207 | 592 | 110 |
| macadamia nuts | | | | | | | | | | | | |
| dried—*1 oz (28 g)* | | 75 | 69 | 131 | 92 | 26 | 27 | 74 | 96 | 91 | 255 | 48 |
| dry roasted, Blue Diamond—*1 oz (28 g)* | 17 | 85 | 82 | 161 | 93 | 82 | 62 | 90 | 138 | 96 | 371 | 59 |
| oil roasted—*1 oz (10-12 nuts) (28 g)* | | 65 | 61 | 115 | 81 | 23 | 24 | 64 | 84 | 80 | 223 | 42 |
| mixed nuts | | | | | | | | | | | | |
| dry roasted[d]—*1 oz (28 g)* | 75 | 170 | 211 | 389 | 202 | 65 | 82 | 271 | 192 | 265 | 637 | 136 |
| oil roasted[e]—*1 oz (28 g)* | 70 | 162 | 206 | 382 | 187 | 96 | 83 | 261 | 186 | 266 | 575 | 134 |
| w/o peanuts, oil roasted[f]—*1 oz (28 g)* | 72 | 161 | 200 | 359 | 194 | 98 | 86 | 233 | 145 | 270 | 565 | 118 |
| nuts, wheat-base formulated | | | | | | | | | | | | |
| flavored[g]—*1 oz (28 g)* | 49 | 157 | 157 | 276 | 252 | 78 | 64 | 166 | 138 | 202 | 279 | 108 |
| macadamia flavored[h]—*1 oz (28 g)* | 39 | 135 | 138 | 242 | 218 | 68 | 53 | 145 | 122 | 176 | 232 | 92 |
| unflavored[i]—*1 oz (28 g)* | 47 | 164 | 158 | 281 | 258 | 79 | 72 | 171 | 137 | 207 | 302 | 112 |
| peanut butter, creamy/smooth—*1 T (16 g)* | 55 | 132 | 177 | 342 | 176 | 47 | 58 | 260 | 219 | 206 | 613 | 133 |
| peanut butter, chunk style/crunchy—*2 T (32 g)* | 75 | 263 | 270 | 499 | 276 | 94 | 99 | 399 | 313 | 323 | 920 | 195 |

[a] Liquid expressed from grated coconut.
[b] Liquid expressed from grated coconut & water.
[c] Liquid from coconuts.
[d] Cashews, almonds, peanuts, filberts & pecans.
[e] Cashews, peanuts, brazilnuts, filberts, almonds & pecans.
[f] Cashews, almonds, brazilnuts, pecans & filberts.

[g] Hydrogenated soybean oil, wheat germ, sugar, sodium caseinate, soy protein, natural & artificial flavors, & artificial color.
[h] Hydrogenated soybean oil, wheat germ, sugar, wheat starch, sodium caseinate, soy protein, natural & artificial flavor.
[i] Hydrogenated soybean oil, wheat germ, fructose, wheat starch, sodium caseinate, soy protein, & salt.

| | TRY | THR | ISO | LEU | LYS | MET | CYS | PHE | TYR | VAL | ARG | HIS |
|---|---|---|---|---|---|---|---|---|---|---|---|---|
| peanut flour | | | | | | | | | | | | |
| defatted—*1 T (4 g)* | 25 | 60 | 81 | 157 | 81 | 21 | 27 | 119 | 100 | 94 | 281 | 61 |
| low-fat—*1 oz (28 g)* | 92 | 324 | 333 | 613 | 340 | 116 | 121 | 491 | 385 | 397 | 1132 | 239 |
| peanuts | | | | | | | | | | | | |
| boiled—*½ cup (32 g)* | 42 | 148 | 152 | 280 | 155 | 53 | 55 | 224 | 176 | 181 | 517 | 109 |
| dried—*1 oz (28 g)* | 88 | 211 | 283 | 548 | 282 | 75 | 93 | 417 | 350 | 330 | 982 | 212 |
| dry roasted—*1 oz (28 g)* | 64 | 227 | 233 | 430 | 238 | 81 | 85 | 344 | 270 | 278 | 793 | 168 |
| oil roasted—*1 oz (28 g)* | 92 | 220 | 295 | 571 | 294 | 78 | 97 | 435 | 365 | 344 | 1024 | 222 |
| peanuts, spanish, oil-roasted—*1 oz (28 g)* | 76 | 269 | 276 | 508 | 281 | 96 | 101 | 407 | 319 | 329 | 938 | 198 |
| peanuts, valencia, oil-roasted—*1 oz (28 g)* | 74 | 259 | 266 | 491 | 272 | 93 | 97 | 393 | 308 | 318 | 906 | 192 |
| peanuts, virginia, oil-roasted—*1 oz (28 g)* | 70 | 248 | 255 | 470 | 260 | 89 | 93 | 375 | 295 | 304 | 866 | 183 |
| pecans | | | | | | | | | | | | |
| dried—*1 oz (31 large nuts) (28 g)* | 57 | 72 | 91 | 148 | 83 | 53 | 59 | 116 | 81 | 110 | 314 | 64 |
| dry roasted—*1 oz (28 g)* | 58 | 74 | 94 | 152 | 85 | 54 | 61 | 120 | 83 | 113 | 323 | 66 |
| oil roasted—*1 oz (15 halves) (28 g)* | 51 | 64 | 82 | 133 | 74 | 47 | 53 | 104 | 72 | 98 | 282 | 58 |
| pilinuts, dried—*1 oz (15 nuts) (28 g)* | | 116 | 137 | 253 | 105 | 112 | | 141 | 108 | 199 | 431 | 72 |
| pine nuts, pignolia, dried—*1 oz (28 g)* | 86 | 216 | 265 | 491 | 256 | 122 | 124 | 261 | 249 | 352 | 1326 | 163 |
| pine nuts, pinyon, dried—*1 oz (28 g)* | 41 | 104 | 128 | 237 | 123 | 59 | 60 | 126 | 120 | 170 | 639 | 79 |
| pistachio nuts | | | | | | | | | | | | |
| dried—*1 oz (47 nuts) (28 g)* | 80 | 205 | 277 | 476 | 363 | 108 | 146 | 336 | 203 | 400 | 621 | 152 |
| dry roasted—*1 oz (28 g)* | 59 | 149 | 201 | 346 | 263 | 78 | 106 | 244 | 147 | 291 | 450 | 110 |
| dry roasted, Blue Diamond—*1 oz (28 g)* | 70 | 249 | 292 | 493 | 345 | 144 | 124 | 306 | 170 | 385 | 637 | 161 |
| pumpkin & squash seeds | | | | | | | | | | | | |
| dried—*1 oz (142 seeds) (28 g)* | 122 | 256 | 359 | 590 | 521 | 156 | 85 | 347 | 289 | 560 | 1145 | 193 |
| roasted—*1 oz (28 g)* | 164 | 344 | 482 | 793 | 699 | 210 | 115 | 466 | 389 | 753 | 1539 | 260 |
| sesame butter (tahini)—*1 T (15 g)* | 56 | 106 | 110 | 195 | 82 | 84 | 51 | 135 | 107 | 143 | 378 | 75 |
| sesame seeds | | | | | | | | | | | | |
| kernels, dried[a]—*1 T (8 g)* | 38 | 94 | 103 | 172 | 66 | 72 | 42 | 122 | 90 | 118 | 266 | 54 |
| kernels, toasted[a]—*1 oz (28 g)* | 105 | 200 | 207 | 369 | 154 | 159 | 97 | 255 | 202 | 269 | 714 | 142 |
| whole, dried—*1 T (9 g)* | 35 | 66 | 69 | 122 | 51 | 53 | 32 | 85 | 67 | 89 | 237 | 47 |
| whole, toasted & roasted—*1 oz (28 g)* | 105 | 200 | 207 | 369 | 154 | 159 | 97 | 255 | 202 | 269 | 714 | 142 |
| soybean nuts | | | | | | | | | | | | |
| dry roasted—*½ cup (86 g)* | 495 | 1478 | 1651 | 2772 | 2265 | 459 | 549 | 1777 | 1287 | 1699 | 2641 | 918 |
| roasted—*½ cup (86 g)* | 440 | 1316 | 1470 | 2466 | 2016 | 409 | 488 | 1581 | 1146 | 1512 | 2350 | 817 |
| roasted & toasted—*1 oz (95 nuts) (28 g)* | 160 | 456 | 535 | 856 | 734 | 142 | 178 | 548 | 417 | 525 | 855 | 283 |
| sunflower seeds | | | | | | | | | | | | |
| dried—*1 oz (28 g)* | 99 | 264 | 323 | 471 | 266 | 140 | 128 | 332 | 189 | 376 | 682 | 179 |
| dry roasted—*1 oz (28 g)* | 84 | 224 | 275 | 400 | 226 | 119 | 109 | 282 | 160 | 317 | 579 | 152 |
| oil roasted—*1 oz (28 g)* | 93 | 247 | 303 | 442 | 250 | 131 | 120 | 311 | 178 | 350 | 640 | 168 |
| walnuts, black, dried—*1 oz (28 g)* | 91 | 207 | 278 | 484 | 205 | 134 | 133 | 314 | 213 | 365 | 1040 | 193 |
| walnuts, english/persian, dried—*1 oz (14 halves) (28 g)* | 54 | 127 | 161 | 282 | 110 | 80 | 98 | 178 | 125 | 205 | 597 | 102 |
| watermelon seeds, dried—*1 oz (95 large seeds) (28 g)* | 111 | 316 | 381 | 610 | 252 | 237 | 124 | 577 | 289 | 442 | 1391 | 220 |

**25. Poultry[b]**
**25.1. Chicken**
**25.1.1. Broiler/Fryer Meat**

| | TRY | THR | ISO | LEU | LYS | MET | CYS | PHE | TYR | VAL | ARG | HIS |
|---|---|---|---|---|---|---|---|---|---|---|---|---|
| dark meat w/ skin, fried—*3.5 oz (100 g)* | 308 | 1123 | 1370 | 1994 | 2202 | 725 | 365 | 1071 | 884 | 1326 | 1681 | 804 |
| dark meat w/ skin, roasted—*3.5 oz (100 g)* | 289 | 1071 | 1288 | 1883 | 2105 | 688 | 348 | 1007 | 832 | 1258 | 1634 | 759 |
| dark meat w/ skin, stewed—*3.5 oz (100 g)* | 261 | 969 | 1167 | 1705 | 1906 | 623 | 314 | 911 | 754 | 1139 | 1477 | 687 |
| dark meat w/o skin, fried—*3.5 oz (100 g)* | 340 | 1221 | 1528 | 2176 | 2441 | 799 | 375 | 1156 | 978 | 1438 | 1742 | 897 |
| dark meat w/o skin, roasted—*3.5 oz (100 g)* | 320 | 1156 | 1445 | 2053 | 2325 | 757 | 350 | 1086 | 924 | 1357 | 1651 | 849 |

[a] Decorticated seeds.

[b] Gram weights are edible portions.

| | TRY | THR | ISO | LEU | LYS | MET | CYS | PHE | TYR | VAL | ARG | HIS |
|---|---|---|---|---|---|---|---|---|---|---|---|---|
| dark meat w/o skin, stewed—*3.5 oz (100 g)* | 303 | 1097 | 1371 | 1949 | 2206 | 719 | 322 | 1030 | 877 | 1288 | 1566 | 806 |
| light & dark meat w/ skin, fried, batter dipped—*3.5 oz (100 g)* | 257 | 922 | 1125 | 1653 | 1765 | 591 | 311 | 899 | 732 | 1100 | 1378 | 655 |
| light & dark meat w/ skin, fried, flour coated—*3.5 oz (100 g)* | 323 | 1181 | 1439 | 2092 | 2320 | 762 | 382 | 1121 | 928 | 1392 | 1766 | 845 |
| light & dark meat w/ skin, roasted—*3.5 oz (100 g)* | 305 | 1128 | 1362 | 1986 | 2223 | 726 | 364 | 1061 | 879 | 1325 | 1711 | 802 |
| light & dark meat w/ skin, stewed—*3.5 oz (100 g)* | 276 | 1020 | 1233 | 1797 | 2011 | 657 | 329 | 959 | 796 | 1199 | 1545 | 726 |
| light & dark meat w/o skin, fried—*3.5 oz (100 g)* | 358 | 1289 | 1612 | 2294 | 2583 | 844 | 393 | 1217 | 1031 | 1516 | 1839 | 947 |
| light & dark meat w/o skin, roasted—*3.5 oz (100 g)* | 338 | 1222 | 1528 | 2171 | 2458 | 801 | 370 | 1148 | 977 | 1435 | 1745 | 898 |
| light & dark meat w/o skin, stewed—*3.5 oz (100 g)* | 319 | 1153 | 1441 | 2048 | 2318 | 755 | 349 | 1083 | 921 | 1353 | 1646 | 847 |
| light meat w/ skin, fried—*3.5 oz (100 g)* | 344 | 1262 | 1537 | 2231 | 2487 | 815 | 405 | 1192 | 991 | 1485 | 1888 | 904 |
| light meat w/ skin, roasted—*3.5 oz (100 g)* | 326 | 1202 | 1458 | 2119 | 2374 | 776 | 385 | 1130 | 940 | 1412 | 1811 | 858 |
| light meat w/ skin, stewed—*3.5 oz (100 g)* | 294 | 1084 | 1316 | 1910 | 2142 | 699 | 347 | 1019 | 848 | 1273 | 1629 | 774 |
| light meat w/o skin, fried—*3.5 oz (100 g)* | 383 | 1386 | 1732 | 2463 | 2784 | 908 | 420 | 1303 | 1108 | 1628 | 1978 | 1018 |
| light meat w/o skin, roasted—*3.5 oz (100 g)* | 361 | 1305 | 1632 | 2319 | 2626 | 855 | 396 | 1226 | 1043 | 1533 | 1864 | 959 |
| light meat w/o skin, stewed—*3.5 oz (100 g)* | 337 | 1220 | 1525 | 2167 | 2454 | 799 | 370 | 1146 | 975 | 1433 | 1742 | 896 |

**25.1.2. Broiler/Fryer Parts**

| | TRY | THR | ISO | LEU | LYS | MET | CYS | PHE | TYR | VAL | ARG | HIS |
|---|---|---|---|---|---|---|---|---|---|---|---|---|
| back w/ skin, fried—*½ back (72 g)* | 266 | 822 | 1001 | 1463 | 1599 | 529 | 272 | 790 | 647 | 973 | 1235 | 587 |
| breast w/ skin, fried—*½ breast (98 g)* | 357 | 1300 | 1599 | 2306 | 2581 | 845 | 410 | 1228 | 1028 | 1531 | 1915 | 940 |
| breast w/ skin, roasted—*½ breast (98 g)* | 333 | 1219 | 1495 | 2154 | 2424 | 791 | 382 | 1146 | 960 | 1432 | 1800 | 879 |
| breast w/ skin, stewed—*½ breast (110 g)* | 343 | 1257 | 1541 | 2221 | 2499 | 815 | 395 | 1181 | 990 | 1476 | 1858 | 906 |
| breast w/o skin, fried—*½ breast (86 g)* | 335 | 1214 | 1518 | 2158 | 2439 | 796 | 368 | 1142 | 970 | 1427 | 1733 | 892 |
| breast w/o skin, roasted—*½ breast (86 g)* | 311 | 1127 | 1409 | 2002 | 2266 | 739 | 341 | 1059 | 900 | 1324 | 1609 | 828 |
| breast w/o skin, stewed—*½ breast (95 g)* | 322 | 1163 | 1454 | 2066 | 2339 | 762 | 352 | 1093 | 929 | 1395 | 1661 | 855 |
| drumstick w/ skin, fried—*1 drumstick (49 g)* | 150 | 549 | 672 | 972 | 1085 | 355 | 174 | 518 | 432 | 646 | 815 | 395 |
| drumstick w/ skin, roasted—*1 drumstick (52 g)* | 158 | 583 | 708 | 1028 | 1152 | 376 | 186 | 548 | 456 | 684 | 876 | 417 |
| drumstick w/ skin, stewed—*1 drumstick (57 g)* | 163 | 599 | 730 | 1057 | 1187 | 388 | 191 | 563 | 470 | 704 | 897 | 429 |
| leg w/ skin, fried—*1 leg (112 g)* | 340 | 1245 | 1520 | 2205 | 2452 | 804 | 400 | 1180 | 980 | 1467 | 1858 | 893 |
| leg w/ skin, roasted—*1 leg (114 g)* | 332 | 1226 | 1487 | 2160 | 2421 | 791 | 393 | 1153 | 959 | 1440 | 1847 | 876 |
| leg w/ skin, stewed—*1 leg (125 g)* | 339 | 1253 | 1520 | 2208 | 2474 | 808 | 401 | 1178 | 980 | 1471 | 1884 | 894 |
| leg w/o skin, stewed—*1 leg (101 g)* | 310 | 1120 | 1401 | 1991 | 2253 | 734 | 339 | 1052 | 896 | 1316 | 1600 | 823 |
| neck w/ skin, fried—*1 neck (36 g)* | 92 | 364 | 403 | 608 | 658 | 218 | 122 | 331 | 264 | 410 | 559 | 237 |
| neck w/ skin, simmered—*1 neck (38 g)* | 76 | 295 | 331 | 510 | 557 | 183 | 107 | 278 | 218 | 347 | 500 | 196 |
| neck w/o skin, simmered—*1 neck (18 g)* | 52 | 187 | 233 | 332 | 375 | 122 | 57 | 175 | 149 | 219 | 267 | 137 |
| thigh w/ skin, fried—*1 thigh (62 g)* | 187 | 685 | 835 | 1214 | 1345 | 442 | 222 | 652 | 539 | 808 | 1027 | 490 |
| thigh w/ skin, roasted—*1 thigh (62 g)* | 174 | 643 | 779 | 1133 | 1269 | 415 | 206 | 605 | 502 | 755 | 971 | 458 |
| thigh w/ skin, stewed—*1 thigh (68 g)* | 177 | 654 | 792 | 1153 | 1291 | 422 | 211 | 615 | 511 | 768 | 990 | 466 |
| thigh w/o skin, roasted—*1 thigh (52 g)* | 158 | 570 | 712 | 1012 | 1146 | 373 | 173 | 535 | 456 | 669 | 814 | 419 |
| wing w/ skin, fried—*1 wing (32 g)* | 90 | 338 | 396 | 592 | 650 | 214 | 116 | 321 | 258 | 398 | 538 | 233 |
| wing w/ skin, roasted—*1 wing (34 g)* | 98 | 370 | 432 | 645 | 714 | 234 | 126 | 348 | 281 | 435 | 592 | 255 |
| wing w/ skin, stewed—*1 wing (40 g)* | 98 | 370 | 434 | 646 | 716 | 235 | 125 | 348 | 282 | 435 | 588 | 256 |

**25.1.3. Capon**

| | TRY | THR | ISO | LEU | LYS | MET | CYS | PHE | TYR | VAL | ARG | HIS |
|---|---|---|---|---|---|---|---|---|---|---|---|---|
| meat w/ skin, roasted—*3.5 oz (100 g)* | 325 | 1200 | 1455 | 2115 | 2370 | 774 | 384 | 1128 | 938 | 1409 | 1806 | 857 |

**25.1.4. Roaster**

| | TRY | THR | ISO | LEU | LYS | MET | CYS | PHE | TYR | VAL | ARG | HIS |
|---|---|---|---|---|---|---|---|---|---|---|---|---|
| dark meat w/o skin, roasted—*3.5 oz (100 g)* | 272 | 982 | 1228 | 1745 | 1975 | 644 | 298 | 923 | 785 | 1153 | 1402 | 722 |

| | TRY | THR | ISO | LEU | LYS | MET | CYS | PHE | TYR | VAL | ARG | HIS |
|---|---|---|---|---|---|---|---|---|---|---|---|---|
| light & dark meat w/ skin, roasted—*3.5 oz (100 g)* | 266 | 989 | 1191 | 1739 | 1945 | 636 | 320 | 929 | 769 | 1162 | 1506 | 701 |
| light & dark meat w/o skin, roasted—*3.5 oz (100 g)* | 292 | 1056 | 1321 | 1877 | 2125 | 693 | 320 | 993 | 844 | 1240 | 1509 | 776 |
| light meat w/o skin, roasted—*3.5 oz (100 g)* | 317 | 1146 | 1433 | 2036 | 2305 | 751 | 347 | 1077 | 916 | 1346 | 1637 | 842 |

**25.1.5. Stewer**

| | TRY | THR | ISO | LEU | LYS | MET | CYS | PHE | TYR | VAL | ARG | HIS |
|---|---|---|---|---|---|---|---|---|---|---|---|---|
| dark meat w/o skin, stewed—*3.5 oz (100 g)* | 329 | 1189 | 1486 | 2112 | 2391 | 779 | 360 | 1117 | 950 | 1396 | 1698 | 874 |
| light & dark meat w/ skin, stewed—*3.5 oz (100 g)* | 301 | 1113 | 1348 | 1961 | 2197 | 717 | 357 | 1046 | 869 | 1307 | 1680 | 793 |
| light & dark meat w/o skin, stewed—*3.5 oz (100 g)* | 356 | 1285 | 1606 | 2283 | 2585 | 842 | 389 | 1207 | 1027 | 1509 | 1835 | 944 |
| light meat w/o skin, stewed—*3.5 oz (100 g)* | 386 | 1396 | 1744 | 2479 | 2807 | 914 | 423 | 1311 | 1115 | 1639 | 1993 | 1025 |

**25.2. Turkey**

| | TRY | THR | ISO | LEU | LYS | MET | CYS | PHE | TYR | VAL | ARG | HIS |
|---|---|---|---|---|---|---|---|---|---|---|---|---|
| dark meat w/ skin, roasted—*3.5 oz (100 g)* | 304 | 1200 | 1379 | 2138 | 2503 | 774 | 302 | 1076 | 1044 | 1432 | 1936 | 828 |
| dark meat w/o skin, roasted—*3.5 oz (100 g)* | 325 | 1271 | 1485 | 2276 | 2693 | 828 | 297 | 1134 | 1129 | 1518 | 1993 | 893 |
| ham, cured thigh meat —*3.5 oz (100 g)* | 215 | 842 | 984 | 1508 | 1784 | 548 | 197 | 751 | 748 | 1006 | 1321 | 591 |
| light & dark meat, w/ skin, roasted—*3.5 oz (100 g)* | 311 | 1227 | 1409 | 2184 | 2557 | 790 | 308 | 1100 | 1066 | 1464 | 1979 | 845 |
| light & dark meat, w/o skin, roasted—*3.5 oz (100 g)* | 333 | 1304 | 1525 | 2336 | 2763 | 849 | 305 | 1164 | 1159 | 1557 | 2045 | 915 |
| light meat, w/ skin, roasted—*3.5 oz (100 g)* | 315 | 1247 | 1432 | 2220 | 2599 | 803 | 314 | 1117 | 1084 | 1487 | 2013 | 859 |
| light meat, w/o skin, roasted—*3.5 oz (100 g)* | 340 | 1330 | 1555 | 2383 | 2818 | 866 | 311 | 1187 | 1182 | 1588 | 2086 | 933 |
| loaf, breast meat—*3.5 oz (100 g)* | 256 | 1001 | 1170 | 1793 | 2120 | 652 | 234 | 893 | 889 | 1195 | 1570 | 702 |

**25.3. Other Poultry**

| | TRY | THR | ISO | LEU | LYS | MET | CYS | PHE | TYR | VAL | ARG | HIS |
|---|---|---|---|---|---|---|---|---|---|---|---|---|
| duck w/ skin, roasted—*3.5 oz (100 g)* | 232 | 773 | 872 | 1465 | 1486 | 475 | 299 | 752 | 640 | 938 | 1284 | 462 |
| duck w/o skin, roasted—*3.5 oz (100 g)* | 327 | 1003 | 1206 | 1983 | 2009 | 635 | 361 | 984 | 894 | 1228 | 1499 | 620 |
| goose w/ skin, roasted—*3.5 oz (100 g)* | | 1123 | 1183 | 2109 | 1988 | 608 | | 1055 | 805 | 1232 | 1566 | 700 |
| pheasant w/o skin, raw—*3.5 oz (100 g)* | 328 | 1180 | 1324 | 1995 | 2157 | 686 | 309 | 920 | 773 | 1305 | 1433 | 939 |
| quail w/o skin, raw—*3.5 oz (100 g)* | 341 | 1090 | 1187 | 1866 | 1905 | 689 | 380 | 944 | 1010 | 1180 | 1379 | 825 |

**25.4. Internal Organs**
**25.4.1. Giblets**

| | TRY | THR | ISO | LEU | LYS | MET | CYS | PHE | TYR | VAL | ARG | HIS |
|---|---|---|---|---|---|---|---|---|---|---|---|---|
| chicken, fried—*3.5 oz (100 g)* | 373 | 1467 | 1630 | 2601 | 2348 | 810 | 437 | 1480 | 1067 | 1737 | 2159 | 759 |
| chicken, simmered—*3.5 oz (100 g)* | 295 | 1172 | 1297 | 2066 | 1886 | 646 | 343 | 1170 | 848 | 1379 | 1727 | 602 |
| turkey, simmered—*3.5 oz (100 g)* | 307 | 1204 | 1339 | 2140 | 1951 | 662 | 354 | 1207 | 877 | 1430 | 1768 | 625 |

**25.4.2. Gizzard**

| | TRY | THR | ISO | LEU | LYS | MET | CYS | PHE | TYR | VAL | ARG | HIS |
|---|---|---|---|---|---|---|---|---|---|---|---|---|
| chicken, simmered—*3.5 oz (100 g)* | 243 | 1251 | 1281 | 1907 | 1877 | 712 | 356 | 1129 | 825 | 1216 | 1950 | 547 |
| turkey, simmered—*3.5 oz (100 g)* | 264 | 1356 | 1389 | 2067 | 2034 | 772 | 386 | 1224 | 895 | 1318 | 2114 | 593 |

**25.4.3. Heart**

| | TRY | THR | ISO | LEU | LYS | MET | CYS | PHE | TYR | VAL | ARG | HIS |
|---|---|---|---|---|---|---|---|---|---|---|---|---|
| chicken, simmered—*3.5 oz (100 g)* | 338 | 1196 | 1415 | 2303 | 2214 | 638 | 359 | 1183 | 946 | 1496 | 1694 | 693 |
| turkey, simmered—*3.5 oz (100 g)* | 343 | 1212 | 1435 | 2333 | 2243 | 646 | 364 | 1199 | 959 | 1516 | 1717 | 702 |

**25.4.4. Liver**

| | TRY | THR | ISO | LEU | LYS | MET | CYS | PHE | TYR | VAL | ARG | HIS |
|---|---|---|---|---|---|---|---|---|---|---|---|---|
| chicken, simmered—*3.5 oz (100 g)* | 343 | 1083 | 1294 | 2198 | 1843 | 577 | 327 | 1212 | 857 | 1535 | 1493 | 647 |
| duck, raw—*3.5 oz (100 g)* | 264 | 833 | 995 | 1691 | 1418 | 444 | 252 | 932 | 660 | 1181 | 1148 | 498 |
| goose, raw—*3.3 oz (94 g)* | 216 | 684 | 818 | 1388 | 1165 | 365 | 207 | 766 | 541 | 970 | 943 | 409 |
| turkey, simmered—*3.5 oz (100 g)* | 338 | 1066 | 1273 | 2163 | 1814 | 568 | 322 | 1193 | 844 | 1511 | 1469 | 637 |

**27. Sauces**

| | TRY | THR | ISO | LEU | LYS | MET | CYS | PHE | TYR | VAL | ARG | HIS |
|---|---|---|---|---|---|---|---|---|---|---|---|---|
| marinara (tomato based) sce—*1 cup (250 g)* | 28 | 93 | 78 | 113 | 115 | 20 | 23 | 85 | 55 | 83 | 80 | 63 |
| soy sce | | | | | | | | | | | | |
| made w/ soy & wheat (shoyu)—*¼ cup (58 g)* | 43 | 121 | 142 | 240 | 171 | 44 | 53 | 158 | 109 | 148 | 207 | 78 |
| made w/ soy (tamari)—*¼ cup (58 g)* | 105 | 236 | 282 | 426 | 424 | 97 | 62 | 310 | 198 | 304 | 235 | 125 |

| | TRY | THR | ISO | LEU | LYS | MET | CYS | PHE | TYR | VAL | ARG | HIS |
|---|---|---|---|---|---|---|---|---|---|---|---|---|
| spaghetti sce, cnd—*1 cup (249 g)* | 32 | 105 | 87 | 127 | 129 | 22 | 27 | 95 | 60 | 92 | 90 | 72 |
| tomato sce, cnd—*½ cup (122 g)* | 11 | 37 | 32 | 45 | 46 | 9 | 10 | 34 | 22 | 33 | 33 | 26 |
| spanish style—*½ cup (122 g)* | 12 | 40 | 34 | 49 | 50 | 9 | 11 | 37 | 23 | 35 | 35 | 28 |
| w/ herbs & cheese—*½ cup (122 g)* | 26 | 72 | 85 | 138 | 135 | 34 | 20 | 85 | 73 | 100 | 109 | 61 |
| w/ mushrooms—*½ cup (122 g)* | 21 | 52 | 45 | 67 | 90 | 17 | 9 | 48 | 28 | 50 | 51 | 34 |
| w/ onions—*½ cup (122 g)* | 20 | 45 | 51 | 60 | 72 | 12 | 22 | 44 | 35 | 41 | 139 | 31 |
| w/ onions, green peppers & celery—*½ cup (122 g)* | 10 | 27 | 26 | 34 | 37 | 6 | 9 | 26 | 17 | 24 | 45 | 18 |
| w/ tomato tidbits—*½ cup (122 g)* | 11 | 37 | 32 | 45 | 46 | 9 | 10 | 34 | 22 | 33 | 33 | 26 |
| **28. Soups** | | | | | | | | | | | | |
| **28.1. Canned, Condensed** | | | | | | | | | | | | |
| celery, crm of—*1 can (305 g)* | 46 | 143 | 189 | 302 | 180 | 73 | 46 | 189 | 131 | 217 | 143 | 95 |
| cheese—*1 can (257 g)* | 144 | 380 | 645 | 1025 | 761 | 234 | 90 | 558 | 499 | 761 | 324 | 293 |
| chicken, crm of—*1 can (305 g)* | 104 | 317 | 415 | 641 | 522 | 195 | 122 | 372 | 287 | 421 | 406 | 223 |
| mushroom, crm of—*1 can (305 g)* | 70 | 189 | 235 | 384 | 265 | 95 | 61 | 226 | 183 | 262 | 204 | 113 |
| tomato—*1 can (305 g)* | 49 | 125 | 143 | 241 | 122 | 55 | 67 | 171 | 104 | 162 | 146 | 88 |
| **28.2. Canned, Condensed, Prep w/ Milk** | | | | | | | | | | | | |
| asparagus, crm of—*1 cup (248 g)* | 84 | 260 | 340 | 558 | 432 | 144 | 67 | 290 | 270 | 384 | 231 | 159 |
| celery, crm of—*1 cup (248 g)* | 74 | 241 | 322 | 518 | 394 | 131 | 55 | 273 | 248 | 360 | 206 | 149 |
| cheese—*1 cup (251 g)* | 128 | 371 | 567 | 906 | 700 | 218 | 83 | 474 | 444 | 650 | 309 | 256 |
| chicken, crm of—*1 cup (248 g)* | 99 | 312 | 414 | 657 | 533 | 181 | 87 | 347 | 312 | 444 | 312 | 201 |
| clam chowder, new england—*1 cup (248 g)* | 117 | 350 | 451 | 719 | 605 | 203 | 102 | 374 | 337 | 489 | 407 | 265 |
| mushroom, crm of—*1 cup (248 g)* | 84 | 260 | 340 | 553 | 429 | 141 | 62 | 288 | 270 | 377 | 231 | 156 |
| pea, green—*1 cup (254 g)* | 130 | 485 | 541 | 1016 | 831 | 206 | 117 | 572 | 447 | 711 | 853 | 279 |
| potato, crm of[a]—*1 cup (248 g)* | 82 | 243 | 320 | 513 | 402 | 131 | 64 | 278 | 255 | 362 | 221 | 149 |
| tomato—*1 cup (248 g)* | 77 | 233 | 303 | 494 | 370 | 124 | 64 | 265 | 238 | 335 | 206 | 146 |
| tomato bisque—*1 cup (251 g)* | 80 | 248 | 321 | 520 | 409 | 131 | 60 | 271 | 254 | 356 | 211 | 153 |
| **28.3. Canned, Condensed, Prep w/ Water** | | | | | | | | | | | | |
| asparagus, crm of—*1 cup (244 g)* | 29 | 78 | 98 | 163 | 112 | 41 | 29 | 95 | 76 | 115 | 85 | 49 |
| bean w/ bacon—*1 cup (253 g)* | 83 | 326 | 385 | 650 | 536 | 99 | 89 | 440 | 235 | 435 | 415 | 205 |
| bean w/ franks—*1 cup (250 g)* | 413 | 488 | 823 | 680 | 125 | 110 | 558 | 298 | 550 | 525 | 260 | 498 |
| beef noodle—*1 cup (244 g)* | 46 | 154 | 188 | 315 | 261 | 90 | 59 | 195 | 124 | 207 | 198 | 112 |
| black bean—*1 cup (247 g)* | 64 | 249 | 287 | 422 | 415 | 62 | 59 | 311 | 173 | 284 | 331 | 163 |
| celery, crm of—*1 cup (244 g)* | 20 | 59 | 78 | 124 | 73 | 29 | 20 | 78 | 54 | 90 | 59 | 39 |
| cheese—*1 cup (247 g)* | 72 | 190 | 321 | 511 | 380 | 116 | 44 | 279 | 249 | 380 | 163 | 146 |
| chicken & dumplings—*1 cup (241 g)* | 53 | 193 | 243 | 407 | 378 | 108 | 72 | 224 | 142 | 277 | 292 | 137 |
| chicken, crm of—*1 cup (244 g)* | 41 | 129 | 171 | 264 | 215 | 81 | 51 | 154 | 117 | 173 | 166 | 93 |
| chicken gumbo—*1 cup (244 g)* | 22 | 83 | 100 | 168 | 161 | 46 | 17 | 98 | 68 | 117 | 122 | 59 |
| chicken noodle[b]—*1 cup (241 g)* | 39 | 128 | 159 | 265 | 219 | 77 | 46 | 164 | 106 | 176 | 166 | 94 |
| chicken rice—*1 cup (241 g)* | 41 | 142 | 178 | 270 | 251 | 92 | 51 | 152 | 123 | 188 | 234 | 101 |
| chicken veg—*1 cup (241 g)* | 31 | 113 | 135 | 231 | 222 | 60 | 24 | 133 | 94 | 159 | 169 | 80 |
| chili beef—*1 cup (250 g)* | 70 | 275 | 328 | 553 | 455 | 85 | 73 | 373 | 200 | 368 | 350 | 175 |
| clam chowder, new england—*1 cup (244 g)* | 54 | 149 | 183 | 288 | 251 | 90 | 56 | 159 | 127 | 195 | 229 | 137 |
| minestrone—*1 cup (241 g)* | 31 | 104 | 130 | 236 | 183 | 43 | 34 | 154 | 84 | 178 | 198 | 72 |
| mushroom, crm of—*1 cup (244 g)* | 34 | 90 | 112 | 181 | 127 | 44 | 27 | 107 | 88 | 122 | 95 | 54 |
| pea, green—*1 cup (250 g)* | 73 | 303 | 298 | 623 | 510 | 105 | 80 | 378 | 250 | 443 | 708 | 170 |
| pea, split w/ ham—*1 cup (253 g)* | 101 | 364 | 435 | 711 | 696 | 139 | 134 | 455 | 319 | 491 | 703 | 215 |
| pepperpot—*1 cup (241 g)* | 41 | 195 | 234 | 402 | 311 | 92 | 60 | 234 | 157 | 299 | 494 | 92 |
| potato, crm of[a]—*1 cup (244 g)* | 24 | 61 | 76 | 117 | 83 | 29 | 27 | 83 | 61 | 93 | 76 | 39 |
| scotch broth—*1 cup (241 g)* | 43 | 154 | 186 | 316 | 304 | 84 | 34 | 181 | 128 | 217 | 231 | 108 |
| stockpot—*1 cup (247 g)* | 42 | 151 | 183 | 311 | 299 | 82 | 35 | 178 | 126 | 215 | 227 | 109 |
| tomato—*1 cup (244 g)* | 20 | 51 | 59 | 100 | 51 | 22 | 27 | 71 | 41 | 66 | 61 | 37 |

[a] Includes vichyssoise.

[b] Includes chicken noodle-o's; chicken w/ stars; curly noodle w/ chicken & chicken alphabet

| | TRY | THR | ISO | LEU | LYS | MET | CYS | PHE | TYR | VAL | ARG | HIS |
|---|---|---|---|---|---|---|---|---|---|---|---|---|
| tomato beef w/ noodle—*1 cup (244 g)* | 41 | 144 | 171 | 290 | 242 | 83 | 54 | 181 | 115 | 193 | 183 | 102 |
| tomato bisque—*1 cup (247 g)* | 22 | 67 | 77 | 126 | 89 | 30 | 25 | 77 | 59 | 86 | 67 | 44 |
| turkey noodle—*1 cup (244 g)* | 37 | 124 | 151 | 254 | 212 | 73 | 46 | 156 | 102 | 168 | 159 | 90 |
| turkey veg—*1 cup (241 g)* | 27 | 96 | 116 | 198 | 190 | 53 | 22 | 113 | 82 | 135 | 145 | 67 |
| veg vegetarian—*1 cup (241 g)* | 14 | 75 | 99 | 147 | 99 | 24 | 24 | 99 | 48 | 99 | 99 | 48 |
| veg w/ beef[a]—*1 cup (244 g)* | 49 | 173 | 210 | 359 | 344 | 95 | 39 | 205 | 146 | 246 | 261 | 122 |
| veg w/ beef broth—*1 cup (241 g)* | 22 | 72 | 92 | 164 | 125 | 31 | 24 | 106 | 58 | 125 | 137 | 51 |
| **28.4. Canned, Ready-to-Serve** | | | | | | | | | | | | |
| beef, chunky—*1 cup (240 g)* | 465 | 592 | 898 | 929 | 248 | 123 | 481 | 353 | 636 | 609 | 275 | 725 |
| chicken, chunky—*1 cup (251 g)* | 123 | 437 | 552 | 924 | 853 | 243 | 163 | 505 | 326 | 628 | 660 | 311 |
| chicken noodle, chunky—*1 cup (240 g)* | | 437 | 552 | 924 | 854 | 245 | 163 | 504 | 326 | 629 | 662 | 312 |
| pea, split w/ ham, chunky—*1 cup (240 g)* | 110 | 391 | 468 | 766 | 749 | 149 | 144 | 490 | 343 | 526 | 758 | 233 |
| turkey, chunky—*1 cup (236 g)* | 99 | 404 | 514 | 781 | 809 | 215 | 106 | 418 | 307 | 552 | 531 | 238 |
| veg, chunky—*1 cup (240 g)* | 26 | 108 | 161 | 271 | 190 | 26 | 26 | 161 | 82 | 190 | 190 | 82 |
| **29. Special Dietary Foods** | | | | | | | | | | | | |
| breakfast bar, Carnation | | | | | | | | | | | | |
|   choc chip—*1.44 oz bar (41 g)* | 76 | 201 | 260 | 405 | 331 | 89 | 50 | 255 | 240 | 282 | | 129 |
|   choc crunch—*1.34 oz bar (38 g)* | 61 | 170 | 224 | 348 | 281 | 74 | 46 | 222 | 205 | 242 | | 112 |
|   peanut butter crunch—*1.35 oz bar (38 g)* | 72 | 202 | 265 | 408 | 332 | 93 | 49 | 257 | 248 | 294 | | 134 |
|   peanut butter w/ choc chips—*1.39 oz bar (39 g)* | 78 | 207 | 270 | 419 | 339 | 93 | 53 | 267 | 251 | 298 | | 136 |
| gluten-free, wheat-free foods, Ener-G Foods | | | | | | | | | | | | |
|   bread | | | | | | | | | | | | |
|     rice, brown—*2 slices (73 g)* | | 112 | 110 | 229 | 140 | 0 | | 158 | 50 | 176 | 267 | 68 |
|     rice, white—*2 slices (51 g)* | | 72 | 63 | 135 | 101 | 0 | | 79 | 27 | 105 | 189 | 36 |
|   nutquik milk powder—*1 oz (28 g)* | 144 | 244 | 230 | 414 | 161 | 69 | 96 | 311 | 180 | 280 | 725 | 142 |
|   pizza shell, rice, low protein—*2 oz (60 g)* | | 10 | 10 | 17 | 13 | 0 | | 10 | 3 | 13 | 9 | 5 |
|   soup, tomato, dry mix—*1⅔ T(15 g)* | | 14 | 12 | 20 | 15 | 4 | | 15 | 7 | 16 | 16 | 9 |
|   soyquix milk powder—*2 T (14 g)* | | 1 | 1 | 1 | 1 | | | 1 | 1 | 1 | 1 | |
| slender bars, Carnation | | | | | | | | | | | | |
|   choc—*2 bars (55 g)* | 175 | 533 | 649 | 997 | 807 | 345 | 138 | 591 | 552 | 742 | | 297 |
|   choc chip—*2 bars (55 g)* | 181 | 527 | 631 | 980 | 812 | 333 | 122 | 569 | 550 | 717 | | 289 |
|   choc peanut butter—*2 bars (55 g)* | 153 | 467 | 583 | 910 | 726 | 289 | 111 | 543 | 524 | 679 | | 288 |
|   van—*2 bars (55 g)* | 186 | 559 | 684 | 1059 | 864 | 346 | 139 | 631 | 595 | 776 | | 320 |
| slender, liquid diet meal, cnd, Carnation | | | | | | | | | | | | |
|   banana—*10 fl oz (313 g)* | 165 | 569 | 761 | 1167 | 961 | 308 | 88 | 590 | 651 | 847 | | 333 |
|   choc—*10 fl oz (313 g)* | 113 | 466 | 498 | 1008 | 804 | 282 | 69 | 538 | 541 | 663 | | 291 |
|   choc fudge—*10 fl oz (313 g)* | 116 | 485 | 545 | 1052 | 834 | 294 | 66 | 563 | 570 | 692 | | 304 |
|   choc malt—*10 fl oz (313 g)* | 116 | 485 | 545 | 1052 | 834 | 294 | 66 | 563 | 570 | 692 | | 304 |
|   milk choc—*10 fl oz (313 g)* | 116 | 485 | 541 | 1048 | 836 | 294 | 78 | 560 | 570 | 692 | | 304 |
|   peach—*10 fl oz (313 g)* | 165 | 569 | 761 | 1167 | 961 | 308 | 88 | 590 | 651 | 847 | | 333 |
|   strawberry—*10 fl oz (313 g)* | 165 | 569 | 761 | 1167 | 961 | 308 | 88 | 590 | 651 | 847 | | 333 |
|   van—*10 fl oz (313 g)* | 119 | 432 | 516 | 1014 | 814 | 250 | 88 | 516 | 504 | 635 | | 263 |
| **31. Spices, Herbs, & Flavorings** | | | | | | | | | | | | |
| basil, ground—*1 t (1 g)* | 3 | 8 | 8 | 15 | 9 | 3 | 2 | 10 | 6 | 10 | 9 | 4 |
| dill seed—*1 t (2 g)* | | 12 | 16 | 19 | 22 | 3 | | 14 | | 24 | 27 | 7 |
| fennel seed—*1 t (2 g)* | 5 | 12 | 14 | 20 | 15 | 6 | 4 | 13 | 8 | 18 | 14 | 7 |
| fenugreek seed—*1 t (4 g)* | 14 | 33 | 46 | 65 | 62 | 13 | 14 | 40 | 28 | 41 | 91 | 25 |
| garlic powder—*1 t (3 g)* | 6 | 13 | 18 | 29 | 16 | 9 | 5 | 14 | 6 | 20 | 47 | 9 |
| ginger, ground—*1 t (2 g)* | 1 | 3 | 5 | 7 | 5 | 1 | 1 | 4 | 2 | 7 | 4 | 3 |
| mustard seed, yellow—*1 t (3 g)* | 17 | 36 | 36 | 59 | 50 | 16 | 19 | 35 | 25 | 44 | 58 | 25 |
| onion powder—*1 t (2 g)* | 3 | 4 | 6 | 7 | 10 | 2 | 4 | 5 | 5 | 5 | 28 | 3 |
| poppy seed—*1 t (3 g)* | 7 | 25 | 25 | 42 | 31 | 13 | 13 | 25 | 19 | 36 | 56 | 15 |

[a] Includes beef; beef veg; barley & veg beef.

| | TRY | THR | ISO | LEU | LYS | MET | CYS | PHE | TYR | VAL | ARG | HIS |
|---|---|---|---|---|---|---|---|---|---|---|---|---|
| **32. Spreads (butter, margarine, mayonnaise, etc.)** | | | | | | | | | | | | |
| butter | | | | | | | | | | | | |
|   —*1 t (5 g)* | 1 | 2 | 3 | 4 | 3 | 1 | 0 | 2 | 2 | 3 | 2 | 1 |
|   —*1 T (15 g)* | 3 | 6 | 9 | 12 | 9 | 3 | 0 | 6 | 6 | 9 | 6 | 3 |
|   whipped—*1 t (4 g)* | 0 | 1 | 2 | 3 | 3 | 1 | 0 | 2 | 2 | 2 | 1 | 1 |
|   whipped—*1 T (11 g)* | 0 | 3 | 6 | 9 | 9 | 3 | 0 | 6 | 6 | 6 | 3 | 3 |
| margarine by form & type of oil | | | | | | | | | | | | |
|   liquid, soybean & cottonseed—*1 t (5 g)* | 1 | 4 | 5 | 9 | 7 | 2 | 1 | 4 | 4 | 6 | 3 | 2 |
|   stick, corn—*1 t (5 g)* | 1 | 2 | 2 | 4 | 3 | 1 | 0 | 2 | 2 | 3 | 1 | 1 |
|   stick, safflower & soybean—*1 t (5 g)* | 1 | 2 | 2 | 4 | 3 | 1 | 0 | 2 | 2 | 3 | 1 | 1 |
|   stick, soybean—*1 t (5 g)* | 1 | 2 | 2 | 4 | 3 | 1 | 0 | 2 | 2 | 3 | 1 | 1 |
|   stick, soybean & cottonseed—*1 t (5 g)* | 1 | 2 | 2 | 4 | 3 | 1 | 0 | 2 | 2 | 3 | 1 | 1 |
|   tub, corn—*1 t (5 g)* | 1 | 2 | 2 | 3 | 3 | 1 | 0 | 2 | 2 | 2 | 1 | 1 |
|   tub, safflower—*1 t (5 g)* | 1 | 2 | 2 | 3 | 3 | 1 | 0 | 2 | 2 | 2 | 1 | 1 |
|   tub, soybean—*1 t (5 g)* | 1 | 2 | 2 | 3 | 3 | 1 | 0 | 2 | 2 | 2 | 1 | 1 |
|   tub, soybean & cottonseed—*1 t (5 g)* | 1 | 2 | 2 | 3 | 3 | 1 | 0 | 2 | 2 | 2 | 1 | 1 |
| margarine, imitation (diet) by form & type of oil | | | | | | | | | | | | |
|   tub, corn—*1 t (5 g)* | 0 | 1 | 1 | 2 | 2 | 1 | 0 | 1 | 1 | 2 | 1 | 1 |
|   tub, soybean & cottonseed—*1 t (5 g)* | 0 | 1 | 1 | 2 | 2 | 1 | 0 | 1 | 1 | 2 | 1 | 1 |
| mayonnaise | | | | | | | | | | | | |
|   safflower & soybean—*1 T (14 g)* | 2 | 8 | 9 | 13 | 10 | 5 | 3 | 8 | 6 | 10 | 10 | 4 |
|   soybean—*1 T (14 g)* | 2 | 8 | 9 | 13 | 10 | 5 | 3 | 8 | 6 | 10 | 10 | 4 |
| vegetable oil spread by form & type of oil | | | | | | | | | | | | |
|   stick, soybean & palm—*1 t (5 g)* | 0 | 1 | 2 | 3 | 2 | 1 | 0 | 1 | 1 | 2 | 1 | 1 |
|   stick, soybean & cottonseed—*1 t (5 g)* | 0 | 1 | 2 | 3 | 2 | 1 | 0 | 1 | 1 | 2 | 1 | 1 |
| **33. Sugars, Syrups & Other Sweeteners** | | | | | | | | | | | | |
| sugar substitute | | | | | | | | | | | | |
|   equal powder[a]—*1 g pkt (1 g)* | | | | | | | | 19 | | | | |
|   equal tablet[b]—*1 tablet ( g)* | | | | 3 | | | | 19 | | | | |
| **34. Vegetables, Vegetable Products & Vegetable Salads** | | | | | | | | | | | | |
| adzuki beans | | | | | | | | | | | | |
|   boiled—*1 cup (230 g)* | 166 | 587 | 690 | 1454 | 1304 | 182 | 161 | 915 | 515 | 890 | 1118 | 455 |
|   cnd, sweetened—*1 cup (296 g)* | 107 | 382 | 447 | 944 | 847 | 118 | 104 | 595 | 334 | 580 | 728 | 296 |
|   w/ sugar (yokan)—*three ¼" thick slices (43 g)* | 14 | 48 | 56 | 119 | 107 | 15 | 13 | 75 | 42 | 73 | 92 | 37 |
| alfalfa seeds, sprouted, raw—*1 cup (33 g)* | | 44 | 47 | 88 | 71 | | | | | 48 | | |
| amaranth, boiled—*½ cup (66 g)* | 18 | 56 | 67 | 110 | 72 | 20 | 17 | 75 | 45 | 78 | 69 | 29 |
| aspargus | | | | | | | | | | | | |
|   boiled—*½ cup (6 spears) (90 g)* | 23 | 65 | 86 | 101 | 111 | 23 | 28 | 55 | 37 | 90 | 109 | 36 |
|   cnd—*½ cup (121 g)* | 25 | 73 | 96 | 113 | 122 | 25 | 30 | 62 | 41 | 99 | 121 | 40 |
|   frzn, boiled—*4 spears (60 g)* | 17 | 49 | 65 | 77 | 84 | 17 | 21 | 42 | 28 | 68 | 83 | 28 |
| avocado, raw | | | | | | | | | | | | |
|   calif—*1 med (173 g)* | 38 | 121 | 130 | 227 | 173 | 67 | 38 | 125 | 90 | 178 | 109 | 52 |
|   florida—*1 med (304 g)* | 52 | 161 | 173 | 301 | 228 | 88 | 52 | 164 | 119 | 237 | 143 | 70 |
| bamboo shoots | | | | | | | | | | | | |
|   raw—*½ cup (76 g)* | 21 | 65 | 67 | 106 | 102 | 23 | 17 | 68 | | 81 | 74 | 32 |
|   boiled—*1 cup (120 g)* | 19 | 60 | 61 | 98 | 95 | 20 | 16 | 64 | | 74 | 68 | 30 |
|   cnd—*1 cup (131 g)* | 24 | 75 | 76 | 122 | 117 | 26 | 18 | 79 | | 93 | 84 | 37 |
| beans, cnd | | | | | | | | | | | | |
|   baked, vegetarian—*1 cup (254 g)* | 145 | 513 | 538 | 973 | 836 | 183 | 132 | 658 | 343 | 638 | 754 | 338 |
|   baked w/ pork & sweet sce—*1 cup (253 g)* | 159 | 564 | 592 | 1073 | 921 | 205 | 147 | 726 | 377 | 703 | 832 | 374 |
|   baked w/ pork & tomato sce—*1 cup (253 g)* | 154 | 549 | 577 | 1042 | 896 | 197 | 142 | 706 | 367 | 683 | 807 | 364 |

[a] Contains dextrose w/ dried corn syrup, aspartame, silicon dioxide, cellulose, tribasic calcium phosphate & cellulose derivatives.

[b] Contains lactose, aspartame, maltodextrin, leucine, cellulose & cellulose derivatives.

| | TRY | THR | ISO | LEU | LYS | MET | CYS | PHE | TYR | VAL | ARG | HIS |
|---|---|---|---|---|---|---|---|---|---|---|---|---|
| beans, baked, homemade[a]—1 cup (253 g) | 170 | 577 | 612 | 1083 | 959 | 218 | 157 | 726 | 392 | 713 | 901 | 387 |
| beans, refried, cnd—1 cup (253 g) | 187 | 663 | 696 | 1260 | 1083 | 238 | 172 | 853 | 443 | 825 | 977 | 438 |
| beet greens, boiled—½ cup (72 g) | 29 | 55 | 38 | 83 | 54 | 15 | 17 | 49 | 44 | 55 | 53 | 28 |
| beets | | | | | | | | | | | | |
| boiled—½ cup slices (85 g) | 10 | 26 | 27 | 38 | 32 | 10 | 11 | 26 | 21 | 31 | 24 | 12 |
| cnd—½ cup slices (85 g) | 9 | 23 | 23 | 33 | 28 | 9 | 9 | 22 | 19 | 27 | 20 | 10 |
| cnd, harvard—½ cup slices (123 g) | 12 | 31 | 31 | 43 | 37 | 12 | 12 | 30 | 25 | 36 | 27 | 14 |
| cnd, pickled—½ cup slices (114 g) | 10 | 27 | 27 | 39 | 33 | 10 | 11 | 26 | 22 | 32 | 24 | 13 |
| black beans, boiled—1 cup (172 g) | 181 | 642 | 673 | 1218 | 1046 | 229 | 165 | 824 | 430 | 798 | 944 | 425 |
| black turtle beans | | | | | | | | | | | | |
| boiled—1 cup (185 g) | 179 | 636 | 668 | 1208 | 1040 | 228 | 165 | 818 | 426 | 792 | 938 | 422 |
| cnd—1 cup (240 g) | 170 | 610 | 638 | 1154 | 994 | 218 | 158 | 782 | 408 | 756 | 895 | 403 |
| broadbeans | | | | | | | | | | | | |
| boiled—1 cup (170 g) | 122 | 459 | 520 | 972 | 826 | 105 | 165 | 546 | 410 | 575 | 1193 | 328 |
| cnd—1 cup (256 g) | 133 | 497 | 566 | 1052 | 896 | 115 | 179 | 591 | 443 | 622 | 1293 | 356 |
| falafel[b]—3 patties w/ 2¼" diameter (51 g) | 68 | 251 | 289 | 481 | 437 | 95 | 93 | 361 | 173 | 287 | 653 | 186 |
| broccoli | | | | | | | | | | | | |
| raw—½ cup chopped (44 g) | 13 | 40 | 48 | 58 | 62 | 15 | 9 | 37 | 28 | 56 | 64 | 22 |
| boiled—½ cup (78 g) | 24 | 75 | 90 | 108 | 117 | 28 | 16 | 70 | 52 | 106 | 120 | 41 |
| frzn | | | | | | | | | | | | |
| chopped, boiled—½ cup (92 g) | 29 | 93 | 111 | 133 | 144 | 34 | 20 | 86 | 64 | 131 | 148 | 51 |
| spears, boiled—½ cup (92 g) | 29 | 93 | 111 | 133 | 144 | 34 | 20 | 86 | 64 | 131 | 148 | 51 |
| brussels sprouts | | | | | | | | | | | | |
| boiled—½ cup (4 sprouts) (78 g) | 22 | 71 | 78 | 89 | 90 | 19 | 12 | 58 | | 91 | 119 | 44 |
| frzn, boiled—½ cup (78 g) | 31 | 101 | 112 | 128 | 129 | 27 | 18 | 83 | | 130 | 170 | 64 |
| burdock root, boiled—1 cup (125 g) | 10 | 44 | 51 | 55 | 115 | 15 | 10 | 56 | 30 | 58 | 180 | 53 |
| cabbage, chinese (pak-choi) | | | | | | | | | | | | |
| raw—½ cup shredded (35 g) | 5 | 17 | 30 | 31 | 31 | 3 | 6 | 15 | 10 | 23 | 29 | 9 |
| boiled—½ cup shredded (85 g) | 13 | 43 | 76 | 77 | 79 | 8 | 14 | 39 | 26 | 59 | 74 | 23 |
| cabbage, green | | | | | | | | | | | | |
| raw—½ cup shredded (35 g) | 4 | 15 | 21 | 22 | 20 | 4 | 4 | 14 | 7 | 18 | 24 | 9 |
| boiled—½ cup shredded (75 g) | 8 | 25 | 36 | 37 | 34 | 8 | 6 | 23 | 12 | 31 | 41 | 14 |
| cabbage, red | | | | | | | | | | | | |
| raw—½ cup shredded (35 g) | 5 | 17 | 25 | 25 | 23 | 5 | 4 | 15 | 8 | 21 | 28 | 10 |
| boiled—½ cup shredded (75 g) | 8 | 27 | 40 | 41 | 38 | 8 | 7 | 26 | 14 | 34 | 45 | 16 |
| cabbage, savoy | | | | | | | | | | | | |
| raw—½ cup shredded (35 g) | 7 | 24 | 35 | 36 | 33 | 7 | 6 | 22 | 12 | 30 | 40 | 14 |
| boiled—½ cup shredded (73 g) | 13 | 45 | 66 | 68 | 62 | 13 | 11 | 42 | 23 | 56 | 74 | 27 |
| carrots | | | | | | | | | | | | |
| raw—1 med (72 g) | 8 | 27 | 30 | 31 | 29 | 5 | 6 | 23 | 14 | 32 | 31 | 12 |
| boiled—½ cup slices (78 g) | 9 | 31 | 34 | 36 | 34 | 5 | 7 | 27 | 16 | 36 | 35 | 13 |
| cnd—½ cup slices (73 g) | 5 | 17 | 18 | 20 | 18 | 3 | 4 | 15 | 9 | 20 | 19 | 7 |
| frzn, boiled—½ cup slices (73 g) | 9 | 31 | 34 | 36 | 34 | 6 | 7 | 27 | 17 | 37 | 36 | 13 |
| cassava, raw—3.5 oz (100 g) | 43 | 65 | 61 | 90 | 100 | 26 | 65 | 60 | 40 | 79 | 314 | 45 |
| cauliflower | | | | | | | | | | | | |
| raw—½ cup pieces (50 g) | 13 | 36 | 38 | 58 | 54 | 14 | 12 | 36 | 22 | 50 | 48 | 20 |
| boiled—½ cup pieces (62 g) | 16 | 42 | 44 | 68 | 62 | 16 | 14 | 42 | 25 | 58 | 56 | 24 |
| frzn, boiled—½ cup pieces (90 g) | 19 | 53 | 55 | 85 | 77 | 21 | 17 | 52 | 32 | 73 | 70 | 30 |
| celery | | | | | | | | | | | | |
| raw—1 stalk (7.5" long) (40 g) | 4 | 8 | 8 | 12 | 10 | 2 | 2 | 8 | 4 | 10 | 8 | 4 |
| boiled—½ cup diced (75 g) | 5 | 11 | 12 | 18 | 15 | 3 | 2 | 11 | 5 | 15 | 11 | 6 |
| celtuce, raw—12 leaves (100 g) | 6 | 39 | 55 | 52 | 55 | 10 | 10 | 36 | 21 | 46 | 46 | 15 |
| chard, swiss, boiled—½ cup chopped (88 g) | 16 | 76 | 136 | 119 | 91 | 18 | | 100 | | 100 | 107 | 33 |
| chayote, boiled—½ cup pieces (80 g) | 6 | 25 | 26 | 46 | 24 | 1 | | 29 | 19 | 38 | 21 | 9 |
| chickpeas (garbanzo beans) | | | | | | | | | | | | |
| boiled—1 cup (164 g) | 139 | 540 | 623 | 1035 | 973 | 190 | 195 | 779 | 361 | 610 | 1369 | 400 |

[a] White beans, onions, salt pork, molasses, brown sugar, vinegar, salt, pepper & dry mustard.

[b] Broadbeans, soybean oil, onions, flour, salt, garlic, coriander & cumin.

| | TRY | THR | ISO | LEU | LYS | MET | CYS | PHE | TYR | VAL | ARG | HIS |
|---|---|---|---|---|---|---|---|---|---|---|---|---|
| cnd—*1 cup (240 g)* | 115 | 442 | 509 | 845 | 794 | 156 | 161 | 636 | 295 | 499 | 1118 | 326 |
| hummus[a]—*1 cup (246 g)* | 116 | 426 | 487 | 905 | 768 | 101 | 155 | 509 | 381 | 536 | 1109 | 308 |
| chickory greens, raw—*½ cup chopped (90 g)* | 28 | 42 | 91 | 67 | 60 | 9 | | 37 | | 69 | 112 | 26 |
| chickory witloof, raw—*½ cup (45 g)* | 8 | 13 | 27 | 20 | 18 | 3 | | 1 | | 20 | 33 | 8 |
| chives | | | | | | | | | | | | |
| raw—*1 T chopped (3 g)* | 1 | 3 | 4 | 5 | 4 | 1 | | 3 | 2 | 4 | 6 | 1 |
| freeze-dried—*¼ cup (0.8 g)* | 2 | 7 | 7 | 10 | 8 | 2 | | 5 | 5 | 7 | 12 | 3 |
| coleslaw, homemade[b]—*½ cup (60 g)* | 10 | 29 | 37 | 49 | 43 | 11 | 9 | 28 | 20 | 37 | 42 | 17 |
| collards | | | | | | | | | | | | |
| boiled—*1 cup chopped (190 g)* | 27 | 74 | 86 | 129 | 101 | 29 | 21 | 74 | 57 | 103 | 106 | 40 |
| frzn, boiled—*½ cup chopped (85 g)* | 32 | 89 | 103 | 156 | 120 | 34 | 26 | 89 | 68 | 123 | 129 | 48 |
| corn, yellow | | | | | | | | | | | | |
| boiled—*½ cup (82 g)* | 19 | 109 | 109 | 294 | 116 | 57 | 22 | 127 | 103 | 157 | 111 | 75 |
| cnd—*½ cup (82 g)* | 15 | 86 | 86 | 233 | 92 | 45 | 17 | 100 | 82 | 124 | 88 | 59 |
| cream style—*½ cup (128 g)* | 15 | 90 | 90 | 241 | 95 | 46 | 18 | 104 | 84 | 128 | 91 | 61 |
| vacuum pack—*½ cup (105 g)* | 18 | 102 | 102 | 273 | 107 | 53 | 21 | 118 | 97 | 145 | 103 | 69 |
| w/ red & green peppers—*½ cup (114 g)* | 19 | 106 | 106 | 280 | 113 | 55 | 23 | 122 | 99 | 150 | 108 | 72 |
| frzn, boiled—*½ cup (82 g)* | 17 | 99 | 99 | 267 | 105 | 52 | 21 | 116 | 94 | 142 | 101 | 68 |
| corn pudding[c]—*1 cup (250 g)* | 133 | 495 | 588 | 1075 | 658 | 293 | 163 | 560 | 455 | 718 | 543 | 288 |
| cornsalad, raw[d]—*½ cup (28 g)* | 7 | 21 | 28 | 37 | 28 | 7 | 6 | 25 | 10 | 28 | 25 | 10 |
| cowpeas, (blackeye peas) | | | | | | | | | | | | |
| boiled—*1 cup (171 g)* | 162 | 503 | 537 | 1012 | 894 | 188 | 145 | 771 | 428 | 629 | 915 | 410 |
| cnd—*1 cup (240 g)* | 139 | 432 | 463 | 871 | 770 | 161 | 125 | 665 | 367 | 542 | 787 | 353 |
| frzn, boiled—*½ cup (85 g)* | 83 | 269 | 387 | 515 | 474 | 103 | 107 | 396 | 296 | 418 | 506 | 233 |
| cowpeas, catjang, boiled—*1 cup (171 g)* | 171 | 528 | 564 | 1065 | 941 | 198 | 154 | 812 | 450 | 662 | 963 | 431 |
| cranberry beans | | | | | | | | | | | | |
| boiled—*1 cup (177 g)* | 196 | 696 | 729 | 1320 | 1135 | 248 | 181 | 894 | 466 | 866 | 1023 | 460 |
| cnd—*1 cup (260 g)* | 172 | 606 | 637 | 1152 | 991 | 216 | 156 | 780 | 406 | 754 | 892 | 400 |
| cucumber, raw—*½ cup slices (1/6 cucumber) (52 g)* | 2 | 8 | 9 | 12 | 11 | 2 | 2 | 8 | 5 | 9 | 18 | 4 |
| dock | | | | | | | | | | | | |
| raw—*½ cup chopped (67 g)* | 63 | 68 | 112 | 77 | 23 | | 76 | 56 | 89 | 72 | 36 | 88 |
| boiled—*3.5 oz (100 g)* | | 86 | 93 | 152 | 105 | 32 | | 104 | 75 | 121 | 98 | 49 |
| eggplant | | | | | | | | | | | | |
| raw—*½ cup pieces (41 g)* | 4 | 16 | 20 | 28 | 21 | 5 | 2 | 19 | 12 | 23 | 25 | 10 |
| boiled—*½ cup (48 g)* | 4 | 14 | 17 | 25 | 19 | 4 | 2 | 17 | 11 | 21 | 22 | 9 |
| endive, raw—*½ cup chopped (25 g)* | 1 | 13 | 18 | 25 | 16 | 4 | 3 | 13 | 10 | 16 | 16 | 6 |
| french beans, boiled—*1 cup (177 g)* | 147 | 526 | 550 | 997 | 857 | 188 | 136 | 674 | 352 | 653 | 773 | 347 |
| garlic, raw—*3 cloves (9 g)* | 6 | 14 | 20 | 28 | 25 | 7 | 6 | 16 | 7 | 26 | 57 | 10 |
| ginger root, raw—*¼ cup slices (24 g)* | 3 | 9 | 12 | 18 | 14 | 3 | 2 | 11 | 5 | 18 | 10 | 7 |
| gourd, calabash (white-flowered), boiled—*½ cup cubes (73 g)* | 2 | 12 | 23 | 26 | 15 | 3 | | 10 | | 19 | 10 | 3 |
| great northern beans | | | | | | | | | | | | |
| boiled—*1 cup (177 g)* | 175 | 621 | 651 | 1177 | 1012 | 221 | 161 | 798 | 416 | 772 | 913 | 411 |
| cnd—*1 cup (262 g)* | 228 | 812 | 852 | 1541 | 1326 | 291 | 210 | 1045 | 545 | 1011 | 1195 | 537 |
| green beans (snap beans)[e] | | | | | | | | | | | | |
| boiled—*½ cup (62 g)* | 12 | 51 | 43 | 72 | 56 | 14 | 11 | 43 | 27 | 58 | 47 | 22 |
| cnd—*½ cup (68 g)* | 8 | 34 | 29 | 48 | 37 | 10 | 7 | 29 | 18 | 39 | 31 | 15 |
| w/ onions, red peppers & garlic—*½ cup (114 g)* | 10 | 41 | 34 | 58 | 46 | 11 | 9 | 34 | 22 | 47 | 39 | 18 |
| frzn, boiled—*½ cup (68 g)* | 10 | 40 | 34 | 57 | 45 | 12 | 9 | 34 | 22 | 46 | 37 | 18 |
| hyacinth beans, boiled—*1 cup (194 g)* | 132 | 611 | 757 | 1341 | 1079 | 126 | 184 | 795 | 565 | 819 | 1160 | 452 |
| jute, potherb, boiled—*½ cup (43 g)* | 10 | 56 | 75 | 132 | 74 | 22 | 14 | 72 | 50 | 84 | 84 | 37 |
| kale | | | | | | | | | | | | |
| boiled—*½ cup chopped (65 g)* | 15 | 55 | 74 | 86 | 74 | 12 | 16 | 63 | 44 | 68 | 69 | 26 |
| frzn, boiled—*½ cup chopped (65 g)* | 23 | 83 | 110 | 129 | 110 | 18 | 25 | 95 | 66 | 101 | 103 | 39 |

[a] Chickpeas, lemon jce, tahini, olive oil & garlic.
[b] Cabbage, celery, table cream, sugar, green pepper, lemon jce, onion, pimiento, vinegar, salt, dry mustard & white pepper.
[c] Yellow corn, whole milk, egg, sugar, butter, salt & pepper.
[d] European herb widely cultivated as a salad plant & potherb.
[e] Includes Italian, green & yellow varieties.

| | TRY | THR | ISO | LEU | LYS | MET | CYS | PHE | TYR | VAL | ARG | HIS |
|---|---|---|---|---|---|---|---|---|---|---|---|---|
| kale, scotch, boiled—½ cup chopped (65 g) | 15 | 55 | 73 | 86 | 73 | 12 | 16 | 63 | 44 | 68 | 68 | 26 |
| kidney beans | | | | | | | | | | | | |
| boiled—1 cup (177 g) | 182 | 646 | 678 | 1227 | 1053 | 230 | 166 | 830 | 432 | 804 | 950 | 428 |
| cnd—1 cup (256 g) | 156 | 561 | 586 | 1062 | 911 | 200 | 146 | 719 | 374 | 696 | 824 | 371 |
| kidney beans, red | | | | | | | | | | | | |
| boiled—1 cup (177 g) | 182 | 646 | 678 | 1227 | 1053 | 230 | 166 | 830 | 432 | 804 | 950 | 428 |
| cnd—1 cup (256 g) | 159 | 566 | 594 | 1073 | 922 | 202 | 146 | 727 | 379 | 701 | 832 | 374 |
| kidney beans, red, california, boiled— 1 cup (177 g) | 191 | 680 | 713 | 1290 | 1110 | 242 | 175 | 874 | 455 | 846 | 1000 | 450 |
| kidney beans, royal, red, boiled—1 cup (177 g) | 198 | 706 | 742 | 1340 | 1152 | 253 | 182 | 908 | 473 | 878 | 1039 | 467 |
| kohlrabi, boiled—½ cup slices (82 g) | 9 | 43 | 68 | 58 | 48 | 11 | 6 | 34 | | 43 | 91 | 16 |
| lambsquarters, boiled—½ cup chopped (90 g) | 26 | 112 | 174 | 240 | 243 | 33 | 61 | 113 | 121 | 155 | 174 | 79 |
| leeks | | | | | | | | | | | | |
| raw—¼ cup chopped (26 g) | 3 | 16 | 14 | 25 | 20 | 5 | 7 | 14 | 11 | 15 | 20 | 7 |
| boiled—¼ cup chopped (26 g) | 2 | 9 | 7 | 14 | 11 | 3 | 4 | 8 | 6 | 8 | 11 | 4 |
| freeze-dried—¼ cup (0.8 g) | 1 | 5 | 4 | 8 | 6 | 1 | 2 | 4 | 3 | 5 | 6 | 2 |
| lentils, boiled—1 cup (198 g) | 160 | 640 | 772 | 1295 | 1247 | 152 | 234 | 881 | 477 | 887 | 1380 | 503 |
| lentils, sprouted, stir-fried—3.5 oz (100 g) | | 322 | 320 | 617 | 698 | 103 | 328 | 434 | 248 | 391 | 600 | 252 |
| lettuce | | | | | | | | | | | | |
| butterhead, rawª—2 leaves (15 g) | 1 | 9 | 12 | 12 | 13 | 2 | 2 | 8 | 5 | 10 | 11 | 3 |
| cos/romaine, raw—½ cup shredded (28 g) | 3 | 21 | 29 | 27 | 29 | 6 | 5 | 19 | 11 | 24 | 25 | 8 |
| iceberg, rawᵇ—1 leaf (20 g) | 2 | 11 | 15 | 14 | 15 | 3 | 3 | 10 | 6 | 12 | 13 | 4 |
| looseleaf, raw—½ cup shredded (28 g) | 3 | 17 | 24 | 22 | 24 | 4 | 4 | 15 | 9 | 20 | 20 | 6 |
| lima beans | | | | | | | | | | | | |
| boiled—1 cup (188 g) | 173 | 634 | 773 | 1265 | 983 | 186 | 162 | 844 | 519 | 882 | 899 | 447 |
| cnd—1 cup (241 g) | 140 | 513 | 624 | 1024 | 795 | 149 | 130 | 684 | 419 | 713 | 728 | 364 |
| lima beans, baby | | | | | | | | | | | | |
| boiled—1 cup (182 g) | 173 | 632 | 770 | 1263 | 981 | 186 | 162 | 843 | 517 | 881 | 897 | 448 |
| frzn, boiled—½ cup (90 g) | 78 | 254 | 385 | 470 | 395 | 97 | 73 | 295 | 193 | 374 | 400 | 203 |
| lima beans, fordhook, frzn, boiled— ½ cup (85 g) | 68 | 218 | 332 | 405 | 341 | 51 | 63 | 254 | 166 | 322 | 345 | 175 |
| lotus root | | | | | | | | | | | | |
| raw—10 slices (81 g) | 16 | 41 | 44 | 56 | 76 | 18 | 18 | 36 | 23 | 45 | 71 | 31 |
| boiled—10 slices (89 g) | 11 | 28 | 29 | 37 | 51 | 12 | 12 | 25 | 15 | 30 | 47 | 20 |
| lupins, boiled—1 cup (166 g) | 208 | 951 | 1154 | 1960 | 1381 | 183 | 319 | 1026 | 971 | 1079 | 2771 | 735 |
| mixed veg | | | | | | | | | | | | |
| cndᶜ—½ cup (82 g) | 21 | 85 | 103 | 141 | 126 | 25 | 20 | 89 | 55 | 111 | 143 | 54 |
| frznᵈ—½ cup (91 g) | 26 | 105 | 126 | 173 | 155 | 31 | 24 | 109 | 67 | 136 | 176 | 66 |
| mothbeans, boiled—1 cup (177 g) | 89 | 687 | 929 | 752 | 133 | 71 | 620 | | 443 | | 466 | |
| mountain yam, hawaii, steamed—½ cup cubes (72 g) | 10 | 44 | 42 | 78 | 48 | 17 | 15 | 58 | 33 | 50 | 104 | 27 |
| mung beans, boiled—1 cup (202 g) | 154 | 465 | 600 | 1099 | 990 | 170 | 125 | 859 | 424 | 735 | 994 | 414 |
| mung beans, sproutedᵉ | | | | | | | | | | | | |
| raw—½ cup (52 g) | 19 | 41 | 69 | 91 | 86 | 18 | 9 | 61 | 27 | 68 | 102 | 36 |
| cnd—½ cup (62 g) | 12 | 25 | 42 | 55 | 53 | 11 | 6 | 37 | 16 | 42 | 63 | 22 |
| ckd—½ cup (62 g) | 17 | 36 | 61 | 81 | 76 | 16 | 7 | 53 | 24 | 60 | 91 | 32 |
| stir-fried—½ cup (62 g) | 36 | 76 | 128 | 171 | 162 | 33 | 16 | 113 | 50 | 126 | 192 | 68 |
| mungo beans, boiled—1 cup (180 g) | 140 | 472 | 693 | 1125 | 900 | 198 | 126 | 792 | 421 | 761 | 884 | 380 |
| mushrooms | | | | | | | | | | | | |
| rawᶠ—½ cup pieces (35 g) | 16 | 33 | 29 | 45 | 74 | 14 | 2 | 28 | 16 | 34 | 36 | 20 |
| boiled—½ cup pieces (78 g) | 40 | 79 | 69 | 107 | 177 | 34 | 5 | 69 | 37 | 80 | 87 | 47 |
| cnd—½ cup pieces (78 g) | 34 | 69 | 60 | 92 | 153 | 29 | 4 | 59 | 33 | 69 | 75 | 41 |
| mushrooms, shitake | | | | | | | | | | | | |
| ckd—4 mushrooms (72 g) | 3 | 49 | 40 | 67 | 34 | 18 | 19 | 48 | 32 | 48 | 64 | 16 |
| dried—4 mushrooms (15 g) | 5 | 75 | 61 | 102 | 51 | 27 | 29 | 73 | 48 | 73 | 97 | 24 |

ª Includes Boston & Bibb types.
ᵇ Includes crisphead types.
ᶜ Carrots, green peas, snap beans & lima beans.
ᵈ Corn, lima beans, snap beans, green peas & carrots.
ᵉ Seeds attached to sprouts.
ᶠ Agaricus bisporus.

| | TRY | THR | ISO | LEU | LYS | MET | CYS | PHE | TYR | VAL | ARG | HIS |
|---|---|---|---|---|---|---|---|---|---|---|---|---|
| mustard greens | | | | | | | | | | | | |
| boiled—½ cup chopped (70 g) | 18 | 42 | 57 | 48 | 72 | 15 | 24 | 42 | 83 | 62 | 116 | 28 |
| frzn, boiled—½ cup chopped (75 g) | 19 | 45 | 62 | 53 | 77 | 16 | 26 | 45 | 90 | 66 | 125 | 31 |
| navy beans | | | | | | | | | | | | |
| boiled—1 cup (182 g) | 187 | 666 | 699 | 1265 | 1087 | 238 | 173 | 855 | 446 | 828 | 981 | 440 |
| cnd—1 cup (262 g) | 233 | 831 | 870 | 1575 | 1355 | 296 | 215 | 1066 | 555 | 1032 | 1221 | 548 |
| okra | | | | | | | | | | | | |
| boiled—½ cup slices (80 g) | 13 | 49 | 52 | 78 | 60 | 16 | 14 | 49 | 65 | 68 | 62 | 23 |
| frzn, boiled—½ cup slices (92 g) | 16 | 63 | 66 | 100 | 77 | 20 | 18 | 63 | 84 | 87 | 80 | 30 |
| onion rings, frzn, heated[a]—7 rings (70 g) | 49 | 105 | 150 | 245 | 106 | 57 | 76 | 170 | 110 | 151 | 228 | 76 |
| onions | | | | | | | | | | | | |
| raw—½ cup chopped (80 g) | 14 | 22 | 34 | 33 | 45 | 8 | 17 | 24 | 23 | 22 | 126 | 15 |
| boiled—½ cup chopped (105 g) | 14 | 23 | 34 | 34 | 45 | 7 | 17 | 24 | 23 | 22 | 127 | 16 |
| cnd—½ cup chopped (112 g) | 13 | 22 | 32 | 31 | 44 | 8 | 17 | 24 | 22 | 21 | 122 | 15 |
| dehydrated flakes—¼ cup (14 g) | 18 | 30 | 44 | 44 | 60 | 10 | 22 | 32 | 31 | 29 | 168 | 20 |
| frzn, boiled—3.5 oz (100 g) | 10 | 17 | 25 | 25 | 34 | 6 | 13 | 18 | 18 | 16 | 95 | 12 |
| onions, spring, raw[b]—½ cup chopped (50 g) | 10 | 34 | 37 | 52 | 44 | 10 | | 28 | 25 | 39 | 63 | 15 |
| onions, welsh, raw—3.5 oz (100 g) | 21 | 74 | 81 | 113 | 95 | 21 | | 61 | 55 | 84 | 137 | 33 |
| parsley | | | | | | | | | | | | |
| raw—½ cup chopped (30 g) | 11 | | | | 66 | 5 | | | | | | |
| freeze-dried—¼ cup (1.4 g) | 7 | | | | 44 | 3 | | | | | | |
| peas, green | | | | | | | | | | | | |
| raw—½ cup (78 g) | 29 | 158 | 152 | 252 | 247 | 64 | 25 | 156 | 88 | 183 | 334 | 83 |
| boiled—½ cup (80 g) | 30 | 161 | 154 | 256 | 251 | 65 | 26 | 158 | 90 | 186 | 338 | 84 |
| cnd—½ cup (85 g) | 26 | 140 | 135 | 224 | 220 | 57 | 22 | 139 | 79 | 163 | 297 | 74 |
| w/ onions, red peppers & garlic—½ cup (114 g) | 24 | 132 | 127 | 210 | 206 | 54 | 21 | 130 | 74 | 153 | 278 | 70 |
| frzn, boiled—½ cup (80 g) | 28 | 154 | 148 | 246 | 242 | 62 | 24 | 152 | 86 | 178 | 326 | 81 |
| peas, mature seeds, sprouted, boiled[c]—3.5 oz (100 g) | | 240 | 221 | 473 | 497 | 89 | 200 | 325 | 164 | 285 | 627 | 217 |
| peas, split, boiled—1 cup (196 g) | 182 | 580 | 674 | 1172 | 1180 | 167 | 249 | 753 | 474 | 772 | 1458 | 398 |
| peppers, hot chili[d] | | | | | | | | | | | | |
| raw—1 pepper (45 g) | 12 | 33 | 29 | 47 | 40 | 11 | 17 | 28 | 19 | 38 | 43 | 18 |
| cnd—½ cup chopped (68 g) | 8 | 22 | 20 | 32 | 27 | 7 | 12 | 19 | 13 | 26 | 29 | 12 |
| peppers, jalapeno, cnd—½ cup chopped (68 g) | 7 | 20 | 18 | 29 | 24 | 7 | 10 | 17 | 12 | 23 | 26 | 11 |
| peppers, sweet[d] | | | | | | | | | | | | |
| raw—½ cup chopped (50 g) | 6 | 16 | 14 | 22 | 19 | 5 | 8 | 13 | 9 | 18 | 21 | 9 |
| boiled—½ cup chopped (68 g) | 5 | 16 | 14 | 22 | 19 | 5 | 8 | 13 | 9 | 18 | 20 | 9 |
| cnd—½ cup halves (70 g) | 7 | 20 | 18 | 29 | 25 | 7 | 11 | 18 | 12 | 24 | 27 | 11 |
| freeze-dried—¼ cup (1.6 g) | 4 | 11 | 9 | 15 | 13 | 3 | 6 | 9 | 6 | 12 | 14 | 6 |
| frzn, boiled—3.5 oz (100 g) | 12 | 35 | 31 | 49 | 42 | 11 | 18 | 29 | 20 | 40 | 45 | 19 |
| pigeonpeas, boiled—1 cup (168 g) | 111 | 402 | 412 | 811 | 796 | 128 | 131 | 973 | 282 | 491 | 680 | 405 |
| pink beans, boiled—1 cup (169 g) | 181 | 644 | 676 | 1222 | 1051 | 230 | 167 | 828 | 431 | 801 | 948 | 426 |
| pinto beans | | | | | | | | | | | | |
| boiled—1 cup (171 g) | 166 | 592 | 621 | 1122 | 964 | 212 | 152 | 759 | 395 | 735 | 870 | 392 |
| cnd—1 cup (240 g) | 130 | 461 | 482 | 874 | 751 | 166 | 120 | 593 | 307 | 574 | 679 | 305 |
| potato | | | | | | | | | | | | |
| raw w/o skin—1 potato (112 g) | 36 | 84 | 94 | 139 | 141 | 37 | 29 | 103 | 86 | 131 | 106 | 50 |
| baked w/ skin—1 potato (202 g) | 73 | 170 | 188 | 279 | 283 | 73 | 59 | 206 | 172 | 263 | 214 | 101 |
| baked w/o skin—1 potato (156 g) | 47 | 111 | 125 | 184 | 186 | 48 | 39 | 136 | 114 | 172 | 140 | 67 |
| boiled w/o skin—1 potato (135 g) | 36 | 84 | 95 | 139 | 140 | 36 | 30 | 103 | 86 | 130 | 107 | 51 |
| cnd w/o skin—½ cup (90 g) | 20 | 46 | 51 | 77 | 77 | 20 | 16 | 57 | 47 | 72 | 59 | 28 |
| cottage fries, frzn, heated[e]—10 strips (50 g) | 23 | 78 | 74 | 104 | 92 | 20 | 11 | 74 | 43 | 88 | 82 | 29 |
| french fried, from restaurant[f]—10 pieces (50 g) | 27 | 92 | 87 | 122 | 107 | 23 | 13 | 86 | 51 | 103 | 96 | 34 |

[a] Breaded & parboiled in veg oil.
[b] Includes tops & bulbs.
[c] Seeds attached to sprouts.

[d] Includes green & red varieties.
[e] Pan-fried in veg oil.
[f] Fried in veg oil.

| | TRY | THR | ISO | LEU | LYS | MET | CYS | PHE | TYR | VAL | ARG | HIS |
|---|---|---|---|---|---|---|---|---|---|---|---|---|
| french fried, frzn, heated[a]—*10 pieces (50 g)* | 24 | 79 | 75 | 105 | 92 | 20 | 11 | 74 | 44 | 88 | 82 | 29 |
| frzn, boiled w/o skin—*3.5 oz (100 g)* | 31 | 72 | 80 | 119 | 120 | 31 | 25 | 88 | 73 | 111 | 91 | 43 |
| hash brown, frzn, prep[b]—*½ cup (78 g)* | 33 | 112 | 106 | 148 | 131 | 27 | 16 | 105 | 62 | 126 | 116 | 41 |
| hash brown, homemade[b]—*½ cup (78 g)* | 26 | 86 | 81 | 114 | 100 | 21 | 12 | 80 | 48 | 96 | 90 | 32 |
| mashed, from flakes[c]—*½ cup (105 g)* | 20 | 89 | 102 | 158 | 140 | 34 | 23 | 95 | 86 | 125 | 88 | 48 |
| mashed, from granules[c]—*½ cup (105 g)* | 32 | 144 | 161 | 247 | 223 | 51 | 39 | 153 | 138 | 200 | 147 | 78 |
| mashed, homemade[d]—*½ cup (105 g)* | 30 | 77 | 91 | 139 | 130 | 37 | 24 | 90 | 80 | 118 | 86 | 46 |
| microwaved w/ skin—*1 potato (202 g)* | 77 | 180 | 200 | 297 | 301 | 79 | 63 | 220 | 184 | 279 | 228 | 109 |
| microwaved w/o skin—*1 potato (156 g)* | 52 | 119 | 133 | 197 | 200 | 51 | 42 | 145 | 122 | 184 | 151 | 72 |
| potato pancakes, homemade[e]—*1 pancake (76 g)* | 72 | 192 | 234 | 337 | 282 | 107 | 86 | 231 | 178 | 286 | 258 | 106 |
| potato salad, homemade[f]—*½ cup (125 g)* | 53 | 145 | 176 | 253 | 214 | 83 | 64 | 169 | 130 | 215 | 190 | 78 |
| potatoes, au gratin, homemade[g]—*½ cup (122 g)* | 85 | 234 | 346 | 540 | 465 | 143 | 54 | 310 | 281 | 397 | 248 | 184 |
| potatoes, o'brien frzn, prep—*3.5 oz (100 g)* | 34 | 80 | 89 | 131 | 132 | 34 | 30 | 95 | 79 | 120 | 111 | 48 |
| homemade[h]—*1 cup (194 g)* | 68 | 173 | 213 | 328 | 279 | 83 | 58 | 206 | 178 | 258 | 211 | 105 |
| potatoes, scalloped, homemade[i]—*½ cup (122 g)* | 51 | 140 | 176 | 275 | 234 | 71 | 41 | 165 | 148 | 212 | 144 | 85 |
| pumpkin boiled—*½ cup mashed (122 g)* | 11 | 26 | 28 | 41 | 48 | 10 | 2 | 28 | 37 | 31 | 48 | 13 |
| cnd—*½ cup (122 g)* | 16 | 39 | 41 | 62 | 73 | 15 | 4 | 43 | 56 | 46 | 72 | 21 |
| pumpkin pie mix, cnd—*½ cup (135 g)* | 18 | 42 | 46 | 68 | 80 | 16 | 4 | 47 | 61 | 51 | 78 | 23 |
| purslane, boiled—*½ cup (58 g)* | 9 | 29 | 31 | 53 | 38 | 8 | 6 | 34 | 14 | 42 | 33 | 13 |
| radish, raw—*10 radishes (45 g)* | 2 | 13 | 14 | 17 | 16 | 3 | 2 | 10 | 6 | 14 | 18 | 6 |
| radish, oriental[j] raw—*½ cup slices (44 g)* | 1 | 11 | 11 | 14 | 13 | 3 | 2 | 9 | 5 | 12 | 15 | 5 |
| boiled—*½ cup slices (74 g)* | 3 | 21 | 21 | 26 | 24 | 4 | 4 | 16 | 10 | 23 | 29 | 10 |
| dried—*½ cup (58 g)* | 25 | 189 | 200 | 240 | 228 | 44 | 36 | 152 | 87 | 212 | 264 | 86 |
| rutabaga, boiled—*½ cup cubes (85 g)* | 10 | 36 | 39 | 30 | 31 | 8 | 9 | 25 | 18 | 37 | 116 | 23 |
| seaweed kelp (kombu/tangle), raw—*3.5 oz (100 g)* | 48 | 55 | 76 | 83 | 82 | 25 | 98 | 43 | 26 | 72 | 65 | 24 |
| laver (nori), raw—*3.5 oz (100 g)* | 43 | 232 | 259 | 501 | 222 | 145 | 100 | 273 | 254 | 402 | 285 | 140 |
| spirulina, raw—*3.5 oz (100 g)* | 96 | 306 | 331 | 509 | 312 | 118 | 68 | 286 | 266 | 362 | 427 | 112 |
| spirulina, dried—*3.5 oz (100 g)* | 929 | 2970 | 3209 | 4947 | 3025 | 1149 | 662 | 2777 | 2584 | 3512 | 4147 | 1085 |
| wakame, raw—*3.5 oz (100 g)* | 35 | 165 | 87 | 257 | 112 | 63 | 28 | 112 | 49 | 209 | 92 | 15 |
| shallots raw—*1 T chopped (10 g)* | 3 | 10 | 11 | 15 | 13 | 3 | | 8 | 7 | 11 | 18 | 4 |
| freeze-dried—*¼ cup (4 g)* | 5 | 17 | 19 | 26 | 22 | 5 | | 14 | 13 | 20 | 32 | 8 |
| soybean products miso—*½ cup (138 g)* | 197 | 882 | 1119 | 1558 | 911 | 206 | 131 | 822 | 500 | 1024 | 1031 | 454 |
| natto—*½ cup (88 g)* | 196 | 715 | 819 | 1328 | 1008 | 183 | 194 | 828 | 489 | 896 | 800 | 451 |
| tempeh—*½ cup (83 g)* | 234 | 639 | 832 | 1358 | 934 | 220 | 265 | 840 | 608 | 813 | 1093 | 413 |
| tofu, dried-frozen (koyadufu)—*1 piece (17 g)* | 127 | 333 | 404 | 619 | 537 | 104 | 113 | 397 | 273 | 411 | 542 | 237 |
| tofu, fried—*1 piece (13 g)* | 35 | 91 | 111 | 170 | 147 | 29 | 31 | 109 | 75 | 113 | 149 | 65 |
| tofu, okara—*½ cup (61 g)* | 31 | 80 | 97 | 149 | 129 | 25 | 27 | 96 | 66 | 99 | 131 | 57 |
| tofu, raw—*½ cup (124 g)* | 156 | 409 | 496 | 761 | 660 | 128 | 139 | 487 | 335 | 506 | 667 | 291 |
| tofu, raw, firm—*½ cup (126 g)* | 310 | 811 | 985 | 1511 | 1309 | 255 | 275 | 968 | 665 | 1003 | 1323 | 578 |

[a] Pan-fried in veg oil.
[b] Prepared w/ veg oil.
[c] Whole milk & butter added.
[d] Whole milk, margarine & salt added.
[e] Potatoes, eggs, onion, margarine, flour & salt.
[f] Potatoes, egg, mayonnaise, celery, sweet pickle relish, onion, green pepper, pimiento, salt & dry mustard.

[g] Potatoes, whole milk, cheddar cheese, butter, flour & salt.
[h] Potatoes, whole milk, onions, green pepper, bread crumbs, salt, butter & black pepper.
[i] Potatoes, whole milk, butter, flour & salt.
[j] Includes daikon (Japanese) & Chinese.

| | TRY | THR | ISO | LEU | LYS | MET | CYS | PHE | TYR | VAL | ARG | HIS |
|---|---|---|---|---|---|---|---|---|---|---|---|---|
| tofu, salted & fermented (fuyu)—*1 block (11 g)* | 14 | 37 | 44 | 68 | 59 | 11 | 12 | 44 | 30 | 45 | 60 | 26 |
| soybeans, green, boiled—*½ cup (90 g)* | 135 | 443 | 489 | 795 | 665 | 135 | 102 | 503 | 399 | 494 | 895 | 299 |
| soybeans, mature, boiled—*1 cup (172 g)* | 416 | 1244 | 1388 | 2331 | 1906 | 385 | 461 | 1495 | 1084 | 1429 | 2221 | 772 |
| soybeans, mature, sprouted[a] | | | | | | | | | | | | |
| steamed—*½ cup (47 g)* | 91 | 231 | 199 | 334 | 278 | 45 | 21 | 159 | 131 | 223 | 191 | 107 |
| stir-fried[b]—*3.5 oz (100 g)* | 300 | 759 | 654 | 1100 | 916 | 147 | 69 | 524 | 432 | 734 | 629 | 352 |
| spinach | | | | | | | | | | | | |
| raw—*½ cup chopped (28 g)* | 11 | 34 | 41 | 62 | 49 | 15 | 10 | 36 | 30 | 45 | 45 | 18 |
| boiled—*½ cup (90 g)* | 36 | 114 | 137 | 208 | 164 | 50 | 32 | 121 | 102 | 151 | 151 | 59 |
| cnd—*½ cup (107 g)* | 41 | 128 | 154 | 234 | 184 | 56 | 36 | 136 | 113 | 169 | 170 | 66 |
| frzn, boiled—*½ cup (95 g)* | 40 | 127 | 152 | 232 | 182 | 55 | 36 | 135 | 113 | 168 | 169 | 66 |
| squash, summer | | | | | | | | | | | | |
| all varieties, raw—*½ cup slices (65 g)* | 7 | 18 | 27 | 45 | 42 | 11 | 8 | 27 | 20 | 34 | 33 | 16 |
| all varieties, boiled—*½ cup slices (90 g)* | 7 | 20 | 30 | 48 | 45 | 12 | 9 | 29 | 22 | 37 | 34 | 18 |
| crookneck, raw[c]—*½ cup slices (65 g)* | 5 | 15 | 22 | 36 | 34 | 9 | 7 | 21 | 16 | 27 | 26 | 13 |
| crookneck, boiled[c]—*½ cup slices (90 g)* | 7 | 20 | 30 | 48 | 45 | 12 | 9 | 29 | 22 | 37 | 34 | 18 |
| crookneck, cnd[c]—*½ cup slices (108 g)* | 5 | 16 | 24 | 39 | 37 | 10 | 6 | 24 | 17 | 30 | 28 | 14 |
| crookneck, frzn, boiled[c]—*½ cup slices (96 g)* | 11 | 30 | 44 | 72 | 68 | 17 | 13 | 43 | 33 | 56 | 52 | 27 |
| scallop, raw—*½ cup slices (65 g)* | 7 | 19 | 28 | 46 | 44 | 11 | 8 | 27 | 21 | 35 | 33 | 17 |
| scallop, boiled—*½ cup slices (90 g)* | 8 | 23 | 33 | 55 | 51 | 14 | 10 | 32 | 25 | 42 | 40 | 20 |
| zucchini, raw—*½ cup slices (65 g)* | 7 | 18 | 27 | 44 | 42 | 11 | 8 | 27 | 20 | 34 | 32 | 16 |
| zucchini, boiled—*½ cup slices (90 g)* | 5 | 14 | 21 | 33 | 32 | 8 | 6 | 20 | 15 | 26 | 24 | 13 |
| zucchini, frzn, boiled—*½ cup slices (112 g)* | 11 | 31 | 46 | 75 | 72 | 18 | 13 | 45 | 35 | 58 | 54 | 28 |
| zucchini, italian style, cnd[d]—*½ cup slices (114 g)* | 10 | 29 | 42 | 68 | 65 | 17 | 13 | 41 | 31 | 52 | 49 | 25 |
| squash, winter | | | | | | | | | | | | |
| all varieties, baked—*½ cup cubes (102 g)* | 13 | 28 | 36 | 51 | 34 | 11 | 8 | 36 | 31 | 39 | 50 | 17 |
| acorn, baked—*½ cup cubes (102 g)* | 16 | 34 | 45 | 65 | 42 | 14 | 10 | 45 | 39 | 49 | 64 | 21 |
| acorn, boiled, mashed—*½ cup (122 g)* | 12 | 24 | 32 | 46 | 31 | 10 | 7 | 32 | 28 | 35 | 45 | 16 |
| butternut, boiled—*½ cup cubes (102 g)* | 13 | 28 | 36 | 52 | 34 | 11 | 8 | 36 | 31 | 40 | 51 | 17 |
| butternut, frzn, boiled—*½ cup mashed (120 g)* | 20 | 44 | 58 | 84 | 54 | 18 | 13 | 58 | 49 | 64 | 82 | 28 |
| hubbard, baked—*½ cup cubes (102 g)* | 21 | 45 | 59 | 86 | 56 | 18 | 13 | 59 | 51 | 65 | 84 | 29 |
| hubbard, boiled, mashed—*½ cup (118 g)* | 25 | 52 | 68 | 99 | 65 | 21 | 15 | 68 | 59 | 76 | 97 | 33 |
| spaghetti, boiled/baked—*½ cup (78 g)* | 7 | 14 | 19 | 27 | 17 | 5 | 4 | 19 | 16 | 20 | 26 | 9 |
| succotash | | | | | | | | | | | | |
| boiled—*½ cup (96 g)* | 55 | 203 | 275 | 428 | 285 | 65 | 53 | 235 | 166 | 296 | 284 | 155 |
| cnd—*½ cup (128 g)* | 37 | 138 | 188 | 293 | 195 | 45 | 36 | 161 | 114 | 202 | 195 | 106 |
| cnd w/ cream style corn—*½ cup (133 g)* | 40 | 146 | 198 | 309 | 205 | 47 | 39 | 169 | 120 | 213 | 205 | 112 |
| frzn, boiled—*½ cup (85 g)* | 41 | 152 | 207 | 322 | 214 | 49 | 40 | 177 | 125 | 223 | 213 | 116 |
| swamp cabbage | | | | | | | | | | | | |
| raw—*1 cup chopped (56 g)* | | 78 | 58 | 82 | 61 | 25 | 16 | 71 | 45 | 76 | 83 | 26 |
| boiled—*½ cup chopped (49 g)* | | 55 | 41 | 57 | 43 | 17 | 11 | 50 | 31 | 53 | 58 | 18 |
| sweet potato | | | | | | | | | | | | |
| baked—*1 sweet potato (114 g)* | 24 | 98 | 98 | 144 | 97 | 48 | 16 | 117 | 81 | 128 | 91 | 36 |
| boiled—*½ cup mashed (164 g)* | 33 | 134 | 134 | 198 | 133 | 67 | 21 | 62 | 112 | 177 | 126 | 51 |
| candied[e]—*1 piece 2½″ long & 2″ diameter (105 g)* | 12 | 45 | 46 | 68 | 46 | 22 | 7 | 55 | 38 | 60 | 42 | 18 |
| cnd—*1 cup pieces (200 g)* | 40 | 164 | 166 | 242 | 162 | 82 | 26 | 198 | 136 | 216 | 154 | 62 |
| syrup pack—*½ cup (98 g)* | 16 | 63 | 63 | 92 | 62 | 31 | 10 | 75 | 52 | 82 | 59 | 24 |
| frzn, baked—*½ cup cubes (88 g)* | 18 | 75 | 76 | 111 | 74 | 37 | 12 | 91 | 62 | 99 | 70 | 28 |

[a] Seeds attached to sprouts.
[b] Stir-fried in veg oil.
[c] Includes straightneck varieties.

[d] Packed in tomato jce.
[e] Canned sweet potato & syrup, brown sugar, butter & salt.

| | TRY | THR | ISO | LEU | LYS | MET | CYS | PHE | TYR | VAL | ARG | HIS |
|---|---|---|---|---|---|---|---|---|---|---|---|---|
| taro, ckd—½ cup slices (66 g) | 5 | 16 | 13 | 25 | 15 | 5 | 7 | 18 | 13 | 18 | 24 | 8 |
| tomato, green, raw—1 tomato (123 g) | 11 | 37 | 36 | 54 | 54 | 12 | 20 | 38 | 26 | 38 | 36 | 22 |
| tomato, red | | | | | | | | | | | | |
|   raw—1 tomato (123 g) | 9 | 27 | 26 | 41 | 41 | 10 | 15 | 28 | 18 | 28 | 27 | 16 |
|   boiled—½ cup (120 g) | 10 | 34 | 32 | 49 | 49 | 12 | 17 | 35 | 23 | 35 | 32 | 20 |
|   cnd | | | | | | | | | | | | |
|     stewed—½ cup (128 g) | 9 | 29 | 28 | 44 | 44 | 10 | 15 | 31 | 20 | 31 | 28 | 18 |
|     wedges in tomato jce—½ cup (131 g) | 8 | 26 | 25 | 38 | 38 | 9 | 13 | 28 | 18 | 26 | 25 | 16 |
|     whole, peeled—½ cup (120 g) | 8 | 29 | 26 | 41 | 41 | 10 | 14 | 29 | 19 | 29 | 28 | 17 |
|     stewed[a]—1 cup (101 g) | 20 | 52 | 63 | 102 | 48 | 23 | 26 | 74 | 45 | 68 | 57 | 35 |
| tomato paste, cnd—½ cup (131 g) | 34 | 113 | 96 | 138 | 141 | 25 | 29 | 105 | 67 | 101 | 100 | 79 |
| tomato puree—1 cup (250 g) | 28 | 95 | 80 | 115 | 120 | 23 | 25 | 88 | 55 | 85 | 83 | 65 |
| turnip | | | | | | | | | | | | |
|   boiled—½ cup cubes (78 g) | 5 | 16 | 23 | 20 | 22 | 7 | 3 | 11 | 9 | 18 | 15 | 9 |
|   frzn, boiled—3.5 oz (100 g) | 15 | 42 | 62 | 57 | 61 | 19 | 9 | 30 | 23 | 51 | 41 | 24 |
| turnip greens | | | | | | | | | | | | |
|   raw—½ cup chopped (28 g) | 7 | 23 | 22 | 38 | 27 | 10 | 5 | 26 | 16 | 29 | 26 | 10 |
|   boiled—½ cup chopped (72 g) | 14 | 45 | 42 | 76 | 53 | 19 | 9 | 50 | 32 | 56 | 52 | 20 |
|   cnd—½ cup (117 g) | 27 | 87 | 82 | 145 | 103 | 36 | 18 | 97 | 62 | 108 | 99 | 39 |
|   frzn, boiled—½ cup (82 g) | 48 | 151 | 142 | 252 | 179 | 62 | 31 | 169 | 107 | 187 | 172 | 66 |
| turnip greens & turnips, frzn, boiled—3.5 oz (100 g) | 31 | 97 | 101 | 156 | 120 | 41 | 20 | 102 | 66 | 120 | 108 | 45 |
| vegetable combinations, cnd | | | | | | | | | | | | |
|   peas & carrots—½ cup (128 g) | 20 | 104 | 101 | 160 | 157 | 40 | 17 | 101 | 58 | 120 | 210 | 54 |
|   peas & onions—½ cup (60 g) | 14 | 72 | 71 | 115 | 114 | 29 | 13 | 71 | 42 | 83 | 162 | 38 |
| vegetable combinations, frzn | | | | | | | | | | | | |
|   peas & carrots—½ cup (80 g) | 18 | 93 | 90 | 143 | 140 | 35 | 15 | 90 | 51 | 107 | 187 | 48 |
|   peas & onions, boiled—½ cup (90 g) | 17 | 84 | 82 | 133 | 132 | 33 | 15 | 83 | 49 | 96 | 188 | 44 |
| vinespinach, raw—3.5 oz (100 g) | 28 | 55 | 53 | 101 | 86 | 19 | 27 | 85 | 48 | 65 | 70 | 39 |
| watercress, raw—½ cup chopped (17 g) | 5 | 23 | 16 | 28 | 23 | 3 | 1 | 19 | 11 | 23 | 26 | 7 |
| waxgourd, boiled[b]—½ cup cubes (87 g) | 2 | | | | 8 | 3 | | | | | | |
| white beans | | | | | | | | | | | | |
|   boiled—1 cup (179 g) | 206 | 732 | 768 | 1389 | 1196 | 261 | 190 | 942 | 490 | 911 | 1078 | 485 |
|   cnd—1 cup (262 g) | 225 | 799 | 838 | 1517 | 1305 | 286 | 207 | 1027 | 534 | 996 | 1176 | 529 |
| white beans, small, boiled—1 cup (179 g) | 190 | 675 | 709 | 1282 | 1103 | 242 | 175 | 868 | 453 | 840 | 993 | 448 |
| winged beans, boiled—1 cup (172 g) | 401 | 619 | 771 | 1311 | 1121 | 187 | 286 | 750 | 765 | 803 | 991 | 415 |
| yam, boiled/baked[c]—½ cup cubes (68 g) | 8 | 35 | 34 | 64 | 39 | 14 | 12 | 47 | 27 | 41 | 84 | 22 |
| yambean, boiled—3.5 oz (100 g) | | 30 | 26 | 40 | 42 | 11 | 10 | 27 | 19 | 35 | 61 | 31 |
| yardlong bean, boiled—1 cup (171 g) | 174 | 540 | 576 | 1086 | 959 | 202 | 156 | 828 | 458 | 675 | 982 | 439 |
| yellow beans, boiled—1 cup (177 g) | 191 | 683 | 717 | 1296 | 1113 | 244 | 177 | 878 | 457 | 848 | 1004 | 451 |
| **35. Miscellaneous** | | | | | | | | | | | | |
| soybean protein concentrate—1 oz (28 g) | 234 | 693 | 824 | 1377 | 1100 | 228 | 248 | 918 | 644 | 858 | 1300 | 442 |
| soybean protein isolate—1 oz (28 g) | 312 | 878 | 1191 | 1899 | 1492 | 316 | 293 | 1286 | 902 | 1147 | 1868 | 645 |
| tomato powder—3½ oz (100 g) | 89 | 295 | 250 | 359 | 370 | 66 | 76 | 273 | 173 | 264 | 258 | 204 |
| whey | | | | | | | | | | | | |
|   acid, dry—1 T (3 g) | 7 | 17 | 17 | 32 | 29 | 6 | 6 | 11 | 9 | 17 | 9 | 7 |
|   acid, fluid—1 cup (246 g) | 38 | 94 | 93 | 178 | 161 | 35 | 34 | 62 | 48 | 92 | 52 | 37 |
|   sweet, dry—1 T (8 g) | 15 | 61 | 54 | 88 | 77 | 18 | 19 | 30 | 27 | 52 | 28 | 18 |
|   sweet, fluid—1 cup (246 g) | 33 | 132 | 116 | 192 | 166 | 39 | 41 | 66 | 59 | 113 | 61 | 38 |
| yeast, tortula, dried, Lake States—3.5 oz (100 g) | 523 | 2565 | 2660 | 4133 | 4133 | 285 | 190 | 2613 | 1663 | 3088 | 2803 | 1093 |

[a] Tomatoes, bread crumbs, margarine, sugar, onions, salt & pepper.

[b] Chinese preserving melon.

[c] This is the true yam of tropical areas (Dioscorea species), not the american yam which is really a sweet potato.

# Alcohol (Ethanol) Content of Alcoholic Beverages

| | weight (g) | volume (%) | | weight (g) | volume (%) |
|---|---|---|---|---|---|
| **ALES, BEERS & MALT LIQUORS** | | | **COCKTAILS & COCKTAIL MIXES** | | |
| ale, Blatz Cream—*12 fl oz (360g)* | 15.5 | | pina colada | | |
| beer—*12 fl oz (356g)* | 12.8 | 4.5 | cnd—*6.8 fl oz can (222g)* | 20.0 | 11.2 |
| Anheuser-Busch—*12 fl oz (355g)* | 13.5 | | pineapple jce, rum, sugar & coconut cream—*4.5 fl oz cocktail (141g)* | 14.0 | 12.3 |
| Black Label—*12 fl oz (360g)* | 12.6 | | screwdriver (orange jce & vodka)—*7 fl oz cocktail (213g)* | 14.1 | 8.2 |
| Blatz—*12 fl oz (360g)* | 13.1 | 4.6 | tequila sunrise | | |
| Coors Premium—*12 fl oz (360g)* | 13.2 | | cnd—*6.8 fl oz can (211g)* | 19.8 | 11.7 |
| Heileman's Old Style—*12 fl oz (360g)* | 13.7 | | orange jce, tequila, lime jce & grenadine—*5.5 fl oz cocktail (172g)* | 18.7 | 13.5 |
| Heileman's Special Export—*12 fl oz (360g)* | 15.5 | | tom collins (club soda, gin, lemon jce & sugar)—*7.5 fl oz cocktail (222g)* | 16.0 | 9.0 |
| Heileman's Special Export Dark—*12 fl oz (360g)* | 15.5 | | whiskey sour | | |
| Herman Joseph's—*12 fl oz (360g)* | 14.2 | 4.95 | cnd—*6.8 fl oz cocktail (209g)* | 19.9 | 11.8 |
| Killian's—*12 fl oz (360g)* | 15.6 | 5.43 | lemon jce, whiskey & sugar—*3 fl oz cocktail (90g)* | 15.1 | 20.6 |
| Rainier—*12 fl oz (360g)* | 13.1 | | prep from bottled mix—*2 fl oz mix & 1.5 fl oz whiskey (106g)* | 14.9 | 17.4 |
| Schmidt—*12 fl oz (360g)* | 13.1 | | prep from powdered mix—*17 g pkt, 1.5 fl oz water & 1.5 fl oz whiskey (103g)* | 15.0 | 18.0 |
| Stroh's American Lager—*12 fl oz (355g)* | 12.0 | | | | |
| beer, light—*12 fl oz (354g)* | 11.3[a] | 4.0 | **DISTILLED SPIRITS** | | |
| Anheuser-Busch—*12 fl oz (355g)* | 11.0 | | gin, 90 proof—*1.5 fl oz jigger (42g)* | 15.9 | 45.0 |
| Blatz—*12 fl oz (360g)* | 11.9 | | gin/rum/vodka/whiskey, 94 proof—*1.5 fl oz jigger (42g)* | 16.7 | 47.0 |
| Coors—*12 fl oz (360g)* | 11.9 | 4.18 | gin/rum/vodka/whiskey, 100 proof—*1.5 fl oz jigger (42g)* | 17.9 | 50.0 |
| Heileman's Old Style—*12 fl oz (360g)* | 10.3 | | rum, 80 proof—*1.5 fl oz jigger (42g)* | 14.0 | 40.0 |
| Heileman's Special Export—*12 fl oz (360g)* | 11.9 | | vodka, 80 proof—*1.5 fl oz jigger (42g)* | 14.0 | 40.0 |
| beer, LA (low alcohol) | | | whiskey, 86 proof—*1.5 fl oz jigger (42g)* | 15.1 | 43.0 |
| Anheuser-Busch—*12 fl oz (355g)* | 6.4 | | | | |
| Blatz—*12 fl oz (360g)* | 6.5 | | **LIQUEURS** | | |
| Heileman's Old Style—*12 fl oz (360g)* | 6.5 | | coffee, 53 proof—*1.5 fl oz (52g)* | 11.3 | 26.5 |
| malt beverages, nonalcoholic—*12 fl oz (360g)* | 0.7 | 0.3 | coffee, 63 proof—*1.5 fl oz (52g)* | 13.5 | 31.5 |
| Kingsbury—*12 fl oz (360g)* | 1.0 | | coffee w/ cream, 34 proof—*1.5 fl oz (47g)* | 6.5 | 17.0 |
| malt liquor | | | creme de menthe—*1.5 fl oz (50g)* | 14.9 | 36.0 |
| Blatz Old Fashioned Private Stock—*12 fl oz (360g)* | 13.7 | | | | |
| Colt 45—*12 fl oz (360g)* | 15.7 | | **WINES & WINE BEVERAGES** | | |
| | | | sparkling cooler, citrus, La Croix—*12 fl oz (360g)* | 12.6 | |
| **COCKTAILS & COCKTAIL MIXES** | | | sparkling cooler, strawberry, La Croix—*12 fl oz (360g)* | 12.6 | |
| bloody mary (tomato jce, vodka & lemon jce)—*5 fl oz cocktail (148g)* | 13.9 | 11.7 | wine, dessert, dry—*2 fl oz (59g)* | 9.0 | 18.8 |
| bourbon & soda—*4 fl oz cocktail (116g)* | 15.1 | 16.1 | wine, dessert, sweet—*2 fl oz (59g)* | 9.0 | 18.8 |
| daiquiri | | | wine, table, all types—*3.5 fl oz (103g)* | 9.6 | 11.5 |
| cnd—*6.8 oz can (207g)* | 19.9 | 11.9 | wine, table, red—*3.5 fl oz (103g)* | 9.6 | 11.5 |
| rum, lime jce & sugar—*2 fl oz cocktail (60g)* | 13.9 | 28.3 | wine, table, rose—*3.5 fl oz (103g)* | 9.6 | 11.5 |
| gin & tonic (tonic water, gin & lime jce)—*7.5 fl oz cocktail (225g)* | 16.0 | 8.8 | wine, table, white—*3.5 fl oz (103g)* | 9.6 | 11.5 |
| manhattan (whiskey & vermouth)—*2 fl oz cocktail (57g)* | 17.4 | 36.9 | | | |
| martini (gin & vermouth)—*2.5 fl oz cocktail (70g)* | 22.4 | 38.4 | | | |

[a] Range from 7.8 to 15.6 mg.

# Biotin (mcg)

**CEREALS, COOKED OR TO-BE-COOKED**

| | |
|---|---:|
| corn grits, inst, white hominy, enr | |
| Quaker—*1 pkt (4/5 cup ckd) (23 g)* | 1 |
| w/ cheddar cheese flavor, Quaker—*1 oz pkt (28 g)* | 1 |
| w/ imit bacon bits, Quaker—*1 oz pkt (28 g)* | 2 |
| w/ imit ham bits, Quaker—*1 oz pkt (28 g)* | 1 |
| corn grits, quick, yellow hominy, enr, Quaker—*3 T (1 oz) (28 g)* | 1 |
| corn grits, reg/quick, white hominy, enr, Quaker/Aunt Jemima—*3 T (1 oz) (28 g)* | 1 |
| farina, dry, quick, creamy wheat, Quaker—*2½ T (1 oz) (28 g)* | 1 |
| oatmeal, inst, Quaker—*1 pkt (¾ cup ckd) (28 g)* | 7 |
| w/ apples & cinn—*1 pkt (¾ cup ckd) (35 g)* | 4 |
| w/ bran & raisins—*1 pkt (¾ cup ckd) (43 g)* | 7 |
| w/ cinn & spice—*1 pkt (¾ cup ckd) (46 g)* | 6 |
| w/ honey & graham—*1 pkt (¾ cup ckd) (35 g)* | 4 |
| w/ maple & brown sugar—*1 pkt (¾ cup ckd) (43 g)* | 7 |
| w/ peaches & cream—*1 pkt (¾ cup ckd) (35 g)* | 4 |
| w/ raisins & spice—*1 pkt (¾ cup ckd) (43 g)* | 6 |
| w/ raisins, dates & walnuts—*1 pkt (¾ cup) (37 g)* | 4 |
| w/ strawberries & cream—*1 pkt (¾ cup) (35 g)* | 4 |
| oatmeal, quick/old fashioned, Quaker—*⅓ cup dry (⅔ cup ckd) (28 g)* | 4 |
| oatmeal, quick/reg, Ralston Purina—*1 oz dry (28 g)* | 4.5 |
| ralston, ckd—*¾ cup (190 g)* | 1.9 |

**CEREALS, READY-TO-EAT**

| | |
|---|---:|
| bran chex, Ralston Purina—*⅔ cup (1 oz) (28 g)* | 3.3 |
| cap'n crunch, Quaker—*¾ cup (1 oz) (28 g)* | 1 |
| cap'n crunch's | |
| choco crunch, Quaker—*¾ cup (1 oz) (28 g)* | 1 |
| crunchberries, Quaker—*¾ cup (1 oz) (28 g)* | 1 |
| peanut butter, Quaker—*¾ cup (1 oz) (28 g)* | 2 |
| cookie crisp, choc chip, Ralston Purina—*1 cup (1 oz) (28 g)* | 0.5 |
| cookie crisp, vanilla wafer, Ralston Purina—*1 cup (1 oz) (28 g)* | 0.8 |
| corn bran, Quaker—*⅔ cup (1 oz) (28 g)* | 3 |
| corn chex, Ralston Purina—*1 cup (1 oz) (28 g)* | 1.1 |
| corn flakes, Ralston Purina—*1 cup (1 oz) (28 g)* | 0.4 |
| crispy oatmeal & raisin chex, Ralston Purina—*¾ cup (1.3 oz) (38 g)* | 1.2 |
| halfsies, Quaker—*¾ cup (1 oz) (28 g)* | 1 |
| king vitamin, Quaker—*1¼ cups (1 oz) (28 g)* | 1 |
| life, cinn, Quaker—*⅔ cup (1 oz) (28 g)* | 6 |
| life, Quaker—*⅔ cup (1 oz) (28 g)* | 6 |
| life w/ raisins, Quaker—*⅔ cup (1 oz) (28 g)* | 6 |
| Mr. T, Quaker—*1 cup (1 oz) (28 g)* | 1 |
| puffed wheat, Quaker—*1 cup (½ cup) (14 g)* | 1 |
| Quaker 100% natural—*¼ cup (1 oz) (28 g)* | 5 |
| w/ apples & cinn—*¼ cup (1 oz) (28 g)* | 3 |
| w/ raisins & dates—*¼ cup (1 oz) (28 g)* | 4 |
| quisp, Quaker—*1 cup (1 oz) (28 g)* | 1 |
| rice chex, Ralston Purina—*1⅛ cups (1 oz) (28 g)* | 0.4 |
| shredded wheat | |
| Quaker—*1 oz (28 g)* | 4 |

**CEREALS, READY-TO-EAT**

| | |
|---|---:|
| sun flakes, corn & rice, Ralston Purina—*1 cup (1 oz) (28 g)* | 0.5 |
| wheat & raisin chex, Ralston Purina—*¾ cup (1.3 oz) (37 g)* | 2.9 |
| wheat chex, Ralston Purina—*⅔ cup (1 oz) (28 g)* | 1.7 |

**CHEESE**

| | |
|---|---:|
| cheddar, med, Kraft—*1 oz (28 g)* | 0.6 |
| cream cheese, light, Philadelphia Brand—*1 oz (28 g)* | 0.7 |
| cream cheese, Philadelphia Brand—*1 oz (28 g)* | 0.5 |
| cream cheese w/ herb & garlic, Cremerie—*1 oz (28 g)* | 0.5 |
| havarti, Casino—*1 oz (28 g)* | 0.5 |

**CHEESE PRODUCTS**

| | |
|---|---:|
| Light n' Lively, singles—*1 oz (28 g)* | 1.0 |
| Velveeta sharp cheese spread—*1 oz (28 g)* | 1.0 |

**DESSERTS**

**Cakes**

| | |
|---|---:|
| coffee cake mix, Aunt Jemima—*1.3 oz dry mix (37 g)* | 1 |

**Frozen Desserts**

| | |
|---|---:|
| bon bon ice cream nuggets, Carnation | |
| bavarian mint—*5 nuggets (48 g)* | 0.5 |
| choc—*5 nuggets (49 g)* | 0.4 |
| choc peanut butter—*5 nuggets (49 g)* | 0.4 |
| van—*5 nuggets (48 g)* | 0.5 |

**Granola Desserts**

| | |
|---|---:|
| caramel nut dipps, Quaker—*1.1 oz bar (31 g)* | 2 |
| caramel nut, Smores—*1 oz bar (28 g)* | 3.5 |
| choc chip, chewy, Quaker—*1 oz bar (28 g)* | 3 |
| choc chip dipps, Quaker—*1 oz bar (29 g)* | 1 |
| choc chip, Smores—*1 oz bar (28 g)* | 2.1 |
| choc, graham & marshmallow, chewy, Quaker—*1 oz bar (28 g)* | 3 |
| chunky nut & raisin, chewy, Quaker—*1 oz bar (28 g)* | 4 |
| honey & oats, chewy, Quaker—*1 oz bar (28 g)* | 3 |
| honey & oats dipps, Quaker—*1 oz bar (28 g)* | 2 |
| mint choc chip dipps, Quaker—*1 oz bar (28 g)* | 2 |
| peanut butter & choc chip, chewy, Quaker—*1 oz bar (28 g)* | 5 |
| peanut butter & choc chip, Smores—*1 oz bar (28 g)* | 4.1 |
| peanut butter, chewy, Quaker—*1 oz bar (28 g)* | 6 |
| peanut butter dipps, Quaker—*1 oz bar (28 g)* | 5 |
| peanut butter, Smores—*1 oz bar (28 g)* | 4.0 |
| raisin & almond dipps, Quaker—*1 oz bar (28 g)* | 2 |
| raisin & cinn, chewy, Quaker—*1 oz bar (28 g)* | 3 |
| rocky road dipps, Quaker—*1 oz bar (28 g)* | 2 |

**EGGS, CHICKEN**

| | |
|---|---:|
| white, fresh/frzn—*white of 1 large egg (33 g)* | 2.6 |
| whole, fresh/frzn—*1 large (50 g)* | 11.0 |
| yolk, fresh—*yolk of 1 large egg (17 g)* | 8.4 |

**ENTREES**

**Box Mix Entrees**

| | |
|---|---:|
| macaroni & cheese deluxe dinner, prep, Kraft—*¾ cup (147 g)* | 3.4 |
| pasta shells & cheese, prep, Velvetta—*¾ cup (150 g)* | 2.1 |

**ENTREES & MEALS**
**Canned Entrees**
chili-mac, Wolf Brand—*scant cup (213 g)* · 4
chili w/ beans
   Wolf Brand—*1 cup (227 g)* · 9
   Wolf Brand, extra spicy—*scant cup (213 g)* · 8
chili w/o beans
   Wolf Brand—*1 cup (227 g)* · 5
   Wolf Brand, extra spicy—*scant cup (213 g)* · 5
tamales, Wolf Brand—*scant cup (213 g)* · 6
**Frozen Entrees**
pizza, canadian style bacon
   Celeste—*7.75 oz pizza (220 g)* · 9
   Celeste—*¼ of 19 oz pizza (135 g)* · 5
pizza, cheese
   Celeste—*6.5 oz pizza (184 g)* · 7
   Celeste—*¼ of 18 oz pizza (126 g)* · 5
pizza, deluxe
   Celeste—*8.25 oz pizza (234 g)* · 12
   Celeste—*¼ of 22 oz pizza (158 g)* · 6
pizza, pepperoni
   Celeste—*6.75 oz pizza (191 g)* · 10
   Celeste—*¼ of 19 oz pizza (135 g)* · 5
pizza, sausage
   Celeste—*7.5 oz pizza (213 g)* · 9
   Celeste—*¼ of 20 oz pizza (142 g)* · 6
pizza, sausage & mushroom
   Celeste—*8.5 oz pizza (241 g)* · 12
   Celeste—*¼ of 25 oz pizza (177 g)* · 6
pizza, suprema
   Celeste—*9 oz pizza (255 g)* · 13
   Celeste—*¼ of 23 oz pizza (163 g)* · 8

**GRAIN FRACTIONS**
barley, pearled
   med, Scotch Brand—*¼ cup (48 g)* · 3
   quick, Scotch Brand—*¼ cup (48 g)* · 3
corn meal mix, Aunt Jemima
   white, bolted—*1/6 cup (1 oz) (28 g)* · 2
   white, buttermilk, self-rising—*3 T (1 oz) (28 g)* · 1
   yellow, bolted—*1/6 cup (1 oz) (28 g)* · 1
corn meal, white, bolted, enr, self-rising, Aunt Jemima—
   *1/6 cup (1 oz) (28 g)* · 2
corn meal, white, degermed
   enr, Quaker/Aunt Jemima—*3 T (1 oz) (28 g)* · 1
   enr, self-rising, Aunt Jemima—*1/6 cup (1 oz) (28 g)* · 2
corn meal, yellow, degermed, enr, Aunt Jemima—*3 T (1 oz) (28 g)* · 1
masa harina de maiz, Quaker—*⅓ cup (37 g)* · 3
masa trigo, Quaker—*⅓ cup (37 g)* · 1
oat bran, Quaker—*⅓ cup (1 oz) (28 g)* · 10
wheat bran, unprocessed, Quaker—*2 T (7 g)* · 2
wheat flour, self-rising, enr, Aunt Jemima—*¼ cup (1 oz) (28 g)* · 1

**GRAIN PRODUCTS**
**Breads & Bread Products**
corn bread, mix, Aunt Jemima—*1.7 oz dry mix (48 g)* · 2
**Crackers**
ry-krisp—*¼ large square (14 g)* · 6.8
   seasoned—*¼ large square (14 g)* · 2.2
   sesame—*2 triple crackers (14 g)* · 0.7

**GRAIN PRODUCTS**
**French Toast**
frzn
   Aunt Jemima—*2 slices (85 g)* · 4
   cinn swirl, Aunt Jemima—*2 slices (85 g)* · 5
   raisin, Aunt Jemima—*2 slices (85 g)* · 4
**Muffins**
corn muffin mix, Flako—*1 oz dry mix (28 g)* · 1
**Pancakes**
from frzn batter, Aunt Jemima
   blueberry—*three 4" pancakes (113 g)* · 2
   buttermilk—*three 4" pancakes (113 g)* · 3
   plain—*three 4" pancakes (113 g)* · 3
frzn, Aunt Jemima
   blueberry—*three 4" pancakes (106 g)* · 3
   buttermilk—*three 4" pancakes (106 g)* · 3
   plain—*three 4" pancakes (106 g)* · 7
pancake/waffle mix, Aunt Jemima
   buckwheat—*¼ cup dry mix (31 g)* · 3
   buttermilk—*⅓ cup dry mix (51 g)* · 2
   buttermilk, complete—*½ cup dry mix (71 g)* · 4
   plain—*¼ cup dry mix (31 g)* · 2
   plain, complete—*½ cup dry mix (74 g)* · 4
   whole wheat—*⅓ cup dry mix (43 g)* · 5
**Pasta**
noodles, enr, ckd—*1 cup (160 g)* · 4
**Rolls**
popover mix, Flako—*1 oz dry mix (28 g)* · 1
**Waffles**
frzn, Aunt Jemima
   apple & cinn—*2 waffles (71 g)* · 1
   blueberry—*2 waffles (71 g)* · 1
   buttermilk—*2 waffles (71 g)* · 1
   plain—*2 waffles (71 g)* · 1
   raisin—*2 waffles (82 g)* · 3

**MEATS, LUNCHEON**
meat spread, Carnation
   chicken—*1.9 oz (53 g)* · 0.6
   ham—*1.9 oz (53 g)* · 0.6
   tuna—*1.9 oz (53 g)* · 0.6
   turkey—*1.9 oz (53 g)* · 0.6

**MILK, COW**
evaporated, cnd, Carnation—*4 fl oz (126 g)* · 7.2
evaporated, skim, cnd, Carnation—*4 fl oz (128 g)* · 7.6

**MILK BEVERAGES**
eggnog, nonalcoholic
   mix in whole milk, Delmark—*1.23 oz mix in 8 fl oz milk (257 g)* · 10
instant breakfast in whole milk
   choc, Delmark—*1.23 oz mix in 8 fl oz milk (279 g)* · 90
   van/strawberry, Delmark—*1.23 oz mix in 8 fl oz milk (279 g)* · 90
instant breakfast, van/strawberry, liquid pack, Delmark—*8 fl oz (279 g)* · 70

**MILK BEVERAGE MIXES**
cocoa mix, powder, Carnation
   choc & marshmallow—*1 oz (28 g)* · 0.4
   milk choc—*1 oz (28 g)* · 0.2
   rich choc—*1 oz (28 g)* · 0.4
   rich choc, 70 cal—*1 pkt (3 hp t) (21 g)* · 2
   sugar-free—*1 pkt (4 hp t) (15 g)* · 3.7

**MILK BEVERAGE MIXES**

instant breakfast, Carnation

| | |
|---|---|
| strawberry—*1.25 oz pkt (35 g)* | 5.0 |
| van—*1.23 oz pkt (35 g)* | 5.0 |

**NUTS**

| | |
|---|---|
| almonds, whole, Blue Diamond—*1 oz (28 g)* | 23 |

**SAUCES**

| | |
|---|---|
| chili hot dog sce, Wolf Brand—*1/6 cup (35 g)* | 2 |

**SPECIAL DIETARY FOODS**

fortified pudding, from mix, Delmark

| | |
|---|---|
| choc—*½ cup (164 g)* | 60 |
| van/lemon—*½ cup (164 g)* | 60 |

gluten-free, wheat-free foods, Ener-G Foods

| | |
|---|---|
| nutquik milk powder—*1 oz (28 g)* | 22 |
| soyquix milk powder—*2 T (14 g)* | 10 |

high protein foods, Delmark

| | |
|---|---|
| broth, beef, from mix—*6 fl oz (183 g)* | 1 |

**SPECIAL DIETARY FOODS**

| | |
|---|---|
| broth, chicken, from mix—*6 fl oz (183 g)* | 1 |
| gelatin dessert, all flavors, from mix—*5 fl oz (175 g)* | 7 |

slender bars, Carnation

| | |
|---|---|
| choc—*2 bars (55 g)* | 75 |
| choc chip—*2 bars (55 g)* | 75 |
| choc peanut butter—*2 bars (55 g)* | 75 |
| van—*2 bars (55 g)* | 75 |

slender, liquid diet meal, cnd, Carnation

| | |
|---|---|
| banana—*10 fl oz (313 g)* | 75 |
| choc—*10 fl oz (313 g)* | 75 |
| choc fudge—*10 fl oz (313 g)* | 75 |
| choc malt—*10 fl oz (313 g)* | 75 |
| milk choc—*10 fl oz (313 g)* | 75 |
| strawberry—*10 fl oz (313 g)* | 75 |
| van—*10 fl oz (313 g)* | 75 |

**MISCELLANEOUS**

| | |
|---|---|
| yeast, torula, dried, Lake States—*3.5 oz (100 g)* | 85 |

# Caffeine (mg)

**BEVERAGES**

**Carbonated Beverages**[a]

| | |
|---|---|
| cherry coke, Coca-Cola—*12 fl oz (370 g)* | 46 |
| cherry cola Slice—*12 fl oz (360 g)* | 48 |
| cherry RC—*12 fl oz (360 g)* | 36 |
| Coca-Cola—*12 fl oz (370 g)* | 46 |
| Coca-Cola Classic—*12 fl oz (369 g)* | 46 |
| cola—*12 fl oz (370 g)* | 37 |
| cola, RC—*12 fl oz (360 g)* | 36 |
| Mello Yello—*12 fl oz (372 g)* | 52 |
| Mr. Pibb—*12 fl oz (369 g)* | 40 |
| Mountain Dew—*12 fl oz (360 g)* | 54 |
| pepper type soda—*12 fl oz (368 g)* | 37 |
| Pepsi Cola—*12 fl oz (360 g)* | 38 |

**Carbonated Beverages, Low Calorie**[a]

| | |
|---|---|
| diet cherry coke, Coca-Cola—*12 fl oz (354 g)* | 46[a] |
| diet cherry cola Slice—*12 fl oz (360 g)* | 48 |
| diet coke, Coca-Cola—*12 fl oz (354 g)* | 46 |
| diet cola, aspartame sweetened—*12 fl oz (355 g)* | 50 |
| diet Pepsi—*12 fl oz (360 g)* | 36 |
| diet RC—*12 fl oz (360 g)* | 48 |
| Pepsi Light—*12 fl oz (360 g)* | 36 |
| Tab—*12 fl oz (354 g)* | 46 |

**Coffee**

| | |
|---|---|
| brewed—*6 fl oz (177 g)* | 103 |
| inst powder—*1 rd t (1.8 g)* | 57 |
| decaffeinated—*1 rd t (1.8 g)* | 2 |
| w/ chicory—*1 rd t (1.8 g)* | 37 |
| prep from inst powder—*6 fl oz water & 1 rd t powder (179 g)* | 57 |

**BEVERAGES**

| | |
|---|---|
| amaretto, General Foods—*6 fl oz water & 11.5 g powder (189 g)* | 60 |
| amaretto, sugar-free, General Foods—*6 fl oz water & 7.7 g powder (185 g)* | 60 |
| decaffeinated—*6 fl oz water & 1 rd t powder (179 g)* | 2 |
| francais, General Foods—*6 fl oz water & 11.5 g powder (189 g)* | 53 |
| francais, sugar-free, General Foods—*6 fl oz water & 7.7 g powder (185 g)* | 59 |
| irish creme, General Foods—*6 fl oz water & 12.8 g powder (190 g)* | 53 |
| irish creme, sugar-free, General Foods—*6 fl oz water & 7.1 g powder (185 g)* | 48 |
| irish mocha mint, General Foods—*6 fl oz water & 11.5 g powder (189 g)* | 27 |
| irish mocha mint, sugar-free, General Foods—*6 fl oz water & 6.4 g powder (184 g)* | 25 |
| orange cappuccino, General Foods—*6 fl oz water & 14 g powder (191 g)* | 73 |
| orange cappuccino, sugar-free, General Foods—*6 fl oz water & 6.7 g powder (184 g)* | 71 |
| suisse mocha, General Foods—*6 fl oz water & 11.5 g powder (189 g)* | 41 |
| suisse mocha, sugar-free, General Foods—*6 fl oz water & 6.4 g powder (184 g)* | 40 |
| vienna, General Foods—*6 fl oz water & 14 g powder (191 g)* | 56 |
| vienna, sugar-free, General Foods—*6 fl oz water & 6.7 g powder (184 g)* | 55 |
| w/ chicory—*6 fl oz water & 1 rd t powder (179 g)* | 38 |

[a] Caffeine-free carbonated beverages & most non-cola carbonated beverages contain no caffeine.

**BEVERAGES**
**Tea, Hot/Iced**

| | |
|---|---|
| brewed 3 min—*6 fl oz (178 g)* | 36 |
| inst powder—*1 t (0.7 g)* | 31 |
|     w/ lemon flavor—*1 rd t (1.4 g)* | 25 |
|     w/ sugar & lemon flavor—*3 rd t (23 g)* | 29 |
|     w/ sodium saccharin & lemon flavor—*2 t (1.6 g)* | 36 |
| prep from inst powder | |
|     *1 t powder in 8 fl oz water (237 g)* | 31 |
|     Crystal Light—*8 fl oz (238 g)* | 11 |
|     w/ lemon flavor—*1 rd t powder in 8 fl oz water (238 g)* | 26 |
|     w/ sugar & lemon flavor—*3 rd t powder in 8 fl oz water (259 g)* | 29 |
|     w/ sodium saccharin & lemon flavor—*2 t powder in 8 fl oz water (238 g)* | 36 |

**CANDY**
chocolate

| | |
|---|---|
|     german sweet, Bakers—*1 oz square (28 g)* | 8 |
|     semi-sweet, Bakers—*1 oz square (28 g)* | 13 |
| choc chips | |
|     Bakers—*¼ cup (43 g)* | 12 |
|     german sweet, Bakers—*¼ cup (43 g)* | 15 |
|     semi-sweet, Bakers—*¼ cup (43 g)* | 14 |
| milk choc, Cadbury—*1 oz (28 g)* | 15 |

**DESSERTS**
**Frozen Desserts**
pudding pops, Jell-O

| | |
|---|---|
|     choc—*1 pop (47 g)* | 2 |
|     choc caramel swirl—*1 pop (47 g)* | 1 |
|     choc fudge—*1 pop (47 g)* | 3 |
|     choc van swirl—*1 pop (47 g)* | 1 |
|     choc w/ choc chips—*1 pop (48 g)* | 3 |
|     choc w/ choc coating—*1 pop (49 g)* | 3 |
|     double choc swirl—*1 pop (47 g)* | 2 |
|     milk choc—*1 pop (47 g)* | 2 |
|     van w/ choc chips—*1 pop (48 g)* | 1 |
|     van w/ choc coating—*1 pop (49 g)* | 1 |

**Pies**

| | |
|---|---|
| choc mousse, from mix, Jell-O—*⅛ pie (95 g)* | 6 |

**DESSERTS**
**Puddings, from inst mix**
choc

| | |
|---|---|
|     Jell-O—*½ cup (150 g)* | 5 |
|     sugar-free, D-Zerta—*½ cup (130 g)* | 4 |
|     sugar-free, Jell-O—*½ cup (133 g)* | 4 |
| choc fudge | |
|     Jell-O—*½ cup (150 g)* | 8 |
|     sugar-free, Jell-O—*½ cup (135 g)* | 9 |
| choc fudge mousse, Jell-O—*½ cup (86 g)* | 12 |
| choc mousse, Jell-O—*½ cup (86 g)* | 9 |
| choc tapioca, Jell-O—*½ cup (147 g)* | 8 |
| milk choc, Jell-O—*½ cup (150 g)* | 5 |

**MILK BEVERAGES**

| | |
|---|---|
| choc flavor mix in whole milk—*2-3 hp t powder in 8 fl oz milk (266 g)* | 8 |
| choc malted milk flavor powder | |
|     in whole milk—*3 hp t powder in 8 fl oz milk (265 g)* | 8 |
|     w/ added nutrients in whole milk—*4-5 hp t powder in 8 fl oz milk (265 g)* | 5 |
| choc syrup in whole milk—*2 T syrup in 8 fl oz milk (282 g)* | 6 |
| cocoa/hot chocolate, prep w/ water from mix—*¾ hp t powder in 6 fl oz water (206 g)* | 4 |

**MILK BEVERAGE MIXES**

| | |
|---|---|
| choc flavor mix, powder—*2-3 hp t (22 g)* | 8 |
| choc malted milk flavor mix, powder—*¾ oz (3 hp t) (21 g)* | 8 |
| choc malted milk flavor mix w/ added nutrients, powder—*¾ oz (4-5 hp t) (21 g)* | 6 |
| choc syrup—*2 T (1 fl oz) (38 g)* | 5 |
| cocoa mix powder—*1 oz pkt (3-4 hp t) (28 g)* | 5 |

**SPECIAL DIETARY FORMULAS, COMMERCIAL & HOSPITAL**

| | |
|---|---|
| ensure, choc, Ross Labs—*8 fl oz (253 g)* | 8 |
| ensure, coffee, ross Labs—*8 fl oz (253 g)* | 8 |
| ensure HN, choc, Ross Labs—*8 fl oz (253 g)* | 8 |
| ensure plus, choc, Ross Labs—*8 fl oz (259 g)* | 10 |
| ensure, plus, coffee, Ross Labs—*8 fl oz (259 g)* | 12 |

**MISCELLANEOUS**

| | |
|---|---|
| baking choc, unsweetened, Bakers—*1 oz (28 g)* | 25 |

# Choline (mg)

**BEVERAGES**
**Alcoholic**
    beer, Stroh's American Lager—*12 fl oz (355 g)*      80

**EGGS, CHICKEN**
white, fresh/frzn—*white of 1 large egg (33 g)*      0.46
whole, fresh/frzn—*1 large (50 g)*      238.4
yolk, fresh—*yolk of 1 large egg (17 g)*      238

**MILK BEVERAGES**
eggnog, nonalcoholic
    mix in whole milk, Delmark—*1.23 oz mix in 8 fl oz milk (257 g)*      48
instant breakfast in whole milk
    choc, Delmark—*1.23 oz mix in 8 fl oz milk (279 g)*      48
    van/strawberry, Delmark—*1.23 oz mix in 8 fl oz milk (279 g)*      50
instant breakfast, van/strawberry, liquid pack, Delmark—*8 fl oz (279 g)*      30

**MILK BEVERAGES**
milk shake mix in whole milk, Delmark
    choc—*.667 oz mix in 8 fl oz milk (263 g)*      30
    strawberry—*.667 oz mix in 8 fl oz milk (263 g)*      30
    van—*.667 oz mix in 8 fl oz milk (263 g)*      30

**SPECIAL DIETARY FOODS**
fortified pudding, from mix, Delmark
    choc—*½ cup (164 g)*      28
    van/lemon—*½ cup (164 g)*      48
high protein foods, Delmark
    broth, beef, from mix—*6 fl oz (183 g)*      0.97
    broth, chicken, from mix—*6 fl oz (183 g)*      1.1

**MISCELLANEOUS**
yeast, torula, dried, Lake States—*3.5 oz (100 g)*      275

# Gluten-Containing & Gluten-Free Grains & Products[a]

**GLUTEN-CONTAINING GRAINS**
barley
buckwheat
oats
rye
wheat

**GLUTEN-FREE GRAINS & PRODUCTS**
corn flour
corn meal
cornstarch
gluten-free wheat starch
lima bean flour
potato flour
rice
rice flour
soy flour

[a] Nontropical sprue and other malabsorption symptoms may be relieved/improved by a restriction of gluten-containing grains.

# Iodine (mcg)

**CHEESE**
cheddar, med, Kraft—*1 oz (28 g)*                                12
cream cheese, light, Philadelphia Brand—*1 oz (28 g)*           11
cream cheese, Philadelphia Brand—*1 oz (28 g)*                   9
havarti, Casino—*1 oz (28 g)*                                    9

**CHEESE PRODUCTS**
Light n' Lively, singles—*1 oz (28 g)*                          25
Velveeta sharp cheese spread—*1 oz (28 g)*                      17

**DESSERTS, FROZEN**
bon bon ice cream nuggets, Carnation
   bavarian mint—*5 nuggets (48 g)*                 3
   choc—*5 nuggets (49 g)*                          3
   choc peanut butter—*5 nuggets (49 g)*           3
   van—*5 nuggets (48 g)*                           3

**EGGS, CHICKEN**
white, fresh/frzn—*white of 1 large egg (33 g)*                  1
whole, fresh/frzn—*1 large (50 g)*                              26

**ENTREES, BOX MIX**
pasta shells & cheese, prep, Velvetta—*¾ cup (150 g)*          52[a]

**MEATS, LUNCHEON**
meat spread, Carnation
   chicken—*1.9 oz (53 g)*                          4
   ham—*1.9 oz (53 g)*                              4
   tuna—*1.9 oz (53 g)*                             4
   turkey—*1.9 oz (53 g)*                           4

**MILK, COW**
evaporated, cnd, Carnation—*4 fl oz (126 g)*                    52
evaporated, skim, cnd, Carnation—*4 fl oz (128 g)*              54

**MILK BEVERAGES**
eggnog, nonalcoholic
   mix in whole milk, Delmark—*1.23 oz mix in 8 fl oz milk (257 g)*                                                122
instant breakfast in whole milk—*1 pkt in 8 fl oz milk (265 g)*                                                           48
   choc, Delmark—*1.23 oz mix in 8 fl oz milk (279 g)*   97
milk shake
   mix in whole milk, Delmark
     choc—*.667 oz mix in 8 fl oz milk (263 g)*   31
     strawberry—*.667 oz mix in 8 fl oz milk (263 g)*   51
     van—*.667 oz mix in 8 fl oz milk (263 g)*   51

**MILK BEVERAGE MIXES**
cocoa mix, powder, Carnation
   choc & marshmallow—*1 oz (28 g)*                 2
   milk choc—*1 oz (28 g)*                         11
   rich choc—*1 oz (28 g)*                          2
   rich choc, 70 cal—*1 pkt (3 hp t) (21 g)*       14
   sugar-free—*1 pkt (4 hp t) (15 g)*              17

**MILK BEVERAGE MIXES**
instant breakfast, Carnation
   choc—*1.25 oz pkt (35 g)*                        3
   choc malt—*1.24 oz pkt (35 g)*                   3
   coffee—*1.26 oz pkt (36 g)*                      3
   eggnog—*1.20 oz pkt (34 g)*                      3
   strawberry—*1.25 oz pkt (35 g)*                  3
   van—*1.23 oz pkt (35 g)*                         3
instant breakfast, no sugar added, Carnation
   choc—*.69 oz pkt (20 g)*                         3
   choc malted—*.71 oz pkt (20 g)*                 3
   strawberry—*.68 oz pkt (19 g)*                   3
   van—*.67 oz pkt (19 g)*                          3

**NUTS**
almonds, whole, Blue Diamond—*1 oz (28 g)*                       4

**SPECIAL DIETARY FOODS**
figurine diet bar, Pillsbury
   choc—*1 bar (21 g)*                             21
   choc caramel—*1 bar (21 g)*                     21
   choc peanut butter—*1 bar (21 g)*              21
   s'mores—*1 bar (21 g)*                         21
   van—*1 bar (21 g)*                             21
fortified pudding, from mix, van/lemon, Delmark—*½ cup (164 g)*                                                           40
high protein foods, Delmark
   gelatin dessert, all flavors, from mix—*5 fl oz (175 g)*   6
slender bars, Carnation
   choc—*2 bars (55 g)*                            38
   choc chip—*2 bars (55 g)*                       38
   choc peanut butter—*2 bars (55 g)*            38
   van—*2 bars (55 g)*                             38
slender, liquid diet meal, cnd, Carnation
   banana—*10 fl oz (313 g)*                       38
   choc—*10 fl oz (313 g)*                         38
   choc fudge—*10 fl oz (313 g)*                   38
   choc malt—*10 fl oz (313 g)*                    38
   milk choc—*10 fl oz (313 g)*                    38
   strawberry—*10 fl oz (313 g)*                   38
   van—*10 fl oz (313 g)*                          38

**SPICES**
salt, iodized—*1 t (6 g)*                                       400
salt, noniodized—*1 t (6 g)*                                   <100
salt substitute, Morton lite salt—*1 t (6 g)*                   400

**MISCELLANEOUS**
yeast, torula, dried, Lake States—*3.5 oz (100 g)*             110

[a] 25 mcg iodine if prepared w/ uniodized salt added to cooking water.

# Pectin (g)

| | |
|---|---|
| **BEVERAGES** | |
| alcoholic | |
| beer—*12 fl oz (356 g)* | 0.712 |
| whiskey sour, prep from bottled mix—*2 fl oz mix & 1.5 fl oz whiskey (106 g)* | 0.106 |
| whiskey sour mix, bottled—*2 fl oz cocktail (65 g)* | 0.130 |
| coffee | |
| inst powder—*1 rd t (1.8 g)* | 0.004 |
| inst powder, mocha flavor, sugar sweetened—*2 rd t (11.5 g)* | 0.104 |
| prep from inst powder, mocha flavor, sugar sweetened—*6 fl oz water & 2 rd t powder (188 g)* | 0.188 |
| fruit juice drinks & fruit flavored beverages | |
| lemonade, from frzn conc—*6 fl oz (240 g)* | 0.248 |
| orange breakfast drink, from frozn conc—*6 fl oz (188 g)* | 0.188 |
| tea, black, inst powder—*1 t (0.7 g)* | 0.026 |
| **FRUITS** | |
| apple | |
| raw, w/ skin—*1 med (138 g)* | 1.48 |
| raw, w/o skin—*1 med (128 g)* | 0.49 |
| boiled, w/o skin—*1 cup (171 g)* | 0.46 |
| cnd, sliced, sweetened—*½ cup (102 g)* | 0.44 |
| cnd, sliced, sweetened, heated—*½ cup (102 g)* | 0.50 |
| frzn, unsweetened—*½ cup (86 g)* | 0.40 |
| frzn, unsweetened, heated—*½ cup (103 g)* | 0.40 |
| micro ckd w/o skin—*1 cup (170 g)* | 0.75 |
| applesce, cnd, sweetened—*½ cup (128 g)* | 0.38 |
| kiwifruit, raw—*1 med (76 g)* | 0.32 |

| | |
|---|---|
| **NUTS** | |
| almonds, dried, unblanched—*1 oz (24 nuts) (28 g)* | 0.38 |
| chestnuts, european | |
| raw, unpeeled—*1 oz (2½ nuts) (28 g)* | 0.34 |
| roasted—*1 oz (3½ nuts) (28 g)* | 0.34 |
| **VEGETABLES** | |
| broccoli, frzn, boiled—*½ cup (92 g)* | 0.92 |
| broccoli spears, frzn, boiled—*½ cup (92 g)* | 0.92 |
| brussel sprouts, frzn, boiled—*½ cup (78 g)* | 1.09 |
| carrots, raw—*1 med (72 g)* | 0.72 |
| corn, sweet, yellow/white, frzn, boiled—*½ cup (82 g)* | 0.33 |
| green beans, frzn, boiled—*½ cup (68 g)* | 0.61 |
| peas, green, frzn—*½ cup (72 g)* | 0.50 |
| peas, green, frzn, boiled—*½ cup (80 g)* | 0.48 |
| spinach | |
| raw—*½ cup chopped (28 g)* | 0.22 |
| boiled—*½ cup (90 g)* | 0.72 |
| frzn, boiled—*½ cup (95 g)* | 1.05 |
| squash, summer, all varieties | |
| raw—*½ cup slices (65 g)* | 0.39 |
| boiled—*½ cup slices (90 g)* | 0.45 |
| squash, summer, crookneck | |
| raw—*½ cup slices (65 g)* | 0.39 |
| boiled—*½ cup slices (90 g)* | 0.45 |
| sweet potato | |
| baked—*1 sweet potato (114 g)* | 0.91 |
| frzn, baked—*½ cup cubes (88 g)* | 0.70 |

# Phytosterol (mg)

| | |
|---|---|
| **CREAM SUBSTITUTES** | |
| powdered, coffee-mate, Carnation—*1 t (2 g)* | 0.6 |
| **ENTREES, BOX MIX** | |
| pizza, cheese, from Contadina Pizzeria Kit | |
| thick crust—*¼ pizza (128 g)* | 3.1 |
| thin crust—*¼ pizza (104 g)* | 3.1 |
| **FATS, OILS & SHORTENINGS** | |
| corn oil, Mazola—*1 T (14 g)* | 140 |
| veg oil spray, Mazola No Stick—*2.5 sec spray (0.7 g)* | 6 |
| **FRUITS** | |
| apple, raw, w/ skin—*1 med (138 g)* | 17 |
| apricots, raw—*3 med (106 g)* | 19 |
| banana, raw—*1 med (114 g)* | 18 |
| cantaloupe, raw—*1 cup pieces (160 g)* | 16 |
| cherries, sweet, raw—*10 cherries (68 g)* | 8 |
| figs, raw—*1 med (50 g)* | 16 |
| grapefruit, raw, white—*½ med (118 g)* | 20 |
| grapes, european (adherent skin), raw—*1 cup (160 g)* | 6 |
| lemon peel—*1 T (6 g)* | 2 |
| lemon, raw w/ peel—*1 med (108 g)* | 13 |

| | |
|---|---|
| **FRUITS** | |
| loquats, raw—*10 med (100 g)* | 2 |
| orange, navel, raw—*1 med (140 g)* | 34 |
| orange peel—*1 T (6 g)* | 2 |
| peach, raw—*1 med (87 g)* | 9 |
| pear, raw—*1 med (166 g)* | 13 |
| persimmon, japanese, raw—*1 med (168 g)* | 7 |
| pineapple, raw—*1 cup pieces (155 g)* | 9 |
| plum, raw—*1 med (66 g)* | 5 |
| pomegranate, raw—*1 med (154 g)* | 26 |
| strawberries, raw—*1 cup (149 g)* | 18 |
| watermelon, raw—*1 cup (160 g)* | 3 |
| **MEATS, LUNCHEON** | |
| meat spread | |
| chicken, Carnation—*1.9 oz (53 g)* | 16.5 |
| ham, Carnation—*1.9 oz (53 g)* | 9.9 |
| tuna, Carnation—*1.9 oz (53 g)* | 16.0 |
| turkey, Carnation—*1.9 oz (53 g)* | 16.3 |
| **NUTS, NUT PRODUCTS & SEEDS** | |
| almonds, dried—*1 oz (24 nuts) (28 g)* | 41 |
| cashews, dry roasted—*1 oz (28 g)* | 45 |

**NUTS, NUT PRODUCTS & SEEDS**

| | |
|---|---:|
| chestnuts, european, raw—*1 oz (2½ nuts) (28 g)* | 6 |
| coconut, raw—*1 piece (2"x2"x½") (45 g)* | 21 |
| coconut milk, raw—*1 cup (240 g)* | 2 |
| peanut butter | |
|    creamy/smooth, Skippy—*1 T (16 g)* | 16 |
|    chunk style/crunchy—*2 T (32 g)* | 33 |
|    chunk style/crunchy, Skippy—*1 T (16 g)* | 16 |
| pecans | |
|    dried—*1 oz (31 large nuts) (28 g)* | 31 |
| pine nuts, pignolia, dried—*1 oz (28 g)* | 40 |
| pistachio nuts, dried—*1 oz (47 nuts) (28 g)* | 31 |
| sesame seeds, whole, dried—*1 T (9 g)* | 64 |
| sunflower seeds, dried—*1 oz (28 g)* | 152 |
| walnuts, english/persian, dried—*1 oz (14 halves) (28 g)* | 31 |

**SAUCES**

| | |
|---|---:|
| pizza sce, cnd | |
|    Contadina—*¼ cup (60 g)* | 3.2 |
|    w/ cheese, Contadina—*¼ cup (60 g)* | 3.2 |
|    w/ pepperoni, Contadina—*¼ cup (60 g)* | 3.2 |
| tomato sce, cnd | |
|    Contadina—*½ cup (124 g)* | 0.1 |
|    italian style, Contadina—*½ cup (124 g)* | 5.3 |
|    refrig, Fresh Chef—*4 oz (113 g)* | 10.6 |

**SPREADS**

| | |
|---|---:|
| margarine | |
|    Mazola—*1 T (14 g)* | 70 |
|    Mazola unsalted—*1 T (14 g)* | 70 |
| margarine, imitation (diet), Mazola diet—*1 T (14 g)* | 58 |
| mayonnaise, Best Foods/Hellmann's—*1 T (14 g)* | 40 |
| sandwich spread, Best Foods/Hellmann's—*1 T (15 g)* | 20 |

**VEGETABLES**

| | |
|---|---:|
| aspargus, raw—*4 spears (58 g)* | 14 |
| bamboo shoots, raw—*½ cup (76 g)* | 14 |
| beet greens, raw—*½ cup (19 g)* | 4 |
| beets, raw—*½ cup (68 g)* | 17 |

**VEGETABLES**

| | |
|---|---:|
| brussel sprouts, raw—*½ cup (44 g)* | 11 |
| cabbage, green, raw—*½ cup shredded (35 g)* | 4 |
| carrots, raw—*1 med (72 g)* | 9 |
| cauliflower, raw—*½ cup pieces (50 g)* | 9 |
| celery, raw—*1 stalk (7.5" long) (40 g)* | 2 |
| celtuce, raw—*12 leaves (100 g)* | 11 |
| chives, raw—*1 T chopped (3 g)* | 0.3 |
| cucumber, raw—*½ cup slices (1/6 cucumber) (52 g)* | 7 |
| eggplant, raw—*½ cup pieces (41 g)* | 3 |
| ginger root, raw—*¼ cup slices (24 g)* | 4 |
| green beans, frzn, boiled—*½ cup (68 g)* | 2 |
| lettuce, iceberg, raw—*1 leaf (20 g)* | 2 |
| lettuce, looseleaf, raw—*½ cup shredded (28 g)* | 11 |
| mung beans, sprouted, raw—*½ cup (52 g)* | 8 |
| okra, raw—*½ cup (50 g)* | 12 |
| onions, raw—*½ cup chopped (80 g)* | 12 |
| parsley, raw—*½ cup chopped (30 g)* | 2 |
| peppers, sweet, raw—*½ cup chopped (50 g)* | 4 |
| potato, raw w/o skin—*1 potato (112 g)* | 6 |
| pumpkin, raw—*½ cup (58 g)* | 7 |
| radish, raw—*10 radishes (45 g)* | 3 |
| shallots, raw—*1 T chopped (10 g)* | 1 |
| soybeans, green, raw—*½ cup (128 g)* | 64 |
| spinach, raw—*½ cup chopped (28 g)* | 2 |
| taro, raw—*½ cup slices (52 g)* | 10 |
| tomato, red | |
|    raw—*1 tomato (123 g)* | 9 |
|    cnd, Contadina | |
|       crushed in tomato puree—*½ cup (119 g)* | 3.1 |
|       italian style (pear)—*½ cup (120 g)* | 8.4 |
|       stewed—*½ cup (123 g)* | 0.2 |
|       whole, peeled—*½ cup (120 g)* | 8.4 |
| tomato paste, cnd, italian, Contadina—*¼ cup (57 g)* | 5.7 |
| turnip, raw—*½ cup cubes (65 g)* | 5 |
| turnip greens, raw—*½ cup chopped (28 g)* | 3 |
| yam, raw—*½ cup cubes (75 g)* | 8 |

# Purine-Yielding Foods[a]

**FOODS HIGHEST IN PURINES (150–825 mg/100 g)**
anchovies (363 mg/100 g)
brains
kidney (beef—200 mg/100 g)
game meats
gravies
herring
liver (calf/beef—233 mg/100 g)
mackerel
meat extracts (160–400 mg/100 g)
sardines (295 mg/100 g)
scallops
sweetbreads (825 mg/100 g)

**FOODS HIGH IN PURINES (50–150 mg/100 g)**
asparagus
breads & cereals, whole grain
cauliflower
eel
fish, fresh & saltwater
legumes, beans/lentils/peas
meat—beef/lamb/pork/veal
meat soups & broths

**FOODS HIGH IN PURINES (50–150 mg/100 g)**
mushrooms
oatmeal
peas, green
poultry—chicken/duck/turkey
shellfish—crab/lobster/oysters
spinach
wheat germ & bran

**FOODS LOWEST IN PURINES (0–50 mg/100 g)**
beverages—coffee/tea/sodas
breads & cereals except whole grain
cheese
eggs
fats
fish roe
fruits & fruit juices
gelatin
milk
nuts
sugars, syrups, sweets
vegetables (except those listed above)
vegetable & cream soups

[a] Purines are normally formed in the body during the metabolic breakdown of nucleoproteins. In certain genetic disorders, including gout, the relatively insoluble purine *uric acid* tends to accumulate and deposit in the toes and in other joints. Drug treatment is generally prescribed for patients with gout; however, dietary restriction of purine-yielding foods may also be advised.

# Salicylates (mg/100 g)[a]

**<.10 mg/100 g**
**FRUITS**
apple (yellow), banana, paw paw, pear w/o skin, plum (green), pomegranate

**VEGETABLES**
bamboo shoots, bean sprouts, blackeyed peas, brown beans, brussels sprouts, cabbage (green/red), celery, chives, garbanzo beans, leek, lentils, lettuce, lima beans, mung beans, peas (green/split), potato w/o peel, shallots, soy beans, summer squash (chayote), swede

**GRAINS & GRAIN PRODUCTS**
arrowroot, barley, buckwheat, maize, millet, oats, rice (brown/white), rye, soy grits, wheat

**NUTS & SEEDS**
cashews, poppyseeds

**ANIMAL PRODUCTS**
beef, cheese, chicken, egg, kidney, lamb, liver, milk, oysters, pork, salmon, scallops, shrimp, tripe, tuna, yogurt

**OTHER**
carob powder, cocoa powder, coffee powder (decaffeinated), gin, maple syrup, Ovaltine powder, parsley leaves, saffron, soy sauce, sugar, tanodri powder, tea bag (camomile), vinegar (malt), vodka, whisky

**.10–.49 mg/100 g**
**FRUITS**
apple (red), apple juice, apricot nectar, cherries (sour), custard apple, figs (fresh/cnd), grapes (light, seedless), grape juice (light), grapefruit juice, kiwi fruit, lemon, loquat, lychee, mango, nectarine, orange juice, passion fruit, peach nectar, pear w/ skin, persimmon, pineapple juice, plum (red), tamarillo, watermelon

**VEGETABLES**
asparagus, beet, carrot, cauliflower, corn (reg/creamed), eggplant w/o peel, green french beans, horseradish, mushrooms (fresh), onion, parsnip, pimentos, potato w/ peel, pumpkin, rhubarb, spinach (frzn), squash (marrow), sweetpotato (yellow), tomato (fresh), tomato juice, turnip

**NUTS & SEEDS**
brazil nuts, coconut (dried), hazelnuts, peanut butter, pecans, sesame seeds, sunflower seeds, walnuts

**OTHER**
beer, brandy, caramels, cereal coffee powder, cider (hard), cola soda, coriander leaves, garlic, molasses, olives (black), sherry (dry), syrup (corn), tabasco sauce, tea bag (decaffeinated/fruit herbal/rose hip), wine (claret/rose/white), vermouth

**.50–.99 mg/100 g**
**FRUITS**
apple (cnd), apple (granny smith), avocado, cherries (sweet), figs (dried), grapes (red), grape juice (dark), grapefruit, mandarin orange, mulberries, peach, tangelo

**VEGETABLES**
alfalfa, broad beans, broccoli, chili peppers (green/yellow-green), cucumber w/o peel, eggplant w/peel, mushrooms (cnd), okra, spinach (fresh), squash, sweetpotato (white), tomato (canned), watercress

**NUTS**
macadamia nuts, pine nuts, pistachios

**OTHER**
coffee powder,[b] fennel powder, sherry (sweet), wine (cabernet/claret riesling/sauvignon)

**1.00–4.99 mg/100 g**
**FRUITS**
apricot, blackberries, blueberries, boysenberries, cantaloupe, cherries (cnd), cranberries, cranberry sauce, currants (black/red), dates (fresh/dried), guava, grapes (sultana), logenberries, orange, pineapple, plum (dark red), raspberries (frzn), strawberries, youngberries

**VEGETABLES**
chicory, chili peppers (red), endive, mushrooms (cnd), peppers (sweet green), radishes, tomato paste, tomato sauce, zucchini

**NUTS**
almonds, peanuts, waterchestnuts

**OTHER**
bay leaves, basil, caraway, champagne, chili flakes, chili powder, ginger root, mints, nutmeg, olives (green), pepper (white), peppermints,[b] pimento powder, port, rum, tea bags/leaves (regular/herbal/peppermint),[b] vanilla flavoring, vinegar (white)

**5.00–10.00 mg/100 g**
**FRUITS**
raisins, prunes (cnd), raspberries (fresh)

**OTHER**
allspice, cardamom, cloves, dill (fresh), licorice, liqueurs,[b] mint (fresh), paprika (sweet), pepper (black), pickles

**>10.00 mg/100 g**
**OTHER**
aniseed, canella powder, cayenne, celery powder, cinnamon, cumin, curry, dill powder, fenugreek powder, garam masala, honey,[b] mace, mustard powder, oregano, paprika (hot), rosemary, sage, tarragon, tumeric, thyme, worcestershire sauce

[a] Adapted from Swain et al, 1985.
[b] Salicylate ranges for these items (mg/100 g) are: coffee powder, .0–.96; honey, 2.5–11.24; liqueurs, .66–9.04; peppermints, .77–7.50; tea bags/leaves, 1.9–7.34.

# Sugars (g)

**BEVERAGES**

**Alcoholic Beverages**

| | |
|---|---|
| ale, Blatz Cream—*12 fl oz (360 g)* | 3.1[a] |
| beer | |
|     Black Label—*12 fl oz (360 g)* | 3.7[a] |
|     Blatz—*12 fl oz (360 g)* | 3.3[a] |
|     Heileman's Old Style—*12 fl oz (360 g)* | 3.2[a] |
|     Heileman's Special Export—*12 fl oz (360 g)* | 3.1[a] |
|     Heileman's Special Export Dark—*12 fl oz (360 g)* | 3.1[a] |
|     Rainier—*12 fl oz (360 g)* | 3.5[a] |
|     Schmidt—*12 fl oz (360 g)* | 4.0[a] |
|     Stroh's American Lager—*12 fl oz (355 g)* | 13.4 |
| beer, light | |
|     Anheuser-Busch—*12 fl oz (355 g)* | 0.1 |
|     Blatz—*12 fl oz (360 g)* | 1.6[a] |
|     Heileman's Old Style—*12 fl oz (360 g)* | 1.7[a] |
|     Heileman's Special Export—*12 fl oz (360 g)* | 1.8[a] |
| beer, LA (low alcohol) | |
|     Blatz—*12 fl oz (360 g)* | 1.8[a] |
|     Heileman's Old Style—*12 fl oz (360 g)* | 1.8[a] |
| brandy, cherry—*2 fl oz (60 g)* | 19.6 |
| distilled spirits, rum/vodka—*1.5 fl oz (42 g)* | 0.0 |
| liqueurs | |
|     coffee—*1.5 fl oz (52 g)* | 20.4 |
|     orange—*1.5 fl oz (52 g)* | 14.7 |
| malt liquor | |
|     Blatz Old Fashioned Private Stock—*12 fl oz (360 g)* | 3.2[a] |
|     Colt 45—*12 fl oz (360 g)* | 3.9[a] |
| sherry, med—*2 fl oz (60 g)* | 2.2 |
| vermouth | |
|     dry—*2 fl oz (60 g)* | 3.3 |
|     sweet—*2 fl oz (60 g)* | 9.5 |
| wine | |
|     rose—*3.5 oz (103 g)* | 2.6 |
|     white—*3.5 oz (103 g)* | 0.6 |

**Carbonated Beverages**

| | |
|---|---|
| all flavors—*12 fl oz (360 g)* | 37.8 |
| diet, all flavors—*12 fl oz (360 g)* | 0.0 |

**Cereal Grain Beverages**

| | |
|---|---|
| prep from powder w/ water, Postum—*6 fl oz (181 g)* | 0.8 |
| prep from powder w/ water, coffee flavored, Postum— *6 fl oz (180 g)* | 0.7 |

**Coffee, Prep From Inst Powder**

| | |
|---|---|
| amaretto, General Foods—*6 fl oz water & 11.5 g powder (189 g)* | 5.6 |
| amaretto, sugar-free, General Foods—*6 fl oz water & 7.7 g powder (185 g)* | 0.2 |
| francais, General Foods—*6 fl oz water & 11.5 g powder (189 g)* | 5.3 |
| francais, sugar-free, General Foods—*6 fl oz water & 7.7 g powder (185 g)* | 0.2 |
| irish creme, General Foods—*6 fl oz water & 12.8 g powder (190 g)* | 6.8 |
| irish creme, sugar-free, General Foods—*6 fl oz water & 7.1 g powder (185 g)* | 0.2 |
| irish mocha mint, General Foods—*6 fl oz water & 11.5 g powder (189 g)* | 6.7 |

**BEVERAGES**

| | |
|---|---|
| irish mocha mint, sugar-free, General Foods—*6 fl oz water & 6.4 g powder (184 g)* | 0.2 |
| mocha flavor, sugar sweetened—*6 fl oz water & 2 rd t powder (188 g)* | 4.9 |
| orange cappuccino, General Foods—*6 fl oz water & 14 g powder (191 g)* | 8.7 |
| orange cappuccino, sugar-free, General Foods—*6 fl oz water & 6.7 g powder (184 g)* | 0.2 |
| suisse mocha, General Foods—*6 fl oz water & 11.5 g powder (189 g)* | 6.6 |
| suisse mocha, sugar-free, General Foods—*6 fl oz water & 6.4 g powder (184 g)* | 0.2 |
| vienna, General Foods—*6 fl oz water & 14 g powder (191 g)* | 9.0 |
| vienna, sugar-free, General Foods—*6 fl oz water & 6.7 g powder (184 g)* | 0.2 |

**Fruit Juice Drinks & Fruit Flavored Beverages**

| | |
|---|---|
| appleberry jce works, Campbell's—*6 fl oz (182 g)* | 23.4 |
| apple jce works, Campbell's—*6 fl oz (182 g)* | 22.0 |
| cherry, cnd—*8 fl oz (240 g)* | 25.7 |
| cherry jce works, Campbell's—*6 fl oz (182 g)* | 21.1 |
| fruit punch drink | |
|     cnd—*8 fl oz (240 g)* | 27.1 |
|     from frzn conc—*8 fl oz (240 g)* | 24.5 |
|     from powder—*2 rd t in 8 fl oz water (240 g)* | 27.8 |
| grape jce works, Campbell's—*6 fl oz (182 g)* | 22.1 |
| kool-aid, from powder, all flavors—*8 fl oz (246 g)* | 25.1 |
| kool-aid, from sugar sweetened powder, all flavors—*8 fl oz (241 g)* | 20.3 |
| kool-aid kooler, from powder, all flavors—*8.5 fl oz (262 g)* | 30.4 |
| lemonade | |
|     from frzn conc—*8 fl oz (240 g)* | 22.1 |
|     from powder—*8 fl oz (240 g)* | 13.2 |
|     from powder, Country Time—*8 fl oz (242 g)* | 20.4 |
| lemonade, pink, from powder, Country Time—*8 fl oz (242 g)* | 20.4 |
| lemon lime, from powder, Country Time—*8 fl oz (242 g)* | 20.4 |
| orange flavor breakfast drink | |
|     from frzn conc—*8 fl oz (240 g)* | 24.0 |
|     prep from powder—*8 fl oz (240 g)* | 25.9 |
| orange, cnd—*8 fl oz (240 g)* | 17.3 |
| orange jce works, Campbell's—*6 fl oz (182 g)* | 20.4 |
| strawberry jce works, Campbell's—*6 fl oz (182 g)* | 22.6 |
| tang, orange, from powder—*6 fl oz (185 g)* | 21.7 |
| thirst-quencher drink, cnd—*8 fl oz (240 g)* | 14.2 |
| malt beverages, nonalcoholic, Kingsbury—*12 fl oz (360 g)* | 4.5[a] |
| tea, herb, brewed—*6 fl oz (178 g)* | 0.0 |

**CANDY**

| | |
|---|---|
| chocolate | |
|     dark, sweet—*1 oz (28 g)* | 13.7 |
|     german sweet, Bakers—*1 oz square (28 g)* | 14.3 |
|     milk—*1 oz (28 g)* | 15.3 |
|     milk w/ almonds—*1 oz (28 g)* | 13.7 |
|     milk w/ crisped rice—*1 oz (28 g)* | 12.9 |

[a] Specified as maltose.

## CANDY

| | |
|---|---|
| semi-sweet—*1 oz (28 g)* | 15.1 |
|    Bakers—*1 oz square (28 g)* | 12.5 |
| chocolate chips | |
|    Bakers—*¼ cup (43 g)* | 28.4 |
|    german sweet, Bakers—*¼ cup (43 g)* | 22.9 |
|    semi-sweet, Bakers—*¼ cup (43 g)* | 23.8 |
| chocolate covered | |
|    coconut center & almonds—*1 oz (28 g)* | 5.6[a] |
|    crunchy peanut butter—*1 oz (28 g)* | 8.3[a] |
|    fudge, caramel & peanuts—*1 oz (28 g)* | 6.6[a] |
|    malt nougat & caramel—*1 oz (28 g)* | 7.9[a] |
|    malted milk balls—*1 oz (28 g)* | 4.0[a] |
|    mint flavored fondant, discs—*1 oz (28 g)* | 12.7[a] |
|    nougat—*1 oz (28 g)* | 15.3 |
|    nougat & caramel—*1 oz (28 g)* | 7.5[a] |
|    peanut butter nougat, caramel & peanuts—*1 oz (28 g)* | 12.6 |
|    peanuts—*1 oz (28 g)* | 9.6[a] |
| hard candy—*1 oz (28 g)* | 18.7 |
| jelly beans—*1 oz (28 g)* | 16.5 |
| licorice—*1 oz (28 g)* | 5.5[a] |
| peanut, caramel & van fudge bar—*1 oz (28 g)* | 9.3[a] |
| sugar-coated | |
|    choc & peanut discs—*1 oz (28 g)* | 13.2 |
|    choc disks—*1 oz (28 g)* | 16.2 |
| toffee—*1 oz (28 g)* | 15.5 |

## CEREALS, COOKED

| | |
|---|---|
| farina, quick/inst—*¾ cup (175 g)* | 0.2 |
| oatmeal, quick/reg—*¾ cup (175 g)* | 0.7 |
| whole wheat, reg—*¾ cup (182 g)* | 0.7 |

## CEREALS, READY-TO-EAT

| | |
|---|---|
| almond delight, Ralston Purina—*¾ cup (1 oz) (28 g)* | 8.0 |
| alpha-bits, Post—*1 cup (1 oz) (28 g)* | 11.1 |
| apple jacks, Kellogg's—*1 cup (1 oz) (28 g)* | 14.9 |
| body buddies, brown sugar & honey, General Mills—*1 cup (1 oz) (28 g)* | 6.0 |
| body buddies, natural fruit flavor, General Mills—*1 cup (1 oz) (28 g)* | 6.0 |
| booberry, General Mills—*1 cup (1 oz) (28 g)* | 13.0 |
| bran, Kellogg's all-bran—*⅓ cup (1 oz) (28 g)* | 5.4 |
| bran, 100%—*½ cup (1 oz) (28 g)* | 6.3 |
| bran chex, Ralston Purina—*⅔ cup (1 oz) (28 g)* | 5.0 |
| bran flakes—*1 oz (28 g)* | 3.4 |
| bran flakes, Post—*⅔ cup (1 oz) (28 g)* | 5.0 |
| bran flakes w/ raisins—*1 oz (28 g)* | 7.4 |
| bran muffin crisp, General Mills—*⅔ cup (1.2 oz) (35 g)* | 12.0 |
| cap'n crunch, Quaker—*¾ cup (1 oz) (28 g)* | 11.4 |
| cap'n crunch's | |
|    crunchberries, Quaker—*¾ cup (1 oz) (28 g)* | 12.5 |
|    peanut butter, Quaker—*¾ cup (1 oz) (28 g)* | 9.1 |
| cheerios, General Mills—*1¼ cups (1 oz) (28 g)* | 1.0 |
| cinnamon toast crunch, General Mills—*¾ cup (1 oz) (28 g)* | 9.0 |
| circus fun, General Mills—*1 cup (1 oz) (28 g)* | 12.0 |
| cocoa krispies, Kellogg's—*¾ cup (1 oz) (28 g)* | 12.6 |
| cocoa pebbles, Post—*⅞ cup (1 oz) (28 g)* | 12.2 |
| cocoa puffs, General Mills—*1 cup (1 oz) (28 g)* | 11.0 |

## CEREALS, READY-TO-EAT

| | |
|---|---|
| cookie crisp, choc chip, Ralston Purina—*1 cup (1 oz) (28 g)* | 13.0 |
| cookie crisp, vanilla wafer, Ralston Purina—*1 cup (1 oz) (28 g)* | 11.0 |
| corn chex, Ralston Purina—*1 cup (1 oz) (28 g)* | 3.0 |
| corn flakes—*1 oz (28 g)* | 1.9 |
|    country, General Mills—*1 cup (1 oz) (28 g)* | 3.0 |
|    Kellogg's—*1¼ cups (1 oz) (28 g)* | 2.0 |
|    Post Toasties, Post—*1 cup (1 oz) (28 g)* | 1.9 |
|    Ralston Purina—*1 cup (1 oz) (28 g)* | 2.0 |
| corn total, General Mills—*1 cup (1 oz) (28 g)* | 3.0 |
| count chocula, General Mills—*1 cup (1 oz) (28 g)* | 13.0 |
| cracklin bran, Kellogg's—*⅓ cup (1 oz) (28 g)* | 8.1 |
| crispy oatmeal & raisin chex, Ralston Purina—*¾ cup (1.3 oz) (38 g)* | 12.0 |
| crispy wheats & raisins, General Mills—*¾ cup (1 oz) (28 g)* | 10.0 |
| fiber one, General Mills—*½ cup (1 oz) (28 g)* | 2.0 |
| fortified oat flakes, Post—*⅔ cup (1 oz) (28 g)* | 5.5 |
| frankenberry, General Mills—*1 cup (1 oz) (28 g)* | 13.0 |
| froot loops, Kellogg's—*1 cup (1 oz) (28 g)* | 13.9 |
| frosted mini-wheats, Kellogg's—*4 biscuits (1 oz) (28 g)* | 7.4 |
| frosted rice krinkles—*⅞ cup (1 oz) (28 g)* | 12.0 |
| fruit & fiber, Post | |
|    harvest medley—*½ cup (1 oz) (28 g)* | 6.9 |
|    mountain trail—*½ cup (1 oz) (28 g)* | 6.8 |
|    tropical fruit—*½ cup (1 oz) (28 g)* | 6.4 |
|    w/ dates, raisins & walnuts—*½ cup (1 oz) (28 g)* | 7.6 |
| fruity pebbles, Post—*⅞ cup (1 oz) (28 g)* | 12.1 |
| golden grahams, General Mills—*¾ cup (1 oz) (28 g)* | 9.0 |
| granola | |
|    hearty, Post—*¼ cup (1 oz) (28 g)* | 6.8 |
|    hearty w/ raisins, Post—*¼ cup (1 oz) (28 g)* | 8.0 |
|    Kretschmer Sun Country | |
|       w/ almonds—*¼ cup (1 oz) (28 g)* | 9.0 |
|       w/ raisins—*¼ cup (1 oz) (28 g)* | 7.7 |
| grape-nut flakes, Post—*⅞ cup (1 oz) (28 g)* | 4.7 |
| grape-nuts, Post—*¼ cup (1 oz) (28 g)* | 3.4 |
| grape-nuts w/ raisins, Post—*¼ cup (1 oz) (28 g)* | 6.1 |
| heartland natural, w/ coconut—*¼ cup (1 oz) (28 g)* | 6.3 |
| heartland natural, w/ raisins—*¼ cup (1 oz) (28 g)* | 7.4 |
| honey buc wheat crisp, General Mills—*¾ cup (1 oz) (28 g)* | 8.0 |
| honeycomb, Post—*1⅓ cups (1 oz) (28 g)* | 10.7 |
| honey nut cheerios, General Mills—*¾ cup (1 oz) (28 g)* | 10.0 |
| ice cream cones, choc chip, General Mills—*¾ cup (1 oz) (28 g)* | 11.0 |
| ice cream cones, vanilla, General Mills—*¾ cup (1 oz) (28 g)* | 10.0 |
| kaboom, General Mills—*1 cup (1 oz) (28 g)* | 6.0 |
| kix, General Mills—*1½ cups (1 oz) (28 g)* | 3.0 |
| life, cinn, Quaker—*⅔ cup (1 oz) (28 g)* | 5.1 |
| life, Quaker—*⅔ cup (1 oz) (28 g)* | 5.1 |
| lucky charms, General Mills—*1 cup (1 oz) (28 g)* | 11.0 |
| oat cereal—*1 oz (28 g)* | 0.8 |
| pac man, General Mills—*1 cup (1 oz) (28 g)* | 12.0 |
| product 19, Kellogg's—*¾ cup (1 oz) (28 g)* | 3.0 |
| puffed rice—*1 cup (½ oz) (14 g)* | 0.1 |
| puffed wheat—*1 cup (½ oz) (14 g)* | 0.7 |

[a] Specified as sucrose.

## CEREALS, READY-TO-EAT

| | |
|---|---|
| Quaker 100% natural—*¼ cup (1 oz) (28 g)* | 6.1 |
| w/ apples & cinn—*¼ cup (1 oz) (28 g)* | 7.1 |
| w/ raisins & dates—*¼ cup (1 oz) (28 g)* | 8.0 |
| quisp, Quaker—*1 cup (1 oz) (28 g)* | 11.5 |
| raisin bran | |
| Kellogg's—*¾ cup (1.3 oz) (37 g)* | 10.9 |
| Post—*½ cup (1 oz) (28 g)* | 8.8 |
| raisin nut bran, General Mills—*½ cup (1 oz) (28 g)* | 8.0 |
| rice chex, Ralston Purina—*1⅛ cups (1 oz) (28 g)* | 2.0 |
| rice crispy—*1 oz (28 g)* | 2.5 |
| rice krispies, Kellogg's—*1 cup (1 oz) (28 g)* | 2.3 |
| rice krispies, frosted, Kellogg's—*1 cup (1 oz) (28 g)* | 10.8 |
| rice toasties, Post—*¾ cup (1 oz) (28 g)* | 2.7 |
| rocky road, General Mills—*⅔ cup (1 oz) (28 g)* | 12.0 |
| shredded wheat—*1 oz (28 g)* | 0.1 |
| shredded wheat—*1 biscuit (24 g)* | 0.1 |
| s'mores crunch, General Mills—*¾ cup (1 oz) (28 g)* | 10.0 |
| special K, Kellogg's—*1⅓ cups (1 oz) (28 g)* | 2.2 |
| sugar corn pops, Kellogg's—*1 cup (1 oz) (28 g)* | 13.2 |
| sugar frosted flakes, Kellogg's—*¾ cup (1 oz) (28 g)* | 11.1 |
| sugar smacks, Kellogg's—*¾ cup (1 oz) (28 g)* | 15.8 |
| sugar sparkled flakes, Post—*¾ cup (1 oz) (28 g)* | 11.3 |
| super golden crisp, Post—*⅞ cup (1 oz) (28 g)* | 13.1 |
| super sugar crisp—*⅞ cup (1 oz) (28 g)* | 12.8 |
| team flakes—*1 cup (1 oz) (28 g)* | 4.5 |
| total, General Mills—*1 cup (1 oz) (28 g)* | 3.0 |
| trix, General Mills—*1 cup (1 oz) (28 g)* | 12.0 |
| wheat & malted barley nuggets—*1 oz (28 g)* | 2.5 |
| wheat & raisin chex, Ralston Purina—*¾ cup (1.3 oz) (37 g)* | 10.0 |
| wheat chex, Ralston Purina—*⅔ cup (1 oz) (28 g)* | 2.0 |
| wheat flakes—*1 oz (28 g)* | 2.2 |
| wheaties, General Mills—*1 cup (1 oz) (28 g)* | 3.0 |

## CHEESE

| | |
|---|---|
| cheddar—*1 oz (28 g)* | 0.5 |
| cottage, creamed—*1 cup (210 g)* | 1.3 |
| cottage, lowfat—*1 cup (226 g)* | 7.2 |
| cream cheese—*1 oz (2T) (28 g)* | 0.5 |
| ricotta, whole/skim—*1 oz (28 g)* | 0.4 |
| swiss—*1 oz (28 g)* | 0.2 |

## CHEESE PRODUCTS

| | |
|---|---|
| cheese food, american—*1 oz (28 g)* | 2.7 |

## CHIPS & SNACK FOODS

| | |
|---|---|
| chex party mix—*⅔ cup (1 oz) (28 g)* | 5.0 |
| chex party mix, nacho—*⅔ cup (1 oz) (28 g)* | 5.0 |
| chex party mix, sweet & nutty—*¾ cup (1 oz) (28 g)* | 6.0 |
| popcorn, oil-popped—*1 cup (9 g)* | 0.1 |
| popcorn w/ caramel—*1 oz (28 g)* | 11.0 |

## CREAMS & CREAM SUBSTITUTES

| | |
|---|---|
| cream, whipping, unwhipped—*1 T (15 g)* | 0.4 |
| whipped topping | |
| from mix, Dream Whip—*1 T (5 g)* | 1.0 |
| from mix, w/ nutrasweet, D-Zerta—*1 T (from 1.112 g dry mix) (5 g)* | 0.3 |
| frzn, Cool Whip extra creamy, dairy—*1 T (5 g)* | 1.2 |
| frzn, Cool Whip non-dairy—*1 T (4 g)* | 0.7 |

## DESSERTS

**Cakes**

| | |
|---|---|
| cheesecake from mix, Jell-O—*⅛ cheesecake (99 g)* | 28.0 |
| fruitcake—*1 piece (43 g)* | 18.5 |
| sponge, jam-filled—*1 piece (66 g)* | 31.5 |

**Cookies**

| | |
|---|---|
| animal crackers—*10 pieces (26 g)* | 5.9 |
| choc wafers, Famous—*5 cookies (28 g)* | 11.3 |
| **Doughnut, cake type**—*1 doughnut (25 g)* | 4.2 |

**Frozen Desserts**

| | |
|---|---|
| fruit jce bar, all flavors, Jell-O—*1 bar (52 g)* | 9.4 |
| gelatin pops, all flavors, Jell-O—*1 pop (44 g)* | 6.8 |
| pudding pops, Jell-O | |
| choc—*1 pop (47 g)* | 9.8 |
| choc caramel swirl—*1 pop (47 g)* | 10.1 |
| choc fudge—*1 pop (47 g)* | 9.9 |
| choc van swirl—*1 pop (47 g)* | 10.1 |
| choc w/ choc chips—*1 pop (48 g)* | 11.2 |
| choc w/ choc coating—*1 pop (49 g)* | 13.0 |
| double choc swirl—*1 pop (47 g)* | 10.1 |
| milk choc—*1 pop (47 g)* | 10.3 |
| van—*1 pop (47 g)* | 10.4 |
| van w/ choc chips—*1 pop (48 g)* | 11.3 |
| van w/ choc coating—*1 pop (49 g)* | 13.1 |

**Gelatin Desserts, from mix**

| | |
|---|---|
| all flavors, Jell-O—*½ cup (140 g)* | 18.7 |
| orange—*½ cup (140 g)* | 17.9 |
| raspberry—*½ cup (140 g)* | 8.7 |

**Granola Desserts**

| | |
|---|---|
| caramel grand slam, New Trail—*1.8 oz bar (51 g)* | 19.7 |
| caramel nut, Smores—*1 oz bar (28 g)* | 9.0 |
| choc chip, New Trail—*1.3 oz bar (37 g)* | 14.5 |
| choc chip, Smores—*1 oz bar (28 g)* | 10.0 |
| choc chip raisin, Smores—*1 oz bar (28 g)* | 10.0 |
| choc fudge, Smores—*1 oz bar (28 g)* | 12.0 |
| cocoa, choc covered, New Trail—*1.3 oz bar (37 g)* | 14.0 |
| honey graham, choc covered, New Trail—*1.3 oz bar (37 g)* | 12.4 |
| peanut butter & choc chip, New Trail—*1.3 oz bar (37 g)* | 10.5 |
| peanut butter & choc chip, Smores—*1 oz bar (28 g)* | 9.0 |
| peanut butter, New Trail—*1.3 oz bar (37 g)* | 10.0 |
| peanut butter, Smores—*1 oz bar (28 g)* | 10.0 |
| peanut, choc covered, New Trail—*1.3 oz bar (37 g)* | 12.3 |
| plain—*1 oz bar (28 g)* | 5.5 |

**Pie, from mix**

| | |
|---|---|
| banana cream, Jell-O—*⅛ pie (92 g)* | 17.7 |
| choc mousse, Jell-O—*⅛ pie (95 g)* | 17.4 |
| coconut cream, Jell-O—*⅛ pie (94 g)* | 20.7 |

**Pies, Snack**

| | |
|---|---|
| apple, baked—*1 snack pie (90 g)* | 27.8 |
| apple, fried—*1 snack pie (90 g)* | 10.4 |

**Pudding, cnd**

| | |
|---|---|
| choc—*½ cup (150 g)* | 20.0[a] |
| van—*½ cup (150 g)* | 22.0[a] |

**Pudding, from inst mix**

| | |
|---|---|
| banana cream, Jell-O—*½ cup (147 g)* | 24.0 |
| banana cream, sugar-free, Jell-O—*½ cup (130 g)* | 6.0 |
| butter pecan, Jell-O—*½ cup (147 g)* | 23.7 |
| butterscotch, Jell-O—*½ cup (147 g)* | 23.9 |
| butterscotch, sugar-free, D-Zerta—*½ cup (130 g)* | 6.0 |

[a] Specified as sucrose.

**DESSERTS**

| | |
|---|---|
| butterscotch, sugar-free, Jell-O—*½ cup (131 g)* | 6.1 |
| choc, Jell-O—*½ cup (150 g)* | 24.7 |
| choc, sugar-free, D-Zerta—*½ cup (130 g)* | 6.0 |
| choc, sugar-free, Jell-O—*½ cup (133 g)* | 6.0 |
| choc fudge, Jell-O—*½ cup (150 g)* | 23.7 |
| choc fudge, sugar-free, Jell-O—*½ cup (135 g)* | 6.1 |
| choc fudge mousse, Jell-O—*½ cup (86 g)* | 14.9 |
| choc mousse, Jell-O—*½ cup (86 g)* | 16.2 |
| choc tapioca, Jell-O—*½ cup (147 g)* | 21.0 |
| coconut cream, Jell-O—*½ cup (147 g)* | 22.1 |
| french van, Jell-O—*½ cup (147 g)* | 24.1 |
| golden egg custard, Jell-O—*½ cup (143 g)* | 23.0 |
| lemon, Jell-O—*½ cup (147 g)* | 24.4 |
| milk choc, Jell-O—*½ cup (150 g)* | 24.8 |
| pineapple cream, Jell-O—*½ cup (147 g)* | 24.2 |
| pistachio, Jell-O—*½ cup (147 g)* | 23.7 |
| pistachio, sugar-free, Jell-O—*½ cup (131 g)* | 6.0 |
| rice, Jell-O—*½ cup (149 g)* | 19.0 |
| van, Jell-O—*½ cup (147 g)* | 24.6 |
| van, sugar-free, D-Zerta—*½ cup (130 g)* | 6.1 |
| van, sugar-free, Jell-O—*½ cup (131 g)* | 6.0 |
| vanilla tapioca, Jell-O—*½ cup (145 g)* | 21.1 |

**Dessert Toppings**

| | |
|---|---|
| choc syrup—*2 T (38 g)* | 25.3 |
| confectioner's coating | |
|   carob—*1 oz (28 g)* | 10.6 |
|   white choc—*1 oz (28 g)* | 17.5 |
| icing/frosting, ready-to-spread | |
|   choc—*amt for 1/12 cake (37 g)* | 20.6 |
|   other flavors—*amt for 1/12 cake (37 g)* | 26.3 |

**ENTREES**
**Canned Entrees**

| | |
|---|---|
| beans, baked | |
|   w/ bacon, Special Recipe—*6.9 oz (195 g)* | 9.4 |
|   w/ beef in bbq sce, Special Recipe—*6.9 oz (195 g)* | 8.4 |
|   w/ chicken in bbq sce, Special Recipe—*6.9 oz (195 g)* | 9.0 |
|   w/ franks, Campbell's—*8 oz (227 g)* | 13.2 |
|   w/ franks in tomato sce, Campbell's—*7.9 oz (223 g)* | 13.0 |
| beef & veg stew, Bounty—*7.6 oz (216 g)* | 1.9 |
| beef & veg stew, Campbell's—*7.5 oz (213 g)* | 1.6 |
| beef ravioli, Franco-American—*7.5 oz (213 g)* | 9.2 |
| beef raviolio's, Franco-American—*7.5 oz (213 g)* | 9.0 |
| beef sirloin w/ onions, Prego Plus—*4 oz (113 g)* | 11.5 |
| chicken a la king, Swanson—*5.3 oz (149 g)* | 1.4 |
| chicken & dumplings, Swanson—*7.5 oz (213 g)* | 0.8 |
| chicken & veg stew, Bounty—*7.5 oz (213 g)* | 1.6 |
| chicken & veg stew, Campbell's—*7.6 oz (216 g)* | 1.4 |
| chicken w/ veg & pasta, Prego—*9.49 oz (269 g)* | 4.9 |
| chili-mac, Bounty—*7.8 oz (220 g)* | 4.3 |
| chili w/ beans, Bounty—*7.8 oz (220 g)* | 2.6 |
| chili w/ beans, hot, Bounty—*7.8 oz (220 g)* | 2.5 |
| dumplings & chicken, Bounty—*7.5 oz (213 g)* | 1.2 |
| linguini w/ white clam sce, Prego—*11 oz (312 g)* | 6.0 |
| macaroni & cheese, Franco-American—*7.4 oz (209 g)* | 1.3 |
| macaroni w/ meat sce, Hearty—*7.5 oz (213 g)* | 8.0 |
| noodles & chicken, Bounty—*7.5 oz (213 g)* | 1.4 |
| pasta twists w/ meat sce, Hearty—*7.5 oz (213 g)* | 18.0 |
| pasta w/ chicken cacciatore sce, Prego—*12.2 oz (347 g)* | 7.7 |

**ENTREES**

| | |
|---|---|
| pizzo's, Franco-American—*7.5 oz (213 g)* | 12.1 |
| potatoes & beef in gravy, Bounty—*7.5 oz (213 g)* | 2.9 |
| ravioli w/ meat sce, Franco-American—*7.5 oz (213 g)* | 10.3 |
| ravioli w/ meat sce, Hearty—*7.5 oz (213 g)* | 10.3 |
| sausage, italian & green peppers, Prego Plus—*4 oz (113 g)* | 10.0 |
| spaghetti 'n beef, Franco-American—*7.5 oz (213 g)* | 7.5 |
| spaghettio's, Franco-American | |
|   w/ franks—*7.4 oz (209 g)* | 8.0 |
|   w/ meatballs—*7.4 oz (209 g)* | 7.7 |
|   w/ tomato & cheese sce—*7.5 oz (213 g)* | 11.1 |
| spaghetti w/ meatballs & tomato sce | |
|   Franco-American—*7.4 oz (209 g)* | 9.9 |
|   Prego—*13 oz (369 g)* | 16.6 |
| spaghetti w/ meat sce | |
|   Franco-American—*7.5 oz (213 g)* | 8.1 |
|   Hearty—*7.4 oz (209 g)* | 12.8 |
|   Prego—*12.5 oz (354 g)* | 8.7 |
| spaghetti w/ tomato sce & cheese, Franco-American—*7.8 oz (220 g)* | 12.5 |
| spaghetti w/ tomato sce, Franco-American—*7.4 oz (209 g)* | 11.9 |
| UFO's, Franco-American—*7.5 oz (213 g)* | 12.5 |
| UFO's w/ meteors, Franco-American—*7.5 oz (213 g)* | 11.4 |
| veal & mushrooms, Prego Plus—*4 oz (113 g)* | 11.0 |

**Frozen Entrees (1-2 items/entree)**

| | |
|---|---|
| beef marsala w/ noodles, Prego—*11.3 oz (319 g)* | 10.2 |
| chicken piccata w/ rice, Prego—*11 oz (312 g)* | 5.3 |

**FAST FOODS**

| | |
|---|---|
| cheeseburger—*1 reg sandwich (112 g)* | 5.8 |
| eggs, scrambled—*1 serving (98 g)* | 0.9 |
| english muffin w/ egg, cheese & canadian bacon—*1 sandwich (138 g)* | 2.9 |
| fish sandwich—*1 sandwich (143 g)* | 4.7 |
| hamburger—*1 reg sandwich (98 g)* | 4.6 |
| ice milk, soft serve in cone—*1 serving (115 g)* | 20.9 |
| shake, all flavors—*1 shake (290 g)* | 52.2 |
| sundae | |
|   caramel—*1 sundae (165 g)* | 41.3 |
|   hot fudge—*1 sundae (165 g)* | 41.7 |
|   strawberry—*1 sundae (165 g)* | 44.6 |

**FRUIT JUICES**

| | |
|---|---|
| apple jce, unsweetened, cnd—*8 fl oz (248 g)* | 27.0 |
| grape jce, from frzn conc—*8 fl oz (253 g)* | 35.9 |
| grapefruit jce, cnd—*8 fl oz (247 g)* | 18.5 |
| lemon jce, fresh—*8 fl oz (244 g)* | 5.9 |
| orange jce, fresh—*8 fl oz (248 g)* | 25.3 |
| orange jce, from frzn conc—*8 fl oz (249 g)* | 26.4 |
| pineapple jce, unsweetened, cnd—*8 fl oz (250 g)* | 31.3 |
| prune jce, bottled—*8 fl oz (256 g)* | 34.3 |
| tomato jce, cnd—*6 fl oz (182 g)* | 5.3 |
| tomato jce, from concentrate, Campbell's—*6 fl oz (182 g)* | 5.3 |
| V-8 vegetable cocktail, Campbell's—*6 fl oz (182 g)* | 5.6 |
|   no salt added—*6 fl oz (182 g)* | 6.2 |
|   spicy hot—*6 fl oz (182 g)* | 6.0 |

**FRUITS**

| | |
|---|---|
| apple, raw—*1 med (138 g)* | 18.4 |
| applesce, cnd, sweetened—*½ cup (128 g)* | 21.1 |

## FRUITS

| | |
|---|---|
| apricots | |
|     raw—*3 med (106 g)* | 9.0 |
|     dried, sulfured—*10 halves (35 g)* | 13.6 |
| banana, raw—*1 med (114 g)* | 17.8 |
| blueberries, raw—*1 cup (145 g)* | 10.6 |
| cantaloupe—*1 cup pieces (160 g)* | 13.9 |
| cherries, sour, raw--*1 cup (114 g)* | 9.2 |
| cherries, sweet, raw—*10 cherries (68 g)* | 9.9 |
| currants—*½ cup (56 g)* | 4.5 |
| dates, dried—*10 dates (83 g)* | 53.3 |
| figs, dried—*10 figs (187 g)* | 124.4 |
| fruit cocktail, cnd, jce pack—*½ cup (124 g)* | 19.0 |
| fruit salad, Fresh Chef | |
|     fruit cooler—*2/5 cup (99 g)* | 8.1 |
|     tropical delight—*4/5 cup (198 g)* | 25.2 |
| grapefruit, raw—*½ med (118 g)* | 7.3 |
| grapes, american, raw—*1 cup (92 g)* | 15.1 |
| kiwifruit, raw—*1 med (76 g)* | 8.0 |
| lemon, raw—*1 med (58 g)* | 1.5 |
| lime, raw—*1 med (67 g)* | 0.3 |
| mixed fruit, frzn in syrup, Birds Eye—*½ cup (142 g)* | 15.9 |
| nectarine, raw—*1 med (136 g)* | 11.6 |
| orange, raw—*1 med (140 g)* | 12.5 |
| peach | |
|     raw—*1 med (87 g)* | 7.6 |
|     cnd, jce pack—*1 cup (248 g)* | 43.2 |
|     dried, sulfured—*10 halves (130 g)* | 58.0 |
| pear | |
|     raw—*1 med (166 g)* | 17.4 |
|     cnd, heavy pack—*1 cup (255 g)* | 38.8 |
|     cnd, jce pack—*1 cup (248 g)* | 24.1 |
|     cnd, water pack—*1 cup (244 g)* | 14.9 |
| pineapple | |
|     raw—*1 cup pieces (155 g)* | 18.4 |
|     cnd, jce pack—*1 cup pieces (250 g)* | 35.5 |
| plum, raw—*1 med (66 g)* | 5.0 |
| prunes, dried—*10 prunes (84 g)* | 37.0 |
| raisins, dried—*⅔ cup (100 g)* | 65.0 |
| raspberries, frzn in lite syrup, Birds Eye—*½ cup (142 g)* | 19.6 |
| strawberries | |
|     raw—*1 cup (149 g)* | 8.6 |
|     frzn, in lite syrup, Birds Eye—*½ cup (142 g)* | 20.6 |
| tangelo, raw—*1 med (170 g)* | 12.6 |
| watermelon, raw—*1 cup (160 g)* | 14.4 |

## GRAIN FRACTIONS

| | |
|---|---|
| wheat bran—*1 oz (28 g)* | 0.6 |
| wheat flour | |
|     white—*1 cup (113 g)* | 1.9 |
|     whole wheat—*1 cup (120 g)* | 2.4 |
| wheat germ, crude/toasted—*¼ cup (1 oz) (28 g)* | 3.4 |

## GRAIN PRODUCTS

| | |
|---|---|
| biscuits, from mix—*1 biscuit (28 g)* | 1.2 |
| bread | |
|     white—*1 slice (24 g)* | 0.9 |
|     white, toasted—*1 slice (21 g)* | 0.8 |

## GRAIN PRODUCTS

| | |
|---|---|
|     whole wheat—*1 slice (25 g)* | 1.0 |
|     whole wheat, toasted—*1 slice (21 g)* | 0.9 |
| crackers, rye—*¼ large square (14 g)* | 0.4 |
| muffin, english, buttered—*1 muffin (57 g)* | 2.2 |
| pasta salad, italian, Fresh Chef—*3.2 oz (92 g)* | 1.2 |
| pasta salad, seafood, Fresh Chef—*4.3 oz (123 g)* | 1.9 |
| roll, hamburger—*1 roll (40 g)* | 3.0 |
| stuffing, from mix, Stove Top | |
|     americana san francisco style—*½ cup (107 g)* | 2.5 |
|     chicken flavored—*½ cup (107 g)* | 2.6 |
|     chicken flavored w/ rice—*½ cup (109 g)* | 2.5 |
|     chicken florentine—*½ cup (102 g)* | 3.2 |
|     cornbread—*½ cup (107 g)* | 2.5 |
|     for beef—*½ cup (108 g)* | 3.2 |
|     for pork—*½ cup (107 g)* | 2.7 |
|     garden herb—*½ cup (95 g)* | 3.2 |
|     homestyle herb—*½ cup (96 g)* | 2.5 |
|     long grain & wild rice flavor—*½ cup (109 g)* | 2.3 |
|     savory herbs flavor—*½ cup (107 g)* | 2.5 |
|     turkey flavor—*½ cup (107 g)* | 2.6 |
|     veg & almond—*½ cup (95 g)* | 3.4 |
|     wild rice & mushroom—*½ cup (95 g)* | 3.1 |
| tortilla, corn—*1 tortilla (30 g)* | 0.2 |

## INFANT FORMULA

| | |
|---|---|
| isomil, 20 cal/fl oz, Ross Labs—*1 fl oz (30 g)* | 1.0[a] |
| isomil, SF, 20 cal/fl oz, Ross Labs—*1 fl oz (30 g)* | 1.0[a] |
| nursoy, 20 cal/fl oz, Wyeth—*1 fl oz (30 g)* | 1.1[a] |

## MEATS

| | |
|---|---|
| pork sausage, ckd—*3.5 oz (100 g)* | 2.6 |

## MEATS, LUNCHEON

| | |
|---|---|
| beef & pork spiced loaf—*1 oz (28 g)* | 0.9 |
| bologna, beef—*1 slice (23 g)* | 0.6 |
| frankfurter, beef & pork—*1 frank (45 g)* | 0.9 |
| ham, smoked, ckd—*1 oz (28 g)* | 0.3 |
| meat spread, chicken, cnd, Swanson—*1.02 oz (29 g)* | 0.3 |
| pastrami, beef—*1 oz (28 g)* | 0.2 |
| salami, beef—*1 slice (23 g)* | 0.3 |

## MILK, COW

| | |
|---|---|
| buttermilk, cultured—*8 fl oz (245 g)* | 11.8 |
| lowfat, dry—*¼ cup (30 g)* | 15.1 |
| skim—*8 fl oz (245 g)* | 10.8 |
| whole—*1 cup (244 g)* | 12.2 |
| whole, dry—*¼ cup (32 g)* | 11.5 |

## YOGURT

| | |
|---|---|
| lowfat, plain—*1 cup (227 g)* | 11.6 |
| lowfat, strawberry—*1 cup (227 g)* | 34.7 |

## MILK BEVERAGES

| | |
|---|---|
| choc malted flavor powder in whole milk—*3 hp t powder in 8 fl oz milk (265 g)* | 18.0 |

## MILK BEVERAGE MIXES

| | |
|---|---|
| choc malted milk flavor mix, powder—*¾ oz (3 hp t) (21 g)* | 11.0[a] |
| cocoa mix, powder, Carnation | |
|     choc & marshmallow—*1 oz (28 g)* | 16.0[a] |
|     milk choc—*1 oz (28 g)* | 16.0[a] |

[a] Specified as sucrose.

## MILK BEVERAGE MIXES

| | |
|---|---|
| rich choc—*1 oz (28 g)* | 17.0[a] |
| rich choc, 70 cal—*1 pkt (3 hp t) (21 g)* | 11.0[a] |
| instant breakfast, Carnation | |
| choc—*1.25 oz pkt (35 g)* | 20.0[b] |
| choc malt—*1.24 oz pkt (35 g)* | 19.0[b] |
| coffee—*1.26 oz pkt (36 g)* | 21.0[b] |
| eggnog—*1.20 oz pkt (34 g)* | 21.0[b] |
| strawberry—*1.25 oz pkt (35 g)* | 22.0[b] |
| vanilla—*1.23 oz pkt (35 g)* | 21.0[b] |

## NUTS, NUT PRODUCTS & SEEDS

| | |
|---|---|
| almonds | |
| blanched, Blue Diamond—*1 oz (28 g)* | 1.6[a] |
| blanched, slivered, Blue Diamond—*1 oz (28 g)* | 1.6[a] |
| chopped, Blue Diamond—*1 oz (28 g)* | 1.6[a] |
| dried/roasted—*1 oz (28 g)* | 1.7 |
| sliced, Blue Diamond—*1 oz (28 g)* | 1.6[a] |
| whole, Blue Diamond—*1 oz (28 g)* | 1.9[a] |
| brazilnuts, oil-roasted—*1 oz (28 g)* | 0.7 |
| cashews, oil-roasted—*1 oz (28 g)* | 1.4 |
| chestnuts, european—*1 oz (2½ nuts) (28 g)* | 3.0 |
| coconut | |
| raw—*1 piece (2″x2″x½″) (45 g)* | 1.6 |
| dried, sweetened, flaked, cnd—*4 oz (114 g)* | 39.2 |
| dried, sweetened, flaked, cnd, Angel Flake—*⅓ cup loosely packed (25 g)* | 7.7 |
| dried, sweetened, flaked, packaged, Angel Flake—*⅓ cup loosely packed (25 g)* | 8.5 |
| dried, sweetened, shredded, Bakers—*⅓ cup loosely packed (28 g)* | 9.8 |
| macadamia nuts, oil-roasted—*1 oz (10-12 nuts) (28 g)* | 1.7 |
| mixed nuts, oil roasted—*1 oz (28 g)* | 1.1 |
| peanut butter, creamy/smooth—*1 T (16 g)* | 1.2 |
| peanuts | |
| dried—*1 oz (28 g)* | 1.2 |
| dry/oil-roasted—*1 oz (28 g)* | 1.3 |
| pecans, dried—*1 oz (31 large nuts) (28 g)* | 1.2 |
| pistachio nuts, dried—*1 oz (47 nuts) (28 g)* | 1.8 |
| pumpkin & squash seeds, dried—*1 oz (142 seeds) (28 g)* | 0.3 |
| sesame seeds, dried/roasted—*1 oz (28 g)* | 0.3 |
| sunflower seeds, dried—*1 oz (28 g)* | 0.9 |
| walnuts, english/persian, dried—*1 oz (14 halves) (28 g)* | 0.6 |

## POULTRY

| | |
|---|---|
| chicken, cnd, Swanson | |
| chunks o'chicken—*2.5 oz (71 g)* | 0.2 |
| chunk, white & dark—*2.5 oz (71 g)* | 0.2 |
| chunk white—*2.5 oz (71 g)* | 0.2 |
| chunk white in water—*2.5 oz (71 g)* | 0.3 |
| mixin chicken—*2.5 oz (71 g)* | 0.2 |
| turkey breast—*3.5 oz (100 g)* | 0.2 |

## SALAD DRESSINGS
**Low Calorie, from mix, Good Seasons**

| | |
|---|---|
| italian, lite—*1 T (15 g)* | 0.4 |
| italian, lite zesty—*1 T (15 g)* | 0.3 |
| italian, no oil—*1 T (17 g)* | 1.3 |

## SALAD DRESSINGS
**Regular, from mix, Good Seasons**

| | |
|---|---|
| bleu cheese & herbs—*1 T (16 g)* | 0.3 |
| buttermilk farm style—*1 T (16 g)* | 0.8 |
| cheese garlic—*1 T (16 g)* | 0.2 |
| cheese italian—*1 T (16 g)* | 0.2 |
| classic herb—*1 T (16 g)* | 0.1 |
| italian—*1 T (16 g)* | 0.3 |
| italian, mild—*1 T (17 g)* | 1.0 |
| italian, zesty—*1 T (16 g)* | 0.3 |
| lemon & herbs—*1 T (16 g)* | 0.3 |

## SAUCES, CONDIMENTS & GRAVIES
**Sauces & Condiments**

| | |
|---|---|
| alfredo fetticini sce, cnd, Prego—*5 oz (142 g)* | 2.4 |
| alfredo sce, refrig, Fresh Chef—*4 oz (113 g)* | 0.6 |
| barbeque sce, Open Pit—*1 T (18 g)* | 4.5 |
| hickory smoke flavor—*1 T (18 g)* | 4.5 |
| hickory thick & tangy—*1 T (18 g)* | 4.5 |
| hot 'n tangy flavor—*1 T (18 g)* | 4.4 |
| mesquite 'n tangy—*1 T (18 g)* | 4.5 |
| sweet 'n tangy flavor—*1 T (18 g)* | 5.1 |
| w/ onions—*1 T (18 g)* | 4.7 |
| bolognese sce, refrig, Fresh Chef—*4 oz (113 g)* | 9.2 |
| catsup (ketchup), tomato, Campbell's—*1 T (14 g)* | 2.4 |
| clam sce, red, refrig, Fresh Chef—*4 oz (113 g)* | 6.1 |
| clam sce, white, refrig, Fresh Chef—*4 oz (113 g)* | 2.0 |
| marinara (tomato based) sce, Prego—*4 oz (113 g)* | 6.9 |
| pesto sce, refrig, Fresh Chef—*1 oz (28 g)* | 0.5 |
| spaghetti sce, cnd | |
| no salt added, Prego—*4 oz (113 g)* | 6.9 |
| Prego—*4 oz (113 g)* | 12.4 |
| w/ meat flavor, Prego—*4 oz (113 g)* | 12.8 |
| w/ mushrooms & chunk tomatoes, Prego—*4 oz (113 g)* | 9.6 |
| w/ mushrooms, Prego—*4 oz (113 g)* | 12.2 |
| tomato sce, cnd | |
| al fresco, Prego—*4 oz (113 g)* | 7.1 |
| refrig, Fresh Chef—*4 oz (113 g)* | 10.6 |
| w/ mushrooms al fresco, Prego—*4 oz (113 g)* | 6.9 |
| w/ red peppers, al fresco, Prego—*4 oz (113 g)* | 6.5 |
| white cream (bechamel) sce, cnd, Campbell's—*2 oz (57 g)* | 0.3 |

**Gravies, cnd**

| | |
|---|---|
| au jus, Franco-American—*2 oz (57 g)* | 0.3 |
| beef, Franco-American—*2 oz (57 g)* | 0.2 |
| brown, Campbell's—*2 oz (57 g)* | 0.7 |
| brown w/ onions, Franco-American—*2 oz (57 g)* | 1.2 |
| chicken, Campbell's—*2 oz (57 g)* | 0.3 |
| chicken, Franco-American—*2 oz (57 g)* | 0.3 |
| chicken giblet, Franco-American—*2 oz (57 g)* | 0.1 |
| mushroom, Franco-American—*2 oz (57 g)* | 0.2 |
| pork, Franco-American—*2 oz (57 g)* | 0.3 |
| turkey, Franco-American—*2 oz (57 g)* | 0.4 |

## SOUPS
**Canned, Condensed, Prep w/ Water**

| | |
|---|---|
| beef broth & barley, Campbell's—*1 cup (233 g)* | 0.6 |
| beef, Campbell's—*1 cup (233 g)* | 0.7 |
| beef noodle homestyle, Campbell's—*1 cup (233 g)* | 0.7 |

[a] Specified as sucrose.

[b] Sucrose is 12 g for choc, 10 g for choc malt, 8 g for coffee, 13 g for eggnog, 9 g for strawberry & 9 g for vanilla.

## SOUPS

| | |
|---|---|
| broccoli, creamy, Campbell's—*1 cup (233 g)* | 0.8 |
| cauliflower, creamy, Campbell's—*1 cup (233 g)* | 1.6 |
| chicken alphabet, Campbell's—*1 cup (233 g)* | 0.7 |
| chicken & stars, Campbell's—*1 cup (233 g)* | 0.6 |
| chicken & wild rice, Golden Classic, Campbell's—*1 cup (233 g)* | 4.1 |
| chicken barley, Campbell's—*1 cup (233 g)* | 0.6 |
| chicken broth & noodles, Campbell's—*1 cup (233 g)* | 0.6 |
| chicken broth & rice, Campbell's—*1 cup (233 g)* | 0.2 |
| chicken, crm of, Special Request (⅓ less salt)—*1 cup (233 g)* | 0.6 |
| chicken creamy mushroom, Campbell's—*1 cup (233 g)* | 0.6 |
| chicken noodle, Special Request, (⅓ less salt)—*1 cup (233 g)* | 0.5 |
| chicken noodle-o's, Campbell's—*1 cup (233 g)* | 0.6 |
| corn potage, Campbell's—*1 cup (233 g)* | 5.8 |
| curly noodle w/ chicken, Campbell's—*1 cup (233 g)* | 0.6 |
| garden veg, Campbell's—*1 cup (233 g)* | 2.3 |
| gazpacho, Campbell's—*1 cup (233 g)* | 5.2 |
| meatball alphabet, Campbell's—*1 cup (233 g)* | 1.2 |
| mushroom, golden, Campbell's—*1 cup (233 g)* | 0.7 |
| nacho cheese, Campbell's—*1 cup (233 g)* | 1.8 |
| noodles & ground beef, Campbell's—*1 cup (233 g)* | 0.8 |
| pea, split w/ ham & bacon, Campbell's—*1 cup (233 g)* | 2.9 |
| spinach, creamy, Campbell's—*1 cup (233 g)* | 0.9 |
| tomato, crm of, Campbell's—*1 cup (233 g)* | 11.7 |
| tomato garden, crispy, Campbell's—*1 cup (233 g)* | 12.3 |
| tomato zesty, Campbell's—*1 cup (233 g)* | 14.0 |
| tortellini & veg, Golden Classic, Campbell's—*1 cup (233 g)* | 5.4 |
| veg, Campbell's—*1 cup (233 g)* | 4.3 |
| veg, Special Request (⅓ less salt)—*1 cup (233 g)* | 4.2 |
| veg, old fashioned, Campbell's—*1 cup (233 g)* | 1.6 |
| won ton, Campbell's—*1 cup (233 g)* | 0.4 |
| **Canned, Ready-to-Serve** | |
| bean, Campbell's—*7.5 oz (213 g)* | 2.3 |
| beef noodle, Campbell's—*7.27 oz (206 g)* | 0.6 |
| beef noodle, Home Cookin, Campbell's—*10.76 oz (305 g)* | 2.6 |
| beef ravioli romano, chunky, Campbell's—*9.49 oz (269 g)* | 12.4 |
| beef w/ mushroom, chunky, low Na, Campbell's—*10.76 oz (305 g)* | 3.3 |
| beef w/ noodles, stroganoff style, chunky, Campbell's—*10.76 oz (305 g)* | 3.6 |
| chicken broth, low Na, Campbell's—*7.27 oz (206 g)* | 0.8 |
| chicken broth, Swanson—*7.27 oz (206 g)* | 0.6 |
| chicken, crm of, Campbell's—*7.27 oz (206 g)* | 0.6 |
| chicken mushroom, creamy, chunky, Campbell's—*9.38 oz (266 g)* | 1.5 |
| chicken noodle, Campbell's—*7.27 oz (206 g)* | 0.6 |
| chicken rice, Campbell's—*7.27 oz (206 g)* | 0.4 |
| chicken veg, chunky, low Na, Campbell's—*10.76 oz (305 g)* | 3.0 |
| chicken veg w/ rice, Home Cookin, Campbell's—*10.76 oz (305 g)* | 3.6 |
| chicken w/ noodles & mushrooms, chunky, Campbell's—*10.76 oz (305 g)* | 1.0 |
| chicken w/ noodles, Home Cookin, Campbell's—*10.76 oz (305 g)* | 1.5 |
| chicken w/ noodles, low Na, Campbell's—*10.76 oz (305 g)* | 2.9 |
| chicken w/ rice, chunky, Campbell's—*9.49 oz (269 g)* | 2.6 |
| chili beef, chunky, Campbell's—*9.74 oz (276 g)* | 2.6 |

## SOUPS

| | |
|---|---|
| clam chowder | |
| manhattan, Campbell's—*7.27 oz (206 g)* | 1.5 |
| new england, chunky, Campbell's—*10.76 oz (305 g)* | 3.1 |
| fisherman chowder, chunky, Campbell's—*9.49 oz (269 g)* | 1.9 |
| ham n' butter bean, chunky, Campbell's—*10.76 oz (305 g)* | 3.9 |
| lentil, Home Cookin, Campbell's—*10.76 oz (305 g)* | 4.9 |
| lentil, Prego—*9.49 oz (269 g)* | 5.8 |
| mediterranean veg, chunky, Campbell's—*9.49 oz (269 g)* | 6.6 |
| minestrone, Campbell's—*7.27 oz (206 g)* | 1.3 |
| minestrone w/ italian sausage, Prego—*9.49 oz (269 g)* | 5.8 |
| mushroom, crm of, Campbell's—*7.27 oz (206 g)* | 0.8 |
| mushroom, crm of, low Na, Campbell's—*7.27 oz (206 g)* | 3.4 |
| mushroom, creamy, chunky, Campbell's—*9.38 oz (266 g)* | 1.7 |
| onion, low Na, Campbell's—*7.27 oz (206 g)* | 4.2 |
| pea, green, Campbell's—*7.5 oz (213 g)* | 3.7 |
| pea, split, low Na, Campbell's—*7.27 oz (206 g)* | 2.9 |
| pea, split w/ ham, Home Cookin, Campbell's—*10.76 oz (305 g)* | 5.4 |
| sirloin burger, chunky, Campbell's—*9.49 oz (269 g)* | 2.5 |
| steak & potato, chunky, Campbell's—*9.49 oz (269 g)* | 0.9 |
| tomato, Campbell's—*7.27 oz (206 g)* | 12.6 |
| tomato w/ tomato pieces, low Na, Campbell's—*7.27 oz (206 g)* | 11.7 |
| tortilla, chunky, Campbell's—*10.76 oz (305 g)* | 6.9 |
| veg, Campbell's—*7.27 oz (206 g)* | 2.3 |
| veg w/ beef | |
| Campbell's—*10.76 oz (305 g)* | 3.9 |
| chunky, Campbell's—*9.49 oz (269 g)* | 3.0 |
| chunky, low Na, Campbell's—*10.76 oz (305 g)* | 5.4 |
| won ton, imperial, chunky, Campbell's—*9.49 oz (269 g)* | 3.9 |
| **Dehydrated** | |
| chicken noodle w/ meat, Campbell's—*0.92 oz (26 g)* | 2.9 |
| chicken rice, Campbell's—*0.85 oz (24 g)* | 0.7 |

## SPECIAL DIETARY FOODS

| | |
|---|---|
| breakfast bar, Carnation | |
| choc chip—*1.44 oz bar (41 g)* | 10.0[a] |
| choc crunch—*1.34 oz bar (38 g)* | 8.0[a] |
| peanut butter crunch—*1.35 oz bar (38 g)* | 7.0[a] |
| peanut butter w/ choc chips—*1.39 oz bar (39 g)* | 10.0[a] |
| gluten-free, wheat-free foods, Ener-G Foods | |
| corn mix—*1 cup (128 g)* | 0.8[a] |
| nutquik milk powder—*1 oz (28 g)* | 1.6[a] |
| rice mix—*1 oz (28 g)* | 0.1[a] |
| soyquix milk powder—*2 T (14 g)* | 0.6[a] |
| slender bars, Carnation | |
| choc—*2 bars (55 g)* | 18.0[a] |
| choc chip—*2 bars (55 g)* | 20.0[a] |
| choc peanut butter—*2 bars (55 g)* | 18.0[a] |
| vanilla—*2 bars (55 g)* | 17.0[a] |
| slender, liquid diet meal, cnd, Carnation | |
| banana—*10 fl oz (313 g)* | 21.0[a] |
| choc—*10 fl oz (313 g)* | 25.0[a] |
| choc fudge—*10 fl oz (313 g)* | 25.0[a] |
| choc malt—*10 fl oz (313 g)* | 23.0[a] |
| milk choc—*10 fl oz (313 g)* | 23.0[a] |
| peach—*10 fl oz (313 g)* | 21.0[a] |
| strawberry—*10 fl oz (313 g)* | 21.0[a] |
| vanilla—*10 fl oz (313 g)* | 21.0[a] |

[a] Specified as sucrose.

## SPECIAL DIETARY FORMULAS, COMMERCIAL & HOSPITAL

| | |
|---|---|
| enrich, Ross Labs—*8 fl oz (255 g)* | 12.2[a] |
| ensure HN, Ross Labs—*8 fl oz (253 g)* | 13.4[a] |
| ensure plus, Ross Labs—*8 fl oz (259 g)* | 10.9[a] |
| ensure plus HN, Ross Labs—*8 fl oz (260 g)* | 10.4[a] |
| ensure, Ross Labs—*8 fl oz (253 g)* | 10.3[a] |
| pulmocare, Ross Labs—*8 fl oz (250 g)* | 13.5[a] |
| vital high nitrogen, Ross Labs—*300 ml (79 g pkt w/ 255 ml water) (326 g)* | 9.4[a] |

## SUGARS, SYRUPS & OTHER SWEETENERS

| | |
|---|---|
| honey—*1 T (21 g)* | 17.2 |
| molasses, reg—*1 T (20 g)* | 12.0 |
| sugar | |
|    brown—*1 cup not packed (145 g)* | 130.2 |
|    powdered—*1 cup (120 g)* | 111.6 |
|    white, granulated—*1 cup (200 g)* | 193.6 |
| syrup | |
|    corn, dark—*1 T (21 g)* | 7.8 |
|    corn, high fructose—*1 T (21 g)* | 15.6 |
|    corn, light—*1 T (21 g)* | 10.7 |
|    maple—*1 T (20 g)* | 12.7 |
|    maple honey, Log Cabin—*1 fl oz (39 g)* | 24.6 |
|    pancake & waffle, Log Cabin | |
|       *1 fl oz (39 g)* | 21.3 |
|       buttered—*1 fl oz (39 g)* | 22.7 |
|       country kitchen—*1 fl oz (39 g)* | 19.5 |
|       lite—*1 fl oz (36 g)* | 15.0 |

## VEGETABLES

| | |
|---|---|
| artichoke | |
|    boiled—*1 med (300 g)*[b] | 3.3 |
|    frzn, boiled—*2.8 oz (80 g)*[b] | 4.7 |
| asparagus | |
|    boiled—*½ cup (6 spears) (90 g)* | 1.4 |
|    frzn, boiled—*4 spears (60 g)* | 1.7 |
| avocado, raw—*1 med calif (173 g)* | 1.6 |
| beans, cnd, baked | |
|    bbq, Canpbell's—*7.9 oz (223 g)* | 10.7 |
|    bbq, Special Recipe—*6.9 oz (195 g)* | 9.4 |
|    garden style, Special Recipe—*6.9 oz (195 g)* | 8.4 |
|    homestyle, Campbell's—*8 oz (227 g)* | 16.0 |
|    new england style, Special Recipe—*6.9 oz (195 g)* | 8.8 |
|    old fashioned, Special Recipe—*6.9 oz (195 g)* | 5.5 |
|    ranchero, Campbell's—*7.7 oz (219 g)* | 5.5 |
|    w/ molasses & brown sugar, Campbell's—*8 oz (227 g)* | 18.1 |
|    w/ pork—*1 cup (253 g)* | 21.0 |
|    w/ pork & tomato sce, Campbell's—*8 oz (227 g)* | 11.5 |
|    w/ tomato sce—*1 cup (253 g)* | 14.4 |
| beans, common, ckd—*1 cup (253 g)* | 5.6 |
| beet, raw—*½ cup (68 g)* | 4.4 |
| broadbeans | |
|    immature, boiled—*1 cup (170 g)* | 0.9 |
|    mature, ckd—*1 cup (170 g)* | 3.1 |
| broccoli | |
|    raw—*½ cup chopped (44 g)* | 0.7 |
|    frzn, chopped, boiled—*½ cup (92 g)* | 1.8 |

## VEGETABLES

| | |
|---|---|
|    frzn, spears, boiled—*½ cup (92 g)* | 1.7 |
|    frzn, w/ cheese sce, Birds Eye—*½ cup (142 g)* | 4.4 |
|    frzn, w/ creamy italian sce, Birds Eye—*½ cup (128 g)* | 2.8 |
| brussel sprouts | |
|    boiled—*½ cup (78 g)* | 1.5 |
|    w/ cheese sce, Birds Eye—*½ cup (128 g)* | 4.1 |
| cabbage, chinese (pak-choi), raw—*½ cup shredded (35 g)* | 0.5 |
| cabbage, green, raw—*½ cup shredded (35 g)* | 1.3 |
| cabbage, red | |
|    raw—*½ cup shredded (35 g)* | 1.9 |
|    boiled—*½ cup shredded (75 g)* | 2.1 |
| cabbage, savoy, raw—*½ cup shredded (35 g)* | 1.0 |
| carrot | |
|    raw—*1 med (72 g)* | 4.8 |
|    boiled—*½ cup slices (78 g)* | 3.4 |
|    cnd—*½ cup slices (73 g)* | 2.4 |
|    frzn, boiled—*½ cup slices (73 g)* | 4.2 |
| cauliflower | |
|    raw—*½ cup pieces (50 g)* | 1.2 |
|    frzn | |
|       boiled—*½ cup pieces (90 g)* | 2.3 |
|       w/ cheese sce, Birds Eye—*½ cup (142 g)* | 5.1 |
| celery, raw—*1 stalk (7.5" long) (40 g)* | 0.4 |
| chickpeas (garbanzo beans), ckd—*1 cup (164 g)* | 7.9 |
| coleslaw, Fresh Chef—*4 oz (113 g)* | 11.4 |
| corn, yellow, sweet | |
|    boiled—*½ cup (82 g)* | 2.1 |
|    cnd—*½ cup (82 g)* | 2.3 |
|    frzn, boiled—*½ cup (82 g)* | 3.1 |
|    frzn, on-the-cob, Birds Eye—*1 ear (125 g)* | 4.9 |
| cucumber, raw—*½ cup slices (1/6 cucumber) (52 g)* | 1.2 |
| eggplant, raw—*½ cup pieces (41 g)* | 1.4 |
| endive, raw—*½ cup chopped (25 g)* | 0.3 |
| green beans (snap beans) | |
|    raw/frzn, boiled—*½ cup (62 g)* | 1.4 |
|    cnd—*½ cup (68 g)* | 1.1 |
|    frzn, Birds Eye | |
|       cut—*½ cup (85 g)* | 2.8 |
|       french style—*½ cup (85 g)* | 2.8 |
|       french style w/ toasted almonds—*½ cup (85 g)* | 4.2 |
|       italian—*½ cup (85 g)* | 3.6 |
|       whole—*4 oz (113 g)* | 3.2 |
| jerusalem artichoke, raw | |
|    freshly harvested—*½ cup slices (75 g)* | 1.9 |
|    stored—*½ cup slices (75 g)* | 7.2 |
| kale, raw—*3.5 oz (100 g)* | 2.2 |
| lentils, boiled—*1 cup (198 g)* | 3.6 |
| lettuce | |
|    cos/romaine, raw—*½ cup shredded (28 g)* | 0.6 |
|    iceberg, raw—*1 leaf (20 g)* | 0.5 |
| lima beans, boiled—*1 cup (188 g)* | 5.5 |
| lima beans, baby, frzn, boiled—*½ cup (90 g)* | 4.5 |
| lima beans, fordhook, frzn, boiled—*½ cup (85 g)* | 2.7 |
| mixed veg, frzn, Birds Eye—*½ cup (95 g)* | 4.2 |
|    w/ onion sce—*⅓ cup (76 g)* | 5.4 |
| mung beans, sprouted, raw—*½ cup (52 g)* | 1.1 |

[a] Specified as sucrose.

[b] Weight w/ refuse.

## VEGETABLES

| | |
|---|---|
| mushroom marinara salad, Fresh Chef—*3.2 oz (92 g)* | 1.2 |
| mushrooms | |
|     shitake, cnd, Campbell's—*4 oz (113 g)* | 1.8 |
|     sovereign, cnd, Campbell's—*4 oz (113 g)* | 0.1 |
| okra, raw—*1 cup (100 g)* | 2.4 |
| onion, raw | |
|     mature—*½ cup chopped (80 g)* | 5.0 |
|     spring—*½ cup chopped (80 g)* | 1.6 |
| onion, frzn, Birds Eye | |
|     small, whole—*½ cup (113 g)* | 6.0 |
|     small w/ cream sce—*½ cup (85 g)* | 6.7 |
| parsley, raw—*½ cup chopped (30 g)* | 0.3 |
| peas, green | |
|     boiled—*½ cup (80 g)* | 4.5 |
|     cnd—*½ cup (85 g)* | 3.0 |
|     frzn | |
|         boiled—*½ cup (80 g)* | 2.8 |
|         w/ cream sce, Birds Eye—*½ cup (76 g)* | 6.6 |
| peas, split, boiled—*1 cup (196 g)* | 1.6[a] |
| peppers, sweet, green, raw—*½ cup chopped (50 g)* | 1.3 |
| potato | |
|     baked—*1 med (202 g)* | 3.4 |
|     french fried—*10 pieces (50 g)* | 0.3 |
|     hashed brown—*½ cup (78 g)* | 0.2 |
| potato salad, Fresh Chef—*4 oz (113 g)* | 6.2 |
| radish, raw—*10 radishes (45 g)* | 1.2 |
| rice, brown, ckd—*1 cup (195 g)* | 0.6 |
| rice, white, enr, ckd—*1 cup (205 g)* | 0.2[a] |
|     parboiled—*1 cup (175 g)* | 0.4[a] |
| rice, white, from mix, Minute—*⅔ cup (124 g)* | 0.3 |
|     for rib roast—*½ cup (117 g)* | 1.7 |
|     fried—*½ cup (97 g)* | 1.4 |
|     w/ chicken flavor—*½ cup (107 g)* | 0.8 |
| rice, long grain & wild, from mix, Minute—*½ cup (115 g)* | 1.0 |
| rutabaga, raw—*1 cup (140 g)* | 7.8 |
| salad, Fresh Chef | |
|     chicken w/ pineapple tidbits—*4.66 oz (132 g)* | 3.9 |
|     ham & cheddar cheese—*4.65 oz (132 g)* | 5.0 |
| soybean product, tofu, raw, firm—*½ cup (126 g)* | 0.5 |
| soybeans, mature, boiled—*1 cup (172 g)* | 5.2 |
| spinach | |
|     raw—*½ cup chopped (28 g)* | 0.1 |
|     frzn, boiled—*½ cup (95 g)* | 1.1 |
|     frzn, creamed, Birds Eye—*⅓ cup (85 g)* | 2.4 |
| squash, summer, all varieties, raw—*½ cup slices (65 g)* | 1.4 |
| squash, winter, all varieties, raw—*¼ squash (122 g)* | 4.6 |
| sweet potato, raw—*1 sweet potato (180 g)* | 10.3 |
| tomato, red | |
|     raw—*1 tomato (123 g)* | 3.4 |
|     cnd—*½ cup (128 g)* | 3.2 |
| tomato paste, cnd—*½ cup (131 g)* | 16.9 |
| turnip, raw—*½ cup cubes (65 g)* | 4.9 |
| vegetable combinations, frzn, Birds Eye | |
|     broccoli & cauliflower w/ creamy italian cheese sce—*½ cup (128 g)* | 3.2 |

## VEGETABLES

| | |
|---|---|
| broccoli, carrots & pasta w/ lightly seasoned sce—*⅔ cup (95 g)* | 2.7 |
| broccoli, carrots & water chestnuts—*¾ cup (113 g)* | 4.5 |
| broccoli, cauliflower & carrots—*¾ cup (113 g)* | 3.4 |
| broccoli, cauliflower & carrots w/ cheese sce—*½ cup (142 g)* | 5.1 |
| broccoli, corn & red peppers—*⅔ cup (113 g)* | 3.0 |
| broccoli, green beans, pearl onions & red peppers—*¾ cup (113 g)* | 3.0 |
| broccoli, red peppers, bamboo shoots & straw mushrooms—*¾ cup (113 g)* | 1.6 |
| brussel sprouts, cauliflower & carrots—*¾ cup (113 g)* | 3.3 |
| carrots, peas & pearl onions—*½ cup (95 g)* | 5.1 |
| cauliflower, carrots & snow peas—*⅔ cup (113 g)* | 4.3 |
| chinese style—*½ cup (95 g)* | 2.8 |
| chinese style, stir-fry—*½ cup (95 g)* | 3.4 |
| chow mein style—*½ cup (95 g)* | 3.7 |
| corn, green beans & pasta curls w/ light cream sce—*½ cup (95 g)* | 3.3 |
| green beans, bavarian style & spaetzle (noodles)—*½ cup (95 g)* | 2.5 |
| italian style—*½ cup (95 g)* | 3.8 |
| japanese style—*½ cup (95 g)* | 3.7 |
| japanese style, stir-fry—*½ cup (95 g)* | 3.2 |
| mandarin style—*½ cup (95 g)* | 3.6 |
| new england style—*½ cup (95 g)* | 2.5 |
| pasta primavera style—*½ cup (95 g)* | 3.9 |
| peas & pearl onions—*½ cup (95 g)* | 5.6 |
| peas & pearl onions w/ cheese sce—*½ cup (142 g)* | 6.9 |
| peas & potatoes w/ cream sce—*½ cup (76 g)* | 6.6 |
| rice & peas w/ mushrooms—*⅔ cup (66 g)* | 1.7 |
| rice, french style—*½ cup (95 g)* | 1.5 |
| rice, italian style—*½ cup (95 g)* | 1.3 |
| rice, spanish style—*½ cup (95 g)* | 2.0 |
| san francisco style—*½ cup (95 g)* | 2.8 |
| yam, boiled/baked—*½ cup cubes (68 g)* | 0.3 |

## MISCELLANEOUS

| | |
|---|---|
| baking choc, unsweetened, Bakers—*1 oz (28 g)* | 4.0 |
| chewing gum—*1 stick (3.2 g)* | 2.2 |
| chewing gum, sugarless—*1 stick (2.7 g)* | 0.0 |
| fruit pectin | |
|     Certo—*1 T (14 g)* | 0.2 |
|     light, sweetened, Sure-Jell—*¼ pkt (12 g)* | 6.7 |
|     sweetened, Sure-Jell—*¼ pkt (12 g)* | 9.3 |
| oven fry, meat/poultry coatings | |
|     extra crispy recipe for chicken—*¼ pouch (29 g)* | 2.5 |
|     extra crispy recipe for pork—*¼ pouch (29 g)* | 1.3 |
|     light crispy homestyle recipe—*¼ pouch (22 g)* | 0.5 |
| shake & bake, meat/poultry coatings | |
|     barbeque for chicken—*¼ pouch (25 g)* | 9.9 |
|     barbeque for pork—*¼ pouch (20 g)* | 7.5 |
|     country mild recipe—*¼ pouch (17 g)* | 0.3 |
|     for chicken—*¼ pouch (19 g)* | 0.9 |
|     for fish—*¼ pouch (19 g)* | 1.4 |
|     for pork—*¼ pouch (21 g)* | 1.5 |
|     italian herb recipe—*¼ pouch (20 g)* | 0.8 |

[a] Specified as sucrose.

# Theobromine (mg)

**BEVERAGES**
tea, hot/iced
    brewed 3 min—*6 fl oz (178 g)*     3.6
    inst powder—*1 t (0.7 g)*     2.1
    prep from inst powder—*1 t powder in 8 fl oz water (237 g)*     2.4

**CANDY**
milk choc, Cadbury—*1 oz (28 g)*     44.0

**MILK BEVERAGES**
choc flavor mix in whole milk—*2-3 hp t powder in 8 fl oz milk (266 g)*     120.0
choc malted milk flavor mix in whole milk—*3 hp t powder in 8 fl oz milk (265 g)*     106.0
choc malted milk flavor mix w/ added nutrients in whole milk—*4-5 hp t powder in 8 fl oz milk (265 g)*     217.0

**MILK BEVERAGES**
choc syrup in whole milk—*2 T syrup in 8 fl oz milk (282 g)*     90.0
cocoa/hot chocolate, prep w/ water from mix—*¾ hp t powder in 6 fl oz water (206 g)*     68.0

**MILK BEVERAGE MIXES**
choc flavor mix, powder—*2-3 hp t (22 g)*     123.0
choc malted milk flavor mix, powder—*¾ oz (3 hp t) (21 g)*     106.0
choc malted milk flavor mix w/ added nutrients, powder—*¾ oz (4-5 hp t) (21 g)*     217.0
choc syrup—*2 T (1 fl oz) (38 g)*     89.0
cocoa mix, powder—*1 oz pkt (3-4 hp t) (28 g)*     67.0

**SPECIAL DIETARY FORMULAS, COMMERCIAL & HOSPITAL**
ensure HN, choc, Ross Labs—*8 fl oz (253 g)*     45.5
ensure plus, choc, Ross Labs—*8 fl oz (259 g)*     62.1
ensure, choc, Ross Labs—*8 fl oz (253 g)*     45.5

# Vitamin D (IU)

**CEREALS, READY-TO-EAT**
bran flakes, Post—*⅔ cup (1 oz) (28 g)*     49
cocoa pebbles, Post—*⅞ cup (1 oz) (28 g)*     49
corn flakes
    Post Toasties, Post—*1 cup (1 oz) (28 g)*     49
    Ralston Purina—*1 cup (1 oz) (28 g)*     40
crispy oatmeal & raisin chex, Ralston Purina—*¾ cup (1.3 oz) (38 g)*     5
fortified oat flakes, Post—*⅔ cup (1 oz) (28 g)*     49
fruit & fiber, Post
    harvest medley—*½ cup (1 oz) (28 g)*     49
    mountain trail—*½ cup (1 oz) (28 g)*     49
    tropical fruit—*½ cup (1 oz) (28 g)*     49
    w/ dates, raisins & walnuts—*½ cup (1 oz) (28 g)*     49
fruity pebbles, Post—*⅞ cup (1 oz) (28 g)*     49
granola, hearty, Post—*¼ cup (1 oz) (28 g)*     49
granola, hearty w/ raisins, Post—*¼ cup (1 oz) (28 g)*     49
grape-nut flakes, Post—*⅞ cup (1 oz) (28 g)*     49
grape-nuts, Post—*¼ cup (1 oz) (28 g)*     49
grape-nuts w/ raisins, Post—*¼ cup (1 oz) (28 g)*     49
honeycomb, Post—*1⅓ cups (1 oz) (28 g)*     49
raisin bran, Post—*½ cup (1 oz) (28 g)*     49
sugar sparkled flakes, Post—*¾ cup (1 oz) (28 g)*     49
sun flakes, Ralston Purina
    corn & rice—*1 cup (1 oz) (28 g)*     40
    wheat & rice—*1 cup (1 oz) (28 g)*     40
super golden crisp, Post—*⅞ cup (1 oz) (28 g)*     49

**CHEESE**
cheddar, med, Kraft—*1 oz (28 g)*     3
cream cheese, Philadelphia Brand—*1 oz (28 g)*     2
cream cheese w/ herb & garlic, Cremerie—*1 oz (28 g)*     3
havarti, Casino—*1 oz (28 g)*     3

**CHEESE PRODUCTS**
cheese food, american, grated, Kraft—*1 oz (28 g)*     8
cheese products, Light n' Lively
    sharp cheddar—*1 oz (28 g)*     1
    singles—*1 oz (28 g)*     2
    swiss—*1 oz (28 g)*     1
cheese spread
    Cheez Whiz, Kraft—*1 oz (28 g)*     1
    Velveeta sharp—*1 oz (28 g)*     3

**CREAMS & CREAM SUBSTITUTES**
whipped topping, from mix, Dream Whip—*1 T (5 g)*     2

**DESSERTS**
**Cakes**
cheesecake, from mix, Jell-O—*⅛ cheesecake (99 g)*     28
**Frozen Desserts**
bon bon ice cream nuggets, Carnation
    bavarian mint—*5 nuggets (48 g)*     8
    choc—*5 nuggets (49 g)*     6
    choc peanut butter—*5 nuggets (49 g)*     6
    van—*5 nuggets (48 g)*     8

[a] Prepared w/ vitamin D fortified milk.

**DESSERTS**

**Pies**

| | |
|---|---|
| banana cream, from mix, Jell-O—⅛ pie (92 g) | 29[a] |
| choc mousse, from mix, Jell-O—⅛ pie (95 g) | 30[a] |
| coconut cream, from mix, Jell-O—⅛ pie (94 g) | 30[a] |

**Puddings, from inst mix**

| | |
|---|---|
| banana cream | |
| Jell-O—½ cup (147 g) | 50[a] |
| sugar-free, Jell-O—½ cup (130 g) | 50[a] |
| butter pecan, Jell-O—½ cup (147 g) | 50[a] |
| butterscotch | |
| Jell-O—½ cup (147 g) | 50[a] |
| sugar-free, D-Zerta—½ cup (130 g) | 50[a] |
| sugar-free, Jell-O—½ cup (131 g) | 50[a] |
| choc | |
| Jell-O—½ cup (150 g) | 50[a] |
| sugar-free, D-Zerta—½ cup (130 g) | 50[a] |
| sugar-free, Featherweight—½ cup (134 g) | 50[a] |
| sugar-free, Jell-O—½ cup (133 g) | 50[a] |
| choc fudge | |
| Jell-O—½ cup (150 g) | 50[a] |
| sugar-free, Jell-O—½ cup (135 g) | 50[a] |
| choc fudge mousse, Jell-O—½ cup (86 g) | 25[a] |
| choc mousse, Jell-O—½ cup (86 g) | 25[a] |
| choc tapioca, Jell-O—½ cup (147 g) | 50[a] |
| coconut cream, Jell-O—½ cup (147 g) | 50[a] |
| french van, Jell-O—½ cup (147 g) | 50[a] |
| golden egg custard, Jell-O—½ cup (143 g) | 55[a] |
| lemon, Jell-O—½ cup (147 g) | 50[a] |
| milk choc, Jell-O—½ cup (150 g) | 50[a] |
| pineapple cream, Jell-O—½ cup (147 g) | 50[a] |
| pistachio | |
| Jell-O—½ cup (147 g) | 50[a] |
| sugar-free, Jell-O—½ cup (131 g) | 50[a] |
| rice, Jell-O—½ cup (149 g) | 50[a] |
| vanilla | |
| Jell-O—½ cup (147 g) | 50[a] |
| sugar-free, D-Zerta—½ cup (130 g) | 50[a] |
| sugar-free, Featherweight—½ cup (134 g) | 50[a] |
| sugar-free, Jell-O—½ cup (131 g) | 50[a] |
| vanilla tapioca, Jell-O—½ cup (145 g) | 50[a] |

**EGGS, CHICKEN**

| | |
|---|---|
| whole, fresh/frzn—1 large (50 g) | 27 |
| yolk, fresh—yolk of 1 large egg (17 g) | 27 |

**ENTREES, BOX MIX**

| | |
|---|---|
| chili con carne, concentrate, Oscar Mayer—1 oz (28 g) | 9 |

**GRAIN PRODUCTS**

**Stuffing, from mix, Stove Top**

| | |
|---|---|
| americana san francisco style—½ cup (107 g) | 9 |
| chicken flavored—½ cup (107 g) | 9 |
| chicken flavored w/ rice—½ cup (109 g) | 9 |
| chicken florentine—½ cup (102 g) | 13 |
| cornbread—½ cup (107 g) | 9 |
| for beef—½ cup (108 g) | 9 |
| for pork—½ cup (107 g) | 9 |
| garden herb—½ cup (95 g) | 13 |

**GRAIN PRODUCTS**

| | |
|---|---|
| homestyle herb—½ cup (96 g) | 7 |
| long grain & wild rice flavor—½ cup (109 g) | 9 |
| savory herbs flavor—½ cup (107 g) | 9 |
| turkey flavor—½ cup (107 g) | 9 |
| veg & almond—½ cup (95 g) | 13 |
| wild rice & mushroom—½ cup (95 g) | 13 |

**MEATS**

| | |
|---|---|
| pork, bacon pieces, bacon bits, Oscar Mayer—¼ cup (7 g) | 4 |

**MEATS, LUNCHEON, OSCAR MAYER**

| | |
|---|---|
| bbq loaf (pork & beef)—1 oz slice (28 g) | 10 |
| bologna—1 slice (23 g) | 9 |
| bologna, beef—1 slice (23 g) | 7 |
| bologna, beef garlic—1 slice (23 g) | 8 |
| bologna, w/ cheese—1 slice (23 g) | 10 |
| braunschweiger (pork liver sausage) | |
| german brand—1 oz (28 g) | 12 |
| in tube—1 oz (28 g) | 9 |
| corned beef loaf, jellied—1 oz slice (28 g) | 5 |
| frankfurter—1 frank (45 g) | 16 |
| beef—1 frank (10 per 1 lb pkg) (45 g) | 11 |
| beef & pork, small, Oscar Mayer—1 frank (9 g) | 5 |
| ham & cheese loaf/roll—1 slice (28 g) | 12 |
| headcheese (pork)—1 slice (28 g) | 13 |
| honey loaf (pork & beef)—1 slice (28 g) | 10 |
| lebanon bologna (beef)—1 slice (23 g) | 11 |
| livercheese, pork fat wrapped, Oscar Mayer—1 slice (38 g) | 19 |
| luxury loaf (pork)—1 slice (28 g) | 8 |
| meat spread—1 oz (28 g) | 10 |
| ham & cheese—1 oz (28 g) | 7 |
| ham salad—1 oz (28 g) | 8 |
| old fashioned loaf (pork & beef)—1 slice (28 g) | 11 |
| olive loaf (pork)—1 slice (28 g) | 11 |
| peppered loaf (pork & beef)—1 slice (28 g) | 9 |
| pickle & pimento loaf (pork)—1 slice (28 g) | 9 |
| picnic loaf (pork & beef)—1 slice (28 g) | 12 |
| salami, hard—1 slice (9 g) | 6 |
| thuringer (cervelat/summer sausage) | |
| beef—1 slice (23 g) | 9 |
| beef & pork—1 slice (23 g) | 11 |

**MILK**

| | |
|---|---|
| evaporated, cnd, Carnation—4 fl oz (126 g) | 100 |
| evaporated, lowfat, cnd, Carnation—4 fl oz (127 g) | 100 |
| evaporated, skim, cnd, Carnation—4 fl oz (128 g) | 100 |

**MILK BEVERAGES**

| | |
|---|---|
| Alba choc flavor nonfat dry milk in water—8 fl oz | 70 |
| choc malted milk flavor mix w/ added nutrients in whole milk—4-5 hp t powder in 8 fl oz milk (265 g) | 278[a] |
| eggnog, nonalcoholic mix in whole milk, Delmark—1.23 oz mix in 8 fl oz milk (257 g) | 140 |
| instant breakfast in whole milk—1 pkt in 8 fl oz milk (265 g) | 100 |
| choc, Delmark—1.23 oz mix in 8 fl oz milk (279 g) | 132 |
| van/strawberry, Delmark—1.23 oz mix in 8 fl oz milk (279 g) | 100 |

[a] Prepared w/ vitamin D fortified milk.

**MILK BEVERAGES**

| | |
|---|---|
| instant breakfast, van/strawberry, liquid pack, Delmark— *8 fl oz (279 g)* | 100 |
| malted milk flavor mix w/ added nutrients in whole milk—*4-5 hp t in 8 fl oz milk (265 g)* | 278[a] |
| milk shake mix in whole milk, Delmark | |
|     choc—*.667 oz mix in 8 fl oz milk (263 g)* | 100 |
|     strawberry—*.667 oz mix in 8 fl oz milk (263 g)* | 100 |
|     van—*.667 oz mix in 8 fl oz milk (263 g)* | 100 |

**MILK BEVERAGE MIXES**

| | |
|---|---|
| cocoa mix, powder, Alba—*19.14 g pkt (19 g)* | 56 |
| dairy light, Alba—*2.8 g pkt (2.8 g)* | 16 |
| fit 'n frosty, Alba | |
|     choc—*21.26 g pkt (21 g)* | 56 |
|     choc marshmallow—*21.26 g pkt (21 g)* | 56 |
|     double fudge—*21.26 g pkt (21 g)* | 56 |
|     strawberry—*21.26 g pkt (21 g)* | 49 |
|     van—*21.26 g pkt (21 g)* | 41 |
| malted milk flavor mix w/ added nutrients, powder—*¾ oz (4-5 hp t) (21 g)* | 178 |

**SALAD DRESSINGS**

| | |
|---|---|
| buttermilk farm style, from mix, Good Seasons—*1 T (16 g)* | 3 |

**SAUCES**

| | |
|---|---|
| horseradish sce, Sauceworks—*1 T (14 g)* | 1 |

**SPECIAL DIETARY FOODS**

| | |
|---|---|
| figurine diet bar, Pillsbury | |
|     choc—*1 bar (21 g)* | 10 |
|     choc caramel—*1 bar (21 g)* | 10 |
|     choc peanut butter—*1 bar (21 g)* | 10 |
|     s'mores—*1 bar (21 g)* | 10 |
|     van—*1 bar (21 g)* | 10 |
| fortified pudding, from mix, Delmark | |
|     choc—*½ cup (164 g)* | 72 |
|     van/lemon—*½ cup (164 g)* | 72 |
| gluten-free, wheat-free foods, Ener-G Foods | |
|     nutquik milk powder—*1 oz (28 g)* | 3 |
| slender bars, Carnation | |
|     choc—*2 bars (55 g)* | 100 |
|     choc chip—*2 bars (55 g)* | 100 |

**SPECIAL DIETARY FOODS**

| | |
|---|---|
|     choc peanut butter—*2 bars (55 g)* | 100 |
|     van—*2 bars (55 g)* | 100 |
| slender, liquid diet meal, cnd, Carnation | |
|     banana—*10 fl oz (313 g)* | 100 |
|     choc—*10 fl oz (313 g)* | 100 |
|     choc fudge—*10 fl oz (313 g)* | 100 |
|     choc malt—*10 fl oz (313 g)* | 100 |
|     milk choc—*10 fl oz (313 g)* | 100 |
|     strawberry—*10 fl oz (313 g)* | 100 |
|     van—*10 fl oz (313 g)* | 100 |

**SPREADS**

| | |
|---|---|
| margarine | |
|     Mazola—*1 T (14 g)* | 60 |
|     Mazola unsalted—*1 T (14 g)* | 60 |
|     Nucoa—*1 T (14 g)* | 60 |
|     Nucoa soft—*1 T (13 g)* | 60 |
| margarine, imitation (diet), Mazola diet—*1 T (14 g)* | 60 |
| miracle whip, light, Kraft—*1 T (14 g)* | 1 |

**VEGETABLES**

| | |
|---|---|
| broccoli, frzn | |
|     w/ cheese sce, Birds Eye—*½ cup (142 g)* | 2 |
|     w/ creamy italian cheese sce, Birds Eye—*½ cup (128 g)* | 1 |
| brussel sprouts, frzn, w/ cheese sce, Birds Eye—*½ cup (128 g)* | 1 |
| cauliflower, frzn, w/ cheese sce, Birds Eye—*½ cup (142 g)* | 2 |
| rice, white, from mix, Minute—*⅔ cup (124 g)* | 2 |
|     for rib roast—*½ cup (117 g)* | 4 |
|     w/ chicken flavor—*½ cup (107 g)* | 4 |
| rice, long grain & wild, from mix, Minute—*½ cup (115 g)* | 4 |
| vegetable combinations, frzn, Birds Eye | |
|     broccoli & cauliflower, w/ creamy italian cheese sce— *½ cup (128 g)* | 1 |
|     broccoli, cauliflower & carrots, w/ cheese sce—*½ cup (142 g)* | 1 |
|     green beans, bavarian style & spaetzle (noodles)— *½ cup (95 g)* | 2 |
|     pasta primavera style—*½ cup (95 g)* | 1 |
|     peas & pearl onions, w/ cheese sce—*½ cup (142 g)* | 1 |

**MISCELLANEOUS**

| | |
|---|---|
| shake & bake, for chicken—*¼ pouch (19 g)* | 6 |

[a] Prepared w/ vitamin D fortified milk.

# Vitamin E (IU)

**BEVERAGES**

coffee, prep from inst powder

| | |
|---|---|
| francais, sugar-free, General Foods—*6 fl oz water & 7.7 g powder (185 g)* | .06 |
| irish creme, sugar-free, General Foods—*6 fl oz water & 7.1 g powder (185 g)* | .06 |
| irish mocha mint, sugar-free, General Foods—*6 fl oz water & 6.4 g powder (184 g)* | .07 |
| orange cappuccino, sugar-free, General Foods—*6 fl oz water & 6.7 g powder (184 g)* | .06 |
| suisse mocha, sugar-free, General Foods—*6 fl oz water & 6.4 g powder (184 g)* | .06 |
| vienna, sugar-free, General Foods—*6 fl oz water & 6.7 g powder (184 g)* | .06 |

**CANDY**

| | |
|---|---|
| chocolate, semi-sweet, Bakers—*1 oz square (28 g)* | .09 |
| choc chips | |
|     Bakers—*¼ cup (43 g)* | .13 |
|     german sweet, Bakers—*¼ cup (43 g)* | .19 |
|     semi-sweet, Bakers—*¼ cup (43 g)* | .19 |
| choc fudgies, Kraft—*1 piece (8 g)* | .10 |

**CEREALS, READY-TO-EAT**

| | |
|---|---|
| king vitamin, Quaker—*1¼ cups (1 oz) (28 g)* | 9.00 |
| Quaker 100% natural—*¼ cup (1 oz) (28 g)* | 1.00 |
|     w/ raisins & dates—*¼ cup (1 oz) (28 g)* | 1.00 |

**CHEESE**

| | |
|---|---|
| cheddar, med, Kraft—*1 oz (28 g)* | .10 |
| cream cheese, Philadelphia Brand—*1 oz (28 g)* | .10 |
| cream cheese w/ herb & garlic, Cremerie—*1 oz (28 g)* | .10 |

**CHEESE PRODUCTS**

| | |
|---|---|
| cheese food, american, grated, Kraft—*1 oz (28 g)* | .20 |
| cheese products | |
|     Light n' Lively, singles—*1 oz (28 g)* | .10 |
|     Light n' Lively, swiss—*1 oz (28 g)* | .10 |

**CREAMS & CREAM SUBSTITUTES**

whipped topping

| | |
|---|---|
|     from mix, Dream Whip—*1 T (5 g)* | .07 |
|     from mix, w/ nutrasweet, D-Zerta—*1 T (from 1.112 g dry mix) (5 g)* | .07 |

**DESSERTS**

**Cakes**

| | |
|---|---|
| cheesecake, from mix, Jell-O—*⅛ cheesecake (99 g)* | .39 |
| coffee cake, mix, Aunt Jemima—*1.3 oz dry mix (37 g)* | .20 |

**Frozen Desserts**

bon bon ice cream nuggets, Carnation

| | |
|---|---|
|     bavarian mint—*5 nuggets (48 g)* | .02 |
|     choc—*5 nuggets (49 g)* | .01 |
|     choc peanut butter—*5 nuggets (49 g)* | .01 |
|     van—*5 nuggets (48 g)* | .02 |
| fruit juice bar, all flavors, Jell-O—*1 bar (52 g)* | .02 |
| pudding pops, Jell-O | |
|     choc w/ choc coating—*1 pop (49 g)* | .20 |
|     van w/ choc coating—*1 pop (49 g)* | .18 |

**DESSERTS**

**Granola Desserts**

| | |
|---|---|
| choc chip, chewy, Quaker—*1 oz bar (28 g)* | 1.00 |
| choc, graham & marshmallow, chewy, Quaker—*1 oz bar (28 g)* | 1.00 |
| chunky nut & raisin, chewy, Quaker—*1 oz bar (28 g)* | 1.00 |
| honey & oats, chewy, Quaker—*1 oz bar (28 g)* | 1.00 |
| mint choc chip dipps, Quaker—*1 oz bar (28 g)* | 1.00 |
| peanut butter & choc chip, chewy, Quaker—*1 oz bar (28 g)* | 1.00 |
| peanut butter, chewy, Quaker—*1 oz bar (28 g)* | 1.00 |
| peanut butter dipps, Quaker—*1 oz bar (28 g)* | 1.00 |
| raisin & almond dipps, Quaker—*1 oz bar (28 g)* | 1.00 |
| raisin & cinn, chewy, Quaker—*1 oz bar (28 g)* | 2.00 |

**Pies, from mix, Jell-O**

| | |
|---|---|
| banana cream—*⅛ pie (92 g)* | 1.07 |
| choc mousse—*⅛ pie (95 g)* | .77 |
| coconut cream—*⅛ pie (94 g)* | .70 |

**Pie Crust**

| | |
|---|---|
| mix, Flako—*1.7 oz dry mix (48 g)* | .20 |

**Puddings, from inst mix**

banana cream

| | |
|---|---|
|     Jell-O—*½ cup (147 g)* | .22 |
|     sugar-free, Jell-O—*½ cup (130 g)* | .01 |
| butter pecan, Jell-O—*½ cup (147 g)* | .29 |
| butterscotch, Jell-O—*½ cup (147 g)* | .22 |
| choc | |
|     Jell-O—*½ cup (150 g)* | .21 |
|     sugar-free, D-Zerta—*½ cup (130 g)* | .03 |
| choc fudge | |
|     Jell-O—*½ cup (150 g)* | .23 |
|     sugar-free, Jell-O—*½ cup (135 g)* | .11 |
| choc fudge mousse, Jell-O—*½ cup (86 g)* | .52 |
| choc mousse, Jell-O—*½ cup (86 g)* | .50 |
| choc tapioca, Jell-O—*½ cup (147 g)* | .19 |
| coconut cream, Jell-O—*½ cup (147 g)* | .12 |
| french van, Jell-O—*½ cup (147 g)* | .22 |
| golden egg custard, Jell-O—*½ cup (143 g)* | .13 |
| lemon, Jell-O—*½ cup (147 g)* | .13 |
| milk choc, Jell-O—*½ cup (150 g)* | .23 |
| pineapple cream, Jell-O—*½ cup (147 g)* | .22 |
| pistachio | |
|     Jell-O—*½ cup (147 g)* | .29 |
|     sugar-free, Jell-O—*½ cup (131 g)* | .08 |
| vanilla, Jell-O—*½ cup (147 g)* | .21 |

**Sauces, Syrups & Toppings for Desserts**

| | |
|---|---|
| fudge topping, Kraft—*1 T (20 g)* | .20 |

**ENTREES**

**Canned Entrees**

| | |
|---|---|
| beef & veg stew, Wolf Brand—*scant cup (213 g)* | 2.00 |
| chili-mac, Wolf Brand—*scant cup (213 g)* | 2.00 |
| chili w/ beans | |
|     Wolf Brand—*1 cup (227 g)* | 2.00 |
|     Wolf Brand, extra spicy—*scant cup (213 g)* | 2.00 |

**ENTREES**
chili w/o beans
  Wolf Brand—*1 cup (227 g)* .......................... 2.00
  Wolf Brand, extra spicy—*scant cup (213 g)* ......... 2.00
tamales, Wolf Brand—*scant cup (213 g)* .............. 2.00
**Frozen Entrees**
pizza, canadian style bacon
  Celeste—*7.75 oz pizza (220 g)* ..................... 4.00
  Celeste—*¼ of 19 oz pizza (135 g)* .................. 3.00
pizza, cheese
  Celeste—*6.5 oz pizza (184 g)* ...................... 2.00
  Celeste—*¼ of 18 oz pizza (126 g)* .................. 1.00
pizza, deluxe
  Celeste—*8.25 oz pizza (234 g)* ..................... 2.00
  Celeste—*¼ of 22 oz pizza (158 g)* .................. 3.00
pizza, pepperoni
  Celeste—*6.75 oz pizza (191 g)* ..................... 4.00
  Celeste—*¼ of 19 oz pizza (135 g)* .................. 3.00
pizza, sausage
  Celeste—*7.5 oz pizza (213 g)* ...................... 4.00
  Celeste—*¼ of 20 oz pizza (142 g)* .................. 3.00
pizza, sausage & mushroom
  Celeste—*8.5 oz pizza (241 g)* ...................... 5.00
  Celeste—*¼ of 25 oz pizza (177 g)* .................. 3.00
pizza, suprema
  Celeste—*9 oz pizza (255 g)* ........................ 3.00
  Celeste—*¼ of 23 oz pizza (163 g)* .................. 3.00

**GRAIN FRACTIONS**
corn germ, Ener-G Foods—*1 cup (100 g)* .............. 6.00
corn meal mix
  white, bolted, Aunt Jemima—*1/6 cup (1 oz) (28 g)* .. 1.00
corn meal, white bolted, enr, self-rising, Aunt Jemima—
  *1/6 cup (1 oz) (28 g)* ............................. 1.00
corn meal, white, degermed, enr, Quaker/Aunt Jemima—
  *3 T (1 oz) (28 g)* ................................. 1.00
corn meal, yellow, degermed, enr, Quaker/Aunt
  Jemima—*3 T (1 oz) (28 g)* .......................... 1.00
wheat germ
  toasted—*¼ cup (1 oz) (28 g)* ....................... 6.00
  toasted w/ brown sugar & honey—*¼ cup (1 oz) (28 g)* . 4.30

**GRAIN PRODUCTS**
**Breads & Bread Products**
corn bread, mix, Aunt Jemima—*1.7 oz dry mix (48 g)* .. .60
**French Toast. frzn**
cinn swirl, Aunt Jemima—*2 slices (85 g)* ............ 3.00
raisin, Aunt Jemima—*2 slices (85 g)* ................ 4.00
**Muffins**
corn, muffin mix, Flako—*1 oz dry mix (28 g)* ........ .20
**Pancakes**
from frzn batter. Aunt Jemima
  buttermilk—*three 4″ pancakes (113 g)* .............. 2.00
  plain—*three 4″ pancakes (113 g)* ................... 1.00
frzn, Aunt Jemima
  blueberry—*three 4″ pancakes (106 g)* ............... 1.00
  buttermilk—*three 4″ pancakes (106 g)* .............. 1.00
  plain—*three 4″ pancakes (106 g)* ................... 1.00
pancake/waffle mix, Aunt Jemima
  buckwheat—*¼ cup dry mix (31 g)* .................... .10
  buttermilk—*⅓ cup dry mix (51 g)* ................... .20

**GRAIN PRODUCTS**
  buttermilk, complete—*½ cup dry mix (71 g)* ......... .50
  plain—*¼ cup dry mix (31 g)* ........................ .20
  plain, complete—*½ cup dry mix (74 g)* .............. .50
  whole wheat—*⅓ cup dry mix (43 g)* .................. 3.00
**Rolls**
popover mix, Flako—*1 oz dry mix (28 g)* ............. .10
**Stuffing**
from mix, Stove Top
  americana san francisco style—*½ cup (107 g)* ....... .59
  chicken flavored—*½ cup (107 g)* .................... .73
  chicken flavored w/ rice—*½ cup (109 g)* ............ .71
  chicken florentine—*½ cup (102 g)* .................. 1.10
  for beef—*½ cup (108 g)* ............................ .73
  for pork—*½ cup (107 g)* ............................ .73
  garden herb—*½ cup (95 g)* .......................... .78
  homestyle herb—*½ cup (96 g)* ....................... 2.11
  long grain & wild rice flavor—*½ cup (109 g)* ....... .71
  savory herbs flavor—*½ cup (107 g)* ................. .73
  turkey flavor—*½ cup (107 g)* ....................... .72
  veg & almond—*½ cup (95 g)* ......................... 1.22
  wild rice & mushroom—*½ cup (95 g)* ................. .82

**MEATS, LUNCHEON**
meat spread, Carnation
  chicken—*1.9 oz (53 g)* ............................. .72
  ham—*1.9 oz (53 g)* ................................. .43
  tuna—*1.9 oz (53 g)* ................................ .70
  turkey—*1.9 oz (53 g)* .............................. .71

**MILK BEVERAGES**
eggnog, nonalcoholic
  mix in whole milk, Delmark—*1.23 oz mix in 8 fl oz
    milk (257 g)* ..................................... .10
instant breakfast in whole milk—*1 pkt in 8 fl oz milk
  (265 g)* ............................................ 7.80
  choc, Delmark—*1.23 oz mix in 8 fl oz milk (279 g)* . 9.90
  van/strawberry, Delmark—*1.23 oz mix in 8 fl oz milk
    (279 g)* .......................................... 9.90
instant breakfast, van/strawberry, liquid pack, Delmark—
  *8 fl oz (279 g)* ................................... 7.50
milk shake
  mix in whole milk, Delmark
    choc—*.667 oz mix in 8 fl oz milk (263 g)* ........ .10
    strawberry—*.667 oz mix in 8 fl oz milk (263 g)* .. .10
    van—*.667 oz mix in 8 fl oz milk (263 g)* ......... .10

**MILK BEVERAGE MIXES**
instant breakfast, Carnation
  choc—*1.25 oz pkt (35 g)* ........................... 7.50
  choc malt—*1.24 oz pkt (35 g)* ...................... 7.50
  coffee—*1.26 oz pkt (36 g)* ......................... 7.50
  eggnog—*1.20 oz pkt (34 g)* ......................... 7.50
  strawberry—*1.25 oz pkt (35 g)* ..................... 7.50
  van—*1.23 oz pkt (35 g)* ............................ 7.50
instant breakfast, no sugar added, Carnation
  choc—*.69 oz pkt (20 g)* ............................ 7.50
  choc malted—*.71 oz pkt (20 g)* ..................... 7.50
  strawberry—*.68 oz pkt (19 g)* ...................... 7.50
  van—*.67 oz pkt (19 g)* ............................. 7.50

## NUTS
almonds

    blanched, Blue Diamond—*1 oz (28 g)*    8.75

    blanched, slivered, Blue Diamond—*1 oz (28 g)*    8.50

    chopped, Blue Diamond—*1 oz (28 g)*    8.50

    sliced, Blue Diamond—*1 oz (28 g)*    8.50

    whole, Blue Diamond—*1 oz (28 g)*    10.10

filberts (hazelnuts), roasted, salted, Blue Diamond—*1 oz (28 g)*    4.40

macadamia nuts, dry roasted, Blue Diamond—*1 oz (28 g)*    .30

pistachio nuts, dry roasted, Blue Diamond—*1 oz (28 g)*    .60

## SALAD DRESSINGS
french, Catalina, Kraft—*1 T (15 g)*    1.00

from mix, Good Seasons

    bleu cheese & herbs—*1 T (16 g)*    .74

    buttermilk farm style—*1 T (16 g)*    4.09

    cheese garlic—*1 T (16 g)*    2.23

    cheese italian—*1 T (16 g)*    7.49

    classic herb—*1 T (16 g)*    2.29

    garlic & herbs—*1 T (16 g)*    2.22

    italian—*1 T (16 g)*    2.26

    italian, lite—*1 T (15 g)*    2.09

    italian, lite, zesty—*1 T (15 g)*    .63

    italian, mild—*1 T (17 g)*    2.30

    italian, zesty—*1 T (16 g)*    2.26

    lemon & herbs—*1 T (16 g)*    2.26

## SAUCES
barbeque sce, Open Pit—*1 T (18 g)*    .12

    hickory smoke flavor—*1 T (18 g)*    .12

    hickory thick & tangy—*1 T (18 g)*    .12

    hot 'n tangy flavor—*1 T (18 g)*    .12

    mesquite 'n tangy—*1 T (18 g)*    .12

    sweet 'n tangy flavor—*1 T (18 g)*    .10

    w/ onions—*1 T (18 g)*    .12

chili hot dog sce, Wolf Brand—*1/6 cup (35 g)*    1.00

## SPECIAL DIETARY FOODS
breakfast bar, Carnation

    choc chip—*1.44 oz bar (41 g)*    7.50

    choc crunch—*1.34 oz bar (38 g)*    7.50

    peanut butter crunch—*1.35 oz bar (38 g)*    7.50

    peanut butter w/ choc chips—*1.39 oz bar (39 g)*    7.50

figurine diet bar, Pillsbury

    choc—*1 bar (21 g)*    4.18

    choc caramel—*1 bar (21 g)*    4.18

    choc peanut butter—*1 bar (21 g)*    4.18

    s'mores—*1 bar (21 g)*    4.20

    van—*1 bar (21 g)*    4.20

fortified pudding, from mix, Delmark

    choc—*½ cup (164 g)*    5.40

    van/lemon—*½ cup (164 g)*    5.40

gluten-free, wheat-free foods, Ener-G Foods

    nutquik milk powder—*1 oz (28 g)*    4.28

slender bars, Carnation

    choc—*2 bars (55 g)*    7.50

    choc chip—*2 bars (55 g)*    7.50

    choc peanut butter—*2 bars (55 g)*    7.50

    van—*2 bars (55 g)*    7.50

slender, liquid diet meal, cnd, Carnation

    banana—*10 fl oz (313 g)*    7.50

    choc—*10 fl oz (313 g)*    7.50

## SPECIAL DIETARY FOODS
    choc fudge—*10 fl oz (313 g)*    7.50

    choc malt—*10 fl oz (313 g)*    7.50

    milk choc—*10 fl oz (313 g)*    7.50

    strawberry—*10 fl oz (313 g)*    7.50

    van—*10 fl oz (313 g)*    7.50

## VEGETABLES
artichoke, frzn, boiled—*2.8 oz (80 g)*    .22

broccoli, frzn

    chopped, boiled—*½ cup (92 g)*    .65

    spears, boiled—*½ cup (92 g)*    .65

    w/ cheese sce, Birds Eye—*½ cup (142 g)*    1.86

    w/ creamy italian cheese sce, Birds Eye—*½ cup (128 g)*    .97

brussel sprouts, frzn

    boiled—*½ cup (78 g)*    1.02

    w/ cheese sce, Birds Eye—*½ cup (128 g)*    1.16

carrots, frzn, boiled—*½ cup slices (73 g)*    .50

cauliflower, frzn

    boiled—*½ cup pieces (90 g)*    .05

    w/ cheese sce, Birds Eye—*½ cup (142 g)*    1.36

corn, yellow, frzn, boiled—*½ cup (82 g)*    .11

green beans (snap beans), frzn

    boiled—*½ cup (68 g)*    .17

    cut, Birds Eye—*½ cup (85 g)*    .21

    french style, Birds Eye—*½ cup (85 g)*    .21

    french style w/ toasted almonds, Birds Eye—*½ cup (85 g)*    .71

    whole, Birds Eye—*4 oz (113 g)*    .28

mixed veg, frzn, Birds Eye—*½ cup (95 g)*    .35

onions, frzn, small, whole, Birds Eye—*½ cup (113 g)*    .21

peas, green, frzn, boiled—*½ cup (80 g)*    .33

rice, white, from mix, Minute—*⅔ cup (124 g)*    .05

    for rib roast—*½ cup (117 g)*    .15

    w/ chicken flavor—*½ cup (107 g)*    .16

rice, long grain & wild

    from mix, Minute—*½ cup (115 g)*    .15

spinach, frzn, boiled—*½ cup (95 g)*    2.70

vegetable combinations, frzn, Birds Eye

    broccoli & cauliflower, w/ creamy italian cheese sce—*½ cup (128 g)*    .70

    broccoli, carrots & pasta w/ lightly seasoned sce—*⅔ cup (95 g)*    1.76

    broccoli, cauliflower & carrots—*¾ cup (113 g)*    .54

        w/ cheese sce—*½ cup (142 g)*    1.45

    broccoli, corn & red peppers—*⅔ cup (113 g)*    .53

    broccoli, green beans, pearl onions & red peppers—*¾ cup (113 g)*    .61

    brussel sprouts, cauliflower & carrots—*¾ cup (113 g)*    .88

    carrots, peas & pearl onions—*½ cup (95 g)*    .51

    chinese style—*½ cup (95 g)*    1.29

    chinese style, stir fry—*½ cup (95 g)*    .67

    corn, green beans & pasta curls w/ light cream sce—*½ cup (95 g)*    1.39

    green beans, bavarian style & spaetzle (noodles)—*½ cup (95 g)*    1.60

    italian style—*½ cup (95 g)*    1.80

    japanese style—*½ cup (95 g)*    1.79

    japanese style, stir fry—*½ cup (95 g)*    .42

    new england style—*½ cup (95 g)*    2.78

    peas & pearl onions—*½ cup (95 g)*    .32

**VEGETABLES**

| | |
|---|---|
| peas & pearl onions w/ cheese sce—*½ cup (142 g)* | 1.32 |
| rice, italian style—*½ cup (95 g)* | .17 |
| rice, spanish style—*½ cup (95 g)* | .15 |
| san francisco style—*½ cup (95 g)* | 1.17 |

**MISCELLANEOUS**

| | |
|---|---|
| baking choc, unsweetened, Bakers—*1 oz (28 g)* | 1.40 |
| meat/poultry coatings | |
|   oven fry | |
|     extra crispy recipe for chicken—*¼ pouch (29 g)* | 1.48 |

**MISCELLANEOUS**

| | |
|---|---|
| extra crispy recipe for pork—*¼ pouch (29 g)* | 1.57 |
| light crispy homestyle recipe—*¼ pouch (22 g)* | .81 |
| shake & bake | |
|   barbeque for chicken—*¼ pouch (25 g)* | .85 |
|   barbeque for pork—*¼ pouch (20 g)* | .68 |
|   country mild recipe—*¼ pouch (17 g)* | 2.03 |
|   for chicken—*¼ pouch (19 g)* | 1.00 |
|   for fish—*¼ pouch (19 g)* | .95 |
|   for pork—*¼ pouch (21 g)* | .52 |
|   italian herb recipe—*¼ pouch (20 g)* | .63 |

# Vitamin E as Alpha-Tocopherol (mg)

**CHIPS & SNACKS**

| | |
|---|---|
| potato chips—*1 oz (28 g)* | 1.20 |
| potato sticks—*1 oz (28 g)* | 2.23 |

**EGGS, CHICKEN**

| | |
|---|---|
| whole, fresh/frzn—*1 large (50 g)* | 0.88 |
| yolk, fresh—*yolk of 1 large egg (17 g)* | 0.87 |

**ENTREES, BOX MIX**

| | |
|---|---|
| pizza, cheese, from Contadina Pizzeria Kit | |
|   thick crust—*¼ pizza (128 g)* | 0.14 |
|   thin crust—*¼ pizza (104 g)* | 0.14 |

**FATS, OILS & SHORTENINGS**
**Animal Fats**

| | |
|---|---|
| beef tallow, raw—*1 T (13 g)* | 0.30 |
| pork fat (lard), raw—*1 T (13 g)* | 0.20 |

**Vegetable Oils**

| | |
|---|---|
| almond oil—*1 T (14 g)* | 5.30 |
| coconut oil—*1 T (14 g)* | 0.10 |
| corn oil—*1 T (14 g)* | 1.90 |
| corn oil, Mazola—*1 T (14 g)* | 3.00 |
| cottonseed oil—*1 T (14 g)* | 4.80 |
| olive oil—*1 T (14 g)* | 1.60 |
| palm oil—*1 T (14 g)* | 2.60 |
| peanut oil—*1 T (14 g)* | 1.60 |
| safflower oil—*1 T (14 g)* | 4.60 |
| sesame oil—*1 T (14 g)* | 0.20 |
| soybean oil—*1 T (14 g)* | 1.50 |
| soybean oil, hydrogenated—*1 T (14 g)* | 1.10 |
| sunflower oil—*1 T (14 g)* | 6.10 |
| veg oil spray, Mazola No Stick—*2.5 sec spray (0.7 g)* | 0.51[a] |
| wheat germ oil—*1 T (14 g)* | 20.30 |

**FRUIT & VEGETABLE JUICES**

| | |
|---|---|
| apple jce, cnd/bottled—*8 fl oz (248 g)* | 0.03 |
| grapefruit jce, cnd—*8 fl oz (247 g)* | 0.10 |
| orange jce, fresh—*8 fl oz (248 g)* | 0.10 |
| tomato jce—*6 fl oz (182 g)* | 0.40 |

**FRUITS**

| | |
|---|---|
| apple | |
|   raw, w/ skin—*1 med (138 g)* | 0.81 |
|   raw, w/o skin—*1 med (128 g)* | 0.35 |
| apricots, cnd, in heavy syrup—*4 halves (90 g)* | 0.80 |
| banana, raw—*1 med (114 g)* | 0.31 |
| blackberries, raw—*½ cup (72 g)* | 0.35 |
| cantaloupe, raw—*1 cup pieces (160 g)* | 0.22 |
| cherries, sour, raw—*½ cup (78 g)* | 0.10 |
| currants, european black, raw—*½ cup (56 g)* | 0.56 |
| currants, red & white, raw—*½ cup (56 g)* | 0.06 |
| gooseberries, raw—*1 cup (150 g)* | 0.56 |
| grapefruit, raw, red & white—*½ med (123 g)* | 0.30 |
| mango, raw—*1 med (207 g)* | 2.32 |
| mixed fruit, frzn, in syrup, Birds Eye—*½ cup (142 g)* | 0.06 |
| orange, navel or valencia, raw—*1 fruit (131 g)* | 0.30 |
| pear, raw—*1 med (166 g)* | 0.83 |
| pineapple, raw—*1 cup pieces (155 g)* | 0.16 |
| raspberries | |
|   raw—*1 cup (123 g)* | 0.37 |
|   frzn, in lite syrup, Birds Eye—*½ cup (142 g)* | 0.27 |
| strawberries | |
|   raw—*1 cup (149 g)* | 0.18 |
|   frzn, in lite syrup, Birds Eye—*½ cup (142 g)* | 0.13 |
|   frzn, sweetened or unsweetened—*1 cup (149 g)* | 0.31 |

**GRAIN PRODUCTS**
**Pasta**

| | |
|---|---|
| macaroni, enr, ckd—*1 cup (140 g)* | 1.03[a] |
| spaghetti, enr, ckd—*1 cup (140 g)* | 1.03[a] |

**NUTS, NUT PRODUCTS & SEEDS**

| | |
|---|---|
| almonds | |
|   dried—*1 oz (24 nuts) (28 g)* | 6.72 |
|   oil roasted—*1 oz (22 nuts) (28 g)* | 1.55 |
|   toasted—*1 oz (28 g)* | 1.41 |
|   whole, Blue Diamond—*1 oz (28 g)* | 1.66 |
| brazilnuts, dried—*1 oz (8 med nuts) (28 g)* | 2.13 |
| cashews, dry roasted—*1 oz (28 g)* | 0.16 |

[a] Specified as tocopherols.

## NUTS, NUT PRODUCTS & SEEDS

| | |
|---|---|
| coconut, raw—*1 piece (2″x2″x½″) (45 g)* | 0.33 |
| filberts (hazelnuts), dried—*1 oz (28 g)* | 6.70 |
| peanut butter, creamy/smooth, Skippy—*1 T (16 g)* | 3.00 |
| peanut butter, chunk style/crunchy, Skippy—*1 T (16 g)* | 3.00 |
| peanuts | |
|     dried—*1 oz (28 g)* | 2.56 |
|     dry roasted—*1 oz (28 g)* | 2.18 |
|     oil roasted—*1 oz (28 g)* | 2.07 |
| pecans, dried—*1 oz (31 large nuts) (28 g)* | 0.87 |
| pistachio nuts, dried—*1 oz (47 nuts) (28 g)* | 1.46 |
| sesame seeds, whole, dried—*1 T (9 g)* | 0.20 |
| walnuts, english/persian, dried—*1 oz (14 halves) (28 g)* | 0.73 |

## SPREADS

| | |
|---|---|
| butter—*1 T (15 g)* | 0.20 |
| margarine by brand | |
|     Mazola—*1 T (14 g)* | 8.00 |
|     Mazola unsalted—*1 T (14 g)* | 8.00 |
| margarine by form & type of oil | |
|     liquid, soybean & cottonseed—*1 t (5 g)* | 0.20 |
|     stick, safflower & soybean—*1 t (5 g)* | 0.80 |
|     stick, soybean—*1 t (5 g)* | 0.10 |
|     stick, soybean & cottonseed—*1 t (5 g)* | 0.30 |
|     tub, corn—*1 t (5 g)* | 0.50 |
|     tub, safflower—*1 t (5 g)* | 0.60 |
|     tub, soybean—*1 t (5 g)* | 0.10 |
|     tub, soybean & cottonseed—*1 t (5 g)* | 0.30 |
| margarine, imitation (diet) by brand | |
|     Mazola diet—*1 T (14 g)* | 3.00 |
|     Parkay, diet soft—*1 T (14 g)* | 0.40 |
| margarine, imitation (diet) by form & type of oil | |
|     tub, soybean & cottonseed—*1 t (5 g)* | 0.40 |
| mayonnaise | |
|     Best Foods/Hellmann's—*1 T (14 g)* | 11.00 |
|     soybean—*1 T (14 g)* | 2.90 |
| miracle whip, Kraft—*1 T (14 g)* | 0.50 |
| miracle whip, light, Kraft—*1 T (14 g)* | 0.40 |
| sandwich spread, Best Foods/Hellmann's—*1 T (15 g)* | 5.00 |

## VEGETABLES

| | |
|---|---|
| asparagus | |
|     cnd—*½ cup (121 g)* | 0.46 |
|     frzn, boiled—*4 spears (60 g)* | 0.81 |
|     raw—*4 spears (58 g)* | 1.15 |
| avocado, raw, calif—*1 med (173 g)* | 2.32 |
| beet greens, raw—*1 cup (38 g)* | 0.57 |
| beets, cnd, harvard—*½ cup slices (123 g)* | 0.04 |
| broccoli, raw—*½ cup chopped (44 g)* | 0.20 |
| brussels sprouts | |
|     raw—*½ cup chopped (44 g)* | 0.39 |
|     boiled—*½ cup (4 sprouts) (78 g)* | 0.66 |

## VEGETABLES

| | |
|---|---|
| cabbage, chinese (pak-choi), raw—*½ cup shredded (35 g)* | 0.05 |
| cabbage, green, raw—*½ cup shredded (35 g)* | 0.58 |
| carrots | |
|     raw—*1 med (72 g)* | 0.32 |
|     boiled—*½ cup slices (78 g)* | 0.33 |
| cauliflower, raw—*½ cup pieces (50 g)* | 0.02 |
| celery, raw—*1 stalk (7.5″ long) (40 g)* | 0.14 |
| corn, sweet, yellow/white, cnd—*½ cup (128 g)* | 0.05 |
| corn, sweet, yellow/white, frzn—*½ cup (82 g)* | 0.02 |
| cucumber, raw—*½ cup slices (1/6 cucumber) (52 g)* | 0.08 |
| dandelion greens, raw—*½ cup chopped (28 g)* | 0.70 |
| eggplant, raw—*½ cup pieces (41 g)* | 0.01 |
| garden cress, raw—*½ cup (25 g)* | 0.18 |
| garlic, raw—*3 cloves (9 g)* | 0.001 |
| green beans (snap beans) | |
|     raw—*½ cup (55 g)* | 0.01 |
|     cnd—*½ cup (68 g)* | 0.03 |
|     frzn—*½ cup (62 g)* | 0.06 |
|     frzn, boiled—*½ cup (68 g)* | 0.09 |
| leeks, raw—*¼ cup chopped (26 g)* | 0.24 |
| lettuce, iceberg, raw—*¼ head (135 g)* | 0.54 |
| mushrooms, raw—*½ cup pieces (35 g)* | 0.03 |
| mustard greens, raw—*½ cup chopped (28 g)* | 0.56 |
| onion rings, frzn, heated—*7 rings (70 g)* | 0.48 |
| onions, raw—*½ cup chopped (80 g)* | 0.25 |
| parsley, raw—*½ cup chopped (30 g)* | 0.52 |
| parsnips, raw—*½ cup (67 g)* | 0.67 |
| peas, green | |
|     raw—*½ cup (78 g)* | 0.10 |
|     frzn—*½ cup (72 g)* | 0.09 |
|     frzn, boiled—*½ cup (80 g)* | 0.10 |
| peppers, sweet, raw—*½ cup chopped (50 g)* | 0.34 |
| potato | |
|     raw w/o skin—*1 potato (112 g)* | 0.07 |
|     baked w/o skin—*1 potato (156 g)* | 0.05 |
|     boiled w/o skin—*1 potato (135 g)* | 0.05 |
|     french fried, frzn, heated—*10 pieces (50 g)* | 0.10 |
| pumpkin, raw—*½ cup (58 g)* | 0.58 |
| rutabaga, boiled—*½ cup cubes (85 g)* | 0.13 |
| seaweed, kelp (kombu/tangle), raw—*3.5 oz (100 g)* | 0.87 |
| spinach | |
|     raw—*½ cup chopped (28 g)* | 0.53 |
|     cnd—*½ cup (107 g)* | 0.02 |
| squash, winter, all varieties, baked—*½ cup cubes (102 g)* | 0.12 |
| sweet potato, raw—*1 med (130 g)* | 5.93 |
| tomato, red, raw—*1 tomato (123 g)* | 0.42 |
| turnip greens, raw—*½ cup chopped (28 g)* | 0.63 |
| watercress, raw—*½ cup chopped (17 g)* | 0.17 |

# Vitamin K (mcg/100 g)

**BEVERAGES**

| | |
|---|---:|
| coffee, dry | 38 |
| tea, green, dry | 712 |

**EGGS**

| | |
|---|---:|
| whole, fresh/frzn | 50 |
| yolk, fresh | 147 |

**FATS & OILS**
**Vegetable Oils**

| | |
|---|---:|
| coconut oil | 10 |
| corn oil | 60 |
| cottonseed oil | 0 |
| olive oil | 0 |
| palm oil | 8 |
| peanut oil | 0 |
| safflower, linoleic | 0 |
| safflower, oleic | 3 |
| soybean oil | 540 |

**FRUITS**

| | |
|---|---:|
| apple, raw w/ skin | 3 |
| orange, raw | 5 |
| strawberries, raw | 14 |

**GRAINS**

| | |
|---|---:|
| oats, dry | 63 |
| wheat bran | 83 |
| wheat flour, whole wheat | 30 |
| wheat germ | 39 |

**INFANT FORMULA[a]**

| | |
|---|---:|
| concentrate, reconstituted | 13 |
| powder, reconstituted | 15 |
| ready-to-feed | 13 |

**MEATS**
**Beef**

| | |
|---|---:|
| ground, regular, raw | 4 |

**Variety Cuts**

| | |
|---|---:|
| heart, beef, raw | 0 |
| kidneys, beef, raw | 0 |
| liver, raw | |
| beef | 104 |
| chicken | 80 |
| lamb | 0 |
| pigeon | 0 |
| pork | 88 |
| rabbit | 35 |
| turkey | 0 |
| veal | 27 |

**MILK, COW**

| | |
|---|---:|
| non-fat dry,reg | 10 |
| skim | 4 |
| whole, 3.7% fat | 4 |

**MILK, OTHER**

| | |
|---|---:|
| human | 2 |

**SWEETENERS**

| | |
|---|---:|
| honey | 25 |

**VEGETABLES**

| | |
|---|---:|
| asparagus spears | |
| frzn, boiled | 27 |
| raw | 39 |
| beet, raw | 5 |
| broccoli | |
| raw | 132 |
| frzn | 68 |
| cabbage, green, raw | 149 |
| carrot, raw | 13 |
| cauliflower, raw | 191 |
| chickpeas (garbanzo beans) | |
| mature seeds, dry | 264 |
| sprouted seeds, raw | 48 |
| corn, yellow, raw | 7 |
| cucumber, raw | 5 |
| green beans (snap beans) | |
| frzn, boiled | 32 |
| raw | 28 |
| lentils, mature seeds, dry | 223 |
| lentils, sprouted seeds, raw | 39 |
| lettuce, iceberg, raw | 112 |
| mung beans | |
| mature seeds, dry | 170 |
| sprouted seeds, raw | 33 |
| mushrooms, raw | 8 |
| nettle leaves, raw | 372 |
| peas, mature seeds, dry | 81 |
| peas, sprouted seeds, raw | 28 |
| potato | |
| raw | 16 |
| baked | 4 |
| seaweed | |
| dulse, dried | 1700 |
| rockweed, dried | 1700 |
| seagrass | 246 |
| sealettuce | 68 |
| soybeans, mature, raw | 190 |
| spinach | |
| raw | 266 |
| frzn | 138 |
| tomato, green, raw | 47 |
| tomato, red, raw | 23 |
| turnip greens, raw | 650 |
| watercress, raw | 57 |

[a] Vitamin K values are listed in the main table for specific infant formulas and for special dietary formulas, commercial and hospital.

# Sources of Data for the Tables

Agriculture Handbook No. 8, Composition of Foods, Raw, Processed, Prepared, U.S. Department of Agriculture, Washington, D.C., 1963.

Agriculture Handbook No. 8, Revised, Composition of Foods, Raw, Processed, Prepared, U.S. Department of Agriculture, Washington, D.C.

8-1 Dairy and Egg Products, November 1976
8-2 Spices and Herbs, January 1977
8-3 Baby Foods, December 1978
8-4 Fats and Oils, June 1979
8-5 Poultry Products, August 1979
8-6 Soups, Sauces and Gravies, February 1980
8-7 Sausages and Luncheon Meats, September 1980
8-8 Breakfast Cereals, July 1982
8-9 Fruits and Fruit Juices, August 1982
8-10 Pork Products, August 1983
8-11 Vegetables and Vegetable Products, August 1984
8-12 Nut and Seed Products, September 1984
8-13 Beef Products, August 1986
8-14 Beverages, May 1986
8-15 Finfish and Shellfish Products, September 1987
8-16 Legumes and Legume Products, December 1986

Agriculture Handbook No. 456, Nutritive Value of American Foods in Common Units, U.S. Department of Agriculture, 1975.

Fletcher, D. C., Do clotting factors in vitamin K-rich vegetables hinder anticoagulant therapy? (Questions and Answers), JAMA, 237(17):1871, 1977.

Swain, A. R., S. P. Dutton and A. S. Truswell, Salicylates in foods, J. Am. Diet. Assoc. 85(8):950–960, 1985.

U.S. Department of Agriculture Provisional Tables, Washington, D.C.
Fatty Acid and Cholesterol Content of Selected Foods, March 1984
Nutrient Content of Bakery Foods & Related Items, August 1981
Nutrient Content of Beverages, September 1981
Nutrient Content of Fast Foods, June 1984
Sugar Content of Selected Foods, October 1986
Vitamin K Content of Foods, June 1986

Information provided upon request by the food industry (individual companies and trade associations)

Previous editions of Food Values of Portions Commonly Used

# Other Sources of Food Composition Data

Additional references are provided in three sections:

■ References by substance (references for one major nutrient/compound in a food or foods)

■ References by food group (references for more than one substance in a food or group of similar foods)

■ References that report various substances in various foods

Most of these references are relatively recent: 74% are from the 1980s, 22% are from the 1970s, and 4% were published prior to 1970.

## REFERENCES BY SUBSTANCE

### Biotin

Evans, R. J., J. A. Davidson, D. Bauer and H. A. Butts, The biotin content of fresh and stored shell eggs, Poultry Sci. 32:680–683, 1953.

Guilarte, T. R., Analysis of biotin levels in selected foods using a radiometric microbiological method, Nutr. Rep. Inter. 32(4):837–845, 1985.

### Caffeine and Theobromine

Ashoor, S. H., G. J. Seperich, W. C. Monte and J. Welty, High performance liquid chromatographic determination of caffeine in decaffeinated coffee, tea, and beverage products, J. Assoc. Off. Anal. Chem. 66(3):606–609, 1983.

Blauch, J. L. and S. M. Tarka Jr., HPLC determination of caffeine and theobromine in coffee, tea, and instant hot cocoa mixes, J. Food Sci. 48:745–747, 750, 1983.

Bunker, M. L. and M. McWilliams, Caffeine content of common beverages, J. Am. Diet. Assoc. 74:28–32, 1979.

Burg, A. W., Effects of caffeine on the human system, Tea and Coffee Trade J. 147:40–42, 88, 1975.

Caffeine and pregnancy, Office of Public Affairs, Food and Drug Administration, Public Health Service, U.S. Department of Health and Human Services, HHS Publication No. (FDA) 81–1081, 1981.

Caffeine: how to consume less, Consumer Reports 46(10):597–599, 1981.

Craig, W. J. and T. T. Nguyen, Caffeine and theobromine levels in cocoa and carob products, J. Food Sci. 49(1):302–303, 305, 1984.

Dulitzky, M., E. de la Tega and H. F. Lewis, Determination of caffeine in tea by high-performance liquid chromatography and a modified digestion procedure, J. Chromat. 317:403–405, 1984.

Graham, D. M., Caffeine—its identity, dietary sources, intake and biological effects, Nutr. Rev. 36(4):97–102, 1978.

Groisser, D. S., A study of caffeine in tea, Am. J. Clin. Nutr. 31:1727, 1978.

Hallal, J. C., Caffeine: is it hazardous to your patients' health?, Am. J. Nurs. 86(4):422–425, 1986.

Hsu, T. J., C. C. Liao and M. Y. Chen, Liquid chromatography of adenine, caffeine, theobromine, theophylline, tannic acid, xanthine and its application to tea analysis, J. Chin. Chem. Soc. 25(3):153–160, 1978.

Hurst, W. J., K. P. Snyder and R. A. Martin Jr., Use of microbore high-performance liquid chromatography for the determination of caffeine, theobromine and theophylline in cocoa, J. Chromatogr. 318(2):408–411, 1985.

Institute of Food Technologists' Expert Panel on Food Safety and Nutrition, Caffeine, Food Tech. 37(4):87–91, 1983.

Kreiser, W. R. and R. A. Martin Jr., High pressure liquid chromatographic determination of theobromine and caffeine in cocoa and chocolate products: collaborative study, J. Assoc. Off. Anal. Chem. 63(3):591–594, 1980.

Lecos, C., The latest caffeine scorecard, FDA Consumer, March 1984 (HHS Publication No. [FDA]84–2184).

Rajasekharan, T., A. S. V. Rao, K. O. Abraham and M. L. Shankaranarayana, Analysis of coffee–chicory blends, Indian Coffee 50(1):19–24, 1986.

Shivashankar, S., C. Balachandran, Y. S. Lewis and C. F. Natarajan, Determination of theobromine in cocoa products, J. Food Sci. Tech., India 15(4):153–161, 1978.

Sjoeberg, A. M. and J. Rajama, Simple method for the determination of alkaloids in cocoa using paper chromatography and UV spectrometry, J. Chromatogr. 295(1):291–294, 1984.

Terada, H. and Y. Sakabe, High-performance liquid chromatographic determination of theobromine, theophylline and caffeine in food products, J. Chromatogr. 291:453–459, 1984.

Trugo, L. C., R. Macrae and J. Dick, Determination of purine alkaloids and trigonelline in instant coffee and other beverages using high-performance liquid chromatography, J. Sci. Food Agr. 34(3):300–306, 1983.

Tyler, T. A., Liquid chromatographic determination of sodium saccharin, caffeine, aspartame, and sodium benzoate in cola beverages, J. Assoc. Off. Anal. Chem. 67(4):745–747, 1984.

Weidner, G. and J. Istvan, Dietary sources of caffeine (letter), N. Engl. J. Med. 313(22):1421, 1985.

What's in soft drinks, National Soft Drink Association, Washington, D.C., September 1982.

Zoumas, B. L., W. R. Kreiser and R. A. Martin, Theobromine and caffeine content of chocolate products, J. Food Sci. 45(2):314–316, 1980.

## Carotenoids

Balasubramanian, T., Studies on quality and nutritional aspects of tomato, J. Food Sci. Tech., India 21(6):419–421, 1984.

Beecher, G. R. and F. Khachik, Evaluation of vitamin A and carotenoid data in food composition tables, J. Nat. Cancer Inst. 73(6):1397–1404, 1984.

Bushway, R. J., Determination of alpha- and beta-carotene in some raw fruits and vegetables by high-performance liquid chromatography, J. Agr. Food Chem. 34(3):409–412, 1986.

Edwards, C. G. and C. Y. Lee, Measurement of provitamin A carotenoids in fresh and canned carrots and green peas, J. Food Sci. 51(2):534–535, 1986.

Ezeala, D. O., Nutrients, carotenoids and mineral compositions of the leaf vegetables *Amaranthus viridis L.* and *A. caudatus L.*, Trop. Agr. 62(2):95–96. 1985.

Hsieh, Y. P. C. and M. Karel, Rapid extraction and determination of alpha- and beta-carotenes in foods, J. Chromatogr. 259(3):515–518, 1983.

Johjima, T. and H. Ogura, Analysis of tomato carotenoids by thin-layer chromatography and a cis-form gamma-carotene newly identified in tangerine tomato, J. Jap. Soc. Hort. Sci. 52(2):200–209, 1983.

Johnson, C. D., R. R. Eitenmiller, D. A. Lillard and M. Rao, Vitamin A activity of selected fruits, J. Am. Diet. Assoc. 85(12):1627–1629, 1985.

Landen, W. O. Jr., D. M. Hines, T. W. Hamill, J. I. Martin, E. R. Young, R. R. Eitenmiller and A. G. Soliman, Vitamin A and vitamin E content of infant formulas produced in the United States, J. Assoc. Off. Anal. Chem. 68(3):509–511, 1985.

Picha, D. H., Crude protein, minerals, and total carotenoids in sweet potatoes, J. Food Sci. 50(6):1768–1769, 1985.

Premachandra, B. R., A simple TLC method for the determination of provitamin A content of fruits and vegetables, Int. J. Vit. Nutr. Res. 55(2):139–147, 1985.

Takahashi, T., Vitamin A in new food composition tables from Japan, J. Nat. Cancer Inst. 73(6):1405–1407, 1984.

## Cholesterol

Feeley, R. M., P. E. Criner and B. K. Watt, Cholesterol content of foods, J. Am. Diet. Assoc. 61:134–149, 1972.

## Choline

Koning, A. J. de, Phospholipids of marine origin. V. The crab— a comparative study of a marine species (*Cyclograpsus punctatus*) and a fresh water species (*Potamon*), J. Sci. Food Agr. 21(6):290–293, 1970.

Parsons, J. G., P. G. Leeney and S. Patton, Identification and quantitative analysis of phospholipids in cocoa beans, J. Food Sci. 34(6):497–499, 1969.

Saucerman, J. R., C. E. Winstead and T. M. Jones, Quantitative gas chromatographic headspace determination of choline

in adult and infant formula products, J. Assoc. Off. Anal. Chem. 67(5):982–985, 1984.

Zeisel, S. H., D. Char and N. F. Sheard, Choline, phosphatidylcholine and sphingomyelin in human and bovine milk and infant formulas, J. Nutr. 116(1):50–58, 1986.

## Chromium

Farre, R., M. J. Lagarda and R. Montoro, Atomic absorption spectrophotometric determination of chromium in foods. J. Assoc. Off. Anal. Chem. 69(5):876–879, 1986.

Smart, G. A. and J. C. Sherlock, Chromium in foods and the diet, Food Addit. Contam. 2(2):139–147, 1985.

## Dietary Fiber

Cummings, J. H., H. N. Englyst and R. Wood, Determination of dietary fibre in cereals and cereal products—collaborative trials. I. Initial trials, J. Assoc. Pub. Anal. 23(1):1–35, 1985.

Holloway, W. D., Composition of fruit, vegetable and cereal dietary fibre, J. Sci. Food Agric. 34(11):1236–1240, 1983.

Holloway, W. D., J. A. Monro, J. C. Gurnsey, E. W. Pomare and N. H. Stace, Dietary fiber and other constituents of some Tongan foods, J. Food. Sci. 50:1756–1757, 1985.

Horvath-Mosonvi, M., J. Rigo and E. Hegedues-Voelgvesi, An investigation into the dietary fibre content of different bread and dietary bran samples, Develop. Food Sci. 5B:1115–1120, 1983.

Kunerth, W. H. and V. L. Youngs, Effect of variety and growing year on the constituents of durum bran fiber, Cereal Chem. 61(4):350–352, 1984.

Lanza, E. and R. R. Butrum, A critical review of food fiber analysis and data, J. Am. Diet. Assoc. 86(6):732–743, 1986.

Lund, E. D., J. M. Smoot and N. T. Hall, Dietary fiber content of eleven tropical fruits and vegetables, J. Agric. Food Chem. 31(5):1013–1016, 1983.

Marlett, J. A. and J. G. Chesters, Measuring dietary fiber in human foods, J. Food Sci. 50(2):410–414, 423, 1985.

McNutt, K. W., Perspective—Fiber, J. Nutr. Ed. 8(4):150–152, 1976.

Patrow, C. J. and J. A. Marlett, Variability in the dietary fiber content of wheat and mixed-grain commercial breads, J. Am. Diet. Assoc. 86(6):794–796, 1986.

Paul, A. A. and D. A. T. Southgate, McCance and Widdowson's The Composition of Foods: Dietary fibre in egg, meat and fish dishes, J. Hum. Nutr. 33:335–336, 1979.

Polizzoto, L. M., A. M. Tinsley, C. W. Weber and J. W. Berry, Dietary fibers in muffins, J. Food Sci. 48:111–113, 1983.

Prosky, L., N. G. Asp, I. Furda, J. W. Devries, T. F. Schweizer and B. F. Harland, Determination of total dietary fiber in foods and food products: Collaborative study, J. Assoc. Off. Anal. Chem. 68(4):677–679, 1985.

Prosky, L., N. G. Asp, I. Furda, J. W. Devries, T. F. Schweizer and B. F. Harland, Determination of total dietary fiber in foods, food products, and total diets: Interlaboratory study, J. Assoc. Off. Anal. Chem. 67(6):1044–1052, 1984.

Ross, J. K., C. English and C. A. Perlmutter, Dietary fiber constituents of selected fruits and vegetables, J. Am. Diet. Assoc. 85(9):1111–1116, 1985.

Saraswathi, G., S. Kanchana and K. S. Shurpalekar, Estimation of dietary fibre of some selected Indian foods by different methods, Indian J. Med. Res. 77:833–838, 1983.

Varo, P., R. Laine, K. Veijalainen, A. Espo, A. Wetterhoff and P. Koivistoinen, Dietary fibre and available carbohydrates in Finnish vegetables and fruits, J. Agr. Sci. in Finland 56(1):49–59, 1984.

Varo, P., K. Veijalainen and P. Koivistoinen, Effect of heat treatment on the dietary fibre contents of potato and tomato, J. Food Tech. 19(4):485–492, 1984.

Visser, F. R. and C. Gurnsey, Inconsistent differences between neutral detergent fiber and total dietary fiber values of fruits and vegetables, J. Assoc. Off. Anal. Chem. 69(4):565–567, 1986.

Wenlock, R. W., L. M. Sivell and I. B. Agater, Dietary fibre fractions in cereal and cereal-containing products in Britain, J. Sci. Food Agric. 36:113–121, 1985.

Zyren, J., E. R. Elkins, J. A. Dudek and R. E. Hagen, Fiber contents of selected raw and processed vegetables, fruits and fruit juices as served, J. Food Sci. 48:600–603, 1983.

## Fatty Acids

Ahn, P. C., N. Kassim and P. V. J. Hegarty, Total fat and fatty acid composition of commercially available chocolate candies, J. Am. Diet. Assoc. 79(5):552–554, 1981.

Anderson, B. A., Comprehensive evaluation of fatty acids in foods, VII. Pork products, J. Am. Diet. Assoc. 69:44–49, 1976.

Anderson, B. A., Comprehensive evaluation of fatty acids in foods, XIII. Sausages and luncheon meats, J. Am. Diet. Assoc. 72(1):48–52, 1978.

Anderson, B. A., G. Fristrom and J. L. Weihrauch, Comprehensive evaluation of fatty acids in foods, X. Lamb and veal, J. Am. Diet. Assoc. 70:53–58, 1977.

Anderson, B. A., J. E. Kinsella and B. K. Watt, Comprehensive evaluation of fatty acids in foods, II. Beef products, J. Am. Diet. Assoc. 67:35–41, 1975.

Brignoli, C. A., J. E. Kinsella and J. L. Weihrauch, Comprehensive evaluation of fatty acids in foods, V. Unhydrogenated fats and oils, J. Am. Diet. Assoc. 68:224–229, 1976.

Chanmugam, P., M. Boudreau and D. H. Hwang, Differences in the omega-3 fatty acid contents in pond-reared and wild fish and shellfish, J. Food Sci. 51:1556–1557, 1986.

Dutta, A. K., P. K. Pal, A. Ghosh, S. Misra, S. Nandi and Y. A. Choudhur, Lipids and fatty acids of the gastropod mollusc *Cerethidea cingulata*, J. Am. Oil Chem. Soc. 63(2):223–225, 1986.

Exler, J., R. M. Avena and J. L. Weihrauch, Comprehensive evaluation of fatty acids in foods, XI. Leguminous seeds, J. Am. Diet. Assoc. 71(4):412–415, 1977.

Exler, J. and J. L. Weihrauch, Comprehensive evaluation of fatty acids in foods, XII. Shellfish, J. Am. Diet. Assoc. 71(5):518–521, 1977.

Exler, J. and J. L. Weihrauch, Provisional table on the content of omega-3 fatty acids and other fat components in selected foods, Nutrient Data Research Branch, Nutrition Monitoring Division, Human Nutrition Information Service, HNIS/PT-103, U.S. Department of Agriculture, May 1986.

Fogerty, A. C., A. J. Evans, G. L. Ford and B. H. Kennett, Distribution of omega-6 and omega-3 fatty acids in lipid classes in Australian fish, Nutr. Rep. Inter. 33(5):777–786, 1986.

Fristrom, G. A., B. C. Stewart, J. L. Weihrauch and L. P. Posati,

Comprehensive evaluation of fatty acids in foods, IV. Nuts, peanuts, and soups, J. Am. Diet. Assoc. 67:351–355, 1975.

Garcia, V. V., J. K. Palmer and R. W. Young, Fatty acid composition of the oil of winged beans, *Psophocarpus tetragonolobus (L.) DC.* J. Am. Oil Chem. Soc. 56:931–932, 1979.

Gibson, R. A., Australian fish—an excellent source of both arachidonic acid and omega-3 polyunsaturated fatty acids, Lipids 18(11):743–775, 1983.

Guild, L., D. Deethardt and E. Rust, Fatty acids in foods served in a university food service, J. Am. Diet. Assoc. 61:149–151, 1972.

Hepburn, F. N., J. Exler and J. L. Weihrauch, Provisional table on the content of omega-3 fatty acids and other fat components of selected foods, J. Am. Diet. Assoc. 86(6):788–793, 1986.

Kinsella, J. E., J. L. Shimp, J. Mai and J. Weihrauch, Fatty acid content and composition of freshwater finfish, J. Am. Oil Chem. Soc. 54:424–429, 1977.

Miljanich, P. and R. Ostwald, Fatty acids in newer brands of margarine, J. Am. Diet. Assoc. 56(1):29–30, 1970.

Ostwald, R., Fatty acids in eleven brands of margarine, J. Am. Diet. Assoc. 39(4):313–316, 1961.

Posati, L. P., J. E. Kinsella and B. K. Watt, Comprehensive evaluation of fatty acids in foods, I. Dairy products, J. Am. Diet. Assoc. 66:482–487, 1975.

Posati, L. P., J. E. Kinsella and B. K. Watt, Comprehensive evaluation of fatty acids in foods, III. Eggs and egg products, J. Am. Diet. Assoc. 67:111–115, 1975.

Sheppard, A. J., J. L. Iverson and J. L. Weihrauch, Composition of selected dietary fats, oils, margarine, and butter, In Handbook of Lipid Research, vol. 1, edited by A. Kuksis, Plenum, New York, 1973.

van den Reek, M. M., M. C. Craig-Schmidt and A. J. Clark, Use of published analyses of food items to determine dietary trans octadecenoic acid, J. Am. Diet. Assoc. 86(10):1391–1394, 1986.

Weihrauch, J. L., C. A. Brignoli, J. B. Reeves III and J. L. Iverson, Fatty acid composition of margarines, processed fats, and oils: A new compilation of data for tables of food composition, Food Tech. 31(2):80–91, 1977.

Weihrauch, J. L., J. E. Kinsella and B. K. Watt, Comprehensive evaluation of fatty acids in foods, VI. Cereal products, J. Am. Diet. Assoc. 68:335–355, 1976.

Williams, G., B. C. Davidson, P. Stevens and M. A. Crawford, Comparative fatty acids of the dolphin and the herring, J. Am. Oil Chem. Soc. 54:328–330, 1977.

Worthington, R. E., The linolenic acid content of peanut oil, J. Am. Oil Chem. Soc. 54:167–169, 1977.

## Fluoride

Marier, J. R. and D. Rose, The fluoride content of some foods and beverages—a brief survey using a modified Zr-SPANDS method, J. Dent. Res. 31:941–946, 1966.

Ophaug, R. H., L. Singer and B. F. Harland, Estimated fluoride intake of 6-month-old infants in four dietary regions of the United States, Am. J. Clin. Nutr. 33:324–327, 1980.

Read, J. I. and R. Collins, Estimation of total fluoride in foodstuffs, J. Assoc. Pub. Anal. 20(4);109–111, 115, 1982.

Moody, G. J., B. Ong, K. Quinlan, A. H. Riah and J. D. R. Thomas, The determination of fluorine in coffee and tea using a microprocessor coupled with a fluoride ion-selective electrode, J. Food Tech. 15(3):335–343, 1980.

Siebert, G. and K. Trautner, Fluoride content of selected human food, pet food and related materials, Z. Ernahrungswiss. 24(1):54–66, 1985.

Smith, G. E., Fluoride, the environment, and human health, Perspect. Biol. Med. 29(4):560–572, 1986.

Taves, D. R., Dietary intake of fluoride ashed (total fluoride) v. unashed (inorganic fluoride) analysis of individual foods, Br. J. Nutr. 49(3):295–301, 1983.

Waldbott, G. L., Fluoride in food, Am. J. Clin. Nutr. 12:455–462, 1963.

Walters, C. B., J. C. Sherlock, W. H. Evans and J. I. Read, Dietary intake of fluoride in the United Kingdom and fluoride content of some foodstuffs, J. Sci. Food Agric. 34(5):523–528, 1983.

## Folate

Huq, R. S., J. A. Abalaka and W. L. Stafford, Folate content of various Nigerian foods, J. Sci. Food Agric. 34(4):404–406, 1983.

Perloff, B. P. and R. R. Butrum, Folacin in selected foods, J. Am. Diet. Assoc. 70:161–172, 1977.

## Gluten

Olson, G. B. and G. R. Gallo, Gluten in pharmaceutical and nutritional products, Am. J. Hosp. Pharm. 40(1):121–122, 1983.

## Iodine

Berg, J. N. and D. Padgitt, Iodine concentrations in milk from iodophor teat dips, J. Dairy Sci. 68(2):457–461, 1985.

Bruhn, J. C. and A. A. Franke, An indirect method for the estimation of the iodine content in raw milk, J. Dairy Sci. 61(11):1557–1560, 1978.

Bruhn, J. C., A. A. Franke, R. B. Bushnell, H. Weisheit, G. H. Hutton and G. C. Gurtle, Sources and content of iodine in California milk and dairy products, J. Food Prot. 46(1):41–46, 1983.

Galton, D. M., L. G. Petersson and H. N. Erb, Milk iodine residues in herds practicing iodophor premilking teat disinfection, J. Dairy Sci. 69(1):267–271, 1986.

Galton, D. M., L. G. Petersson, W. G. Merrill, D. K. Bandler and D. E. Shuster, Effects of premilking udder preparation on bacterial population, sediment, and iodine residue in milk, J. Dairy Sci. 67(11):2580–2589, 1984.

Gushurst, C. A., J. A. Mueller, J. A. Green and F. Sedor, Breast milk iodide: reassessment in the 1980s, Pediatrics 73(3):354–357, 1984.

van Ryssen, J. B., S. van Malsen and J. G. van Blerk, The iodine content of fresh milk samples in Natal and the effect of iodophor teat dips on milk iodine content, J. S. Afr. Vet. Assoc. 56(4):181–185, 1985.

Wenlock, R. W., D. H. Buss, R. E. Moxon and N. G. Bunton, Trace nutrients. 4. Iodine in British foods, Br. J. Nutr. 47:381–390, 1982.

Wheeler, S. M., G. H. Fleet and R. J. Ashley, Effect of processing upon concentration and distribution of natural and iodophor-derived iodine in milk, J. Dairy Sci. 66(2):187–195, 1983.

## Inositol

Clements, R. S. Jr. and B. Darnell, *Myo*-inositol content of common foods: development of a high-*myo*-inositol diet, Am. J. Clin. Nutr. 33:1954–1967, 1980.

Olano, A., Presence of trehalose and sugar alcohols in sherry, Am. J. Enology Viticulture 34:148–151, 1983.

Sandberg, A. S. and R. Ahderinne, HPLC method for determination of inositol tri-, tetra-, penta-, and hexaphosphates in foods and intestinal contents, J. Food Sci. 51(3):547–550, 1986.

## Nickel

Smart, G. A. and J. C. Sherlock, Nickel in foods and the diet, Food Addit. Contam. 4(1):61–71, 1987.

Solomons, N. W., F. Viteri, T. R. Schuler and F. H. Nielsen, Bioavailability of nickel in man: effects of foods and chemically defined dietary constituents on the absorption of inorganic nickel, J. Nutr. 112(1):39–50, 1982.

Veien, N. K. and M. R. Andersen, Nickel in Danish food, Acta. Derm. Venereol. (Stockholm) 66(6):502–509, 1986.

## Nitrate and Nitrite

Crosby, N. T., J. K. Foreman, J. F. Palframan and R. Sawyer, Estimation of steam-volatile N-nitrosamines in foods at the 1 ug/kg level, Nature 238:342–343, 1972.

Eggers, N. J. and D. L. Cattle, High-performance liquid chromatographic method for the determination of nitrate and nitrite in cured meat, J. Chromatogr. 354:490–494, 1986.

Fiddler, W., R. C. Doerr, R. A. Gates and J. B. Fox Jr., Comparison of chemiluminescent and AOAC methods for determining nitrite in commercial cured meat products, J. Assoc. Off. Anal. Chem. 67(3):525–538, 1984.

Hotchkiss, J. H., Sources of N-nitrosamine contamination in foods, Adv. Exp. Med. Biol. 177:287–298, 1984.

Hunt, J. and D. J. Seymour, Method for measuring nitrate-nitrogen in vegetables using anion-exchange high-performance liquid chromatography, Analyst 110(2):131–133, 1985.

Jackson, P. E., P. R. Haddad and S. Dilli, Determination of nitrate and nitrite in cured meats using high-performance liquid chromatography, J. Chromatogr. 295(2):471–478, 1984.

Jancar, J. C., M. D. Constant and W. C. Herwig, Determination of inorganic anions in beer by ion chromatography, J. Am. Soc. Brew. Chem. 42(2):90–93, 1984.

Kikugawa, K., T. Kato and H. Hayatsu, Mutagenicity of smoked, dried bonito products, Mutat. Res. 158(1-2):35–44, 1985.

Kleijn, J. P. de and K. Hoven, Determination of nitrite and nitrate in meat products by high-performance liquid chromatography, Analyst 109(4):527–528, 1984.

Kok, S. H., K. A. Buckle and M. Wootton, Determination of nitrate and nitrite in water using high-performance liquid chromatography, J. Chromatogr. 260(1):189–192, 1983.

Revelle, R., Toxins in the human food system, Basic Life Sci. 34:11–26, 1985.

Ross, H. D. and J. H. Hotchkiss, Determination of nitrate in dried foods by gas chromatography–thermal energy analyzer, J. Assoc. Off. Anal. Chem. 68(1):41–43, 1985.

Tanaka, A., N. Nose, H. Masaki, Y. Kikuchi and H. Iwasaki, Gas–liquid chromatographic determination of trace amounts of nitrite in egg, egg white, and egg yolk, J. Assoc. Off. Anal. Chem. 66(2):260–263, 1983.

White, J. W. Jr., Relative significance of dietary sources of nitrate and nitrite, J. Agric. Food Chem. 23(5):886–891, 1975.

Wooton, M., S. H. Kok and K. A. Buckle, Determination of nitrite and nitrate levels in meat and vegetable products by high-performance liquid chromatography, J. Sci. Food Agr. 36(4):297–304, 1985.

## Oxalic Acid

Awadalla, M. Z., N. S. Bassily and N. H. Saba, Oxalate content of some common Egyptian food stuffs, J. Egypt. Public Health Assoc. 60(3–4):41–51, 1985.

Bushway, R. J., J. L. Bureau and D. F. Mcgann, Determinations of organic acids in potatoes by high-performance liquid chromatography, J. Food Sci. 49:75–77, 1984.

Kozukue, E., N. Kozukue and T. Kurosaki, Organic acid, sugar and amino acid composition of bamboo shoots, J. Food Sci. 48:935–938, 1983.

Ohkawa, H., Gas chromatographic determination of oxalic acid in foods, J. Assoc. Off. Anal. Chem. 68(1):108–111, 1985.

Oxalic acid content of selected vegetables, Vegetables and Vegetable Products, Agriculture Handbook No. 8-11, Composition of Foods, Raw, Processed, Prepared, p. 11, U.S. Department of Agriculture, Washington, D.C., August 1984.

Pilac, L. M., I. C. Abdon and E. P. Mandap, Oxalic acid content and its relation to the calcium present in some Philippine plant foods, Philippine J. Nutr. 24(1):21–36, 1971.

Ramasastri, B. V., Calcium, iron and oxalate content of some condiments and spices, Qual. Plan.—Plant Foods for Human Nutr. 33(1):11–15, 1983.

Sachde, A. G., A. Y. Al-Bakir, M. A. A. Aziz and J. A. Faris, Oxalic acid content of some common Iraqi vegetables, Iraqi J. Agr. Sci. (Zanco) 2(3):33–38, 1984.

## Phytate

Faridi, H. A., P. L. Finney and G. L. Rubenthaler, Effect of soda leavening on phytic acid content and physical characteristics of Middle Eastern breads, J. Food Sci. 48:1654–1658, 1983.

Harland, B. F. and D. Oberleas, Anion-exchange method for determination of phytate in foods: collaborative study, J. Assoc. Off. Anal. Chem. 69(4):667–670, 1986.

Harland, B. F. and D. Oberleas, Phytate and zinc contents of coffees, cocoas, and teas, J. Food Sci. 50:832–842, 1985.

Kim, W. J., N. M. Kim and H. S. Sung, Effect of germination on phytic acid and soluble minerals in soymilk, Korean J. Food Sci. Tech. 16(3):358–362, 1984.

Oberleas, D. and B. F. Harland, Phytate content of foods: effect on dietary zinc bioavailability, J. Am. Diet. Assoc. 79:433–435, 1981.

Ologhobo, A. D. and B. L. Fetuga, Investigations on the trypsin inhibitor, hemagglutinin, phytic and tannic acid contents of cowpea *Vigna unguiculata*, Food Chem. 12(4):249–254, 1983.

O'Neill, I. K., M. Sargent and M. L. Trimble, Determination of phytate in foods by phosphorus-31 fourier transform nuclear magnetic resonance spectrometry, Anal. Chem. 52:1288–1291, 1980.

Phillippy, B. Q. and M. R. Johnston, Determination of phytic acid in foods by ion chromatography with post-column derivatization, J. Food Sci. 50(2):541–542, 1985.

Reddy, N. R., S. K. Sathe and D. K. Salunkhe, Phytates in legumes and cereals, Adv. Food Res. 28:1–92, 1982.

Tan, N. H., Z. H. Rahim, H. T. Khor and K. C. Wong, Winged bean (*Psophocarpus tetragonolobus*) tannin level, phytate content, and hemagglutinating activity, J. Agric. Food Chem. 31(4):916–917, 1983.

Tangkongchitr, U., P. A. Seib and R. C. Hoseney, Phytic acid, II. Its fate during breadmaking, Cereal Chem. 58(3):229–234, 1981.

Teklenburg, E., M. E. Zabik, M. A. Uebersax, J. Deitz and E. W. Lusas, Mineral and phytic acid partitioning among air-classified bean flour fractions, J. Food Sci. 49(2):569–572, 584, 1984.

Vinh, L. T. and E. Dworschak, Phytate content of some foods from plant origin from Vietnam and Hungary, Nahrung 29(2):161–166, 1985.

## Purines

Burns, B. G. and P. J. Ke, Liquid chromatographic determination of hypoxanthine content in fish tissue, J. Assoc. Off. Anal. Chem. 68(3):444–448, 1985.

Savaiano, D. A., L. M. Salati, W. D. Rosamond, J. Salinsky and B. W. Willis, Nucleic acid, purine and proximate analyses of mechanically separated beef and veal, J. Food Sci. 48:1356–1357, 1983.

Shinoda, T., Y. Aoyagi and T. Sugahara, Contents of purine bases in fishes and fish products, J. Jap. Soc. Food Nutr. 34(2):153–162, 1981.

Shinoda, T. E., Y. Aoyagi and T. Sugahara, Purine base contents in foods and effects of cooking methods (sautéing, broiling, boiling), J. Jap. Soc. Food Nutr. 35(2):103–109, 1982.

Tiemeyer, W., M. Stohrer and D. Giesecke, Metabolites of nucleic acids in bovine milk, J. Dairy Sci. 67(4):723–728, 1984.

Warthesen, J. J., P. T. Waletzko and F. F. Busta, High-pressure liquid chromatographic determination of hypoxanthine in refrigerated fish, J. Agric. Food Chem. 28(6):1308–1309, 1980.

## Selenium

Amer, M. A. and G. J. Brisson, Selenium in human food stuffs collected at the Ste-Foy (Quebec) food market, J. Inst. Can. Sci. Technol. Aliment 6(3):184–187, 1973.

Arthur, D., Selenium content of Canadian foods, Can. Inst. Food Sci. Technol. J. 5(3):165–169, 1972.

Cappon, C. J. and J. C. Smith, Chemical form and distribution of mercury and selenium in edible seafood, J. Anal. Toxicol. 6:10–21, 1982.

Cappon, C. J. and J. C. Smith, Chemical form and distribution of mercury and selenium in canned tuna, J. Appl. Toxicol. 2(4):181–189, 1982.

Cappon, C. J. and J. C. Smith, Mercury and selenium content and chemical form in fish muscle, Arch. Environ. Contam. Toxicol. 10:305–319, 1981.

Ferretti, R. J. and O. A. Levander, Effect of milling and processing on the selenium content of grains and cereal products. J. Agric. Food Chem. 22(6):1049–1051, 1974.

Ferretti, R. J. and O. A. Levander, Selenium content of soybean foods, J. Agric. Food Chem. 24(1):54–56, 1976.

Hadjimarkos, D. M. and C. W. Bonhorst, The selenium content of eggs, milk, and water in relation to dental caries in children, J. Pediatr. 59(2):256–259, 1961.

Hahn, M. H., R. W. Kuennen, J. A. Caruso and F. L. Fricke, Determination of trace amounts of selenium in corn, J. Agric. Food Chem. 29:792–796, 1981.

Higgs, D. J., V. C. Morris and O. A. Levander, Effect of cooking on selenium content of foods, J. Agric. Food Chem. 20(3): 678–680, 1972.

Koivistoinen, P. and J. K. Huttunen, Selenium in food and nutrition in Finland: An overview on research and action, Ann. Clin. Res. 18(1):13–17, 1986.

Landsberger, S. and E. Hoffman, Rapid determination of selenium in various marine species by instrumental neutron activation analysis, J. Radioanal. Nucl. Chem. 87(1):41–50, 1984.

Lane, H. W., B. J. Taylor, E. Stool, D. Servance and D. C. Warren, Selenium content of selected foods, J. Am. Diet. Assoc. 82:24–28, 1983.

Levander, O. A., A review: selenium and chromium in human nutrition, J. Am. Diet. Assoc. 66:338–344, 1975.

Luten, J. B., A. Ruiter, T. M. Ritskes, A. B. Rauchbaar and G. Riekwel-Booy, Mercury and selenium in marine- and freshwater fish, J. Food Sci. 45:416–419, 1980.

Martin, R. F., V. R. Young and M. Janghorbani, Selenium content of enteral formulas, J. Parenter. Enteral. Nutr. 10(2):213–215, 1986.

Morris, V. C. and O. A. Levander, Selenium content of foods, J. Nutr. 100:1383–1388, 1970.

Moxon, A. L. and D. L. Palmquist, Selenium content of foods grown or sold in Ohio, Ohio Report 65(1):13–14, 1980.

Olson, O. E. and I. S. Palmer, Selenium in foods purchased or produced in South Dakota, J. Food Sci. 49:446–452, 1984.

Olson, O. E., I. S. Palmer and M. Howe Sr., Selenium in foods consumed by South Dakotans, Proc. S. D. Acad. Sci. 57: 113–121, 1978.

Robberecht, H., O. Van Schoor and H. Deelstra, Selenium and chronium content of European beers as determined by AAS, J. Food Sci. 49:300–301, 1984.

Schroeder, H. A., D. V. Frost and J. J. Balassa, Essential trace metals in man: Selenium, J. Chronic Dis. 23:227–243, 1970.

Schubert, A., J. M. Holden and W. R. Wolf, Selenium content of a core group of foods based on a critical evaluation of published analytical data, J. Am. Diet. Assoc. 87(3):285–299, 1987.

Shum, G. T. C., H. C. Freeman and J. E. Uthe, Flameless atomic absorption spectrophotometry of selenium in fish and food products, J. Assoc. Off. Anal. Chem. 60(5):1010–1014, 1977.

Snook, J. T., D. Kinsey, D. L. Palmquist, J. P. DeLany, V. M. Vivian and A. L. Moxon, Selenium content of foods purchased or produced in Ohio, J. Am. Diet. Assoc. 87:744–749, 1987.

Taussky, H. H., A. Washington, E. Zubillaga and A. T. Milhorat, Selenium content of fresh eggs from normal and dystrophic chickens, Nature 200(4912):1211, 1963.

Thompson, J. N., P. Erdody, P. Smith and D. C. Smith, Selenium content of food consumed by Canadians, J. Nutr. 105: 274–277, 1975.

Thorn, J., J. Robertson and D. H. Buss, Trace nutrients: selenium in British food, Br. J. Nutr. 39:391–396, 1978.

## Sugars

Kozukue, E., N. Kozukue and T. Kurosaki, Organic acid, sugar and amino acid composition of bamboo shoots, J. Food Sci. 48:935–938, 1983.

Li, B. W. and P. J. Schuhmann, Sugar analysis of fruit juices: Content and method, J. Food Sci. 48:633–635, 1983.

Li, B. W., P. J. Schuhmann and J. M. Holden, Determination of sugars in yogurt by gas-liquid chromatography, J. Agric. Food Chem. 31(5):985–989, 1983.

Southgate, D. A. T., A. A. Paul, A. C. Dean and A. A. Christie, Free sugars in foods, J. Hum. Nutr. 32:335–347, 1978.

## Tin

Dabeka, R. W., A. D. McKenzie and R. H. Albert, Atomic absorption spectrophotometric determination of tin in canned foods, using nitric acid–hydrochloric acid digestion and nitrous oxide–acetylene flame: collaborative study, J. Assoc. Off. Anal. Chem. 68(2):209–213, 1985.

Sherlock, J. C. and G. A. Smart, Tin in foods and the diet, Food Addit. Contam. 1(3):277–282, 1984.

## Tyramine

Buteau, C., C. L. Duitschaever and G. C. Ashton, High-performance liquid chromatographic detection and quantitation of amines in must and wine, J. Chromatogr. 284(1): 201–210, 1984.

Chang, S. F., J. W. Ayres and W. E. Sandine, Analysis of cheese for histamine, tyramine, tryptamine, histidine, tyrosine, and tryptophane, J. Dairy Sci. 68(11):2840–2846, 1985.

Chin, K. D. H. and P. E. Koehler, Identification and estimation of histamine, tryptamine, phenethylamine and tyramine in soy sauce by thin-layer chromatography of dansyl derivatives, J. Food Sci. 48(6):1826–1828, 1983.

Hui, J. Y. and S. L. Taylor, High-pressure liquid chromatographic determination of putrefactive amines in foods, J. Assoc. Off. Anal. Chem. 66(4):853–857, 1983.

Jalon, M., C. Santos-Buelga, J. C. Rivas-Gonzalo and A. Marine-Font, Tyramine in cocoa and derivatives, J. Food Sci. 48: 545–547, 1983.

Joosten, H. M. L. and C. Olieman, Determination of biogenic amines in cheese and some other food products by high-performance liquid chromatography in combination with thermo-sensitized reaction detection, J. Chromatogr. 356(2):311–319, 1986.

McCabe, B. J., Dietary tyramine and other pressor amines in MAOI regimens: a review, J. Am. Diet. Assoc. 86(8):1059–1064, 1986.

Reuvers, T. B. A., M. M. de Pozuelo, M. Ramos and R. Jimenez, A rapid ion-pair HPLC procedure for the determination of tyramine in dairy products, J. Food Sci. 51(1):84–86, 1986.

Santos-Buelga, C., M. J. Pena-Egido and J. C. Rivas-Gonzalo, Changes in tyramine during chorizo sausage ripening, J. Food Sci. 51(2):518–513, 1986.

Sayem-El-Daher, N., R. E. Simard and L. L'Heureux, Determination of mono-, di- and polyamines in foods using a single-column amino acid auto-analyzer, J. Chromatogr. 256(2):313–321, 1983.

Sem, N. P., Analysis and significance of tyramine in foods, J. Food Sci. 34:22–26, 1969.

Sullivan, E. A. and K. I. Shulman, Diet and monoamine oxidase inhibitors: A re-examination, Can J. Psychiatry 29(8):707–711, 1984.

Voigt, M. N., R. R. Eitenmiller, P. E. Koehler and M. K. Hamdy, Tyramine, histamine, and tryptamine content of cheese, J. Milk Food Technol. 37(7):377–381, 1974.

Zee, J. A., R. E. Simard and L. L'Heureux, Evaluation of analytical methods for determination of biogenic amines in fresh and processed meat, J. Food Prot. 46(12):1044–1049, 1054, 1983.

### Vitamin D

Berg, H. van den, P. G. Boshuis and W. H. P. Schreurs, Determination of vitamin D in fortified and nonfortified milk powder and infant formula using a specific radioassay after purification by high-performance liquid chromatography, J. Agr. Food Chem. 34(2):264–268, 1986.

Kunz, C., M. Niesen, H. von Lilienfeld-Toal and W. Burmeister, Vitamin D, 25-hydroxy-vitamin D and 1,25-dihydroxy-vitamin D in cow's milk, infant formulas and breast milk during different stages of lactation, Int. J. Vitam. Nutr. Res. 54(2-3):141–148, 1984.

Okano, T, K. Yokoshima and T. Kobayashi, High-performance liquid chromatographic determination of vitamin D-3 in bovine colostrum, early and later milk, J. Nutr. Sci. Vitaminol. (Tokyo) 30(5):431–439, 1984.

Sertl, D. C. and B. E. Molitor, Liquid chromatographic determination of vitamin D in milk and infant formula, J. Assoc. Off. Anal. Chem. 68(2):177–182, 1985.

Takeuchi, A., T. Okano, M. Ayame, H. Yoshikawa, S. Teraoka, Y. Murakami and T. Kobayashi, High-performance liquid chromatographic determination of vitamin D-3 in fish liver oils and eel body oils, J. Nutr. Sci. Vitaminol. (Tokyo) 30(5):421–430, 1984.

### Vitamin E (Tocopherols)

Atuma, S. S., Electrochemical determination of vitamin E in margarine, butter and palm oil, J. Sci. Food Agric. 26(4):393–399, 1975.

Bunnell, R. H., J. Keating, A. Quaresimo and G. K. Parman, Alpha-tocopherol content of foods, Am. J. Clin. Nutr. 17(1):1–10, 1965.

Candlish, J. K., Tocopherol content of some Southeast Asian foods, J. Agric. Food Chem. 31(1):166–168, 1983.

Herting, D. C. and E. E. Drury, Alpha-tocopherol content of cereal grains and processed cereals, Agr. Food Chem. 17(4):785–790, 1969.

Koehler, H. H., H. C. Lee and M. Jacobson, Tocopherols in canned entrees and vended sandwiches, J. Am. Diet. Assoc. 70(6):616–620, 1977.

Lambertsen, G., H. Myklestad and O. R. Braekkan, Tocopherols in nuts, J. Sci. Food Agric. 13:617–620, 1962.

Landen, W. O. Jr., D. M. Hines, T. W. Hamill, J. I. Martin, E. R. Young, R. R. Eitenmiller and A. G. Soliman, Vitamin A and vitamin E content of infant formulas produced in the United States, J. Assoc. Off. Anal. Chem. 68(3):509–511, 1985.

Lehmann, J., H. L. Martin, E. L. Lashley, M. W. Marshall and

J. T. Judd, Vitamin E in foods from high and low linoleic acid diets, J. Am. Diet. Assoc. 86(9):1208–1216, 1986.

McLaughlin, P. J. and J. L. Weihrauch, Vitamin E content of foods, J. Am. Diet. Assoc. 75:647–665, 1979.

Syvaoja, E. L., V. Piironen, P. Varo, P. Koivistoinen and K. Salminen, Tocopherols and tocotrienols in Finnish foods: human milk and infant formulas, Int. J. Vitam. Nutr. Res. 55(2):159–166, 1985.

### Vitamin K

Doisy, E. A., Availability of vitamin K in human diets (abstract), Fed. Proc. 31(2):713, 1972.

Fletcher, D. C., Do clotting factors in vitamin K-rich vegetables hinder anticoagulant therapy? (questions and answers), JAMA 237(17):1871, 1977.

Geigy Scientific Tables, Vol. 1, Units of Measurement, Body Fluids, Composition of the Body, Nutrition, 8th ed., Ciba-Geigy, 1981.

Haroon, Y., M. J. Shearer, G. McEnery, V. E. Allan and P. Barkhan, Assay of vitamin K-1 (phylloquinone) by high-performance liquid chromatography: values for human and cow's milk, Proc. Nutr. Soc. 39(2):49A, 1980.

Haroon, Y., M. J. Shearer, S. Rahim, W. G. Gunn, G. McEnery and P. Barkhan, The content of phylloquinone (vitamin K-1) in human milk, cows' milk and infant formula foods determined by high-performance liquid chromatography, J. Nutr. 112(6):1105–1117, 1982.

Howard, P. A. and K. N. Hannaman, Warfarin resistance linked to enteral nutrition products, J. Am. Diet. Assoc. 85(6):713–715, 1985.

Hwang, S. M., Liquid chromatographic determination of vitamin K-1 trans- and cis-isomers in infant formula, J. Assoc. Off. Anal. Chem. 68(4):684–689, 1985.

Kempin, S. J., Warfarin resistance caused by broccoli (letter), N. Engl. J. Med. 308(20):1229–1230, 1983.

Kutsop, J. J., Vitamin K-1 content of enteral products (letter), Am. J. Hosp. Pharm. 40(12):2120, 2123, 1983.

Matschiner, J. T. and E. A. Doisy, Vitamin K content of ground beef, J. Nutr. 90:331–334, 1966.

O'Reilly, R. A. and D. A. Rytand, "Resistance" to warfarin due to unrecognized vitamin K supplementation (letter), N. Engl. J. Med. 303(3):160–161, 1980.

Parrish D. B., Determination of vitamin K in foods: a review, Crit. Rev. Food Sci. Nutr. 13(4):337–352, 1980.

Schneider, D. L., H. B. Fluckiger and J. D. Manes, Vitamin K-1 content of infant formula products, Pediatrics 53(2):273–275, 1974.

Seifert, R. M., Analysis of vitamin K-1 in some green leafy vegetables by gas chromatography, J. Agric. Food Chem. 27(6):1301–1304, 1979.

## REFERENCES BY FOOD GROUP

### Beverages

Meranger, J. C., K. S. Subramanian and C. Chalifoux, Survey for cadmium, cobalt, chromium, copper, nickel, lead, zinc, calcium, and magnesium in Canadian drinking water supplies, J. Assoc. Off. Anal. Chem. 64(1):44–53, 1981.

Ough, C. S., E. A. Crowell and J. Benz, Metal content of California wines, J. Food Sci. 47:825–828, 1982. (Ca, Cu, Fe, K, Mg, Na, Pb, Zn)

## Chips and Other Snack Foods

Khan, M. A. and J. A. Martin, Salt content of selected snack foods, J. Food Sci. 48:656–657, 1983.

## Eggs

Naber, E. C., The effect of nutrition on the composition of eggs, Poult. Sci. 58(3):518–528, 1979.

Robel, E. J., The effect of age of breeder hen on the levels of vitamins and minerals in turkey eggs, Poult. Sci. 62(9): 1751–1756, 1983.

Sivell, L. M., R. W. Wenlock and P. A. Jackson, Determination of vitamin D and retinoid activity in eggs by HPLC, Hum. Nutr. Appl. Nutr. 36A:430–437, 1982.

## Entrees and Meals

De Ritter, E., M. Osadca, J. Scheiner and J. Keating, Vitamins in frozen convenience dinners and pot pies, J. Am. Diet. Assoc. 63(4):391–397, 1974. (vitamin A, carotene, vitamin E, thiamin, riboflavin, vitamin B-6, vitamin B-12, niacin, ascorbic acid)

Porrini, M., S. Ciappellano, P. Simonetti and G. Testolin, Chemical composition of Italian cooked dishes, Int. J. Vitam. Nutr. Res. 56(3):263–268, 1986.

Wiles, S. J., P. A. Nettleton, A. E. Black and A. A. Paul, The nutrient composition of some cooked dishes eaten in Britain: A supplementary food composition table, J. Hum. Nutr. 34:189–223, 1980.

## Fast Foods

Appledorf, H. and L. S. Kelly, Proximate and mineral content of fast foods, J. Am. Diet. Assoc. 74(1):35–40, 1978. (Ca, P, Na, K, Mg, Fe, Zn, Mn, Cu)

Bowers, J. A., J. A. Craig, T. J. Tucker, J. M. Holden and L. P. Posati, Vitamin and proximate composition of fast-food chicken, J. Am. Diet. Assoc. 87:736–739, 1987.

Li, B. W., J. M. Holden, S. G. Brownlee and S. G. Korth, A nationwide sampling of fast-food fried chicken: Starch and moisture content, J. Am. Diet. Assoc. 87:740–743, 1987.

Young, E. A., E. H. Brennan and G. L. Irving, Update: Nutritional analysis of fast foods, Public Health Currents (Ross Labs) 21(3), May–June 1981. (proximate nutrients, 8 vitamins, 8 minerals)

## Fats and Oils

Buss, D. H., P. A. Jackson and D. Scuffam, Composition of butters on sale in Britain, J. Dairy Res. 51:637–641, 1984.

Elson, C. M., R. G. Ackman and A. Chatt, Determination of selenium, arsenic, iodine and bromine in fish, plant and mammalian oils by cyclic instrumental neutron activation analysis, J. Am. Oil Chem. Soc. 60(4):829–838, 1983.

Peart, J., A comprehensive study on the composition of margarines on the market, J. Can. Diet. Assoc. 39(1):11–15, 1978.

## Fish, Shellfish and Crustacea

Ahamad, I. H., R. M. Rao, J. A. Liuzzo and M. A. Khan, Comparison of nutrients in raw, commercially breaded and hand-breaded shrimp, J. Food Sci. 48:307–308, 1983. (proximates, thiamin, riboflavin, niacin, Ca, Fe)

Anthony, J. E., P. N. Hadgis, R. S. Milam, G. A. Herzfeld, L. J. Taper and S. J. Ritchey, Yields, proximate composition and mineral content of finfish and shellfish, J. Food Sci. 48:313–314, 316, 1983. (Ca, P, Mg, Na, K, Cu, Fe, Zn, Mn)

Berg, C. J. Jr., J. Krzynowek, P. Alatalo and K. Wiggin, Sterol and fatty acid composition of the clam, *Codakia orbicularis,* with chemoautotrophic symbionts, Lipids 20(2):116–120, 1985.

Crawford, D. L., D. K. Law and J. K. Babbitt, Nutritional characteristics of marine food. Fish carcass waste and machine-separated flesh, J. Agr. Food Chem. 20(5):1048–1051, 1972. (proximates, 14 minerals)

Grieg, R. A., Comparison of atomic absorption and neutron activation analyses for the determination of silver, chromium, and zinc in various marine organisms, Anal. Chem. 47(9):1682–1684, 1975.

Iwasaki, M. and R. Harada, Proximate and amino acid composition of the roe and muscle of selected marine species, J. Food Sci. 50:1585–1587, 1985.

Jhaveri, S. N., P. A. Karakoltsidis, J. Montecalvo Jr. and S. M. Constantinides, Chemical composition and protein quality of some southern New England marine species, J. Food Sci. 49:110–113, 1984. (protein, lipid, moisture, amino acids, Ca, Mg, Na, Zn, Fe, Cu, Mn, Ni, Cd)

Jhaveri, S. N., P. A. Karakoltsidis, S. Y. K. Shenouda and S. M. Constantinides, Ocean pout (*Macrozoarces americanus*): Nutrient analysis and utilization, J. Food Sci. 50:719–722, 1985. (amino acids, fatty acids, Ca, Mg, Na, Zn, Fe, Cu, Mn, Ni, Cd)

Lopez, A., D. R. Ward and H. L. Williams, Essential elements in oysters (*Crassostrea virginica*) as affected by processing method, J. Food Sci. 48:1680–1691, 1983. (Ca, Cl, Cr, Co, Cu, Fe, Mg, Mn, Mo, Ni, P, K, Si, Sn, Zn)

Lucas, H. F. Jr., D. N. Edgington and P. J. Colby, Concentrations of trace elements in Great Lakes fishes, J. Fisheries Res. Bd. Can. 27(4):677–684, 1970. (15 elements)

Mustafa, F. A. and D. M. Medeiros, Proximate composition, mineral content, and fatty acids of catfish (*Ictalurus punctatus, Rafinesque*) for different seasons and cooking methods, J. Food Sci. 50:585–588, 1985. (Na, K, P, Mg, Ca, Zn, Fe, Cu)

Seet, S. T. and W. D. Brown, Nutritional quality of raw, precooked and canned albacore tuna (*Thunnus alalunga*), J. Food Sci. 48:288–289, 1983. (amino acids, thiamin, riboflavin, niacin, Na, K, Ca, Fe, Cu)

Sidwell, V. D., P. R. Foncannon, N. S. Moore and J. C. Bonnet, Composition of the edible portion of raw (fresh or frozen) crustaceans, finfish, and mollusks. I. Protein, fat, moisture, ash, carbohydrate, energy value and cholesterol, Marine Fisheries Review 36(3):21–35, 1974.

## Fruits

Bushway, R. J., D. F. McGann, W. P. Cook and A. A. Bushway, Mineral and vitamin content of lowbush blueberries (*Vaccinium angustifolium Ait.*), J. Food Sci. 48:1878–1880, 1983. (11 minerals, 5 vitamins)

Edem, D. O., O. U. Eka and E. T. Ifon, Chemical evaluation of nutritive value of the fruit of African starapple (*Chrysophyllum albidum*), Food Chem. 14(4):303–311, 1984.

Edem, D. O., O. U. Eka and E. T. Ifon, Chemical evaluation of the nutritive value of the raffia palm fruit (*Raphia hook-*

*eri*), Food Chem. 15(11):9–17, 1984. (proximates, 10 minerals, phytate, oxalate)

Johnson, C. D., R. R. Eitenmiller, J. B. Jones Jr., V. N. M. Rao and S. E. Gebhardt, Composition of red delicious apples, J. Food Sci. 49:952–953, 1984. (7 vitamins, 9 minerals)

## Grains and Grain Products

Albrecht, J. A., E. H. Asp and I. M. Buzzard, Content and retention of sodium and other minerals in pasta cooked in unsalted or salted water, Cereal Chem. 64:106–109, 1987.

Burk, R. F. and N. W. Solomons, Trace elements and vitamins and bioavailability as related to wheat and wheat foods, Am. J. Clin. Nutr. 41(5 suppl.):1091–1102, 1985.

Douglass, J. S. and R. H. Matthews, Nutrient content of pasta products, Cereal Foods World 27(11):558–561, 1982. (proximate nutrients, 10 minerals, 5 vitamins)

Englyst, H. N., V. Anderson and J. H. Cummings, Starch and non-starch polysaccharides in some cereal foods, J. Sci. Food Agric. 34:1434–1440, 1983.

Morgan, D. E., Note on variations in the mineral composition of oat and barley grain grown in Wales, J. Sci. Food Agr. 19(7):393–395, 1968. (Ca, Mg, K, Na, P, Cl, Cu, Co, Mn, Zn)

Schweizer, T. F., W. Frolich, S. del Vedovo and R. Besson, Minerals and phytate in the analysis of dietary fiber from cereals. I. Cereal Chem. 61(2):116–119, 1984.

Simwemba, C. G., R. C. Hoseney, E. Varriano-Marston and K. Zeleznak, Certain B vitamin and phytic acid contents of pearl millet (*Pennisetum americanum (L.) Leeke*), J. Agric. Food Chem. 32(1):31–34, 1984.

Singh, B. and L. M. Dodda, Studies on the preparation and nutrient composition of bulgur from triticale, J. Food Sci. 44(2):449–452, 1979.

Sivell, L. M. and R. W. Wenlock, The nutritional composition of British bread: London area study, Hum. Nutr. Appl. Nutr. 37A:459–469, 1983.

Tarone, C. M. and R. H. Matthews, Proximate and mineral content of selected baked products, Cereal Foods World 27(7):308–313, 1982. (Ca, Fe, Mg, P, K, Na, Zn, Cu)

Wenlock, R. W., The nutrient content of UK wheat flours between 1957 and 1980, J. Sci. Food Agric. 33:1310–1318, 1982.

Wenlock, R. W., L. M. Sivell, R. T. King, D. Scuffam and R. A. Wiggins, The nutritional composition of British bread—a nationwide study, J. Sci. Food Agric. 34:1302–1318, 1983.

Zook, E. G., F. E. Greene and E. R. Morris, Nutrient composition of selected wheats and wheat products, VI. Distribution of manganese, copper, nickel, zinc, magnesium, lead, tin, cadmium, chromium, and selenium as determined by atomic absorption spectroscopy and colorimetry, Cereal Chem. 47:720–731, 1970.

## Meat

Bentley, R., A fresh look at lamb, J. New Zealand Diet. Assoc. 40:81–88, 1986. (proximates, 10 vitamins, 9 minerals, amino acids, fatty acids)

Marchello, M. J., D. B. Milne and W. D. Slanger, Selected macro and micro minerals in ground beef and longissimus muscle, J. Food Sci. 49:105–106, 1984. (K, Na, P, Ca, Cu, Fe, Mg, Zn, Mn)

Ono, K., B. W. Berry, H. K. Johnson, E. Russek, C. F. Parker, V. R. Cahill and P. G. Althouse, Nutrient composition of lamb of two age groups, J. Food Sci. 49:1233–1257, 1984. (proximates, cholesterol, 8 vitamins, 8 minerals, fatty acids)

Paul, A. A. and D. A. T. Southgate, A study on the composition of retail meat: dissection into lean, separable fat and inedible portion, J. Hum. Nutr. 31:259–272, 1977.

Riss, T. L., P. J. Bechtel, R. M. Forbes, B. P. Klein and F. K. McKeith, Nutrient content of special fed veal ribeyes, J. Food Sci. 48:1868–1871, 1983. (proximates, cholesterol, 8 minerals, 8 vitamins, amino acids)

Young, L. L., G. K. Searcy, L. C. Blankenship, J. Salinsky and D. Hamm, Selected nutrients in ground and mechanically separated veal, J. Food Sci. 48:1576–1578, 1983. (proximates, cholesterol, purines, nucleic acids)

## Milk, Cream and Cheese

Ahmed, A. A., Y. L. Awad and F. Fahmy, Studies on some minor constituents of camel's milk, Vet. Med. J. 25:51–56, 1977.

Dang, H. S., D. D. Jaiswal, C. N. Wadhwani, S. Somasunderam and H. Dacosta, Breast feeding: Mo, As, Mn, Zn, Cu concentrations in milk of economically poor Indian tribal and urban women, Sci. Total Environ. 44(2):177–182, 1985.

Department of Health and Social Security, The composition of mature human milk, Report on Health and Social Subjects No. 12, London, HMSO, 1977.

Florence, E., D. J. Knight, J. A. Owen, D. F. Milner and W. M. Harris, Nutrient content of liquid milk as retailed in the United Kingdom, J. Soc. Dairy Technol. 38:121–127, 1985.

Florence, E., D. F. Milner and W. M. Harris, Nutrient composition of dairy products. I. Cheeses, J. Soc. Dairy Technol. 37:13–16, 1984.

Florence, E., D. F. Milner and W. M. Harris, Nutrient composition of dairy products. II. Creams, J. Soc. Dairy Technol. 37:16–18, 1984.

Goldsmith, S. J., R. R. Eitenmiller, R. T. Toledo and H. M. Barnhart, Effects of processing and storage on the water-soluble vitamin content of human milk, J. Food Sci. 48:994–997, 1983. (9 vitamins)

Larson, L. L., S. E. Wallen, F. G. Owen and S. R. Lowry, Relation of age, season, production, and health indices to iodine and beta-carotene concentrations in cow's milk, J. Dairy Sci. 66(12):2557–2562, 1983.

Pennington, J. A. T., D. B. Wilson, B. E. Young, R. D. Johnson and J. E. Vanderveen, Mineral content of market samples of fluid whole milk, J. Am. Diet. Assoc. 87:1036–1042, 1987.

Sawaya, W. N., J. K. Khalil and A. F. Al-Shalhat, Mineral and vitamin content of goat's milk, J. Am. Diet. Assoc. 84(4):433–435, 1984. (Na, K, Ca, Mg, P, Fe, Cu, Zn, Mn, vitamin A, thiamin, riboflavin, vitamin B-6, vitamin B-12, folacin, niacin, pantothenic acid, ascorbic acid)

Sawaya, W. N., J. K. Khalil, A. Al-Shalhat and H. Al-Mohammad, Chemical composition and nutritional quality of camel milk, J. Food Sci. 49:744–747, 1984. (proximates, Ca, Mg, P, Na, K, Fe, Cu, Zn, Mn, 9 vitamins, fatty acids, amino acids)

Scott, K. J. and D. R. Bishop, Nutrient content of milk and milk products: water soluble vitamins in baby milk formulae, J. Dairy Res. 52:521–528, 1985.

Scott, K. J. and D. R. Bishop, The nutrient content of milk

and milk products. Vitamins of the B complex and vitamin C in retail market milk and milk products, J. Soc. Dairy Technol. 39:32–35, 1986.

Scott, K. J., D. R. Bishop, A. Zechalko and J. D. Edwards-Webb, Nutrient content of liquid milk. II. Content of vitamin C, riboflavin, folic acid, thiamin, vitamins B-12 and B-6 in pasteurized milk as delivered to the home and after storage in the domestic refrigerator, J. Dairy Res. 51:51–57, 1984.

Scott, K. J., D. R. Bishop, A. Zechalko, J. D. Edwards-Webb, P. A. Jackson and D. Scuffam, Nutrient content of liquid milk. I. Vitamins A, D-3, C, and of the B complex in pasteurized bulk liquid milk, J. Dairy Res. 51:37–50, 1984.

## Nuts and Nut Products

Galvao, L. C. A., A. Lopez and H. L. Williams, Essential mineral elements in peanuts and peanut butter, J. Food Sci. 41: 1305–1307, 1976. (Ca, Cl, K, Mg, Na, P, Co, Cr, Cu, Fe, Mn, Mo, Zn)

## Poultry

Mast, M. G., R. M. Leach and J. H. MacNeil, Performance, composition, and quality of broiler chickens fed dried whole eggs, Poultry Sci. 63(10):1940–1945, 1984.

## Vegetables

Abdullah, A. and R. E. Baldwin, Mineral and vitamin contents of seeds and sprouts of newly available small-seeded soybeans and market samples of mungbeans, J. Food Sci. 49: 656–657, 1984. (Cu, Fe, Mg, Mn, Mo, P, K, Na, Zn, ascorbic acid, thiamin, riboflavin, niacin)

Bradbury, J. H. and U. Singh, Thiamin, riboflavin, and nicotinic acid contents of tropical root crops from the South Pacific, J. Food Sci. 51:1563–1564, 1986.

Finglas, P. M. and R. M. Faulks, Nutritional composition of UK retail potatoes, both raw and cooked, J. Sci. Food Agric. 35:1437–1356, 1984.

Kadam, S. S. and D. K. Salunkhe, Nutritional composition, processing, and utilization of horse gram and moth bean, CRC Crit. Rev. Food Sci. Nutr. 22(1):1–26, 1985.

Lopez, A., H. L. Williams and F. W. Cooler, Essential elements, cadmium and lead in fresh and canned corn (*Zea mays L.*). J. Food Sci. 50:1760–1761, 1985. (Ca, Cl, Cr, Co, Cu, Fe, Mg, Mn, Mo, Ni, P, K, Si, Na, Sn, Zn)

Sawaya, W. N., A. Al-Shalhat, A. Al-Sogair and M. Al-Mohammad, Chemical composition and nutritive value of truffles of Saudi Arabia, J. Food Sci. 50:450–453, 1985. (moisture, protein, fat, amino acids, ascorbic acid, Ca, Mg, P, Na, K, Fe, Mn, Cu, Zn)

Singh, U., K. C. Jain, R. Jambunathan and D. G. Faris, Nutritional quality of vegetable pigeonpeas (*Cajanus cajan (L.) Mill sp.*): Dry matter accumulation, carbohydrates and proteins, J. Food Sci. 49:799–802, 1984. (dietary fiber, starch, sugars, amino acids)

Singh, U., K. C. Jain, R. Jambunathan and D. G. Faris, Nutritional quality of vegetable pigeonpeas (*Cajanus cajan (L) Mill sp.*): Mineral and trace elements, J. Food Sci. 49: 645–646, 1984. (P, K, Ca, Mg, Zn, Cu, Fe, Mn)

Singh, U., M. S. Kherdekar, D. Sharma and K. B. Saxena, Cooking quality and chemical composition of some early, medium and late maturing cultivars of pigeon pea (*Cajanus cajan (L.) Mill*)., J. Food Sci. Tech., India 21(6):367–373, 1984.

Slater, G. G., S. Shankman, J. S. Shepherd and R. B. Alfin-Slater, Seasonal variation in the composition of California avocados, J. Agr. Food Chem. 23(2):468–474, 1975. (proximates, fatty acids, 11 vitamins, 17 minerals)

Thomas, B., J. A. Roughan and E. D. Watters, Cobalt, chromium and nickel content of some vegetable foodstuffs, J. Sci. Food Agric. 25:771–776, 1974.

Yao, J. J., L. S. Wei and M. P. Steinberg, Effect of maturity on chemical composition and storage stability of soybeans, J. Am. Oil Chem. Soc. 60(7):1245–1249, 1983.

## Miscellaneous Foods

Glass, L. and T. I. Hedrick, Nutritional composition of sweet- and acid-type wheys, II. Vitamin, mineral, and calorie contents, J. Dairy Sci. 60(2):190–196, 1977.

Sarwar, G., B. G. Shah, R. Mongeau and K. Hoppner, Nucleic acid, fiber and nutrient composition of inactive dried food yeast products, J. Food Sci. 50:353–357, 1985. (purine, pyrimidine, nucleic acids, amino acids, dietary fiber, Ca, Mg, P, Na, K, Fe, Zn, Cu, Mn, folacin, pantothenic acid, biotin)

## REFERENCES FOR VARIOUS SUBSTANCES IN VARIOUS FOODS

Davies, N. T. and S. Warrington, The phytic acid, mineral, trace element, protein and moisture content of UK Asian immigrant foods, Hum. Nutr. Appl. Nutr. 40(1):49–59, 1986.

Gormican, A., Inorganic elements in foods used in hospital menus, J. Am. Diet. Assoc. 56:397–403, 1970. (P, K, Ca, Mg, Na, Al, Ba, Fe, Sr, B, Cu, Zn, Mn, Cr)

Holak, W., Analysis of foods for lead, cadmium, copper, zinc, arsenic, and selenium using closed-system sample digestion: Collaborative study, J. Assoc. Off. Anal. Chem. 63(3):485–495, 1980. (strained chicken, strained applesauce, reference materials)

Koehler, H. H. and M. M. Hard, Protein, fat, and amino acid content and protein quality of selected pre-prepared foods, J. Am. Diet. Assoc. 82(3):241–245, 1983.

Monro, J. A., W. D. Holloway and J. Lee, Elemental analysis of fruit and vegetables from Tonga, J. Food Sci. 51(2): 522–523, 1986. (Ca, K, Mg, P, S, B, Cu, Fe, Mn, Na, Zn)

Pennington, J. A. T., B. E. Young, D. B. Wilson, R. D. Johnson and J. E. Vanderveen, Mineral content of foods and total diets: The selected minerals in foods survey, 1982–84, J. Am. Diet. Assoc. 86(7):876–891, 1986. (Na, K, Ca, P, Mg, Fe, Zn, Cu, Mn, Se, I)

Tan, S. P., R. W. Wenlock and D. H. Buss, Second supplement to McCance and Widdowson's 'The composition of foods': immigrant foods. London, HMSO, 1985.

Wolnik, K. A., F. L. Fricke, S. G. Capar, G. L. Braude, M. W. Meyer, R. D. Satzger and R. W. Kuennen, Elements in major raw agricultural crops in the United States. 2. Other elements in lettuce, peanuts, potatoes, soybeans, sweet corn, and wheat, J. Agric. Food Chem. 31(6):1244–1249, 1983. (Ca, Cu, Fe, K, Mg, Mn, Mo, Na, Ni, P, Se, Zn)

# Index